Jeremiah 1

A Commentary on the
Book of the Prophet Jeremiah
Chapters 1—25

by William L. Holladay

Edited by Paul D. Hanson

**Fortress
Press**

Philadelphia

Library of Congress Catalog Card Number 85-45498
ISBN 0-8006-6017-X

Printed in the United States of America
Design by Kenneth Hiebert
Type set on an Ibycus System at Polebridge Press
1807J85   20-6017

Contents
Jeremiah 1

The name *Hermeneia*, Greek ἑρμηνεία, has been chosen as the title of the commentary series to which this volume belongs. The word *Hermeneia* has a rich background in the history of biblical interpretation as a term used in the ancient Greek-speaking world for the detailed, systematic exposition of a scriptural work. It is hoped that the series, like its name, will carry forward this old and venerable tradition. A second entirely practical reason for selecting the name lies in the desire to avoid a long descriptive title and its inevitable acronym, or worse, an unpronounceable abbreviation.

The series is designed to be a critical and historical commentary to the Bible without arbitrary limits in size or scope. It will utilize the full range of philological and historical tools, including textual criticism (often slighted in modern commentaries), the methods of the history of tradition (including genre and prosodic analysis), and the history of religion.

Hermeneia is designed for the serious student of the Bible. It will make full use of ancient Semitic and classical languages; at the same time, English translations of all comparative materials—Greek, Latin, Canaanite, or Akkadian—will be supplied alongside the citation of the source in its original language. Insofar as possible, the aim is to provide the student or scholar with full critical discussion of each problem of interpretation and with the primary data upon which the discussion is based.

Hermeneia is designed to be international and interconfessional in the selection of authors; its editorial boards were formed with this end in view. Occasionally the series will offer translations of distinguished commentaries which originally appeared in languages other than English. Published volumes of the series will be revised continually, and eventually, new commentaries will replace older works in order to preserve the currency of the series. Commentaries are also being assigned for important literary works in the categories of apocryphal and pseudepigraphical works relating to the Old and New Testaments, including some of Essene or Gnostic authorship.

The editors of *Hermeneia* impose no systematic-theological perspective upon the series (directly, or indirectly by selection of authors). It is expected that authors will struggle to lay bare the ancient meaning of a biblical work or pericope. In this way the text's human relevance should become transparent, as is always the case in competent historical discourse. However, the series eschews for itself homiletical translation of the Bible.

The editors are heavily indebted to Fortress Press for its energy and courage in taking up an expensive, long-term project, the rewards of which will accrue chiefly to the field of biblical scholarship.

The editor responsible for this volume is Paul D. Hanson of Harvard University.

January 1986   *Frank Moore Cross*   *Helmut Koester*
                    For the Old Testament   For the New Testament
                    Editorial Board   Editorial Board

The editorial board of *Hermeneia* has decided to issue the two volumes of the commentary on Jeremiah separately, in order that the material on chapters 1—25 become available as soon as possible. That decision involves a postponement of all indexes, and of the introduction to the commentary (and thus the accompanying bibliography of general works on Jeremiah) until *Jeremiah 2* appears, I hope not too many years in the future. Readers of the present volume must accept cross-references to material in *Jeremiah 2* with patience.

I am delighted to share my detailed work on the first twenty-five chapters of Jeremiah at this time, but I regret that those chapters must appear unsupported by an introduction, because that introduction will offer a full account of what I have concluded in regard to two crucial matters in the book, a chronology of the prophet's career (and thus to some degree the assignment of dates for specific passages), and a scheme for the literary history of the book—even for a delimitation of the contents of the first two scrolls dictated by the prophet (chap. 36). Until that introduction appears, readers must be content here with a preliminary essay on these questions, "A Chronology of Jeremiah's Career," which follows.[1]

There are several distinctive matters in this work to which attention should be called. The first is in regard to the two abbreviations Jer and Jrm: Jer refers to the *book* of Jeremiah, and Jrm to the *man* Jeremiah.

Second, a distinction is made in the symbols for an emended text between single diagonal brackets ⟨ ⟩ and double diagonal brackets ⟪ ⟫. The first is used for the revocalization of an acceptable consonantal text (with the exception of the possible presence or absence of *matres lectionis*); the second for instances in which the consonantal text itself has been emended. (See further Editor's Note.)

Third, the bibliography within a given section often contains bibliography that ranges farther than the span of that section: thus the section 1:1–3 begins with bibliography on chaps. 1—25 and continues with bibliographies for steadily shortening spans (for chaps. 1—24, chaps. 1—10, and so on), before the bibliography of 1:1–3 proper is reached. It has appeared easier to arrange bibliography in this way than to set up special bibliographical sections before the treatment of a given short section (in the case of the example, 1:1–3). This means, for example, that Hermisson's treatment of 22:24–30, much of which concerns vv 28–30, is found under 22:24–27, since vv 24–27 and 28–30 make up separate sections here; there is no fresh citation of Hermisson's article under 22:28–30.

Fourth, before the discussion of "Form" for each passage is a section called

---

1   This essay is adapted from my "The Years of Jeremiah's Preaching," *Int* 37 (1983) 146–59, used here by permission; it supersedes my earlier publications on these questions, "The Identification of the Two Scrolls of Jeremiah," *VT* 30 (1980) 452–67, and "A Coherent Chronology of Jeremiah's Early Career," *Le Livre de Jérémie* (ed. Pierre-Maurice Bogaert; BETL 54; Leuven: Leuven University, 1981) 58–73.

"Structure." In this section three related questions are discussed. (1) What is the delimitation of the passage in question? (2) Why is the passage in its present location? (3) What is the inner structure of the passage?

The inner structure of a passage may be relevant for prose, but it is particularly relevant for poetry. The question of the contrast between "prose" and "poetry," and the lineation and typography of "poetry," are crucial matters in Jer. I have been influenced in these questions by two recent studies which at several points do not agree with each other, that of Michael O'Connor[2] and that of James Kugel.[3] In Jer the contrasting styles of "poetry," with consistent parallelism, and "prose," where parallelism is intermittent and less structured, merit the use of the traditional terms "poetry" and "prose" without apology or quotation marks.

As to the typography of poetry, the ordinary bicolon causes no trouble, and the occasional tricolon; in these instances I have indented the second colon and double-indented any third colon. But consistency then demands that I continue the chain of indentations for what only can be called a hexacolon (4:22)! From time to time, however, one finds circumstances in which it is not at all clear where the division into cola occurs. One particular difficulty arises where a colon seems to consist of a single word: O'Connor will not allow a colon containing a single word (i.e., a verb),[4] but Kugel disagrees.[5] In one such instance in 3:5 I propose a convincing solution to the problem, and in 2:5 I at least raise the question whether the text has not suffered haplography. My solutions to such puzzles may not in all cases be the best ones, but I have tried to stay with common sense and to maintain agnosticism where certainty is out of the question. Even after many centuries of work on these problems, I suspect more light may yet dawn: the fact that two verses of precisely the same highly unusual structure can appear in Jrm's poetry (2:6 and 5:15) suggests that behind these congruences are patterns which were perceived by the ancient hearer, even if not recoverable by us.

Several other matters should be noted here. First, Ugaritic texts are cited according to the Herdner numeration.[6]

Second, I have used "Yahweh" to translate the tetragrammaton in most instances: Jrm himself surely pronounced the name, and I trust I do not offend anyone by its use. But by the same token I have translated the tetragrammaton by "the LORD" in passages that appear to have originated in the postexilic period (e.g., 3:6, 16–17; 9:11–14; 23:34–38); just as surely the common use of the original pronunciation was proscribed by then.

Finally, the translation style adopted here is sometimes excessively wooden. One reason for this is an effort at concision in English that will match the concision of the Hebrew. But the most substantial reason is the impulse to translate identical words and identical phrases consistently throughout the book, in order to further a comparison of the parallel passages which are such a prominent feature of the book. In this regard I regret all the examples where I have felt forced to use masculine-dominated language. I have racked my brain to find a more acceptable rendering

2   Michael Patrick O'Connor, *Hebrew Verse Structure* (Winona Lake, IN: Eisenbrauns, 1980).
3   James L. Kugel, *The Idea of Biblical Poetry* (New Haven and London: Yale University, 1981).
4   O'Connor, *Structure*, 74–75.
5   Kugel, *Poetry*, 319.
6   Andrée Herdner, *Corpus des tablettes en cunéiformes alphabétiques* (Paris: Imprimerie Nationale, 1963).

for אָדָם וּבְהֵמָה than "man and beast" when "human being and animal" is meant; I am not at all pleased with the solution to which I have come in these instances.

I regret not having read everything available on Jer; the field is immense. I apologize in advance for presenting, as my own, suggestions arrived at by others unbeknownst to me, or for not having read suggestions which might justifiably have modified some conclusion offered here. What follows are my conclusions at this time on some of the most astonishing passages of Scripture.

My son David F. Holladay designed for my use a word-processing program which has saved me many months of work in the preparation of this volume, and he has processed my data disks to render them usable for publication. For all this help, grateful thanks.

Spring 1985   *William L. Holladay*

1. Sources and Abbreviations

The abbreviations used for biblical books are in common use. The abbreviations of names of Dead Sea Scrolls and related texts conform to the sigla in Joseph A. Fitzmyer, *The Dead Sea Scrolls: Major Publications and Tools for Study* (SBLSBS 8; Missoula, MT: Scholars, 1975) 3–53. Note also the form for rabbinic literature: *m. Ta'an.* refers to the Mishna, tractate Ta'anit; *b. Šabb.* refers to the Babylonian Talmud, tractate Šabbat; *Midr. Cant.* refers to the Midrash on Canticles.

a'	Aquila
AB	Anchor Bible
AJSL	*American Journal of Semitic Languages*
AJT	*American Journal of Theology*
AnBib	Analecta biblica
ANEP	*Ancient Near East in Pictures* (ed. J. B. Pritchard)
ANET	*Ancient Near Eastern Texts* (ed. J. B. Pritchard)
AnOr	Analecta orientalia
Anton	*Antonianum*
AOAT	Alter Orient und Altes Testament
ARW	*Archiv für Religionswissenschaft*
ATANT	Abhandlungen zur Theologie des Alten und Neuen Testaments
ATD	Das Alte Testament Deutsch
AusBR	*Australian Biblical Review*
BA	*Biblical Archaeologist*
BAG	W. Bauer, W. F. Arndt, and F. W. Gingrich, *Greek-English Lexicon of the New Testament*
BAR	*Biblical Archaeologist Reader*
BASOR	*Bulletin of the American Schools of Oriental Research*
BASP	*Bulletin of the American Society of Papyrologists*
BBB	Bonner biblische Beiträge
BDB	F. Brown, S. R. Driver, and C. A. Briggs, *Hebrew and English Lexicon of the Old Testament*
BDF	F. Blass, A. Debrunner, and R. W. Funk, *A Greek Grammar of the New Testament*
BeO	*Bibbia e oriente*
BETL	Bibliotheca ephemeridum theologicarum lovaniensium
BFCT	Beiträge zur Förderung christlicher Theologie
BHH	*Biblisch-Historisches Handwörterbuch* (ed. B. Reicke and L. Rost)
BHK	R. Kittel, *Biblia hebraica*
BHS	*Biblia hebraica stuttgartensia*
Bib	*Biblica*
BibLeb	*Bibel und Leben*
BibOr	Biblica et orientalia
BKAT	Biblischer Kommentar: Altes Testament
BLit	*Bibel und Liturgie*
BO	*Bibliotheca orientalis*
BTB	*Biblical Theology Bulletin*
BZ	*Biblische Zeitschrift*
BZAW	Beiheft zur *ZAW*
ca.	*circa,* approximately
CBQ	*Catholic Biblical Quarterly*
CChr	Corpus Christianorum
ConB	Coniectanea biblica
DISO	C.-F. Jean and J. Hoftijzer, *Dictionnaire des inscriptions sémitiques de l'ouest*
DJD	Discoveries in the Judaean Desert
EBib	Etudes bibliques
ed(s).	editor(s), edited by, edition
EncJud	*Encyclopaedia Judaica* (1971)
EstBib	*Estudios bíblicos*
ETR	*Etudes théologiques et religieuses*
EvQ	*Evangelical Quarterly*
EvT	*Evangelische Theologie*
ExpTim	*Expository Times*
FRLANT	Forschungen zur Religion und Literatur des Alten und Neuen Testaments
G	Septuagint; note also G^B = codex Vaticanus, etc.
GKC	*Gesenius' Hebrew Grammar* (ed. E. Kautzsch; tr. A. E. Cowley)
Greg	*Gregorianum*
HALAT	W. Baumgartner et al., *Hebräisches und aramäisches Lexikon zum Alten Testament*
HAT	Handbuch zum Alten Testament
HDR	Harvard Dissertations in Religion
HKAT	Handkommentar zum Alten Testament
HSM	Harvard Semitic Monographs
HTR	*Harvard Theological Review*
HUCA	*Hebrew Union College Annual*
IB	*Interpreter's Bible*
ICC	International Critical Commentary
IDB	*Interpreter's Dictionary of the Bible* (ed. G. A. Buttrick)
IDBSup	Supplementary volume to *IDB*
IEJ	*Israel Exploration Journal*
Int	*Interpretation*
JA	*Journal asiatique*
JAOS	*Journal of the American Oriental Society*
JB	*Jerusalem Bible* (ed. A. Jones)
JBL	*Journal of Biblical Literature*
JJS	*Journal of Jewish Studies*
JNES	*Journal of Near Eastern Studies*
JQR	*Jewish Quarterly Review*
JSOT	*Journal for the Study of the Old Testament*

JSS	*Journal of Semitic Studies*		*T*	Targum
JTS	*Journal of Theological Studies*		*θ'*	Theodotion
KAI	H. Donner and W. Röllig, *Kanaanäische und aramäische Inschriften*		*TBl*	*Theologische Blätter*
			TBü	Theologische Bücherei
KAT	Kommentar zum A.T. (ed. E. Sellin)		*TDNT*	*Theological Dictionary of the New Testament* (ed. G. Kittel and G. Friedrich)
KB	L. Koehler and W. Baumgartner, *Lexicon in Veteris Testamenti libros*			
KD	*Kerygma und Dogma*		*TDOT*	*Theological Dictionary of the Old Testament* (ed. G. J. Botterweck and H. Ringgren)
LCL	Loeb Classical Library			
LD	Lectio divina		*TGl*	*Theologie und Glaube*
LSJ	Liddell-Scott-Jones, *Greek-English Lexicon*		*TPQ*	*Theologisch-Praktische Quartalschrift*
			tr.	translation, translated by
M	Masoretic Text		*TToday*	*Theology Today*
McCQ	*McCormick Quarterly*		*TWAT*	*Theologisches Wörterbuch zum Alten Testament* (ed. G. J. Botterweck and H. Ringgren)
MS(S).	manuscript(s)			
MUSJ	*Mélanges de l'université Saint-Joseph*			
NAB	*New American Bible*		*TZ*	*Theologische Zeitschrift*
NEB	*New English Bible*		*UF*	*Ugarit Forschungen*
NF	Neue Folge, new series		Ug.	Ugaritic texts, Herdner numbers (see Foreword)
NICOT	New International Commentary on the Old Testament			
			UT	C. H. Gordon, *Ugaritic Textbook*
NJV	*New Jewish Version* (The Jewish Publication Society of America)		VD	*Verbum domini*
			VSpir	*Vie spirituelle*
NorTT	*Norsk Teologisk Tidsskrift*		*VT*	*Vetus Testamentum*
NRT	*La nouvelle revue théologique*		VTSup	Vetus Testamentum, Supplements
NS	New Series		WMANT	Wissenschaftliche Monographien zum Alten und Neuen Testament
NT	New Testament			
OrAnt	*Oriens antiquus*		ZAW	*Zeitschrift für die alttestamentliche Wissenschaft*
OT	Old Testament			
OTS	*Oudtestamentische Studiën*		ZDMG	*Zeitschrift der deutschen morgenländischen Gesellschaft*
PEFQS	*Palestine Exploration Fund, Quarterly Statement*			
			ZDPV	*Zeitschrift des deutschen Palästina-Vereins*
PEQ	*Palestine Exploration Quarterly*		ZTK	*Zeitschrift für Theologie und Kirche*
PJ	*Palästina-Jahrbuch*			
PL	J. Migne, *Patrologia latina*			
PRU	*Le Palais royal d'Ugarit*			
RB	*Revue biblique*			
rep.	reprinted			
RevQ	*Revue de Qumran*			
RevScRel	*Revue des sciences religieuses*			
RHR	*Revue de l'histoire des religions*			
RivB	*Rivista biblica*			
RSO	*Rivista degli studi orientali*			
RSR	*Recherches de science religieuse*			
RSV	*Revised Standard Version*			
RTP	*Revue de théologie et de philosophie*			
S	Syriac version (Peshitta)			
s'	Symmachus			
SBLDS	SBL Dissertation Series			
SBLMS	SBL Monograph Series			
SBT	Studies in Biblical Theology			
sec(s).	section(s)			
SEÅ	*Svensk exegetisk årsbok*			
SOTSMS	Society for Old Testament Study Monograph Series			
SSS	Semitic Study Series			
ST	*Studia theologica*			
s.v.	*sub verbo* or *sub voce*, under the word (entry)			

2. Short Titles of Commentaries, Studies, and Articles Often Cited

Alonso Schökel, "Esperanza"
Luis Alonso Schökel, "'Tú eres la esperanza de Israel' (Jer 17,5–13)," *Künder des Wortes, Beiträge zur Theologie der Propheten* (ed. Lothar Ruppert et al.; Würzburg: Echter, 1982) 95–104.

Alonso Schökel, "Jeremías como anti-Moisés"
Luis Alonso Schökel, "Jeremías como anti-Moisés," *De la Tôrah au Messie, Mélanges Henri Cazelles* (ed. M. Carrez, J. Doré, and P. Grelot; Paris: Desclée, 1981) 245–54.

American Translation
J. M. Powis Smith et al., and Edgar J. Goodspeed, *The Complete Bible: An American Translation* (Chicago: University of Chicago, 1939).

Bach, *Flucht*
Robert Bach, *Die Aufforderungen zur Flucht und zum Kampf im alttestamentlichen Prophetenspruch* (WMANT 9; Neukirchen: Neukirchener, 1962).

Bailey-Holladay
Kenneth E. Bailey and William L. Holladay, "The 'Young Camel' and 'Wild Ass' in Jeremiah ii 23–25," *VT* 18 (1968) 256–60.

Baltzer, *Biographie*
Klaus Baltzer, *Die Biographie der Propheten* (Neukirchen: Neukirchener, 1975).

Baly, *Geography*
Denis Baly, *The Geography of the Bible* (New York: Harper, 1974).

Barnett, *Nimrud Ivories*
Richard D. Barnett, *A Catalogue of the Nimrud Ivories, with other examples of Ancient Near Eastern Ivories in the British Museum* (London: Trustees of the British Museum, 1957).

Bauer-Leander
Hans Bauer and Pontus Leander, *Historische Grammatik der hebräischen Sprache des Alten Testaments* (Halle: Niemeyer, 1922; rep. Hildesheim: Olms, 1965).

Baumgartner, *Klagegedichte*
Walter Baumgartner, *Die Klagegedichte des Jeremia* (BZAW 32; Giessen: Töpelmann, 1917).

Berridge
John M. Berridge, *Prophet, People, and the Word of Yahweh, An Examination of Form and Content in the Proclamation of the Prophet Jeremiah* (Zurich: EVZ, 1970).

Berridge, "Jeremia und die Prophetie des Amos"
John M. Berridge, "Jeremia und die Prophetie des Amos," *TZ* 35 (1979) 321–41.

Beuken and van Grol
W. A. M. Beuken and H. W. M. van Grol, "Jeremiah 14,1—15,9: A Situation of Distress and Its Hermeneutics, Unity and Diversity of Form—Dramatic Development," *Le Livre de Jérémie, Le prophète et son milieu, Les oracles et leur transmission* (ed. Pierre-Maurice Bogaert; BETL 54; Leuven: Leuven University, 1981) 297–342.

Bodenheimer, "Fauna"
Friedrich S. Bodenheimer, "Fauna," *IDB* 2:246–56.

Bright
John Bright, *Jeremiah* (AB 21; Garden City, NY: Doubleday, 1965).

Bright, "Apodictic Prohibition"
John Bright, "The Apodictic Prohibition: Some Observations," *JBL* 92 (1973) 185–204.

Bright, *History*
John Bright, *A History of Israel* (Philadelphia: Westminster, 1981).

Brongers, "Zornesbecher"
Hendrik A. Brongers, "Der Zornesbecher," *OTS* 15 (Leiden: Brill, 1969) 177–92.

Brueggemann, "Crisis"
Walter A. Brueggemann, "The Epistemological Crisis of Israel's Two Histories (Jer 9:22–23)," *Israelite Wisdom, Theological and Literary Essays in Honor of Samuel Terrien* (ed. John G. Gammie et al.; Missoula, MT: Scholars, 1978) 85–105.

Budde, "Erste Kapitel"
Karl Budde, "Über das erste Kapitel des Buches Jeremia," *JBL* 40 (1921) 23–37.

Calvin
John Calvin, *Commentaries on the Book of the Prophet Jeremiah and the Lamentations* (Calvin Translation Society, 1850–55; rep. Grand Rapids: Eerdmans, 1950).

Castellino, "Observations"
Giorgio R. Castellino, "Observations on the literary structure of some passages in Jeremiah," *VT* 30 (1980) 398–408.

Childs, *Exodus*
Brevard S. Childs, *The Book of Exodus, A Critical, Theological Commentary* (Philadelphia: Westminster, 1974).

Childs, *Isaiah and the Assyrian Crisis*
Brevard S. Childs, *Isaiah and the Assyrian Crisis* (SBT 2d Series 3; Naperville, IL: Allenson, 1967).

Christensen, "Terror"
Duane L. Christensen, "'Terror on Every Side' in Jeremiah," *JBL* 92 (1973) 498–502.

Christensen, *Transformations*
Duane L. Christensen, *Transformations of the War Oracle in Old Testament Prophecy* (HDR 3; Missoula, MT: Scholars, 1975).

Cogan, "Sentencing"
Morton Cogan, "Sentencing at the Gate in Jeremiah 1:15–16," *Gratz College Annual* 1 (1972) 3–6.

Condamin
Albert Condamin, *Le Livre de Jérémie* (EBib; Paris: Gabalda, 1936).

Cooke, *Inscriptions*
George A. Cooke, *A Textbook of North-Semitic Inscriptions* (Oxford: Clarendon, 1903).

Cornill

Carl H. Cornill, *Das Buch Jeremia* (Leipzig: Tauchnitz, 1905).

Cross, *CMHE*

Frank M. Cross, *Canaanite Myth and Hebrew Epic* (Cambridge: Harvard University, 1973).

Cross, "Scripts"

Frank M. Cross, "The Development of the Jewish Scripts," *The Bible and the Ancient Near East* (ed. G. Ernest Wright; New York: Doubleday, 1961) 133–202.

Curtis and Madsen, *Chronicles*

Edward L. Curtis and Albert A. Madsen, *A Critical and Exegetical Commentary on the Books of Chronicles* (ICC; New York: Scribner's, 1910).

Dahood, "Hebrew-Ugaritic Lexicography II"

Mitchell Dahood, "Hebrew-Ugaritic Lexicography II," *Bib* 45 (1964) 393–412.

Dahood, "Jeremiah 17,13"

Mitchell Dahood, "The Metaphor in Jeremiah 17,13," *Bib* 48 (1967) 109–10.

Dahood, "Jer 18,14–15"

Mitchell Dahood, "Philological Notes on Jer 18,14–15," *ZAW* 74 (1962) 207–9.

Dahood, *Psalms I, II, III*

Mitchell Dahood, *Psalms 1—50*, AB 16; *Psalms 51—100*, AB 17; *Psalms 101—150*, AB 17A (Garden City, NY: Doubleday, 1966, 1968, 1970).

Dahood, "Two Textual Notes"

Mitchell Dahood, "Two Textual Notes on Jeremia," *CBQ* 23 (1961) 462–64.

De Roche, "Contra Creation"

Michael De Roche, "Contra Creation, Covenant and Conquest (Jer. viii 13)," *VT* 30 (1980) 280–90.

Driver, "Jeremiah"

Godfrey R. Driver, "Linguistic and Textual Problems: Jeremiah," *JQR* 28 (1937/38) 97–129.

Duhm

Bernhard Duhm, *Das Buch Jeremia* (Kurzer Hand-Commentar zum Alten Testament 11; Tübingen and Leipzig: Mohr [Siebeck], 1901).

Ehrlich, *Randglossen*

Arnold B. Ehrlich, *Randglossen zur hebräischen Bibel* 4 (Leipzig: Hinrichs, 1912).

Eichrodt, *Theology 1, 2*

Walther Eichrodt, *Theology of the Old Testament* (Philadelphia: Westminster, 1961, 1967).

Eissfeldt, *Introduction*

Otto Eissfeldt, *The Old Testament, An Introduction* (Oxford: Blackwell, 1965).

Elliger, *Deuterojesaja*

Karl Elliger, *Deuterojesaja* (BKAT 11/1; Neukirchen: Neukirchener, 1978).

Fishbane, "Revelation and Tradition"

Michael A. Fishbane, "Revelation and Tradition: Aspects of Inner-Biblical Exegesis," *JBL* 99 (1980) 343–61.

Fohrer, "Gattung der Berichte über symbolische Handlungen" = *Studien*

Georg Fohrer, "Die Gattung der Berichte über symbolische Handlungen der Propheten," *ZAW* 64 (1952) 101–20 = *Studien zur alttestamentlichen Prophetie (1949–1965)* (BZAW 99; Berlin: Töpelmann, 1967) 92–112.

Forbes, "Extracting, Smelting, and Alloying"

Robert J. Forbes, "Extracting, Smelting, and Alloying," *A History of Technology* I (ed. Charles Singer, E. J. Holmyard, and A. R. Hall; Oxford: Oxford University, 1954) 572–99.

Forbes, *Metallurgy*

Robert J. Forbes, *Metallurgy in Antiquity* (Leiden: Brill, 1950).

Forbes, *Studies 8*

Robert J. Forbes, *Studies in Ancient Technology* VIII (Leiden: Brill, 1964).

Freedman

Harry Freedman, *Jeremiah* (Soncino Books of the Bible; London: Soncino, 1949).

Gemser

Berend Gemser, "The *rîb*- or controversy-pattern in Hebrew Mentality," *Wisdom in Israel and in the Ancient Near East, Presented to Professor Harold Henry Rowley by the Society for Old Testament Study in Association with the Editorial Board of Vetus Testamentum in Celebration of his Sixty-Fifth Birthday, 24 March 1955* (ed. Martin Noth and D. Winton Thomas; VTSup 3; Leiden: Brill, 1955) 120–37.

Giesebrecht

Friedrich Giesebrecht, *Das Buch Jeremia* (HKAT 3,2; Göttingen: Vandenhoeck & Ruprecht, 1907).

Gray, *Kings*

John Gray, *I & II Kings* (Philadelphia: Westminster, 1970).

Guillaume, *Prophecy and Divination*

Alfred Guillaume, *Prophecy and Divination Among the Hebrew and Other Semites* (London: Hodder & Stoughton, 1938).

Habel, "Call Narratives"

Norman C. Habel, "The Form and Significance of the Call Narratives," *ZAW* 77 (1965) 297–323.

Harper, *Amos and Hosea*

William R. Harper, *A Critical and Exegetical Commentary on Amos and Hosea* (ICC; New York: Scribner's, 1905).

Harris "Linguistic Structure"

Zellig S. Harris, "Linguistic Structure of Hebrew," *JAOS* 61 (1941) 143–67.

Hatch-Redpath

Edwin Hatch and Henry A. Redpath, *A Concordance to the Septuagint and the Other Greek Versions of the Old Testament* (Oxford: Clarendon, 1897).

Held, "Action-Result"

Moshe Held, "The Action-Result (Factitive-Passive) Sequence of Identical Verbs in Biblical Hebrew and Ugaritic," *JBL* 84 (1965) 272–82.

Herr, *Scripts*

Larry G. Herr, *The Scripts of Ancient Northwest Semitic Seals* (HSM 18; 1978).

J. Herrmann, "Jer 22,29; 7,4"
Johannes Herrmann, "Zu Jer 22,29; 7,4," *ZAW* 62 (1949–50) 321–22.

Heschel, *The Prophets*
Abraham J. Heschel, *The Prophets* (New York: Harper, 1962).

Hillers, *Treaty-Curses*
Delbert R. Hillers, *Treaty-Curses and the Old Testament Prophets* (BibOr 26; Rome: Pontifical Biblical Institute, 1964).

Holladay, *Architecture*
William L. Holladay, *The Architecture of Jeremiah 1—20* (Lewisburg, PA: Bucknell University, 1976).

Holladay, "Background"
William L. Holladay, "The Background of Jeremiah's Self-Understanding: Moses, Samuel, and Psalm 22," *JBL* 83 (1964) 153–64.

Holladay, "Coherent Chronology"
William L. Holladay, "A Coherent Chronology of Jeremiah's Early Career," *Le Livre de Jérémie, Le Prophète et son milieu, les oracles et leur transmission* (ed. Pierre-Maurice Bogaert; BETL 54; Leuven: Leuven University, 1981) 58–73.

Holladay, "Deuteronomic Gloss"
William L. Holladay, "The So-Called 'Deuteronomic Gloss' in Jer. viii 19b," *VT* 12 (1962) 494–98.

Holladay, "Identification"
William L. Holladay, "The Identification of the Two Scrolls of Jeremiah," *VT* 30 (1980) 452–67.

Holladay, "Jer 20:1–6"
William L. Holladay, "The Covenant with the Patriarchs Overturned: Jeremiah's Intention in 'Terror on Every Side' (Jer 20:1–6)," *JBL* 91 (1972) 305–20.

Holladay, "Jeremiah and Moses, Further Observations"
William L. Holladay, "Jeremiah and Moses: Further Observations," *JBL* 85 (1966) 17–27.

Holladay, "Lawsuit"
William L. Holladay, "Jeremiah's Lawsuit with God," *Int* 17 (1963) 280–87.

Holladay, "On Every High Hill"
William L. Holladay, "'On Every High Hill and Under Every Green Tree,'" *VT* 11 (1961) 170–76.

Holladay, "Prototype"
William L. Holladay, "Prototype and Copies: A New Approach to the Poetry-Prose Problem in the Book of Jeremiah," *JBL* 79 (1960) 351–67.

Holladay, "Recovery"
William L. Holladay, "The Recovery of Poetic Passages of Jeremiah," *JBL* 85 (1966) 401–35.

Holladay, *Spokesman*
William L. Holladay, *Jeremiah, Spokesman Out of Time* (New York: Pilgrim, 1974).

Holladay, "Style"
William L. Holladay, "Style, Irony and Authenticity in Jeremiah," *JBL* 81 (1962) 44–54.

Holladay, *Šûbh*
William L. Holladay, *The Root Šûbh in the Old Testament, With Particular Reference to Its Usages in Covenantal Contexts* (Leiden: Brill, 1958).

Holm-Nielsen, "Shiloh"
Svend Holm-Nielsen, "Shiloh (City)," *IDBSup*, 322–23.

Hubmann, *Untersuchungen*
Franz D. Hubmann, *Untersuchungen zu den Konfessionen, Jer 11,18—12,6 und Jer 15,10–21* (Forschung zur Bibel 30; Würzburg: Echter, 1978).

Hyatt
J. Philip Hyatt, "Introduction and Exegesis, Jeremiah," *IB* 5:775–1142.

Jacob, "Mourning"
Edmond Jacob, "Mourning," *IDB* 3:452–54.

Janzen
J. Gerald Janzen, *Studies in the Text of Jeremiah* (HSM 6; Cambridge: Harvard University, 1973).

Jastrow
Marcus Jastrow, *A Dictionary of the Targumim, the Talmud Babli and Yerushalmi, and the Midrashic Literature* (New York: Putnam, 1903).

Jerome
(S.) Hieronymi Presbyteri in Hieremiam Prophetam, Libri Sex (ed. Siegfried Reiter; CChr, Series Latina 74; Turnhout: Brepols, 1960).

Johnson, *Vitality of the Individual*
Aubrey R. Johnson, *The Vitality of the Individual in the Thought of Ancient Israel* (Cardiff: University of Wales, 1949).

Joüon, *Gramm.*
Paul Joüon, *Grammaire de l'Hébreu Biblique* (Rome: Pontifical Biblical Institute, 1947).

Kelso, "Pottery"
James L. Kelso, "Pottery," *IDB* 3:846–53.

Knox
Ronald Knox, *The Holy Bible, A Translation from the Latin Vulgate in the Light of the Hebrew and Greek Originals* (New York: Sheed & Ward, 1954).

König, *Syntax*
Eduard König, *Historisch-Comparative Syntax der hebräischen Sprache* (Leipzig: Hinrichs, 1897).

Kraus, *Psalmen*
Hans-Joachim Kraus, *Psalmen* (BKAT 15; Neukirchen: Neukirchener, 1961).

Kraus, *Worship*
Hans-Joachim Kraus, *Worship in Israel* (Richmond: Knox, 1966).

Kugel, *Poetry*
James F. Kugel, *The Idea of Biblical Poetry* (New Haven and London: Yale University, 1981).

Kumaki
F. Kenro Kumaki, "A New Look at Jer 4,19–22 and 10,19–21," *Annual of the Japanese Biblical Institute* 8 (1982) 113–22.

Lévi
Israel Lévi, *The Hebrew Text of the Book of Ecclesiasticus, Edited with Brief Notes and a Selected Glossary* (SSS 3; Leiden: Brill, 1904).

Limburg
James Limburg, "The Root ריב and the Prophetic Lawsuit Speeches," *JBL* 88 (1969) 291–304.

Lindblom, *Prophecy*
Johannes Lindblom, *Prophecy in Ancient Israel* (Oxford: Blackwell, 1963).

Lindblom, "Wisdom in the OT Prophets"
Johannes Lindblom, "Wisdom in the Old Testament Prophets," *Wisdom in Israel and in the Ancient Near East Presented to Professor Harold Henry Rowley by the Society for Old Testament Study in Association with the Editorial Board of Vetus Testamentum in Celebration of his Sixty-Fifth Birthday, 24 March 1955* (ed. Martin Noth and D. Winton Thomas; VTSup 3; Leiden: Brill, 1955) 192–204.

Lipiński, "באחרית הימים"
Edouard Lipiński, "באחרית הימים dans les textes préexiliques," *VT* 20 (1970) 445–50.

Lohfink, "Der junge Jeremia"
Norbert Lohfink, "Der junge Jeremia als Propagandist und Poet, Zum Grundstock von Jer 30—31," *Le Livre de Jérémie, Le Prophète et son milieu, les oracles et leur transmission* (ed. Pierre-Maurice Bogaert; BETL 54; Leuven: Leuven University, 1981) 351–68.

Long, "Reports of Visions"
Burke O. Long, "Reports of Visions Among the Prophets," *JBL* 95 (1976) 353–65.

Long, "Schemata"
Burke O. Long, "Two Question and Answer Schemata in the Prophets," *JBL* 90 (1971) 129–39.

Luckenbill, *ARAB*
Daniel D. Luckenbill, *Ancient Records of Assyria and Babylonia* (2 vols.; Chicago: University of Chicago, 1927; rep. New York: Greenwood, 1968).

Lundbom, *Jeremiah*
Jack R. Lundbom, *Jeremiah, A Study in Ancient Hebrew Rhetoric* (SBLDS 18; Missoula, MT: Scholars, 1975).

Malamat, "Twilight of Judah"
Abraham Malamat, "The Twilight of Judah," *Congress Volume, Edinburgh 1974* (VTSup 28; Leiden: Brill, 1975) 123–45.

March, "Prophecy"
W. Eugene March, "Prophecy," *Old Testament Form Criticism* (ed. John H. Hayes; San Antonio: Trinity University, 1974) 141–77.

Mayes, *Deuteronomy*
Arthur D. H. Mayes, *Deuteronomy* (Grand Rapids: Eerdmans, 1979).

Mays, *Micah*
James L. Mays, *Micah* (Philadelphia: Westminster, 1976).

McKane, "Jeremiah 13:12–14"
William McKane, "Jeremiah 13:12–14: A Problematic Proverb," *Israelite Wisdom, Theological and Literary Essays in Honor of Samuel Terrien* (ed. John

G. Gammie et al.; Missoula, MT: Scholars, 1978) 107–20.

McKane, "משא"
William McKane, "משא in Jeremiah 23$_{33-40}$," *Prophecy, Essays Presented to Georg Fohrer on His Sixty-fifth Birthday, 6 September 1980* (ed. John A. Emerton; BZAW 150; Berlin: de Gruyter, 1980) 35–54.

McKane, "Poison"
William McKane, "Poison, trial by ordeal and the cup of wrath," *VT* 30 (1980) 474–92.

McKane, *Prophets and Wise Men*
William McKane, *Prophets and Wise Men* (SBT 44; Naperville, IL: Allenson, 1965).

McKane, *Proverbs*
William McKane, *Proverbs, A New Approach* (Philadelphia: Westminster, 1970).

Mendenhall, *Tenth Generation*
George E. Mendenhall, *The Tenth Generation, The Origins of the Biblical Tradition* (Baltimore: Johns Hopkins, 1973).

Meyer, *Jeremia*
Ivo Meyer, *Jeremia und die falsche Propheten* (Göttingen: Vandenhoeck & Ruprecht, 1977).

Michaelis
Johann D. Michaelis, *Observationes Philologicae et Criticae in Jeremiae Vaticinia et Threnos* (Göttingen: Vandenhoeck & Ruprecht, 1793).

Moffatt
James Moffatt, *A New Translation of the Bible, Containing the Old and New Testaments* (New York: Harper, 1934).

Montgomery, *Kings*
James A. Montgomery, *A Critical and Exegetical Commentary on the Books of Kings* (ICC; New York: Scribner's, 1951).

Muilenburg, "Covenantal Formulations"
James Muilenburg, "The Form and Structure of the Covenantal Formulations," *VT* 9 (1959) 347–65.

Naegelsbach
C. W. Eduard Naegelsbach, *The Book of the Prophet Jeremiah, Theologically and Homiletically Expounded* (New York: Scribner's, 1886).

Nicholson, *Jer. 1—25*
Ernest W. Nicholson, *The Book of the Prophet Jeremiah Chapters 1—25* (The Cambridge Bible Commentary on the New English Bible; Cambridge: Cambridge University, 1973).

Nicholson, *Preaching*
Ernest W. Nicholson, *Preaching to the Exiles, A Study of the Prose Tradition in the Book of Jeremiah* (Oxford: Blackwell, 1970).

Niditch, *Symbolic Vision*
Susan Niditch, *The Symbolic Vision in Biblical Tradition* (HSM 30; Chico, CA: Scholars, 1983).

Noth, *Könige*
Martin Noth, *Könige I. 1-16* (BKAT 9/1; Neukirchen: Neukirchener, 1968).

Nötscher
Friedrich Nötscher, *Das Buch Jeremias* (Die Heilige Schrift des Alten Testaments 7, 2; Bonn: Hanstein, 1934).

O'Connor, *Structure*
Michael Patrick O'Connor, *Hebrew Verse Structure* (Winona Lake, IN: Eisenbrauns, 1980).

Oosterhoff, "Detail"
Berend J. Oosterhoff, "Ein Detail aus der Weisheitslehre (Jer. 9,11ff.)," *Travels in the World of the Old Testament, Studies Presented to Professor M. A. Beek on the Occasion of his 65th Birthday* (ed. M. S. H. G. Heerma van Voss; Assen: Van Gorcum, 1974) 197–203.

Ottosson, *Gilead*
Magnus Ottosson, *Gilead, Tradition and History* (ConB, OT Series 3; Lund: Gleerup, 1969).

Overholt, *Falsehood*
Thomas W. Overholt, *The Threat of Falsehood, A Study in the Theology of the Book of Jeremiah* (SBT 2d Series 16; Naperville, IL: Allenson, 1970).

Overholt, "Idolatry"
Thomas W. Overholt, "The Falsehood of Idolatry: An Interpretation of Jer. x. 1—16," *JTS* NS 16 (1965) 1–12.

Pedersen
Johannes Pedersen, *Israel, Its Life and Culture* (Copenhagen: Branner; London: Oxford University, 1926, 1940).

Percy, *Lead*
John Percy, *The Metallurgy of Lead, Including Desilverization and Cupellation* (London: Murray, 1870).

Percy, *Silver and Gold*
John Percy, *Metallurgy: The Art of Extracting Metals from Their Ores, Silver and Gold, Part I* (London: Murray, 1880).

Petersen, *Late Prophecy*
David L. Petersen, *Late Israelite Prophecy: Studies in Deutero-Prophetic Literature and in Chronicles* (SBLMS 23; Missoula, MT: Scholars, 1977).

Pohlmann, *Studien*
Karl-Friedrich Pohlmann, *Studien zum Jeremiabuch, Ein Beitrag zur Frage nach der Entstehung des Jeremiabuches* (FRLANT 118; Göttingen: Vandenhoeck & Ruprecht, 1978).

Pope, *Song of Songs*
Marvin H. Pope, *Song of Songs* (AB 7C; Garden City, NY: Doubleday, 1977).

Porten, *Elephantine*
Bezalel Porten, *Archives from Elephantine, The Life of an Ancient Jewish Military Colony* (Berkeley and Los Angeles: University of California, 1968).

Post, *Flora*
George E. Post, *Flora of Syria, Palestine and Sinai* (Beirut: American, 1932–33).

Preuss, *Verspottung*
Horst Dietrich Preuss, *Verspottung fremder*

Religionen im Alten Testament (BWANT 92; Stuttgart: Kohlhammer, 1971).

von Rad, *Deuteronomy*
Gerhard von Rad, *Deuteronomy* (Philadelphia: Westminster, 1966).

von Rad, *OT Theology 1, 2*
Gerhard von Rad, *Old Testament Theology 1, 2* (New York: Harper, 1962, 1965).

von Rad, *Studies in Deuteronomy*
Gerhard von Rad, *Studies in Deuteronomy* (SBT 9; Naperville, IL: Allenson, 1953).

von Rad, *Wisdom*
Gerhard von Rad, *Wisdom in Israel* (Nashville: Abingdon, 1972).

Ramsey, "Speech-Forms"
George W. Ramsey, "Speech-Forms in Hebrew Law and Prophetic Oracles," *JBL* 96 (1977) 45–58.

Reventlow, *Liturgie*
Henning Graf von Reventlow, *Liturgie und prophetisches Ich bei Jeremia* (Gütersloh: Gütersloher [Gerd Mohn], 1963).

Rietzschel, *Urrolle*
Claus Rietzschel, *Das Problem der Urrolle, Ein Beitrag zur Redaktionsgeschichte des Jeremiabuches* (Gütersloh: Gütersloher, 1966).

de Rossi
Giovanni B. de Rossi, *Variae Lectiones Veteris Testamenti, III* (Parma: Bodoni, 1786).

Rudolph
Wilhelm Rudolph, *Jeremia* (HAT 12; Tübingen: Mohr, 1968).

Sakenfeld
Katherine D. Sakenfeld, *The Meaning of Ḥesed in the Hebrew Bible* (HSM 17; Missoula, MT: Scholars, 1978).

Sawyer, "Partridge"
John F. A. Sawyer, "A Note on the Brooding Partridge in Jeremiah xvii 11," *VT* 28 (1978) 324–29.

Scharbert, "ארר"
Josef Scharbert, "ארר," *TDOT* 1:405–18.

Sebastian Schmidt
Sebastian Schmidt, *Commentarii in Librum Prophetiarum Jeremiae* (Frankfurt am Main, 1706).

Schmidt, *Exodus*
Werner H. Schmidt, *Exodus* (BKAT 2; Neukirchen: Neukirchener, 1974–).

Skinner
John Skinner, *Prophecy and Religion, Studies in the Life of Jeremiah* (Cambridge: Cambridge University, 1922).

Skweres, "Strafgrunderfragung"
Dieter E. Skweres, "Das Motiv der Strafgrunderfragung in biblischen und neuassyrischen Texten," *BZ* NF 14 (1970) 181–97.

Soggin, *Joshua*
J. Alberto Soggin, *Joshua* (Philadelphia: Westminster, 1972).

Speiser, *Genesis*
Ephraim A. Speiser, *Genesis* (AB 1; Garden City, NY: Doubleday, 1964).

Stoebe, "Seelsorge"
Hans Joachim Stoebe, "Seelsorge und Mitleiden bei Jeremia, Ein exegetischer Versuch," *Wort und Dienst* NF 4 (1955) 116–34.

Tawil, "Lexicographical Note"
Hayim Tawil, "Hebrew צלח/הצלח, Akkadian *ešēru/ šūšuru*: A Lexicographical Note," *JBL* 95 (1976) 405–13.

Thiel, *Jer 1—25*
Winfried Thiel, *Die deuteronomistische Redaktion von Jer 1—25* (WMANT 41; Neukirchen: Neukirchener, 1973).

Thomas, "מלאו"
D. Winton Thomas, "מלאו in Jeremiah IV.5: A Military Term," *JJS* 3 (1952) 47–52.

Thompson
John Arthur Thompson, *The Book of Jeremiah* (NICOT; Grand Rapids: Eerdmans, 1980).

Toy, *Proverbs*
Crawford H. Toy, *A Critical and Exegetical Commentary on the Book of Proverbs* (ICC; New York: Scribner's, 1899).

de Vaux, *Ancient Israel*
Roland de Vaux, *Ancient Israel, Its Life and Institutions* (New York: McGraw-Hill, 1961).

Volz
Paul Volz, *Der Prophet Jeremia* (KAT 10; Leipzig: Deichert, 1928).

Wanke, *Baruchschrift*
Gunther Wanke, *Untersuchungen zur sogenannten Baruchscrift* (BZAW 122; Berlin: de Gruyter, 1971).

Weinfeld, *Deuteronomy*
Moshe Weinfeld, *Deuteronomy and the Deuteronomic School* (Oxford: Clarendon, 1972).

Weinfeld, "Metamorphosis"
Moshe Weinfeld, "Jeremiah and the Spiritual Metamorphosis of Israel," *ZAW* 88 (1976) 17–55.

Weippert, *Prosareden*
Helga Weippert, *Die Prosareden des Jeremiabuches* (BZAW 132; Berlin: de Gruyter, 1973).

Weiser
Artur Weiser, *Das Buch Jeremia* (ATD 20/21; Göttingen: Vandenhoeck & Ruprecht, 1969).

Westermann, *Basic Forms*
Claus Westermann, *Basic Forms of Prophetic Speech* (Philadelphia: Westminster, 1967).

Westermann, *Genesis*
Claus Westermann, *Genesis* (BKAT 1; Neukirchen: Neukirchener, 1974–82).

Westermann, *Isaiah 40—66*
Claus Westermann, *Isaiah 40—66* (Philadelphia: Westminster, 1969).

Whybray, *Intellectual Tradition*
Roger N. Whybray, *The Intellectual Tradition in the Old Testament* (BZAW 135; Berlin: de Gruyter, 1974).

Wildberger, *Jesaja*
Hans Wildberger, *Jesaja* (BKAT 10; Neukirchen: Neukirchener, 1972–82).

Wilson, *Prophecy and Society*
Robert R. Wilson, *Prophecy and Society in Ancient Israel* (Philadelphia: Fortress, 1980).

Wiseman, *Chronicles*
Donald J. Wiseman, *Chronicles of Chaldaean Kings (626–556 B.C.)* (London: British Museum, 1956).

Wisser
Laurent Wisser, *Jérémie, Critique de la vie sociale, Justice sociale et connaissance de Dieu dans le livre de Jérémie* (Geneva: Labor et Fides, 1982).

Wolff, *Anthropology*
Hans Walter Wolff, *Anthropology of the Old Testament* (Philadelphia: Fortress, 1974).

Wolff, *Hosea*
Hans Walter Wolff, *Hosea* (Hermeneia; Philadelphia: Fortress, 1974).

Wolff, *Joel and Amos*
Hans Walter Wolff, *Joel and Amos* (Hermeneia; Philadelphia: Fortress, 1977).

Wolff, *Micha*
Hans Walter Wolff, *Micha* (BKAT 14/4; Neukirchen: Neukirchener, 1982).

van der Woude, *Micha*
A. S. van der Woude, *Micha* (De Prediking van het Oude Testament; Nijkerk: Callenbach, 1976).

Yadin, *Warfare*
Yigael Yadin, *The Art of Warfare in Biblical Lands* (New York: McGraw-Hill, 1963).

Zimmerli, *Ezekiel 1, 2*
Walther Zimmerli, *Ezekiel 1, 2* (Hermeneia; Philadelphia: Fortress, 1979, 1983).

Zimmerli, *Hope*
Walther Zimmerli, *Man and His Hope in the Old Testament* (SBT 2d Series 20; Naperville, IL: Allenson, 1971).

Zorell
Franz Zorell, *Lexicon Hebraicum et Aramaicum Veteris Testamenti* (Rome: Pontifical Biblical Institute, 1962).

The translation of Jeremiah 1—25 presented by
Professor Holladay in this volume is new, and is based
on a thorough study of the ancient texts. Words of the
translation enclosed within parentheses ( ) amplify
the sense of the literal Hebrew, while angle brackets
⟨ ⟩ or ⟪ ⟫ indicate emendations of *M* discussed in
the textual notes (see Author's Foreword, p. xi). Words
of the biblical text enclosed by square brackets [ ] are
regarded by the author as secondary interpolations or
redactional supplements to the Book of Jer; within
these supplements, braces { } enclose segments of text
considered to be even later interpolations. Reverse
angle brackets ⟩ ⟨ are occasionally used to set off
material less certainly deemed to be secondary.

Pictured on the endpapers is a fragment of 4Q Jer[b]
containing Jeremiah 9:22—10:18 in the "short
edition" of Jeremiah known elsewhere only from the
Old Greek (*G*) Version. The MS. is written in a
Hasmonean script (mid-first century B.C.E.). (Cf. Frank
M. Cross, *The Ancient Library of Qumran,* rev. ed. [New
York: Doubleday Anchor Books, 1961], 187, esp. n.
38. Photo: courtesy of the Department of Antiquities
and Museums, State of Israel.)

I have become convinced that the data for a reconstruction of the chronology of Jrm's career, and for the establishment of fairly secure settings for his words and actions, are attainable, and this commentary is based upon such a reconstruction. A thorough presentation of the data must await the Introduction in *Jeremiah 2*, but a preliminary survey[1] is called for here (see Foreword).

Almost every suggestion that I offer here could be challenged, and some are quite different from anything heretofore proposed. At the outset I part company with those who assume that Jrm began to prophesy in 627,[2] and with those who assume that much of the prose material in the book was shaped by a circle of Deuteronomistic editors.[3] Of course modest expansions in the tradition were made during and after the exile, but I have a different explanation for the so-called Deuteronomistic prose of the book (see sec. 2 below).

1. Birth (627); Josiah's Reform (622)
I take it that the "thirteenth year of Josiah" (1:2) is the date of the prophet's birth, 627, not the date of the beginning of his career.[4] The theological burden of the call in 1:5 suggests it—that Yahweh's action through Jrm began in the womb—and many other bits of evidence point in the same direction (see sec. 6, and the exegesis of 15:16).[5] If 627 is his birth date, then the puzzle of why we find in the book no clear judgment for or against

Josiah's reform in 622 is clear: Jrm's proclamations lie years in the future. I propose, then, that the prophet was born when the kingship of Josiah was well along, a time when that king was beginning to feel free of the pressure of Assyria.

Jrm would have been a boy of five years at the time of Josiah's reform, a reform (so the consensus) triggered by the discovery of an early form of Deuteronomy.[6] Since his father Hilkiah was a priest in Anathoth (1:1), and since as a consequence of the reform the cult became centralized in Jerusalem, one can imagine the impression made on the boy by the shift of his father's activity from Anathoth to Jerusalem.

2. The Septennial Reading of Deuteronomy
Now I assume that the injunction of Deut 31:9–13 was taken seriously, that the form which Deuteronomy took in those days was recited every seven years at the feast of booths (tabernacles), thus at the end of September or the beginning of October. If the proclamation of Deuteronomy was initially in 622, then subsequent readings would have taken place in the autumn of 615, 608, 601, 594, and 587. It is my proposal that these occasions offer a chronological structure for the career of Jrm, and most specifically that several of the parade examples of Deuteronomistic prose in the book are Jrm's various counterproclamations at those times when Deuteronomy

---

1 Note that this essay does not deal with every text, only a selection. It should also be noted that I assume a spring (Nisan) new year; for arguments cautiously in favor of the Nisan new year see David J. A. Clines, "The Evidence for an Autumnal New Year in Pre-exilic Israel Reconsidered," *JBL* 93 (1974) 22–40, against Simon J. De Vries, "Chronology of the OT," *IDB* 1:594–98, and "Chronology, OT," *IDBSup*, 163–64. David J. A. Clines, "New Year," *IDBSup*, 626–27, tries to weigh the arguments.

2 Most scholars, e.g., John Bright, *Jeremiah* (AB 21; Garden City, NY: Doubleday, 1965) LXXXVII.

3 On this assumption see, e.g., Winfried Thiel, *Die deuteronomistische Redaktion von Jer 1—25* (WMANT 41; Neukirchen: Neukirchener, 1973), and *Die deuteronomistische Redaktion von Jer 26—45* (WMANT 52; Neukirchen: Neukirchener, 1981); Ernest W. Nicholson, *Preaching to the Exiles, A Study of the Prose Tradition in the Book of Jeremiah* (Oxford: Blackwell, 1970), and Robert P. Carroll, *From Chaos to Covenant, Prophecy in the Book of Jeremiah* (New York: Crossroads, 1981).

4 So also J. Philip Hyatt, "Introduction and Exegesis, Jeremiah," *IB* 5:779, 798. For full bibliography for and against the proposal see exegesis of 1:1.

5 See William L. Holladay, *Jeremiah, Spokesman Out of Time* (New York: Pilgrim, 1974) 17–22, "A Fresh Look at 'Source B' and 'Source C' in Jeremiah," *VT* 25 (1975) 409–10, and "A Coherent Chronology of Jeremiah's Early Career," *Le Livre de Jérémie, Le Prophète et son milieu, les oracles et leur transmission* (ed. Pierre-Maurice Bogaert; BETL 54; Leuven: Leuven University, 1981) 58–73.

6 See, e.g., John Bright, *A History of Israel* (Philadelphia: Westminster, 1981) 317–22.

1

was recited. This proposal, as I shall show, is most convincing for 594 and is plausible for 587; beyond those dates I have suggestions for Jrm's proclamations in 608 and 601[7] (as well as at times other than those occasions when Deuteronomy was read, of course).

3. A Propagandist for Josiah (615–609)

As I have already indicated, Deuteronomy would have been recited again in the autumn of 615; by our reckoning Jrm would have been twelve years old. With hesitation I suggest the possibility that this was the occasion for his responding to his call (1:4–10): vv 7 and 9 are very similar to Deut 18:18, the word to Moses about a prophet like Moses in time to come. Is this not a likely occasion? Jrm himself protests that he is "only a youth [נַעַר]" (v 6). I have elsewhere proposed that Jrm's perception of his call was shaped by traditions regarding Moses and Samuel.[8] As for Samuel, there is the tradition, doubtless known to Jrm, of Yahweh's speaking to the boy Samuel: 1 Sam 2:18, 11, 16; 3:1, 8 all refer to him as a "boy" [נַעַר]. (And one may recall that Jesus is recorded as discussing matters with the teachers in the temple when he was twelve years old [Luke 2:41–47].) In any event it is clear to me now[9] that during a period of time before Josiah was killed on the battlefield of Megiddo in the spring of 609, the youthful Jrm acted to support the king's program of cultic and political reunion between the north and south (2 Kgs 23:15–18).

Some of the evidence for this activity of the young Jrm is laid out in a recent study by Norbert Lohfink.[10] It has long been recognized that some at least of chapters 30—31 may have been directed to the north;[11] Lohfink has subjected these chapters to careful analysis and isolates 30:5–7, 12–15, 18–21; 31:2–6 and 15–22 as having that setting.[12] He suggests, then, that the young Jrm pro-

claimed Yahweh's initiative in Josiah's effort to win the north ("Ephraim") back to political and religious union with Jerusalem.[13]

I would only add that there are traces of the prophet's words to the north in chapters 2—3 as well, specifically in 2:4–9 ("families" in v 4 is really "tribes," a word which he uses more than once for the northern tribes); 3:1–2, 4–5, 12, 14–15 (one notes "north" in v 12 and "family" [= tribe] in v 15), portions of 18, 19, 21a, 22–23, the core of 24–25, and 4:1–2. Of course the material in chapters 2—3 and 30—31 directed to the north was incorporated later by the prophet in the context of addresses to the south.[14]

4. From the Temple Sermon (609) to the Battle of Carchemish (605)

In the year 609 events moved quickly. King Josiah was killed at Megiddo in the spring in a three-cornered fight. Assyria had been defeated by Babylonia in 612, and Assyria had only the remnant of an army left in the field. Egypt, recognizing Babylon to be the new enemy, marched north through Palestine to bolster the fading Assyrian force. Josiah tried to interpose his own army to prevent the passage of the Egyptians and was killed. His second son, Jehoahaz, was put on the throne of Judah but ruled for only three months; the victorious Egyptian army deposed him and took him to Egypt where he disappeared from history (compare 22:10–12), and his older brother, Jehoiakim, was placed on the throne as an Egyptian vassal. By the end of that September, then, Judah had seen three kings on the throne in the year,[15] and in the swirl of these events Jrm proclaimed the first dated utterance of his career, the so-called temple sermon, 7:1–12.[16]

This sermon may be dated by the narrative account in

---

7   See now William L. Holladay, "A Proposal for Reflections in the Book of Jeremiah of the Seven-Year Recitation of the Law in Deuteronomy (Deut 31,10–13," *Deuteronomium, Entstehung, Gestalt und Botschaft* (ed. Norbert Lohfink; BETL 68; Leuven: Leuven University, 1985) 326–28.

8   William L. Holladay, "The Background of Jeremiah's Self-Understanding: Moses, Samuel, and Psalm 22," *JBL* 83 (1964) 153–64; "Jeremiah and Moses: Further Observations," *JBL* 85 (1966) 17–27; *Spokesman*, 26–28.

9   Against Holladay, *Spokesman*, 23–24.

10   Norbert Lohfink, "Der junge Jeremia als Propagandist und Poet, Zum Grundstock von Jer 30—31," *Le Livre de Jérémie, Le Prophète et son milieu, les oracles et leur transmission* (ed. Pierre-Maurice Bogaert; BETL 54; Leuven: Leuven University, 1981), 351–68.

11   See, for example, Bright.

12   I agree, only adding 31:1aαb and 9b to this material.

13   Compare Bright, *History*, 322.

14   For this process see Holladay, *Spokesman*, 111–14.

15   Bright, *History*, 324–25.

16   The "sermon" is usually reckoned to continue

chapter 26: it was uttered in the "beginning" of the reign of Jehoiakim (v 10), thus evidently sometime between September 609 and March 608, probably at the feast of booths in September/October 609.[17] By the reckoning adopted here the prophet would be eighteen years old.

The sermon is a call to repentance: "make good your ways and your doings" (7:3, 5); if the people do make their ways good, then Yahweh will let them dwell in the land (v 7). Such a call to repentance is implied in three other verses in the first part of the book—4:4, 4:14, and 6:8. Of these, 4:14 says it straight out: "O Jerusalem, wash your heart from wickedness, that you may be saved." The other two say it with "lest" (= "so that . . . not"): "Circumcise yourselves to Yahweh . . . lest my wrath go forth like fire" (4:4); "Be warned, O Jerusalem, lest I be alienated from you" (6:8). If the people repent, Yahweh will stay his hand and not bring destruction upon them.

This is also the purpose of the first scroll that Jrm dictated to his scribe Baruch in the course of 605 (36:1–8)—the purpose is to preserve Yahweh's words of judgment on Israel and Judah which are to warn the people: it is possible they may repent, in which case Yahweh will stay his hand (36:3, 7). One must, therefore, understand the words of judgment from Yahweh during the period from 609 at least through 605 to be scenarios of destruction, a proclamation of what Yahweh is capable of doing to his people.

By a variety of paths I have concluded that in the first dictated scroll were included the following: the call of 1:4–10 and an early recension at least of 1:11–16; 2:1–25, 29–37;[18] 3:1–2, 4–5, 12–15, portions of 18; 3:19, 21–23, the core of 24–25, 4:1–4, 5–8, 13–18, 29–31; 6:1–8; and 7:1–12.[19] Beyond the call, these are words of accusation and scenarios of punishment all of which

imply the call to repentance expressed in 4:4, 4:14, 6:8, and 7:1–12. These passages, then, by my proposal, would have been heard in the period 609–605.

By content and style I locate another noteworthy unit from this period, the visit to the potter's workshop (18:1–12). In this passage I submit that רֶגַע (vv 7 and 9) does not carry the meaning "at any time" (*RSV*) but its normal meaning "suddenly." Yahweh has plans for ill and for good for nations and for kingdoms. But he can suddenly change his mind if the behavior of such a nation or kingdom makes the change appropriate: he can change his mind about the evil he intends to do with nation A, and he can change his mind about the good he intends to do with nation B. Will he call off the mobilization plans he has in mind for Babylon against Judah? Repent, repent!

I have already indicated (sec. 2) that in the autumn of 608 there would have been a recitation of Deuteronomy. The little poem in 2:2–3 carries overtones of the festival of booths: thus both Lev 23:39 and Deut 16:13–15, which make provision for that festival, use the term "harvest" (תְּבוּאָה) which occurs in 2:3. The introductory words, literally "Go call out in the ears of" (2:2), suggest an audience at a festival: the instructions for reciting Deuteronomy use the same phrase (Deut 31:11). If 2:2–3 was proclaimed by Jrm in the autumn of 608, it cannot be all he uttered at that time: perhaps much or all of the material above listed from 2:1 to 4:4 was proclaimed—one notes the likeness of 4:4 to Deut 10:16.

One cannot ascertain why in 605 Jrm was debarred from the temple area (36:5), but events in that year had put a new face on the political map of Judah: in May or June of 605 the Egyptian army was dealt a stunning defeat by the Babylonian army under the command of Nebuchadrezzar, who was still crown prince, at the city

---

through v 15, but on stylistic and rhetorical grounds I conclude that vv 13–15 were added at the time of the second scroll: see sec. 6.

17 "Beginning" is evidently a technical term for "accession year," the partial year of a reign before the new year, which I assume was in the spring (see n. 1, and see Bright, p. 169). The feast of booths is a natural occasion during this interval when a large crowd would assemble for worship (7:2; 26:2).

18 I take "Assyria" in vv 18 and 36 to be the poetic designation of the power in Mesopotamia at the time (i.e., Babylon); so also John M. Berridge, *Prophet,*

People, and the Word of Yahweh, An Examination of Form and Content in the Proclamation of the Prophet Jeremiah (Zurich: EVZ, 1970) 81. Compare Zech 10:10, 11.

19 This list differs slightly from the one in William L. Holladay, "The Identification of the Two Scrolls of Jeremiah," *VT* 30 (1980) 452–67, esp. 464–65.

of Carchemish, in northern Syria; and later in the same year the remnant of the Egyptian army was defeated in central Syria. If the leadership of Judah had been convinced after Megiddo (609) that Egypt was invincible, they now thought so no more: sometime during this period Jehoiakim switched sides and became a vassal of Babylon (2 Kgs 24:1), probably in 604.[20]

If Jrm's first scroll was dictated in 605, and if, as I believe, it included material about the foe from the north (passages including 4:14 and 6:8), then the most plausible context for such utterances would be in the weeks just after the results of Carchemish became known in Judah.

5. The Drought Begins; The King Burns the Scroll (601)

Eventually Jrm's scroll came to the attention of the king, who burned it (36:23). But there is a chronological difficulty with that event which is crucial to my reconstruction.

The text of *M* states that the scroll was burned in the ninth month of Jehoiakim's fifth year (36:9), that is, November/December 604. The text of *G*, however, gives a date in the ninth month of the eighth year,[21] that is, November/December 601. Lohfink has pointed out[22] that the historical circumstances of 601 make that date far more plausible than 604 for the burning of the scroll. Thus, in November/December 604, the Babylonian army had marched west to the Mediterranean Sea and south along the Palestinian coastal plain, sacking the Philistine city of Ashkelon.[23] This event clearly threatened Judah, and a scroll that included words of warning about Yahweh's sending a foe from the north would hardly have been burned even by so insensitive a king as Jehoiakim. But in November/December 601 the Babylonian army, by then fighting in the Egyptian delta, was dealt a defeat by the Egyptian forces and withdrew to Babylon.[24] If the defeat suggested that Babylon was nothing but a "paper tiger," then one has a plausible

motive for the king's contemptuous burning of the scroll.

Text-critically, too, we must choose "eighth" rather than "fifth"; it is the more difficult reading: one could well imagine a scribe consciously or unconsciously changing "eighth" (השמנית) to "fifth" (החמשית), thus assuming a gap of only one year from the "fourth year" mentioned in v 1, but one cannot imagine a motive for the reverse change.

If the burning of the scroll is to be dated in 601 rather than in 604, then the occasion of that fast called by the king (36:9), in the context of which the scroll was burned, was not the threat signaled by the sacking of Ashkelon;[25] it must have been for another reason. I propose with Wilhelm Rudolph[26] that the fast was proclaimed because of a drought, indeed that this is the date for the great drought presupposed by 14:1—15:9; one notes that that passage likewise mentions a fast (14:12). One must imagine, then, perhaps a spring without rain, certainly a hot summer and an autumn without rain, a drought lasting until the "ninth month"; Rudolph cites a passage from the Mishna, "If the first of Chislev [= November/December] was come and no rain had fallen, the court enjoins on the congregation three days of fasting."[27]

Now the autumn of 601 is the next occasion for a recitation of Deuteronomy. If my reasoning to this point is correct, then that celebration of the festival of booths already suffered under the drought. Is there a passage of Jer suggestive both of a recitation of Deuteronomy and of a drought? There is: it is 8:4–10a + 13.[28] In v 8 the prophet mocks those who assume that "the law of Yahweh is with us," and in v 13 we hear that "there are no grapes on the vine, nor figs on the fig tree; even the leaves are withered." I submit that this passage was recited on the occasion of the festival of booths in the autumn of 601. Such a dating in turn suggests that the similar passage 6:9–15 has a setting in the same period. A variety of evidence suggests that 5:20–29 is from the same period (v 25 indicates a drought), and since the

---

20 Bright, *History*, 327.
21 The passage is 43:9 in the LXX.
22 Norbert Lohfink, "Die Gattung der 'Historischen Kurzgeschichte' in den letzten Jahren von Juda und in der Zeit des Babylonischen Exils," *ZAW* 90 (1978) 324–28.
23 Bright, *History*, 326.
24 Ibid., 327.

25 Against Bright, *History*, 327, and *Jeremiah*, 180–82.
26 Wilhelm Rudolph, *Jeremia* (HAT 12; Tübingen: Mohr [Siebeck], 1968), 233.
27 *m. Ta'anit* 1:5.
28 Verses 10b–12 are a doublet of 6:13–15 and are lacking in *G*; they are thus secondary here. See Bright, *Jeremiah*, 50.

refrain of 5:29 is found also in 5:9 and 9:8, one may assume the same period as the appropriate setting for 5:1–9 and 8:14—9:9 (does 8:20 have a background in the same drought in the same season?).

6. The Word of Irrevocable Punishment; Jrm's Announcement of Celibacy (601–600)

The king burned Jrm's scroll. The consequence was a word of judgment from Yahweh to the king (36:29–31), a detail which has not generally been noticed. The king is to be without successors on the throne, and his dead body is to be denied burial, but in addition "I will punish . . . his offspring and his servants for their iniquity; I will bring upon them, and upon the inhabitants of Jerusalem, and upon the men of Judah, all the evil that I have pronounced against them, but they would not hear." That is to say, the king's burning the scroll was the catalyst that led the prophet to the conviction that Yahweh's words of judgment against the people were no longer simply scenarios for warning, but rather plans to be carried out: repentance was no longer to be expected, and the people stood under irrevocable judgment.

This is a crucial change in Jrm's perception, and we can date it to November/December 601. Then and for many years thereafter the prophet insisted that Yahweh's judgment was inevitable. After the king burned the scroll, Jrm took a second scroll and dictated to Baruch all the words of the first scroll and new words as well (36:28, 32). The new words would be ones he had delivered since 605, and words that came to him in the light of the new situation after the king burned the scroll. But even the old words, those from the period 609–605, would be seen in the light of his new understanding, that Yahweh's punishment is now irrevocable. Was this the occasion when he broke the flask (19:1–15), when he was locked in the stocks overnight (20:1–6)?

I have already cited the long section 14:1—15:9, a passage that has the drought for a background. It is in the form of a liturgy; it is probable indeed that it is a "counter-liturgy" in the context of the fast proclaimed by the king (36:9). There it is said that Yahweh will not listen to the intercessory prayers for the people (15:1–4); nothing is ahead but destruction (15:5–9). The word that

Yahweh will not listen to Jeremiah's intercession is found elsewhere as well: 7:16–20 is a striking example.

I have pointed out that Jrm felt called to be the prophet like Moses of Deut 18:18 (see sec. 3). In contrast, Alonso Schökel in a recent study[29] suggests that Jrm was an anti-Moses figure: Moses had been the great intercessor, while Jrm is bidden not to intercede (15:1). I propose that it is precisely at this point in his career that Jrm shifted in his self-understanding.

The conviction that Yahweh is determined to punish his people is new at this point; one may thus conclude that the call to Jrm to abstain from marriage (16:1–4) cannot be dated before this time, since it is the sign par excellence of the extinguishing of hope for the people. If the prophet was born in 627, he would now be twenty-six years old. (Here is one more argument against the assumption that 627 was the date when he began to prophesy; by that assumption he would be so old by 601 as to make the date less than plausible for such a declaration.)[30]

Jrm declared his celibacy, and he uttered words declaring the extinguishing of hope for the people. The result, as one might expect, was persecution by the optimistic prophets; this is suggested by 14:13–16, and by the collection of material on those prophets in 23:9–32 (one notes a word about the drought in 23:10). The rhetoric of these passages bespeaks a prophet whose credentials are being challenged both by the optimistic prophets and by historical events; if Babylon was a "paper tiger" in the struggle with Egypt, then Jrm is a false prophet and must die—so the optimistic prophets would have read Deut 18:20!

There is another passage that speaks both to the crisis in Jrm's vocation and to the drought, and that is 4:9–12: Yahweh is deceiving the people through the optimistic prophets (compare 4:10 with 14:13), and a desiccating wind (both a physical wind and the metaphorical wind of the Babylonian army) is bearing down on the people (4:11–12).

I conclude that 4:9–12 was an addition in the second

---

29   Luis Alonso Schökel, "Jeremías como anti-Moisés," *De la Tôrah au Messie, Mélanges Henri Cazelles* (ed. M. Carrez, J. Doré, and P. Grelot; Paris: Desclée, 1981)

245–54.
30   See Holladay, "Coherent Chronology." Rudolph struggles with the same problem, pp. 111–12.

scroll; its companion 4:19–28 was as well.[31] The terrible vision of cosmic chaos in 4:23–26 is really completed by vv 27–28, and the diction of v 28a is close to that of 14:2a: that vision finds its origin in the drought.[32] And as in sec. 4 above, I must confine myself to listing other additions in the second scroll—2:26–28; 3:2b–3 and 20; 5:10–17; 6:9–15, 16–26, 27–30—without justifying my decisions.[33]

7. The First Confessions (601–600)

The opposition of the optimistic prophets at the end of 601 and early in 600 gave rise to some of the so-called confessions of Jrm; one notes in the first confessional sequence (11:18—12:6) a sudden word about the drought (12:4).

The whole set of issues involved in the setting of the confessions, the laments of Jrm to Yahweh, and the perceived answers from Yahweh is too complex for treatment here (see the essay "Jeremiah's Confessions: Introduction," before 11:18, below). It is sufficient to say that I believe a few of these passages emerged during this period, that they were expanded by more confessions in a similar crisis in the prophet's career in the summer of 594 (see sec. 9), and that it was in that latter crisis that Jrm "went public" with this material.

The idea that those persecuting Jrm were the optimistic prophets is not a new one,[34] but it has been demonstrated with fresh cogency in the dissertation of Franz D. Hubmann.[35] One notes, to take a single datum, the resemblance between 11:23 and 23:12.

By my analysis the passages that find their setting at this time are 11:18–23 (minus "the men of Anathoth" in v 21 and "upon the men of Anathoth" in v 23); 12:1–5; 15:15–19; 17:5–8 (plus perhaps vv 9–10) and 18:18–23.[36] In these words Jrm pours out to Yahweh his sense of abandonment over against his persecutors: rather than being destined for slaughter himself (11:19), he affirms that it is his persecutors who should be slaughtered (12:3). He is puzzled why his circumstances turn the norms of Psalm 1 upside down (12:1b) so that it is the "wicked" (or "guilty") who thrive. His opponents he calls "merrymakers" (15:17), another clue that they are optimistic in their view of the nation's future. He describes Yahweh in terms appropriate to an outer drought as well as an inner one (15:18). Yahweh calls him to repent (15:19), and, by my analysis, he affirms his repentance (17:5–8), again in a variation of Psalm 1, but using words appropriate to a period of drought.

8. The First Siege of Jerusalem (598–597)

If the Babylonian army paused in its depredations in the year 600, leaving Jrm puzzled, the pause did not last long; in December 598 Jehoiakim died (was he assassinated?),[37] his son Jehoiachin came to the throne, Nebuchadrezzar besieged Jerusalem, the city fell in March 597, and the young king, members of the royal family, and other leading citizens were led off to exile.

Beyond words from Jrm about the fate of Jehoiachin (22:24–30), is there any material datable to this siege of the city? There is: 10:17–22.[38] There the city is contemptuously addressed by Yahweh as a refugee woman: I would translate v 17 "Gather up your bundle from the

31 On this matter see in more detail Holladay, "Identification," 460–61.

32 I revocalize the first word of v 27b from וְכָלָה to וְכָלֹה; the resultant line will read "And none of it [i.e., the earth] will I (re)make." This terrible utterance is thus consistent with the rest of the passage. I assume that the negative is secondary in the similar 5:10a to bring it into line with Jrm's word in 30:11 which he uttered before Jerusalem fell in 587 (see sec. 10).

33 See n. 18.

34 It was suggested by the Jewish commentator Isaac Abrabanel in the fifteenth century and by the Christian commentator Sebastian Schmidt at the end of the seventeenth.

35 Franz D. Hubmann, *Untersuchungen zu den Konfessionen, Jer 11,18—12,6 und Jer 15,10–21* (Forschung zur Bibel 30; Würzburg: Echter, 1978), *passim*, esp. 136, 279–81.

36 For the judgment that "men of Anathoth" is secondary in 11:21 and 23, and that 12:6 and 15:20–21 are secondary, see Hubmann, *Untersuchungen*, 75–107, 169–75, 290–95; for argumentation in favor of linking 17:5–8 with 15:18–19, see Holladay, *Spokesman*, 98–100.

37 Bright, *History*, 327.

38 So also Bright, 73.

ground, O you enthroned under siege!" Jerusalem is "enthroned" (יֹשֶׁבְתִּי) geographically above her valleys, but she must get down from her throne to pick up her knapsack like any other refugee. If there is anything like a chronological sequence to many of the passages in this portion of the book (and I now believe there is), then dating 8:14—9:8 to the time of the drought in the latter part of 601 and dating 10:17–22 to the siege of early 597 suggest that 9:16–21 is to be dated some time before the siege, perhaps just before the siege.

9. The Jerusalem Conference and Its Consequences (594)

The Babylonians put Zedekiah on the throne, and we hear nothing further from Jrm for three years. Then a chain of incidents took place which brought Jrm into the second crisis in his prophetic vocation.

There was an uprising against Nebuchadrezzar from within his own army in December 595 or January 594: he boasts of killing the ringleader with his own hands.[39] This attempted coup d'état must have excited the Jewish exiles into a hope that Nebuchadrezzar could fall, and the news stimulated Zedekiah to call a conference of ambassadors from Edom, Moab, Ammon, Tyre, and Sidon in Jerusalem in the late spring or early summer of 594;[40] that meeting is presupposed by chapter 27.[41]

Jrm was convinced that the optimism of the conference was misplaced; he not only wore a collar of thongs and yoke-pegs[42] but gave similar collars to all the ambassadors—everyone[43] must be ready to submit to the yoke of Nebuchadrezzar. Indeed Jrm sent a letter to the exiles instructing them to submit and be prepared for a long stay in Babylon (29:1–23).

Then in late July or early August 594 he was confronted by the optimistic prophet Hananiah in the temple area (28:1–16);[44] Jrm was still wearing his collar. Hananiah proclaimed good news: the exile would be over within two years (28:3). Jrm expressed his doubts (28:5–9). Then Hananiah broke the pegs of Jrm's collar in a symbolic act, and Jrm, dejected, could only go his way (28:10–11). Later Jrm heard Yahweh say that the wooden pegs would be replaced by iron ones, since Nebuchadrezzar's yoke would also be one of iron (28:12–14). And Jrm's final word to Hananiah was that the latter was an illegitimate prophet and would die within a year. This was not simply Jrm's personal curse; the prophet who prophesies falsely was to die (Deut 18:20).

This opposition from Hananiah was reinforced by opposition from other quarters which we may discern or surmise. Thus there was opposition from optimistic prophets in Babylon who objected to Jrm's word that the exile would be long; these prophets asked the priest in charge of the temple police to lock him up in the stocks (29:24–32) as he had been locked up years before (20:1–6). Though the priest did not accede to the request, it is clear that Jrm's word brought enmity.

In this crisis I would find the setting for the rest of the confessions, specifically the addition of "men of Anathoth" in 11:21 and 23, the addition of 12:6, the passage 15:10–14, the addition of 15:20–21, then 17:14–18 and 20:7–12. The warrant for such a setting for the passages is indirect but suggestive. I believe that the addition of "men of Anathoth" in 11:21 and 23 and the addition of 12:6 come from Jrm himself:[45] these additions (particularly 12:6) are not likely to have been devised by someone unacquainted with his circumstances. If there was opposition by his fellow villagers and his family, and if it did not take place in the crisis of 601–600, and further if opposition by his family is unlikely

---

39 Compare Bright, *History*, 329. For Nebuchadrezzar's boast, see Donald J. Wiseman, *Chronicles of Chaldaean Kings (626–556 B.C.E.)* (London: British Museum, 1956) 72–73, lines 21–22.

40 Bright, *History*, 329.

41 The date in 27:1 is erroneous; on this see Bright, pp. 199, 201–2.

42 The Hebrew מֹטוֹת, 27:2, are evidently the pegs fitted into a yoke which rest on either side of the neck of each ox; the pegs are tied with thongs underneath the neck so that the oxen cannot dislodge the yoke. Jrm wore the thongs and pegs, not the yoke itself

(against the assumptions of most commentators, e.g., Bright, p. 199).

43 The Hebrew reads "send them" in 27:3, that is, the collars, not "send word," the emended text of the *RSV*.

44 For the date see Bright, 200.

45 Against Hubmann, *Untersuchungen*; see n. 35.

when he bought the field at Anathoth (32:1–15), evidently in the summer of 588, then this is the most likely time. Hananiah was from Gibeon (28:1), eight kilometers west of Anathoth; was there some reason why the folk in these villages thought Jrm was too extreme? I have dated the call to abstain from marriage (16:1–4) in the crisis of 601–600 (see sec. 6). But the associated command to abstain from attending funerals and weddings (16:5–9), more extreme even than the abstention from marriage, doubtless dishonored Jrm's family and brought opposition on him from that quarter.

It appears, in any event, that the confessions of 601–600 were useful once more, and those that seem to have been added in 594 have overtones that link them to the encounter with Hananiah. Thus I would now translate the puzzling 15:10–12 as follows: (10) Woe is me, my mother, that you ever bore me, a man of lawsuit and strife for the whole land! I have not lent, nor have they lent to me, yet all of them have treated me with contempt. (11) Yahweh has said,[46] I swear I have armored you[47] well,[48] I swear I have intervened with you[49] in a time of trouble and a time of distress![50] (12) Can he break iron, iron from the north, and bronze?

By this understanding the subject of the verb in v 12 is not the indefinite "one" (*RSV*) but "he," that is, Hananiah; the three terms are the "iron" of the hypothetical iron yoke-pegs (28:13), the "iron from the north" of Nebuchadrezzar's yoke (28:14), and the "bronze" wall into which Yahweh would make Jrm (15:20); and the vocabulary of metals is anticipated by the "armored" of v 11. Jrm's complaint in v 10 is an apostrophe to his mother; is this evidence of family opposition? Yahweh's answer to Jrm's complaint in v 10 is that the prophet has been satisfactorily armored for the crisis, and that Hananiah is bound to fail when he tries to break the iron and bronze.

I thus date 15:20–21 to this period as well, and 20:7–12 likewise, for reasons that will become clear in a moment.

The autumn of 594 is the occasion once more to hear the recitation of Deuteronomy. I propose that 11:1–17 is Jrm's counterproclamation on that occasion. The resemblance of "cursed is" in 11:3 and "so be it" (= "Amen") in 11:5 to the "curses" and "Amens" of Deut 27:15–26 has long been noted.[51] And Jrm has "iron" on his mind (11:4). But most crucially he says (v 9) that "there is revolt among the men of Judah and inhabitants of Jerusalem." The word "revolt" (or "conspiracy," קֶשֶׁר) does not otherwise appear in Jer (or Deuteronomy); it is typically used of an attempted revolt by a vassal against his overlord (as Hoshea against the king of Assyria, 2 Kgs 17:4). And this word precisely fits the situation of 594: a conference to revolt against Nebuchadrezzar. But, says Yahweh, Nebuchadrezzar's yoke is my will, so that the revolt is against me: so Jrm at the festival of booths in late September or early October 594.

But something else happened that month, perhaps even during the festival: Hananiah dropped dead (28:17). What a stunning validation of Jrm's prophetic word (Deut 18:20)! The event must have made a great impression on everyone: the identity of the month is carefully preserved. I suggest that the event of Hananiah's death explains two puzzles. The first is the meaning of 20:13, a verse otherwise so out of the emotional context; I propose that it is Jrm's praise to Yahweh that the conspiracy against him has been broken and that in effect his prophetic standing has been validated. The second is why the confessions are part of the public record at all. They are after all private transactions between Jrm and Yahweh; no one in those days was interested in the "psychology of prophetism." But these prayers and answers were made public by Jrm to affirm his validity as a true prophet of Yahweh. Yahweh had answered his prayers. Note well: one has 10:17–22 dated to 598, then 11:1–17 from the autumn of 594, followed immediately by the whole confessional collection from 11:18 through chapter 20: Hananiah dropped dead. The material was thus collected in

---

46 So *M* against *G*.

47 Reading the qere' שֶׁרִיתִיךָ as a pi'el denominative from שִׁרְיוֹן "armor," a suggestion of Franz Hubmann in personal consultation.

48 For "well" as a rendering of לְטוֹב compare Robert Gordis, "A Note on טוֹב," *JTS* 35 (1934) 187.

49 This is the meaning of the verb in 36:25 and Isa 53:12.

50 I take "the enemy" as a gloss; compare the same diction in Isa 7:17 and Mic 3:8.

51 E.g., Rudolph, p. 77.

chronological order.

But if 20:13 marks Jrm's response to the death of Hananiah, 20:14–18 suggests that the prophet's depression continued, and the diction suggests that it was family opposition that continued. One may surmise that the struggle between the optimistic prophets and a pessimistic prophet in Jerusalem meant less to his family in Anathoth than his actions which continued to dishonor them.

10. The Second Siege of Jerusalem (588–587)

The events of the prophet's career in 588 and 587 are better known (though some details remain obscure), since we have the biographical material of chapters 37—44.[52] In January 588 Nebuchadrezzar began a second siege of Jerusalem. During the spring or summer the Egyptian army forced the Babylonians to withdraw temporarily, but then the siege was renewed and Jrm was imprisoned. Two or three times King Zedekiah asked Jrm to intervene or to give news of any change of heart on Yahweh's part (21:1–10; 37:1–21; 38:14–28), but the prophet continued to insist that resistance to Babylon was futile. In July 587 the city fell; Zedekiah tried to escape but was captured near Jericho, taken to Nebuchadrezzar's headquarters and sentenced (39:1–7). In August of that year the Babylonian general destroyed the walls of the city and burned the palace and temple;[53] Gedaliah was appointed governor, administering from Mizpah a few kilometers north of Jerusalem (40:7–12).

In the midst of these terrible events Jrm was bidden to speak optimistically of a new beginning for the people after the exile. This new turn in his message may have been triggered by the purchase of the field at Anathoth (32:1–15), which perhaps occurred during the respite from the siege in 588 (compare the puzzling 37:12). Such a gesture by the prophet would at least have helped heal the breach with his family.

That new beginning was embodied most signally in a new scroll Jrm was bidden to prepare (30:2–4) with optimistic words for the future. That scroll evidently contained the old words which in his youth he had directed to the north (see sec. 3), plus fresh words more particularly shaped for the south (I believe 30:10–11, 16–17, and 31:7–9a). I further propose that the scroll, whose last word of poetry was 31:21–22, was rounded off by 31:27–28. This scroll, then, would have been proclaimed between the summer of 588 and the summer of 587.

11. The New Covenant (587)

But there is one more step. In the autumn of 587 it was time to recite Deuteronomy once more. Could one imagine the priests embarking on this ritual at the appointed time, when the temple itself had been burned a scant six weeks before? I submit that they did. I submit that this was the goal of the pilgrims from the north, from Shechem, Shiloh, and Samaria, who were coming to present their offerings at the temple "in the seventh month" (41:1–5). The year of that pilgrimage is not mentioned, but if these pilgrims had remained loyal to Josiah's program of cultic and political reunion between north and south, as their action indicates, then the occasion of the recitation of Deuteronomy was an appropriate one.[54] I pass by the assassination of Gedaliah and the massacre of those pilgrims who could not bribe their way to freedom (41:1–10).

Is there an utterance of Jrm's that would fit the occasion of the recitation of Deuteronomy in the autumn of that year? I propose that it is the "new covenant" passage, 31:31–34. Note that it is placed after what I take to be the close of the scroll of hope (see the end of sec. 10), that its diction is strongly reminiscent of Deuteronomy,[55] and that it states that the old covenant is obsolete. If this is its setting, then its pure vision of a new initiative by Yahweh is all the more astonishing.

12. The Flight to Egypt

Soon after the assassination of Gedaliah, those loyal to the governor fled to Egypt, taking Jrm and Baruch with them (chaps. 42—43). If it was late in the year 587, and if the prophet proclaimed 31:31–34 in the autumn of 587, then that was his last word in Jerusalem. It must have been horrid for Jrm to see himself going to Egypt,

---

52   See for example Bright, pp. 219–66.
53   Bright, *History*, 329–30.
54   Compare Bright, pp. 253–54.

55   See Hyatt, p. 1038.

whence Moses had led the people out (compare Deut 17:16); if he were an anti-Moses figure (see sec. 6), then this is the crowning deed of an anti-Moses! No wonder his last recorded word to the travelers was "Behold I have sworn by my great name, says Yahweh, that my name shall no more be invoked by the mouth of any man of Judah in all the land of Egypt, saying, 'As the Lord Yahweh lives'" (44:26).[56] If Yahweh had taught Moses the divine name and enjoined him to teach the name to his people, then Jrm would announce the extinguishing of the divine name in Egypt. The hope for the future of the people lay in Babylon, not in Egypt (29:7; see sec. 9). It is the last we hear of the prophet; by my reckoning he would have been forty years old. Perhaps Baruch died first, since we have no notice of the prophet's death.

13. Conclusion

If this is a valid reconstruction of the prophet's career, it exposes the shifts of his perception of Yahweh's will through several decades: a prophetic career which we can come to know in unparalleled detail.

Some years ago Stanley Brice Frost suggested that the book of Jer is a memorial to a childless man.[57] It is ironic that some of the wealth of detail which we have of Jrm's career may thus be due to Yahweh's command that he not marry and have children. Though a book may be a poor substitute for sons to carry on one's name, Jrm's sacrifice is our gain.

56   See Alonso Schökel, "Jeremías como anti-Moisés," 248.

57   Stanley Brice Frost, "The Memorial of a Childless Man, A Study in Hebrew Thought on Immortality," *Int* 26 (1972) 446–47.

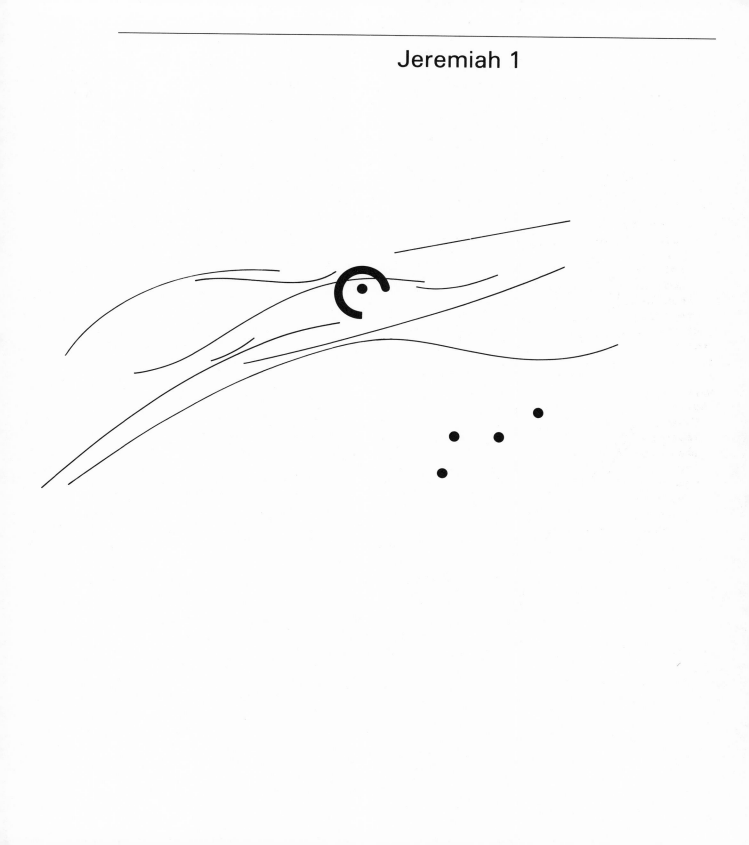

The Title of the Book

Bibliography

On chaps. 1—25:

Neumann, Peter K. D.
"Das Wort, das geschehen ist . . . , Zum Problem der Wortempfangsterminologie in Jer. i—xxv," *VT* 23 (1973) 171–217.

Thiel, Winfried
Die deuteronomistische Redaktion von Jer 1—25 (WMANT 41; Neukirchen: Neukirchener, 1973).

On chaps. 1—24:

Rietzschel, Claus
Das Problem der Urrolle, Ein Beitrag zur Redaktionsgeschichte des Jeremiabuches (Gütersloh: Gütersloher, 1966) 122–26.

On chaps. 1—20:

Holladay, William L.
The Architecture of Jeremiah 1—20 (Lewisburg, PA: Bucknell University, 1976).

On chaps. 1—10:

Loretz, Oswald
"Die Sprüche Jeremias in Jer 1,17—9,25," *UF* 2 (1970) 109–30.

Torrey, Charles C.
"The Background of Jeremiah 1—10," *JBL* 56 (1937) 193–216.

On chaps. 1—6:

Berridge, pp. 74–113.

On 1:1–19:

Budde, Karl
"Über das erste Kapitel des Buches Jeremia," *JBL* 40 (1921) 23–37.

Renaud, Bernard
"Jer 1: Structure et Théologie de la Redaction," *Le Livre de Jérémie* (ed. Pierre-Maurice Bogaert; BETL 54; Leuven: Leuven University, 1981) 177–96.

Stade, Bernhard
"Streiflichter auf die Entstehung der jetzigen Gestalt der alttestamentlichen Prophetenschriften, 1) Jer c. 1," *ZAW* 23 (1903) 153–57.

Stade, Bernhard
"Der 'Völkerprophet' Jeremia und der jetzige Text von Jer Kap. 1," *ZAW* 26 (1906) 97–123.

On 1:1–3:

Vogt, Ernst
"Verba Jeremias Filii Helciae," *VD* 42 (1964) 169–72.

1

1   The words of Jeremiah, the son of Hilkiah,
of the priestly family at Anathoth in the
land of Benjamin, 2/ what came as the
word of Yahweh to him in the days of
Josiah the son of Amon, king of Judah, in
the thirteenth year of his reign, 3/ and
came in the days of Jehoiakim son of
Josiah, king of Judah, until the
completion of the eleventh year of
Zedekiah son of Josiah, king of Judah,
(that is) until the exile of Jerusalem, in
the fifth month.

Form and Setting

The diction contained in this superscription is typical of
that of superscriptions found at the beginning of other
prophetic books, indeed of superscriptions scattered
through the Book of Jer. Such headings, with similar
diction, are also found at the head of inscriptional
material in the ancient Near East, for example, at the
head of the Ešmunʿazar stele (early third century B.C.E.):
"In the month Bul, in the fourteenth year . . . of the
reign of King Ešmunʿazar king of the Sidonians, son of
King Tabnit king of the Sidonians, spoke King
Ešmunʿazar king of the Sidonians, saying. . . ."[1]

But a close inspection of the text suggests that these
verses were shaped in two or even three stages; the
transitions are less smooth than the English translations
indicate, and the joins are found at the junctions of the
three verses.

Verse 1, beginning "The words of Jeremiah," followed
by his lineage, matches most closely Amos 1:1, "The
words of Amos, who was among the shepherds of
Tekoa. . . ." Verse 2, however, is a different matter. The
sequence is אֲשֶׁר הָיָה דְבַר־יהוה אֵלָיו בִּימֵי . . . ; its syntax is
unclear. It is closely analogous to the headings of 14:1;
46:1; 47:1; and 49:34: all of these read אֲשֶׁר הָיָה דְבַר־יהוה
אֶל־יִרְמְיָהוּ, and these are independent clauses, evidently
to be translated "What has come as the word of Yahweh
to Jeremiah"—peculiar as the syntax is, it is evidently not
a reading due to scribal error[2] but a form peculiar to the
Book of Jer. This form is thus not, strictly speaking,
comparable to the form of superscription found in Hos
1:1, Joel 1:1, Mic 1:1 and Zeph 1:1: Hos 1:1 reads דְּבַר־

יהוה אֲשֶׁר הָיָה אֶל־הוֹשֵׁעַ בֶּן־בְּאֵרִי בִּימֵי "The word of Yahweh
which came to Hosea the son of Beeri in the days of. . . ."
The most logical assumption is that vv 1 and 2 (the latter
originally reading "to Jeremiah" instead of "to him")
were alternative superscriptions, and that what we have
before us is a conflate text, with v 2 secondarily altered
to read "to him" instead of "to Jeremiah." The
combination of the two then makes v 2 a dependent
rather than an independent clause, the אֲשֶׁר referring to
"Jeremiah" in v 1, so that v 2 is now construed to read,
"to whom the word of Yahweh came in the days of. . . ."[3]
An alternative solution is to reject the parallel between v
2 and the form found in 14:1 and to assume that v 2
originally had the form found in Hos 1:1 but that it was
subsequently altered to its present form when v 1 was
affixed.[4] The decision between these two solutions is
complicated by the G text of the first two verses, "The
word of God which came to Jeremiah the son of
Hilkiah . . . , as the word of God came to him in the days
of Josiah. . . ." The G rendering of v 2 is evidence that
the translator perceived אֲשֶׁר not to refer to the antecedent "Jeremiah"; but the form of G in v 1 is evidence
either of a secondary revision of the text represented by
M to bring it into conformity with most other prophetic
superscriptions, or else evidence of the lateness of the
shaping of the material in v 1, so that both text forms
emerged after the Palestinian/Babylonian and Egyptian
text traditions diverged.

The problem of the intentionality of the material in v
2 is complicated by the question of the event in Jrm's life
to which the "thirteenth year" of Josiah refers. By the

1   *ANET*, 505; George A. Cooke, *A Textbook of North-Semitic Inscriptions* (Oxford: Clarendon, 1903) 30–31.
2   GKC, sec. 138e, note.
3   So Bernhard Stade, "Streiflichter auf die Entstehung der jetzigen Gestalt der alttestamentlichen Prophetenschriften," *ZAW* 23 (1903) 153–55.
4   So Bernhard Duhm, *Das Buch Jeremia* (Kurzer Hand-Commentar zum Alten Testament 11; Tübingen and

Leipzig: Mohr [Siebeck], 1901); Rudolph; Bright; so Budde, "Ernste Kapitel," 23–28.

chronology accepted in the present study this date refers to the year of his birth (see "A Chronology of Jeremiah's Career," sec. l, and in more detail "Life and Proclamation of Jeremiah" in the Introduction in Vol. 2). Verse 2 could have been prefixed to the first and second scrolls described in chapter 36, dating from 605 and 601/600 (see "A Chronology of Jeremiah's Career," secs. 4 and 6); v 3 could have been added to an enlarged collection of oracles, including the hopeful scroll (30:1–3) which begins with 30:4 and ends with 31:28 (note in v 3 "until the exile of Jerusalem, in the fifth month," compare 2 Kgs 25:8–12), and v 1 could have been prefixed, and v 2 reshaped, after the biographical material was added (since "words" in v 1 may refers to "acts" as well, see Interpretation). It should also be noted that if the thirteenth year of Josiah does refer to the year of Jrm's birth, then the scribe who compiled the data must have had access to testimony that went back to Jrm himself; the most logical person of course is Baruch (see 32:12) for both vv 2 and 3.

Interpretation

■ **1** Our understanding of דִּבְרֵי, whose primary meaning is "words of," depends on our understanding of the point at which this verse of the superscription came into the tradition. If it was as early as the dictated scrolls (chap. 36), then clearly "words of" is correct. But if (as is proposed here: see Form and Setting) it was at the time when the biographical material was added, or later, then "words and deeds of" is implied.[5] David Qimḥi suggested something like our modern word "history" (compare "the rest of the acts of [דִּבְרֵי] Jeroboam," 1 Kgs 14:19, and many other such phrases), and Wilhelm Rudolph concurs; such a translation certainly fits the contours of the present Book of Jer.

The name "Jeremiah" was borne by ten men in the OT;[6] even within Jer the name is borne by two men other than the prophet (35:3; 52:1). The name also appears on three inscribed Hebrew seals—one from Beth-Shemesh from the mid-eighth century;[7] another, of unknown provenience, from the mid-eighth century;[8] and a third, from the Lachish hoard, dated to the late seventh century[9]—and it occurs in one of the Lachish ostraca.[10] In every instance in this extrabiblical material the name is spelled in the "long form" יִרְמְיָהוּ. It was thus not an uncommon name during this period. The derivation of the name is, however, uncertain, and this uncertainty has raised questions about the correct vocalization of the name. The name of the prophet appears approximately 120 times within the Book of Jer in the long form יִרְמְיָהוּ, and 4 times for the prophet outside Jer in the long form; and it appears 9 times in Jer in the short form יִרְמְיָה—these 9 occurrences falling within 27:1—29:3 (see the section "Peculiarities of Spelling, 27:1—29:3" before treatment of chap. 27), and twice with the short form outside Jer. The G transliteration is ιερεμιας. The name is clearly a compound of an imperfect verb form and (וֹ)יָה, a short form of "Yahweh."[11] The imperfect is best understood as a jussive ("May Yahweh do so-and-so"). There are two possible verbs to which to refer the name. The first, already anticipated by Jerome,[12] is רום hip'il, "May Yahweh lift up";[13] the vocalization would then be yĕrēmyāh(û) or yĕramyāh(û). Such a derivation would be supported by the G transliteration (compare yĕqamyāh, ιεχεμιας, 1 Chr 2:41, no doubt from yĕqēm, קום hip'il). The second is רמה qal, which may have a variety of meanings (see below). If this is the verb, the vocalization in Jrm's day would have been yirmyāh(û), later yiremyāh(û); the latter vocalization could give rise to the G

---

5   See Werner H. Schmidt, "דָּבָר,"*TDOT* 3:104–6.
6   Bruce T. Dahlberg, "Jeremiah," *IDB* 2:822.
7   Elihu Grant and G. Ernest Wright, *'Ain Shams Excavations 5* (Haverford, PA: Haverford College, 1939) 80; Larry G. Herr, *The Scripts of Ancient Northwest Semitic Seals* (HMS 18; 1978) no. 45, p. 103.
8   Herr, *Scripts*, no. 108, p. 129.
9   Ibid., no. 23, p. 93.
10 I 4; see Harry Torczyner et al., *Lachish I (Tell ed Duweir): The Lachish Letters* (London: Oxford University, 1938) 20–31. These ostraca date from the early sixth century, according to most authorities;

see conveniently Richard W. Hamilton, "Lachish," *IDB* 3:56–57.
11 See Bernhard W. Anderson, "God, names of," *IDB* 2:409.
12 "Ieremia excelsus domini": *Liber Interpretationis Hebraicorum Nominum*, ed. Paul de Lagarde, in CChr Series Latina 72 (Turnhout: Brepols, 1959) 127.
13 Martin Noth, *Die israelitischen Personennamen im Rahmen der gemeinsemitischen Namengebung* (BWANT 3, 10; Stuttgart: Kohlhammer, 1928), 201. Noth compares names like "Jehoiakim," where the verb is the hip'il of קום, and points to poetic expressions like

vocalization, and the present *M* vocalization could well be the result of breaking up the original consonant cluster differently. The verb רמה appears with "Yahweh" in Exod 15:1, 21 in the meaning, "throw, cast," and such an action of the divine warrior is an altogether likely basis for the name—"May Yahweh cast." The Akkadian cognate *ramū*, however, offers other possibilities of meaning: "May Yahweh loosen (the womb?)";[14] "May Yahweh found (a dwelling? a lineage?)."[15]

There was a Hilkiah who was high priest in Jerusalem in 622 (2 Kgs 22:4), and it is attractive to identify that high priest with Jrm's father (Qimḥi notes that his father Joseph made the identification). By the reading of *M* in 20:15, a messenger brought to Jrm's father the news of Jrm's birth, and that datum might lend credence to the identification; but the present study proposes a fresh understanding of that passage. The proposal has further been made that if Josiah embarked upon his reforms earlier than the time of the finding of the Deuteronomic scroll (so 2 Chr 34:3), then Jrm's father, a priest in touch with northern traditions, may have entered the Jerusalem priesthood with the king's reform.[16] But it is unlikely that the present superscription would omit the designation "high priest" if such were the case; here the identification is "of the priests of Anathoth," probably to distinguish him from the high priest.

The text then says "from the priests in Anathoth"; "from" (מִן) is frequently used of descent from a tribe or people (Num 3:12). It is unlikely that there was more than one priestly family in a village the size of Anathoth, so that "from the priests" may be understood as "of the priestly family."

The village of Anathoth (עֲנָתוֹת) bears a name no doubt originally derived from the Canaanite goddess ʿAnat,[17] with the same formation as the place-name Ashtaroth (עַשְׁתָּרוֹת) from the goddess ʿAštart. The pagan association of the name of the village at least suggests a pre-Israelite settlement. It was located near its present-day namesake, the Arab village of ʿanātā, situated four kilometers northeast of Iron Age Jerusalem (*Atlas of Israel* grid 175–135). Albrecht Alt first suggested[18] that biblical Anathoth is to be located on the rocky promontory which the Arabs call *rās el-ḥarrūbeh* ("summit of the carob-beans"), a few hundred meters to the southwest of the present Arab village, and this identification is virtually certain. Soundings at the site indicate that settlement began with the Israelite monarchy.[19] From this promontory the Mount of Olives is visible to the southwest.

Whether the archeological evidence is complete, or whether the site identification is correct for all periods, biblical memory insists that Anathoth was no new settlement in Solomon's time. It is mentioned as a Levitical city in Josh 21:18, and though some scholars have thought the list in which it appears to be utopian,[20] we learn in 1 Kgs 2:26 that Solomon told the deposed priest Abiathar to go "to your own field" in Anathoth—in short, that he had had a field there for some time, perhaps by inheritance.

The association of Abiathar with Anathoth is important in a way other than simply to establish the antiquity of the locality, for Abiathar, it is implied, was the last survivor in Solomon's day of the house of Eli the priest who had ministered at Shiloh until its destruction (1 Kgs 2:27).[21] It is quite possible, then, that in this way the priestly family at Anathoth preserved the religious traditions of Shiloh, where the ark of the covenant had been kept in the time of the judges—it would seem to be no accident that Jrm is the only prophet who mentions Shiloh (7:12, 14; 26:6, 9) and Samuel (15:1). Here, then,

1 Sam 2:8 = Ps 113:7 for the use of that latter verb in the context of divine elevation.

14   So BDB.

15   Compare *HALAT*.

16   Robert R. Wilson, *Prophecy and Society in Ancient Israel* (Philadelphia: Fortress, 1980) 223.

17   Compare Edward R. Dalglish, "Anath," *IDB* 1:125.

18   Albrecht Alt, "Anathoth," *PJ* 22 (1926) 23–24.

19   A. Bergman, "Soundings at the Supposed Site of Old Testament Anathoth," with an Additional Note by William F. Albright, *BASOR* 62 (1936) 22–26, and see further A. Bergman and William F. Albright, "Anathoth?" *BASOR* 63 (1936), 22–23. Compare Menaḥem Haran, "Studies in the Account of the Levitical Cities, I. Preliminary Considerations," *JBL* 80 (1961) 52.

20   See J. Alberto Soggin, *Joshua* (Philadelphia: Westminster, 1972) 203–4.

21   See Richard W. Corney, "Abiathar," *IDB* 1:6–7.

is one possible clue to the religious milieu into which Jrm entered.

"In the land of Benjamin." Jrm singles out the Benjaminites when he urges folk to leave Jerusalem (6:1), and he envisions Rachel, mother of Benjamin, weeping for her children (31:15). In these ways he perhaps expresses his own tribal affiliation.

■ **2** For the question whether the אֲשֶׁר-clause is to be construed as independent or dependent, see Form and Setting. The phrase הָיָה דְבַר־יהוה אֶל־ or its equivalent is a technical term for the onset of prophecy: היה does not mean "come," strictly speaking, but "happen, occur," and דָּבָר does not mean "word" alone but more generally "revelatory activity" (compare the remarks on דִּבְרֵי in v 1).[22] The expression is a standard one,[23] not only in superscriptions but in first-person testimony of the prophets as well (e.g., vv 4, 11, 13; 2:1), and, before the prophetic literature proper, in Gen 15:1 (JE), 1 Sam 15:10. See on v 4 for a more extended discussion of the expression.

On the assumption that Judah reckoned its years beginning with the month Nisan (March/April),[24] the thirteenth year of Josiah will be 627/626. Though most scholars have assumed this datum to refer to the onset of Jrm's prophetic career,[25] the present study, as already noted (see Form and Setting), takes the datum to refer to the prophet's birth.

■ **3** This verse continues the listing of subsequent kings. The wording "until the completion of the eleventh year of Zedekiah" is curious, since Jerusalem fell on the ninth day of the fourth month of the eleventh year of Zedekiah (39:2; 52:5–6), at which time of course his reign came to an end. Since the verse governs material delivered by Jrm until the fifth month, that is, one month after the fall of the city, the "completion of the eleventh year of Zedekiah" must not be pressed mathematically but must mean "until the end of the reign of Zedekiah, in his eleventh year" (compare Rudolph). By the assumption of the present work Jerusalem fell on 18 July 587; "the fifth month" would then be in August of that year, when the Babylonian officer destroyed the walls and burned the temple and palace (2 Kgs 25:8–12).

Aim

The immediate purpose of the superscription is clearly to set the material concerning Jrm in time and space; but theologically it affirms that the words and deeds come from Yahweh to this particular man at a specific time in history. The superscription thus becomes a paradigm of the biblical understanding of revelation: that in the fullness of time the word becomes flesh.

---

22   See W. H. Schmidt, "דָּבָר," *TDOT* 3:112–14.
23   Compare the study of Peter K. D. Neumann (see bibliography for chaps. 1—25).
24   For bibliography on the Nisan new year see "A Chronology of Jeremiah's Career," n. 1.
25   So Rudolph, Bright.

The Call, and Associated Visions

Bibliography

On 1:4–19:
Bewer, Julius A.
  "Historical Criticism of Jeremiah 1:4–19," *AJT* 6
  (1902) 510–18.
Cornill, Carl H.
  "Die literarhistorische Methode und Jeremia Kap.
  1," *ZAW* 27 (1907) 100–110.
García-Moreno, Antonio
  "Vocación de Jeremías," *EstBib* 27 (1968) 49–68.
Marks, John
  "The Imagery of Jeremiah's Call," *McCQ* 16 (1963)
  29–38.
Michaud, Henri
  "La vocation du prophète des nations," *Maqqél
  Shâqqédh, La Branche d'Amandier, Hommage à
  Wilhelm Vischer* (Montpellier: Causse, Graille,
  Castelnau, 1960) 157–64.
Mottu, Henry
  "Aux sources de notre vocation: Jérémie 1,4–19,"
  RTP 114 (1982) 105–19.
Schreiner, Josef
  "Prophetsein im Untergang, Aus der Verkün-
  digung des Propheten Jeremias: Jer 1,4–19,"
  BibLeb 7 (1966) 15–28.
Vogt, Ernst
  "Vocatio Jeremiae," *VD* 42 (1964) 241–51.

**On 1:4–10; call narratives in general;
office and call of the prophet in general:**
Baltzer, Klaus
  "Considerations Regarding the Office and Calling
  of the Prophet," *HTR* 61 (1968) 567–81.
Clements, Ronald E.
  Prophecy and Tradition (Atlanta: Knox, 1975).
Gouders, Klaus
  "Zu einer Theologie der prophetischen Berufung,"
  BibLeb 12 (1971) 79–93.
Habel, Norman C.
  "The Form and Significance of the Call Narra-
  tives," *ZAW* 77 (1965) 297–323.
Henry, Marie-Louise
  Prophet und Tradition, Versuch einer Problemstellung
  (BZAW 116; Berlin: de Gruyter, 1969).
Kilian, Rudolf
  "Die prophetischen Berufungsberichte," *Theologie
  im Wandel, Festschrift zum 150-jährigen Bestehen der
  Katholisch-Theologischen Fakultät an die Universität
  Tübingen* (Tübinger Theologische Reihe 1;
  Munich: Wewel, 1967) 356–76.
Kraus, Hans-Joachim
  Worship in Israel (Richmond: Knox, 1966) 108–11.
Muilenburg, James
  "The 'Office' of the Prophet in Ancient Israel,"

The Bible in Modern Scholarship, Papers Read at the 100th Meeting of the Society of Biblical Literature, December 28–30, 1964 (ed. J. Philip Hyatt; Nashville: Abingdon, 1965) 74–97.

Olmo Lete, Gregorio del
La Vocación del Líder en el antiguo Israel, Morfología de los Relatos Bíblicos de Vocación (Salamanca: Universidad Pontificia de Salamanca, 1973).

Richter, Wolfgang
Die sogenannten vorprophetischen Berufsberichte (FRLANT 101; Göttingen: Vandenhoeck & Ruprecht, 1970).

Ross, James F.
"The Prophet as Yahweh's Messenger," Israel's Prophetic Heritage, Essays in Honor of James Muilenburg (ed. Bernhard W. Anderson and Walter Harrelson; New York: Harper, 1962) 98–107.

Vogels, Walter
"Les récits de vocation des prophètes," NRT 95 (1973) 3–24.

Westermann, Claus
Basic Forms of Prophetic Speech (Philadelphia: Westminster, 1967).

Zimmerli, Walther
Ezekiel 1 (Hermeneia; Philadelphia: Fortress, 1979) 97–100.

On Jeremiah and Moses:

Alonso Schökel
"Jeremías como anti-Moisés."

Broughton, P. E.
"The Call of Jeremiah: The Relation of Deut. 18,9–22 to the Call of Jeremiah," AusBR 6 (1958) 37–46.

Childs, Brevard S.
The Book of Exodus, A Critical, Theological Commentary (Philadelphia: Westminster, 1974) 53–60.

Holladay
"Background," 153–64.

Holladay
"Jeremiah and Moses: Further Observations."

On 1:4–10 specifically; individual verses:

Bach, Robert
"Bauen und Pflanzen," Studien zur Theologie der alttestamentlichen Überlieferungen (ed. Rolf Rendtorff and Klaus Koch; Neukirchen: Neukirchener, 1961) 7–32.

Berridge
pp. 26–62.

Gilula, M.
"An Egyptian Parallel to Jeremia i 4–5," VT 17 (1967) 114.

Gouders, Klaus
"'Siehe, ich lege meine Worte in deinem Mund,' Die Berufung des Propheten Jeremia (Jer 1,4–10)," BibLeb 12 (1971) 162–86.

Gunneweg, Antonius H. J.
"Ordinationsformular oder Berufsbericht in

Jeremia 1," Glaube, Geist, Geschichte, Festschrift für Ernst Benz (ed. Gerhard Müller and Winfried Zeller; Leiden: Brill, 1967) 91–98.

Holladay, William L.
"Prototype and Copies: A New Approach to the Poetry-Prose Problem in the Book of Jeremiah," JBL 79 (1960) 335–67, esp. 363–64.

Reventlow, Henning Graf von
Liturgie und prophetisches Ich bei Jeremia (Gütersloh: Gütersloher [Gerd Mohn], 1963) 24–77.

Schultes, Josef L.
"Gott nimmt ganz in seinen Dienst, Bibel Meditation zu Jer 1,4–10," BLit 48 (1975) 180–83.

Stade, Bernhard
"Emendationen—Jer. 1,4 [sic, for 1,5]," ZAW 22 (1902) 328.

Vischer, Wilhelm
"Vocation of the Prophet to the Nations, An Exegesis of Jer. 1:4–10," Int 9 (1955) 310–17.

Voegelin, Eric
Order and History, 1: Israel and Revelation (Baton Rouge: Louisiana State University, 1956) 467–70.

Weippert, Helga
Die Prosareden des Jeremiabuches (BZAW 132; Berlin: de Gruyter, 1973) 193–99.

On 1:11–19, and prophetic visions in general:

Horst, Friedrich
"Die Visionsschilderungen der alttestamentlichen Propheten," EvT 20 (1960) 193–205.

Long, Burke O.
"Reports of Visions Among the Prophets," JBL 95 (1976) 353–65.

Niditch, Susan
The Symbolic Vision in Biblical Tradition (HSM 30; Chico, CA: Scholars, 1983).

On Jeremiah's visions in general:

Zimmerli, Walther
"Visionary Experience in Jeremiah," Israel's Prophetic Tradition, Essays in Honour of Peter R. Ackroyd (ed. Richard Coggins, Anthony Phillips and Michael Knibb; Cambridge: Cambridge University, 1982) 95–118.

On the foe from the north; Scythians:

Vaggione, Richard P.
"All Over Asia? The Extent of the Scythian Domination in Herodotus," JBL 92 (1973), 523–30, with full bibliography on the problem.

See further:

Cazelles, Henri
"Zephaniah, Jeremiah, and the Scythians in Palestine," A Prophet to the Nations, Essays in Jeremiah Studies, Leo G. Perdue and Brian Kovacs (Winona Lake, IN: Eisenbrauns, 1984) 129–49 = "Sophonie, Jérémie, et les Scythes en Palestine," RB 74 (1967) 24–44, with full bibliography.

Childs, Brevard S.
"The Enemy from the North and the Chaos Tradition," *JBL* 78 (1959) 187–98.
Lauha, Aarre
Zaphon der Norden und die Nordvölker im Alten Testament (Annales Academiae Scientiarum Fennicae 49; Helsinki: Ständerhuset, 1943).
Vaggione, Richard P.
"Scythians," *IDBSup*, 797–98.

On 1:11–16:
Berridge
pp. 63–72.
Bode, Edward L.
"The Seething Caldron—Jer. 1:13," *Bible Today* 42 (April 1969) 2898–2903.
Cogan, Morton
"Sentencing at the Gate in Jeremiah 1:15–16," *Gratz College Annual* 1 (1972) 3–6.
Guillaume, Alfred
Prophecy and Divination Among the Hebrews and Other Semites (London: Hodder & Stoughton, 1938) 153–54.
Harris, Scott L.
"The Second Vision of Jeremiah: Jer 1:13–15," *JBL* 102 (1983) 281–82.
Irwin, William A.
"The Face of the Pot, Jeremiah 1:13b," *AJSL* 47 (1930–31) 288–89.
Lindblom, Johannes
"Der Kessel in Jer i, 13f.," *ZAW* 68 (1956) 223–24.

Niditch
Symbolic Vision, 41–52.
Reventlow
Liturgie, 77–87.
Sauer, Georg
"Mandelzweig und Kessel in Jer 1:11ff," *ZAW* 78 (1966) 56–61.
Williams, Walter G.
"Jeremiah's Vision of the Almond Rod," *A Stubborn Faith, Papers on Old Testament and Related Subjects, Presented to Honor William Andrew Irwin* (ed. Edward C. Hobbs; Dallas: Southern Methodist University, 1956) 90–99.
Wood, Pearle S.
"Jeremiah's Figure of the Almond Rod," *JBL* 61 (1942) 99–103.

On 1:17–19:
Berridge
pp. 198–201.
Jüngling, Hans-Winfried
"Ich mache dich zu einer ehernen Mauer, Literar-kritische Überlegungen zum Verhältnis von Jer 1,18–19 zu Jer 15,20–21," *Bib* 54 (1973) 1–24.
Talmon, Shemaryahu
"An Apparently Redundant MT Reading—Jeremiah 1:18," *Textus* 8 (1973) 160–63.

1

4　The word of Yahweh came to me as follows:

5　Before I summoned[a] you,
　　in the belly I knew you,
　and before you came forth,
　　from the womb I dedicated you,
　　a prophet to the nations I made you.

6　But I said, "Ah, Lord Yahweh, look, I do not know how to speak, for I am (only) a youth."

7　But Yahweh said to me,
　Do not say, "I[a] am (only) a youth";
　but to everyone to whom I send you you shall go,
　and everything I command you you shall speak;

8　do not be afraid of them,
　　for I am with you to rescue you,
　　　　　　oracle of Yahweh.

9　And Yahweh extended his hand and touched[a] my mouth; and Yahweh said to me,
　Look, I have put my words in your mouth;

Text

5a　The qere', *G*, *V*, *T*, and *S* all read אֶצָּרְךָ "formed you" (יצר qal), and the ketib אצורך is usually taken as אֲצוּרְךָ, identified with a by-form צור "form, fashion" (Franz Zorell, *Lexicon Hebraicum et Aramaicum Veteris Testamenti* [Rome: Pontifical Biblical Institute, 1962]; cf. BDB). But Dahood suggests a root צור "summon" in Ps 77:3 (Mitchell Dahood, *Psalms 51—100* [AB l7; Garden City, NY: Doubleday, 1966] 225–26) on the basis of parallelism there, and he further suggests the presence of that root here. There is then the strong possibility of a "near miss" here: one expects "form" but hears "summon," preserved in the ketib. It is striking that in Isa 49:1, 5 we have מִבֶּטֶן קְרָאָנִי "from the womb he has called me" and יֹצְרִי מִבֶּטֶן "shapes me from the womb," two phrases within Isa 49:1–6 which may reflect the expected verb and the actual verb in the present phrase. (For another "near miss," see the first word of v 12.) See further Interpretation. For the possible occurrence of a related noun צָרָה "appeal," see 4:31.

7a　A few MSS., *G* and *S* add כִּי after תֹאמַר, thus "Do not say, 'For I am (only) a youth.'" Either reading is possible.

9a　There is uncertainty whether the vocalization should be וַיַּגַּע (נגע qal) "touch" or וַיַּגַּע (נגע hip'il) "let

10

see, I have appointed you this day
    over nations and over kingdoms,
to uproot and to demolish [and to destroy
        and to overthrow,]ᵃ
    to build and to plant.

it touch." *M* here is vocalized as a hip'il, as it is in the parallel account of Isaiah's call in Isa 6:7. *G* and *V* in both passages read "touched," suggesting that the Hebrew of both passages originally read the qal and the vocalizers softened the word to the hip'il to avoid too harsh an anthropomorphism, or else that the original reading was a hip'il and the Versions did not find the distinction significant. *S* is uncertain; the Walton Polyglot edition offers a pe'al ("touch") in both passages, while the Urmia edition offers a pe'al in Jer 1:9 and a pa'el ("let touch") in Isa 6:7: hardly a basis for establishing the meaning of the Hebrew here.

10a   Omitting וּלְהַאֲבִיד וְלַהֲרוֹס as prosaicizing synonyms added under the influence of the diction of 18:7, 9, and 45:4 (so also Paul Volz, *Der Prophet Jeremia* [KAT 10; Leipzig: Deichert, 1928], and Rudolph). Three parallel passages in Jer have a selection of four of the six verbs in symmetrical patterns (24:6; 42:10; 45:4), indirect evidence that the call also contained a selection of four; the last-named passage is particularly significant, since the usage of the four verbs in chapter 45 is different than in the remaining passages: the building and planting are what Yahweh has done in the past, not what he will do in the future. If we omit the middle pair of verbs in the present passage, as suggested, what remains is a chiasmus of four verbs, two negative ones from the realms of planting and building respectively, and two positive ones from the realms of building and planting respectively, a chiasmus furthermore that offers a pleasing assonance (Volz; Holladay, "Prototype," 363–64). The rightness of this choice of verbs is rendered slightly more convincing by the distribution of the conjunction "and" before the verbs in *M* (but not in the Versions). The literary and Versional history of the verbs in this and in parallel passages is a complex problem. Relevant parallel passages are Jer 12:14–17; 18:7–9; 24:6; 31:38, 40; 42:10; 45:4; and Sir 49:7. In the present passage *T* and *S* reflect the present *M*; so does *V*, though Jerome translates the verb הרס by *dissipes* "scatter." *G* offers only five verbs here instead of six (and offers two instead of three in 18:7, and four instead of six in 31:28 [*G* 38:28]). These five are: the first, then the third, then either the second or the fourth, then the fifth and sixth. The uncertain translation is κατασκάπτειν, which may render either נתץ or הרס; the Greek verb translates נתץ seven times in the OT, but not otherwise in the Latter Prophets, and translates הרס fourteen times, including six times in the Latter Prophets (and of these, one other instance in Jer, 27:15 [*G* 50:15]). On this basis one assumes that *G* translates הרס here and omits נתץ (against J. Gerald Janzen, *Studies in the Text of Jeremiah* [HSM 6; Cambridge: Harvard University, 1973] 35). But Janzen is correct that the present *M* is an attempt at completeness in depicting

11	The word of Yahweh came to me as follows: What do you see, Jeremiah?[a] And I said, I see a twig of the almond tree (*šāqēd*).
12	And Yahweh said to me, You have seen right, for I am watchful (*šōqēd*) over my word to carry it out.
13	And the word of Yahweh came to me a second time, as follows: What do you see?[a] And I said, I see a pot being fanned, whose rim is away from the north.
14	And Yahweh said to me, From the north, disaster will be opened upon all the inhabitants of the land.
15	Look! I am going to summon all the [a]⟨tribes⟩ [kingdoms][a] of the north, oracle of Yahweh, and they shall come in and each place his throne at the entrance of the gates of Jerusalem, [and upon all its walls around, and over all the cities of Judah.][b]
16	And I shall pronounce my judgments on them[a] for all their crime in abandoning me, in sacrificing to other gods, and in worshiping the work[b] of their hands.

- - - -

| 17 | For your part, you shall gird up your loins,
arise and speak to them [all that [b]I
command[b] you;][a]
do not be panicked by their presence,
or I will panic you in their presence. |

Jrm's call, beyond the concision of the original text.

11a, 13a *G* omits the vocative "Jeremiah" in v 11, like *M* in v 13; in contrary fashion a Hebrew MS. fragment from the Cairo Geniza adds the vocative in v 13 like *M* in v 11. Given the fact that the stereotyped question may appear either with or without the vocative (see Form), either the minus of *G* or the plus of the Cairo fragment is possible. In these circumstances it is best to stay with *M*.

15a—a *M* reads "tribes of the kingdoms," and *G* reads simply "kingdoms." The construct מִשְׁפְּחוֹת can easily be revocalized as the absolute מִשְׁפָּחוֹת, in which case the two nouns are parallel variants (so Janzen, p. 10), and *M* is a conflate text; this view is accepted here. Carl H. Cornill, *Das Buch Jeremia* (Leipzig: Tauchnitz, 1905), Friedrich Giesebrecht, *Das Buch Jeremia* (HKAT 3,2; Göttingen: Vandenhoeck & Ruprecht, 1907), Volz, Albert Condamin, *Le Livre de Jérémie* (EBib; Paris: Gabalda, 1936), Bright, and Rudolph believe that "tribes of" is a secondary insertion from 25:9, but the word "tribes" offers assonance with מִשְׁפְּטֵי in v 16 (compare the similar word-play in 10:25, and see Preliminary Observations). It is better, then, to delete "kingdoms," though there remains the possibility that "kingdoms" was substituted for "tribes," or added to "tribes," in the first or second scroll (see again Preliminary Observations). One may also note that 10:25 offers "tribes" in most MSS. but "kingdoms" in a few, and "kingdoms" in *T* to that passage and in the parallel Ps 79:6.

b   A later expansion (so Giesebrecht); see Preliminary Observations and Interpretation.

16a   *M* reads אוֹתָם but many MSS. read אֶתָּם. It is uncertain whether this idiom demands the preposition or the *nota accusativa*: 4:12 and 12:1 use the latter, 39:5 and 52:9 the former. The meaning in any event is clear.

b   Following many MSS. and *V S*, reading מַעֲשֵׂה (singular) for *M* "works" (plural). Both forms of the idiom occur often, and there is much MS. variation between the singular and plural in given instances, but earlier occurrences (Isa 2:8; Hos 14:4; Mic 5:12; Ps 135:15) favor the singular.

17a   The phrase is probably a gloss from v 7 (so Volz); see Interpretation.

b—b   *M* אָנֹכִי אֲצַוֶּךָ is evidently a conflate text: the verb is a variant vocalization of the form in v 7, אֲצַוֶּךָ; but some MSS. read a participle מְצַוֶּךָ, a reading reflected in *S* and *T*, and the present tense in *V* (*praecipio*) points in the same direction. The participle of course demands the pronoun that is present in *M* but unnecessary with the *M* finite verb (it does not carry the emphatic function as do the pronouns that begin vv 17 and 18).

18   For my part, see, I have made you today
         into a fortified city,
             an iron bolt
             and a bronze wall
         [{against all the land,}b
             to the kings of Judah andc her officials,
             {to her priests}d
             and to the people of the land.]a

19   Though they shall fight against you,
         they shall not overcome you,
             for I am with you,
                           oracle of Yahweh,
             to rescue you.

18a   The bracketed words are evidently a secondary expansion of "city"; there is nothing like them in the parallel 15:20 (compare the expansion in 2:26, and see further Preliminary Observations and Interpretation).

b   For "against all the land, to the kings of Judah" G reads "to all the kings of Judah." The phrase "against all the land," with עַל־, fits oddly with the specific terms following, each of which is introduced by the more idiomatic לְ. Omit "against all the land" with Volz as evidence of a conflate doublet or late gloss.

c   A few MSS., G, and S read "and" here; M omits.

d   A few MSS. and S read "and to her priests"; G, however, omits the whole phrase, which should be deleted as an expansionist addition (so Cornill; Janzen, pp. 35–36). Compare 34:19.

Preliminary Observations

The literary-critical problems posed by the remainder of the chapter are intricate and far from easy of solution. Among them are the following: (1) What is the relation of vv 4–10 to vv 11–19? Is Jrm's call confined to vv 4–10? In this case vv 11–19 will represent supplemental material, including the visions. Or are the visions to be understood as part of the call from the beginning? In the latter case, is the reassurance to Jrm in vv 17–19 to be understood as supplemental, or part of the call from the beginning? (2) The first vision (vv 11–12) offers wording that is balanced and restrained; by contrast the second vision (vv 13–16) offers wording that is prolix. Does this circumstance suggest (a) that the second vision was added later to the first vision, or (b) that the two visions were originally a balanced pair but that the second has undergone later expansion, or (c) is the prolixity of the second vision in fact irrelevant? (3) Why is there mention of "nations" in v 5 and of "nations" and "kingdoms" in v 10, since the bulk of Jrm's oracles, at least in the early years, appear to have been directed against Judah? (4) What, after all, is one to make of the second vision, both the general meaning of it and the specific words in it?

Form criticism can offer no direct help in these matters. Thus visions such as those recorded in vv 11–16 might well be understood in the context of a call (see Form on those verses), but there is no necessary connection between call and vision. The only possibility of a solution lies in a rhetorical-structural analysis of the text; it is fortunate that the original layer of material gives evidence of careful structure. Thus it is likely that "youth" (נַעַר) in 1:6, 7 is linked to "(time of) youth" (נְעוּרִים) in 2:2 and 3:4 (and perhaps 3:25), and that the striking word "tribes" (מִשְׁפָּחוֹת), v 15, is linked to its

occurrence in 2:4. These data suggest a unity between vv 4–10 and at least the visions of vv 11–16. (For further considerations reinforcing this conclusion, see Structure.) The first task then is a rhetorical-structural analysis of vv 4–19.

We begin with the double reading "tribes (of) kingdoms of" (מִשְׁפָּחוֹת מַמְלְכוֹת) in v 15; evidence is given in Text for understanding this to be a conflate reading. The word "tribes" (מִשְׁפָּחוֹת) is the *lectio difficilior*, and two points about it are noteworthy. First it is linked assonantally with "my judgments" (מִשְׁפָּטַי) in v 16 (the same assonantal association of "tribes" with the root "judge" is found in 10:24–25). Second, the association of "tribes" in 2:4 and 3:14 (and 31:1) is with the tribes of Israel, not of the enemy. Whether the "tribes" in 2:4 and 3:14 are intended to refer to all twelve tribes or only the ten tribes of the north is not immediately clear, but the instructions at the beginning of 3:12 indicate that it is at least possible that the reference in 3:14 is to the ten northern tribes. This line of reasoning suggests in turn the possibility that the first clause of v 15 and the first clauses of vv 15–16 here are part of an original stratum of material directed to the northern tribes of Israel: "Look! I am going to summon all the tribes of the north, and I shall speak my judgments on them for all their crime." This surmise, it is here proposed, is correct; it is consistent with the diction of 2:4–9; 3:1–2, 4–5, 12, 14–15, 18, 19, 21a–25; 4:1–2, which likewise emerge as early utterances directed to the northern tribes (see 2:1—4:4, Preliminary Observations).

The rest of v 15 clearly refers to the foe from the north, however, who were ultimately (if not originally) the Babylonians. The meaning of the vision of the pot then appears to have undergone an adaptation to refer to

23

the foe from the north. So what might be made of the vision of the pot?

Critical understanding of the meaning of that vision (vv 13–14) has always centered on the foe from the north because of the wording of most of v 15, and therefore the assumption has been that the pot is about to boil over, spilling water toward the south and scalding its inhabitants. But this interpretation ignores three data: (1) Nothing in the vision is said about water. (2) A pot, filled with water and put on to boil, is unlikely to be in a tipped position. (3) The verb "will be opened" (תִּפָּתַח) is an odd expression for the spilling of water. The exegesis given in detail in the Interpretation of vv 13–14 clarifies the situation. The pot is lying empty on its side, heated by coals to clean off baked-on organic material; Ezek 24:11 uses the same image. In that passage the heat applied to the pot is a symbol of the judgment on Jerusalem, and since an analogous figure is used in Jer 6:27–30 of heat applied to crude lead to extract the silver as a symbol of the refining of the covenant people, we may conclude that the original meaning of the vision of the pot is that it is a symbol of the judgment of Yahweh on the tribes of (northern) Israel. It is true that the word to the northern tribes in vv 15–16 is ambiguous; it is bad news in that Yahweh will "pronounce" his "judgments" and that "disaster" will come, but good news is at least suggested by the verb "will be opened." This study will propose that the "judgments" on the northern tribes are embodied in the portions of chapters 2:1—4:4 which were directed to the north, and that the possibility of good news comes in the appeal to "return" which carries with it the possibility of reunion with the south (3:12, 14–15, 18). (Compare the association of bad news and good news in the original stratum of material, directed to the north, in chaps. 30—31.)

But there is a problem to this analysis: the words "and they shall come in and each put his throne at the entrance of the gates of Jerusalem" (v 15) give every evidence of being genuine to Jrm. Thus "entrance" (פֶּתַח) shares the same root with "will be opened" (תִּפָּתַח) in v 14 and lacks a preposition, characteristic of poetic diction; and more generally the structure of "and they shall come in and each put his throne" is identical with 51:9aβ—again the diction of poetry. (By contrast the rest of v 15, "and upon all its walls around, and over all the cities of Judah," is an awkward prose addition.)

Now if the two lines "and they shall come in and each put his throne at the entrance of the gates of Jerusalem" are genuine words of Jrm, then it was evidently the prophet himself who reinterpreted the vision of the pot to refer to the foe from the north. At this point the word "kingdoms" as well as "tribes" becomes appropriate at the beginning of the verse (so G); perhaps Jrm substituted "kingdoms" for "tribes" at some point in the dictation process. Jrm became convinced: Yahweh is not summoning the tribes of Israel from the north but rather the foe from the north. Since the foe is (at least potentially) besieging the cities of Judah in 4:5–8, 13–18, and 6:1–8, material in the first scroll triggered by the battle of Carchemish (by the hypothesis of the present study), these two lines of v 15 are best understood as an expansion at that point.

The words beginning with אֲשֶׁר in v 16 ("in abandoning me" to the end of the verse) likewise suggest the poetry of Jrm. The words are not integrated into the original stratum of the meaning of the pot vision, but detailed evidence is given in Interpretation that the wording is genuine to Jrm, indeed that it is his poetic rendering of the words of Huldah to the delegation from the temple (2 Kgs 22:17). Two considerations suggest that these words too were added at the time of the dictation of the first scroll. First, the phrase "in abandoning me" is an echo of "me they have abandoned" in 2:13, part of the material (by the hypothesis of the present study) of the first scroll. Second, Jrm's first scroll was clearly modeled on the scroll found in the temple in 622 (see Interpretation on chap. 36), and words echoing Huldah's judgment on that earlier scroll would suggest to Jrm and his hearers that parallel. The judgment that vv 15–16 are a Deuteronomistic expansion (see Interpretation) is therefore incorrect, but the impression of secondary additions here is a sound one.

Verses 17–19 represent another problem. Unquestionably the passage (excluding the bracketed words) are genuine to Jrm; the material is analyzable as poetry, and the pairing of the two stems of חתת (qal or nip'al; hip'il) is typical of him. A variant of vv 18–19 is found in 15:20–21; the existence of a doublet elsewhere does not demonstrate that the verses are genuine to Jrm, but at the same time it does not rule out the possibility either.

From the point of view of literary structure the passage does not share any semantic or assonantal links with vv 11–16; the structural ties with preceding material are of another sort. Thus "I (have) made you" (נְתַתִּיךָ) in v 5 is repeated in v 18; the only other occurrences of this form in Jer are 6:27 (see Structure) and 49:15. The occurrence of "today" in vv 10 and 18 is perhaps not significant in itself, but the repetition adds to the integration of the two passages. The most striking parallel, however, is that between "do not be panicked by their presence" (אַל־תֵּחַת מִפְּנֵיהֶם) in v 17 and "do not be afraid of them" (אַל־תִּירָא מִפְּנֵיהֶם) in v 8 (compare the parallelism in Isa 51:7) and between the two occurrences of "for I am with you to rescue you" in vv 8 and 19. There is also a possible parallel between the "fortified city," metaphorically applied to Jrm in v 18, and "Jerusalem" in v 15. The material in 15:20–21 is part of the "confessional" material; data will be offered that these verses in chapter 15 were shaped by the crisis in Jrm's vocation in the summer of 594 (see Confessions, Setting, after 11:17). There is no reason to conclude otherwise than that these verses in chapter 1 entered the tradition at the same time, perhaps even as a rhetorical balance to the growing collection of "confessions" at the end of the second scroll.

The question then might arise whether v 8 was a late addition along with vv 17–19. The answer must be, probably not; form-critically v 8 is a part of Yahweh's reassurance to the prophet, a normal part of the call; the phrase "I will be with you" appears in Exod 3:12 in the call to Moses and in Judg 6:16 in the call to Gideon.

Structure

It has already been stated (Preliminary Observations) that vv 4–19 must be considered as a unit; it appears that the original stratum of the call is to be found in vv 4–16 and that vv 17–19, though original to Jrm, were added at a later point.

The material is tightly integrated into the series of units that follows by a series of inclusios: (1) There is the link of "youth" (נַעַר) here in vv 6 and 7 and "(time of) youth" (נְעוּרִים) in 2:2 and 3:4 (and probably 24 and 25) and the link of "tribes" (מִשְׁפָּחוֹת) here in v 15 and in 2:4 and 3:14 (see Preliminary Observations). (2) "I (have) made you" (נְתַתִּיךָ) appears with "prophet" here in v 5

and with "fortified city" in v 18, and then with "assayer" in 6:27 (the only other occurrence of this verb form is in 49:15). (Both these sets of parallels have already been discussed in Preliminary Observations.) (3) "The nations" and "I knew you" occur here in v 5, and "the nations" and "do not know you" in 10:25. (4) Verses 18–19 are virtually a doublet of 15:20–21 (see Preliminary Observations). "Come forth from the womb" occurs both in v 5 and in 20:18. These inclusios may well give indication of the steps by which the present collection of written material took shape.[1] The call narrative, then, has been part of the growing collection of Jrm material from the beginning, beginning with the first scroll (as a means to legitimate the prophet?—see further Setting).

Form-critically verses 4–16 divide easily into two sections, vv 4–10, the call proper, and vv 11–16, the two visions; but the time-markers indicate a contrast between vv 4–5, with the "before"-clauses, referring to the time before Jrm's birth, and vv 6–10, marked by "this day" (v 10). There are no further time-markers for the two visions, and the assumption is therefore that they are subsumed under the same time period as that represented by "this day" in v 10.

Several considerations suggest a basic unity between vv 4–10 and vv 11–16: (1) There is the integration of both vv 4–10 and vv 11–16 with adjoining material in chapter 2; this is the most immediate inclusio and has already been noted above. (2) There seems to be an integration between "word(s)" in vv 9 and 12, and between "nations" and "tribes/kingdoms" in vv 5, 10, and 15. (3) There is an identity in the introductory words in vv 4, 11, and 13 (except for "a second time" in v 13); see further Form. (4) The phraseology of 20:18 offers both "come forth from the womb" and "see," suggesting at least that "seeing" is integrated with the call from the womb.

The speech of Yahweh's in v 5 is carefully balanced. Now all translations and commentaries that take the division into cola seriously divide it into three cola. But the question arises whether it should not rather be construed in five cola. Two considerations lead to this conclusion: (1) The "before"-clause (introduced by בְּטֶרֶם) in Isa 42:9b seems to form a colon of its own, and the

---

1   For the last-named inclusio, see Jack R. Lundbom, *Jeremiah: A Study in Ancient Hebrew Rhetoric* (SBLDS 18; Missoula, MT: Scholars, 1975) 28; and for the general approach to the process by which chaps. 1—20 were built up, see Holladay, *Architecture*.

diction of that verse is very close to those here; cf. further Jer 13:16. (2) The prepositional expressions "in the belly," "from the womb," and "to the nations" appear to be parallel; each is followed by a verb expressing Yahweh's appointment of Jrm. These two considerations lead to our understanding the first two independent clauses to be "in the belly I knew you" and "from the womb I dedicated you" rather than simply the bare verbs "I knew you" and "I dedicated you."[2] The difference from the conventional understanding is not great, but it is nice nevertheless: the prepositional phrases are not buried in their clauses, but highlighted (see further Interpretation).

Yahweh's speeches in vv 7–8 and 9–10 are also (coincidentally?) five cola each. In vv 7–8 the first and fourth cola begin with אַל־תֹּאמַר and אַל־תִּירָא respectively, cola two and five are both introduced by כִּי, and cola two and three are closely parallel. In vv 9–10 the first colon is parallel with the second (deictic words followed by perfect first singular verbs), cola four and five show inner parallelism and chiasmus in their infinitives (see Text, Interpretation), and the third colon stands alone, completing the thought of the second but offering the same kind of inner parallelism found in the fourth and fifth cola.

These speeches are united by the congruence of diction between the last colon of v 5, "a prophet to the nations I made you," and the first two cola of v 10, "I have appointed you . . . over nations and over kingdoms," and by the contrast of time reference already referred to, "before . . ." in v 5 and "this day" in v 10.

Jrm's speech in v 6 can be divided into three parts, but it manifests no striking parallelism: Klaus Baltzer points out that the contrast between the poetry of Yahweh's speeches and the prose of Jrm's speech conforms to courtly protocol.[3]

The two visions in vv 11–16 divide easily: v 11, the vision of the almond-twig; v 12, its explanation; v 13, the vision of the fanned pot; vv 14–16, its explanation. The relation between the vision and the explanation of the almond-twig depends on the word-play of שָׁקֵד and שֹׁקֵד. The relation between the vision and the explanation of the fanned pot is more complicated, playing upon (1)

"north" (vv 13, 14, 15), (2) "fanned" (נָפוּחַ) and "will be opened" (תִּפָּתַח) (vv 13, 14), and (3) "calamity" and "crime," two translations of רָעָה (vv 14, 16). And the original clauses of vv 15 and 16 are parallel (the assonance of מִשְׁפָּחוֹת and מִשְׁפָּטַי, as already noted: see Preliminary Observations).

The additions in vv 15 and 16 are not in tight parallelism. Thus in v 15 one might close a colon with "his throne" and another with "Jerusalem." The gloss that closes v 15 likewise divides into two phrases. The added words in v 16 make up three clauses; the last two ("in sacrificing to other gods" and "in worshiping the works of their hands") may be construed as two cola. But "in abandoning me" (אֲשֶׁר עֲזָבוּנִי) is uncomfortably short; conceivably in the earliest stage (the words to the north) the only colon of v 16 ended with "for all their crime," and when the further three clauses were added in the next stage (the first scroll) "for all their crime" was understood to begin a colon that is closed by "in abandoning me" (so the typography of *BHS*); but that is purely speculative.

The first bicolon of v 17 has a structure very much like 4:5a or 5:1aα, a verb clause in the first colon balanced by two parallel verbs in the second; and this resemblance is not surprising, given the fact that all of them are in form a battle call. The second bicolon in v 17 offers a nice contrast between two stems of "panic" (חתת) and two occurrences of "their face/presence" (פְּנֵיהֶם: see Interpretation). The form of the first colon of v 18 should conform to the first colon of v 10 (thus including "this day"/"today"), and the following three phrases, each of two words, make up three cola. Verse 19 should evidently be construed as three cola—the doublet in 15:21 must evidently be four (the addition of "to save you and" with "rescue you" makes the fourth), but the present text is hardly deficient, since 30:11a has the same colon as the third here.

Form
Verses 4–19 embody the call narrative of Jrm. Analysis of the passage is rendered difficult by the fact that the various prophetic call narratives in the OT differ from each other in their constitutive elements. They are,

---

2 For a treatment of clauses with בְּטֶרֶם see Michael Patrick O'Connor, *Hebrew Verse Structure* (Winona Lake, IN: Eisenbrauns, 1980) 248–49 (for Zeph 2:2)

and 323 (on the pattern in general).

3 Klaus Baltzer, *Die Biographie der Propheten* (Neukirchen: Neukirchener, 1975) 115.

beside the present one, that of Isaiah (Isaiah 6) and Ezekiel (Ezek 1:1—3:11); in addition there are elements of a call narrative in Isa 40:1–11. Walther Zimmerli has pointed out[4] that the calls of Isaiah and Ezekiel show vivid visual features wherein those called perceive themselves present in the heavenly council (compare also Micaiah's vision, 1 Kgs 22:19). These features are absent, however, in Jrm's call.

The call of Jrm by contrast is closely comparable to the narrative of Moses' call, both in the JE form (Exod 3:1—4:17, particularly 3:10–12) and in the P form (Exod 6:2–13, 28; 7:1–5), and to that of Gideon's call (Judg 6:11–23, particularly vv 11–17). Now it is true that some traditions in the OT attribute prophetic status to Moses (by implication, Num 12:5–8 [JE?]; more directly in Deut 18:18; 34:10 [D]; Hos 12:13), but Gideon was not called to be a prophet. One is left, then, with the question whether we have to do with a general pattern of a call to leadership,[5] or whether, in view of the particularly close parallels between the call of Jrm and that of Moses (see below), the resemblance to Moses is not deliberate, and, if it is deliberate, whether the modeling of the call of Jrm after that of Moses is due to the sensibility of Jrm himself (whether conscious or unconscious) or is due to a redactor who wished to underline the resemblance between Jrm and Moses. Given the paucity of our models, form criticism is able to give only tentative answers to these questions.

Norman Habel[6] has attempted to present parallels in the constitutive elements of the calls of Isaiah, Jrm, Ezekiel, Moses, and Gideon; these are six, "divine confrontation," "introductory word," "commission," "objection," "reassurance," and "sign." But his scheme is too artificial for all the passages in question. Thus he locates a single "objection" for Isaiah, namely "How long, O Lord?" in Isa 6:11; but surely there is an earlier one, "Woe is me, for I am lost . . . ," Isa 6:5. Ezekiel manifests no objection at all, the item fading behind the reassurance of Ezek 2:6. Gideon offers two objections, Judg 6:15, "Pray, Lord, how can I deliver Israel?" and Judg 6:22, "Ah, Lord Yahweh, for now I have seen the angel of Yahweh face to face." Habel further leaves one uncertain of his first two elements, particularly with respect to Jrm's call. So it is best to stay with his last four elements, and to omit the calls of Isaiah and of Ezekiel from any parallel table.[7] We have then:

commission:	Jer 1:5	Exod 3:10	Judg 6:14
objection:	Jer 1:6	Exod 3:11	Judg 6:15
reassurance:	Jer 1:7–8	Exod 3:12	Judg 6:16
sign:	Jer 1:9	Exod 3:12	Judg 6:17–22

The calls of both Moses and Gideon are prefaced by a description of the circumstances in which the call was heard: Moses was keeping his father-in-law's flock, he saw the burning bush, Yahweh declares he has seen the affliction of his people (Exod 3:1–9); Gideon was beating out the wheat in the wine-press when the angel came and sat under the oak (Judg 6:11). But in the case of Jrm we are given no circumstance—simply the bare statement that the word of Yahweh came to him as follows . . . (v 4).

The commission to Jrm in v 5 is to be a prophet to the nations. Curiously enough the call of Isaiah does not use the term "prophet" (נָבִיא), and the call of Ezekiel uses the term only once, and there in a quite indirect fashion (Ezek 2:5); nor do either of those calls employ the related verb "prophesy." Further, no phrase like "to the nations" is to be found in those calls, though the books that bear their names do contain oracles against the nations in the same way as Jer does. "To the nations" suggests a call to kingship (compare Pss 2:8; 72:11) and implies sovereignty over other nations.

The call to be a prophet from before one's birth is likewise unparalleled among other prophetic calls, though such an affirmation would be extended later in the biblical tradition: by Deutero-Isaiah to Israel and to Yahweh's servant (Isa 44:4, 24; 49:5), and in the NT by Paul to himself (Gal 1:15) and by Matthew and Luke to Jesus Christ (Matt 1:18–25; Luke 1:26–38). Indeed the

4   Zimmerli, *Ezekiel 1*, 98–99.
5   Gregorio del Olmo Lete, *La Vocación der Líder en el antiguo Israel, Morfología de los Relatos Bíblicos de Vocación* (Salamanca: Universidad Pontificia de Salamanca, 1973).
6   Habel, "Call Narratives."
7   So also Werner H. Schmidt, *Exodus* (BKAT 2; Neukirchen: Neukirchener, 1977) 123–29; Berridge, pp. 27–62.

matter is pressed back to the foundation of the world in Wisdom's self-designation (Prov 8:22–31) and in the prologue of John about Jesus Christ (John 1:1–18). But there is material of such a sort earlier than Jrm: an angel told Samson's mother that "the boy shall be a Nazirite to God from birth" (Judg 13:5), and the stories of the infancy of Moses and of Samuel imply a destiny directed by Yahweh from their birth (Exodus 2; 1 Sam 1:1—2:10). As is well known, the narrative of the infancy of Moses is paralleled in the far earlier account of the infancy of Sargon of Akkad,[8] and the specific wording of the call from birth is closely paralleled by several royal self-descriptions from both Mesopotamia and Egypt. Thus we have the opening words of a self-description of King Shulgi of the Third Dynasty of Ur (c. 2050 B.C.E.) in a royal hymn, "A king am I; from the womb I have become a hero";[9] the self-description of Assurbanipal (668–627), "I am Assurbanipal, offspring (creature) of Assur and Bêlit, the oldest prince of the royal harem, whose name Assur and Sin, the lord of the tiara, have named for the kingship from earliest days, whom they formed in his mother's womb, for the rulership of Assyria; whom Shamash, Adad and Ishtar, by their unalterable decree, have ordered to exercise sovereignty";[10] and, most strikingly, part of a speech of the god Amun, set forth in a stele of Pianchi, pharaoh of the Twenty-fifth Dynasty (ca. 751–730), "It was in the belly of your mother that I said concerning you that you were to be ruler of Egypt; it was as seed and while you were in the egg, that I knew you, that (I knew) you were to be Lord."[11]

Verse 6 embodies Jrm's "objection": he seeks some way to avoid Yahweh's commission. The precise wording, with "Ah, Lord Yahweh" (אֲהָהּ אֲדֹנָי יהוה), is not found at this point in other calls, though it expresses a second objection at a later point in the narrative of

Gideon (Judg 6:22). Likewise, the suggestion that the one called to be God's spokesman does not know how to speak is not part of Moses' objection at this precise point in his call, but both the JE and P traditions recall such an objection at a later point (Exod 4:10; 6:12, 30). Indeed each of the "objections" recorded for those called is quite distinctive (cf. Exod 3:11 and Judg 6:15). One is reminded, too, of Saul's reaction when told of his destiny to be king, "Am I not a Benjaminite, from the least of the tribes of Israel?" (1 Sam 9:21), and David's "Who am I . . . ?" in the course of a prayer (2 Sam 7:18).[12]

There are of course many other instances of "objections" in the OT: as we might expect, there are those spoken by one human being to another (Gen 24:39; 1 Sam 18:18; 23:3) as well as those in response to a commission from God. Jrm's words "for I am only a youth" (כִּי־נַעַר אָנֹכִי) echo the words of Solomon's dismay in his prayer on entering into kingship, "but I am a mere youth" (וְאָנֹכִי נַעַר קָטֹן, 1 Kgs 3:7 NAB). Though that prayer is part of the Deuteronomic history, there is some opinion that this passage belongs to an earlier tradition,[13] so that it is possible that the model was available to Jrm.[14]

Given the existence of royal models in the phrases of both the commission and the objection, one is led at this point to ask whether the fact is significant. Is it only an accident that the analogies are often royal ones?—might any person sensible of a call be likely to verbalize it as a call from the womb and then offer an expression of modesty or dismay? Or is the call of Jrm shaped with some deliberateness on royal models? The role of both king and prophet varied greatly in the course of the history of the united and divided monarchies, but this much seems clear: Samuel was the last leader to maintain the functions both of civil leadership and of prophet in

8 See conveniently ANET, 119.

9 Samuel N. Kramer, "The Oldest Literary Catalogue," BASOR 88 (December 1942) 14 n. 1.

10 The Rassam Cylinder, col. 1; see Daniel D. Luckenbill, Ancient Records of Assyria and Babylonia (Chicago: University of Chicago, 1927, rep. New York: Greenwood, 1968) 2:291, sec. 765.

11 M. Gilula, "An Egyptian Parallel to Jeremia i 4–5," VT 17 (1967), 114.

12 Some of these correspond to the form analyzed by George W. Coats, "Self-Abasement and Insult Formulas," JBL 89 (1970) 14–26, but Jrm's objection

does not fit that form.

13 Martin Noth, Könige I. 1–16 (BKAT 9/1; Neukirchen: Neukirchener, 1968) 46; compare Otto Eissfeldt, The Old Testament, An Introduction (Oxford: Blackwell, 1965) 288.

14 For a discussion of Solomon's objection as a possible model for Jrm see Berridge, pp. 45–49.

one person; after him the functions were divided between king and prophet. The balance may have been lost at the time of Solomon and thereafter, but in the south the balance was righted by Isaiah's time, and the balance had been maintained in the northern kingdom of Israel.[15] If, then, Jrm understood himself to be a successor to Moses and Samuel (15:1; see below on Jrm and Moses), if he saw the prophet's role to be analogous to that of the king, if he saw in the law of Deuteronomy guidelines for the king (Deut 17:14–20) laid alongside guidelines for the prophet (Deut 18:15–22), then he may well have been impelled to perceive his own calling to be verbalized in a way analogous to those of kings.

Yahweh's "reassurance" comes in vv 7–8. It begins by his rejecting Jrm's objection: "Do not say, 'I am (only) a youth.'" There is no parallel in any other call narrative for the form "Do not say . . .": the phrase appears nowhere else in the OT when God is speaker, only of Moses to Israel (Deut 9:4) and in the wisdom literature (Prov 3:28; 20:22; 24:29; Eccl 5:5).

The function of the conjunction כִּי after the rejected words is uncertain. The reassurance in Exod 3:12 and Judg 6:16 both begin the same way, כִּי (אֵלָיו יהוה) וַיֹּאמֶר אֶהְיֶה עִמָּךְ "and he/Yahweh said (to him) כִּי 'I am with you.'" The conjunction could either mean "for," its normal translation (so *RSV*, *NEB*), or (following the negative of the prohibition) mean "but (rather)" (*NJV*). In the present case the second alternative is more likely: it is intended to overcome the hesitation expressed in the previous verse.

The best parallels for the next two phrases are to be found in Deut 18:18, "And he shall speak to them whatever I command him" (referring to the prophet like Moses who is to come), and Exod 7:2 (P), "It is you who will speak whatever I command you." The first parallel is not form-critically significant at this point, but the second is the form of reassurance in the P-narrative, following an objection of Moses (6:30).

The words "do not fear" (אַל־תִּירָא) in v 8 clearly

embody the quintessence of reassurance: the words are found in a second reassurance to Gideon (Judg 6:23) after his second objection ("Ah, Lord Yahweh," Judg 6:22—see see above on v 6).

The phrase "for I am with you" (כִּי אִתְּךָ אָנִי)[16] reminds one of the analogous phrase in both Exod 3:12 and Judg 6:16—the phrase called a "support formula" (*Beistandsformular*) by Werner H. Schmidt.[17] The linking of these two phrases, "Do not fear, for I am with you," is often repeated in oracles of salvation (30:10–11; Isa 41:10; 43:5), though it is hardly fair to say that a speaker is conscious of using the forms of the oracle of salvation whenever it is stated that Yahweh is present with someone.[18] The precise wording of "for I am with you" in the present passage, and the addition of "to rescue you," seem to be confined to Jer and will be repeated in v 19 (and its doublet 15:20); but the theme of Yahweh's rescue is obviously a traditional one (Exod 3:8; Ps 22:9, 21). Compare the format of the oracle of salvation in vv 17–19.

The call continues with the sign, "And Yahweh extended his hand and touched my mouth" (v 9). Analogous signs were perceived by both Isaiah and Ezekiel: in Isaiah's case, the seraph touched his mouth with a burning coal taken from the temple altar (Isa 6:6–7), while in Ezekiel's case Yahweh commanded him to eat a written scroll (Ezek 2:8—3:3). In the cases of both Moses and Gideon the word "sign" (אוֹת) is used (Exod 3:12; Judg 6:17); for Moses the sign will simply be that when he has brought Israel out of Egypt they shall serve God on Mount Sinai (Exod 3:12), while for Gideon the sign is the assurance by the angel of his continued presence (Judg 6:18) and ultimately by the fire from the rock (Judg 6:21). Gideon's calling is not primarily centered around speaking, but Moses' is. There is, however, no attention to Moses' mouth in the context of Exod 3:12: Moses' objections that he cannot speak well come later in the narrative, as we have seen (Exod 4:10 [JE]; 6:12, 30 [P]), and Yahweh's response is to remind

---

15 Frank M. Cross, *Canaanite Myth and Hebrew Epic* (Cambridge: Harvard University, 1973) 223–24; Baltzer, *Biographie*, 71–87.

16 Manfred Görg, "'Ich bin mit Dir,' Gewicht und Anspruch einer Redeform im Alten Testament," *TGl* 70 (1980) 214–40, esp. 224.

17 Schmidt, *Exodus*, 126–27.

18 Compare Berridge, pp. 52–53 and n. 145.

Moses that he, Yahweh, created Moses' mouth (Exod 4:11–12 [JE]) and that Aaron can be an intermediary (both traditions, Exod 4:14–17 [JE]; 7:1–5 [P]).

The sign concludes with words that accompany the action, "Look, I have put my words in your mouth" (v 9), the beginning of a speech that continues through v 10. This phraseology is not duplicated in the other prophetic calls: Ezekiel describes most elaborately how he ate the written scroll, but what God then says is not a description of what has been done but a command for the prophet to speak; God's words to Isaiah are to declare the prophet's guilt to be taken away and his sin forgiven (Isa 6:7). The close verbal parallel is with Deut 18:18, as was the case with one of the phrases in v 7; on the significance of the parallel with Deut 18:18 see below on Jrm and Moses.

The remainder of Yahweh's speech (v 10) reinforces the shape of Jrm's call in v 5; this diction is not paralleled in other call narratives.

Now what can be made of all this variety in vv 4–10? Brevard S. Childs says, "The striking parallels of Ex. 3 with Judg. 6 and Jer. 1 have long been noticed and confirm a stereotyped structure."[19] This is doubtless true to a degree. There is a widespread conviction that the phrasing of Judg 6:16 ("And Yahweh said to him, 'I will be with you'") is deliberately based on Exod 3:12.[20] But I would suggest that given the variety of form among the calls of Jrm, Isaiah, and Ezekiel, and the closeness of the parallels between the call of Jrm and the call of Moses— most especially given the fact that the parallels with Moses are taken not only from Exodus 3 but from Exodus 4, 6, 7, and Deut 18:18—we are dealing here not so much with a stereotyped structure as with a deliberate parallel with the model of Moses primarily, and with the models of Gideon, Samuel, and kings secondarily. And the freedom that we perceive in recasting the various elements of the call into a fresh unity is best understood as the work of Jrm himself, whether done consciously or unconsciously (see Setting).

A final question that must be addressed here is a closer specification of the nature of this office to which Jrm was called, the office presupposed by the form of this call narrative. Parallels with kingship ideology, especially parallels with Mesopotamian and Egyptian royal self-designations, by which the king is called by the deity, are striking, and account has already been taken of these; but such models are clearly not the most important for Jrm. There have been attempts to typify the prophet as a covenant mediator,[21] but the designation seems restrictive. Baltzer has suggested the model of the commissioning of the vizier of a king,[22] but this is not persuasive: the vizier offers no objection to being named. It has long been popular to understand the prophet as Yahweh's messenger;[23] but models of prophetic activity which go back to Mari (eighteenth century) make it clear that there were persons functioning in ways analogous to that of Israel's prophets for centuries, and therefore that it may be fruitless to inquire too specifically into the secular models for a prophetic call.[24]

The vision narratives of vv 11–16 are evidently integrated with vv 4–10 as part of the call (see Preliminary Observations, Structure). In both the calls of Isaiah and of Ezekiel visionary experience is integral; the

19 Childs, *Exodus*, 54.
20 George F. Moore, *A Critical and Exegetical Commentary on Judges* (ICC; Edinburgh: Clark, 1895) 186; Robert G. Boling, *Judges* (AB 6A; Garden City, NY: Doubleday, 1975) 132.
21 James Muilenburg, "The 'Office' of the Prophet in Ancient Israel," *The Bible in Modern Scholarship, Papers Read at the 100th Meeting of the Society of Biblical Literature, December 28–30, 1964* (ed. J. Philip Hyatt; Nashville: Abingdon, 1965) 74–97; Kraus, *Worship*, 108–12.
22 Baltzer, *Biographie;* and Klaus Baltzer, "Considerations Regarding the Office and Calling of the Prophet," *HTR* 61 (1968) 567–81.
23 Westermann, *Basic Forms*, 98–115; Habel, "Call Narratives"; but see more generally Klaus Koch, *The Growth of the Biblical Tradition, The Form-Critical Method* (New York: Scribner's, 1969) 189, and James F. Ross, "The Prophet as Yahweh's Messenger," *Israel's Prophetic Heritage, Essays in Honor of James Muilenburg* (ed. Bernhard W. Anderson and Walter Harrelson; New York: Harper, 1962) 98–107.
24 See on this matter W. Eugene March, "Prophecy," *Old Testament Form Criticism* (ed. John H. Hayes; San Antonio: Trinity University, 1974) 153–54.

verb in the present passage is "see" (ראה) (vv 11, 12, 13) as it is in Isa 6:1 and in Ezek 1:1 (and five more times through Ezekiel 3). In this way the call of Jrm resembles more closely those of Isaiah and Ezekiel (compare the contrast of the call of Jrm with those two prophets noted above). For a thorough treatment of the experience of vision as a part of the call see Zimmerli, *Ezekiel 1*, 97–110.

As already noted, the introductory phrases of vv 11 and 13 repeat that of v 4. After those phrases in both vv 11 and 13 comes the question from Yahweh, "What do you see, Jeremiah?" That same question is found in 24:3, with the vocative "Amos" in Amos 7:8 and 8:2, and, without a vocative, in Zech 4:2 and 5:2; it is then a fixed expression introducing some of the vision narratives in the OT. Johannes Lindblom notes, "It seems likely that behind this form of question and answer lies the the normal didactic method in the teaching of 'the wise'."[25]

Jrm received a "sign" (v 9; see above). But just as Moses received more than one "sign" in the course of his call (Exod 3:12; 4:1–19), so it is plausible to see the visions of vv 11–16 as further signs to Jrm.[26]

The fixed form here has been called the "oracle-vision."[27] But the form as found in Amos 8:1–2 is more extended, having an "announcement of the vision" ("thus the Lord Yahweh showed me"), a "transition" ("and behold"), and the "image" ("a basket of summer fruit"), before the "question by Yahweh" ("and he said, 'Amos, what do you see?'") equivalent to the questions with which vv 11 and 13 here begin. One notes that the vision-report in 24:1–10 offers the full format analogous to that in Amos 8:1–2. But the structure here is simply: (1) the question by Yahweh (vv 11a, 13a); (2) the answer by the prophet (vv 11b, 13b); and (3) the oracle by Yahweh (vv 12, 14–16). The format of the vision report

is used here, at the beginning of the collection of material in Jer, programmatically to set forth some of the themes of the prophet's message: the vindication of Yahweh's word, and his judgments and offer of reconciliation (first with the north and then) with Judah.[28]

Verses 17–19 are in the form of a pure salvation oracle.[29] Originally the salvation oracle seems to have been delivered to charismatic leaders before a holy war;[30] the phrase "gird your loins" indicates preparation for hard physical action, such as battle (for such a salvation oracle, see 2 Chr 20:15–17). Jrm is being equipped by Yahweh for lifelong battle as a warrior in holy war against his people.[31] All the components of a salvation oracle are here:[32] (1) address, "and you" (v 17); (2) exhortation of salvation, "do not be panicked" (v 17); (3) substantiation, "I have made you today a fortified city . . ." (v 18), "I am with you to rescue you" (v 19b); (4) result, "though they fight against you, they shall not overcome you" (vv 19a).[33] The parallel to a passage like Isa 41:8–13 is very close. One notes the way the context of holy war has been adapted for prophetic use; the war imagery of v 17 shifts to the diction of prophetic activity ("speak to them").[34]

Setting

Questions of setting have already been addressed in Preliminary Observations, but they must now be examined more systematically.

Form critics who are struck by the close parallels in form between the call of Jrm and earlier calls in the OT will assume that the call here is simply the formalization of a pattern and does not represent Jrm's personal perception of his call. Thus Schmidt writes, "Jer 1:4ff. too scarcely reproduces Jeremiah's call in the historical sense";[35] so also Henning Graf von Reventlow.[36]

25 Johannes Lindblom, "Wisdom in the Old Testament Prophets," *Wisdom in Israel and in the Ancient Near East Presented to Professor Harold Henry Rowley by the Society for Old Testament Study in Association with the Editorial Board of Vetus Testamentum in Celebration of his Sixty-Fifth Birthday, 24 March 1955* (ed. Martin Noth and D. Winton Thomas; VTsup 3; Leiden: Brill, 1955) 192–204, esp. 202.
26 See on this Long, "Reports of Visions," 358–59.
27 Ibid., 357.
28 Ibid., 358.
29 Berridge, p. 198.
30 Reventlow, *Liturgie*, p. 58; Berridge, p. 199.
31 Berridge, p. 200.
32 Joachim Begrich, "Das priesterliche Heilsorakel," *ZAW* 52 (1934) 81–92 = his *Gesammelte Studien zum Alten Testament* (Theologische Bücherei 21; Munich: Kaiser, 1964) 217–31.
33 Berridge, p. 200.
34 Ibid., 201.
35 Schmidt, *Exodus*, 124.
36 Reventlow, *Liturgie*, 26.

Zimmerli suggests that Jrm reports his call in a stylized way.[37] On the other hand, though recognizing the formal elements in Jrm's call, John M. Berridge affirms that the prophet used these in an individual manner.[38]

Both the form-critical and rhetorical-structural analyses of the passage which are here offered lead to the conclusion that Berridge is correct. Thus the verbal linkages between chapters 1 and 2 ("youth," 1:6, 7, and "[time of] youth," 2:2; "tribes," 1:15; 2:4—see Structure) suggest strongly that the call was integrated with the material of chapter 2 as early as the dictation of the first scroll in 605. There is no reason to doubt that the verbalization of vv 4–16 represents Jrm's own perception of his call.

If this is the case, then the contrast of time-reference between "before . . ." (v 5) and "this day" (v 10) raises the question whether the lines of v 5 were not in Jrm's consciousness for some time before his acceptance of the call; but there is obviously no way to determine this. There is no way, either, to determine when Jrm accepted his call, if the datum of 627/626 (1:1) is assumed to be the date of his birth, as here proposed. Jrm evidently proclaimed early material to the north shaped by Josiah's program of reunion between north and south (see especially 3:12–15 and 18, and portions of chaps. 30—31), so that he must have been functioning as a prophet before the king's death in 609. I propose that if Josiah's reform, based on an early recension of Deuteronomy, took place in 622, the next occasion for a recitation of Deuteronomy would have been at the feast of booths in late September or early October of 615. Since Jrm's call was strongly shaped by Deut 18:18, I propose that occasion for Jrm's acceptance of his call; by the chronology proposed here, he would have been only twelve years old (see further "A Chronology of Jeremiah's Career").

If the analysis given in Preliminary Observations is correct, the two visions in vv 11–12 and 13–16 were associated with the call from the beginning. The flow-ering almond would have been seen by him in late January or early February (four months after his acceptance of the call?!).

The analysis in Preliminary Observations has suggested that the additions in vv 15–16 are the words of Jrm himself. They transform words about the northern kingdom of Israel to the foe from the north, a circumstance that suggests a setting at the time of the battle of Carchemish (May or June 605). This is also the year when Jrm dictated his first scroll (36:1); and the added words in v 16 are reminiscent of Huldah's words to the delegation of King Josiah with regard to the Deuteronomic scroll (2 Kgs 22:17)—the the parallel is doubtless intentional.

Verses 17–19 are paralleled by 15:20–21; evidence is given in the treatment of the confessions in the present study (see "Jeremiah's Confessions," Introduction [before the treatment of 11:18—12:6], and 15:10–21, Setting) that those verses have their setting in Jrm's vocational crisis in the summer of 594, and there is every reason therefore to view vv 17–19 here as Yahweh's reinforcement of Jrm's call at that time.

Interpretation

■ **4** The first-person introduction to Jrm's call is expressed in the same idiom as that which appears (in the third person) in the superscription, "the word of Yahweh came to me/Jrm" (v 2). As already indicated (v 2), this formula was a standard one to describe Yahweh's revelatory communication to the prophet. The verb היה in this context means "happen, occur, be extended to."[39] The prophet perceived the onslaught of Yahweh's word as the formative impact of his career.[40] This phrase is repeated in vv 11 and 13, passages concerned with vision-experience; the phrase therefore covers both verbal and visionary material.[41] The phrase carries with it the whole paradoxical experience of the overwhelming inbreaking of God's revelation into the consciousness of the one who is to speak and act for God.

37 Zimmerli, *Ezekiel 1*, 97–98.
38 Berridge, p. 27.
39 Carl H. Ratschow, *Werden und Wirken, Eine Untersuchung des Wortes hajah als Beitrag zur Wirklichkeitserfassung des Altes Testamentes* (BZAW 70; Berlin: Töpelmann, 1941) 34–35.
40 Sigmund Mowinckel, *Die Erkenntis Gottes bei den alttestamentlichen Profeten* (Tilleggshefte til *NorTT*; Oslo: Grøndahl, 1941) 19-20; and for a careful examination of the phrases, Hans Wildberger, *Jahwewort und prophetische Rede bei Jeremia* (Zurich: Zwingli, 1942) 19–30.
41 Compare Berridge, pp. 31–32.

■ **5** Evidence has been given in Structure for a division of the verse into five cola, the first and third being the "before"-clauses and the other three being the parallel main clauses. In this case "in the belly" and "from the womb" are to be construed with their respective main verbs that follow rather than with the "before"-clauses, or at least they will be heard with what comes after as much as with what comes before.

The repetition of "before" (בְּטֶרֶם) is quite striking (note that the same repetition occurs again in 13:16). This expression "before" occurs particularly in contexts of birth or creation and death (compare Isa 42:9; 48:5; 66:7; Pss 39:14; 90:2).

Evidence has been given in Text for reading the first verb not according to the qere' as "I formed you" (אֶצָּרְךָ), but according to the ketib as "I summoned you" (אֱצוּרְךָ). Of course "formed" is what one would expect, given the diction of Ps 139:13; doubtless then the expected verb lingers behind "summoned" (compare the diction of Isa 49:1 and 5, which offers both meanings). All five verbs then point toward Jrm's being called. In Jrm's case his birth and his vocation are coterminous: there was never a time he was not summoned.

The nouns "belly" (בֶּטֶן) and "womb" (רֶחֶם) are often in parallelism (Isa 46:3; Pss 22:11; 58:4; Job 3:11; 10:18–19; 31:35), though "belly" does not occur otherwise in Jer. Behind this diction may also lie Ps 22:10–11.[42]

As already noted, the three main verbs are all parallel: "I knew you" (יְדַעְתִּיךָ), "I designated you" (הִקְדַּשְׁתִּיךָ), "I made you" (נְתַתִּיךָ); they must be understood together. "Know" (ידע) carries with it here two nuances that carry it beyond the meaning of "be acquainted with" familiar in modern European languages. The first is the intimacy of husband and wife; in Gen 4:1 we are told that "Adam knew Eve his wife, and she conceived," and the sexual connotation of "know" is often present in the OT. At least this possibility reminds us that "knowledge" in the OT is likely to be personal and relational. Since Jrm will be called not to marry (16:2) and since there is indication

more than once that he understood his prophetic calling to have an intimacy analogous to that of a wife with her husband (15:16; 20:7), it is not illegitimate to see at the beginning of his call an intimation of that metaphor. The second is that of the relationship of suzerain to vassal. In both the OT and extrabiblical sources, "know" implies the suzerain's recognition of the legitimacy of the vassal's relationship to him.[43] Thus (to stay within the OT) God says of Abraham in Gen 18:19, "For I knew him (יְדַעְתִּיו)," that is, I recognized him as my legitimate servant; and similarly David, in responding to Nathan's oracle, says, "What more can David say, for you have known your servant, O Lord God" (2 Sam 7:20). "Know" here then implies both intimacy and a covenantal bond; Yahweh chooses Jrm to be his spokesman and obligates him thereby.

The verb "I designated you" (הִקְדַּשְׁתִּיךָ) is similar. The root קדש has to do with what is "holy," that is, what is the inherent realm of God, what is at his disposal, what belongs to him. Thus in 2:3 Israel is stated to be קֹדֶשׁ to Yahweh, that is, his possession, at his disposal; the passages are thus analogous. The hip'il stem here means "designate someone to be consecrated, set someone aside for God's purposes." The older translations (*KJV*: "sanctified"; *RSV*: "consecrated") are correct but imply to the modern reader that Jrm was made pure, whereas the accent is on his being designated for God's task. This verb then carries covenantal overtones just as "know" does.

What is indicated in general in v 5a is made specific in v 5b: Jrm is made a "prophet" (נָבִיא). One notes that the verb נתן, literally "give," means "make" when occurring with two accusatives (compare the close parallel Exod 7:1); the same verb will mean "put" in v 9.

It is a daring affirmation to make, that Jrm is called to be a prophet from his birth. It is intimated that Moses, Samson, and Samuel were each called to their tasks from their birth, but the closest parallels in existence in Jrm's time are royal ones from Mesopotamia and Egypt (see

---

42   See Holladay, "Background," 156–57.
43   Herbert B. Huffmon, "The Treaty Background of the Hebrew יָדַע." *BASOR* 181 (February 1966) 31–37; Herbert B. Huffmon and Simon B. Parker, "A Further Note on the Treaty Background of Hebrew יָדַע." *BASOR* 184 (December 1966) 36–38; James Muilenburg, "Intercession of the Covenant Mediator (Exodus 33:1a, 12-17)," *Words and Meanings, Essays*

Presented to David Winton Thomas (ed. Peter R. Ackroyd and Barnabas Lindars; Cambridge: Cambridge University, 1968) 180–81.

Form). The diction will be used later by Deutero-Isaiah and by NT writers (Paul about himself, Matthew and Luke about Jesus Christ: see again Form). Whether the royal models were at the forefront of Jrm's perception or not, it remains true that the experience of the providence of God attracts men and women throughout history to such language of predestination. Jrm may have grappled with the call to be a prophet when he was only a youth, but he became convinced that Yahweh had been calling him from the beginning of his existence.

The literature on the role of "prophet" is immense;[44] beyond such general literature see particularly the remarks in Form and in the Introduction in *Jeremiah 2*.

But Jrm is called specifically to be a prophet "to the nations," plural. It is again a daring word to find in the call. (Bernhard Stade's suggestion to emend the word to "to my nation"[45] is to be rejected.) Earlier prophets never felt themselves confined simply to Israel and Judah, and Amos and Isaiah offered oracles destined for various nations that impinged upon Israel and Judah; but no other prophet perceived in his call that specific far extent of his office. And it is reinforced by the words "over nations and over kingdoms" in v 10. Does it begin by Jrm's perception of the two entities, Israel and Judah? In any event, it is a true internationalizing of the prophetic office: Jrm may be destined to speak largely to the local necessities of Judah, but there will be no limitation to the effectiveness of the word he speaks. Wilhelm Vischer may be overimaginative to suggest that in order to be called to the nations Jrm had to be called before birth;[46] still, the reach of both the extent of time for his call and the extent of space over which he is called are stretched beyond what is expected. We are alerted to Jrm's unique set of perceptions as to the nature of his prophetic call. What was it like to hear these lines

hammering in one's ear? The call must have seemed self-validating to Jrm.

■ **6** If Jrm perceived his call to be part of the providence of Yahweh from the beginning, we might have expected him to accede to it gladly, but instead he tries to refuse it. The phrase "Ah, Lord Yahweh!" (אֲהָהּ אֲדֹנָי יהוה) appears ten times in the OT (beyond the present passage: 4:10; 14:13; 32:17; Josh 7:7; Judg 6:22; Ezek 4:14; 9:8; 11:13; 21:5) to express dismay or alarm. Form-critically the most important parallel is Judg 6:22, one of Gideon's objections to Yahweh's call (see Form); and though the phrase is a different one, it is the functional equivalent of Moses' בִּי אֲדֹנִי in his objections (Exod 4:10, 13).

He begs Yahweh that he is too young (so G νεώτερος, and so Luther; James Moffatt, *A New Translation of the Bible, Containing the Old and New Testaments* [New York: Harper, 1934]; *NAB*), a phrase which is reminiscent of Solomon's dismay on entering into kingship (1 Kgs 3:7—see again Form).

The word נַעַר (here "youth") covers a large range of meaning; it may refer to a male infant, such as Moses in the basket (Exod 2:19), but it may also refer to the weapon-bearer of Jonathan (1 Sam 14:1).[47] One recent study has suggested that in the second example the reference is to someone in domestic or military service for a lord, much like the early European "squire."[48] It has been proposed more than once that the word implies Jrm's unmarried state (compare 16:2);[49] but if the chronology proposed in the present study is correct (see v 2, and "A Chronology of Jeremiah's Career"), then Jrm was only eighteen years old at the time of the temple sermon in 609 and younger during the reign of Josiah, when according to the tradition he was already prophesying—certainly young enough so that he would be referring to his age when he used the term. It was a

44 One may refer conveniently to B. Davie Napier, "Prophet," *IDB* 3:894–919, and Martin J. Buss, "Prophecy in Ancient Israel," *IDBSup*, 694–97, both with extensive bibliographies.

45 Bernhard Stade, "Emendationen," *ZAW* 22 (1902) 328.

46 Wilhelm Vischer, "Vocation of the Prophet to the Nations, An Exegesis of Jer. 1:4–10," *Int* 9 (1955) 311–12.

47 Hans-Peter Stähli, *Knabe, Jüngling, Knecht, Untersuchungen zum Begriff* נער *im Alten Testament* (Frankfurt am Main: Lang, 1978).

48 James Macdonald, "The Status and Role of the Na'ar in Israelite Society," *JNES* 35 (1976) 147–70, esp. 149.

49 For the literature on this suggestion see Berridge, p. 45 n. 110.

society that valued the wisdom of the elders; Cornill points out that Jrm had in mind the social reversal by which boys talk back to the elders (compare Isa 3:4; Eccl 10:16a + 15b + 16b, where נְעָרִים is used). He felt retiring and fearful (Rudolph); "Jeremiah believed that his words would neither meet with respect nor be given credence."[50] Jrm identified with both Moses and Samuel (15:1); at this point he is like Moses in his objection to the call (see Form), and like Samuel in his youth (1 Samuel 3: note the resemblance between 1 Sam 3:11 and Jer 19:3, and see further the remarks about Anathoth, v 1). Though there is no reason why a prophet should always accept his call without objection, as Isaiah (Isa 6:8) and Ezekiel (Ezek 1—3) are portrayed as doing, nevertheless Jrm's hesitation sets the stage for his laments to Yahweh (the "confessions" in chaps. 11—20).

■ 7 Yahweh answers Jrm's objection by forbidding him to speak as he does and then reassuring him (see Form). Given the preponderance of occurrences of "do not say" (אַל־תֹּאמַר) in the wisdom literature (Prov 3:28; 20:22; 24:29; Eccl 5:5), the impression left by the phrase is that of homely advice—its mood matches the reassurance of the parallel "do not be afraid" in v 8. Jrm's self-image is irrevelant to Yahweh's intention.

The phrase "Do not say, 'I am (only) a youth'" is followed by the conjunction כִּי; it is normally translated "for (to all to whom I send you . . .)," but given the fact that Yahweh's reassurances in Exod 3:12 and Judg 6:16 begin with כִּי, the conjunction here doubtless carries the same force, "but (rather)" (see Form).

The precise denotation of the next clause (עַל־כָּל־אֲשֶׁר אֶשְׁלָחֲךָ) is puzzling. For poetic reasons there is no concluding עָלָיו or עֲלֵיהֶם (so C. W. Eduard Naegelsbach *The Book of the Prophet Jeremiah, Theologically and Homiletically Expounded* [New York: Scribner's, 1886]); but does עַל mean "concerning," or "against," or is it the equivalent of אֶל "to"? And does the object of the preposition, כָּל־אֲשֶׁר, mean "everyone who" (G) or "everything which" (V, T, S)? Given the neuter meaning of the second כָּל־אֲשֶׁר in the verse, one could argue either for a parallel or contrast here. The verb שׁלח is not normally followed by עַל, but 26:15 offers a fine parallel with עַל, and there its object is personal. In other instances אֶל is used in

what appear to be similar contexts (25:15; 43:1). Either there is no discernible difference of meaning between the two prepositions (so most commentators), or there is. The context in 26:15 is clearly a hostile situation, and the present passage implies the possibility of future hostility in the fear Jrm manifests; so "against" does not seem to press the meaning too far. The interpretation of *T* ("for everywhere I send you you shall go") is thus too weak.

This line is modeled on the following one, and that in turn is modeled on the last clause of Deut 18:18, "and he shall speak to them whatever I command him" (וְדִבֶּר אֲלֵיהֶם אֵת כָּל־אֲשֶׁר אֲצַוֶּנּוּ) which refers to the prophet like Moses to come (see Form). Like that other formulation (and a similar phrase in Exod 7:2, if known to Jrm), this verse, with its repeated כָּל־, underlines the totality of the commitment to which Yahweh is calling Jrm. Yahweh does not ride roughshod over Jrm's integrity, but he does overwhelm the prophet's own hesitation by the call to serve. Jrm must respond! The two cola impressively dovetail Yahweh's will ("send," "command") and Jrm's will ("go," "speak") and further dovetail action ("send," "go") and spoken word ("command," "speak") which make up the effective "word" (דָּבָר: compare Isa 55:10–11).

■ 8 The "do not be afraid" with which the verse begins matches "do not say . . ." in v 7. The sequence "Ah Lord Yahweh" followed by "do not be afraid" is identical with that in Judg 6:22, 23, when the angel of God reassures Gideon (see above, and Form). "Fear" is followed by the expression מִפְּנֵי, literally "from the face (or appearance) of," but this literal meaning is not to be pressed, given the simple מִן in the same context in Josh 10:8.

The formulation "for I am with you to deliver you" (כִּי־אִתְּךָ אֲנִי לְהַצִּלֶךָ) and its variants is evidently a formula confined to Jer (see v 19 and 15:20), but it is of a type of reassurance normal in the genre of the oracle of salvation (see Form).

The expression נְאֻם־יהוה, translated in this study "oracle of Yahweh," occurs 168 times in Jer, usually in quite specific patterns. The phrase does not participate in the parallelism of poetry; here, as often, it closes an independent word from Yahweh.[51]

---

50   Ibid., 45.
51   Rolf Rendtorff, "Zum Gebrauch der Formel *ne'um* *jahwe* im Jeremiabuch," *ZAW* 66 (1954) 27–37; for the present context, see p. 31.

■ **9** Word and action are still intertwined: "Yahweh said to me" (v 7) is matched by "Yahweh extended his hand and touched my mouth" here. The action is similar to that in Isaiah's call: there the seraph took a live coal in his hand with tongs and touched Isaiah's mouth (Isa 6:6–7). In both instances the prophet's mouth is readied for taking in and giving out Yahweh's word. And the action of touching Jrm's mouth is linked to the word of explanation, "Look, I have put my words in your mouth."

It would be tempting to vocalize דברי as "my word" (singular) rather than "my words" (plural); this reading would bring the expression into congruence with that in v 12, which is clearly singular.[52] But *G*, *V*, and *T* are all plural, and the word in *S* carries the seyome (plural sign), so there is no warrant for the change.

The more expected word for "put" in such an action is שׂים: so "Yahweh put a word in Balaam's mouth" (Num 23:5), "I have put my words in your mouth" (Isa 51:16), and eight other instances with "word(s)" and "mouth."[53] But the word here for "put" is נתן (literally "give"), which appears in this context in only two other passages, 5:14 and Deut 18:18. It is thus appropriate to Jrm's diction, and there is strong presumption that Deut 18:18 stimulated the present passage.

In a way the last colon of the verse, together with the first two cola of v 10, are an expansion of the last colon in v 5 ("a prophet to the nations I made you"). Thus this colon of v 9 repeats the verb נתן of that colon in v 5: having "given" Jrm at his birth as a prophet to the nations, Yahweh now "gives" his words into Jrm's mouth.

Jrm, like Isaiah, understands his prophetic task to be centered in his mouth: Yahweh takes the initiative in putting his words into Jrm's mouth so that his mouth in turn might give forth those words. The wording of other lines of Jrm's likewise attest to this understanding of his experience: "I am going to make my words in your mouth into fire" (5:14); "your words were found, and I ate them" (15:16); "you shall be as my mouth" (15:19).

■ **10** The expansion of the last colon of v 5 continues: "See, I have appointed you this day over nations and over kingdoms." The imperative "see" functions as a parallel to "look" (הִנֵּה) in v 9. "Appoint" (פקד hipʿil) is normally an administrative term: the king "appoints" someone to an office. Thus Nebuchadrezzar appointed Gedaliah governor (40:11). In only two other passages in the OT is God the subject: Ps 109:6, "appoint a wicked man against him," and Lev 26:16, "I will appoint over you sudden terror." There is something awesome about Yahweh's making an appointment over the whole world.

Given the likeness of diction between "a prophet to the nations I made you (נתן)" in v 5 and "I have appointed you over nations and over kingdoms (פקד)" here, the question arises whether נתן and פקד are perceived as different actions or analogous ones. It is clear that נתן may mean "appoint": 1 Sam 12:13 may mean "God has set a king over you" or "appointed a king over you." It is also clear that with two accusatives נתן may mean both "appoint (someone to be something)" and "make (someone something)"—the two shade into each other. Thus Isa 3:4 can mean "I shall appoint boys (to be) their princes" or "I shall make boys (into being) their princes." It is equally clear that פקד cannot mean "make someone into something." So it is conceivable that the contrast in the present passage between v 5 and v 10 is that in the womb Yahweh made Jrm (into being) a prophet, while on the day of his acceptance of the call Yahweh installed him in the office of prophet; but this is doubtless an overfine distinction, so that it is better to be content with the basic contrast between the verses, that in v 5 the reference is to the time before Jrm's birth, while the reference in v 10 is to "this day," the day he accepted his call. On those two occasions Yahweh does analogous actions: before Jrm's birth he made him a prophet potentially, made him a prophet by anticipation, while on the day he accepted the call Yahweh made him a prophet in actuality.

The word "nations" in v 5 is now expanded to the parallelism of "nations" and "kingdoms" (compare Isa 60:12; Ps 46:7).

There is no reason to doubt that the four infinitives posited for the original text are authentic ("uproot, smash, build, plant"); Jrm understands his task to be constructive as well as destructive. If the conclusions set forth in Preliminary Observations (both above and in the parallel section in 2:1—4:4) are correct, that the earliest material in 2:1—4:4 was directed to the north, then in

---

52 So Budde, "Erste Kapitel," 30.
53 Exod 4:15; Num 22:38; 23:12, 16; Deut 31:19; 2 Sam 14:3, 19; Isa 59:21.

that material one hears both the destructive and constructive task of the prophet. Yet his early optimism about the north faded as he turned to address the south, and after King Jehoiakim burned his scroll, he understood his task to be the bringing of words of judgment to the exclusion of words of restoration (compare 28:8). Yet he returned to words of hope at the end of his career: he bought the field at Anathoth (32:6–15) and then proclaimed words of hope gathered in a new scroll (chaps. 30—31). The opinion then of some scholars at the turn of the century that the last two verbs are unauthentic is to be rejected.[54]

The four verbs that form the original text make up a chiasmus with fine assonances (see Text). "Uproot" (נתש) is the opposite of "plant" (נטע) (Amos 9:15), though except for Ezek 19:12 the verb in the OT is used only metaphorically (and in that passage the verb, a qal passive or hopʻal, has "vine" as subject, itself a metaphor for Israel). God "uproots" the Asherim (Mic 5:13) or the nation from its territory (1 Kgs 14:15).

"Demolish" (נתץ) is equally destructive. But while the subject of "uproot" is almost always God (at least eleven cases out of fourteen) and the meaning almost always metaphorical, "demolish" is rarely metaphorical and rarely has God as subject (three cases out of thirty-one).[55] More commonly various Israelites smash altars (Gideon, Judg 6:23; Josiah, 2 Kgs 23:7, 8, 12) or a whole city (Abimelech, the city of Shechem, Judg 9:45). The verb is strong enough so that it is translated "raze" in Judg 9:45 (*RSV*, *JB*, *NJV*). It was perhaps the very specificity of the verb which in similar passages in Jer encouraged synonyms more appropriate to God's action, verbs which were then imported secondarily into the present passage (see again Text). These verbs are אבד hipʻil, which essentially means "put to death" (subject either God or human beings) but moves into the metaphor of "destroy" (nations, or even objects like chariots, Mic 5:9); and הרס, which means either "pull down" (an altar; even Shebna from his office, Isa 22:19) or "break" (Ps 58:7, a prayer that God will "smash" the teeth of the enemy) and moves into the metaphor of "ruin" (the land, by high taxes, Prov 29:4).

The two positive verbs "build" and "plant" need little

comment: both are used of both God and human beings in a great range of concrete and metaphorical contexts. Inevitably the two appear side by side in many contexts (Deut 6:10–11; 28:30; Isa 5:2). They form the base for Jrm's task of construction after the destruction is completed.

■ **11–14** For the introductory words "The word of Yahweh came to me as follows" (vv 11, 13) see v 4. For the fixed form of the question "What do you see?" (vv 11, 13) see Form. "See" may refer without specification to the perception of both external objects and inner visions. Thus Micaiah reports seeing Yahweh on his throne (1 Kgs 22:19), as does Isaiah (Isa 6:1). The verb in these verses, however, doubtless records Jrm's seeing external (photographable) objects.

■ **11–12** The word מַקֵּל may be used of a walking-stick (1 Sam 17:40, compare 43) and of the sort of staff used in divination (Hos 4:12). Here it means the twig of a tree, presumably in bloom (against Hyatt and Bright, who assume a "stick"); Gen 30:37 uses the word to mean "twig." The word שָׁקֵד is used twice of the almond tree (beyond the present passage, in Eccl 12:5) and twice of the nut (Gen 43:11; Num 17:23). There is no doubt that the word is related to the verb "watch" (שֹׁקֵד, v 12), so the word association in the two verses is that of a true etymology, not of a folk etymology or simple word-play. It was noted in ancient times that the almond was the first to bloom in the spring. Thus Pliny so states, specifying that the almond blooms in January.[56] One may further cite Ahikar 2:7: "My son, be not in a hurry, like the almond-tree whose blossom is the first to appear, but whose fruit is the last to be eaten; but be equal and sensible, like the mulberry-tree whose blossom is the last to appear, but whose fruit is the first to be eaten."[57] The present writer will never forget the experience of seeing the white blossoms of almond trees in early February, through a thick morning fog, at *el-jīb* (Gibeon, eight kilometers west of Anathoth). The almond thus "watches" for the spring.

The suggestion has been made that the narrative of Aaron's rod, which sprouted ripe almonds (Num 17:23,

---

54 See Karl Grimm, *Euphemistic Liturgical Appendices in the Old Testament* (Leipzig: Hinrichs, 1901) 51–52, with further references.

55 Pss 52:7; 58:7; Job 19:10.

56 *Hist. Nat.* 16.42.

57 Syriac version: see *APOT* 2.728.

P?), may have played a role in Jrm's vision.[58] But this is unlikely; the emphasis in the vision is not on "twig" (or "rod") but on "almond," and the association of that word with "watch." It is worth noting that both *V* and *T* reflect a tradition vocalizing שָׁקֵד as שָׁקַד and thus miss the word-play. *V* reads "a rod watching" (*virgam vigilantem*). *T* evidently interprets the rod as a scepter and thus metonymy for a ruler, for it renders "a king intent on displeasure," thus accommodating it to the meaning of the vision in vv 13–14; this interpretation is remarkable enough to merit mention by Rashi. One may conclude that, given an unvocalized text, it is difficult to preserve a tradition of word-play when the variation is only in the vowels.

Verse 12 begins "You have seen right," literally "You have done well to see"; יטב hip'il often carries this nuance (compare 1 Sam 16:17).

The verb "watch" here (שקד) seems indistinguishable from the more common שמר: the two verbs are synonyms in Ezra 8:29 and are found in the same context in Ps 127:1. In 5:6 the verb is used of the leopard keeping watch over the cities of Judah, cities which do not (yet) belong to the leopard, so that "keep an eye on" is implied: Yahweh promises to keep an eye on his word "to carry it out" (לַעֲשֹׂתוֹ). The same usage, with God as subject of עשׂה and דָּבָר as object, is found in Joel 2:11: God carries out his word, accomplishes it, executes it. The "word" again is not an utterance only but an utterance in process of being actualized (compare v 2). Yahweh will back up his word: Jrm's utterances on Yahweh's behalf will not be empty utterances (compare Isa 55:10–11), though Jrm will accuse Yahweh later of breaking this promise (see 17:15). But we must bear in mind that Yahweh's word includes not only words spoken through Jrm but earlier words spoken by other prophets[59] or found in the Deuteronomic scroll (see on 15:16).

The assurance came to Jrm, as already indicated, by the association of the words "almond" and "watch."

Word association is known elsewhere as a source of revelation for the prophets (see 13:4, 7, and Amos 8:1–2).[60] There are two striking aspects to this revelatory conviction. The first is that Jrm should gain a sense of conviction regarding Yahweh's trustworthiness from an object and by a process of word association that appears so casual. But it is clear that trust in God is never based upon data which are intrinsically convincing to someone who does not share an openness to conviction; as a NT writer would say, "Faith is the assurance of things hoped for, the conviction of things not seen" (Heb 11:1). "This association of ideas came to [Jrm] as an answer to the question he was just pondering. Had not Yahweh let him see this almond tree in order to show him that He at all events would watch over the accomplishment of His words spoken by His prophets? . . . The whole had for the prophet the character of a revelation. The trivial impression was by inspiration from God lifted up to a higher level."[61]

The second striking aspect of this vision is that Jrm should have pondered the question at all. Why should Yahweh not watch over his word to carry it out? The whole tradition of Israel was such that it was taken for granted Yahweh would fulfill his word. For Amos Yahweh utters his voice and the top of Carmel withers (Amos 1:2); for Isaiah God has send a word against Jacob, and it will fall and do its work and people will recognize it (Isa 9:7–8). But Jrm needs to have the reassurance that Yahweh is faithful to reinforce his word by action, and in that need there is betrayed the prophet's uneasiness with the experience of that word of Yahweh which he is to have. There is no reason to doubt that that hesitation was there from the beginning (see Setting); so its presence here is a reminder that Jrm's hesitation was not altogether laid to rest by Yahweh's reassurance in vv 8–10.

■ **13–14** The precise denotation of Jrm's answer as to what he sees has raised great uncertainty among scholars. The words are chosen partly for their alliterative quality

58   Pearle S. Wood, "Jeremiah's Figure of the Almond Rod," *JBL* 61 (1942) 99–103; Walter G. Williams, "Jeremiah's Vision of the Almond Rod," *A Stubborn Faith, Papers on Old Testament and Related Subjects, Presented to Honor William Andrew Irwin* (ed. Edward C. Hobbs; Dallas: Southern Methodist University, 1956) 90–99. Though Aaron's rod is called a מַטֶּה, not a מַקֵּל, the words appear to be synonymous; see

      Lawrence E. Toombs, "Rod," *IDB* 4:102–3.
59   See Berridge, p. 69 and the bibliography in his n. 26.
60   Guillaume, *Prophecy and Divination*, 149–50.
61   Johannes Lindblom, *Prophecy in Ancient Israel* (Oxford: Blackwell, 1963), 139.

—the repeated *n* and *p* in both נָפוּחַ and צָפוֹנָה. The solution reached in the present study has already been outlined in Preliminary Observations, but the question must now be explored in more detail.

A סִיר is a cooking-pot (2 Kgs 4:38–41 describes a large one).[62] Though such a pot might be of earthenware, it could well be of metal, either iron or copper; the parallel in Ezek 24:11, cited below, offers a copper pot.

The modifier נָפוּחַ is the qal passive participle of נפח "blow, fan"; the related noun מַפֻּחַ is a "bellows" (6:29). A similar phrase is found in Job 41:12 with a synonymous noun and the same modifier: "Out of (the crocodile's) nostrils comes forth smoke, like a fanned pot and rushes." That passage offers its own difficulties in exegesis: the word "rushes" may be in error—*V* translates "a pot kindled and boiling." The probable assumption of the Job passage is that a pot is filled with water and steaming, though if "rushes" is correct, the assumption is not a necessary one: that pot, like the one here (if the present proposal is correct) may be empty of water. In any event נָפוּחַ by itself does not imply that water is involved; *G* in the present passage translates the participle "with a fire under it" (ὑποκαιόμενον).

The universal assumption of commentators, however, is that the pot is filled with water, that it is tipped, and that the water is about to boil out toward the south. This assumption is natural, given the present form of the text in which the tribes of the north are to come down to invade and judge Jerusalem (v 16). But if the phrases of v 16 are viewed as a reinterpretation at the time of Carchemish (see Preliminary Observations), then the necessity of visualizing a pot filled with water falls away.

That there is no water in the pot becomes likely when one encounters the following phrase "and its rim is away from the north" (וּפָנָיו מִפְּנֵי צָפוֹנָה: see below). Because it has always been assumed that there is water in the pot, it is further assumed that the pot is tipped, doubtless only slightly. But no one in his or her right mind places a pot in a tipped position before filling it with water to boil: no one wants the water to spill when it boils, and in any event the vibration of boiling water is liable to tip the pot all the way over. "Its rim is away from the north" suggests a quite striking sight: that the pot is lying completely on its side, empty.

The first occurrence of פָּנִים (literally "face") refers to the surface or rim of the pot. The word is often used of the surface of water (Gen 1:2) and once of the surface of a dish that is wiped and then turned "on its face," that is, upside down (2 Kgs 21:13).[63] Thus the efforts of earlier commentators to translate it "front" (Bernhard Duhm, Cornill, Giesebrecht, Volz), explaining it as the side facing the spectator, is simply wrong—a pot has no "front" or "back" (Duhm suggests it is the side from which the fuel is inserted under the pot). The second occurrence of פָּנִים, namely מִפְּנֵי, means "away from." The form of "north," with he *locale*, is normal idiom.[64]

One concludes, then, that the pot is lying on its side with coals underneath it that are being fanned. The situation is precisely that of Ezek 24:11: the empty pot is being heated in order to get rid of baked-on food remains or other carbonaceous material (in the manner of a modern self-cleaning oven). The passage in Ezekiel mentions both "filthiness" (טֻמְאָה), a word which in his metaphor has cultic associations, and חֶלְאָה (translated "rust"). The process in question would get rid of organic material but not "rust" (or verdigris, since it is a matter in Ezekiel of a copper pot). But the word חֶלְאָה is cognate with a Semitic word for "dirt," so that Ezekiel may not have used the word in our sense of the oxide of the metal. In any event, the situation described in Ezek 24:11 makes explicable the fact that the pot is empty.

The nearest parallel is in Jer 6:27–30, in which the "bellows" (מַפֻּחַ) heats crude lead in order that silver be extracted; that passage portrays a judgment of the people by purification. Given that parallel and the one in Ezek 24:11, one must assume that the same process is envisaged here: the covenant people are subject to the heat of Yahweh's judgment for their purification.

---

62   For recent descriptions see James L. Kelso, "Pottery," *IDB* 3:846–53, esp. 850, and, in more detail, Ruth Amiran, *Ancient Pottery of the Holy Land* (New Brunswick, NJ: Rutgers University, 1970) 227–32 and plates 75–76.

63   Compare Ernst Vogt, "Vocatio Jeremiae," *VD* 42 (1964) 250.

64   GKC, sec. 90e.

Ezekiel's pot symbolizes Jerusalem, the "bloody city" (Ezek 24:6); Jrm's pot, facing away from the north, evidently represents the northern tribes, turning toward the south (compare 3:14; 31:6), waiting to return.

The second word of Yahweh's reply in v 14 momentarily suggests hope: "(from the north) there shall be opened" (תִּפָּתַח). What shall be opened? The prison-gate, liberation for the captives (Isa 51:14)? No, "calamity," a judgment for all their crime (v 16). This "calamity" (רָעָה) will fall on "all the inhabitants of the land." (Conceivably one might argue that the expression means "all the inhabitants of the earth," but the exegesis here of the original intention of the vision suggests an application to Israel alone: see vv 15–16.) One concludes that the vision communicates either a judgment on the northern tribes or a summoning of those tribes to stand judgment along with the south. Of course when the original two clauses of vv 15–16 are expanded by fresh words (authentic to Jrm at the time of the battle of Carchemish, by the proposal of this study), the vision of the pot shifted its signification: now it signaled the irruption of the foe from the north (for both significations see further vv 15–16).

■ 15–16 If the conclusion in Preliminary Observations is correct, the original recension (directed to the tribes of the north) consisted of the first clause of v 15 and the first clause of v 16.

Verse 15 opens with כִּי followed by הִנְנִי and a participle, not a common sequence in Jer.[65] Since הִנְנִי tends to be first in its clause, it is preferable to avoid the routine translation "for" (RSV, NEB, NJV) in favor of a deictic rendering like "lo" (NAB) or "look."[66]

The noun מִשְׁפָּחָה has a varied usage. Most precisely it denotes a subdivision of a tribe (שֵׁבֶט, Josh 7:14–18);[67] several times, however, it is used for שֵׁבֶט to refer to one of the twelve tribes of Israel (Judg 13:2; 17:7; 18:2, 19), and since this is the meaning proposed in 2:4 and 3:14, it is the meaning proposed here also for the earliest recension (see Preliminary Observations). For Jrm's

reinterpretation of this clause in the second recension, see below.

If the proposal of the present study is correct, the first clause of v 16 (in the early recension to the north) declares that Yahweh will summon the northern tribes to stand trial for their misdeeds, either alone or alongside the south. The phrase דִּבֶּר מִשְׁפָּטִים אֶת occurs only five times in the OT, and only in Jer;[68] it is uncertain whether the idiom calls for the preposition אֶת or the *nota accusativa* (see Text). The clearest context for the phrase is 39:5, where Nebuchadrezzar passes judgment and sentence upon Zedekiah. The constituents of the idiom suggest the meaning "pronounce judgments on," so that the phrase evidently denotes the specific accusations in a lawsuit.

In this context Yahweh will bring "calamity" (רָעָה, v 14) by putting the covenant people on trial for their "crime" (again רָעָה): the latter translation is appropriate in a legal context. The same shift of meaning of רָעָה is found from 2:3 (where the calamity came upon the enemy in Israel's honeymoon period) to 2:13 (where Israel is brought to trial for her double crime).

The remaining phrases in these verses were (by the present hypothesis) added by Jrm at the time of the battle of Carchemish. These additions involved a reinterpretation of the first clause of v 15. Since מִשְׁפָּחָה may refer not only to the divisions of Israel but occurs in poetic texts for the nations of the world (10:25 and Amos 3:2), the words could be reconstrued by Jrm to refer to the foe from the north: the armies of Assyria and Babylonia were made up of contingents from their various vassal states.[69]

Commentators have been uncertain whether the added material in vv 15–16 describes a siege, a judicial hearing, or (in some fashion) both. Qimḥi long ago cited 39:3 as a parallel for the phrase "put his throne at the entrance of the gates of Jerusalem," and that verse of course describes the situation after the city has fallen; one must conclude that we have a description of the

---

65 Of about sixty instances of הִנְנִי plus participle in Jer only five are preceded by כִּי (beyond the present passage: 8:17; 30:10; 45:5; 46:27).

66 Compare the treatment of Amos 6:14, which offers the same sequence, in Hans Walter Wolff, *Joel and Amos* (Hermeneia; Philadelphia: Fortress, 1977): "Indeed [it shall be] so!"

67 See C. Umhau Wolf, "Tribe," *IDB* 4:699 and

bibliography, 701; Roland de Vaux, *Ancient Israel, Its Life and Institutions* (New York: McGraw-Hill, 1961) 7–8.

68 Beyond the present passage, in 4:12; 12:1; 39:5 = 52:9; the last passage is also paralleled in 2 Kgs 25:6, where (erroneously) the singular מִשְׁפָּט is read (though some MSS. offer the plural).

69 For Assyria, so the implication of Isa 10:8, and see

defeat of the city and its submission to the judicial acts of the victor. The two phrases introduced by עַל with which v 15 ends fit awkwardly with what has preceded (see Text) and are doubtless glosses intended to expand the notices of the extent of Chaldean authority at the time of the fall of Jerusalem. Such a judicial situation as is here described is depicted in the reliefs of Nineveh showing the Assyrian siege of Lachish: an enthroned Sennacherib is seen receiving Judahite captives, bowed low in obeisance at the feet of their Assyrian overlord. But this scene is part of a relief, other scenes of which show the siege of the city; so that the additional phrases at the end of v 15, implying a siege or at least military activity, are the verbal equivalent of the "montage," on the relief, of the sequence of events which take place, one after the other.[70]

If the basic assumption of the phrases genuine to Jrm here is that the city will have fallen, then וּבָאוּ does not mean the colorless "and they shall come" of recent translations but rather implies that the enemy will enter the city (note the same verb in 39:3 preceding the mention of the "sitting" of the Babylonian authorities). To "place one's throne" implies the assertion of royal authority (2 Kgs 25:28 = Jer 52:32); for the use of "throne" implying the giving of judgment see Pss 9:5; 122:5; and for the "entrance of the gate(s)" of a city as the place of judicial decision see Josh 20:4, and, with "gate" alone, Isa 29:21; Amos 5:10 and 15. The image of these words then is that of the terrifying variety of foreigners who will enter Jerusalem and settle down to decide the fate of its inhabitants, indeed decide the fate of the inhabitants of the whole land.

At first glance there seems no close connection between the conquerors' dispensing their mode of justice at the gate (v 15) and Yahweh's pronouncement of judgment (v 16) except for the obvious—that Yahweh expresses his judgment against Jerusalem by his bringing the kings against it (so Qimḥi). But a recent study suggests a more substantial connection after all. It was the policy of Assyria to despoil the images of deities in conquered realms; thus Sargon's Letter to the Gods reads, "Respecting the god Ḥaldia, in whom Urartu trusted, I gave orders to take him out. I, as victor, placed him in front of his town gate." The chief deity of Urartu, thus seated at the gate, publicly oversaw the carrying-off of his treasures.[71] Verse 16 is thus ironic in two ways: the foe from the north would of course expect to bring the image of Yahweh out to the gate of the city to be humiliated (compare Isaiah's depiction of the casual assumption of Assyria about the images of Samaria and Jerusalem, Isa 10:10–11), whereas in the case of Yahweh there is no image to bring out. And further Yahweh will not sit mute and humiliated; to the contrary, it is he who is directing the foe from the north to victory over Jerusalem ("I am going to call all the tribes of the north," v 15).

It has been stated that the last three clauses of v 16 are authentic to Jrm and not the product of a Deuteronomistic editor (see Preliminary Observations), but this assertion must now be substantiated, since the assumption of Deuteronomistic redaction here is widespread.[72]

"Abandon me (= Yahweh)" is found repeatedly in the genuine poetry of Jrm (2:13, 17, 19; 5:7, 19; compare 9:1, where subject and object of this verb are reversed); the expression is found in Deuteronomy only in 28:20 and 31:16, both passages likely to be part of late redactional work on Deuteronomy.[73] The verb קטר pi‘el "sacrifice (in a pagan rite)" is not found in Deuteronomy at all but is found in the prose of Jer's temple sermon (7:9) and elsewhere in Jer. "Other gods" is found in

---

the inscriptions of Sargon II in *ANET*, 284–85; for Nebuchadrezzar's army see 25:9.

70 For the scene of Sennacherib on the throne see *ANEP*, fig. 371; for the whole relief in which this scene is a part see Yigael Yadin, *The Art of Warfare in Biblical Lands* (New York: McGraw-Hill, 1963) 430–31; for the comparison of the depiction of the relief with the verbal expression in these lines see Cogan, "Sentencing," 4–5.

71 For the connection with Jer 1:15–16, see Cogan, "Sentencing," 5–6; for the text of Sargon's Letter, with explanation, see Morton Cogan, *Imperialism and*

Religion: Assyria, Judah and Israel in the Eighth and Seventh Centuries B.C.E. (SBLMS 19; Missoula, MT: Scholars, 1974) 23.

72 Hyatt assumes that all of vv 15–16 are Deuteronomic; the last two clauses of v 16 are listed as Deuteronomic phraseology in Moshe Weinfeld, *Deuteronomy and the Deuteronomic School* (Oxford: Clarendon, 1972) 321, no. 9, and 324, no. 7.

73 Arthur D. H. Mayes, *Deuteronomy* (Grand Rapids: Eerdmans, 1979) 350, 376.

Deuteronomy (eighteen times), it is true, but it is also found in the prose of Jrm (7:9, 18 and often). The phrase "work(s) of one's hands" for idols occurs three times in Deuteronomy, but again in passages that appear to be secondary additions.[74] It may be affirmed that there are two specific passages behind the wording here: 2 Kgs 22:17, part of Huldah's answer to the delegation who asked her judgment on the genuineness of the scroll found in the temple, "because they abandoned me and sacrificed to other gods so that they provoked me to anger with all the work of their hands"; and Isa 2:8, "The works of their hands they worship." In regard to Huldah's answer it is not necessary to assume that the wording is simply conventional Deuteronomistic wording;[75] there is evidence that this was indeed the diction of her answer.[76] And there is no question about the wording of Isa 2:8. The format of this phraseology is very similar to Jer 2:13 (see above), where the double crime of the people is defined as (1) abandoning Yahweh and (2) digging for themselves broken cisterns, a reference to idols made by human hands. We may conclude that the diction of these three clauses reflects Jrm's understanding of the crime of the covenant people: Jrm sees the judgment of Huldah on the words of Moses as operative now on the people as he carries on the work of Moses.

"Abandon" (עזב) is used in general of "leaving" something behind, but it is used in particular of "forsaking"—with human subject and object, of abandoning orphans (49:11); of an animal's forsaking her young (14:5); and in particular of Israel's forsaking Yahweh. The word in Jrm's diction stands alongside the earlier נטש (Deut 32:15; so Jer 15:6). There must have been a note of irony in these verbs when first used in this context: if the verb were typically used of abandoning children, then it is proper to speak of Yahweh's never abandoning his children (Ps 9:11), or on the contrary to speak of his abandoning them (Isa 2:6; Ps 22:2); but how can one understand the people's "abandonment" of their pro-

tecting deity?

The verb קטר pi'el is not found from Genesis through Judges. Except for Amos 4:5, where it carries the object "thank-offering," it is always used of pagan or illegitimate cults (and occurs only in the historical books and in the prophets). Cognates in other Semitic languages are related to a root "rise" (from the altar, as of smoke or incense), but the traditional translation "burn incense" (*RSV, JB, NAB*) is too specific: Jrm uses it to mean "offer pagan sacrifices" (see Hos 11:2).[77] The phrase "other gods" inevitably reminds the hearer of the First Commandment (Exod 20:3; Deut 5:7): the accusation goes to the very heart of Israel's covenant obligation, and the phrase is often found elsewhere as well (Hos 3:1).

"Worship" (וַיִּשְׁתַּחֲווּ), given the Ugaritic evidence,[78] is now to be analyzed as חוה hištap'el;[79] it means essentially "prostrate oneself" (Gen 18:2), and in cultic contexts "worship." It, too, occurs in the Ten Commandments—the Second (Exod 20:5, Deut 5:9), which forbids the making of a graven image. Here Judah stands accused of worshiping the work of human hands: it is as implausible to worship what one has made oneself as to abandon God (see above), and the foolishness of such a venture was made clear again and again to Israel (10:3–5; Isa 44:4–20).

Excursus: The Problem of the Identity of the Foe from the North

The present shape of the text of vv 14–16 raises the question, who is the foe from the north of which Jrm speaks? The advent of this foe is mentioned often in subsequent passages (4:6–7; 6:1–5, 22–23; 10:22 and elsewhere). The chronology adopted in the present study renders the question no longer a problem (see below), but since most scholars have assumed that Jrm began to exercise his prophetic vocation in 627, the problem has been acute and some account of the discussion becomes necessary. What foe would have been active in the years after 627?

---

74 Deut 4:28; 27:15; 31:29; for these passages see Mayes, *Deuteronomy*, 148, 346, 379.

75 As is the assumption of John Gray, *I & II Kings* (Philadelphia: Westminster, 1970) 727.

76 Jack R. Lundbom, "The Lawbook of the Josianic Reform," *CBQ* 38 (1976) 295–98.

77 And see Hans Walter Wolff, *Hosea* (Hermeneia; Philadelphia: Fortress, 1974) 86, on 4:13.

78 *UT*, glossary, no. 847.

79 So *HALAT*.

The suggestion that the foe was the Scythians was evidently first made by Hermann Venema in 1765,[80] and this identification has been an attractive one to scholars; it is based on a report in Herodotus[81] of an incursion by the Scythians in the years around 625 through Asia as far as the frontier of Egypt, and this reported incursion appeared to fit Jeremiah's descriptions (so Duhm, Cornill, John Skinner).[82]

More recently commentators have shied away from this identification (Volz, Condamin) or have rejected it altogether (Rudolph, Bright). Herodotus's report has been widely challenged, notably by Fritz Wilke[83] and J. Philip Hyatt,[84] and it has been dealt a death-blow by the recent work of Richard P. Vaggione.[85]

Since the discovery of Ugaritic literature it has become clear that "north" carries mythological connotations,[86] so that some scholars have come to see the foe from the north in this book as a mythological figure, a kind of enemy from "never-never land": thus the north is "the direction out of which the demonic enemy descends."[87] By this view the enemy is not to be identified with a specific national group but, like Gog and Magog in Ezekiel 38—39, is simply God's instrument, coming from beyond the known historical realm, to judge the covenant people.

Others have viewed the descriptions of the foe to have been shaped first under the stimulus of the Scythians and later adapted to refer to the Babylonians.[88]

The problem is that though the foe is described metaphorically (he is a lion, 4:7; a leopard or a wolf, 5:6, perhaps a sirocco wind, 4:11–12), he is also described concretely: he has chariots and horses (4:13; 6:23; 8:16), he is an ancient nation (5:15). The description of the foe in 5:15 resembles Isaiah's description of Assyria in Isa 5:26–29, and the description in 4:13 resembles the description of the Chaldeans in Hab 1:8.

The lower chronology for Jrm's career adopted in the present study obviates the difficulties. If Jrm began to exercise his prophetic office a few years before 609, then the foe from the north is the Babylonians from the beginning. It is perhaps significant that Ezek 26:7 describes God as bringing upon Tyre Nebuchadrezzar from the north, with horses and chariots.

■ **17–19** These verses are genuine to Jrm, but were added late in his career (see Preliminary Observations, Setting).

They are a word from Yahweh of encouragement to Jrm (see Form). The opening pronoun "for your part" (וְאַתָּה) is balanced by "for my part" (וַאֲנִי) at the beginning of v 18 (not, note well, by "I" [אָנֹכִי] in the second line of v 17, which is evidence of textual confusion).

Jrm is told to gird up his loins. This phrase denotes tying a belt or the like around one's waist so as to confine the tunic or other long garment, or to tuck up the extremities of one's tunic into the belt, so as to free the legs for running, physical work, doing battle, or the like (1 Kgs 18:46; Isa 5:27); a modern expression with similar connotation is "roll up your sleeves." The opposite idiom

80   Hermann Venema, *Commentarius ad librum prophetiarum Jeremiae* (Leeuwarden: de Chalmot, 1765), pars prior, 142, according to Richard P. Vaggione, "All Over Asia? The Extent of the Scythian Domination in Herodotus," *JBL* 92 (1973) 523.

81   *Hist.* 1.103–6.

82   John Skinner, *Prophecy and Religion, Studies in the Life of Jeremiah* (Cambridge: Cambridge University, 1922) 39–44.

83   Fritz Wilke, "Das Skythenproblem im Jeremiabuch," *Alttestamentliche Studien Rudolf Kittel zum 60. Geburtstag dargebracht von A. Alt, G. Beer, F. Böhl [etc.]* (Beiträge zur Wissenschaft vom Alten Testament 13; Leipzig: Hinrichs, 1913) 222–54.

84   J. Philip Hyatt, "The Peril from the North in Jeremiah," *JBL* 59 (1940) 499–513.

85   Richard P. Vaggione, "All Over Asia? The Extent of the Scythian Domination in Herodotus," *JBL* 92 (1973) 523–30; "Scythians," *IDBSup*, 797–98.

86   See notably Otto Eissfeldt, *Baal Zaphon, Zeus Kasios und der Durchzug der Israeliten durchs Meer* (Beiträge zur Religionsgeschichte des Altertums 1; Halle:

Niemeyer, 1932) 13–30; Aare Lauha, *Zaphon der Norden und die Nordvölker im Alten Testament* (Annales Academiae Scientiarum Fennicae; Helsinki: Ständerhuset, 1943); William F. Albright, "Baal-Zephon," *Festschrift Alfred Bertholet zum 80. Geburtstag gewidmet von Kollegen und Freunden, herausgegeben durch Walter Baumgartner, Otto Eissfeldt, Karl Elliger, Leonhard Rost* (ed. Walter Baumgartner; Tübingen: Mohr [Siebeck], 1950) 1–14; Brevard S. Childs, "The Enemy from the North and the Chaos Tradition," *JBL* 78 (1959) 187–98.

87   Brevard S. Childs, *Myth and Reality in the Old Testament* (SBT 27; Naperville, IL: Allenson, 1960) 87.

88   James Muilenburg, "Jeremiah the Prophet," *IDB* 2:825–26.

is found in Isa 45:1: to "ungird the loins of kings" is to disarm them.[89] The idiom is often metaphorical, indicating a preparation for verbal argumentation (Job 38:3; 40:7). The usage of the idiom in the present passage suggests that Jrm is to prepare for conflict with his enemies (see Form, which explores the imagery of holy war here). The command "and arise" (וְקַמְתָּ) continues the forward movement into action[90] (compare a similar sequence in 13:4). Indeed that verb may continue the metaphor of holy war[91] (compare Judg 4:1; 7:9; and often). The clause "and speak to them" is thus a displacement of the diction for activity in holy war (see again Form).

The command "do not be panicked" (אַל־תֵּחַת) is a variation of "do not be afraid" (אַל־תִּירָא, v 8); the two verbs are often found in parallelism in the OT.[92] This verb, and its counterpart אֲחִתְּךָ in the next clause, share in the assonance of ḥ and t which begins with תִּפְתַּח in v 14 and continues in v 15, just as the occurrence of פְּנֵיהֶם (twice) and of פֶּן here matches the assonance of v 13. The verb in question is חתת, in its second occurrence a hip'il, in its first occurrence either qal or nip'al—there is no distinction of meaning, and the qal and nip'al of this type of verb may be indistinguishable.[93] Though the verb functions as a synonym of "be afraid," the traditional translation "be dismayed" (RSV, JB) is too weak; the hip'il verb is used of physical shattering in Isa 9:3, and it appears to be used of psychological paralysis, or inability to function at all (note the use of the qal stem in 14:4 of the soil which is "stricken" for lack of rain), so that "be panicked" is not too strong. The collocation of two stems of a verb is already found in Ugaritic poetry[94] and in the biblical Psalms,[95] but it is particularly common in Jrm's style.[96] Yahweh tells Jrm not to be paralyzed by the threat of his enemies among the people, but that reas-

surance is joined by a kind of threat that Yahweh himself will paralyze him if his courage breaks down. Jrm is free to exercise his own integrity, but that integrity is intimately wrapped in Yahweh's own sovereignty (and that same blend of reassurance and threat is found in 15:19). The double occurrence of פְּנֵיהֶם perhaps means little more than the pronoun ("Do not be panicked by them, or I will panic you by them"); but the word implies "their face, their presence": it is their faces that threaten Jrm with paralysis.[97] The verb "be panicked" is often used for the collapse of warriors (Isa 8:9; 37:27; Obadiah 9); Jrm is to be a warrior who does not collapse, on behalf of Yahweh against his opponents.

The focus in v 17 has been on Jrm's task as a prophetic warrior; in v 18 the focus is on what Yahweh will do to empower him for that task ("for my part," וַאֲנִי). Note that the verb "I have made you" (נְתַתִּיךָ) reflects the same word in 1:5, and "today" (הַיּוֹם) echoes "this day" in v 10.

Jerusalem is vulnerable to the foe from the north called forth by Yahweh (v 15); by contrast, Jrm becomes by Yahweh's will an invulnerable city. A city is by definition fortified, and the term accompanying "city" here, literally "fortification" (מִבְצָר), only reinforces that characteristic.[98]

The question about the originality to the passage of the phrases here translated "an iron bolt and a bronze wall" is difficult. G reads a shorter text ("a strong bronze wall") which simply duplicates the phrase in 15:20. Given the fact that G omits "iron bolt," one might well conclude that it is a late gloss.[99] On the other hand the phrase is unique to the OT, a circumstance suggesting its validity.[100] Furthermore "iron" and "bronze" are correlative in 15:12 (and, with a different reference, in 6:28).

Shemaryahu Talmon[101] suggests that עַמּוּד בַּרְזֶל means

---

89 Karl Elliger, *Deuterojesaja* (BKAT 11/1; Neukirchen: Neukirchener, 1978) 492.

90 Berridge, p. 200.

91 Ibid., 201.

92 Fifteen times, e. g., 30:10.

93 GKC, sec. 67g.

94 Moshe Held, "The Action-Result (Factitive-Passive) Sequence of Identical Verbs in Biblical Hebrew and Ugaritic," *JBL* 84 (1965) 272–82.

95 Ibid.; Mitchell Dahood, *Psalms 101—150* (AB 17A; Garden City, NY: Doubleday, 1970) 414.

96 William L. Holladay, "Style, Irony and Authenticity in Jeremiah," *JBL* 81 (1962) 44–54, esp. 46.

97 Compare Aubrey R. Johnson, *The Vitality of the Individual in the Thought of Ancient Israel* (Cardiff: University of Wales, 1949) 42–44.

98 Frank S. Frick, *The City in Ancient Israel* (SBLDS 36; Missoula, MT: Scholars, 1977) esp. 31.

99 Francis S. North, "Textual Variants in the Hebrew Bible Significant for Critical Analysis," *JQR* 47 (1956) 78; Berridge, p. 199 n. 82.

100 So Rudolph and Janzen, and so Shemaryahu Talmon, "An Apparently Redundant MT Reading— Jeremiah 1:18," *Textus* 8 (1973), 160–63.

an "iron bolt" for the city gate. He notes the repeated triad of "walls, gates and bars" in the description of a city (Deut 3:5; 2 Chr 8:5; 14:6) and the use of the phrase "bars of iron" both literally and figuratively (Isa 45:2; Ps 107:16). It is true, the normal word for the bar of a city gate is בְּרִיחַ, not עַמּוּד, which normally means a "column." But עַמּוּד occurs occasionally in postbiblical Hebrew for a cylinder in any position (e.g., a cylinder around which a scroll is rolled).[102] In any event, whether the phrase here means "iron column" or "iron bolt," it and the "bronze wall" would be inconceivably strong (compare the "wall of tin" in Amos 7:7);[103] Jrm is now rendered symbolically invincible by Yahweh.

The list of classes of people who will fight against Jrm (the balance of v 18) does not accord well with poetic style; it is doubtless an expansion of the text. Who were the "officials" (שָׂרִים)? In the premonarchical period the term referred to "chiefs" (see Judg 8:14); during the monarchy the term was used for military commanders (2 Kgs 11:4 and often), palace officials (1 Kgs 22:26) and for the governors of cities or districts (1 Kgs 20:14). They are deputies of the king, but it is not possible to be more specific.[104]

"Her priests" is omitted by G. The sequence of M is also found in 34:19, and it is certainly true that there were priests opposed to Jrm (20:1–6; 26:7–9). But since "priests" are so often linked with "prophets" in such lists (see 4:9), given the omission in G it is better to bracket the expression here.

The precise denotation of "people of the land" (עַם הָאָרֶץ) is difficult, and opinions vary widely. Ernest W. Nicholson believes that the term had no fixed meaning but was used in a fluid manner with varying meaning from context to context.[105] The general meaning is the body of free men enjoying civic rights in a given terri-

tory;[106] the term is thus used here for the citizens of the nation outside the orbit of the palace and temple in Jerusalem. Jrm will not be the spokesman for a struggle of the rural citizenry against the city: the totality of his fellow citizens will be against him.

The last verse of the chapter rounds off the affirmations of v 18: "they [Jrm's fellow citizens] shall fight against you, but they shall not overcome you," a sequence with striking assonance of ', l, and k. Curiously, for all the wording in these verses which implies holy war and the besieging of cities, this is the first word connoting combat. But Jrm's opponents will not be the victors in the struggle. (The verb "overcome" [יכל] is central in one of the "confessions" [20:7–11]: there Jrm accuses Yahweh of overcoming him and affirms that his enemies are plotting to overcome him. Both vv 17–19 here and 20:7–13 are given the same setting in the present study.) Finally there comes the reassurance of Yahweh to Jrm which repeats the last line of v 8: "For I am with you to deliver you."

Aim

The call narrative embodies Jrm's testimony that he is a legitimate prophet commissioned by Yahweh to speak and act on his behalf. The fact that Jrm includes a frank statement of his objection to the call underlines his affirmation that his career is in no sense something he devised for himself but was something laid upon him. Indeed the content of his objection, "I am only a youth," merely anticipates what unsympathetic hearers are likely to say, that he is too young to be a prophet. The whole narrative then serves the purpose of self-legitimation.

In contrast to his great predecessor Isaiah and his great successor Ezekiel, Jrm is offered no glimpse of a vision of the heavenly court: the visions he is offered are

---

101 See n. 100.

102 Marcus Jastrow, *A Dictionary of the Targumim, the Talmud Babli and Yerushalmi, and the Midrashic Literature* (New York: Putnam, 1903).

103 Gilbert Brunet, "La Vision de l'étain, Réinterprétation d'Amos VII 7–9," *VT* 16 (1966) 387–95; William L. Holladay, "Once More, אֲנָךְ—'Tin,' Amos vii 7–8," *VT* 20 (1970) 492–94.

104 De Vaux, *Ancient Israel*, 69.

105 Ernest W. Nicholson, "The Meaning of the Expression עם הארץ in the Old Testament," *JSS* 10 (1965) 66.

106 De Vaux, *Ancient Israel*, 70; Marvin H. Pope, "'Am Ha'arez," *IDB* 1:106–7 with bibliography; and, recently, Antonius H. L. Gunneweg, "עם הארץ—A Semantic Revolution," *ZAW* 95 (1983) 437–40.

homely ones that reassure him of Yahweh's faithfulness and suggest to him what Yahweh is about to do. Otherwise he receives only the bare words of Yahweh. And the content of these words is astonishing in two respects. First, they resemble the call to Moses and therefore make the claim, overtly or covertly, that Jrm is the legitimate successor to Moses, an awesome comparison even given the warrant of Deut 18:18 (one is reminded of the way Jesus set himself up alongside Moses at a later time—see Mark 10:3–9, for example). Second, in stating (twice!) that Jrm is specifically called to exercise his prophetic office over nations, and in insisting that Jrm was called from before his birth, the words beg comparison with the claims made by the kings of neighboring empires: and this at a time when the sovereignty of the kings of Judah was waning and would finally be extinguished. Jrm in speaking for Yahweh would offer an authority which would rival and finally replace that of monarchs, and such a claim would become an important source of continuity and authority when Jerusalem fell. When other institutions crumbled, the words of Jrm's call, audacious though they seemed on first hearing, would invite the trust of those in the Jewish community who preserved them. And the continuity which Jrm's call offered is symbolized by the four verbs that sum up his task to exercise judgment and restoration: to uproot and demolish, then to build and plant (v 10).

The call narrative received expansions from Jrm himself: his expectation of the return of the northern tribes is swallowed up by the advent of the foe from the north, and still later that reverse of holy war is balanced by a salvation-oracle of reassurance (vv 17–19) to the prophet himself: the nation is helpless before the foe from the north, but Jrm will be invulnerable to his enemies among the citizens of Judah. Jrm's hesitation in accepting his commission (v 6) to be Yahweh's spokesman in the lawsuit Yahweh is bringing against his people (v 16) is overcome by Yahweh's promise to him to guarantee his effectiveness in that task: the promise in vv 17–19 reinforces that given in v 8. The promise becomes an implied covenant between Yahweh and Jrm, and the time will come when Jrm will take Yahweh to court even as Yahweh takes Israel to court (12:1).[107] But for now we have simply been allowed to hear Yahweh's assurance to Jrm that the prophet will be strong enough to withstand whatever opposition is coming.

---

107 See William L. Holladay, "Jeremiah's Lawsuit with God," *Int* 17 (1963) 280–87.

The Accusation of Harlotry
and the Appeal to Repent

Bibliography

On 2:1—6:30:
Albertz, Rainer
    "Jer 2—6 und die Frühzeitverkündigung
    Jeremias," *ZAW* 94 (1982) 20–47.

On 2:1–37, and the covenant lawsuit (rîb):
De Roche, Michael
    "Yahweh's *rîb* Against Israel: A Reassessment of
    the So-Called 'Prophetic Lawsuit' in the Preexilic
    Prophets," *JBL* 102 (1983) 563–74.
Gemser, Berend
    "The *rîb*- or Controversy-Pattern in Hebrew
    Mentality," *Wisdom in Israel and in the Ancient Near
    East, Presented to Professor Harold Henry Rowley by the
    Society for Old Testament Study in Association with the
    Editorial Board of Vetus Testamentum in Celebration of
    his Sixty-Fifth Birthday, 24 March 1955* (ed. Martin
    Noth and D. Winton Thomas; VTSup 3; Leiden:
    Brill, 1955) 120–37.
Harvey, Julien
    "Le Rîb-Pattern: Réquisitoire prophétique sur la
    rupture de l'Alliance," *Bib* 43 (1962) 172–96.
Huffmon, Herbert B.
    "The Covenant Lawsuit in the Prophets," *JBL* 78
    (1959) 285–95.
Limburg, James
    "The Root ריב and the Prophetic Lawsuit
    Speeches," *JBL* 88 (1969) 291–304.
Nielsen, Kirsten
    *Yahweh as Prosecutor and Judge: An Investigation of the
    Prophetic Lawsuit (Rîb-Pattern)* (JSOT Supplement
    Series 9; Sheffield: Sheffield University, 1978).
Ramsey, George W.
    "Speech-Forms in Hebrew Law and Prophetic
    Oracles," *JBL* 96 (1977) 45–58.
Suganuma, Eiji
    "The Covenant *Rib* Form in Jeremiah Chapter 2:
    A Form Critical Study," *Journal of the College of
    Dairy Agriculture* 4 (Nopporo, Hokkaido, Japan:
    1972) 121–54.

Other studies:
Milgrom, Jacob
    "The Date of Jeremiah, Chapter 2," *JNES* 14
    (1955) 65–69.
Overholt, Thomas W.
    "Jeremiah 2 and the Problem of 'Audience
    Reaction,'" *CBQ* 41 (1979) 262–73.

On 2:1–3:
De Roche, Michael
    "Jeremiah 2:2–3 and Israel's Love for God during
    the Wilderness Wanderings," *CBQ* 45 (1983) 364–
    75.

Fox, Michael V.
  "Jeremiah 2:2 and the 'Desert Ideal,'" *CBQ* 35
  (1973) 441–50.
Schottroff, Willy
  "Jeremia 2,1–3: Erwägungen zur Methode der
  Prophetenexegese," *ZTK* 67 (1970) 263–94.
Watson, Wilfred G. E.
  "Symmetry of Stanza in Jeremiah 2,2b–3," *JSOT*
  19 (1981) 107–10.
Wiéner, Claude
  "Jérémie ii, 2: 'Fiançailles' ou 'Épousailles'?" *RSR*
  44 (1956) 403–7.

On ḥesed:
Glueck, Nelson
  Ḥesed in the Bible (Cincinnati: Hebrew Union
  College, 1967).
Sakenfeld, Katherine D.
  The Meaning of Ḥesed in the Hebrew Bible (HSM 17;
  Missoula, MT: Scholars, 1978).
Stoebe, Hans Joachim
  "Die Bedeutung des Wortes ḥäsäd im Alten
  Testament," *VT* 2 (1952) 244–54.
Zobel, Hans-Jürgen
  "חֶסֶד," *TWAT* 3, cols. 48–71.

On 2:4–13:
De Roche, Michael
  "Israel's 'two evils' in Jeremiah ii 13," *VT* 31 (1981)
  369–71.
Williams, Prescott
  "The Fatal and Foolish Exchange; Living Water
  for 'Nothings': A Study of Jeremiah 2:4–13,"
  Austin Seminary Bulletin, Faculty Edition 81 (1965)
  3–59.

On 2:20–25:
Bailey, Kenneth E., and William L. Holladay
  "The 'Young Camel' and 'Wild Ass' in Jeremiah ii
  23–25," *VT* 18 (1968) 256–60.
Holladay, William L.
  "'On Every High Hill and Under Every Green
  Tree,'" *VT* 11 (1961) 170–76.
McKane, William
  "Jeremiah ii 23–25: Observations on the Versions
  and History of Exegesis," *The Witness of Tradition*
  (*OTS* 17; Leiden: Brill, 1972) 73–88.
Soggin, J. Alberto
  "'Your Conduct in the Valley,' Note on Jeremiah
  2,23a," *Old Testament and Oriental Studies* (BibOr
  29) 78–83 = "'La tua condotta nella Valle,' Nota a
  Geremia ii, 23a," *RSO* 36 (1961) 207–11.

On 2:26–28:
Fishbane, Michael A.
  "Revelation and Tradition: Aspects of Inner-
  Biblical Exegesis," *JBL* 99 (1980) 343–61, esp.
  351–52.

On 2:29–32:
Hoffmann, Y.
  "Jeremiah 2:30," *ZAW* 89 (1977) 418–20.
Köhler, Ludwig
  "Jer 2,31," *ZAW* 44 (1926) 62.
Loewenclau, Ilse von
  "Zu Jeremia ii 30," *VT* 16 (1966) 117–23.

On 2:33–37:
Fishbane
  "Revelation and Tradition," 351–52.
Holladay, William L.
  "Jeremiah ii 34bβ—A Fresh Proposal," *VT* 25
  (1975) 221–25.
Soggin, J. Alberto
  "Einige Bemerkungen über Jeremias ii 34," *VT* 8
  (1958) 433–35.
Strobel, Albert
  "Jeremia 2,34 im Rahmen des Gedichtes 2,29–37,"
  Kirche und Bibel, Festgabe für Bischof Eduard Schick
  (Paderborn: Schöningh, 1979) 449–58.

On 3:1—4:4:
Jobling, David
  "Jeremiah's Poem in III 1—IV 2," *VT* 18 (1978)
  45–55.
Muilenburg, James
  "A Study of Hebrew Rhetoric: Repetition and
  Style," *Congress Volume, International Organization
  for the Study of the Old Testament, Copenhagen, 1953*
  (VTSup 1; Leiden: Brill, 1953) 104–5.
Raitt, Thomas M.
  "The Prophetic Summons to Repentance," *ZAW*
  83 (1971) 30–49.

On 3:1–5:
Fishbane, Michael A.
  "Torah and Tradition," *Tradition and Theology in
  the Old Testament* (ed. Douglas A. Knight; Phila-
  delphia: Fortress, 1977) 284–86.
Fishbane
  "Revelation and Tradition," 351.
Hobbs, Trevor R.
  "Jeremiah 3:1–5 and Deuteronomy 24:1–4," *ZAW*
  86 (1974) 23–29.
Long, Burke O.
  "The Stylistic Components of Jeremiah 3:1–5,"
  ZAW 88 (1976) 386–90.
Martin, James D.
  "The Forensic Background to Jeremiah III 1," *VT*
  19 (1969) 82–92.
Wurz, Heinrich
  "Die Möglichkeit der Umkehr nach Jer 3,1; War
  nach Jeremia der von menschlicher Seite
  gebrochene Bund mit Gott durch neuerliche
  Gehorsamsleistung wiederherstellbar?" *Erbe als
  Auftrag, Zur Theologie- und Geistesgeschichte des 19.
  Jahrhunderts, Joseph Pritz zum 60. Geburtstag*

(Wiener Beiträge zur Theologie 40; Vienna: Dom, 1973) 259–73.

On 3:6–11:

McKane, William
"Relations Between Poetry and Prose in the Book of Jeremiah with Special Reference to Jeremiah III 6–11 and XII 14–17," *Congress Volume, Vienna, 1980* (VTSup 32; Leiden: Brill, 1981) 220–37.

On 3:12–18:

Cazelles, Henri
"Israël du nord et Arche d'Alliance (Jér. III 16)," *VT* 18 (1968) 147–58.

Haran, Menaḥem
"The Disappearance of the Ark," *IEJ* 13 (1963) 46–58, rep. in *Israel Exploration Journal Reader 1* (New York: Ktav, 1981) 262–74.

Petersen, David L.
Late Israelite Prophecy (SBLMS 23; Missoula, MT: Scholars, 1977) 32.

Soggin, J. Alberto
"The Ark of the Covenant, Jeremiah 3,16," *Le Livre de Jérémie* (ed. P.-M. Bogaert; BETL 54; Leuven: Leuven University, 1981) 215–21.

Weinfeld, Moshe
"Jeremiah and the Spiritual Metamorphosis of Israel," *ZAW* 88 (1976) 19–26.

On 3:19–25:

Paul, Shalom M.
"לשונות אימוץ (Adoption Formulae)," *Eretz-Israel* 14 (1978) 31–36, English summary, 123.

On 4:1–4:

Berridge
p. 77.

Le Déaut, Roger
"Le Thème de la Circoncision du Coeur (Dt. xxx 6; Jér. iv 4) dans les Versions anciennes (LXX et Targum) et à Qumrân," *Congress Volume, Vienna 1980* (VTSup 32; Leiden: Brill, 1981) 178–205.

2

1 The word of Yahweh came to me as follows: 2/ Go and call out in the ears of Jerusalem as follows:
Thus Yahweh has said:
I have recalled in your favor the loyalty of your youth,
  the love of your bridal days,
    your walking after me in the wilderness,
    in a land unsown.

3 Israel has been Yahweh's possession,
  the first-fruits of [a]his harvest,[a]
all who ate of him were held guilty,
  disaster would come upon them,
               oracle of Yahweh.
- - - -

4 Hear the word of Yahweh, household of Jacob,
  and all the tribes of the household of Israel!

5 Thus Yahweh has said:
What did your fathers find wrong with me?
  Look: they distanced themselves from me,
    and walked after a nothing,
      shared in nothingness ⟪. . . (?)⟫[a]

6 They did not say, "Where is Yahweh?—
he who brought us up from the land of Egypt,
  who led us in the wilderness,
    in a land of waste and ravine,
      in a land of drought and [a]utter darkness,[a]
        in a land where no one crossed,
        where nobody lived."

7 And I brought you into the land of gardens
  to eat its fruit and its bounty;

Text

2:3a—a Reading with the qere' and some MSS. תְּבוּאָתוֹ. The ketib תבואתה can be read, and some MSS. do read, תְּבוּאָתָהּ ("its harvest," feminine possessor), the feminine presumably referring to the "land" mentioned in the last line of v 2. On the other hand, final ה occasionally occurs for the third singular masculine suffix (GKC, secs. 7c, 91e), and the masculine was surely intended here by the text tradition which preserved ה.

5a One may suspect that a verb closely resembling ויהבלו has dropped out by haplography, but if so, it is lost without a trace; see Interpretation.

6a—a Instead of the noun G reads the adjective ἀκάρπῳ "barren." Since a' and s' use ἄκαρπος in Job 15:34 to render גַּלְמוּד "barren," Wilhelm Rudolph (*BHS*) and John Bright suggest that G knew a reading גַּלְמוּדָה here. This is plausible, but the assonance offered by צַלְמָוֶת and its association with its synonyms in similar contexts (see Interpretation) makes *M* the preferable reading.

but you came in and defiled my land,
and my inheritance you made
loathsome.

8 The priests—they have not said, "Where
is Yahweh?"—
those dealing with the law have not
known me,
the shepherds have rebelled against
me,
the prophets have prophesied by
Baal:
after useless things they have
walked.

9 That is why I shall once more enter suit
with you,
oracle of Yahweh,
and with ªyour childrenª I shall enter suit.

- - - -

10 Look—cross to the shores of the Cypriots
and see,
and to Kedar send and make careful
inquiry [and see.]ª
⟨Has it (ever) been done⟩ᵇ like this?

11 Has any nation exchanged gods?—
though those are non-gods!
But my people have exchanged
ªtheir gloryª for something
useless.

12 Be horrified, O heavens, at this,
stand aghast ⟪and⟫ª be utterly dry,
oracle of Yahweh,

13 look—a double crime my people have
committed:
me they have abandoned,
the spring of running water,
to dig themselves cisterns,
broken cisterns,
that hold no water.

14 Is Israel a slave,
or a bondman by birth?
Why then has he become a victim?

15 Over him lions have been roaring,
have uttered their cry;
they have made his land a desolation,
his cities ªhave been burned,ª without
inhabitant.

9a—a So 3 MSS. and *V*; the majority of MSS. (and the other Versions) insert "children of" before the expression. The short reading is suggested by the contrast with "your fathers" in v 5 (compare "your children" in v 30). The majority reading is thus dittographic.

10a One of the two occurrences of וּרְאוּ in this verse is dittographic. Against Rudolph, I excise the second occurrence rather than the first; its insertion here became plausible when the following sequence was wrongly vocalized (see textual note "b"). The rightness of the first occurrence is undergirded by the phrasing of Amos 6:2.

b *M* הֵן הָיְתָה "if there was (anything)" is most dubious, and Rudolph's suggestion (*BHS*) to read הֲנִהְיְתָה is undoubtedly right. This brings two occurrences of הֲ in parallel verses. For נִהְיְתָה (היה nip'al) see 5:30.

11a—a Reading *M* כְּבוֹדוֹ in spite of the tradition that this is a *tiqqun sopherim* for כְּבוֹדִי "my (i.e., God's) glory." In lists of *tiqqune sopherim* this passage is listed along with Hos 4:7 and Ps 106:20: these three passages all have the verb מור hip'il "exchange" with the object כְּבוֹדוֹ or כְּבוֹדָם in *M*, and in each case the tradition is that the original reading was כְּבוֹדִי. (For the rabbinic citations, see Christian D. Ginsburg, *Introduction to the Massoretico-Critical Edition of the Hebrew Bible* [London: Trinitarian Bible Society, 1897; rep. New York: Ktav, 1966] 348, 350; for the discussion of each passage, see pp. 356, 357, 360–61.) The matter is not simple, and space precludes a treatment here of the three passages together. What is clear is that either a third-person suffix or a first-person suffix may raise theological difficulties: the third-person suffix, that God was the people's glory and therefore somehow under their control; and the first-person suffix, that the people could dispose of God's own glory. The double tradition of text thus becomes understandable. But the possibility that the third-person suffix in these passages is valid is supported by the diction of Ps 3:4, where "my glory" is spoken by the psalmist: he said, "God is my glory," and the surrounding phrases protect the integrity of the text. The tradition that Jer 2:11; Hos 4:7; and Ps 106:20 were altered by the scribes is then erroneous. For Hos 4:7, see Hans Walter Wolff, *Hosea*, 71; for Ps 106:20, see Mitchell Dahood, *Psalms III*, 72. The judgment here given on the present passage concurs with Paul Volz, Albert Condamin, and Rudolph against Bright. For the *tiqqune sopherim* in general see Carmel McCarthy, "Emendations of the Scribes," *IDBSup*, 263–64, and the bibliography there.

12a Adding וְ with *S* and in parallel with the diction of v 10; haplography with preceding waw.

15a—a Reading with the qere' and some MSS. נִצְּתוּ (יצת nip'al). The ketib נצתה may have been a feminine singular with plural subject, or it may have been intended as a perfect feminine third plural

16   **Even the sons of Memphis and**
        Tahpanhes^a ⟨have been breaking⟩^b
        your skull.

17   ^a**Don't you know what's really**
         responsible^a—
       that you abandoned Yahweh your God
         ^b**at the time he was leading you on**
          the road?^b

(compare Aramaic, and see the discussion on this matter in GKC, sec. 44m, and Paul Joüon, *Grammaire de l'Hébreu Biblique* [Rome: Pontifical Biblical Institute, 1947] sec. 42f). Other MSS. offer נִתְּצוּ (נתץ nipʻal) "be demolished." The Versions scatter: *G* κατεσκάφησαν "are broken down" suggests נתץ nipʻal; *V exustae sunt* must be יצת nipʻal; *S nṣdyn* and *T* צדרין "are desolate" reflect נצה nipʻal (compare their rendering of 4:7). Since the similar phraseology of 4:7 has נצה and 4:26 has נתץ, it is plausible to see the third of these sound-alikes in the present verse; hence the choice of יצת.

16a   The qereʼ is וְתַחְפְּנֵחֶם, and this reading is represented in several MSS.; the ketib וְתַחְפַּנֵס, like the תְּחַפְנְחֵס of Ezek 30:18, represents a variant writing (or miscopying) of this Egyptian place-name. See Interpretation.

b   *M* (רעה qal) יִרְעוּךְ "have been pasturing you" is plainly wrong. Other MSS. and *G* read יְדָעוּךְ "know you," and *V* (*constupraverunt te*, "have debauched you") may have used this reading as well, understanding "know" as "sexually violate"; but these Versions diverge in their treatment of "forehead," and the reading is doubtless the simplification of a difficult set of consonants. *S* reads *nrʻwnky*, that is, "they will break you" (*rʻʻ* peal), thus assuming a Hebrew root רעע of this meaning (cited in BDB and KB as רעע II), and this reading is accepted by Bright; the form would then be יְרֹעוּךְ. But this verb is poorly attested in the OT for the qal, and it may be that *S* is simply translating with the same consonants in its own (and Aramaic) vocabulary. (Note that 15:12, usually cited for this verb, is probably better understood otherwise: see there.) As a safer suggestion I would propose יָרֵעוּךְ "they will harm (you)" (רעע I hipʻil), a verb stem common to Jrm (see for example 2:33 and 3:5 as here revocalized). Either of these revocalizations is more economical than the emendation (Bernhard Duhm, Carl H. Cornill, Rudolph) to יְעָרוּךְ "lay bare" (ערה piʻel), understood as "shaved bald."

17a—a   Literally, "Isn't this what is working on you?—(namely)"; reading *M* תַּעֲשֶׂה, construed as third singular feminine with זֹאת as subject. Two MSS. read תַּעֲשִׂי, second singular feminine; by that reading זֹאת must be construed as object: "Isn't this what you are doing to yourself?" In the light of v 19a (see Interpretation) *M* as here read is surely correct. Rudolph's emendation to עָשָׂה "Has not your abandonment of Yahweh your God done this to you?" is unnecessary, though this reading is suggested by *G. V, S,* and *T* seem to read the nipʻal תֵּעָשֶׂה "Is this not done to you?"

b—b   *G* omits this colon, and it has been judged secondary by most commentators (Duhm, Friedrich Giesebrecht, Cornill, Volz, Rudolph; Bright also tends to the view that it is secondary). By this view it is dittographic with the first syllables of v 18; so, most recently, J. Gerald Janzen, p. 10, with careful

18   So now why should you be on the road to
          Egypt
          to drink the water of the Nile?
             Or why should you be on the road to
                Assyria
                to drink the water of the
                   Euphrates?

19   Let your wrongdoing punish you
          ªand your turningsª reprove you,
       so you know and see
          how bad and bitter
             that you abandoned Yahweh your God
                and ᵇdid not hold me in awe,ᵇ
                   oracle of the Lord Yahweh of hosts.

20   Look, long ago ªyou brokeª your yoke,
          ªyou tore awayª your cords
             and said, ᵇ"I will not serve!"ᵇ

discussion. One suspects that this judgment is reinforced by a hesitation to accept a tricolon; but if v 16 consists of only a single colon, vv 16–17 together make up a tetracolon (see Structure). Condamin is right to raise the question whether, to the contrary, *G* does not have a haplographic text. This colon does not resemble the first colon of v 18 too closely; one could argue that Jrm is offering assonance between this colon and the first and third cola of v 18. The participle מוֹלִיכֵךְ is grammatically difficult, but הַמּוֹלִיךְ in v 6 encourages the genuineness of the participle here. On the other hand, the diction of 6:15 suggests that הוֹלִיכֵךְ is what we might expect here; perhaps that is the correct reading (compare GKC, sec. 116g, n. 1). In any event the line seems valid.

19a—a   Reading *M* וּמְשֻׁבוֹתַיִךְ. It is tempting to read the noun without waw and yod as the singular וּמְשֻׁבָתֵךְ "your turning, waywardness," and thus to read תּוֹכִחֵךְ as תּוֹכַחֵךְ. It is to be noted that the verb is written defectively and so open to that vocalization, and further that the verb as presently vocalized must be construed as an imperfect third plural feminine (thus תּוֹכַחְנָה plus suffix): this passage is one of three in the OT in which the form of the second plural masculine serves for second or third plural feminine imperfect before a suffix (see GKC, sec. 60a). The temptation to read a singular here is reinforced by two MSS. which so read, and three Versions (*G*, though with the reversal of the terms of the first two cola, *V* and *S*; *T* is periphrastic). On the other hand, *M* is the *lectio difficilior* and is to be preferred: Jrm uses the noun in three other instances in the plural (3:22; 5:6; 14:7) and once in the singular (8:5).

b—b   Reading פָּחַדְתִּי אֵלַי, with the archaic spelling of the second singular feminine perfect with the first hand of one MS. (Giovanni B. de Rossi, *Variae Lectionis Veteris Testamenti, III* [Parma: Bodoni, 1786] 715) and *S*, for the dubious *M* פַּחְדָּתִי אֵלַיִךְ "(and not) my fear [or, fear of me] in you." For the archaic spelling compare vv 20, 33, and 3:4, 5, and elsewhere, and GKC, sec. 44h. The preposition אֶל is what one expects with the verb פָּחַד; see Hos 3:5; Mic 7:17. For the finite verb after an infinitive construct see GKC, sec. 114r, and further Interpretation. Though I believe (with Rudolph) that this is the correct reading, the understanding of this line with אֵלַיִךְ is so widespread as to raise the question whether the readings of both de Rossi's MS. and *S* are not secondary recorrections.

20a—a   Though *M* vocalizes these verbs as first singular, נָתַקְתִּי שָׁבַרְתִּי, and though *S* and *T* so understand them, the context clearly demands that the consonantal text be taken as representing the archaic second singular feminine (so *G*); compare the *M* vocalization in v 33 and 3:4, 5, and compare note b to v 19. *V*, puzzled by it all, reads "You broke my yoke, tore away my fetters."

b—b   Reading ketib אֶעֱבֹד; qere' אֶעֱבוֹר "I will not

> Again, on every high hill
> and under every leafy tree,
> there you are sprawling, whoring.

21 But it was I who planted you choice
> grapes,
> wholly sound stock,
> so how could you turn 《 putrid? 》[a]
> [—a foreign vine.][b]

22 Again, even if you scrub with soda,
> even go over and over yourself with
> ashes,
> your guilt stays stained before me,
> oracle of the Lord Yahweh.

23 How can you say, "I am not defiled,
> and[a] after the Baals I have not
> walked!"?
> Look at your way in the Valley,
> recognize what you have done,
> a skittish young camel interlacing her
> tracks;

24 [a]a wild ass[a] trained [b]to the wilderness,[b]
> in the passion of her[c] desire ⟨sniffing⟩[d]
> the wind;
> in her season who can turn her back?
> None who seek her need tire,
> in her month they will find her.

25 Don't run your foot bare
> or [a]your throat[a] dry!

transgress" is a mitigation, though attested by many MSS. and by the Cairo Genizah material (and by *T*).

21a *M* is unacceptable: לִי סוּרֵי הַ "to me those turning aside (= those degenerate of?)" (the foreign vine). Read with Duhm and Rudolph לְסוּרִיָה; this word is not otherwise cited in Hebrew, but the Aramaic and Syriac *sry* "become putrid," and noun and adjective derivatives, render the reconstruction plausible. *G* πῶς ἐστράφης εἰς πικρίαν "how have you turned to bitterness?" is a convincing translation of the text as here reconstructed. Since Jrm is offering a variation on Isa 5:1–7 (see Interpretation), one looks here for a synonym for Isaiah's word בְּאֻשִׁים; it is well to note, therefore, that *S* and *T* for Exod 7:18 and 16:20 translate באש "become foul" by *sry*. One wonders, was the text originally נהפכתי ל (archaic second feminine singular), misconstrued as נהפכת לי?

b *M* הַגֶּפֶן נָכְרִיָּה "foreign vine" offers the anomalous article on the noun without a corresponding article on the adjective; the article is explicable as the conclusion of the previous word (see note a). The phrase is unimaginative and must be taken as an early gloss on the *hapax legomenon* just before. The matter has not been noticed because of a hesitation to perceive tricola; see Structure.

23a Reading with many MSS., *G*, *S*, and *T* וְאַחֲרֵי for *M* (and *V*) אַחֲרֵי.

24a—a The Hebrew text tradition is confused about this word, and correspondingly about the gender of the suffix on נֶפֶשׁ (see note c). *V*, *S*, and *T* all agree on "onager" here (*G* reads quite another text), the spelling for which is consistently פֶּרֶא in nine instances in the OT; this is the only passage with פֶּרֶה, and many MSS. do offer פֶּרֶא. But פֶּרֶא is ordinarily masculine (Hos 8:9) and לִמֻּד is masculine; there is a shift to a feminine reference in the next colon, however (שׁאפה, whatever the vocalization [compare note d], and the ambiguous suffix of נֶפֶשׁ [compare note c]), and this reference is continued in the following colon. It may be that a scribe, aware of the feminine references in the following cola, slipped and wrote פרה "heifer." But the description of the wild ass is secure, and she is female (see Interpretation).

b—b Some MSS. read the more prosaic בַּמִּדְבָּר for the *status absolutus* מִדְבָּר, and the Versions are favorable to this paraphrase; but the construct phrase is tighter poetry.

c Reading the qere' נַפְשָׁהּ for the ketib נַפְשׁוֹ; the references are now consistently feminine (see note a—a).

d Vocalizing as a participle שֹׁאֲפָה instead of the *M* perfect שָׁאֲפָה "she sniffed." *T* offers a participial phrase, שתיא רוחא "drinking the wind," and though this might be periphrastic, one expects a parallel to the participle modifying "young camel."

25a—a Reading the qere' וּגְרוֹנֵךְ for the ketib וגרונך, presumably a slip of the pen influenced by גֹּרֶן "threshing-floor."

So you said, "I don't care! Yes,
   I did love strangers,
      and after them I will walk!"

26   Like the shame of a thief when he's
      caught,
     so the children[a] of Israel have behaved
      shamefully;
they [their kings, their officials, and their
     priests, and their prophets][b]
     27/ keep saying
   to the tree, "you are my father!"
    and to the stone, "It is you [a]gave me
     birth!"[a]
Yes, they have turned their back to me and
   not their face,
   but in the time of their disaster they will
    say,
     "Arise and save us!"

28   Where are your gods which you made for
     yourself?
   Let them arise if they can save you
    in the time of your disaster!
Yes, as many as your cities are your
    gods, O Judah,
  《 and as many as your streets, O
    Jerusalem, have they sacrificed to
    Baal. 》[a]

26a   Reading בְּנֵי with G and S for M בֵּית "house(hold)" (compare v 4). The ironic collocation with "father" in v 27 makes the reading appropriate here.

b   This listing is a gloss that does not fit the poetic sequence. Duhm, Giesebrecht, Volz, and Rudolph also perceive a gloss here, but they excise הֵמָּה as well. A colon, however, can hardly begin with אֹמְרִים (compare the diction of 17:15). The nouns appear to be an expansion of the sequence in 4:9. MSS. and Versions differ in their distribution of "and" in the sequence.

27a—a   Reading the ketib יְלִדְתִּנִי in preference to the qere' (and many MSS.) יְלִדְתָּנוּ "you have given us birth." G and V read "me"; S offers "me" but reads the previous colon as "you are our father"; T reads "our," "us" in both cola. With regard to the form of the qere', GKC, sec. 59h cites Josh 2:17, 20; Cant 5:9 as three passages using הִשְׁבַּעְתָּנוּ, understood as הִשְׁבַּעְתְּ second singular feminine plus suffix; BHS suggests emending each of these three texts, but a form found in separate books is perhaps valid. The parallelism with וְהוֹשִׁיעֵנוּ in v 27 suggests the qere' here, while the parallelism with אָבִי here suggests the ketib; either is plausible.

28a   There is general agreement among commentators that a line like this needs to be restored here on the basis of G καὶ κατ᾽ ἀριθμὸν διόδων τῆς ιερουσαλημ ἔθυον τῇ βααλ and of the wording of 11:13, which offers a version of the line with prose diction: וּמִסְפַּר חֻצוֹת יְרוּשָׁלַםִ שַׂמְתֶּם מִזְבְּחוֹת לַבֹּשֶׁת מִזְבְּחוֹת לְקַטֵּר לַבָּעַל "and (by) the number of the streets of Jerusalem you have set up altars to Shame, altars to offer sacrifice to Baal." I propose the reconstruction: וּכְמִסְפַּר חֻצוֹת יְרוּשָׁלַיִם קִטְּרוּ לַבָּעַל. Several details need consideration. This is essentially the reconstruction of Heinrich Ewald (*Commentary on the Books of Nahûm, Ssephania, Habaqqûq, "Zakharya" XII—XIV, Yéremyá with Translation*, tr. J. Frederick Smith [London: Williams & Norgate, 1878] 102) and Cornill; they omit, however, the article with בַּעַל and do not use כְּ with מִסְפַּר (so similarly Janzen, p. 121). Volz, Condamin, and Rudolph reconstruct with מִזְבְּחוֹת instead of קִטְּרוּ; but θύω is a frequent rendering of קטר pi'el, and מִזְבְּחוֹת is part of the prose diction of 11:13. Rudolph rightly adds the article with בַּעַל, however (compare G and the vocalization in v 8). One is left unsure about the use of כְּ; there is a כְּ in v 26, and of course the κατ᾽ of G, but there is κατ᾽ in both cola, required by Greek syntax, and one cannot be sure of the necessities of Hebrew poetic diction here. I propose that חֻצוֹת was intended to mean "your streets," the suffix of "your cities" doing double duty, and that "Jerusalem" is vocative, matching "Judah," and that G, misunderstanding the double-duty suffix, reconstrued the syntax. If there was a double-duty suffix from the next-to-last colon, was there a single כְּ in the last colon also doing double duty for both lines?—Dahood offers instances where the preposition is missing in the first

29 《Why do you speak against me,》[a]
      why argue with me?
    《All of you have been guilty,
      and》[b] all of you have rebelled against
        me,
                                oracle of Yahweh.
30 In vain have I beaten your children,
      correction they did not accept;
    《a sword》[a] ate 《of you》[b]
      like a destructive lion.
31 〈Are you a community?〉[a]
      Then see the word of Yahweh!
    Have I become a wilderness to Israel,
      or a land of supreme darkness?
        Why then have my people said, "We
          have roamed,[b]
      we shall no longer come to you!"?
32 Can a virgin forget her ornaments,
      a bride her breast-band?
        But my people have forgotten me
          days beyond number.

rather than the second colon (*Psalms III*, 437, Ps 89:2 with לְ). No other Version offers the missing line, which could have dropped out because of haplography with מִסְפָּר.

29a The text of this verse has evidently suffered haplography in both v 29a (both *M* and *G* differently) and v 29b (*M*). In v 29a *M* reads "Why do you argue with me?" while *G* reads lamely "Why do you speak to me?" (ἵνα τί λαλεῖτε πρός με); λαλέω πρός means simply "speak to," not "argue with, talk back to" or the like, and λαλέω is the steady rendering of דבר pi'el. Further πρός με = אֵלַי fits *M* רִיב well, but hardly דבר pi'el. These considerations, and the fact that *G* offers a bicolon in v 29b (see note b), suggests that there were two lines here, the first being לָמָּה תְּדַבְּרוּ בִי: דבר pi'el and רִיב are linked in 12:1. This is essentially the reconstruction of Volz, though I suggest לָמָּה in the first line to explain *G* ἵνα τί. *M* will then have arisen by haplography with לָמָּה, while *G* will have arisen by a jump from תְּדַבְּרוּ in the first line to אֵלַי in the second. The assonance of these two verbs matches a similar assonance in the verbs of v 29b (see note b).

b Reading כֻּלְּכֶם רְשַׁעְתֶּם וְ, the text presupposed by *G* (so also Cornill and Volz; Janzen also allows this possibility, p. 30). The matter is not altogether simple; *G* reads, "All of you have been guilty (ἠσεβήσατε), and all of you have rebelled against me (ἠνομήσατε εἰς ἐμέ)." *G*[A] reads only the second clause, leading to the possibility that *G* reads a conflate text; but the repeated "all of you" is striking and argues against conflation. A retrojection into Hebrew is not easy: ἀσεβέω translates רשע about ten times and פשע about nine times; and ἀνομέω translates רשע seven times and פשע three times. I assume that רשע occurs in the first colon and פשע in the second; the haplography will have arisen from כֻּלְּכֶם. The two verbs offer assonance (compare v 29a).

30a Reading חֶרֶב with *G* for *M* חַרְבְּכֶם "your sword"; see Interpretation.

b Reading בָּכֶם for *M* נְבִיאֵיכֶם "your prophets" (Y. Hoffmann); for justification for the reading, and a suggestion of the sequence of alterations which produced *M*, see Interpretation.

31a Reading הֲדוֹר אַתֶּם for *M* הַדּוֹר אַתֶּם "O generation (?), you." For this meaning of דוֹר and for an explication of this climactic bicolon see Interpretation. *G* at this point is καὶ οὐκ ἐφοβήθητε "and you did not fear" = וְלֹא יְרֵאתֶם, which appears to be a secondary corruption (though a plausible one!) of the *lectio difficilior* adopted here; note the likeness of the last three letters in the sequence אתם.

b Though the Versions only guess at the meaning of רַדְנוּ here, there is no need to emend the text to מָרַדְנוּ (Rudolph) or יָרַדְנוּ (Mitchell Dahood, *Psalms 51—100* [AB 17; Garden City, NY: Doubleday, 1968] 81; *S* favors this reading). Arabic *rāda* is common and the meaning ("walk about, prowl") fits the context admirably.

33 How good you make your way—
  to seek 《illicit》[a] love!
    〈In fact you've done ill,〉[b] 〈you've been
      trained〉[c] (in) your ways!
34 Indeed 《on your palms》[a] is found
    《blood》[b] of lives of the innocent
      [the poor;][c]
    not in burglary [d]did you find them[d]—
      〈your yoke〉[e] certainly 〈becomes a
        curse!〉[e]
35 But you said, "I've certainly been
    innocent;
  his anger will surely turn back from
    me!"
Look, I am going to law with you
  because you said, "I have not sinned!"

33a Reading לֹא־כֵן with G (οὐχ οὕτως) for M לָכֵן
  "therefore"; the expression, however, is better
  understood adjectivally than adverbially as G does
  ("not thus"). If הרעות is to be read as רעע hip'il in
  parallelism with יטב hip'il (see note b), then "therefore" cannot be right. For לֹא־כֵן as an adjective at
  the end of a colon see 23:10; for other instances in
  which it seems necessary to correct לָכֵן to לֹא־כֵן with
  G see Gen 4:15 and perhaps 1 Kgs 22:19 = 2 Chr
  18:18.

b Reading הֲרֵעוֹת (רעע hip'il perfect second singular
  feminine) with G for M הָרָעוֹת "the wicked"
  (feminine plural, construed either as "wicked
  women" or as an adjective with דְּרָכָיִךְ). The contrast
  between יטב hip'il in the first colon and the proposed רעע hip'il here is persuasive. The same
  parallelism is found in 4:22, and the same revocalization for this verb will be proposed in 3:5, note b.
  The M particle את is either to be read as אַתְּ ("you,"
  feminine singular subject), or else it was added
  secondarily; compare note c.

c Vocalizing a pu'al, לֻמַּדְתִּי אַתְּ, for M pi'el "you
  have taught"; "teaching" is not at issue—habitual
  conduct is the problem. Note that the ketib uses the
  archaic spelling for the second person feminine
  singular; compare vv 19 and 20. As in the previous
  instance, the M particle את is either to be revocalized as the subject pronoun אַתְּ (see note b), or else it
  may have been inserted secondarily.

34a Reading בְּכַפַּיִךְ "on your palms" with G and S for
  M בִּכְנָפַיִךְ "on your skirts." It is difficult to choose
  between the two readings (so also Rudolph). The
  noun כָּנָף (literally "wing") does mean "skirt"
  elsewhere (e.g., Hag 2:12), but the word does not
  occur elsewhere in Jer, while כַּף does—in poetry in
  4:31; 12:7; and 15:21. "Blood" is associated with כַּף
  in Isa 1:15; כָּנָף when used metaphorically has sexual
  connotations (Deut 23:1; Ezek 16:8), and this would
  particularly be the case with the mention of blood;
  such connotations are inappropriate here.

b Reading the plural construct דְּמֵי with G for M
  singular דַּם; this solves the inconsistency of a
  singular subject with plural verb and brings the
  diction closer to Exod 22:1 (see Interpretation).
  There are other possible solutions to the inconsistency (that דַּם is a gloss, that the verb is plural by
  attraction to נפשות), but this solution seems simplest
  (so also Duhm, Cornill, Giesebrecht, Condamin).

c Omitting אֶבְיוֹנִים with G as a gloss (so also
  Rudolph). For the syntax of what remains see
  Interpretation.

d—d Construing מְצָאתִים as second feminine singular
  with S rather than as first singular with G and V.

e Revocalizing this sequence as עֻלֵּךְ לְאָלָה for M עַל־
  כָּל־אֵלֶּה "on (or against) all these." M is impossible;
  see William L. Holladay, "Jeremiah ii 34bβ," VT 25
  (1975) 221–25. Compare 23:10, where M reads אָלָה
  but a few MSS., G and S read אֵלֶּה. For other
  restorations of אָלָה see 4:12; 5:25; 14:22.

36
How very ⟨casually you act⟩[a]
    to change your way;
      《 indeed you've done it a hundred
           times! 》[b]
Indeed by Egypt you will be shamed
    as you were shamed by Assyria!—

37/ [. . . .][b]
    you will go out with hands on your head,
    for Yahweh has rejected your mainstays,
    and you will not succeed with[a] them.

3

1
    . . .[a] as follows:[a]
Suppose a husband sends away his wife,
    and she goes off from him,
      and marries another man,
would he return to her again?—
    would that land not really be profaned?
But you have whored with many
        partners,[b]
and to think you would return to me!
             oracle of Yahweh.

2
Lift your eyes onto the caravan-tracks
    and see,
    where have you not been ravished?[a]
    On the paths you have sat (waiting)
      for them
      [b] like an Arab[b] in the wilderness.
So you profaned the land
    with your whorings[c] and your
      wickedness;[c]

36a   For M תֵּזְלִי, interpreted as a contraction from זלל (אזל) תֵּאזְלִי "go [about]"), read תֵּזַלִּי זלל hip'il "make light of") with G, V, S (and Rashi); so most recent commentators.

b   The sequence גַּם מֵאֵת זֶה at the beginning of v 37, understood as "from (with) this one also" (= "from here"?), must be reconstrued as containing a verb, מאה pi'el, denominative from מֵאָה "hundred" (proposed by Mitchell Dahood for Ps 22:26 [*Psalms 1—50* (AB 16; Garden City; NY: Doubleday, 1966) 142], 66:20 [*Psalms II*, 125], and 109:20 [*Psalms III*, 107]) and transferred to a position just before the existing גַּם in v 36. The displacement may be explained by assuming the omission of the sequence by haplography (two occurrences of גַּם), by its restoration in the margin and subsequent reinsertion at the wrong spot. I propose this verb also for 13:25. This verb would likewise be vocalized מֵאֵת for the perfect second singular feminine; זֶה might better be vocalized as the feminine זֹה (Ezek 40:45 and elsewhere). See further Interpretation.

37a   Reading בָּהֶם with one MS., G and S for M לָהֶם "in regard to them" (?).

3:1a—a   This seemingly truncated expression is not to be emended (against Rudolph and Bright); it is proposed here that in the early collection of material destined for the north 2:4–9 was followed directly by 3:1–5; thus the legal case discussed here in v 1 is the nucleus of the lawsuit into which Yahweh enters with the "children" (2:9). The intervening material has made the expression less plausible here.

b   Reading רֵעִים with M; a few MSS., G and S read רֹעִים "shepherds" (compare v 3, note a).

2a   The verb שׁגל was considered obscene by the Masoretes and the corresponding stem of שׁכב "lie (with)" was substituted in the qere' in all four occurrences in the OT (beyond the present passage: Deut 28:30; Isa 13:16; Zech 14:2), and a few MSS. read the qere' instead of the ketib. Compare *b. Meg.* 25b: "Whenever an indelicate expression is written in the text, we substitute a more polite expression in reading" (compare Christian D. Ginsburg, *Introduction to the Massoretico-Critical Edition of the Hebrew Bible* [London: Trinitarian Bible Society, 1897; rep. New York, Ktav, 1966] 346).

b—b   There is significant textual variation here. One MS. and T read the plural כַּעֲרָבִים "like Arabs," but this is surely a prosaic secondary reading. G and S read "like a crow," כְּעֹרֵב, a not implausible reading; but it is better to stay with M. Note the possibility of the reverse in 1 Kgs 17:4, 6, where some commentators suggest that Elijah was fed by "Arabs" rather than by "ravens"; see John Gray, *Kings*, 378–80.

c—c   There is much variation in the number of these two nouns: M reads (1) plural, (2) singular, but a few MSS. read a singular in both, and a few read a plural in both. Both G and V read a plural in both; S reads a singular in both (though it groups the second noun with the next verse). T follows M,

3   ªand the showers have been withheld,
    and the latter rain has not fallen;ª
you have had the forehead of a whore,
    have refused to be humiliated.

4   Is not ⟪ "my mainstay" ⟫ª what ᵇyou have
    calledᵇ me? ["My father,"]ᶜ
    "you are the companion of my youth!"

5   "Will he bear a grudge forever,
    or keep watch endlessly?"
    See: ª you have spokenª and acted,
    ⟨you have done wrong⟩ᵇ and prevailed.

6/ [And the LORD said to me in the days of
    King Josiah, "Have you seen what
    Turncoat Israel did? — she used to go
    onto every high mountain and off
    under every leafy tree and whoredᵇ
    there! **7/** And I thought, 'After she
    does all these things, she will turn
    back to me'; but she did not. And
    her sister Traitor Judah sawª (it);
    8/ ªand she sawª that precisely

though the first noun is interpreted as "idols." Since
the Versions work toward consistency in number, *M*
is to be preferred.

3a—a   *G* reads altogether differently, and Duhm,
    Giesebrecht, and Condamin adopt it here; for a
    judgment in favor of *M*, see Preliminary
    Observations.

4a   *M* here reads מֵעַתָּה, literally "from now (on)," an
    expression which in no way fits the context (Volz),
    nor does it fit the perfect verb; to translate it "just
    now" (*RSV*, *NJV*, compare *NEB*) is to force a very
    dubious interpretation on it. The Versions struggle
    with the problem in various ways. "My father" is a
    gloss from v 19 and overloads the line (see note c),
    so that the present expression masks the original
    appellation of Yahweh in this colon. *G* reads ὡς οἶκον
    "like a house." *G* also carries "father" at the end of
    the clause, so that if the latter word is an intruder in
    the original text, "like" in *G* may be a secondary bit
    of editing. Since *G* uses οἶκος to render מָעוֹן in Deut
    26:15, I propose that מְעֹנִי be read here: תה is a
    plausible misreading of ני in the Old Aramaic script
    of the early postexilic period. Jrm may have had in
    mind an expression like Ps 90:1. The word will then
    give pleasing assonance with מֵאַנְתְּ in the previous
    colon.

b—b   The ketib offers the archaic spelling of the second
    singular feminine (compare 2:20, 33).

c   The word overloads the line; it is an intrusive
    gloss from v 19 and does not comport easily with
    the metaphor of husband and wife basic to vv 1–5,
    and certainly does not comport with "companion of
    my youth" (so also Duhm, Giesebrecht, Volz,
    Rudolph, though for varying reasons).

5a—a   The ketib offers the archaic spelling of the
    second feminine singular verb (compare v 4, note b).

b   Vocalizing הֲרֵעוֹת (רעע hip'il, compare 2:33, note
    b) for *M* הָרָעוֹת "(you have done) evil things"; see
    Structure, Interpretation.

6—11a   This is an exilic or postexilic midrash on themes
    in the poetry of chapter 3; see Interpretation.

b   *M* reads וַתְּזְנִי, a form which appears to be a second
    singular feminine, though the context demands a
    third singular feminine וַתִּזֶן (so v 8), and the
    Versions all offer third-person verbs (*G*, *T*, mas-
    culine plural; *V*, *S*, feminine singular). The final yod
    is characteristic of Aramaic verbs of this type for the
    third feminine singular, but the waw-consecutive
    imperfect is not Aramaic idiom. The form is
    probably a simple copyist's error, but it is odd that it
    should have been preserved; compare GKC, sec.
    75ii.

7a   The ketib reads וַתִּרְאֶה and the qere' וַתֵּרֶא; the
    qere' is the expected form, but they are simply
    orthograpic variations.

8a—a   Reading with one MS., the corrector of *G*ᴼ, some
    Lucianic minuscules and *S* וַתֵּרֶא for the *M* (and *T*)
    וָאֵרֶא "and I saw." This verb was attracted to the
    first-person verb at the beginning of v 7;

because Turncoat Israel committed adultery, I sent her off and gave her a bill of divorce, yet Treacherous Judah her sister had no fear and herself went off and whored. 9/ And it happened because of her casual[a] whoring that she ⟨profaned⟩[b] the land and committed adultery with stone and tree. 10/ But even in all this her sister Traitor Judah did not turn back to me with all her heart, but insincerely"—oracle of the LORD. 11/ And the LORD said to me, "Turncoat Israel made herself more innocent than Treacherous Judah."]ª

12 Go and call out these words to the north and say:
  Turn a turning, Israel,
          oracle of Yahweh,
  I will not frown at you,
  for I am faithful,   oracle of Yahweh,
  I will not bear a grudge forever.

13 Just admit your guilt,
  that against Yahweh your God you rebelled
    and scattered your strengthª among strangers [under every leafy tree]ᵇ
  and my voice did not obey,ᶜ
        oracle of Yahweh.

14 Return, turnable children,
  《 one from a city
  and two from a tribe, 》ª
        oracle of Yahweh,
  for it is I who am your master,
  and I shall take you [. . .]ª
  and bring youᵇ to Zion.

conceivably, however, it is dittographic and with *V* should be omitted altogether (Volz).

9a All the Versions (and Rashi and David Qimḥi) understand מִקֹּל to derive from קלל "be light, frivolous," and thus "from the lightness of," rather than "from the noise (or rumor) of." This noun קֹל would then be a hapax word here. The commentators have not been so sure; Condamin accepts the emendation to מִקְּלוֹן "from the dishonor of" proposed by earlier scholars, and earlier C. W. Eduard Naegelsbach defended the meaning "cry." But the unanimity of the Versions and the plausibility of the meaning all commend this interpretation.

b With *V*, *S*, and *T* vocalizing וַתַּחֲנֵף (hipʻil) for *M* וַתֶּחֱנַף (qal) "and it was profaned." Conceivably the qal might be correct if the אֶת־ following the verb were omitted (or if אֶת־ is to be construed with a "passive," so Volz, compare GKC, sec. 121a) so that הָאָרֶץ could be construed as subject, but then the transition to what follows is difficult.

13a Accepting *M* דְּרָכַיִךְ, which ordinarily means "your paths," in a meaning of the noun which evidently fits a few other passages in the OT and is attested in Ugaritic. The Versions all support *M*, in spite of the seeming oddity of the phrase. Commentators have suggested emendations: Cornill, Artur Weiser (*Das Buch Jeremia* [ATD 20/21; Göttingen: Vandenhoeck & Ruprecht, 1969]), and Rudolph read דּוֹדַיִךְ "your loves"; Duhm ingeniously suggested that the phrase is וַתְּפַשְּׂקִי בִרְכַּיִךְ "and you spread your knees (= legs)," comparing Ezek 16:25. But there are Ugaritic texts in which *drkt* (feminine) is parallel to *mlk* "kingship" and thus means "dominion, authority" (e.g., 49.5.5–6; 49.6.34–35); and one notes also that the Hebrew verb דרך means "tread" (compare 4:11; 9:2). Many scholars who wish to find this meaning for the noun in the OT point to Hos 10:13, but Wolff (*Hosea*) doubts the meaning there. However, the parallelism points to the meaning "strength" in Prov 31:3, and Ps 138:5 is also convincing. Other suggested passages are at least plausible (see Dahood, *Psalms* volumes, indices *s.v.*). Note that in Prov 31:3 and Ps 138:5 the word is plural, as in the present passage, so there appears to be no need to emend to the singular דַּרְכֵּךְ (the suggestion in *HALAT*, 223a). See also 16:17, Interpretation.

b A gloss from 2:20 (Rudolph); see Interpretation.

c *M* shifts from singular to plural here (as do *S* and *T*); *G* and *V*, however, save the shift to plural until v 14; the latter reading may be correct.

14a With some hesitation I propose shifting "one from a city and two from a tribe" from the second half to the first half of the verse. The verse is poetry, and there are a number of considerations that make the suggestion plausible: see Structure.

b The second occurrence of אֶתְכֶם may be dittographic; see Structure.

15 And I shall give you shepherds according
　　to my desire,
　　and they shall pasture you
　　《constantly》[a] and skillfully.
16/ [And when you become many and
　　fruitful in the land in those days,
　　oracle of the LORD, they shall no
　　longer say "the ark of the covenant
　　of the LORD," and it will not be
　　thought of, nor shall they remem-
　　ber it,[b] nor miss it, nor will it be
　　made again. 17/ At that time they
　　shall call Jerusalem "the throne of
　　the LORD," and all the nations shall
　　gather toward her for the name of
　　the LORD at Jerusalem, and they
　　shall no longer walk after the
　　stubbornness of their evil heart.
　　18/ In those days the household of
　　Judah shall walk together with the
　　household of Israel, and they shall
　　come in together from the land of
　　the north][a]
　　on the land which I gave [c]your
　　　　fathers[c] to inherit.

19 But I for my part thought,
　　"How (gladly) will I treat you like
　　　　sons!"
　　So I gave you a lovely land,
　　　　the [a]most glorious[a] inheritance of the
　　　　nations;
　　and I thought, "[b]You will call[b] me 'My
　　　　father,'
　　　　and from me [b]you will not draw back."[b]

20 《But as》[a] a woman 《betrays》[a] her lover,

15a　For *M* דֵעָה read רָעֹה with *G* (ποιμαίνοντες); this
sequence is a plausible one (compare the structure of
1 Sam 6:12, and see GKC, sec. 113s); for two
infinitives absolute in a poetic passage, see 22:19. *M*
may be understood to offer two nouns here ("with
knowledge [and skill]"), and this text has almost
equal claim to plausibility.

16—18a　One or more exilic or postexilic expansions:
see Preliminary Observations and Interpretation.

b　For בּוֹ, an unusual expression (זכר normally takes
the accusative), a few MSS. read עוֹד, thus "nor will
they remember (it) again," and one MS. has both בּוֹ
and עוֹד (a reading reflected in *T*). The readings are
equivalent in any case.

c—c　The pronoun reference of "your fathers" fits the
diction of v 15, of which this colon is a continuation;
one MS., *G* and *S* read "their fathers," accommodating to the insertion.

19a—a　*M* read צְבִי צִבְאוֹת, an expression which appears
to mean "glory of the hosts of," thus literally "the
inheritance of the glory of the hosts of the nations."
G has understood the phrase differently, seeing in
צִבְאוֹת the designation of God, the equivalent of
אֱלֹהֵי צְבָאוֹת "inheritance of Almighty God of
nations," a reading which can hardly be original. *V*
and *S* read צְבָאוֹת as "armies of," while *T* seems to
read it as a form of צְבִי "the inheritance of joy of the
delight of the peoples." The present interpretation,
with most commentators, accepts the understanding
of *T*: there are several examples of nouns in -*y* which
dissimilate to -'*îm* in the plural, and this plural in -*ôt*
could be an analogical formation (Hans Bauer and
Pontus Leander, *Historische Grammatik der hebräischen
Sprache des Alten Testaments* [Halle: Niemeyer, 1922;
rep. Hildesheim: Olms, 1965] sec. 72p'). The
singular construct plus the plural of the same noun
is one way to express a superlative (GKC, sec. 133i),
and *T* thus recognizes this idiom here. It is not
impossible, however, that we have a deliberate
ambiguity which then cannot be translated.

b—b　Reading the qere' תִּקְרָאִי and תָּשׁוּבִי (feminine
singulars) with many MSS. and with *V* and *T*; the
ketib תִּקְרָאוּ and תָּשׁוּבוּ (masculine plurals) are read
by *G* and *S*. (Note that de Rossi's listing of MSS.
manifesting the feminine singular readings is not
quite identical for the two verbs: pp. 68–69.) In *M*
the masculine plural appears unequivocally in v 20
(בְּגַדְתֶּם), and Rudolph wishes to read the ketib of
both verbs here to correspond with v 20, but he also
wishes to emend the vocalization of the feminine
singular references in אֲשִׁיתֵךְ and לָךְ earlier in the
verse to masculine singular forms. None of this is
necessary, and it is best to stay with feminine
singular forms through the whole verse.

20a—a　Reading אַךְ כְּבָגַד with *G* and *V* for *M* אָכֵן בָּגְדָה;
the latter would mean something like "to the
contrary, a woman has betrayed her lover." On the
meaning of אָכֵן see v 23, Interpretation. Given the
כֵּן in v 20, a word like "just as" must be assumed at

so you have betrayed me, O household
of Israel,

              oracle of Yahweh.

21 A sound out on the caravan-tracks may
be heard,

    supplicant weeping for the children of
Israel,

since they have deflected their course,
forgotten Yahweh their God:

22 "Turn, turnable children,
I want to heal[a] your turnings!"

"Here we are, [b]we have come[b] to you,
for you are Yahweh our God!"

23 "No! To delusion from the hills,
[a](to) confusion (from) the mountains!"[a]

"No! In Yahweh our God is the rescue of
Israel,

24   while Shame has eaten the increase of
our fathers: [from our youth—][a]
[their flocks and their herds,
[c]their sons[c] and their
daughters—][b]

25 let us lie in our shame,
and let our dishonor cover us;

how we have sinned against [Yahweh][a]
our God [we and our fathers][b] from
our youth [down to this day,][c]
nor obeyed the voice of Yahweh! [our
God]."[d]

4

1 If you turn (at all), Israel,

              oracle of Yahweh,

(then) to me you should turn;

and if you remove [a]your vile things ⟪ from
your mouth,

and from my presence ⟫[a] do not wander,

---

the beginning of the first colon, and both *S* and *T*
have supplied such a word. But אָכֵן does not fit the
context: the rhetoric here is analogous to that of
2:26, and *G* and *V* translate the two passages
similarly (note: for *G* πλήν = אַךְ see 10:24; 12:1). So
also Giesebrecht, Volz, Rudolph. The nun would be
an easy reading mistake for kap in the Old Aramaic
script, and the misreading would be stimulated by
the double occurrence of אָכֵן in v 23. The he at the
end of בָּגְדָה is easily explicable as a secondary
correction, but one wonders if the original text
might have been הָאִשָּׁה with generic article (compare
Eccl 7:26; GKC, sec. 126m).

22a   Many MSS. offer the spelling אֶרְפָּא, which is the
expected form, but *M* gives אֶרְפֶּה, with he, though
with the vocalization of a III-'alep verb. For such
mixed forms see GKC, sec. 75pp.

b—b   If the reading אָתָנוּ is correct and to be understood as the verb אתה, the expected form would be
*אָתִינוּ. The vocalization is that expected for a III-
'alep verb, and indeed many MSS. read אָתָאנוּ give
the possible assonance with אַתָּה in the next colon,
the vocalization is likely to be correct. For such
forms see GKC, sec. 75rr.

23a—a   Though many MSS., *G*, *V*, and *S* read הֲמוֹן הָרִים
"turmoil of the mountains," the absolute form הָמוֹן is
the *lectio difficilior* and explicable by the device of the
double-duty preposition; see Interpretation.

24a   Prose expansion from v 25; see Preliminary
Observations.

b   This listing as a gloss explaining "increase," taken
perhaps from 5:17; note the oddity of the third-
person references instead of first-person ones. See
further Interpretation.

c   Some MSS., *G*, and *S* insert וְ "and" before "their
sons."

25a   Omit with *G* as an expansion; compare Janzen, p.
80.

b   Omit as an expansion (so also Rudolph).

c   Omit as a gloss (so also Volz, Rudolph).

d   Omit as a gloss; compare the diction of Isa 1:10.
The pattern here is that of the "breakup of com-
posite divine names" (Dahood, *Psalms III*, xxxix–xli);
compare my treatment of the matter in 8:14, and
from a different perspective see the material in
Janzen, pp. 80–81.

4:1a—a   The textual problems of this sequence are
complex. There are three text traditions. (1) *M*
reads שִׁקּוּצֶיךָ מִפָּנַי וְ; this sequence is ambiguous,
depending on whether the following "you will not
wander" is (a) construed as part of the protasis,
"your vile things from my presence, and [you will
not wander]," or (b) construed as an apodosis, "your
vile things from my presence then [you will not
wander]." The question of delimiting protasis and
apodosis here is part of that question on a larger
scale in vv 1–2 (see Interpretation). (2) *V*, *S*, and *T*
omit וְ; by this reading, "you will not wander" must
be an apodosis. Ten MSS. of the Hebrew have

2
and swear "By the life of Yahweh"
    truly, justly and rightly,
then nations will bless themselves in
    him,
    and in him congratulate themselves.

3
For thus Yahweh has said to the men of
    Judah and to 《 the inhabitants of 》[a]
    Jerusalem:
"plow yourselves unplowed ground,"
    and do not sow among thorns;

4
be circumcised to Yahweh,
    and remove "the foreskin[a] of your
    heart,"
        O men of Judah and inhabitants of
        Jerusalem,
or my wrath will go forth like fire
    and burn with none to quench
        from the presence of the evil of your
        doings.

yielded the same reading (Volz), and so has a Cairo Genizah MS. (*BHS*); it is adopted by most commentators (Duhm, Volz, Rudolph). The basic difficulty with both (1) and (2) is that of the integrity of poetic cola; enjambment is hardly possible, and "you will not wander" alone in a colon is dubious alongside the longer expressions on either side (compare the typography of *BHS*). (3) *G* has shifted the vocative "Israel" to become the subject of third-person verbs, which continue consistently through the end of v 2 (compare the twofold "in him" and see Interpretation); its reading of the sequence in question is "his vile things from his mouth, and from my presence." If one assumes that the shift to third person is an inner Greek development, the antecedent Hebrew would be שִׁקּוּצֶיךָ מִפִּיו וּמִפָּנַי, and this is the reading adopted here. The movement of וְ from before "you shall not wander" to before "from my presence" is attractive, and Bright seems to have adopted that shift, but not the Septuagintal "from my mouth." However, the assonance produced by the addition of "from my mouth" is even more attractive, and the association with "vile things" (presumably "idols") with Israel's "mouth" rather than with Yahweh's "presence" makes it the *lectio difficilior* (see again Interpretation). It would be difficult, then, to explain *G* as a doublet reading, as Janzen does (p. 30). I propose that the reading adopted here is the best suited to explain the three existent readings: (3) by the shift to third person; (2) by haplography in the two expressions for "from," and (1) by reinsertion of וְ as a partial correction.

3a   *M* lacks the bracketed words, but they are found in five MSS., in *G, S,* and *T;* I restore them here, assuming they dropped out by haplography (so also Janzen, p. 119). On the other hand, it is possible that they are an expansionist addition from the phraseology of v 4; it is difficult to be sure in the case of such an introductory rubric. It is perhaps significant that *G*[A] omits the whole rubric; Volz therefore omits it all.

4a   *M* reads "foreskins" (עָרְלוֹת), but many MSS., *G* and *S* read the singular עָרְלַת: this is the preferred reading, with "heart" (singular) following. The similar passage Deut 10:16 likewise has the singular.

Preliminary Observations

Introduction. One begins with the assumption that 2:1— 4:4 forms a self-contained collection. Though not all of the material deals with the harlotry of the nation, much of it does; and in 4:5 and beyond, the emphasis is on the foe from the north. And though there appears to be a rhetorical break between chapters 2 and 3, it will become apparent that both chapters contain early material destined for the north which formed a continuous sequence; there is therefore no reason to subdivide.

The analysis of the stages by which 2:1—4:4 came to be, and consequently of the structure and setting for these stages, is one of the most baffling and intricate problems in the book. Some of my own efforts have been published, and many more have been drafted and then rejected. The solution presented here must inevitably offer some details that remain tentative. I propose three recensions by Jrm himself: (1) an early one destined for the north; (2) a large expansion of that first recension, which was then dictated as a part of the first scroll dictated by the prophet (36:2, 6), and (3) a slight expansion of the second recension which was then dictated as a part of the second scroll (36:32). Though the analysis of structure and setting will be offered in full detail in those specific sections, it is necessary to give a preliminary account of the whole matter here with as much coherence and as little circular reasoning as possible.

Historical References Within the Passage. There are few of these, and those that exist are not unequivocal.

The assumption of scholars that Jrm's prophetic career began in the thirteenth year of Josiah (i.e., 627; see the discussion on 1:2) and the mention of "Assyria" in 2:18 and 36 have led to the conclusion that the years before Josiah's reform (627–622) are the setting for these early chapters of the book; but evidence given below (see Setting) indicates that "Assyria" is simply the poetic designation for the current political power in Mesopotamia, the counterpart of "Egypt." The reference to Egypt in 2:16 fits events in 609, and the swing between Egypt and Mesopotamia implied in 2:18 and 36 best fits the events of 609–601.

The reference to the killing of the prophets in 2:30 is evidently a spurious text (see Interpretation). The references to Baal worship are too unspecific to be helpful. The reference to the drought in 3:3 is indeed helpful, but only for the lines in question (see below). This line of inquiry is not productive.

The Rubrics; 2:1–3; 4:3–4. There are four rubrics within the material, 2:1–2aα; 2:4; 3:12aα; and 4:3aα. It is conceivable that these are secondary interpretations of the words that follow, glosses subsequently added; this is the assumption of some commentators on 3:12, e.g., J. Philip Hyatt and Ernest W. Nicholson.[1] But they are different enough from each other to lay claim to authenticity. "Jerusalem" is the audience named in 2:1–2 and 4:3, a datum suggesting that an inner core was expanded both at the beginning and the end by material destined for Jerusalem. The words of 4:3–4 assume an appeal to repentance, material appropriate to the first scroll (36:2–3, 6–7, compare 7:3–12); it is plausible then to assign 2:1–3 and 4:3–4, with the matching expression "to Yahweh" (לַיהוה, 2:3; 4:3) to the first scroll.

The inner core just referred to, it is proposed here, is material destined for the north. Such material must be viewed alongside material in chapters 30—31 destined for the north. The present study accepts the proposal of Lohfink[2] that the basic stratum of chapters 30—31 was directed to the north by the youthful Jrm in the years just before 609, when Josiah was killed. There is material within 2:1—4:4 which matches that setting, as will become clear.

In contrast to the rubrics in 2:1–2 and 4:3, that in 3:12 speaks specifically of the "north"; and 2:4, it appears, implies the north (at least in the earliest recension), since the "tribes" of the house of Israel refer in Jrm's earliest diction to the northern tribes (see on 1:15, and compare 3:14 and 31:1). An initial task, then, is to locate within 2:4—4:2 the material belonging to that early recension directed to the north, and because of the literary-structural problems posed by 3:1—4:2, we shall begin there.

The Present State of 3:1—4:2. There are two related problems in this sequence: the tracing of the redactional history of the material, which consists of both poetry and prose, and the understanding of the intention of Jrm in some key expressions, notably "(re)turn" (שׁוב): is it geographical return, covenantal repentance, a combination of these, or a shift between them? The verb "(re)turn" is used repeatedly in the passage.[3]

The most urgent issue is the place of 3:6–18 in the sequence. Volz, Rudolph, and Bright are impressed by the way v 19 appears to continue the diction of vv 1–5, and they therefore see vv 6–18 as a collection which intrudes on the continuity of the material before and after; by this analysis, vv 6–18 need to be shifted to another position. Other commentators leave vv 6–18 in place, but the variety of opinion on the literary and rhetorical divisions within this sequence suggests the

1   Ernest W. Nicholson, *The Book of the Prophet Jeremiah Chapters 1—25* (The Cambridge Bible Commentary on the New English Bible; Cambridge: Cambridge University: 1973) 45–46.
2   Lohfink, "Der junge Jeremia," 351–68.
3   James Muilenburg, "A Study of Hebrew Rhetoric: Repetition and Style," *Congress Volume: Copenhagen* (VTSup 1; Leiden: Brill, 1953) 104–5.

difficulty of the problem. Thus Volz divides the verses into vv 6–15 plus 18bβ on the one hand and vv 16–18ba on the other; the latter sequence, in his view, is secondary. Condamin divides the sequence into vv 6–10, 11–13, and 14–18; Rudolph combines the first two, dividing the passage into vv 6–13 and 14–18. Hyatt, by contrast, divides the sequence into vv 6–11, 12–14a, and 14b–18.

Now it is clear that v 19 is in continuity with *something* preceding it ("and/but I for my part," וְאָנֹכִי). Volz, Rudolph, and Bright, who conclude that vv 6–18 are intrusive, perceive a unity between the occurrences of the phrase "call me 'My father'" (vv 4, 19) and a logical movement from the people's fatuous remarks in vv 4–5 to Yahweh's hopes for Israel in vv 19–20. There are difficulties, however, with this theory of intrusion; there are at least three considerations. (1) One may as easily see a continuity between vv 1–5 and whatever poetic core there is in vv 12ff; the phrase "bear a grudge forever" appears in both vv 5 and 12. (2) Exegetes have misunderstood the opening phrase in the poem of v 12, שׁוּבָה מְשֻׁבָה יִשְׂרָאֵל, translating it "Return, faithless Israel" (*RSV*) or the like. The linking of מְשֻׁבָה and יִשְׂרָאֵל in that phrase is based upon the diction of vv 6–11, where the two words are so linked. But evidence offered in the present study indicates that the phrase in v 12 embodies a cognate accusative ("turn a turning, Israel") and that the diction of vv 6–11 is a misunderstanding of the syntax of the poetic phrase (for the details see Interpretation on v 12). If this suggestion is correct, then one must assume a significant time-lapse between the poetic line in v 12 and the shaping of the prose material in vv 6–11; this assumption in turn suggests an independent existence for the poetic material in vv 12ff. If this reasoning is sound, then it becomes plausible to view the poetic material in vv 12ff as always having had a position between vv 1–5 and vv 19–25. (3) Textual analysis of 3:4 indicates that "My father" is a gloss from v 19 (see Text note c); if that observation is correct, there is less reason to insist that v 19 follows directly on v 5. In short, I suggest that vv 6–11 is one prose sequence, and the prose material after the poetry of vv 12ff is another: they must be dealt with independently, and the poetry of vv 12ff is in its rightful position in the sequence.

Analysis of 3:12–18. Let us consider first v 14; commentators differ in their assessment of it. Hyatt maintains that only v 14a is authentic. But v 14b, with its word that Yahweh will bring the northerners to Zion, is certainly part of the ideology of Josiah's program (compare 31:6), the numerical parallelism of one/two suggests poetry, and the word "tribe" is part of Jrm's vocabulary to the north (compare 1:15; 2:4). It must be admitted that finding a poetic structure for the verse is uncertain, but I have a suggestion for a slight rearrangement of the phrases that may help to restore the poetry (see Structure).

There is no reason to question v 12aβγb: the first line of the poetry, שׁוּבָה מְשֻׁבָה יִשְׂרָאֵל, offers good counterpoint to the first line of v 14, שׁוּבוּ בָנִים שׁוֹבָבִים.

But v 13 is jarring: the address suddenly shifts from masculine plural to feminine singular. It is appropriate to consider this verse an addition in the first scroll, along with the bulk of chapter 2 (note that "strangers" [זָרִים] occurs both here and in 2:25).

The reference of "(re)turn" in v 14 is that of geographical return from exile; the reference of the verb in the parallel sequence in vv 22–23 is that of repentance. The reference in v 12 is ambiguous, doubtless intentionally so.

Now what about v 15? It may be construed as poetry. "And I shall give" at the beginning of the verse is easily parallel with "and I shall take" in v 14. I suspect that the *G* reading of the next-to-last word of the verse is correct (רָעָה; see Text note a); the two infinitives absolute could then make up a colon. The message of the verse continues the program of Josiah, and (as we shall see below) the mention of "shepherds" is parallel with the negative assessment of "shepherds" in 2:8, part of a coordinate sequence in the early recension to the north.

Verses 16–17 are clearly a later prose addition.

Verse 18 is difficult. It begins with "in those days," hardly a part of Jrm's diction to the north. The rest of v 18a could be translated "the household of Judah will walk with the household of Israel," an expression appropriate to the program of Josiah, but the words of v 18ba, "and they shall come in together from the land of the north," hardly fits: when Jrm addressed the north, Judah was not in exile. But the closing phrase, "on the land which I gave your fathers to inherit," closes v 15 well (Volz) and serves also as a correlative for "your fathers" in 2:5, part of a coordinate sequence in the early recension to the north (see again below). It is best then to bracket v 18abα along with vv 16–17 as secondary.

To summarize: in the early recension to the north were vv 12, 14–15, 18bβ; v 13 was added in the first scroll, and vv 16–18bα were added by later expansionists.

Analysis of 3:19—4:2. Verse 21a is closely parallel with 31:15, and v 25 with 31:19b. Both those verses in chapter 31 are part of early material directed to the north, and this circumstance suggests that some at least of the material within 3:19—4:2 belongs in the early recension to the north.

We begin with vv 22–23. This material may be assigned to that early recension: the first colon of v 22 is identical with the first colon of v 14. And v 23 belongs with v 22; both verses involve expressions of the people's return to Yahweh, evidently specious (see Interpretation).

As to vv 24–25, they evidently have a poetic core ("Let us lie down in our shame, and let our dishonor cover us," v 25), and, given the parallel with 31:19b already noted, this poetic core must be included in the early redaction to the north.

Commentators all trim these verses down to locate the poetic core, but they differ in their solutions. What conclusions may be drawn from the evidence? (1) The listing in v 24 ("their flocks and their herds, their sons and their daughters") is a gloss based on 5:17 (so Rudolph); compare the similar gloss in 2:26. (2) "Down to this day" is a clear gloss (Volz, Rudolph). (3) There is no need to emend "Shame" in v 24 to "Baal" as Volz and Rudolph do; "Baal" appears in the text of 2:8 and 23 without being altered to a euphemism. "Shame" is here because of the play on "shame" in v 25. (4) There is no way to divide the long clause of v 24a into two cola as Rudolph does (the object cannot be separated from the verb). One can only conclude that "from our youth" is added secondarily here, perhaps by dittography from v 25. "From our youth" does belong in v 25, where it is associated with expressions of "shame" (compare once more 31:19b). (5) "We and our fathers" is expansionistic in v 25 (so also Rudolph): "our fathers" belongs in v 24, but not here. (6) *G* omits "Yahweh" in v 25a: I propose that it is an expansion here.[4] Note that the parallel

expression in 8:14 uses "Yahweh" but not "our God." Conversely I propose that "our God" in v 25b is a gloss; there is a strong tendency to expand these liturgical terms[5]—one notes the separation of "Yahweh" and "her king" in 8:19, and the possibility of separation of "our God" and "Yahweh" in 8:14 (see Text there). The repeated double term is correct in vv 22 and 23 (poetic structure of v 23b!), but I propose that they are separated here. The result is a satisfactory five-colon sequence beginning with "Shame" and ending with "Yahweh," in which "our fathers" is parallel with "our youth," and in which the double use of "shame" in the first two cola balances "our God" and "Yahweh" in the last two. This five-colon sequence, then, was part of the early recension to the north.

This (specious) expression of repentance on the part of the people in vv 22–25 is answered by Yahweh's own prescription for return to him in 4:1–2: these verses fit nicely at the close of this sequence to the north.

Verses 19–21 are difficult. Verse 19 resumes the diction of vv 4–5 (the perception of Volz, Rudolph, and Bright cited above); Israel is addressed as feminine singular, and there is a concern about what she is to "call" (קרא) Yahweh; vv 4–5 will be assigned to the early recension to the north (see below), and therefore v 19 likewise belongs in that recension.

Verse 20 shifts diction, however; at least in *M* the address shifts to the masculine plural. Furthermore the verb "betray" (בגד) appears otherwise in additions in the second scroll, 5:11; 9:1; 12:1—5:11 is particularly close in diction, and the passage in which that verse appears clearly belongs to the period of the second scroll when there is no longer hope for repentance (5:14; compare the purpose of the second scroll, 36:31). Verse 20 is thus to be assigned to the second scroll.

Verse 21a resembles 31:15, part of early material directed to the north; one can have no hesitation then in including this half-verse in that early recension. But there are two related matters in this verse that need attention, the question of whose voice is "heard" in v 21a, and the question of the place and meaning of v 21b in the sequence. Beyond the present passage there are eight other occurrences of "voice" (קול) in a context similar to

---

4   This possibility is also discussed in Janzen, p. 80.
5   Ibid., 80–81.

the use here (4:15, 19, 31; 8:19; 9:18; 18:5; 30:5; 31:15), and in all of them the present study detects a quotation following (in 4:16, 20; and otherwise within the same verse); in three of these there is general agreement among commentators that a quotation follows (4:31; 8:19; 9:18), but there are telling arguments for the existence of quotations in the remainder (see Interpretation on the respective passages). As already noted, the parallel with 31:15 is particularly close: there Rachel is calling for her lost children, and it would be surprising then if the present passage indicated that the lost sons are calling Yahweh: my proposal is that the "suppliant weeping" (בְּכִי תַחֲנוּנֵי) introduces an objective genitive, that it is suppliant weeping *for* Israel's sons (compare 6:26, "mourning for an only son . . . lamentation of bitterness"; for the objective genitive in general see GKC sec. 128h) on the part of Yahweh. The "weeping" of Yahweh is a striking figure but is found also in 9:9, if the analysis there is correct. The natural continuation of v 21a is then v 22; even if the conjunction כִּי at the beginning of v 21b were to mark the beginning of a quotation (compare 4:8b and elsewhere), the third-person reference is an odd way for Yahweh to begin his speech. The best solution is to see v 21b as an addition which to some degree interrupts the material destined for the north. I propose that this half-verse is appropriate for the first scroll: "way" (דֶּרֶךְ) occurs in the singular as object of a verb in 2:23, 33 and 36, and "forget" (object "Yahweh") is found in 2:32; this material will likewise be assigned to the first scroll (see below).

To summarize: the early recension to the north included 3:19, 21a, 22–23, the poetic core of 24–25, and 4:1–2; for the first scroll Jrm added v 21b, and for the second scroll he added v 20.

Analysis of 3:1–5. The steady use of "(re)turn" (שׁוּב) in portions of 3:12—4:2 already assigned to the early recension to the north makes plausible the assignment of (at least the major portion of) this sequence, too, to the northern recension. This passage begins with a legal case implicating the divorce law of Deut 24:1–4 (see Form, Interpretation).

I would propose that the seemingly truncated expression "as follows" (לֵאמֹר) at the beginning of v 1 originally was a bridge from 2:9, which announces Yahweh's entering suit with "your children." It will be proposed (see below) that 2:9 is the closing of 2:4ff, the only

portion of chapter 2 to be included in the early recension to the north, so that the discussion of the legal case in 3:1–5 is Yahweh's legal complaint (2:9).

Verse 3 brings special problems. *M* for v 3a speaks of a drought ("and the showers have been withheld, and the spring rain has not come"): this is phraseology suggesting the drought which not only forms the background of 14:1—15:9 but of other passages as well (5:24–25; 8:13; 23:10). The present study associates this great drought with the fast proclaimed by Jehoiakim (36:9, compare 14:12), circumstances which gave rise to the second scroll (36:32). Now *G* reads an altogether different text for v 3a ("and you had many shepherds for a stumbling block for yourself"), and some commentators follow *G* here (Duhm, Giesebrecht, Condamin); if this text is read, then of course any decision involving the drought is irrelevant. But there are good reasons to retain *M* (see Interpretation), so that v 3a at least should be assigned to the second scroll.

Verse 3b ends "you have refused to be humiliated," a phrase very close to "nor did they know how to be humiliated" in 6:15, part of a passage whose setting is in the period of the second scroll, when punishment was irrevocable (6:11–12). This circumstance suggests then that v 3b, like v 3a, was added in the second scroll.

To summarize: 3:1–2, 4–5 was part of the early recension to the north; v 3 was added for the second scroll.

Analysis of 2:4–37. The rubric of 2:4 suggests that what follows was originally destined for the north (see above). I propose that the sequence intended for the north extends through v 9. First, it is noteworthy that "your fathers" (v 5) is matched by "your children" (v 9). Second, the expression "as follows" at the beginning of 3:1 makes a nice transition from 2:9 (see above). Third, there are several correlations between 2:5–8 and 3:12, 14–15, 18bβ. One notes "shepherds" (רֹעִים) in both 2:8 and 3:15: these are the only two occurrences of the word until 6:3 (where it refers to leaders of the foe from the north); in 2:8 there is an accusation against unfaithful shepherds, while in 3:15 Yahweh will supply shepherds who obey his will. There are less dramatic parallels: if 2:9 ("your children") is one counterpart to 2:5 ("your fathers"), then 3:14 is another ("your fathers went far from me," 2:5; "return, turnable children," 3:14), and 3:18bβ in turn supplies a correlative to 3:14 ("to the land which I gave your fathers to inherit"). In 2:7 Yahweh has "brought in" the nation to a plentiful land, and in 3:14 Yahweh will "bring in" the exiles to Zion (both בוא hip'il). And it may be significant that in 2:5 there occurs the verb הבל qal, a rare denominative verb from הֶבֶל "nothingness," while in 3:14 there occurs the verb בעל qal, whose meaning is here surely denominative from בַּעַל "Baal": Bright has pointed out that the noun and related verb הבל may have been chosen in 2:5 at least in part because of assonance with בַּעַל, which itself appears in 2:8. One more point: 23:13 states of the prophets of Samaria, "they prophesied by Baal," a phrase also found here in 2:8: this circumstance renders plausible the suggestion that this sequence really did apply first to Samaria. (One notes that the operative word in 23:14, "commit adultery," נאף qal, is found in 5:7, part of a sequence whose setting is completely within the orbit of Jrm's proclamation to Jerusalem: see Setting on 5:1–9.)

I propose then that 2:4–9 was in the original collection destined for the north.

Verses 10–13, by contrast, do not appear to have been a part of that recension for the north. There are no links of vocabulary between vv 10–13 and 3:1–2, 4–5, 12, 14–15, 18, 21a, 22–25; 4:1–2; in particular there is no imagery of water in that material.

There is no way to certainty, but the most probable conclusion is that the bulk of vv 10–37 was part of the first scroll; the only possible exception, explored below, is vv 26–28, perhaps added in the second scroll; vv 26–28 are the only sequence here offering second-person references in the masculine singular. Verses 10–25 and 29–37 divide into two groups, those sequences with second-person references in the feminine singular (vv 14–19, 20–25, 33–37) and those with second-person references in the masculine plural (vv 10–13, 29–32). The masculine plural passages both deal with the identity of Yahweh (the spring of running water, v 13; a wilderness, v 31) and refer to what "my people" (עַמִּי) have done (vv 11, 13, 31, 32: there are no other references to "my people" in 2:1—4:4). The feminine singular passages share references to "Assyria" and "Egypt" (vv 18, 36) and underline the accusation of harlotry (vv 20, 23–25, 33, 36). It is possible that vv 29–32 were uttered on the same occasion as were vv 1–3 ("forget," "bride," v 32; "remember," "[time of] bride," v 2), and thus that vv 1–3, 10–13, and 29–32 share a common setting, and that

setting may possibly be the autumn of 608 (see Setting); certainly (if v 31a is here understood correctly) it was a time when Jrm conceived repentance to be possible still. There is reason to believe that the feminine singular material (vv 14–19, 20–25, 33–37) fits the time of the Battle of Carchemish (the changing of loyalty between Egypt and "Assyria," understood here to be Babylon— see Setting), and therefore somewhat later than the masculine plural material. But both groups were doubtless added to vv 4–9 (destined for the north) at the time of the dictation of the first scroll, the year of the Battle of Carchemish.

Verses 26–28 differ from this material not only in being the only sequence with second-person references in the masculine singular; there are other contrasts. The analysis of vv 26–28 in Structure suggest that many of the cola are long in comparison to cola in the surrounding sequences. More substantially, whereas the surrounding material uses metaphors for Israel (vv 14, 20–24), this passage uses an elaborate simile (v 26). Though it is difficult to find clues for a setting in so short a passage, four bits of data point to a setting in the period when the second scroll was dictated, or thereafter. (1) The same format of simile with כְּ and כֵּן appears in the text of 3:20 (as emended following G: see Text); this verse has already been dated to the time of the second scroll (see above). (2) "Time of trouble" (עֵת רָעָה), beyond vv 27 and 28, appears in 11:12, 14, and 15:11; both 11:1–17 and 15:11 are dated in the present study to 594. (3) A prose version of the passage is to be found in 11:12–14, dated again to 594. (4) The verb "save" (ישׁע nip'al and hip'il) with "Israel" as object appears, beyond vv 27, 28, and 11:12, in three relevant passages, 4:14; 8:20; and 14:9 (30:7, 10, 11, and 31:7 bring their own issues of setting). In 4:14 we have an appeal to Jerusalem to be saved (first scroll), while in 8:20 and 14:9 we have the words of the people that they are *in extremis* and are in fact not saved (implication: second scroll). Verses 26–28 are thus to be assigned to the second scroll, and a guess for their setting would be 594 (compare 7:21–28, Setting).

Summary. By this analysis the early recension to the north consisted of: 2:4–9; 3:1–2, 4–5, 12, 14–15, 18bβ, 19, 21a, 22–23, the poetic core of vv 24–25, and 4:1–2. In the first scroll the following were added: 2:1–3, 10–25, 29–37; 3:13, 21b; and 4:3–4. In the second scroll the following were added: 2:26–28; 3:3 and 20. Later expansionists were responsible for 3:6–11 and 16–18bα.

Structure

The Recension to the North: General Shape. If the analysis in Preliminary Observations is sound, then it is useful to focus first on the recension to the north. What is its shape? The subdivisions long accepted by the commentators are our best guide. The passage falls into five sections: (1) Yahweh's historical review and accusation of unfaithfulness, 2:4–9; (2) Yahweh's legal argument with Israel, 3:1–2, 4–5; (3) Yahweh's appeal to the north to return to Zion, 3:12, 14–15, 18bβ; (4) Yahweh's intention, and the pattern of imagined repentance, 3:19, 21a, 22–23, and the poetic core of 24–25; and (5) the shape of true repentance, 4:1–2.

The relation among these sections is sequential and logical, not symmetric: that is to say, there is no relation among them like ABCB'A', nor is there a discernible pattern among them as to number of cola or the like. But following sections reflect earlier ones in a complex network, as has already been noted in Preliminary Observations. Thus (2), the argument with Israel, emerges out of the end of (1) ("enter suit with your children"). At the same time (3) grows both out of (1) ("children," "shepherds," "inheritance," "fathers") and out of (2) ("[re]turn"). Section (4) grows out of (1) (the contrast between "Yahweh," 2:6, 8; 3:22, 23, 25, and "Baal," 2:8, or "Shame," 3:24), out of (2) (what Israel is to "call" Yahweh); and (4) and (5) grow out of (2) and (3) in the constant repetition of "(re)turn."

The Recension in the First Scroll: General Shape. Again, if the analysis in Preliminary Observations is correct, the sequence destined for the north was expanded greatly by the time of the dictation of the first scroll: by an introduction (2:1–3) and conclusion (4:3–4), more heavily by the addition of 2:10–25 and 29–37, and lightly by the addition of 3:13 and 21b. Is there symmetry here? Perhaps.

It is likely that the introduction and conclusion match, not only in their respective rubrics which mention "Jerusalem," but in their use of the verb "sow" (זרע, 2:2; 4:3; the verb does not otherwise appear until 12:13).

The large insertion in chapter 2, namely vv 10–25, 29–37, extends greatly the accusations against Israel. It is divisible of the basis of the shifts in second-person reference: masculine plural (vv 10–13), feminine singular (vv 14–25), masculine plural (vv 29–32), feminine singular (vv 33–37). Further, vv 14–25 seem to divide between vv 14–19 and 20–25 on the basis of subject matter. We may refer to these then as (1), vv 10–13; (2), vv 14–19; (3), vv 20–25; (4), vv 29–32, and (5), vv 33–37. Numbers (1) and (4) are correlative, in referring to "my people" (vv 11, 31, 32) and in the metaphors for Yahweh ("spring of running water," v 13; "wilderness," v 31). Numbers (2) and (5) are likewise correlative ("Egypt" and "Assyria," vv 18 and 36). This leaves (3) a central section, a cascade of metaphors for Israel. It is of course impossible to determine whether these five sections took shape in Jrm's mind at once or whether they were built up by stages, but this symmetry does not appear implausible.

Whether the brief insertions within 3:12–18 (namely v 13) and within 3:19–25 (namely v 21b) were perceived to participate in a structural pattern would be hard to say.

Additions in the Second Scroll. The same observation must be made in regard to these later additions: 2:26–28 is inserted just after the centerpoint in the additions in chapter 2 for the first scroll; and 3:3 and 3:20 are inserted in the midst of 3:1–5 and 3:19–25 respectively, but it would be difficult to insist that these additions participate in structural patterns.

2:1–3. The rubric in 2:1–2aα governs everything through 4:4, if the analysis in Preliminary Observations is correct. The poem in 2:2aβ–3 is composed of a tetracolon (v 2) in what might be call "end-expanded" form, wherein successive cola expand on elements at the end of previous cola (compare v 6 below), and two bicola (v 3). The poem shifts in reference to Yahweh from first person (v 2) to third person (v 3), and Wilfred G. E. Watson has pointed out[6] that the six nouns in v 2aβb match the six nouns in v 3 in gender symmetry (masc., masc.; fem., fem.; masc., fem.).

2:4–9. In the present context this passage is linked to what precedes by the repetition of "land not" (vv 2, 6), and it contrasts the disloyalty of Israel in the immediate

---

6   Wilfred G. E. Watson, "Symmetry of Stanza in Jeremiah 2,2b–3," *JSOT* 19 (1981) 107–10.

past with her primal loyalty in the wilderness (vv 1–3), a contrast underlined by the repetition of "go after" (הלך אַחֲרֵי, vv 2, 5, 8).

The poem (vv 5–9) is bracketed by "your fathers" (v 5) and "your children" (v 9) (see Preliminary Observations). But its inner form is not obvious; perhaps it is deliberately nonsymmetrical. If "your fathers" and "your children" bracket the passage, then the general form may be chiastic: "not say, 'Where is Yahweh?'" begins vv 6 and 8, and the rest of v 6 and all of v 7 deal with the action of Yahweh to "bring us out" of the land of Egypt through the desert and to "bring you in" to the land of orchards.

The pattern of number of cola in the verses of this passage is obscured by several details. It is doubtful if the last word of v 5, וַיֶּהְבָּלוּ, makes up a colon of its own[7] (Rudolph thinks it was delivered slowly and emphatically),[8] and it surely is not part of the previous colon; the text then may have suffered haplography (see Interpretation). Further, Rudolph assumes that "They did not say, 'Where is Yahweh?'" at the beginning of v 6 is a single colon, while "The priests have not said, 'Where is Yahweh?'" is a bicolon;[9] the latter, however, is probably a single colon. Such considerations lend uncertainty to any attempt to discern a pattern in this passage.

Verse 4 is a simple bicolon. Verse 5, after the messenger formula, seems to consist of four cola; the first is explicated by the following three. The second and third cola of the verse offer verbs of motion, and the verb in the fourth echoes the noun at the end of the third. The verse therefore hints at "end-expansion," for which see v 2 and, more elaborately, v 6. (If a verb has dropped out at the end by haplography, it perhaps echoes the word "wrong" in the first colon; see Interpretation.) Verse 6 is an elaborate example of "end-expansion" (compare v 2): "Yahweh" in the first colon generates two hip'il participles in the second and third cola, "wilderness" in the third colon generates the fourth, fifth, and sixth cola with the repeated "in a land," and "where no one crossed" at the end of the sixth colon brings the parallel "where nobody lived" in the seventh. (For the same format see 5:15.) Verse 7 is made up of two bicola in a more "normal" pattern, but v 8, like vv 5 and 6, seems to be deformed from a "normal" pattern: the first colon

reflects the first in v 6, as already noted, the first four cola have a subject, while the last line has no fresh subject but is closely parallel to the fourth colon—one has thus a true pentacolon. Verse 9 is a single bicolon, with an exact repetition of the verb.

2:10–13. This sequence breaks into two formal sections, vv 10–11 and vv 12–13; each begins with masculine imperatives, evidently commands to the witnesses (see Form), and ends with מְאֹד, and each section continues with an accusation of disloyalty. The commands are each bicola (vv 10a, 12). The first accusation section (vv 10b–11), as here reconstructed, is an interwoven tetracolon: the first two cola are both questions, the first a general one, the second specific; the third colon is a parenthetical contrast to the second (linked by "gods"), and the fourth reflects the second in using "exchange" (הֵמִיר). The first colon of the second set of commands (v 12a) reflects the first line of the first accusation (v 10b) in offering a prepositional expression with "this" (זֹאת)—"like this," "at this." The second accusation (v 13) has six cola, the first colon an initial summary ("double crime"), followed by two parallel cola expressing the first half of the "double crime," and by three parallel cola expressing the second half. These last three cola are tightly knit: the first two repeat the noun ("cisterns"), and the last two are synonymous ("broken," "hold no water"). Note also that the third and sixth cola in the verse offer "water."

2:14–19. This sequence is closely linked to vv 10–13 in two respects: v 18 picks up the metaphor of "water" from v 13, and "abandon Yahweh your God" (עָזְבֵךְ אֶת־יהוה אֱלֹהָיִךְ, vv 17 and 19) picks up "me they have abandoned" in v 13.

In spite of Rudolph's assumption, v 14 is not a bicolon but a tricolon: the threefold question form מַדּוּעַ, אִם־, הֲ־ elsewhere demands three cola (v 31, for example); though each line is short, the nominal clauses of the first two cola and the use of היה in the third line are normal.[10]

---

7 See Foreword, nn. 4, 5.
8 Rudolph, p. 15: *also langsam und schwer zu sprechen ist.*
9 So *BHS*.

10 To use the terminology of O'Connor, *Structure*, the first line is a single verbless clause line of two constituents, predicate-subject (see p. 176, Gen

I follow Rudolph in analyzing v 15 into four cola. One notes that he is inconsistent with the phrase מִבְּלִי יֹשֵׁב, counting it as only a part of a colon here but as a full colon in 9:10. I follow Michael Patrick O'Connor, however, in disregarding "particles" (such as מִבְּלִי and מֵאֵין) in the "fine structure of the verse,"[11] so that the phrase cannot stand alone. Verse 16 must be a single colon: subject cannot be separated from predicate into two cola (against Rudolph). If the "lions" in v 15 refer to "Assyria" (see Interpretation), then we have "Assyria" and "Egypt" side by side here, preparing for "Egypt" and "Assyria" in v 18. Formally then it is likely that the three cola of v 17 must be seen to belong with v 16: v 15 and vv 16–17 will then each contain four cola. At the same time the three cola of v 17 help to generate vv 18–19, not only in the phrase "that you abandoned your God" but also in the word "road," which is expanded in v 18, and in the question of responsibility, which is expanded in v 19. Verse 18 is a tetracolon. There is no reason to follow Rudolph and construe "know and see how bad and bitter" as a single colon; note that רַע וָמָר may be construed as two perfect verbs just as well as two adjectives: these two words are formally parallel with the two verbs "know and see." The long expression "oracle of the Lord Yahweh of hosts" stands outside the poetic structure. As a result v 19 emerges as six cola in three pairs.

2:20–25. This sequence is held together by the three occurrences of "say," second singular feminine: in the third colon of v 20 and the third-from-last colon of v 25 (וַתֹּאמְרִי) and at the beginning of v 23 (אֵיךְ תֹּאמְרִי). Indeed one could propose that the bicolon at the beginning of v 23 is the midpoint, not only in the word "say" but in both the word "how" (אֵיךְ, last colon of v 21, first colon of v 23) and in the phrase "walk after" (הָלַךְ אַחֲרֵי, second colon of v 23, last colon of v 25).

Verses 20–22 offer a remarkable series of four tricola, each a fresh metaphor for the errant people: the refractory farm animal (v 20a), the whore (v 20b), the

vine gone bad (v 21), and the person with bloody hands (v 22). This structure is obscured in *BHS* by the gloss at the end of v 21, which of course is not integral to the passage, and by the phrase "oracle of the Lord Yahweh" at the end of v 22, which again is not part of the poetic structure. Each tricolon begins with a marker (vv 20a, 20b and 22, כִּי; v 21, subject pronoun), and in each tricolon the first two cola parallel each other closely, while the third colon is less closely parallel, being in every case an accusation.

The bicolon at the beginning of v 23 points in both directions (see above): the first colon, with "I am not defiled," suggests the metaphors of vv 20–22, especially that of v 22, while the second colon, with "walk after," points toward the metaphors of the following cola and is rounded off by the last colon of v 25.

The analysis of the rest of vv 23–25 is more difficult. Verse 23 continues with a bicolon with two imperatives ("look," "recognize") and this is balanced by the bicolon of v 25a with its single prohibition ("don't run"). This leaves the descriptions of the camel and the wild ass. The description of the camel could be taken as a bicolon ("skittish" parallel with "interlacing her tracks"), but the first description of the wild ass contains only three words, indivisible into a bicolon. It is best to see here three participles morphologically parallel ("interlacing," "trained," "sniffing," the last with revocalization). Now what to do with "In her season who can turn her back?" "In her season" looks back to "in the passion of her desire" and forward to "in her month," and the rhetorical question "Who can turn her back?" implies the answer "no one" reflected in the colon just after. Thus the six cola from "a skittish young camel" to the end of v 24 can be grouped in a variety of ways, either as 2 + 2 + 2 or as 3 + 3.

2:26–28. This is not an easy sequence to analyze. Let us begin at the end, with v 28b. In spite of Rudolph, one cannot split "Yes, as many as your cities are your gods, O Judah" (it would mean the separation of subject and

49:22a and b); the second line is a zero clause, one constituent and two units (see p. 356 no. 1, and in general on "nominal lines" there); for the third line, see the treatment of היה on p. 303—the line contains one clause, two constituents, and two units (compare p. 317).

11   Ibid., 300, 305.

verb), and therefore the balancing clause (supplied by *G*) must again be a single colon: v 28b is thus a long bicolon.[12] One suspects then that the opening bicolon (v 26a), with a mention of "children of Israel," matches the closing bicolon, with vocatives "Judah" and "Jerusalem."

In vv 26–27 I construe "they" (הֵמָּה) with the participle "keep saying" (אֹמְרִים). One assumes that this participial clause makes a separate colon from the quotation that follows (against Rudolph);[13] compare v 27b, where "they will say" must be separated from the quotation. What emerges then is that "they" plus v 27aα makes up a tight tricolon.

Verse 27aβb must likewise be a tricolon: "Yes, they have turned their back to me and not their face" cannot be split (against Rudolph), since the negative "not" cannot count as a unit.[14]

The foregoing analysis in turn suggests that v 28a is a tricolon (against Rudolph): "arise and save" makes up the second colon here as it makes up the third colon of the tricolon at the end of v 27, and "in the time of your disaster" makes up the third colon here as it forms a substantial part of the second colon at the end of v 27.

The result, if this analysis is correct, is a sequence with opening and closing bicola and three tricola in the center.

2:29–32. The analysis here depends, as often, on the soundness of the textual reconstruction. If the reconstruction here is correct, vv 29 and 30 each consist of two bicola. Verse 32 is a tetracolon. Verse 31aβb is likewise a tetracolon: the threefold question form offers three cola, and the parallel "we shall no longer come to you" makes up the fourth. With eight cola before and eight cola after, the remaining bicolon (v 31aα) becomes the centerpiece, the striking challenge to the people.

2:33–37. Again textual questions render the analysis difficult. Verse 33, by the understanding offered here, is a tricolon in which the first and last cola are closely parallel: "make good" (יטב hip'il) and "do ill" (רעע hip'il), "way" and "ways." (Rudolph's analysis of 33b is not convincing even for *M*: הרעות cannot stand alone, whatever the vocalization.) Verse 34 is likewise a tricolon, though the parallelism is quite loose; the first colon is long because of the gloss—the remaining five

units are within the limit for a colon (compare the two cola in v 28b). The analysis gains slightly in plausibility when one notices that "seek" is the verb in the second colon of v 33 and "find" the verb in the same position in v 34. One might be tempted to bracket the two cola introduced by גַּם- (here translated "indeed"), but vv 36–37a (as here reconstructed) offer an analogous structure (see below). Verse 35 is made up of two bicola. Verses 36–37a, by the reconstruction offered here, make up two tricola which structurally are closely analogous to the tricola in vv 33–34. Thus both sequences begin with "how" (מָה), both have third and fourth cola beginning with גַּם- ("indeed"), and both have second cola containing an infinitive phrase ("to seek illegitimate love," "to change your way"). The first tricolon of each sequence is concerned with the false "way" of the people, and the second tricola of both sequences are subtly linked: "find" (in a criminal act, v 34) and "shame" (v 36b) are associated in the later v 26; "palms" (v 34) is synonymous with "hands" (v 37), and one implication of "yoke" in v 34 is the vassalage suggested by vv 36b–37a. Verse 37b is a simple bicolon. The passage is then precisely symmetrical: vv 33–35a (two tricola and a bicolon) and vv 36–37 (two tricola and a bicolon) surround v 35b, a central bicolon which is the climactic outburst from Yahweh explaining his rhetoric.

3:1–5. If the analysis offered in Preliminary Observations is sound, the original recension (directed to the north) omitted v 3. Verse 1 contains seven cola (Rudolph tries to achieve eight by dividing "Would not that land really be profaned?"—but, as in other instances, the subject cannot be separated from its predicate). These cola are tightly woven together in several ways but are doubtless best grouped into a tricolon and two bicola. Thus the first five discuss the legal question implied by Deut 24:1–4; the fourth and fifth are parallel questions growing out of the legal situation. The sixth and seventh cola are an accusation, yet the seventh colon is closely parallel to the fourth.

Verse 2a is a tetracolon; one might view it as a chiasmus, the first and fourth cola paralleling "caravan-tracks" and "wilderness," the second and third paralleling the two perfect verbs שֻׁגַּלְתְּ and יָשַׁבְתְּ. Verse 2b is a

---

12 Ibid., 347, "constellation #21, with one clause, four constituents, five units."

13 Ibid., 245, on Zeph 1:12e and f.

14 See ibid., 255, on the negatives in Zeph 3:2.

bicolon.[15] Verses 4 and 5a are each bicola; v 5b (as reconstructed) is also a bicolon—one might propose that "you have spoken" refers to vv 4–5a and that "you have acted" refers to vv 1b–2.

If that is the case, then the sequence divides between vv 1b–2 and vv 4–5a, and into that division v 3 was inserted for the second scroll, a verse consisting of two bicola.

3:12–15, 18bβ. If the analysis in Preliminary Observations is sound, the original recension of this sequence (directed to the north) omitted v 13. After the prose command at the beginning of v 12, the balance of the verse consists of two bicola.

Verse 14 is a puzzle as it stands in *M*. The first half can easily be a bicolon, but v 14b, though seemingly an expression of Josiah's ideology, hardly seems poetry (compare Preliminary Observations, especially the opinion of Hyatt cited there). But in v 12 the conjunction כִּי introduces the second half of the verse (and so also in 2:27, 28, and the reconstruction here of 3:25). One wonders then whether "one from a city and two from a tribe" is not misplaced; if it is inserted after "Return, turnable children," then כִּי will introduce the half-verse stating Yahweh's action. This suggestion gains slightly in plausibility by a comparison with the phraseology in 23:14aβ "so as not to turn, each from his evil," where a distributive expression follows שׁוּב, and similar expressions in prose passages (e.g., 18:11). If this proposal is correct, then the verse consists of two tricola, the second and third cola of each of which offer close parallelism ("one" and "two," and the verb phrases "take you" and "bring you").[16]

And again if the analysis is sound, we have in vv 15 + 18bβ a tetracolon which reflects the structure of the two bicola in v 14: "fathers" in the last colon reflects "children" in the first colon of v 14, the internal parallelism of "one" and "two" in the restored second colon of v 14 is balanced by the two infinitives absolute in the third colon of vv 15 + 18bβ, and "I shall take" in v 14 is balanced by "I shall give" in v 15. The sequence, then, emerges as twelve cola in three groups of four.

3:19–25. Again an analysis of structure depends on the soundness of the reconstruction of the literary history of the passage (see Preliminary Observations): by the proposal offered here, vv 24–25 have been expanded by prose additions; the poetic material of this passage essentially took shape as part of the early appeal to the north, but v 21b was added for Jrm's first scroll and v 20 for Jrm's second scroll.

The early appeal to the north then is a general counterpoise to vv 1–5: "but I for my part" (וְאָנֹכִי) in v 19 seems to contrast with "but you" (וְאַתְּ) in v 1, the mention of the "land" Yahweh gave the people balances the mention of the "land" which the people profaned (v 1), Yahweh's hope that the people would "call" him "My father" (v 19) contrasts with what the people have "called" Yahweh (v 4), and the "caravan-tracks" where, it is implied, Yahweh calls the errant people to return (evidently: see Preliminary Observations), are the same "caravan-tracks" where the people commit harlotry (v 2). At the same time the use of "(re)turn" (שׁוּב) in the passage picks up that verb not only in vv 1–5 but more particularly in vv 12–14 (the identity of the opening cola in vv 14 and 22).

This early recension to the north is a simple succession of ten bicola. The first three (v 19) seem to be separate from what follows—they are Yahweh's word to himself; the first bicolon begins with "but I for my part thought" and the third with "and I thought" (both אמר). These are followed (in the present analysis) by an introduction to the interchange between Yahweh and the people (bicolon 4, v 21a), then by the quick speeches of Yahweh, the people and Yahweh (bicola 5, 6, and 7 respectively, vv 22–23a), then by the longer speech of the people (bicola 8 through 10, vv 23b–25). In a fashion then the three bicola of this long speech of the people at the end of the sequence balance the three bicola of Yahweh's thoughts at the beginning (does the expression "our fathers" in v 24 echo "My father" in v 19?). The last three bicola of the sequence (if the poetry of vv 24–25 is correctly reconstructed) open with "Yahweh our God" (v 23b) and close with "our God" and "Yahweh" (v 25).

The two additions in the sequence are each bicola: that in the first scroll (v 21b) and that in the second scroll (v 20).

4:1–2. Verse 1a is a bicolon united by the two occur-

---

15 For "with your whorings and your wickedness" compare ibid., 247, on Zeph 1:16b.

16 The object pronoun "you" (אֶתְכֶם) counts as a "unit" in the cola (so also 8:17b); compare the treatment of "in them" (בָּהֶם) in Deut 32:28b in ibid., 202.

rences of "(re)turn" (שוב). Verse 2b is likewise a bicolon consisting of two synonymous clauses. The cola of vv 1b–2a, however, are not so easily analyzed; but v 1b cannot be other than a bicolon, with "from your mouth" balancing "from my presence," and this leaves v 2a a bicolon, to be divided as the Masoretic accent zaqep qaṭon does, after "By the life of Yahweh," rather than as Rudolph does in *BHS*, after "truly." If the distribution of protases and apodoses in these verses is correctly analyzed (see Interpretation), then the first bicolon (v 1a) embodies the first protasis-apodosis pair, and vv 1b–2 make up a second set, two bicola of protases (vv 1b–2a) and one bicolon of an apodosis (v 2b).

4:3–4. After the rubric (v 3aα) v 3 consists of a single bicolon. As the text of v 4 stands, the vocatives make up all of the third colon; it is a surprising structure, but Ps 35:23 is comparable. The verse then consists of two tricola.

Form

Early Recension to the North (2:4–9; 3:1–2, 4–5, 12, 14–15, 18bβ, 19, 21a, 22–23, the poetic core of 24–25; 4:1–2). The first two sections (2:4–9; 3:1–2, 4–5) embody the accusation speech of a *rîb*, a covenant lawsuit initiated by Yahweh against his people;[17] note the use of the verb "enter suit" (ריב) in 2:9. This genre is a theological extension of the accusation speech in a true lawsuit; but, as A. S. van der Woude points out, in a true lawsuit the plaintiff addresses the judge (1 Kgs 3:17),[18] while in the theological adaptation Yahweh is both plaintiff and judge,[19] so that what one has here is a prophetic oracle using the terminology of a lawsuit. Yahweh's accusation will be greatly extended in the additions of the first scroll (2:10–25, 29–37): see below.

The closest parallel to 2:4–9 is Mic 6:1–8: one has the verb "enter suit" (v 9, compare Mic 6:1), the summons to the defendant to hear the word of the plaintiff (v 4, compare Mic 6:1), the rhetorical question how Yahweh might have offended (v 5, compare Mic 6:3), the review of Yahweh's saving acts in the exodus and thereafter (vv 6–7, compare Mic 6:4–5). Hos 9:10–13; 13:4–8; and Isa 5:1–7 are more distant in content, but they too offer a view of the close relation of Yahweh to Israel in the past, contrasting with the present circumstance that will call forth Yahweh's judgment. Compare also the short oracle in Isa 1:2–3: "Sons have I reared and brought up. . . ." In such passages the basic accusation speech has been expanded by a review of prior history, especially by a review of Yahweh's benefits.[20]

Yahweh quotes the people in 3:4 (see below); prophetic oracles serve to reinforce the divine accusation.[21] But the opening passage here portrays Yahweh as citing words which his opponents did *not* use (vv 6, 8).

Normally a lawsuit speech begins with an appeal to the cosmic witnesses (Mic 6:1; 1:2; Isa 1:2; Deut 32:1); that word is missing here (but will be supplied in the recension in the first scroll, 2:12).

After the summons to the defendant in 2:4, the speech opens in v 5 with a rhetorical question addressed to the defendant. The parallel in Mic 6:3 has been cited; other similar rhetorical questions are found in Isa 1:5, 11; 5:4; and Deut 32:6. Rhetorical questions directed to the defendant were part of ordinary rhetoric in legal procedure (Judg 8:2; 11:12; 25–26),[22] and may have been characteristic of a "pre-trial encounter."[23]

It is difficult to locate the question "Where is Yahweh?" form-critically. A good parallel is 2 Kgs 2:14, where Elisha asks the question in the context of the departed Elijah. Job 35:10 is another, but not one to give form-critical help. Judg 6:13 is less close. The closest parallel is

17   For the classic study of the *rîb*, see Gemser, pp. 120–37; and see further in the Bibliography under this topic.

18   A. S. van der Woude, *Micha* (De Prediking van het Oude Testament; Nijkerk: Callenbach, 1976) 207.

19   Kirsten Nielsen, *Yahweh as Prosecutor and Judge: An Investigation of the Prophetic Lawsuit (Rîb-Pattern)* (JSOT Supplement Series 9; Sheffield: Sheffield University, 1978).

20   Westermann, *Basic Forms*, 182–83; Ramsey, "Speech-Forms," 45.

21   Hans Walter Wolff, *Das Zitat im Prophetenspruch*

(BEvT 4; Munich: Kaiser, 1937) = *Gesammelte Studien zum Alten Testament* (TBü 22; Munich: Kaiser, 1973) 36–129.

22   On these see Westermann, *Basic Forms*, 112–15, and Limburg, pp. 297–99.

23   So Ramsey, "Speech-Forms," 49–50.

Isa 63:11–13, where (evidently) the worshiping community[24] raises this question and then follows it with participles referring to Yahweh's saving acts. It is clear that Isa 63:11–13 is in the context of a community lament,[25] so that one is led to community laments within the Psalter, like Psalm 44, which combines a recitation of Yahweh's salvific acts in the past (Ps 44:2–9) with questions as to why Yahweh now neglects his people (Ps 44:24, 25: "Why do you sleep, O Yahweh?"; "Why do you hide your face?") But one wonders whether both Elisha's question and the questions raised in the context of community lament are not secondary evidences of normal oracular inquiry on the part of the priest, perhaps associated with the procedure signified by the phrase "inquire of Yahweh" (שאל ביהוה)—compare, for example, Judg 1:1; one notes that it is specifically the priests (v 8) who no longer pose the question. But all we can conclude is that the earnest inquiry represented by the question is, in Jrm's view, now absent.

The recitation of Yahweh's mighty acts in times past is a feature of covenant lawsuits: we have already noted Mic 6:4–5, but Deut 32:10–14 is another parallel. And the ungracious response of Israel to Yahweh's gracious acts, found in v 7b, is paralleled in Deut 32:15–18. In v 8 Jrm becomes specific in naming categories of leaders who are particularly culpable: parallels are Hos 4:4–6 and Isa 1:23. Verse 9 brings a statement of Yahweh's determination to pursue the lawsuit.

The specificity of the lawsuit is unfolded in 3:1–2, 4–5, argumentation based on the law reflected in Deut 24:1–4 (see Preliminary Observations, Interpretation). The argument of v 1b is that of "how much more" (Hebrew: qal weḥomer);[26] compare 2:11 (below) and 12:5. In v 2 there is a call to view the evidence (compare 2:23). In vv 4–5a, as already noted, we hear quotations of Israel cited by Yahweh the plaintiff. Such quotations are the common stuff of public argumentation; compare the device in the quite secular context of the argument between Delilah and Samson in Judg 16:15. Two fine examples in prophetic oracles are the mockery of the counselors of Pharaoh in Isa 19:11, and Yahweh's chiding of Israel in Isa 40:27.[27] Verse 5b embodies summary indictments.

The last three sections (3:12, 14–15, 18bβ, 19, 21a, 22–23, the poetic core of 24–25, and 4:1–2) embody a summons to repentance,[28] examples of which occur in earlier prophetic material (Amos 5:4–5, 6–7, 14–15; Hos 14:2). The summons to repentance is heard four times, 3:12a, 14a, 22a, and 4:1a. The first occurrence is associated with a reference to Yahweh's character (v 12b) as a motivation for return (compare Joel 2:12–13). The second (3:14a) is followed (vv 14b–15 + 18bβ) by an announcement (= proclamation) of salvation.[29]

Verse 19 offers a surprise, a declaration by Yahweh of his own thought, his historic intention for Israel: the adverb "how (gladly)" (איך) underlines the poignancy and thoughtfulness of the expression (for which compare Yahweh's laments over his people in 9:9–10 and 12:7–13, and his meditation on his affection for Ephraim in 31:20). Even the words of Deutero-Isaiah which declare Yahweh's intention from the beginning (Isa 41:9) are words addressed directly to Israel. But though the first two cola and last two in the verse might be construed as words delivered long ago to Israel, they are more probably to be understood as words now spoken in disputation with Israel about what Yahweh had thought to himself long ago (compare the negative fantasy expressed in 9:1a). The third and fourth cola add a bit to the array of the gracious acts of Yahweh in bringing Israel into Canaan such as are expressed in the "Where is

---

24 Paul D. Hanson, *The Dawn of Apocalyptic* (Philadelphia: Fortress, 1975) 84, note c, and 89; Claus Westermann, *Isaiah 40–66* (Philadelphia: Westminster, 1969) 385, note b.

25 Compare v 15 there, and see Westermann, *Isaiah 40—66*, 388.

26 See Louis Jacobs, "Hermeneutics," *EncJud* 8:367. This form of argument is common in the NT as well; note Matt 6:30 = Luke 12:28; Matt 7:11 = Luke 11:13; Rom 11:12.

27 See Hans Wildberger, *Jesaja* (BKAT 10; Neukirchen: Neukirchener, 1972–82) 717; Elliger, *Deuterojesaja*,

94; Westermann, *Isaiah 40—66*, 59–60.

28 See Thomas M. Raitt, "The Prophetic Summons to Repentance," *ZAW* 83 (1971) 30–49; March, "Prophecy," 168–69.

29 For this genre see March, "Prophecy," 163–64.

Yahweh?" sequence in 2:7.

Verses 21a + 22–25 evidently present a hypothetical sequence of repentance; this presumption is confirmed by a careful comparison with 31:18–19, a closely analogous passage (note "for you are Yahweh our God," 3:22bβ, and "for you are Yahweh my God," 31:18bβ). In 31:18–19 the repentance is genuine ("Bring me back, and let me come back," 31:18ba, a plea for help), while in 3:22ba the word is "Here we are, we have come to you," an assertion of loyalty (*Treuebeteuerung*) lacking the humility found in 31:18. What we have then in 3:21–25 is Yahweh's scenario for repentance, or his description of what the people are likely to do in response to his appeal, and therefore continues the private, meditative mood of v 19, a mood in strong contrast with the public realism of 4:1–2. Verse 21a is an astonishing passive-voice statement about Yahweh's pleading to his errant sons (if the passage is understood here correctly: see Preliminary Observations, Interpretation): a divine report about Yahweh himself. Following Yahweh's appeal for repentance (v 22a) comes the people's positive response to the appeal: they do appear to repent, and offer an assertion of loyalty in Yahweh (see above). In v 23a Yahweh confronts the people with a denial to test their sincerity (see Interpretation, and compare Josh 24:19–20), but the people insist on their sincerity and offer an admission of guilt (vv 23b–25). The passage is not, then, a communal lament, as has been assumed.[30]

Though 4:1–2 embodies a final appeal to repentance, its form is rather that of parenesis (moral exhortation) wherein the rhetoric of covenant speech is used to urge adherence to covenant norms;[31] for a more elaborate example see 7:1–12. Verses 1–2a are an exhortation, and v 2b is a promise.

Additions in the First Scroll (2:1–3, 10–25, 29–37; 3:13, 21b; 4:3–4). Though the opening unit, 2:1–3, may have been prefixed to 2:4–9 at a later time, it shares with the verses which follow it the genre of the accusation-speech of a *rîb* (see above). Thus if Mic 6:1–8 offers similarities to Jer 2:4–9, it also offers similarities to 2:1–3 (the motif of "remembering" the events of the past, Mic 6:5). The word "remember" in the mouth of Yahweh also occurs in a disputational speech in Hos 7:2. The diction of Jer 2:2–3 point in the direction of covenantal vocabulary (see Interpretation), a fact reinforcing this identification of genre (see further Bibliography).

Verses 10–25 and 29–37 extend greatly the negative material of vv 4–9, displaying many rhetorical devices associated with the *rîb*-pattern. Verses 10–11a constitute a (rhetorical) question in a search for precedents for Israel's covenant breaking. The comparison with foreign peoples is found elsewhere, notably in Amos 6:2, and, in the mouth of foreigners arguing with Israel, in Isa 10:9–11 and 2 Kgs 18:34–35, so that such disputational style fits public argumentation, even though there are no parallels for such diction in other covenant lawsuits. For the "how much more" argumentation in v 11 compare the remarks above on 3:1. Verses 11b and 13 offer accusations against the defendant which extend the particulars of vv 7b–8. Verse 12, a modification of the summoning of cosmic witnesses, is an appeal to them to be aghast at the crimes here specified. This summons names the "heavens," and ultimately it is to be heard in counterpoise to the summons to the "earth" in 6:19. Such a summons is likewise found in Isa 1:2; Mic 1:2; 6:1; and Deut 32:1.[32] There are extrabiblical parallels for the invocation of heaven and earth; in Ugaritic they are invoked as witnesses to an international agreement between Ugarit and Amurru.[33]

Verse 14 brings an occurrence of the threefold question formula introduced by מַדּוּעַ, אִם־הֲ.[34] The formula is employed to pose a common type of question found not only within the OT but more generally: the land is suffering—why has this happened? Such a genre is found outside the prophets in Deut 29:22–28 and 1 Kgs 9:8–9. It is likewise found in Ashurbanipal's annals: "Whenever the inhabitants of Arabia asked each other: 'On account of what have these calamities befallen

30 Berridge, p. 168.
31 See James Muilenburg, "The Form and Structure of the Covenantal Formulations," *VT* 9 (1959) 347–65.
32 For the matter see Gemser, pp. 129–30; G. Ernest Wright, "The Lawsuit of God: A Form-Critical Study of Deuteronomy 32," *Israel's Prophetic Heritage, Essays in Honor of James Muilenburg* (ed. Bernhard W. Anderson and Walter Harrelson; New York: Harper,

1962) 44–49, and further literature in commentaries on these parallel passages.
33 Jean Nougayrol, *PRU IV*, 137.6; see further Dennis J. McCarthy, *Old Testament Covenant, A Survey of Current Opinions* (Richmond: John Knox, 1972) 38 n. 7.
34 William L. Holladay, "The So-Called 'Deuteronomic Gloss' in Jer. viii 19b," *VT* 12 (1962) 494–98.

Arabia?' (they answered themselves:) 'Because we did not keep the solemn oaths (sworn by) Ashur, because we offended the friendliness of Ashurbanipal, the king, beloved by Enlil!'"[35] The form found in Deuteronomy 29 and 1 Kings 9 and in certain passages in Jer is analyzed intensively by Burke O. Long;[36] but he does not discuss the present passage, which is associated with this question-and-answer scheme by Delbert R. Hillers.[37] Jrm is using the question-and-answer form conventional in public dispute, whether posed simply with rhetorical motive or sincerely to seek clarification, as part of the argumentation of the covenant lawsuit. This section uses the metaphors of "lions" (v 15) and "water" (v 18), comments on the news of the day (v 16) and raises the question what the cause of the present disaster is (vv 14, 17, 19); no "pure" genre is employed here but rather the expected rhetoric of public dispute to set forth for the people what is really happening to them.

The transitional "so now" (וְעַתָּה) at the beginning of v 18 serves to introduce the present situation in the light of the antecedent circumstances referred to in the previous verses: in covenantal formulations it introduces the statement of substance after the antecedent history.[38] Verse 19, suddenly, is an announcement of the consequence of wrongdoing, not directly Yahweh's judgment, but an inevitable outgrowth of the people's sin, and the announcement is couched as a plea to admit guilt (compare v 23b), using wisdom vocabulary ("know and see").

Verses 20–25 continue the diction of legal disputation. Thus the expression "But it was I who" (וְאָנֹכִי) in v 21 (compare 3:19) emphasizes Yahweh's former action in contrast to Israel's present deeds; the same diction may be found in Amos 2:9 and Hos 11:3. Again the expression "How can you say?" (אֵיךְ תֹּאמְרִי) in v 23a is found also

in 8:8 and 48:14, and outside Jer in Judg 16:15 and Isa 19:11; 40:27. This rhetorical quoting of what Israel says is now a counterpoise to what Israel has not said (in 2:6, 8); for the device of quoting one's opponent in disputation, see the discussion of 3:4–5 above. What we have here are thus fragments of typical disputation language woven together by the structure of these verses, beginning with an appeal to Israel to admit her guilt (v 23b) and culminating in argumentation that presses Israel into the admission that she is indeed guilty but intends to continue on her erring way (v 25).

The language of disputation continues in vv 29–32 ("argue," רִיב, v 29; "why then have my people said . . . ?" v 31); rhetorical questions (vv 31aβ, 32a). There is the suggestion in v 30 of a wisdom motif: "correction they did not accept"—the people were disobedient, whereas children or pupils should accept the chastisement of him who is charged with their training. If the text of v 31aα is correctly understood, it is a rhetorical question to the people reminding them of their identity, followed by a consequent summons to pay attention to the word and action of Yahweh. Verse 32b closes with another accusation.

The last sequence of chapter 2 (vv 33–37) continues the language of the covenant lawsuit as the plaintiff continues to quote the defendant ("But you said," "because you say," v 35). He mocks the pretensions of the defendant by an ironic restatement of her claims ("How good you make your way to seek illegitimate love!" v 33). The double use of the particle גַּם in vv 33 and 34, and again in vv 36 and 37 appears to reinforce the rhetoric of dispute (as in Isa 57:6–7; see Interpretation), and v 34 argues that Israel has resorted to violence without legal justification such as the offense of housebreaking would present. Verse 35 by the use of the verb "go to law" (שׁפט

35   *ANET*, 300a.
36   Burke O. Long, "Two Question and Answer Schemata in the Prophets," *JBL* 90 (1971) 129–39, and compare the earlier literature cited there.
37   Delbert R. Hillers, *Treaty-Curses and the Old Testament Prophets* (BibOr 16; Rome: Pontifical Biblical Institute, 1964) 65 n. 60.
38   Klaus Baltzer, *The Covenant Formulary in Old Testament, Jewish, and Early Christian Writings* (Philadelphia: Fortress, 1971) 21; compare, more generally, Muilenburg, "Covenantal Formulations," 352–65; André Laurentin, "We'attāh—Kai nun.

Formule caractéristique des textes juridiques et liturgies (à propos de Jean 17,5)," *Bib* 45 (1964) 168–97; H. A. Brongers, "Bemerkungen zum Gebrauch des Adverbialen wĕ'attāh im Alten Testament," *VT* 15 (1965) 289–99, esp. 297. For another use in prophetic material see Hos 2:12 and the remarks by Wolff, *Hosea*, 37, on that passage.

nip'al) underlines the disputation; then, once more "how!" (מָה) in v 36 mocks the conduct of the defendant, and the double use of the particle גַּם־ rounds off the sequence.

By the analysis offered here, there are two brief additions in the first scroll in chapter 3, vv 13 and 21b. Verse 13, like 2:23, is a plea to Israel that she admit her guilt; the diction is very much like 2:19, which is analogous. Verse 21b is a brief accusation.

This sequence in the first scroll was evidently completed by 4:3–4. After the rubric in v 3a, vv 3b–4a embody a call to repentance, couched in imperatives like the calls to repentance in 3:12, 14, 22; it thus reinforces the softer tone of 4:1–2, adding further reminiscences of divine words known to the community (see Preliminary Observations). Verse 4b is a final threat.

Additions in the Second Scroll (2:26–28; 3:3, 20). In 2:26–28 we meet further disputational material associated with the *rib*-pattern. Verse 26 embodies a simile the form of which appears to be drawn from the orbit of proverbs: for "as ... so" (כְּ ... כֵּן) compare Prov 10:26; 26:1.[39] The passage continues with an accusation of covenant breaking by quotations of pagan devotion (v 27aα), followed by a mocking prediction of inconsistent behavior (v 27b) reminiscent of Hos 2:9b ("Then she shall say, 'I will set out and return to my first husband'"). Then comes the mocking rhetorical question "Where are your gods?" (a nice counterpoise to the question "Where is Yahweh?" which Israel had forgotten to say, vv 6, 8!) and the challenge that these gods might manifest their power to save (v 28a). This challenge is reminiscent of Deut 32:37–38, Josh 10:14, and, with the same intent though different wording, 2 Kgs 3:13, and anticipates similar expressions in Deutero-Isaiah (Isa 41:23; 45:20). The passage closes with a final accusation of polytheism (v 28b).

The first addition in chapter 3 (v 3) consists of two parts: the first (v 3a) a report of God's punitive act in sending a drought, the second (v 3b) a renewed accusation of Israel's refusal to repent. A close analogy is found in the repeated pattern in Amos 4:6–11. The second addition in the chapter (v 20), if the text is correctly reconstructed, consists of a simile derived from

the milieu of wisdom (compare 2:26 above) embodying an accusation of unfaithfulness.

Later Prose Additions (3:6–11, 16–18bα). The prose sequence in 3:6–11 is a monologue of Yahweh to the prophet, a description of the conduct of Israel (that is, the northern kingdom) and Judah; they are personified ("Turncoat Israel" and "Treacherous Judah") and their conduct compared. It is really an allegory,[40] and as such it is a midrash on vv 12–13, given the initial instructions in v 12 indicating that these are words directed to the north. The character "Turncoat Israel" was developed from a misunderstanding of the syntax of the first colon of poetry in v 12, and the phraseology is pieced out from other material in chapters 2 and 3 (for the details see Setting and Interpretation).

The prose additions in 3:16–18bα render the material eschatological ("in those days," vv 16, 18; "at that time," v 17) and stress the restoration of Jerusalem as a cultic center with the ark of the covenant. They are thus proclamations of salvation. Verse 16 announces a change of speech-pattern of the people; similar announcements of a change in speech-pattern are to be found in 23:7–8 and 31:29–30. The change of speech-pattern is related to the change in names of places or persons (compare 7:32 = 19:6 and 20:3).

Setting

A solution for the settings of the material in 2:1—4:4 proposed in the present study has already been set forth in Preliminary Observations in order that the problems of Structure and Form might be dealt with in an orderly fashion; and some of the evidence for this solution has likewise been presented. But the evidence must now be examined in a more systematic way, since the general consensus of scholars on the question has been different; it will not do to fall prey to circular argumentation.

Settings for 3:6–11 and 16–18bα will be offered below. These passages are generally agreed to be late and unauthentic to Jrm. The rest of the material in these chapters are by common consent accepted as authentic to the prophet; it is this material that must now be examined in detail.

The Poetry. Unfortunately the specific clues for dating

---

39 See Trevor R. Hobbs, "Some Proverbial Reflections in the Book of Jeremiah," *ZAW* 91 (1979) 64–65; compare Daryl Schmidt, "The LXX *Gattung*

'Prophetic Correlative,'" *JBL* 96 (1977) 519.
40 Compare Zimmerli, *Ezekiel 1*, 334–35 and 481–82, on chaps. 16 and 23.

these material are few: one can count three. First, there is the mention of "lions" as military enemies in 2:15, of Egyptian cities which humiliate Israel in v 16, and of "Assyria" and "Egypt" in vv 18 and 36. Second, there is the presumed reference to the killing of prophets with the sword in the *M* text of 2:30. Third, there is the mention of a drought in 3:3. Beyond these clues are more general accusations of apostasy and Baal worship that are too vague to be of direct help. Otherwise one must deal as one can with the rubrics of 2:1, 4; 3:12; and 4:3, with the rhetorical structure of the total sequence, and with one's understanding of the chronology of Jrm's career, and it is these that supplement the information to be derived from the specific clues and bring one to the solution already proposed.

Let us deal first with the specific clues of chapters 2 and 3. These are enticing, but there is an interlocking set of uncertainties which renders the evidence difficult to use. It is clear first of all that the parallelism of "Assyria" and "Egypt" is to be found in Hosea (Hos 7:11; 9:3, 6; 11:5, 11; 12:2): in Hosea's day Assyria was the great threat, and there was always the hope of Egyptian help against Assyria.[41] The same parallelism is found in Zech 10:10–11; there the commentators recognize that the terms reflect traditional parallelism rather than the political reality of the period in which the passage originated; the same may be said of Isa 19:23–25. It is therefore possible that the parallelism in 2:18 and 36 may be based on poetic tradition and not be pressed as evidence that the Assyrian Empire was in existence at the time.

It is also clear that various words for "lion" had long been used for Assyria (Amos 3:12; Isa 5:29; Nah 2:12–13). Jrm uses the metaphor of "lion" in 4:7 for the foe from the north (4:6), and 4:7 offers diction similar to that in 2:15. The identification of the foe from the north which one makes is to some degree dependent on the chronology which one adopts for Jrm's career: by the low chronology adopted in this work the foe will be Babylon

(compare Interpretation of 1:14–15). But even if the traditional high chronology were correct, by which Jrm would have begun to speak out in 627, there is no way the foe could be Assyria as a military power:[42] that power was by then waning, and one would be forced to assume, if passages concerned with the foe from the north (i.e., 1:14–15; 4:6–7; and others) were delivered during the period 627–622, that the foe is a mythological figure whose characteristics would come to fit Babylon later on. But the low chronology, I submit, is sound; the most telling bit of evidence is the declaration of celibacy (16:1–4), which, by my understanding of the implications of chapter 36, can only have been made after Jehoiakim burned the first scroll.[43] The foe in 4:6–7 and elsewhere is thus Babylon, and the "lion" in 4:7 is therefore Babylon.

This leaves one in perplexity regarding the "lions" in 2:15 and the mention of Egyptian cities in v 16 and of "Assyria" and "Egypt" in vv 18 and 36. If one assumes that v 16 is an interpolation, as Rudolph and Bright do,[44] then the "lions" in v 15 are counterposed to "Assyria" and "Egypt" in v 18. If the "lions" were Babylon (4:7), then it is possible that we have depicted here the kind of three-cornered fight which prevailed in 612 and thereafter: the Assyrians were ejected from Nineveh by the Babylonians, and the Egyptians sent an army into the field in northern Syria. But this conclusion is hard to sustain: Assyria was no real political entity by the time the Egyptians took the field to aid her, offering neither aid (compare v 18) nor threat (compare v 36) to Judah. The only way in which this interpretation could be sustained is if the aid from Egypt were a present possibility and the aid from Assyria were part of the historical past; v 18 offers nominal clauses, not specific for time, and v 36 offers a perfect ("as you were shamed by Assyria"). But these assumptions are alike unlikely. A three-cornered fight is hard to depict in Hebrew poetry, and there are no triple structures here appropriate to such a depiction; only two nations are named in v 36, and

---

41 Bright, *History*, 272; compare 2 Kgs 17:4.
42 Against Jacob Milgrom, "The Date of Jeremiah, Chapter 2," *JNES* 14 (1955) 65–69.
43 Holladay, "Coherent Chronology," 58–62; and see "A Chronology of Jeremiah's Career," above.
44 It must be stressed, however, that they believe the interpolation to be genuine to Jrm himself, inserted in the sequence at a later period in his career;

Rudolph, it may be added, is also concerned about v 36.

v 16 is introduced by the particle גַּם־ precisely as the clause of "Egypt" is in v 36. Furthermore, the assumption that v 16 is an interpolation is an ad hoc one based upon the high chronology which this study finds unconvicing. All these considerations suggest that v 16 belonged from the beginning where it is, and therefore that vv 15–16 are parallel to v 18 and to v 36, so that "lions" in v 15 means whatever "Assyria" means in vv 18 and 36.

Now (to recapitulate) if the term "Assyria" in vv 18 and 36 means "political Assyria," then either or both of the following assumptions are correct: (1) the references to Assyria are to the historical past (to Manasseh's time, say): but then the "lions" in v 15 cannot refer to Assyria, since they are a present threat to Judah; (2) the low chronology espoused in the present study is wrong, since there is no way that the rump power Assyria, by 609–605 little more than a group of refugees west of the Euphrates, can be pictured as roaring over the victim Judah. But if 2:15 sounds like 4:7, and if 4:7 refers to Babylon, then the way is open to understand the "lions" of 2:15 as Babylon, and "Assyria" in vv 18 and 36 as the poetic equivalent of Babylon,[45] that is, the ruling power in Mesopotamia at the time of the utterance of the passage; Jrm would then be imitating Hos 7:11. This approach would even allow the possibility that "Assyria" in v 18 refers to Babylon and that "Assyria" in v 36 refers to political Assyria at a time earlier than the time when the oracle was first delivered, or even that "Assyria" in v 36 referred to political Assyria at an earlier time and was later in Jrm's career reinterpreted to refer to Babylon.

By far the most economic conclusion to these interlocking problems, then, is to see 2:14–19 and the material associated with 2:36 as having poetic integrity (thus without interpolations) in a setting in the last decade of the seventh century, when Babylonia and Egypt were alternative great powers imposing vassalage on Judah (2 Kgs 23:31—24:2).[46] (We may note in passing that Rashi places 2:36 in the days of Jehoiakim and Zedekiah!)

There is the possibility that 2:16 refers specifically to the death of Josiah at Megiddo in 609, if "your skull" (= "your head") refers to him, and even the possibility that the verse refers both to the death of Josiah and to the deposition of Jehoahaz three months later, if the verb is imperfect and that imperfect is frequentative (see the discussion in Interpretation).

In regard to the reference to the killing of the prophets in M of 2:30, that clue is valid only if the text is correct. But once one is persuaded, as the present study is (see Interpretation), that the text is faulty, then the clue vanishes; at the most, the present altered form of text might indicate the understanding (or misunderstanding) of a copyist. The reference in M is unlikely to be the killing of prophets in Elijah's time (so Volz), nor is it likely to be a vague reference to the killing of prophets in earlier times (Neh 9:26, compare Matt 23:30–31, thus Rudolph); rather it would be to the specific incident of the killing of the prophet Uriah (26:20–23) which took place during the reign of Jehoiakim, doubtless early in that reign (see Setting of chap. 26). Though only a single martyrdom, such an event would arouse in the copyist a memory of prophets killed in earlier centuries. But (to repeat) the text as here reconstructed would not carry such a clue.

The reference in 3:3 to a drought is understood here to refer to the great drought (14:1—15:9, so also 5:25; 8:13; 12:4; 23:10), but it seems to break the flow of thought in 3:1–5 and is thus taken here as a genuine word from Jrm but added later to vv 1–2, 4–5 (see Preliminary Observations).

Is the repeated accusation in these chapters of fertility-cult worship any aid in establishing a setting? Rudolph believes that chapter 2 describes circumstances which are pre-Deuteronomic.[47] But there was surely a resurgence of Baalism under Jehoiakim and Zedekiah, or at least Jrm so testified. Thus the word from Yahweh prohibiting Jrm from any further intercession on behalf of the people (7:16–20) was, by the analysis presented here, a reflection of the prophet's convictions after Jehoiakim burned the first scroll; and the main burden of that prohibition was that the fathers, mothers, and children each had their allotted tasks in preparation of cakes for the queen of heaven. And the last preaching of the prophet which is recorded, his words to the refugees from Babylonian occupation who had fled to the Egyptian delta (if there is validity to the narrative), makes

---

45   So also Berridge, p. 81, and compare further the discussion in Interpretation of 2:18.

46   See the reconstruction in Bright, *History*, 324–26.

47   Rudolph, p. 13.

the same accusation (44:15–28). But the evidence for the semipagan religious practices before the time of Josiah's reform suggests a slightly different picture: that evidence may be discerned in the word of the Deuteronomic historian for the period of the reign of Manasseh (2 Kgs 21:3–9) and in the words of Zephaniah for the early years of Josiah's reign. In both bodies of material there is indeed mention of Baalism, but there is also mention of the pagan priests (כְּמָרִים, 2 Kgs 23:5; Zeph 1:4; compare Hos 10:5), and Zephaniah mentions the god Milcom (Zeph 1:5) associated with the Ammonites (compare 2 Kgs 23:13). But in the mention of Baalism in Jrm's oracles there is no mention of the pagan priests, nor of Milcom or other deities associated with foreign powers with whom Judah was involved in vassalage to Assyria. Such argumentation is of course *e silentio*, but it does appear that Josiah had rid Judah of pagan practices which were specifically associated with foreign powers, and what reappeared in Jehoiakim's reign was the fertility worship which had always been associated with Canaanite Palestine; that is the situation which chapter 2 seems to reflect.[48]

The question of the evidence offered by the rubrics of 2:4 and 3:12, and in general the setting which the words of 3:12, 14–15, 18bβ imply, has already been discussed in Preliminary Observations, but it is necessary to discuss the contrasting conclusions of other commentators on these matters. Hyatt assumed that the words of the poetic lines in 3:12ff are an appeal to Judah to "repent" and that those words were secondarily misunderstood by an editor who thought they were words directed to the north to "return" to the south;[49] he also assumes that the reference to "Ephraim" and "Samaria" in chapter 31 betoken a setting at the time of the governorship of Gedaliah in 587 and thereafter. Hyatt's views were shaped by his chronology for Jrm: he proposed not only that Jrm was born in 627 but that his career began only in the reign of Jehoiakim;[50] there is therefore no room, in his estimation, for an early appeal to the north, for by Jehoiakim's time reunion with the north was a dead issue. On the other hand, most commentators (Duhm, Cornill, Rudolph, Bright) take both 3:12ff and the material in chapter 31 to be from the period in Jrm's

career during the reign of Josiah, when reunion with the north was a live issue; their high chronology, by which Jrm's public career began in 627, allows this possibility. The present study, as already noted, proposes a low chronology but assumes that the prophet's career began a few years before the death of Josiah.

What is likewise new here is the proposal to link 2:4–9 with 3:1–2, 4–5, 12, 14–15, 18bβ, both because of the specific occurrence of the word "tribes" in 2:4 and 3:14, and because of more general parallels of diction between the two sequences. If that linking is sound, then it only remains to try to determine, by rhetorical links, the extent of that early word to the north; thus the proposal set forth in Preliminary Observations.

If this rhetorical analysis of the material is sound, then the prefixing of 2:1–3 signals a reuse of that message to the north for the prophet's audience in Judah. What would have been the setting of that reuse? The diction of 2:1–3 offers two hints. First, there is the wording of the poem of 2:2–3. Thus both Lev 23:39 and Deut 16:13–15, which make provision for the feast of booths, use the term "harvest" (תְּבוּאָה) which occurs in 2:3. And it is to be noted that the feast of booths was early associated both with the vintage (Deut 16:13) and with the exodus from Egypt (Lev 23:43), and it is probable that the vintage is the assumed "harvest" in our Jer passage: when the theme of the foe's "eating" Israel occurs again, in 5:17, it is "your vines and fig trees" specifically which are eaten. The possibility is then open of a setting at the feast of booths.

Second, there is the phrase in the rubric of 2:1, literally "call out in the ears of" (קְרָא בְאָזְנֵי). The phrase occurs in the book again only in chapter 36 (vv 6, 10, 13, 14, 15, 21) for a reading to an audience from Jrm's scroll. The prophet is told to "call out" (קְרָא) the words of Yahweh in four other passages in the book; in all of these a place is named—in 7:2 it is the gate of the temple, in 19:2 it is the Potsherd Gate, and in 3:12 it is in a northerly direction, while in 11:6 and the present passage no precise location is given but it is clear that a general audience in Jerusalem is assumed. A large audience, then, is implied. And when it is noted that "call out in the ears of" occurs only once in Deuteronomy,

48   Holladay, "Coherent Chronology," 67–68.
49   Hyatt, p. 826.
50   Ibid., 779b.

precisely in Deut 31:11, in the instructions for the seven-year recitation of the Deuteronomic law, and that in 2:1ff material expresses Yahweh's accusation of covenant disloyalty (the *rîb*), then a setting at one of the septennial recitations of Deuteronomy suggests itself. That which (by the reckoning here adopted) took place in September/October 608 suggests itself: Jehoiakim has completed one year of his reign, and the religious and social circumstance of Judah was very different from that which prevailed seven years previously. This is the setting, then, which I propose for 2:1–3, the reuse of the material in 2:4—4:2 used earlier in the prophet's appeal to the north, and for (at least) some (if not all) of 2:10–25, 29–37. Question: Is there a clue in the curious word "community" (דּוֹר) in 2:31?—it may suggest a cultic assemblage (Ps 24:6: "This is the assemblage (דּוֹר) of those who seek [Yahweh]"). Does this sequence have the same setting? Several of the sequences in chap. 2 seem more appropriate, however, after the battle of Carchemish in 605 (2:14–19? 2:33–37?). In any event, material in these chapters which Jrm proclaimed between 608 and 605 he dictated in his first scroll in 605 (36:1) (see Preliminary Observations).

A few passages, by the analysis offered here, Jrm added in his second scroll (here dated 601/600 and thereafter). For 3:3 one can offer a setting during the great drought. For 2:26–28 it is possible to suggest a setting in 594 (see Preliminary Observations, and compare 7:21–28, Setting). For 3:20 it is not possible to be specific.

3:6–11. These verses are very late; the passage shares no characteristic with the conventional prose of Jer except for the short phrase "with all her heart" (v 10, compare 24:7; 29:13; 32:41). Admittedly the passage is short, so that the lack of such conventional phrases is not too significant; but at the same time the style is careless and inelegant and may show Aramaic influence (see Interpretation for the details). If the analysis given in Interpretation is correct, that the personification of

"Turncoat Israel" (מְשֻׁבָה יִשְׂרָאֵל) is based upon a misunderstanding of the syntax of v 12, then some time would have had to pass for that misunderstanding to arise. Its point of view contrasts with that of the Deuteronomic historian (2 Kgs 17:34–40),[51] and we would not be far wrong to assign the passage to the Persian period and understand it to have been stimulated by the allegories of Ezekiel 16 and 23 (see again Interpretation).

3:16–18bα. These verses likewise do not share the characteristics of the conventional prose of Jer except for the phrase "walk after the stubbornness of their evil heart" (v 17, compare 7:24; 9:13; 11:8; 13:10; 16:12; 18:12). The passage is similar in idiom and theme to 23:34–40; both passages doubtless belong in the Persian period.[52] The passage is also linked form-critically to 23:7–8 and 31:29–30 (the change of speech-pattern) and to 31:35–37, and there are hints in these passages that point to a setting in Nehemiah's time (fifth century: see Setting for each passage). On the other hand, the message that the ark of the covenant will not be missed may well be based on Jeremianic tradition; Jrm's interest in Shiloh (7:12; 26:6, 9) and Samuel (15:1) might well have focused his attention on the fate of the ark.

Interpretation

■ **2:1–2aα** *G* omits "The word of Yahweh . . . in the ears of Jerusalem as follows" entirely, substituting simply "and say" (καὶ εἶπε). Janzen suggests that chapter 2 originally had a shorter opening and that *M* expanded the text secondarily on the basis of 1:4, 11, 13; 3:12 and the like.[53] This view is to be rejected; each introductory rubric has its own integrity—Rudolph states correctly, "The LXX has shortened the whole introduction to καὶ εἶπε."[54]

The same form of instruction to a prophet, with "go" (infinitive absolute of הלך) followed by a waw-consecutive perfect is found twice outside Jer (2 Sam 24:12; Isa 38:5) and occurs in nine further instances within Jer.[55] Though the text of Isaiah 38 has varied 2 Kings 20 and

51 See Mordechai Cogan, "Israel in Exile—The View of a Josianic Historian," *JBL* 97 (1978) 43.
52 Petersen, *Late Prophecy*, 27–32.
53 Janzen, p. 113.
54 Rudolph, p. 14.
55 Jer 3:12; 13:1; 17:19; 19:1; 28:13; 34:2; 35:2, 13; 39:16; there is one further instance if one credits *G* in 22:1.

therefore might be a later reshaping, there is no reason to doubt the antiquity of the diction in 2 Samuel 24.[56] The second occurrence of "as follows" (לֵאמֹר) might seem excessive to modern tastes, but precisely the format of the present passage is also found in 28:13 and 39:16. We may conclude then that the present wording is a standard form for the beginning of a prophetic utterance and in its full solemnity stands here at the beginning of Jrm's words to the people of Judah.

The infinite absolute of "go" (הָלֹךְ) functions here as an emphatic imperative (compare 2 Kgs 5:10).[57] The phrase "call out in the ears of" suggests an address or a reading to a large assemblage (for details see Setting). The messenger formula "Thus Yahweh has said" appears here for the first of dozens of times in Jer; the formula belongs exclusively to prophetic literature and prophetic narratives.[58] The perfect tense ("has said") is preferable to render אָמַר.[59]

If this rubric serves to open the recension for the south, then it serves to supersede the very similar rubric in 3:12 (see there, and see Preliminary Observations).

■ **2:2aβb** The phrase normally translated "I remember" (זָכַרְתִּי לָךְ) carries several nuances which are unexpected for the modern reader. First, the verb is perfect; the imperfect is used when steady or permanent memory is intended (31:20), but the perfect of this verb appears to emphasize a particular past action with present consequences ("I have recalled and so now remember": compare Hos 7:2).[60] Second, the act of remembering is the act of calling to mind an image from the past which assists in determining action or influencing action;[61] "The act of remembrance is not simply inner reflection, but involves an action, an encounter with historical events."[62] In Jrm's diction the verb carries the nuance of "give attention to something,"[63] so that the present

phrase suggests "I have put my attention to the loyalty of your youth." The expression "in your favor" (literally "for you," לָךְ, disregarded, incidentally, in *G*) suggests with the verb a forensic nuance (compare Lev 26:45); the phrase refers to the legal situation of the defendant.[64] Far from being an expression of Yahweh's idle recollection, then, the phrase describes Yahweh's laying the image of the covenantal solidarity of the past alongside the covenantal rupture of the present, implying the necessity of taking action to rectify the rupture.

The second-person references here are feminine singular: Yahweh is addressing the people as his erstwhile bride.

The noun חֶסֶד (*ḥesed*, here "loyalty") is central to OT theology (*RSV* normally "steadfast love"; see Bibliography). The present discussion will deal with three issues: (1) the general meaning of *ḥesed*; (2) its ambiguity in the present passage in referring both to Israel's loyalty to Yahweh and to Yahweh's loyalty to Israel; and (3) the participation of both marriage imagery and suzerain-vassal imagery in its usage here.

(1) Typically it is the action by a superior to an inferior in a relationship to effect protection or deliverance for the latter; this action is perceived as a moral rather than a legal right, so that from the viewpoint of the inferior it implies a gift received.[65] In theological contexts, then, it refers to Yahweh's action to deliver or protect his covenant people Israel, perceived as a gracious gift. But just as Israel cannot force the saving action of Yahweh, so Yahweh cannot force gratitude or loyalty from Israel, so that the word may be used of Israel's faithful response to Yahweh as well.[66]

(2) The nuance of *ḥesed* in the present passage is not self-evident; is it Yahweh's *ḥesed* for Israel (so most commentators) or Israel's for Yahweh?[67] The Versions

56 Compare Hans W. Hertzberg, *I & II Samuel* (Philadelphia: Westminster, 1964) 415–16.

57 See GKC, sec. 113bb.

58 Westermann, *Basic Forms*, 34–36.

59 See Siegfried Wagner, "אָמַר," *TDOT* 1:339, and Wolff, *Joel and Amos*, 128.

60 See more generally GKC, sec. 106g.

61 Johannes Pedersen, *Israel, Its Life and Culture* (2 vols.; Copenhagen: Branner; London: Oxford University; 1926) 106–7.

62 Brevard S. Childs, *Memory and Tradition in Israel* (SBT 37; Naperville, IL: Allenson, 1962) 88.

63 Pieter A. H. de Boer, *Gedenken und Gedächtnis in der Welt des Alten Testaments* (Stuttgart: Kohlhammer, 1962) 36.

64 Hans J. Boecker, *Redeformen des Rechtslebens im Alten Testament* (WMANT 14; Neukirchen: Neukirchener, 1964) 105–11; compare his "Anklagereden und Verteidigungsreden im Alten Testament," *EvT* 20 (1960) 411–12.

65 Sakenfeld, pp. 3, 233–34.

66 Ibid., 235.

67 So Michael V. Fox, "Jeremiah 2:2 and the 'Desert Ideal,'" *CBQ* 35 (1973) 441–50.

afford no help. A close parallel is 31:3, where the same parallelism of ḥesed and אַהֲבָה ("love") occurs; there it is the ḥesed and love of Yahweh for Israel. Further, the description in v 3b here implies Yahweh's steady care for Israel. On the other hand, the immediate context of v 2b implies the loyalty of Israel for Yahweh. One may conclude that the expression is deliberately ambiguous, referring to the ḥesed and love of both Yahweh and Israel for each other within the covenant.

The parallel "love" (אַהֲבָה) has encouraged translators to find a rendering for ḥesed in the realm of the affections (Duhm: *Huld*, "grace, favor"; *RSV:* "devotion"). On the other hand, the root אהב "love" itself carries a political nuance in many contexts (see below), so that the hearer is pressed again into the context of covenant.

(3) Katharine D. Sakenfeld, in discussing the present passage, cites Hos 4:1 and 6:6 as well. Though she assumes that in Jer 2:2 ḥesed refers only to Israel's loyalty to Yahweh, her conclusions are still germane.

> The term can be used both in the context of "primary," personal relationship (marriage imagery) and of "secondary," political relationship (suzerain-vassal imagery . . .) . . . , just as in the pre-exilic secular usage. . . . As has been pointed out, Israel can never be in a position of power with respect to Yahweh so that she would be free from reprisal if she failed to meet her treaty obligations. In the secular usage both parties must maintain their responsibilities within a political relationship, but only the circumstantially superior party is said to do ḥesed. And even in the personal imagery of the marriage relationship one cannot escape Israel's subordination to Yahweh. . . . In its use with respect to Yahweh, Israel's ḥesed is abstracted from specific actions and moves toward faithfulness or loyalty, sole recognition of the suzerain.[68]

To summarize: the conclusion here is that ḥesed refers both to Yahweh's gracious love and support of Israel and to Israel's glad fidelity to Yahweh. In both directions the term designates outer conduct which goes beyond the minimum necessity, so that it indicates an inner attitude of affection as well. The word resonates strongly both with marriage and political imagery. No one English word is adequate, but "loyalty" will have to do.

Its parallel אַהֲבָה "love" covers as wide a spectrum of contexts as does the English word; the root may cover both Yahweh's love for Israel (31:3, already cited) and Israel's for Yahweh (Exod 20:6 and often), and not only the expected marriage imagery (Hos 3:1 and often) but the political one as well. The marriage imagery is obvious; "love" in vv 33–36, however, clearly has a political nuance. This use of "love" in a political sense is pre-Israelite: in the Amarna correspondence the Akkadian *rāmu* (cognate with רחם "be compassionate") is used of the "love" of princes for each other, the "love" of vassals to the pharaoh, the "love" of pharaoh to his vassals.[69] It continues in Israelite diction; Hiram, king of Tyre, "always loved David" (1 Kgs 5:15), and the expression "love God" in Deuteronomy is clearly within the orbit of covenantal language, sharing the political overtone of "love."[70] Jrm's use of the term here then suggests, as much as ḥesed does, a love of Yahweh for Israel marked by fidelity and a love of Israel for Yahweh marked by adherence to covenantal stipulations.[71] The covenant assumed here is of course that of Sinai associated with the exodus from Egypt, that exodus hinted at in the next line, "your walking after me in the wilderness."

The noun נְעוּרִים means "youth" (as a stage of life); compare the discussion of "youth" (נַעַר) in 1:6. For a woman it implies her situation before marriage (Lev 22:13), so that it is an apt parallel for כְּלוּלֹת, the time when one is a "bride" (כַּלָּה, v 32). It is probable that Jrm's diction here is stimulated by the phrasing of Hos 2:17: in a time of restoration Yahweh says that he will bring her into the wilderness, "and there she shall

---

68   Sakenfeld, pp. 173, 175, 176–77.
69   Alfred O. Haldar, "אָהַב," *TDOT* 1:101.
70   William L. Moran, "The Ancient Near Eastern Background of the Love of God in Deuteronomy," *CBQ* 25 (1963) 77–87.
71   See further John Arthur Thompson, "The Significance of the Verb *love* in the David-Jonathan Narratives in 1 Samuel," *VT* 234 (1974) 334–38; and "Israel's 'lovers,'" *VT* 27 (1977) 475–81.

willingly follow as in the days of her youth (כִּימֵי נְעוּרֶיהָ), as at the time when she came out of the land of Egypt." Both Hosea and Jrm are idealizing the honeymoon time, the time of the exodus.

The phrase הָלַךְ אַחֲרֵי is literally "walk behind, follow (someone)." A woman walks after a man with whom she is associated (Gen 24:5; 1 Sam 25:42); it thus suggests human loyalty. But it is also used in religious contexts: Israel is to "walk after" Yahweh (Deut 13:5) but instead has "walked after" her lovers, the Baals (Hos 2:7; Jer 2:5). Specifically, the phrase may have cultic overtones: in 1 Kgs 18:21 Elijah says, "If Yahweh is God, follow him; but if Baal, then follow him." The present passage thus may imply "your worshiping me in the wilderness."[72]

The מִדְבָּר "wilderness" is perfectly defined by its parallel "a land unsown," the area receiving insufficient rainfall for rain-fed farming. It is not necessarily the sand desert but includes the parched area of Sinai, the Negeb, the steppes of the Transjordan that produce nothing but thorns and briers (Judg 8:7; Isa 41:18–19; 55:13);[73] see further 9:9. It is a fearful place, unfit for human habitation (v 6). That Israel should have been loyal to Yahweh through the wilderness is loyalty indeed.

■ 2:3 Israel is identified as קֹדֶשׁ to Yahweh. The normal translation for the line, "Israel was holy to Yahweh," is somewhat misleading, for קֹדֶשׁ is a noun, not an adjective, and further "holy" suggests moral purity, a nuance not central to the passage. Both קֹדֶשׁ and its parallel "first fruits" (רֵאשִׁית) are words drawn from the cult, and this is surprising—the preexilic prophets did not ordinarily use cultic language to define Israel's calling. The noun קֹדֶשׁ refers to what is within Yahweh's sphere, particularly his cultic sphere. Priests who are disobedient fail to make a distinction between what is appropriate to Yahweh (קֹדֶשׁ) and what is fit only for ordinary use, common, "profane" (חֹל, Ezek 22:26). The primeval holy mountain, identified with Zion, is קֹדֶשׁ (Ezek 28:14), and so are the garments of priests (Ezek 42:14). The merchandise of

Tyre (Isa 23:18) will in the end time be at Yahweh's disposal. And this is no doubt the basic meaning of the word in the present passage: Israel has been Yahweh's possession (so also Rudolph: "Jahweh's Eigentum was Israel"). "Holiness is always most closely connected with the concept of the property of God."[74] Because it is here parallel with "first fruits," Johannes Lindblom translates it here by "consecrated gift."[75] Israel was a gift given to Yahweh, so that she was completely at Yahweh's disposal, just as thoroughly as the first fruits given by a farmer to Yahweh, or indeed as thoroughly as the merchandise of Tyre in the end time. Israel is no longer her own, free to pursue the ordinary goals of life.

The shift of reference to Yahweh from the first person in v 2 ("after me") to the third person appears odd but is not; 5:10–11, displaying a similar semantic field, offers the opposite shift.

Israel is the "first fruits of his harvest" (רֵאשִׁית תְּבוּאָתֹה). Such a phrase appears in Prov 3:9 as a general term for whatever is the first of the yield, whether of grain, wine, oil, or fruits (Num 18:12–14). "In Israel these רֵאשִׁית dedications . . . were presented as signs of gratitude and of dependence on the Lord of the land."[76] Here, then, Israel is depicted as herself being given as a gift of gratitude to Yahweh. Given the likeness of diction of 5:10–11 to the present passage, it is likely that the metaphor Jrm had in mind here was specifically the vineyard harvest; תְּבוּאָה is used of the vineyard in Deut 22:9 (and the root קֹדֶשׁ appears in that context). For the whole image of Israel as the "possession" of Yahweh, compare the use of "property" (נַחֲלָה) of Yahweh to designate Israel in 12:7.

There are one or two antecedent passages in the prophets that may throw light on Jrm's diction here. The more secure one is Hos 9:10: "Like grapes in the wilderness I [Yahweh] found Israel; like a first fruit on a fig tree (כְּבִכּוּרָה בִתְאֵנָה)[77] I discovered your fathers." Then if an emendation I have suggested for Amos 6:1 is valid, that verse may also be relevant.[78] My suggestion is

72 So *HALAT*, 237a.

73 Denis Baly, *The Geography of the Bible* (New York: Harper, 1974) 101–5.

74 George E. Mendenhall, *The Tenth Generation, The Origins of the Biblical Tradition* (Baltimore: Johns Hopkins, 1973) 207.

75 Lindblom, *Prophecy*, 327.

76 Kraus, *Worship*, 117.

77 The following word בראשיתה is surely a gloss; see Wolff, *Hosea*, 160.

78 William L. Holladay, "Amos vi 1bβ: a suggested solution," *VT* 22 (1972) 107–10.

to read תְּבֻאַת לָהֶם for the puzzling וּבָאוּ לָהֶם; by this reading those who are at ease in Zion are sarcastically described as "the pick of the first (fruits) of the nations, the cream of the crop of the house of Israel," and the occurrence of רֵאשִׁית and *תְּבֻאַת in parallel cola would be an example of the break-up of stereotyped phrases.[79] One may suspect, therefore, that Jrm in v 3a is using liturgical phrases otherwise unknown to us to remind Israel of her calling. Victor Maag makes a similar point on the passage: "Jeremiah could scarcely have invented this formulation—he found it present among the people."[80]

Matching the shift in personal reference to Yahweh from v 2 (first person) to v 3 (third person) is the shift in reference to Israel from v 2 (second singular feminine) to v 3 (third singular masculine): the suffix on אֹכְלָיו matches the masculine "Israel." The use of "eat" (אכל) meta-phorically for miliary conquest is old:[81] Balaam in one of his oracles described Israel as one who "shall eat up . . . his adversaries" (Num 24:8), and Jrm may have had this phraseology in mind when he refers to the enemies of Israel in those early days who attempted to conquer Israel (compare further 5:17). The verb אשם means more than "became guilty" (*RSV*); it means "make oneself culpable, punishable."[82] Thus *NEB* "no one who devoured her went unpunished," and *JB* "anyone who ate of this had to pay for it."

For "disaster" (רָעָה) see 1:14; the verb "come" (בוא) occurs often with the noun in such a context (Mic 3:11 and repeatedly in Jer). The verbs are imperfects here, suggesting that such disasters were a steady feature of past history.[83]

■ **2:4** The appeal to listen, coming on the heels of the earlier introductory words in v 2, appears odd but is not to be excised (Rudolph, against Giesebrecht and Volz). Jrm could use "tribes" (מִשְׁפָּחוֹת) to indicate the northern tribes (see 1:15), and it is the proposal of the present study that this verse originally introduced Jrm's word to the north (see Preliminary Observations). The fact that

the references of "tribes" and "Israel" could be shifted from the north to the south allowed the words to stand when vv 1–3 were prefixed. The verse is a summons to the accused (see Form; Mic 6:1 is comparable).

"Household of Israel" was the designation of the tribal league at the time of the judges (1 Sam 7:2, 3) and of the kingship of Saul and David (2 Sam 1:12; 6:5), and "household of Jacob" is a poetic synonym (Amos 3:13) functioning as a reminder of Israel's election.[84]

■ **2:5** The passage begins with a rhetorical question; for the syntax see Joüon, *Gramm.*, sec. 144d, and for parallels to such rhetorical questions see Form.

The noun עָוֶל is an antonym of צְדָקָה (Ezek 18:24); it is thus "injustice" or "wrong" in the ethical sense. Behind the present shocking question are two sorts of expressions. First there is the expression for the basis for divorce, Deut 24:1, כִּי מָצָא בָהּ עֶרְוַת דָּבָר "because he has found in her some indecency." But of course in Israelite society a wife may not divorce her husband in the way a husband may divorce his wife: so in Jrm's metaphor it is a shocking thing that Israel should consider divorcing her husband Yahweh (compare 3:1). Second, there is the affirmation of the Song of Moses, Deut 32:4, "The Rock, his work is sound, / for all his ways are justice (מִשְׁפָּט); / a God of faithfulness (אֱמוּנָה) and without wrong (וְאֵין עָוֶל), / just (צַדִּיק) and right (וְיָשָׁר) is he." Of course!—there is no blemish in Yahweh. But now Israel has chosen the Baals rather than Yahweh. The notion of comparing Yahweh with the Baals is an old one; Elijah forced a comparison (1 Kgs 18:21), and Hosea pictures Israel as saying that Yahweh offers a better subsistence for Israel than do the Baals (Hos 2:9). But Jrm by his rhetorical question forces the listener to conceive the inconceivable—that Yahweh might have a defect. And though the question is a rhetorical one, the fact that Jrm perceives Yahweh to be raising it at all suggests a kind of capacity of kenosis (compare Phil 2:7) on God's part, a (theoretical) willingness to admit fault which is hinted at again in the "new covenant" passage (31:31–34), that

79 Ezra Z. Melamed, "Break-up of Stereotype Phrases as an Artistic Device in Biblical Poetry," *Scripta Hierosolymitana* 8 (1961) 115–53; Dahood, *Psalms I*, xxxiv and often.

80 Victor Maag, *Text, Wortschatz und Begriffswelt des Buches Amos* (Leiden: Brill, 1951) 192.

81 The Akkadian cognate was used in the same way; Magnus Ottosson, "אָכַל," *TDOT* 1:236.

82 Wolff, *Hosea*, 89, on 4:15; and, more generally, Diether Kellermann, "אָשַׁם," *TDOT* 1:435–36.

83 GKC sec. 107e.

84 Wolff, *Joel and Amos*, 201 and n. 7. For a survey of "house(hold)" in such contexts, see Harry A. Hoffner, "בַּיִת," *TDOT* 2:114.

Yahweh has learned from the failure of the earlier covenant and will plug the loopholes next time (v 32 there).

The "fathers" are the forebears of the audience, as often (e.g., 2 Kgs 21:17; compare the same usage in Jer 7:22). These are the Israelites after the exodus from Egypt (v 6) who turned to Baal worship.

The second colon is introduced by כִּי, not necessarily "that," but the beginning of the accusations.[85] The verb רחק means "become distant." There are evidently no instances earlier than Jrm for this verb in the context of Israel's distancing herself from Yahweh; Ezek 11:15 and 44:10 are doubtless dependent on the present passage. But the plea that Yahweh not distance himself from the worshiper is found five times in the Psalms.[86] What the worshiper asks Yahweh not to do, Israel as a whole has done to Yahweh.

Israel's wandering from Yahweh means her walking "behind" his rivals, in contrast to her walking "behind" Yahweh in the time of loyalty (v 2). The rivals are here called "emptiness" (הַהֶבֶל). These lines are full of assonance (וַיֶּהְבָּלוּ, בִּי עָוֶל, הַהֶבֶל מֵעָלַי and the related verb), but more pertinent is that fact that the word הַהֶבֶל is evidently chosen as a pun on "Baal" (הַבַּעַל: so Bright)—compare v 8. The term basically means "breath" (Isa 57:13),[87] but its usual meaning in the OT is "nothingness." It occurs in the plural in 8:19 (as it does in Deut 32:21) for nonexistent deities. One may conclude that though Jrm was not the first to use the term this way, he exploited its potential. It may be noted in passing that 2 Kgs 17:15 borrows the whole of this line to indict Samaria in part of a passage attributed to the later Deuteronomistic redactor.[88]

In the present form of text the verse ends with the single verb וַיֶּהְבָּלוּ, related to "a nothing" (הֶבֶל). Aside from the present passage and its imitation in 2 Kgs 17:15 הבל qal appears only twice in the OT, Ps 62:11 and Job 27:12. The question arises whether the verb here means "become nothing" or "devote oneself to what is nothing";

both meanings have been proposed. But the latter meaning is doubtful: if it were the case, it would result in a tautology. The translation offered here, "shared in nothingness," covers both nuances (compare the implication of "walking in the Lie," 23:14). The idea that one becomes like what one worships is found in Hos 9:10: "But they came to Baal-peor, and consecrated themselves to shame [= Baal? see the commentaries], and became detestable like their 'friend' [see again the commentaries]"; compare Ps 115:8 = 135:8. Theologically the passage resembles 7:19: "Is it I they are offending? Is it not themselves so that they are left shamefaced?"

A colon consisting of a single word is dubious,[89] so that the text may have suffered haplography (see Text, Structure): the colon may originally have consisted of the present verb followed by another resembling it closely (compare the sequence of verbs in the reconstructed text of 3:5 and in 5:27b–28a). One possibility is וַיֵּחָבְלוּ, "and were ruined" (חבל nip'al);[90] Prov 13:13 cites this form, though the pu'al may be preferable there (and here?), וַיְחֻבְּלוּ. Another possibility is the qal stem of that verb, וַיַּחְבְּלוּ, "and offended" (compare Job 34:31). Still another possibility is וַיִּבָּהֲלוּ, "and were terrified" (בהל nip'al: compare the semantic field of 4:9). But obviously there is no sure way to reconstruct the text.

■ 2:6 The first colon is parallel with the first colon of v 5: what the fathers neglected to say is intertwined with what they did. The verb אמר may mean "ask oneself" (NJV). The question "Where is Yahweh?" is not ironic, as "Where is your God?" so often is (2:28; Ps 42:4, 11); the question is posed in earnest concern (see Form). The use of the participles הַמַּעֲלֶה and הַמּוֹלִיךְ suggest the constant possibility of acts of rescue (compare Job 35:10).

"Who brought us up from the land of Egypt" is a traditional formula; similar phrasing, with participle, is found in Deut 8:15; Josh 24:17; and elsewhere. The parallel participle "who led" (הַמּוֹלִיךְ) is not cited elsewhere.

Following "from the land of Egypt" come three

---

85   Gemser, p. 129; for the translation "look," compare Pedersen, I/II 118.
86   Pss 22:12, 20; 35:22; 38:22; 71:12.
87   Klaus Seybold, "הֶבֶל," *TDOT* 3:315.
88   James A. Montgomery, *A Critical and Exegetical Commentary on the Books of Kings* (ICC; New York: Scribner's, 1951) 469; Gray, *Kings*, 645–49.
89   Michael Patrick O'Connor will not allow it, while

James Kugel will; see Foreword, nn. 4 and 5, and the remarks there.
90   J. J. Glück suggests that by paronomasia this verb was the real verb intended here, "Paronomasia in Biblical Literature," *Semitics* 1 (University of South Africa, 1970) 68.

repetitions of "in the land of" (בְּאֶרֶץ), entailing an elaborate description of the wilderness; it may be an expansion of Isa 30:6. The poetic structure of the verse is very close to that of 5:15 (see Structure). The words are chosen for their assonance (the sibilants š and ṣ; 'ărābâ and 'ābar) as well as synonymy. The double genitive construction, which occurs here twice, is usually avoided but does occur;[91] the present example is baroque in extent.

"Waste" (עֲרָבָה, "Arabah") refers to the depression formed by the Dead Sea and the rift valley from the Dead Sea to the Gulf of Aqaba;[92] it is mentioned as being on the path of the Israelites in their wilderness wanderings (Deut 2:8). "Ravine" (שׁוּחָה) is a "pit" (compare 18:20, 22). It is not so much that it is a "land of pits" (RSV) as that the Arabah is itself a pit, a trap out of which it is difficult to come;[93] "ravine" is the rendering of Bright.

On the noun צַלְמָוֶת (here "utter darkness") there is a large literature. Given the Arabic ẓalima "be dark" and cognates in Ethiopic and Akkadian, critical scholarship has assumed recently that the traditional understanding of the expression as צֵל מָוֶת "shadow of death" (so already T and S) is a folk-etymology and that the true form is *צַלְמוּת or *צַלְמֹת.[94] But recently, given compound nouns in Ugaritic, particularly those with 'il,[95] there has been a swing to the view that the traditional interpretation is correct[96] (compare "supreme darkness," מַאְפֵּלְיָה, v 31).

The verse is completed by two dependent clauses related genitivally to the preceding "land."[97] The normal diction for the expression of uninhabitability uses a participle (4:29; 9:11); the perfect verbs here then suggest action completed before the time of the exodus (thus: never before crossed); so KJV, NEB, NJV, but not RSV or JB. NEB: "where no man ever trod, no man made his home."

But this description of the empty land is not simply geographical; it is ontological. This is the realm farthest from history, since no one has lived there. The impossible has happened: the God of history has taken our ancestors through realms untouched by history before; where no one crosses, God led them across (compare the rhetoric of Isa 43:1–2, regarding a new exodus from Babylon). For the association of "wilderness" and "darkness" as realms at the edge of God's reach, see Ps 107:4–5, 10.[98] Question: Does שׁוּחָה "pit" suggest Sheol?—its cognate שַׁחַת does (Ps 30:10 and often). Jrm is then piling up synonyms here not only to tell of the horrors of the wilderness but of the grace of God in leading the forebears through an area as chaotic and as destructive as that wilderness.

The quotation ends with the verse, as the opening clause of v 7 makes clear.

■ 2:7 A hint of contemporaneity was achieved in v 6 by the participles; a similar hint is given here by the use of "you" rather than "them": "I brought you in," for you, the hearers, are still the recipients of the land. "Bring in" (בוא hip'il) is traditional in this context (Deut 26:9); hip'il (causative) verbs constantly underline the guidance of Yahweh. He had brought the ancestors through the nightmare land described so fully in v 6, and now he has "brought you" into another sort of land, אֶרֶץ הַכַּרְמֶל, here "land of gardens." This land, with the definite article, is set over against הַמִּדְבָּר (so the vocalization), "the wilderness," v 6; so again 4:26. The noun כַּרְמֶל appears to be related to כֶּרֶם "vineyard," but is contrasted not only with "wilderness" but with "forest" (e.g., Isa 29:17; 32:15), so that it means land that is fertile and productive. In the desert one is thirsty; here one can eat, and in plenty: what a miraculous contrast!

Verse 7a is in contrast to v 6 in the shift from the nightmare land to the land of gardens; but in v 7b there is a new contrast, "I brought you in," but then "you came in" and ruined the land of gardens. And the land was not given to Israel, it is "my land," Yahweh's land. This view of the land is consonant with Lev 25:23 and is rather different from the more common affirmation that the

91   GKC sec. 128a; Joüon, Gramm., sec. 129b.
92   Simon Cohen, "Arabah," IDB 1:177–79; Baly, Geography, 202–9.
93   "It is well-nigh impassable," Baly, Geography, 208.
94   So Zorell and KB.
95   E. g., tlḥn 'il, "magnificent [divine] table," 4.1.39.
96   So D. Winton Thomas, "צַלְמָוֶת in the Old Testament," JSS 7 (1962) 199–200; Dahood, Psalms

I, 147.
97   GKC sec. 130d.
98   For these themes see Pedersen, I/II 462–64.

land is a gift (Exod 20:12, and constantly in Deuter-onomy and elsewhere).[99] The parallel, "inheritance" (נַחֲלָה), means "land, (inalienable) property," usually family property gained by inheritance; compare 3:19; 12:7–10.[100] The hearers defiled Yahweh's land and made it loathsome. These terms are strong and come out of the orbit of the cult. Lev 18:19–30 lists offenses that "defile" (טמא pi'el) the land: incest, sodomy, child sacrifice; Num 35:34 mentions murder, and Deut 21:23 the leaving of the corpse of a criminal to hang from a tree overnight. The land has thus been made loathsome (תּוֹעֵבָה), a term again occurring repeatedly in Lev 18:22–30; it is a term used not only in reference to sexual sins but to pagan idols, everything offensive to Yahweh and his community. Jrm considers the present situation to be a parade example of Lev 18:19–30; though the gross crimes of Leviticus may not have been evident, the situation is as gross in Yahweh's eyes as if these crimes were committed daily. (One notes in passing the chiastic structure of v 7b which is both semantic and assonant.)[101]

■ **2:8** Exegesis and analysis of the structure of this verse are mutually dependent. How many groups are referred to here? How does the last colon fit with the rest? Commentators who have analyzed the verse as con-taining six cola (assuming "Where is Yahweh?" to be a separate line)[102] are wrong; there must be five cola. At least five solutions have been proposed.

(1) Because "priests" and "prophets" are so often parallel (e.g., 5:31), it is tempting to see these two as bracketing the verse. By this understanding "those dealing with the law" are the priests (compare 18:18), so that the first two cola balance the last two, and the "shepherds" (= rulers) take up the unparalleled third colon. This seems to be the analysis of Bright (followed by John Arthur Thompson).[103] (2) Volz assumes there are four groups referred to; the fifth colon, by his analysis, describes the people's action (subject simply "one"). (3) Rudolph assumes three groups, identifying the priests and "those dealing with the law," but other-wise agrees with Volz. (4) John M. Berridge assumes two groups, the priests (the first two cola) and the prophets, proposing that the "shepherds" in the third colon is synonymous with "prophets."[104] Though he claims he is construing the verse "in parallel fashion throughout," he bypasses the problem of the last colon altogether. (5) Daniel Grossberg has recently pointed out the climactic function of the fifth colon:[105] it differs from the previous four in offering a finite verb after a preposition in place of the expected noun, and (obviously) in not specifying a subject. He concludes that there are four classes of leaders indicted (so Volz) and that the fifth colon refers to all the four classes just named (not "the people" as Rudolph and Volz assume). This thesis is convincing.

It is striking that each subject precedes its verb; this in itself indicates that four different classes are referred to.

Though the verb in the first colon of v 8 (אָמְרוּ) is identical with that in the first colon of v 6, it must be translated as an English perfect: the "fathers" were in a previous generation, but the priests are part of the present. If the priests are the cultic mediators between Yahweh and the community, and then they do not seek Yahweh, ask about him, look for him, then they have failed their task.

Who are "those dealing in the law"? The verb תפש means "take hold of, seize"; "handle the law" (RSV) is good, "administer the law" (JB) is correct but a bit abstract. NJV translates "the guardians of the Teaching." There is much evidence to identify this group with the priests (see above): the priests have to do with תּוֹרָה

99 Gerhard von Rad, "The Promised Land and Yahweh's Land in the Hexateuch," *The Problem of the Hexateuch and Other Essays* (New York: McGraw-Hill, 1966) 79–93; Walter Brueggemann, *The Land: Place as Gift, Promise and Challenge in Biblical Faith* (Philadelphia: Fortress, 1977) esp. 122.

100 Harold O. Forshey, "The Construct Chain *naḥalat YHWH / 'elōhîm*," *BASOR* 220 (December 1975) 51–53.

101 John S. Kselman, "Semantic-Sonant Chiasmus in Biblical Poetry," *Bib* 58 (1977) 222–23.

102 So Volz and Rudolph (*BHS*).

103 John Arthur Thompson, *The Book of Jeremiah* (NICOT; Grand Rapids: Eerdmans, 1980).

104 Berridge, p. 140.

105 Daniel Grossberg, "Noun/Verb Parallelism: Syntactic or Asyntactic," *JBL* 99 (1980) 486–87; "Canticles 3:10 in the Light of a Homeric Analogue and Biblical Poetics," *BTB* 11 (1981) 75.

(torah), normally translated "law" (18:18), though the term is broader and more generally means "instruction."[106] On the other hand Jrm seems to refer in 8:8 to a scribal group who claim mastery of Yahweh's law; if this group is distinct from the priests, then Jrm may have in mind the cultic concerns of the priests and the teaching and interpreting functions of the scribes. The verb "know" (ידע) is a word of intimacy, or personal relation (1:5), but its use in political contexts makes it appropriate in covenant lawsuits.[107] Those who are charged with mediating Yahweh's instructions, then, have broken covenant with him.

The "shepherds" are the rulers, as often; the Assyrian cognate rē'û was so used.[108] The passage in 23:1–4, from a later period of the prophet's career, is a useful parallel. The rulers have rebelled against Yahweh. The expression פשע ב is frequently used of transgressing against God (Isa 1:2; Hos 7:13), but its political overtones (compare 1 Kgs 12:19, where it refers to political revolt) makes it useful here in the colon following "have not known me," with its own political nuance.

The prophets are trafficking not with Yahweh but with "the Baal"—the deity carries the definite article. What was only hinted at in the word הֶהָבֶל in v 5 is now made explicit. Jrm elsewhere uses both the singular "the Baal" (23:13) and the plural "the Baals" (2:23) without seeming differentiation. Baal was the Canaanite god of fertility, conceived of both in general and in particular local manifestations.[109]

The last line of the verse is climactic (see above). As the first four cola have the stressed subjects before their respective verbs, so in this last colon a prepositional phrase precedes the verb, and the object of the preposition is the unexpected verb phrase "they do not profit" (לֹא־יוֹעִלוּ). The phrase "walk after" is a repetition of the same phrase in vv 2 and 5, bringing this portion of the oracle to a close: instead of worshiping Yahweh (v 2) the leaders worship "those who do not profit," those who are of no use. It is another pun on "Baal" (Bright), parallel to "a nothing" (הֶהָבֶל) in v 5. But since the singular לֹא־יוֹעִיל would have made a better word-play (and since this singular does appear in v 11), one can only conclude that the plural here, alongside the singular of "the Baal" just above, is deliberate, as if to say that the devotees of Baal cannot count and do not know the difference between monotheism and polytheism. (Assonance, however, might have played a part in the use of the syllable -û here.) If there is an echo of Isa 30:6 in v 6 just above, then there is surely an echo of Isa 30:5 in the present verse: Isaiah there accuses Judah of depending on Egypt, a "useless people" (עַם לֹא־יוֹעִילוּ).

The people in general may have become disloyal to Yahweh (vv 5–7), but it is specifically the leaders who have turned their back on their calling.

■ 2:9 The conjunction "therefore, that is why" (לָכֵן) normally introduces the announcement of judgment after the accusation (so 5:14);[110] here, however, it announces Yahweh's consequent legal pursuit of his people (see Preliminary Observations, Form, Setting). The adverb עד is curious; it evidently means "once more." But what was the first time? By the proposal of the present study, this verse was originally part of Jrm's word to the north (see Preliminary Observations). In that context, then, the original confrontation of Yahweh with Israel was in 721, so there will be a fresh confrontation. But Jrm made fresh use of this material to address the south; in that context, the original confrontation was with the north, and the fresh confrontation is with the south.

There is a parallel between the first colon of v 9 ("I

---

106 For Torah as "instruction," and its connection with the priests, see Walter J. Harrelson, "Law in the OT," *IDB* 3:86a, and the bibliography, 89b; and de Vaux, *Ancient Israel*, 353–55.

107 See Interpretation on 1:5 and n. 43 there.

108 So BDB, KB.

109 There is an enormous literature on the topic, particularly since the decipherment of the Ugaritic literature; see conveniently G. Ernest Wright, *Biblical Archaeology* (Philadelphia: Westminster, 1962) chap. 7; John Gray, "Baal," *IDB* 1:328–29, with bibliography; William F. Albright, *Yahweh and the Gods of*

Canaan, A Historical Analysis of Two Contrasting Faiths (New York: Doubleday, 1968); Cross, *CMHE*; Martin J. Mulder, "בַּעַל," *TDOT* 2:192–200.

110 Westermann, *Basic Forms*, 149; March, "Prophecy," 160.

shall enter suit with you," אָרִיב אֶתְכֶם) and the first colon of v 7 ("and I brought you [into a land of gardens]," וָאָבִיא אֶתְכֶם): Yahweh continues to take action with his hearers, if not in grace, then in judgment. It is not easy to find a good English equivalent for רִיב; our words tend either to be too specific in their legal denotation or too general to communicate the forensic context. It means "argue out in public," particularly in the context of legal dispute.[111] Many translations use "accuse" for this passage (*NAB*, *NJV*), which is good if one understands by it a formal legal accusation. Yahweh is putting Israel on trial (compare *JB*) for breaking the covenant. And it is the hearers who must face Yahweh's lawsuit, not simply the religious leaders named in v 8: the leaders may set the pace in disobedience, but everyone is responsible to Yahweh. And he will continue the lawsuit to later generations until he gains satisfaction.

■ **2:10–11** Verse 10 begins with כִּי which does not mean "for" (*RSV*), since what follows is not in any sense a reason for what has preceded; instead it marks a beginning (or the renewal) of argumentation (see Form)—for the translation "look," compare v 5 above. The immediate antecedent for "cross (עִבְרוּ) to the shores of the Cypriots and see" is Amos 6:2, "go off (עִבְרוּ) to Calneh and see." Who is addressed in the plural imperatives? Doubtless the witnesses to the public disputation. There is a vocative, "heavens," mentioned in v 12. It is grotesque to visualize the heavens crossing to Cyprus; instead we must simply understand conventional diction in the lawsuit context, by which the assemblage is asked whether there is any precedent anywhere else for the defendant's conduct.

The first destination is the אִיֵּי כִתִּיִּים. The אִיִּים are coastlands and islands, land next to water, land available to sea-going trade. The כִתִּיִּים are, strictly speaking, the inhabitants of *כִתִּי (compare Phoenician *kt, kty*), the city the Greeks called Kition, present-day Larnaca on Cyprus. So the term refers to the Cypriots in general, and, more generally still, the population of the islands

and coastlands of the eastern Mediterranean, later of the Greeks in general (compare 1 Macc 1:1) and of the Romans (Dan 11:30).[112] Jrm intends no geographical precision here, but "the Cypriots" is not misleading.

The second destination is "Kedar," an important Arab tribe (Gen 25:13) located in general east of Transjordan in northern Arabia (compare the oracle against Kedar in 49:28–33).[113] The kingdom of Kedar traded widely (Ezek 27:21), as did the Cypriots. The two peoples represent the extremes of west and east for Jrm. The verb הִתְבּוֹנְנוּ (בִּין hitpoʻlel) means "study, take a good look" (1 Kgs 3:21).

The mention of the foreign peoples of Cyprus and Kedar in v 10 and the mention of "my people" in v 11 enclose a tightknit tricolon which raises the theoretical question: Is there any precedent anywhere for a nation to decide to trade gods?—foreign nations do not do it, even when their gods are nonexistent! (For the expression "non-gods," compare the parallel expressions in Deut 32:17 and 21.) The verb הָיָה nipʻal (Text, v 10, note b) occurs occasionally, in the meaning "occur, be done" (5:30). For the impersonal feminine in the case of both *נִהְיְתָה and כָּזֹאת see GKC sec. 144b. The verb הֵמִיר, analyzed as the hipʻil of either מוּר or יָמַר[114] means "exchange, barter." Trading peoples like the Cypriots and the tribe of Kedar are masters of barter and exchange, but they certainly do not exchange their own gods for others.

For the hearer of the first colon of v 11 אֱלֹהִים is ambiguous, "a god" or "gods." The ambiguity is cleared up in the second colon with "they" (הֵמָּה), but the touch of ambiguity makes a good parallel for "their glory" (= Yahweh) in the third colon. Other nations have many gods, but "my people" have only me, "their glory," and that glory they have bartered away.

The immediate precedent for this diction is Hos 4:7, which evidently originally read "their glory for dishonor they exchanged" (כְּבוֹדָם בְּקָלוֹן הֵמִירוּ).[115] Hosea evidently intended "their glory" not to apply to God himself but to

111 See Gemser, pp. 120–25; Limburg, pp. 291–304; and, for a summary of various views on the verb, Eiji Suganuma, "The Covenant *Rib* Form in Jeremiah Chapter 2: A Form Critical Study," *Journal of the College of Dairy Agriculture* 4 (Nopporo, Hokkaido, Japan, 1972) 123–25.

112 For the details see Jonas C. Greenfield, "Kittim," *IDB* 3:40–41.

113 John Alexander Thompson, "Kedar," *IDB* 3:3–4.

114 BDB: מוּר; Zorell and *HALAT*, both verbs.

115 See v 11, Text note a—a, see Wolff, *Hosea*, 4:7, Text note i.

the position of the priests (William R. Harper)[116] or to their calling to cultivate the knowledge of God (Wolff). But if Jrm knew Hosea's phrase (and he doubtless did), then he took it to apply to Yahweh himself, and the phraseology of Ps 3:4 would encourage this. "Their glory," then, in the present context, is their (object of) adoration,[117] him in whom they are to glory, and him they have bartered away for לוֹא יוֹעִיל, something worthless (for the theological challenge of the diction see the Text note, and for a similar expression see v 32). The plural appeared at the end of v 8; now we have the singular. There is a kind of ultimate horror in the fact that Israel should barter away her sovereign Lord, who brought her out of Egypt, through the desert and into the land, bartered him away for some god or other of nature, a will-o'-the-wisp Baal who claimed much but brought nothing to the worshiper.

■ **2:12** Yahweh's address to the heavens begins with שֹׁמּוּ שָׁמַיִם "be horrified, O heavens," surely a parody of Isaiah's phrase שִׁמְעוּ שָׁמַיִם "hear, O heavens" (Isa 1:2; compare Mic 1:2; 6:1). The phrasing is effective not only in the word-play and the fact that the emotional content of שֹׁמּוּ is extreme alongside of שִׁמְעוּ, but also in that Jrm has postponed the address beyond the beginning of the accusation. The translation "be horrified" is an attempt to mimic "hear" a bit. The verb שׁמם (and related nouns) appears frequently in Jer; it means both to be paralyzed by a physical or psychic blow or deprivation[118] and to be desolate or depopulated—it thus indicates the state of a person or city when all liveliness has vanished. And it is the heavens whom Yahweh is addressing as the representative of the cosmic powers who are witnesses at the law-court scene: the background is the metaphor of Yahweh's council.[119] There are a whole array of such possible witnesses: heaven and earth (Isa 1:2), mountains and hills (Mic 6:1–2), the peoples of the earth (Mic 1:2). One expects Jrm to name the "earth" as a correlative to "heavens" here, but it may be that eventually 6:19 was perceived to be that correlative. So: only the heavens are

addressed, and how ironic that they should be told to "be appalled" (*RSV*, *NJV*), to "be desolate" like some depopulated area (Ezek 33:28)! The phrase "at this" (עַל־זֹאת) echoes "like this" (כָּזֹאת) in v 10: this is an unprecedented situation. The verb שׂער is parallel to שׁמם: it is a denominative from שֵׂעָר "hair" and means "bristle, be struck with terror so that the hair stands on end" (for the parallelism compare Ezek 27:35; 32:10). One may note that the verb שׂער occurs in Deut 32:17, a verse which may be antecedent to Jer 2:11 (see above); that verb is normally translated "know, be acquainted" (BDB, KB) and thus assumed to be homonymous with the verb here. One wonders: is a double meaning involved here in this verb?

The third verb, חָרְבוּ, has caused trouble to the Versions: *G* reads ἐπὶ πλεῖον "exceedingly," thus הַרְבֵּה while *S* reads *wdḥlw* "and fear," therefore perhaps חִרְדוּ; these renderings have attracted the commentators, to say nothing of emendations unsupported by the Versions. But there is no need to emend the text. The arrangement of the verbs in these two cola reflects in general the arrangement of verbs in the first two cola of v 10, completed in both cases by מאד (see Structure). The verb חרב is double in meaning, "be dry" and "be desolate."[120] Both directions of meaning are involved here: the notion of "desolation and depopulation" is shared with שׁמם, and clearly a land that suffers from drought will eventually be depopulated; and the idea of "drought" leads in the direction of the dry land implied in v 13 when the people abandon the spring of running water and dig leaky cisterns. (The two verbs שׁמם and חרב are associated in Amos 7:9; Zeph 3:6; and Ezek 12:20 and 29:12.) The heavens are to be dry, since the people have made themselves dry (compare the heavens without light as a result of covenant disloyalty, 4:23, 28).[121]

■ **2:13** The emphatic word in the first colon is the object, "a double crime"; the English equivalent might well be a passive, "Two crimes have been committed by my people." The noun רָעָה carries the meaning "crime" as it

---

116 William R. Harper, *A Critical and Exegetical Commentary on Amos and Hosea* (ICC; New York: Scribner's, 1905) 257.

117 Dahood, *Psalms III*, 72, on Ps 106:20.

118 Compare Pedersen, I/II 457–58.

119 Cross, *CMHE*, 186–90.

120 BDB and Zorell assume two homonymous verbs, while *HALAT* posits one verb.

121 For a depiction of the circle of meaning that is encompassed by depopulation, dryness, and emotional horror, represented by שׁמם and חרב, see Pedersen, I/II 457–58 and 542 (note on p. 458).

does in 1:16 (so also *JB*), but "evils" (*RSV*) is also correct—indeed these are "disastrous acts" as well, in that they have consequences for the people in metaphorically taking away the people's water supply. The number שְׁתַּיִם (literally "two") here implies "double" (compare Exod 22:3), since in reality only one act is involved, the exchange of one deity for another; indeed it is something of a puzzle to locate the "two crimes," since one involves the other. But Jerome nicely parallels the two, the abandoning of God and the adhering to a deity of fertility, with the first clauses of the Ten Commandments: "I am the Lord your God, who brought you out of the land of Egypt, out of the house of bondage" (Exod 20:6) and "You shall have no other gods before me" (Exod 20:3). It is ironic: in the honeymoon time of Israel's life with Yahweh other nations set one disaster going against themselves (v 3), but now Israel has set two disasters going against herself.

One wonders whether Hos 10:10 does not lie behind this expression. But the text of that verse is by no means clear; the qere' of *M*, many MSS., and *G*, *V*, and *S* read לִשְׁתֵּי עֲוֹנֹתָם "for their double iniquity," but the ketib reads the second word as עֵינֹתָם "their springs," leading commentators to ask whether לִשְׁתֵּי is not an infinitive of שׁתה, thus "to drink (from) their springs."[122] Clearly Jrm had "drink" in mind (compare v 18). Did Hosea intend a word-play in his phrase? Again, was Jrm aware of a double tradition in the interpretation of Hosea's phrase?

The second colon again offers an inversion, "me they have abandoned"; Jrm offers parallels elsewhere where the object pronoun referring to the deity precedes the verb ("me they do not know," 4:22; "me shall they not fear?" 5:22). For "abandon" (God) see 1:16.

Yahweh is depicted metaphorically as a "spring of running water" (מְקוֹר מַיִם חַיִּים). A מָקוֹר is a natural spring, and מַיִם חַיִּים is normal idiom for "running water" (Gen 26:19; Lev 14:5; and often). The adjective חַי does mean "living," and Yahweh is the "living God" (אֱלֹהִים חַיִּים, Deut 5:26 and often), and Jrm plays on the double

meaning of חַיִּים here; nevertheless, "fountain of living water" (*RSV* and other translations) is misleading, for the contrast is between the running water of this spring and the collected water in the reservoirs which must come from some other source even if the reservoirs were tight. Behind Jrm's metaphor could well be Isa 8:6–8: there Israel has refused the waters of Shiloah which supply Jerusalem, so that God must bring over them the waters of the river (the Euphrates). Shiloah was an aqueduct from the spring of Gihon; that spring gushes several times a day[123] and served Isaiah as a metaphor for Yahweh's word[124] or for Yahweh himself as a helper in trouble.[125] On the other hand, מְקוֹר חַיִּים "spring/ fountain of life" is a standard phrase (Ps 36:10; Prov 10:11; 13:14; 14:27; 16:22) for "source of life," and one wonders whether this is not some otiose phrase with mythological overtones like "tree of life."[126] All these intersecting images—running water, source of life, living God, and a spring as symbol for Yahweh or his word in Isaiah 8—coalesce in Jrm's phrase, which recurs in the book (17:13).[127]

And the people have forsaken the only source of water only to go off and dig cisterns. For Israel's alternative to Yahweh we have had a plural (v 8), then a singular (v 11), now a plural again, "cisterns." And they have dug cisterns "for themselves" (לָהֶם): rarely has an ethical dative (GKC sec. 119s) carried so much irony—they dig the cisterns by themselves and for their own benefit, while the spring which they abandoned produces water of itself. And this ethical dative, usually a dative of advantage, is occasionally a dative of disadvantage (e.g., Ezek 37:11), so that the question remains whether the cisterns are to the advantage of the excavators. A בְּאֵר is a cistern; there is orthographic uncertainty about the word(s) בְּאֵר/בּוֹר (see the lexica, and compare the Text note in 6:7), but as here vocalized the word is assumed to be the equivalent of בּוֹר, an excavation in the soil, sometimes for the storage of grain, but usually for the storage of water. The major rock west of the Jordan is

122 See the commentaries, notably Harper, *Amos and Hosea*, 353, and Wolff, *Hosea*.
123 Georges A. Barrois, "Gihon," *IDB* 2:396.
124 Wildberger, *Jesaja*, 324.
125 Otto Kaiser, *Isaiah 1—12, A Commentary* (Philadelphia: Westminster, 1972) 113.
126 Compare Prov 10:11 with 3:18, and see the discussion of William McKane, *Proverbs, A New*

Approach (Philadelphia: Westminster, 1970) 296 and 418, against Crawford H. Toy, *A Critical and Exegetical Commentary on the Book of Proverbs* (ICC; New York: Scribner's, 1899) 206.
127 Note the NT application of the image in John 4:10 and 7:38.

porous limestone,[128] so that cisterns, to be watertight, need to be plastered, and a thick lime plaster was developed for the purpose.[129] But in Jrm's metaphor the cisterns leak! The verb יָכִלוּ (כול hip'il) means "contain, not let run out."[130] These cisterns, dug out with such care by the effort of the people, were expected to hold what drains into them (not, of course, to produce water as the spring does); but they are unplastered and do not even retain the water coming into them. The parallel diction of 1:16 underlines the reality behind this metaphor: the Baals are idols constructed by human beings. Those deities which promise fertility do not produce it but to the contrary drain it away. And the ultimate irony is that Yahweh took the people through the (dry) desert and brought them into the garden land, only to see them digging away foolishly in an enterprise that will only lead to dryness once more.

■ **2:14–19** Verses 4–9 (+ 10–13) have offered a contrast between Israel's present disloyalty to Yahweh and her original loyalty (vv 2–3): she walks now after worthless gods (v 8), while then she walked after Yahweh (v 2). The present passage offers a contrast between Israel's identity now (she appears to be a slave, v 14) and her original identity (Yahweh's possession, v 2).

■ **2:14** The diction of this verse hovers between two metaphors: Israel is depicted as a captive slave, and Israel's enemies are depicted as lions capturing their prey. The two metaphors are united by the circumstance of war; defeat can lead to slavery, and the depiction of the Mesopotamian enemy as a lion had antecedents in Isaiah's oracles.

The word עֶבֶד is a general term for "slave" or "servant"; the OT made no terminological distinction between a slave who was owned by a master and a servant who was free to terminate his relation to his master. The יְלִיד בַּיִת was a "house-born slave," that is, one born in the house of the master rather than one acquired through purchase, captivity in war, or the like. The distinction is found in Lev 22:11, though there נֶפֶשׁ

is found instead of עֶבֶד; in the present passage, however, the two terms are simply poetic parallels.[131]

The form of threefold question with מַדּוּעַ, אִם, הֲ is distinctive to Jrm.[132] The questions are in contrast to Israel's status announced in v 3: Israel has been Yahweh's own possession, a free partner in the covenant, a witness to the victories over all her enemies accomplished by Yahweh her suzerain. Now the unthinkable has occurred—Israel appears to be reduced to slavery, carried off captive in war. How could this have happened?

The word בַּז means "booty, plunder," normally in war (see, for example, Isa 10:6) or raiding parties. Human beings could become booty in war or raids (Num 14:3); indeed it is too easily forgotten for present-day readers for whom the goal of war is the destruction of the enemy that in biblical times one of the main goals of war was plunder (again Isa 10:6; compare Judg 5:30). This reality has so faded today as to encourage the use of the translation "victim" instead of "plunder." The thrust of the question here is this: how did Israel lose her independence so as to become the prey of her enemies?

■ **2:15** The word בַּז (v 14) is not associated with an animal's prey; that is טֶרֶף (Amos 3:4; Isa 5:29). Thus, choice of בַּז before the metaphorical "lions" is a stretching of normal diction, emphasizing that what is intended here is Israel's military foe. It is the conclusion of the present study that "lions" here, like "Assyria" in vv 18 and 36, refers to Babylon, which had taken Nineveh in 612 and defeated the remainder of the Assyrian army again at Haran in 610. Egypt marched through Palestine in 609 to help what was left of the Assyrians against the Babylonians; Josiah was killed at Megiddo, and the Egyptians had de facto control of Palestine—they deposed Jehoahaz after three months of rule and placed Jehoiakim on the throne as an Egyptian vassal. Thereupon the Babylonians defeated the Egyptians at Carchemish in 605 and routed them southward, defeating them again near Hamath, so that Jehoiakim

---

128 Denis Baly, "Palestine, geology of," *IDB* 3:643b, and, in more detail, *Geography*, 19, 174, 181, and often.

129 Ovid R. Sellers, "Plaster," *IDB* 3:825; Chester C. McCown, "Cistern," *IDB* 1:631; Martin Noth, *The Old Testament World* (Philadelphia: Fortress, 1966) 154–55.

130 Rudolph's emendation to כלא = כלה, יְכִלוּ, is unnecessary.

131 For slavery in the OT, see Isaac Mendelsohn, "Slavery in the OT," *IDB* 4:383–91; Walther Zimmerli, "Slavery in the OT," *IDBSup*, 829–30; de Vaux, *Ancient Israel*, 80–90, compare 219.

132 Walter Brueggemann, "Jeremiah's Use of Rhetorical Questions," *JBL* 92 (1973) 358–74; for this passage see there 359, 360, 371.

transferred his vassalage to Babylon.[133] The Babylonians have "roared" against Judah.

The expression "over him" (עָלָיו) is emphatic: "it is over him that the lions have been roaring." (The suffix on אָרְצוֹ in the third colon renders unlikely Rudolph's contention that the expression means "over it," i.e., the plunder.) The specific word for "lions" here, כְּפִרִים, is usually distinguished by translators from other words for lion, in that the present word means "young lions."[134] But it is not necessary to stress the youngness of the lions at every occurrence of the word, and in any case it is clear that the כְּפִיר is able to hunt for himself, so that one doubtless has here simply a poetic synonym.[135] Rudolph is unjustified in emending the imperfect of שׁאג; the pairing of imperfect and perfect verbs is now recognized as a standard feature of OT poetry.[136] (Question: Is it any more than coincidence that another example of imperfect-perfect parallelism, 5:6, also offers the metaphor of animals?) It is to be noted that a lion roars over his catch when the catch is dying, or already dead.[137] The lions are not threatening Israel, they have caught Israel. The bad news is not potential but actual.

In v 15b "they," ostensibly the lions, destroy the cities of Judah—though it may be noted that if, poetically, v 16 balances v 15a, then "Assyria" and "Egypt" both destroy the cities. One might think that the metaphor of the "lions" fades here (Rudolph), but the same movement of thought from the lion to military destruction is found even more insistently in 4:7.

The diction of this half-verse is similar to that of Isa 1:7. The noun שַׁמָּה is related to the verb שׁמם (v 12): as that verb means "be horrified, desolate," so the noun means "(place of) horror, desolation." The verb in the fourth colon is best understood as יצת nip'al "be burned" (see Text); for other occurrences see Neh 1:3 and (in the

qal) Isa 9:17. (But it is to be noted that other textual choices do not seriously shift the meaning of the colon.) The last phrase, "without inhabitant" (מִבְּלִי יֹשֵׁב), is a variation of the phrasing of v 6. It is terrible irony that the lovely land into which Yahweh brought the people (v 7) has been rendered like the uninhabited wilderness through which Yahweh had brought them (v 6). The diction implies a holy war against Judah.[138]

■ 2:16 Though on first reading this verse gives the impression of being an insertion,[139] the data of the present study point to its belonging here from the beginning (see Structure, Setting). The particle גַּם does not mean "moreover" (RSV) but "even" (see, notably, 12:6: in both passages the subject precedes the verb). Given the roaring of the lions over dying Judah, even the Egyptians, once thought to be a potential help to the nation, will add insult to injury.

The place-name נֹף is given (more correctly) as מֹף in Hos 9:6: it is Memphis, about twenty kilometers south of Cairo on the west bank of the Nile. It had been the capital in the Old and Middle Kingdoms, and though no longer the capital, it retained its importance.[140] Tahpanhes is the modern Tel Defneh on Lake Menzaleh in the east of the Nile Delta; the Greeks called it "Daphne" (but to be distinguished from a place of that name near Antioch). Herodotus names it as an important Egyptian city in the seventh century,[141] and it was the place of refuge for Jews fleeing from the Babylonian occupation of Judah (43:7–9).[142] Both cities, in fact, held Jewish refugees at that time (44:1), and both, no doubt, would have been cities to which emissaries would have gone during this period (609–604) to negotiate with Egyptian officialdom. The word בְּנֵי "sons of" governs both nouns (compare the same construction with אֶרֶץ in v 6).

133 On all this see, conveniently, Bright, *History*, 316, 324–26.

134 Compare the G σκύμνος "cub" for כפיר in Amos 3:4 and elsewhere.

135 W. Stewart McCullough and F. S. Bodenheimer, "Lion," *IDB* 3:136–37, minimize the connotation of youngness, while G. Johannes Botterweck, "אֲרִי, etc.," *TDOT* 1:376, stresses it.

136 See, recently, James F. Kugel, *The Idea of Biblical Poetry* (New Haven and London: Yale University, 1981) 17–19, with references; and, conveniently, Dahood, *Psalms III*, 420–23.

137 See Amos 3:4, and the comments in Wolff, *Joel and Amos*, 185.

138 Berridge, pp. 92–94.

139 Rudolph and Bright presume so, though Rudolph believes the addition was made by Jrm himself.

140 Thomas O. Lambdin, "Memphis," *IDB* 3:346–47.

141 Herodotus 2.30.

142 Thomas O. Lambdin, "Tahpanhes," *IDB* 4:510.

For the difficult verb יָרֹעוּ see Text. The two objects (the verb suffix and "skull") may be analyzed variously, as a dative and accusative respectively, or as two accusatives the second of which specifies the part of the body affected (GKC sec. 117 ll). The noun קָדְקֹד is, strictly speaking, the "crown" of the head, but it is sometimes used in parallelism with the normal word for "head" (רֹאשׁ: Gen 49:26 and elsewhere) so that it may be considered here a poetic synonym for "head." Since רֹאשׁ itself sometimes implies the king or other leader (Hos 2:2; Isa 7:8, 9), it is plausible to see the word here referring to the king. (Compare 48:45, where קָדְקֹד almost surely refers to the royal house of Moab.) Condamin sees a reference in this verse to the tragedy at Megiddo in 609; the suggestion here then is that the verse refers to the death of the "head" of the people, Josiah. Indeed, since the verb is imperfect, one might speculate that it refers not only to the death of Josiah but to the deposition of Jehoahaz as well.

If the verse is not an interpolation, it must nevertheless be admitted that it does come on oddly, without parallelism. That impression was doubtless Jrm's intention; "the lions, who are Babylon, have been roaring over you, and mangling you, and, by the way, the Egyptians have been doing their share lately too." This casual abruptness adds greatly to its effect in the context.

■ **2:17** The first colon has given commentators trouble. I propose (see Text) that *M* is correct, that the verb is third singular feminine, and that זֹאת is its subject, anticipating the infinitive construct in the next colon: "Is this not what what is acting [or working] on you?—(namely), that you abandoned. . . ." The analysis of structure here has indicated that the three cola in this verse are the climax of the sequence and that this colon is in balance with the first in v 14, "Is Israel a slave?" The point of that question in v 14 was: Why has Israel become a victim of events? The point of the question here is: Do not blame others for these events, you have only yourself to blame; it is your abandonment of Yahweh that has caused all your trouble. The verse thus anticipates v 19: your own wrongdoing is the only cause of your difficulties—do not look for any external cause. The oddly idiomatic diction in this line is unexpected; it is no wonder that the

Versions have reconstrued the phrase in various ways.

The infinitive phrase עָזְבֵךְ אֶת־יהוה אֱלֹהָיִךְ "that you abandoned Yahweh your God" reflects v 13. The third colon, here accepted as genuine (see Text), ironically parallels the second: he did not abandon you but led you; at the very time he was leading you, you abandoned him. The participle here points back to the diction of v 6: he is the one who has always been able to lead you, and particularly in the wilderness (compare Deut 8:2, 15).

■ **2:18** For the transitional "so now" (וְעַתָּה) see Form. The idiom of the first and third cola, מַה "what" with two substantives introduced by לְ, is odd. The closest parallel is Hos 14:9, אֶפְרַיִם מַה־לִּי עוֹד לָעֲצַבִּים: commentators generally read לוֹ there with *G*, "Ephraim, what has he any more to do with idols?"[143] Without the second substantive, but with the following לְ and the infinitive construct (as in the second and fourth cola here) is Ps 50:16, where the nuance is, "How can you recite my commandments?" One is left uncertain whether the idiom here is identical with the more common occurrence with וְ between the two phrases with לְ (e.g., 2 Kgs 9:18), but one may suspect that the piling up of six occurrences of לְ in the four cola is deliberate, giving an impression of a constant scurrying and rearranging now that Judah is out from under Yahweh's patronage. In any event, the translation given, "Why should you be on the road to Egypt?" etc., is Jrm's intention, given the train of thought of the passage.

Judah has abandoned the one who would lead them on the road to Canaan, so now they must take the road to Egypt or Assyria; and since Yahweh, whom they have abandoned, is the spring of running water, they must seek water where they can, be it in Egypt or Assyria. "Water" here implies security, specifically foreign military aid. One cannot be certain whether specific covenantal language is found here or not,[144] but the metaphor implies some kind of treaty obligations.

The word שִׁחוֹר is not the normal word for "Nile" in the OT (that is יְאֹר); this word, which appears three times otherwise,[145] is derived from the Egyptian *P'-š-Ḥr* "Pool of Horus" and refers to a body of water on the eastern edge of Egypt, either one of the eastern arms of the Nile or a lake like Lake Menzaleh.[146] The general location

---

143 Wolff, *Hosea*, 236–37, and n. 32.
144 Delbert R. Hillers, *Covenant, The History of a Biblical Idea* (Baltimore: Johns Hopkins, 1969) 40, makes this

suggestion.
145 Josh 13:3; Isa 23:3; 1 Chr 13:5.
146 See Thomas O. Lambdin, "Shihor," *IDB* 4:328, and

would then be close to Tahpanhes (v 16); but, as is the case with other geographical terms in this chapter, the name is not to be taken in any exact sense but may have been intended by Jrm as a poetic synonym for the Nile (compare Isa 23:3).[147]

The word נָהָר, "river," normally carries the article in the meaning "Euphrates," but occasionally (as here) omits the article.[148] The only occurrence of the word in reference to the Tigris is Dan 10:4, where "Tigris" is surely an erroneous gloss;[149] the use of the noun here is another clue that "Assyria" here really means Babylon (see Setting). Jrm's phrasing here is modeled on Hos 7:11.

If the imagery here reflects that of v 13, and if Isa 8:6–8 was part of the background of Jrm's thinking as he delivered v 13, then that Isaiah passage could equally have been in the background in the present instance: there, for Isaiah, the waters of the Great River (= the Euphrates) and the king of Assyria will flood Judah; here, by contrast, Judah goes off to the Great River to drink. And is there further irony?—in the honeymoon days other nations would try to "eat" of Israel and were punished for the attempt (v 3); now Israel needs to go off to other nations to "drink," and she undergoes punishment in the process. (In 5:17 the foe from the north will come to "eat" of Israel with impunity.)

■ 2:19 The first two cola are chiastically arranged, the two verbs enclosing their respective subjects. The two imperfects must be construed as jussives, given the link (with וְ) with the following two imperatives (so Volz and NJV).[150] The verb יסר pi'el is common in wisdom diction; the cognate noun מוּסָר "discipline, correction" is found in v 30 and often in Jrm's oracles, and the verb occurs elsewhere in his lines, though less often. It means "chastise, discipline, train, correct"; "punish" is the appropriate meaning here. Its parallel יכח hip'il has a wide range of meanings, "reprove, reproach, settle quarrels";[151] it thus comes out of the semantic fields of both legal disputes and of wisdom (occurring ten times in

Proverbs). But Jrm's use of these two verbs with these subjects is striking: only in these two cola in all the OT does either verb carry a subject other than God, the head of a family, or another personal authority figure. Here it is Judah's wrongdoing which is to cause the punishment; it is Judah's acts of apostasy which are to bring on her suffering. What is hinted at in v 17 here becomes explicit: there it was said that your abandoning Yahweh is what is "working on you," but now it is spelled out— you have brought it all on yourselves. The expected point of view, that it is Yahweh who will punish the people, is constant through Jrm's oracles, but occasionally, as in v 17 and here, Jrm suggests that it is most particularly the wrongdoing of the people that sets in motion, quite directly, the present miserable situation, and this idea is underlined by verbs whose subject one would expect to be God. (The same idea will recur in 5:25.)

The subject of the first verb, "your wrong, evil," could also be translated "your disaster" (compare vv 3, 13), and since Jrm is suggesting here that the present disaster is the direct result of their wrongdoing, the ambiguity aids the thought. The subject of the second verb, מְשֻׁבוֹתַיִךְ, appears to intend a meaning of plurality of number rather than a plural of abstract such as is described in GKC sec. 124f (against Rudolph). The basic meaning of the word here is "acts of turning (away), instances of unfaithfulness," but the veering and turning of Judah's foreign policy in these years in being in vassalage first to Egypt and then to Babylonia such as is implied in v 18, and the double meaning of the verb שׁוב indicated in 4:1 and 8:4, both suggest that the noun here may have implications of "constant turning back and forth."

The verbs "know" and "see" are favorite correlatives for Jrm (v 23; 5:1; 11:18; 12:3), but the two are linked elsewhere as well.[152] The conjunction כִּי here, before adjectives, must be translated "how" (so also 4:18).[153] The adjective רַע "bad" is ironically collocated with רָעָתֵךְ "your wrongdoing": it is your badness that has made your

---

the bibliography in Rudolph, p. 18.

147 Curiously G translates γηων, which = Gihon in Gen 2:13, which latter river was sometimes identified with the Nile; see the discussion in Claus Westermann, *Genesis* (BKAT 1; Neukirchen: Neukirchener, 1974– 82) I.297.

148 See BDB for a listing.

149 James A. Montgomery, *A Critical and Exegetical*

Commentary on the Book of Daniel (ICC; New York: Scribner's, 1927) 407; Louis F. Hartman and Alexander A. Di Lella, *The Book of Daniel* (AB 23; New York: Doubleday, 1978) 263.

150 See GKC sec. 110i.

151 See Gemser, pp. 124–25 and n. 4 for an extended discussion of the verb and particularly the participle מוכיח "arbitrator, admonisher."

situation bad. The fifth colon, "that you abandoned Yahweh your God" is obviously repeated from v 17. The last colon offers a perfect verb parallel with the infinitive construct of the fifth colon; the sequence is not impossible, particularly when the second verb is negated (see Text; so also 9:12). The phrase פָּחַד אֶל "stand in awe of" is also found in Hos 3:5; the phrase there appears to be genuine,[154] though there are later Judean glosses in that verse. The verb means "come with fear and trembling." The complement with the first singular reference to Yahweh strikes one as odd alongside the third singular reference in the previous colon, but this is likewise the sequence in vv 2–3 (see above) and may well be intended to balance it.

The sequence ends with an elaboration of the more normal rubric (נְאֻם־יהוה), namely נְאֻם־אֲדֹנָי יהוה צְבָאוֹת; this sequence is found only twice otherwise in Jer (46:26; 50:31), though three of the terms are found together from time to time, with either אֲדֹנָי or צְבָאוֹת missing. There is no discernible significance to these variations.

■ 2:20 If v 19 rounds off vv 14–19 (and its structure, not to mention the closing rubric, suggests that it does), then it will not do to translate כִּי at the beginning of the present verse by "for" (RSV; compare the same observation above on v 10). "Look" may not be far off the mark, or the current "as a matter of fact." The expression "long ago" (מֵעוֹלָם) appears in the book only otherwise at 5:15, where it describes a nation "of long standing, from early times." But if one understands the perfect verbs here to express historical narrative, then it must carry the meaning found in Josh 24:2, "a long time ago."

The expression "break one's yoke" (שָׁבַר עֹל) occurs frequently in the book.[155] "Yoke" usually implies political servitude: in 1 Kgs 12:4 it is used for the impositions of Solomon in comparison with what

Rehoboam might do. But except for the present passage and 5:5 (and perhaps one implication of 2:34 as reconstructed; see there) there seem to be no other passages in the OT where "yoke" is used of Yahweh's covenant (but compare Hos 10:11, discussed below): it is striking that Jrm should use the same expression for Israel's servitude to Yahweh as for her servitude to Pharaoh or Babylon. The question then is not the presence or absence of a yoke, but which yoke is to be present.[156]

The verb נתק, both in the qal and (as here) in the pi'el, means "tear away, tear up," and is used of tearing up bowstrings or a cord, or of lacerating the breasts. The "cords" (מוֹסֵרֹת) may be any restraints, whether of metal, leather, or fiber. The linking of the word with "yoke-pegs" (מֹטוֹת) in 27:2 suggests that the word here refers to the collar-cords securing the oxen to the yoke; for a thorough discussion of the Palestinian yoke see 27:2.

The images here are strong ones: the covenant is a real imposition of the will of Yahweh upon Israel, understood in the image of a domesticated animal (compare Hos 10:11, where the prophet speaks in different vocabulary of Yahweh's disciplining Ephraim and Judah by putting them to pulling the wagon and plowing and harrowing).

Israel's words in the third colon come almost to "I will not be a slave!"—an ironic expression, given the situation described by the question in v 14, "Is Israel a slave?" There it is a description of her misery; she has become slave to Egypt or Babylon because she has refused to be a slave to Yahweh. The verb עבד then has political overtones (see 27:8, of serving Nebuchadrezzar) as well as religious ones (Exod 3:12; 20:5; and often).[157] "I will not devote myself to you!" In sum, the metaphor here is that of a domesticated animal (compare 31:18 and Deut 32:15 along with Hos 10:11) blended with the politico-religious metaphor of covenant: on the level of the

152 1 Sam 12:17; 14:38; and other passages.
153 William F. Albright, "The Refrain 'And God Saw kî ṭôb' in Genesis," Mélanges bibliques rédigés en l'honneur de André Robert, Travaux de l'Institut Catholique de Paris (Paris: Bloud et Gay, 1957) 22–26; Dahood, Psalms III, 405–6.
154 Wolff, Hosea.
155 Beyond the present passage: 5:5; 28:2, 4, 11; and in a late prose addition, 30:8.
156 For a general discussion of the yoke on draught animals see C. Umhau Wolf, "Yoke," IDB 4:924–25.
157 See in general Johannes Peter Floss, Jahwe Dienen—

Göttern Dienen, Terminologische, literarische und semantische Untersuchung einer theologischen Aussage zum Gottesverhältnis im Alten Testament (BBB 45; Köln: Hanstein, 1975), and Ingrid Riesener, Der Stamm עבד im Alten Testament, Eine Wortuntersuchung unter Berücksichtigung neuerer sprachwissenshaftlicher Methoden (BZAW 149; Berlin: De Gruyter, 1979).

animal metaphor Israel says, "I will not work!" and on the level of covenant Israel says, "I will not submit!"

The verse continues with a second כִּי: the three occurrences of this conjunction in vv 20 and 22 are correlative, ticking off one by one the metaphors of covenant breaking. "Item: long ago you broke your yoke . . . ; item: on every high hill . . . ; item: even if you scrub. . . ." For the second and third occurrences "again" would be an English equivalent. The two phrases in the fourth and fifth cola are Jrm's summary of the phraseology of Deut 12:2, itself a summary of Hos 4:13.[158] Where Deut 12:2 says עַל־הֶהָרִים הָרָמִים וְעַל־הַגְּבָעוֹת, with assonance on "mountain," Jrm says עַל־כָּל־גִּבְעָה גְּבֹהָה, with assonance on "hills." The adjective גָּבֹהַ has overtones of "haughty" (Isa 5:15), a striking description of "hills." The phrase וְתַחַת כָּל־עֵץ רַעֲנָן is identical to that in Deut 12:2; רַעֲנָן means "luxuriant, leafy."[159] Question: Is there sexual imagery, perhaps unconscious, for the male in the fourth colon and for the female in the fifth?

In the syntax of v 20b it is noteworthy that the participial clause waits for the last colon; the emphasis on the phrases of locality in the fourth and fifth cola justifies the repetition of "there" in the translation. And due weight must be given to the fact that the last colon is a participial construction, the description of a steady circumstance. The verb צעה is used of "tilting" a wine vat (48:12) or "stooping" under a burden (Isa 51:14); "sprawling" (*NEB*) is excellent. (It might well be pointed out that sexual intercourse was evidently taken in the ancient Near East not only face to face but from the rear.)[160] The last word, וֹנָה does mean "prostitute," but its rime with צֹעָה reminds the hearer that it, too, is a participle, so that it is best to translate it so.

The high hills and leafy trees were the site of fertility-cult worship: this is clear from the fuller description in Hos 4:13. But as elsewhere in prophetic descriptions of this sort, it is not only that specific Israelites resorted to fertility rites in the Canaanite fashion, but that Israel as a whole is personified as a prostitute who had abandoned her true husband Yahweh in favor of Baal deities (so, in more details, 3:1–5). As Israel is called an unruly animal in v 20a, so she is called a whore in v 20b.

■ **2:21** The opening word וְאָנֹכִי "but I" is contrastive with אַתְּ "you" (feminine singular) in the last colon of v 20. Here is still another metaphor, Israel as a vine. Though Hosea used it (Hos 10:1), these three cola draw specifically on Isa 5:1–7, indeed serve as a summary reminder of that passage. Isaiah said וַיִּטָּעֵהוּ שֹׂרֵק, "and he planted it as *śōrēq* grapes" (Isa 5:2), and Jrm says נְטַעְתִּיךְ שֹׂרֵק, "I planted you as *śōrēq* grapes"; these are the only two passages where this variety of grape is mentioned in the OT. The root שרק is associated with the bright redness of the sun,[161] so that the word here evidently refers to a particularly luscious variety of red grapes.[162] The word then does not refer primarily to the appearance of the vine but of the grape (the word "putrid," reconstructed in the third colon, points in the same direction). Vines are not usually propagated by "seed," so that זֶרַע in the second colon must be understood in a nonliteral sense (compare Ezra 2:59, where זַרְעָם means "their descent"). The word אֱמֶת means "reliability"; in the metaphor it refers to the sound, trustworthy stock of grapes, but not far from the center of attention would be the fact that Yahweh's intention is that the people of Israel be a people of אֱמֶת; thus in 4:2 Israel is told that Yahweh intends them to swear by him "truly."

The third colon brings the kind of rhetorical question already heard in vv 14 and 18. The verb הפך nip'al is regularly used of "turning (into something else)" (compare 30:6, "[Why have I seen] every face changed?"). A noun *sōriyyâ (or a formation like it)[163] which would be in assonance with *śōrēq* and which will have a meaning similar to בְּאֻשִׁים (Isa 5:2, 4) is what is required here, and the proposed word suits the context admirably (see Text); it will then mean "putrid, stinking." Since בְּאֻשִׁים occurs last in its cola in Isa 5:2, 4, one expects the corresponding word here to be last in the colon, and the structure leads one to view the verse as a

---

158 Holladay, "On Every High Hill," 170–76.

159 D. Winton Thomas, "Some Observations on the Hebrew Word רענן," *Hebräische Wortforschung, Festschrift zum 80. Geburtstag von Walter Baumgartner* (VTSup 16; Leiden: Brill, 1967) 387–97.

160 Compare plates IV and V in Marvin H. Pope, *Song of Songs* (AB 7C; New York: Doubleday, 1977) after p. 360.

161 Sir 50:7, משרקת, "(the sun) shining (red)"; compare Zech 1:8, where the word is used of the color of a horse (*RSV*: "sorrel").

162 But for the inexactitude of words for color in the OT see Athalya Brenner, *Colour Terms in the Old Testament* (JSOT Supplement Series 21; Sheffield: JSOT, 1982).

163 Compare אָנִיָה from אנה II.

tricolon. The words גֶּפֶן נָכְרִיָּה "foreign vine" are then an early gloss on the rare word "putrid." (The metaphor in Deut 32:32–33 is doubtless in the background.) Jrm is thus repeating here what Isaiah had declared in his Song of the Vineyard, except that Jrm, by using a rare word in assonance with *śōrēq*, no doubt manages to stretch Isaiah's diction (compare the remarks above on v 12 in comparison with Isa 1:2); or else Jrm, aware of Isaiah's two pairs of puns in Isa 5:7, wished to parallel such word-play here.

■ **2:22** For כִּי see the remarks on the second כִּי in v 20. In washing in ancient times one used such detergents as were available: any translation of this verse using "soap" (*RSV, NEB, NAB*) is anachronistic, since soap as we know it came into use much later—"it may have been a Teutonic or Tatar invention."[164] Jrm names two detergents here, נֶתֶר and בֹּרִית. Though they are of course poetic synonyms, they may be distinguished. The first is the Greek *nitron*, Latin *natrum*, terms applied most often to mineral deposits of sodium carbonate. Since there are no such natural deposits in Palestine, the material was no doubt imported from Egypt, where there were several centers of production.[165] By contrast בֹּרִית was a plant product obtained locally (both *G* and *V* specify a grass), an alkali made from the ashes of the "soda" plant (*Salsola kali*).[166] "Ashes" is not too accurate a translation (it is that of Condamin), but many people know that soap may be made from wood-ashes.

Though the verb כבס is normally used for washing clothes, its use in Ps 51:5, 9 for God's washing the worshiper of his guilt is the background of its use here. Indeed it becomes clear that Jrm has both Psalm 51 and Isa 1:15–20 in mind in offering this passage. The psalmist may ask God to scrub him of his guilt, but Israel may not be able to do it herself.

It is difficult at first hearing to grasp the implication of the second colon, וְתַרְבִּי־לָךְ בֹּרִית: the assonance of *t-r-b b-r-t* is nice, but how are the words to be understood? One notes that the waw is nonconsecutive, so that the first two cola are correlative;[167] the verb (רבה hip'il) means "do much" or "do more," but it will not be "do more" of what the first verb means. Further, it is easy to assume that בֹּרִית is the object of the verb (*G, V*, "increase grass for yourself"), but the parallelism makes it more likely that the בְּ in the first colon governs both nouns (double-duty preposition; see, for example, v 24; 3:23; 5:14),[168] leaving one uncertain what the nuance of the verb is here. But again, Ps 51:4 is the background: it reads הֶרֶב כַּבְּסֵנִי מֵעֲוֹנִי—the conventional translation is "wash me thoroughly from my iniquity," but Dahood suggests that הרבה means "again and again," that is, that the number of washings should equal the number of God's mercies.[169] Whether that translation is certain in the present passage, it is clear that the experience of using a cleanser again and again on a stain is an obvious one.

The verb כתם is a *hapax legomenon* in the OT, though interestingly the Aramaic equivalent (pe'al passive participle) occurs in *T* to Isa 1:18, one of the passages from which Jrm draws his imagery here. Since the related noun כֶּתֶם occurs in postbiblical Hebrew for the menstrual stain on a woman's clothes, one is led to assume that the phrase here implies bloodstains (compare v 34). The metaphor of this verse then is the man of violence, one who has shed blood, who is trying to remove bloodstains from himself, scouring the stains as one scours stained clothes. But the stain is not really blood, rather it is the people's עָוֹן, their offense and consequent guilt. All the imagery of Isa 1:15–17 and 18–20 lies behind these words. God may succeed in washing the worshiper clean in the words of Psalm 51, but now

164 F. Sherwood Taylor and Charles Singer, "Pre-Scientific Industrial Chemistry," *A History of Technology* II (ed. Charles Singer et al.; New York and London: Oxford University, 1956) 355; see the discussion, 355–56.

165 H. Neil Richardson, "Lye," *IDB* 3:192; Robert J. Forbes, "Chemical, Culinary, and Cosmetic Arts," *A History of Technology* I (ed. Charles Singer, E. J. Holmyard, and A. R. Hall; New York and Oxford: Oxford University, 1954) 259–60.

166 H. Neil Richardson, "Soap," *IDB* 4:394–95; Robert J. Forbes, "Chemical, Culinary, and Cosmetic Arts," *A

History of Technology I (ed. Charles Singer, E. J. Holmyard, and A. R. Hall; New York and Oxford: Oxford University, 1954) 260–61.

167 Joüon, *Gramm.*, sec. 115a.

168 Dahood, *Psalms III*, 435–37.

169 Dahood, *Psalms II*, 3.

Israel cannot accomplish it. The guilt remains, and thus the stain.

■ **2:23** Disputation language emerges again: for the question "How can you say . . . ?" see Form. The purported claim of the people, "I am not defiled," reflects the metaphor of the man with bloodstains in v 22, and the verb reminds one further of its use in v 7, where the people "defiled" the land. Once they defiled the land; now, alas, they have defiled themselves. The next colon, "and after the Baals I have not walked," reflects the metaphor of the whore in v 20b and mimics most precisely the diction of v 8b. The word order is striking, as if to say, "Baals? I have not gone after *them*!" One notes also that as Israel has declared she will not serve (Yahweh) in v 20, she is heard to declare here that she has not followed the Baals: as there was an imperfect verb in v 20, there is a perfect verb here, and the direction of devotion is opposite. What a tangle of contradictions Israel has woven!

"Way" (דֶּרֶךְ) suggests not only the path that Israel takes to the valley (compare vv 17, 18) but "habit," almost "style of life" (thus v 36).

One is uncertain what is referred to by "in the valley" (בַּגַּיְא). *G* translates by ἐν τῷ πολυανδρείῳ "in the cemetery." Curiously both *T* and thus Rashi identify it as the valley opposite Beth-Peor, an identification doubtless encouraged by the fact that Moses is buried "in the valley opposite Beth-Peor" (Deut 34:6) and because of the incident recorded in Num 25:3, where Israel "yoked himself to Baal of Peor," and perhaps also because of the images of the young camel and wild ass of the desert in the next cola. Jerome, in his commentary, rightly identifies the valley as that of the sons of Hinnom (compare 7:31–32; the description in that passage of that location as a vast burial place in time to come may have encouraged the translation in *G*). To speak in Jerusalem of "the valley" without further designation meant this valley (compare the expression "Valley Gate" in 2 Chr 26:9; Neh 2:13, 15). It is difficult to specify the nature of the cult practices in the Valley of the Sons of Hinnom; 7:31–32 and 2 Kgs 23:10 describe child sacrifice, and 2 Chr 28:3 adds that Ahaz offered pagan sacrifice there. One has the impression of illicit activities of many sorts

that lodged outside the immediate walls of Jerusalem, tolerated at times by officials willing to look the other way, and the object of a "clean-up campaign" in Josiah's time (again 2 Kgs 23:10, and see further Interpretation in 7:31–32). In the parallel colon "know" (ידע) means "recognize, perceive, understand."

And now the two animals! Both are depicted as female, but the two animals have different patterns of behavior, and the sexual hunger of the בִּכְרָה (young female camel) is not at issue, for the behavior of cow-camels is not changed when the male comes on rut;[170] the camel is female here only for consistency, and because Israel is being addressed as female. At issue is her youth; a young camel "is ungainly in the extreme and runs off in any direction at the slightest provocation, much to the fury of the camel-driver. . . . A young camel never takes more than about three steps in any direction."[171] In Jrm's description, then, the young camel is קַלָּה, "swift-footed" (compare Isa 18:2), literally "light(-footed)." She is described as מְשָׂרֶכֶת דְּרָכֶיהָ. The verb שׂרך is a *hapax legomenon*, but a שְׂרוֹךְ is a sandal-thong, so that "interlace" is the right rendering. "To this day the young camel provides a dramatic illustration of anything unreliable. Thus 'interlacing her paths' is an accurate description of a young camel."[172] Israel has no pattern to her steps (is this one more reflection of the constant changes of direction in Judah's foreign policy?). One notes the assonance *k-r*, *r-k*, *r-k*.

■ **2:24** "In contrast to the female camel, however, the habits of the female ass in heat are dramatic and vulgar. When in heat, she sniffs the path in front of her, trying to pick up the scent of a male (from his urine). When she finds it, she rubs her nose in the dust and then straightens her neck and, with head high, closes her nostrils and 'sniffs the wind.' What she is really doing is *snuffing* the dust which is soaked with the urine of a male ass. With her neck stretched to the utmost she slowly draws in a long, deep breath, then lets out an earth-shaking bray and doubles her pace, racing down the road in search of the male."[173] The depiction in the first three cola of this verse perfectly matches that description, and the widespread decision of commentators to excise the mention of the wild ass (Cornill, Giesebrecht, Volz,

---

170 Bailey-Holladay, p. 258.
171 Ibid.
172 Ibid., 258–59.

173 Ibid., 259.

Bright), a practice which has spread to recent translations (*JB*, *NEB*, *NAB*), or otherwise to emend the text, is simply unjustifiable.

The פֶּרֶא (here פֶּרֶה; see Text) is the onager (wild ass); four verses in Job describe his ability to roam the steppes, far from habitation (Job 39:5–8).[174] The wild ass is לִמֻּד מִדְבָּר, "trained (or taught) to the desert." The description is ironic, because Israel was struck by the utter freedom of the wild ass to be himself (see the Job passage just cited, and Hos 8:9); how can such an animal be "trained" to be free or wild? (For the masculine adjective here, see Text.) Further, if the wild ass is a metaphor for Israel, how could Israel imagine herself at home in the wilderness, the nightmare land (v 6)? The construct chain בְּאַוַּת נַפְשָׁהּ is a standard phrase, used of appetite for food (Deut 12:15, 20, 21) and more generally for eagerness or passionate desire (Deut 18:6; 1 Sam 23:20).[175] But given the parallelism with "throat" suggested in v 25 (see there), is there not the possibility to localize the נֶפֶשׁ to the throat (compare Isa 5:14; Ps 63:6)? The associated verb is שׁאף, which refers to rough or heavy breathing, "gasp, pant" (and one notes again assonance: *b-', p-š, š-'-p*). The object רוּחַ may be either "breath" or "wind," so the phrase may mean either "gasp for breath" or "sniff the wind," or both. The only parallel is 14:6, where the wild asses are dying of thirst in the drought. A dying animal may be labored in breathing, but here the female in heat is sniffing rapidly and audibly for the scent she seeks.

The noun תַּאֲנָתָהּ is another *hapax legomenon*, and the word and its syntax have called forth a great variety of suggestions from the earliest period. *G* renders "she is given up" (παρέδοθη), presumably assuming a reading like תֻּנְתַּן or נִתְּנָה; *T* and *S* read as if the Hebrew were תַּנִּים or the like (*T*: "like a dragon"; *S*: "like a jackal"). Rashi mentions the rendering of *T* but adds two other suggestions, תַּאֲנִיָּה "grief" in Lam 2:5 and תַּאֲנַת־שִׁילֹה in Josh 16:6. *V* reads *amoris sui* "of her love" but assumes (wrongly, from the point of view of the present study) that the noun is dependent on רוּחַ just preceding. This rendering has suggested the emendation of the word to תַּאֲוָתָהּ "her desire" (e.g., Giesebrecht), but though one might expect assonance with בְּאַוַּת in the previous colon, the repetition of the same root is not necessary. There is

no reason to doubt the soundness of the reading; a derivation from אנה III "encounter opportunely" is fitting. The word will not then mean so much "her lust" as "her season (of heat)" and will be poised semantically between בְּאַוַּת נַפְשָׁהּ "in the passion of her desire" in the previous colon and בְּחָדְשָׁהּ "in her month" two cola later. The syntax of the word has also caused difficulty: is it "(In) her season who can hold her back?" or "Her season, who can hold it back?" Rudolph holds for the latter, while Bright elects the former, though without reference to what is probably the solution, namely a double-duty preposition (see v 22). This is a more persuasive solution than to see the suffix on יְשִׁיבֶנָּה as appositional with the noun,[176] as Rudolph does. When her season is upon her, who can turn her back? "Let the rider beware—one can easily be thrown by such a she-ass in heat."[177] If the young camel cannot walk straight, then the female wild ass in heat walks only too straight, so impetuously that one cannot deal with her. Both animals in their different ways are perfect symbols for Israel's tracks to Baal, her tracks specifically to the Valley of the Sons of Hinnom where cults to illicit gods existed: who can turn her back? One cannot deal with either animal responsibly, and Yahweh cannot deal responsibly with Israel.

The last two cola of the verse refer to the potential mates of the female in heat. The verb יעף means "tire oneself out," here by a fruitless or unnecessary task (exactly the slang phrase "knock oneself out"); a good parallel context is Hab 2:13. The verb in the present passage must no doubt be construed as a jussive: "let none . . . tire themselves." The verb in the last colon exhibits the rare suffix *-ûnhā*,[178] in part to be in assonance with *-ennā* two cola before. The expression בְּחָדְשָׁהּ troubled some of the Versions, not so much because of the identity of the word itself but because of its unexpectedness here. *G* mysteriously translates "in (her) humiliation," which α' corrects to "in her new moon" (!); *S* offers "in her paths." *T* softens to "in her time," while *V* says "in her monthly period." Though there is no other citation for חֹדֶשׁ in the meaning of "season (of heat)," the reference is immediately clear to the hearer. John Calvin (*Commentaries on the Book of the Prophet Jeremiah and the Lamentations* [Calvin Translation Society, 1850–55, rep.

---

174 W. Stewart McCullough, "Wild Ass," *IDB* 4:843.
175 For a good explication of the phrase see Pedersen, I/II 147.
176 GKC sec. 131m.
177 Bailey-Holladay, p. 259.
178 GKC sec. 60e.

Grand Rapids: Eerdmans, 1950]) assumes that it is her month of foaling, when she is less mobile and can be caught more easily, but this assumption is artificial. The word to potential mates is simply: "Relax, you will have your chance!" An animal caught by the instinct of mating is helpless, but Israel should not have become prey simply to her blind instinct to rebel.

■ **2:25** After the description of the wild ass and the eagerness of her mates, Israel is addressed in a feminine singular imperative matching the two imperatives in the third and fourth cola of v 23. The word יָחֵף is strictly speaking an adjective, "barefoot," but it functions here in parallel with the noun צִמְאָה "thirst." Since both *V* and *S* rightly translate "bare(footed)ness" here, it is possible that the word should be vocalized as יַחַף, a noun extant in postbiblical Hebrew. The two cola are literally "keep your foot from barefootness and your throat from thirst," but it is not clear what these commands imply. It *is* clear that the first colon has reference to the young camel and the second to the wild ass, and that Israel is bidden not to follow the pattern of these animals. But what is the tone of the command?—is it a sincere call to Israel to stop her irresponsible running around, or is it a bit ironic, like the slang phrase "Keep your shirt on!" meaning "Do not get frantic!"? There is no doubt that the comparison of Israel to these animals is the stuff of humor. One notes the striking resemblance of these cola to 31:16a, and one notes assonance once more: מִיָּחֵף mimics יִּעֵפוּ, and מִצִּמְאָה reflects יִּמְצָאוּנְהָ.

The third colon of the verse begins the last tricolon. The expression נוֹאָשׁ is the nip'al participle of יאשׁ, presumably "it is hopeless" or the like. But any word occurring as an interjection (and parallel passages are 18:12 and Isa 57:10) needs precision in its connotation. *V* renders the word in all three passages as an expression of hopelessness,[179] but curiously both *G* and *S* translate the word in the two Jer passages with expressions of defiance.[180] Rashi explains the word with "no apprehension" (אין מיחוש), adds "I put no hope at all in your

words," and finally offers the vernacular expression נונקלייר,[181] which = modern French *non chaloir*, from which the noun "nonchalance" is derived; in short, Rashi sees the expression as one of contempt and indifference. Thus the translation here, "I don't care!"

One is left uncertain whether לֹא belongs to the first colon of the tricolon (so most recent commentators) or at the beginning of the second colon (so the accentuation of *M*). The כִּי is doubtless intended to highlight the second colon, picking up the repeated occurrences of כִּי in vv 20 and 22, but לֹא must be interpreted in the light of כִּי. The adverb לֹא occasionally is used either alone or with כִּי to mean "No!"[182] Of the relevant passages in the OT with כִּי לֹא, two of them are concerned with identities (Josh 5:14; 1 Kgs 3:22); only Gen 18:15 really parallels the present passage, but it does provide the perfect model. In the Genesis verse לֹא כִּי contradicts a previous denial: Sarah denies having laughed, but the divine guest contradicts her, לֹא כִּי צָחָקְתְּ, "No, but you did laugh" (*RSV*), "Yes you did" (Ephraim A. Speiser,[183] *NAB*). In the present passage Israel is finally forced by Yahweh's evidence to admit what she has done. (This interpretation nullifies the proposal of Duhm and Rudolph to excise the words לֹא הָלַכְתִּי from v 23 because of a contradiction with the wording of v 25; the contrast between the self-deceit in v 23 and the complacent admission in v 25 is the whole point at issue.)

The verb "love" reflects its usage in v 2, continuing to carry both religious and political overtones (see there). The "strangers" (זָרִים) will then be both "alien gods" (compare Deut 32:16, a passage which may hang in the background of the passage here) and "foreigners" (so Isa 1:7; Hos 7:9; and often in the preexilic prophets). If Israel does not embrace Yahweh, perforce she will embrace the political might of foreigners and their deities. The last colon reverses normal word order for emphasis: "And they are the ones after whom I am going to walk!" This colon then echoes both v 23 and v 2, rounding off this section of the discourse. The colon

---

179 Here *desperavi*, in 18:12 *desperavimus*, in Isa 57:10 *quiescam*.

180 *G* "I/we shall act like a man," here ἀνδριοῦμαι, in 18:12 ἀνδρούμεθα; *S* with *ḥyl* etpe'el "be sturdy, resolute." Both Versions translate otherwise in Isa 57:10.

181 According to another MS., נונקלוייר; see Solomon ben Isaac, *Commentarius hebraicus in Biblia latinè*

versus, cum notis, J. F. Breithaupto, III (Gotha, 1714) 336 n. 51.

182 GKC sec. 152c; *HALAT* 486b, no. 10.

183 Ephraim A. Speiser, *Genesis* (AB 1; Garden City, NY: Doubleday, 1964) 130.

contradicts Hos 2:9, "I will set out and return to my first husband" (Yahweh). In Jrm's perception the willfulness of Israel is now more unyielding than in Hosea's day.

■ **2:26** The form כְּבֹשֶׁת is surely to be construed as כְּ plus an infinitive: 6:7 offers the same structure. The form בֹּשֶׁת is listed as the infinitive construct of בוש by Franz Zorell (and as a noun as well), though not by BDB and *HALAT*. (For another proposed example of בֹּשֶׁת as an infinitive construct see 7:19.)

A thief is shamed, chagrined, humiliated when he is caught; he is helpless and cannot act.[184] The thief is "caught" (מצא nip'al), not simply "found out," as one might expect from the qal meaning of the verb; the law in Exod 22:1 is doubtless behind the present phrasing (and compare v 34 below). Now what does הֹבִישׁוּ mean in the second colon?—does the hip'il carry the same meaning as the qal here (so the Versions), or virtually the same meaning as the qal (BDB: qal, "be ashamed"; hip'il, "be put to shame"), or, to the contrary, does the hip'il carry a distinctive meaning here, "act shamefully," as it clearly does in Hos 2:7 (so also *G* there)? The qal is used in a similar context, with Israel as subject, in v 36. Is the hip'il in the present passage purely a matter of stylistic contrast, or is a shift of meaning evident? I suggest that there really is a distinction here and propose the same translation as in Hos 2:7. (The same qal/hip'il pairing of this verb is found in 6:15 [= 8:12]; see there.) It is not simply that the children of Israel are ashamed, chagrined, or the like; they have acted shamefully, committed shameful acts by what they say to tree and stone, by the gods they claim to have made with their own hands. And their shame derives not only from their pagan worship but from their being caught in inconsistency (the last two cola of v 27): they are caught as surely as a thief is.

The quartet of ranks of leadership in the gloss in this verse is taken from the poetry of 4:9 and must be understood in the first instance as an explication of הֵמָּה, which is taken here as original, necessary with אֹמְרִים in v

27 (see Text). The four nouns appear in the prose of 8:1 and 32:32. Pagan worship was not something which was indulged in only by the common people (compare 5:4) but was specifically sponsored by various ranks of leaders (compare then 5:5!). If the words of the gloss are not authentic to Jrm, the thought is. It must be noted, however, that now that the gloss is part of the text, the four nouns become part of a listing alongside הֵמָּה, so that the pronoun by exclusion must be taken to mean "the people in general."

The pronoun הֵמָּה, with its accompanying participle אֹמְרִים at the beginning of v 27, parallels the participial phrase in the last colon of v 20; and the pronoun contrasts with the second singular pronouns in v 27a.

■ **2:27** The participle אֹמְרִים implies steady habit, in contrast to the future prediction with יֹאמְרוּ in the last half of the verse. These two instances of "say" (אמר) continue the drumfire of quotation which Yahweh employs in disputation (compare vv 20, 23, 25, and see Form).

Though the general meaning of the first two cola is clear, one would wish to know precisely the nuance of the articles assumed in the vocalization of עֵץ and אֶבֶן. The choices are several. The articles could be understood demonstratively: "They say to this tree . . . and to that stone. . . ." Or, since the article is often used with materials,[185] the implication might be, "They say to wood . . . and to stone. . . ."[186] Or the article may suggest "any at all": in Job 14:7 this appears to be the implication: "There is hope for the tree" means "Any tree offers more hope than any man." Given the occurrence of "every leafy tree" for pagan worship in v 20, this last alternative may be the most plausible.

What significance are we to give to the masculine and feminine references of these cola? Duhm pointed out that "tree" (עֵץ) is grammatically masculine and "stone" (אֶבֶן) feminine in Hebrew; Hyatt, however, suggests that if the "stone" was a massebah, an upright stone[187] which would be interpreted as a phallic symbol here, and if the

---

184 For an exposition of what is involved in "shame" see Pedersen, I/II 239–44; for a thorough survey of passages see Martin A. Klopfenstein, *Scham und Schande nach dem Alten Testament, Eine begriffsgeschichtliche Untersuchung zu den hebräischen Wurzeln bôš, klm und ḥpr* (ATANT 212; Zurich: Theologischer, 1972) esp. 39 for the present passage.

185 GKC sec. 126n.

186 The *RSV* of Hab 2:19 handles the idiom in much this way: "Woe to him who says to a wooden thing. . . ." Compare also the commentaries on Hos 4:12.

187 "Massebah," *IDB* 3:299; Georges A. Barrois, "Pillar," *IDB* 3:815–17; Carl F. Graesser, "Standing Stones in Ancient Palestine," *BA* 35 (1972) 34–63.

"tree" was an Asherah,[188] a symbolic wooden object standing for female fertility, then Jrm would have been reversing the sexual imagery here for the sake of sarcasm, casting contempt on the whole wretched business of fertility worship. On the other hand, Volz and Rudolph reject the fertility reference here and instead see the phrases to be describing the worship of local deities, stone and tree cults representing primitive numina or demons. Though possible, I think this suggestion unlikely; the linking of "wood" and "stone" is standard in the OT polemic against the idolatries of Assyria and Babylonia (e.g., Deut 4:28; Isa 37:19; Ezek 20:32), so that Jrm is not speaking here of autochthonous cults. And his polemic against fertility cults is so steady as to render any other implication here unlikely (especially given the reference to Baal at the close of v 28 and the closeness of the present verse to v 20). Indeed one is tempted to see a general parallel of sexual imagery between the "high hill" in v 20 and the "stone" here, as well as between the references to "trees" in both verses (see on v 20). On the other hand, though the link with types of massebah and Asherah is likely (compare their association in Deut 16:21–22 and 2 Kgs 23:14), the massebah functions in a variety of ways in OT life, and we know far too little about the Asherah. In any case a discussion of what kind of paganism is involved here is beside the mark; Jrm is mocking paganism in general, and many sorts of practice may be subsumed under his biting words. The diction of this passage is close to that of Deuteronomy 32 (compare vv 37–38 there); that chapter is concerned about all kinds of paganism, and so is Jrm.

The verse in Deuteronomy 32 which lies specifically behind these words is v 18: "You were unmindful of the Rock that gave you birth, you forgot the God who was in travail with you." That chapter uses the birth image in the context of metaphors for the rescue and nurturing of Israel in the desert (Deut 32:10–14), and Jrm uses the fatherhood of Yahweh (3:19) in the context of his steady

capacity for historical rescue (the participles of 2:6). But the people have taken these powerful sexual and family metaphors, "You are my father," "You have given me birth," and have applied them to any wood and stone. The people have forgotten Yahweh (v 5) just as Deut 32:18 says they have; instead of remembering the massive Rock (צוּר) that really gave Israel birth, they have said "You gave me birth" to any "stone" (אֶבֶן). Wood and stone, it will appear, cannot save in the emergencies of history (the last half of the verse), so to bestow metaphors of family and sexuality to these surrogate deities is simply foolishness.

It represents, in fact, a 180-degree turn away from Yahweh; the people are no longer face to face with him but offer him the back of their neck (עֹרֶף)[189] (compare 18:17, where Yahweh will turn the back of his neck, not his face, to Israel on the day of their disaster). The assonance of the third colon is striking (pānû, 'ōrep, pānîm).[190] In Josh 7:12 Israel is unable to stand before her enemies but has turned (פנה) the back of her neck to them; here Israel is unable to face Yahweh and has turned away. How can Yahweh carry on a relationship with the back of a neck? (Compare the similar diction of 7:24.)

"In the time of their disaster": formerly it was the enemy who would suffer disaster (v 3); now it is Israel's turn. Is there an echo here of Ps 37:19, "They [the blameless] are not put to shame in the time of disaster"? During the course of the present chapter one has heard what Israel has not said (vv 6, 8), what she has said (vv 20, 23, 25), and what she continues to say (the first half of the present verse). Now we hear what she will say: she will offer a Yahwistic psalm. The words here, קוּמָה וְהוֹשִׁיעֵנוּ, "Arise and save us," are very close to Ps 3:8, קוּמָה יהוה הוֹשִׁיעֵנִי אֱלֹהַי, "Arise, O Yahweh, save me, my God," and "save us" occurs in Hezekiah's prayer when Jerusalem was besieged (2 Kgs 19:19) as well as elsewhere. The singular imperatives, coming after the double mention of tree as father and stone as mother,

---

188 William L. Reed, "Asherah," *IDB* 1:250–52.

189 For a brief discussion of some of the implications of this word see Johnson, *Vitality of the Individual*, 66–67 n. 3.

190 The consonant *p* normally occurs in less than 2 percent of the aggregate consonants of a Hebrew consonantal text.

make it clear that the prayer is to Yahweh, quite aside from the association with Yahwistic prayers. The tension between the double mention of tree and stone and the singular address to Yahweh will grow in v 28. In good weather Israel resorts to pagan deities, but when the storm blows up she is impelled to return to Yahweh. The pagan deities are nothing but fair-weather gods.

■ **2:28** "Where are your gods which you made for yourself?" The Hebrew here, taken without regard to context, is ambiguous: "your gods" could be construed as "your God." To say אַיֵּה אֱלֹהֶיךָ, "Where is your God?" or "Where are your gods?" is to use a standard form of mockery; the psalmist complains that his enemies say continually, "Where is your God?" (Ps 42:4, 11), and others complain that the nations say of Israel, "Where is their God?" (Ps 79:10; 115:2; Joel 2:17). But Israel can play the same game with pagans and mock their gods, and so Deut 32:37 states, "Then he [God] will say, 'Where are their gods . . . ?'" The question, as always, is: What deity can rescue effectively? The plurality here is only implied by the theological implication of the clause "which you made for yourself," a reference back to the tree and stone. The question posed by Yahweh is particularly ironic here, since it is not a question of where to find evidence of deities who have not been visible or active in the life of the worshiper, as the mocking question usually implies—we have just seen these gods of wood and stone! And surely there is irony also in the present context, since we have heard just recently (vv 17, 19) of Yahweh as "your God" whom Israel has abandoned, and earlier, that Israel has not said, "Where is Yahweh?"

The second colon of the verse reverses the elements of the two parts of v 27b. It is not clear how the first half of the colon is to be understood; both the modal nuance of יָקוּמוּ and the function of אִם is at issue. As for אִם, the particle is occasionally used to introduce a question, as הֲ does (so Gen 38:17), and G has so construed the present phrase: "Will they arise and save you?" As for the modal nuance of יָקוּמוּ, the verb could theoretically be construed as an indicative with ironic intent, "Oh, they will arise, most assuredly!"—but the context of Deut 32:38 is jussive, and the verb here must surely be so understood.

On the other hand, Deut 32:38 has וְ where the present passage has אִם and *V*, *S*, and *T* all understand the colon here as Deut 32:38 is expressed. Rudolph assumes that אִם introduces an indirect question: "They should arise (so one might see) whether they can help you."[191] The *NAB* takes the clauses as quite separate: "Let them rise up! Will they save you . . . ?" I propose that the simplest solution is to take אִם simply to mean "if," Jrm's little twist of the knife: in your panic you turn back to Yahweh and pray to him to arise; good, but why do you not pray that your idols might arise in your hour of desperation, if indeed they have any power to save at all!

And the verbs are plural; the polytheism that was only implied by "which you made for yourself" now becomes explicit. You have tried to go back to the singularity of Yahweh; why do you not remain consistent and stay with the plurality of your deities? Of course you are really the folk to whom Yahweh said long ago he would speak (Deut 32:37–38), and now he says it: the old words have been fulfilled.

The particle כִּי at the beginning of v 28b scarcely means "for" (the usual translation). It is not because your gods are many that you should call upon them; the multiplicity of deities is a fact of your life, as the plural number of the verbs has just indicated, so a reinforcing particle like "indeed" or "yes" is what is needed. The particle כִּי functions in the same way as it does in the third colon of v 27, with which it is correlative (see Structure). The noun מִסְפַּר "number" may be construed as a predicate nominative of the thing numbered, but a better solution would be to propose *וּכְמִסְפַּר in the last (reconstructed) colon of the verse and assume a double-duty preposition (compare v 22); in this way the proposed כְּ would balance the כְּ which begins v 26. In any event the meaning is clear.

For the last (reconstructed) colon see Text; that reconstruction uncovers a nice interlocking structure in the parallelism of v 28b. For קטר pi'el see 1:16.

The plurality of the deities is now the focus of Yahweh's scorn. How many cities in Judah?—that is how many gods you have. How many streets in Jerusalem?—that is how many Baal altars you maintain. For the multiplicity of altars implied in the last colon and spelled

---

191   *Sie sollen aufstehen, ob sie dir helfen können.*

out in the prose version of 11:13 compare Hos 10:1. By the message of these lines these cults are not some marginal peccadillo of Judah, a hobby of ill-bred folk off in the Valley of the Sons of Hinnom: paganism is rife, it is everywhere, it is all around you.[192]

■ **2:29** *M* offers a good text for two cola in the verse, and the two additional cola suggested in the textual reconstruction do not shift the meaning. Yahweh insists that he will pursue the legal case against Israel by continuing to argue it out (v 9), but now comes his question, Why do you try to argue back with me?—you have a weak case, the evidence is all against you! The *JB* has caught the connotation of the colon of *M* in v 29a: "What case can you make against me?" The verb ריב appears with אֶל in three other passages: 12:1, where it appears to mean "I pursue a case against (you)"; Judg 21:22, where it means "complain to you," and Job 33:13, where the context is almost exactly that of the present passage: "Why then plead your case against him?" (*NEB*). You have no case to present! And if a colon has been lost before the *M* text of v 29a, it will be synonymous: "Why do you speak against me?"

The *M* text of v 29b enlarges on the accusation against the "shepherds" in v 8 ("the shepherds have rebelled against me"): now it is "all of you" that have rebelled (for פשע see v 8). And if the reconstruction from *G* of a fourth colon in the verse is correct, it contains רשע; this verb is not cited elsewhere in Jer, but the prophet uses the related adjective elsewhere (5:26; 12:1), and the fact that that adjective occurs in 12:1 in the context of ריב אֶל is a modest encouragement for the reconstruction.

Whatever the solution for the textual questions of the verse, the thought is clear: you have no legal case against me, because all of you are in rebellion against the covenant between us.

■ **2:30** Something is wrong with *M*, which reads: "In vain have I beaten your children, correction they did not accept; your sword ate your prophets like a destructive lion." Though this text gives some sense and is accepted by a few (Weiser, Bright), there is widespread uneasiness among commentators. Though *G* is slightly different, reading "you did not accept" for "they did not accept" and "a sword" for "your sword," these variations do not affect the general direction of the text reflected in *M*. It is unnecessary to list all the suggested emendations which various scholars offer, but Duhm, Giesebrecht, Volz, Condamin, and Rudolph all differ from each other, and Ilse von Loewenclau[193] and Hoffmann[194] offer further suggestions.

The basic difficulty is centered around "your prophets," an expression which brings historical, literary, and poetic problems. Historically one is uncertain what prophets are meant; there is no reference nearer than the slaughter of Yahwistic prophets in Elijah's time more than two centuries before, though of course it is conceivable that Jrm has reference here to one or more incidents otherwise unknown to us. Literarily this condemnation is unparalleled either elsewhere in Jer or in any of the other prophetic writings (Hoffmann), and the indictment is serious enough that the lack of reference or parallel elsewhere is disturbing. It is of course conceivable that Jrm has reference here to the killing of Uriah (26:20–23) and is linking his martyrdom to the murder of prophets in earlier times, but since the general context of the present passage is an accusation of covenant disloyalty, the normal concomitant of which is the oppression of the poor (v 34), the specificity of killing the prophets here is odd. And poetically the oddity is increased by the fact that "children" and "prophets" are not normally parallel, a fact which has encouraged the variety of proposed emendations. And the inconcinnity of "children" and "prophets" is part of a larger disjunction, because the first and third cola of the verse are not parallel, as one might expect. Further the diction of v 30b is no longer in focus: the metaphor of the lion is used when speaking of the punishment to be visited upon the people, not of their crimes (4:7; 5:6); and the sword most commonly appears in Jrm's prophecies as a tool in the

---

192 The proposal of Dahood, that עריך here means not only "your cities" but "your protectors," *Psalms I*, 55–56, is dubious; there is evidently no corresponding double meaning to "streets."

193 Ilse von Loewenclau, "Zu Jeremia ii 30," *VT* 16 (1966) 117–23.

194 Y. Hoffmann, "Jeremiah 2:30," *ZAW* 89 (1977) 418–20.

hand of Yahweh with which he punishes the disobedient (12:12 and frequently in the foreign nations oracles, and in prose) (again Hoffmann).

The adoption of G "a sword" for M "your sword" and the emendation of "your prophets" (נְבִיאֵיכֶם) to "of you" (בָּכֶם) solves these problems. (The emendation is a suggestion of Hoffmann's; his other emendations, of "your children" to "my children" and "your sword" to "my sword" are unnecessary and unlikely.) Conceivably the G reading "you did not accept" in the second colon is correct, but the meaning is the same in either case. "Your children" then has the same reference as the same expression did in v 9, namely a poetic synonym for the citizens of Judah. Now the parallelism is restored: "your children" and "you" are parallel in the first and third cola, just as "you" and "your children" are parallel in v 9. One also notes that v 31 offers "you" (אַתֶּם), so that when "of you" in the present verse is linked with "you" in v 31, "your children" becomes associated with "community" (דּוֹר) in v 31, just as "his children" (בָּנָיו) and "community" (דּוֹר) are parallel in Deut 32:5, material stimulating the diction of the present passage (compare vv 28 and 31). Now the first and third cola both refer to Yahweh's punishment.

The text may have been altered in the following way: "your prophets" may have been added as a gloss on בָּכֶם by a copyist who had the tragedy of Uriah in mind, and then חֶרֶב בָּכֶם "corrected" to חַרְבְּכֶם (see Setting).

By this reading, then, Yahweh has "beaten" his children by the advent of a sword, clearly the threat of foreign invasion. Isa 1:2 + 5 offers a similar sequence from פשע "rebel" to נכה hip'il "beat," again in the context of foreign invasion and devastation (vv 7–9 there). Children are "beaten" to teach them a lesson (מוּסָר "chastisement, correction"): see Prov 23:12–14 for the association of this verb with this noun. The noun is a general word covering everything from a "warning" (Ezek 5:15) to physical punishment.[195] "Take correction" is a favorite phrase in Jer (5:3; 7:28; 17:23; 32:33;

35:13), evidence that Jrm drew on the wisdom tradition.[196] But these "children" do not learn their lesson; Yahweh chastises them "in vain." (For other cola in which "in vain" comes first see 4:30; 6:29; 18:15; 46:11; it is a favorite emphatic expression for Jrm.)

A lion devours, a lion destroys (compare again 4:7); Yahweh's warning is as destructive as a lion on the loose.

■ 2:31 Verse 31aα is almost universally taken as a gloss and thus laid aside (Duhm, Rudolph, Bright; NEB also omits the words). But a gloss should clarify (like "foreign vine," v 21) rather than mystify, and the diction of these words in M is strange indeed: הַדּוֹר with article is dubious as a vocative ("O generation," or the like), certainly in the first position in a colon, and the subject pronoun (אַתֶּם "you") is even odder afterward; "see the word of Yahweh" is extreme (though see below), certainly strange for a gloss. The Versions are not reassuring: G reads a different text (see Text) and S, though keeping the wording of M, has reversed אַתֶּם and הַדּוֹר ("You, O generation"), evidently in a secondary effort to extract meaning from the words. But the problem is solved if one vocalizes הַדּוֹר, parallel with הֲמִדְבָּר הָיִיתִי just following and with הֲתִשְׁכַּח at the beginning of v 32. The noun דּוֹר does not always mean "generation";[197] it occurs in Deut 32:5 in parallel with בָּנִים, and the occurrence there is likely the trigger for Jrm's use of the word here (compare v 30): "They are no longer children to him . . . ; they are a perverse and crooked דּוֹר," that is, "community."[198] The word here then seems to mean a company of people who are akin by virtue of a common characteristic—in this case, the covenantal responsibility of mutual care; conceivably the word means "the assemblage" at the temple (see Setting). If the covenant is broken, then solidarity is broken. "Are you are community with solidarity? If you are, then see the word of Yahweh!"

The diction of "seeing" with "word of Yahweh" is extreme though comprehensible. The phrase may appear in 23:18 (though the text has evidently under-

---

195 Compare the remarks on the related verb יסר, v 19, and see Georg Bertram, "παιδεύω, κτλ.," TDNT 5:603–7, and Paul E. Davies, "Discipline," IDB 1:846.

196 Lindblom, "Wisdom in the OT Prophets," 203; and, more generally, William McKane, Prophets and Wise Men (SBT 44; Naperville, IL: Allenson, 1965) 102–12.

197 David N. Freedman, Jack Lundbom, and G.

Johannes Botterweck, "דּוֹר," TDOT 3:171–74.

198 See also Pedersen, I/II 490.

gone conflation: see there); one finds analogous diction in Amos 1:1 ("The words of Amos . . . which he saw [חזה]"). "See" implies acknowledgment as well as perception, and "word" implies deed as well as spoken word. This striking bicolon is the centerpiece in vv 29–32 (see Structure).

Yahweh had been identified as a spring of running water (v 13); Yahweh had taken Israel through the wilderness (v 6). Now, however, the identities are so scrambled that not only has Israel forgotten she is a community, but she has begun to treat Yahweh as the wilderness to be avoided at all costs. Hosea had indicated that Yahweh threatened to make Israel a wilderness (Hos 2:5); now this is what Israel has done with Yahweh. The question might also be raised: If Israel is a wild ass (v 24), and if that wild ass is "trained to the wilderness" (v 24), then is this not more evidence that Yahweh has become a wilderness to Israel?[199] The wilderness is the land of death and chaos; is Yahweh then perceived as the source of death and chaos?

The parallel colon is "land of מַאְפֵּלְיָה"; this word is a *hapax legomenon* in the OT and not fully understood. The root אפל suggests "be dark," and מַאְפֵּל appears once (Josh 24:7) for the (supernatural) darkness which Yahweh put between the Israelites and the Egyptians. The traditional rabbinic interpretation is to understand the word as מַאְפֵּל plus יָה "Yah," the shortened form of Yahweh, thus "darkness of Yahweh," meaning superlative darkness; so also BDB, *HALAT*, and D. Winton Thomas.[200] On the other hand, Zorell explains the words as a feminine adjective modifying אֶרֶץ "land," meaning either "arid" or "dark." Rudolph, following a suggestion of Eduard König, revocalizes the word to מַאְפֵּלְיָה, but such a vocalization would not shift the meaning perceptibly. One can say that if the word is a superlative with "Yah," then there is irony here: does Israel perceive Yahweh to be nothing but that darkness which he once put between the Israelites and the Egyptians? Further, if both צַלְמָוֶת in v 6 and מַאְפֵּלְיָה here

are compound nouns, is there an intended contrast between מָוֶת "Death," indeed the god Mot, and "Yahweh"? (For another collocation between Yahweh and "Death" or Mot, see 9:19–20.) For the association of "wilderness" and "darkness" see v 6.

The questions in these two cola have been introduced by הֲ and אִם, and the third question in the sequence (see v 14 for the formula) is, "Why then have my people said, רַדְנוּ?" We have heard much of what Israel has or has not said (vv 5, 23, 25, 27), and this is another quotation in the series; for "my people" compare vv 11, 13. But the meaning of רַדְנוּ is uncertain. The Versions only guess: G "we will not be ruled over" is evidently periphrastic from רדה; V "we have withdrawn"; S "we have gone down" = יָרַדְנוּ; T "we have wandered" may have understood the verb correctly, or may have read נַדְנוּ. As it stands, M implies a verb רוד; the same verb appears to be used in Hos 12:1, a passage with its own share of difficulties.[201] The simplest solution after all seems to be the one offered by the lexica, identifying the verb here as רוד, cognate with the Arabic *rāda* "walk about, roam," a meaning which fits the parallelism of the last colon. (The suggestion is made in the present study to reconstruct a difficult word in 17:3 to be a hip'il of this verb; see there.)

"We shall no longer come to you!" The expression of both these cola reflects that thrust of v 25 very closely; having tasted the excitement of wandering, Israel is in no mood to approach Yahweh again. The phrase בוא אֶל is used in so many contexts it is impossible to specify the nuance here, but given the bridal image in the next verse, and given the use of the phrase of a bride's entering a husband's house (Josh 15:18 = Judg 1:14), it is possible that the implication here is of "going to" the center of power or protection. Israel's now spurns such protection.

■ **2:32** And another question with הֲ: "Can a virgin forget her ornaments?" The עֲדִי are ornaments of silver or gold and clearly a source of pride (2 Sam 1:24); there is a fine

199 Oral suggestion of my former student the Rev. Mr. Raymond A. Squibb.

200 Both Qimḥi and Jehiel Hillel ben David Altschuler (מקראות גדולות in מצודת ציון, Warsaw, 1874–77) compare this word to שַׁלְהֶבֶתְיָה in Cant 8:6. See D. Winton Thomas, "Unusual Ways of Expressing the Superlative," *VT* 3 (1953) 211–14.

201 See Wolff, *Hosea*, 205–6, 210, for a full discussion.

description of bridal ornamentation in Ezek 16:10–13.[202] And the parallel is that the bride cannot forget her קִשֻּׁרֶיהָ. This is a word of uncertain meaning, since it appears only here and in the list of finery in Isa 3:20. The verb קשר means "bind," and therefore it has been suggested that the word means "breast-band, stomacher" (so *G*, *V*), and this is as good a guess as any.[203] In the Israelite context the high moment of a woman's life is her wedding day, and her mode of dress proclaims her status: virginity, bridehood. There is no way that a woman can take her mind off her only self-identity, any more than a domestic animal can forget his feeding-trough or who his master is (Isa 1:3). But, says Yahweh, "my people have forgotten me for days innumerable." The contrast here is with the image of primal devotion in v 2. Yahweh remembers Israel's primal love, but Israel has forgotten Yahweh long since (compare the diction of Deut 32:18). When one thinks about it, the comparison here between the bride who cannot forget and the people who do is really startling, for one would have thought that the image controlling these passages is Israel the bride of Yahweh. But the verse does not say, "Can a virgin forget her fiancé, a bride her bridegroom?" This is the comparison one would expect, to fit the terrible conclusion, "But my people have forgotten me." Instead Jrm has the bride's attention not on the bridegroom but on her own finery. Is Yahweh to be compared to the finery of a bride? Do we have a metaphor here comparable to that in v 11, where Yahweh is called "their glory," that is, the glory of the people? At least the intensity of the bride's pride in her bridal dress gives some indication of the intensity of devotion which Yahweh craves from his people but does not receive and has not received for many years now.

■ **2:33** This verse, which begins the last sequence of the chapter, is evidently a striking sarcastic statement about the people's disobedience, but several textual difficulties need to be dealt with.

The key to unlocking the verse is the contrast between תֵּיטְבִי (יטב hip'il) "you do well" and הרעות, to be vocalized with *G* as הֲרֵעוֹת "you have done ill" (Text, b). The two verbs are correlative in 4:22 and 13:23; the latter passage is particularly close in diction, given the association with למד (see below) there as well. (The two verbs also appear in 10:5, though commentators have doubted the authenticity of that passage to Jrm.)

If there is a contrast between "do well" and "do ill," then לָכֵן "therefore" is impossible (Rashi strains to make it mean "verily" here). Again the key is in *G*, which reads οὐχ οὕτως "not thus" (= לֹא־כֵן). I propose, however, that the text does not intend a contradiction, such as would be implied by "not thus," but that the original לֹא־כֵן is adjectival, meaning "illicit";[204] this adjective appears in 23:10, there too at the end of a colon. So understood, the first two cola of the verse are a terrible commentary on the appeal of 7:3 and 5, "Make good (יטב hip'il) your ways (דַּרְכֵיכֶם): "How good you make your way," Yahweh says, "to seek illicit love!" For מַה "how" with יטב hip'il compare the same exclamation with the qal stem in Num 24:5. The phrases play on diction one has met earlier in vv 23–25: "your way" (v 23), "seek" (v 24), the verb "love" (v 25) (and note that "trained," proposed in v 33b, occurs in v 24). Israel, as always, is seeking love, that is to say, religious devotion which is satisfying and political security which is dependable (see the discussion on v 2).

If הרעות is to be revocalized as a verb, then the particle אֶת must either be revocalized as the subject pronoun אַתְּ or (more likely) explained as a secondary addition when the verb was misconstrued.

The vocalization of the last verb לִמַּדְתִּי, thus "you have taught," cannot be right; teaching is not at issue, but rather habitual conduct. The clue is 13:23, where one reads לִמֻּדֵי הָרֵעַ "trained to do ill," so that the verb needs to be vocalized as a pu'al, לֻמַּדְתִּי; compare the same thought in 4:22, "They are wise in doing ill." (It may be noted that *G* reads a quite different text, τοῦ μιᾶναι τὰς ὁδούς σου = לְטַמֵּא אֶת־דְּרָכָיִךְ, "to pollute your ways." If this text is correct, the verb would echo its appearance in

---

202 For a general notice of women's ornaments see Jacob M. Myers, "Dress," *IDB* 1:871, with references to further articles concerning specific ornaments. Elizabeth E. Platt's (unpublished) dissertation (Harvard University), *Palestinian Iron Age Jewelry from Fourteen Excavations*, is summarized in "Palestinian Iron Age Jewelry," *American School of Oriental Research 1973–74 Newsletter No. 10* (June 1974) 1–6;

see her further articles, "Triangular Jewelry Plaques," *BASOR* 221 (February 1976) 103–11; "Bone Pendants," *BA* 41 (1978) 23–28.

203 For a recent discussion see Wildberger, *Jesaja*, 143.

204 BDB 467a, II כֵּן, l; Zorell, 362b, ²כֵּן, 2; *HALAT* 459b, I כֵּן 2c.

vv 7 and 23. The reading is a plausible one and may be correct even though unattested by any other Version and even though it would be hard to imagine, if correct, how *M* could have arisen.) If the puʿal revocalization is sound, the particle אֶת is a problem; it is conceivable that it is a preposition; conceivably one could revocalize it as the subject pronoun אַתְּ, but it is most likely a secondary addition (compare the remarks above on the earlier occurrence of the same particle). What is the force of the particle גַּם in the verse? There is a sequence in Isa 57:6–7 which is much like the present one, a context of accusation, and in that passage the particle appears to heighten the accusations—"in fact," "indeed," or the like.

One would wish for a translation as pungent as Jrm's eight words, but one must be content with a paraphrase. "Make good your way?—oh, you've made it best, if illicit love is what you want. Actually, you've made it bad, addicted to your ways as you are!"

■ **2:34** The first colon of this verse offers several problems. Either "on your skirts" (*M*) or "on your palms" (*G*, *S*) is possible, but given the implication of v 22, and the diction of Isa 1:15, that the stain is on the person rather than the clothing, "on your palms" is more likely (see Text). The word אֶבְיוֹנִים is missing in *G*, overloads the line and is best understood as a gloss (see again Text). This leaves a triple construct chain ("blood of the lives of the innocent") which is heavy but possible (compare 8:21, literally "wound of the daughter of my people"). Jrm uses דָּם הַנָּקִי "blood of the innocent" elsewhere (22:17, compare 26:15), and the variant דָּם נְקִיִּם occurs in 19:4. This phraseology suggests that נְפָשׁוֹת, too, is a gloss, but its presence in *G* leads one to leave it in the text (unless there were two glosses, one lodged in both *G* and *M* and one only in *M*!). The situation is complicated by the fact that Deut 27:25 reads נֶפֶשׁ דָּם נָקִי in one of the Twelve Curses (i.e., literally "a person, that is, innocent blood"); perhaps Jrm is here playing with that old phrase. In any event, innocent people have suffered violent death, and this line reminds the hearer of the "guilty stain" in v 22.

The noun מַחְתֶּרֶת "housebreaking" is found only here and in Exod 22:1: "If a thief is caught housebreaking (בַּמַּחְתֶּרֶת יִמָּצֵא) and is struck so that he died, there shall be no bloodguilt (דָּמִים) for him." The verb מְצָאתִים may be construed either as "I found them" (*G* and *V*) or as "you [feminine singular] found them" (*S*); either is possible, but given the rhetorical flow, the second person

is preferable. Why kill these poor people?—you did not catch them breaking into your house, did you? There is justifiable homicide, but these instances do not fall in that category.

The last colon gives sense when revocalized as here (see Text). The expression "your yoke" is found in v 20 to denote the yoke imposed upon you by Yahweh: and that yoke has to you become a curse. However, "your yoke" may also mean "the yoke which you impose on others" (1 Kgs 12:4 offers both this subjective genitive, "his yoke [which he imposed on us]," and an objective genitive, "our yoke [which we have endured]"), and that nuance is appropriate in the present context of social oppression. Finally Jrm might well have had in mind the yoke which the foe from the north would impose upon the people (chaps. 27—28), and in the light of the prediction that the people would soon march off with hands on head (v 37) this nuance is appropriate. In all three senses, then, your yoke becomes a curse. The word אָלָה "curse" is also found in 23:10, a poetic passage (though with Versional support there for the reading וְאֵלֶּה). One notes in passing that the same 23:10 offered an example of adjectival לֹא־כֵן as has been reconstructed here in v 33. For the syntax of the subject plus לְ and noun in the predicate of a nominal clause compare Lam 4:3, בַּת־עַמִּי לְאַכְזָר "The daughter of my people becomes (someone) cruel."

How is כִּי to be construed? Given the negative in the previous colon, one's first thought is "but rather," but given the possible triple ambiguity of the reference of the phrase, one is safest with a corroborative expression like "certainly."

■ **2:35** The verb וַתֹּאמְרִי brings with it the same kind of self-justification as it did in v 25. It is followed by כִּי, and one has the impression that the conjunction here matches its use in the last colon of v 34. The verb נִקֵּיתִי "I have been innocent" picks up נְקִיִּם "innocent" in v 34. Israel, fatuous as ever, says "I've certainly been innocent!" or even "To the contrary, I've been innocent!"; my conscience is clear. The expression "wrath (of Yahweh)" (אַף) with "turn back" (שׁוּב) is a common one (compare the refrain in Isa 5:25; 9:11, 16, 20; 10:4); the three other occasions in which it appears in Jrm's poetry (4:8; 23:20; 30:24) contain the negative—Yahweh's wrath will not turn back. In this single occurrence without the negative we catch the false hope of Israel.

This brief quotation is answered by Yahweh. For הִנְנִי plus participle see 1:15. The nip'al of שׁפט is used both in legal contexts (Ezek 17:20, "go to law with him") and nonlegal ones (Prov 29:9, "argue with someone"). It means "argue one's case"—Isa 43:26 is a good verse to compare. Here the phrase is virtually identical with רִיב אֶל in v 29: in that verse Yahweh declared Israel had no case, and now we hear that Yahweh is pursuing *his* case. He is pursuing his case precisely because Israel keeps saying she is innocent: "I have not sinned."

■ **2:36–37** The first two cola of this sequence nicely mimic the first colon of v 33, more closely in Hebrew than can easily be indicated in translation: you make cheap the changing of your way, just as you presumed to make good your way. The verb זלל hip'il appears only otherwise in Lam 1:8, where it means "treat contemptuously, cheaply." But Jrm uses the qal stem in 15:19: זוֹלֵל is the opposite of יָקָר "what is precious"; the cognate there then means "what is of little worth, cheap." In Lam 1:8 the verb is in contrast to כבד pi'el "honor, give high estimation to." The verb in the present passage then means "give low estimation to." To change her way is something Israel does quite casually; is there the suggestion here that she is available to the highest bidder? "Change one's way" recalls the phrasing of v 18—to be on the road to Egypt, to be on the road to "Assyria." The reference, in short, is to Israel's changing her political course; she does it so easily, so casually. "Be shamed" (בוש) may carry a forensic meaning here ("be shown to be in the wrong").[205]

At the beginning of v 37 the expression מֵאֵת זֶה is puzzling, though the commentators are not troubled by it. There is no parallel for the expression. *G* translates "from here" (ἐντεῦθεν), a rendering which is either periphrastic or a translation as if the expression were מִזֶּה. *V* gives "from it" (*ab ista*), i.e., from Egypt, and *S* and *T* both translate "from the presence of Egypt," thus personifying Egypt rather than referring primarily to its land. It is a curiously colorless expression to receive the reinforcement of גַּם "even, also."

The proposal may appear bold, but I submit that we have here an example of a verb מאה pi'el "do (something) a hundred times," denominative from מֵאָה "hundred."

This verb is proposed by Dahood for Pss 22:26; 66:20; and 109:20,[206] though the present proposal does not imply approval of all his proposed citations of this verb, only that such a verb exists (I propose it also for 13:25, which see). One must be careful that the context really makes a numerical expression plausible, but the present context does. The first colon of v 36 has מְאֹד "very," an expression of degree, and the second colon has שׁנה pi'el "change," literally "do twice, do for the second time."[207] The phrase גַּם מֵאֵת זֶה (or זֹה) will then mean "In fact you have done it a hundred times" and makes a perfect third colon for v 36. (Note that no revocalization is necessary.) One must assume that the phrase was displaced because of the second גַּם phrase: the phrase in question would have been omitted by haplography, notated in the margin and then reinserted at the wrong place, an error that would have been particularly easy if and when the meaning was misunderstood. We would have then a symmetrical sequence: an imperfect verb ("you change"), a perfect verb ("you have done it a hundred times"), an imperfect verb ("you will be shamed"), and a perfect verb ("you were shamed").

The verb זלל "treat cheaply" moves in the semantic field of dishonor (Lam 1:8 once more): if she changes her way cheaply, then she will be treated cheaply by Egypt as well as by "Assyria": thus the train of thought of the next two cola. For "be shamed" (בוש) see v 26; for the references to Egypt and "Assyria," see v 18 and Setting.

For וְ "and" before "hands" see GKC, sec. 154a, note b. What does the expression "hands on your head" mean? It is perhaps fortuitous, but the only direct parallel is the narrative of Amnon's rape of Tamar in 2 Samuel 13, and there are enough direct parallels to make it plausible that Jrm has that scene in mind. After Tamar is violated, Amnon hates her; she is "sent away" (v 16 there), the door is bolted against her, she "goes off" (הלך) with her

---

205 J. W. Olley, "A forensic connotation of *bôš*," *VT* 26 (1976) 230–34.

206 Dahood, *Psalms I*, 142; *Psalms III*, 107.

207 Compare the Ugaritic *ṯn* "two" and *ṯny* "repeat," and compare Hebrew שׁלשׁ pi'el "do a third time," 1 Kgs 18:34.

hands on her head (v 19 there).[208] The "hands on your head" in the present passage is then an expression of humiliation and despair; does Jrm imply that Egypt will rape Israel as Amnon took advantage of Tamar?

"For Yahweh has rejected your mainstays." The "mainstays" (מִבְטַחִים) are the things on which you rely, the people in whom you put your trust. In 5:17 Israel puts her trust in fortified cities; here she has put her trust in foreign alliances. Neither will do. The verb צלח hip'il means "succeed, prosper." There is uncertainty regarding the preposition here. M has לָהֶם, but de Rossi cites one MS. with בָּהֶם; G and S appear to support בְּ and T לְ. The passages elsewhere in which בְּ occurs with this verb (Dan 8:25; 2 Chr 32:30) are not appropriate to the meaning of the preposition which fits this context: in the present verse בָּהֶם would presumably mean "by means of them" and would parallel the occurrence of the same preposition in the previous colon. On the other hand לָהֶם would presumably mean "in regard to them" (Rudolph). With hesitation I choose בְּ. Foreign alliances will bring no success to Israel.

■ 3:1 This verse, beginning with the curious expression "as follows" (לֵאמֹר), was originally (by the proposal of the present study) a continuation of 2:9 (see Preliminary Observations). The first poetic expression is introduced by הֵן, a word which can mean either "behold" (= הִנֵּה) or "if" (as in Aramaic). Here it means "if"; that is, it is a particle introducing a hypothetical situation on which a question is based:[209] a close parallel to the present passage is Hag 2:12.[210] Perhaps the Aramaic usage, known in this period (see the remarks on 10:11 and 20:1–6), encouraged its use in these contexts, since most if not all of the passages in which הֵן occurs are later ones in the OT.

The first five cola of the poem set forth a legal case of divorce modeled on Deut 24:1–4. Since Hosea 2 also presupposes the Deuteronomy passage (see Hos 2:9),[211] Jrm is doubtless stimulated by both here.

Jrm has made remarkably free use of the Deuter-

onomy 24 passage.[212] The passage in Deuteronomy is framed as an address of Moses to Israel, and thus Yahweh is referred to in the third person (v 4; compare Deut 5:1). In the Jer passage, by contrast, Yahweh is the speaker. In both the Deuteronomy passage and the Jer passage the protasis (the "when"- or "suppose"-clause) states the circumstance, but in the Deuteronomy passage the apodosis ("then"-clause) states the law, while in the Jer passage the apodosis is a rhetorical question (the fourth colon). In the present passage, then, Yahweh is himself raising a question about the (Deuteronomic) law; this brings a startling rhetorical effect, given that Yahweh himself is the author of Torah. The law in Deuteronomy deals with the case of a man who divorces his wife; the wife then remarries, whereupon her new husband either divorces her or dies: her first husband is forbidden to remarry her. The Jer passage has used the law metaphorically to comment on the relation between Yahweh (the husband) and Israel (the wife), the same metaphor which prevailed in chapter 2, beginning with vv 2–3 there. And Jrm has gone beyond the text in Deuteronomy in both occurrences of the verb "return" (שׁוב) in the fourth and seventh cola (see below).

In the first colon the verb שׁלח pi'el does not quite mean "divorce," but it implies it by reference to the phraseology of the Deuteronomic law, which says, "if . . . he writes her a bill of divorce (סֵפֶר כְּרִיתֻת) and puts it in her hand and sends her out (שׁלח pi'el) of his house. . . ."

As already indicated, Jrm presses the verb "return" (שׁוב) in the fourth colon beyond the usage in Deuteronomy. In Deut 24:4 we read, "Her first husband . . . cannot turn (שׁוב) to take her [i.e., cannot again take her] to be a wife to him": the verb שׁוב carries here the idiomatic meaning "do something again." But Jrm says, "Would he (re)turn to her again?" Here is the adverb "again" (עוֹד), implied by שׁוב in Deuteronomy, while שׁוב carries its full value "(re)turn." The result in Jrm's metaphor is that Yahweh is the active agent, as the husband is in the Deuteronomic law, but the meaning of

---

208 G, V, and S there all read "hands," plural, against the singular in M; the plural is likely to be correct.
209 So BDB, 243, b.
210 Compare C. J. Labuschagne, "The particles הֵן and הִנֵּה," OTS 18 (1973) 9.
211 Wolff, Hosea, 36.
212 See Michael A. Fishbane, "Torah and Tradition," Tradition and Theology in the Old Testament (ed. Douglas A. Knight; Philadelphia: Fortress, 1977) 284–86.

the verb here suggests a kind of humbling action on Yahweh's part, as if Israel is the stable one and Yahweh contemplates moving back to her (compare the remarks on Yahweh's rhetorical question in 2:5). The perspective is so startling, given the status of women in the culture, that G reverses the gender references, μὴ ἀνακάμπτουσα ἀνακάμψει πρὸς αὐτὸν ἔτι, "Will she really return again to him?" (הֲשׁוֹב תָּשׁוּב אֵלָיו עוֹד). M is thus clearly the *lectio difficilior* and is followed by V and T (S paraphrases a bit, translating "if she returns to him again," and taking the fifth colon as a statement rather than a question). Many commentators (Cornill, Duhm, Giesebrecht, Rudolph) elect to follow G and emend the text to הֲשׁוֹב אֵלָיו עוֹד; this reading is more "logical" but leaves unanswered how the M text could have arisen if secondary, unless by the most unlikely of *lapsus calami*. M is thus to be accepted; in the last colon the gender references are the expected ones, so that Jrm has directed the hearer to the assumption of parity between Yahweh and Israel in "turning" (compare a similar parity between Jrm and Yahweh in 15:19).

The fifth colon, with "land," seems odd at first hearing, and both G and V read "woman" (and Volz and Condamin accept that reading). But again "land" is the *lectio difficilior* and follows the thought of Deut 24:4 ("and you shall not bring guilt upon the land"); the reading "woman" may have begun in G and been reinforced both by the "natural" train of thought and by the likeness of "land" (Greek γῆ) and "woman" (Greek γυνή) (Rudolph). The verb חנף qal means "be polluted"; it seems to be a more extreme term than טמא (which occurs in 2:7 and 23)—Johannes Pedersen states that it denotes that which "resists" what is sacred.[213] The verb is associated with blood-guilt (Num 35:33; Ps 106:38). While the law in Deut 24:4 simply states that for the first husband to take back a wife who had had a second husband would bring "guilt" (חטא hip'il) upon the land, Jrm uses חנף and so associates the situation with that in which violent blood has been shed. (For a similar law with slightly different vocabulary see Lev 19:29.)

But Israel, it seems, has done worse than the hypothetical wife in the legal case: she has not become a wife to another husband but has "whored" with "many partners." For "whore" see 2:20; רֵעִים may imply "lovers" (so *RSV* and other translations)—it carries that meaning in Cant 5:16, but since it is a general term for "fellows, partners," it is best here to stress that connotation (compare v 20 and Hos 3:1; the latter passage doubtless stands behind the present phrase).

The last colon of the verse offers a simple infinitive absolute without accompanying finite verb; Jrm uses this idiom to put some distance between the speaker and the action (English: "And imagine returning to me!" or "And to think you would return to me!"): compare the same usage in 4:18 and 8:15 (Rashi already compares the usage here to that of 4:18).

This verse offers an example of "how much more" (compare 2:10–11; 12:5): it is against the law for a wife to return to her first husband after a second marriage—how much more impossible for Israel to imagine returning to Yahweh after her affairs with the Baals![214] Jrm may be attempting here to oppose any complacency that the people might derive from the more reassuring message of Hos 3:1–5.

■ **3:2** In diction much like that in 2:23 Israel is invited to look squarely at her own behavior. The meaning of שְׁפָיִם has occasioned much debate.[215] Joüon first proposed the translation adopted here, "caravan-tracks,"[216] and that definition has been accepted in KB. On the other hand, the traditional rendering "bare heights" (so already Ibn Ezra on Isa 41:18 and Qimḥi on the present passage—*KJV*, Luther) has been defended recently by Karl Elliger.[217] The Versions are divided and uncertain; for the present passage G and V offer "straight ahead," while T renders "on the paths" and S "to the track." Rashi explains the word in this passage as "watercourses, wadis" (יבלי מים), in contrast to Qimḥi. The word appears six times in Jer (besides the present passage, 3:21; 4:11; 7:29; 12:12; 14:6) and three times elsewhere (Num 23:3;

---

213 Pedersen, III/IV 271.

214 So Lundbom, *Jeremiah*, 38.

215 For a full account of the renditions of the word in the Versions and commentators see William McKane, "*špy(y)m* with Special Reference to the Book of Jeremiah," *Mélanges bibliques et orientaux en l'honneur de M. Henri Cazelles* (ed. André Caquot and Matthias Delcor; AOAT 212; Neukirchen: Neukirchener,

1981) 319–35.

216 Paul Joüon, "Le sens du mot hébreu שְׁפִי," *JA* 7 (1906) 137–42.

217 Karl Elliger, "Der Sinn des hebräischen Wortes שְׁפִי," *ZAW* 83 (1971) 317–29.

Isa 41:18; 49:9).[218] These passages offer the following data: there is a specific association with "wilderness" (מִדְבָּר) in Jer 4:11; 12:12; and Isa 41:18, an association likewise implied in Jer 14:6 and perhaps in the present passage; there is an association with "path" (דֶּרֶךְ) in Isa 49:9 and perhaps in the present passage and 3:21; the word connotes the route of an invader in 12:12 and metaphorically in 4:11. The only passage where "height" is arguable is Isa 41:18, but "track" there is just as appropriate. I suggest that the word, clearly derived from שׁפה "sweep bare," refers to the beaten path where no plants grow, and that the association with "height" derives from the association of the present passage with the diction of 2:20. But it is unlikely that the fertility cult was pursued in the wilderness—no one seeks fertility there; the ruling metaphor here is that of the nation's waylaying economic and political partners as Arabs waylay caravans (see below).

The verb שָׁגַלְתְּ (שׁגל puʿal or qal passive) has traditionally been considered obscene and שָׁכַבְתְּ "been lain with" substituted in public reading (see Text). The other three occurrences of this verb are in the context of sexual violence (Deut 28:30; Isa 13:16; Zech 14:2), so it is likely that the connotation here is not simply that of sexual intercourse expressed crudely but of ravishment. Though Israel seeks lovers, she is ill-treated by those who take her.

"On the paths you have sat for them"—is there an ironic echo here of ישׁב לְ "sit for, stay at home for" in Hos 3:3? One has the impression that the Hosea passage implies that Gomer must sit rather than lie with Hosea; here, by contrast, Israel is depicted as sitting waiting for partners to lie with. The word כַּעֲרָבִי has caused difficulty (see Text), since both the "Arab" (M; T plural) and the "crow" (G, S) are associated with the desert and with pillaging or scavenging (V translates quasi latro "like a thief"!). Jerome cites the story of the man going down from Jerusalem to Jericho who fell among thieves (Luke 10:30).[219] For the association with עֹרְבִים "crows, ravens"

east of the Jordan, on the other hand, see 1 Kgs 17:4, 6.[220] Since M makes sense, it is better to stay with it, though it must be admitted that the image of the crow is an appropriate one as well (compare the young camel and wild ass in 2:23–24). For the prostitute waiting by the roadside compare Gen 38:14–16.

Verse 2b summarizes vv 1–2a: "profaned the land" reflects the fifth colon of v 1, and "with your whorings" (בִּזְנוּתַיִךְ) recalls the verb "whore" (זָנִית) in the sixth colon of that verse. Rudolph[221] suggests that בִּזְנוּתַיִךְ is a singular noun, in spite of the plural suffix, but this seems unnecessary. The RSV and NAB take the nouns in the last colon as a hendiadys (RSV: "your vile harlotry"), and this is certainly possible: the nouns are equivalent.

■ 3:3 Verse 3a reads altogether differently in M and G. The present study chooses M, but G is a plausible alternative (chosen by Duhm, Cornill, Giesebrecht, Condamin); it reads "And you had many shepherds for a stumbling-block to yourself" (καὶ ἔσχες ποιμένας πολλοὺς εἰς πρόσκομμα σεαυτῇ), which could be retrojected into וּמֵרֵעַיִךְ הָרַבִּים וּמוֹקֵשׁ לָךְ הָיָה (Duhm). The diction of the clause in G is of a piece with its surroundings; M, on the contrary, is the lectio difficilior (moving in an unexpected direction as it does), and the analysis in Preliminary Observations, by which v 3 is seen to be an addition by Jrm at the time of the second scroll, renders the reading of M the plausible one.

The consequence of Israel's whoring is the withdrawal of rain; "withhold" (מנע) is used with "rain" in Amos 4:7. The use of the nipʿal stem of the verb suggests not so much that Yahweh brought on the drought as that the drought came on its own because of Israel's disloyalty; such a thought is congruent with that of 2:19 (see there). The רְבִבִים "showers" cannot be specified more closely; the word is a poetic one (otherwise: 14:22; Deut 32:2; Mic 5:6; Pss 65:11; 72:6). The מַלְקוֹשׁ, on the other hand, is specifically the "latter rain" (compare the rendering in G of the first gloss in 5:24), occurring in April or early May.[222]

---

218 The ketib of Job 33:21 is textually dubious and unhelpful.
219 For reference to such brigands in the Christian era see Alfred Plummer, *A Critical and Exegetical Commentary on the Gospel According to St. Luke* (ICC; New York: Scribner's, 1896) 286.
220 On this bird in general see W. Stewart McCullough, "Raven," *IDB* 4:13.
221 Following Bauer-Leander, sec. 76k.
222 See Baly, *Geography*, 50–51; R. B. Y. Scott, "Palestine, climate of," *IDB* 3:625.

Volz accepted a suggestion of Ehrlich[223] to read "bronze (forehead)" (נְחֻשָּׁה) for "(forehead of) a whoring woman" (אִשָּׁה זוֹנָה), citing Isa 48:4 as a parallel. But אִשָּׁה זוֹנָה occurs in Josh 2:1, and the double expression may be useful here to pick up אִשְׁתּוֹ in v 1.

The "forehead" (מֵצַח) is the seat of obstinacy (Isa 48:4; Ezek 3:7), and Israel is offering Yahweh a whore's forehead. Though the expression is usually taken simply as an expression synonymous with that of the last colon, it is possible that it refers to some kind of phylactery worn by a prostitute; Herodotus mentions that Babylonian women resorting to cult prostitution sit "with a crown of cord around the head,"[224] and there is some evidence from carvings to that effect.[225]

The last colon completes the thought: Israel refuses to evidence any humiliation. The verb כלם nip'al evidently refers both to an inner emotional state and to an outer social situation. As to the inner emotional state, the diction of 31:19 suggests that it is more profound or intense than "be ashamed" (בוש). V translates here "blush" (*erubescere*), and this rendering is followed by many; but the Hebrew verb refers to a state that may continue for seven days (Num 12:14) and was the reaction of David's envoys to the Ammonites when their skirts were slit and beards half-shaved (2 Sam 10:5). Though blushing can be a sign of humiliation, it is safer to remain with "be humiliated." On the other hand, the verb also betokens an outward situation, "stand accused, stand incriminated"[226] (compare the inner and outer components of "were held guilty" in 2:3). The verb is a normal parallel to בוש (on which see 2:26, 36), so 6:15. Israel has forgotten how to be aware of humiliation.

■ **3:4** The second expression in *M* of this verse, מֵעַתָּה (literally "from now"), is scarcely explicable, in spite of the effort of commentators. The meaning "just now" seems forced, but the perfect verb קָרָאתִי would require some such meaning. The meaning "from now on" would require a rendering of what Yahweh hopes to hear from Israel, but then the perfect verb is puzzling, and the

expression "companion of my youth" would appear odd as something Yahweh wants to hear. From the point of view of poetic expression אָבִי "my father" would be possible if מֵעַתָּה is correct, but there is no parallel in the OT for "my father" as a wife's designation for a husband, and again "companion of my youth" would be an odd expression. For these reasons I propose to emend מֵעַתָּה and omit "my father" as a gloss (see Text).

If the reconstructed word מְעֹנִי is correct, it is a dramatic expression; the rendering "mainstay" is the proposal of Dahood for Ps 90:1,[227] a passage which Jrm may have had in mind. But to Jrm such a psalmic expression is open to grave misuse: the temptation for the people is to take Yahweh for granted, as if he were always available (compare another instance in which Jrm indicates a misuse of psalm language, 10:25, and compare, too, his insistence that Yahweh is transcendant as well as immanent, 23:23).

The phrase "companion of my youth" (אַלּוּף נְעֻרַי) is also found in Prov 2:17 as an expression for one's husband.[228] The word אַלּוּף means "someone trusted": it is parallel with רֵעַ in a wisdom passage in Mic 7:5 (compare the occurrence of that word in Jer 3:1, here "partners") and with מְיֻדָּע "confidant" in Ps 55:14. It is nowhere else used as a designation for God, and it would appear intended to shock by its familiar tone.

Israel may have had many "partners," but she persists in using cultic and familiar terms for Yahweh, as if he were completely at her disposal. Israel should be at Yahweh's disposal (2:3).

■ **3:5** The verb נטר "keep, watch" appears five times in the OT in the meaning "keep one's anger, bear a grudge"—beyond the present passage and in v 12 it appears in Lev 19:18; Nah 1:2; Ps 103:9. This last passages states, "He [God] will not bear a grudge for ever." The parallel colon uses שמר without an object; this idiom is found in a

223 Ehrlich, *Randglossen,* 243. The suggestion is also noticed by Rudolph.

224 Herod. 1, 199: στέφανον περὶ τῇσι κεφαλῇσι ἔχουσαι θώμιγγος.

225 Richard D. Barnett, *A Catalogue of the Nimrud Ivories, with other examples of Ancient Near Eastern Ivories in the British Museum* (London: Trustees of the British Museum, 1957) 145–51, esp. 148–49.

226 Martin A. Klopfenstein, *Scham und Schande nach dem Alten Testament, Eine begriffsgeschichtliche Untersuchung zu den hebräischen Wurzeln bôš, klm und ḥpr* (ATANT 212; Zurich: Theologischer, 1972) 143–44, 158.

227 Dahood, *Psalms II,* 172 (on 71:3) and 322 (on 90:1).

228 Toy, *Proverbs,* 46–47, suggests that the phrase in Proverbs may be dependent on the present passage, but this does not appear necessary.

similar context in Amos 1:11.[229] Israel counts on Yahweh's grace, counts indeed on his losing interest in keeping track of her sins (compare Job 7:11–21 for Job's expression of the wish that God would stop keeping track of him).

Analysis of the structure of this verse suggests that the present vocalization of הרעות needs to be altered to the appropriate form of רעע hip'il, like the revocalization in 2:33 (see Text). If this change is sound, then the four verbs are Yahweh's summary of the situation, arranged symmetrically in two pairs, perfect and waw-consecutive imperfect. For the last verb one would expect for the second singular feminine not וַתּוּכַל but וַתּוּכְלִי. The matter is discussed in GKC, secs. 69r and 145t, where other examples are given in which the imperfect second singular feminine is missing the suffix -î in a series: this may be a valid though rare pattern (see the remarks on 13:27, Text, Interpretation). The verb means "be victor"; the translation "gone unchallenged" is that of the *NEB*, and the *NJV* offers "and had your way" (compare וַתּוּכַל in the same meaning in 20:7 in Jrm's accusation to Yahweh).

■ 3:6–11 These six verses offer an early prose midrash (see Setting) on several phrases and words from the poetry of chapters 2—3, notably the words שׁוּבָה מְשֻׁבָה יִשְׂרָאֵל (3:12; see below). Other words and expressions which the passage picks up are: "on every high mountain, under every leafy tree," v 6 (see 2:20); "I sent her off," v 8 (see v 1); "commit adultery," נאף qal or pi'el, vv 8 and 9 (see 9:1); "betray," בגד, vv 8 and 11 (see v 20); "profane the land," v 9 (see vv 1, 2); "stone and tree," v 9 (see 2:27).

The passage takes "Israel" in v 12 to refer to the northern kingdom, and compares the conduct of the northern and southern kingdoms, just as Ezek 16:44–63 and 23:1–49 do, raising the question, Who is more guilty? The relation between the present passage and these chapters in Ezekiel is disputed: those who assume that vv 6–11 reflect the meaning of v 12 will hold to its

authenticity to the Jeremianic tradition, and therefore assume that Ezekiel 16 and 23 are dependent upon it (Cornill, Giesebrecht, Bright);[230] while those who are impressed by the lateness of the language of vv 6–11, viewing vv 6–11 as a reinterpretion of v 12, assume that the passage is dependent upon Ezekiel 16 and 23 (Duhm, Hyatt). The present study takes the latter position (see below; and see Setting, Interpretation on v 12).

It is proposed here that the midrash misconstrued the intended syntax of the words שׁוּבָה מְשֻׁבָה יִשְׂרָאֵל in v 12, that this clause was originally a verb with a cognate accusative, "Turn a turning, Israel!" (for a detailed defense of this proposal see v 12). The midrash assumed instead that מְשֻׁבָה there was either a kind of feminine adjective describing Israel personified as a young woman ("Turn, turnable Israel!"), or else an abstract noun for the concrete embodiment of that noun ("Turn, Turncoat Israel!").[231] This regrouping of the words may have been stimulated by v 22, where שׁוֹבָבִים is an adjective, and 8:5, where שׁוֹבֵבָה is an adjective. But the pseudoadjective in the present instance, preceding the noun and without the expected definite article, was perceived to be a kind of appositional proper name.[232] On this assumption, and under the further stimulus of both the introductory words in v 12 and the occurrence of the verb בגד in v 20, the writer of the midrash constructed a second character, referred to either as בָּגוֹדָה אֲחוֹתָהּ יְהוּדָה "her sister Traitor Judah" (vv 7, 10) or as בֹּגֵדָה יְהוּדָה "Treacherous Judah" (vv 8, 11, with the added appositive אֲחוֹתָהּ "her sister" in v 8).

There are many oddities in the Hebrew of this midrash in the form in which it has reached us. The vocalizations of בָּגוֹדָה and בֹּגֵדָה are odd: are they intended to be the same word with uncertain vocalization, or is there some difference here which escapes us? If there is an adjective בָּגוֹר otherwise unattested, why is the feminine not בְּגוֹדָה?[233] And if בֹּגֵדָה is to be construed as a feminine participle of בגד, why is it not בֹּגֶדֶת?[234] Neither form carries the definite article, though modi-

229 See the careful analysis in Wolff, *Joel and Amos*, 130–31.

230 See also Zimmerli, *Ezekiel 1*, 482.

231 Volz compares "he was made sin" in 2 Cor 5:21.

232 GKC, sec. 132b; so also Volz.

233 Compare Bauer-Leander, sec. 26t'.

234 Compare ibid., sec. 26t.

fying or referring to "Judah," no doubt because its parallel מְשֻׁבָה, whether construed as a kind of adjective or not, carries no article either. The feminine gender of מְשֻׁבָה, as well as the feminine references in vv 1–5, elsewhere in these chapters, and in Ezekiel 16 and 23, would encourage the personifications of the midrash, but surely the masculine imperative שׁוּבָה in v 12 would jar the sensibilities of those who saw cogency in the midrash.

The style of the passage is careless and appears late. If the final yod of וַתְּזְנִי in v 6 is stimulated by parallel Aramaic forms (see Text), then it is possible that the curious וְהָיָה in v 9 is also an expression influenced by Aramaic (Hebrew usage would suggest וַיְהִי).[235] The verb נאף shifts from pi'el in v 8 to qal in v 9 (if the vocalization is correct) without discernible reason. Other oddities include the unique sequence עַל־כָּל־אֹדוֹת אֲשֶׁר "precisely because" in v 8—one is reminded of such periphrastic conjunctions in Aramaic, such as the common כָּל־קֳבֵל דִּי "because" in Dan 2:8—and one may include here also the compound preposition אֶל־תַּחַת in v 6.[236] The use of the participle in v 6 is also suggestive of a later style (Duhm); compare the narrative use of the participle in the Aramaic of Dan 3:3–4.

In the matter of the misconstruction of the syntax of v 12 by the writer of the midrash, a modern parallel might be useful. The *KJV* and American Revised Version rendered πίετε ἐξ αὐτοῦ πάντες in Matt 26:27 by "Drink ye all of it." There "all" of course was intended to be construed with the subject "ye"; but more recent English would misunderstand the syntax and take "all" to refer to the contents of the cup, so that one finds a devotional poem[237] based on this misunderstanding: "'"Drink ye all of it," *all*, not just a sup—/ Drink my faith, my love,' said Jesus, / Drink the fullness of my cup. . . ." (Three more stanzas follow.) The *RSV* translates, "Drink of it, all of you."

The understanding of מְשֻׁבָה embodied in the midrash is understandably underlined by the medieval commentators; Rashi identified מְשֻׁבָה with הַשּׁוֹבֵבָה in 31:22 and

49:4, and Qimḥi says, "An adjective, and its meaning is 'rebelling,' from שׁוֹבוּ בָנִים שׁוֹבָבִים [vv 14, 22]." But if such an understanding of מְשֻׁבָה commended itself to the writer of the midrash and thus to the medieval exegetes (and to V, one may add; both here and in v 12 the word is rendered *adversatrix*), G and S perceived the word to be related to ישׁב "dwell" (G renders מְשֻׁבָה יִשְׂרָאֵל by ἡ κατοικία τοῦ ισραηλ "the house of Israel," as if the first word were מוֹשָׁב; and S translates "inhabitant [fem.] of Israel," as if the word were יֹשֶׁבֶת. T is periphrastic).

■ **3:6** The passage is set in the days of Josiah, but the combination "And the Lord said to me" with "in the days of" is curious and not paralleled elsewhere in Jer, one more indication that the passage is late and imitative: in the attribution to the days of Josiah the writer is trying for verisimilitude (compare 1:2, 3; 36:2). The translation "the LORD" for יהוה is appropriate for the postexilic period, when the tetragrammaton was no longer commonly pronounced.[238] For the question-form "Have you seen what . . . ?" see Form. One notes also that the writer has shifted from "hill" (גִּבְעָה), the word in 2:20, to "mountain" (הַר) here (so also Isa 30:25; 57:7).[239]

■ **3:7** For "think" to translate אמר see v 19; just as God originally expected Israel to stay faithful to him (v 19), so now in the situation of the disobedience of the northern kingdom God looks for Israel's return to him—"return" (שׁוב) being a steady motif of 3:1—4:4. "But she did not"; the evidence, of course, is that that nation was destroyed by Yahweh. The designation בָּגוֹדָה for Judah is derived, as we have seen, from the diction of v 20, where the corresponding verb appears; the verb means "betray," not only in the marriage relation but in covenantal relations generally (for further discussion of the verb see v 20). Judah saw the wicked behavior of Israel.

■ **3:8–9** The verb נאף (pi'el here, qal in v 9) means (in both stems) "commit adultery"; it is the verb in the Ten Commandments (Exod 20:14; Deut 5:18) and occurs in poetic passages of Jrm (5:7; 9:1; 23:10, 14), though not in 2:1—4:4. The verb "send off" is picked up from v 1,

---

235 Note that T at this point reads וַהֲוָה; but see GKC, sec. 112ss.

236 For the few further instances of this combination see BDB, p. 1066a, III, 1.

237 The poem is by E. Dent Lackey, appearing in *The Christian Century* (February 14, 1940) 57:210.

238 See Helmer Ringgren, *Israelite Religion* (Philadelphia: Fortress, 1966) 308.

239 Holladay, "On Every High Hill," 174.

but what follows here is not what v 1 says but what the legal source behind v 1, namely Deut 24:1, says: "I gave her a bill of divorce," that is, God sent the northern kingdom into exile. All of this Judah saw, but she did not draw the lesson. She "had no fear," and profaned the land and worshiped stone and tree.

■ **3:10** "But even in all this" (וְגַם־בְּכָל־זֹאת) sounds like a phrase typical of later Hebrew, but a very similar phrase, again with שׁוב (though the verb carries the opposite sense), begins the "refrain" in Isa 5:25; 9:11, 16, 20; 10:4. The phrase "with all one's heart" occurs in the prose of Jer (24:7; 29:13; 32:41) and is common in Deuteronomy and the Deuteronomistic editorial passages.[240] Bright has a nice translation of כִּי אִם־בְּשֶׁקֶר "but insincerely": "but only pretended to do so." If Judah speaks of coming back to God, there is no substance to the notion.

■ **3:11** Judah did not take advantage of the lesson offered by the northern kingdom, and in ignoring the lesson and repenting insincerely she has made herself more guilty than the north.

■ **3:12** The section begins with the introductory command, "Go and call out these words to the north and say." The infinitive absolute הָלֹךְ followed by a waw-consecutive perfect verb is a common pattern in Jer (eight times beyond the present passage), but only 2:2, like the present passage, has הָלֹךְ וְקָרָאתָ "go and call out." The present study accepts these words as identifying the original context of the words that follow, directed by Jrm to the north (see Preliminary Observations, Setting). In that case the word "(re)turn" (שׁוב) in v 14 carries the primary meaning of geographical return from exile and of return in loyalty from political and cultic schism, and in this meaning the word echoes the dream of Josiah for a reunion of the north and the south in loyalty to Jerusalem. Behind these meanings is the assumption that it is a "return" to Yahweh, and that is the meaning of the same verb in the present verse. Jrm's adaptation of these words by the addition of further material in 2:1—4:4 will reapply the words to the south, where the emphasis is on "return" to Yahweh, that is, repentance. Only when Judah experienced an exile would the word again shift weight to the connotation of "return" from exile.

The first colon of poetry offers an imperative in the masculine singular to conform to the gender of "Israel"; it is doubtless an expansion of "Return, O Israel" (שׁוּבָה יִשְׂרָאֵל) in Hos 14:2 (compare below on v 22). As already noted above (on vv 6–11), the present study proposes that the expression שׁוּבָה מְשֻׁבָה יִשְׂרָאֵל is an instance of cognate accusative, "Turn a turning, Israel." There are cognate accusatives elsewhere in Jrm's poetry: "and a flight they fled" (וּמָנוֹס נָסוּ), and two instances of "plead a pleading" (דִּין דִּין, 5:28 and 22:16). One notes that the first parallel (46:5), like the present instances, involves an intransitive verb of motion. The cognate accusative has not heretofore been recognized in the present passage because of the reconception of the expression in vv 6–11, whether a particular commentator has believed those previous verses to present Jrm's thinking or not. Negatively it must be said that there is no parallel elsewhere in Jrm's lines for the kind of personification of an action noun such as is presupposed by the writer of the midrash. (In passing it may be noted that one might have expected the feminine imperative שׁוּבִי if there were a feminine personification here; S, as a matter of fact, does have the feminine singular imperative here.) Positively it must be said that the colon makes sense as a cognate accusative; the closest parallel is 8:5, where מְשֻׁבָה is likewise singular, unsuffixed, as best construed as a cognate accusative (see there). It is to be noted that elsewhere in Jrm's poetry מְשֻׁבָה is plural and suffixed (2:19; 3:22; 5:6; 14:7), and that in the plural it seems to mean "acts of apostasy" (see particularly the contexts of 5:6 and 14:7). Jrm elsewhere exploits the double direction of שׁוב (4:1; 8:4), and that double direction may be implicit here as well, since in the context the imperative שׁוּבָה suggests "repent" and מְשֻׁבָה suggests "apostasy": the two are placed side by side in a tension that is far from easy to reproduce—"make a turning from apostasy" is surely implied.

If these poetic verses belong in the present sequence of poetry (see Structure), then this colon is in strong contrast to the ironic exclamation at the end of v 1, "And to think you would return to me!" That exclamation was a reflection of Israel's casual assumption that she could go back to Yahweh's good graces at any time: "Will he

---

240 Weinfeld, *Deuteronomy*, 334, nos. 9 and 9a.

bear a grudge for ever?" (v 5). Now, by contrast, comes the passionate appeal from Yahweh that the people return to him, but return thoroughly and sincerely.

The first two cola are separated from each other by the expression "oracle of Yahweh" (נְאֻם־יהוה); so are the last two cola of the verse, and the two cola of v 14;[241] note that by the proposal of the present study vv 12 and 14 are part of the original proclamation to the north, and v 13 was added by Jrm when he proclaimed the words to the south (Preliminary Observations). "Oracle of Yahweh" appears once earlier in the poetry of the chapter (v 1) and appears in v 20, and these appearances represent what one assumes to be the normal frequency of the use of the expression. But why three times in the six cola of vv 12 and 14?—is it a mark of particular intensity in prophetic expression?

The second colon curiously shifts the address to the plural (and G, V, and S agree on the shift). "I will not frown at you" is literally "I will not let my face fall for you." There is no strict parallel for this expression (נפל hip'il with פָּנִים), though Job 29:24 has "they did not let fall the light of my face," and Gen 4:5–6 offers נפל qal with פָּנִים subject.[242] Yahweh will not be angry.

In the third colon Yahweh declares himself to be חָסִיד, "faithful, dependable." This adjective is used thirty-two times in the OT, but as a description of God it appears only here and in Ps 145:17 (and, according to Marvin H. Pope, is never applied to God in the Talmud or later Jewish literature).[243] One who is חָסִיד is one who does חֶסֶד, ḥesed (on which see 2:2); thus Yahweh is saying, "I keep my promises." The tone of this statement is warm and reassuring; compare the diction of Ps 86:2, where the worshiper begs God to preserve his life and save him, כִּי־חָסִיד אָנִי, "for I am steadfast in my loyalty." One would expect Yahweh by definition to keep his loyalty, so this language reveals the kind of condescension to the level of human discourse which is implicit in 2:5 and 3:1.

Parallel to this colon is the last in the verse, "I will not bear a grudge for ever," the answer to the frivolously posed question in v 5: of course Yahweh will not hold a grudge for ever (if the change of heart of the people is sincere, a proviso set forth in v 13). The theology is quite compatible with that of Exod 34:6–7. But what a contrast between the frivolity of the wayward wife, Israel, and the steady purpose of Yahweh!

■ **3:13** The feminine singular address in this verse picks up the diction of vv 1–5 but interrupts the diction of vv 12 and 14; for a discussion of this and other evidence that the verse is a later addition by Jrm, see Preliminary Observations.

The particle אַךְ restricts the meaning of the imperative which follows: "Just admit your guilt" (compare אַךְ with the imperative in Gen 27:13 and Judg 10:15). The verb ידע usually "know," here means "recognize, acknowledge," as in 2:23. For "guilt" (עָוֺן) see 2:22.

"That against Yahweh your God you rebelled": similar passages in 2:8, 29 offer "against me" (first person), while here we have the third person. The shift is analogous to that between 2:2 and 3.

The following phrase is odd (see Text); assuming the text is correct, "scatter your strength among strangers" can only refer to the way Judah has dissipated her resources to Egypt and Babylon. The verb פזר pi'el occurs only seven times: Ps 147:16 states that God scatters hoarfrost like ashes, and Joel 4:2 refers to those who have scattered Israel among the nations. The word דְּרָכִים (normally "ways") in the meaning of "strength" evidently means "virility" in Prov 31:3[244] and "dominion" in Ps 138:5.[245] One may surmise, then, that the reference here is to "sovereignty" or "wealth," which has been sent out broadside to gain favor and security. Jehoiakim, we read in 2 Kgs 23:35, "gave the silver and the gold to Pharaoh, but he taxed the land to give the money according to the command of Pharaoh. He exacted the silver and the gold of the people of the land, from every one according to his assessment, to give it to Pharaoh Neco." But then after the battle of Carchemish (605), Judah passed under Babylonian control, and

---

241 Compare the discussion in Rolf Rendtorff, "Zum Gebrauch der Formel ne'um jahwe im Jeremiabuch," ZAW 66 (1954) 29.

242 On such expressions for "face" see Johnson, *Vitality of the Individual*, 43.

243 Marvin H. Pope, "Hasidim," *IDB* 2:528–29.

244 So Toy, *Proverbs*, 540.

245 So Dahood, *Psalms III*, 278.

Jehoiakim became Nebuchadrezzar's "servant" (2 Kgs 24:1). This is a fitting background for the colon (compare 16:17). For "strangers" (וָרִים) see 2:25. The verse is rounded off by the clause "and my voice [you] did not obey." The idiom שמע בְּקוֹל "obey the voice (of Yahweh)"[246] occurs eighteen times in Deut (e.g., Deut 4:30) and just as often in Jer, largely as a recurrent prose phrase, but it occurs twice in Jrm's poetry, here and in 22:21, as well as in 7:23, part of the second scroll. The present passage is distinctive in its inversion of verb and complement. The fact that the expression later became a cliché in the prose of the book should not blind us to its distinctiveness here; its appearance in Jrm's poetry marks its first recorded occurrence in the prophets, and, though a standard legal phrase, it must have been striking in the context.

■ **3:14–15** These two verses offer three reminiscences of 2:8–9: "children" in v 14 (compare 2:9); the verb בעל "be master" in v 14, related to "Baal" (2:8); and "shepherds" in v 15 (2:8). It must be borne in mind that according to the conclusions of the present study 2:9 in the original recension to the north was immediately followed by 3:1–2, 4–5, 12 and then the present two verses (see Preliminary Observations); the present material was therefore originally in close proximity to 2:8–9.

■ **3:14** The first colon (repeated as the first colon of v 22) offers prodigious assonance: שׁוּבוּ בָנִים שׁוֹבָבִים, "Return, turnable children," offering not only the permutation of š and b but a pleasing succession of seven long vowels. As already stated (see v 12), the context of "return" in the earliest recension (words to the north) was geographical return, return in loyalty from political and cultic schism.

"Children" repeats that word in 2:9 (see above). Yahweh wishes not only to confront the northerners with his accusations (2:9) but with the opportunity for restoration as well.

The adjective שׁוֹבָב appears only here (and in the identical v 22) and in Isa 57:17, and one must presume that Isa 57:16–18 is a later reflection on the material in

Jer. The Versions are of little help in pinpointing the meaning of the word, but a translation of "apostate" or "disloyal" would fit.

In the present study the text of the verse is rearranged so that the second colon is the phrase "one from a city and two from a tribe" found in the second half of the verse (for this rearrangement see Text). Yahweh will bring the northerners home; for "tribe" (מִשְׁפָּחָה) in reference to the north, see 1:15. The numbers "one" and "two" form standard parallelism,[247] but the implication of these numbers is that only a remnant will return.

The following colon, כִּי אָנֹכִי בָּעַלְתִּי בָכֶם, "for it is I who am your master," implies, by its use of the verb corresponding to the noun בַּעַל "Baal," that Yahweh is the only true ba'al, "lord, master" to Israel: again the diction is reminiscent of the material in chapter 2, this time in v 8 there. (This verb will be used once more in Jer, in 31:32; see there.)

"I will take you and bring you to Zion" expresses the hope of Josiah to bring the north back into unity with the south (compare the same implication in 31:6). But of course these words would have fresh usefulness at a time when the south would be threatened with exile, and a time thereafter when the exile had taken place; that God could bring the exiles of Judah back to Zion would be good news indeed.

■ **3:15** For "shepherds" see 2:8; Yahweh will replace the unfaithful shepherds with his own faithful ones.

■ **3:16–17** For the translation "the LORD" for the tetragrammaton, see on v 6. God assures his people that the ark of the covenant will no longer be needed: it is thus God's intention that the ark disappear. One cannot avoid the impression that these verses reflect the hunger of the exiles that God bless the inevitable. Whether the ark was restored to the temple by Josiah after it was in eclipse during Manasseh's reign, as 2 Chr 33:7 and 35:3 suggest,[248] there is no doubt that it was lost sight of in the destruction of Jerusalem, and the disappearance of so central an object was a crucial matter; hence the burden

---

246 "Hear" (שמע) implies "obey": one notes the frequency with which the Hebrew verb is rendered in G by ὑπακούειν "obey": see Gerhard Kittel, "ἀκούω, κτλ.," *TDNT* 1:217–18, 224.

247 Wolfgang M. W. Roth, "The Numerical Sequence x/x+1 in the Old Testament," *VT* 12 (1962) 301.

248 On the meaning of the latter verse see Edward L. Curtis and Albert A. Madsen, *A Critical and Exegetical*

Commentary on the Books of Chronicles (ICC; New York: Scribner's, 1910) 512–13.

of the verse.[249] The narrative of 2 Macc 2:1–18, by which Jrm was told to go up on Mount Nebo and take there the tent, the ark, and the altar of incense and seal them in a cave, is clearly a later legend dependent on the present passage. (Compare *2 Apoc. Bar.* 6:7–10, in which an angel from heaven, during the siege of Jerusalem, takes away the veil, the holy ark, the mercy-seat, the two tables, the holy raiment of the priests, the altar of incense, and other objects, and hides them; or *m. Šeqal.* 6.1–2, in which the ark is hidden in the temple.) The innovativeness of the message is reflected elsewhere in affirmations of the period: compare Isa 43:18, "Remember not the former things."

Whatever the appearance and function of the ark, some traditions indicated it to have been a "throne" for the invisible Yahweh: the ark was deposited under the cherubim in the holy of holies (1 Kgs 8:6), and Hezekiah began a prayer to Yahweh in the temple, "O Yahweh, God of Israel, who art enthroned above the cherubim" (2 Kgs 19:15).[250] Verse 17 is a prime datum to reinforce the thesis that the ark was understood to be a throne for Yahweh; the verse indicates that in time to come *all* Jerusalem (implication, not merely the ark) will be called "the throne of the LORD."[251] Further it is said that all nations shall stream to Jerusalem to worship there; the theme of the gathering of the nations to Jerusalem became a convention in the postexilic period.[252] That the nations are understood to be "gathered" or "collected" (קוה II nipʿal) for the "name" of the LORD suggests a reflection of the "name"-theology of Deuteronomy, by which the immanent presence of Yahweh is in the central place where he "makes his name dwell" (Deut 12:11).[253] It may be noted in passing that the phrase "for the name of the LORD in Jerusalem" is omitted in *G* and is perhaps a secondary addition to the text.

The noun שְׁרִרוּת, occurring often in Jer (see below), is normally translated "stubbornness." But it may not necessarily imply unreasonable obstinacy: the *NJV* has "willfulness," the *JB* (perhaps influenced by *G*) has

"dictates," and a recent study suggests "self-reliance."[254] The phrase "walk after/in the stubbornness of their evil heart" occurs nine times: Deut 29:18; Jer 23:17 (poetry); the present passage; and six more times in the prose of the book (7:24; 9:13; 11:8; 13:10; 16:12; 18:12). In all these passages except possibly the present one the "evil heart" is that of Israel. It is startling, then, that it is said here that stubbornness will no longer be manifested by "the nations," and Rudolph wonders whether the text should not be emended from כָּל to מִכָּל, thus "(and they [i.e., Israel] shall gather toward her) from all (the nations)," etc. But there is no real warrant for such a change, and one has best see the present passage as the author's adaptation of a stock phrase in the tradition, an adaptation in a universalistic direction.

■ **3:18** The meaning of עַל here must be "in addition to" (as in 1 Kgs 15:20);[255] this is the understanding of *S* and *T*. "North" here carries a quite general sense: historically Israel was both in the north of Palestine and (along with Judah) in Mesopotamia (compare the message of Ezek 37:21).

■ **3:19** This verse resumes the diction of vv 4–5 (see Preliminary Observations); there is a contrast between what Israel had called Yahweh (v 4) and what Yahweh had desired to happen, a contrast signaled by the opening words וְאָנֹכִי אָמַרְתִּי, translated here "But I for my part thought." The verb אמר is often used for inner speaking, thinking, and desiring (2 Kgs 5:11).[256]

The implication of desire carries over into אֵיךְ "how" with which the second colon begins; the emotion of the word must be seen from the context, in this case "how much, how gladly" (compare Prov 5:12, וְאָמַרְתָּ אֵיךְ שָׂנֵאתִי מוּסָר "But you say, 'How I hate discipline!'"). *G* has interpreted אֵיךְ spectacularly, taking the consonants איך as an abbreviation for אָמֵן יהוה כִּי "so be it, Yahweh,

---

249 Compare Gerhard von Rad, *Old Testament Theology 2* (New York: Harper, 1965) 272.

250 For a discussion of the ark as a throne see typically Gerhard von Rad, "The Tent and the Ark," *The Problem of the Hexateuch and Other Essays* (New York: McGraw-Hill, 1966) 108.

251 See n. 250.

252 See for example Gerhard von Rad, "The City on the

Hill," *The Problem of the Hexateuch and Other Essays* (New York: McGraw-Hill, 1966) 232–42.

253 See Gerhard von Rad, *Studies in Deuteronomy* (SBT 9; Naperville, IL: Allenson, 1953) 38–39.

254 Aída Besançon Spencer, "שרירות as Self-Reliance," *JBL* 100 (1981) 247–48.

255 See BDB, 755, 4c.

256 See ibid., 56, qal 2.

for,"[257] but this is not the original intention of the wording.

The implication of the next two words, אֲשִׁיתֵךְ בַּבָּנִים, literally "I will place you among the sons," is not self-evident. The same idiom, שִׁית בְּ, appears in 2 Sam 19:29; there Mephibosheth (Meribaal) says to David, "You included me among those who eat at your table." But this meaning is baffling here; who would the "sons" be with whom the "wife" is included? Jewish exegesis (e.g., Rashi) assumes the "sons" to be other nations; but the phrase may intend something slightly different. There are no "sons" separate from the "wife" in the metaphor. Does it mean "I will put you in the status of sons," that is, give you inheritance rights such as sons have? Widows had no inheritance rights, while sons did;[258] this explanation makes sense, given the word "inheritance" (נַחֲלַת) in the fourth colon. (There is no warrant to think of inheritance rights of a daughter here [Duhm, Cornill]; the metaphor has been of a "wife," v 1, and by the conclusion of the present study "my father" in v 4 is a gloss.) There is a similar passage in Job 30:1, where שִׁית עִם (not בְּ) is used in a hypothetical situation: "But now they make sport of me, men who are younger than I, whose fathers I would have disdained to set with the dogs of my flock." Here "set with" could easily be "treat like." So in the present passage, given the vocative "sons/children" in v 22, it is best to translate "treat as" (so also *NAB*). Yahweh wants to bequeath to the people land, just as a father bequeaths land to his sons. (For the image of Israel as the sons of Yahweh, see Deut 32:5, and see further below on "father.")

"So I gave you a lovely land": the feminine suffixes must have sounded striking to ears not accustomed to hearing of a woman heir! (compare the inheriting of property by the daughters of Zelophehad in Numbers 27 and 36). The word חֶמְדָּה "excellence, loveliness" is not common in Jer; it does appear in 12:10 in a similar context, where Yahweh mourns the destruction of his own lovely portion (or land). For the expression אֶרֶץ

חֶמְדָּה here compare אֶרֶץ הַכַּרְמֶל "the garden land" in 2:7.

The fourth colon offers נַחֲלָה "(inalienable) property, inheritance"; in 2:7, the passage just referred to, this word is likewise in parallel with "land." For the understanding of צְבִי צְבָאוֹת as a superlative, "most glorious," see Text. The general turn of phrase here is reflected in Ezek 20:6, 15; there צְבִי is not repeated, but the diction implies a superlative nevertheless: צְבִי הִיא לְכָל־הָאֲרָצוֹת, "It is the most glorious of all lands." The third colon of Amos 6:1 likewise expresses the thought that Israel is the most privileged of all nations.

The fifth colon continues the "thought" of Yahweh: if Israel, formerly understood as a "wife," is to be treated by him like sons, then he expects Israel to call him "my father." The image of God as father is of course very old in the Near East, antedating Yahwism. There are Mesopotamian names compounded with "father," e.g., Shamash-abi, "Shamash is my father," and in the Ugaritic text Danel calls El his father. Similarly the OT theophoric names compounded with אָב/אֲבִ "father" are common in all periods. But texts are loath to call Yahweh "father," doubtless because of the prevalence of such imagery in Canaanite religious diction. In Exod 4:22 (J), however, Yahweh calls Israel his first-born son, and in Deut 32:6 we read, "Is not he your father, who created you . . . ?" Closer to Jrm's time is Isa 1:2, "Sons have I reared and brought up, but they have rebelled against me."[259]

With מֵאַחֲרֵי the verb שׁוּב carries the specific meaning "withdraw (often under pressure)"; it is used spatially in passages like 2 Sam 11:15, "Put Uriah on the forefront of the hardest fighting, and draw back," and figuratively of withdrawing from God. This is the only instance in Jer of שׁוּב with this preposition.[260] If Yahweh is to be treated as a father, then Israel would not back away from him as one backs away from the military pressure of an enemy.

■ 3:20 The root בגד has already occurred in v 7; it has the general meaning "betray, act faithlessly against," whether in marriage, as in the first colon here, or in the covenant,

---

257 See Bauer-Leander, sec. 5a'; Rudolph; and compare Michael A. Fishbane, "Abbreviations, Hebrew texts," *IDBSup*, 4, d.
258 Otto J. Baab, "Inheritance," *IDB* 2:701–2.
259 For a survey of the image in the ancient Near East and in the OT see Helmer Ringren, "אָב," *TDOT* 1:4–5, 6–7, 16–18.
260 On this idiom see William L. Holladay, *The Root Šûbh in the Old Testament, With Particular Reference to Its Usages in Covenantal Contexts* (Leiden: Brill, 1958) 64, 80, 129.

as in the second, or in breaking other kinds of human agreements or rebelling against the created order.[261] The contrast of preposition between the two cola appears deliberate—as a woman betrays (מֵ) her lover, so you have betrayed (בְּ) me; but it is not easy to give an account of the contrast. The verb does not appear with מִן in any other passage of the OT, and the expression here may simply be linked with the occurrence of מִן in מֵאַחֲרֵי in the previous line. By contrast, בְּ is common with the verb. On רֵעַ for a sexual partner see v 1. Yahweh had had a great plan to treat Israel like sons and to enter into a relation as solid as that between a father and sons in a human family, only to see Israel shatter the plan.

The background of Jrm's diction here is the marriage law in Exod 21:8—though there it is the husband who has betrayed his wife; and more particularly Hos 5:7 and 6:7, where it is stated that Israel has betrayed Yahweh. The phrase "house of Israel" is a final vocative. It sounds stiff and formal: is Yahweh suddenly abandoning the language of intimacy for the language of forensic accusation once more?

■ **3:21** Is קוֹל to be construed as the subject of the clause ("A sound [on the paths may be heard, the suppliant weeping]") or, with Volz, Rudolph, *NEB*, *NJV*, as an interjection ("Hark! [on the paths may be heard the suppliant weeping]")? Though the earlier lexica posit the exclamatory use of קוֹל,[262] KB cites the usage only with a query,[263] and it seems more economical in the present instance to maintain the parallelism of "sound" and "weeping." For שְׁפָיִים = "caravan-tracks" see v 2. The participle נִשְׁמָע is to be understood here as potential, "may be heard."[264]

Evidence has already been given that the long construct chain, בְּכִי תַחֲנוּנֵי בְּנֵי יִשְׂרָאֵל, literally "the weeping of the supplication of the children of Israel," contains an objective genitive, that it means "suppliant weeping for Israel's sons." The wording is very close to 31:15, where Rachel is weeping for her lost children. By this understanding, then, it is not that the Israelites are

weeping to Yahweh, but rather that Yahweh is weeping for his lost children, the Israelites (for detailed argumentation, see Preliminary Observations). For another passage where Yahweh is evidently weeping over his people, see 9:9.

Since קוֹל תַּחֲנוּנִים "sound of weeping" is a standard phrase in the Psalms (Pss 28:2, 6; 31:23; 86:6; 130:2; 140:7; compare 116:1), the usage here is an example of the break-up of a stereotyped phrase.[265] One also notes that בְּכִי and תַחֲנוּנִים are in parallelism in Jer 31:9, so that the two Jer passages represent a set of variations on normal phraseology. The noun תַּחֲנוּנִים means "supplication, cries for favor."[266] If the interpretation here is correct, that Yahweh is weeping for his children, then this diction clearly sets forth a poignant image of God, lowering himself to deal with Israel on a human level (compare the remarks on 2:5; 3:1, 12).

Verse 21b is an addition in the first scroll (see Preliminary Observations); כִּי here must mean something like "given the fact that, inasmuch as." The noun דֶּרֶךְ, singular, carries the meaning it does in 2:23, 33, 36, "way, course of life." We have been told that Israel "changed" her way (2:36); now we hear that she has "deflected" her way: עוה hip'il means "twist, pervert." For "forget Yahweh" see 2:32.

■ **3:22** For the first colon, with the two occurrences of the root שׁוּב, see v 14.

The second colon brings a third word with שׁוּב, מְשׁוּבֹתֵיכֶם; for its meaning see 2:19. "I want to heal your turnings" reflects "I want to heal their turnings" in Hos 14:5. These two cola thus represent a climax to the chapter, building on vv 12 and 14, and ultimately on Hos 14:2, 5 (see above on v 12). The turnings, the acts of apostasy, Yahweh wants to heal (for this meaning of the imperfect see Giesebrecht, Weiser, *JB*). Whatever the nation manifests that takes it away from Yahweh, he can cure.

Then the people, in Yahweh's scenario, answer, "Here we are!" The word אָתָנוּ is evidently a verb (אתה) used

---

261 Seth Erlandsson, "בָּגַד," *TDOT* 1:470–73.
262 BDB, 877a, 1f; Zorell, 716b, end of sec. 2; see also GKC, sec. 146b.
263 *HALAT*, 1015a, end of entry.
264 GKC, sec. 116e.
265 See the discussion on 2:3, and n. 79.
266 David N. Freedman and Jack Lundbom, "חָנַן," *TWAT*, III, col. 27.

only in poetic diction. In 2:31 the people denied being willing to come to Yahweh ("We shall no longer come to you!"); here, by contrast, the scenario includes a willingness to come (Rudolph), a willingness to recognize Yahweh for who he is ("for you are Yahweh our God"). The latter phrase is repeated (except for a change of suffix) in 31:18: indeed the material in 31:15–18 is close to the diction of vv 21a + 22 here. Since the passage in vv 15–18 represents actual repentance and the present passage hypothetical repentance, the two should be read side by side.

■ **3:23** The implication of the double occurrence of אָכֵן has been misunderstood: the Versions uniformly translate with an expression for "truly," and the commentators and modern translations have followed them in this. Furthermore, the syntax of the first half of the verse is not clear, and commentators have tended to follow the Versions in reading "the hills" (הַגְּבָעוֹת) for "from hills" (מִגְּבָעוֹת) (Volz, Rudolph, Bright: Bright suggests the text has a mem enclitic) and reading "confusion of" (construct, הֲמוֹן) for "confusion" (absolute, הָמוֹן). Some basic reassessment is in order.

The lexica assume tht אָכֵן means either "truly" or "nevertheless," but it is not at all clear how a single word can be alternatively asseverative and contrastive. There are eight passages cited as asseverative ("truly") in BDB and *HALAT* (the lists are identical): Gen 28:16; Exod 2:14; 1 Sam 15:32; Isa 40:7; 45:15; Jer 3:23; 4:10; and 8:8. The line in Isa 40:7 is universally judged to be a gloss; all the remainder except Isa 45:15 can (and, I submit, must) be understood as contrastive. Thus in Gen 28:16, Jacob clapped himself on the head, so to say, when he woke from his dream, and said, "Oh, no!— Yahweh is in this place, but I certainly did not know it." In Exod 2:14, Moses, confronted by his fellow Hebrew who reminds him of his murder of the Egyptian overseer, says, "Oh, no!—the affair is known about." Admittedly 1 Sam 15:32 is a difficult text, but conceivably Agag, confronted by his death, says, "Oh, no!—

here comes a bitter death." (The verb סור qal often means "turn in at.") The occurrence in Jer 4:10 is analyzed as contrastive below; and 8:8, like the first occurrence in the present verse, is associated with לְשֶׁקֶר (literally "to falsehood") and may be explained as I propose to do for the present passage. It is true, Isa 45:15 does seem asseverative, but there may be a nuance which is unclear (does it contrast with v 14?). These suggested renderings, added to the list of passages in which אָכֵן is generally accepted to be contrastive, make an impressive array. The word ordinarily opens a speech that indicates a sudden recognition in contrast to what was theretofore assumed.[267] In its double use here one has, I suggest, the same kind of quick interchange of one-line or half-line speeches which Greek tragedy sometimes offers, where the nuance hangs on a single particle like γε. The first two cola of the present verse, by this understanding, are a contrastive speech of Yahweh's, and the last two a consequent contrastive speech of the people: each is contradicting the previous speaker.

The first noun expression, לְשֶׁקֶר, picks up the preposition לְ from לָךְ in the third colon of v 23: "Rather, it is to falsehood (that you are coming) from the hills (of fertility worship), not to me!" Yahweh is testing out the sincerity of the people's repentance. Is the repentance too easy? Does Israel really understand what she is saying? (Josh 24:19–20 offers exactly the same kind of denial to test sincerity; compare Form.) I have closed Yahweh's speech with a question mark because Yahweh is in his mind trying to establish how thoroughgoing Israel's change of heart is.

The second colon, with its two bare nouns, must be understood by the prepositions of the first colon: two double-duty prepositions.[268] This diction is not only archaic but perhaps conversational (compare the remark on the diction of Greek tragedy above). This analysis brings into parallelism שֶׁקֶר and הָמוֹן, a fascinating collocation. Jrm uses שֶׁקֶר "falsehood," as a key term in his theology;[269] "falsehood" is what is without basis in the

---

267 Compare Frederick J. Goldbaum, "Two Hebrew Quasi-Adverbs לכן and אכן," *JNES* 23 (1964) 135; he does not emphasize the contrastive meaning, but he does stress the element of realization and surprise (he suggests "ah!").

268 See, conveniently, Dahood, *Psalms III*, 435–37.

269 Thomas W. Overholt, *The Threat of Falsehood, A Study in the Theology of the Book of Jeremiah* (SBT 2d Series 16; Naperville, IL: Allenson, 1970) esp. 86–104.

soul, what is hollow and rootless[270]—specifically, for Jrm, the realm of that which lulls people into spurious security apart from Yahweh, pagan, idolatrous worship and the parallel seeking for purely political solutions in foreign alliances. In the present passage "falsehood" focuses no doubt on the false solution of fertility worship. There is an interesting colon in Hos 12:2 (even if it is a gloss):[271] "lies (כָּזָב) and violence (שֹׁד) he multiplies"—here what is false and what is violent are linked, because both are a betrayal of the maintenance of the covenant.[272] The noun הָמוֹן indicates both the steady noise of a crowd, the confusion that a crowd manifests, and the large numbers of people in a crowd. It normally has a negative connotation and is clearly the expression of a culture accustomed to the quiet order of clan and village life. In 2 Sam 18:29 a messenger has run to David's court from the battlefront where Absalom had died, and he reported, "I saw a great tumult (הֶהָמוֹן הַגָּדוֹל), . . . but I did not know what it was." The noun is used of the crowd of carousing lovers of Oholah and Oholibah in Ezek 23:42, and though the text of that verse is corrupt, it is clear that the noun describes the wildness as well as the multiplicity of their followers. The two words "falsehood" and "confusion" in the present passage then refer to the insubstantiality and the orgiastic wildness respectively of fertility worship. But surely the "hills" and the "mountains" are to be understood as the place of such worship (2:20); how then is one to understand the thought here? Is it "from pillar to post," "out of the frying pan, into the fire"? Is Yahweh suggesting that the "turning" from Baal can as easily be a "returning" to Baal (compare 4:1)?—it would seem so.

But the people contradict Yahweh's probing with another אָכֵן: "No!—in Yahweh our God is the rescue of Israel." Thus they repeat "Yahweh our God" from the end of v 22. This is the only occurrence of תְּשׁוּעָה "deliverance, rescue" in Jer; it is frequent in the Psalms, and the connotation here is of a liturgical exclamation (compare Ps 37:39, וּתְשׁוּעַת צַדִּיקִים מֵיהוָה "and the rescue

of the righteous is from Yahweh").

■ **3:24** The speech of the people continues. In the first colon the subject precedes the verb, הַבֹּשֶׁת "shame": this figure is set in contrast with Yahweh. Against some commentators (Duhm, Volz, Rudolph) who suggest emending הַבֹּשֶׁת to הַבַּעַל "Baal," one must affirm that Jrm intends the word הַבֹּשֶׁת here, in order to play on the word in v 25 (see below). Jrm uses הַבַּעַל "Baal" elsewhere (e.g., 2:8), and if the tradition preserves "Baal" there, there is no reason for a censored text in the present passage. As is well known, there is a close association of the name *ba'al* "Baal" with *bōšet* "shame"—witness the existence of the alternative proper names Ishbosheth/Eshbaal (2 Sam 2:8; 1 Chr 8:33) and Mephibosheth/Meribaal (2 Sam 4:4; 1 Chr 8:34). But the view (since the nineteenth century) that these proper names were simply censored by those who wanted to avoid the use of the term Baal[273] may be too simple; Matitiahu Tsevat has suggested that Bosheth may be a divine name in its own right (Akkadian *baštu* "pride, guardian angel").[274] In any event, there is no doubt that *bōšet* and *ba'al* are associated, given the tradition of double names in Saul's household and in the diction of Hos 9:10, and the very use of הַבֹּשֶׁת in the present passage is indication that Jrm saw in the association one more way to mock Baal worship, since the word appears in v 25 in its ordinary meaning of "shame."

Baal promised fertility to his devotees; how ironic then that Shame should eat up produce instead of lavishing it! The word יְגִיעַ means "toil," and then the gain that comes from toil, normally agricultural produce (Deut 28:33) but also the riches that accumulate in a city (Jer 20:5). It is what one should expect to receive from successful agricultural and mercantile endeavors. In the Deuteronomy passage just cited (28:33) it is said that a foreign nation will eat up your gain, and that thought is repeated in Jer 5:17 (without יְגִיעַ); in the present passage it is said that Shame has accomplished the same thing: another instance in which wrong worship and wrong politics are

---

270 Pedersen, I/II 412.
271 See Wolff, *Hosea*, 206.
272 Pedersen, I/II 413.
273 See for example Richard W. Corney, "Ishbosheth," *IDB* 2:747.
274 Matitiahu Tsevat, "Ishbosheth and Congeners, The Names and Their Study," *HUCA* 46 (1975) 71–87,

esp. 76, 85. For the nineteenth-century literature see 72.

parallel in Jrm's mind. (The gloss at the end of the verse explaining יָגִיעַ—flocks and herds, sons and daughters—could well have been taken from 5:17; one notes the oddity of the repeated third plural suffixes instead of first plural ones.) And it is not only current gain: the people sense that Shame has always been eating up the gain of the nation, from the time of the fathers, from our youth: and here the material picks up in an inclusio the "fathers" from 2:5 and "youth" from 2:2 and 3:4.

■ **3:25** The verse begins with "let us lie" (נִשְׁכְּבָה), which surely carries a sexual connotation: the only other occurrence of the cohortative of this verb is in Gen 19:32, where Lot's daughters say of their father, "And let us lie with him." But instead of "let us lie with Baal" or the like, we hear "let us lie in our shame." Shame personified, instead of being a bed-partner, becomes depersonalized, simply the bed itself on which we lie in humiliation; and in parallel, "humiliation" becomes the blanket above (compare Ps 69:8, כִּסְּתָה כְלִמָּה פָנָי "disgrace has covered my face"). For another metaphor of bed and cover note Isa 14:11, "Maggots are the bed beneath you, and worms are your covering." Volz and Rudolph translate "we must lie" here; the cohortative can be so understood (compare 4:19, 21), but such a rendering would lose the sexual innuendo.

Finally the people are able to admit the true situation, "How we have sinned against Yahweh our God!"—that which they deny in 2:35 ("because you say, 'I have not sinned!'"), an admission not only for the present generation but for generations past. The translation "how" for כִּי here needs justification. The combination כִּי חָטָאנוּ occurs several times in Jer (beyond the present passage: 8:14; 14:7, 20; and compare 30:15), leading one to raise the question whether כִּי does not carry a particular force in confessions of sin. In Lam 5:16 that combination follows אוֹי־נָא לָנוּ "woe to us!" and justification for the translation "oh!" or "how!" after "woe to us!" is offered in 4:13 (compare 6:4). One notes also that in Gen 18:20 כִּי means "how!" in the context of vocabulary for sin. Thus

כִּי would seem to be part of confession of sin.[275]

The remainder of the verse contains prose expansions; commentators differ in what they omit and what they retain (for a justification of the reconstruction offered here, see Preliminary Observations). The phrase "sins of my youth" (Ps 25:7) may lie behind the diction here;[276] compare also "You have cut short the days of his youth, you have covered him with shame" (Ps 89:46).

■ **4:1–2** The syntax of these two verses offers a bewildering problem: where are the protases ("if"-clauses) and where are the apodoses ("then"-clauses)? *M* offers seven verbs; the first and third are introduced by אִם "if" and are thus protases; the fourth, fifth, sixth, and seventh are introduced by וְ, literally "and," either attached to the verb directly—waw-consecutive perfects (the fourth and fifth verbs), or attached to other elements, in which case the verbs are imperfects (the third and seventh verbs). It is clear that the parallel sixth and seventh verbs must be apodoses, since they end the immediate sequence, but it is unclear whether the second, fourth, and fifth verbs are variously protases or apodoses (compare GKC, secs. 112kk and 112ff[a] for such instances of protasis and apodosis respectively). A table will make the matter clear:

G RSV	V, S Cond.,[277] Rud.[278]	T Duhm, Gies.,[279] Volz, JB	NEB, NJV	NAB	Bright
1. if you turn					
prot.	prot.	prot.	prot.	prot.	prot.
2. to me turn					
apod.	apod.	apod.	prot.	apod.	prot.
3. and if you remove					
prot.	prot.	prot.	prot.	prot.	prot.
4. you do not wander					
prot.	apod.	apod.	prot.	prot.	prot.
5. and swear					
prot.	apod.	prot.	prot.	apod.	apod.

---

275 Compare Isa 59:12; Dahood translates כִּי as "indeed" in Ps 38:19 (*Psalms I*, 234) and in Isa 59:12 (*Psalms II*, 3).

276 And Ps 90:8 as well, if the understanding of *T* there is correct: see Charles A. Briggs and Emilie G. Briggs, *A Critical and Exegetical Commentary on the Book of Psalms* (ICC; New York: Scribner's, 1906–7) II, 274, and Dahood, *Psalms II*, 325.

277 Condamin.

279 Rudolph.

279 Giesebrecht.

6. and will bless

    apod.   apod.   apod.   apod.   apod.   apod.

7. and congratulate

    apod.   apod.   apod.   apod.   apod.   apod.

Each of these analyses may be defended by appropriate argumentation. In addition there are other Versional readings in v 1 each of which has its plausibility and adds uncertainty to the analysis of the passage (see Text).

Two considerations, neither conclusive but both suggestive, lead one to see the second colon of v 1 as an apodosis rather than as a parallel protasis. The first is the usage in 8:4, where the two occurrences of יָשׁוּב are clearly contrastive ("Will he turn [away] and not turn [back]?"); one suspects then that the two occurrences of תָּשׁוּב here are likewise contrastive. Second, the fact that "and if" (וְאִם) begins the third colon suggests that it begins a fresh conditional sequence—that is, that there is both a protasis and an apodosis before the third colon. One is moved, then, to understand the first two cola as "If you turn (at all), (then) to me you should return." Parallels to such a sequence are difficult to locate—a protasis followed by the identical verb is not common; one would expect an imperative in any case, as in 1 Sam 21:10. The imperfect is often used to express obligation (Ruth 3:4: "And he will tell you what you are to do," אֵת אֲשֶׁר תַּעֲשִׂין),[280] or used where we would expect an imperative (Isa 18:3).

The three actions referred to in the third, fourth, and fifth clauses ("if you remove your vile things from my presence," "you do not wander" [i.e., from me], "you swear 'as Yahweh lives' truly") are all analogous. It is certainly conceivable to see the second and/or the third of these as apodoses ("if you remove your vile things . . . then you will not wander," or "if you remove your vile things . . . then you will swear . . . truly"), but the great shift comes from these second-person clauses to the last two, whose verbs are in the third person; therefore the most plausible understanding is to see the last two verbs as apodoses and the third, fourth, and fifth verbs as protases ("if you do this, that and the other, then nations will bless themselves," etc.).

There are two further general considerations. First,

נוּד, here translated "wander," means "wobble, oscillate, flutter, move aimlessly"; the nearest parallel to its usage here is Gen 4:14, where Cain affirms that he is to be a fugitive and "wanderer" on earth. Since the sixth clause is modeled on Gen 22:18, a word of God to Abraham (see below on v 2), the implication here seems to be, "If you stop being like Cain, you can begin to be like Abraham"; and this contrast in turn reinforces the plausibility of the division proposed here between protases and apodoses. Second, the two "if . . . then" sequences here are really of two different sorts. The first says, "If you do it at all, then you should do it this way," while the second says, "If you do this, then nations will do that." In the latter case, the action of the second party ("nations") is consequent or dependent on the action of the first party ("you"), while in the former case, one action is not consequent on another but is the obligational clarification of a more general action—since the subject in both cases is the second person. And since the protases of the second group are essentially equivalent to the apodosis in the first group ("you do not wander" is really equivalent to "you turn to me"), what we have in these two verses is a reference to three levels of action, which may be paraphrased as follows: "If you continue to be able to turn this way and that, then to me you should turn; and if, by doing so, you remove your vile things from my presence . . . then nations will bless themselves in him. . . ."

This interpretation thus agrees with that of the first column of the table above, that of *G* (for all its differences of textual detail: see Text) and of the *RSV*.

■ 4:1 If the second colon is an apodosis (see above), then the first occurrence of שׁוּב (in the first colon) is potentially ambivalent: Israel is capable of turning to evil from Yahweh, or from evil to Yahweh (compare the usage in 3:19 and 22, and compare the opposites in 8:4).[281] These occurrences of שׁוּב here thus sum up in a nutshell the repeated expressions of the concern for repentance that occur in chapter 3.

The noun שִׁקּוּצִים appears to mean "filth" in Nah 3:6 (so the translations), but it became a conventional term in this period for pagan gods and idols. Since a related noun (שֶׁקֶץ) is used of what is ceremonially unclean (Lev

---

280 See Joüon, *Grcmm.*, sec. 113m.
281 See Holladay, *Šûbh*, 78–81, 130.

7:21), especially of creatures forbidden for food, like creeping vermin (Lev 11:41), it is clear that the noun here serves as a kind of cover-word for pagan deities, a word carrying a high level of repugnance.[282] It occurs once in Hosea (Hos 9:10), in a slightly different context (people became repugnant because they devoted themselves to Baal), but otherwise the word occurs in our text only in Jrm's period and thereafter (frequently in Ezekiel); the only other occurrence in Jrm's poetry is in 13:27. If the phrase "from your mouth" is original (see Text), then the line refers to Israel's calling on the name of pagan gods, or to Israel's calling on Yahweh in a way that is perceived to be the equivalent of worshiping pagan gods (compare "swear 'by the life of Yahweh' truly," v 2). The verb סור hip'il is common for "take away, remove" (compare v 4); for an object as disgusting as שִׁקּוּצִים it implies "get rid of." For נוד see the discussion of vv 1–2 above: moving off from Yahweh's presence means "wandering" aimlessly.

■ **4:2** There appears to be a pairing of the images in vv 1–2a: "wander" and "turn" are both verbs of motion, and (again, if "from your mouth" is correct) "swear 'by the life of Yahweh' truly" is parallel to "get rid of your vile things from your mouth." The expression חַי יהוה (here translated "by the life of Yahweh") is a set expression occurring forty-three times in the OT, nine times in the Book of Jer. There is some uncertainty how the phrase is to be construed; Moshe Greenberg has argued recently that חַי is a noun,[283] and Walter Baumgartner concurs.[284] By this understanding the phrase will mean "by the life of Yahweh" rather than "as Yahweh lives," as most translations have it. In either event, what is clear is that oaths were frequently resorted to in OT times to ensure the speaking of the truth in crucial situations, and that the only valid oath for an Israelite was an oath invoking Yahweh. It is equally clear that there was a tendency to invoke God's name in unworthy ways (Exod 20:7, the Third Commandment) and that the phrase here struggles with the problem of how to ensure that an oath taken in Yahweh's name was serious and sincere.[285] The seriousness and sincerity which are to be expected in such oaths are betokened by the three qualifiers בֶּאֱמֶת בְּמִשְׁפָּט וּבִצְדָקָה ("truly, justly, and rightly"). In meaning these three are scarcely to be distinguished and indeed are intended as mutual reinforcement. The last two are conventional parallels (22:3, 15) and are concerned with what is just and right, while אֱמֶת has to do with what is trustworthy or dependable; this word is parallel with צְדָקָה only in Isa 48:1 and Zech 8:8, and there is no other instance to my knowledge where all three appear together. The triplet is then profoundly impressive and functions with something of the solemnity that an oath itself would. The theme of these two lines is reflected again in 5:2. It is so easy to repeat words, even solemn words, without inner conviction: can the nation be urged to fill its words with content once more, so that an oath in the name of Yahweh carries all the integrity of Yahweh himself?

Verse 2b, the final apodosis, is a chiasmus with the centerpiece "nations" (גּוֹיִם). The chiasmus is deliberate: the verbs, which stand at the extremes of the bicolon, are both hitpa'el stems. There is no other passage in the OT where these two verbs are parallel, but it is clear that they are similar in meaning. The first imitates the diction of Gen 22:18 (E), a word of God to Abraham after the intended sacrifice of Isaac: "And all the nations of the earth shall bless themselves in your offspring," diction repeated in Gen 26:4 (J) in a word to Isaac. Both these passages are associated with שבע nip'al "swear" (Gen 22:16; 26:3). The second verb in the passage, הלל hitpa'el, is often found in liturgical contexts (eight times in the Psalms) meaning "boast" (in one's riches, for example, Ps 49:7) or "exult." A passage which could well be the archetype for our text is Ps 63:12, a passage in which the verb is associated with "swear": "But the king shall rejoice in God, all who swear by him shall exult (בּוֹ יִתְהַלֵּל כָּל־הַנִּשְׁבָּע)." Jrm appears deftly to have combined the features of both the Genesis texts and the Psalm text

---

282 Compare Pedersen, III/IV 252, and Marc H. Lovelace, "Abomination," *IDB* 1:12–13.

283 Moshe Greenberg, "The Hebrew Oath Particle Ḥay/Ḥē," *JBL* 76 (1957) 34–39.

284 See *HALAT*, 295, in contrast to KB, 292, where the word was construed as an adjective.

285 Compare Marvin H. Pope, "Oaths," *IDB* 3:575–77.

in the present bicolon. It is natural to ask who the "him" is here: the assumption is that it is Yahweh, yet the antecedent passage in Genesis has the nations blessing themselves in Abraham's offspring, so that Rudolph is moved to emend "in him" in both instances in the present text to "in you" (so also *JB*). In the Psalm passage the "him" is superficially ambiguous, capable of referring either to the king (so Hans-Joachim Kraus)[286] or to God (so most); but it would seem clear that in that passage בּוֹ reflects בֵּאלֹהִים "in God" in the same position in the previous colon and therefore must refer to God.[287] This consideration reinforces one's impression that the text of the present passage is sound: it is odd that the diction of Yahweh should have shifted from first person (v 1) to the third person, but the third person of the oath has doubtless attracted the diction here, and in any event such a shift is found elsewhere (2:2–3). What Jrm has done, then, is to shift the focus of the promise to Abraham from Israel's glory to Yahweh's glory: if Israel is able to fulfill her calling given first to Abraham, by returning to Yahweh in integrity, then the nations of the world will bask in their good fortune under Yahweh. The translation "congratulate themselves" is intended to match "bless themselves," but is not inaccurate (compare the meaning "boast" in Ps 49:7). But there is no trace here of mockery in the notion that the nations should start boasting and congratulating themselves: there is nothing reprehensible in boasting—the point is that they are boasting in God. *Deo soli gratia!*

■ **4:3** For the fresh rubric see Preliminary Observations.

The poetry of vv 3–4 offers two metaphors, that of plowing fallow ground and of circumcising the heart. The first colon, נִירוּ לָכֶם נִיר, "plow yourselves unplowed ground," is identical in wording with a colon in Hos 10:12, and since these are the only two occurrences of the verb ניר, there is strongly likelihood that Jrm intended the words as a reminiscence or even a direct quotation of Hosea. The noun נִיר refers to land which either has never been plowed or has lain fallow for a period of time, and the cognate verb ניר then means "plow, break up" such fallow soil. Fallow ground may by careful working bring a good yield (so, evidently, the meaning of Prov 13:23),[288] and the context of the line in Hosea suggests that Israel break ground not touched lately by returning to Yahweh.[289] One must assume then a similar understanding in the present context if the words are a quotation. And Jrm reinforces it by a synonymous line, "Do not sow among thorns." Plowing fallow ground rids the soil of the thorns that grow there otherwise (compare Isa 5:6; 32:13; Prov 24:31)—the sower in Jesus' story sowed seed among thorns (Matt 13:7) growing in ground that clearly had not been plowed. The temptation is to ask what Jrm had in mind when he used the term "thorns" (BDB: "[the line is] said of a few righteous deeds amid much wickedness")[290]—in short, to resort to allegory. But Jrm simply intends to suggest that one plow what needs to be plowed, that one not cut corners like a foolish farmer who sows among thorns. This line may even be proverbial for foolish action. Jerome nicely compares it to Jesus' "Do not give dogs what is holy, and do not throw your pearls before swine" (Matt 7:6).[291]

■ **4:4** The first colon appears ambiguous: הִמֹּלוּ לַיהוה can mean either "be circumcised [or circumcise yourselves: the passive and reflexive are hardly to be distinguished] to Yahweh," where "Yahweh" is the goal or recipient of the action, or "be circumcised by Yahweh," where "Yahweh" is the agent of the action. The former interpretation is taken by the Versions (*G, V, S*) and recent translations, and is favored by the antecedent passage in Deut 10:16, "and you shall circumcise the foreskin of your heart," and by the parallelism here, "remove the foreskin of your heart": in both Deut 10:16 and the parallel colon here the emphasis is on the initiative of the people. Yet the second interpretation hangs in the background;[292] it is clear that with a passive verb לְ may introduce the agent.[293] Such a meaning is at least compatible with the parallel expression, "remove the

---

286 Hans-Joachim Kraus, *Psalmen* (BKAT 15; Neukirchen: Neukirchener, 1961) 443.

287 So Dahood, *Psalms II*, 101.

288 Compare McKane, *Proverbs*, 462–63.

289 Compare Wolff, *Hosea*, 185–86.

290 BDB, 281b.

291 *S. Hieronymi Presbyteri in Hieremiam Prophetam, Libri Sex* (ed. Siegfried Reiter; CChr Series Latina 74; Turnhout: Brepols, 1960) p. 41.

292 Robert Althann, "*mwl*, 'Circumcise' with the *lamedh* of Agency," *Bib* 62 (1981) 239–40.

293 GKC, sec. 121f; BDB, 514a, *e*; *HALAT*, 485a, 24.

foreskin of your heart": the question is, who rules the "heart" of Judah? In 31:33 Yahweh will write his law on the people's heart, and in 15:19 the initiative of "returning" lies in tension between Yahweh and Jrm.

The two parallel clauses are an expansion of the clause in Deut 10:16 already cited. Jrm prefers the form לֵב for "heart," while Deuteronomy prefers לֵבָב;[294] thus the choice of לְבָב here would remind the hearer of Deuteronomy. In addition the form may have been chosen here partly because of the vowel-parallelism between lĕbabkem and lĕyahweh.

Whether the circumcision is to be "for Yahweh" or "by Yahweh," it must make a genuine difference in the life of the people. Many nations circumcise (9:24–25), but Israel is to do it for Yahweh, so that her heart, which is the center of planning and decision making, of action as well as emotion and thought, may be conformable to his will.[295] The same sort of diction as that found in Deut 10:16 and the present passage is to be found in Deut 30:6 and Lev 26:41, so that the image of the "circumcision of the heart," though striking to the modern reader, became a kind of convention in the OT (though G felt the awkwardness of the wording: in Deut 10:16 and here it softens the phrase to "circumcise your hardheartedness" and offers other periphrases in the remaining relevant passages). Jrm, however, extended the metaphor in 6:10 to "their ear is uncircumcised," a usage that is indeed unique.

There is no need to excise the words "men of Judah and inhabitants of Jerusalem" as do Cornill, Duhm, Giesebrecht, Condamin, and Rudolph. The words appear in 2 Kgs 23:2, doubtless part of the first Deuteronomic historical work,[296] in the narrative of the reading of the Deuteronomic scroll to the assemblage in 622, so that their occurrence here, closing this section of Jrm's preaching to Judah, would reinforce that association with the earlier occasion.

Verse 4b is duplicated in 21:12b, but there is a strong feeling that 21:12–14 is a kind of pastiche of lines from

elsewhere (see there).

The diction of the first two cola, "or my wrath will go forth like fire and burn with none to quench," has no precise parallels elsewhere in the prophetic literature, though there are of course partial models. Thus one finds "with none to quench" at the end of Isa 1:31, part of a passage genuine to Isaiah,[297] and one finds "or the house of Joseph will ignite like fire and devour with none to quench" in Amos 5:6, though that verse appears to be an insertion into the text of Amos, perhaps a bit of exegesis added just before Jrm's time (Wolff suggests the circumstance of Josiah's destruction of the sanctuary at Bethel, 2 Kgs 23:15–16).[298] One also finds "his wrath is poured out like fire" in Nah 1:6.

"Wrath" (חֵמָה) is found elsewhere in Jrm's poetry with "go forth" (יצא, 23:19 = 30:23) as well as with other verbs of motion. Though the noun is used of human anger elsewhere (Gen 27:44), its frequent occurrence in Jer is confined to God's anger; in meaning it is not to be distinguished from אַף or חֲרוֹן אַף (v 8: see 44:6 for a hendiadys of the two terms). Yahweh's wrath can burn— this is a frequent metaphor; indeed God himself can burn (Lam 2:3). And when Yahweh's wrath burns, there is no remedy, none to quench.

The last colon, "from the presence of the evil of your doings," has models in earlier prophetic material, though not with "from the presence of" (מִפְּנֵי): Isa 1:16, "remove the evil of your doings"; Hos 9:15, "because of (עַל) the evil of their doings." Given the models of earlier prophets, there is no warrant to excise this colon (with Cornill, Duhm, Giesebrecht) as the gloss of an editor.

Aim
If the proposal of this study is correct, Jrm was pre-occupied from the earliest years of his career by the process of "returning": during the reign of Josiah it was the northerners who were called to "return" from exile, but that return was at the same time a return to union with Judah, return to the cult in Jerusalem, return to the

---

294 For the statistics see KB, 468b.
295 For "heart" see Pedersen, I/II *passim*; Johnson, *Vitality of the Individual*, 77–88; and Hans Walter Wolff, *Anthropology of the Old Testament* (Philadelphia: Fortress, 1974) 40–58, esp., on the present passage, 53–54.
296 Gray, *Kings*, 728.
297 Wildberger, *Jesaja*, 70.

298 Wolff, *Joel and Amos*, 228, 240.

covenant with Yahweh—a return which was to be in the context of Yahweh's accusation to the north of covenant disloyalty (the first recension to the north: see Preliminary Observations).

Jrm portrays Yahweh as using a dazzling variety of rhetorical turns in his appeal: he poses the rhetorical question, "What did your fathers find wrong with me?" (2:5), he raises a specific issue in Israelite law between husband and wife as a parallel for the monstrous broken relation between Israel and himself (3:1), he quotes what Israel is supposed to have called him (3:4), he states what his hope from the covenantal relation has been (3:19), and spins out his expectation of the way in which Israel might find her way back to his embrace once more (3:22–25), all this punctuated by appeals to return (3:12, 14, 22) which suggest that his hope for the restoration of his relation to the people might not be altogether forlorn. He portrays Israel as harlotrous (3:2) and complacent (3:4–5) and depicts her attempts to return as superficial (3:22–25). And the rhetoric is crowned by Yahweh's specific requirements for Israel's repentance, requirements couched in the form of reminiscences of the Decalogue and of the promise to Abraham (4:1–2). These verses are optimistic, but they will later be overlaid by others that are not so optimistic; Yahweh may hope for a change of heart, but in the long run it will prove an impossible possibility.

Both appeal and accusation (especially the latter) were expanded and made more specific when the audience of Yahweh's words became Judah; after all, Judah was still an intact political entity, whereas the northern kingdom was a thing of the past.

Yahweh (in Jrm's understanding) appealed to Judah by depicting the wilderness period as an ideal time, the time when Israel had been loyal to Yahweh (2:1–3), in contrast to the more recent period of apostasy: here he is in contrast to Ezekiel, who was convinced that Israel was always in rebellion against Yahweh, even in the wilderness (Ezek 20:13).

As for accusation, the theme of harlotry is still there (2:20b, 24–25), but to it is added the theme of vulnerability in war (2:14–19, 36–37). Israel is portrayed as denying her wrongdoing (2:23), without chagrin even

when faced with evidence of wrongdoing (2:25, 31). Yahweh is puzzled, even hurt (2:32): the language is frequently warm and emotional. In all this there is astonishing realism in the depiction of Israel the defendant: self-defensive, self-contradictory (2:23 against 2:25), self-defeating (2:13, 18); indeed it will be Israel's own actions that may do her in, not Yahweh's primarily (2:19). The variety of rhetorical technique manifested in the material to the north is expanded here: Yahweh quotes the presumed remarks and thoughts of Israel (2:20, 23, 25, 31), challenges her to face the consequences of her search for foreign aid (2:18). At bottom the issue is disloyalty to Yahweh, rebellion in fact (2:29), so that Israel no longer understands her identity as the possession of Yahweh (2:3) but misperceives herself (2:20–25, 31) and so, ultimately, misperceives Yahweh (2:31). Sometimes Yahweh is not only hurt but angry (2:35), so that he mocks Israel (2:33, 36).

The address to Judah is rounded off by further reminiscences of words of the past—a word from Hosea, a tradition about circumcision in Deuteronomy, ending with a dire threat (4:3–4).

This array of accusations is deepened even further by additions in the second scroll, notably the accusation that Judah worships idols and the challenge that she face the consequences of that worship (2:26–28).

The set of accusations that Yahweh hurls at Israel in these chapters is awesome; those accusations, and the associated appeal to return, are basic for an understanding of the prophet's message. Hosea in the eighth century explored in depth the distorted relationship between Yahweh and Israel, largely in terms of the metaphor of harlotry, and Ezekiel would explicate that broken relationship in extended allegories (Ezekiel 16, 23). But the richness of Jrm's presentation of that relationship is unsurpassed. Not until the hearing of the series of Jesus' parables, particularly the parables of the kingship of God, would Jews be offered such variety and depth of insight on the nature of the relationship between God's people and their God.

Wars and Rumors of Wars

Bibliography

On holy war in general:
Gottwald, Norman K.
   "War, holy," *IDBSup* 942–44, with full
   bibliography.

On holy war in its relation to prophecy:
Ackerman, James S.
   "Prophecy and Warfare in Early Israel: A Study of
   the Deborah-Barak Story," *BASOR* 220 (December
   1975) 5–13, esp. the bibliography.
Bach, Robert
   *Die Aufforderungen zur Flucht und zum Kampf im
   alttestamentlichen Prophetenspruch* (WMANT 9;
   Neukirchen: Neukirchener, 1962).

Foe from the North: see 1:14.

Preliminary Observations

Within the compass of these seven chapters there is a
steady series of passages containing references to the
coming of the foe from the north (4:5–8, 13–18, 29–31;
5:6, 15–17; 6:1–6, 11–12, 22–26; 8:10a, 14–17; 9:9–
10; 10:17–22; for "north" see specifically 4:6; 6:22;
10:22). These passages are form-critically announcements of judgment, a genre not prominent in 2:1—4:4
(only 2:19, 37 there) or, if not announcements of
judgment, at least warnings (specifically 4:14; 6:8).

In 11:18 the series of "confessions" of Jrm begins, and
it is those "confessions" which evidently form the skeleton of the material in the book from that point on
through chapter 20. One is left uncertain, therefore,
whether to include 11:1–17 with what precedes or what
follows; that is to say, those prose verses resemble what
precedes in that there is a similar prose sequence in
7:1—8:3, but on the other hand there seems to be a
connection between the motif of "tree" in 11:16 and in
11:19. It will become apparent that the setting for 11:1–
17 can be determined quite specifically and that it is not
connected closely either with what precedes or what
follows. It is appropriate therefore to cut off a discussion
of the "foe from the north" material at 10:25.

Three interlocking sets of questions emerge when one
attempts to analyze 4:5—10:25 in detail. The first
involves general considerations of structure. What is the
organizing principle of the individual units of discourse
here? Clearly some material is alien and doubtless added
at a late stage (notably 10:1–16), but just as clearly there

are parallel passages that suggest some kind of organizing principle (for example, compare 4:5–8; 6:1; and
8:14; or 6:12 and 8:10a). Indeed what is the demarcation of the individual units of discourse here? Glaringly, why
does the prose sequence 7:1—8:3 seem to interrupt the
flow of poetry? If the organization of the units in these
chapters is discernible, is it rhetorical or thematic? Or is
it chronological? Or is it in some way both?—for
example, is there material in the first scroll to which
material in the second scroll has been added in some
symmetrical way?

This last consideration leads to the second set of
questions, which involve a determination of settings. Can
one determine the settings of each unit? If one can, then
these have a bearing on the questions of structure.

Third, there seem to be shifts of speaker within the
units of discourse. For example, the "I" of Yahweh in 4:6
shifts to "us" in 4:8; the speaker of 8:23 is ordinarily
taken to refer to Jrm, whereas the "me" in 9:2 is Yahweh.
Can these shifts be specified and the various speakers
identified in the material? Are the shifts patterned, and if
so, can such patterns in turn help in identifying the
speaker in ambiguous passages?

The details of these questions will be discussed for
each unit, but a preliminary look at them is appropriate
here. Though it is difficult to avoid circular reasoning, I
shall attempt to offer the data in as open a way as
possible.

The Units of 4:5—10:25. As already noted, there are
repeated motifs within the series of utterances regarding

the foe from the north. Thus 6:1 parallels 4:5–6 in speaking of trumpet and visual signal, 5:10 and 6:9 both refer to Israel as a vine, 4:8 and 6:26 both appeal for lamentation. After the long prose passage (7:1—8:3) there is material in 8:14 and beyond which parallels material in 4:5—6:30. Thus 8:14 closely mimics 4:5, the same refrain in 5:9 and 29 is found once more in 9:8, the curious parallelism of "tent" and "curtains" in 4:20 occurs again in 10:20.[1] The long prose passage in 7:1—8:3 tempts the modern reader to assume a basic division at the end of chapter 6 (so, for example, William Rudolph, who divides chapters 1—20 into two large blocs, chaps. 1—6 and 7—20, and 7—20 in turn into four sections of which the first is 7—10);[2] but this assumption (by the analysis offered here) is erroneous, as the recurrence of the refrain of 5:9 and 29 in 9:8 might suggest.

Commentators have differed in their demarcation of units within this collection. Rudolph is content simply to deal with 4:5—6:30 essentially chapter by chapter (4:5–31; 5:1–31; 6:1–26, 27–30), while 8:4—9:25 he breaks up into nine "individual sections"; other commentaries are equally unsatisfactory. If one tries to lay 4:5 and what follows alongside 6:1 and what follows to see whether typical diction or form-critical categories continue parallel, the attempt fails.

The most satisfactory procedure, it appears, is to find in the clusters of imperatives or prohibitions the beginnings of respective units;[3] one concludes then that 4:5; 5:1; 5:10; 5:20; 6:1; 6:9; 6:16; 8:14; 9:16; and 10:17 will mark beginnings. Among these, as already noted, 4:5; 6:1; and 8:14 match closely, as do 5:10 and 6:9 (Israel as the vine). One may surmise further that 5:9, 29; and 9:8, embodying a repeated "refrain," mark endings of respective units. In this way one may confidently conclude that 5:1–9 is a unit, built around the diction of Yahweh's "pardoning" the people (vv 1, 7), that 5:20–29 is a unit, and that 6:1–8 is a unit: these sequences are of comparable length. Tentatively one may presume that 5:10–17 and 6:9–15 are likewise single units (see above), but the presumption must be tested because of shifts of speaker and consequent form-critical complexity within these two sequences. It is equally clear, on the other hand, that both 4:5–31 and 8:14—9:8 need to be analyzed into smaller units. With regard to 6:16–30, one may confidently call vv 27–30 a coda and divide what remains into two sections—vv 16–21 (v 21 is similar to v 15) and vv 22–26 (these verses resemble 4:5–8). And with regard to 10:17–25, vv 23–25 is a coda and vv 17–22 (which resemble 4:5–8) are a unit. Now what remains among the poetry? The two verses 5:30–31 are a small fragment evidently added secondarily. The sequence 8:3–13 is a puzzle (even after vv 10b–12 are excised as a secondary doublet of 6:13–15): is it single or double (with a boundary between vv 7 and 8)? Likewise, is 9:16–21 single or double?

Patterns emerge from a close inspection of this material. Thus the units after 8:3 appear to be united by the catchword "gather" (אסף): 8:13, at the end of a sequence; 8:14, at the beginning of another; 9:21, at the end of a sequence; and 10:17, at the beginning of another. But further analysis is best pursued in a search for settings of the individual units.

Settings. The present study accepts as historical the contrast between the purpose of Jrm's first scroll and that of the second (36:2–3, 31–32): the first scroll was intended to warn, while the second scroll, dictated after Jehoiakim burned the first one, was to declare Yahweh's irrevocable sentence of punishment on the people. It has been shown that the bulk of the material in 2:1—4:4 is appropriate to the purpose of the first scroll and is assumed to have been contained in that scroll.

By the same token, the foe from the north material, which forms the bulk of 4:5—10:25, describing the destruction of Judah as it does, would appear to be appropriate for the second scroll. But there are two obvious difficulties. The first is that given units of material may fall into any of three groups: the first (hereafter "Group A") would consist of material included in the first scroll, the *terminus ad quem* for which is the end of the fifth year of Jehoiakim (March 604: see 36:1); the second ("Group B") would be material taking shape in Jrm's mind and delivered between the time of the dictation of the first scroll and the king's burning of that scroll in December 601; and the third ("Group C") would be material taking shape in Jrm's mind and delivered

---

1   For a full list of the parallels between 4:5—6:30 and 8:14—10:25 see Holladay, *Architecture*, 108–9.

2   Compare Rietzschel, *Urrolle*, 125.

3   Holladay, *Architecture*, 62–71.

after the king burned the scroll. Both Group A and Group B would thus embody material intended to warn; only Group C would have material implying irrevocable punishment. The second scroll will thus have taken Group A material and enlarged it with Group B and Group C material (compare 36:32). But the second difficulty is equally obvious: a description of destruction may be intended as a statement of punishment (thus appropriate for Group C), but on the other hand it may be intended only as a warning (thus appropriate for Group A or Group B) which could later be reused as a statement of punishment. Therefore the assignment of a given unit to a group is a matter of delicacy.

There are two verses of poetry which must be taken as warning, 4:14 and 6:8; 4:14 is an appeal for repentance, "Wash your heart, that you may be rescued!" and 6:8 offers "Be warned!" (or punishment will follow). The temple sermon, 7:1–12, is a prose passage which is quintessentially an appeal for repentance (7:13–15 turns out to be an appendix added for the second scroll; see there). There is nothing from 7:16 to 10:25 which is specifically a warning or an appeal for repentance. On the other hand, 4:28 suggests the inevitability of punishment: "On this account the earth shall mourn, and the heavens be dark above, inasmuch as I have spoken and will not relent, I have decided and will not turn back from it" (clauses rearranged according to *G*). One concludes that 4:5–31 contains a mixture of material from both Group C and either Group A or Group B, and that 4:14 and 6:8 (and 7:1–12, if one allows prose as well) are fixed points in the process of assigning the various units.

Can absolute dates be helpful for the quest at this point? Let us work from later units to earlier ones. As will become clear later, 11:1–17 must be assigned to the early autumn of 594. The poetry just preceding, which describes a siege in progress (10:17–18), is appropriate to the siege of Jerusalem in 597. It is assumed here that Jehoiakim burned Jrm's first scroll in December 601, and that the great drought had been under way for some time. Indications of the drought may be found in 8:13 and possibly in 8:20. And (it is again assumed here) there was a recitation of the Deuteronomic law in the autumn of 601; 8:8 is appropriate to that event. It would appear, then, that the material in this part of the book was added in roughly chronological order. Now if material asso-

ciated with the refrain in 9:8 took shape in the historical period under discussion, then we must assume that the material assocated with the same refrain, 5:1–9 and 5:20–29, took shape in the same period.

The battle of Carchemish is to be dated to May or June 605, and Jrm dictated his first scroll in the fifth year of Jehoiakim (April 605 to March 604). There is no way to determine which came first, Carchemish or the dictation of the scroll, or, indeed, if one were to assume that Carchemish came first, whether that battle was a stimulus for the dictation of the scroll; but the fact that 4:14; 6:8; and 7:1–12 serve the purposes of warning and the fact that 4:14 and 6:8 are associated with battle scenes suggests that at least initially the material describing the foe from the north was stimulated by Carchemish.

Now 26:3 (part of the narrative of the preaching the temple sermon) bears a close resemblance to 36:3 (the purpose of the first scroll). And if, as the present study maintains, this resemblance represents more than simply the repetitions of a Deuteronomistic editor, then one may conclude that 7:1–12, the temple sermon, closed the first scroll: it would certain make a splendid ending to it. Further, if 6:1–8 immediately preceded the temple sermon, then the latter becomes the "warning" implied in 6:8—a nice transition. Indeed one may see the threat that the land would become "uninhabited" (6:8) leading to Yahweh's promise that if the people repent "I shall let you dwell in this place" (7:7), and the threat that Yahweh's heart "will wrench away" from his people (again 6:8) leading to the parallel promise that if the people repent "I may dwell with you in this place" (7:3). Tentatively then one may conclude that the Group A comprises some portion of chapter 4 (a portion which includes 4:14); 6:1–8; and 7:1–12.

The next step is to try to define that portion of chapter 4 that includes 4:14. The immediate context of 4:14 is clearly vv 13–18 (compare Rudolph). Indeed there are close resemblances between 4:13–18 and 6:1–8: the cry of the people "woe to us" (4:13; 6:4), the image of foreign invaders surrounding the territory of Judah (עָלֶיהָ מִסָּבִיב or עָלֶיהָ סָבִיב, 4:17; 6:3), the vocative "O Jerusalem" in 4:14 and 6:8.

But vv 13–18 hardly stand alone; three considerations lead to the conclusion that vv 13–18 must be taken with vv 5–8 and 29–31 to form one stratum (Group A; see above), and that 4:9–12 and 19–28 are a later stratum, Group C. The first is that the diction of 6:1 parallels that of 4:5–6, suggesting in turn that it is actually 4:5–8 + 13–18 which is matched by 6:1–8. The second is a seeming symmetry of speakers between vv 5–8 and 29–31 (see the following section), a symmetry suggesting that these two sequences belong together. The third is that 4:9–12 and 19–28 give evidence both of being parallel to each other and of having characteristics of Group C which thus set them apart from the rest of 4:5–31. As for their being parallel to each other: the same sequence of catchwords is found in each, and each appears to divide between a "battle" section and a "drought" section (for the details see 4:5–31, Structure, in the section *Structure Within the Unit*). As for the characteristics which suggest an assignment to Group C, v 10 implies an opposition between Jrm and the optimistic prophets; vv 11–12 may imply a drought, and v 28, as already noted, implies the irrevocability of Yahweh's decision. One concludes therefore that the first scroll included 4:5–8, 13–18, and 29–31, and that these were expanded by 4:9–12 and 19–28 in the dictation of the second scroll.

It is appropriate to examine next 5:1–9 and 20–29; both these passages end with the same refrain. They share not only the refrain but descriptions of various specific contraventions of the covenant: false swearing (5:2), swearing by false gods (5:7), adultery (5:8), seizing of household goods (5:26), neglect of justice for the poor (5:28), all violations against which the people have been warned in the temple sermon (7:9). These passages do not belong in Group C: The refrain implies that Yahweh will punish, but there is a still a possibility (though perhaps only a theoretical one) that he can pardon—the issue is posed as a double rhetorical question. Do the passages belong in Group A, or not rather in Group B? Do the words in 5:24–25 suggest the great drought that was evidently under way in the autumn of 601? Do the words in 5:5, "Just let me go off to the leaders and let me speak with them," reflect the event of Baruch's reading of the scroll to the courtiers before it came to the ear of the king (36:10–11)? Both the rhetorical questions of the refrain and these last two considerations point to a date in the period just before the king burned the scroll.

This likelihood is increased to some degree by an examination of the material preceding the third occur-

rence of refrain (9:8). But how much material belongs with that refrain? There is no clear division from 8:14 to 9:8 (compare Structure on that passage). Though the long sequence begins with diction close to that of 4:5–6, it continues with motifs reminiscent of 5:1–9 and 20–29: acts of covenant breaking (here sins of the tongue, 9:2–5), a possible reference to the drought (8:20), rhetorical questions posed by Yahweh that express exasperation (8:19; 9:6; compare 5:7). Though the diction of 8:14, as already noted, mimics that of 4:5–6, it deepens the threat by the words "and meet our doom there." All these considerations point toward a setting for the three passages in the period 605–601, quite possibly in the autumn of 601 (thus Group B).

One turns next to 8:4–7; it is true, those verses have a likeness to 4:1–2 (here assigned to the first scroll) in that both passages use "(re)turn" in a double sense. But closer resemblances are found rather with 5:1–9 and 20–29. Thus the colon "they refuse to return" is found in both 8:5 and 5:3, rhetorical questions are found in 8:4–5 and in 5:7, and the people are found to be less obedient to Yahweh's will than the birds (8:7) or the sea (5:22). One is led, then, to assign this passage also to Group B. It may be added that its diction has strong resemblances to that found in 23:10 and 23:25–27, passages about the optimistic prophets, suggesting in turn a date in the autumn of 601 or the winter of 600.

The same may be said of 8:8–13. It is true, 8:10a closely resembles 6:11, and the latter is part of a passage to be assigned to Group C (see below). But on the other hand the rhetorical question of Yahweh in 8:8 resembles such questions in other Group B material (such as 5:7), and the diction of 8:13 strongly suggests the drought which in the chronology of the present study began in the autumn of 601. So it is appropriate, if 8:4–7 and 8:14—9:8 belong in Group B, to assign 8:8–13 to Group B as well.

The rest of the poetic material in the basic stratum of these chapters, and much of the rest of the prose in chapter 7, will be appropriate to the purpose of the second scroll (that is, Group C material). Of 4:9–12, 19–28 little more need be said here; some of the main points of evidence have already been cited, and more will be given under Setting for each passage. The assignment of 4:19–28 implies the same assignment for 10:17–22: both passages offer words of lament from the people of the destruction of the "tent" and "curtains" (4:20; 10:20), evidently a reference to the envisaged destruction of the temple (see Interpretation on those verses). As will be shown, 10:23–25 is analogous to 4:3–4: both close off large blocs of material, and both cite earlier scripture; one must conclude that these last verses of chapter 10 belong in the same setting as do vv 17–22.

The same setting (second scroll, thus Group C) may be proposed for 5:10–17 and 6:9–15, two passages with close similarities. Both begin with images of destruction of the vine Israel (5:10; 6:9; for the difficulty of the negative in the second colon of 5:10, see Text; and for the implication of "glean" in 6:9, see Interpretation), and both imply that there are prophets who have falsely preached optimism (5:12–13; 6:14). In 5:14b Jrm himself becomes the agency of Yahweh's destruction of the people, and the same role is implied in 6:11. For "peace, peace" in 6:14 compare 14:13, and see the Setting on 14:1—15:9.

The passage 6:16–26 must likewise be assigned to the second scroll (for the unity of this sequence see Structure on that passage). Three data point in this direction. First, the use of "terror on every side" here (6:25) is generalized from its specific use with respect to Pashhur (20:1–6), and the incident with Pashhur appears to be consequent on Jrm's smashing of the earthenware flask at the Potsherd Gate (19:1–15), a public declaration that must be subsequent to the king's burning of the scroll (see Setting of 19:1—20:6). Second, 6:21 closely resembles 6:11 (the classes of people to be destroyed) and 6:15 ("stumble" twice, v 21; "fall" twice, v 15). Third, "watchmen" (6:17) suggests "prophets, early and constantly" in 7:25 (see Setting on that passage).

There is no reason to come to a different conclusion for 6:27–30: Jrm himself is involved in the process of judgment, as is the case in 5:14 and 6:10; Yahweh's rejection of the people (6:30) matches their rejection of his torah (6:19).

One can reach less certainty with regard to 9:9–10 and 16–21. The difficulty with 9:9–10 revolves around the textual uncertainty regarding the first verb in v 9: if M is correct ("I shall lift up"), and if the speaker is Yahweh, as

is the case in v 10, then the passage must be Yahweh's own lament over the demise of his people. Form-critically the closest parallel is 12:7–13, and the association there of drought and military invasion suggests once more the period of 601–600. There are few clues within 9:16–21, but the demise of the people is assumed and the parallelism of "children" and "youth" resembles the parallelism of 6:11. We will not be wrong to assign both these passages to the second scroll.

The other prose sequences within chapter 7 (i.e., vv 16–20, 21–29, and 30–34) all give evidence of having arisen after the king burned the scroll (see Setting for each passage). Whether these prose passages entered the second scroll at the time of its dictation, or later (attracted by the prose of 7:1–12 + 13–15) would be difficult to say.

The remainder of the passages in 4:5—10:25 were lodged in their present position secondarily; each has its own history (notably 10:1–16).

Structural Organization of the Sequence of Units. If the foregoing analysis is correct, the first scroll contained 4:5–8, 13–18, 29–31; 6:1–8; and 7:1–12. The question arises what the pattern is for the enlarged sequence in the second scroll. One may surmise that 8:4–13; 8:14—9:8; 9:16–21; and 10:17–25 were added roughly in chronological order (see Setting for these units). But the organization for 4:5—6:30 is more complex. The solution may be beyond reach, but I have made one proposal which is at least plausible:[4]

A. Battle Orders (4:5–31)
B. Orders That Turn Attention to Wisdom (5:1–9)
C. Metaphorical Orders, to Destroy the Vineyard Israel (5:10–17)
D. The "Lesson" of Yahweh the Schoolmaster (5:20–29)
A'. Again Battle Orders (6:1–8)
C'. Again Metaphorical Orders, to Glean the Vineyard Israel (6:9–15)
B'. Again Orders That Turn Attention to Wisdom (6:16–30)

There is another possibility for the three units of chapter 5: the same sequence of images is found there as in 2:20–21: the refractory animal (5:5), the harlot (5:7b–

---

4   See ibid., 64–71.

8), the vine gone bad (5:10), the man of violence (5:26–28).

Identification of Speakers. A striking feature of the material on the foe from the north in these chapters is the variety of speakers, and analysis suggests that the interchange of speakers plays a role in the poetic structure of the individual units. The identity of the speaker in specific verses has not been dealt with systematically by the commentators heretofore, so that the methodology for such identifications becomes an important part of the exegetical task.

Any careful reader becomes aware of frequent shifts of speaker in these passages. All commentators have noted, for example, that Jrm speaks in 4:19–21 and that Yahweh speaks in v 22, and translations that employ quotation marks (for example, *RSV*) take notice of that shift. But it is equally clear that there is a shift from 4:6, where Yahweh speaks, to 4:8b, where the people speak (in the first-person plural), yet only Rudolph marks v 8b as an inner quotation, and no commentator notes what is proposed here, namely that the speaker shifts from Yahweh in vv 5–7 to Jrm in v 8 (see below).

There are those who solve the problem of perceived shifts of speaker by positing a kind of homogenized blending of voices. Thus Rudolph says of 4:6, "The divine and the prophet 'I' run off into each other" like watercolors in a painting;[5] and Abraham J. Heschel assumes that the "us" at the end of 6:26, analogous to the "us" in 4:8, represents God's word through the prophet to the people in which he is mourning for himself as well as for the people.[6] If the voice of Yahweh blends with the voice of Jrm, as Rudolph believes, or if the voice of Yahweh and the voice of Jrm blend with the voice of the people, as Heschel believes, then there is no problem; but it would be prudent to ask if we have understood the text rightly. If, to the contrary, the voices do not blend but are distinct, and if they can be distinguished, then what emerges will be a fresh understanding of the text. And our suspicions that all is not well increase when a commentator emends the text to fit his identification of the speaker (Rudolph wishes to read "Yahweh" instead of "me" in 9:2 on the assumption that Jrm is speaking in that verse as he does in 8:23). The proposal of the

present study is that systematic analysis of the question yields such identifications with a high degree of probability.

The only evidence, of course, is internal clues of diction and analogies of such clues in comparable passages. The rubric "oracle of Yahweh" or "for thus Yahweh has said" may not be dependable, since they stand outside the poetic structure of the lines; in Jer they usually do match the identifications made from evidence within the poetic lines themselves, but occasionally they are in error (for example, 17:5).

The process of the specific identification of speakers is best left to the individual passages; the details will usually be found in Structure, sometimes in Interpretation. It must be said in anticipation, however, that the identifications will elicit some pleasing symmetries of structure and some fresh understandings of the use of כִּי (see 4:8, 15, 22, 31; 6:4, 26; 10:21) and of the isolated infinitive absolute (4:18). The identification of speakers will afford us a more secure grasp on Jrm's understanding of his task and his attitude toward Yahweh (compare the general discussion of Setting, above).

If the emergence of a systematic interchange of speakers is a surprise to the modern reader, it must have been an equal surprise to the first hearers. To hear Yahweh speaking, then Jrm himself, then interruptions from the people and even from the enemy (6:4–5) must have been stunning to these hearers: nothing in the OT record indicates that prophetic oracles in Israel had been heard like these before. Micah offers hints of a dialogue between himself and God, and so does Habakkuk; but to add a third or fourth speaker to that dialogue is a quantum jump. There is a similar quantum jump in Greek drama: Aeschylus had been able to stay within the pattern of two speaking actors at a time, beyond the chorus, but Sophocles on occasion added a third actor speaking with the other two, an example being the messenger scene in *Electra*, where the messenger, Electra, and Clytemnestra interchange lines (lines 673–79). One wonders how Jrm managed it; how did he make plain in his recitation or his chanting who was speaking a given sequence of cola? Was it a shift of rhythm, or the pitch of his voice, or were there different modes or

---

5 *Das göttliche und das prophetische Ich gehen ineinander über,* 32.
6 Abraham J. Heschel, *The Prophets* (New York: Harper, 1962) 111, compare 113.

harmonies or gestures associated with the different speakers? There is no hope to learn, but one must assume that such shifts were apparent to Jrm's audience, however painfully we ourselves must tease them back to life.

Yahweh Can and Will Impose the Sentence of Death

Bibliography

On 4:5—6:30:
Gailey, James H., Jr.
    "The Sword and the Heart, Evil from the North—
    and Within, An Exposition of Jeremiah 4:5—
    6:30," *Int* 9 (1955) 294–309.

On 4:5–18:
Castellino, Giorgio R.
    "Observations on the literary structure of some
    passages in Jeremiah," *VT* 30 (1980) 401–3.

On 4:5–12:
Berridge
    pp. 91–113.
Reventlow
    Liturgie, 94–121.

On 4:5–8:
Christensen, Duane L.
    *Transformations of the War Oracle in Old Testament
    Prophecy* (HDR 3; Missoula, MT: Scholars, 1975)
    188–90.
Thomas, D. Winton
    "מלאו in Jeremiah IV.5: A Military Term," *JJS* 3
    (1952) 47–52.

On 4:9–12 in general:
Althann, Robert
    "Jeremiah iv 11–12: Stichometry, Parallelism and
    Translation," *VT* 28 (1978) 385–91.
Holladay, William L.
    "Structure, Syntax and Meaning in Jeremiah iv
    11–12a," *VT* 26 (1976) 28–37.
Meyer, Ivo
    Jeremia und die falsche Propheten (Göttingen:
    Vandenhoeck & Ruprecht, 1977) 81–85.
Robinson, Theodore H.
    "Note on the Text of Jer. iv 11," *JTS* 23 (1922) 68.
Soggin, J. Alberto
    "Zum wiederentdeckten altkanaanäischen Monat
    ṣḥ," *ZAW* 77 (1965) 83–26; and "Nachtrag zu *ZAW*
    77 (1965) S. 83–86," *ZAW* 77 (1965) 326.

On 4:9–12 and the sirocco:
Baly
    Geography, 51–53.

On 4:13–18:
Rabin, Chaim
    "Noṣerim," *Textus* 5 (1965) 44–52.

On 4:19–31:
Castellino
    "Observations," 399–401.

On 4:19–22:

Berridge
  pp. 169–70.
Kumaki, F. Kenro
  "A New Look at Jer 4,19–22 and 10,19–21,"
  Annual of the Japanese Biblical Institute 8 (1982)
  113–22.
McKane
  Prophets and Wise Men, 88–89.

On 4:23–28:

Berridge
  pp. 191–93.
Eppstein, Victor
  "The Day of Yahweh in Jer 4:23–28," *JBL* 87
  (1968) 93–97.
Fishbane, Michael A.
  "Jeremiah iv 23–26 and Job iii 3–13: A Recovered
  Use of the Creation Pattern," *VT* 21 (1971) 151–
  67.
Holladay, William L.
  "The Recovery of Poetic Passages of Jeremiah,"
  JBL 85 (1966) 404–6.
Holladay
  "Style," 47–48.

Lindblom
  Prophecy, 126–27.
Soggin, J. Alberto
  "The 'Negation' in Jeremiah 4,27 and 5,10a, cf.
  5,18b," *Old Testament and Oriental Studies* (BibOr
  29; 1975) 179–83 = "La 'negazione' in Geremia
  4,27 e 5,10a, cfr. 5,18b," *Bib* 46 (1965) 56–59.

On 4:29–31:

Beer, Georg
  "Miscellen—4. Zu Jeremiah 4,31," *ZAW* 31 (1911)
  153–54.
Efros, Israel
  "An Emendation of Jer. 4.29," *JAOS* 41 (1921) 75.
Levitan, Isidor S.
  "Dr. Efros' Emendation of Jer. 4.29," *JAOS* 41
  (1921) 316.

4

5 Yahweh:

> **Declare in Judah,**
> > **and in Jerusalem announce (it) [and
> > say,]**[a]
> > **sound**[b] **the trumpet in the land;**
> **call out, "Form up!" and say,**
> > **"Gather and let us get in
> > to the fortified cities!"**

6

> **Raise a signal**[a] **in Zion,**
> > **get (folk) to shelter, don't stand there,**
> **for disaster I am bringing from the north,**
> > **and great collapse.**

7

> **A lion has come up from his thicket,**
> > **and a destroyer of nations has set out,**
> > **he has come out from his place,**
> **to make your land a desolation—**
> > **your cities shall be in ruins, without
> > inhabitant.**

8 Jeremiah:

> **On this account gird on sackcloth,**
> > **lament and wail:**
> > > **"Oh, the hot anger of Yahweh has not
> > > turned back from us!"**

- - - -

9 Yahweh:

> **And it will happen on that day,**
> > > **oracle of Yahweh:**
> **The heart of the king will fail,**
> > **and the heart of the officials,**
> > > **and the priests shall be made desolate,**
> > > **and the prophets stunned.**

10 Jeremiah:

> [a] **Then I said,**[a] **Oh, Lord Yahweh, no!—you
> really did deceive this people and
> Jerusalem, saying, 'You shall have
> peace,' while a sword has reached
> the (very) throat!"**

- - - -

Text

5a Omitting וְאָמְרוּ with Rudolph; this verb is repeated at the end of the third colon and appears dittographic here, or else is a secondary attempt to sort out where the beginning of a quotation occurs. See Interpretation.

b Reading תִּקְעוּ with qere', many MSS., G, S, T; ketib וְתִקְעוּ "and sound."

6a For נֵס G reads φεύγετε "flee" = נָס. This is a plausible variant, particularly in view of the context of a call to flight (see Form); but a similar context in 6:1 has a parallel noun מַשְׂאֵת "fire signal," so M is to be preferred.

10a–a For the expected G καὶ εἶπα "and I said" G[A] has καὶ εἶπαν = וַיֹּאמְרוּ "and they said." Bernhard Duhm (hesitantly), Friedrich Giesebrecht, Paul Volz, Albert Condamin, Rudolph, and Artur Weiser read וְאָמְרוּ "and they said" (with nonconsecutive וְ); Volz goes further and excises the following words "Ah, Lord Yahweh," which are more appropriate on the lips of Jrm (compare 1:6). All this is on the assumption that the optimistic prophets (of v 9) speak here. But this assumption is erroneous (so also John Bright) and is based in part on a misunderstanding of the meaning of אָכֵן, here translated "no!" (see Interpretation). In spite of Rudolph's insistence, it appears that Jrm assumed at the time this passage was uttered that the optimistic prophets were indeed sent from Yahweh (against 23:21) but that thereby Yahweh intentionally deceived the people. It is probable that the G[A] reading is a seeming *lectio*

11 Jeremiah: **At that time it will be said to this people and to Jerusalem,**
"A wind is glowing on the caravan-tracks,
in the wilderness ⟨it has trodden⟩ᵃ my fair people;
not for winnowing and not for cleansing;

12 **the wind is ⟨full of curse,⟩ᵃ**
it comes for me."
Now I too will pronounce judgments on them.

- - - - -

13 Yahweh: **See, like clouds he comes up,**
and like the whirlwind are his chariots,
swifter than eagles his horses;
people: **Woe to us, oh, we are ruined!**
14 Jeremiah: **Wash from evil your heart,**
O Jerusalem, that you may be rescued!
How long will your baneful schemes lodgeᵃ in your inner self?
15 Yahweh: **Yes, a voice declares from Dan**
and announces bane from Mount Ephraim:
16 **"Proclaim to the nations, ⟨'(Right) this way!'⟩ᵃ**
announce (it) over Jerusalem";
shouters come from the distant land
and have uttered over the cities of Judah their cry,
17 **like guards of a field they have closed in around her,**
for it is I she has defied,
oracle of Yahweh.
18 Jeremiah: ᵃ **To thinkᵃ ᵇyour wayᵇ ᵃhave doneᵃ these (things) to you!**
Such is your ruin,
for ⟪your defiance⟫ᶜ reaches toᵈ your (very) heart!

- - - - -

19 Jeremiah: **My bowels, my bowels,**
ᵃ**I cannot help churning!**ᵃ

facilior which arose within the *G* tradition. On Jrm's attitude toward the optimistic prophets, see further Interpretation.

11a Vocalizing *M* דֶּרֶךְ "(on) the way of (?)" as דָּרַךְ; see William L. Holladay, "Structure, syntax and meaning in Jeremiah iv 11–12a," *VT* 26 (1976) 28–37. For parallel uses of this verb in Jer and elsewhere, see Interpretation.

12a Vocalizing מָלֵא מֵאֵלֶּה for *M* מָלֵא מֵאֵלֶּה "fuller than these, too full for these" (compare Condamin). The word אָלָה "curse" is appropriate here in the context of drought; compare 23:10, where it is associated with מָלֵא (and מִדְבָּר "wilderness"), and note that in that passage a few MSS. and *G* and *S* read אֵלֶּה "these" for *M* אָלָה. Note also the revocalization of אֵלֶּה אָלָה as אָלָה אֵלֶּה proposed in 2:34. After I came to the proposal myself, I found it in the seventeenth-century commentator L. Cappellus (see Jacobus Cappellus, *Ludovici Cappelli Commentarii et Notae Criticae in Vetus Testamentum* [Amsterdam: 1689]) and in the translation and notes of Benjamin Blayney (*Jeremiah and Lamentations, A New Translation; With Notes Critical, Philological and Explanatory* [Oxford: 1784]). Michaelis called the suggestion "ingenious" (Johann D. M. Michaelis, *Observationes Philologicae et Criticae in Jeremiae Vaticinia et Threnos* [Göttingen: Vandenhoeck & Ruprecht, 1793]) but rejected it. Part of the difficulty is construing the preposition מִן; it is proposed here that the adjective מָלֵא may take מִן as the related verb does.

14a The incongruity of feminine singular verb with plural subject is acceptable (GKC, sec. 145k); but I would propose that the consonants be vocalized as *tālênnā* (compare תֵּשַׁבְןָ, Ezek 16:55). The suggestion in *HALAT* to construe the verb as hip'il ("How long will you lodge your baneful schemes within yourself?" p. 503a) is dubious (the verb would appear to be masculine).

16a Vocalizing הַנֵּה for *M* הִנֵּה "behold" with Condamin; compare the revocalization in 31:8 of הִנֵּה to הַנֵּה.

18a—a MSS. divide whether to read the infinitive absolute עָשׂוֹ or the perfect עָשׂוּ. Form-critically the verse is similar to 8:15, where the infinitive absolute also appears; this, then, is the preferable reading.

b—b A few MSS., *G*, *V*, *S*, and *T* read דְּרָכַיִךְ "your ways." In 17:10, where the two nouns appear again in hendiadys, the ketib is singular, the qere' is plural; in 23:22 the noun is singular. In prose Jrm prefers the plural (7:3, 5). Read the singular, as the stronger expression.

c Following the suggestion of Rudolph (*BHS*) read מֶרְיֵךְ for *M* מַר כִּי "(how) bitter, for"; see Interpretation.

d Many MSS. read עַל "upon"; but normal usage with this verb is the majority reading עַד "(up) to"; compare the same expression in v 10.

19a—a Reading with ketib, many MSS., *G* and *V* אָחוּלָה, cohortative of חוּל qal; the MS. variant אָחִילָה is

141

⟨You are chilled (?)⟩[b] O my heart, in
  turmoil for me!
My heart I cannot silence,
for the sound of the trumpet [c]you have
  heard,
O my soul,[c] the blast of battle!
"Crash upon crash!" is shouted,[a]
  "Oh, the whole land is devastated!

20

simply a by-form. For the translation see Structure
and Interpretation. The words "my bowels, my
bowels" will have to be construed either as an
accusative of specification (Joüon, *Gramm.*, sec.
126g) or as an independent exclamation (compare 2
Kgs 4:19; see Joüon, *Gramm.*, sec. 162c). A less
likely reading is אֲחִילָה (hip'il, transitive, with "my
bowels, my bowels" the direct object). The qere'
reads אוֹחִילָה "let me wait" (יחל hip'il); this is clearly
a mitigating reading which neither the Versions nor
the medieval commentators have taken seriously.

b   *M* reads קִירֹות "walls of" (my heart); such a phrase
would have to be construed as another exclamation,
parallel with "my bowels, my bowels." But the
phrase is not paralleled elsewhere, and *G* and *V*
paraphrase ("feelings of": αἰσθητήρια; *sensus*).
Structural analysis of the verse lends plausibility to a
verb here. With hesitation I propose קָרֹות, קרר qal;
the yod will then have arisen secondarily as an
erroneous *mater lectionis*. The verb קרר is not
attested in the qal, but its antonym חמם is. If the
hip'il stem, which is attested, can carry an intransitive meaning, then one could borrow the he from
the cohortative just preceding, rendering that verb
noncohortative, and read הַקִּירֹות. This proposal
leads to a pattern of verbs in the verse wherein the
first and third are imperfect first singular, and the
second and fourth perfect second singular. See
further Structure, Interpretation.

c—c   Reading with the qere' שָׁמַעַתִּי, perfect second
singular feminine (compare 22:21; 1 Kgs 1:11; Ruth
2:8) with archaic spelling (compare 2:20, 33; 3:4, 5),
and construing "my soul" as a vocative; so also
Bright. The Versions all read a third singular
feminine verb ("my soul has heard"), though *T* by
vocalization only; this implies the participle שֹׁמַעַת,
and at least one MS. does read שומעת. Some commentators prefer to read the ketib as שָׁמַעְתִּי "I have
heard," and are then inclined to delete "my soul," or
to substitute it for the second occurrence of "my
heart" (thus reading הֹמֶה־לִּי; so Volz, Rudolph).
Such a shift is uncalled for; for the two occurrences
of "my heart" see Structure.

20a   Understanding נִקְרָא as the nip'al participle of קרא
"call"; the identical perfect verb would carry
virtually the same meaning ("has been the shout").
In favor of construing a participle is the participle
נִשְׁמָע in similar contexts (3:21; 31:15). The Versions
and commentaries divide equally between understanding קרא I "call" and קרא II "meet"; by the latter
alternative the line would read "crash overtakes
crash" (compare *NJV*). In favor of "call": *G*, *V*,
Giesebrecht, Condamin, Rudolph; in favor of
"meet": *S*, *T*, Duhm, Volz, Bright. It is conceivable
that some ambiguity is intended here, but in favor
of "call" is that fact that diction regarding "tent" and
"curtains" must be spoken by the people (so,
inevitably, from 10:20: note there "my children,"
and compare that diction with 31:15, spoken by

(Oh,) suddenly [b] ⟨my tent⟩ 《is
     devastated,》[b]
     [c]in an instant,[c] my curtains!"

21 How long must I see the ⟨fugitive,⟩[a]
     hear the sound of the trumpet?

22 Yahweh: Well, my people are foolish,
     me they do not know,
          they are stupid children,
          they have no sense,
               they are wise in doing ill,
               but how to do good they do not
                    know.

- - - - -

23 Jeremiah: I looked at the earth, to see a formless
     waste,
          and to the heavens, and their light was
               no more;
24 I looked at the mountains, to see them
     quaking,
          and all the hills rocked to and fro;
25 I looked, to see no man,
          and all the birds of the heavens had
               fled;
26 I looked, to see the garden-land a wilder-
     ness,
          and all its cities demolished[a] before
               Yahweh,
               before[b] his hot anger 《made
                    desolate.》[c]
27 For thus Yahweh has said,
     Yahweh: All the earth shall be a desolation,
          ⟨and none of it⟩[a] will I remake;

Rachel for Ephraim; see further Structure and
Interpretation).

b—b   Reading the singular שָׁדַד אָהֳלִי with *G* and *S* for
M plural, שֻׁדְּדוּ אֹהָלַי "my tents are destroyed." In
favor of the singular is not only the reading of two
Versions but the parallel in 10:20 and the phraseology of Isa 54:2; the metaphor is evidently a
reference to the temple: see Interpretation.

c—c   For *M* רֶגַע *G* reads "are torn," probably נִתְּקוּ. This
is a plausible reading, and רֶגַע and פִּתְאֹם are not in
parallel elsewhere in Jer; but they do appear in a
common context in Isa 47:9, 11, and it is therefore
better to stay with *M*.

21a   Reading נָס with *V* and *S*; *G* has the same reading
but paraphrases with a plural; *M* reads נֵס "signal"
(see v 6). These readings are by themselves equally
plausible. What tips my balance in favor of "fugitive"
is reading of both *V* and *S*, since both of them know
נֵס "signal" in v 6; both traditions, then, know the
vocalization נָס here, and given Jrm's penchant for
word-play, one must conclude that *M* has leveled the
variation.

26a   Reading *M* נִתְּצוּ, נתץ nip'al. *G* reads ἐμπεπυ-
ρισμέναι "are burned" = נִצְּתוּ, יצת nip'al; and
Rudolph states that several MSS. of *M* read the same
(*BHS*), though they are not listed in Giovanni B. De
Rossi, p. 71. It should be noted that *V* and *S* agree
with *M*, while *T* assumes נצה nip'al "are brought to
ruin." The problem appears in the opposite
direction in 2:15 (see Text there): the majority of
MSS. read the qere' נִצְּתוּ "are burned" (ketib נִצְּתָה),
from יצת or נצה, while *G* reads κατεσκάφησαν "are
demolished" = נִתְּצוּ as so some Hebrew MSS. Since
M and *G* seem to agree in 4:7 that the verb is נצה
nip'al "be brought to ruin," and since all three
passages offer "cities" as subject of their respective
verbs, one can only conclude that Jrm is ringing the
changes on the possibilities, so it must be assumed
that each passage uses a different verb. It is most
economical, then, to accept *M* here and *M* qere' in
2:15. See Holladay, *Architecture*, 179 n. 17.

b   Many MSS., *G*, *V*, *S* read וּמִפְּנֵי "and before."
Either reading is satisfactory.

c   Restoring נָשַׁמּוּ (שמם nip'al) from *G* ἠφανίσθησαν.
G preserves the chiasmus of these two cola and the
presence of the verb here is intrinsically plausible. In
G ἀφανίζω renders שמם about twenty-nine times; in
Jer the rendering occurs in 12:11 and 50:45—the
diction in 12:11 is particularly close to the context
in the present passage. Since Yahweh's speech in v
27 begins with שְׁמָמָה, and since the occurrence of
נָשַׁמּוּ in v 9 may be perceived to interact with the
present passage (see Structure), the reconstruction
becomes convincing.

27a   Revocalizing *M* וְכָלָה to וְכֻלָּהּ "all of it" (feminine:
that is, the earth). The colon in *M* must be
translated "but I shall not make a full end," wording
which does not fit the context. I suggest that the
negative in 5:10 is a gloss (see Text there) and that

28
on this account the earth shall mourn,
  and the heavens be dark above,
    [a]inasmuch as[a] I have spoken [. . . .][b] and
      have not retracted,
        《I have decided》[b] and will not turn back
          from it.

- - -

29 Yahweh: From the shout, "Horseman [a]and
            archer!"[a]
    every 《region》[b] is fleeing;
    they have gone 《into the caves,
      and have hidden》[c] in the thickets,
        and into the rocks have gone up;
    《every city》[d] is deserted,
      and no one is dwelling in them,
        [e]each one 《is slain.》[e]

5:18 as a whole is a mitigating gloss, given the statement in 30:11. For a justification of the reading in the present verse see Interpretation.

28a—a There is no warrant to delete עַל with Duhm, Volz, Rudolph, and Weiser; the expression עַל כִּי is found also in Deut 31:17; Judg 3:12; Mal 2:14; and Ps 139:14. The word עַל resonates with עַל־זֹאת in the first colon of v 28 and with מִמַּעַל in the second.

b Moving זַמֹּתִי "I have decided" from its present position after "I have spoken" with *G*; so also Duhm, Giesebrecht, Condamin, Rudolph, Bright (against Volz). The restored order remedies the curious distribution of "and"; it also matches the pattern of "A and not B" found in 5:21, 22; 17:11; and 30:19 as well as elsewhere in the OT: the last-cited passage is particularly appropriate for comparison, given the similarity of diction (note also the shape of Isa 46:11b).

29a—a *M* וְרֹמֵה קֶשֶׁת literally "shooter of an arrow"; many MSS. read וְרֹמֵי קֶשֶׁת "shooters of an arrow," plural. The singular, parallel with "horseman," is to be preferred; see further Interpretation.

b Reading *G* χώρα = אֶרֶץ for *M* הָעִיר "(all) the city." The noun עִיר appears correctly in the sixth colon of the verse but is incorrect here. The curious *G* here, πᾶσα χώρα, without the article, really does suggest the striking Hebrew כָּל־אֶרֶץ (contrast 8:16, כָּל־הָאָרֶץ = *G* πᾶσα ἡ γῆ). The analysis of the text for the sixth colon (see d) suggests the balancing כָּל־עִיר there. The expression כָּל־אֶרֶץ in the absolute state is unparalleled in the OT, though Ezek 19:7, with אֶרֶץ וּמְלֹאָהּ "(the) land and all who were in it" suggests that the noun without article could serve in such contexts.

c Restoring בְּמְעָרוֹת וַיַחְבְּלוּ from *G* εἰς τὰ σπήλαια . . . ἐκρύβησαν, omitted in *M*. Duhm, Volz, Rudolph, and Bright all agree; Carl H. Cornill and Giesebrecht disagree. Volz points out a homoioteleuton that would account for the haplography: באו במערות ויחבאו בעבים, in which the sequence באו appears twice. J. Gerald Janzen discusses the two readings carefully (p. 31) and cautiously declares for *G*. The proposed tricolon in v 29b makes a tricolon here more plausible: the two match each other closely in diction (see Structure).

d Reading כָּל־עִיר with *G* (πᾶσα πόλις) for *M* כָּל־הָעִיר "all the city." The occurrence of the plural בָּהֶן "in them" in the next colon reinforces the rightness of this correction; note also כָּל־עִיר in a similar context in 48:8.

e—e Constructing the third colon in a tricolon with אִישׁ, construed in *M* closely with "dwelling in them," and closing the verse, and with שָׁדוּד, a masculine participle which in *M* is the second word of v 30 but which does not agree with the feminine pronoun there (וְאַתְּ). Duhm acutely remarks that אִישׁ overloads the colon and should be expected directly after וְאֵין "and no one" anyway; compare 8:6 and 12:11, where the word order is אֵין אִישׁ plus

144

30 ᵃAnd you,ᵃ [. . . .]ᵇ what are you doing? —
    that you should dress in scarlet,
        adorn yourself with ᶜornaments ofᶜ
        gold,
            enlarge with paint your eyes:
    in vain you try to beautify yourself!
        Paramours reject you,
        your life they seek!

31 Jeremiah: Instead ᵃa shout like a woman writhingᵃ I
        have heard,
        ᵇan appealᵇ like one bearing her first,
            the sound of fair Zion panting,ᶜ
                extending her hands:

participle. The word שָׁדוּד ends a verse in the Song of Deborah, Judg 5:27; compare also Isa 33:1. The word was doubtless inadvertently omitted in copy, a stage represented by *G*, which omits the word, then entered in the margin and later reinserted in the body of the text at the wrong spot; compare the misplaced word in v 28.

30a—a The ketib ואתי offers the archaic spelling of the second singular feminine pronoun (so six other times: Judg 17:2; 1 Kgs 14:2; 2 Kgs 4:16, 23; 8:1; Ezek 36:13). Some MSS. read the qere' וְאַתְּ, which is the normal spelling.

b   See v 29 e.

c—c Commentators differ as to whether עֶדְיֵ is dittographic from the verb just preceding (תַּעְדִּי: so Volz and Rudolph), or whether the word is original. There is no way to be sure, hence it is better to retain *M* (see further Interpretation).

31a—a *M* כְּחוֹלָה with waw appears to represent a feminine participle of חלה (thus "someone weak, sick"); but the parallelism suggests a feminine participle of חיל "shake, whirl," which would be חָלָה. *G*, *V*, and *T* translate with expressions for "giving birth" or "pregnant," while *S* stays with "weak." The participle may have been irregular (compare the lexica) or the copyist may have slipped. Note the similar problem with the same root in v 19 (note a—a).

b—b Both the parallelism here (with קוֹל twice) and *G* (τοῦ στεναγμοῦ σου, "of your groaning") suggest a word here for a sound, and the normal meaning of צָרָה "distress" seems too unspecific. Accordingly several commentators have accepted the suggestion of Arnold B. Ehrlich, *Randglossen*, 251, to read here a noun צָרָה from צרח "shriek, raise a war-cry" (so Volz, Rudolph, Bright). Such a noun is probably to be read in Ezek 21:27 (so George A. Cooke, *A Critical and Ezegetical Commentary on the Book of Ezekiel* [ICC; New York: Scribner's, 1936] 233, 239; Walther Zimmerli, *Ezekiel 1*, 437), but the use of צָרָה in contexts associated with labor-pains in 6:24 and 49:24 suggests that the text may be correct after all. Mitchell Dahood has suggested (*Psalms II*, 225–26) that there is a second noun צָרָה associated with a root צור (not recognized in the lexica) meaning "beckon" (see 1:5, Text, a); the noun would then mean "appeal, imploring." If there is such a meaning to צָרָה, then the occurrences of the noun in 6:24 and 49:24 will carry a double meaning.

c   The verb תִּתְיַפַּח, יפח hitpa'el, is a *hapax legomenon* in the OT. The Versions appear to offer guesses: *G* "shall be faint" and *V* "who is fainting"; *T* "who is prostrating herself"; *S* "who is working to exhaustion." The root יפח is perhaps a by-form of פוח I and נפח "blow," but it is by no means certain how to analyze the various scattered evidences of יפח elsewhere (see the lexica on יָפֵחַ in Hab 2:3 and Jastrow on יְפַח). In any event the meaning "panting"

"Woe is me! How my life ^dhas ebbed away^d before murderers!"

fits the context admirably, and the general semantic range is hardly in doubt.

d—d The verb עֵיפָה, perfect feminine of עִיף, is striking if correct: the perfect of this verb is not otherwise attested. Since נֶפֶשׁ appears twice elsewhere with the feminine adjective (or participle) עֲיֵפָה (31:25; Prov 25:25), some have suggested that vocalization (BDB with a query). However, since G, V, and S all offer a finite verb in translation, only T offering a participle, it would seem that the vocalization of M is correct.

Structure

Extent of Unit. Three conclusions have emerged already in Preliminary Observations. (1) Verses 5–31 evolved in two stages: vv 5–8, 13–18, and 29–31 were part of the first scroll, and vv 9–12 and 19–28 were added in the second scroll. (2) There is structural congruence between vv 9–12 and vv 19–28. (3) The first nine verses of chapter 5 form a separate unit. And evidence will be adduced below, in the discussion of structure within the unit, that there is congruence among 4:5–8, 13–18, and 29–31. Thus even though vv 5–31 reflect more than one setting, it is best to deal with the whole sequence as a single unit (so also Duhm, Volz, Rudolph, Bright).

Structure Within the Unit. The three sections that were part of the first scroll share common characteristics. In each of them are vivid descriptions of the coming of the enemy (vv 5–7, 13a, 15–17, 29); within these are occasional first-person references identifying Yahweh as the speaker ("disaster I am bringing from the north," v 6; "for it is I she has defied," v 17). Yahweh's speeches each contain quotations of battle shouts (vv 5, 15, 29). The first and third sections end with a despairing cry of the people (vv 8b, 31b), and though it is not immediately apparent to the modern reader, these cries are each set within a speech of Jrm's (vv 8, 30–31; see below). The central section is more elaborate; it likewise ends with a speech of Jrm's (v 18), but it has a more complicated structure, since Yahweh's speech in vv 13a, 15–17 is interrupted by a cry of the people (v 13b, similar to v 31b) and by an appeal of Jrm's (v 14).

Interwoven with these three sections are two sequences of second-scroll material (vv 9–12, 19–28), and it will become apparent that each of these sequences is twofold, so that one is dealing with four units (vv 9–10, 11–12, 19–22, 23–28), of which the first and third match in catchword ("heart" [לֵב] twice in both v 9 and 19; "throat/soul" [נֶפֶשׁ], in v 10 and 19), and the second and fourth likewise, this time in word-play: "wilderness"

(מִדְבָּר, vv 11, 26), and "speak" (דבר pi'el, vv 12, 28). Thematically they are also set up in parallel fashion, with images of "sword" (specifically in v 10; by implication in the battle imagery of vv 19–20) and of drought (vv 11–12a; by implication, vv 25–26, 27–28: see especially Interpretation on v 28); this pairing is likewise the basic feature of the organization of the liturgy on drought and battle in 14:1—15:9 (see there).

It may also be significant that the patterning of speakers in vv 13–18, the central section, finds its closest parallel in the patterning of 6:22–26; in this way the sequence of oracles on the foe from the north in the second scroll achieves a kind of inclusio.

Verses 5–8. It is clear that Yahweh speaks at least through v 6 ("disaster I am bringing"). Jrm speaks in v 8: it is the task of the prophet to call people to repentance (7:1–12), and Mic 1:8 (which also opens with עַל־זֹאת, "on this account") begins a lament spoken by the prophet. Verse 7 is a problem. On the one hand, the diction is very much like that of 5:6, which, for a variety of reasons, appears to be spoken by Jrm (see there); on the other hand, the verse seems to continue the "war news" spoken by Yahweh in vv 5–6, and the diction and structure are much like that found in v 29, which will be assigned to Yahweh (see below). On balance, it is more plausible to understand v 7 to close Yahweh's speech: in this way his war news will be continued in v 13.

Verse 5 appears to separate into six cola. It would be easy to perceive here three bicola (the parallelism of "declare" and "announce," the quotation in the last two cola), but two considerations lead to the solution of two tricola. First, "in Judah," "in Jerusalem," and "in the land" are strongly parallel in the first tricolon; second, "to the fortified cities" in the sixth colon parallels "in the land" in the third. Is it significant that the number of stressed words (Michael Patrick O'Connor: "units")[1] is symmetrical in the six cola: 2 + 2 + 3; 3 + 2 + 2?

Verse 6 is made up of two bicola. Verse 7 is made up

of five cola (the last colon is exactly analogous to that in 2:15: see there). The first three cola all embody verbs of motion, and thus v 7a is a tricolon; but these clauses point immediately to the expressions of result in v 7b, so that the tricolon and bicolon belong closely together. Is it significant that in Yahweh's speech two tricola and two bicola are followed by one tricolon and one bicolon?

Verse 8 must be a tricolon: there is no way to divide the utterance of the people (Rudolph tries, by rearranging the words, but the subject and verb cannot be in separate cola).[2] Finally it must be noted that the three imperatives calling to lament in v 8a are in ironic balance with the military imperatives in vv 5–6.

Verses 9–12. Verse 9 opens with introductory words and continues with a divine word, four cola which may be analyzed either as two bicola (the first united by the repetition of "heart," the second by a chiasmus—verb, "the priests," "the prophets," verb) or as a tetracolon each colon of which names a category of leaders. Verse 10 (Jrm's response to the oracle: see Interpretation) is prose (compare the remarks in Structure on 1:6).

The introductory words in v 11 appear to be parallel to those in v 9 ("at that time," parallel to "in that day") and v 10 ("this people and Jerusalem"). Verses 11–12a make up a short poem. It is clear that v 11aβ makes up two cola; v 11b ("not for winnowing and not for cleansing") must make up a single colon, since the negatives are not "units." Verse 12a must be understood as two cola ("for me" [לִי] counts as a "unit").[3] The first colon of the poem then matches the first colon of v 12a ("wind" twice), and the (reconstructed) verb דָּרַךְ "it has trodden" in the second colon of the poem parallels בוא "it comes" in the second colon of v 12a (the same parallelism occurs in Mic 5:4, 5). The third colon ("not for winnowing and not for cleansing") thus resonates both with the two cola before it and the two after it.

Verses 13–18. Verse 13a continues the war news and is thus spoken by Yahweh; the lines form a tight tricolon, the first and second cola paralleling "like clouds" and "like the whirlwind," the second and third paralleling "his chariots" and "his horses." This is followed (v 13b) by a single line spoken by the people (compare the single line spoken by the people in vv 8b and 31b). Verse 14 must

be assigned to Jrm, whose task is to call the people to repentance (compare the remarks above on v 8). The verse must be a tricolon (against Rudolph): again, subject cannot be separated from predicate. The first colon parallels the third ("your heart," "within you" [literally "in your entrails"]). The people's interruption (v 13b) thus stands poised between two tricola: v 13b not only summarizes v 13a, but the passive verb "we are ruined" (v 13b) is answered by the passive "you may be rescued" in the middle colon of v 14.

Verses 15–17 embody eight cola; the war news continues, and the sequence is spoken by Yahweh ("for it is I she has defied," v 17). They make up four bicola. The first (v 15) offers two hip'il participles, the second (v 16aα) two hip'il imperatives, the second of which is the same verb as that in v 15b. The third bicolon (v 16aβb) loosely parallels both the first bicolon (participle in the first colon, "come," parallel with "declares" and "announces") and the second bicolon ("Judah" parallel with "Jerusalem," and, more loosely, "from the distant land" with "to the nations"). The last two cola are not directly parallel with each other; v 17a parallels the third bicolon ("guards" parallels נֹצְרִים, here translated "shouters": a double meaning is evidently involved—see Interpretation on v 17), while v 17b is an isolated colon giving a final accusation (see Form).

The section closes with three cola (v 18) which must be attributed to Jrm (compare the diction of the last colon here with the last clause in v 10). The parallelism of the three lines is not close; the text evidently needs repair. In any event "these" in the first colon is parallel with "this" in the second. And emending the text of the last colon (see Interpretation), כִּי מָרֵךְ parallels the last colon of v 17, with כִּי אֹתִי מָרָתָה. Does this tricolon structurally reflect those of v 13a and 14?

Verses 19–22. Verse 22 is spoken by Yahweh ("me they do not know"). Verses 19–21, by contrast, are assumed to be spoken by Jrm (T even prefixes to v 19 the words "the prophet said"); indeed Yahweh is unlikely to voice the cohortatives of v 21. The contrast of mood between the two speeches is stunning: Jrm voices his own reaction of panic and cites the panicked shouting of the people (v 20), but Yahweh speaks simply as a schoolmaster would,

---

1   O'Connor, *Structure,* 87.
2   For analogous cola see ibid., 229, on Judg 5:28b, and 286, on Ps 106:40a.
3   See ibid., 257, on Zeph 3:8a.

marking his students: *doing ill*, pass with honors; *doing good*, fail! Yet it is possible that they are linked by a word-play between "my bowels," מֵעַי, and "my people," עַמִּי: Jrm is concerned about his symptoms, Yahweh about his people.

There is no way to arrange v 19a satisfactorily into cola; something must be wrong with the text. "I cannot silence" (לֹא אַחֲרִישׁ) at the end of v 19a cannot stand alone (against Rudolph); "my heart" just preceding, however, can stand as an object. This expression will then balance the first-person verb at the beginning, "I cannot help churning" (אָחוּלָה). But what remains in the middle is neither grammatical nor convincing as a colon. With hesitation therefore I suggest that "walls of" be reconstrued as a second singular verb, and that "my heart" is therefore addressed, as "my soul" is in v 19b, but "chill" with "heart" is otherwise unattested, and the solution may be beyond our reach (see further Interpretation). So reconstructed, however, the half-verse is a tricolon. Verse 19b is clearly a bicolon.

Verse 20 is a tetracolon, the second and third cola of which offer "is ruined," the third and fourth the parallelism of "my tent" and "my curtains." Verse 21 is just as clearly a bicolon, which echoes the bicolon of v 19b.

Yahweh's speech in v 22 cannot be analyzed as other than a hexacolon. It is true that the last two cola are especially close ("do ill," "do good"), but then again "they do not know" occurs in both the second and the sixth cola and a third expression with the negative in the fourth colon, "they" (הֵמָּה) occurs in the third, fourth, and fifth cola, which are nominal clauses like the first colon. Parallelism runs in every direction; it is simply meant to box the compass of pedagogical reporting.

Verses 23–28. Verses 27–28 are spoken by Yahweh (the diction of v 28, not to mention the rubric at the beginning of v 27). Conceivably vv 23–26 might also be spoken by Yahweh: the diction reminds one of Genesis 1 (see below), where Yahweh is the subject of the repeated occurrences of "see," but two considerations render it almost inevitable that Jrm is the speaker here. The first is form-critical: the closest analogy to vv 23–28 is Amos 7:7–9, a vision report of the prophet followed by Yahweh's confirmation of that vision report (see Form). The second is more subtle, the preposition אֶל "to" in the phrase "to the heavens" (v 23), a hint that the speaker is a human being and not Yahweh (see Interpretation). On

that assumption two patterns emerge. (1) What Jrm "sees" is analogous to what he "sees" and "hears" in vv 19 and 21. (2) Diction in Jrm's speech is picked up in Yahweh's speech: not only "earth" and "heavens" (vv 23, 27–28a), but more particularly the last verb in v 26, נָשַׁמּוּ (reconstructed from *G*), is picked up in v 27 by שְׁמָמָה. And one notes further the way "all" functions in the two speeches: one has "all the earth" in the first verse of Yahweh's speech (and a second "all," here, with the negative, translated "none," if the revocalization is correct); Jrm had not said "all the earth," but "all the hills," "all the birds of the heavens," and "all its cities," so that "all the earth" in v 27 denotes "all creation." Thus one has in vv 23–28 a longer speech of Jrm's and a shorter speech of Yahweh's, just as one has in vv 19–22.

Verses 23–26 each open with "I looked" (רָאִיתִי); the repetition in this sequence is similar to that in 50:35–37 and 51:20–23. These verses are (until the last phrases of v 26) of steadily decreasing length (one notes the typography of *BHS*): the verb רָאִיתִי has an object in vv 23 and 24, but no object in vv 25 and 26. Verse 25 must be a bicolon, and vv 23 and 24, which are parallel, must be bicola as well. And if the closing verb in v 26 is correct (see Text), then that verse cannot be other than a tricolon.

The first two verses deal with the realm of nonlife (earth, heavens; mountains, hills) while the second two deal with the realm of life (man, birds; fruitful land, cities). And not only are the nouns within each verse parallel, but those within v 23 are congruent with those in v 25 (man lives on the earth, birds live in the heavens). Further the references in v 23 are clearly to Genesis 1 ("formless void," תֹהוּ וָבֹהוּ, Gen 1:2; "light," Gen 1:3), and in v 25 "no man" (אֵין הָאָדָם) seems to reflect "no man" (וְאָדָם אַיִן) in Gen 2:5. The movement of the vision is thus from creation in Genesis 1—2 to the settlement in Canaan, "fruitful land" (הַכַּרְמֶל, v 26) being found in the context of the settlement in 2:7, and "cities demolished" there reflecting similar phrasing in 2:15 and 4:7. But then the steadily decreasing length of lines suddenly opens out into the extra material at the end of v 26, material which underlines Yahweh's anger.

Yahweh's speech in vv 27–28 consists of three bicola; the third is the climax, with four first-person verbs.

Verses 29–31. The battle warnings of v 29 can safely be assigned to Yahweh. The end of v 31 offers a quotation of the people, here personified as a woman in childbirth, but who quotes the people? Jrm quotes the people in vv 8 and 20; one is then on safe ground in assigning v 31 to Jrm (compare a similar sequence in 6:26). But there is a shift from v 30 to v 31: in v 30 the speaker addresses the people (second singular feminine) contemptuously as a whore, while in v 31 the speaker describes the people (third singular feminine) compassionately as a woman in childbirth. The diction of v 30 is thus similar to that of 2:23 and 25, where of course Yahweh speaks, so that it is plausible to assign v 30 as well as v 29 to Yahweh. The structure of speakers in these three verses is thus parallel to that in vv 5–8. One must conclude that the כִּי is strongly contrastive (here "instead"), as is the כִּי at the beginning of v 22. And not only is the metaphor of the woman shifted, but one has a nice contrast between the whore "trying to beautify herself" (תִּתְיַפִּי) and fair Zion "panting" (תִּתְיַפֵּחַ), and between the "shout" in v 29 and the "shout" in v 31.

As the text of v 29 is reconstructed, the verse consists of a bicolon and two tricola. The first tricolon (v 29aβ) offers close parallelism (verbs of motion, the list of hiding places). The parallelism in the second tricolon (v 29b) is equally close (the words of totality "all," "none," "each"; participles), and the first colon there ("every city is deserted") parallels the second colon of the verse ("every region is fleeing," again with "every" and a participle). This leaves the first colon without a close parallel, though "shout" is picked up at the beginning of v 31 (see above). The structure of this verse is comparable with that of v 7: v 7a, a tricolon, likewise has three verbs of motion like those in the tricolon of v 29a here, and v 7b has diction very close to that of v 29b here.

The second, third, and fourth cola of v 30 are closely parallel (actions of self-beautification); similarly the last two cola of the verse are closely parallel (the paramours). This allows the first colon and the fifth to be heard together ("And you, what are you doing?"—"In vain you try to beautify yourself!"). In general, then, the pattern of the seven cola in v 30 resemble the second through eighth cola in v 29, reassurance that one is correct to assign both verses to Yahweh. (For simplicity's sake, however, it is best to display v 30 as a tetracolon and

tricolon.)

Verse 31 is a finely wrought pentacolon (against Rudolph, who divides the last colon). The first and third cola are united by קוֹל "shout," "sound," the first and second by feminine participles, and the third and fourth by imperfect feminine verbs; the last colon is of course the content of the "shout" referred to in the first. The existence in vv 29–31 of structures more intricate than bicola would seem to contribute to the high emotion of the passage.

Form

Contents of the First Scroll, vv 5–8, 13–18, 29–31. The purpose of the first scroll is warning (see Preliminary Observations), even though there is explicit warning only once in these three passages (v 14). It follows that for the purpose of the first scroll all the announcements of judgment must be understood as merely potential; it is in the second scroll that the announcements become actual.

Each of the three passages opens with Yahweh's report of the coming battle, and indeed these battle reports make up eight of the thirteen verses (vv 5–7, 13, 15–17, 29).

Verses 5–8 begin with plural imperatives, "Declare!" "announce!": the address is to messengers or heralds.[4] These messengers are to fan out through the land to urge the nation (vv 5b–6a) to prepare for war; it is thus a call to alarm. Specifically it is a call to escape destruction by seeking the protection of the cities. Beyond analogous passages (6:1; 8:14), this appeal to escape is found in the oracles against foreign nations (48:6; 49:8; 50:6–10; 51:27–29) and is common in other prophetic collections.[5] The form evidently began as a warning to a third party to get out of the way of the battle that is coming (compare 1 Sam 15:6).[6] That pattern prevails in the passages in Jer 50 and 51 just cited, but in the present passage the inhabitants who are being warned are part of the population to be punished: holy war is to break out against the covenant people. That ironic situation becomes acute as Yahweh announces that the cities (heretofore a sanctuary) shall be uninhabited (vv 7, 29), an announcement which the people eventually recognize (8:14). The appeal to escape is logically followed by the

---

4   See Frank Crüsemann, *Studien zur Formgeschichte von Hymnus und Danklied in Israel* (WMANT 32; Neukirchen: Neukirchener, 1969) 50–55, and Wolff,

5   *Joel and Amos*, 191–92 on Amos 3:9.

6   Bach, *Flucht*, 19–20.
     Ibid., 40, 48.

reason for the appeal, his bringing of the enemy (v 6b).[7] This in turn is followed by a description of the enemy (v 7) in the metaphor of a lion. It is thus remarkable in these verses that the enemy is not directly called an "army" or a "nation" (compare 5:15).

Jrm then issues a call to communal lamentation (v 8a), a genre that is found elaborately in Joel 1:5–14.[8] Now "blow the trumpet" (which occurs in the present passage in v 5) is found in Joel 2:15 in the context of a call to communal lament, and in Joel 2:1 in the context of a cry of alarm at the approach of the enemy; it is therefore possible to see Jrm as using the military imperatives in a fresh way by the genre of v 8.[9] The call to lamentation anticipates an act of worship that will take place at some time in the future.[10] Commentators differ in their assessment of v 8b: most have assumed that here Jrm offers the reason for the call to lamentation (so that there is no quotation, and כִּי means "for"),[11] but the present study follows Volz and Rudolph in taking כִּי to introduce an inner quotation of the people, prescriptive speech, what the content of their wail is to be.

Verse 13 continues the description of the enemy begun in vv 6a–7, now not in metaphor but similes (v 13a); this description is interrupted (v 13b) by a lament of the people, now not prescriptive speech but actual, beginning with a cry of anxiety, "Woe to us!"[12] Verse 14 is a summons to repentance (compare 3:14), issued this time not by Yahweh but by Jrm.[13] Verses 15–17 continue Yahweh's description of the enemy, now in elaborate specifics; v 15 embodies a divine report (compare 3:21), and v 17b is a final accusation, the reason for the divine judgment. Verse 18 is a summary appraisal by Jrm, his reflection on the meaning of the invasion that is envisaged (compare Isa 14:26–27).[14]

Verse 29 reverts to Yahweh's description of the invasion: now, however, one does not hear an appeal to flight (vv 5–6a) but a description of flight. In v 30 Yahweh offers a taunt-song addressed to the nation personified as a whore; perhaps the best parallel is the taunt-song to Tyre personified as a whore in Isa 23:16. Expressions of mockery often involve a rhetorical question (compare Ps 42:4 and 11, and Isa 14:16–17), and so in this case.[15] Finally v 31 offers Jrm's counter-image of the nation, personified as a woman in childbirth; it suggests an audition,[16] but that diction may simply be a rhetorical device. The quotation begins with the cry of anxiety "Woe is me!" (compare v 13b above).

Additions in the Second Scroll: vv 9–12, 19–28. Verse 9 begins with a "connection formula"[17] and continues with Yahweh's declaration of the panic of all the leaders of the nation, an implication of holy war.[18] Verse 10 is spoken by Jrm (for the refutation of the contrary view, see Interpretation). He expresses his dismay to Yahweh at the leaders' panic, the result of Yahweh's sending false prophets (compare Jrm's other expressions of dismay, 1:6; 14:13). Henning Graf von Reventlow is hardly correct in calling this verse a lamentation.[19]

Verses 11–12 are difficult; they are a prediction (v 11aα) about what will be said in the future. The difficulty is partly textual and partly a question of the identification of who is speaker; for both these matters see Interpretation. From the discussion there one concludes that (1)

---

7 On the form of vv 5–6 see further Berridge, pp. 94–99; Bach, *Flucht*, 22, 92–95.

8 Hans Walter Wolff, "Der Aufruf zur Volksklage," *ZAW* 76 (1964) 48–56 = his *Gesammelte Studien zum Alten Testament* (Munich: Kaiser, 1973) 392–401, and the summary in his *Joel and Amos*, 21–22.

9 Compare also Hos 5:8, taken by some to be a call to alarm (Wolff, *Hosea*, 112), but by Good as a call to a cultic rite (Edwin M. Good, "The Composition of Hosea," *SEÅ* 31 [1966] 37).

10 Berridge, p. 100. For the form criticism of v 8 in general see Berridge, pp. 99–107.

11 Ibid., 101.

12 Wolff, *Joel and Amos*, 242.

13 See on Form of 3:14 and n. 28 there.

14 Brevard S. Childs, *Isaiah and the Assyrian Crisis* (SBT 2d Series 3; Naperville, IL: Allenson, 1967) 128–36.

15 Eissfeldt, *Introduction*, 91–94.

16 For a discussion of audition see Lindblom, *Prophecy*, 135–37; and see further below in vv 19–21.

17 Compare Wildberger, *Jesaja*, 418, on Isa 10:27a.

18 See Bach, *Flucht*.

19 Reventlow, *Liturgie*, 127–28. For further discussion on the form of this verse see Berridge, pp. 107–11.

the quotation (vv 11aβ–12a) is a divine word of judgment analogous to v 7 and other such expressions in the chapter, so that the prediction is perceived to be in the mouth of Jrm, and that (2) after the prediction the prophet affirms (v 12b) that his own activity of judgment is added to that of Yahweh.

Verses 19–21 are spoken by Jrm, an emotional outburst the diction of which goes beyond anything preserved from contemporary or earlier prophets. While vv 23–26 are a vision report (see below), these present verses are not so much a report of audition (v 19) and vision (v 21) as words spoken during audition and vision; Gustav Hölscher thought them to be evidence of prophetic ecstasy.[20] If the syntax and text are here rightly understood, Jrm addresses his soul and perhaps his heart as well (v 19); such an address reminds one of the genre of the dialogue of a man with his soul, such as is found in Pss 42:6 and 116:7 (compare Luke 12:19), but those parallels are calm in mood, while Jrm's words here are violent. The burden of v 20 is quotations of words Jrm hears, and in v 21 the rhetorical question (addressed to whom?—his soul? Yahweh?) continues the same emotional pitch. By contrast, Yahweh's speech in v 22 moves within the orbit of wisdom[21] and is evidently a report by Yahweh the schoolmaster concerning his refractory pupils, the nation. God often "teaches" in the OT, beginning with his pupil Moses (Exod 4:12),[22] but except for the comparable 5:21 (which see) I am not aware of an analogous passage in which God speaks so specifically in the diction of a schoolmaster, and I am not aware of another passage that represents the genre of a schoolmaster's report, whether he be human or divine.

In vv 23–26 Jrm speaks (see Structure); these verses are a vision report,[23] more elaborate this time than those in which Yahweh validated his call of the prophet. This vision report is of Yahweh's judgment, like those in Amos 7:1–9 and 8:1–2 but more elaborate than these. To the vision report is added (vv 27–28) Yahweh's confirmation of the vision, a confirmation analogous to

that in Amos 7:8–9: vv 27–28a are analogous to Amos 7:9, a description by Yahweh of the destruction, and v 28b is analogous to Amos 7:8bβ, a statement of a determination not to retract the punishment.[24]

Setting

The question of a date for the components of this passage (and analogous passages placed afterward in the book) is inextricably bound up with general questions of the chronology of the prophet's life, the boundaries of the components, and the identity of the foe from the north.

Many commentators (e.g., Rudolph) have assumed that the material was first spoken between the thirteenth and eighteenth years of Josiah (i.e., 627/626 and 622/62l), under the assumption that Jrm accepted his prophetic call in the thirteenth year (1:2) and that appeals to repentance must antedate Josiah's reform (2 Kgs 22:3); others (e.g., Bright) leave the question open.[25] The lower chronology proposed in the present work (see "A Chronology of Jeremiah's Career") rules out altogether a date before Josiah's reform. It may be pointed out that the phrase "disaster I am bringing" (4:6) is found in Huldah's prophecy (2 Kgs 22:16); Jrm may then see the carrying out of the prophecy after Josiah's death in 609.[26]

For the question of the identity of the foe from the north in the present study, see the Excursūs after Interpretation of 1:16. And much evidence has already been given above (4:5—10:25, Preliminary Observations) for the setting proposed for the components of the present passage; little more need be said here.

A large proportion of the material preceding the present passage (that is, 2:1—4:4) has been here assigned to the first scroll. In that material there is little sense of the immediacy of battle (even 2:37 is vague). Now it is likely that any first-scroll material found in 4:5 and thereafter will have been uttered after the first-scroll material within 2:1—4:4. As already noted, the *terminus*

20 Gustav Hölscher, *Die Profeten, Untersuchungen zur Religionsgeschichte Israels* (Leipzig: Hinrichs, 1914) 7, 32.

21 McKane, *Prophets and Wise Men*, 88–89.

22 Joseph Kaster, "Education, OT," *IDB* 2:33–34.

23 See bibliography of 1:11–19, "prophetic visions," especially Long, "Reports of Visions."

24 For the Amos passage see Wolff, *Joel and Amos*, 294–95.

25 For a survey of recent literature see Berridge, pp. 74–80.

26 Ibid., 99.

ad quem for the first scroll is March/April 604 (the end of the fourth year of Jehoiakim, 36:1). That year had seen the battle of Carchemish (May or June 605) and the consequent eclipse of Egyptian power; Babylon was the new power to reckon with. All signs therefore point to Carchemish as the stimulus for vv 5–8, 13–18, 29–31; news of the outcome of the battle would hardly have taken more than a month to reach Jerusalem, so that a safe guess for these sections is the early summer of 605.

If vv 9–12, 19–28 were added for the second scroll, one must still determine whether one or more of the sections took shape between the dictation of the first scroll (605/604) and the burning of that scroll (December 601), or to the contrary whether they took shape after the scroll was burned. Verses 9–10 suggest a conflict between Jrm and the optimistic prophets such as emerged during the drought—see 14:13–16; but in 14:14 Yahweh tells Jrm that the optimistic prophets had no divine legitimacy, while in 4:10 Jrm assumes Yahweh sent them; it is plausible then to date that passage very early in the conflict, directly after the king burned the scroll. Verses 11–12 seem to assume the sirocco wind associated with drought, and the parallel of "sword" (v 10) and words associated with drought reflects that parallel in 14:1—15:9, so that again one is pointed to a period close to that for vv 9–10.

Verses 19–22 and 23–28 offer no specific clues for dating, but both passages are fuller and more elaborately worked out, and coming after vv 9–12 are likely to have taken shape afterward, but not long afterward: perhaps during the early weeks of 600.

Interpretation

■ **5–6a** Verses 5–6a offer a whole series of imperative verbs, seven in v 5 (omitting the first וְאִמְרוּ in *M* as dittographic; see Text), or eight if one includes the cohortative "and let us go in," וְנָבוֹאָה; and three more in v 6a. All the imperatives are masculine plural, and several are verbs of saying or shouting; the question then arises whether one has a hierarchy of quotations. It is clear that "Gather and let us get in to the fortified cities!" is a quotation introduced by "and say," but Bright (who accepts the genuineness of the first "and say" in *M*) sees

"sound the trumpet" as the beginning of a larger outer quotation (which he does not close until the end of v 8).

If the imperatives at the beginning of v 5 are a summons to heralds (see Form), the question is how many of the verbs are addressed to those heralds. "Raise a signal" in v 6a is parallel with "sound the trumpet" in v 5; "call out" is hardly other than parallel with "declare" and "announce." It is likely that מַלְאוּ (whatever its meaning—here rendered "Form up!"; see below) is an inner quotation after "call out" (compare a similar sequence in 12:6). This allows "Gather . . . fortified cities" to be a parallel quotation introduced by "say"; this is the most economic solution.

The shouts come thick and fast: without warning we are in the midst of a battle under way or perceived to be under way; this long array of imperatives in the midst of battle is hardly paralleled in prophetic literature, though one may note Nah 2:2, and, in another genre, commands to do justice, Isa 1:16–17.

■ **5** The first two cola offer agreeable assonance, *-idū + -i-ūd-*, and *-ūšā-m + -ašm-ū*; these stirring words announce holy war declared against the covenant people (compare Form).

The sound of the trumpet suggests the military emergency (so Amos 3:6; Joel 2:1); more specifically, the sounding of the trumpet accompanied holy war (Judg 7:15–22), arousing panic in the enemy to be vanquished, who in the present instance is Judah. On the other hand, the sound of the trumpet marks a summons to repent (Joel 2:15). The imperative here thus carries several connotations (see further Form).

It has already been suggested (see above) that מַלְאוּ, the imperative following "call out," is a quotation, but its precise meaning escapes us. The traditional rendering of the two verbs (*G, V, S*) is "call in a loud voice" or the like; *T* "call, multiply" is little help. Several scholars think that קִרְאוּ אַחֲרֶיךָ מָלֵא in 12:6 is a parallel; there is a resemblance, but there מָלֵא is an adjective rather than a verb, and that passage requires its own interpretation (which see). D. Winton Thomas has suggested[27] that the phrase has a military connotation; he proposes for the two verbs "assemble an assembly" = "declare a mobilization, proclaim a muster (of troops)." Though Rudolph and

---

27   Thomas, "מלאו," 47–52.

John M. Berridge reject the suggestion, I accept it with the further proposal, as already stated, that the second verb is a quotation (so similarly after נִקְרָא in v 20; compare further the solution proposed for 12:6). "Form up!" may not be right, but with data available at present there can be no certainty on the precise meaning of the expression.

For "fortified city" see 1:18. The fortified cities are understood to be places of safety: a good parallel is Josh 10:20, where the remnant of the Amorite forces "entered into the fortified cities" to escape the Israelite forces under Joshua. Though the sanctuary of Jerusalem will fail (6:1) and all the fortified cities will become a deathtrap (8:14), here the shout is still innocent; the population of Judah is simply bidden to drop everything and get to safety.

■ **6** *M* reads "raise a signal" (שְׂאוּ נֵס), while *G* ἀναλαβόντες φεύγετε seems to mean "gathering up (your wares), flee" (see Text). Since most of the appeals to flight (see Form) exhibit the word נֻסוּ "flee" (48:6; 49:8, 30; 51:6; Zech 2:10), which *G* offers here, we may conclude (assuming *M* is correct) that Jrm intends a variation on that expected word in the wording before us. The trumpet was an auditory signal; the נֵס is a visual signal (so explicitly 4:21; Isa 18:3; 30:17).[28] For the form צִיּוֹנָה (with he *locale*), "in Zion," compare צָפוֹנָה "north" in 1:13.[29]

The verb עוז hip'il occurs only once with an object (Exod 9:19, where the parallel is אסף nip'al: "Get (your cattle and all that you have in the field) to shelter." The meaning is thus clear here and in 6:1, where the same verb appears. The imperative of "stand still" (עמד) will occur in 6:16, "stand still, halt" on the old paths; here, to the contrary, there is no time to lose; the people must be on their way.

For the imagery of disaster from the north, which may suggest a certain "uncanniness," see the Excursus after 1:16. For the possibility that Jrm took over the phrase "disaster I will bring" from Huldah's prophecy (2 Kgs

22:16) see Setting. The phrase שֶׁבֶר גָּדוֹל (here "great collapse") is a favorite one for Jrm (6:1; 14:17; 48:3; 50:22; 51:54); it is also found in Zeph 1:10, and one wonders whether Jrm took it over from Zephaniah.[30] The noun שֶׁבֶר in Jrm appears to center around three usages: the fracture of a bone (metaphorically in 6:14; 8:21; 10:19; compare Lev 21:19); the shattering of pottery (compare Isa 30:14) and the breaking of walls (compare Isa 30:13). When a village or city is destroyed, walls collapse, roof-beams fall and break pottery storage jars, and these images are here in the forefront: the nation crashes with the totality of numberless crashes and so itself collapses in a heap.

■ **7** Yahweh continues to speak (see Structure), describing the enemy in the metaphor of a lion (see Form); that metaphor has occurred already, in 2:15 (which see), though there the word for "lions" is כְּפִרִים, while here "lion" is אַרְיֵה. Indeed there is a very close likeness between the present verse and 2:15: the first colon of 2:15 begins with *'ālāyw*, the first colon here begins with *'ālâ*; and the last half of both verses resemble each other closely: "make [synonymous verbs] his/your land a desolation, his/your cities have been burned/shall be in ruins [closely assonantal verbs with *n*, *t*, and *ṣ*], without [synonyms] inhabitant." Is there some significance to the resemblance? Why is there a shift from masculine plural address to feminine singular address here? (Jrm will revert to masculine plural in his speech in v 8.) Is there an intention to hear Yahweh as recalling the earlier words?

The word "thicket" (סְבֹךְ) is rare; it might be an intentional variation on "lair" (סֹךְ: compare 25:38!), used with regard to a lion not only in 25:38 but in Pss 10:9; 76:3 ("his thicket" is *subběkô*, "his lair" is *sukkô*). Since "destroying lion" (אַרְיֵה מַשְׁחִית) occurs in 2:30, and "destroyer" (מַשְׁחִית) occurs in the second colon here, one wonders if this is an example of the break-up of a stereotyped phrase.[31] The word means not only a "destroyer" in general, but a "raider" in particular (1 Sam

---

28   Bernard Couroyer, "Le *nēs* biblique: signal ou enseigne?" *RB* 91 (1984) 5–29.

29   GKC, sec. 90d.

30   For a recent discussion of the date of Zephaniah see Frank Charles Fensham, "Zephaniah, Book of," *IDBSup*, 983–84.

31   See 2:3, and n. 79 there.

13:17; 14:15), so that this destroyer of nations is understood as one who plunders the nations at will. (Compare a similar suggestion for 5:26.) The verb נסע "set out" is rare in the prophets (in Jer only otherwise in 31:24). Its connotation is of schedules and itineraries, being used of nomads starting out, of the Israelites moving out from one camping spot to another in the wilderness. But never elsewhere is it used for a wild animal; this lion moves not as a wild animal does, by impulse, but deliberately, by plan, for this lion is the foe from the north.

"Shall be in ruins" (תִּצֶּינָה) is from נצה qal. "Cities" seems to have three different verbs that closely resemble each other in 2:15, here, and in 4:26 (for the details see Text on 2:15 and 4:26). For the general imagery in v 7b see 2:15.[32] The final irony is that the cities will be in ruins, after they have been looked to as refuge (v 5).

■ **8** Jrm makes a brief speech (see Structure, Form). For "on this account" (עַל־זֹאת) in the context of dismay see 2:12; here, as there, we have three imperatives. "Sackcloth" was rough fabric of goat's or camel's hair worn (perhaps, in the present phrase, as a loincloth: "gird on" suggests it) in times of mourning or public lamentation.[33] The imperatives (masculine plural, as in vv 5–6) are addressed to the people of Judah; the diction in v 8a is close to that in Mic 1:8 and Joel 1:13 (the call to collective lamentation; see Form).

As already stated (see again Form) I follow Volz and Rudolph in taking v 8b as a quotation[34] (for another example of כִּי introducing a lament see Gen 37:35). I thus propose that כִּי not only introduces the quotation but serves as an emotional expression of emphasis (here "Oh!": for a full treatment of כִּי in the laments of these chapters see below on v 13).

The combination "(Yahweh's) anger" and "turn (back)" (שׁוב + אַף־יהוה) appeared in 2:35 (see there); in that verse the people blithely assumed that Yahweh's anger has turned back from them, but now they are instructed to admit that it has not turned back from them at all. The phrase in our verse is close to that in the

first half of the refrain in Isa 5:25b; 9:11b, 16b, 20b; 10:4b. Berridge points out[35] the phrase "Yahweh has not turned from his great hot anger" in the context of Josiah's reform (2 Kgs 23:36) and the phrase "that his hot anger may turn back from us/you" in the context of Hezekiah's form (2 Chr 29:10; 30:8) and suggests that the phrase in the present passage may be a convention from Josiah's reform (compare the remarks above on "disaster I am bringing," v 6).

■ **9-10** This little passage gives few inner clues by which to understand the circumstance out of which it comes; only an analysis of the structure of vv 5–31 and comparison with passages elsewhere in the book can bring any certainty. It is proposed here that the fast declared by Jehoiakim in December 601 was on the occasion of a drought, while in that same month the Babylonians suffered a setback at the hands of the Egyptians in the Egyptian delta; optimistic prophets thus prevailed, while Jrm was pessimistic and bewildered at the prevalence of these optimists (see Structure, Setting for details).

■ **9** The verse begins with "And it will happen on that day, oracle of Yahweh." The words stand outside the structure of the poetry, and because the phrase "on that day" is a constant one in OT diction, Peter A. Munch considered it to be a secondary addition.[36] But the phrase is not "eschatological" in the postexilic sense here, and Rudolph rightly retains it; the phrase has the same function as do the opening words of v 11: both of them place the poems they introduce into their contexts (see Form).

In the poem four ranks of leadership will be equally demoralized: the king, the officials (for which see 1:18), the priests, and prophets; the totality of the nation's leadership will collapse. Here the "heart" (לֵב) is not so much the character, as it was in v 4, as morale or courage: the "heart" of both king and officials will (literally) "perish" (אבד). In the days of Ahaz more than a century before, Isaiah was to reassure the king regarding the Syro-Ephraimitic crisis: "Do not let your heart be

32   For implications of holy war, see Berridge, pp. 92–94.
33   William L. Reed, "Sackcloth," *IDB* 4:147.
34   Compare James Muilenburg, "The Linguistic and Rhetorical Usages of the Particle כִּי in the Old Testament," *HUCA* 32 (1961) 144, no. 5.
35   Berridge, p. 102 n. 165.
36   Peter A. Munch, *The Expression Bajjôm Hāhū', Is It an Eschatological Terminus Technicus?* (Oslo: Dybwad, 1936) 45.

faint (or timid)," Isa 7:6; indeed his heart and the heart of his people had shaken like trees (Isa 7:2) at the emergency. But now the king's heart will fail altogether, and his courtiers will stand no sturdier than he.

The priests shall be made "desolate," "horrified," made to "shudder" (שׁמם nip'al): the qal of this verb was used in 2:12 of the heavens as they contemplate what the people have done. And the prophets shall be "stunned" (תמה qal): the best context for this verb is Ps 48:6, where it is in parallelism with בהל nip'al ("be in panic") and חפז nip'al ("take to flight"). Both verbs in v 9b are vivid ones; the religious leaders are in no better shape than the civil ones, for they too are in psychic collapse. One of the expectations in holy war is that the enemy will experience loss of courage: in Josh 5:1, "When all the kings of the Amorites . . . heard that Yahweh has dried up the waters of the Jordan . . . , their heart melted, and there was no longer any spirit in them, because of the people of Israel" (compare Josh 7:5). But in this passage it is the leaders of Judah whose heart fails; it is against Judah that holy war has been declared.[37]

■ 10 Earlier commentators have assumed that v 10 must have been spoken by the (false) prophets, revocalizing "Then I said" (וָאֹמַר) to "And one shall say" (וְאָמַר) or emending with G^A to "And they shall say" (וְאָמְרוּ) under the assumption that bewilderment can only be expressed by the false prophets (so Duhm, Cornill, Giesebrecht, Volz, Condamin, Rudolph); Volz suggests excising "Oh, Lord Yahweh!" None of this is necessary; Jrm is protesting that the optimistic prophets were sent by Yahweh to confuse the people (compare Form).

His dismay begins with the same words found in 1:6, "Oh, Lord Yahweh!" This fixed expression occurs twice more in Jer (14:13; 32:17), four times in Ezekiel, and in Josh 7:7 and Judg 6:22. The situation in Josh 7:7 is a good comparison; Joshua tears his clothes and says, "Oh, Lord Yahweh, why have you brought this people over the Jordan at all, to give us into the hands of the Amorites, to destroy us?"

It is followed by אָכֵן, a conjunction implying a strong contrast of point of view: "to the contrary," or "yes, but . . ." (compare 3:23 on this word). And the conjunction is followed in turn by the infinitive absolute

reinforcing its finite verb; the infinitive absolute here does not intensify the action (*RSV* "utterly," Rudolph "grievously" [*schwer*]), but affirms the certain occurrence of something announced (Hab 2:3),[38] or the contradiction of a denial or affirmation. That both אָכֵן and the infinitive absolute are used here suggests strong emotion: Jrm expresses dismay in the midst of denial, as if he is reflecting part of an argument, with Yahweh, presumably.

The verb נשׁא II hip'il "deceive, beguile" is used in Gen 3:13 by Eve ("The serpent beguiled me"); it is used in 2 Kgs 18:29 (= Isa 36:14) by the Rabshakeh of Assyria to the people of Jerusalem ("Do not let Hezekiah deceive you, for he will not be able to deliver you out of my hand"), and similarly by the king of Assyria (2 Kgs 19:10 = Isa 37:10) to Hezekiah ("Do not let your God . . . deceive you"). That Jrm should use the verb associated with the serpent in Genesis 3 and with Yahweh only in the mocking mouth of the king of Assyria shows the depth of Jrm's emotion. (A different verb is used in 20:7; see there.)

In the context of community well-being "peace" (שָׁלוֹם) suggests "safety" and "security,"[39] so that "you shall have peace" suggests more generally "it shall go well with you." It is the word spoken by the false prophets (14:13).

But to the contrary, says Jrm, the sword has touched (נגע) the very *nepeš*. The last-named word ordinarily means "life," "self," but here it means "breath, throat," a meaning found also in Isa 5:14 and now well attested in Ugaritic.[40] Jrm is bewildered because the religious leadership has misled—not only the prophets of weal, but priests as well; one notes two other passages from this historical context, 6:14; 14:18 (compare 14:13), in which priest is paralleled with prophet. These leaders doubtless have the best credentials (compare Hananiah seven years later, 28:1–2, who uses the same norms of prophetic speech as does Jrm himself), and there is thus no reason to doubt that they are who they say they are, spokesmen

---

37 Berridge, pp. 91–92.
38 Carl Brockelmann, *Hebräische Syntax* (Neukirchen: Erziehungsverein, 1956) sec. 93a.
39 See Pedersen, I/II, 263–335; Gerhard von Rad, "εἰρήνη, κτλ.," *TDNT* 2:402–6.
40 *HALAT*, 672b, 1.

for Yahweh, mediators with Yahweh.[41] If their word is a misleading word, then this must be Yahweh's doing (infinitive absolute: "you really did deceive"). Yahweh is closing off the great experiment he has begun with his covenant people, and in so doing he intends to beguile and deceive his people. But why should he want to do that?

■ **11–12** The introductory words echo phrases from v 9 ("at that time" parallels "on that day") and v 10 ("this people and Jerusalem").

What follows has often been emended, though I submit the passage needs less emendation than some have proposed; my own reading demands only two revocalizations (see Text). By this reading the poem is a compact one of five interlocking cola.

The word רוּחַ, which meant "breath" in 2:24, means "wind" here. The wind referred to is the sirocco, the dry wind from the east, in contrast to the normal moist wind in Palestine, from the northwest. The temperature rises steeply (as much as ten degrees centigrade) and the relative humidity falls by as much as 40 percent. Denis Baly describes it: "Tourists find the sirocco especially frustrating, for not only does travel become fatiguing, but the fine yellowish dust which fills the air drains it of all color, blots out all but the immediate vicinity, and makes photography a mockery. Even in the house one is aware of it, for the dust penetrates everywhere, and the soap dries on one's face in the interval of putting down the brush and picking up the razor."[42] The adjective צַח means "dazzling," "glowing": it is used of "dazzling" heat in Isa 18:4, and the description fits the desert wind precisely. For "caravan-tracks" for שְׁפָיִם see 3:2. The syntax of the noun is clarified by the preposition בְּ in the next colon; it does double duty.

I propose the verb דָּרַךְ "has trodden" for M דֶּרֶךְ ("path of"? "toward"?). Jrm uses this verb in 9:2 (where it is doubtless to be vocalized as a qal: see Text there) in the related sense of "drawing (i.e., exerting force on)" an arrow (see Interpretation there), but it is used in a context comparable to the present one in Mic 5:4, 5, where it is likewise parallel to בוא "come (in)" in describing the invasion of the land by the Assyrian army. The sirocco wind thus treads the inhabitants down. I propose that the wind described here is a real one but that the description is open as well to interpretation as a metaphor for an invading army (Volz, compare Bright).

The phrase בַּת־עַמִּי, literally "my daughter people," is best translated by a term of endearment, "my fair people" (*NJV*: "my poor people"). The traditional rendering "daughter of my people" is misleading, since the genitive is appositional;[43] such phrases serve the same function in Hebrew rhetoric as personifications like "John Bull" and "Uncle Sam" in political rhetoric and cartoons in our tradition.

The sirocco is not a wind for winnowing or cleansing: we have already noted the yellowish dust it brings. It is not a blessing but a curse (for Hosea's use of the sirocco for Yahweh's judgment see Hos 13:15). The noun "curse" (אָלָה), proposed (most recently by Condamin) in place of *M* "these" (אֵלֶּה), is appropriate in contexts of drought (see Text, and note particularly 23:10). For the phrase "full of curse" compare Deut 33:23, where Naphtali is described as "full of the blessing of Yahweh" (מָלֵא בִּרְכַּת יהוה).

The meaning of the last colon, "It comes to/for me," depends on who is speaking. Berridge discusses the identity of the speaker thoroughly and concludes that the poem is spoken by Jrm.[44] If this is the case, then "it comes toward me" is the natural interpretation (so Condamin); but if Yahweh speaks, then "it comes for me," that is, "at my behest" is the connotation (so Rudolph: *auf mein Geheiss*). I propose that the clue is in v 12b, גַּם־אָנִי, the most plausible meaning for which is "I too." The problem of who speaks this line is likewise a problem,[45] but if the line begins "I too," then Jrm would appear to be placing himself (reluctantly?) alongside Yahweh to utter judgment on the people. If this is the case, then the poem of vv 11–12a is spoken by Yahweh,

41   See James L. Crenshaw, "Prophecy, false," *IDBSup*, 701–2 with bibliography.

42   Baly, *Geography*, 52.

43   GKC, sec. 122i; BDB 123b, under בַּת 3: "with name of city, land, or people, poet. personif. of that city or inhabitants, etc." See more specifically William F. Stinespring, "No Daughter of Zion, A Study of the Appositional Genitive in Hebrew Grammar,"

Encounter 26/2 (Spring 1965) 133–41.

44   Berridge, pp. 111–12.

45   Ibid., 112–13.

and the wind comes "at my behest."

■ **13** Though this verse is not implausible as a continuation of v 12 (compare the presentations of Condamin and Bright), the proposal here is that the first three cola are a continuation of the divine speech of vv 5–7 (see Structure).

They begin with the deictic particle הִנֵּה, "See!" In the mouth of God this particle is usually הִנְנִי (5:14, 15; 6:21) or הִנֵּה אָנֹכִי (6:19) to introduce a declaration about himself; but here (and in the analogous 6:22) Yahweh's word directs the hearer's attention not to himself but to the enemy. The tricolon is a marvel of concision (see Structure). Even so the components are variations of the conventional building-blocks of poetry; thus the second colon, "like the whirlwind are his chariots," resembles Isa 5:28, "and his wheels are like the whirlwind," and the third, "swifter than eagles his horses," resembles Hab 1:8 (again a description of the Chaldeans [= Babylonians]), "swifter than leopards are his horses," and 2 Sam 1:23, where Saul and Jonathan are described as "swifter than eagles." "Like the whirlwind are his chariots": nothing is so demoralizing to a peasant people as to be overwhelmed by chariotry and horses.

Then the people interrupt with their cry of despair. The verb שׁדד is a favorite in the book: the qal and the pu'al (or qal passive) of this verb occur a total of twenty-six times in Jer out of fifty in the OT as a whole. It may be used of the violent killing of a single person (Judg 5:27, thus the reconstructed last colon of v 29 below) or of the ruin of a whole land (v 20). An occurrence of the verb in Mic 2:4 is close to the context of the present passage: "Wail with bitter lamentation, 'We really are ruined!' (שָׁדוֹד נְשַׁדֻּנוּ)." The use of the conjunction כִּי following "Woe to us!" (אוֹי לָנוּ) is noteworthy. It is useful to lay out the full array of the people's interjections of panic in chapters 4—6:

4:8	כִּי . . .
4:13	אוֹי לָנוּ כִּי שֻׁדָּדְנוּ
4:20	כִּי שֻׁדְּדָה כָל־הָאָרֶץ
	. . . פִּתְאֹם שֻׁדְּדוּ
4:31	אוֹי־נָא לִי כִּי . . .
6:4	. . . אוֹי לָנוּ כִּי
6:26	. . . . כִּי פִתְאֹם יָבֹא הַשֹּׁדֵד

Form-critically the expressions in 4:8 and 6:26 are lamentations, and the context of 4:31 (a woman in birth-pangs with her firstborn) implies it. As we have just seen,

Mic 2:4 specifically introduces as a lamentation an expression parallel to that found here. The passage in 4:20 seems to be a shout (נִקְרָא: see there). All these expressions are those of panic in the context of holy war (see v 8). The conjunction כִּי seems to introduce the substance of the lament in each case, and the fact that 6:26 has כִּי פִתְאֹם suggests that the כִּי in 4:20 does double duty for two cola, given the פִתְאֹם which follows. The translation "Oh!" or "How!" then appears to be justified by the emotion of these phrases and preferable to the flat "for" usually used. (For כִּי = "How!" see further 2:19, and compare אֵיךְ שֻׁדַּדְנוּ in 9:18.)

This single-colon lament of the people is unique in the collection in that it follows directly on a speech of Yahweh's. The lament in 6:4 is sandwiched between two shouts of the enemy, but all the rest of them follow words of Jrm's. It is Jrm who is perceived to be the mediator between Yahweh and the people, and the impact of the three sudden compact cola from Yahweh's mouth describing the enemy, followed immediately by the helpless panic of the people, is stunning.

■ **14** Now, after the lament of the people, comes the mediating word from Jrm: now the prophet acts to intercede with the people. "Wash" (כבס pi'el) occurred in 2:22; there the image was of the hopelessness of people's washing of their hands. Here, by contrast, there is an image which is (at least theoretically) more hopeful, that the people, by an inner washing, an interior cleansing of their lives, can stay the hand of Yahweh. Ps 51:4, 9 has similar vocabulary, but there the prayer is that God wash the worshiper of his evil, while here the people are bidden to do their own washing. This passage is unique in the OT in taking the object "heart" with this verb; in all other instances where the object has personal reference (i.e., when the object is not "garments" or the like) the object is simply a pronoun suffix (like the Psalm references just given). This unusual expression then attracts comparison with that in v. 4, "Be circumcised to Yahweh, remove the foreskin of your heart." Both expressions call for radical renovation of the character, the will, to render it fit for covenant with Yahweh.

The phrase "that you may be rescued," which in a way is a counterpoise to the despairing cry of the people at the end of v 13, is the clearest expression that at this point Jrm maintains hope that the people may repent. The verb "rescue" occurred in 2:27–28 to express the fatuity of expecting the false gods to rescue the people (that passage, by the conclusions reached in the present study, has a later setting). Here, by contrast, genuine rescue is within reach.

The last colon is a rhetorical question, "How long will your baneful schemes lodge in your inner self?" One would wish for a better translation than "in your inner self," since the expression קִרְבֵּךְ is directly parallel to לִבֵּךְ "your heart." "Your entrails" is too specific and anatomical; the קֶרֶב is one's "insides," as children say; but this phrase, like "your heart," is ambiguous, referring both to the interior intentionality of persons within the total community and to the center of the community ("within your walls" or the like): compare the two uses of the word in 6:1, 6 and the similar ambiguity in 17:1. This tension in the imagery is reinforced by the verb: לין means "lodge, spend the night," and the model for Jrm's phrase may be Isa 1:21, "Righteousness lodged in her [i.e., the city], but now murderers." But Jrm plays on the image of baneful schemes lodging both in the geographical middle of the city and also of their lodging deep within the character of the city.

The מַחְשְׁבוֹת are "schemes," often good and constructive schemes, especially when referring to Yahweh's schemes, but often evil and destructive ones, especially when referring to those of Yahweh's enemy or of his people: compare the collocation of the two nuances in Ps 33:11. The completion of the phrase here is אָוֶן: אוֹנֵךְ is a description of what is strong and evil, with implications of magical power;[46] "baneful" (Bright) is then an excellent word in English. The combination occurs elsewhere in the OT (Isa 55:7; 59:7; Prov 6:18). Jrm is struck by the way Jerusalem's evil persists within her: he asks here how long these schemes are going to stay, and in 6:7 he perceives Yahweh to accuse the city of preserving her evil fresh and cool like well water. "How long" will the situation continue?

■ **15–16a** Yahweh will not be denied his announcement of doom from the hand of the enemy! His new speech begins with כִּי: this conjunction evidently indicates a change of speaker, but it may also pick up the כִּי of the people's lament at the end of v 13 (there translated "Oh!"): the neutral translation "Yes" here indicates at the

very least the resumption of the train of thought before the interruptions of Yahweh's earlier speech. A "voice" declares and announces bane from Dan and from Mount Ephraim. The same verbs were used in addressing heralds in v 5; here, then, a single herald is evidently assumed (in v 29 the same word קוֹל seems to be no more than an anonymous "shout"). The same word אָוֶן appears here as at the end of v 14, and these are the only two occurrences of the word in Jer. If the people harbor their baneful schemes, then Yahweh has his own bane to bring over the land. Berridge discusses this collocation and compares it to a similar sequence with רָעָה in 23:10, 12;[47] he might have added רָעָה in 1:14, 16. Dan is the conventional reference to the northernmost Israelite locality in Galilee (thus the frequent "from Dan to Beersheba" to express "from north to south," e.g., 1 Sam 3:20). The phrase "Mount Ephraim" (הַר אֶפְרַיִם) refers to the region centering at Shechem (Josh 20:7). The two terms simply express northern territory within the purview of Judah, a sign that the enemy is close.

The first two cola of v 16 bring problems of text and interpretation, so much so that Volz, Condamin, and Rudolph have embarked upon a number of emendations, and Bright omits the last portion of the first colon as untranslatable. I propose to the contrary that the consonantal text is sound but that at several points the commentators and translations have missed the direction of the bicolon.

The first problem is M הִנֵּה "See!" "Look!" at the end of the first colon. The word means nothing in the context and is implausible at the end of the colon; revocalizing (with Condamin) to הֵנָּה (literally "Hither!" here "Right this way!") yields admirable sense, and if the meaning of this bicolon is consistent with that of the next bicolon (as I argue), then the utterance is a call to a group like the "shouters/scouts" of the third colon.

The previous word in that line, לַגּוֹיִם, "to the nations," is odd: what nations? The "nations" are addressed in 6:18 as witnesses in a cosmic law-court scene, indeed "nations" are frequent in Jer for the nations of the world in general (1:5, 10). Here, however, the denotation is evidently the foe summoned against Judah. Bright mentions a suggestion of D. N. Freedman to read a singular "to the nation"

---

46 Pedersen, I/II, 421.
47 Berridge, p. 78.

with a mem-enclitic, but I am not aware of any passage in Jer in which the hypothesis of a mem-enclitic is the best solution. Since the Babylonian army had many ethnic contingents within it (compare the discussion on 1:15–16), it is better so to understand the word here (so also 25:11). The vocalization with the article is doubtless correct: the expression is in parallelism with מֵאֶרֶץ הַמֶּרְחָק in the third colon, and in both instances the article has almost the force of a demonstrative, "to those nations," "from that distant land," expressions of the awesomeness of the enemy. (For another instance of parallel definite articles see 5:13.)

Other emendations have been proposed for v 16a, but they are not necessary. Thus Condamin wishes to revocalize the imperatives הַשְׁמִיעוּ, הַזְכִּירוּ to perfect forms, הִזְכִּירוּ and הִשְׁמִיעוּ ("they have proclaimed," "they have announced"); but once v 16a is seen to be a quotation introduced by "declares," "announces" in v 15, such revocalization becomes unnecessary. Again the repetition of the same verb "announce" in both v 15 and v 16a is explicable in that the second is within the quotation; they are not really parallel. Rudolph's suggestions in the first colon, "Warn Benjamin!" (הַזְהִירוּ לְבֶנְיָמִן) or "Announce in Judah!" (הַגִּידוּ בִיהוּדָה), are wide of the mark. A proper noun is not necessary here to parallel "Jerusalem": the latter word is paralleled by "cities of Judah" in the fourth colon (as the two phrases with the article are parallel in the first and third cola; see above).

The verb זכר hip'il carries a variety of nuances in the OT, but Isa 12:4 offers a relevant context; there the verb is parallel with ידע hip'il "make known," so that "proclaim" is a suitable translation. The verb שמע hip'il על in v 16a, however, is ambiguous. In Amos 3:9 the expression occurs in the same form-critical context, and there the object of על is the addressee; the translation "announce to Jerusalem" is thus appropriate.[48] On the other hand in 51:27 we have . . . הַשְׁמִיעוּ עָלֶיהָ מַמְלָכוֹת, where the balancing colon is קַדְּשׁוּ עָלֶיהָ גוֹיִם; the latter colon means "consecrate (for holy war) against her the nations," so that the former colon must means "summon against her the kingdoms of. . . ." In the present passage the translation "announce" is appropriate to "proclaim" just preceding, but "summon against" is appropriate both

to the reconstructed expression "Right this way!" and to "shouters/scouts are coming" which follows.

The question arises how far the quotation continues. The third colon of v 16 offers the participle בָּאִים, which is most naturally perceived as parallel with the participles in v 15. This being the case, it is likely that the quotation ends with v 16a.

■ **16b** The subject נֹצְרִים carries the conventional translation "watchers," but this meaning here is widely distrusted. Duhm proposed נְמֵרִים "leopards," but this is impossible, there being no diction pertaining to animals in this context; Rudolph and Bright adopt צָרִים "enemies" (so *JB*). The verb נצר does mean "watch, guard"; on the basis of the passive participle in Isa 1:8, where the expression presumably means "besieged city," some translations render "besiegers" here (*RSV, NAB*).

I propose that the word here carries a double meaning. The fact that v 17 begins with "like guards of a field" suggests that "watchers" ("scouts," perhaps) is intended here. But the immediate parallel is "utter a shout" (נתן קול), and another occurrence of נֹצְרִים in 31:6 is in the context of "merrymaking" and "calling"; one's attention is therefore drawn to a second verb נצר occurring in Akkadian, Ugaritic, and Syriac, associated with weeping and lamentation, covering the range of "howl," "shriek," and the like.[49] The men referred to here may be "scouts," but they "shout" their way into the land. These scouts are the vanguard of the invading army from that distant land of whom the people stand in dread, but the scouts are not secret spies but the self-confident advance guard of the foe. And, given קוֹל ("voice," "shout") in both v 15 and here, may we conclude that the "voice" of v 15 is the shout of these scouts?

■ **17** The "shouters/scouts" of v 16b are compared to "guards of a field" (שֹׁמְרֵי שָׂדָי). There is no parallel for this phrase, but שֹׁמְרֵי הַחֹמוֹת in Cant 5:7 are guards on the city walls, and שֹׁמֵר הַפַּרְדֵּס in Neh 2:8 is the keeper of the king's park. The "guards of a field" need not be "officials"; they may simply be those responsible for keeping thieves or birds away from ripening crops.[50]

---

48   Wolff, *Joel and Amos*, 191; Wolff suggests "proclaim over."

49   Chaim Rabin, "Noṣerim," *Textus* 5 (1965) 44–52;

John F. Healey, "Syriac *nṣr*, Ugaritic *nṣr*, Hebrew *nṣr* II, Akkadian *nṣr* II," *VT* 26 (1976) 429–37.

50   Compare H. Neil Richardson, "Watchtower," *IDB*

The point is, the guards of a field belong there; they are responsible for the field. But the scouts of the enemy that are moving in upon Judah act already as if they owned the place, in no way like spies that skulk and hide. The term may in addition carry a second meaning: in 51:12 we have הָקִימוּ שֹׁמְרִים הָכִינוּ הָאֹרְבִים "set up watchmen, prepare ambushers," so that שֹׁמְרִים, in addition to its domestic use, may have a military meaning like "sentries," in which case the scouts that are acting as if they were already responsible for the fields of Judah are also sentries watching for the fields to fall into their hands.

The verb הָיוּ is dynamic, not static, so that a translation is erroneous which assumes it is the equivalent of הֵמָּה (like the *RSV*); it is not that they "are" against her on every side but that they "have turned out to be" against her; a verb is thus necessary which captures the process (Bright: "they have ringed her round about"; *NEB*: " . . . are closing in all round her"; *NJV*: "they surround her on every side," similarly *NAB*). Like those who work together to move through a vineyard to clear it of foxes (Cant 2:15), so these scouts move in together from every direction.

Why is this happening? Because, says Yahweh, "It is I she has defied." The verb מרה occurs in Jer only here and in 5:23 (לֵב מוֹרֶה, "obstinate heart"), but there is a line much like it in Hos 14:1, כִּי מָרְתָה בֵּאלֹהֶיהָ, "for she defied her God." The verb means "be obstinate against." The reason for all this military incursion is expressed in three words in Hebrew with six long vowels: *kî 'ōtî mārātâ*; for that reason the enemy scouts are moving in upon the land with clarion voice and sure step.

■ 18 For the translation "to think" for the infinitive absolute see 3:1. The general import of Jrm's response in this verse is clear: "Your conduct and your deeds have brought all this upon you." But details of the text give difficulty.

Let us begin with v 18b. The phrase זֹאת רָעָתֵךְ "such is your ruin" is sound, comparable to זֶה גוֹרָלֵךְ "such is your lot" in 13:25. But the words כִּי מָר which follow are dubious. The *NAB* translates "How bitter is this disaster of yours," but this would surely demand רָעָתֵךְ הַזֹּאת, which would be unlikely in poetry, and in any event the

masculine gender of מָר (and נָגַע) is implausible. Rudolph translates, "It is your evil which makes it so bitter," but this is simply periphrastic.

On the positive side it must be affirmed that כִּי מָר here closely resembles the diction of 2:19 (indeed the diction of this verse resembles 2:19 in more ways that one: see below). Negatively it must be admitted that beyond the question already mentioned of the gender of מָר and נָגַע is that of the syntax of the sequence. One can hardly take כִּי מָר and כִּי נָגַע as parallel: the first offers an adjective (or the pausal form of the perfect of a stative verb), the second a nonstative verb. But to posit a structure in which the second clause is subordinate to the first is to move away from the concision of poetry. With some hesitation then I conclude that the text has been damaged. Conceivably something drastic might have happened (for example, the difficult קִירוֹת in v 19 or something like it may have been displaced from v 18). But the most economical solution is to accept the proposal noted by Rudolph in *BHK* and *BHS*, reading מֶרְיֵךְ "your defiance" for מָר כִּי; this noun will then pick up the related verb in v 17b, and the last colon of v 18 will thus mimic the last colon of v 17 (see Structure).

The meaning of רָעָתֵךְ in the second colon oscillates between "your wickedness" (v 14, and so parallel with "your way and your doings" here) and "your disaster," the disaster coming upon you from the north (v 6). Jrm is convinced that the internal covenant breaking and the external punishment are one and the same, that the wickedness of Judah has brought the punishment inevitably and automatically (so 2:19). Therefore it is the defiance of Judah that threatens the very core of her being (compare the diction of v 10).

■ 19 The entire speech of Jrm's, vv 19–21, maintains a high pitch of emotion. It begins with the repetition מֵעַי מֵעַי, literally "My bowels, my bowels!" an expression which carries none of the distasteful overtones of the English—but the term is not so specifically psychological as the *RSV* "My anguish, my anguish!" It is both psychological and physical turmoil centered in the viscera; similar phraseology involving מֵעַי is found in Lam 1:20; 2:11; Job 30:27.[51] David Qimḥi appropriately compares the expression "My head, my head," spoken by

4:806b and illustration there.
51   Compare Johnson, *Vitality of the Individual*, 76 and n. 5.

the boy to his father in 2 Kgs 4:19. The words seem to stand in no close relation with what follows and must therefore be understood as an exclamation.

The text that follows is uncertain at several points. If one accepts the consonantal text, the next word is a cohortative, vocalized with the ketib as אָחוּלָה; the verb חול means "writhe" or the like. Eduard König pointed out long ago that the cohortative indicates strong volition[52] either of the subject or of someone else, and cites this verb and the corresponding two verbs in v 21 (אֶרְאֶה must be construed as cohortative, as אֶשְׁמָעָה is; see there); these three verbs clearly parallel each other and must be seen together. Rudolph translates the present verb as "ich muss mich winden," and he uses "ich muss . . ." again in v 21, but "I must writhe" is not English: Jrm of course means "I am impelled, forced to writhe," not "I insist on writhing." Further, one must understand this verb in the light of לֹא אַחֲרִישׁ at the end of v 19a: "I am not keeping still" = "I cannot keep still." Hence the rendering here, "I cannot help churning." But if the letter he at the end of the verb is the remnant of a following hip'il verb, then the verb is not cohortative, and "I am churning" is all that is meant (see below).

The next expression in M is קִירוֹת לִבִּי, understood as "the walls of my heart," again as an exclamation. The word קִירוֹת is not otherwise cited in such an expression, occurring elsewhere only for architectural walls or the like. Hans Walter Wolff thinks of angina pectoris in the phraseology here,[53] but this is surely too specifically medical. Jrm's heart is in an uproar, as are his viscera, because of the impact on him of the vision of war.

But the uniqueness of the expression and the difficulty of dividing v 18a into cola lead me to doubt the soundness of the text here, and I propose with hesitation the reading of the verb קרר "be chilled" here, either the qal or hiphil, and construing "my heart" as vocative like "my soul" in v 19b (for the details see Text). This verb is found in a different context in 6:7. Admittedly there is no good parallel for "You are chilled, O my heart," so the

suggestion must simply remain a possibility. "My heart" is repeated in the following sequence in M; Rudolph calls the repetition "unsightly" (unschön) and follows the suggestion of Volz to read נַפְשִׁי "my soul" here. But structurally it is plausible to see the repetition of "heart" as parallel with the repetition of "heart" in v 9 (see Structure), and if the first "my heart" were construed as vocative, then the repetition is not so unsightly at all. (Compare the repetition of the verb שׁדד in v 20.)

One turns now to the last verb phrase in v 19a, לֹא אַחֲרִישׁ, "I cannot keep still" (see above). The verb (חרשׁ hip'il) is normally intransitive, but once it is transitive (Job 11:2). Since לֹא אַחֲרִישׁ cannot stand alone in a colon (see Structure), one is pressed to construe it transitively with the previous "my heart" (so a suggestion of Bright). By this analysis the participial expression הֹמֶה־לִּי must be construed with what precedes, not what follows (against the typography of BHK and BHS). The verb המה is used with "heart" in 48:36 and with מֵעִים "viscera" in 31:20 (and Isa 16:11; Cant 5:4); it is also used with "waves," "waters" in 5:22 (compare 6:23) and elsewhere. It thus means "be in an uproar": in Hebrew the heart pounds as waves do, just as in English.

For the syntax of v 19b see Text. The vocative "O my soul" is the equivalent, of course, to the first-person singular but functions in the genre of a dialogue of a man with his soul (see Form). The diction of this half-verse recapitulates that of v 5—"sound of the trumpet," "blast of battle." The word order is noteworthy: "sound of the trumpet" before the verb. "Blast of battle" (תְּרוּעַת מִלְחָמָה) occurs also in 49:2: it is the intense shouting of combatants augmented by the blowing of trumpets[54] and was an integral part of holy war.[55] Jrm and his soul are responding not in the confidence that they are situated alongside Yahweh grandly watching the destruction of Judah, but in the terror which holy war elicits in the demoralized enemy (compare the implication of v 12b).

■ 20 The sound of the trumpet and the blast of battle in v 19 are sounds that Jrm has heard from the enemy side;

52 Eduard König, *Historisch-Comparative Syntax der hebräischen Sprache* (Leipzig: Hinrichs, 1897) sec. 199: "eine starke Willensregung."

53 Wolff, *Anthropology*, 41–42.

54 Wolff, *Joel and Amos*, 161.

55 Berridge, p. 96; Paul Humbert, *La "Terou'a"— Analyse d'un Rite Biblique* (Neuchâtel: Secrétariat de l'Université, 1946) 29–30.

now in this verse he hears the sounds from Judah's side. The Versions and commentators divide as to whether the nip'al verb נִקְרָא is to be understood from the first root, "call, shout" or from the second, "meet"; for justification for taking it from the first root see Text. One may say further that since v 19b referred to auditory stimuli, the way is prepared for the meaning "is shouted" here. I follow Rudolph in taking שֶׁבֶר עַל־שֶׁבֶר as a quotation; compare 20:8, חָמָס וָשֹׁד אֶקְרָא "'Violence and destruction' I call." For שֶׁבֶר "crash" see v 6.

For שדד pu'al "be devastated" see v 13. For justification for taking the last three cola as a quotation see again Text.

The nuance of "my tent(s)" and "my curtains" is not immediately apparent. The parallelism sometimes has a literal meaning (49:29), but here one assumes some kind of poetic extension of meaning: Klaus Koch has suggested "one's hearth and home" for some occurrences of "tent."[56] But F. Kenro Kumaki[57] makes the happy suggestion, which I believe correct, that the people are here lamenting the fall of the Jerusalem temple. "Tent of meeting" is of course the designation in E and P for the tabernacle (compare "the tent," Exod 26:9), and the "curtain(s)" of the tabernacle figure repeatedly in the descriptions of P (Exod 26:1 and often). Frank M. Cross has recently shown that the P tradition of the tabernacle is not a late construct,[58] and Richard E. Friedman has recently proposed that the tabernacle was actually erected inside the holy of holies in the temple.[59] Kumaki points out that in Ezekiel 23 Jerusalem is called "Oholibah = 'my tent is in her,'" and more particularly that in Isa 54:2–3, where "tent" and "curtains" are part of an oracle of restoration, the curtains are those of מִשְׁכְּנוֹתַיִךְ, a word which may be translated not only "your habitations" but also "your tabernacles."[60] M reads "my

tents" here, and it is conceivable that the plural suggests the plurality of temple buildings, like the plural in 7:4; but in the light of the foregoing and of the singular "my tent" in 10:20 it is better follow G here and read the singular (see Text). Is it significant that Yahweh's answer in v 22, "They are wise in doing ill, but how to do good they do not know," is reminiscent of the appeal in 7:3 in the temple sermon, "Make good your ways and your doings"? If so, the reference is to the people's reaction to Yahweh's punishment on them for their not having listened to the temple sermon.

For the translation "Oh!" for כִּי at the beginning of the second colon, and its presumed double-duty function in the following colon as well, see the discussion on v 13; and further compare the two occurrences of כִּי in 9:18. The adverb פִּתְאֹם "suddenly" is used especially in contexts of calamity or invasion;[61] compare Isa 47:11; Prov 24:22. It occurs four times elsewhere in the book (6:26; 15:8; 18:22; 51:8). Its parallel רֶגַע "(in a) moment" occurs otherwise in the book only in 18:7, 9. The people are in despair and call out in dismay at the repeated shattering of the roofs and walls and storage jars of their homes and of their sanctuary: the whole land is shattered. What an appalling thing to hear in the mind's ear these tortured, despairing cries from here and there across the land of Judah!

■ 21 The verb אֶשְׂמְעָה is cohortative, and therefore its parallel אֶרְאֶה is also to be so construed.[62] The appropriate translation for the cohortatives here is the modal auxiliary "must" (see the discussion on v 19).[63]

Though the expression עַד־מָתַי "how long" is normally construed as an interrogative, it is at least possible to construe it as exclamatory ("How long I must see the signal . . . !"); so the translation of Ronald Knox: "Always the sight of men fleeing, always the sound of the trumpet

56 Klaus Koch, "אֹהֶל, etc.," *TDOT*, 1:120.
57 Kumaki, pp. 113–22.
58 Frank M. Cross, "The Priestly Tabernacle in the Light of Recent Research," *Temples and High Places in Biblical Times: Proceedings of the Colloquium in Honor of the Centennial of Hebrew Union College—Jewish Institute of Religion, Jerusalem, 14–16 March 1977* (ed. Avraham Biran; Jerusalem: The Nelson Glueck School of Biblical Archaeology of Hebrew Union College—Jewish Institute of Religion, 1981) 169–78.
59 Richard E. Friedman, "The Tabernacle in the Temple," *BA* 43 (1980) 241–48.
60 Kumaki, pp. 118–19.
61 BDB, 837b.
62 See GKC, sec. 75l on the lack of special cohortative forms for III-he verbs.
63 Joüon, *Gramm.*, sec. 114c, n. 3.

in my ears!"[64] If "fugitive" is the correct reading (see Text), then it is implied by cries of the people cited in v 20; if "signal" is correct, it is an echo of v 6. "Sound of the trumpet" of course picks up that phrase in v 19b.

■ **22** The function of כִּי here is to mark the change of speaker, as at v 15; here it is rendered by the neutral "Well." Not only does the speaker change, but there is the strongest contrast in mood between Jrm's demoralized speech in vv 19–21 and Yahweh's calm speech here, a shift marked as well by the play on words between מֵעַי "my bowels" (v 19) and עַמִּי "my people" here (see Structure).

Yahweh speaks like a schoolmaster: the vocabulary here is very much in the orbit of wisdom (see Form).[65] Thus "foolish" (אֱוִיל) appears in Proverbs nineteen times and in Job twice; "stupid" (סָכָל) appears in 5:21, but otherwise only in Ecclesiastes (six times); the participle "having sense" (בין nipʿal) appears nine times in Proverbs and once in Ecclesiastes.

"My people are foolish": Wolff points out[66] that an אֱוִיל is a "blockhead," especially a "foolish talker" (Prov 10:8, 10). The second colon begins with a striking inversion, the object pronoun coming first, "me they do not know"; the phrase recurs in 9:2 (compare a similar inversion with "fear" in 5:22). For "know" with God as object see 2:8.

"They are stupid children": "stupid" (סָכָל) occurs as the antonym of "wise" (חָכָם) in Eccl 2:19, as does the corresponding verb סָכַל in Isa 44:25. "They have no sense": the participle means "perceptive," but there is no way to distinguish the various synonyms and antonyms in this verse: they are meant to offer crushing parallelism. And not only semantic parallelism, but assonance as well—note the association of בָּנִים and נְבוֹנִים, and the thrice-repeated הֵמָּה. The last two cola are closely parallel, with a hint of chiasmus in the central infinitives: "They are wise in doing ill, but how to do good they do not know." (For a possible link here with the temple sermon, 7:1–12, see v 20.) The last colon is likewise

closely parallel with the second, both ending with "they do not know," and that parallel is crucial, since to know Yahweh is to know how to do good: ethical decisions flow from the knowledge of Yahweh. It is a nice anticipation of Augustine's maxim, "Dilige, et quod vis fac" ("Love [God], and do what you like").[67] It would be hard to imagine a more damning report on the people than this monotonous, cold assessment of six clauses.

■ **23–26** The stark sublimity of this poem is hardly to be matched in the OT. The translation offered here is modeled on that of *JB*, which alone among recent translations attempts to replicate something of the repetitions and parallels of the original. Each of the four verses begins with רָאִיתִי, literally "I saw," and continues in each first half of the verse with וְהִנֵּה, literally "and behold"; here, to avoid the archaism of "behold," the translation uses "I looked (at)" and "to see" respectively. The parallels within the poem are precisely organized (for the details see Structure).

One matter needs more attention, the possible parallel intended between Gen 1:2, 3 in v 23 and Gen 2:5 in v 25.[68] If that parallelism is valid, it suggests that the P account and the J account of creation were both available to the prophet at this time (for another possible reference to the P material in Genesis see on 20:3–6, and for another destructive reference to creation, compare 8:13 and its antecedent passage, Zeph 1:2–3).[69]

The poem moves from the categories of creation in vv 23–25 to those concerned with settlement in Canaan in v 26: the mention there of "the wilderness" (הַמִּדְבָּר) and "the garden-land" (הַכַּרְמֶל) remind the hearer of the movement from "the wilderness" in 2:6 into "the garden-land" in 2:7. Beyond the possible antecedents of the diction of this passage in Genesis 1 and 2 there are other passages offering resemblances; in the kind of climactic contrast with וְהִנֵּה, literally "and/but behold," compare Isa 5:7, "He longed for justice, but behold bloodshed, for righteousness, but behold a cry." And there are passages in other seventh-century prophets offering similar

64 Ronald Knox, *The Holy Bible, A Translation from the Latin Vulgate in the Light of the Hebrew and Greek Originals* (New York: Sheed & Ward, 1954).

65 Lindblom, "Wisdom in the OT Prophets," 199.

66 Wolff, *Hosea*, 156.

67 Augustine, *In epistolam Joannis ad Parthos* vii.8, in *PL* 35, col. 2033.

68 So Holladay, "Recovery," 406.

69 For a recent study of the date of P, compare Menahem Haran, "Behind the Scenes of History: Determining the Date of the Priestly Source," *JBL* 100 (1981) 321–33; for Zeph 1:2–3 see Michael De Roche, "Zephaniah i 2–3: The 'Sweeping' of Creation," *VT* 30 (1980), 104–9.

vocabulary and content, not only Zeph 1:2–3, already referred to, but Nah 1:5, "The mountains quake before him, the hills melt." But though there are phraseological parallels, the passage is unique in power.

Jrm speaks (see both Structure and Form). He envisages a "de-creation" of the cosmos, the world again become the chaos before creation began: not a retroversion, turning the clock back, but a moving ahead to a state identical with that before Yahweh's creative activity began; in the most terrible way *Endzeit ist Urzeit*.[70] The covenant has been a failure (compare the covenantal language of 2:5–13, similar to the vocabulary here), and therefore creation itself is dispensable, since creation serves as a first step toward the covenant.[71] There are other subtle links in the poem to motifs connected with the covenant. Thus the earth and heavens, mountains and hills are the traditional witnesses in a cosmic law-court scene (2:12; 6:19; Mic 1:2; 6:1–2); now they are to be removed from the scene. Other diction reminds one of holy war expanded to the nth degree: thus in 8:16 one hears that the whole land quakes (רָעֲשָׁה) from the neighing of enemy stallions, while here the mountains are quaking (רֹעֲשִׁים) in the ultimate catastrophe; in 9:9 "all the birds of the heavens had fled" in the context of a historical defeat (compare 9:10), while here "all the birds of the heavens had fled" in a cosmic destruction.[72]

One's understanding of vv 23–26 is shaped in part by an understanding of the meaning of Yahweh's response to the vision in vv 27–28; but some preliminary questions may be posed. Is this apocalyptic?—or, to pose the question more precisely in Paul D. Hanson's terminology,[73] is this apocalyptic eschatology? Clearly not:[74] there is here no scheme of God's intervention for the favored righteous by which to compensate them for the exclusion from power and freedom in the historical

context, only an image of total destruction of the created world, a destruction hardly more total than that envisaged by Jrm's contemporary Zephaniah (Zeph 1:2–3, see above), but couched not in "historical" categories, as Zephaniah's vision is, but in cosmic, partly mythic categories. It is clear that the poem is genuine to Jrm.[75] Hanson affirms, "The transformation of prophetic eschatology into apocalyptic eschatology was the gradual result of community crisis and national disintegration, circumstances which led prophets like Jeremiah and Ezekiel to envision redemption increasingly on a cosmic level through the use of motifs drawn from myth (Jer. 4:23–28; Ezek. 47),"[76] though one may add that by the interpretation of the passage offered here it is hardly redemption which is envisioned. It may be added that the imagery here owes much to the concept of the "day of Yahweh."[77]

One final general observation: if what is striking in vv 19–21 is the "subjectivity" of Jrm's experience, his description of his physical and emotional response to the cataclysm to come, then what is striking here is the "objectivity" of the vision. There is no hint of the prophet's own involvement with the events: they are removed utterly from his grasp, this in spite of the four-times repeated "I looked." He is reporting without emotion. He is uninvolved. The poem is appalling enough in itself, but its impact is heightened by its collocation with the earlier emotional outburst.

■ 23 The verb רָאִיתִי, "I looked," which begins each verse, picks up אֶרְאֶה "must I see" in v 21. One wonders, why does the particle אֶת־ appear in this first colon, and nowhere else? It does not appear in v 24, before הֶהָרִים. Perhaps we have to do here with syllable count: in Jrm's day הָאָרֶץ was a disyllable;[78] perhaps אֶת־ filled out a third syllable to parallel the three syllables of הֶהָרִים.

70 Compare Brevard S. Childs, *Myth and Reality in the Old Testament* (SBT 27; Naperville, IL: Allenson, 1960) 76–77.
71 Compare the remarks of Eichrodt on the inner coherence of creation and history, Walther Eichrodt, *Theology of the Old Testament* (Philadelphia: Westminster, 1961, 1967) 100–101.
72 For an extended discussion of holy-war motifs in this passage see Berridge, pp. 191–93.
73 Paul D. Hanson, "Apocalypticism," *IDBSup*, 29–31.
74 So Lindblom, *Prophecy*, 127, against Volz, p. 50.
75 See Holladay, "Style," 47–48.

76 Paul D. Hanson, "Apocalypticism," *IDBSup*, 32a.
77 For this passage see Victor Eppstein, "The Day of Yahweh in Jer 4:23–28," *JBL* 87 (1968) 93–97, and Jörg Jeremias, *Theophanie, Die Geschichte einer alttestamentlichen Gattung* (WMANT 10, 2d ed.; Neukirchen: Neukirchener, 1977) 99–100; for the day of Yahweh in general see Ernst S. Jenni, "Day of the Lord," *IDB* 1:784–85, and A. Joseph Everson, "Day of the Lord," *IDBSup*, 209–10, and bibliography in both articles.
78 Zellig S. Harris, "Linguistic Structure of Hebrew," *JAOS* 61 (1941) 145, par. 13.

The phrase תֹהוּ־וָבֹהוּ is a hendiadys; it occurs only here and in Gen 1:2 (there is a break-up of the stereotyped phrase in Isa 34:11). Beyond these three occurrences of בֹהוּ the word תֹהוּ occurs another seventeen times in the OT, but not otherwise in Jer. There is a large literature on the meaning of the expression and its constituents.[79] The words rime, and this rime reinforces the uncanniness of the expression. The Versions tend to translate by words suggesting "emptiness" or "void" (G οὐθέν "nothing"; V vacua erat et nihili "it was empty and worthless"), but this understanding may have been influenced by the doctrine of creatio ex nihilo in Genesis. The word תֹהוּ is parallel with מִדְבָּר "wilderness" in Deut 32:10, an early poem. Johannes Pedersen describes the desert as follows: "The wilderness is a land of chaos, because the law of life does not operate there; we hear several times that the desert is tōhū or tōhū wābhōhū, the characteristic expressions of chaos, the lawless, the empty. He who wanders there may suddenly be led astray, for there is no road; how should a road leading to a goal be found in a 'land' the essence of which is disorder and confusion?"[80] To see the earth, the arena of Yahweh's creative order, with its roads and fields, villages and cities, reduced to trackless, hideous confusion is appalling.

"And to the heavens": the preposition is אֶל rather than the nota accusativi אֶת־, as was the case with "the earth." Jrm is no cosmic spectator; he is rooted to the ground and looks toward the heavens. In Genesis 1:3–5 the creation of light is not associated specifically with the heavens but is thoroughly appropriate here. It is a puzzle to our scientific mentality that the Israelites should separate the notion of light from that of the presence of the light-giving sun and moon and stars, but it is clear that the sky is light long before the sun comes up. According to one late apocalyptic vision one characteristic of the end time will be continuous day rather than the alternation of day and night (Zech 14:7). But Jrm's vision is the contrary: permanent darkness, without any hope that light might come again.

■ **24** Though the mountains and the hills may be addressed as witnesses in a cosmic law-court scene (Mic 6:1: see above on vv 23–26), they are not primary in

creation in the way the earth and heavens are. Nevertheless we hear often in the OT of the strength necessary for God to establish the mountains (Ps 65:7) or of the antiquity of the mountains and hills, being created at the very beginning (Ps 90:2; Prov 8:25). There are other passages in which the mountains are envisaged as disappearing ("I will not fear even if the mountains shake in the heart of the sea," Ps 46:3; in a theophany the mountains melt under God, Mic 1:4), but the context of v 23 shapes one's understanding of the present verse as an expression of the ultimate collapse of the stability of the mountains and hills. The participle רֹעֲשִׁים is of a verb whose noun derivative (רַעַשׁ) means "earthquake" (47:3). The parallel verb here, used of the hills, is הִתְקַלְקָלוּ, the hitpalpel stem of קלל and as such a hapax legomenon in the OT; but the root קלל means "be light, trifling, swift," and the pilpel stem of the verb in Ezek 21:26 means "shake" (arrows in divination); the form here is clearly reflexive and perhaps iterative as well: "rock to and fro."

What does it mean when the earth is a formless waste, without landmarks, when there is no light by which to see—when indeed there is no stability underfoot, even in the sturdiest elements of the world, the mountains and hills?

■ **25** Now, as we have noted, the diction becomes more abrupt (see Structure): "I looked" lacks a complement. "I looked, to see" what?—no one at all (אָדָם means "human being"). Here אֵין (literally "there is not") parallels its occurrence in v 23b (there "was no more"). Folk of the present age, crowded in overpopulation, crave solitude from time to time, but solitariness for the Israelites was a nightmare: they craved above all the companionship of family, clan, village. Lot's first-born daughter, after the destruction of Sodom, said, "Our father is old, and there is not a man on earth [וְאִישׁ אֵין בָּאָרֶץ] to come to us after the manner of all the earth," so the two daughters contrived to have intercourse with him to preserve offspring (Gen 19:31): incest is preferable to the horror of solitariness and the end of the human race. But now, in Jrm's vision, it is come to that.

And then: why birds? One might have expected "beast" as the correlative of "man" (7:20; 21:6; and often). Mainly, of course, because of the parallel habitat

---

79 See Westermann, Genesis 1:105–6, 142–44.
80 Pedersen, I/II, 456.

of "the heavens" specified here, a reference tied to v 23b; but there is also the fact that even when in another passage of Jrm's poetry the destruction of beasts is named, a phrase very close to the present one is used ("both bird of the heavens and beast have fled, have gone," 9:9), so that it appears that Jrm was fond of birds, mentioning them more than once (8:7). The phrase here lends poignancy to the vision of total destruction: even off in the desert one sees birds (49:16); what is it like when even the birds are gone?

■ **26** Still the abruptness of lack of complement after "I looked," and what now has Jrm seen? Quite strikingly, two nouns both carrying the article: "the garden-land" has now become "the desert," though English idiom will not allow "desert" to carry the article here. Both nouns carried the article in 2:6–7, and the presence of the articles in the present passage ensures that the specific historical desert experience by the Israelites, the specific garden-land into which they entered in Canaan, are what is understood. The desert was the horrifying place (see on 2:6), the garden-land a gracious gift from Yahweh, and now that gracious gift is turned into a place of horror like that from which he had delivered them. The garden-land is not only a pleasant place, it is a place of sustenance, the place producing grain, wine, oil, fruit to sustain body and spirit.

And the cities that in the vision lie demolished are not only evidences of civilization, of trade and political power, they are above all secure places in time of war: cities have walls and one seeks them out for safety (v 5), but now they are destroyed. This theme was explored in 2:15 and 4:7, where similar diction is to be found, but in the present context the destruction of the cities makes particular in the failure of the covenantal community what has already been said on a cosmic scale.

The verb נִתְּצוּ "lie demolished" might well be expected to close the poem: the second colon of v 24 offered only the single verb הִתְקַלְקָלוּ for predicate, and the second colon of v 25 the single verb נָדָדוּ; but when the poem is

at its tightest and most extreme expression, it suddenly opens out again, not in a coda or afterthought, as *M* gives it ("before Yahweh, before his hot anger"), but in a chiastic structure that includes a third colon with its own verb (for the identification of the verb, and justification for restoring it, see Text). "Before Yahweh" is literally "from the presence of Yahweh," and "presence" (literally "face") here implies "fury": for this nuance see the discussion in 9:6. For שמם nip'al "made desolate" see v 9. Now, suddenly, one understands the agent of the whole array of destruction we have glimpsed: it is the word of Yahweh in חֲרוֹן אַפּוֹ "his hot anger" (for the phrase see v 8). As Yahweh was the only agent for creation, so now he is the only agent of destruction. It is his righteous wrath, elicited by the covenantal disobedience of his people, that has brought on this smashing of creation.

■ **27–28** These two verses bring a major set of interpretational problems, particularly v 27b, וְכָלָה לֹא אֶעֱשֶׂה, "and/but an annihilation I shall not make." This colon appears to contradict the first colon of the poem, "and the earth/land shall be a desolation," and it certainly contradicts the general direction of v 28, "On this account the earth shall mourn," and the rest. Various solutions have been proposed. (1) It means what it says. Berridge, for example, states that עשה כלה generally refers to the destruction of the people (except Nah 1:8, 9), so that the colon means that the land will be destroyed but not the people.[81] In view of the Nahum passage this judgment seems arbitrary. The general expectation of parallelism and the tone of the two verses are against this understanding. (2) The colon is a mitigating gloss similar to that at the end of Amos 9:8;[82] or the word לֹא "not" is secondarily added,[83] or should be emended to לָהּ "to it" (feminine, referring to the earth),[84] or should be emended to the lamed *emphaticum*.[85] None of these solutions commends itself.

I propose to revocalize וְכָלָה to וְכֻלָּהּ (see Text), a reading that does fit the context: "and none of it [feminine = the earth] shall I (re)make" (compare the

81   Berridge, p. 191.
82   Hyatt, citing Arthur S. Peake, *Jeremiah* (New Century Bible; New York: Frowde, 1910, 1912) 124.
83   Volz.
84   Rudolph: but surely the idiom demands אֶת־, not לְ, see 5:18; 30:11.
85   J. Alberto Soggin, "The 'Negation' in Jeremiah 4,27 and 5,10a, cf. 5,18b," *Old Testament and Oriental*

Studies (BibOr 29; 1975) 179–83 = "La 'negazione' in Geremia 4,27 e 5,10a, cfr. 5,18b," *Bib* 46 (1965) 56–59.

same revocalization, supported by Westermann, for Gen 18:21).[86] Phrasing by which a noun introduced by כָּל־ ends one line of a bicolon and כֹּל with suffix begins the next colon is found elsewhere in Jrm's poetry (20:7; see there). For the idiom כָּל־ with לֹא = "none," compare 2:24; 9:3.[87] The meaning "remake" is not cited elsewhere for עשׂה "make" (unless with עוֹד "again," 3:16), but בנה "build" may certainly mean "rebuild" (1 Kgs 12:25). The verb עשׂה "make" occurs often in contexts of creation (e.g., Gen 1:31) and so is appropriate in this context. The two verses share vocabulary with 18:1–10 to the degree that this passage must be considered the reverse of that one; compare the use of שׁוב "turn" and עשׂה "make" in 18:4 and נחם pi'el "change one's mind" in 18:8, 10 with the use of those verbs here. The vocalization suggested here makes possible an understanding of Yahweh's speech appropriate to the starkness of Jrm's vision.

■ **27** The verb begins with the solemn messenger formula "Thus Yahweh has said" (see 2:2). This is the first occurrence in the book of that formula introduced by כִּי.

The word שְׁמָמָה is common in Jer. "Desolation" is the rendering here, but the word also suggests uncanniness and the effect of stupefaction.[88] There are two relevant antecedents to the phrase here, Exod 23:29, פֶּן־תִּהְיֶה הָאָרֶץ שְׁמָמָה, "lest the land become a desolation," part of an addition to the Covenant Code (recent discussion suggests this to be part of a parenetic epilogue, perhaps arising in Deuteronomistic circles),[89] and Isa 1:7, אַרְצְכֶם שְׁמָמָה, "Your land is a desolation." Both these passages use אֶרֶץ for the local land of Israel in a historical sense, but if the revocalization suggested for v 27b is valid, then there is no need to conclude that the passage uses אֶרֶץ in the local sense as the commentators and translations have assumed:[90] we can understand הָאָרֶץ here as "the earth," the meaning it carries in v 28 and v 23. By this understanding the traditional phrase will have been expanded into the sphere of the whole cosmos, in accordance with the tone of the passage from v 23 onward.

The noun שְׁמָמָה picks up the verb נָשַׁמּוּ restored in the last colon of v 26: this first colon of Yahweh's speech then simply affirms in a single clause what Jrm's whole vision has stated.

General justification for the reconstruction of v 27b, "and none of it shall I remake," has already been offered in the discussion of vv 27–28 above. But it may be added that עשׂה כָלָה, with or without a negative, may have been a standard phrase (note its occurrence twice in 30:11 and once in Ezek 11:13), so that if the proposed revocalization is correct, part of the horror of the phrase may be that it is a "near miss" on a phrase that the people would much prefer to have heard, a phrase into which the M in its vocalization slipped. To mock deliverance in this way must have been excruciating: so near to deliverance, and yet so far.

■ **28** For עַל־זֹאת "on this account" see 2:12; "this is why" the earth shall mourn. There is a colon very much like it in Hos 4:3: עַל־כֵּן תֶּאֱבַל הָאָרֶץ.

It is not clear whether אבל represents two homonymous verbs, "mourn" and "wither,"[91] or whether it is a single verb with two foci of meaning,[92] but it is clear that "wither" is a potential meaning, certainly in cases where the parallelism suggests it. So 14:2, in the drought passage (see there), and so in Hos 4:3 just cited. There it is said that fertility will be withdrawn because the commandments of Yahweh have been broken. Here too the suggestion of fertility withdrawn is implicit (thus all the birds of the heavens are gone, v 25), because of covenant disobedience ("before the hot anger of Yahweh," v 26). But stressed far more is "mourn," given the parallel קדר "be dark" in the following colon. "Mourn" suggests a permanent situation: one mourns for someone who is dead, with all the finality that death implies.

The verb קדר "be dark" is often associated with mourning, not perhaps so much that one wears specific dark clothes in time of mourning as that in dismay one neglects to wash face and clothes (compare 2 Sam 19:25;

---

86   Westermann, *Genesis* 2:345, 346; compare John Skinner, *A Critical and Exegetical Commentary on Genesis* (ICC; New York: Scribner's, 1930) 304. According to Skinner, the suggestion was made by Julius Wellhausen.
87   See GKC, sec. 152b.
88   For a description see Pedersen, I/II, 457–58.
89   Childs, *Exodus*, 460–61.
90   See Rudolph and Bright, and, in more detail, Lindblom, *Prophecy*, 127.
91   So *HALAT*.
92   So Zorell; see further Arnulf Baumann, "אָבֵל," *TDOT* 1:45.

Job 30:28). Here the expression nicely dovetails with the extinguishing of the light of the heavens in v 23. In a way the whole cosmos is in mourning for itself. Such expressions will feed later into the mentality of apocalyptic (Joel 2:10; 4:15). This is the only occurrence of מִמַּעַל "above" in Jrm's poetry, though it is often associated with "the heavens" elsewhere (for example, Isa 45:8).

The translation "inasmuch as" in the third colon seems appropriate for the rare and perhaps archaic expression עַל כִּי (for the phrase see Text). It is difficult to find an adequate rendering for נחם; it means "be sorry," but more than that, "change one's purpose out of pity,"[93] because thought and word and deed are unified in Israelite expression. Many times God is depicted in the OT as regreting a decision and changing his mind: for making humankind (Gen 6:6–7), for making Saul king (1 Sam 15:11, 35).[94] Often the verb means "retract" in a forensic context,[95] and that is perhaps the best rendering here. Thus in the narrative of potter's workshop (18:1–12) we hear that Yahweh can retract his decision about the disaster or (ironically!) about the blessing that he plans (18:8, 10). Particularly comparable is the sequence in Amos 7:1–9: twice Yahweh retracts his decision (vv 3, 6 there) and then is determined, and the high places of Isaac shall be made desolate (v 9 there: the verb is נָשַׁמּוּ, the same verb restored in Jer 4:26). Now one hears the worst: Yahweh has pronounced his decree, and there is no way he will retract.

The verb זַמֹּתִי (זמם) expresses thinking that leads directly to action:[96] a זִמָּה is a "plan" or "plot," so this is a decision on Yahweh's part. The expression מִמֶּנָּה "from it" (feminine) is a vague reference to the parallel feminine עַל-זֹאת at the beginning of the verse. The verb נחם is parallel with שׁוב in Jon 3:9; the four verbs in v 28b make a collection that involves thinking, saying, and doing.

By the reading offered here Yahweh's decree matches the final desolation that Jrm has envisaged. From the viewpoint of these lines Yahweh's last word is

destruction.

■ 29 Yahweh speaks in vv 29–30 (see Structure).

There are two questions to be faced in the first colon. (1) Does פָּרָשׁ mean "horse" or "horseman"? (2) Does one have here a quotation, "From the shout, 'Horse(man) and archer!'" or a construct chain, "From the shout/noise of horse(man) and archer"?

As to פָּרָשׁ, it is clear the the word usually means "horseman" (= an original *parrāš) but occasionally means "horse" (= an original pārāš).[97] Sigmund Mowinckel suggests "horse" in our passage.[98] Against this suggestion are two considerations. (1) Yigael Yadin remarks, "In the Assyrian chariots of this period [early first millennium] there were two men in the crew, a driver and an archer."[99] Assyrian *cavalrymen* also rode in pairs, the horseman holding the reins of *both horses*, leaving the bowman free to shoot.[100] It is altogether likely, therefore, that two men in a team are referred to here, whether in a chariot or riding free. (2) The companion passage in v 13 speaks of the "chariots" and the "horses" of the enemy, so that symmetry would suggest that another reference to "horses" is out of place here. One is safe to stay with "horsemen," the translation affirmed in the Versions.

As to whether one has here a quotation or a construct chain, the construct chain is possible, but symmetry with vv 5–8 suggests that as that passage had quotational material (at least one quotation, perhaps two) in the first part of Yahweh's speech and another quotation to round off Jrm's speech, so here: a quotation rounds off Jrm's speech at the end of v 31, and it is appropriate to find a quotation here toward the beginning of Yahweh's speech. It is noteworthy also that קוֹל "voice, shout" is associated with the quotation in v 31 and thus may suggest one here. (Volz, Rudolph, and Bright accept a quotation here, as does *JB*.)

The noun פָּרָשׁ "horseman" is found in Jer otherwise only in 46:4, and the phrase רֹמֵה קֶשֶׁת "archer" is found only here in the book.

---

93 Johannes Behm in Johannes Behm and Ernst Würthwein, "νοέω, κτλ.," *TDNT* 4:989.
94 Eichrodt, *Theology* 1:266.
95 Compare Sylvia Huberman Scholnick, "The Meaning of *mišpaṭ* in the Book of Job," *JBL* 101 (1982) 528.
96 Pedersen, I/II, 126.
97 See Zorell, 671–72 (two lexemes) and *HALAT*, 919–20 (one lexeme).
98 Sigmund Mowinckel, "Drive and/or Ride in O.T.," *VT* 12 (1962) 291 n. 5; compare his discussion of the matter, 289–95.
99 Yadin, *Warfare* 2:298; see the illustration, 300.
100 Ibid., 297, and illustration, 384–85.

One must next take note of the remarkable fact that the three nouns in the third, fourth, and fifth cola all have the definite article; that is to say, the vocalization of *M* of the nouns "in the thickets" and "into the rocks" (which survive in a text that I propose is defective) assumes the presence of the definite article, though the consonantal text does not necessitate it; and the three nouns in *G* all have the article (εἰς τὰ σπήλαια, εἰς τὰ ἄλση, ἐπὶ τὰς πέτρας): surely cumulative evidence. And this is remarkable because one would expect in poetry to have the places of refuge anonymous, "into caves, in thickets, into rocks." Instead one has specific, well-known places of refuge: these are the focus of one's attention.

And by contrast, the second and sixth cola, which are parallel, appear in the original text to have been without article, "every region," "every city." This is difficult to assert with certainty, but the evidence points in this direction. True, *M* has כָּל־הָעִיר in both lines. But *G* has πᾶσα πόλις, without article, in the second instance, and the context demands כָּל־עִיר (see Text); and *G* offers different wording in the first instance (πᾶσα χώρα, without article), suggesting a Hebrew antecedent כָּל־אֶרֶץ (see Text). If this reconstrucion is correct, Jrm offers the article here where one does not expect it and offers no article where one would ("city and country flee to the caves," rather than "the city and the country flee to caves"). The former places of habitation have become anonymous.

In regard to כָּל־אֶרֶץ "every region," most commentators agree that *G* offers the valid text, but their retranslation has wrongly included the article. It is admitted (see Text) that אֶרֶץ in the absolute state in the meaning proposed, "rural region," is not unequivocally cited elsewhere, though Ezek 19:7 appears to be a good candidate; but it is clear that אֶרֶץ can refer to a tribal territory ("land of Zebulun," Judg 12:12) and that הָאָרֶץ may refer to the countryside in general (compare עַם הָאָרֶץ in 1:18 and the discussion there), so the usage here is by no means implausible.

When someone shouts "Horseman and archer!" then every region flees; but ironically they do not flee to the fortified cities (v 5)—"Every city is deserted." Instead they flee to places of refuge out in the open.

These places of refuge are described in a tricolon (as the text is reconstructed following *G*, or in a bicolon, if one follows *M*): caves, thickets, rocks; one is reminded of the words about flight to the mountains in Mark 13:14. The noun suggested in the reconstruction, מְעָרוֹת "caves," is found in the singular in 7:11, but not otherwise in Jer. The noun עָבִים "thickets" is a *hapax legemenon* in the OT, but the root of the word means "thick," and there is no doubt of its meaning (the Versions are not helpful: *G* "groves" is too civilized, and *V ardua* "steeps" is perhaps guesswork). The word כֵּפִים "rocks" is found only otherwise in Job 30:6, where it is also the haunt of refugees (the Aramaic singular is כֵּפָא, whence "Cephas," John 1:42). One has the impression here not only of tight parallelism but of unusual vocabulary: strange places for the population of a countryside.

And now another tricolon (again if the reconstruction is correct; see Text). The first colon, "every city is deserted," is, as already stated, ironic, given the function of the city to take in refugees from the countryside in time of siege; and this clause, together with that in the second colon, includes the totality of the population. The whole impact of the verse is of a deserted land: the shout that the chariots are coming is enough to depopulate the place (Volz).

For the phrase וְאֵין יוֹשֵׁב בָּהֵן "and no one is dwelling in them" compare מִבְּלִי יֹשֵׁב (2:15) and מֵאֵין יוֹשֵׁב (4:7). Duhm acutely remarks that אִישׁ overloads the line in *M,* and it should be added that if the word belongs with what precedes then it should appear directly after וְאֵין (compare the diction of 8:6 and 12:11 on this point). A third colon of a tricolon may plausibly be reconstructed from אִישׁ and the masculine שָׁדוּד, which clearly does not belong in its present position in *M* with the feminine diction of the first colon of v 30. The noun אִישׁ is parallel to יֹשֵׁב in 4:4, and שָׁדוּד ends a colon in Judg 5:27, describing Sisera's death. Active forms of the verb שׁדד appear in 5:6 and 6:26; the passive participle שָׁדוּד means a victim of violence. The flight of refugees has left no sign of human life.

■ **30** Yahweh continues to speak, mocking Jerusalem as a whore (see Form). The expression וְאַתְּ מַה־תַּעֲשִׂי, with subject pronoun followed by a question, is so far as I know unique in the OT. Rhythmically it is comparable to 2:23, דְּעִי מֶה־עָשִׂית "know what you have done," but there seems to be no close parallel to the present diction. It is the equivalent of the colloquial English "So what do you think *you're* doing?" The accent is thus not only on "what" but also on "you," the implication being that you are no longer in a position to act as you are doing. The "in vain" of the fifth colon affirms that the question is rhetorical; what you are doing is pointless (compare remarks on this sequence in Structure). The sudden feminine singular address is startling; in v 14 one had such address, but there the emotional tone was compassionate, and Jrm was assigned as the speaker, while here the emotional tone is contemptuous, and Yahweh is assigned as the speaker. He is addressing the personified nation as a whore, as in chapters 2—3 (see esp. 2:33). The transition from lost battle to the harlotry of the nation is a startling one, but we have met this association of ideas in those earlier chapters.

The threefold כִּי in the second, third, and fourth cola has been translated here simply as a threefold "that," but the conjunction could well be deictic: "So: you dress in scarlet; so: you adorn yourself . . ." etc.[101] The word שָׁנִי "scarlet" appears only here in Jer; it refers to a dye obtained from the female kermes insects (*Coccus ilicis*), which attach themselves to the leaves of the kermes oak (*Quercus coccifera*). Clothing of such a dye was considered elegant and precious (compare 2 Sam 1:24).[102] It is uncertain whether עֲדִי "ornaments of" is original in the third colon (see Text), but the assonance of *š* in the second colon and *k* in the fourth, and the presence of two words following the verb in the fourth colon, suggest that the repetition of ' and *d* in two words here is correct. Reference has already been made to "scarlet" in 2 Sam 1:24, but the resemblance continues with mention of "gold": these two words may function as a fixed pair. For עֲדִי "ornament" see 2:32. The verb עדה "adorn" occurs in the book only otherwise in 31:4. The noun פּוּךְ means "eye-paint"; it evidently refers to one of several compounds, notably galena (lead sulfide, PbS, which is dark gray) and stibnite (antimony trisulfide, Sb_2S_3, which is bluish gray).[103] The verb קרע literally means "tear out," but its implication here is far from clear. There is doubtless an association here between "eyes" and "windows," given the same verb with "windows" in 22:14 and given the sequence in 2 Kgs 9:30, in which Jezebel "painted her eyes, and adorned her head, and looked out the window." "Windows" are associated with whores; beyond Jezebel one thinks of Rahab (Josh 2:15) and perhaps the implication in the description of the mother of Sisera (Judg 5:28) and Prov 7:6–7a *G*, if that is the original form of text.[104] It is possible that the verb here means simply "enlarge" (compare 22:14), but since 2 Kgs 9:30 uses another verb (שִׂים, "attend to"), it is also possible that the verb is ironically meant: "that you tear out your eyes with paint," ruining them.

For לַשָּׁוְא "in vain" see 2:30. The verb תִּתְיַפִּי, the hitpaʿel stem of יפה "be beautiful," is a *hapax legomenon*, so there is no way to be sure of the nuance, but one may suspect it means "try to beautify yourself": compare the remarks on "claim to be king," 22:15 (and compare further Dan 11:36, where וְיִתְגַּדֵּל means "consider himself greater [than the gods]").

In the sixth colon current translations offer "your lovers," treating עֹגְבִים as if it were אֹהֲבַיִךְ (2:25) or מְאַהֲבַיִךְ (30:14), but one has the impression the word has a different set of connotations. It is a participle without suffix; the finite verb appears otherwise only in a series of six instances in Ezekiel 23, where Oholah and Oholibah "lusted" after various metaphorical sexual partners. It is possible that the word was considered obscene; a noun derivative in post-biblical Hebrew was used for the genitals. In any event, the contexts in Ezekiel 23 give the word an ugly cast; the translation suggested here ("paramours") may be too elegant, but other words have even less to commend them—"partners" suggests too much parity, "clients" too much of business and not enough of sex. These are lusty males out for satisfaction.

The verb מאס "reject" has occurred before (2:37); Jrm seems to use it often to close off a unit (not only 2:37 and here, but 6:19, 30; 7:29; 8:9). It is said elsewhere that Yahweh has rejected Israel (2:37; 6:30); it is ironic, then, that Judah's "gentlemen friends" should reject her too! Indeed they are trying to kill her; so much for her efforts

---

101 Compare James Muilenburg, "The Linguistic and Rhetorical Usages of the Particle כי in the Old Testament," *HUCA* 32 (1961) 148, no. 20.

102 For details of the process of extracting and employing the dye see Chester L. Wickwire, "Scarlet," *IDB* 4:233–34 and bibliography there.

103 For details of the archeological evidence see John Alexander Thompson, "Eye paint," *IDB* 2:202–3,

and bibliography there.

104 For the theme of the "woman at the window" see in detail Barnett, *Nimrud Ivories*, 145–51.

to find allies or supporters in her political and military struggle.

■ **31** For the shift of speaker to Jrm, and the consequent translation "instead" for כִּי see Structure. The "shout" here like that of a woman in labor echoes the "shout" in the midst of battle that occurs in the first colon of Yahweh's speech, v 29. One finds here the same word order as in v 19b, with the object before the verb "hear." It is noteworthy that though Yahweh uses a metaphor in v 30 (implying that the nation is a whore), Jrm more circumspectly uses a simile here (the nation is like a woman in labor). The comparison of the panic of a nation subjected to holy war with the agony of a woman in labor was evidently a standard one (50:43; see also Isa 13:8; Nah 2:10);[105] that this conventional comparison should be turned on Judah is part of the horror of Jrm's message (so also 6:24). But the comparison elsewhere, whether used of Judah's enemy or of Judah herself, uses the participle יֹלֵדָה "one giving birth"; the participles here are far more vivid. (For the identity of the verb represented by חוֹלָה see Text; see v 19 for an earlier use not implying labor pangs.)

If the noun צָרָה is correctly discerned here to mean "appeal" (see Text), then it is a touching image that emerges—the woman in birth pangs cries out for help.

The participle כְּמַבְכִּירָה "like one bearing her first" is the only instance in the OT of בכר hip'il "bear a first-born." What might the comparison imply? First, clearly, fear of the unknown: a woman giving birth for her first time is caught up by physical pangs she has never before experienced; she is risking her life in the birth process and is involuntarily, helplessly swept along—no wonder the shout comes, "Woe is me! how my life ebbs away before murderers!" Judah is panicked as she is swept along in the maelstrom of historical events she cannot control, and the panic of a woman giving birth for the first time is the perfect comparison. Second, a woman giving birth for the first time is full of pride; God has opened her womb! (compare Gen 30:1). And she looks forward eagerly for the new life she hopes to bring forth: will the child be alive and normal? will it live? All the agony is worth it if only the child will grow and prosper. The cruel disappointment of a birth process that comes

to nothing is reflected in the metaphor of Isa 26:18: "We conceived and writhed in pain, giving birth to wind" (*NAB*; "wind" = רוּחַ). Does the simile here suggest that Jrm hopes for a happy issue out of present events?—one might compare the symbolism found in the incident in the potter's workshop (18:1–12). Third, though a firstborn daughter is indeed precious (compare the story of Jephthah's daughter, Judg 11:34), there is hope particularly for a בְּכוֹר, a firstborn son who can inherit the blessing of the father and carry on the family name.[106] One can imagine the pride of a father in his firstborn son (compare 20:15; 31:9); we have only hints of how a mother feels about her firstborn son (the only son is "delicate," Prov 4:3!), but one can extrapolate: women must have internalized the values of the male-dominated society (compare Hannah's prayer, 1 Sam 1:11). If the child born, then, is a son, the new mother will have fulfilled her ultimate destiny (when Rachel finally bore a son, she said, "God has taken away my reproach," Gen 30:23). Is Judah approaching the climactic event in her life?

For the expression "fair Zion" for בַּת־צִיּוֹן, literally "daughter Zion," compare "my fair people," v 11. Though the verb תִּתְיַפֵּחַ is a *hapax legomenon*, the meaning "panting" suits the comparison of a woman in birth pangs (see Text); for the assonance with תִּתְיַפִּי in v 30 see Structure. The phrase "extending her hands" finds a parallel in Isa 1:15: there "your extending your hands" is a gesture of prayer to Yahweh, while here it is a gesture of entreaty to those around her. The noun כַּף "hand," literally "palm," was restored in 2:34 and discussed there. Judah is now really helpless and is imploring the mercy of any who can help—a hopeless gesture.

The last colon is the "shout" mentioned in the first colon. The phrase אוֹי־נָא לִי "woe is me" echoes in idiom (and in assonance) אוֹי לָנוּ "woe to us" in v 13. The particle נָא reinforces the mood of entreaty already indicated in "extending her hands" (Duhm). The phrases both in v 13 and here are followed by כִּי in an expression of lamentation, and the translation "how" is appropriate here as it was in v 13 (see there), though "that" would be equally appropriate (15:10; 45:3). The verb עיף "become

105   Delbert R. Hillers, "A Convention in Hebrew Literature: The Reaction to Bad News," *ZAW* 77 (1965) 86–90; Berridge, pp. 88–91.

106   On the institution of the firstborn see Vernon H. Kooy, "First-born," *IDB* 2:270–72 and bibliography; and de Vaux, *Ancient Israel*, 41–42.

faint" is not common as a verb, though the corresponding adjective עָיֵף "faint" is. If the perfect verb is correct here (see Text), then it means "has become fainter." Yahweh's harsh word to the whore that her paramours are really trying to kill her is matched ironically by the cry of the nation that her life ebbs away before murderers: the match extends beyond semantics to assonances: in v 30 the paramours (עֹגְבִים) were seeking the "life" (נֶפֶשׁ) of Judah, while here the nation says that her life ebbs away before murderers (הֹרְגִים). The irony, then, works in several directions: Jrm has replaced Yahweh's metaphor of the whore with the simile of a woman in labor; the woman in labor brings forth new life, yet screams she is being murdered; the life of nation *is* ebbing away before murderers, however, so that Yahweh may be right after all. Yet the woman in labor may be bringing forth something very fine, and the hope lingers that the agony of the present may foreshadow something better to emerge in the future.

When all is said and done, however, one must take account of the curious way in which Jrm "corrects" Yahweh's imagery by his own. Jrm has offered the tenderer image of the woman in labor instead of the more brutal image of the whore perceived to be voiced by Yahweh. But both images are communicated to us through Jrm's perception, both his perception of Yahweh's utterance and his perception of his own utterance. What does it mean that a prophet who is commissioned to speak for Yahweh senses such a contrast between his own sensibility and that of the God whom he serves? Psychologically it would be easy to recognize here some kind of split in consciousness (compare Rudolf Bultmann's discussion of the split in Paul between the two manifestations of his "self" expressed in Rom 7:17, "So then it is no longer I that do it, but sin which dwells within me").[107] But one is duty-bound to listen to Jrm's perception and become aware of the tension within him between what he would like to say and what he hears Yahweh say.

Aim

If, as proposed here, vv 5–8, 13–18, and 29–31 make up material in the first scroll, then these verses must be heard first as warning, intended to move the people to repentance (v 14). Yahweh may stay his hand: but all the scenarios of battle, with the bewildering variety of voices, represent possibilities within Yahweh's will. They offer *in nuce* the themes of Jrm's preaching: the harlotry of the people (v 30), the possibility of a holy war declared by Yahweh against his people, Jrm's role as mediator to Yahweh on behalf of his people (vv 14, 31). These themes will be expanded in subsequent chapters.

Upon this come the additions in the second scroll (vv 9–12, 19–28). These additions in themselves speak of the irrevocability of Yahweh's judgment on the people (v 28), of Jrm's unavoidable role as mediator of that judgment (v 12), of his tormented emotions when he contemplates the destruction to come (vv 19–21), of his stark sense that the cosmos has turned to ashes (vv 23–26); but these additions signify that the scenarios of possible judgment in the first scroll are now activated and become part of the announcement of inevitability.

The nation faces the sentence of death; and the issues that this sentence sets forth will only be soluble, Jrm ultimately became convinced, in the light of a new covenant: compare "they will all know me," 31:34, with "me they do not know" in 4:22 (and there will be another parallel between the new covenant passage and a phrase in 5:1–9; see Aim there). We are very much in the center of Jrm's depiction of the people's situation, poised as they are on the brink of disaster.

---

107 Rudolf Bultmann, *Theology of the New Testament* (New York: Scribner's, 1951, 1955) 245.

**Even the Leaders
Have Broken the Yoke**

Bibliography
Berridge
    pp. 77–80, 83.
Holladay
    Architecture, 85–86.
Jastrow, Marcus
    "Jeremiah 5:8," *AJSL* 13 (1896/7), 216–17.
Lundbom
    Jeremiah, 75–78.
May, Herbert G.
    "Individual Responsibility and Retribution," *HUCA* 32 (1961) 115–16.
Sutcliffe, Edmund F.
    "A Note on Jeremiah V.3," *JSS* 5 (1960) 348–49.
Wisser, Laurent
    Jérémie, Critique de la vie sociale, Justice sociale et connaissance de Dieu dans le livre de Jérémie (Geneva: Labor et Fides, 1982) 31–33.

5

1 Yahweh: **Search through the streets of Jerusalem,
    just look and learn,
        and seek in her squares,
    whether you find a man,
        whether there is anyone doing justice,
        anyone seeking honesty,
    so that I can pardon her.**[a]

3aα Jeremiah: 《 **Your eyes look for honesty, Yahweh, do
    they not?** 》[a]

2   **And (people) say, "by the life of
            Yahweh," do they not?
        No!**[b] **—they are swearing falsely.**

3   **[. . . .]**[a]
    **You struck them, but they did not feel
        pain,**[c]
    **you destroyed them, they refused to
        take correction;**
        **they made their face harder than
            rock,**
            they refused to return.

4   **I myself thought,
        "But these are poor folk without sense,
        for they do not know the path of
            Yahweh,
            the justice of their God.**

5   **Just let me go off to the leaders
        and let me speak** [a]**with them;**[a]

Text

1a   *G* adds λέγει κύριος = נְאֻם־יהוה "oracle of Yahweh"; it is a plausible reading.

2–3a With Rudolph (and *JB*) bringing the first four words of v 3 before v 2; this shift solves the difficulty of the presence of וֹ at the beginning of v 2 and generally makes plausible the movement of thought of these lines. In addition I propose to rearrange the order of the four words to הֲלוֹא לֶאֱמוּנָה יהוה עֵינֶיךָ. Two considerations form the basis for this proposal. (1) The expression הֲלוֹא appears seven other times in the poetry of the book, always as the first word in a bicolon (2:17; 3:1, 4; 13:21; 14:22; 23:24, 29); compare also the phrase וְלֹא לֶאֱמוּנָה in 9:2 and the grouping of words proposed there. (2) The vocative rarely appears in first position: of approximately twenty instances of "Yahweh" as vocative in the poetry of chapters 1—31, only two instances offer the word as first in the verse (11:20; 20:12; both וַיהוה); one more begins the second half of a bicolon (14:7). Much more typically the vocative appears second or third in a colon (10:23, 24; 12:1, 3; and often). Though it would be difficult to offer an unchallengeable proposal how the text became dislocated as I assume it now is, the sequence אִם . . . אִם . . . וְאִם in vv 1–2 doubtless contributed to the omission of the four words, their insertion in the margin or between the lines, and their later restoration in the wrong sequence.

b   Read אָכֵן with twenty-six MSS. (so de Rossi) and *S*. Note also the association of אָכֵן with לַשֶּׁקֶר in 3:23 and 8:8.

c   As accented, from חוּל "writhe" (as 4:19 ketib, 4:31); but *S* and many commentators refer the verb to חלה "be sick."

5a—a אוֹתָם may be a slip of the pen for אִתָּם (compare 9:7); but *M* may be correct, echoing אֹתָם in v 3. This

they are the ones to know the path of
　　　　Yahweh,
　　　　　　the justice of their God!"
　　　　But they likewise have broken the yoke,
　　　　　　have shattered the bonds.

6　　That is why a lion from the thicket has
　　　　　　struck them,
　　　　　　a wolf of the deserts has been devas-
　　　　　　　tating them,
　　　　　　　a leopard keeps watch over their
　　　　　　　　cities:
　　　　　　anyone going out from them will be torn
　　　　　　　up—
　　　　　　　how many are their sins,
　　　　　　　numerous their turnings!

7 Yahweh:　On what basis ᵃcan I pardonᵃ you?
　　　　Your children have left me
　　　　　　and swear by non-gods.
　　　　Though I fed them full, they committed
　　　　　　adultery,
　　　　　　and in a brothel ᵇthey slash them-
　　　　　　　selves;ᵇ

8　　ᵃtrappedᵃ stallions ᵇfrom Meshechᵇ they
　　　　　　have been,
　　　　　　each for his neighbor's wife neighs;

9　　with these (folk) shall I not deal?ᵃ
　　　　　　　　　　oracle of Yahweh,
　　　　and upon a nation like this shall my soul
　　　　　　not gain satisfaction?

verb seems to take an accusative of person in Gen
37:4 as well.

7a–a　Ketib אֶסְלוֹחַ, qere' אֶסְלַח. The former represents
only a variation of writing or pronunciation (GKC,
sec. 65b): indeed it may be nothing more than a slip
of the pen.

b–b　For יִתְגֹּדָ֫רוּ two MSS. read יִתְגֹּרָ֫רוּ "they reside as a
sojourner" (גור hitpolel), compare 1 Kgs 17:20; so *G*
κατέλυον "lodge" (accepted by Rudolph, Bright). For
a discussion see Interpretation.

8a　　*M* מְיֻזָּנִים has given steady difficulty; the Versions
are of no help. Read with Marcus Jastrow (see
Bibliography) the pu'al participle of יון, "well
provided," a form appearing in *b. Giṭ.* 67a. See
further Interpretation.

b–b　This adjective too has given steady difficulty, and
again the Versions are of no help. Read with Jastrow
(see Bibliography) the masculine plural of a gentilic
adjective מָשְׁכִי from the ethnic name מֶשֶׁךְ; see
further Interpretation.

9a　　Several MSS. add here and/or in v 29 בָּם as *M*
reads in 9:8; for the meaning see Interpretation.

Structure

Extent and Placement of Unit. Clearly vv 1–9 make up the
unit; the passage begins with a burst of imperatives
(compare 4:5–6) and ends (v 9) with the "refrain" which
also appears in v 29 and 9:8 (see the discussion on 4:5–
10:25, Preliminary Observations). As to the placement of
the unit, see above, 4:5—10:25, Preliminary Observations, *Structural Organization of Units*.

　　Structure Within the Unit. The passage breaks easily into
three sections according to speaker. Yahweh speaks in v
1 ("so that I can pardon her"). Jrm speaks beginning in vv
3aα + 2 (the vocative to Yahweh) and continues in v 3
(the second-person addresses to Yahweh) and at least
through v 5 ("let me go off to the leaders and . . . speak
with them"). By v 7 Yahweh speaks again ("On what basis
can I pardon you?") and that speech continues through v
9. Verse 6, however, is without immediate clues; Bright
states that it could be assigned to either speaker.
Rudolph assigns the verse to Jrm,[1] rightly I believe;[2] the
general content and mood parallels 10:21, where עַל־כֵּן
("that is why") likewise appears in the middle of a speech,
dividing a judgment about the stupidity of leaders from
the consequent punishment of the people. If Jrm's

speech continues through v 6, then Yahweh's speech in v
7 begins where it ended in v 1, with the verb "pardon." Is
it significant that Yahweh's first speech contains seven
cola, and his second speech seven cola plus the refrain?

　　Verse 1 is best analyzed as two tricola plus an orphan
colon (note the position of the 'atnaḥ at the end of the
sixth colon!). The first tricolon consists of four imperatives, two in the second colon and one each in the first
and third; the first and third likewise balance in paralleling "streets of Jerusalem" and "her squares." The
second tricolon offers the particle אִם in the first and
second cola and participles in the second and third. The
two tricola are united by "seek" (last colon of the first
tricolon), "find" (first colon of the second tricolon), and
"seeking" (third colon of the second tricolon). The
orphan last colon in the verse remains suspended until it
is picked by the first colon of v 7 (see above).

　　The beginning of Jrm's speech, verses 3aα + 2, make
up a tricolon; the first two cola are introduced by the two
interrogative particles הֲ + וְאִם (compare v 9) and offer
the name "Yahweh"; the second and third deal with
"swearing"—the second by an oath-phrase, the third by
the verb "swear" itself; and the first and third offer the

1　　Lundbom, *Jeremiah*, 77.
2　　Against my analysis in Holladay, *Architecture*, 85–86.

174

contrast of "honesty" with "falsehood" (see Interpretation). Verse 3aβb makes up a tetracolon: the first two cola are closely parallel (each with two clauses contrasting the subjects "you" and "they"), as are the last two (single clauses with subject "they"), but the second and fourth cola are likewise closely parallel, with "they refused" (מֵאֲנוּ). Verses 4 and 5a are closely parallel to each other: the third colon of each verse offers "know the path of Yahweh," and the fourth colon of each is identical ("the justice of their God"). But the first part of v 4 gives a problem. The Masoretic punctuation marks אָמַרְתִּי "I thought" with a zaqep qaṭon and הֵם "they" with the atnaḥ, therefore reading, "But I myself thought, / they are only poor folk; / they have no sense, for they do not know the path of Yahweh. . . ." Cornill proposed that אַךְ־דַּלִּים "poor folk" is an exclamation; by this understanding הֵם נוֹאֲלוּ "they are without sense" makes up a colon of its own; subsequent commentators have followed this understanding, and so have current translations (so the typography of *BHK* and *BHS*). But I cannot locate elsewhere a context in which אַךְ and the following word make up an exclamation; and in the meantime the first two words of 3:19, namely וְאָנֹכִי אָמַרְתִּי "but I for my part thought," make up a single colon (see Structure there), so that one is pressed to see וַאֲנִי אָמַרְתִּי "I myself thought" here likewise making up a single colon, and thus to understand אַךְ־דַּלִּים הֵם נוֹאֲלוּ "but these are poor folk without sense" as the second colon (נוֹאֲלוּ may be construed as subordinate, as if introduced by אֲשֶׁר: see Interpretation). By this analysis the first two cola of vv 4 and 5a are chiastically related: the first colon of v 4 offers אָמַרְתִּי, "I thought" (literally "I said"), and the second colon of v 5a offers "let me speak"; the second colon of v 4 has "poor folk," and the first colon of v 5a has "the leaders." Since the second and third cola of v 4 are parallel ("without sense," "they do not know") one is moved to take v 4 as a tetracolon, and therefore v 5a as well.

Jrm's musing began with the second colon of v 4; but the question (which is both structural and form-critical) arises, where does the quotation end? John Arthur Thompson[3] ends it with v 4; Bright (with *JB* and *NEB*) with v 5a, and Rudolph with v 5b. One must conclude

that the parallelism between the second bicolon of v 4 and the second bicolon of v 5a demands that the musing continues through v 5a. But the tone changes in v 5b; the diction reverts to the same level as that in v 3b. One must answer then that Bright is correct; but then one must go on to affirm that the אַךְ at the beginning of v 5b is ironic in standing outside the quotation, since the same particle began the quotation in v 4 (see further Interpretation).

Verse 5b is an obvious bicolon, but אַךְ הֵמָּה "but they" in the first colon picks up אַךְ + הֵם in the second colon of v 4, tying this bicolon closely with vv 4–5a.

The first three cola of v 6, with the successive mention of the three animals, make up a tricolon. The last two cola of the verse are likewise closely parallel, leaving the fourth colon somewhat isolated. But the subject of the verb in that colon refers to the people and in that way is to be heard with the last two cola, making up a second tricolon.

Verse 7 begins with an orphan colon that picks up the last colon of v 1 (see above). The balance of v 7 and all of v 8 make up three bicola, each colon of which offers a third plural verb describing the people's behavior. And the refrain (v 9) is a bicolon, a double rhetorical question that balances the rhetorical question in the first colon of v 7.

Jrm's speech (vv 2–6) builds on Yahweh's speech in v 1 with the repetition of "honesty" (v 3aα) and justice (vv 4, 5a). And Yahweh's second speech (vv 7–9) builds on Jrm's speech by the rhetorical questions of vv 7 and 9 that pick up those in vv 3aα + 2a, by the repetition of "swear" (v 7, see v 2), and perhaps subtly by the response of the people to Yahweh's grace in v 7b ("though I fed them full, they committed adultery") over against the response of the people to Yahweh's judgment in v 3 ("you struck them, but they did not feel pain . . .").

Form

Though the imperatives of v 1 appear to be battle orders (they are masculine plural; compare 4:5–6a), they turn out to be an ironic appeal to the hearers to look for an honest man in Jerusalem. Yahweh speaks; who are the hearers?—evidently witnesses at a cosmic law court who are to produce evidence sufficient for acquittal. In this

---

3   Thompson, p. 233.

the form is analogous to the command in 2:10 to search for evidence, where the hearers were likewise the cosmic witnesses (2:12).

Jrm's speech is addressed to Yahweh, the prophetic equivalent of the report of a messenger to his master. It begins with rhetorical questions (vv 3aα + 2a) and continues (vv 2b–3) with the report proper. The format of an address to Yahweh shifts beginning in v 4: Jrm soliloquizes on the people's conduct, proposing to himself a contrast in culpability between those of low station and those high in society. The analysis in Structure concludes that the soliloquy ends with v 5a. Verse 5b then concludes the prophetic report: those of high station stand equally guilty. Verse 6 closes his speech, bringing the metaphor of the wild beast that Yahweh has used elsewhere (4:7), to ponder the impending doom of the people.

Yahweh had spoken of the people in the third-person feminine singular in v 1. Now, however, he turns to address her in the second person (v 7), first in a rhetorical question, then in an accusation ("your children have left me"). But the ensuing accusations stay with references to the "children" in the third person. The closing refrain (v 9) is a double rhetorical question of self-justification. Is it to be perceived as a word to Jrm rather than to the people?

Setting

Evidence has already been given for a setting late in the period 605–601, most probably the autumn of 601 (see 4:5—10:25, Preliminary Observations, Setting). Thus the passage hints at Yahweh's law ("the path of Yahweh," "the justice of their God"), material appropriate to a season in which the Deuteronomic law was recited (by the chronology offered here, the early autumn of 601). And the phraseology of v 5 may well be applicable to the time when Baruch read the contents of Jrm's first scroll to the courtiers and then to the king (36:10–26).

Interpretation

■ **1** The opening imperative, שׁוֹטְטוּ (שׁוּט polel) is not a common verb; it occurs four times otherwise, twice of God's eyes "ranging" or "roaming" through the whole

earth (Zech 4:10; 2 Chr 16:9) and once (Amos 8:12) of people wandering from north to east to seeking the word of Yahweh (the fourth instance, Dan 12:4, is difficult and thus does not aid a definition). The qal stem is used once in the imperative, in 2 Sam 24:20, where David commands Joab to go through (i.e., work through) all the tribes of Israel to take a census. In short, the impression given by the first colon is of military orders for a "search" mission, and this grim impression is shifted only in the second tricolon, when it becomes clear that Yahweh wants not prisoners of war but an honest man.

The רְחֹב is an "open place, plaza," often near the gate, a gathering-place for the population.[4]

The word אֱמוּנָה is not "truth" with most translations, but trustworthiness, integrity; it is the trait that enables one to keep one's word, to be counted on; "and seeks to be faithful" (*NAB*).[5] As to the parallel in the previous colon, the phrase "do justice" is common; מִשְׁפָּט moves from "justice" in specific instances (Ps 9:17, "Yahweh . . . has executed judgment") to "justice" in general; Abraham, who was chosen to "do justice," points out to Yahweh that the judge of all the earth should "do justice" (Gen 18:19, 25). "Doing justice" is one of the three requirements God exacts in the well-known verse of Micah (Mic 6:8). The parallel of "justice" (מִשְׁפָּט) and "honesty" (אֱמוּנָה) is found also in Deut 32:4; that passage may well be in the background of Jrm's diction here. Elsewhere אֱמוּנָה is the object of "do" (Prov 12:22), but here Jrm speaks not of "acting honestly" but of "seeking honesty"; he does this partly to echo "seek" earlier in the verse (see Structure), but he thereby underlines the dynamic of covenantal obedience: it is a question not simply of adherence to rules ("do justly") but of wanting, craving, seeking integrity as well.

The singularity of אִישׁ "a man" is not underlined here (the number "one" is not used), but it is surely implied. Those familiar with ancient Greek traditions will recall the story of the Cynic Diogenes (fourth century B.C.E.), who is said to have gone around Athens with a lantern in broad daylight looking for an honest man: here is a striking case of cultural convergence on a single theme. But the background for Jrm's words is clearly Gen 18:23–32 (so already Jerome): Abraham bargained with

---

4   Chester C. McCown, "City," *IDB* 1:636a.
5   Pedersen, I/II, 338–39, 347.

God over the number of righteous men who could stay the sentence of destruction on Sodom. Abraham bargained God from fifty down to ten; now, Jrm implies, one will do. (And is there thus the implication that Jerusalem is ten times as wicked as Sodom?) But there may be a further implication here: Jrm has said that Josiah did justice (22:15); now (assuming the setting proposed here is correct) where is Josiah when we need him?—one Josiah would be enough, but instead the king is Jehoiakim, who works "by injustice" (22:13). This possibility lends resonance to the reference to "the leaders" in v 5.

In the poetry of Jrm the verb "pardon" (סלח) appears only otherwise in the matching line in v 7 and in 31:34; the implication of the new covenant passage is then that only such an innovation will solve the problem posed here.

■ **3aα** For the arrangement of the words in the colon, and the position of the colon before v 2, see Text. The syntax of this first clause of Jrm's speech is puzzling to non-Semites, and most translations follow V in adding a verb (*Domine oculi tui respiciunt fidem*, "O Lord, your eyes behold truth")—Giesebrecht wished to restore a verb in the Hebrew text. But לֹא plus לְ without verb has parallels elsewhere (e.g., v 10; Ps 33:18a is even closer to the diction here). The phrase then means "Do your eyes, Yahweh, not belong to honesty?" The mention of "eyes" is unexpected but perhaps triggered by the opening verb in v 1 (see the discussion above).

■ **2** The ordering of v 3aα before v 2 brings וְאִם into correlation with הֲ there, so that a translation like "though" (*RSV*, *NAB*) is not called for. The negative לֹא does double duty (as in Isa 28:27).[6]

For "by the life of Yahweh" see 4:2. The implication of the two questions is that the constant swearing by Yahweh's name in the streets of Jerusalem is surely an evidence of sincerity and honesty (אֱמוּנָה), but Jrm's hearers instead hear a strong denial (for אָכֵן see 3:23). The word שֶׁקֶר (literally "falsehood"; in the present expression the rendering is "falsely") is the opposite of "honesty"; the same contrast is found in 9:2. The casual oaths of the people are insincere, really dishonest. (For a more extended discussion of the diction here see on 7:9.)

■ **3aβb** The identity of the verb חָלוּ (here "feel pain"), whether from חוּל "writhe" or חלה "be ill, incapacitated," is unclear. The Masoretic accent indicates "writhe," and so V; S translates "be ill" (G is ambiguous, T periphrastic). Commentators have always been divided. Jrm has used חוּל more than once (4:19, 31); on the other hand there is a nice parallel with חלה in Prov 23:35, "They struck me, but I was not hurt" (note also Isa 1:5 in a similar prophetic context, הִכּוּ "you are struck" followed by לָחֳלִי, a cognate of חלה). It is more than possible that Jrm intended an ambiguity here, and in any event they are relatively close in meaning.

Earlier commentators were uneasy about the verb כִּלִּיתָם "you destroyed them": it seemed illogical to affirm it when the people are still in existence. Thus Duhm and Volz wished to delete the verb (and Volz would delete "but they did not feel pain" as well); Rudolph would emend to כֻּלְּהֶם (for כֻּלָּם) "all of them." But כלה pi'el "destroy" is associated with נכה hip'il "strike" in Deut 28:21–22, and הִכִּיתָה אֹתָם and כִּלִּיתָם offer assonance here; the text should be retained. The verse is then an expansion of 2:30a; see the discussion there for this diction, and for "take correction."

The phrase "they have made their face harder than rock" is without immediate parallel. Of course Exod 4:21, and similar passages, speak of God's hardening (חזק pi'el) Pharaoh's heart; Jer 3:3 speaks of the whore's brow without shame. Here the people harden their own face. Is there irony here in that the Psalms frequently refer to God as the "rock" (the same word, סֶלַע)? Jrm's phrase is developed in Ezek 3:7[7] and Isa 48:4. "They refused to return" (מֵאֲנוּ לָשׁוּב): the phrase is already found in Hos 11:5. The implication is: "They refused to repent," but in the light of 4:1 (and 8:5) one may understand "They refused to make a change."

■ **4** For the division of the first two cola see Structure.

The verse begins with an emphatic pronoun; in v 3 Jrm had been reflecting Yahweh's will and work; now he is separating himself from Yahweh in order to attempt to find a mitigation for the people's obduracy. For "(I) thought" for אָמַרְתִּי see 3:19.

If אַךְ־דַּלִּים הֵם נוֹאֲלוּ makes up a single colon, how might it be understood? The *JB* and *NAB* make a general

---

6   Joüon, *Gramm.*, sec. 160q; see further the suggestions in Dahood, *Psalms III*, 438.

7   Ezek 2:4a is evidently secondary; see Zimmerli,

Ezekiel 1, 90.

statement about poor folk; *JB*: "Only the ordinary people . . . behave foolishly"; *NAB*: "It is only the lowly . . . who are foolish." But these translations appear to neglect the force of the pronoun הֵם. I propose that אַךְ־דַּלִּים הֵם be understood as a nominal clause, and that נוֹאֲלוּ then be understood as a subordinate clause (as if introduced by אֲשֶׁר). The *NEB* and *NJV* follow this line, though they translate as if נוֹאֲלוּ is coordinate; *NEB*: "After all, these are the poor, these are stupid folk"; *NJV*: "These are just poor folk; they act foolishly." The particle אַךְ here thus carries its normal restrictive force, "but":[8] "But these are (just) poor folk!"—that would explain it all. Jrm is looking for an excuse against the evidence (compare the use of the same particle in v 5b).

One notices in v 5 that the גְּדֹלִים, "leaders," are graced with the definite article, while in the present verse the דַּלִּים, "poor," do not: even grammatically the poor remain anonymous. Who are the דַּלִּים? Sometimes they are simply the opposite of the rich (Ruth 3:10), but not always; sometimes they are simply the powerless and insignificant, as opposed to those with power and influence (Lev 19:15), and so here. In the city streets and squares (v 1) they would be the petty merchants and peddlers, craftsmen and porters crowding and shouting.[9] Such folk are always likely to use oaths casually (v 2), but one can hardly blame them; how can they know any better? The verb יאל nip'al (here "without sense") occurs otherwise only three times (Num 12:11 is the best parallel); it means "prove foolish, turn out to be stupid."

"Justice" was joined with "honesty" in v 1, while here it is associated with "path," a word likewise found in Deut 32:4. This is the first use of דֶּרֶךְ in Jer for Yahweh's path: earlier it had been either a physical road (2:18) or the false way of the people (2:23). But Yahweh offers a way, a norm of life, a set of habits by which one lives; this notion will be expanded in 6:16. "Justice" here is sponsored by Yahweh: it is the pattern of just treatment of neighbor that he has enjoined on his people, so much so that Rudolph (and *NAB*) translate the phrase here as

"their duty to their God." It is a marvelous expectation to hope that a whole people will be responsive to Yahweh's will, but these are just the common people, too busy earning a living to pay much attention to what Yahweh wants. They take their cues from the leaders, so it is to the leaders that Jrm undertakes to go.

■ **5** The phrase אֵלֲכָה־לִּי ("just let me go off") is striking. The ethical dative is not common with verbs of motion in the first singular, and the ethical dative is not common with cohortatives of any sort, so that parallels are difficult to locate; but one may cite Num 22:34 (Balaam to the angel: "If you disapprove, then just let me go back again") and 1 Sam 26:11 (David to Abishai over Saul's sleeping body, "So now take the spear that is at his head . . . and let us go our way"). In both these passages the speaker feels somewhat uneasy, so that the translation here is appropriate.[10]

The word "leaders," as already noted (v 4), carries the article, and the article is not common in Jrm's poetry. He refers, then, to what is currently called "the establishment," the shapers of opinion, those who set the pace for the whole community. Jrm says, "Let me go off to the leaders"; one wonders, do they live in a different part of the city? In v 4 the pronoun הֵם appears to function as the subject in a nominal clause (see there), but here, where it appears again, it is emphatic: the leaders are surely the ones to know Yahweh's path.

The first three words in v 5b need attention, אַךְ הֵמָּה יַחְדָּו, since grammatically none of them is necessary for the clause. The particle אַךְ began the quotation in v 4 and now begins the resumption of normal speech outside the quotation; in this way it is more than a little ironic (for the discussion see Structure, Form); again it means "but," contrasting Jrm's musing, his hope, against the evidence (compare the use of the particle in v 4). The pronoun הֵמָּה is of course emphatic, as it was in the third colon of the verse; that colon said, "They are the ones to know the path of Yahweh," while this colon implies, "But they are precisely the ones who do not know." The

---

8   Against BDB; see Norman H. Snaith, "The Meaning of the Hebrew אַךְ," *VT* 14 (1964) 223, but note that Snaith is wrong when he states that the particle is used of the same people in v 5.

9   See C. Umhau Wolf, "Poor," *IDB* 3:843–44, with bibliography, and Leander E. Keck, "Poor," *IDBSup*, 672–75, with bibliography.

10   Rudolph: *Ich will einmal zu den Grossen gehen.*

adverb יַחְדָּו reinforces the pronoun; it does not suggest "all together, unanimously" (Bright: "to a man," so similarly Volz) but rather "likewise, together (with the poor)"; the word in Jrm normally adds another social grouping to the one already named (6:11, 12).

For "broken the yoke, shattered the bonds," see 2:20; but note that מוֹסֵרוֹת ("bonds") is a nice play on מוּסָר ("correction") in v 3.

■ 6 There is the hint of a refractory domestic animal in v 5b; does this trigger the mention of the triplet of wild animals here?

The verse begins with עַל־כֵּן. In contrast to לָכֵן, which is used to open the announcement of judgment (see 2:9), this conjunction introduces established facts:[11] it is not that the determination has been made to send wild animals upon Judah, but rather that the animals are already on their way simply as a consequence of breaking of the covenant.

In 2:15 and 4:7 we hear of lions as a metaphor for the invader; now Jrm speaks of three animals, the lion, the wolf, and the leopard. Given those metaphorical uses one assumes that the animals here are likewise a metaphor for the invader, but it is possible that the animals are intended as real and not metaphorical (Lev 26:22).[12]

There is no other passage with the triple parallelism of these three animals. There are of course pairs, "lions" with "wolves" in Zeph 3:3, "leopard" with "wolf" in Hab 1:8. For the imagery of "lion" and "thicket" see 4:7; this first colon here is a variation of the first colon there, though the word for "thicket" (here יַעַר) is different. The term refers to anything from true "forest" to "scrub";[13] it is associated with "lion" again in 12:8 (and in Amos 3:4). The verb "has struck them" reflects "you have struck" in v 3.

This is the only occurrence of "wolf" (זְאֵב) in Jer. The word עֲרָבוֹת refers to dry, desert lands, but since Zeph 3:3 has a phrase of similar sound, זְאֵבֵי עֶרֶב "evening wolves" (with a balancing contrast of "morning" there), it is possible that Jrm has a word-play in mind here. For

"devastate" see 4:30. "Leopard" (נָמֵר) appears in the book only otherwise in 13:23. For "keep watch" (שׁקד) see 1:12: Yahweh may be "watching" over his word, but the leopard is watching over the cities of Judah.[14] It is noteworthy that the triple parallelism here involves a perfect verb, an imperfect verb, and a participle. There is a parallelism of perfect and imperfect verbs in 2:15; is it only a coincidence that both verses offer diction involving animals?

Yahweh is sending wild animals (whether real or metaphorical) to destroy the population of the cities: "Anyone going out from them will be torn up." The verb טרף is normal to describe the action of a wild beast—of the wolf in Gen 49:27, of the lion in Mic 5:7 and Nah 2:13.

The cities have been places of refuge (4:5) but will be destroyed (4:7), indeed we are told that city-dwellers will flee for safety to the caves (4:29). There is no safety.

"How many are their sins, numerous their turnings!" The noun פֶּשַׁע "sin" occurs only here in Jer, but a possible model for this colon is Amos 5:12, רַבִּים פִּשְׁעֵיכֶם. The verb עצם "be numerous" is found with חַטֹּאת "sins" in 30:14, 15. For "turnings" see 2:19; 3:22. For the translation "how" for כִּי see 2:19 and the discussion there.

■ 7a The phrase אֵי לָזֹאת "on what basis?" is found only here, though אֵי "where?" is found elsewhere with other prepositional phrases of specification (e.g., Gen 16:8, אֵי מִזֶּה "from where?"); so here: "to what?" means "on what basis?" The rhetorical question echoes the last colon of v 1 and by its form implies the near-impossibility of pardon. For "pardon" see further the new covenant passage, 31:34. One notes further that לָזֹאת is rounded off by עַל־אֵלֶּה "with these (folk)" and כָּזֶה in v 9.

"Swear" of course echoes its occurrence in v 2. "Your children have left me" does not pick up anything earlier in the passage, but the existence of the bicolon in 2:30a, "In vain have I beaten (= struck) your children, correction they did not take," which is mimicked in 5:3 by "you

---

11   BDB, 487a, f, against Wolff, *Hosea*, 233 n. 1; see R. Frankena, "Einige Bemerkungen zum Gebrauch des Adverbs 'al-ken im Hebräischen," *Studia Biblica et Semitica Theodoro Christiano Vriezen* (Wageningen: Veenman, 1966) 94–99, esp. 98–99.

12   Compare Hillers, *Treaty-Curses*, 54–55.

13   Baly, *Geography*, 105–7.

14   For these animals see Friedrich S. Bodenheimer, "Fauna," *IDB* 2:249 and 250; W. Stewart McCullough, "Wolf," *IDB* 4:864, and "Leopard," *IDB* 3:111.

have struck them . . . they refused to take correction," suggests that one continues to move in the same circle of discourse as material in v 3. One other curiosity: "non-gods" also occurred in 2:11: there it is preceded by כָּזֹאת (2:10b) as it is preceded here by לֹזֹאת this pattern leads one to speculate about likeness of tune or rhythm when the prophet uttered his oracles. For עזב "leave" see 1:16. It was stated in v 2 that the people swear in Yahweh's name but do it insincerely; now we learn the contrary, that people's sincere oaths are taken in the name of nonexistent gods.

■ **7b–8** These four cola bring vivid imagery and thereby several problems of interpretation.

"Feed full" (שבע hip'il) offers word-play on "swear" (שבע nip'al) in vv 2 and 7a; indeed many MSS. read וָאַשְׁבִּע "I adjured" for "I fed full." The presence of אוֹתָם "them" suggests a parity with "you struck them" (הִכִּיתָה אֹתָם) in v 3; there Yahweh's work was of judgment, while here it is of blessing. It would be hard to imagine a more succinct summary of the people's desertion of Yahweh, who gives fertility, and her consequent liaison with the gods who purport to give fertility but do not: "I fed them to satiety, and they committed adultery." There is no particle here to underline contrast, beyond one's awareness that waw-consecutive clauses may be so related; the terrible contrast comes from our perception of the ingratitude and insensitivity of the people. The verb שבע hip'il "feed full" does not otherwise occur in Jer, but there is stimulus from earlier prophetic words, notably Hos 4:10, "They shall eat and not be satisfied, play the harlot and not multiply," and Hos 13:6, "God led them into the land, and they were satisfied" (both שבע qal). For נאף "commit adultery" see 3:8.

Curiously בֵּית זוֹנָה "brothel" is unparalleled in the OT, though בֵּית הָאִשָּׁה הַזּוֹנָה occurs in Josh 6:22.

The accompanying verb, יִתְגֹּדָדוּ, is a problem. The textual alternative יִתְגֹּרָרוּ (see Text) is the *lectio facilior*: "they lodged at the brothel" (*G*) is a plausible though hardly a striking phrase. The verb with dalet is then undoubtedly right (against *HALAT*, Rudolph, Bright), but it is not clear what it means. The verb (גדד hitpolal) is well cited (five or six times) meaning "slash oneself": the Baal prophets "slashed themselves" on Mt. Carmel (1 Kgs 18:28). Those loyal to Yahweh evidently did the same on occasion in humiliation and abasement (Jer 41:8), and the practice was evidently the practice also in

funeral rites (16:6), in spite of legislation against it (Deut 14:1). The problem obviously is that "slash themselves at the brothel" makes little sense on first hearing. Both *V* and *S* evidently reflect this verb; they assume a violent meaning—"they fought" or "rioted" at the brothel. *T* tries to derive the verb from the root connected with גְּדוּד "a troop," and Rashi and Qimḥi follow this interpretation, as do most commentators and translators who stay with this verb (*RSV*: "they trooped to the houses of harlots"). The problem is that the verb with this meaning has no clear occurrence elsewhere, and it does have strong attestation in the meaning "slash oneself," an action which is specifically associated with Baal worship (1 Kgs 18:28): indeed Jrm might well have this incident in mind. Zech 13:6 seems to have the same kind of reference.

The point of v 7b is the tension between images for literal sexual misconduct and images for the religious orientation of the people. The first verb, "fed full," occurs almost invariably with God as subject: clearly the reference here is to Yahweh's blessing on the people. The words "and they committed adultery" and "in a brothel" are references to literal sexual misconduct, so that chiastically one expects the last element in the bicolon to refer to religious orientation, and this is what one hears: a verb referring to Baal worship. The phrase then means not that men "troop," or "riot," or "lodge" at a brothel, but that their Baal worship results in nothing but a vast whorehouse. The center of gravity of the bicolon then is on theological prostitution, not on prostitution per se.

This tension between sexual misconduct and religious orientation evidently continues in v 8. For the moment let us bypass the two adjectives describing the "stallions." The people are said to be "stallions neighing each for his neighbor's wife." The verb "neigh" (צהל) turns up elsewhere in Jrm's poetry in association with "adultery" and other references to fertility-cult worship (13:27), and since the verb can also be used of ecstatic cries in (legitimate) worship (31:7), Jrm doubtless refers here to the ecstatic cries of Baal worshipers. But horses do not mate for life, so that "each stallion neighing for his neighbor's wife" is nonsense. Indeed the stallions cannot be expected to control themselves, any more than the female wild ass could (2:24), so that Jrm forces the hearer to think about human adultery, and past it to theological adultery—all utterly irresponsible.

Now the adjectives to describe the stallions! Both are unique words in the OT. Though *G* offers only one rendering ($\theta\eta\lambda\upsilon\mu\alpha\nu\epsilon\hat{i}s$, "mad for the female"), both words should be retained (note that the young camel in 2:23b also has two modifiers). The other Versions follow *G* in assuming that the descriptions are of sexual desire, but the translations appear to be guesswork (*V*: "paramours and stud-horses"; *S*: "stud-horses, lustful"; *T* obscure). Rudolph follows this lead, declaring that both attributes mean "ruttish."[15]

The first word has two readings; the Oriental reading and Occidental qere' is מְיֻזָּנִים; the Occidental ketib reads מוּזָנִים. The latter reading would be a hop'al participle of זון "feed," a verb otherwise known in postbiblical Hebrew as well as in Aramaic and Syriac; this is the reading that gives rise to the traditional translation "fed (horses)" (*KJV*); so Cornill, Giesebrecht, Volz, Condamin. The former reading would be a pual participle of יזן, but the question is what that root means. Long ago Albert Schultens (eighteenth century)[16] suggested a cognate in the Arabic *wazana* "weigh," therefore "heavy" (of testicles); so Duhm.

The second attribute מַשְׁכִּים is even more puzzling. Jerome in his commentary favors the vocalization מֹשְׁכִים "dragging" (i.e., the phallus), comparing the expression to Ezek 23:20, and this interpretation is preferred by Michaelis, but has fallen out of favor. In the meantime *KJV* accepted the interpretation of the medieval Jewish exegetes to construe the word as if from מַשְׁכִּימִים "(rising early) in the morning." Hermann Arnheim[17] and Heinrich Graetz[18] suggested in the nineteenth century that the form was a contraction for מַאֲשְׁכִים, a hip'il participle, "those displaying אֲשָׁכִים, testicles," and this has been accepted by Duhm, Cornill, Condamin, and Rudolph. But the omission of the 'alep is dubious.

Jastrow's solution for both words seems to me best.[19] There is one significant occurrence of the participle מְיֻזָּן in the Talmud, namely in *b. Giṭ.* 67a, where Rabbi

Yishmael was characterized as being a חָנוּת מְיוּזֶּנֶת "well-stocked shop," so that the participle means "equipped, supplied" (evidently יון is a by-form of זון). The stallions will then be "equipped" or "attrapped." As for מַשְׁכִּים, he points out that this can be construed as the plural of a gentilic מָשְׁכִּי, pertaining to מֶשֶׁךְ "Meshech," a people and region in Anatolia.[20] It is implied in Ezek 27:13–14; 38:3–4 that Meshech, Tubal, and Togarmah are regions producing war-horses, and this fact is amply documented in Assyrian sources.[21] The phrase here will then be "attrapped stallions of Meshech," and the Masoretic vocalization as well as the consonantal text will be correct. If this understanding is sound, the attributes of the stallions in this colon are not sexual; the sexual reference comes only in the second colon. War-horses become aroused and excited when ready for battle (compare 8:6); if this interpretation is correct, Jrm is associating martial excitement with sexual excitement.

■ **9** This refrain is repeated identically in v 29 and with the variant אֶפְקָד־בָּם in 9:8; there is some MS. evidence for that variant here and in 5:29 as well (see Text), and Volz and Rudolph wish to accommodate both passages to 9:8. There are two interrelated issues here, that of text and that of the meaning of the prepositions עַל and בְּ. As to the text, *G*, *V*, and *S* have identical translations in 5:9, 29, and 9:8; there is no evidence of בָּם at any point (*T* is periphrastic). One wonders then how secure the addition of בָּם is, and whether it radically shifts the meaning of the clause. As to the meaning of the prepositions, the lexica assume that עַל governs the sin and (when dealt with) that בְּ in 9:8 governs the person (and the translations reflect this; *RSV*: "Shall I not punish them for

15 Rudolph, p. 38.
16 Albert Schultens, cited in Michaelis, 50.
17 Hermann Arnheim, *Grammatik der hebräischen Sprache* (Berlin: Gerschel, 1872) 139.
18 Heinrich Graetz, *Emendationes in plerosque Sacrae Scripturae Veteris Testamenti libros* (Fasc. 1; Breslau: Schlesische Buchdruckerei, 1892) 41.
19 Marcus Jastrow, "Jeremiah 5:8," *AJSL* 13 (1896/97)

216–17.
20 Machteld J. Mellink, "Meshech," *IDB* 3:357–58.
21 See Zimmerli, *Ezekiel 2*, 66, on 27:13–14. Assurbanipal speaks several times of the tribute of large horses laid on Mugallu, king of Tabal: see Luckenbill, *ARAB*, 297, sec. 781; 325, sec. 848; and 352, sec. 911. Note also Morris Jastrow, Jr., "Mešek and Tabal," *AJSL* 13 (1896/97), 217.

these things?").[22] But in an overwhelming number of instances of this verb עַל is used with the person (eleven times in Jer: 9:24; 11:22; 21:14; 23:34; 27:8; 29:32; 30:20; 44:13, 29; 46:25; 51:44), and in two of these (27:8; 44:13) בְּ occurs as well, followed by the punishment; and there are further instances from other books. Given the parallelism of "a nation like this" in the second colon, it would seem far better to understand עַל־אֵלֶּה to mean "with these (folk)"; the addition of בָּם in 9:8, if valid, would suggest "by these (offenses/punishments)" (compare Interpretation of 2:17; 4:18; and see further 9:8).

The parallelism of פקד and נקם is found also in 11:20, 22, and 15:15; the range of these words is not simple to state. George E. Mendenhall makes clear[23] that נקם, far from meaning "avenge," has to do with Yahweh's exercise of legitimate sovereignty: here Yahweh calls his own people a גוי ("nation" like other nations) and says he will treat Judah just as he is accustomed to treating the rest of the world, by enforcing law and order upon them. There is no talk here of grace or of special concern; Judah is long past that. Judah is cast adrift in a world of nations.[24] And the hitpaʻel stem here suggests "for Yahweh's benefit"; Mendenhall: "gain satisfaction."

The verb פקד has a wide range of meanings; here it means "deal with" or "take care of" (for reward or punishment as the occasion demands). Amos, in a well-known passage (3:2), represents Yahweh as declaring that he would "take care of you [Israel] for all your iniquities." The Decalogue indicates that Yahweh will "deal with" the children to the third and fourth generation for the sins of the fathers (Exod 20:5). Jrm's verse then offers rhetorical questions that suggest an answer to the rhetorical question of v 7: "How can I pardon her?" I cannot, for "with these folk shall I not deal, and upon a nation like this shall my soul not gain satisfaction?" ("My soul" as a circumlocution for "I" occurs in the mouth of God rather frequently in Jer: compare 6:8.)

Aim

There are many surprises in these verses. What sounds like a barked military command by Yahweh quickly becomes a search for an honest man in Jerusalem (v 1), so that he might pardon her as he might have pardoned Sodom of old. Jrm for his part marvels at the intransigence of his people but tries to excuse it on the ground that poor people do not know any better (v 4). But the leaders themselves are no better, and Jrm sees wild animals tearing them apart. Yahweh replies that they are nothing more than stallions pawing for the fight, indeed frantic for mates (v 8), so that he has little choice but to pronounce sentence (v 9).

The end of the new covenant passage (31:33–34) will offer several echoes of this passage. Whereas now each male neighs for his neighbor's wife, then no one will need to teach his neighbor; whereas now the people do not know the law of their God, neither poor nor great, then the law will be written on the heart so that they will all know God, from the least of them to the greatest; whereas there is little hope now that Yahweh will pardon Israel, then he will pardon their sins. If we are to understand the new covenant in chapter 31 as a description of Yahweh's solution in the future to the present tangle between himself and Israel, then we must understand the present passage as a central description of that tangle.

---

22   Thus BDB, 823b, line 5; *HALAT*, 901a, line 25.
23   Mendenhall, *Tenth Generation*, 97–98.
24   See Ephraim A. Speiser, "'People' and 'Nation' of Israel," *JBL* 79 (1960) 157–63; Ronald E. Clements, "גוי," *TDOT* 2:427–31.

Jeremiah Will Mediate
the Fire of Yahweh
on the Nation

Bibliography
Lundbom
Jeremiah, 39–41.
Meyer
Jeremia, 85–93.
Schmuttermayr, Georg
"Beobachtungen zu Jer 5,13," *BZ* Neue Folge 9 (1965) 215–32.
Sutcliffe, Edmund F.
"A Note on לא הוא Jer 5,12," *Bib* 41 (1960) 287–90.
Westermann
Basic Forms, 169–76.

5

10 Yahweh: **Climb through her terraces and destroy,**
and [do not][a] **make a full end,**
take away her shoots,
for they are not Yahweh's,

11 **for the household of Israel [and the**
household of Judah][a] **did betray**
me,

oracle of Yahweh.

12 Jeremiah: **They have denied Yahweh**
and have said, "He is nothing!"
"Disaster shall not come upon us!"
and "We will not see sword and
famine!"

13 Yahweh, to Jeremiah:
But the prophets shall become wind,
and revelation[a] **is not in them,**
⟨scorching⟩[b] **《 it shall become 》**[c] **to**
them!

(14a) **[. . . .**
. . . .][a]

14b **I am going to make my words in your**
mouth into fire,
and this people into sticks, and it will
eat them.

14a Jeremiah:
《 Therefore thus Yahweh God of hosts has
said:
Yahweh, to people:
Inasmuch as you speak this word, 》[a]

15 **I am going to bring upon you a nation**
from afar, [O household of Israel,][a]

Text

10a Omit אֵל־ as a secondary mitigating gloss (so Rudolph; Hyatt: "probably"). There are several considerations. (1) The context of the second half of v 10b ("Remove her shoots, for they are not Yahweh's") denotes a message of total destruction; Bright's attempt to assume that v 10a refers to pruning founders on this fact. Note that the inconcinnity of "do not make a full end" and v 10b cause *G* and *S* to understand "remove" as "leave" and to omit the negative in the last colon ("leave her supports/foundations, for they are Yahweh's"). (2) Verse 18, another mitigating gloss, is cogent only if the present text lacked the negative. I propose that 30:11 (where the negative is original) encouraged the reconception of 4:27 (see there) and the insertion of the negative here. For another inserted אֵל־ see 18:18.

11a The bracketed words overload the colon and are an expansionist gloss (so Volz and Rudolph; so also *JB*). The antecedent for this verse is evidently 3:20, where only "household of Israel" appears.

13a Some MSS. read וְהַדִּבֵּר "and the word," but וְהַדִּבֵּר is the *lectio difficilior*; *G* καὶ λόγος κυρίου "the word of the Lord."

b Reading כֹּה for M כֹּה "thus," as Volz and Rudolph do in 23:29, a similar context (see there; and see further Structure and Form, and Interpretation).

c Reading יִהְיֶה with *G* and *V* for M יֵעָשֶׂה "shall be done." As to *V eveniet*, it is to be noted that Jerome uses *evenio* to render היה "happen" elsewhere (e.g., 2 Kgs 7:20), while his standard equivalent for עשה nip'al is *fio*. See further Preliminary Observations, Interpretation.

14a Shifting v 14a after v 14b; the words were evidently omitted by haplography (two occurrences of הִנְנִי) and reinserted before the first הִנְנִי instead of the second: see Structure and Form.

15a Delete (with Volz) as a gloss. A vocative cannot alone make up a colon (against *NAB*), nor can an

oracle of Yahweh,
 it is a perennial nation,
  it is a nation from long ago,
   a nation whose tongue you do not
    know,
    whose speech you do not under-
     stand;

16 his quiver is like an open tomb,
 《he destroys more than locusts;》[a]

17 and he will eat your harvest and your
  food,
  [a] he will eat[a] your sons and your
    daughters,
   he will eat your flock and your herd,
    he will eat your vine and your fig-
     tree,
 he will shatter your fortified cities,
  in which you trust, [with a sword.][b]

object and a vocative make up a colon (against Rudolph, Bright, and *JB*). The words are doubtless taken from v 11, an insertion to identify the audience after v 14a was misplaced. See Structure.

16a   Emending to כָּלֹה מְגוֹבִים; *M* כֻּלָּם גִּבּוֹרִים, "all of them are champions." The plural "all of them" jars with the singular "his" in the first colon and with the continued third singular references in v 17, and the phrase, though itself plausible, is slack in parallelism and lacks specificity. The emendation is an adaptation from the suggestion of Bruno, כֻּלּוֹ מְגוֹבִים or כֻּלּוֹ מְגֵבִים (Arvid Bruno, *Jeremiah, Eine rhythmische Untersuchung* [Stockholm: Almqvist & Wiksell, 1954] 252). The suggestion would bring כָּלֹה into the orbit of כָּלָה "full end" in v 10 and the image of locusts prepares the way for the repetitive "eat" in v 17. It is also noteworthy that there is the close association of "fire" and "locusts" in Amos 7:1–6 and of "fire," "eat" and "locusts" in Nah 3:15–17; indeed Amos 7:1 has גֹּבַי and 7:2 has כִּלָּה לֶאֱכוֹל.

17a—a   *M* for this one verb is יֹאכְלוּ "they shall eat"; read the singular with one MS., *V* and *S*.

   b   Omit as a gloss (so Volz and Rudolph); the word is out of place in this colon.

Structure and Form

Extent of Unit. The commentators vary where they place the boundaries of the units in this chapter. Volz and Hyatt, having perceived a unit in vv 1–14, see vv 15–17 as a new unit. Rudolph, having found units in vv 1–6 and 7–11, sees another unit in vv 12–17. Condamin carries a unit from vv 10 to 18 (seeing in "not a full end" an inclusio).

Both vv 18 and 19 are prose extensions and are not integral with the poetry that precedes. It is clear that there is a shift of speaker from vv 10–11 (Yahweh) to v 12 (Jrm), and it is also clear (if the present order of v 14a and 14b is left untouched) that there is a shift of audience from v 14b (Jrm) to v 15 (the people); these discontinuities elicit the various analyses already cited. But against these discontinuities are two considerations. (1) Verse 10 begins with a series of imperatives; so do vv 20–21a. It has already been suggested that this is a mark of the beginning of each unit in the oracles on the foe from the north within chapters 4—10 (see 4:5—10:25, Preliminary Observations, *The Units of 4:5—10:25*). (2) Verse 14b implies the destruction of the people by fire; so does v 13, if the emendation of v 13b is accepted. Verse 10 likewise implies the destruction of the people (particularly if the negative is excised in v 10a). Verse 12, offering the diction of the optimistic prophets, resembles

14:13 closely, and 14:1—15:9 have a secure setting in the time the king burned the scroll and Jrm perceived Yahweh to be announcing irrevocable judgment. Verses 15–17 are not alien to this setting. In short, the evidence suggests that vv 10–17 are a unit with a striking set of shifts of speaker and audience appropriate to the needs of the hour. (For ways in which the passage is united, see below, *Internal Structure*.)

Placement of Unit. See 4:5—10:25, Preliminary Observations, *Structural Organization of the Sequence of Units*.

Speaker, Audience, and Form. Verses 10–11 are spoken by Yahweh. This is clear even if one disregards the rubric "oracle of Yahweh" at the end of v 11. Thus one has the first-person reference "me" in v 11 (and this takes precedence over the third-person reference to "Yahweh" in v 10: one has the same situation of shift between first and third person as in 2:2–3). The audience (plural) would appear to be the heavenly court (compare vv 1–9, Form). The command to destroy the covenant people (v 10) here serves implicitly as an announcement of judgment; v 11 then gives the reason for the judgment.

In v 12 one again has a third-person reference to Yahweh. Who speaks here: does it continue to be Yahweh, or is it Jrm reporting (or complaining) to Yahweh? "They" are specifically the optimistic prophets (compare 14:13; 23:17), so that there is a modest shift from "the household of Israel" (v 11). Of the two parallel verses just cited, 14:13 is clearly spoken by Jrm, and though the rubric at the beginning of 23:16 suggests that 23:17 is spoken by Yahweh, the analysis given there indicates that the rubric is a false secondary addition and that in fact Jrm speaks vv 16–20 (see 23:16–20, Structure and Form). One concludes that v 12 here is spoken by Jrm. Given the fact that v 13 will be assigned to Yahweh and linked with v 14b, wherein Jrm is addressed, one cannot call v 12 a "rebuke" (as Rudolph does: *Scheltrede*); it is rather a prophetic report (or complaint) to Yahweh. One other question must be dealt with here: Does the verse contain one quotation or more than one? Commentators who punctuate either carry a single quotation to the end of the verse (Bright) or carry the quotation through the end of v 13 (on which see below). But "Disaster shall not come upon us" is found in Mic 3:11 (and, with adjustment for person, in Jer 23:17); "We shall not see sword and famine" is found (with adjustments) in 14:13; "He is nothing" is found nowhere else. Given these scattered parallels and given the occurrence elsewhere of more than one quotation from a speaker within a single verse (4:20), I propose three quotations here.

Assuming the validity of the emendations proposed here for v 13b, the whole of v 13 must be understood as spoken by Yahweh; the "scorching" anticipates the "fire" of v 14b. The verse thus begins Yahweh's answer to Jrm and does not (as Volz, Rudolph, and others have assumed) continue the quotational material of v 12. The word of v 14b (and thus of v 13) is reassurance to Jrm, an announcement of divine intervention, which is at the same time an announcement of judgment on the people[1] (for the rearrangement of the two halves of v 14, see Text).

Verse 14a begins an address of Yahweh to the people, an announcement of divine punishment that continues through v 17. It is proclaimed by Jrm: v 14aα is the messenger formula. Verse 14aβ begins the divine speech proper, offering the immediate reason for the Yahweh's activity ("inasmuch as you speak this word"). Verses 15–17 are the announcement of punishment, here modeled on a traditional curse (Lev 26:16; Deut 28:30–33). The curious shift from second plural in vv 14a + 15a to second singular in vv 15b and 17 may have been an effort to distinguish the people in v 14a + 15a from Jrm in v 14b, but it is impossible to be sure: see further Interpretation, vv 15–17.

Internal Structure of the Passage. The foregoing analysis of speaker, audience, and form of the successive verses indicates that the passage falls into three sections: (1) Yahweh's speech (to the heavenly host?), vv 10–11; (2) Jrm's complaint to Yahweh, and Yahweh's response, vv 12, 13 + 14b; and (3) Jrm's proclamation of Yahweh's announcement to the people of punishment, vv 14a, 15–17. These three sections are united in several ways. They are united by the reference to a vine (vv 10, 17) and to "eating" (vv 14b, 17). But more substantially, each of the three subsections offers a shift from phrases in 2:3: "They are not Yahweh's" (v 10), "Disaster shall not come upon us" (v 12), and the enemy's "eating" of Israel (v 17) (for the details see Interpretation for each verse).

Verses 10–11 are to be analyzed as a tricolon (the commands) and a bicolon (the two כִּי clauses). Verse 12 offers four cola, either two bicola (reference to Yahweh, reference to "us") or a tetracolon. Verse 13 is a tricolon with interlocking parallelism ("prophets" and "revelation"; "in them" and "to them"). Verse 14b is a puzzle. Rudolph and Bright divide it into four cola, but this will not do: "in your mouth into fire" cannot stand alone, and it is the assumption of this study that a single word cannot stand alone ("and it will eat them"). It is a bicolon with complicated parallelism ("my words into fire" is parallel with "my people into sticks," and "eat" reflects "in your mouth"). Verse 14a, with the messenger formula and the divine statement of the reason for the punishment, offers no specific structure. Verse 15 can only be a pentacolon: the pattern here is almost exactly that of the last five cola in 2:6[2] (see Structure there for a discussion of "end-expansion"). Verse 16 is a bicolon. Verse 17a is a tetracolon with strong repetition (compare 50:35–38 and 51:20–23 for similar repetition). There is a hint of chiasmus in these cola, the outer two dealing with plant life, the inner two with livestock and children.[3] Verse 17b is a bicolon.

1 For the form criticism of vv 10–14 see Westermann, *Basic Forms*, 175.

2 See Holladay, *Architecture*, 61–62.

3 Lundbom, *Jeremiah*, 156 n. 80.

Setting

The setting for this passage proposed in the present study is soon after the king burned Jrm's first scroll in December 601. "Burning" was on his mind (v 14b), as was the issue of the optimistic prophets (vv 12–13) and his own role (v 14b). It was a time of drought in which the image of "eating" (v 17) is central. (For a more extended treatment of the setting of this and parallel passages, see above, 4:5—10:25, Preliminary Observations, *Settings*.)

Interpretation

■ **10–11** The first words, "Climb through her terraces," balance the first words of v 1, "Work through the streets of Jerusalem"; if the words of v 1 sound like an urban search-and-destroy mission, these words seem to be a rural counterpart.

The word here translated "terraces," שָׁרוֹת, occurs only here in the OT, and both it and the companion word "shoots" (נְטִישׁוֹת) gave trouble to the Versions (*G* "ramparts" and "supports" [buttresses?] respectively; *S* "walls" and "foundations" respectively; *T* "cities" and "palaces" respectively). *V* has the second word right but translates the first as "walls." Both *V* and *S* thus assume a relation to שׁוּר "wall." But there is now agreement that the word means "terraces" here. Conceivably the word is misvocalized and should be שֻׁרוֹת, thus related to שׁוּר,[4] but it is equally possible that it is related to the root שׁרר "be firm"; a pronunciation *šarrōteyhā* would go well with the following verb, pronounced *šaḥḥētū*.

The hill country of Judah is so broken up by little hillocks and wadis that terracing becomes the only practical way to prevent erosion and practice agriculture; terraces are particularly appropriate for rows of vines.[5] One of the tasks of the vinegrower in Isaiah's poem of the vineyard was to clear the fertile hill of stones (Isa 5:2): it is these stones that make up the terraces. Yahweh commands his audience to climb the terraces and then destroy. There is no mitigation in the latter verb, which appears again in 12:10, "Many shepherds have destroyed my vineyard."

The verb is reinforced by the next colon, "And make a full end" (omitting the negative; see Text). The noun

(כָּלָה) means "annihilation"; it occurs in *M* of 4:27, but evidently needs emendation there (see Text there); its occurrence in Ezek 11:13 offers a typical context. The third colon reinforces the command even more: the people are to remove even the "tendrils" or "shoots" of the vine. The diction here is likely to be dependent on Isa 18:5, "For before the harvest . . . the shoots he will remove, cut away"; the verb "take away" is not necessarily gentle.

The last colon of v 10 is literally "For they are not to Yahweh." It is the reverse of the situation in the first colon of 2:3, which is literally "Israel is holiness to Yahweh." In the honeymoon time Israel was loyal to Yahweh and was his possession, but that time is past. (Note that both cola refer to Yahweh in the third person, though they are in the midst of divine speeches; on this matter see 2:3.) For Israel as a vine, see 2:21.

For the phraseology of v 11, see the discussion in 3:20.

■ **12** Jrm responds to Yahweh's statement in v 11 by his own restatement of the same fact: "They have denied Yahweh." This is the only occurrence of the view כחש pi'el, though it occurs twice in Hosea; it refers to verbal rejection ("deny, disown"), though in Israel verbal rejection is always substantive rejection. The people, by denying him, are living as if he does not matter. The second colon says it: "They have said, 'He is nothing!'" The phrase לֹא־הוּא is uncertain of meaning. It is not theoretical or practical atheism, "He does not exist" (*NEB*), which would be אֵין־הוּא or אֵינֶנּוּ (Gen 5:24). Many translations, assuming that לֹא implies a verb, translate "He will do nothing" (*RSV*)—compare Zeph 1:12 "Yahweh will not do good, nor will he do ill"; but though this thought is implied, such a translation goes too far. Volz and Rudolph suggest "There is nothing to him," that is, he does not matter (Rudolph: *mit ihm ist's nichts*). Edmund F. Sutcliffe[6] suggests that הוּא is neuter and that the phrase means "It's not so," but the parallel implied with לוֹא לַיהוה (v 10) speaks against the suggestion. The present study accepts Dahood's proposal that לֹא is a noun, "nothing," translating "He is nothing";[7] Job 6:21 ketib implies such a meaning, and *HALAT* accepts the meaning in the latter passage.

"Disaster shall not come upon us" continues the

---

4 So KB.
5 For an analysis of ancient terracing in Judah see Gershon Edelstein and Mordechai Kislev, "Mevas- seret Yerushalayim: Ancient Terrace Farming," *BR* 44 (1981) 53–56; for terracing today see Baly, *Geography*, 116, 183.

variations on 2:3 to be found here: in that earlier passage disaster came upon those who ate of Israel; now the optimistic prophets and other complacent folk insist that no disaster will come upon them. But the colon is a direct quotation of Mic 3:11, where Micah is quoting the optimistic prophets of his own day. Jrm matches this quotation with another, "We will not see sword and famine" (compare 12:4 and 14:13).

■ **13** Some commentators (Volz, Condamin, Rudolph) have assumed that this verse continues the speech of Jrm, and that the words are a continuation of the quotational material in v 12 (so *RSV, NEB, JB, NAB, NJV*). By this understanding the "prophets" are those like Jrm whom the people hold in contempt. A difficulty with this view is the word order of the first colon of the verse: "the prophets" precedes the verb, so that a contrast is implied with what has come before. Other commentators (Bright, Thompson), though assuming that v 13 continues the speech of Jrm, close the quotational material with v 12; by this understanding the "prophets" are the optimistic prophets whom Jrm opposes. But if the emendation proposed here for the third colon of the verse (see Text) is correct, then the prophets are indeed the optimistic ones, but Yahweh is the speaker (see Structure and Form, *Speaker, Audience, and Form*).

The definite article with both "prophets" and "revelation" is almost demonstrative: "those prophets," "that revelation." "Wind" (רוּחַ, compare 4:11) often means "spirit": it is Yahweh's spirit which animated the prophets in early times (e.g., 1 Sam 10:6–10), and Ezekiel's diction revived the idea (Ezek 2:2 and often). Here, however, the meaning is turned around: those who claim to be filled with the spirit will become nothing but wind. If the noun of the second colon is correctly vocalized (הַדִּבֵּר) and not (with Condamin, KB) to be emended to הַדָּבָר, then it carries the meaning found in postbiblical Hebrew, "revelation." The word of Yahweh is not in them (*G*).

The last colon, if here correctly emended, evidently implies that "it" (that is, the revelation) "will become scorching to them"; that is to say, the colon continues the theme of ironic reversal implied in the first colon: revelation, which should go outward to bring insight to others, instead will backfire and burn the erstwhile

prophets. The verb proposed here, כוה qal, does not occur in the qal in *M*, but it is proposed by Volz and Rudolph in the same context in 23:29 and occurs in the qal in postbiblical Hebrew.

■ **14** This verse, as it stands in *M*, needs repair: the shift from second plural, addressing the people (v 14a), to second singular, addressing Jrm (v 14b), is implausible. The solution proposed by Duhm and accepted by Cornill, Volz, Condamin, Rudolph, and Bright, to emend "you speak" (דִּבֶּרְכֶם) in v 14a to "they speak" (דִּבְּרָם) does not explain how such a strange reading arose. The best solution is to assume a haplography with הִנְנִי (vv 14b, 15) in which v 14b dropped out and was reinserted after v 14a instead of before it (see Text).

■ **14b** Yahweh continues to address Jrm. The first colon, "I am going to make my words in your mouth into fire" (הִנְנִי נֹתֵן דְּבָרַי בְּפִיךָ לְאֵשׁ), is an extension of the words of his call in 1:9, "Look, I have put my words in your mouth." Those words in 1:9 were to have both a destructive and a constructive effect (1:10). But the occasion here is one for destruction only, and the image of God's word as fire (implied in the emended text of v 13 here) will recur: the word like fire or a hammer to smash rocks (23:29), the fire in the bones (20:9).

The plural עֵצִים indicates sticks for firewood (compare 7:18, which also offers a plural); the usual translation "wood" suggests the material only. Is there a continuity with the imagery of the vine in v 10? The vine which is the people is to be broken up into pieces of fuel, to be consumed by the fire of Yahweh's word in Jrm's mouth. Yahweh's word is an accomplishing word (Isa 50:10–11). It is ironic that a mouth, which should eat food, should instead hold the fire which eats something else.

■ **14a** By the understanding of the present study, this half-verse begins Yahweh's judgment word to the people, and Jrm begins it with the messenger formula, the first time the full formula is found in Jer (for "Yahweh of hosts" see 2:19, and for "Thus Yahweh has said" see 2:2). One has the impression therefore of a particularly solemn opening to the speech, and that impression is reinforced by the opening word of the speech proper, יַעַן, here translated "inasmuch as." The word is not common in Jer,[8] though it is more frequent in Isaiah and

6   Edmund F. Sutcliffe, "A Note on לא הרא Jer 5,12," *Bib* 41 (1960) 287–90.

7   Dahood, *Psalms II,* 371–72, with other proposed

occurrences.

8   When followed by an infinitive, only here, in 7:13; 23:38; and 48:7.

Ezekiel. Paul Joüon remarks that it is used in "lofty style,"[9] and Donald E. Gowan has analyzed its occurrences form-critically:[10] it introduces a description of the human action which is the reason for a forthcoming divine activity. "This word" of course refers to the words of v 12, but ironically it reflects "the revelation" in v 13 and "this people" in v 14b.

■ **15–17** These verses take the image of "eating" (v 14b) and use it not of fire but of the nation from afar; behind this sequence of thought may lie Isa 5:24–26, which first describes a consuming fire and then the nation from afar.

The text traditions offer inconsistencies in the second-person references in this speech. *M* offers a second plural in v 15a and a second singular in the verbs of v 15b, and then consistent second singulars again in v 17; and *V, S,* and *T* all reflect this shift. But while *G* reflects the shift in v 15, it reverts to second plural in v 17. The parallel material in Deut 28:49, 51–52 uses second singular throughout. Given these data there is no way to be sure how the inconsistencies evolved (for a further suggestion see Structure and Form, *Speaker, Audience, and Form*).

■ **15** Indeed the concision and repetition of images in v 15 reminds one of Isa 5:27. For "afar" (מֵרָחָק) see 4:16. The word אֵיתָן is found again in Jer only in the twice-repeated phraseology of 49:19; 50:44; it means "steady, perennial," being used in the phrase "ever-flowing stream" (Amos 5:24). For "from long ago" see 2:20. One wonders if the repeated הוּא ("he," translated here "it") does not echo לֹא־הוּא in v 12: if the people persist in saying "He is nothing," then a "he" will be brought upon them who will truly be something!

Fearsome descriptions of the enemy are found in Deut 28:49–52; Isa 5:26–29; 28:11; 33:19; and Hab 1:6–11, stressing the distance from which they come, the strangeness of their language, their swiftness and brutality. One could imagine that Jrm had at least Isa 5:26–29; 28:11; and Hab 1:6–11 in mind, but descriptions like this were doubtless traditional stereotypes.[11] It is utterly terrifying to be subjected to the barked orders

of military invaders which are incomprehensible.

■ **16** The first colon is an odd phrase. Volz and Rudolph therefore emend "his quiver" (אַשְׁפָּתוֹ) to "whose mouth" (אֲשֶׁר פִּיהוּ) in the light of Ps 5:10. That emendation is reinforced slightly by the rendering of *S,* "his throat," and if the emendation of the second colon is correct, the mention of locusts (to say nothing of the repeated "eat" in v 17) makes a mention of "mouth" here plausible. But the phrase should not be emended; Jrm had another perception. The quiver of the enemy, which normally gives forth arrows, yawns like an open tomb. A tomb lies open to receive the dead. Where are the dead? Where are the arrows from that quiver? Are they already flying through the air? Why does the quiver have to be so big, how many arrows has it held, how many men will have to die?

The terrible answer is in the second colon, "He destroys more than locusts" (for the emendation see Text). After locusts have come through the land, there is nothing left; such will be the fate of the victims of the invading nation.

■ **17** The enemy will eat everything in sight. If "they are not Yahweh's" in v 10 reflects "Israel has been Yahweh's possession" in 2:3, then the image here of the enemy's eating everything that belongs to Israel is the opposite of the situation in 2:3 in which everyone who ate of Israel was punished. The image of the enemy's eating what belongs to the people is old: compare Isa 1:7, "Aliens devour your land."

The last half of the verse reverts to the military image of v 16b. The pol'el stem of רשש ("shatter") does not appear otherwise in the OT, though the pu'al does, in Mal 1:4. For "fortified cities" see 4:5. Earlier prophets had offered words of scorn for the way in which Israel "trusted" (בטח) in military preparedness (Isa 31:1; Hos 10:13).

Aim

Jrm has here adapted the classic judgment against the

9 *Style revelé*: Joüon, *Gramm.,* 522–23.
10 Donald E. Gowan, "The use of *yaʿan* in Biblical Hebrew," *VT* 21 (1971), 168–85; compare also Martin J. Mulder, "Die Partikel יַעַן," *Syntax and Meaning: Studies in Hebrew Syntax and Biblical Exegesis* (*OTS* 18; Leiden: Brill, 1973) 49–83, esp. 53–56.
11 Gottfried Seitz, *Redaktionsgeschichtliche Studien zum Deuteronomium* (BWANT 93; Stuttgart: Kohlhammer, 1971) 295–97.

nation: a formal set of speeches that make up the description of the offense and the announcement of Yahweh's punishment. Israel has been Yahweh's vine: now Yahweh commands its destruction. And here Jrm serves no longer as a representative of Israel, doing his best to find some mitigating feature within the life of the community by which to urge the forbearance of Yahweh (see vv 4–5); now he is the agent of Yahweh in effecting the punishment. The people have been led hopelessly astray by the false prophets, who are reduced to empty wind, while Jrm is being equipped to mediate the fire of Yahweh, the fire of the word of punishment. Suddenly that word comes forth, an avalanche of phrases describing the nation from afar who will consume all the life of the nation. The decision has been made, and there is no hope of staying the execution of that decision.

Two Brief Reflections
on Judgment

Bibliography
Long
  "Schemata," 129–39.
Skweres, Dieter E.
  "Das Motiv der Strafgrunderfragung in biblischen
  und neuassyrischen Texten," *BZ* NF 14 (1970)
  181–97.

5

18   [But even in those days, oracle of Yahweh,
     I will not make of you a full end.]ᵃ

19   And when 《 they say, 》ᵃ "For what (offense)
     has Yahweh our God done all these
     things to us?" then you shall say to them:
     Just as you abandoned me and served
     alien gods in your land, so shall you serve
     strangers in a land not yours.

Text

18a   These words are a later gloss: see Setting, Form,
     Interpretation.

19a   Reading יאמרו with the commentators for *M*
     תאמרו "you say"; the verb needs to agree with
     אֲלֵיהֶם. The present text is doubtless influenced by
     אִתְּכֶם in v 18.

Setting

The setting of these two verses must be settled before a
consideration of form, and v 19 must be dealt with first.
Verse 19 is a reflection on the terrible words of vv 10–17
which are evidently genuine to Jrm. One notes first the
unique expression תַּחַת מֶה, which may be ironic, and the
possible double meaning of "strangers"; on these see
Interpretation. Further the mind-set of the answer in v
19 is analogous to that in 16:13: in the present passage it
is hinted (as it is said explicitly in 16:13) that the people
will have to serve alien gods in exile. The present study
finds 16:10–13 to be authentic to Jrm and proposes a
setting in the context of Jehoiachin's exile, in 598 or
soon thereafter; the same setting is appropriate here.

The setting of v 18 is one in which it was appropriate
to mitigate the terrible finality of vv 10–17. It reflects a
text of v 10 without the negative now present: the
terrible weight of Yahweh's judgment lay upon the
people, and the question must have been severe whether
the word of v 10 was the last word from Yahweh. There
was, however, the counterbalancing perception that the
people were not quite destroyed and the conviction that
Yahweh did not intend them to be (a conviction reinforced by 30:11). This word of mitigation is inserted
here as a current word from Yahweh. A setting early in
the exilic period is appropriate.

It is therefore not legitimate to argue the inauthenticity of v 19 (as Rudolph, Hyatt, and Bright do) because
of the inauthenticity of v 18.

Form

Each verse is form-critically distinct. Verse 18 is a brief
proclamation of salvation (*Heilsankündigung*). Verse 19 is
the first example in Jer of a question-and-answer schema
couched as an oracle from Yahweh to the prophet with a
prescribed answer (Burke O. Long's "Type B");[1] other
examples of this type are 13:12–14; 15:1–4; 16:10–13;
23:33; Ezek 21:12; and 37:19, and, more distantly, Jer
9:11–15; 23:37–40 (*G*); Ezek 12:9–12; and 24:19–21.
An oft-quoted extrabiblical parallel is one found in the
annals of Ashurbanipal, but that conforms more closely
to Long's "Type A," a narrative (for which see 22:8–9,
Form).

Interpretation

■ **19** The expression תַּחַת מֶה "for what (offense)" is unique
in the OT; the nearest parallel in an interrogative
context is perhaps 2 Sam 19:22: "Shall not Shimei be put
to death for this (הֲתַחַת זֹאת), that he cursed Yahweh's
anointed?" The preposition תַּחַת, which normally means
"under," appears here meaning "in exchange for, in
return for." The expected question instead in this
question-and-answer scheme is עַל־מֶה "because of what?"
(16:10); it is to be noted that the spatial meaning of the

---

1   Long, "Schemata," 134–39.

latter preposition ("over") is the opposite of what appears in the present verse. It is conceivable that there is a nuance here that everything is turned upside down, but it is more likely that it is a reminiscence of the phraseology of Huldah's reply to the delegation from the temple (2 Kgs 22:17): there the conjunction תַּחַת אֲשֶׁר introduces the phrases "they have abandoned me and sacrificed to other gods," diction which is close enough to the present passage to suggest a connection.

The answer to be given falls into three phrases; one might display the answer as poetry (compare 1:16). Cornill, Volz, Rudolph, and Janzen[2] omit "abandoned me and" with G, but this is not acceptable: it would mean construing the first occurrence of the imperfect תַּעַבְדוּ as a present (thus "just as you serve alien gods in your land"), but the pattern of 16:11 is that the imperfect for "serve" there is waw-consecutive, and "abandoned" also occurs in that verse.

The phrase "alien gods" (אֱלֹהֵי נֵכָר) does not otherwise occur in Jer, though the synonymous "alien vanities" (הַבְלֵי נֵכָר) does (8:19); but the phrase is typical of "E" (Gen 35:2, 4) and other early material. One may suspect here the immediate influence of Deut 32:12 (אֵל נֵכָר), in

that "strangers" (זָרִים) occurs in Deut 32:16 with the meaning of "strange gods"; it likewise occurs in Jer 2:25 with the same implication. Further, the parallel in 16:13, which is explicitly "you will serve other gods (in a strange land)," implies that "strangers" here betokens "strange gods." On the other hand, it is just as clear that "strangers" here may mean "strange masters" (as in 30:8), and the verb "serve" (עבד) may take as object either a deity or a human master. It is a nice double meaning. One also notes the assonance of עבד with עזב "abandon."

Aim

These two verses represent two reactions to the appalling news set forth in vv 10–17. Verse 19 deals with the people's inevitable question "why?" which the word of Yahweh's judgment elicits; v 18, on the other hand, affirms that his judgment, though severe, will not be total annihilation. Both verses offer indications of the integrity of the people over against the horrors of their historical experience, the sense that they must comprehend what is going on and must hear an affirmation of hope for the future.

---

2   Janzen, p. 36.

The Rich Oppress the Poor

Bibliography

Emerton, John A.
"Notes on Some Problems in Jeremiah v 26," *Mélanges bibliques et orientaux en l'honneur de M. Henri Cazelles* (ed. André Caquot and Matthias Delcor; AOAT 212; Neukirchen: Neukirchener, 1981) 125–33.

Gaster, Theodor H.
"Jeremiah v. 28," *ExpTim* 56 (1944–45) 54.

Holladay
Architecture, 88–89.

Tawil, Hayim
"Hebrew צלח/הצלח Akkadian *ešēru/šūšuru*: A Lexicographical Note," *JBL* 95 (1976) 405–13, esp. 409–11.

Thomas, D. Winton
"Jeremiah v. 28," *ExpTim* 57 (1945–46) 54–55.

Wisser
pp. 41–64.

5

20 Declare this in the household of Jacob,
and announce it in Judah:

21 "Just hear this,
(you) stupid and senseless people,
who have eyes but do not see,
who have ears but do not hear:

22 Me do you not fear?
oracle of Yahweh,
and in my presence do you not tremble?
(I) who have set the sand as a bound for the sea,
a limit forever, and it shall not pass away for it:
《its waters》[a] are convulsed, but they shall not prevail,
and its waves roar, but they shall not pass over it.

23 But this people has had a stubborn [and rebellious][a] heart,
they have turned and gone away,

24 and have not said in their heart,
[a] 'Let us just fear[a] Yahweh our God,
who gives rain [[(both)[c] early rain and latter rain][b] in its season,

Text

22a Restoring as subject of the plural verbs the noun מֵימָיו, which I propose has dropped out of the text; this is a possibility suggested by Bright. *G* and *S* offer singular verbs here, and Rudolph accepts those as original, assuming the plurals arose by dittography. To the contrary I propose that the singular verbs are a secondary correction of the text. Condamin wishes to transfer גַּלָּיו "its waves" to the preceding colon. This is a good solution, but I suggest that the emendation proposed here is more plausible: note that the verb געש occurs in 46:7 with מֵימָיו as subject. The noun, if restored, would fit the consonant pattern nicely, giving a verb with *g* and a subject with *m* in this colon, and in the following a parallel verb with *m* and a subject with *g*.

23a Omitting וּמוֹרֶה with Rudolph. The adjective is a gloss from Deut 21:18, 20, and Ps 78:8 and overloads the colon (by the constrictions defined by Michael Patrick O'Connor, *Structure*, 75, 87, a colon cannot contain more than five "units" [roughly, words], and היה counts as a unit, p. 299).

24a—a The form נִירָא must be construed as a cohortative, as both *G* and *V* indicate: in III—'alep verbs the cohortative in *-â* is avoided (Joüon, *Gramm.*, 307 n. 1).

b The words יֹרֶה וּמַלְקוֹשׁ must be omitted with Rudolph (who cites Johann Wilhelm Rothstein's judgment that the words are a "pedantic gloss"); for the prefixed וּ see below, c. They were perhaps inserted as antecedents to אלה in v 25 when the latter was read as אֵלֶּה. The phrase is found in Deut

25   **[weeks of]ᵈ fixed times of harvest he**
keeps for us.´

25   **Your iniquities have extended ⟨a curse,⟩ᵃ**
and your sins have withheld the bounty
from you.

26   **Indeed among my people criminals are**
found;
⟨they seize goods;
like fowlers⟩ᵃ they set up a raiding-
party,
men they catch.

27   **Like a basket full of birds,**
so their houses are full of fraud;
that is how they have grown great and
rich,

28   **ᵃ grown fat, grown sleek.ᵃ**
Further ⟪they have vouched for⟫ᵇ the
claims of the wrongdoer,
⟪so that they make successful⟫ᶜ

11:14 with "in its season" (בְּעִתּוֹ), and the two nouns are found (in reverse order) associated with גֶּשֶׁם ("rain") in Hos 6:3.

c   The ו of the ketib appears to be a still later attempt to smooth over the problem of the syntax. The Versions read the qere', without the conjunction.

d   שָׁבֻעוֹת is to be omitted with Rudolph. He suggests that it may be dittographic with the sequence of שבעת just preceding; on the other hand, given the unique meaning of חֻקּוֹת "fixed times" in this passage, the word could well be a gloss ("[feast of] weeks") on the following two words, understood as "ordinances of harvest" (compare Exod 34:22).

25a   Revocalizing אֵלֶּה "these" as אָלָה. For the same revocalization see 2:34; 4:12. The parallelism with "bounty" (הַטּוֹב) makes this reading appropriate; see Interpretation.

26a   *M* as vocalized is really incomprehensible: יָשׁוּר כְּשַׁךְ, "He shall watch like the abating of (?)." The Versions give no help; commentators have resorted to elaborate emendations (Bright gives up the effort). I propose to retain the consonants but to regroup them and vocalize as יַשּׁוּ רֶכֶשׁ פִּיקוּשִׁים, the verb being נשׁה hip'il. The meaning proposed for the verb ("seize") is not unambiguously extant in biblical Hebrew, though the by-form נשׁא hip'il in Ps 89:23 may carry the meaning (*G* there affirms it). It is possible that Deut 15:2 is to be so understood, "A creditor shall let go of what he has seized from his neighbor," instead of the usual interpretation, "A creditor shall release what he has loaned to his neighbor." But it is clear that the proposed meaning does occur in postbiblical Hebrew. In the Midrash on Cant 2:7 we read that the torturers heated iron bars white-hot and placed them under the armpits of the martyrs, ומשיאים נפשותיהם מהם "And (so) they seized their lives from them." (The text is found in ספר מדרש רבה על שיר השירים [Warsaw: 1863]; for a translation see August Wünsche [ed.], *Der Midrasch Schir ha-Schirim*, [Bibliotheca Rabbinica 6; Leipzig: Schulze, 1880].)

28a—a   Though this colon is omitted by *G* and *S*, there is no reason to omit it (as Condamin does). It is tempting to propose וַיַּעֲשֵׂתוּ (compare the sequence of tenses in 3:5b, as there emended), but the text is probably sound, imitating the diction of Deut 32:15aβ.

b   Reading עָרְבוּ for *M* עָבְרוּ "they have crossed" or "transgressed." The latter verb occurs twice in v 22 ("pass away," "pass over") but gives no sense here. The legal term fits the context perfectly and is clearly in assonance with עבר in v 22, a circumstance that led the copyist astray. With the emendation the colon has the remarkable consonant sequence '-r-b d-b-r r-'. (For a similar suggested metathesis see 11:15.)

c   Inserting וַיַּצְלִיחוּ after "wrongdoer" from its present position in *M* after "orphan." The word

they have not pled the pleading of the
    orphan [. . . ,]ᶜ
and the judgment of the needy they have
    not upheld.
29   **With these (folk) shall I not deal?ᵃ**
           oracle of Yahweh,
uponᵇ a nation like this shall my soul
    not gain satisfaction?"

could have been erroneously omitted, placed in the
margin, and then reinserted at the wrong spot
(compare 4:30; 5:2–3, 14; and often). The verb
gives little sense in its present position (explanations
of the meaning from remoter Semitic cognates
[Theodor H. Gaster, Hayim Tawil] seem forced)
and admirable sense in the position proposed. See
Interpretation.

d   I propose reading רִיב for the synonymous דִין of
M. Given the two occurrences of the root שפט in the
last colon of the verse and two occurrences of the
root דין in the next-to-last colon (as the words are
here grouped), the third occurrence of the root דין
is inappropriate in the poetic structure. The noun
רִיב accords with the consonantal permutations of *r*
and *b* in the fourth colon from the end of the verse.
But if דִין is retained, the meaning is identical.

29a   Some MSS. read אֶפְקֹד בָּם like 9:8 (compare 5:9).

b   A few MSS. prefix וְ "and" with v 9.

Structure

Extent of the Unit. Verse 20 begins with repeated imperatives as do the other large units within 4:5—6:30 (see
4:5—10:25, Preliminary Observations), and v 29 is the
refrain with which vv 1–9 also concluded; I propose then
that vv 20–29 make up a unit. This analysis contrasts
with that of Volz and Rudolph, who divide the passage
after v 25 on the basis of the contrast of subject matter.
But a fresh oracle can scarcely begin with כִּי and an
accusation, as v 26 does. The word "basket" (כְּלוּב, v 27)
makes a nice balance with "bound" (גְּבוּל, v 22). Form-
critically there is a break between vv 25 and 26, but Jrm
has incorporated genres into larger structures.

Placement of the Unit. Within the second scroll this unit,
the only one in which Yahweh speaks from beginning to
end, appears to have a central position (see 4:5—10:25,
Preliminary Observations, *Structural Organization of the
Sequence of Units*), but whether this datum is the explanation for its placement here cannot be proved.

Internal Structure. Most of the passage consists of
simple bicola or tetracola. The only exception is vv 23–
24, which make up two tricola: the first tricolon consists
of v 23 and the first colon of v 24, united by "heart" (the
first and third colon) and by the word-play of סוֹרֵר
("stubborn") and סָרוּ ("have turned") in the first and
second; the second tricolon is the quotation in the
remainder of v 24. The two tricola are thus roughly at
the center of the passage. As to the sequences before and
after the tricola, at several points one is left uncertain
whether a given series of four cola make up two bicola or
a tetracolon (v 21; v 22αβb; v 26; the last four cola of v
28). There are some striking effects within the passage,
for example the play on the forms of עבר in the fourth
and sixth cola of v 22 and the balancing ערב (if the
emendation is correct) in second colon of v 28, but the
basic structure is simple. The only curiosity is the second
colon of v 21, which consists entirely of a vocative.
O'Connor does not cite any such cola,[1] but they appear
in Deutero-Isaiah (Isa 40:9; 54:11).

Form

This is the only extended unit in 4:5—6:30 in which
Yahweh speaks from beginning to end. Verse 20, with its
plural imperatives, is very similar to 4:5aα (see there):
here too one has commands to messengers or heralds.
What follows in v 21 begins the messengers' speech: but
how far does it extend? Second-person address continues
in vv 22 and 25 (vv 23–24 receding to third-person
description), but there is none thereafter. Further, in vv
26–28 Yahweh cites specific sins of social injustice,
whereas the accusations in vv 23–25 are more general,
referring to the people's unfaithfulness to and lack of
reverence for Yahweh. One could conclude either that
the speech ends with v 25 or continues through v 28 or

---

1   For his treatment of vocatives see O'Connor,
    Structure, 306; for typical examples see p. 261, on
    Zeph 3:16.

29; it is safest to assume it continues to the end (see further the remarks below on the function of כִּי in v 26).

The messengers' speech, particularly in vv 21–23, is heavy with wisdom vocabulary, and in this respect it is comparable to 4:22 (which see). One finds "foolish" (סָכָל) in 4:22 and 5:21, and one notes the inversion of verb and the object pronoun referring to Yahweh in both the second colon of 4:22 and the first colon of 5:22. The phrase "senseless" (אֵין לֵב) is paralleled in Prov 17:16 (see Interpretation). And there is a likeness of vocabulary between this section and 6:27–30, a passage in which Jrm is asked to supervise a kind of final exmination of the people ("stubborn," סוֹרֵר, 5:23 and 6:28). The messengers, then, announce the lecture of Yahweh the schoolmaster to his refractory people;[2] here is a vivid reuse by Jrm of the vocabulary of wisdom.[3] The discourse begins with an elaborate vocative (compare Structure). There is irony in asking people who do not hear to hear.[4] Verse 22 begins with a bicolon of rhetorical questions: Yahweh reminds his people that their basic stance should be fear of him: again a theme of wisdom.[5] The discourse then offers an analogy from nature, the control of the sea; analogies from nature are part of the stock of wisdom.[6] Verses 23–24 make up an accusation. For v 24, in which the people are accused of not having said what they should have, compare 2:6; here what they should have said is an expression of the fear of Yahweh, portrayed again as Lord of nature. Verse 25 is didactic: Yahweh's explanation of the reason why the rains have not come, but again this instruction is taken up in the larger context of accusation (for similar discourse see 2:19; 30:15b).

In vv 26–28 the accusation suddenly lists specific offenses of social injustice; the כִּי with which v 26 begins therefore means something like "specifically," as it does in 2:13, or in 2:20–22 (three times there following the generalities of 2:19).

Setting

Evidence has already been given for a setting for this passage in the autumn of 601 (see 4:5—10:25, Preliminary Observations, *Settings*). The drought is already under way (vv 24b–25), and Yahweh has virtually determined on the destruction of his people (the refrain in v 29).

Interpretation

■ 20 This verse is a permutation on the first two cola of 4:5. The phrase "household of Jacob" appears in Jer only otherwise in the introductory instructions of 2:4.

■ 21 "Just hear this" has an impatient air. "In nearly all instances in MT, the combination שִׁמְעוּ נָא is hostile, minacious."[7] The phrase picks up the word "this" from the first colon of v 20 and the verb שׁמע from the second colon (there the hip'il stem, "announce," here the qal stem, "hear"). The second colon must be construed as a vocative (see Structure). The last two cola of the verse are implicitly relative clauses modifying the vocative, as *V* already recognized, even though in Hebrew they are paratactic and have third-person instead of second-person references; such a shift in personal reference occurs elsewhere in extended vocatives (e.g., Isa 47:8a; 54:1a).[8] The vocabulary here is reminiscent of 4:22 (see there). The "stupid and senseless people" is Jacob: Laban had accused Jacob of doing stupidly (the same root, סכל, Gen 31:28). As Jacob did then, so he does now. "Senseless" is literally "without heart" (Hos 7:11, compare Prov 17:16); since the "heart" is the seat of the mind, the will, the understanding, "senseless" is a good rendering. "Heart" will occur again in vv 23 and 24; indeed Jrm speaks of the "heart" in many contexts: the people are to circumcise the heart (4:4); the heart is devious and perverse (17:9); Yahweh is to write his torah on the people's heart (31:33). This indictment is therefore central. They have no heart. They have eyes and ears, but, having eyes and ears, still they do not see or hear, any more than idols do (Pss 115:5–7; 135:16–17). One is reminded of the sequence of "heart," "ears," and "eyes" in Isa 6:10: the terrible call to Isaiah to deaden the

2   Holladay, *Architecture*, 88–89.
3   Compare McKane, *Prophets and Wise Men*, 86–93, though he does not refer to the present passage.
4   Lundbom, *Jeremiah*, 53.
5   Gerhard von Rad, *Wisdom in Israel* (Nashville: Abingdon, 1972) 53–73.
6   See ibid., 115–24, and James L. Crenshaw, "Wisdom," *Old Testament Form Criticism* (ed. John H.
          Hayes; San Antonio: Trinity University, 1974) 260.
7   Frank Zimmermann, "The Immanuel Prophecy," *JQR* 52 (1961/62) 158 n. 14.
8   König, *Syntax*, sec. 344l.

sensibilities of the people has come all too true.

■ 22 The first colon of this verse offers a striking sequence: the interrogative particle הַ, followed by the object pronoun, followed by the negative and the verb (and the parallel second colon is the equivalent, with a prepositional phrase replacing the object pronoun). The same inversion (but without the interrogative particle) appears in 4:22, "Me they do not know." Current commentaries and translations reflect the interrogative but not the inversion (*RSV*: "Do you not fear me?" and *NAB* "Should you not revere me?"). But the inversion should be honored: the phrasing is parallel both to that in 4:22 and to that in 5:29 (and in 5:9), hence the translation proposed here, "Me do you not fear, and in my presence do you not tremble?"

The parallel verb in the second colon is startling; חיל/חול means "writhe" (4:19). There is no way, then, that the meaning of "fear" can be watered down to some idea of general dependence. Given the word play on חול "sand" in the third colon, one may legitimately raise the question whether the second colon is not a deformation of an expected אִם אֶת־פָּנַי לֹא תְחַלּוּ "and my favor do you not entreat?"—this is the parallel in 26:19 (for the meaning see there). If this is the case, one has here another instance of Jrm's distortion of an expected phrase (compare 2:12 for the device). The verb means "writhe" of Jrm's bowels in 4:19 and describes labor pangs in 4:31; here it means "tremble" before Yahweh's presence (compare Ps 96:9 and Joel 2:6). Yahweh's "presence" here implies his "fury": for this nuance see the discussion in 9:6.

Then suddenly Yahweh defines himself as he who has set a boundary for the sea: though the sea writhes, it respects the boundary—the people have less respect for Yahweh than does the mighty sea. The boundary is the "sand" (חול), a word in assonance with "tremble" (תָּחִילוּ); the same verb is used to describe the action of the waters of the primeval deep in Ps 77:17. The theme of setting a bound for the sea is very old; the story is the background

of Job 38:8–11 and Prov 8:29 (and compare *Enuma Êliš* 4.139–40, where Marduk does the same thing).[9] The phraseology here is particularly close to Ps 104:9, גְּבוּל־שַׂמְתָּ בַּל־יַעֲבֹרוּן, "A bound you have set lest they should pass over." But it is nice that in Jrm's line the barrier should be the sand, something so seemingly insignificant; how remarkable that sand should keep the sea in bounds (Rudolph). The next colon begins with חָק־עוֹלָם "a permanent limit," or "a limit forever," in assonance with לַיָּם . . . חוֹל in the previous colon. The phrase defines "bound" more exactly.

The two verb forms יַעַבְרֻנְהוּ and יַעַבְרֻנְהוּ offer unusual suffix forms;[10] are they evidence of elevated diction?

With the verb phrase וְלֹא יַעַבְרֻנְהוּ one reaches an ambiguity. The standard translation, "and it will not pass over it" (or a purpose clause, "so that it may not pass over it"),[11] is certainly correct; עבר plus accusative does mean "cross, pass over, transgress," and the parallel in Ps 104:9 implies this meaning. It is clear, further, that the last verb phrase in the verb, יַעַבְרֻנְהוּ, does mean "pass over it." But the other element in the colon, "a limit forever" (חָק־עוֹלָם), suggests an inner parallelism, so that the verb may mean "pass away" with a dative suffix. Dative suffixes occur sporadically,[12] for example in 9:1, and there may be more than the traditional grammarians have admitted.[13] Further indication that the suffix here may be construed as dative is the occurrence of לָנוּ "for us" after חֻקּוֹת "fixed times" in v 24. The verb here is ambiguous in just the way עבר is in Ps 148:6b: "He fixed a limit and one shall not pass over it," and "He fixed a law and it shall not pass away" (compare the *RSV* and *RSV* margin there, and the translations of various commentators; in that verse, too, one finds חֹק "limit" and עוֹלָם "forever," which pull the line in two directions). If "pass away" is the alternative under consideration in the present colon, then English idiom would demand a subordinate clause, "a limit forever which shall not pass away for it."

The present study assumes the restoration of "its

---

9   See conveniently *ANET* 67b. For the myth in general see Theodor H. Gaster, "Cosmogony," *IDB* 1:706, and bibliography, p. 709, sec. 9.

10   GKC sec. 58i, k.

11   König, *Syntax*, sec. 154.

12   GKC sec. 117x.

13   See Dahood, *Psalms III*, 377–78.

waters" as the subject of the verb in the fifth colon: in Ps 77:17, a parallel in which יָחִילוּ appears, "waters" (מַיִם) appears, and the diction in Jer 46:7 is even closer (see Text).

The last two cola are closely parallel. It is perhaps significant that the same parallel of חיל/חול "tremble, writhe" and המה "be in an uproar" which occurs here occurs also in 4:19 with Jrm's bowels and heart. One is pressed to see the terrible contrast between the people, who do not tremble before Yahweh, and the waves of the sea, which do indeed roar and yet do not surpass their limits.

■ **23–24** For the way in which the two cola of v 23 and the first colon of v 24 are linked in a tricolon, see Structure. The first colon of v 23 is tied closely with the first two cola of v 21: there is the link of "this" and "people," and there is the tension between the assertion in v 21 that the people are "senseless" (literally "without heart") and the assertion here that though they have a heart, it is stubborn. The addition of "rebellious" (evidently secondary: see Text) reinforces the association with Deut 21:18–20: a "stubborn and rebellious" son deserves to be stoned to death; what does a people with a "stubborn and rebellious" heart deserve?

In the second colon the first verb, סָרוּ "have turned," mimics סוֹרֵר "stubborn" in the first colon. Rudolph, following Ehrlich, wishes to emend the second verb, וַיֵּלֵכוּ "and gone away," to וַיָּכֹלוּ "and prevailed," to match the fifth colon of v 22. But this is unnecessary: the verb is in resonance with that earlier verb but need not repeat it. The diction is reminiscent of Judg 18:21, וַיִּפְנוּ וַיֵּלֵכוּ "So they turned and departed." Off they have gone, there is no stopping them; the people are in contrast to the sea, which is stopped by its barrier.

"Say in one's heart" means "say to oneself" (compare 13:22). For the translation of נִירָא נָא as a cohortative ("let us just fear") see Text. The people have not said, "Let us fear Yahweh": this colon of course reflects the peremptory question which opens v 22.

Yahweh is the giver of the rain, and it comes dependably in its time. There is an awareness of the regularity of the seasons in the OT (Hos 2:11; Ps 1:3), but it must be said that Jrm had a keen eye for it (8:7). When Israel is

faithful to Yahweh, Yahweh is dependable and one can count on the gifts of the seasons.[14] The gloss "early rain and latter rain" further defines "rain" (see Text); "early rain" (יוֹרֶה) occurs only here in Jer, while for "latter rain" see 3:3.

The word חֻקּוֹת, normally "things prescribed, statutes," is unique in this passage in referring to the harvest, though the term is used for the "fixed order" of moon and stars in 31:35 and of the "ordinances" of heaven and earth in 33:25 (compare Job 38:33). The perception here, then, is that the pattern for the harvest is as dependable as the pattern for moon and stars. Yahweh himself, it would seem, is under the obligation to maintain for his people (יִשְׁמָר־לָנוּ) the regularity to which they are accustomed. Yahweh is the true author of fertility, not the Baals. The gloss "weeks" is prompted by the striking phrase "statutes of harvest" (see Text). The use of the term חֻקּוֹת "fixed times, statutes" reminds one of the חוֹק, the "limit" of the sea, as לָנוּ "to us" reminds one of the possibility of a dative meaning for the suffix of the verb in that fourth colon of v 22. Indeed is there a parallel movement between vv 22 and 24, from "fear" to the waters of the sea in v 22, and from "fear" to the water of rain here in v 24?

■ **25** The meaning of the first colon has caused difficulty; the parallelism between "your iniquities" and "your sins" moves us to understand the predicates as synonymous (compare 30:14, 15). The second colon is clearer, so one turns there first. The word טוֹב ("good," here "bounty") occurs in the context of fertility (Deut 30:9), so much so that Dahood proposes the translation "rain" in this and several other passages.[15] "Your sins have withheld bounty/rain from you." Yahweh gives the rain in its season, but your sins have prevented it from coming (compare 3:3 and Amos 4:7); for the idea that the sins of the people are the immediate cause of disaster, without the direct intervention of Yahweh, see 2:19.

Now the first colon: if אלה is vocalized with M as "these," then a plural becomes necessary for the "rains" in v 24 (hence the first gloss there: see Text), and the verb must mean "turn away," as the Versions have it (compare this verb in this meaning in 1 Kgs 11:2: "turn away" someone's heart). But given the association of אָלָה

---

14 See Eichrodt, *Theology* 2:152–62, esp. 157.
15 Mitchell Dahood, "Hebrew-Ugaritic Lexicography II," *Bib* 45 (1964) 411, and *Psalms I*, 25, on Ps 4:7.

"curse" with drought in 4:11–12 (as reconstructed) and 23:10a and the occurrence of that noun alongside טוב in Deut 30:7, 9, I propose it here and therefore the meaning "have extended" for the verb. By this reading the two cola form a powerful parallel.

■ **26** The verb מצא nip'al is often used in legal contexts, "be discovered, caught" (see 2:26, 34). The רְשָׁעִים are not so much "wicked folk" (compare *RSV*) as "criminals" (*NAB*); the word means "the guilty" in legal contexts (Deut 25:1–2), and it is a legal situation here.

The second colon has always been unintelligible, and the Versions give no help. The clue is to recognize the word רְכֻשׁ "(household) goods" in the consonantal text. The verb, reconstructed as יַשּׁוּ (נשה hip'il; see Text) is used in the OT in the sense of "be a creditor" to someone, but here I suggest it has the meaning of "collect" on a loan, specifically "distrain" or "seize" goods pledged where a debt remains unpaid: this is the meaning carried by the verb in postbiblical Hebrew.[16] Ps 109:11 and Prov 22:26–27 provide an exact background for the passage. The first reads, "May the creditor [נוֹשֶׁה, נשה qal] seize [or "ensnare"!] all he has"; the second, "Be not one of those who give pledges, who become surety [עֹרְבִים] for debts [מַשָּׁאוֹת, from נשא, a by-form of נשה]; if you have nothing with which to pay, why should your bed be taken from you?" The practice was forbidden in Deut 24:6, 10–13, and more restrictively in Exod 22:25–27 (regarding a garment given in pledge).[17] The seizure of goods pledged for debt could thus be considered criminal, but it was evidently practiced widely nevertheless, for it might be asked, what good is a pledge if it cannot be seized for nonpayment?

"Like fowlers" anticipates "like a basket full of birds" in v 27. The word מַשְׁחִית is normally translated "trap," but this is an unparalleled meaning for it. It is used of a "destroyer" in many general contexts (4:7); it appears (in the singular) in 1 Sam 13:17; 14:15 for a raiding-party, and similarly the phrase אִישׁ מַשְׁחִית is rightly translated "brigand" in Prov 28:24 by the *NAB* and *NEB*. In short, the noun appears in situations of war. In the present context a term for war is applied to a domestic situation: it is war between the rich and the poor as the law is twisted to favor the rich. It must be borne in mind that one great purpose of war in OT times was the enrichment of the victor by prisoners and booty. The phrase "raiding-party" is chosen here as a term appropriate both to war and to domestic violence; in the present day the police can stage a raid. The verb נצב hip'il is curious: it is normally used of "setting up" a pillar (Gen 35:14) or the like (compare Jer 31:21), or of "setting apart" something special (Gen 21:28, 29). The agent or agents for the raid would be deliberately designated by the wealthy, set up for the task. Here then is the symbolism of war mixed with that of domestic violence, both compared to the purposeful work of a bird-catcher, snaring birds one after the other. Bird-catchers catch birds; these exploiters catch men. The verb לכד can be used of the capture of prisoners in battle (6:11) but can also be used figuratively of getting a person in one's power (18:22).

■ **27–28aα** The comparison continues; the bird-catcher returns, his basket full of birds. (One notes that כְּלוּב "basket" is a nice reminder of גְּבוּל "bound" in v 22.) In the same way the houses of the exploiters are full, not of the men they catch, but of their substance, their possessions (compare Isa 3:14, "Goods stolen from the poor are in your houses"). The word מִרְמָה "fraud" is used by metonymy for the goods gained by fraud; a good parallel is Zeph 1:9, "And I will punish . . . those who fill their master's house [or "the house of their Lord"] with violence and fraud [מִרְמָה]," and compare a similar metonymy in Amos 3:10.

For the conjunction עַל־כֵּן (here "that is how") see 5:6. The sequence of four verbs is striking. The first two are in assonance with words in v 26, גדל "grow great" with לכד "catch," and עשר "grow rich" with רְשָׁעִים "criminals" (for the latter assonance see also Isa 53:9). The fourth verb (עָשְׁתוּ) is uncertain of meaning; Qimḥi explained it as "be smooth," and its derivatives would lend support to the definition.

■ **28aβb** The text of this sequence is in poor shape, and one must proceed with caution. *M* in the first colon makes no sense: literally "They transgress the words of the evil man"—there is no way to stretch these words into meaning. The word wanted is not עָבְרוּ but עָרְבוּ: ערב here would mean "guarantee, vouch for, become surety for."[18] This verb is in the same semantic field as נשה

---

16 See Jastrow, and see above, Text.
17 Georges A. Barrois, "Debt, Debtor," *IDB* 1:809–10 and bibliography there.

18 These consonants represent several homonymous verbs: this is II ערב in BDB and I ערב in *HALAT*.

hip'il, restored in v 26: see Prov 22:26, cited there. As criminals seize the goods of the poor put up in guarantee, so they themselves guarantee the witness of their fellow wrongdoers in court. Jrm is playing with the verbs עבר (v 22) and ערב (restored here) just as עֶרְבָה and עָבַר are found in 2:6 and עֶרְבִי and בְּרָעָתֵךְ in 3:2. The phrase דִּבְרֵי־רָע must be understood in the legal sense, given the parallels of דִּין and מִשְׁפָּט below. "Claims [or legal case] of the wrongdoer" is what is meant; for a good parallel see Deut 16:19, and for דְּבָרִים in this sense elsewhere see Exod 24:14; Josh 20:4; 2 Sam 15:3. Bribery, perjury, and other irregularities in court were a steady problem, clearly.

I read the second colon as וְיַצְלִיחוּ רִיב. I thus reinsert the verb from its position in M after "orphan"; the substitution of רִיב for M דִּין is less urgent but appears plausible in the poetic sequence (on both emendations see Text). For צלח hip'il see 2:37. The clause here is one of result.[19] A רִיב here (if the restoration is correct) is a case in law; for a similar context see Isa 1:23.[20]

The phrase דִּין דִּין is unique to Jrm; Josiah "judged the cause of the poor and needy," dispensed justice to them, upheld their cause (22:16); in a time of hopelessness, "there is no one to uphold, or support your [Israel's] cause" (30:13). So no one looks after the orphan or supports his rights, and with no adult male to protect him his rights are violated. One would expect the last line to speak of the widow (and so G reads; and compare Isa 1:23), but there is no reason to doubt the M reading here, אֶבְיוֹנִים "the needy" (plural). The sequence began with "criminals," plural, and ends with "the needy," plural. These words are pairs in the Psalms (Pss 9:17–19; 37:14), though they are not always plural. And one notes the contrast between "the needy" and "grow rich" (v 27).

It would be interesting to raise the question of the relationship between the דַּלִּים "poor" or "powerless" in v 4 and the אֶבְיוֹנִים "needy" here. The two words are found in poetic parallelism often enough,[21] so they are not two separate social classes. In v 4 Jrm expresses a kind of sad sympathy for them: they do not know the path of Yahweh, but then how could they? They participate, then, in the general breakdown of covenant solidarity because they are simply following the lead of the leadership. In the present passage they are victimized by the powerful. Here is no romanticizing of the proletariat: they may be victimized, but they share in the breakdown of covenant solidarity. No one is innocent now, though the powerful prey on the powerless.

■ **29** See v 9. Verse 9 closed a description of the breakdown of covenant solidarity (there, specifically, the breakdown of sexual integrity), and here it functions similarly, to close a description of economic and legal injustice visited by the powerful upon the powerless in the community.

Aim

The passage centers on two descriptions, of the sand-dune barrier effective against the sea (v 22) and of evidences of social disintegration, really class warfare, within the community (vv 26–28), a disintegration attributed to the people's lack of fear of Yahweh (vv 22a, 23–24a). Whereas the passages of Amos and Micah and Isaiah are filled with descriptions of social injustice, there is much less of it in Jer. This passage is a sterling description of social injustice as Jrm saw it;[22] it is a pity that the text of vv 26 and 28 has become so corrupt, and it is to be hoped that the reconstruction presented here is valid. The passage reveals Jrm to have had as keen an eye for social injustice as did his eighth-century predecessors. Still, there is the question why there are not more such descriptions in his oracles. Is it that Jrm felt the hour to be so late that repentance, though theoretically possible, was hardly a realistic hope?[23]

The sea is not calm in Jrm's description, it is convulsed. So it is not wrong for the people to manifest their passions—what is wrong is for them to turn on each other so that community is destroyed; no wonder, Yahweh says, the fertility of the fields has been withdrawn!

Yahweh begins his speech as a schoolmaster would; but in the context of the rest of Jrm's oracles, one does not have the feeling the people can learn from him (compare 6:27–30).

---

19   Joüon, *Gramm.*, sec. 116e.
20   See Gemser.
21   BDB, 195b: ten times, e.g., Amos 4:1; 8:6; Pss 72:13;
82:4; 113:7.
22   See Wisser, pp. 41–64.
23   For the same point see Weippert, *Prosareden*, 61–62.

**The Prophets and Priests
Reject Their Calling**

Bibliography

Dahood, Mitchell
    "Jer 5,31 and UT 127:32," *Bib* 57 (1976) 106–8.
Holladay
    Architecture, 90.
Holladay, William L.
    "'The Priests Scrape Out on their Hands,' Jer. v
    31," *VT* 15 (1965) 111–13.
Meyer
    Jeremia, 93–99.
Overholt
    Falsehood, 73–74.

5

30   **A frightful and horrible thing has been
        done in the land:**
31   **The prophets—they prophesy by a lie,
      and the priests—[a] they deconsecrate
        themselves,[a]
      and my people—they love it that
        way:
      but what will you (all) do at her
        end?**

Text

31a–a   Literally, "scrape off their hands" (II רדה
"scrape"). See Interpretation.

Structure

This short unit does not belong directly with what
precedes; the refrain in v 29 closes off that oracle. And
6:1 begins a new unit. It is not obvious why this unit is
placed here. If the proposal made here is correct, that
the verb in the second colon of v 31 is an ad hoc antonym
of the formula of consecration of a priest, that they "fill
his hand(s)" (see Interpretation),[1] then it is possible that
the unit was inserted here in association with "full" (מָלֵא),
which appears twice in v 27. Indeed the possibility of that
association reinforces slightly the plausibility of this
explanation of the verb.

    The unit must be analyzed in five cola. The first is the
entirety of v 30 (against Rudolph: the subject cannot be
separated from the predicate).[2] The first three cola of v
31 are closely parallel. The concluding colon refers back
to the colon of v 30 in a general sort of way: the possessive "her" evidently refers to "the land" (see Interpretation). The five cola thus offer an inclusio.

Form

Though the first four cola, speaking of the people in the
third person, could be construed either as a report of the
prophet to Yahweh, or as a meditation by Yahweh on the
wickedness of his people (who is speaking, when "my
people" is mentioned?), the last colon, with second plural
address to the people, makes it clear that the first four
cola are in fact an accusation. The last colon is a rhetorical question such as might be posed by a prosecutor in a
legal proceeding (compare Hos 9:5), but by the use of
"her end" (אַחֲרִיתָה) a pronouncement of judgment is
implied.

Setting

There are no direct clues within the unit to determine its
setting. But parallel diction in other passages whose
setting is more secure gives indirect data. Thus the
linking of "prophet" and "priest" in corruption is found
in 14:18, part of the cycle on the drought and battle, and
in 23:11, part of a passage which describes a drought
(23:10); and "horrible thing" (שַׁעֲרוּרָה) appears only
otherwise in 23:14, part of a passage associated with
23:9–12. The best guess, then, would be a setting in the
autumn of 601 or the winter of 600; if a narrower range
is possible, it is more likely to be before Jehoiakim
burned Jrm's scroll in December 601 than after: the

---

1   Holladay, *Architecture*, 90.
2   See O'Connor, *Structure*, 171, on Gen 49:5a, with a
    compound subject, and 261, on Zeph 3:18b, for an

analogous "single clause line of four constituents";
and see further p. 355.

rhetorical question (last colon) reminds one of 5:9, 29.

Interpretation

■ **30** The two synonymous subjects, שַׁמָּה "frightful thing" and שַׁעֲרוּרָה "horrible thing" are linked by sound as well and make up a hendiadys, so that the singular verb is natural. The noun שַׁמָּה is frequent in Jer (see 2:15), but שַׁעֲרוּרָה appears only here and in 23:14, there again of the behavior of false prophets; a related word is used of figs too rotten to be edible (29:17). For היה nip'al "be done" see 2:10 (as emended).

■ **31** The three cola of v 31a each begin with the subjects of their verbs and are thus stressed (compare 2:8). The triad of "prophets, priests, people" occurs also in 26:7–9; one gathers that in Jrm's perception the two wings of the religious establishment worked in parallel fashion and that the people were a kind of passive claque content with the destructive leading of the establishment.

The phrase "prophesy by a lie" is ambiguous; it may mean on the face of it, "prophesy falsely" (instrumental בְּ), but שֶׁקֶר "lie" may be a reference to Baal, the "Lie" par excellence; note that 2:8, a verse much like this one, has נִבְּאוּ בַבַּעַל "prophesy by Baal."[3]

The second colon is troublesome. It is dubious to take יִרְדּוּ as I רדה "rule," and insist that "rule on their hands" means "rule at their [the prophets'] direction," with Rashi and many recent commentators and translations. There is no evidence elsewhere that the priests took their cues from the prophets, and the possessive reference of "their hands" must surely be the same as the subject of the verb. As indicated in the note in Text, I take the verb to be II רדה "scrape" (Judg 14:9, where Samson scrapes honey out of the lion's carcass) and suggest that the priests are rejecting their consecration: at a priest's installation it is said, "They have filled your hand(s)."[4]

The priests are rejecting their consecration; this phrase is an admirable parallel to the first colon.

And the people love it that way! The expression אהב כֵּן (literally "love thus") is found also in 14:10.

The expression "at her end" (לְאַחֲרִיתָהּ) is puzzling. The noun means "outcome (of a matter), end result" (compare 23:20). To whom or what does the feminine possessive suffix refer? Rudolph claims it is neuter, but surely the reference is to "the land" in v 30, which is feminine. The parallels, given the preposition לְ, are to Isa 10:3, "What will you do on the day of reckoning?" and to Hos 9:5, "What will you do on the day of meeting?"

Aim

It is the same old story: a religious establishment and a populace rejecting the hard word of judgment from God. The passage speaks of a time of reckoning, and it is a theme with which the whole Bible is concerned. Micaiah ben-Imlah challenged the quick "yes" of the court prophets over against his own "no" (1 Kgs 22:1–28), Micah spoke out against the venality, and Isaiah against the drunkenness of priests and prophets in their time (Mic 3:11; Isa 28:7), and Jesus challenged the priestly authority in Jerusalem. There is something about a religious establishment that renders it virtually impervious to fresh truth; the priests and prophets have so much of the truth to begin with that it is almost impossible for them to see the urgent priority of fresh judgment from God.

---

3   Compare 13:25; 23:14. For a discussion of the matter see Rudolph, with bibliography; Overholt, *Falsehood*, 73–74 n. 6; Meyer, *Jeremia*, 95.

4   For this phrase see de Vaux, *Ancient Israel*, 346–47.

Can the People Change and So Avoid Destruction?

Bibliography

Berridge, John M.
"Jeremia und die Prophetie des Amos," *TZ* 35 (1979) 321–41, esp. 335–40.

Christensen
Transformations, 190–92.

Holladay
Architecture, 90–91.

Lundbom
Jeremiah, 78–79.

Soggin, J. Alberto
"Der Prophetische Gedanke über den heiligen Krieg, als Gericht gegen Israel," *VT* 10 (1960) 79–83 = "The Prophets on Holy War as Judgement against Israel," *Old Testament and Oriental Studies* (BibOr 29; Rome: Biblical Institute, 1975) 67–71.

6

1 Yahweh:

Get (folk) to shelter, (you) Benjaminites,
    from the midst of Jerusalem,
and in Tekoa sound the horn,
    and on Beth-haccherem raise a fire-
        signal,
for disaster looms from the north,
    and great collapse.

2

  [a] ⟨You are like⟩ ⟪ the most delicate ⟫[a]

Text

2a—a The whole first colon needs remedy. *G* reads quite differently, and it is not possible from it to retroject an antecedent Hebrew text. The other Versions reflect a text similar to *M*; from the latter a satisfactory text can be derived. The first two words of *M* appear as two feminine attributes, הַנָּוָה וְהַמְּעֻנָּגָה; *V*, *S*, and *T* all read these words as closely synonymous, so that the first is understood as the feminine of נָאוֶה "comely." The first word, however, is to be read as נְוֵה, feminine by-form of נָוֶה "pasture," implied by the diction of v 3 (compare Cornill, Volz, Rudolph, Bright). The ו is to be omitted as a secondary addition after "pasture" was misconstrued as a feminine adjective. Volz, Rudolph, and Bright construe the initial he as interrogative; this means that the he of the second word is a secondary addition. While an interrogative is possible, it is preferable to see both he's as the definite article understood as an expression of the superlative (Joüon, *Gramm.,* sec. 141j); Deut 28:54 is an almost exact parallel. Now the verb! Translations have divided as to whether to refer it to דמה "be like," causative "compare," or to a homonymous verb "cease," causative "destroy"; *V* and *S* take the former alternative, and so *KJV*, Volz, Rudolph, and Bright; the latter alternative is taken by *RSV*, *NAB*, *NJV*, and Condamin. The former ("be like/compare") is more likely, though there is one problem: the second noun, to which the first is compared, should be introduced by לְ or אֶל. The text may be defective, the preposition having dropped out or been omitted; there may be poetic license here of the omission of the preposition (compare "sickness and injury" before v 8); or אֵלֶיהָ in v 3 may do double duty. But it still remains to establish the personal reference of the verb and with

3
        pasture, fair Zion!—
        into her come shepherds and their
             flocks,
          they pitch tents all around her,
          each grazes his own area;

4 enemy: **Prepare battle against her,**
          arise, let us attack at noon!
  people: **Woe to us, how the day is waning!**
          How the shadows of evening lengthen!

5 enemy: **Arise, let us attack at night**
          and destroy her strongholds!

6
      〉**For thus Yahweh of hosts has said:**〈[a]
  Yahweh: **Cut down**[b] **her trees,**[b]
         and throw up against Jerusalem a siege-
          mound!
        《 **Woe, licentious city!** 》[c]
        There is nothing but extortion in her
         midst;

7
        as a well[a] [b]**keeps fresh**[b] **its water,**

it the syntax of בַּת־צִיּוֹן. One may render "Fair Zion is like the most delicate pasture" (דָּמְתָה) so Volz and Rudolph; "I have likened fair Zion to . . ." (דִּמִּיתִי, pi'el, so V, KJV, JB, and so Bright as an alternative possibility); or "You are like the most delicate pasture, fair Zion" (דָּמִית, archaic spelling of second singular feminine, so S, and so the preference of Bright). The proposal of Volz and Rudolph is to be rejected, since it involves an emendation of the consonantal text; the question is then whether "fair Zion" is a vocative or the object of a first-person verb. Either is possible, but the otherwise unparalleled vocative "Jerusalem" in v 8 invites us to see a parallel vocative here (see Structure, Interpretation); the last alternative is therefore the most likely.

6a   This rubric interrupts the flow of the poem, and Volz is likely to be correct in judging it secondary. On the other hand, it is a plausible indication of the distinction between Yahweh's words and those of the enemy just preceding.

b—b Reading עֵצָה with the Oriental qere' and G, V, T, and S for M עֵצָהּ, traditionally understood as a by-form of עֵץ "trees."

c   M reads הִיא הָעִיר הָפְקַד, an impossible phrase (in spite of Rudolph), literally "That is a city (of which?) it is established." The rendering of RSV, "This is the city which must be punished" (compare NAB), is hardly possible: the nip'al stem might carry such a meaning, but the hop'al is unattested in this meaning (and in any event the masculine verb would hardly fit with the feminine noun). Volz has suggested what must be the correct solution; it is supplied by the G ὦ πόλις ψευδής = הוֹי עִיר הַשֶּׁקֶר: for ὦ = הוֹי compare 22:13, 18. A reading of the last word as הֶפְקֵר would explain both the G הַשֶּׁקֶר and M הָפְקַד; indeed Volz cites two MSS. which read הֶפְקֵר. The word may be referred to the postbiblical root פקר "lead a carefree, licentious life"; the vocalization is perhaps הַפְקֵר. This word would be in excellent assonance with קִרְבָּהּ in the next colon. One notes further the close parallel with Nah 3:1, הוֹי עִיר דָּמִים כֻּלָּהּ כַּחַשׁ פֶּרֶק מְלֵאָה, "Woe to the bloody city, all full of lies and booty"; the present colon in Jer may well be a deliberate variation on the line of Nahum, with word-play on פֶּרֶק.

7a   There is textual confusion on this word not only in the present passage but often more generally where בְּאֵר or בּוֹר appears. These two words (and cognate in various forms in other languages) evidently come from one root, *b'r: Walter Baumgartner (HALAT) suggests that בּוֹר is derived from *bu'r, while בְּאֵר retains the 'alep. The word בּוֹר means "pit, cistern," while בְּאֵר, a feminine noun, means "well, water source." In the present passage the ketib is בּוֹר; the qere' appears to be בַּיִר, a word otherwise unattested: it would appear to be for *bayr = *bēr = בְּאֵר. In any event, the word here is feminine (מֵימֶיהָ), and the translation "well" fits the context.

so [b]she keeps fresh[b] her evil;
    violence and destruction are heard in her,
      before me ⟨she measures (them) out⟩;[c]
(in) sickness and injury 8/ take warning,
    Jerusalem,
    or my heart will wrench away from
      you,
      and I will make you a desolation,
        a land uninhabited.

b—b The verb in question occurs twice in this verse: infinitive construct הָקֵר, perfect third singular feminine הֵקֵרָה. The perfect verb suggests the hip'il of קרר; the infinitive construct suggests the hip'il of *קור, but there is much contamination of forms of the double-'ayin verbs by hollow verbs (Joüon, *Gramm.*, sec. 82o), and it seems clear that קרר is the verb here, though this is the only passage in the OT where forms of this verb appear. Its meaning is clarified by derived nouns and adjectives (compare קָרִים in Prov 25:25): the hip'il verb means "make/keep cool, cold." The alternative "flow" assumed by Rudolph, *NAB*, and *NJV* seems to be ruled out: those who take this direction assume a root קור from which מָקוֹר "spring, fountain" would be derived, but the root קור occurs in the qal, 2 Kgs 19:24 = Isa 37:25, meaning "dig," so that that noun is best explained not as "what produces a flow" but "what is dug."

c *M* and all Versions read תָּמִיד "continually," but this word has no parallel in the context and lacks strength. I propose תָּמוֹד, מדד qal; the colon would then be a variation on Amos 3:10b (see Interpretation).

Structure

Extent of the Unit. A new unit begins with 6:1 (which is very similar to 4:5–6), and still another with 6:9 (where the diction is similar to that in 5:10); these eight verses form a rhetorical unity (see below).

Placement of the Unit. The conclusion of the present study (see 4:5—10:25, Preliminary Observations, *Settings*) is that this passage was part of the first scroll and accompanied its preceding companion piece in that scroll, 4:5–8, 13–18, 29–31. Both in diction and form-critically the two passages are closely similar (the battle orders, 4:5–6; 6:1; the people's expression of dismay, 4:13, 31; 6:4; the appeal for repentance, 4:14; 6:8), so that no further explanation of the placement of the present passage within the first scroll is necessary. It was separated from its companion by the interposition of fresh material in the second scroll.

Internal Structure. The speeches of Yahweh, vv 1–3 and 6–8, enclose a short sequence of shouts—the enemy (v 4a), the people (v 4b), and the enemy once more (v 5), each a single bicolon (see further Form and Interpretation; for another sequence of rapid shifts of speaker see 8:19). The interruptions of vv 4–5 are therefore the centerpiece of the passage, and one notes the repeated "Arise, let us attack!" arranged chiastically in the enemy's speeches (vv 4a, 5). The two speeches of Yahweh are in general congruence with each other: (1) vv 1a and 6a embody battle orders; and (2) there is a vocative (Zion, Jerusalem) in the first colon of each of the tetracola (vv 2–3, v 8), and those tetracola involve the action of shepherds, metaphorically in vv 2–3, by implication in the empty land in v 8 (for the motif compare Isa 5:17; 17:2). Two more observations: "Jerusalem" in v 8 is balanced not only by the vocative "Zion" in v 2 but by the nonvocative "Jerusalem" in v 1 as well. And one notes the congruence of וּבְתְקוֹעַ תִּקְעוּ (v 1), תָּקְעוּ (v 3) and תֵּקַע (v 8).

For the grouping of "(in) sickness and injury" with the first words of v 8 see Interpretation.

Beyond vv 2–3 and v 8 the poetry of the passage consists in general of bicola; the only exception is v 1a, which must be construed as a tricolon (against Rudolph).

Form

In form as well as content this passage is comparable to 4:5–8, 13–18, 29–31; both are an announcement of judgment presented (in the first scroll) as warning. The plural imperatives in vv 1a and 6a are evidently addressed to the cosmic courtiers; v 1a initiates a call to flight (compare 4:5–6); v 1b is the reason for the call to flight, a variant of 4:6b. Verses 2–3 are a description of the invaders, couched in the metaphor of shepherds (compare 4:16–17); if v 2 is understood correctly, there may be a tone of mockery analogous to that in 4:30 (and compare 10:17).

The announcement of the coming battle is underlined by the three battle shouts in vv 4–5, that of the enemy complacently preparing holy war against Yahweh's people (vv 4a, 5), that of the people in panic-stricken lament (v 4b)—for the latter phraseology compare 1 Sam 4:7, 8 (where it is spoken by the Philistines) and Lam 5:16 (where it is spoken by Judah). See further Interpretation.

Yahweh continues to give battle orders (v 6a). Verses 6b–7 offer an accusation against the city. If the third colon is correctly reconstructed, it begins with the interjection הוֹי, found in both accusation (22:13) and lamentation (22:18).[1] Verse 7a is couched in a form appropriate to a proverb ("as . . . so") (כְּ . . . כֵּן).[2]

The passage ends (v 8) with a call to repentance (compare 4:14); the passage most resembling this one is 4:3–4, where the threatened punishment is likewise introduced by פֶּן.

Setting

The conclusion of the present study is that this passage is a companion piece to 4:5–8, 13–18, 29–31, warning to the nation to repent, else the foe from the north will invade; the setting must therefore fall between the battle of Carchemish (May or June 605) and the dictation of the scroll (at the latest, March 604) (for the discussion see 4:5—10:25, Preliminary Observations, *Settings*). There is no way to be more precise, but it may be noted that the verb קרר, "keep fresh, cool," is appropriate to the heat of summer, so that a guess of summer 605 would perhaps not be far from the mark.

Interpretation

■ **1–8** John Berridge has pointed out that the present passage has Amos 3:9–11 as a background;[3] and that parallel is strengthened if the revocalization suggested here for v 7 ("she measures them out") is correct.

■ **1** For the imperative "get to shelter" (הָעִזוּ) see 4:6. Conceivably the first colon might be construed as "Get the Benjaminites to shelter," but both *G* and *V* construe "Benjaminites" as vocative, and all the Versions translate the verb intransitively; this verb is intransitive in 4:6 and Isa 10:31 (it is transitive in Exod 9:19). It is striking that Jrm should refer to the Benjaminites here; "Benjamin" does not otherwise appear in his poetry. But it is the tribe to which the prophet himself belonged (1:1), so he is telling those from his own tribe who were to seek refuge in Jerusalem to leave while they could. The message of 4:5–6 implies that people should get to Jerusalem, while in 4:29 and here they are to flee the city. Where is there safety?

Benjamin is north of the city, Tekoa south. For "sound the horn" (תִּקְעוּ שׁוֹפָר) see 4:5. In 4:6 we have שְׂאוּ־נֵס "raise a signal," while here we have שְׂאוּ מַשְׂאֵת "raise a fire-signal"; it is instructive to see how Jrm rings the change on poetic patterns. One notes the triple play on pairs of words in this verse, *bĕnê binyāmîn, bitqŏa' tiq'û, śĕû maś'ēt* (Rudolph); and a fourth may be added, *hakkerem* and *miqqereb*, which completes the symmetry of the four cola. The word מַשְׂאֵת, literally "lifting," is used of a smoke signal in Judg 20:38, 40 and on the basis of the occurrence of the word in the Lachish ostraca (IV, 10) is translated "fire-signal"; but it must be admitted that it could be any signal visible from a distance, smoke by day or fire by night.[4]

What is the significance of Beth-haccherem here, aside from assonance with "from the midst" just noted? Neither its location nor its significance here is sure. Yohanan Aharoni has proposed Ramat Raḥel, between Jerusalem and Bethlehem, where he believes Jehoiakim built his palace (22:13–17),[5] but a seventh-century dating for the installations in question at that site has now been refuted;[6] for other suggestions see Rudolph.

Verse 1b is a variation on 4:6b. The verb שׁקף nip'al is very strong; its subject is usually either a person who "looks down over" a location, or else a geographical

1   See the extensive discussion of the matter in Wolff, *Joel and Amos*, 242–45.
2   See Trevor R. Hobbs, "Some Proverbial Reflections in the Book of Jeremiah," *ZAW* 91 (1979) 64, 66.
3   Berridge, "Jeremia und die Prophetie des Amos," 335–40.
4   So Zorell.
5   Yohanan Aharoni, "Excavations at Ramath Raḥel,

1954, Preliminary Report," *IEJ* 6 (1956) 152–55; "Excavations at Ramat Raḥel," *BA* 24 (1961) 114–18; "Beth-haccherem," *IDBSup*, 97. Ramat Raḥel is located at Israel grid 171–127.
6   Yigael Yadin, "The 'House of Ba'al' of Ahab and Jezebel in Samaria, and that of Athalia in Judah," *Archaeology in the Levant, Essays for Kathleen Kenyon* (ed. Roger Moorey and Peter Parr; Warminster: Aris

entity ("the road . . . overlooks the valley," 1 Sam 13:18). But the diction here reminds one strongly of Ps 85:12, "And Justice from heaven looks down." In that passage "Justice" is a quasi personification of an attendant of God;[7] so here (and in the light of the parallel in 4:6) "disaster" is a quasi personification, a negative expression of Yahweh; Bright: "Evil peers down from the north."

■ **2–3** Though the general thrust of the first colon, v 2, seems to be clear, there is some uncertainty regarding details (see Text). With shocking quickness the imagery appears to change from dark to light, but it will be only for a moment, and the tone is undoubtedly ironic: "You are like the most delicate pasture, fair Zion!" The reading נָוֶה "pasture" is clarified by "shepherds" and "flocks" in v 3; this less common feminine by-form of the masculine נָוֶה may have been chosen because of the address of the personification "fair Zion." The pu'al participle of ענג is otherwise unattested in the OT, but other forms of the root suggest the meaning "exquisitely cared for" or the like. If the definite article here is original, it implies a superlative (see again Text). For "fair Zion" (literally "daughter Zion"), see 4:31. The simile is comparable to that of the people as a lovely green olive-tree (11:16). Yahweh's likening of the people to a delicate pasture is not a matter of words only but of action (v 3)!

Here come shepherds to encamp against her. It is doom. What kind of "shepherds" are these? "Shepherd" here renders the Assyro-Babylonian term for ruler (see 2:8). These shepherds come with their flocks to lay siege to Jerusalem. The phrase "into her come" (יָבֹאוּ אֵלֶיהָ) has sexual overtones (out of many examples, note 2 Sam 16:21); the invaders will ravish fair Zion.

For "around" (סָבִיב) and the general imagery involved see 4:17. The verb "pitch" (tents) is the same as "sound" (the horn) in v 1 (תקע)—the verb means both "give a blast" (on the horn) and "drive" (tent-stakes); but it is ironic that those in Jerusalem should have to "strike" a long note on the horn because foreigners are "striking" their tent-stakes into the soil of the lovely homeland.

Each of the shepherds (רֹעִים, literally "grazers") is "grazing" (רָעוּ) his area, and these words are imitative of "disaster" (רָעָה) in v 1. For this use of יָד (literally "hand") for "area," compare Num 2:17, "So they shall set out, each in his position (אִישׁ עַל־יָדוֹ)." And what kind of "grazing" will these shepherds do? The Book of Micah describes "shepherds" who will "graze" with a sword (Mic 5:4–5), and the same image is implied in our passage— no gentle pastoral scene here.

■ **4–5** Here for the only time in chapters 4—6 one hears the shouts of the enemy (vv 4a, 5). Bright believes that v 4b continues the speech of the enemy ("Too bad— daylight is waning . . . never mind, we'll attack at night"). But this cannot be: the enemy might have said, "It's hopeless!" (נוֹאָשׁ, 2:25; 18:12), but hardly "Woe to us!" (אוֹי לָנוּ); v 4b represents the panic of Yahweh's people, against whom holy war is waged (compare Form).

The enemy twice says "Arise, let us attack!" (literally, "Arise, let us go up!"—קוּמוּ וְנַעֲלֶה) (see Structure). Those words under other circumstances are words of joyous pilgrims going up to Jerusalem to the temple (31:6), so there is bitter irony to hear those words on the lips of the enemy. The irony of cultic language in this context is anticipated by the verb "prepare (battle)": it is literally "consecrate" (קדשׁ pi'el). The enemy is undertaking holy war against Judah in the same way Israel once consecrated herself to do holy war against her enemies and Yahweh's (for the diction compare Mic 3:5; Joel 4:9). Alberto Soggin suggests that the phrase specifically refers to holy war in the prophets;[8] it is thus a striking example of Jrm's use of holy-war imagery against his own people (against Rudolph, who assumes the verb here is a faded metaphor).

Why would the enemy wish to attack at noon? Any battle would ordinarily begin as soon after daybreak as possible, so that one could take advantage of all the daylight possible (compare the well-known passage in Josh 10:12–14, and a similar motif in the Iliad, 2.412– 18, where Agamemnon prays Zeus not to let the sun go

& Phillips, 1978) 130–32.

7   On this point see Dahood, *Psalms II*, 289–90.

8   J. Alberto Soggin, "Der prophetische Gedanke über den heiligen Krieg, als Gericht gegen Israel," *VT* 10 (1960) 81 = "The Prophets on Holy War as Judgement against Israel," *Old Testament and Oriental Studies* (BibOr 29; Rome: Biblical Institute, 1975) 69.

down before the Achaeans have been victorious).[9] Further, noon is hot, a time for rest if possible (Gen 18:1). But this enemy can do anything, wait casually until the day is half gone before mounting the attack!—how could anyone withstand him? (Compare Rudolph: any time of day is right for them; or Harry Freedman:[10] a surprise attack.)

The people respond in panic. If the enemy can attack at noon, the folk in Judah see their chances slipping away; Jrm has nicely caught in his use of words for the passage of time the contrast of mood between the opposing sides—the phrase "the day is waning" (פָּנָה הַיּוֹם) suggests hopelessness and transitoriness (compare Ps 90:9). For panic compare the discussion on 4:13 and 31, and for "how" (כִּי) in this context see again 4:13.

In v 5 the enemy shouts once more: not only are they able to attack at noon, they can attack at night. A night attack is as unlikely as an attack at noon; for such a night attack (which was also holy war) see Judg 7:9, 15. The mode of attack is uncanny, and the enemy is invincible. Indeed they are about to destroy the "strongholds" of the city. It is not altogether certain, but it is quite probable that the אַרְמְנוֹת are the inner citadels within a walled city which are themselves fortified as a last defense of the king and his courtiers,[11] so the impression is created that the enemy has already breached the city walls and is making a last attack on the inner fortress. It is hopeless.

■ 6 For the messenger formula see 5:14.

Background for v 6a is afforded by Deut 20:19–20. There it is forbidden to cut down the fruit trees of an enemy whose city is being besieged: fruit trees take many years to mature and begin to bear, and it is considered inadmissible to destroy them, as was done by many ancient peoples during war.[12] The present passage makes no specification between fruit trees and trees not bearing fruit, nor is it said specifically that the trees are to be cut down to serve as siege-works: the "siege-mound" (סֹלְלָה) consists of loose soil. But the commands given here do suggest a terrible picture of the intensity

and destruction of ancient warfare; compare Josephus's description of the siege of Jerusalem in the first century c.e.: "The Romans, meanwhile, though sorely harassed in the collection of timber, had completed their earthworks in one and twenty days, having, as already stated, cleared the whole district around the town to a distance of ninety furlongs. Pitiful too was the aspect of the country, sites formerly beautified with trees and parks now reduced to an utter desert and stripped bare of timber."[13]

If the reconstruction of the third colon in the verse is correct ("Woe, licentious city!"), it is a striking phrase, implying not only judgment but lament (see Form). The diction is very close to Nah 3:1 and may be modeled on that verse (see Text); note that both passages continue with כֻּלָּה, literally "all of it." The root פקר (reconstructed here) appears in postbiblical Hebrew to describe the conduct of heretics and pagans, conduct governed by no norms or standards whatever. The word עֹשֶׁק appears in Jer only otherwise in the description of Jehoiakim's policies (22:17); though it carries the general meaning of "oppression," in some contexts (e.g., Lev 5:23) it appears to refer to the seizing of goods, so that "extortion" seems a justifiable translation. The phrase is doubtless modeled on Amos 3:9, וַעֲשׁוּקִים בְּקִרְבָּהּ "and the oppressed in her midst."[14] It moves in a semantic field close to that of the distrainment of goods mentioned in (the emended text of) 5:26. There is a nice repetition of קֶרֶב "midst" in this passage: the Benjaminites are to flee from the "midst" of Jerusalem (v 1), where there is nothing but extortion to be found.

■ 7 A well keeps its water cool and fresh and available, a concern particularly in the context of a siege (v 6a);[15] in the same way this city keeps fresh and available her evil. But evil is something the city should get rid of: compare 4:14, "Wash your heart of evil, Jerusalem, that you may be saved!" To the contrary, the city holds onto her evil as something intrinsic and precious, as precious as cool water is in a thirsty land: compare Prov 25:25: "Like cold water (מַיִם קָרִים) to a thirsty person, so is good news from

9   See Soggin, *Joshua*, 122.
10 Harry Freedman, *Jeremiah* (Soncino Books of the Bible; London: Soncino, 1949) 43.
11 See Wolff, *Joel and Amos*, on Amos 1:4; and Yadin, *Warfare*, 23–24.
12 Samuel R. Driver, *A Critical and Exegetical Commentary on Deuteronomy* (ICC; Edinburgh: Clark, 1895) 240.
13 *J.W.* 6.1.1. (sec. 5–6); the translation is that of H. St. J. Thackeray, *Josephus* (LCL; London: Heinemann; New York: Putnam, 1928).
14 Berridge, "Jeremia und die Prophetie des Amos," 338.
15 This association was suggested to me by my former student the Rev. Mr. Paul R. Davis.

a far country." Why should evil become so intrinsic to the city?

One is left uncertain how to construe the phrase "violence and destruction," whether what is heard is the event of violence (*RSV*: "violence and destruction are heard within her," and so also other recent translations), or whether what is heard is the shout "Violence and destruction!" (so Rudolph and Bright). In favor of the former alternative are two considerations: (1) the phrase "sickness and injury," two cola later, refers to outer manifestations, leading one to construe the present phrase as parallel; and (2) if the reconstruction of the last colon of v 7 is correct, then "violence and destruction" is metaphorically understood as some kind of treasure (see below). In this case the singular verb "is heard" (יִשָּׁמַע) forces one to construe the phrase as a hendiadys. In favor of the latter alternative are two considerations: (1) the verb is singular, and (2) the same phrase is a quotation in 20:8. But against (2) one may argue that 20:8 quotes 6:7 just as 20:10 quotes 6:25 ("terror on every side"); that is to say, by this reasoning neither phrase in chapter 6 is a quotation. On balance the present study chooses the former alternative.

It is difficult to distinguish clearly between חָמָס ("violence") and שֹׁד ("destruction"); Wolff proposes that the former is violence against the person and the latter violence against property.[16] But the matter is not so simple; a recent study shows that חָמָס (here "violence") involves brutality which may involve violent words, or bloodshed, and that שֹׁד (here "destruction") may involve violent theft and pillage as well as devastation. The former is the larger semantic field and tends to refer to violence that lasts, while the latter is the smaller field and tends to refer to violence that is passing.[17] But the words here are a hendiadys; one notes that Isa 60:18 offers them in parallel cola, an example of the break-up of a stereotyped phrase.

If the reconstruction of the last colon of the verse is correct, it is a variation of Amos 3:10, "those who store up violence and destruction in their strongholds." People have hoarded violence and destruction like treasure in their keeps; now like treasure they carefully dole them out. One notes in passing that there may be assonance

between שֹׁד and the reconstructed תָּמֹד (probably pronounced *šōdd* and *tāmōdd*).[18]

For "sickness and injury" see below, v 8.

■ **8** The understanding of "sickness and injury" is not immediately clear. *M* construes the words with what precedes: "before me continually are sickness and injury" (see Text, v 7, c). *G* and *S* construe them with what follows: *S* reads "With pains and injuries be instructed, O Jerusalem," and Volz has followed that understanding. While "violence and destruction" is a phrase describing Jerusalem's evil (20:8; Amos 3:10; Ezek 45:9), the pair "sickness and injury" is evidence (at least in Jer) of Yahweh's warning of possible judgment (10:19; 30:12, 15; compare Isa 1:5–6). Though the nouns carry no preposition in *M*, both *G* and *S* construe them as if introduced by בְּ "with," which one would expect with this verb; given the text, this is the solution which offers itself.

"Sickness" and "injury" are thus the disciplinary or warning blows which the people have suffered from Yahweh; they are hints: "Take warning, Jerusalem!" The verb יסר nip'al suggests discipline (compare Lev 26:23; Prov 29:19). Jrm uses this stem of the verb only otherwise in 31:18, "You punished me and I took the punishment."

The next colon is a vivid phrase. The subject is נַפְשִׁי, literally "my soul," that is, Yahweh's self (compare 4:19). The verb is a vivid one (יקע); it is used three times in Genesis 32 of the dislocation of Jacob's thigh and so seems to mean "pop out." It is used in Ezek 23:17, 18, there (as here) with נֶפֶשׁ as subject, but it is uncertain whether the passages in Ezekiel are imitative of Jrm's diction here or whether we have to do with an unusual idiom. I have chosen to translate it as if it were a fresh coinage of Jrm's; since it clearly refers to emotion, "my heart" is justifiable for נַפְשִׁי, but a translation like "or I will loathe you" (*NJV*) is a good rendering if the phrase were an established idiom. Yahweh threatens to turn away in disgust from his people (compare the people's turning the back of their neck to Yahweh in 2:27).

The last words, "and I will make you a desolation, a land uninhabited," are a variation on 4:7 (which see); "make . . . a desolation" is found again in 10:22. Both the

---

16 Wolff, *Joel and Amos*, 194.
17 Jacques Pons, *L'Oppression dans l'Ancien Testament* (Paris: Letouzey et Ané, 1981) 27–66.
18 Compare Harris, "Linguistic Structure," 145, sec. 11.

last two clauses are introduced by the conjunction פֶּן, literally "lest." There is a divine "if" here: Yahweh will not punish if the people "take warning." The terrible scenarios here are not inevitable (compare 4:4, likewise with פֶּן and compare 4:14).

Aim

As in 4:5–8, 13–18, 29–31, the threat of total annihilation is held over Judah, mitigated only by Yahweh's openness to a change of mind (4:14; 6:8). The details of battle are vivid, punctuated by the shouts of the enemy himself in vv 4–5, as day wanes into night. There is little love expressed here by Yahweh for his people; how could there be, given their propensity for keeping fresh their evil? Yahweh's anger with them is serious and not to be ignored; still, he waits for a change of heart from the people with whom he has covenanted.

Yahweh's Wrath
Will Be Poured on
Young and Old Alike

Bibliography
Berridge
    pp. 78–79.
Holladay
    Architecture, 91–92.
Meyer
    Jeremia, 99–110.
Overholt
    Falsehood, 74–79.

6

9
Yahweh:

Thus Yahweh of hosts has said:
  ᵃ Glean, 《 glean 》ᵃ as (with) a vine the
      remnant of Israel;
  bring back your hand like a grape-
      harvester over the tendrils.

10 *Jeremiah:*

Against whom am I to speak,
  so that I admonish, and they may hear?
Look: their ear is uncircumcised,
  so they are unable to pay attention;
look: the word of Yahweh has become for
    them a reproach,
  ᵃ so that they take no pleasure in it;ᵃ

11

but of the wrath of Yahweh I am full,
  I am tired of holding it in.

Yahweh:

Pour (it) out on the children in the street,
  and on the circle of youths as well;
yes, both husband 《 and 》ᵃ wife shall be
    caught,
  the elder with him who is aged.

12

And their houses shall be turned over to
    others,
  fields and wives as well,
    for I shall stretch out my hand
        against the inhabitants of the
        land,
            oracle of Yahweh.

13

For from the least of them to the greatest
    each is getting his own cut,
  and from prophet to priest each
    practices falsehood;

14

they have treated the fracture of ᵃ my

Text

9a—a *M* reads עוֹלֵל יְעוֹלְלוּ "indeed they shall glean" or
(jussive) "indeed let them glean." Given the diction
of the second colon in *M*, with second singular
masculine address (in the context, to Jrm), the text
must be remedied. *G*, by contrast, reads plural
imperatives in both cola, and omits "your hand"
altogether. Following this lead, Giesebrecht and
Condamin read עוֹלְלוּ עוֹלְלוּ; then in the second
colon they assume that the suffix on "hand" is
dittographic and that the present singular imperative "bring back" was secondarily shifted to singular
from an original plural because of "like a grape-
harvester" (unless the verb is to be construed as an
isolated infinitive absolute!). Form-critically the
plural imperative would suggest that Yahweh is
addressing the divine messengers (compare 5:9).
This solution, following *G*, is plausible but is more
attractive for the first colon than for the second. A
second solution, adopted here, is to read עוֹלֵל עוֹלֵל,
imperative singular masculine (so Volz, Rudolph,
Bright). This brings the first colon into congruence
with the second and with v 11aβ; Yahweh is
consistently addressing Jrm. For the question
whether the syntax of the double occurrence of
"glean" is a repeated imperative or an imperative
with infinitive construct, see Interpretation.

10a—a Reading with many MSS., and *V* and *S* וְלֹא
before the verb phrase, for *M* לֹא. The difference is
slight, but the reading preferred here suggests a
parallel with the result clause "so that they are
unable to pay attention" above, while the reading
without וְ suggests a relative clause, "in which they
take no pleasure."

11a Reading גַּם for *M* עִם "with" (Rudolph); גַּם before
אִישׁ hardly makes sense without a second גַּם, so that
a copyist doubtless anticipated the עִם of the next
colon. The double גַּם here would then balance the
double גַּם in v 15 (see Structure).

14a—a Many MSS. here read בַּת־עַמִּי "my poor people"
(literally "daughter of my people") for עַמִּי; so does

people[a] offhandedly,
saying, "Peace, peace,"
      [b] when there is no peace.[b]
15 They have behaved shamefully when
      committing abomination,
yet they were not at all ashamed,
      nor did they know how to ⟨be
      humiliated;⟩[a]
therefore they shall fall among the fallen:
      at the time [b]I deal with them[b] they shall
      stumble,
                    Yahweh has said.

the doublet in 8:11, the Hexaplaric recension of *G*, and *V* and *S*. The same construct chain is found in 8:21 and similar diction in 14:17. Either reading is possible.

b—b   For *M* שָׁלוֹם וְאֵין *G* has καὶ ποῦ ἐστιν εἰρήνη; = וְאַיֵּה שָׁלוֹם "but where is peace?"—a change of only a single consonant. It is a striking and attractive reading, accepted by Duhm and Cornill, but it is safer to stay with *M*.

15a   For *M* הַכְלִים (hip'il) read הִכָּלֵם (nip'al) with the doublet in 8:12. The nip'al appears in 3:3; 22:22; and 31:19 and is the standard parallel with בוש qal. The hip'il stem of this verb elsewhere means "humiliate," a meaning that hardly yields sense here.

b—b   For *M* פְּקַדְתִּים the doublet in 8:12 reads פְּקֻדָּתָם "(of) their being dealt with"; the latter expression is quite frequent in Jer (compare 10:15; 46:21) and is reflected also by some MSS. traditions of *G* and by *V*. But since *M* is less common, it is the *lectio difficilior*.

Structure

Extent of the Unit. Volz analyzes this material in a complicated fashion, one unit being made up of vv 9–11a, another by 8:8–9 plus 6:11b–15. This analysis, which divides the four cola of Yahweh's words in v 11 between two units, is unlikely: it is difficult to imagine how such dislocation could have taken place.

By contrast Condamin, Rudolph, and Bright rightly take vv 9–15 as a unit. It is true, from the form-critical point of view vv 9–15 are complex: the sequence is made up of (1) a speech of Yahweh's, (2) a query by Jrm to Yahweh, and (3) Yahweh's answer. It is likewise true that by the analysis of the present study fresh units in these chapters begin with imperatives, while one finds in vv 9–15 not only the two imperatives in v 9 but another in v 11 at the beginning of Yahweh's answer to Jrm. But these considerations do not necessitate a division of the sequence. The passage is similar to 5:10–17 in several respects (the nation is metaphorically depicted as a vine, 5:10; 6:9; Jrm plays a crucial role in the coming destruction by the power of the word he transmits, 5:14; 6:11), so it is not surprising that the sequence of speakers in 5:10–17 is found in the present passage also. Finally, the soundness of the analysis is reinforced by the rubrics at the beginning of vv 9 and 16. (See further below, *Internal Structure.*)

Placement of the Unit. It has already been determined that this passage was added in the second scroll; the passage will therefore participate in whatever symmetry of sequence was appropriate in that scroll (for the details see 4:5—10:25, Preliminary Observations, *Settings,* and *Structural Organization of the Sequence of Units*).

Internal Structure. The passage breaks into three unequal sections: Yahweh's speech (v 9), Jrm's speech (vv 10–11aα), and Yahweh's speech (vv 11aβ–15). The two speeches of Yahweh appear to be united by internal repetitions and near-repetitions within a given colon: "glean, glean" (עוֹלֵל עוֹלֵל as reconstructed, v 9), "is getting his own cut," (בּוֹצֵעַ בָּצַע, v 13), "peace, peace" (שָׁלוֹם שָׁלוֹם, v 14), "they shall fall among the fallen" (יִפְּלוּ בַנֹּפְלִים, v 15).

Verse 15 rounds off the passage in several respects. The double גַם there balances the double גַם at the beginning of Yahweh's speech in v 11 (as reconstructed: see Text); the infinitive absolute בוֹש there balances the possible infinitive absolute עוֹלֵל in v 9 (see Interpretation); the double לֹא there balances the double לֹא in Jrm's speech in v 10.

Yahweh's first speech (v 9) can only be a bicolon (against Rudolph and Bright).[1] Jrm's speech (vv 10–11aα) consists of four bicola arranged chiastically: the central two are a report on the inability of Israel to hear, each being introduced by הִנֵּה, while the outer two deal with Jrm's personal situation (first-person singular verbs).

---

1   See O'Connor, *Structure,* 75, for cola of five words (O'Connor: "units").

(Note that Rudolph's two attempts to divide the third bicolon, v 10b, in his commentary and in *BHS,* are both unacceptable.) Yahweh's second speech (vv 11aβ–15) consists of a sequence of bicola and tricola. It breaks form-critically into four subsections: the instruction to Jrm to destroy, a single bicolon (v 11aβ); an announcement of judgment, a bicolon and a tricolon (vv 11b–12); an accusation, a bicolon and two tricola (13–15ba), and a final announcement of judgment, a single bicolon (v 15bβ). Yet it must also be said that these first two subsections (vv 11aβ–12) are rhetorically one, in that one hears a sequence of age-groups within the population (v 11aβb), followed by a summary statement that extends to property as well (houses, fields: v 12). Further the last colon of the first judgment subsection (in v 12) is linked with the last colon of the second judgment subsection (in v 15): these are the only cola in which the judgment is expressed by first singular verbs.

The only sequence giving trouble here is v 14: Rudolph agrees on a tricolon but divides after "people" and "saying"; Bright follows Rudolph but divides his third colon in two, making a tetracolon ("peace, peace" / when there is no peace). And there is complete lack of unanimity among recent translations. But the Masoretic accents are surely correct here.

Finally one notes that the tricolon v 15aba is interlocking, with בוש in the first and second cola and גַם . . . לֹא in the second and third.

Form
Formally the entire sequence is a private interchange between Yahweh and Jrm on Jrm's function on the occasion in question: Yahweh's address is singular (vv 9, 11aβ), and in that respect it is comparable to the half-verse 5:14b. But this private interchange becomes the vehicle for the public proclamation of divine accusation and judgment.

Jrm is addressed with divine commands to mediate punishment in vv 9 and 11aβ. His speech (vv 10–11aa) begins (the first bicolon) with a rhetorical question, "Against whom am I to speak?"—a question which is really the equivalent of "How can I speak to them?" The central two bicola report to Yahweh on the inability or unwillingness of the people to listen, and the last bicolon is a lament to Yahweh that the prophet is weary of trying to contain the divine wrath. The totality of Jrm's speech is closely comparable both in diction and in form to the phraseology of 20:8–9, part of one of the "confessions."

The form of Yahweh's second speech (vv 11aβ–15) has already been set forth in Structure (see above): Yahweh's command to Jrm to destroy (v 11aβ), which shifts to a judgment speech introduced by כִּי (vv 11b–12), an accusation speech introduced by כִּי (vv 13–15ba), and a closing judgment speech introduced by "therefore" (לָכֵן, v 15bβ). The splitting of the announcement of judgment by accusation surely contributes to the impact of the speech.

Setting
Commentators have attempted to find a setting for the present passage on the basis of the implication of "glean" in v 9. The word suggests a second and more thorough harvest; and since the image of harvest is one of judgment (see Interpretation), the question arises which two judgments are referred to. Are they the fall of Samaria and then the fall of Jerusalem, or the death of Josiah and then the fall of Jerusalem, or the first and second sieges of Jerusalem? Scholars have differed: Volz and Rudolph, adhering to a higher chronology, opt for the period 625–622 here,[2] so that the second and third options are eliminated; Bright, with hesitation, suggests a time after 597 for all of chapter 6.[3] But an inquiry in this direction does not bring assurance.

It has already been determined that this passage was one of the additions in Jrm's second scroll (see above, 4:5—10:25, Preliminary Observations, *Settings*). The data may be summarized as follows. The present passage is closely parallel to 5:10–17: Israel is depicted as a vine, 5:10; 6:9; there are falsely optimistic prophets, 5:12–13; 6:14; Jrm is given a role in mediating the coming disaster, 5:14b; 6:11aβ. The setting for the present passage must therefore be close to that determined for 5:10–17 (see there). Further, one may note a likeness between 5:12 and 14:13a, and between 6:14 and 14:13b: that is to say, both 5:10–17 and 6:9–15 share motifs with 14:13, "sword and famine" in 5:12 and 14:13a, and

2   Volz, p. 75; Rudolph, p. 45.
3   Bright, p. 51.

"peace" in 6:14 and 14:13b. One is led therefore to the setting to be determined for 14:1—15:9, namely the drought culminating in the king's burning of the scroll in December 601 (see there).

There are one or two more hints that point in the same direction. Thus it is possible that the phrase "from the least of them to the greatest" (v 13) is an indirect reference to the sequence of events leading to the reading of the first scroll to the king (36:9–26), given the reference in 22:17 to the king's concern for his own "cut" (בֶּצַע), the same term that appears here. And it is possible that the linking of corrupt prophet and priest in v 13 can be tied to the setting of 5:30–31 and 23:13–14 (see those passages). All these data suggest a setting in December 601 or early in 600. The two judgments are therefore likely to be the fall of Samaria and the fall of Jerusalem.

Interpretation

■ 9 The opening words of Yahweh's first speech (as emended, see Text) begins with the repetition עוֹלֵל עוֹלֵל, which may be construed either as a repeated singular imperative or as an imperative reinforced by the infinitive absolute (note that with an imperative the reinforcing infinitive absolute comes second: compare 22:10).[4] The commentators are not clear about the syntax: Volz implies a repetition of imperatives and Rudolph a reinforcing infinitive absolute, while Bright is unclear (he offers a translation that suggests a repetition and a footnote that specifies an infinitive absolute). One indication that an infinitive absolute may be present is the infinitive absolute בּוֹשׁ in v 15 which could balance it (see Structure). An infinitive absolute normally affirms by denying a negative (again compare 22:10), so that a translation like "thoroughly" (RSV) is misleading. If an infinitive absolute is implied, then the negative which is denied is the prohibition against gleaning one's vineyard (Lev 19:10; Deut 24:21). In this case the words would imply "in your case do glean; even though it has been forbidden, do it anyway." On the other hand, the passage has other repetitions, notably "peace, peace" in v 14, so the repetition of the imperative is likely; for a repeated imperative in the context of judgment compare Hos 2:4

[2]. One must even be open to the possibility of a deliberate ambiguity in syntax.

The preposition כְּ ("as") in the first colon implies "as with."[5]

The previous passage dealing with Israel as a metaphorical vine was 5:10–17, and there it was indicated that there are parallels with 2:3. Are there parallels between the present passage and 2:3? There is a possibility that Jrm perceives שְׁאֵרִית "remnant" as the reversal of רֵאשִׁית "first-fruits": in 2:3 Israel was the first fruits of Yahweh's harvest, and it has been suggested (Interpretation on 5:10) that the harvest must be understood as that of the vineyard. It would be a temptation, then, to translation "remnant of Israel" here as "last-fruits of Israel." On the other hand, "remnant (of Israel)" is a traditional phrase (Mic 2:12).

Jrm is to glean the vineyard Israel as a grape-harvester is tempted to glean his own vineyard. Bright and Berridge insist that the image is a positive one, that "glean" suggests rescue: "As a gleaner scrutinizes the vine in order that he might find those grapes which are at least good enough for his own use, so is Jeremiah to search diligently for a possible point of connection for Yahweh's essential will of salvation for Judah. A close correspondence thus exists between the 'gleanings' of 6:9 and the 'one' of 5:1."[6] Berridge further points out that if "glean" were negative, Jrm would not ask to whom he should speak and give warning (v 10).[7] But the negative implications are persuasive: the image of "harvest" elsewhere is negative—the harvest is judgment. An excellent parallel is Isa 17:4–6, a passage doubtless genuine to Isaiah: the reaping (v 5) is a judgment on Israel (v 4), and the gleanings (v 6) represents a small remnant. So here: the gleaning process represents, as one would say, a "mopping-up operation" upon a people already previously punished. The whole passage is negative in direction, and Jrm's question in v 10 is rhetorical in the same way as the diction of 5:1 was; one notes the negative implication of עַל־מִי "against whom?" (see on v 10).

The verb הָשֵׁב suggests "bring once more"; it is to repeat the action, as "gleaning" is the second action after the main harvest. The word בּוֹצֵר is the participle of בצר

---

4 König, *Syntax*, sec. 329p.
5 GKC, sec. 118t.
6 Berridge, p. 79.

7 Ibid.

"harvest grapes"; it appears in Deut 24:21 in the law forbidding the gleaning of one's vineyard (see above).

The word סַלְסִלּוֹת occurs only here in the OT, and its meaning is far from certain. *G* and *V* translate "basket," doubtless on the basis of the existence of the word סַל "basket," and traditional translations have followed this (Luther, *KJV*). But such a meaning has seemed inappropriate in the movement of the oracle (Giesebrecht), so since Heinrich Ewald commentators have rendered "tendrils," seeing in the word a by-form of זַלְזַלִּים (Isa 18:5).[8] This meaning is doubtless correct, but it may be more germane to refer to postbiblical Hebrew סִלְסֵל "braid, curl the hair."

■ **10** Jrm responds with a question, Where shall I direct my speech? The sequence begins with עַל־מִי אֲדַבְּרָה וְאָעִידָה. What is the nuance of the first cohortative here? The same problem is dealt with in the discussion of 4:21. Rudolph here translates "To whom am I to speak?";[9] Bright's "To whom can I speak?" is not quite right.

Is the preposition עַל any different from אֶל? Rudolph thinks not. There is no doubt that עַל substitutes for אֶל in many texts (Hos 12:11: *M* עַל, *G* πρός), but on the other hand it is equally clear that דבר pi'el + עַל does sometimes mean "speak against" (Hos 7:13). If Jrm intended to say "speak against," then עַל would be the most natural preposition to use. If "glean" is a negative image, then the nuance of "against" is surely present. The verb וְאָעִידָה is the only occurrence in Jrm's poetry of עוד hip'il "admonish, attest," but it occurs in his prose (11:7) and in other early texts.[10] A pretty problem is the force of the second cohortative here. At first glance one would assume that it is coordinate with the first cohortative: "Against whom am I to speak and admonish?" (the commentators and translations unanimously). But a second cohortative can be subordinate (expressing purpose) to a previous one (Exod 3:3, compare 4).[11] It is clear that וְיִשְׁמָעוּ (with ו) is a jussive, expressing purpose;[12] given the division of cola, between "speak" and "admonish," it is better to take "admonish" as likewise subordinate.

The rest of the verse lists reasons why people cannot hear, or are unwilling to hear, so that Jrm's question at the beginning of the verse is rhetorical: Who is there to whom I might direct my words? His question is about speaking, in response to Yahweh's command to glean. The figurative "gleaning" is an action, but Jrm perceives the action to be the action of speaking: speaking has power for judgment (Isa 9:7 and often).

The verb ערל "circumcise" appears metaphorically in 4:4 with the "heart" (see there); here, with עָרֵל, we hear of the "uncircumcised ear." If the heart is the seat of the will, the ear is the seat of obedience:[13] the ear of the people is no longer suited for the hearing of Yahweh's word. Rudolph notes that Johann Gottfried Eichhorn translated this line somewhat drastically, "They have skin over their ears,"[14] but Jrm's expression is indeed drastic. Because circumcision was the act of initiation into the covenant community, the expression would have struck an Israelite as it would to say of a Christian community, "their ear is unbaptized." If the ear of a people is plugged, how can Jrm speak? The people are unable to pay attention; with the verb "be able" Jrm underlines their incapacity. The clause, וְלֹא יוּכְלוּ לְהַקְשִׁיב, is one of result, parallel with the purpose clause "so that I admonish and they may hear." For the notion of inability to hear compare 5:21.

The noun חֶרְפָּה is first of all the taunt that an enemy levels against one, but then by metonymy it refers to the object of scorn and contempt. In the parallel in 20:8 it is implied that Yahweh's word has become a matter of contempt to Jrm himself (see there)! In 15:16 Jrm expresses the opposite experience: there Yahweh's word is a source of joy and delight to him—these are words pertaining to the delights of marriage (16:9), and חפץ "take pleasure," the verb that appears in the present verse, often refers to sexual desire (Gen 34:19; Deut 21:14). The people should be as attracted to Yahweh's word as Jrm is—as one is attracted to one's beloved; but

---

8   *HALAT*, 715b.
9   *"Zu wem soll ich reden?"*
10   See Wolff, *Joel and Amos*, 200–201, on Amos 3:13.
11   Joüon, *Gramm.*, sec. 116b (3).
12   GKC, sec. 109f.
13   Johnson, *Vitality of the Individual*, 52.
14   Rudolph, p. 45: *sie haben ein Fell vor den Ohren.*

they are not.

For the syntax of the last colon see Text.

■ **11** The verse begins, most strikingly, with וְאֵת (the conjunction with the sign of the definite object); it is the only verse in the poetry of Jrm with this beginning. (The emendation of Rudolph, following Ehrlich, to emend to וַאֲנִי, "but I for my part," on the analogy of Mic 3:8, is to be rejected; if this reading were correct, the verb would surely have followed immediately.) For "wrath" (חֵמָה) see 4:4. It is the wrath of Yahweh that is underlined, and that is the manifestation of the word of Yahweh (v 10). The wrath of Yahweh is rarely described as something within the prophetic orbit of control; one may compare 15:17, "for with indignation (זַעַם) you have filled me." In contrast with the people, who have no passion for the word of Yahweh, Jrm is filled with Yahweh's wrath; he is bottled up with it, since he cannot express it in a way calculated to communicate to his people, who are deaf to it. As 20:8 is a commentary on 6:10, so 20:9 is a commentary on the present verse. Beyond 20:9 and 15:17 (cited above) the only other passage employing מלא "be full" with verbal expression is Job 32:18–20, part of Elihu's speech; it is possible that that passage in Job is dependent on Jeremianic diction.

Beyond the present passage and its parallel in 20:9, לאת nip'al appears in 9:4 (the people are tired of repenting) and 15:6 (Yahweh is tired of changing his mind). The verb כיל/כול hip'il occurs in 2:13, of cisterns that cannot "hold in" their water; Jrm's inner self is so filled with the passion of Yahweh's wrath that he is beginning to leak. He cannot keep silent; unavoidably he must speak (compare again Mic 3:8).

Then Yahweh replies. Jrm had asked (v 10), Against whom am I to direct my speaking, which is the channeling of your wrath? The answer comes, Against everyone: children playing in the street, youths approaching manhood squatting together, husband and wife, elder of the city and those feeble with age. All ages, both sexes, everyone: the time is long since past delicately to sort out who is less, and who more guilty (5:4–5). The judgment is gross and will strike everyone down.

The verb כיל/כול hip'il was used (v 10) of containing bulk or liquid; שׁפך here is used of "pouring out" bulk or

liquid (compare Hos 5:10, עֲלֵיהֶם אֶשְׁפּוֹךְ כַּמַּיִם עֶבְרָתִי "upon them will I pour out like water my fury"). The nouns עוֹלָל "child" and בַּחוּרִים "youths" appear in parallel again in 9:20, a passage which offers a variation on the same theme. The two words offer a marvel of assonance: עוֹלָל resonates with both instances of עַל in the two cola as well as with עוֹלָל in v 9, and בַּחוּרִים with בַּחוּץ "in the street." For "street" see 5:1. The noun בַּחוּר implies both "young man" and "warrior."[15] The conjunction כִּי here is clearly asseverative: "yes . . ." (*NAB*, *NJV*). The verb לכד "catch, capture" is used in 5:26 of the capture of the poor by the rich; here the wrath of Yahweh will catch everyone.

The phrase here translated "him who is aged" is literally "one full of days." Since the previous pairs are contrastive, the text has seemed awry in this last colon: "elder" and "one full of days" appear synonymous. Indeed Rudolph has suggested reading עִם לֹא־מְלֵא יָמִים "with one not full of days," a phrase subsequently misread by haplography. This is ingenious but unnecessary. Wolff assumes that the one "full of days" is older than the "elder",[16] while John MacDonald has suggested that the זָקֵן is the "elder" in social rank, while the מְלֵא יָמִים is one who is really "elderly."[17] One senses the poignancy of Jrm's perception of Yahweh's work of punishment when he lays out all the categories of the population to be touched; Deut 32:25 has similar diction. It is to be noted that lists of this sort are not common in Jrm, in comparison for example with Isaiah (see Isa 2:13–16; 3:2–3, 24; 10:9; 11:6–7; 14–15).

■ **12** A variant form of vv 12–15 appears in 8:10–12, but those verses are missing in chapter 8 of *G* and must be judged a secondary variant;[18] for a detailed listing of textual variations see Text there. But 8:10a is a genuine word reminiscent of 6:12, and the contrast between the doublets has stimulated commentators to emend the present passage, so some account of the matter must be given here. Verse 12a here reads, "Their houses shall pass to others, fields and wives as well," while 8:10a reads, "I shall give their wives to others, their fields to dispossessors." Rudolph, convinced that the category "wives" has been named in v 11, combines these readings, emending to "And their houses shall pass to others,

---

15 Ze'eb Weisman, "The Nature and Background of *bāḥūr* in the Old Testament," *VT* 31 (1981) 441–50.

16 Wolff, *Anthropology*, 120.

17 John MacDonald, "The Status and Role of the Na'ar in Israelite Society," *JNES* 35 (1976) 168.

18 See Janzen, pp. 95–96.

their fields to dispossessors." But this is illegitimate argumentation: if 6:12a says "houses, fields, wives," and 8:10a says "wives, fields," one can hardly argue for "houses, fields": "wives" represents the *lectio difficilis*. Volz is unhappy about "wives," too, but for a different reason; he points out that the normal parallel for "fields" is "vineyards." And this is true (at least sixteen times in the OT); indeed Jer 32:15 has "houses, fields, vineyards." But surely one must stay with the text. Jrm's hearers expect him to say "fields and vineyards as well," but instead he says "fields and wives as well"; he has in mind the collection of curse-forms like that in Deut 28:30: "You shall betroth a wife, and another man shall lie with her; you shall build a house, and you shall not dwell in it; you shall plant a vineyard, and you shall not see the fruit of it."[19] (Compare Jesus' linking of house, family members, and lands, Mark 10:29–30.) Thus יַחְדָּו means "as well," not "together" (the latter giving the impression in English that "fields and wives" specifies "houses").

The verb וְנָסַבּוּ (סבב nip'al) clearly means "be turned over (to someone)" here, though there is no other passage with this nuance of the verb (the qal is used once for the corresponding active meaning, Num 36:9). Since the nip'al stem is twice used of this verb with "house" in the predicate (אַנְשֵׁי הָעִיר נָסַבּוּ עַל־הַבַּיִת, "the men of the city surrounded the house," Gen 19:4; Judg 19:22), it is tempting to wonder whether Jrm did not intend a kind of topsy-turvy effect here: as bullies took a turn around the outside of a house in these old episodes of sexual violence, so these houses will take a turn and fall into the hands of strangers in violent sexual episodes to come.

For נטה hip'il "stretch out" with "hand," see also 15:6 (and Isa 31:3: these are the only instances in the OT). The last colon resonates with Yahweh's initial instructions to Jrm, "Bring back your hand again . . . over the tendrils," and with the drumfire of objects of the preposition עַל "on, over, against" in subsequent lines: "against" whom am I to speak? asks Jrm; "on" the children in the street, "on" the circle of youths, everyone; so this colon summarizes what Yahweh has said up to this point.

■ 13 The idiom "from the least to the greatest" expresses totality, from the bottom to the top of the community. The idiom, in variations, occurs often in the OT, e.g.,

Gen 19:11 (one wonders, is the phrase in the present passage another resonance with the Sodom episode?— compare v 12). In Jrm's words it occurs in 16:6 and 31:34, and in prose passages in 42:1, 8; 44:12.[20] The verb בצע with cognate accusative evidently is not concerned with "making a profit" in an approving sense, nor should one translate it "taking an unjust profit" (*RSV*: "greedy for unjust gain," compare *JB*); בֶּצַע is literally a "cut," and the American slang phrase "take a cut" matches it exactly. This is the world of baksheesh and worse, palms greased, expenses padded. The context is made clear by 22:17: there we must not understand the king to be "taking a profit"; no, he is "in on the take" and so, by the evidence of the present passage, is everybody else (compare Hab 2:9; Prov 1:19; 15:27).

And not only is the craving to "get in on the action" one that infects society generally from bottom to top, but analogous impulses infect the religious leadership as well: "from prophet to priest." What do they do, these religious leaders?—what does עשׂה שֶׁקֶר "do a lie" mean? Thomas W. Overholt suggests[21] that it is defined by the phrases that follow. But "peace, peace" (when there is no peace) is an utterance of the false prophets (so also, by implication, 4:10; see there) and not necessarily of the priests as well. (It is noteworthy that *G* and *S* translate "false prophet" for "prophet" here.) No, the phrase "do a lie" is a general but at the same time basic diagnosis of the destructive activity of the religious leadership. Besides the parallel 8:10 the phrase is found in 2 Sam 18:13, a somewhat opaque text; there it seems to mean "do a treacherous act." To offer an English translation that transfers "lie" to an adverb (*RSV*: "deal falsely"; *NJV*: "act falsely") appears to miss the mark a bit; it is not how these people act but what they do. The *NAB* rendering "practice fraud" is good, but "fraud" is too narrow; it is best to leave the translation open. The phrase appears to parallel עשׂה תוֹעֵבָה "practice abomination" in v 15. Hos 4:4–5 indicts Ephraim similarly, using the phrase פעל שֶׁקֶר.

■ 14 The context of this verse is close to that of 4:10: the phrase "saying, 'peace'" is in the context of a threat to life (see there). For שֶׁבֶר (here "fracture") see 4:6; in 6:1 it suggests the collapse of roof-beams of a house onto

19   Hillers, *Treaty-Curses*, 29, 63.
20   Holladay, "Prototype," 358–59.
21   Overholt, *Falsehood*, 74–79.

pottery storage-jars; here, given the medical connotation of רפא pi'el "heal, treat," it is best to translate "fracture," as a metaphor for the violent break-up of community. One notes in passing the assonance between שֶׁבֶר and שֶׁקֶר in the previous colon. The verb רפא does not always mean "heal": healing is a procedure implying success, but in this instance success is not predicted. For "my poor people" see 4:11. The translation of עַל־נְקַלָּה is suggested by the *NJV* "offhand"; קלל nip'al means "appear trifling," thus literally "as a trifle." For שָׁלוֹם "peace" see 4:10—safety and security are implied, and in the context of medicine and health, the expression means "he is fine" (Gen 43:28). The religious leaders are false messengers, "quack" doctors.

■ **15** For בוש hip'il "act shamefully" see 2:26. For תּוֹעֵבָה "abomination" see 2:7 and 4:1; it must be noted that "commit abomination" is an extremely strong term in Hebrew—in Lev 18:27 and 20:13 it is in the context of forbidden sexual relations, acts considered abhorrent and taboo. Jrm appears to be using the phrase here symbolically (much as Trito-Isaiah will accuse the religious leaderships of his day of fertility worship and child sacrifice, Isa 57:7–8), but its impact must on no account be heard as less than a scathing accusation.

The nuance of גַּם plus infinitive absolute plus לֹא (and with גַּם and לֹא in the next colon) is not clear. The infinitive absolute here stresses the negative, hence the translation "yet . . . not at all." (For a close parallel see Num 23:25, with the repeated series גַּם plus infinitive absolute plus לֹא: *RSV*: "Neither curse them at all nor bless them at all." Unfortunately that passage offers contrastive rather than synonymous verbs.)

For a discussion of כלם (revocalized here to nip'al) see 3:3; as in that passage, it does not seem specifically to mean "blush," in spite of many translations, so that "be

humiliated" is safer.

"Fall" and "stumble" are a traditional pair (Isa 31:3 and often); and נפל qal is also paired with כשל nip'al in Prov 24:17, so that it would be difficult to specify a nuance of meaning for the nip'al of כשל other than simply "stumble." Since 18:23 offers the hop'al stem of כשל in the context of בְּעֵת "at the time . . . ," it is tempting to vocalize both "fall" and "stumble" here as hop'al: "they will be made to fall among the fallen," "they will be made to stumble," but there is no warrant to this revocalization except ingenuity, since the present vocalization gives sense.

The participle הַנֹּפְלִים occurs in three contexts in the OT: "the fallen" (thus not, note well, "the falling"), in statistics of the dead after battle (Josh 8:25; Judg 8:10; 20:46; Ezek 32:22, 24); "the deserters," with עַל plus the kings of Babylon (2 Kgs 25:11; Jer 39:9; 52:15); and generally "those in low condition or morale" (Ps 145:14). The context here is plainly that of battle slaughter.

For פקד "deal with" see 5:9. For a finite verb after עֵת compare Deut 32:35.

Aim

The new covenant passage (31:31–34) offers some phraseological parallels to 5:1–9 and to the present passage as well. If each one is out for his own gain, from the least to the greatest (v 13), then in the new covenant "they shall all know me, from the least of them to the greatest" (31:34). This congruence reminds one of the dark strokes with which the accusation against the people is drawn here: the covenant is broken, nobody cares, Jrm cannot even find anyone to listen. So Yahweh will have to pour out his wrath on young and old alike. No one is exempt, and it will take the miracle of a new start initiated by Yahweh himself to bring light in the darkness.

Yahweh Rejects Their Sacrifices

Bibliography
Berridge
  pp. 88–91.
Emerton, John A.
  "A Problem in the Hebrew Text of Jeremiah vi. 23 and l. 42," *JTS* NS 23 (1972) 106–13.
Holladay
  Architecture, 75–83, 93–97.

6

16   Thus Yahweh has said:

Yahweh: **Stand on the roads and look
           and ask the paths of old,
               "Where is the road to good?"—
           and walk in it,
               and find repose for yourselves.**

witness: **But they said, "We won't walk!"**

17 Yahweh: **And I have been appointing over you
           watchmen:
               "Pay attention to the sound of the
                   trumpet!"**

witness: **But they said, "We won't pay
                   attention!"**

18 Yahweh: **Therefore hear, O nations, [. . .]**[a] **what** ⟨⟨**I
           shall do**⟩⟩[b] **against them;**

19   **hear, O earth,** ⟨⟨**and know the
                   testimony:**⟩⟩[a]
           **I am going to bring disaster on this people,
               the fruit of** [c] **their schemes,**[c]
           **for they paid no attention to my words,
               and my law—they rejected it.**

20   **Why** [a]**does**[a] **frankincense from Sheba**
               [a]**come**[a] **to me,**
           or [b]**sweet cane**[b] **from a land afar?**
           **Your burnt offerings are not acceptable,
               nor are your sacrifices pleasing to me.**

21   **Therefore thus Yahweh has said:**
           **I am going to put among this people
               obstacles,**
           **and they shall stumble on them,
               parents and children as well,
                   neighbor and friend** [a]**shall perish.**[a]

Text

18–19a   Verses 18b–19aα need remedy; Bright omits v 18b altogether as insoluble. The parallelism "nations" and "earth" is sound (compare Mic 1:2). The most economical solution is to transfer ודעי עדה after "hear, O earth"; the feminine imperative "know" will then parallel "hear." The word עֵדָה in that case will not be a vocative, "O congregation" (*RSV*, and other translations similarly), since the other two vocatives carry the definite article; the noun will be an object, "testimony." (It is better to retain the text than to emend to דֵּעָה, construed as an infinitive absolute, with Giesebrecht and Rudolph.) See further Interpretation.

b   For *M* אֶת־אֲשֶׁר־בָּם "what is in them" read אֵת־אֲשֶׁר אֶעֱשֶׂה־בָּם "what I shall do against them," with Rudolph. He cites 1 Kgs 11:25, where עָשָׂה appears to have dropped out of the text but is retained by *G* and *T* (compare *S*). A good parallel for this phrase is 7:12, וּרְאוּ אֵת אֲשֶׁר־עָשִׂיתִי לוֹ "see what I did to it."

c—c   *G* reads ἀποστροφῆς αὐτῶν "their faithlessness" for *M* מְחֻשְׁבוֹתָם. Both nouns are common in Jrm's vocabulary, though מַחֲשָׁבָה with personal suffix is more likely to be in the plural (2:19; 3:22; 5:6; 14:7). Though Giesebrecht and Condamin accept *G*, *M* gives good sense and should be retained.

20a—a   *M* reads תָּבוֹא, but *G*, *V*, and *S* read תָּבִיאָ, thus "Why do you bring frankincense?" This is impressive Versional support but represents the *lectio facilior*. Since the qal verb turns up again in v 22a (בָּא, participle), seemingly in ironic contrast, it is best to stay with *M*.

b—b   Though this is the only occurrence of this phrase in the OT, its meaning is not in doubt, but there is some doubt about the vocalization of קָנֶה and the status of טוֹב. GKC, sec. 126x, suggests that the first element should be construed as a construct, קְנֵה; the phrase יֵין הַטּוֹב in Cant 7:10 is certainly comparable. This suggestion renders unnecessary Rudolph's excision of the he of הַטּוֹב as dittographic. Again the lexica are uncertain whether to understand טוֹב as a separate lexeme "perfume" (*HALAT*) or the frequent noun "goodness" (Zorell).

21a—a   The ketib reads יֹאבֵדוּ, and so, evidently, *G*, *T*, and *S*; the qere' and a few MSS. read וְאָבְדוּ, and so, evidently, *V*. Given the syntax, the difference is

22   **Thus Yahweh has said:**
       See, a people is coming from the land of
           the north,
          and a great nation is aroused from the
             extremes of the earth;
23   **bow and spear they grip,**
        [a] **they are cruel**[a] **and show no mercy,**
    their sound roars like the sea,
        and on horses they ride,
        [b] **drawn up for battle like footsoldiers**[b]
        against you, fair Zion!
24 people: **We have heard a rumor of it,**
        our hands fall slack,
           misery has gripped us,
              writhing like a woman in labor.
25 Yahweh: [a] **Do not go out**[a] **in the field,**
        and on the path [a]**do not walk,**[a]
    for the enemy has a sword,
        terror is all around!
26 Jeremiah: **My poor people, gird on sackcloth**
        and roll in the dust,
    mourning for an only son prepare for
        yourself,
        lamentation of bitterness:
           "How suddenly the devastator comes
              against us!"

scarcely translatable; the *qere'* is probably the *lectio difficilior* and to be preferred.

23a—a   Hebrew says literally "he is cruel" (אַכְזָרִי הוּא); many MSS. and the parallel in 50:42 read "they are cruel" (אַכְזָרִי הֵמָּה). The Versions vary greatly: in *G* the verse offers "they grip," "he is cruel," "he has no mercy," "his sound"; its rendering of 50:42 offers all plurals except "he is cruel." *V* in the present verse offers all singulars until "they ride," but in 50:42 all plurals. *S* and *T* are uniformly plural in both passages. Jrm evidently wanted to emphasize both the unity of the enemy ("people," "nation") and his numerousness (the various plurals). But the difficulty in the phrase at issue is whether אַכְזָרִי is invariable or not. Thus some authorities assume a *singulare tantum* for 50:42 and Prov 12:10 (Rudolph regarding 50:42; GKC, sec. 145h, regarding Prov 12:10), while others suggest it is indeclinable (*HALAT*, 44b): these references offer still more literature on the question. In any event English idiom does not allow a translation of the singular here.

b—b   See Interpretation.

25a—a   Both verbs in the first two cola are contrastive for ketib and qere': the ketib reads feminine singular (תֵּצְאִי, תֵּלְכִי), while the qere', many MSS. and the Versions read masculine plural (תֵּצְאוּ, תֵּלְכוּ). Yahweh addresses the people in the feminine singular in v 23, as does Jrm in v 26; economy of diction would therefore lead one to favor the qere'. Battle orders to the people elsewhere have been couched in the masculine plural (4:5–6; 6:1), but in those passages there have been no instances nearby of address in the feminine singular. The ketib is therefore the *lectio difficilior* and is to be preferred (against the other commentators).

Structure

Extent of the Unit. It is clear that v 16 begins a new unit (see vv 9–15, Structure), and that vv 27–30 form a unit of their own (Yahweh's call to Jrm to be a tester, and the prophet's report). But it is difficult to discern whether vv 16–26 form one unit or more than one. Condamin breaks vv 16–26 into vv 16–20, 21–23, and 24–26. Rudolph and Bright divide vv 16–26 between vv 21 and 22. But in answer to Condamin: form-critically v 21 is a judgment speech surely dependent upon the implied accusation of v 20, and v 24 bears the same relation to vv 22–23 as 4:8b does to 4:5–7. And in answer to Rudolph and Bright: 31:8–9a is a late word of Jrm's (see there) which reverses many of the terms of 6:21–22, a circumstance which suggests that vv 21–22 formed a continuity in Jrm's mind. Therefore even though vv 16–26 are a complex sequence form-critically, one concludes that it forms a single unit of discourse.

Placement of the Unit. It is possible that this passage follows vv 9–15 in a chiastic arrangement with 5:1–9 and 5:10–17 ("streets," 5:1; the vine Israel, 5:10; the vine Israel, 6:9; "paths," 6:16); on this matter see in detail 4:5—10:25, Preliminary Observations, *Structural Organization of the Sequence of Units.*

Internal Structure. The passage is best subdivided on the basis of considerations of form criticism and the identity of speakers (see Form). Verses 16 and 17 make up three tricola; otherwise bicola predominate.

Form

The passage offers a variety of forms, recombined in fresh ways. As before, it is crucial at each point to identify speaker and addressee.

Verses 16–17 belong together. Yahweh speaks in v 17a and therefore in v 16a. In v 16a the people are addressed and instructed (second-person plural). It is therefore inappropriate for Volz, Rudolph, and Bright to read "over them" (עֲלֵיהֶם) for "over you" (עֲלֵיכֶם) in v 17a with two MSS. The speaker in vv 16b and 17b reports in the third person about the people; but who is the speaker? Bright assumes it is still Yahweh, but then "they said" is inappropriate. One therefore deduces a shift of speaker in vv 16b and 17b. It could be Jrm, who speaks in v 26 (compare vv 28–30, where he reports on the intransigence of the people). If the present passage is analogous to 5:1–9 (see Structure), then Jrm's report to Yahweh in 5:3b–5 would suggest that that identification is correct here. On the other hand, the "nations" and "the earth" are addressed in vv 18–19aα as witnesses in Yahweh's covenant lawsuit with the people, so that it is more economical to assign vv 16b and 17b to them. (Question: Does the conjunction "therefore" in v 18 point in the same direction?)

For the question how the word "ask" is to be understood in the second colon of Yahweh's speech in v 16, and whether the third colon is a direct question, see Interpretation. But there is a further problem to be raised here: Is the second colon of v 17 a quotation or a further command from Yahweh? The first and second cola are not directly parallel, and one concludes that the second colon is better construed as a quotation of the watchmen.

Though the diction in vv 16a and 17a at first suggests what is appropriate in the emergency of battle ("stand on the roads," "pay attention to the sound of the trumpet"), the words ultimately are an appeal to wisdom ("ask where is the road to good"), and Yahweh's words therefore embody didactic commands (compare Job 8:8; Sir 8:9), while the witnesses briefly report the people's refusal to obey (for the report, compare 5:2b–3; for the refusal compare 2:20a).

Verses 18–19aα are a summons to the cosmic witnesses of Yahweh's quarrel with Israel (compare 2:12); these witnesses are the "nations" and the "earth" (compare "peoples" and "earth" in Mic 1:2). The witnesses are to hear Yahweh's announcement of judgment (v 19aβ) and the concluding characterization of that judgment (v 19b).[1] These two elements are now expanded (in the reverse and normal order) in vv 20–23. Thus v 20 is

Yahweh's accusation speech to the people. Its first half is an accusatory question, its second half Yahweh's statement of rejection of sacrifices (for the question in an accusation compare 2:29a). Verse 21 begins the announcement of judgment; it is introduced by "therefore" and the messenger formula. In this verse the people are spoken of in the third person. Verses 22–23 continue the announcement of judgment; since there is a fresh messenger formula and the people are addressed in the second-person feminine singular (end of v 23), it is possible that we have here a secondary combination of two units that were discrete at an earlier stage (but vv 21 and 22 were evidently associated in Jrm's mind: see Structure, *Extent of the Unit*).

The response of the people (v 24) is dismay and anguish, the conventional reaction of people subjected to bad news;[2] for the vocabulary compare 4:31; 30:5–7.

Yahweh's speech in v 25 is something of a reprise: battle commands to avoid the enemy, followed by the explanation introduced by כִּי (for the form compare 4:5–6; 6:1).

Finally, Jrm addresses the people in an appeal to lament, closed by a citation of the lamentation to be used (precisely like 4:8).

Setting
Several pieces of evidence point to a time after the king burned the scroll (December 601). The first is the reference to "watchmen" rejected by the people (v 17). "Watchmen" is here a designation for prophets (see Interpretation), so that the accusation that the people have rejected the prophets must be associated with 7:25 and parallels (see there): the setting for the passage suggests the setting here. Again, the diction of v 21 resembles that in vv 11–12 and 15, so that the setting proposed for that passage will be comparable to the setting here. Finally, "terror is all around" (v 25) appears to be a generalization of its specific use in the incident with Passhur (20:1–6). As to that incident, the preponderance of evidence suggests that it was the immediate consequence of Jrm's smashing of the earthenware flask, narrated in chapter 19 (see 19:1—20:6, Preliminary Observations). The smashing of the flask must have

---

1   For "concluding characterization" see Klaus Koch, *The Growth of the Biblical Tradition, The Form-Critical Method* (New York: Scribner's, 1969) 193–94.

2   See Delbert R. Hillers, "A Convention in Hebrew Literature: The Reaction to Bad News," *ZAW* 77 (1965) 86–90, esp. 87; Berridge, pp. 88–89.

taken place after the king burned the scroll (see Setting there), and therefore this present passage as well. A time early in the year 600 is appropriate.

Interpretation

■ **16–17** Volz, Rudolph, and Bright seek in various ways to rectify a text that they feel offers a confusion of personal references. Thus Volz and Bright would insert "I said" (אָמַרְתִּי) before "stand," and Volz, Rudolph, and Bright would read "over them" (עֲלֵיהֶם) for "over you" (עֲלֵיכֶם) in v 17. Neither change is called for (for a critique of the latter see Form).

The verb "stand" (עמד) carries the connotation of a military command (in Nah 2:9 the *RSV* translates עָמְדוּ עֲמֹדוּ as "Halt, halt!"). Volz and Rudolph are doubtful about "and look," Volz emending "roads and look" (דְּרָכִים וּרְאוּ) to "roads of the founders" (דַּרְכֵי הָרִאשֹׁנִים), while Rudolph, following Godfrey R. Driver,[3] reads "roads from the beginning" (דַּרְכֵי מֵרֹאשׁ).[4] Though these suggestions give good parallelism with "paths of old," "look" gives parallelism with "ask," and 5:1, in a similar context, likewise offers "and look," so emendation is not necessary.

The expression שאל לְ can mean either "ask about, ask for" (15:5) or "ask (someone something)" (Job 8:8, a close parallel to the present passage: see Form). A decision between these depends partly on whether one takes the next colon as a direct question (so the translation here) or as an indirect question, "Ask for the paths of old, (ask) where the road to good is." The second colon of v 17 is probably a direct quotation, the call of the watchmen (see Form), so that a direct quotation in v 16 commends itself on the basis of poetic balance. And as to the related problem whether "where . . ." is a direct or indirect quotation, the expression אֵי־זֶה suggests that it is direct,[5] and the direct question in v 20, introduced by "why" (לָמָּה־זֶּה) echoes it.

What are the "paths of old" (נְתִבוֹת עוֹלָם)? J. Philip Hyatt suggests they are the ways of Moses. If the

chronology of the present study is valid, they could well be the ways of Moses made known through the Deuteronomic law. The phrase דֶּרֶךְ הַטּוֹב does not mean "the good way" (*RSV, JB,* which would require either two articles or no article), but rather "the way to good" (so, with variations in phrasing, *NEB, NAB, NJV*). Yahweh begs the people to find the road back to healthy community: if the people walk on that road, they will find "repose" (מַרְגּוֹעַ). This word is a *hapax legomenon* in the OT, but the related מַרְגֵּעַ in Isa 28:12 carries the same meaning: these nouns and the related verb רגע refer to surcease from international pressure; it is close to the current phrase "national security," the ability to live without constant tension and uneasiness before the threat of disaster from abroad. (The reflection of this phrase in Matt 11:29 has moved the center of meaning beyond purely national security!) The people refuse, however.

The verb וַהֲקִמֹתִי appears to refer to repeated action in the past (GKC, sec. 112dd); one notes the Masoretic accent on the last syllable (GKC, sec. 49h). The participle צֹפִים is the standard term for "watchmen" (2 Sam 18:24–27). Since the object of "pay attention to" here is "the sound of the trumpet," while in v 19 it is "my words and my law," it is clear that "watchmen" is a metaphor for prophets (as in Hos 9:8; Ezek 3:17; 33:1–7). For "pay attention" see 6:10. The people pay no heed to the prophets' warning.

■ **18–19a**α *M* for these four cola is not convincing, but I submit that Volz emends too much, and Rudolph as well; Bright, for his part, abandons the attempt for the second and third cola. Volz proposes "hear, O heavens" (שִׁמְעוּ שָׁמַיִם, compare Isa 1:2), but the collection of Jrm's oracles has already offered "be appalled, O heavens" (שֹׁמּוּ שָׁמַיִם, 2:12, without a mention of "earth"), and given "hear, O earth" in the present passage, that suggestion cannot be right. Mic 1:2, a similar form-critical context, offers a parallel between "peoples" (עַמִּים) and "earth," so "nations" is convincing here.

---

3   Godfrey R. Driver, "Linguistic and Textual Problems: Jeremiah," *JQR* 28 (1937/38) 103.

4   For a preposition in a construct chain, see GKC, sec. 130a.

5   Though that expression in 1 Sam 9:18 is assumed in the translations to introduce an indirect question, it may be direct (compare the Masoretic accent zaqep qaṭon).

Both "heavens" and "earth" carry the article, evidently a marker for the vocative (GKC, sec. 126e) even though similar vocatives elsewhere (2:12; 22:29; Isa 1:2; Mic 1:2; 6:2) do not carry the article.

The second colon (וּדְעִי עֵדָה) is traditionally translated "and know, O congregation" (*RSV*). But this is suspect: (1) there is no article on the noun as there is on the other two vocatives, and (2) "congregation" (or "assembly") is an odd designation for the addressees. Conceivably the word is the miscopying of an infinitive absolute דְעָה (so Giesebrecht, Rudolph); one notes that the infinitive absolute follows a related imperative (GKC, sec. 113r). But there is no particular call for a reinforcing infinitive absolute along with the other imperatives in the passage. Since Mic 1:2, a passage similar to the present one, uses "witness" (עֵד) as a designation for Yahweh, one is led to a noun homonymous with "congregation," namely עֵדָה "testimony," construed as the object of "know"; the word evidently appears in postbiblical Hebrew with a similar connotation.[6] But if the substantive is an object and not a vocative, the feminine imperative of the verb becomes a problem, best solved by shifting the colon to a position after "hear, O earth," so that "and know" is a parallel imperative (see Text), and "testimony" is perceived as a parallel to "what I shall do against them," itself a restored reading (see again Text).

The assembled nations of the earth are thus summoned to hear the sentence pronounced against the people; for the general context compare again 2:12. The verb phrase "do against" (עשׂה בְ) is used mostly of executing judgment; a close parallel, part of an "assemble and hear" speech, is found in Isa 48:14.

■ **19aβb** For parallels and variations on the phrase "I am going to bring disaster" see 2:3; 4:6; 5:12, 15; for "this people" see 4:10.

"Fruit of their schemes" is a striking phrase (compare Text); the only comparable phrase with "fruit of" in the metaphorical sense is "fruit of their doings" in 17:10 (compare Isa 3:10). For "schemes" (מַחְשְׁבוֹת) see 4:14.

The schemes of the people bring disaster in their own train (compare 2:19), but they also move Yahweh himself to bring disaster.

"They paid no attention" of course picks up the occurrences of that verb in v 17. For "my [i.e., Yahweh's] words" see 5:14; for "law" (תּוֹרָה) see 2:8.

The last colon of the verse is best construed as a *casus pendens*[7] (compare 28:9; 33:24). For "reject" (מאס) see 2:37: but there Yahweh is the one who rejects, while here it is the people who have rejected Yahweh's word and law.

■ **20** The diction of v 19aβb is conventional; one expects such prophetic judgments (compare Isa 5:24). But the rhetorical question of v 20a comes like a bolt from the blue: "Why does frankincense from Sheba come to me . . . ?" And "Why?" is not just לָמָּה but לָמָּה־זֶּה, almost "Why in the world?" One has been thinking of disaster "coming" upon the people from Yahweh's hand, but while he is preparing the disaster, look at what is "coming" on camel-back from the far south, intended for Yahweh: frankincense, sweet cane!

In a subtle way "sweet cane from a land afar" has been prepared for in the diction of v 16. There the parallelism of "paths of old" (נְתִבוֹת עוֹלָם) and "road to good" (דֶּרֶךְ הַטּוֹב) is skewed, so that a repetition of טוֹב (here "sweet") and an occurence of "afar" (מֶרְחָק) is appropriate (compare the parallel of "from far away," מִמֶּרְחָק, and "from long ago," מֵעוֹלָם, 5:15). Therefore "sweet cane [קָנֶה הַטּוֹב] from a distant land [מֵאֶרֶץ מֶרְחָק]."[8]

Frankincense is the fragrant white gum resin from certain trees (genus *Boswellia*) in Arabia; it was one of the major ingredients of the incense prepared to be set before Yahweh according to the P-Code (Exod 30:34–38), and it functioned in other ways in the cult. Sheba is, strictly speaking, the home of the Sabeans in the southwest corner of the Arabian Peninsula, but the frankincense forests were located both there and in what is now called Somaliland, on the mainland of Africa opposite that corner of Arabia.[9] The frankincense came by both

---

6   See Jastrow, s.v.
7   See GKC, sec. 143d; Joüon, *Gramm.*, sec. 176o.
8   Holladay, *Architecture*, 95.
9   Gus W. Van Beek, "Frankincense and Myrrh," *BA* 23 (1960) 70–94 = David Noel Freedman and Edward F. Campbell, Jr., eds., *The Biblical Archaeologist Reader, 2* (Garden City, NY: Doubleday, 1964) 99–126; Harrell F. Beck, "Frankincense," *IDB* 2:324–25;

Nigel St. J. Groom, *Frankincense and Myrrh: A Study of the Arabian Incense Trade* (London and New York: Longman; Beirut: Librairie du Liban, 1981).

sea and land, and the distance rendered it very expensive.[10] It was an immense effort, this importation of frankincense; and why?—Yahweh wants to know.

As to the companion phrase "sweet cane," this commodity was also used in the cult, in the holy anointing oil (Exod 30:23), and was evidently imported from India.[11] The use of "afar" (מֶרְחָק) here is in contrast to the use in 5:15: there Yahweh uses an exotic nation to punish his own people, while here his people use exotic goods in an attempt to keep his favor.

It is clear from the rhetorical question that Jrm perceives Yahweh to affirm that the importation of frankincense and sweet cane is of no use whatever: for Jrm's seeming rejection of the cult see below.

The frankincense and sweet cane are in a way marginal to the cult: important items, but brought in small quantities at great cost from abroad. But burnt offerings and sacrifices are central; these were offered steadily, daily. The terms for types of sacrifice shifted with the period and are notoriously difficult to make precise. The two terms occurring here, עֹלָה and זֶבַח (here "burnt offering" and "sacrifice" respectively), are often paired, and one has the impression that for the early period these two covered the totality of sacrifices, or at least of animal sacrifices (compare Hos 6:6; Ps 50:8).[12] The "burnt offering" (עֹלָה) was an animal offering which was totally consumed on the altar; the "sacrifice" (זֶבַח) was an animal offering in which only the inedible parts were burned, the rest being shared among the participants.[13] The expression "acceptable" (לְרָצוֹן) embodies the noun רָצוֹן "acceptance." This is the only occurrence of this noun in the book. Jrm must have had the laws of Leviticus in mind: in those laws anything with a blemish should not be sacrificed, "for it shall not be acceptable to you" (כִּי־לֹא לְרָצוֹן יִהְיֶה לָכֶם, Lev 22:20). (Note also the use of the related verb רצה "accept" in Hos 8:13.) "To me" in the last colon does double duty for the previous colon as well: "Your burnt offerings are not acceptable to me." The verb "be pleasing" (ערב) is evidently a technical term in the cult;[14] the present passage may be imitative of Hos 9:4, where much the same phraseology is found. It appears then that both "acceptance" (רָצוֹן) and "be pleasing" (ערב) are technical terms from the cult and may have been the terms used by the priests in pronouncing the sacrifice worthy.[15] In this case Jrm perceives Yahweh to be contradicting the specific cultic procedure.

The implication of the verse is that Jrm affirms the rejection of the sacrificial system altogether, and it then takes its place alongside 7:21–22; Isa 1:10–17; Hos 6:6; 8:13; 9:4; Amos 5:21–24; and Mic 6:6–8 (and, beyond the prophetic literature, 1 Sam 15:22–23; Pss 40:7; 50:8–15; and 51:18–19, and perhaps Prov 15:8; 21:3; and 21:27, at least by implication). The literature on the issue is widespread.[16] The prophets, including Jrm, did not so much have in mind a cultless religion as they were insistent that personal and community responsiveness takes priority, and that any cultic act unaccompanied by loyalty and sensitivity was meaningless. There is no question but that cultic practice had become more elaborate by Jrm's day: any religious establishment (one might say almost "any religious bureaucracy") tends to increase both staff and work as time goes on. To center on this is not what Yahweh has in mind: so one must understand these passages.

■ 21 Now the announcement of punishment: Yahweh is to put obstacles amongst his people on which they shall stumble. The word "obstacle" (מִכְשֹׁל) is normally translated "stumbling-block," but the translation must express something physical, not merely metaphorical: compare the law in Lev 19:14. That law forbids placing an obstacle before a blind person: and it was suggested in 5:21 that the people are metaphorically blind; does the passage then imply that Yahweh has been moved to break the law?

The verse ends with a listing of groups in the population, a sequence much like that in v 11. The phrase שָׁכֵן וְרֵעוֹ is difficult to render literally. The שָׁכֵן is a "resident (somewhere)," usually a "neighbor," but his place of

---

10 See Van Beek (n. 9, above) for estimated cost in terms of current prices.

11 John C. Trever, "Sweet Cane," *IDB* 4:468–69.

12 For a listing of parallels and contrasts in terminology alongside זֶבַח see *HALAT*, 252, no. 3.

13 For a full account of these matters see Kraus, *Worship*, 115–21.

14 So von Rad, *OT Theology 1*, 261.

15 See ibid.

16 See Eichrodt, *Theology* 1:364–68, and the literature cited in Wolff, *Joel and Amos*, 258, and Wildberger, *Jesaja*, 32.

residence (usually "next door" or the like) is normally expressed (Exod 12:4; Prov 27:10). The רֵעַ is one's peer (5:8). The expression here then means "people next door to each other." All these folk shall not only stumble but perish.

■ 22 For the description of the enemy beginning with "See!" (הִנֵּה) compare 4:13. The diction here is reminiscent of 5:15. It is ironic that frankincense comes from the far south, from Sheba, while the enemy is coming from the distant north. (For the identity of the enemy see 4:6.) It is striking that Jrm uses "people" (עַם) for the enemy. This word is in the first instance a poetic synonym for "nation" (גּוֹי) in the next colon, yet "people" carries overtones of kinship and common cause. To this point the word has occurred seventeen times in the book, but always of Israel; is there a hint here that Yahweh may be dealing with that foreign people now rather than Israel?

The verb "be aroused" (עוּר nip'al) is not common, occurring only twice otherwise in Jer (25:32, of the whirlwind, and 50:41, of kings); the word is used of waking from sleep, and being aroused to love. And the noun "extremes" (יַרְכָּה, dual) is not common either (otherwise in Jer: 25:32; 31:8; 50:41). The repetition of conventional phraseology for the enemy ("north," so far seven times in the book, and "nation") here stimulates fresh vocabulary. (For synonymous expressions, see further Isa 5:26.)

■ 23 Now a description of the enemy. First, they grasp their weapons. Of course, one agrees, the enemy does this by definition; still, it is a terrible thing to see the enemy coming on fully armed. They are armed with a "bow" (קֶשֶׁת) and a second weapon (כִּידוֹן), the identity of which needs clarification. The word occurs only nine times: Josh 8:18 (twice); 8:26; 1 Sam 17:6, 45; Jer 6:23 = 50:42; Job 39:23; 41:21. The passages in Job are poetic, those in Joshua are concerned with the battle for Ai (Joshua extended his כִּידוֹן in a symbolic gesture), and those in 1 Samuel are concerned with the weapon of the

Philistine giant. In short, all the passages except those in Jer have to do with an exotic weapon, or a weapon described in poetic terms. Now the word turns up in a passage of the War Scroll of Qumran (1QM v 7, 11, 12, 14, vi 5). The description in these passages is of a short weapon a cubit and a half in length (thus about 75 centimeters: see 1QM v 13), evidently envisioned as a sickle-sword or cutlass.[17] The problem is that Assyrian bas-reliefs show infantrymen who are (1) bowmen and (2) spearmen;[18] the bas-reliefs also depict slingmen and shield-bearers,[19] but they are irrelevant to the discussion. The length of the spears in these depictions appears to be about the same as the height of the spearmen; if one assumes a height of roughly five and a half feet (1.65–1.70 meters), then one is left with a spear more than twice as long as that envisaged at Qumran. The Qumran community was using archaic language to describe an apocalyptic vision, and I propose that the bas-reliefs take precedence over the Qumran descriptions as evidence. The parallel to "bow" is often "arrows," as one might expect (Isa 5:28), and also "sword" (Isa 41:2). In one instance the parallel is "spear" (חֲנִית, Ps 46:10). Jrm may well have intended an exotic term here (and it is possible that Babylonian spears were longer than those usual in Palestine), but the simple translation "spear" seems best in this passage.

The second colon offers two synonyms for mercilessness: one cannot expect kindness from these troops; nothing will turn their heads. And their sound (third and fourth cola)! One has heard the roar of the waves of the sea (5:22): that is what this army sounds like. And they ride horses. That colon is by no means anticlimactic, as one might today assume; if one is a Palestinian villager or a foot-soldier, then horsemen are terrifying. The reference here is evidently to cavalrymen. Assyrian bas-reliefs depict cavalrymen in pairs, one with bow, the other on his own horse beside the first, grasping the reins of both horses;[20] compare 4:29. Later Assyrian bas-reliefs depict lone riders.[21] Though cavalry was suited

17 For bibliography on the discussion of the Qumran description see conveniently HALAT, 450a.
18 See the reproductions in Yadin, Warfare, 430–31, 434–35, 436–37, 443, 444–45.
19 See ibid., 294–95, 430.
20 Ibid., 384–85.
21 Ibid., 384.

for warfare on the open field rather than for siege operations,[22] they were certainly useful for opening battle before the infantrymen were engaged.

Commentators doubt the soundness of *M* in the fifth colon. *G* reads ὡς πῦρ "like fire" = כְּאֵשׁ for *M* כְּאִישׁ; this reading has no claim to authenticity but does indicate the antiquity of the preposition כְּ, so that Rudolph's suggestion, כָּל־אִישׁ "every man (drawn up for battle)," or John A. Emerton's, to omit כְּ, "each (drawn up for battle),"[23] needs to be very convincing to be accepted. But "like a man" seems to balance "like the sea" in the third colon; and the text in 50:42 reads exactly as here, suggesting at least that one does not have some *lapsus calami* for this passage alone. It is likely that Jrm is blending two phrases, אִישׁ מִלְחָמָה "warrior, footsoldier" (compare Isa 3:2) and עָרוּךְ לַמִּלְחָמָה "drawn up for battle" (compare 46:3; Joel 2:5). The phrase then suggests that the enemy has cavalry drawn up as closely and numerously as Judah is wont to have infantry (compare the boast of the king of Assyria, 2 Kgs 18:23). All this is bearing down on "poor Zion."

■ **24** Now the people speak, "We have heard a rumor of it." The phrase is very much like Josh 9:9, כִּי שָׁמַעְנוּ שָׁמְעוּ, "for we have heard talk of him [Yahweh]." "Report" (*RSV, NAB, NJV*) is not quite right, suggesting in our day verified news reports. This is rumor, talk in the village squares, but one such rumor is enough to cause panic. The reaction described in this verse is the convention of the panic among victims of holy war (see Form), but the fact remains that such descriptions are based on the real reactions of people.

"Our hands fall slack." The verb רפה qal occurs fourteen times, nine times with "hands"; it is a standard phrase for panic (compare Ezek 7:17–18, where the phrase appears in a colorful series of descriptions). The next phrase, "misery has gripped us," is ironic in two respects. First, the enemy "grips" his weapons (v 23, the same verb, חזק), but misery has gripped us. Second, our hands, which should "grip" weapons, have fallen slack

(note Neh 6:9, where "their hands will fall slack" appears alongside "strengthen [חזק pi'el] my hands"). "Misery" (צָרָה) is associated with childbirth in 4:31 and 49:24, but the context in 4:31 suggests that one may have a double meaning there, not only "misery" but "imploring" or the like (see there); the same situation may prevail here. Yahweh has declared holy war against his people, and the people respond as their enemies did in times past when subjected to holy war.

■ **25** "Don't go out to the field"—to do one's work of cultivation, of course; but what alternative is there? Huddle in the village? What contradictory orders we have heard! "Flee to the walled cities!" (4:5)—but the enemy will destroy those cities (5:17). "Get out of Jerusalem!" (6:1)—but then refugees will have nowhere to turn but thickets and caves (4:29). It does not appear that Yahweh has provided any escape for folk who want to stay alive. "Don't even go out for a walk!" (One notes in passing the chiasmus of the two cola, in which the predicates are sandwiched by the two verbs.) It was learned in 5:6 that everyone who "goes out" from the cities will be torn by the lion (that is, the enemy), and in 4:7 that the destroyed of nations has "gone out" from his own place. The world outside belongs to the enemy, and the third colon here says it: the enemy has a sword. Curiously, this is the first time the word "enemy" (אֹיֵב) has appeared in Jer; commentators are accustomed to speak about the "foe from the north," but it has always been a "nation" (5:15), or, even more indirectly, "disaster" (4:6). But it is clear who it is, and now it is stated straight out—the enemy.

The phrase "terror all around" has a quite specific relevance in the incident with Pashhur, the officer-priest at the temple (20:1–6), and I have given evidence elsewhere[24] that the phrase in the present passage is a generalization of Jrm's threat to Pashhur (compare Setting). Now the people in general will share the fate of that priest. Is the expression here connected with the

22   Ibid., 297.

23   John A. Emerton, "A Problem in the Hebrew Text of Jeremiah vi. 23 and l. 42," *JTS* NS 23 (1972) 106–13.

24   William L. Holladay, "The Covenant with the Patriarchs Overturned: Jeremiah's Intention in

'Terror on Every Side' (Jer 20:1–6)," *JBL* 91 (1972) 305–20, esp. 318.

word on the rejection of cult in v 20?

■ **26** Now Jrm speaks (compare 4:8, 14: see Form). He appeals to the people to lament in chagrin and repentance; the diction is very close to that in 4:8: for "gird on sackcloth," see that verse. The verb here translated "roll" (פלש hitpa'el) occurs only four times, once otherwise in Jer (25:34). An antecedent passage, with a more common word for "dust" (עָפָר) than the word which appears here (אֵפֶר), is Mic 1:10, part of a sequence of word-plays on village names, and that passage is doubtless part of the background of the phrase in the present verse. The Versions vary: *G, V* "sprinkle (oneself)"; *T* "cover one's head"; *S* "roll." Both Rashi and Qimḥi translate "roll," and since the verb seems to have that meaning in post-biblical Hebrew;[25] it is to be translated "grovel" in 25:34.[26] Perhaps the Versions did not understand the more violent reaction to death that the verb denotes.

The word "dust" here (אֵפֶר) is elsewhere associated with the more common synonym עָפָר (so Gen 18:27), so that Jrm's variation of the phrase in Micah (see above) is plausible; it is associated with "sackcloth" in Isa 58:5. But whereas עָפָר sometimes seems to suggest "mud" (Lev 14:41–42),[27] אֵפֶר is sometimes used for "ashes" (Num 19:9–10). In the context of mourning, however, such distinctions make little difference.

"Mourning for an only son" is a phrase found in Amos 8:10; Jrm may be quoting it.[28] Clearly the mourning for an only son lost is not only mourning the lost child himself, but for all hope of descendants: it means extinction, it is the end, the mourning to end all mourning. "Only son" (יָחִיד) occurs only here in Jer. "Bitterness" (תַּמְרוּרִים) occurs only otherwise in 31:15; that passage is a good parallel to the present one—there Rachel weeps for her lost children, for "not one is left."

The conjunction כִּי here introduces a direct quotation, the content of the lamentation, just as in 4:8 (so Rudolph also in both instances). This passage is very close in diction to both 4:13 and 4:20, so that כִּי doubtless also carries the nuance of "how" (see there). "Comes" reflects "is coming" in v 22, and "against us" reflects "against you" in v 23.

Aim

The contents of every speech in this passage are appalling, but on the other hand almost everything here has been said earlier in chapters 4—6; the passage serves, in a way, as a summary of the news of the coming of the foe from the north. One verse does offer new material, v 20, the rejection of the centrality of the cult. The matter is discussed above (Interpretation), but another word must be said here, especially in view of the opposition Jrm exerted on the priestly establishment of the temple.

Jrm preached a sermon in the court of the temple in 609 (26:1–2); the sermon is recorded in 7:1–12, and the consequences of his preaching it—he narrowly escaped a death sentence—are recounted in 26:7–24. In 605, we learn, he was restricted from going to the temple (36:1, 5), so he was at least then persona non grata to the Jerusalem priesthood. And it was perhaps in December of 601 or early in 600 when Pashhur locked him in the stocks at the temple overnight (20:1–3). The Deuteronomic reform in 622 had resulted in the rediscovery of Moses and the purification of the cult, but that reform had no doubt brought its share of complacency in its train. It would be a shock, then, for worshipers to learn that the sacrifices prescribed in the law should be unacceptable to Yahweh. What kind of God is it who tells his people to put all their eggs in one basket and then tells them that that one basket is unworthy?

Jrm thus allied himself with other prophets and wise men in Israel who taught Yahweh's hatred of religious routine, of "standard operating procedure," of every gesture that was empty rather than filled with glad responsiveness to him. This tradition of tension with the cult would find its culmination in the astonishing words of Trito-Isaiah (Isa 66:1–4) and its New Testament seal in Jesus (Mark 11:15–18) and his interpreters (Heb 9:11—10:18).

---

25 See Jastrow.

26 Godfrey R. Driver, "Studies in the Vocabulary of the Old Testament," *JTS* 31 (1929/30) 275–76.

27 Compare Dahood, *Psalms I, II, III*, passim.

28 Berridge, p. 101.

Jeremiah the Assayer

Bibliography
Dahood, Mitchell
  "Hebrew-Ugaritic Lexicography I," *Bib* 44 (1963) 298.
Driver, Godfrey R.
  "Two Misunderstood Passages of the Old Testament: Jeremiah vi. 27–30," *JTS*, NS 6 (1955) 84–87.
Holladay
  Architecture, 93–97.
Loretz, Oswald
  "'Verworfenes Silber' (Jer 6,27–30)," *Wort, Lied und Gottesspruch 2, Beiträge zu Psalmen und Propheten, Festschrift für Joseph Ziegler* (ed. Josef Schreiner; Forschung zur Bibel 2; Würzburg: Echter, 1972) 231–32.
Robinson, Theodore H.
  "The Text of Jeremiah vi 27–30, in the Light of Ezekiel xxii 17–22," *JTS* 16 (1914/15) 482–90.
Soggin, J. Alberto
  "Jeremias vi 27–30, Einige textkritische Bemerkungen," *VT* 9 (1959) 95–98.

On the metallurgy of lead and silver:
Aitchison, Leslie
  A History of Metals (London: Macdonald & Evans, 1960) 182–83.
Forbes, Robert J.
  Metallurgy in Antiquity (Leiden: Brill, 1950).
Forbes, Robert J.
  "Extracting, Smelting, and Alloying," *A History of Technology* (ed. Charles Singer, E. J. Holmyard, and A. R. Hall; Oxford: Oxford University, 1954) 582–85.
Forbes, Robert J.
  "Metallurgy," *A History of Technology* (ed. Charles Singer et al.; Oxford: Oxford University, 1956) 2:43–46, and see 66 and 67 for the illustrations of furnaces from fifteenth-century Germany.
Forbes, Robert J.
  Studies in Ancient Technology 8 (Leiden: Brill, 1964).
Percy, John
  The Metallurgy of Lead, Including Desilverization and Cupellation (London: Murray, 1870).
Percy, John
  Metallurgy: The Art of Extracting Metals from Their Ores, Silver and Gold, Part I (London: Murray, 1880).
Wertime, Theodore A.
  "Man's First Encounters with Metallurgy," *Science* 146 (December 4, 1964) 1257–67.
Wertime, Theodore A.
  "Beginnings of Metallurgy: A New Look," *Science* 182 (November 30, 1973) 875–87.

See further conveniently:

Gale, Noël H., and Zofia Stos-Gale

  "Lead and Silver in the Ancient Aegean," *Scientific
  American* 244/6 (June 1981) 176–92, and
  bibliography, 202.

On archeology regarding the present
passage:

Barrois, Augustin-Georges

  Manuel d'Archéologie Biblique 1 (Paris: Picard, 1939)
  372.

6

27 Yahweh: **An assayer I have made you among my
  people [⟨rather than a grape-
  harvester⟩],[a]**

  **so that you may know and assay their
  way.**

28 Jeremiah: **They are all princely[a] rebels,**
  bearers of slander,
  bronze and iron, all of them,
  destroyers they are;

29 **[a] the bellows are scorched by the fire,[a]**

Text

27a   *M* reads מִבְצָר, seemingly "fortification" (4:5), a
word that makes no sense in the context. It is not
fruitful to attempt, as Karl H. Graf and Duhm have
done, to revocalize the word as מְבַצֵּר, assuming an
otherwise unattested pi'el stem of בצר "gather
grapes," thus "a searcher" or the like, or to assume
(Volz) a derivative of בֶּצֶר "gold" (Job 22:24). It is
most simply explained as a gloss, מִבֹּצֵר "rather than
a grape-gatherer"; for מִן "rather than" compare
15:19; Hos 6:6; Hab 2:16. It appears to overload
the colon and is best attributed to a glossator who
noted that Jrm's role had changed from that in v 9,
where בּוֹצֵר appears.

28a   Read with a minority of MSS. and *V*, *S*, and *T*
שָׂרֵי for the majority reading סָרֵי "swervers of
[rebels] (?)." The majority reading may have been
influenced by the sequence סָרוּ . . . סוֹרֵר in 5:23. See
further Interpretation.

29a—a   Verse 29a raises many problems. The ketib
(followed by *S*) is hardly comprehensible (though see
the discussion in Rudolph, p. 48 n. 1). Many MSS.,
the qere' and *G* and *V* read the third word as two,
מֵאֵשׁ תַּם, and this is the text here translated. There
are several interlocking questions to be solved. (1)
What is the root and meaning of the verb נָחַר? (2) Is
the expression מֵאֵשׁ to be construed with the first
colon or the second? (3) Is the text sound for the
verb תַּם, and is it to be translated "is used up"
(Rudolph) or "comes whole" (Bright)? The answer to
(3) depends to a large degree on an understanding
of the metallurgy involved; see Excursus. As to (1),
commentators since Michaelis have with virtual
unanimity derived the verb on the basis of an Arabic
cognate from a root נחר "blow," but the root is cited
only for this passage in the lexica. The traditional
derivation, however, from חרר nip'al, "be scorched,"
is preferable (so also BDB). As C. W. Eduard
Naegelsbach points out (p. 86), the meaning "is on
fire, is red hot" is "required by the connection, for it
is to be declared, that an extreme degree of heat
was applied, which is here denoted by the burning
of the bellows. . . . The other explanation [the
meaning "blow"] . . . gives an unsatisfactory sense;
for it is not declared generally that the bellows
works, but that it has done its best." It may further
be noted that if "from the fire" is construed with the
first colon (see below), then the meaning "blows" is
hardly likely. As to question (2), in general when
five words are to be divided between two cola, the

30

the lead ᵃis consumedᵃ—
in vain ᵇ the refinerᵇ has refined,
but the evil are not separated out
"reject silver" they are called,
for Yahweh has rejected them.

division of three plus two prevails (thus so v 29b).
And as to (3), תַּם may be construed as the masculine
third singular perfect qal of תמם, but this requires
that עֹפֶרֶת "lead" be masculine. Since nouns in
unaccented -et are normally feminine, Duhm may be
correct in suggesting a haplography here for תַּתָּם or
תֻּתַּם. But since נְחֹשֶׁת "bronze" is masculine in at least
one passage (1 Kgs 7:45), it may be that עֹפֶרֶת is
masculine and that תַּם is correct here after all.

b—b צָרוֹף is normally construed as an infinitive
absolute of צרף qal, but such an expression hardly
makes sense with "in vain." It is better to understand
the word as an agent noun with a formation like
בָּחוֹן "assayer" in v 27 (see GKC, sec. 84ᵃk; Bauer-
Leander, sec. 61 ja, ka); so Rudolph.

Structure and Form

This little passage serves as a kind of coda to vv 16–26; as
a "final report" by Jrm to Yahweh on the people it is
appropriate at the end of (a particular stage of) the
poetic sequence on the foe from the north. The call to
the prophet in v 27, "an assayer I have made you among
my people" (בָּחוֹן נְתַתִּיךָ בְעַמִּי), may offer an inclusio to "a
prophet to the nations I have appointed you" (נָבִיא לַגּוֹיִם
נְתַתִּיךָ) in 1:5. In this way its placement here is appropriate.

The structure of the passage is simple: Yahweh
addresses Jrm in the bicolon of v 27, and then Jrm speaks
(at least one presumes so: see below) in the remaining
verses. The division into cola of v 28 has been uncertain
because of perceived textual difficulties: both Rudolph
and Bright omit material, and thus Rudolph posits a
bicolon and Bright a tricolon. But it is the conclusion of
the present study that the text of the verse is sound. If so,
the verse is a symmetrical tetracolon ("all of them"
beginning the first colon and ending the third). Furthermore, the tetracolon itself renders vv 28–30 symmetrical: thus the tetracolon of v 28 balances the two bicola
in vv 29b–30, both sequences offering a report on the
people's conduct, while the middle bicolon (v 29a) sets
forth the metallurgical metaphor anticipated in v 27.

The form of v 27 is a prophetic call parallel to 1:5 (see
above); this call, that Jrm be an assayer, is the delegation
to him of a function ordinarily characteristic of Yahweh
(9:6 and often). This is the only passage within 4:5—6:30
offering a prophetic call: the closest parallel is 6:9, the
resemblance to which has occasioned the gloss in this
verse.

There is no absolute indication that vv 28–30 are
Jrm's reply; Yahweh could continue to speak (the third-

person reference to Yahweh does not rule out this
possibility: compare 2:3). But the metaphor of "assayer"
strongly suggests that these verses are Jrm's report (so
also Rudolph, Bright). The messenger-prophet has full
authority to assess the situation as Yahweh would do and
to report back the details. The situation is then similar to
that presupposed by the report of the spies to Canaan in
Num 13:27–29. But one wonders, to whom is Jrm
reporting?—to Yahweh, or to the witnesses in a cosmic
law-court scene? One might compare here the report of
Yahweh the schoolmaster (4:22).

Setting

The people are here "reject silver"; Yahweh has no way
to salvage them. And Jrm is involved in the process of
judgment (v 27). Both data suggest that this material was
part of the additions made in the second scroll (36:32);
for Jrm's involvement in the process of judgment
compare 5:14; 6:11 (and see further 4:5—10:25,
Preliminary Observations, *Settings*). A date early in 600 is
appropriate.

Interpretation

■ 27 The noun "assayer" (בָּחוֹן) occurs only here in the
OT, but the verb "assay" (בחן) occurs not only in the
second colon but five more times in Jer (9:6 and four
times in the "confessions"—11:20; 12:3; 17:10; 20:12),
each time with Yahweh as subject. This passage is then
the only occurrence in the book where a human being
serves as the assayer; and the occurrences of the verb in
other books carry God as subject eleven out of eighteen
times. The verb occurs both in the technical sense of
assaying or testing metals and in the metaphorical sense
of "testing" the character of the people; for passages

where the connotation of metal-testing is used metaphorically see Zech 13:9 and Job 23:10. The standard metaphorical use is enlarged here quite elaborately. One notes that Isa 1:23 speaks of rebellious princes (in diction similar to that here in v 28) and Isa 1:25 of refining metal (though not with the verb "assay," בחן), so that the association of ideas was ready at hand. For "I have made you" (נְתַתִּיךָ) see 1:5 (and compare Structure and Form). For the gloss "rather than a grape-harvester" see Text, and Structure and Form.

The second colon begins with a simple וְ and an imperfect: the colon is thus a final clause (GKC, sec. 165a). The verb usually translated "know" (ידע) may have as here the meaning "learn, find out" (compare Job 21:19; Esth 2:11). The verb "assay" is here established in the orbit of a final examination. For "way" (דֶּרֶךְ) in the meaning of "conduct" see 2:33.

■ **28** The text not only of v 29a but of the present verse has occasioned doubt among the commentators, but it is plausible to take the text as it is. Thus there is no need to excise the words "bronze and iron" with Giesebrecht, Volz, Rudolph, and Bright; these metals may appear in the unsuccessful refining process (see Excursus below). But the present position of the 'atnaḥ with "and iron" (וּבַרְזֶל) is wrong: it is a reading which leaves "all of them are destroyers" (כֻּלָּם מַשְׁחִיתִים הֵמָּה) as one colon. If, on the contrary, "all of them" is construed with "bronze and iron," then "destroyers they are" becomes the last colon and one is left with a tetracolon with nice parallelism (see Structure and Form).

The phrase "princely rebels" (שָׂרֵי סוֹרְרִים) is Jrm's twist on phrases in the eighth-century prophets: Isa 1:23, "your princes are rebels" (שָׂרַיִךְ סוֹרְרִים), and Hos 9:15, "all their princes are rebels" (כָּל־שָׂרֵיהֶם סֹרְרִים). In the eighth century the princes were rebels; now, says Jrm, all the people are princes of rebels—everyone is now what only the leadership had been a century before. (Compare the democratization by Jrm in 9:21 of Elijah's word regarding Jezebel, 2 Kgs 9:37, and compare also the more extreme version which Jrm offers in 2:12 of Isaiah's address to the heavens, Isa 1:2.) Jrm is undoubtedly expanding on Isaiah's word in 1:23 (see the discussion above on "assayer," v 27). At the same time the

association of "rebellious" (סוֹרֵר) in 5:23 with "they have turned away" (סָרוּ) opens the possibility of a word-play here on סָרֵי, participle of "turn away" (סור), thus "swervers of rebels" or the like (hence the majority reading in M: see Text).

The phrase "bearers of scandal" (הֹלְכֵי רָכִיל) offers inner consonant harmony, as does the parallel phrase in the first colon, "princely rebels" (שָׂרֵי סוֹרְרִים), and there is likeness of vowel pattern as well between the two phrases. The law in Lev 19:16 associates "go, walk" (הלך) and "slander" (רָכִיל): "You shall not go about a talebearer among your people," and indeed Prov 11:13 and 20:19 offer the singular participial phrase הֹלֵךְ רָכִיל (and note that the two words are also associated in Jer 9:3). The noun רָכִיל means "slander," but the singular participial phrase appears to mean "talebearer" (compare GKC, sec. 118q). The plural participle הֹלְכֵי may resonate with the pun on *סָרֵי "swervers of" in the first colon (see above): their action of walking here and there is destructive.

The phrase "bronze and iron" suggests stubbornness (compare the metaphor of the unyielding sky and earth in Deut 28:23, and see further the discussion on Jer 15:12). Yet the possibility of a deposit of copper, tin, and iron on the top of the "reject silver" in the refining process must not be ruled out (see Excursus below).

The word "destroyer" (מַשְׁחִית) seems to carry the specific meaning of "raider" in 5:26; everywhere it carries overtones of the enemy (compare 22:7). In 5:26 the rich man had become the enemy of the poor man; here, it would seem, the whole people is in mutual enmity. The phrase echoes Isa 1:4, where בָּנִים מַשְׁחִיתִים suggests "children who are mutually destructive."

■ **29a**

Excursus: The Cupellation of Silver

There is no doubt that the metaphor in v 29a is that of the cupellation of silver, so that attention must be given at this point to the metallurgy of lead and silver.

Silver is rarely found free in nature but is bound commonly in association with lead ores;[1] and the converse is equally true—almost all lead ore contains a small percentage of silver.[2] Lead ore is commonly distributed in the Middle East.[3] The lead itself had no particular economic value at the time[4] but was simply

---

1   Percy, *Lead*, 95–97.
2   Forbes, *Metallurgy*, 179–80; *Studies 8*, 203.
3   Forbes, *Metallurgy*, 180; *Studies 8*, 204.

4   Forbes, *Metallurgy*, 173; *Studies 8*, 197–98.

present in the process of refining silver (see below).

Silver was extracted in two stages: (1) the smelting of the ore, and (2) the refining of silver from crude lead. It is the second stage that is at issue in v 29a, but a word must be said first about smelting.

The most common lead ore is galena (lead sulfide, PbS); since other lead ores are by comparison insignificant, it was galena that was ordinarily smelted for silver,[5] though no doubt cerussite (lead carbonate, $PbCO_3$) and anglesite (lead sulfate, $PbSO_4$), often associated with galena deposits, were exploited for silver as well.[6] It must be understood, however, that galena for the ancient metallurgist was rarely pure lead sulfide but carried copper, iron, antimony,[7] and tin[8] in small proportions as well; and the presence of these metals greatly complicated the refining process. The proportion of silver in galena varies from .05% to 1.0%,[9] and it is this silver which was to be extracted.

The production of crude lead (containing the silver) is accomplished by the smelting of galena in two processes which ideally occur in sequence: (a) roasting and (b) reduction. The galena is roasted (heated gently in a blast of air): it decomposes into sulfur dioxide (SO_2) gas, which escapes, leaving a mixture of intact galena, lead sulfate ($PbSO_4$) and litharge (lead oxide, PbO). Ideally the roasting continues until practically all the galena has been transformed into litharge. The litharge is then reduced (deoxidized) by the burning of charcoal (or coke or wood) at a higher temperature and a (relative) absence of air; the litharge and lead sulfate interact to form sulphur dioxide, and what is left is molten lead.[10] But "it should . . . always be remembered that the deliberate differentiation and recognition of several reactions is the modern phase and the 'simple' method of primitive metallurgy is really a complicated mess of reactions which could only be duplicated with much practical skill and keen observation of product and process, because the reactions were not understood as they are today."[11] The smelting process could take place in a simple hearth-furnace or even in a sloping trench.[12] Since the process of smelting is not at issue in the Jer passage, no

more need be said about it here.

Silver was extracted in ancient times by "cupellation."[13] This was the case whether the silver was to be extracted from the crude lead produced by smelting, or whether a small amount of metal purporting to be silver was to be assayed (metal which may have been contaminated by fraud or by accident, or alloyed by previous working—in jewelry, for example), or whether a large amount of used metal containing silver was to be refined. A "cupel" (French *coupelle*, a small cup) is a shallow vessel made of some porous substance, usually bone-ash; but marl or other clays were also used.[14] Bone-ash was used because it is unaffected by the very corrosive molten litharge that is produced by the process. In assaying metal of dubious silver content, one or more cupels were placed under a clay muffle in the furnace, the metal to be assayed was placed in the cupel under ten to twenty times the weight of lead (less if the silver appeared to be nearly pure) and the process begun. If larger amounts of impure silver were to be refined, or if crude lead was to be treated to extract the silver, then the silver combined with lead, or argentiferous lead, was treated in a hearth prepared of bone-ash pounded fine.

The furnace was heated until the molten lead became bright red (between 900 and 1000 degrees centigrade).[15] A blast of air was then blown across the molten lead, converting it to litharge (lead oxide), which was then absorbed into the porous cupel, leaving the silver intact.[16] Silver is not oxidized by temperatures far beyond its melting-point;[17] rather, molten silver absorbs oxygen and gives it off again during solidification.[18] It is not certain what sort of furnace was used in the Middle East for cupellation; the basic requirements are a hearth for the achievement of the necessary heat and a source of air to urge the fire and to be blown over the lead to oxidize it. "In the primitive furnaces pre-heating may have been used and after the fire had been lit, the correct temperature obtained and the lead melted, the fire must have been raked toward the sides, the blast introduced and the lead oxidized."[19]

5   Percy, *Lead*, 94.
6   Ibid., 70, 98, 99; Forbes, *Metallurgy*, 180–81; *Studies 8*, 204.
7   Percy, *Lead*, 95.
8   Forbes, *Metallurgy*, 203; *Studies 8*, 229.
9   Forbes, *Metallurgy*, 180; *Studies 8*, 203.
10   Forbes, *Metallurgy*, 202; *Studies 8*, 227–28.
11   Forbes, *Metallurgy*, 202; *Studies 8*, 227.
12   Forbes, *Metallurgy*, 124–29; *Studies 8*, 117–26; "Extracting, Smelting, and Alloying," 584.
13   Forbes, *Metallurgy*, 158, 206; *Studies 8*, 172–73, 231.
14   Forbes, *Metallurgy*, 158; *Studies 8*, 172–73.

15   Percy, *Silver and Gold*, 271; Leslie Aitchison, *A History of Metals* (London: Macdonald & Evans, 1960) 182.
16   Percy, *Lead*, 177.
17   Ibid., 177.
18   Percy, *Silver and Gold*, 8.
19   Forbes, *Metallurgy*, 212; *Studies 8*, 238.

If the process was a simple assay, the bone-ash of the cupel absorbed the litharge; if larger quantities of lead were involved, the litharge flowed away through a notch cut in the side of the hearth. The litharge has the further property of dissolving the oxides of some of the other metals which might be present in the smelted crude lead, or with which the silver may have been adulterated or mixed (antimony, copper, arsenic), and so serves as a flux to carry them off:[20] but not the oxides of tin and iron.

However, iron oxide (Fe_3O_4) does serve as a flux for silica (silicon dioxide, SiO_2), and it was thus usually added to lead ores in the primary smelting operation. But if that smelting operation was done under too-reducing conditions and at too high a temperature, then there would form a spongy metallic iron mixed with the lead, and this mixture would render the subsequent refining far more complicated: cupellation was unlikely to succeed. It would not succeed, either, if there was too much tin in the crude lead, or if the furnace was considerably overheated. Further, in refining impure silver there was always an uncertainty how much lead to introduce, since the quantity of course depends on the quantity of impurities in the silver.[21] So if not enough lead was added to the impure silver, then copper oxide or tin would form on the top of the silver, leaving a scummy mess.[22] It was, in short, a process only partially under the control of the ancient metallurgist.[23]

The type of bellows used in ancient times may well resemble that familiar in the present day.[24]

The present study accepts the traditional analysis of the verb נָחַר as חרר nip'al "be scorched" rather than the proposal of Michaelis, almost universally accepted by recent commentators, of a root נחר qal, "blow" (see Text, particularly Naegelsbach's argument there). The fire has been heated so hot (see Excursus) that the bellows themselves are scorched.

The metallurgist John Percy recognized that the process described by Jrm was cupellation[25] in spite of his employment of the somewhat misleading *KJV*, and other authorities concur.[26] The text of the half-verse

established here, and the translation, suits the situation admirably.

"The lead is consumed." Conceivably תמם could be translated "is intact" (so Bright; compare 1 Sam 16:11), if the product of the unsuccessful refining operation is still perceived as "lead" (see below). But the verb is much commoner in the meaning "is used up," and that meaning certainly fits the process in suggesting that all the lead has become litharge without effecting a satisfactory result.

What is not clear is whether Jrm is describing the extraction of silver from crude lead or the refining of impure silver by the use of lead as a flux. It is clear that pure silver is the goal, and the "silver" is a metaphor for the people who are devoted to Yahweh's covenant (see v 30). In favor of the former alternative is the word in 5:1: "[See] whether you can find a man, whether there is anyone doing justice . . . so that I can pardon her." The implication there is that in all the mass of evil folk (6:28) one might find a single representative to redeem the mass: the extraction of one bead of silver from the mass of lead, at the ratio of 100 or 1000 to 1, would be an admirable illustration of the pronouncement in 5:1. In favor of the latter alternative is the parallel in Isa 1:22 + 25; there, clearly (in different vocabulary), the refining of impure silver is at issue. Since one of the crucial mistakes that the refiner can make in the refining of silver is not to introduce enough lead (see Excursus), and since it is likely that Jrm is following the imagery set forth in Isaiah, the second alternative is the more probable. The lead is used up, and the result is a mess. It is even possible that the "bronze" (tin?!) and "iron" of v 28 are to be understood as part of the metallic "mess" in vv 29–30 (see again Excursus).

■ **29b** As the assayer will assay, so the refiner refines; but the refiner refines in vain. Who is the refiner? The assayer in v 27 was to be Jrm. The verbs "assay" (בחן) and "refine" (צרף) are in parallelism in 9:6 and in Zech 13:9; Pss 17:3; 26:2; and 66:10; and in each of these passages

---

20 Percy, *Lead*, 177.

21 Percy, *Silver and Gold*, 280–81.

22 Percy, *Lead*, 177; *Silver and Gold*, 280–81.

23 I am deeply indebted to Professor Cyril Stanley Smith of the Massachusetts Institute of Technology for bibliographical help, and for personal conversation and subsequent correspondence with me in clarifying the processes of smelting and cupellation.

24 Robert W. Funk, "Bellows," *IDB* 1:378; Forbes, *Metallurgy*, 112–19; *Studies 8*, 110–17.

25 Percy, *Lead*, 177.

26 Forbes, *Metallurgy*, 213.

God is both the "assayer" and the "refiner." One will have to assume, then, that if the task of assaying is given to Jrm in v 27, the refiner is likewise he; since the metallurgical process is identical, the verbs are used equivalently. He, the prophet, is putting them to the test on behalf of Yahweh (see Form). But the test proves the people a failure: they are refined in vain. In Jrm's poetry the word "in vain" (לַשָּׁוְא) always comes first in the colon (2:30; 4:30); it is strongly emphatic. And in the second colon of the half-verse there is another inversion of normal word order—the subject precedes the verb: "The evil are not separated out." Now we are back to the character of the people once more, the metaphor has receded; just as in the metaphor the impure metals have not been extracted, so in the analysis of the people of Israel those who rebel against Yahweh are not extracted from the mass. The verb נתק nipʻal has a good parallel in Job 18:14: "He was pulled [or snatched] from his tent."

There is another passage in Jer where a failed process is a metaphor for the state of the people, 18:1–12; the crucial verse there is v 4: "And whenever the vessel which he was making was spoiled, as happens with clay in the hand of the potter, then he would remake it into another vessel, as seemed right in the eyes of the potter to make." In this passage there is redemption, help for a new shape of the people on the far side of destruction. Here, by contrast, the process is an utter failure, and there is no talk of reworking the "refuse silver" (v 30). "In vain the refiner has refined." (One might also think to compare the parable of the good and bad figs, 24:1–10; but there the metaphor is not of a process but simply of two different groups that do not interact with each other.)

■ **30** And once more an inversion: literally, "'Reject silver' they call them." The subject of "call" is a vague "they"; 30:17 offers the same idiom, the equivalent of an English passive. There is no secure parallel for נִמְאָס ("reject") as an adjectival participle (Ps 15:4 may offer a textual problem). But the thought is clear enough: Yahweh has rejected them. In 6:19 the people rejected Yahweh's law; now Yahweh has rejected them. Jrm's report is as gloomy as one could imagine.

Aim

The constant question before Jrm was whether there was any redeeming minority among the people. The rhetorical question in 5:1 suggested that there was not. The metaphor of the potter's work suggests that for the moment there was not but that the potter might still reshape the material into something useful (18:4). The word of Yahweh's rejection of his people is found elsewhere in Jrm's words (7:29), and indeed in earlier prophetic material (Hos 9:17); it became a part of the Deuteronomistic affirmation about God's attitude (2 Kgs 23:27). But ultimately it must be balanced against the more hopeful word for the future declared in Deutero-Isaiah: "You are my servant, I have chosen you and not rejected you" (Isa 41:9).

The Temple Sermon

Bibliography

On 7:1—8:3:
Isbell, Charles D., and Michael Jackson
  "Rhetorical criticism and Jeremiah vii 1—viii 3,"
  VT 30 (1980) 20–26.

On 7:1–15:
Eichrodt, Walther
  "The Right Interpretation of the Old Testament:
  A Study of Jeremiah 7:1–15," *TToday* 7 (1950/51)
  15–25.
Fohrer, Georg
  "Jeremias Tempelwort 7, 1–15," *TZ* 5 (1949) 401–
  17 = *Studien zur alttestamentlichen Prophetie* (BZAW
  99; Berlin: De Gruyter, 1967) 190–203.
Hadey, Jean
  "Jérémie et le temple. Le conflit de la parole
  prophétique et de la tradition religieuse, Jér 7/1–
  15; 26/1–19," *ETR* 54 (1979) 438–43.
Pákozdy, Laszlo M. von
  "Der Tempelspruch des Jeremia," *Zeichen der Zeit*
  12 (1958) 372–81.
Reventlow, Henning Graf von
  "Gattung und Überlieferung in der 'Tempelrede
  Jeremias,' Jer 7 und 26," *ZAW* 81 (1969) 315–52.
Schreiner, Josef
  "Sicherheit oder Umkehr? Aus der Verkündigung
  des Propheten Jeremias, Jer 7,1–15; 26,1–6 (II.
  Teil)," *BibLeb* 7 (1966) 98–111.
Schulz, Hermann
  Das Todesrecht im Alten Testament (BZAW 114;
  Berlin: De Gruyter, 1969) 123–27.
Smith, Eustace J.
  "The Decalogue in the Preaching of Jeremias,"
  CBQ 4 (1942) 197–209.
Weippert
  Prosareden, 26–48.
Wilcoxen, Jay A.
  "The Political Background of Jeremiah's Temple
  Sermon," *Scripture in History and Theology: Essays in
  Honor of J. Coert Rylaarsdam* (ed. Arthur L. Merrill
  and Thomas W. Overholt; Pittsburgh Theological
  Monograph Series 17; Pittsburgh: Pickwick, 1977)
  151–66.
Wright, G. Ernest
  "Security and Faith: An Exposition of Jeremiah
  7:1–15," *The Rule of God, Essays in Biblical Theology*
  (Garden City, NY: Doubleday, 1960) 77–92.

On specific verses and problems:
Day, John
  "The Destruction of the Shiloh Sanctuary and
  Jeremiah vii 12, 14," *Studies in the Historical Books of
  the Old Testament* (VTSup 30; Leiden: Brill, 1979)
  87–94.

Görg, Manfred
  "Das Tempelwort in Jer 7,4," *Biblische Notizen* 18
  (1982) 7–14.
Herrmann, Johannes
  "Zu Jer 22,29; 7,4," *ZAW* 62 (1949–50) 321–22.
Pearce, R. A.
  "Shiloh and Jer. viii 12, 14 and 15," *VT* 23 (1973)

7

105–8.
Sutcliffe, Edmund F.
  "A Gloss in Jeremiah vii 4," *VT* 5 (1955) 313–14.
Whitley, Charles F.
  "A Note on Jeremiah 7:4," *JTS* NS 5 (1954) 57–59.

[7:1 **The word which came to Jeremiah from
Yahweh, as follows: 2/ Stand at the gate
of the house of Yahweh and call out there
this word, and say:]ᵃ Hear the word of
Yahweh, all (you of) Judah, [who enter
these gates to worship Yahweh:]ᵇ
3/ Thus Yahweh [of hosts,]ᵃ the God of
Israel has said: Make good your ways and
your doings, so that I may ⟨dwell with
you⟩ᵇ in this place; 4/ do not put your
trust in false words ⟩which do not avail
you at all,⟨ᵃ as follows: "They are the
temple of Yahweh, the temple of
Yahweh, ᵇ the temple of Yahweh!"ᵇ 5/
Indeed if you do make good your ways and
your doings—if each of you does do justice
between himself and his neighbor, 6/ (if)ᵃ
you do not oppress the stranger, orphan
or widow, [(then) do not shed innocent**

Text

1–2a   These words of vv 1–2 are lacking in *G*. Volz and
Rudolph accept them, but Janzen gives careful
argumentation in favor of rejecting them. (1) In
general there is no reason why *G* should mutilate an
easily understood text. (2) The common content of
chapters 7 and 26 and their verbal parallels invite
secondary harmonization (Janzen, pp. 36–37); for
bibliography see Weippert, *Prosareden*, 27 n. 3.

b   These words are likewise lacking in *G*, and again
Volz and Rudolph follow *M* (compare note a above).
Argument (1) there is relevant here as well. Further,
the words are somewhat out of place, since the
temple sermon was delivered not in the gate(s) but
in the temple court (26:2). The words are similar to
those found in 17:20; 22:2; and 26:2 (Janzen, pp.
36–37); for bibliography see again Weippert,
Prosareden, 27 n. 3.

3a   Omit with *G* as an expansionist gloss; see Janzen,
pp. 75–76.

b   Reading וְאֶשְׁכְּנָה אִתְּכֶם (qal verb) with *V* and *a'*
(Syro-Hexapla) for *M* וַאֲשַׁכְּנָה אֶתְכֶם (pi'el verb) "so
that I may let you dwell." The proposal of the
present study is that the phrase uses a qal verb here
but that *M* correctly reads a pi'el in v 7 (see note a
there, and see further the discussion in Preliminary
Observations).

4a   These words are in *G*, ὅτι τὸ παράπαν οὐκ
ὠφελήσουσιν ὑμᾶς, but are missing in *M* and the
other Versions. Arguments can be adduced either
for inclusion or exclusion of the phrase. It is possible
that a Hebrew antecedent would be לְבִלְתִּי הוֹעִיל,
though לְבִלְתִּי is usually rendered by *G* τοῦ μή plus
the infinitive. But τὸ παράπαν (τοῦ) μή renders לְבִלְתִּי
in 1 Kgs 11:10 and Ezek 20:9, 14, 15, 22, and
46:20; ὅτι and ὑμᾶς might then be an inner Greek
development. On the other hand, לְבִלְתִּי הוֹעִיל does
occur in v 8; *G* there is ὅθεν οὐκ ὠφεληθήσεσθε; if the
presumed Hebrew in the present verse were
identical with *M* in v 8, then one must explain why
the *G* translator rendered them differently; so that a
Hebrew antecedent here might be וְהוֹעֵל לֹא יוֹעִילוּ.
Alternatively *G* may simply represent in this verse
and in v 8 alternate ways of rendering the idiom in v
8, and the presence of the extra phrase here may be
due to secondary expansion. See Janzen, p. 211 n.
78.

b—b   The third occurrence of the phrase is lacking in
G; clearly there is no way to be sure whether the
original text carried two or three occurrences.

6a   The negative in this clause is לֹא in *M*, but many

blood in this place,][b] and (if) you do not walk after other gods to your own hurt, 7/ then I shall [a] let you dwell[a] in this place, in the land which I gave to your fathers from of old for ever. 8/ But you keep putting your trust in false words to no avail! 9/ Do you think to steal, murder, commit adultery, swear falsely, make sacrifices to Baal, and walk after other[a] gods whom you have not known?—10/ and then you come and stand before me in the [*M*: this][a] house which bears my name and say, "We have been rescued!"—(rescued) to commit all these abominations! 11/ Has the [*M*: this][a] house which bears my name become a robbers' cave in your eyes? Very well: I have kept my eyes open too!—oracle of Yahweh. 12/ In fact, just go to my place at Shiloh,[a] where I let my name dwell at first, and see what I did to it in the face of the evil of my people Israel!

- - - -

13 So now, inasmuch as you have done all these deeds [—oracle of Yahweh,][a] and though I have spoken to you [early and constantly][b] you have not listened, and though I have called you you have not answered, 14/ I shall do to the house which bears my name, in which you trust, and to the place which I have given to you and to your fathers, as I did to Shiloh,[a] 15/ and I shall fling you away from my sight as I flung away [all][a] your brothers, all the offspring of Ephraim.

MSS. offer אַל; the latter negative could not occur in the protasis, but would imply a prohibition: that is, the clause would be rendered "then do not oppress the stranger, the orphan or the widow." The latter reading, however, is clearly wrong.

b   The negative in this clause is אַל, which must be translated as a prohibition (compare note a), "and do not shed innocent blood in this place." The syntax is clearly wrong (see again note a), and on this basis the clause is to be rejected as secondary (so also Volz, Rudolph). *G, V,* and *S* accept the passage but take it as a protasis. If the words are not secondary, then at the least the אַל must be corrected to לֹא (compare Bright).

7a—a   Retaining the *M* reading וְשִׁכַּנְתִּי אֶתְכֶם; see v 3, note b, and Preliminary Observations.

9a   A few MSS. omit "other."

10a   Reading בַּבַּיִת with *G* for *M* בַּבַּיִת הַזֶּה "in this house." The *M* plus is secondary from 26:6, 9, 12; compare v 14. See Janzen, p. 37.

11a   Reading הַבַּיִת for *M* הַבַּיִת הַזֶּה "this house." *G* here reads οἶκός μου "my house"; the possessive μου seems to be dittographic from "my name" five words later (against Janzen, p. 37). Compare v 10, note a.

12a   *M* spells the name שִׁילוֹ in v 12 and שִׁלוֹ in v 14; in both verses several MSS. read שִׁילֹה and a few read שִׁלֹה; the differences are purely orthographic.

13a   The rubric is lacking in *G* and should be omitted as expansionist; see Janzen, pp. 82, 84.

b   The phrase is lacking in *G* and is secondary here: two similar expressions, "I have spoken to them and they have not listened, I have called to them and they have not answered" (35:17) and "I have spoken to you early and constantly but you have not listened" (35:14) have here become contaminated (Janzen, p. 37).

14a   See 12a.

15a   Omit with *G* (so Duhm, Cornill, Giesebrecht). *M* frequently inserts "all" secondarily (Janzen, pp. 65–67).

Preliminary Observations

On the surface the passage offers no difficulty for exegesis, but two matters need to be explored here. (1) The vocalization of the occurrences of "dwell" (שׁכן) and of the second plural expressions which follow (vv 3 and 7) has substantial consequences for the analysis of structure and setting for the passage as well as for the interpretation of the verses in question. (2) The assumption of the present study is that the temple sermon served to close off the first scroll which Jrm dictated to Baruch, indeed that it followed directly on 6:1–8, serving as the "warning" implied in 6:8. Yet the closing verses of the present passage (vv 13–15) imply that Yahweh's punishment is irrevocable; the possibility is

then that vv 13–15 were appended at the time of the dictation of the second scroll, so that the original temple sermon closes with v 12.

The first question is that of the verbs in question in vv 3 and 7. *M* vocalizes both verbs as pi'els, reading "so that I may let you dwell" (וַאֲשַׁכְּנָה אֶתְכֶם) in v 3 and "then I shall let you dwell" (וְשִׁכַּנְתִּי אֶתְכֶם) in v 7, and in these readings *G, S,* and *T* concur. But *V* reads both verses as qals and the second-person expression that follows as "with you," thus "so that I may dwell with you" (וְאֶשְׁכְּנָה אִתְּכֶם) in v 3 and "then I shall dwell with you" (וְשָׁכַנְתִּי אִתְּכֶם) in v 7; Aquila agrees with this reading v 3 (according to the Syro-Hexapla) and there are nine Hebrew MSS. that offer this reading in v 7 (so Volz).

Commentators and recent translations divide between those following *M* (Duhm, Giesebrecht, and Condamin; *NEB* and *NAB*) and those following *V* (Volz, Rudolph, and Bright; *JB* and *NJV*). Both readings have cogency and each can be argued from context (see below).

It is the proposal of the present study that both readings are correct, the reading of *V* in v 3 ("so that I may dwell with you") and the reading of *M* in v 7 ("then I shall let you dwell"). To my knowledge this proposal has not been made elsewhere, and one reason may be the assumption that the prose style of the passage is "stereo-typed"[1] and the conviction of many that the prose of this passage and others like it is the work of a Deuteronomistic redactor (see Setting). Given these assumptions about the nature of the passage, one is not likely to sense a shift from one verb stem to another, and given the lack in the consonantal text of any clue for such a shift, there has never been a perception of such a possibility. To entertain this proposal thus entails viewing the passage as a more subtle discourse than many commentators do. The proposal anticipates other subtleties in the passage that will be discussed in Setting, but though it is consistent with such data, it is not dependent on them.

The clear implication of vv 3-4 is that "in this place" refers to the temple area (so both Rudolph and Bright); "place" often refers to a sacred precinct (see Interpretation). This implication is likewise found in v 12. If that is the case, then the passage cannot mean that Yahweh lets Judah dwell there; rather it is Yahweh who is to dwell there, and the wording is close to the idiom in Deuteronomy of the "place" where Yahweh "causes his name to dwell" (Deut 12:11; 14:23), which is the temple (1 Kgs 8:29-30, 35). It is understandable that *M* would have reconceived the expression to mean "so that I may let you dwell," not only because of the attraction of the expression in v 7 (see below) but also because of a theological aversion to making Yahweh's action dependent on the action of the people (the cohortative with וְ in v 3 implies a result clause).[2]

On the other hand there is the evidence of the parallel in 25:5-7: "Return each from his evil way and from the evil of your doings, and remain on the soil [וּשְׁבוּ עַל־הָאֲדָמָה] which I have given to you and to your fathers,

from of old, for ever, and do not walk after other gods . . . to your own hurt." This passage, part of a summary of the first scroll (see Setting on that passage), is a variant of vv 5-7 here. In particular 7:7 and 25:5 are the only passages in the OT which offer the expression "from of old, for ever" (לְמִן־עוֹלָם וְעַד־עוֹלָם). And the occurrence of the verb "remain" in 25:5 suggests strongly that *M* is correct here in v 7, "then I shall let you dwell in this place, in the land which I gave to your fathers from of old, for ever." And the fact is that "in this place" is defined by "in the land" in this verse and thus shifts from the meaning of the expression in v 3. One has, then, a deliberate shift from v 3 to v 7, not only in the meaning of "in this place" but in the stem of "dwell" and in the two second plural expressions "with you" (אִתְּכֶם) and "you," direct object (אֶתְכֶם). Verses 5-7 are not then an expansion of vv 3-4 at all but a second sort of statement; this means that the conjunction כִּי at the beginning of v 5 cannot mean "for," as ordinarily construed, but "indeed": "Make good your ways and your doings, so that I may dwell with you in this place [i.e. in the temple]; . . . . Indeed if you do make good your ways and your doings, . . . then I shall let you dwell in this place, in the land which I gave to your fathers." In both actions Yahweh is sovereign, but both actions are to some some degree contingent on the adherence of the people to his covenant. If they are faithful, then he will dwell with them in the temple area, indeed he will let them dwell in the whole land.

This double view is reinforced by the diction of the summary in 26:4, 6: "If you do not listen to me, to walk in my law which I have set before you, then I shall make this house like Shiloh, and the city I shall make an object of contempt for all the nations of the earth." The punishment will be upon both the temple and the city.

The two modes of verbal understanding are combined in v 12 of the present passage in a kind of rhetorical flourish; here (as has been noted) "my place" again means a sacral area, this time at Shiloh, but here also the verb is שכן pi'el ("let dwell"), as in v 7. The object of the verb, however, is not "you" as in v 7 but "my name," so that the causative expression "let my name dwell" is the semantic equivalent of the simple "dwell" found in v 3.

---

1   Bright, p. 58; Thompson, p. 273.
2   Joüon, *Gramm.*, sec. 116b [1].

And it is to be noted that in v 14 (which, it is suggested below, is part of an addition in the second scroll) the two expressions are set side by side (as they are in 26:6): "I shall do to the house which bears my name, in which you trust, and to the place which I have given to you and to your fathers. . . ." Both the temple and the land are the foci of the passage, twin concerns, and the fate of both can be like Shiloh if the people do not repent.

The second question to be dealt with here concerns the relation of vv 13–15 to what precedes. Through v 7 the words are clearly warning, an appeal to repentance. Verses 8–12 make accusations of present behavior and mention Shiloh as an example of what Yahweh did in the past. Verses 13–15 announce punishment because the people have not listened.

On the surface, therefore, it would seem that we have in the last three verses diction appropriate to the second scroll (36:31). But one must be cautious: 26:9 reports that Jrm prophesied on the occasion of the temple sermon a pure judgment on temple and city: "Why have you prophesied in the name of Yahweh, saying, 'Like Shiloh this house shall be, and this city shall lie in ruins without an inhabitant'?" Conceivably, then, vv 13–15 might belong with the original temple sermon and simply be a final rhetorical flourish indicating what Yahweh's judgment will be in the future if people do not listen. The only way to solve the question is to compare vocabulary in vv 13–15 with comparable material elsewhere, and discern the general rhetorical and form-critical shape of the sequences.

It is convenient to begin at the end. "Fling away" (שלך) occurs twice in v 15. There are no other instances in Jer of this verb with Yahweh as subject, but it appears three times in the passive (hophal) where Yahweh is the agent: in 14:16 of the people who listen to the optimistic prophets (in the context of the drought, here dated to December 601); in 22:28 of Jehoiachin (dated to 598), and in 36:30 of Jehoiakim (in the context of the burning of the scroll, again in December 601). These data suggest that the verb "fling away" here is at least appropriate to the period of the second scroll.

The expression "your brothers" also appears in v 15, of the exiles of the northern kingdom. This expression does not otherwise appear with such a connotation in Jer; the only comparable expression is in 29:16, where the address is to the exiles in Babylon and the reference is to

"your brothers" who were not exiled from Jerusalem— the date is 594. This datum is not substantial but again points in the direction of later diction.

The sequence "speak, not listen, call, not answer" is found otherwise in v 27 and 35:17; both these passages have settings in the period of the second scroll (see the respective passages).

Finally one has the conjunction "inasmuch as" (יַעַן): other instances of this word are 5:14; 19:4; and 25:8, and again all these are to be dated to the period of the second scroll.

One may conclude that vv 13–15 are an addition at the time of the second scroll; these verses have the same function as 26:5, likewise a second scroll addition (see there). Verse 12 may appear to be an abrupt close to the original version of the sermon, but this may be partly because one is accustomed to reading vv 13–15 in continuity with vv 3–12. It is no more abrupt than 6:8, which closes off 6:1–8.

Structure

Extent of the Unit. The unit closes with v 15; vv 16–20 shift from second plural to address Jrm personally (second singular). But vv 13–15, though to be heard as part of the temple sermon, are evidently an appendix added for the second scroll (see Preliminary Observations).

Placement of the Unit. Evidence has already been given (see 4:5—10:25, Preliminary Observations, *Settings*) that the first scroll that Jrm dictated contained 6:1–8, followed immediately by the early form of the present passage (i.e., vv 3–12); these passages in turn were rounded off by the first recension of 25:1–7 (see there). By this understanding the "warning" to Jerusalem (6:8) is embodied in vv 3–12 of the present passage. This conclusion explains the placement of the passage here; additions of further poetic material in the second scroll then separated 6:1–8 from the present passage.

Internal Structure. The simplest analysis of vv 3–12 is four sections, vv 3–4, 5–8, 9–11, and 12. The first and second sections are parallel (see Preliminary Observations), the first referring to the temple, the second referring to the land given to the fathers: both have "make good your ways and your doings" and "put your trust," and the diction moves from "I dwell with you" (v 3) to "I let you dwell" (v 7). Verse 8 (the close of the second section) and v 11b (the close of the third) each begin with a combination of הִנֵּה and a subject pronoun. Verses 9–10 and v 11a are each introduced by the interrogative particle followed by an expression for violence, followed by the expression "house which bears my name"; by this means the third section divides in two. Verse 12, the last section, nicely picks up "place" and "let . . . dwell" from the earlier sections, and "my name."

The addition in vv 13–15 recapitulates earlier material of the chapter in terms of judgment: "house which bears my name" (v 14) reflects that phrase in vv 10 and 11, "in which you trust" reminds the hearer of vv 4 and 8, and the expansion of "you have done all these deeds" in v 13 into the specific verbs of v 14 may parallel the expansion of "your ways and your doings" in v 5 into the specifics of the rest of vv 5 and 6. Finally the reference to "the house" and "the place" in v 14 reflects the references to the temple in vv 3–4 and to the land in vv 5–8 (see again Preliminary Observations), and the pairing of Shiloh and Ephraim in v 15 parallels the pairing of Shiloh and Israel in v 12.

Form

This discourse offers a genre that has carried several names: the most common current one perhaps is parenesis (that is, moral exhortation), but one must understand that it is parenesis based upon covenant formulations, so that perhaps "covenant speech" is the most accurate term. The covenant mediator (in the present instance, Jrm) reminds the hearers of their covenant obligations and urges them to adhere to that which they have promised.

Deuteronomy is the covenantal formulation par excellence,[3] but the genre is found in the introduction to the Covenant Code (Exod 19:3–6) and elsewhere.

The form has been analyzed in detail by James Muilenburg.[4] The present passage begins with the normal messenger formula (v 3a) and continues with an exhortation and divine promise (v 3b); the exhortation is then linked to a prohibition (v 4). Then the words of the exhortation are taken up in an expanded covenant condition (vv 5–6) which names some of the covenant stipulations and concludes with a second divine promise (v 7). Verse 8 is a declaration of the breaking of the prohibition of v 4. Verses 9–12 offer the rhetoric of legal dispute—two rhetorical questions (vv 9, 11), an accusation of wrongdoing (v 10) like that of v 8, and a challenge to the hearers to search for evidence (v 12); for the rhetorical flourishes compare the covenant lawsuit presupposed in chapter 2 (e.g., for the search for evidence, compare 2:10).

Verse 13 begins what appears to be an addition at the time of the second scroll (see Preliminary Observations); it begins with the climactic "so now" (וְעַתָּה), which, Muilenburg points out, introduces the final proclamation in the covenant speech,[5] wherein one hears the consequences of the breaking of divine law (compare 2:18). The verse then continues with "inasmuch as" (יַעַן), which introduces a description of the human action that is the reason for the forthcoming divine action (compare the same form in 5:14). That divine action is set forth in vv 14–15. Jrm has thus adapted the formulas of the covenant speech for a proclamation of Yahweh's judgment.

The same form, according to Muilenburg, is to be found not only in the introduction to the Covenant Code in Exod 19:3–6, but also in the narrative of the covenant ceremony at Shechem (Joshua 24) and the covenant mediated by Samuel narrated in 1 Samuel 12 (presumably at Gilgal). All of these cultic acts are associated with sanctuaries, and in view of Jrm's self-understanding as one standing in the tradition of Moses and Samuel (15:1),[6] it is altogether fitting that Jrm's similar parenetic address be in the forecourt of the temple.

For the divine summons added secondarily (vv 1–2) see the remarks on Form in 26:2–3.

Setting

There are two passages reflecting the so-called temple sermon, 7:1–12 (see Preliminary Observations) and chapter 26. Thus chapter 26 offers a narrative of Jrm's standing in the court of the temple and declaring that Yahweh will make the temple like Shiloh, and then describes subsequent events—Jrm is threatened with death by the religious authorities, a threat averted when some elders cite the precedent of the prophet Micah. That chapter offers in two verses (4 and 6; v 5 there is

3   Compare von Rad, *Studies in Deuteronomy*, 12–24.
4   Muilenburg, "Covenantal Formulations."
5   For bibliography see 2:1—4:4, n. 38.

6   Jer 15:1; compare Holladay, "Background."

redactional) a short form of that address. The present passage offers a long form of the address (vv 3–12) and gives no historical context or narrative. The question then arises of the literary relation between the two passages.

The general assumption of many scholars is that the present passage is the product of a "Deuteronomistic redactor."[7]

But a close look at the phrases of the passage makes it clear that these phrases are not specifically "Deuteronomistic"[8] but make up a carefully wrought discourse with distinctive diction having a close relation to the poetry of Jrm; and the detailed evidence given verse by verse in Interpretation brings one to the same conclusion. Thus "make good" (יטב hip'il, vv 3, 5) is not Deuteronomistic but is part of Jrm's vocabulary; "ways" paired with "doings" is likewise not Deuteronomistic but is part of Jrm's vocabulary. It is true, the triad "stranger, orphan and widow" (v 6) is found in Deuteronomy, but if Jrm wished to cite a legal norm of this sort, it would be hard to avoid using the phrase. The phrase "walk after other gods" (vv 6, 9) is Deuteronomistic, but then the component phrases "walk after" (in religious contexts) and "alien gods" are found in Jrm's poetry (2:5, 23, 36; 5:19) as well. The phrase "house which bears my name" (vv 10, 11, 14) is not found in Deuteronomy. In short, there is some overlap in phraseology between this passage and Deuteronomistic material but not to a significant degree.

The passage contains some highly unusual syntactic constructions. One finds the interrogative particle followed by independent infinitive absolutes in v 9; there is no parallel for this construction elsewhere in the OT (the interrogative particle is followed by one independent infinitive absolute in Job 40:2, if the text there is correct; see further Interpretation on v 9). At the end of v 11 one finds גַם־ plus the subject pronoun plus הִנֵּה plus a perfect verb (translated here "Very well: I have kept my eyes open too!"); the only parallel that is at all useful is Gen 42:22.

There is the shift of diction (proposed here) from "so that I may dwell with you" (v 3) to "then I shall let you dwell" (v 7), on which see Preliminary Observations.

One cannot therefore call the passage "monotonous" or "repetitive," as "Deuteronomistic" prose is often thought to be;[9] rather it is carefully crafted and precise. There is nothing here that suggests exilic authorship or late reflection on an earlier event[10] and much that suggests immediacy and emotion (notably irony; the quotations in vv 4 and 10; the rhetorical questions in vv 9 and 11, the first of which, as has already been noted, is presented in highly unusual syntax; and the unusual construction at the end of v 11). It is difficult to avoid the conclusion that the phraseology of the present passage reflects what Jrm said on that occasion, or at least what he himself recalls having said on that occasion:[11] it must be reiterated that evidence has already been given for the presence of vv 3–12 in the first scroll dictated by Jrm (see Structure).

If these conclusions are sound, then 26:4 and 6 must be viewed as a summary of the longer passage before us. The logic of 26:4 and 6 is by itself not clear: why should the temple be destroyed because of the sins of the people? It is the present passage which supplied the missing link: the people have put false trust in the temple, so the temple must be destroyed.[12] That is, the abbreviated narrative in chapter 26 assumes the availability of the text of 7:3–12 and refers to it in summarizing fashion.

That parallel texts exist gives an indication of the importance of Jrm's temple sermon. The date for the event is given in 26:1—it was sometime in 609/608, probably in late summer or early autumn of 609 (for a thorough discussion see on that verse); there is no reason to doubt the datum.

By the conclusion already reached (see Preliminary Observations) vv 13–15 will have been added for the second scroll, which was dictated soon after December 601 (see "A Chronology of Jeremiah's Career").

---

7 Mowinckel's "Source C": see Sigmund Mowinckel, *Zur Komposition des Buches Jeremia* (Kristiania: Dybwad, 1914) 31. See more recently Rudolph, pp. 51–52; Weinfeld, *Deuteronomy*, passim, esp. 325, 352; Nicholson, *Preaching*, 34, 68–69; Thiel, *Jer 1—25*, 105–15.

8 So also Weippert, *Prosareden*, 26–48.

9 On this see ibid., 38.

10 Ibid., 41, 45–46.

11 Ibid., 41.

12 Ibid., 32.

Interpretation

■ **1–2** The short form of text in these verses, found in *G*, is original (see Text): "Hear the word of Yahweh, all (you of) Judah." In form it is parallel to the summons in 2:4, but while the summons there is to the "house of Jacob and all the tribes of the house of Israel," here it is to "all (you of) Judah." The contrast is appropriate; though all Israel has broken the covenant, the question of temple worship in Jerusalem is of particular concern to Judah. The vocative "all (you of) Judah" is striking: with an appeal like "hear the word of Yahweh" it occurs in Jer only otherwise in 44:26 (the occurrence in v 24 there is a secondary expansion).

The wording of the expansion in v 1 in *M* is found identically in 11:1; 18:1; and 30:1, and six more times in the book without the closing "as follows" (לֵאמֹר); it is a typical effort to enlarge the wording of this text tradition. Similarly the introductory words of v 2 in *M*, "Stand at the gate of the house of Yahweh and call out there this word and say," are not too different from the wording found in the related narrative, 26:2, "Stand in the court of the house of Yahweh and speak . . . all the words. . . ." Finally the additional expressions in *M* at the end of v 2 are likewise found elsewhere in Jer—for "who enter these gates" compare 22:2 (and 17:20, which is evidently quite late); for "to worship" compare the wording in 26:2.

■ **3–12** Here is the temple sermon. It was a notable event in Jrm's ministry. Though the style has struck many as "Deuteronomistic" (see Setting), it is a style Jrm found appropriate to his critique of the use made of Deuteronomy by his hearers; the diction in vv 21–29 and 11:1–17 has the same character (see there).

■ **3** For the messenger formula compare 2:2.

The imperative clause is all-embracing in its generality; it may be paraphrased, "Whatever it is you do, make it good instead of bad." The verb יטב hip'il in general means "do good." The assumption has existed since Luther and the *KJV* that the verb here carries a comparative meaning ("make better your ways and your doings: *KJV*, *RSV*: "amend"). This is a theoretical possibility but is not warranted here: Jrm elsewhere uses the verb contrastively with "do ill" (רעע hip'il: 2:33 as emended; 4:22; 13:23), so it is better to stay with his bipolar mode of expression—one does either good or bad.

The pairing of "way(s)" and "doings" is standard (in poetry: 4:18; 17:10; 23:22; in prose, beyond the present passage: 7:5; 18:11; 25:5; 26:13; 32:19). One has the impression that the singular "way" is commoner in poetry when the parallel occurs, but the plural is standard for prose. For "way" for style of life see 2:23. It is to be stressed that the phrase is not Deuteronomistic (see Setting).

For the revocalization of "so that I may dwell with you" see Preliminary Observations; as stated there, the cohortative after the imperative expresses purpose. If the people do right, then Yahweh will be able to continue to dwell with them. This syntax of course suggests that Yahweh's sovereignty is in this instance dependent on the conduct of the people, and this perception of a dangerous limitation on his independence must have stimulated the vocalization of *M*. Since this verb (שׁכן qal) often appears in parallel with the more common verb "dwell" (ישׁב, e.g., Isa 18:3), "dwell" here is an appropriate rendering. But in some early passages it implies temporary dwelling, "encamp" (Num 24:2); it may carry the connotation of the portable ark and tabernacle of the wilderness in the context of which Yahweh dwells with his people (compare Lev 16:16, of the tent of meeting, and Josh 22:18, of the tabernacle, both P; Isa 8:18; Ps 135:21 and elsewhere in the Psalms).[13] Thus Jrm affirms here that Yahweh will honor the temple in Jerusalem by his presence if the people are loyal to their covenant obligations. The word "place" (מָקוֹם) has the nuance of a holy place (so Gen 12:6; Deut 12:2, 5): the usage may have had a northern origin.[14]

Jrm here mediates Yahweh's expectation that people

---

13 See Jan Dus, "Ein Versuch zur deuteronomischen Kultformel," *Volume du Congrès, Genève 1965* (VTSup 15; Leiden: Brill, 1966) 113–21, and further Baruch Halpern, "The centralization formula in Deuteronomy," *VT* 31 (1981) 20–38.

14 See the review by Baruch A. Levine of Menahem Haran, *Temples and Temple-Service in Ancient Israel: An Inquiry into the Character of Cult Phenomena and the Historical Setting of the Priestly School* in *JBL* 99 (1980) 451.

can repent (see Form). There is no reason to doubt that Jrm was sincere, however much it stands in contrast with the (later) pessimistic word in v 16 (and elsewhere).

■ **4** The command "make good your ways and your doings" in v 3 is matched by the prohibition here, "do not put your trust in the deceptive words . . . ," and there is even the hint of a connection by assonance: *ṭ* + *b* in the verb of v 3, and *b* + *ṭ* in the verb here. "Trust" (בטח) has occurred earlier in the book—in 5:17 Jrm speaks of the "fortified cities in which you trust," while here it is another false item of security, "deceptive words." But in 5:17 the preposition is the expected בְּ, while here it is the less common אֶל, which occurs with this verb ten times in the OT, seven times with the object God, once for persons, and twice (here and in v 8) for things; the impression then left is that people are enjoined not to trust deceptive words when they should trust Yahweh. The phrase "deceptive words" (דִּבְרֵי הַשֶּׁקֶר) occurs only here and in v 8 in the OT; the phrase appears to be a striking one. The explanatory phrase "which do not avail you at all" hardly adds much.

And what are the deceptive "slogans of security"?[15] Literally "They are the temple of Yahweh, the temple of Yahweh, the temple of Yahweh!" Questions cluster around the expression: Did Jrm intend to utter "the temple of Yahweh" three times (*M*) or twice (*G*)? If three times, does he intend a kind of mimicking of the trisagion in Isa 6:3, or is he simply mocking "vain repetitions" (compare Matt 6:7), or what? And what does "they" (הֵמָּה) really mean?—since one would assume that the temple is singular.

Triple utterances are found here and in Isa 6:3, and further in Jer 22:29 and Ezek 21:32 (Neh 1:2 modifies a triple utterance slightly). The repetition in Isa 6:3 is part of a liturgy, but Johannes Herrmann acutely compares the remaining three passages to the triple expressions that occur at the beginning of magical texts at several points in the Babylonian collection of such texts called Maqlû.[16] It is possible then that Jrm intended reference both to the trisagion in the liturgy, where the threefold description of Yahweh is proper, and to the "vain repetitions" of magical texts, where such diction is foolish.

As for the word "they," the traditional explanation,

namely that the plural refers to the several buildings that made up the temple complex, seems the most likely. In 2 Chr 8:11 the place to which the ark of Yahweh came is referred to in the plural (the same plural pronoun), and the plurals "sanctuaries of God" (מִקְדְּשֵׁי־אֵל, Ps 73:17) and "your dwelling-places" for the temple (מִשְׁכְּנוֹתֶיךָ, Ps 84:2 and elsewhere) point in the same direction.[17] So does the reading of *S* here, "you [plural] (are)" ('*antūn*), though of course the person is different.

The word "temple" (הֵיכָל) occurs, beyond this verse, in only three other passages in Jer (24:1; 50:28; 51:11). Elsewhere the temple is referred to as "house" (בַּיִת: vv 10, 11, 14, and 23:11). The choice of the word "temple" may be governed both by the fact that that word appears in Isa 6:1 (if there is an echo here of the trisagion of Isa 6:3) and that the phrase "temple of Yahweh" appears in 1 Sam 1:9; 3:3 for the sanctuary at Shiloh (see v 12 below).

The OT understanding of the power of the word to effect change must have rendered it peculiarly difficult for the people to perceive the phrase "temple of Yahweh" as a deceptive word: all that they had heard within the temple precincts echoed with Yahweh's mighty acts and his faithfulness; yet Jrm insists that to put one's security in such words is vain.

■ **5** This verse picks up the command of v 3, now as an "if"-clause, and reinforces the verb with an infinitive absolute, "if you really do make good your ways and your doings," and then fills in the generality with some specifics.

The original text of vv 5–6 offers three specifics: doing justice to one's peer, not oppressing the powerless beneath, and not following other deities above.

The first of these is likewise reinforced by the infinitive absolute, "if each of you really does do justice between himself and his neighbor. . . ." Why the infinitive absolute?—is it too easy to claim one does justice without really doing so? For "do justice" see 5:1; for the poetic use of the idiom for the reciprocal, "each other" (רֵעֵהוּ + אִישׁ) see 3:20; 5:8.

■ **6** The first "if"-clause (the end of v 6) is emphatic in the presence of an infinitive absolute; the other clauses (in the present verse) are emphatic in the deferment of the verb.

---

15   So Overholt, *Falsehood*, 68.

16   J. Herrmann, "Jer 22,29; 7,4."

17   Compare Dahood, *Psalms II*, 192.

The verb "oppress" (עָשַׁק) is found both in the eighth-century prophets (Amos 4:1; Mic 2:2) and in Deuteronomy (Deut 24:14); it often suggests extortion (so the cognate noun עֹשֶׁק, 6:6). The parallelism of "orphan" and "widow" is already found in Ugaritic[18] and is found frequently in the OT, beginning in the Covenant Code (Exod 22:21; see also Isa 1:17; 10:2; Ps 68:6). The triad "stranger, orphan and widow" is suggested by the contiguity of Exod 22:20 to 22:21 and is found in Ps 146:9 and five times in Deuteronomy (Deut 16:11, 14; 24:19, 20, 21). "Orphan" is not paired with either of the others in Jrm's poetry (in 5:28 the parallel is "the poor"). The noun traditionally translated "sojourner" (גֵּר) refers to a resident alien, "a foreigner who lives more or less permanently in the midst of another community, where he is accepted and enjoys certain rights."[19] The noun יָתוֹם is here translated "orphan," though it is clear in none of the OT passages in which the word appears that both parents are dead: the word may in a given instance mean "fatherless" (hence the customary translation in the KJV and RSV)—in Lam 5:3 the parallel is "without a father" (אֵין אָב), and Ps 109:9, though part of a rhetorical flourish, points in the same direction. The child without a father, the widow without a husband, and the resident alien all lack a natural spokesman to defend their legal rights within Israel and therefore need special consideration.[20]

The clause which follows in M seems to be a second expansion (see Text, and compare the diction of the poem in 22:17). For the shedding of "innocent blood" see 2:34; for "in this place," see v 3 above.

The last "if"-clause is concerned with religious loyalty. Jrm uses similar phraseology in his poetry: for "other gods" compare "alien gods" in 5:19; for "walk after" see 2:5, 23, 36. But "other gods" is a traditional term, found already in the Decalogue (Exod 20:3; Deut 5:7), and the combination "walk after other gods" is found frequently in Deuteronomy (Deut 6:14; 8:19; 11:28; 13:3; 28:14).[21] But there is nothing in Deuteronomy or elsewhere to

match the assonance of this clause ('ḥr 'lm 'ḥrm l' lk lkm). The simple phrase sums up a whole world of experience with pagan religious patterns: to walk after other gods is to be loyal to the Baals, to Mesopotamian deities, to other exotic imports, and thus to be disloyal to Yahweh, to whom Israel properly belongs. The last phrase means literally "for harm to yourselves" (לְרַע לָכֶם); the best parallel is Eccl 8:9: "Man lords it over man to his hurt [לְרַע לוֹ]." No one pursues a religious loyalty deliberately to hurt himself; thus if he pursues Baal it is to gain economic security. But ultimately such pursuits result only in the downfall of the covenant people.

■ 7 Now the apodosis, after the three clauses of the protasis: "then I shall let you dwell in this place," a variation on the phrase of v 3 (see Preliminary Observations). Thus "in this place" has shifted meaning: it is now the land given to the fathers. Deut 12:1–5 makes the same close connection between the "land which Yahweh the God of your fathers has given you to possess" (Deut 12:1) and the destruction of all "places" except the one "place" for a valid sanctuary (Deut 12:2, 5). The phrase regarding the land is traditional (the Decalogue in Exod 20:12 and Deut 5:16), occurring about eighty times in the legal and historical material. For the association between the "fathers" and the land given by Yahweh see 2:5, 7. The phrase "from of old, for ever" (לְמִן־עוֹלָם וְעַד־עוֹלָם) is a startling one in the context of the giving of the land; the only parallel in this context is the reflection on the present passage in 25:5, part of the closing statement for the first scroll (see there): otherwise the phrase is used of Yahweh himself (Ps 90:2) or of his steadfast love (Ps 103:17). Modes of expression regarding the giving of the land to Israel vary greatly in the OT, from the statement that the Israelites are simply "sojourners" (גֵּרִים) on Yahweh's land (Lev 25:23)—compare the possessive "my [Yahweh's] land," "my [Yahweh's] heritage" (2:7)—to the statement given here. It is the paradox of Yahweh's limitless grace to Israel, linked with the necessity for Israel to obey Yahweh:

---

18 Ugaritic texts 17.5.8; 16.6.49–50.
19 De Vaux, *Ancient Israel*, 74, and see in general 74–75; Theodor M. Mauch, "Sojourner," *IDB* 4:397–99.
20 On this whole matter see Pedersen I/II, 355–57. For the triad see now Thomas Krapf, "Traditionsgeschichtliches zum deuteronomischen Fremdling-Waise-Witwe-Gebot," *VT* 34 (1984) 87–91.
21 Weippert, *Prosareden*, 215–18.

Yahweh gave the land to the fathers without any limit of time, yet only by covenant obedience will Israel expect to be blessed by Yahweh in that land.[22]

■ 8 This verse offers a rephrasing of v 4a. It is difficult to state precisely the force of the combination הִנֵּה אַתֶּם with participle: both *JB* and *NAB* are similar (*JB*: "Yet here you are, trusting in delusive words, to no purpose!"; *NAB*: "But here you are, putting your trust in deceitful words to your own loss!"). The *NEB*, however, inverts the order and thus suppresses the vividness of the הִנֵּה: "You gain nothing by putting your trust in this lie." There is a similar sequence, with "they" rather than "you," at the beginning of 17:15, and there *JB* translates, "Look, they keep saying to me. . . ." I propose that "keep putting your trust" fits the context here, just as "keep saying to me" fits 17:15. The mood clearly shifts from the positive words in vv 5–7; hence the necessity for a "but" at the beginning. The preposition in the phrase of this verse is עַל, in contrast to אֶל in v 4, but there is little difference of nuance (only that there are more instances of עַל with this verb when the object is a thing; compare the discussion above on v 4).

The phrase here translated "to no avail" is literally "so as not to profit" (לְבִלְתִּי הוֹעִיל), that is, with unprofitable results; its only other occurrence is in Isa 44:10. For יעל hip'il see 2:8, 11.

■ 9 The precise nuance of the interrogative particle הֲ with the sequence of isolated infinitive absolutes is difficult. The only parallel instance of this combination is Job 40:2, where the Versions differ in their interpretation of the consonantal text; on the assumption that *M* is correct there in reading an infinitive absolute, one has the same context of indignant or excited argumentation that is presupposed in the present passage.[23] The isolated infinitive absolute elsewhere in Jer appears to give a

distance between the action and the speaker (see 3:1; 4:18). The result, then, is something like "How dare you steal, murder . . . ?" or (as offered here) "Do you think to steal, murder . . . ?" Joüon proposes that the interrogative particle carries "an exclamatory nuance"[24] and translates, "Quoi! voler, tuer . . . !"[25] In any event the diction here is striking and emotional.

The series of infinitives in this verse reflects several of the prohibitions in the Decalogue, just as a corresponding series of infinitive absolutes does in Hos 4:2; and the abbreviated listing both here and in Hosea encourages scholars to believe that the original form of the laws in the Decalogue was more abbreviated than the form presently found in Exodus 20 and Deuteronomy 5.[26] The first three verbs are the fourth, third, and fifth respectively of Hosea's list, and the fourth phrase here ("swear falsely") is synonymous with Hosea's first, "curse" (אלה). Both prophets thus cite various commandments, but there is no discernible pattern either between the lists of the two prophets or in the order of choice that either prophet makes from the longer list of the Decalogue.[27]

Though the prohibitions are familiar ones, the precise range of meanings of each prohibition is far from self-evident; and it is clear that there was a development of meaning of the prohibitions as time passed. Thus Albrecht Alt was convinced that the original reference of "steal" (גנב) in the Decalogue (Exod 20:15; Deut 5:19) was to kidnaping,[28] but certainly by Jrm's time the word had broadened to include the stealing of goods (compare the activities of "thieves," גַּנָּבִים, 49:9).[29]

The verb here translated "murder" (רצח, Exod 20:13; Deut 5:17) is difficult to pinpoint. Though it is applied to premeditated murder (Hos 6:9), it is used also of involuntary manslaughter (Deut 4:42): Wolff is then

---

22   On these themes see the literature in 2:1—4:4, n. 99.

23   Compare GKC, sec. 113ee.

24   "Une nuance exclamative," Joüon, *Gramm.*, sec. 161b.

25   Ibid., 123w.

26   See Eduard Nielsen, *The Ten Commandments in New Perspective* (SBT 2d Series 7; Naperville, IL: Allenson, 1968) 110–12; Childs, *Exodus*, 393–401; and compare Johann J. Stamm and Maurice E. Andrew, *The Ten Commandments in Recent Research* (SBT 2d Series 2; Naperville, IL: Allenson, 1967) 56.

27   The bibliography on OT law in general, and on the Decalogue in particular, is of course enormous; see

conveniently Childs, *Exodus*, 385–86.

28   Albrecht Alt, "Das Verbot des Diebstahls im Dekalog," *Kleine Schriften zur Geschichte des Volkes Israel* (Munich: Beck, 1953) 1:333–40; so also Eduard Neilsen, *The Ten Commandments in New Perspective* (SBT 2d Series 7; Naperville, IL: Allenson, 1968) 91.

29   See Childs, *Exodus*, 423–24.

incorrect in his remark on the verb in Hos 4:2.[30]
Brevard S. Childs discusses the matter carefully,[31]
concluding that the verb originally referred to blood
vengeance, killing which is inimical to the community;
but he suggests that by the time of the prophetic
literature, the term "invariably carries the connotation of
intentional and evil violence"[32]—good examples are Isa
1:21 and the Hos 6:9 already cited. It follows that the
prohibition does not encompass killing that is sanctioned
by the community (i.e., the imposition of the death
penalty); see on this Num 35:16–34. In spite of the lack
of complete congruence with our term "murder," that
translation is functionally the best.

"Commit adultery" translates a verb (נאף) meaning
"break marriage" (so, earlier, 3:8, 9; 5:7). Because a wife
is understood to be under the control of her husband, a
man who has sexual intercourse with the wife of another
man breaks the marriage of that second man, while the
woman in question breaks her own marriage. The
prohibition does not refer to intercourse between a man
(married or otherwise) and an unbetrothed or unmarried
woman. It follows that only a betrothed or married
woman is bound to faithfulness. In spite of this double
standard, the law required both parties in adultery to be
put to death (Lev 20:10).[33]

"Swear falsely" (שבע nip'al + לַשֶּׁקֶר) has already
occurred in 5:2. Beyond these two occurrences in Jer the
phrase occurs in Lev 5:24; 19:12; Zech 5:4; and Mal 3:5;
it is thus not a Deuteronomistic phrase but appears to
come out of priestly rhetoric. It has already been noted
that the corresponding expression in Hos 4:2 is a
different one, and it must also be pointed out that the
Decalogue offers neither expression. Nevertheless there
is reason to connect the prohibition here and in Hos 4:2
with the commandment in the Decalogue, "You shall not
take the name of Yahweh your God in vain" (Exod 20:7;
Deut 5:11): S translates the law in the Decalogue with
"You shall not swear falsely by the name of the Lord
your God," and this tradition is found in Jewish circles as

well[34] and is followed in the NJV. It is difficult to
pinpoint the abuse of Yahweh's name at various periods
that gave rise to these contrasting formulations; "swear
falsely" (that is, swear an oath insincerely or dishonestly)
may have been one center of meaning, but the implication may have broadened later to include "curse someone by a misuse of Yahweh's name" (so, evidently, the
implication of the word in Hos 4:2).[35]

For "offer sacrifices to Baal" (לַבַּעַל + pi'el קטר) see
1:16, and for "walk after other gods" see v 6 above. The
phrase "whom you have not known" (אֲשֶׁר לֹא־יְדַעְתֶּם),
referring to gods, is found twice more in the book (19:4;
44:3), and beyond the book, repeatedly in Deuteronomy
(Deut 11:28; 13:3, 7, 14; 29:25). But a poetic equivalent
is found already in Deut 32:17, part of an old poem, so
that Jrm here is not necessarily imitating the use of the
prose of Deut (compare his use in 2:28 of Deut 32:37–
38). Since "know" may carry overtones of the covenant
(see 1:5), the implication here is that these other gods are
ones with whom Israel does not have a valid covenant.

Here then, in a nutshell, is Jrm's reference to covenant
law, broken on all sides by the people of Judah.

■ 10 The infinitive absolutes of v 9 are followed by וְ and
the perfect in a consecutive sense, "and then you
come."[36] The phrase "stand before" (עמד לִפְנֵי) suggests
standing with respect before (a king), presenting oneself
before (Yahweh), as a servant might; 1 Kgs 17:1 is a good
parallel. One stands before Yahweh with reverence and
awe, or at least one should; but Judah stands casually
before Yahweh after having broken covenant with him.

The phrase "house which bears my name" raises many
issues. The phrase occurs here and in vv 11 and 14, in v
30, in 32:34 and 34:15, and the related phrase "city
which bears my name" is found in 25:29. In the poetry of
Jrm the clause refers to the people Israel ("we bear your
name," 14:9) or to the prophet himself ("for I bear your
name," 15:16). The clause modifies "this house" in 1 Kgs
8:43, part of the Deuteronomistic editorial work,
modifies "all the nations" in a redactional addition to

---

30 Wolff, *Hosea*, 68.
31 Childs, *Exodus*, 419–21.
32 Ibid., 421.
33 On these details and specific references to texts in
    this regard see Johann J. Stamm and Maurice E.
    Andrew, *The Ten Commandments in Recent Research*
    (SBT 2d Series 2; Naperville, IL: Allenson, 1967)
    100; for general bibliography see Otto J. Baab,

"Marriage," *IDB* 3:287, and Charles R. Taber,
    "Marriage," *IDBSup*, 576.
34 E.g., in Obadiah ben Jacob Sforno (sixteenth
    century) on Exod 20:7 in the rabbinic Bibles.
35 On Hos 4:2 see Wolff, *Hosea*, 67; on the more
    general question see Childs, *Exodus*, 409–12.
36 Joüon, *Gramm.*, sec. 119s.

Amos (Amos 9:12) and occurs in scattered later material. It occurs once in Deuteronomy, describing Israel (Deut 28:10). Verse 12 of the present passage reflects Deuteronomistic diction—"where I let my name dwell," for the theology of the name of Yahweh is characteristic of Deuteronomy.[37] This name-theology is reflected in only a single occurrence in Deuteronomy of the phrase in question, and it seems impossible to establish whether that occurrence is dependent on the usage in Jer or is prior to it.[38] The phrase implies ownership;[39] the temple (at least in the minds of its devotees) belongs to Yahweh. But is there an ironic contrast here between "I may dwell with you" (v 3), an expression of genuine covenantal solidarity, and "the house which bears my name" here— as if the latter phrase implies "the house of which the people claim I am in charge"? Who proposes that Yahweh's name be pronounced over the temple, and with what justification? The whole tone of the passage implies a complacency that is anathema to Yahweh (and thus to Jrm).

"Rescue" (נצל) has occurred in the hip'il stem (active) in 1:8 and 19; this is the only occurrence in Jer of the nip'al (passive). (S vocalizes נִצַּלְנוּ "rescue us," accepted by Ewald, but this is dubious.) Though the expectation of being rescued is part of the vocabulary of the Psalms (Ps 69:15), Amos once used the verb ironically (Amos 3:12) of the destructive "rescue" which the people in Samaria might expect, and other memories of the use of the verb must have raised uneasy images (see 2 Kgs 19:11). To say "we have been rescued" is unwarranted optimism.

The Versions diverge in their interpretation of the syntax of the last phrase. Thus T paraphrases M ("'We have been rescued!' in order that you may commit . . ."), as does S; but G reads "'We have refrained from committing . . . ,'" and V reads, curiously, "'We have been rescued because we have committed. . . .'" There is no way to understand the subordinating conjunction לְמַעַן other than to express purpose, but it is not at all clear that the quotation ends with "We have been rescued!"—

conceivably it should be understood as "'We have been rescued to commit all these abominations!'" (so Luther, John Calvin). In this case the whole expression is ironic: "You appear to say, 'We have been rescued to commit . . . !'" The M 'atnaḥ, however, favors closing the quotation with "'We have been rescued!'": but in this case the final phrase is still ironic—the ultimate purpose of rescue is still to continue as you have done. (Compare Hos 8:4, where likewise לְמַעַן introduces an infinitive to express an ironic purpose: "From their silver and their gold they make idols for themselves, so that it shall be destroyed.")

The phrase "commit abomination(s)" (עשׂה תוֹעֵבָה) is a strong one, often having sexual overtones; see 6:15.

■ 11 The verse begins, after the interrogative particle, with the phrase "robbers' cave" (מְעָרַת פָּרִצִים); the emphasis, then, is, "Is a robbers' cave what my house . . . has become in your eyes?" Other than the instance in 4:29 where "caves" is restored in the text, neither word in the phrase appears again in the book. Elsewhere in the OT a "cave" (מְעָרָה) is a refuge for man or animal (e.g., 1 Kgs 19:1). A פָּרִיץ is a brigand, not a thief but a man of violence, who will kill to rob; the word occurs only six times (beyond the present passage: of men—Ezek 7:22; 18:10; Ps 17:4; Dan 11:14; of wild animals—Isa 35:9). A robbers' cave is then a den for brigands. Many parts of Palestine are honeycombed with caves, notably in the Shephelah:[40] one thinks of the cave of Adullam in which David and his men took refuge when he was an outlaw (1 Sam 22:1). It is noteworthy that as we find "commit abominations" in v 10 and "robbers" here, so in the listing of the sins of the son of a righteous father in Ezekiel 18 one finds the same two phrases in vv 10 and 12 there: just as Jrm used a term associated with sexual atrocities in v 10 to describe the breaking of covenant norms, so here he describes the temple as the headquarters of thugs. He means to use strong language; his phrase must have been even more shocking to his first hearers than was Jesus' adaptation of the phrase in the

37 See von Rad, *Studies in Deuteronomy*, 37–41; Weinfeld, *Deuteronomy*, 193–94, and more generally Helga Weippert, "'Der Ort, den Jahwe erwählen wird, um dort seinen Namen wohnen zu lassen,' Die Geschichte einer alttestamentlichen Formel," *BZ* NF 24 (1980) 76–94.

38 Compare Weinfeld, *Deuteronomy*, 325; Ernest W. Nicholson, *Deuteronomy and Tradition* (Philadelphia:

Fortress, 1967) 21.

39 Weinfeld, *Deuteronomy*, 195.

40 Compare the description in George A. Smith, *The Historical Geography of the Holy Land* (London: Hodder & Stoughton, 1931; rep. Collins, 1966) 162–70.

temple area in a later century (Mark 11:17 and parallels).

If the text "the house which bears my name" is correct, then Jrm is using the diction now without irony. If the house is to bear the name of Yahweh, then the conduct of those within should befit the name it bears.

The phrase "in your eyes" suggests both "in your sight" (you ought to know better, even if you do not) and "in your good judgment" (you do know better, but you have deliberately distorted the purpose of the temple), and it is balanced by Yahweh's "seeing" referred to in the last phrase.

This last phrase offers highly unusual diction, literally, "I also, behold, I have seen" (גַם plus the subject pronoun plus הִנֵּה plus a perfect verb). A close parallel is the last clause in Gen 42:22; if one may paraphrase that verse, "Reuben answered, 'Didn't I tell you not to do anything wrong to the boy?—but you did not listen, so now we are brought to account for his blood! [וְגַם־דָּמוֹ הִנֵּה נִדְרָשׁ].'" The present verse, like that in Genesis, begins with the interrogative הֲ, so there is evidently a common rhetorical sequence. The speaker grants the validity of the statement implied by the rhetorical question (Gen 42:22: "Didn't I tell you not to do anything wrong to the boy? All right, but you didn't listen"; The present passage, "Have you decided to make the temple a headquarters for thugs? All right. . . ."), but he counterposes the unwelcome consequence (Gen 42:22: "So now we have to face up to it. . . ."). If the pattern of thinking is consistent, then the phraseology here would mean, "All right, but I have eyes too."

In what sense must one understand the reference to "seeing" here? Volz has laid out three possibilities, two of which are affirmed in the medieval Jewish exegetes. (1) "But look, I can see too!"—that is, "I am not blind: you may use your eyes for what you have done, but I see what is in your heart" (so Qimḥi, Calvin; so Rudolph, Bright). And the perfect verb (רָאִיתִי) may carry such a present ("stative") meaning.[41] (2) "I too have seen it (that is, how you regard the temple)!" (so Rashi; so Duhm, Giese-

brecht). (3) "(If you consider the temple to be a robbers' cave,) look, I think so too!" (so Rothstein). The third option is possible but unlikely, given the rhetorical pattern of counterclaim already proposed. The first and second options are very close, and it is not possible to make a decision between them (compare Rudolph); but the general import of the clause is clear.

■ 12 The conjunction כִּי with which the verse begins is clearly not "for," but instead emphatic, corroborative (so already Calvin; Bright: "Yes, go. . . ."). The modal נָא after the imperative "go" suggests that looking for evidence is quite simple (compare the same nuance in 18:13). For "(holy) place" (מָקוֹם) see v 3.

Shiloh is the present site of ḥirbat saylūn (Israel grid 177–162), thirty kilometers north (and a bit east) of Jerusalem, east of the main road from Jerusalem to Shechem and about halfway between Bethel and Shechem.[42] It was of course the central Israelite sanctuary in the period just before the monarchy, where the ark of the covenant was lodged (Judg 21:19; 1 Sam 3:3).

The implication of the present verse and v 14, the parallels in 26:6, 9 and a similar reference in Ps 78:60, is that the sanctuary at Shiloh was destroyed at some time past. The most likely destruction is that of the Philistines. It is true, the narrative in 1 Samuel 4 does not describe such a destruction, but it does describe the capture of the ark of the covenant during a battle at Aphek on the coastal plain west of Shiloh; and inasmuch as the ark was not returned to Shiloh but stored at Kiriath-jearim until installed in Jerusalem, the assumption is easy that the Shiloh sanctuary was destroyed in the same military struggle.

The archeological evidence has not been altogether conclusive. A Danish team excavated Shiloh during several seasons, but no sanctuary was found: the top of the tell, where it might have been located, has been both eroded and then artificially leveled during the Roman period.[43] Their first expedition, in 1929, concluded that evidence had been found for a destruction of the city

---

41   See Joüon, *Gramm.*, sec. 112a.
42   See conveniently Norman K. Gottwald, "Shiloh," *IDB* 4:328–30, and Svend Holm-Nielsen, "Shiloh (City)," *IDBSup*, 322–23. The archeological evidence is to be found in Marie-Louise Buhl and Svend Holm-Nielsen, *Shiloh; The Danish Excavations at Tall Sailūn, Palestine, in 1926, 1929, 1932 and 1963* (Copenhagen: National Museum of Denmark, 1969).

43   Holm-Nielsen, "Shiloh."

about 1150 B.C.E., and this was of course linked to the assumption of a Philistine destruction.[44] But they revised that conclusion during further excavation in 1963:[45]—they could find no clear-cut evidence for a destruction of the site at a period appropriate to the Philistines, and much evidence for continued occupation down to about 600. Recent excavation by Bar-Ilan University (1981) has, however, reversed the judgment once more: The city was occupied early in the Israelite settlement period (Iron Age I), and this stratum was destroyed in a fierce fire. The evidence is thus consistent with the assumption of a Philistine destruction, probably in the mid-eleventh century.[46] In any event it remains true that Jrm spoke of Shiloh as the place of a sanctuary where Yahweh let his name dwell, that is, where his presence was manifest. Such an expression at least implies the presence of the ark, and the fact that the ark was taken from Shiloh during the Philistine wars and not returned to Shiloh suggests strongly that this is the period to which Jrm is referring.[47]

There is another line of reasoning that is relevant here, and that is the possible connection between the traditions at Anathoth and the house of Eli at Shiloh, mediated through the priest Abiathar (see 1:1). If that connection existed, then again it takes one back to sacral institutions at Shiloh associated with the time just before the ark was removed. On balance, then, it is best to see the reference here to Shiloh as a reference to the Philistine destruction of the shrine.

The mode of Jrm's expression indicates that there is no doubt that Yahweh sponsored the shrine at Shiloh: it was "my place," where "I let my name dwell at first." The latter phrase links the references to Yahweh's name in vv 10 and 11 with the use of "dwell" (שׁכן) in vv 3 and 7; the present study accepts the vocalization of M in v 7 and

here, to read the pi'el stem (factitive, causative); here, then, the nuance is "I saw to it that my name dwelt there." The logic of the proposal is: if the temple here in Jerusalem is understood to bear my name, then look at the earlier shrine where I put my name—if I could destroy it, then you cannot assume automatic safety here. "See what I did to Shiloh in the face of the evil of my people Israel!"

■ 13 Verses 13–15, by the conclusion of the present study, are an appendix to the temple sermon added by Jrm after the king burned the scroll (see Preliminary Observations).

For "so now" (וְעַתָּה) and "inasmuch as" (יַעַן) see Form, and the parallels cited there. The conjunction controls the balance of the verse, the equivalent of a long protasis.

There follows then the infinitive "do" (עשׂה) followed by its cognate accusative "deeds" (מַעֲשִׂים). This combination is unusual in the OT;[48] in particular it does not occur elsewhere in Jer.

The verse is completed by four clauses in parallel pairs, "And though I have spoken to you you have not listened, and though I have called you you have not answered." There is no other instance, so far as I am aware, of the parallelism of these four verbs together in previous or contemporary passages, but the sequence is imitated in Trito-Isaiah (Isa 65:12 = 66:4; 65:24); single pairings, however, are common, for example "speak" and "listen" in 6:10. Communication has broken down completely.

Into this symmetrical set of clauses M has secondarily inserted the pair of infinitive absolutes translated "early and constantly" (see Text); this is an expansion from phraseology elsewhere and adds nothing to the passage.

■ 14 This verse, with its threefold "which" (אֲשֶׁר) and one occurrence of "as" (כַּאֲשֶׁר), picks up diction from earlier

---

44   Hans Kjaer, "Shiloh. A Summary Report of the Second Danish Expedition, 1929," *PEQ* 31 (1931) 76–77.

45   Holm-Nielsen, "Shiloh," 822; Marie-Louis Buhl and Svend Holm-Nielsen, *Shiloh; The Danish Excavations at Tall Sailūn, Palestine, in 1926, 1929, 1932 and 1963* (Copenhagen: National Museum of Denmark, 1969) 62.

46   Israel Finkelstein, Zvi Lederman, and Shlomo Bonimovitch, "Shiloh 1981," in "Notes and News," *IEJ* 32 (1982) 148–50, esp. 149b; see further [Gordon Garner], "Shiloh and its Destruction,"

Buried History 19 (1983) 23–27.

47   So, recently, John Day, "The Destruction of the Shiloh Sanctuary and Jeremiah vii 12, 14," *Studies in the Historical Books of the Old Testament* (VTSup 30; Leiden: Brill, 1979) 87–94.

48   I find only Gen 20:9 (E), Num 16:28 (J?), and Isa 28:21, leaving aside about eight further instances in which the verb is in a relative clause modifying "deeds," e.g., "See the deeds which he did."

verses: "house which bears my name" (vv 10, 12), "trust" (v 8), "place which I gave to your fathers" (v 7), "I did to Shiloh" (compare v 12).

■ **15** As v 14 speaks of the destruction of the temple and surrounding area, this verse speaks of the exile of the people of Judah. For this reason some earlier commentators have seen the verse as an exilic addition (Giesebrecht, Volz), to be excised; but this is not justified —there is no reason why Jrm could not have anticipated exile for the people. It had been Assyrian policy, and would be Babylonian policy in time to come. The syntax and diction of the verse match that of v 14 nicely: the main clause followed by "as" (כַּאֲשֶׁר) using the same verb, the use of "your brothers" as a balance to "your fathers" (though the clauses in which the nouns are found do not balance). Jrm was concerned for "Ephraim" (note the four occurrences of the name in 31:6, 9, 18, 20: see the discussion there); the verse gives every evidence of authenticity.

"Fling away" (שׁלך hip'il) appears here for the first time in the book; with the phrase "from my [etc.] sight" (מֵעַל פָּנַי) it is used of Yahweh's banishing men and women from his presence. The expression may have been an old one current in the north[49] and in the temple cult (Ps 51:13). It later became current in Deuteronomistic circles in the south (see 2 Kgs 17:20; 24:20), perhaps stimulated by Jrm's use here.[50]

The expression "brothers" for the people of the northern kingdom is rare; conceivably Mic 5:3 was in the background of Jrm's thinking, but there is no other parallel of which I am aware, so the parallelism here, "your brothers" and "the offspring of Ephraim," is striking conclusion. Yahweh will exile this people as he had exiled those in the north; there is no longer safety in Jerusalem, in spite of the assurance that had come from adherence to Josiah's reform.

Aim

There were in Judah powerful reinforcements for the view that the temple in Jerusalem was the ultimate refuge: the marvelous survival of Jerusalem, and thus of the temple, through the siege of Sennacherib in 701, which Isaiah had foreseen; the steady recitation of

Yahweh's mighty acts by psalmists; and above all, the reform of Josiah, which in response to the words of Deuteronomy centralized the cult in the Jerusalem temple to the exclusion of outlying shrines in the countryside. If the cry "we have been rescued" (v 10) seems fatuous, we must be reminded of the many psalm-verses which assure the hearers that Yahweh rescues the righteous out of all their afflictions (Ps 34:18, 20, and often); if the assumption of ultimate refuge in the temple seems naive, we must be reminded of psalms that assure the hearers that Yahweh hears the cry for help from his temple (Ps 18:7).

But what is this search for security and protection? Jrm asks; why center one's attention on the holiness of the temple? Only if our lives are lived in radical obedience to the demands of Yahweh's covenant, the ethical expectations of the Decalogue, will Yahweh continue to sponsor us and protect us.

Jrm was of course challenging the religious "establishment" of his time by challenging the assumption that the temple was Yahweh's ultimate asylum for the people. There is a special difficulty a religious establishment has in understanding itself to stand under the judgment of God, and when that religious establishment is identified with the political power of a state, as Judah's was, then it is even more difficult to persuade it of its liability to judgment. This was the radical task that Jrm undertook, as Jesus would in a later century when he ejected the money changers from the temple court and in so doing used words adapted from Jrm's sermon (v 11; see Mark 11:15–19 and parallels).

Shiloh had been destroyed: this was not a fact of which people enjoyed being reminded. Jerusalem can be destroyed. And ultimately, Jrm was constrained to say, Jerusalem will be destroyed. And then it was destroyed: it was Jrm's terrible destiny to be vindicated by the destruction of his nation. "The holy stones lie scattered at the head of every street" (Lam 4:1); "this was for the sins of her prophets and the iniquities of her priests" (Lam 4:13).

---

49   Compare Gray, *Kings*, 601–2 on 2 Kgs 13:23.
50   Weinfeld, *Deuteronomy*, lists it as Deuteronomic phraseology: 347, no. 11a.

No More Intercession

Bibliography

Balentine, Samuel E.
  "The Prophet as Intercessor: A Reassessment,"
  JBL 103 (1984) 161–73.
Boer, Pieter A. H. de
  De Voorbede in het Oude Testament (*OTS* 3; Leiden:
  Brill, 1943) esp. 157–70.
Dahood, Mitchell
  "La Regina del Cielo in Geremia," *RivB* 8 (1960)
  166–68.
Delcor, Matthias
  "Le Culte de la 'Reine du Ciel' selon Jer 7,18;
  44,17–19. 25 et ses survivances," *Von Kanaan bis
  Kerala: Festschrift für Prof. Mag. Dr. Dr. J. P. M. van
  der Ploeg O. P. zur Vollendung des siebzigsten
  Lebensjahres am 4. Juli 1979* (ed. W. C. Delsman et
  al.; AOAT 211; Neukirchen-Vluyn:
  Neukirchener, 1982) 101–22.
Gray, John
  "Queen of Heaven," *IDB* 3:975.
Hertzberg, Hans W.
  "Sind die Propheten Fürbitter?" *Tradition und
  Situation, Studien zur alttestamentlichen Prophetie A.
  Weiser zum 70. Geburtstag am 18.11.1963 darge-
  bracht* (ed. Ernst Würthwein and Otto Kaiser; Göt-
  tingen: Vandenhoeck & Ruprecht, 1963) 63–74.
Macholz, Georg C.
  "Jeremia in der Kontinuität der Prophetie,"
  *Probleme biblischer Theologie, Gerhard von Rad zum
  70. Geburtstag* (ed. Hans W. Wolff; Munich: Kaiser,
  1971) 306–34.
Rast, Walter E.
  "Cakes for the Queen of Heaven," *Scripture in
  History and Theology: Essays in Honor of J. Coert
  Rylaarsdam* (ed. Arthur L. Merrill and Thomas W.
  Overholt; Pittsburgh Theological Monograph
  Series 17; Pittsburgh: Pickwick, 1977) 167–80.
Rhodes, Arnold B.
  "Israel's Prophets as Intercessors," *Scripture in
  History and Theology: Essays in Honor of J. Coert
  Rylaarsdam* (ed. Arthur R. Merrill and Thomas W.
  Overholt; Pittsburgh Theological Monograph
  Series 17; Pittsburgh: Pickwick, 1977) 107–28.
Stade, Bernhard
  "Miscellen—13. Die vermeintliche 'Königin des
  Himmels,'" *ZAW* 6 (1886) 123–32.
Stade, Bernhard
  "Das vermeintliche aramäisch-assyrische
  Aequivalent der מלכת השמים Jer 7. 44," *ZAW* 6
  (1886) 289–339.
Stoebe, Hans Joachim
  "Jeremia, Prophet und Seelsorger," *TZ* 20 (1964)
  385–409.
Stoebe, Hans Joachim
  "Seelsorge und Mitleiden bei Jeremia, Ein

exegetischer Versuch," *Wort und Dienst* NF 4 (1955) 116–34.

Weinfeld, Moshe
"The Worship of Molech and of the Queen of Heaven and Its Background," *UF* 4 (1972) 149–54.

7

16 As for you, do not pray for this people, do not lift up for them cry or prayer, do not press me: I will not listen to you. 17/ Do you not see what they are doing in the cities of Judah and the streets of Jerusalem? 18/ The children are collecting sticks, the fathers kindling the fire, and the wives kneading dough to make cakes ªfor the queen ofª heaven and to pour out libations to other gods, so as to offend me. 19/ Is it I they are offending?— oracle of Yahweh. Is it not themselves, so that they are left shamefaced? 20/ Therefore thus says 〉the Lord〈ª Yahweh: My anger and my wrath are going to be poured out on this place, on man and beast, on the tree of the field and fruit of the ground, and it shall burn ᵇand not go out.ᵇ

Text

18a—a The Hebrew למלכת must be understood as "for the queen of"; it is so understood by α', s' and θ', and *V*, and by *G* in the parallel expressions in 44:17, 18, 19, and 25. The correct vocalization must therefore have been לְמַלְכַּת. A wish to avoid reference to Astarte in this text, however, led to a euphemistic reading: *M* is vocalized לִמְלֶכֶת, as if understood as לִמְלֶאכֶת, "for the (handi)work of [heaven]," i.e., the heavenly bodies, and many MSS. so read the word with an 'alep; *G* reads τῇ στρατιᾷ "for the host [of heaven]," and so also *S*, while *T* reads "for the stars of." This euphemistic reading is the preferred traditional Jewish one: see Freedman, p. 55, and R. P. Gordon, "Aleph Apologeticum," *JQR* 69 (1978–79) 112. A. P. Chastoupis raises an interesting possibility, that *G* originally read τῇ στρατείᾳ, an epithet of Aphrodite, identified with Astarte (see the reference in Rudolph, p. 52 n. 1).

20a *G* omits אֲדֹנָי. This passage is the only one in Jer which offers כֹּה אָמַר אֲדֹנָי יהוה, against 153 passages which offer כֹּה אָמַר יהוה. Though *M* is plausible, it is likely that it represents an expansion and that it is *G* which is correct (so also Janzen, pp. 81–82).

b—b A few MSS. read וְאֵין מְכַבֶּה "with none to quench," like 4:4 and 21:12, instead of *M* וְלֹא תִכְבֶּה; and one MS. even mixes the text forms, וְלֹא מְכַבֶּה (see de Rossi, p. 74). *M* is preferable as a plausible variation of the poetic phrase of 4:4; so also the Versions.

Structure, Form, Setting

There are two related questions that arise with this passage. First, is the passage in some sense authentic, or is it to be attributed to a redactor (Deuteronomistic or whatever)? Second, how does the prohibition against intercession fit into Jrm's career?

What was said about the striking diction of vv 3–15 (see Setting there) is equally valid here. Thus one finds אֵין with suffix and participle in vv 16 and 17, הֲ (the interrogative particle) in vv 17 and 19, the contrasting use of כעס hip'il in vv 18 and 19, and the precise phrasing of the announcement of judgment in v 20. None of this is routine stereotyped prose; it commends itself as a deposit of genuine material from Jrm.

Form-critically these five verses appear to make up a unit, but the sequence is not altogether simple (see below). Yahweh begins by addressing Jrm (second-person singular references in vv 16–17); v 16 is a prohibition against his exercising a function of his prophetic office, namely interceding for his people. No objection from Jrm is stated (as there is in 1:6 and 4:10), but, as if he had expressed one, vv 17–19 are Yahweh's justification for the prohibition, namely the conduct of the people. This justification of the prohibition, addressed to Jrm, is at the same time an accusation against the people. That accusation then gives rise to v 20, an announcement of judgment beginning with the messenger formula. But if vv 16–20 are a single unit, then one must understand v

20 to continue the address to Jrm; in this case the announcement of judgment is presumably vouchsafed to the prophet for subsequent proclamation to the people.

As to the second question: a divine prohibition against Jrm's interceding for the people can be dated only after the king burns the scroll, at which time Jrm perceives Yahweh to be irrevocably determined to punish the people; for the prohibition compare 14:11; 15:1. The punishment (which is only threatened in 4:4) is thus activated (v 20). The setting for the passage will then be directly after the burning of the scroll in December 601. (For further discussion of the prohibition see Interpretation on v 16.)

Since the present study concludes that the present passage shares the same setting with vv 13–15 and with vv 21–29 and 30–34, the question of the organizing principle for this sequence of prose units must be raised. In an earlier publication I attempted to solve the problem: I proposed essentially that 7:1–34 was united by the word "place" (מָקוֹם: 7:3, 6, 7, 12, 14, 20, 32), by pronouns ("they," v 4; "you," plural, v 8; "you," singular, v 16; "they," vv 17, 19); and by "fathers" (vv 18, 22, 25, 26) and "children" (vv 18, 30, 31).[1] More recently Charles D. Isbell and Michael Jackson have elaborated this analysis, finding a whole series of words and phrases that bind the sequence together.[2]

The difficulty with such analyses is manifest. The chapter as a whole deals with various aspects of false worship; given, then, the repetitions of vocabulary the chapter offers, it is easy to find "patterns," but these may be adventitious, or it may be that the ordering process in the mind of the compiler was simpler than seems apparent to the scholar today. (Thus the arrangement of "fathers" and "children" mentioned above may have real validity.)

But as a matter of fact the arrangement of the units in this chapter may simply be chronological. Yahweh's prohibition against Jrm's interceding was certainly intrinsic to the drought sequence, dated here to the time of the burning of the scroll (compare again 14:11 and 15:1, and see 14:1—15:9, Setting), so that once the threat to make Jerusalem like Shiloh (v 12) was set into motion (vv 13–15), it would be appropriate to reinforce

this by the prohibition against intercession. Indeed if at a particular moment the present passage was added to the end of the second scroll, it makes an appropriate inclusio with the call narrative in chapter 1. (See further Structure for vv 21–29 and 30–34.)

Interpretation

■ **16** The transitional expression "as for you" (וְאַתָּה, masculine singular) begins the verse, shifting the address from the people of Judah to Jrm.

There follow three synonymous clauses, all prohibiting Jrm from praying for the people, each manifesting striking terminology. It is noteworthy that the negative in each case is אַל (the temporary negative which implies "do not do it at this time"), not לֹא (the permanent negative which implies "never do it");[3] the implication then is that on other occasions it was proper for Jrm to pray for the people (on this see below).

The first verb (פלל hitpa'el with the preposition בְּעַד) quite specifically means "intercede for." It occurs seven times in Jer: the present prohibition is repeated in 11:14 and 14:11, while the verb is used positively with Jrm as subject and the people as object in 37:3; 42:2 and 20, and with the people as subject and Babylon as object in 29:7.

The object of the second clause (רִנָּה) denotes a loud cry of any sort, whether of joy or (as here) of entreaty; therefore the parallel "prayer" (תְּפִלָּה, from the same root as the verb in the first clause) creates a hendiadys, "a prayerful cry." The phrase "lift up your prayer for" is found in 2 Kgs 19:4 = Isa 37:4: Isaiah is asked to intercede for the remnant of Jerusalem. The preposition in the first two clauses is identical: the first two clauses are completely synonymous.

The verb in the third clause is פגע; its basic meaning is "meet, encounter (with consequences)." Sometimes the consequences are good (Isa 64:4), often they are bad and the word implies "attack"; one may here translate "confront"—Yahweh asks Jrm not to "confront" him with a request for the people, that is, not to "press" him too hard (*NAB*: "urge").

The last clause is startling, literally "for I am not listening to you," or "for I do not hear you" (כִּי־אֵינֶנִּי

1   Holladay, *Architecture*, 102–5.
2   Charles D. Isbell and Michael Jackson, "Rhetorical criticism and Jeremiah vii 1—viii 3," *VT* 30 (1980) 20–26.
3   See John Bright, "The Apodictic Prohibition: Some Observations," *JBL* 92 (1973) 185–204.

שָׁמֵעַ). This participial idiom with "hear" occurs in the two other duplicate passages in the book (11:14; 14:12), in Isa 1:15, where God declares that he does not listen to the people's prayers when their main concern is sacrifice, in Deut 21:18, 20, where the law describes a rebellious son who does not listen to his parents, and with plural subjects in Jer 32:33; 44:16; and Ezek 20:39. In all these passages the connotation is a refusal to listen, a determination not to listen. One might ask if there is a discernible contrast with the negative of the imperfect (לֹא אֶשְׁמָע), but the answer seems to be no: Amos 5:23, with that expression, is so close to the present text as to lead one to conclude the expressions are virtually identical in meaning. But one may at least conclude that the present phrase implies that Yahweh has already made up his mind: "I have already determined not to listen." The rebellious son in Deuteronomy 21 is perverse: he is the opposite of what a son should be. The situation in Isa 1:15 is shocking: God is determined not to listen to the prayers of the people because they have their priorities wrong. In the present passage, similarly, though Jrm is obedient to his calling as a prophet, to be a mediator between Yahweh and the people, yet Yahweh suddenly states that half his function is to be denied him. He will continue to speak Yahweh's word to the people but will no longer be able to speak the people's word to Yahweh.

It is clear that one of the functions of the prophet is to intercede to God on behalf of the people.[4] In the E-tradition Abraham is called a "prophet" in that he is an intercessor (Gen 20:7, 17); similarly Moses is portrayed as an intercessor (Num 11:2; 21:7). Jeroboam asked the anonymous "man of God" to pray that the king's hand be healed (1 Kgs 13:6); Elisha prayed that the dead son of the Shunammite woman might be restored to life (2 Kgs 4:33). Amos interceded three times to Yahweh to ask that the sentence of Jacob be lifted (Amos 7:1–9); Hezekiah's officials asked Isaiah to pray for the remnant (2 Kgs 19:4 = Isa 37:4).

There are several instances in which Jrm clearly intercedes: there is a clear statement in 18:20 that he had stood before Yahweh and "spoke good for them" (the wording in 15:11 and 17:16 will not bear this interpretation; see those passages). In the prose accounts King Zedekiah asked Jrm to pray to Yahweh on behalf on the people (21:1, 2; 37:3). The date of the occasion in 37:1–10 is indicated by the notation that the army of Pharaoh had come out of Egypt (v 5)—that is, a little over a year before the final fall of the city; the occasion of 21:1–2 is not given, but may be a duplicate account of the same incident as in 37:1–10 (see those passages). When the king asks Jrm to pray on behalf of the people, the prophet does not answer that Yahweh has forbidden him to do this, though he does bring a negative message to the king. Then in 42:1–6, after the assassination of the governor Gedaliah, Jrm is asked by the group under Johanan to intercede with Yahweh and find out what they should do, and Jrm agrees to do so.

The chronology of Jrm's career proposed in the present study makes the situation plausible. Jrm was free to intercede for the people until he was convinced repentance was impossible, when the king burned the scroll. At that point Jrm understood himself to be an "anti-Moses" figure (compare 15:1).[5] On the eve of the final fall of Jerusalem, however, when he was convinced there was a hopeful future for Judah (30:1–3), he could be released to intercede once more, only finally to revert to being the anti-Moses figure when forced to go down to Egypt with the refugees (44:24–27).[6]

There may be a parallel in the tradition of Ezekiel's dumbness. Robert Wilson has examined this matter:[7] Ezekiel is called to prophesy and is immediately struck dumb (Ezek 3:22–27), a hindrance that is lifted only when the city of Jerusalem falls (Ezek 24:25–27; 33:21–22). Wilson concludes that Ezekiel's dumbness represents his being hindered from acting as a mediator for the people; when Jerusalem falls he may presumably act again as an arbitrator for the people. "The editor of these verses thus indicates that from the time of Ezekiel's call to the fall of Jerusalem the prophet could speak only Yahweh's word of judgment against the city and the people. Not until after the fall was any other prophetic

---

4 Pieter A. H. de Boer, *De Voorbede in het Oude Testament* (OTS 3; Leiden: Brill, 1943) esp. 157–70.

5 Alonso Schökel, "Jeremías como anti-Moisés."

6 Ibid., 249.

7 Robert R. Wilson, "An interpretation of Ezekiel's dumbness," *VT* 22 (1972) 91–104.

function possible."[8] Given the parallels between Ezekiel and Jrm, this model is cogent for Jrm as well. The passage then marks the onset of Jrm's cessation from interceding for the people (see Setting), a word from Yahweh reversed only when Jerusalem is about to fall.

■ **17** There is a nice balance between "I will not listen to you" at the end of v 16 and "Do you not see?" here—both offer the same diction (אֵין with suffix plus participle). The diction of this clause is unique: there is no other instance in the OT of the interrogative particle הֲ prefixed to אֵין with suffix, nor of הֲ prefixed to unsuffixed אֵין in a participial construction; this rarity may be fortuitous, but the phrasing is certainly unusual.

The construction of the balance of the verse is most naturally taken as an indirect question ("Do you not see what they are doing . . . ?"), though the Hebrew (and *G*) conceivably can be construed as a parallel direct question ("Do you not see? What are they doing . . . ?"). The Masoretic 'atnaḥ implies an indirect question, and *V* must be so construed (subjunctive).

Conceivably מָה הֵמָּה עֹשִׂים can be more loosely translated "how they are acting" (Volz) as well as the stricter "what they are doing," but it is better to stay with the latter. The phrase "cities of Judah and streets of Jerusalem" is found in the reconstructed text of 2:28; in that passage the implication was that paganism is everywhere, and so here as well. There is no spot where fertility worship does not go on.

■ **18** The participial phrases continue: the people are busy with their pagan activity, busy constantly, busy this very minute. Everyone has a special chore, fathers, mothers, children. The choice of "wives" (נָשִׁים) instead of "mothers" (אִמּוֹת, compare 16:3) is curious; "children" (בָּנִים) correlates with "fathers" (אָבוֹת), but "wives" does not.

The children are collecting sticks; this is the only occurrence in Jer of this verb (לקט pi'el), which means "collect, pick up," sometimes "glean": it suggests gathering what one has to look for to find. The "sticks" (עֵצִים,

compare 5:14) are for fuel. The fathers are kindling the fire (בער pi'el). The wives are kneading dough; the same vocabulary is found in Hos 7:4.

All this activity is in order to make כַּוָּנִים for the queen of heaven. And what is this object? The word occurs only here and in 44:19. In both passages *G* transliterates χαυῶνας. Since the context indicates that one has to do with some kind of baked goods, it is understandable that *V* should offer "cakes" (*placentas*); but it is equally clear that they are a special kind of cake: *S* transliterates in 44:19 as *G* does, but here uses a Persian loan-word, *zaotrē'*, defined by Carl Brockelmann as "cakes offered to demons."[9] *T* in both passages uses the loan-word כַּרְדִּיטִין, explained by Jastrow as a corruption of the Greek χονδρίται, which is bread made of groats. The only further clue within the text is the expression in 44:19, לְהַעֲצִבָה, literally "to fashion her" (compare עָצַב "idolatrous image"); the expression appears to mean "to make an image of her" or "to mark her image (on it)," but we lack an exact understanding of the expression (see on that verse).

Lexicographers understand the Hebrew word to be a loan-word from the Akkadian *kamānu*, which is a sweetened cake, often baked with honey or figs and often used for cultic purposes.[10] The word occurs in the Gilgamesh epic.[11] It is a type of cake specifically offered to the Babylonian-Assyrian goddess Ishtar.[12] Since the "queen of heaven" is doubtless the Palestinian manifestation of Ishtar (see below), it is appropriate that an Akkadian word used for cakes in her cult should be used in the present passage. Hosea's reference to "cakes of raisins" (Hos 3:1) may well be the same item, though the term is different.

What sort of "image" is borne by the cake? Most authorities assume that the cake is made in a mold in the shape of the figure of the goddess; such a mold was discovered in the palace kitchen at Mari.[13] There are eleven centuries between the palace at Mari and Jrm, but religious tradition is doggedly conservative, and this

8   Ibid., 102.
9   Carl Brockelmann, *Lexicon Syriacum* (Halle: Niemeyer, 1928) 208b.
10   *CAD* 8, 110b–11a.
11   Gilgamesh XI, 216; see *ANET*, 95, and n. 221 there.
12   Eberhard Schrader, *Die Keilinschriften und das Alte Testament* (3d ed.; Berlin: Reuther & Reichard, 1902) 441–42.

13   See the illustration in Pope, *Song of Songs*, Plate I, opposite p. 360, or in Abraham Malamat, "Mari," *BA* 34 (1971) 21, figure 9.

remains the best understanding. But in the nineteenth century Graf proposed that the cake was star-shaped, since Ishtar/Astarte was associated with the astronomical Venus—he compares the moon-shaped cakes called σελῆναι offered to Artemis; and this view is attractive to Volz and Rudolph. Least likely is the suggestion of Harris H. Hirschberg,[14] that the cakes were in the shape of the female sexual organs; his linguistic analysis is unconvincing.

The "queen of heaven" is assumed by most to be a reference to Astarte. The Babylonian-Assyrian equivalent Ishtar was called "queen of heaven" (šarrat šamē).[15] The phrase has turned up in a sixth-century Aramaic papyrus in Hermopolis (Egypt), "house of the queen of heaven" (בית מלכת שמין),[16] but not in a context that identifies the goddess. (For the association with Egypt, see the discussion on 44:17.) It has been proposed[17] that Jrm is referring to the goddess Anat rather than Astarte; but these two goddesses shared functions at Ugarit,[18] and it would be difficult to contrast them on the basis of such an epithet as the present one. Much less likely is the suggestion of Dahood that the sun-goddess Shapash is intended here.[19] A great number of clay figurines of a nude goddess have been excavated from Israelite sites,[20] and it is clear that practices associated with a fertility goddess were widespread in this period.[21]

The verse continues with the parallel "and to pour out libations to other gods." "Pour out libations" (נסך hip'il with cognate accusative נֶסֶךְ) may denote an offering to Yahweh (Num 28:7), but all occurrences of the phrase in Jer refer to pagan offerings. Elsewhere it is indicated that such libations were offered on the roofs of houses (19:13 and the imitative 32:29); such a location suggests the worship of deities represented by astronomical bodies.[22] For "other gods" see v 6.

The verse concludes with the phrase לְמַעַן הַכְעִסֵנִי, which literally seems to mean "in order to provoke me." The word לְמַעַן with an infinitive normally expresses purpose but sometimes (as here) implies what naturally follows, especially when a culpable action has been described that has the effect (if not the purpose) of offending God.[23] Yet there is a Jewish tradition that the expression here does involve purpose: "They are doing all these pagan practices deliberately to provoke me";[24] Calvin has the same opinion.

The verb כעס hip'il is traditionally translated "provoke to anger" (so both G and V here, and so RSV); given the meaning "anger, vexation" for the noun כַּעַס this is plausible. But Jrm makes a special point in v 19, and there "provoke oneself to anger" is impossible (in spite of RSV). In English there is the expression "cut off your nose to spite your face," and "spite" is close (so Bright, and so JB), but that rendering connotes a petty action not appropriate to what erring people do to God: the verb is a catchword in both Deuteronomy and Jer as well as in the Deuteronomistic historical work for the provocation of Yahweh by pagan worship,[25] and "spite" will not fit. One also finds in English the expression "This hurts me worse than it hurts you," but the notion of "hurting" Yahweh is foreign to the OT in the connotation it carries of hurt feelings—though NAB uses the verb here (and compare Rudolph, Wehe tun). "Afflict" has some of the

14 Harris H. Hirschberg, "Some Additional Arabic Etymologies in Old Testament Lexicography," *VT* 11 (1961) 376.

15 Eberhard Schrader, *Die Keilinschriften und das Alte Testament* (3d ed.; Berlin: Reuther & Reichard, 1902) 425–26.

16 Herm W 4:1. See conveniently Joseph A. Fitzmyer, "The Aramaic Language and the Study of the New Testament," *JBL* 99 (1980) 10, and, in detail, Jozef T. Milik, "Les papyrus araméens d'Hermoupolis et les cultes syro-phéniciens en Égypte perse," *Bib* 48 (1967) 583 (text) and 560–64 (discussion).

17 Geo Widengren, *Sakrales Königtum im Alten Testament* (Stuttgart: Kohlhammer, 1955) 12.

18 John Gray, "Ashtoreth," *IDB* 1:256.

19 Mitchell Dahood, "La Regina del Cielo in Geremia," *RivB* 8 (1960) 166–68.

20 See, for example, *ANEP*, 162, figure 469; G. Ernest Wright, *Biblical Archaeology* (Philadelphia: Westminster, 1962) 118.

21 For a good summary of the problem and the evidence through about 1960 see John Gray, "Queen of Heaven," *IDB* 3:975.

22 Compare William Robertson Smith, *Lectures on the Religion of the Semites* (3d ed. with introduction and additional notes by Stanley A. Cook; London: Black, 1927) 230 n. 4, and 580.

23 Joüon, *Gramm.*, sec. 169g; so also Zorell, p. 459a, on this verse.

24 So Jehiel Hillel ben David Altschul(er), *Meṣudat David* (seventeenth century), in מקראות גדולות (Warsaw, 1874–77).

25 Wolff, *Hosea*, 216–17, on Hos 12:15.

same difficulty (Volz: *betrüben*; Condamin: *affliger*); Yahweh hardly carries afflictions. *NJV* uses "vex," but again that implies something petty. I suggest "offend," which suggests that the people have performed wrong actions and that something of Yahweh's honor is at stake, as well as the fact that the people are diminishing their own well-being by their actions (v 19). "We have offended against thy holy laws."[26]

■ **19** This verse brings an unexpected rhetorical flourish to the diction of v 18. Whom are they really offending? Am I the one? The same sequence of הַאֹתִי is found in 5:22 (see there). No, indeed; they are offending themselves. The use of the pronoun אֹתָם for a reflexive is quite rare[27] but is understandable, given the contrast to אֹתִי.

The verse ends with the phrase לְמַעַן בֹּשֶׁת פְּנֵיהֶם; it must thus be understood as a parallel with the last phrase of v 18, "so as to offend me," so that בֹּשֶׁת must be construed as an infinitive construct, as this word is in 2:26 (see there), and לְמַעַן must likewise be understood as in v 18, to signal the consequence of the previous action. The phrase then is literally "so as to shame their face." There are many texts associating shame with the face; in 2 Sam 19:6 the hip'il of the verb appears ("you have shamed the faces of your servants"), and Isa 29:22 and Ps 44:16 offer similar contexts.[28] Pagan worship would appear to be offensive to Yahweh, but its ultimate offense is to the folk who practice such worship, and it is not something they can hide; their humiliation and confusion are plain to the world.

The thought that the people are hurting themselves by false worship is close to that of other passages: 2:5, that when one worships an empty phantom one becomes empty; 2:17 (note the use of הֲלֹא there also), that international humiliation is the fault of the people themselves; 2:19, that the punishment that comes on the people is the work of the wrong acts themselves. Jrm's play on the conventional verb כעס hip'il is a fresh approach to that verb.[29]

■ **20** Yahweh's judgment carries much of the force of 4:23–28—the same sense of the universality of destruction from Yahweh's "anger" (אַף). The diction of this verse has much in common with Nah 1:6: the linking of "anger" and "wrath" (חֵמָה), the verb "be poured out" (נתך nip'al), the comparison to fire.[30] (This stem of the verb in question appears in Jer only otherwise in 42:18 and 44:6, again with the double subject "anger" and "wrath.") This link between the diction of that portion of Nahum and that of Jrm calls into question the assumption that the truncated acrostic poem in Nahum is late.[31]

The phrase "this place" here suggests the whole land (compare v 7). The parallel between "man" (אָדָם) and "beast" (בְּהֵמָה) is a commonplace, particularly in the J and P traditions (e.g., Exod 8:13, 14); it occurs in Jer and in the prophets who followed, but one wonders whether its occurrence in Zeph 1:3 did not encourage Jrm to use it here. Curiously there is no parallel elsewhere in the OT for the paired phrases "tree of the field" and "fruit of the ground," though Joel 1:12 offers similar diction. Yahweh's wrath is to be poured out on both city and country.

For the diction "burn and not go out" see 4:4. There is no hope that Yahweh's judgment will be stayed.

Aim

Jrm is forbidden to exercise one of his functions, to intercede on behalf of the people. He perceives in this pronouncement that the judgment of Yahweh on the people is sure; at this point in his career he sees no hope for the future—he must stand aside and watch the inevitable disaster unfold. When, in the future, he will announce Yahweh's new start with his people, it will be on the other side of destruction.

---

26 Anglican *Book of Common Prayer*, Confession of Sin.
27 GKC, sec. 135k.
28 Pedersen, I/II, 241.
29 Weippert, *Prosareden*, 227.
30 Holladay, "Prototype," 366.
31 Charles L. Taylor, Jr., "Introduction and Exegesis of Nahum," *IB* 6:954a; Eissfeldt, *Introduction*, 416; and compare again Holladay, "Prototype," 366.

Sacrifices Have Never Been Yahweh's Will

Bibliography

Caspari, Wilhelm
"Jeremia und der Priesterkodex," *TBl* 3 (1924) 66–67.

König, Eduard
"On the Meaning and Scope of Jeremiah 7:22–23," *The Expositor* 6th Series 6 (1902) 135–54, 208–18, 366–77.

Milgrom, Jacob
"Concerning Jeremiah's Repudiation of Sacrifice," *ZAW* 89 (1977) 273–75.

Reymond, Philippe
"Sacrifice et 'spiritualité' ou sacrifice et alliance? Jér. 7, 22–24," *TZ* 21 (1965) 314–17.

Strobel, Albert
"Jeremias, Priester ohne Gottesdienst? Zu Jer 7,21–23," *BZ* NF 1 (1957) 214–24.

Weinfeld
"Metamorphosis," 52–55.

Würthwein, Ernst
"Kultpolemik oder Kultbescheid? Beobachtungen zu dem Thema 'Prophetie und Kult,'" *Tradition und Situation, Studien zur alttestamentlichen Prophetie, Artur Weiser zum 70. Geburtstag am 18.11.1963 dargebracht von Kollegen, Freunden und Schülern* (Göttingen: Vandenhoeck & Ruprecht, 1963) 115–31.

7

21 Thus Yahweh [of hosts, the God of Israel][a] has said: Your burnt offerings add to your sacrifices, and eat meat! 22/ No: I did not speak with your fathers nor command them, on the day I[a] brought them out of the land of Egypt, on matters of burnt offerings and sacrifice; 23/ what I commanded them instead was this: Obey my voice, so that I may become God to you and you may become a people to me; walk in exactly the way I command you, so that it may go well with you. 24/ But they did not listen nor turn their ear; they walked [in (their own) counsels,][a] in the stubbornness of their own evil heart, and they turned[b] backward rather than forward. 25/ From the day when [a]your fathers[a] came out of the land of Egypt to this day I have sent [b] to you[b] all my

Text

21a These words are missing in *G* and represent an expansionist gloss in *M*; see Janzen, pp. 75–76.

22a Reading with the *qere'*, many MSS. and the Versions הוֹצִיאִי, literally "(day) of my bringing (them) out," for the ketib הוֹצִיא "(day) of bringing (them) out."

24a בְּמֹעֵצוֹת is lacking in *G*; omit (with Cornill and Rudolph) as a gloss from Ps 81:13; see Janzen, pp. 11, and 193 n. 7. *M* may well have a conflate text here, where בְּמֹעֵצוֹת and בִּשְׁרִרוּת are alternate readings: "in the counsels of their own evil heart" and "in the stubbornness of their own evil heart."

b A few MSS. here read וַיֵּלְכוּ "walked" for *M* וַיִּהְיוּ; *M* is clearly the *lectio difficilior*, the phraseology matching הלך + היה in v 23. The alternative reading is thus a *lapsus calami*.

25a—a Reading *M* אֲבוֹתֵיכֶם (so also *T*) in preference to *G*, *V*, *S* אֲבוֹתֵיהֶם "their fathers." The third-person reference would help the transition to v 26, but it seems better to stay with the second-person reference (compare v 22) and see the third-person references in v 26 as indicating previous generations as well as the present one. Bright follows *G*; Rudolph emends the text of v 26.

b—b Reading *M* אֲלֵיכֶם in preference to the reading of one MS., a few MSS. of *G*, and *S* אֲלֵיהֶם "to them."

servants the prophets [daily,]ᶜ early and
constantly, 26/ but they did not listen to
me nor turn their ear; they stiffened their
neck [and did]ᵃ worse than their fathers.
27/ [And you shall speak to them all
these words, but they will not listen to
you, and you shall call to them, but they
will not answer you.]ᵃ 28/ [. . . .]ᵃ This is
the nation which has not obeyed the
voice of Yahweh [her God],ᵇ and they
have not accepted correction; honesty
[has perished and]ᶜ has been cut off ᵈ
from their mouth.ᵈ

For the problem see note a; Bright again prefers
"them."

c   *M* here has יוֹם, which can hardly mean "daily"
alone: it appears to be dittographic from the
beginning of the verse (so also Rudolph), since the
parallel in 25:4 does not have it. One MS., however,
and *S* read יוֹם יוֹם "daily" here, and this reading is
accepted by Condamin and others.

26a   *M* reads literally "They stiffened their neck, they
did worse than their fathers." *G* omits הֵרֵעוּ, reading
"They stiffened their neck more than their fathers."
The plus in *M* appears to be a secondary expansion
on the basis of 16:12. *G* in 17:23 has a plus over *M*,
adding "more than their fathers," thus indirectly
supporting *G* here. So Janzen, p. 37.

27a   This verse is missing in *G*, and the words, present
in *M*, do not fit the context. Thus the verb sequence
"speak," "listen," "call," "answer" is found in 7:13;
35:17 (lacking in *G*); Isa 65:12; and 66:4; in each of
those passages the combination is in a subordinate
clause introduced by יַעַן and the concluding clause
expresses a punishment by Yahweh; and further, in
each of those passages it is Yahweh's words that fall
on deaf ears. The parallel passage 17:23 suggests
that v 28 follows v 26 better than v 27; see Janzen,
p. 38. Verse 27 is thus a secondary intrusion
modeled on v 13, perhaps serving as a bridge
between vv 21–26 and v 28 after the introductory
words of v 29 were accidentally reinserted before v
28 (see v 28, note a, and v 29, note a).

28a   The introductory words "and you shall say to
them" need to be restored to the beginning of v 29
(see Structure and Form). The words had evidently
dropped out from v 29 by haplography (confusion
of אֲלֵיהֶם with מִפִּיהֶם, at that stage just preceding, at
the end of v 28), inserted in the margin, and
reinserted at the wrong spot. Janzen discusses the
textual difficulties here, p. 38, but does not arrive at
this solution.

b   *G* omits אֱלֹהָיו; *M* has evidently expanded the text
to the more usual form found eleven times in
Deuteronomy. So Janzen, p. 80.

c   *G* translates only one of the synonymous verbs
("has perished," "has been cut off"); the translation
ἐξέλιπεν no doubt stands for נִכְרְתָה (there are ten
other instances of ἐκλείπειν = כרת in *G*, according to
Edwin Hatch and Henry A. Redpath, *A Concordance
to the Septuagint and the Other Greek Versions of the Old
Testament* [Oxford: Clarendon, 1897], but no other
instance of that verb translating אבד). The perfect
with waw is odd for וְנִכְרְתָה, and it is better to
understand *M* as a conflate text than as original
parallel phrases; note the interchangeability of the
two verbs when תִּקְוָה is subject in Prov 10:28; 11:7;
23:18; 24:14.

d—d   For מִפִּיהֶם Oriental MSS. read מִפִּיכֶם "from your
mouth," but the reading is clearly not convincing.

Structure and Form

Verse 21 begins a new unit; while vv 16–20 are an address in the second-person singular to Jrm (see there), vv 21 and 22 shift to the plural to address the people.

There is a small tangle of interrelated textual, form-critical, and literary problems between vv 27 and 30. (1) The rubric in v 21 introduces words addressed to the people, yet the present text of v 28 begins with Yahweh's address to Jrm (as does v 27, which is associated with v 28 secondarily). This datum suggests the beginning of a new unit at vv 27–28. (2) On the other hand, form-critically v 28 embodies a "summary-appraisal,"[1] a genre that appears elsewhere at the end of oracles of accusation and judgment without an introductory rubric (see 13:25; Isa 14:26; 17:14b). (3) The poem of v 29, beginning with feminine singular imperatives, appears suddenly, without warning. A solution that takes account of these data is to restore "and you shall say to them" to the beginning of v 29: it is noteworthy that in 17:20 the same introductory words ("and you shall say to them") are likewise followed immediately by an imperative. The displacement of these words was evidently due to haplography (see Text). Verses 29–34 in this way embody a separate unit with consistent diction: Yahweh's introductory words to Jrm, followed by the words he is to deliver to the people (the present totality of vv 29–34). The present unit is therefore made up of vv 21–28.

It is proposed here that the settings of vv 21–28 and 29–34 are different: that the setting of vv 29–34 is 600 or soon thereafter, and the setting of vv 21–28 is 594 (see Setting for each unit). One must therefore envision vv 29–34 as having been added in its present position directly after vv 16–20, a continuation of Yahweh's address to Jrm in 16–20. Verses 21–28 may have been inserted before vv 29–34 in order not to break an inclusio between chapter 2 and vv 29–34 (see vv 29–34, Structure). The two units may be associated on the basis of "fathers" (vv 22, 25, 26) and "sons/children" (v 31), given the association of "children" and "fathers" in v 18; or they may be associated in that the present passage reverses Deut 12:6, as vv 29–34 reverse Deut 12:5.

Verses 21–23 offer a parody of priestly torah: cultic instructions in the imperative plural, followed by an evaluative concluding statement introduced by כִּי (v 22). The key verb סְפוּ in v 21 may mean "sweep away," in which case כִּי carries its normal meaning "for," but the verb may also mean "add" (so translated here), in which case כִּי must be an emphatic "no" or "specifically." Jrm parodies cultic instructions in a complicated way, partly because of the uncertainty of meaning of the verb and the uncertainty of the relation between devotion to Yahweh and filling one's stomach (see Interpretation), partly because priestly torah itself promised life as its goal (Lev 18:5a; Amos 5:4), and "eating" is a prerequisite to life (the passage is surely a parody of Deut 12:6–7, 15, 20, 27), and partly because the כִּי clause in v 22 does not offer a reinforcement of the command in v 21 by a grounding in the will of Yahweh, but rather a contradiction of the command.[2] Yahweh's denial in v 22 is almost a declaration of innocence (compare 14:14; 23:21; for Jrm's declarations of innocence see 15:17a; 17:16a). Verse 23 is an affirmation of Yahweh's previous acts of revelation (compare 22:21aα). For the form of the covenant formula, "I shall become God to you, and you shall become a people to me," see Interpretation.

Verses 24–26 offer an accusation report, a statement by Yahweh of the disobedience of the covenant people in both past and present: it is noteworthy that the parody of priestly torah in Amos 4:4–5 is continued by an accusation report in Amos 4:6–11. But whereas the accusation report in Amos stresses the many prior punitive acts of Yahweh, the present report stresses the disobedience of the people in spite of Yahweh's effort to communicate to them; a similar recollection of Yahweh's effort is found in Amos 2:11. Verse 28 is a summary-appraisal (see above); it is a form that appears to have its origin in wisdom circles. It functions here as a concluding judgment on the people: Yahweh has excluded all possibility

---

1 Childs, *Isaiah and the Assyrian Crisis*, 128–36.

2 For a close parallel see Wolff, *Joel and Amos*, 211–12, on the form of Amos 4:4–5; on "priestly torah" see Joachim Begrich, "Die priesterliche Tora," *Werden und Wesen des Alten Testaments* (ed. Paul Volz, Friedrich Stummer, and Johannes Hempel; BZAW 66; Berlin: Töpelmann, 1936) 63–88 = Joachim

Begrich, *Gesammelte Studien zum Alten Testament* (Munich: Kaiser, 1964) 232–60.

of hope—it is almost an epitaph on the career of the people.

Setting

Verse 21 is highly ironic: the first verb is ambiguous and the message of v 22 is so opposed to the general content of priestly torah as to leave commentators struggling for an explanation (see Interpretation). There is therefore no doubt that these verses offer Jrm's word. Verse 23, too, would be difficult to deny to him, given the emphatic reversal at the beginning. Volz judges vv 21–23 to be genuine but vv 24–28 to be secondary. Verse 28, the summary-appraisal (see Structure and Form), is used by Jrm elsewhere in a poem (13:25); as for v 27, that verse is clearly secondary, given its omission by G (see Text). Verses 24–26 do appear typical of the stereotyped prose associated with a redactor. There are, however, countervailing considerations. Thus the phrase in v 24, "turn backward rather than forward" (הָיָה לְאָחוֹר וְלֹא לְפָנִים, literally "become backward and not forward"), is unique to the OT: סבב ("turn") appears with לְאָחוֹר ("backward") with a similar meaning in Ps 114:3, 5, but otherwise that adverbial expression is not used in this way. Further, though v 25 looks to be filled with the stereotypical prose associated with a redactor, the verse serves as a necessary transition between the judgment on the ancestors (v 24) and the judgment on the present generation (v 26). It is better to conclude that the whole passage is authentic to Jrm.

The judgment on the ancestors (v 24) is darker than that expressed in 2:2–3, 5: there the pristine loyalty of the ancestors was contrasted with the apostasy of the present generation, while here the ancestors are also apostate.[3] According to the analysis proposed in this study, this message of Yahweh's judgment is to be dated in the period after the king burned the prophet's scroll in December 601.

There are no direct clues within the passage for a more specific date, but there are some indirect hints. There is a close parallel in diction between this sequence and that of 11:1–17, and there is a parallel between these two passages in content as well. Thus both parody Deuteronomy (see Form on both), and both attack the people's dependence on sacrifice (vv 21–22; 11:15). The setting proposed for 11:1–17 is that of the recitation of Deuteronomy in 594 (see there), and the same setting is appropriate for the present passage.

Beyond the shared characteristics with 11:1–17, there appear to be shared characteristics among these two passages and 2:26–28 and 16:10–13. (1) Verse 26 has "They stiffened their neck worse than their fathers," and 16:12 has "You have done worse than your fathers"; these are the only two passages in the book in which such phraseology appears. Further, there is a comparison of generations implied in the strange expression "earlier fathers" in 11:10. (2) The striking verb "hurl" (טול hip'il or hop'al) occurs in 16:13 in the context of the people's going into exile; this usage appears to be a generalization of its specific use with Jehoiachin in 22:26, 28, and therefore subsequent to 597. (3) "Backward rather than forward" (v 24) is a unique expression with the accompanying verb (see above), but the thought is close to "they have turned their back to me and not their face" (2:27). (4) In Jrm's early oracles the pagan gods are assumed to do nothing (2:8), but in both 2:28 and 16:13 it is implied that pagan gods may have power (16:13, "gods . . . who will show you no mercy," emended text: see Text there). The community of diction in these four passages lends plausibility to the setting proposed here, namely 594. (For the setting of 2:26–28, see in detail 2:1—4:4, Preliminary Observations, *Analysis of 2:4–37*.)

Interpretation

■ **21–22** For the messenger formula see 2:2.

The word-order object + imperative in v 21 is rare; in Jer I can locate otherwise only 6:26 (with the similar 46:19) and 39:12 (2:10 could be added if one includes an accusative of location).

For the pair "burnt offering" and "sacrifice" see 6:20.

The phrase סְפוּ עַל is ambiguous. It may mean "add onto, pile up on" (יסף qal, though with this meaning there may be a ספה II as well).[4] But it may also mean "sweep away onto" (ספה). Jrm evidently intends the hearers to be in doubt whether they are to pile up burnt offerings or get rid of them. This uncertainty is compounded by the fact that the burnt offering was entirely

---

3   Rudolph, p. 59.
4   So Zorell.

consumed on the altar and therefore unavailable to supply meat to the worshipers: does Jrm say that the burnt offerings are to be snatched off the altar so the worshipers will have more meat to eat, or does he say they are to be piled up on the altar on top of the sacrifices (וְבָחִים), since it is all "meat" to Yahweh anyway and of no ultimate significance to him?[5] Even if the intention of Jrm was that the verb means simply "add," the verse is heavily sarcastic; one thinks of Amos 4:4–5, a passage that speaks with equal sarcasm of the piling up of sacrifices, or Hos 8:13, where the emphasis likewise seems to be on the appetite of the worshipers, or Isa 29:1, where סְפוּ also appears—"add year to year"—with equal sarcasm regarding the festal calendar. (For further exploration of the irony of the verse, and in particular of the verse as a parody of Deuteronomy 12, see Form.) Ultimately, says Yahweh, sacrificial observance is for you simply a pretext for eating meat: "Eat, then, and stuff your stomachs; nothing of this belongs to me" (Calvin). The word in 11:15 is similar. Paul will have an analogous word for the church in Corinth when its members used the Lord's Supper as an occasion for eating and drinking (1 Cor 11:20–22).

If the first verb in v 21 is heard as "snatch away," then the conjunction that begins v 22 is translated (as normally) "for"; but if the verb in v 21 means "add," the conjunction is corrective, "no" or "rather."

The phraseology of "I did not . . . command them" suggests that Jrm is trying to correct a false understanding that people might have gained from a legal tradition such as the Covenant Code (see Exod 20:24; 23:18); for the matter see further Interpretation on v 31.

But the bald statement that these sacrifices were not a part of the instruction to Israel at the time of the exodus raises great difficulties. It is paralleled by the implication of the rhetorical question in Amos 5:25 and of the linking of sacrifice with kingship in Hos 3:4; these passages stand in stark contrast to the presentation of the total Pentateuch as it now stands. Some of the polemic

against sacrifice in the prophets can be explained as a way of saying, "I would rather have righteousness than sacrifice": this would be plausible for Isa 1:11–14; Hos 6:6; 8:13; Amos 5:21–24; and Mic 6:6–8. This relativizing of the attitude toward sacrifice is taken by a number of authorities[6] and has even been maintained for the present text.[7]

But the present verse, and the analogous texts in Amos and Hosea already cited, do not lend themselves to this interpretation without violence. The words certainly press the hearer to the conclusion that Jrm believed that the Sinaitic covenant had nothing at all to do with "burnt offering and sacrifice"; and given the assumption that Jrm must have known the Covenant Code, the evidence that he knew (at least part of) Deuteronomy and (at least some parts of) the P tradition (on the latter compare 4:23 and 20:3–6), the problem becomes severe.

It was already an issue for the rabbinic commentators. Thus Rashi affirmed that the basis of the relation with Yahweh is "If you will obey my voice and keep my covenant, you shall be my own possession among all peoples" (Exod 19:5), and so, by implication, that basis is the Decalogue (which follows Exodus 19) rather than the sacrificial law, which is not part of the Decalogue; and Qimḥi also cites Exod 19:5 and mentions the Decalogue explicitly, noting as well that individuals were not in fact commanded to offer burnt offerings—they were optional for the individual and obligatory only on the community as a whole.[8] Moshe Weinfeld's recent study essentially follows the same line: Jrm followed the outlook of Deuteronomy, that only the Decalogue was given by Yahweh at Sinai, while other prescriptions, including those regarding sacrifice, were given by Moses later, just before his death.[9]

Roland de Vaux has wisely pointed out that the passages in question no more condemn the cult than Isa 1:15 suggests a condemnation of prayer;[10] the problem is the formalism of exterior worship without any corresponding interior disposition (compare Isa 29:13).[11]

---

5   See Hyatt on this matter.

6   See in particular Guillaume, *Prophecy and Divination*, 369–81; J. Philip Hyatt, *Prophetic Religion* (New York: Abingdon-Cokesbury, 1947) 118–32; Harold H. Rowley, *The Unity of the Bible* (Philadelphia: Westminster, 1953) 30–43 = *The Unity of the Bible* (New York: Meridian Books, 1957) 38–48. Rudolph gives further bibliography (57 nn. 1 and 2).

7   Albert Strobel, "Jeremias, Priester ohne Gottesdienst? Zu Jer 7,21–23," *BZ* NF 1 (1957) 214–24.

8   For Qimḥi on the question see Weinfeld, "Metamorphosis," 53–54.

9   Ibid., 52–55.

10   De Vaux, *Ancient Israel*, 454.

11   Ibid., 454–55.

Recently Jacob Milgrom has made a fresh proposal for the present text. He rejects Weinfeld's view, insisting instead that the words of Jrm have no reference to the temple cult, but rather to voluntary individual sacrifices: in the P-code the "burnt offering" (עוֹלָה) and "sacrifice" (זֶבַח) are named only in the context of such individual offerings (Lev 17:8; 22:17–25; Num 15:1–16).[12] In his view then Jrm is not addressing the priests at all but individuals who are bringing offerings. In v 21 he brackets "burnt offerings" (which were completely consumed on the altar) with "sacrifices" (the edible portions of which were consumed by the worshiper), saying in effect, "You might as well eat meat from the burnt offering as offer it on the altar." The worshiper should thus renounce individual offerings because their ritual piety is vitated by immoral behavior.

Milgrom's interpretation is convincing, but underneath any interpretation of the verse must be an awareness of the emotion it carries. The irony of v 21 continues in v 22. Jrm perceives Yahweh to be angry. His worshipers have turned their backs on his will (v 24); obviously it is not his will to offer burnt offering and sacrifice, not when those who offer it are so deaf to him.

■ 23 The first phrase of this verse follows closely the diction of the previous verse, though a literal translation is awkward: "Rather, it is this matter which I commanded them, as follows."

For "obey my voice" see 3:13. It is a basic command of the covenant God—compare Exod 19:5.

The command is followed here by the covenant formula, "I shall become God to you, and you shall become a people to me." That formula seems to be at home in priestly diction, taken from legal terminology used in marriage and adoption;[13] Wolff makes the point that the negative phraseology of Hos 1:9, "For you are not my people, and I am not there for you," is a formula of divorce,[14] so that marriage phraseology may well stand behind the formula here.

Jrm elsewhere links "listen/obey" and "walk": in 6:16–17 one finds "walk" (הלך) parallel with "pay attention" (קשׁב hip'il: note that קשׁב hip'il and שׁמע, the verb in the present passage, are synonyms in 6:10 and 8:6). The Book of Deuteronomy stresses both, though I am not aware of a passage there that offers them in parallel. The phrase "the whole way" (כָּל־הַדֶּרֶךְ), translated here "exactly the way," is not common: this is the only occurrence in Jer, and it occurs only seven other times in the OT. The only parallel to the present phraseology is a very close one, Deut 5:33 (30), part of a parenetic appeal appended to the Decalogue; it is likely that the Deuteronomy verse is derived from the present passage in Jer.[15] "Walk in the way of Yahweh" or the like is a standard phrase for loyalty in the covenant.[16] The linking here of "way" and "go well" (יטב qal) may be an echo of vv 3 and 5, "make good your ways." Yahweh expects loyalty from his covenant people; if they walk in his way, then all will be well.

■ 24 The parallel of "turn one's ear" (נטה hip'il with אֹזֶן) and "listen" is a standard one (Ps 45:11); for the thought that the people have refused to listen see 6:10, 17. The linking of "listen" and "walk" is parallel to that in v 23.

The phrase "stubbornness of one's heart" (שְׁרִרוּת לִבּוֹ) is repeated often in Jer; for a discussion see 3:17 (where, however, it is part of a secondary insertion).

The parallelism of "ear" and "heart" is nice.

The phrase "turn (out to be) backward rather than forward" occurs only here in the OT (for a discussion see Setting); for the thought, however, compare 2:27, "They have turned their back to me and not their face." In the final analysis the people are facing backward rather than forward: it is no way to walk. This judgment on the ancestors is darker than that in 2:2–3, 5 (see the discussion in Setting).

■ 25 Not only did the generation at Sinai not listen, but neither has any generation since. The first half of the verse modifies the phrasing of v 22. Though the last half of the verse offers phrasing that is duplicated several times elsewhere in the book (25:4; 26:5; 29:19; 35:15; 44:4), it appears to be original here (see Setting).

The phrase "send one's servants" implies the action of a king sending an official representation for diplomatic, commercial, or military purposes (2 Sam 10:3; 11:1; 1 Kgs 5:15; 20:6; 2 Chr 8:18; 32:9). "Send my servants the prophets" then suggests that Yahweh the heavenly king sends the equivalent of his courtiers to the people. "The honour of the envoy is bound up with the honour of the

---

12   Jacob Milgrom, "Concerning Jeremiah's Repudiation of Sacrifice," *ZAW* 89 (1977) 273–75.

13   Weinfeld, *Deuteronomy*, 80–81.

14   Wolff, *Hosea*, 21.

15   Compare Mayes, *Deuteronomy*, 174.

16   Weinfeld, *Deuteronomy*, 333–34.

king. . . . The history of Yahweh is . . . present among men in the fully authorised messenger of His Word."[17] The same image is implied by 23:1, "I did not send the prophets, yet they ran." What is emphasized here in the present verse is the steady, persistent effort of Yahweh to communicate with his people through a long series of prophets: "from the day when your fathers came out . . . to this day"; "all my servants the prophets"; "early and constantly." For the idiom with the infinitive absolute הַשְׁכֵּם, literally "rise early," see GKC, sec. 113k.

■ **26** In v 24 the ancestors are judged; in the first half of the present verse the same judgment is leveled against the present generation. But (if the text of v 25 is correct: see Text) there is a shift from the second person to the third person; Calvin: "There is then no doubt but that it was an evidence of indignation, that he changed the person, and that he was wearied in addressing them."

The phrase "stiffen the neck" is in the context here of refusal to bend the ear, and that may be the connotation of the phrase.[18] It is not found outside Jer; within the book it is found only otherwise in 19:15 and the secondary 17:23. But the phrase "stiff-necked people," applied to the generation of Moses, is found four times in the JE tradition of Exodus 32—34 (e.g., 32:9) and twice in Deuteronomy 9 (vv 6, 13). Thus Jrm seems to have offered his own variation on the traditional description of the generation of Moses; bad as that generation was, the later generation was worse.

■ **27–28** Verse 27 is a secondary insertion (see Text); it reinforces the hopelessness of Jrm's role in speaking to the people. In v 28 they are not called by the normal biblical designation a "people" (עַם) but a "nation" (גּוֹי), one among many (see the discussion on 5:9). "Obey Yahweh's voice" repeats "obey my voice" from v 23, but the first person has now become third person. For "accept correction" see 2:30. For "honesty" (אֱמוּנָה) see 5:1. The verb "be cut off" does not occur elsewhere with "honesty"; "courage" (literally "heart") is cut off (4:9), and "hope" (Prov 10:28), but not such a trait as honesty. For the same thought, however, see 9:2, 4. Qimḥi suggests that "cut off from their mouth" implies they even stopped pretending (compare 12:2b).

Aim

Jrm here proclaims that the people's sacrifices have no place in the will of Yahweh, and that the people both past and present have refused to be sensitive to that will. As a result they are no longer considered by Yahweh to be his covenant people, but are simply one nation among many, a nation that did not respond to its mandate and therefore by implication may simply be lost among the nations. Indeed the summary-appraisal in v 28 reads like an epitaph.

The distance from the darkness of this word to the light of the new covenant, in the context of which the old covenant formula (v 23) will become valid once more (31:33), is as far as the east is from the west (Ps 103:12).

---

17 Walther Zimmerli, "παῖς θεοῦ," *TDNT* 5:664–65.
18 Bernard Couroyer, "Avoir la nuque raide: ne pas incliner l'oreille," *RB* 88 (1981) 216–25.

Child Sacrifice
Will Bring Total Destruction

Bibliography

On human sacrifice in Israel:

Kraus
  Worship, 117–18, and bibliography in n. 73.
Plataroti, D.
  "Zum Gebrauch des Wortes *mlk* im Alten
  Testament," *VT* 28 (1978) 286–300.
Smith, Morton
  "A Note on Burning Babies," *JAOS* 95 (1975) 477–
  79.
Soggin, J. Alberto
  "Child Sacrifice and Cult of the Dead in the Old
  Testament," *Old Testament and Oriental Studies*
  (BibOr 29) 84–87 = "A proposito di sacrifici di
  fanciulli e di culto dei morti nell'Antico
  Testamento," *OrAnt* 8 (1969) 215–17.
De Vaux
  Ancient Israel, 441–46.
Weinfeld, Moshe
  "Burning Babies in Israel, A Rejoinder to Morton
  Smith's Article in *JAOS* 95 (1975), pp. 477–79,"
  UF 10 (1978) 411–13.
Weinfeld, Moshe
  "The Worship of Molech and of the Queen of
  Heaven and Its Background," *UF* 4 (1972) 133–
  54.

7

29   《 And you shall say to them: 》[a]
         Shear your hair and throw it away,
         and raise on the caravan-tracks a
         lament:
         "Oh, Yahweh has rejected and
         forsaken the community of
         his rage!"
30   For the children of Judah have done evil in
      my eyes—oracle[a] of Yahweh; they have
      put their vile things in the house which
      bears my name, to defile it, 31/ [a]and they
      keep building[a] [b]high places[b] at [c]The Fire-

Text

29a   See v 28, Text note a.
30a   The Leningrad MS. reads נאום here for the
       normal נאם; the meaning is unaffected.
31a—a The perfect וּבָנוּ here is startling and appears
       again in the parallel passage in 19:5; the parallel in
       32:35 has the expected imperfect וַיִּבְנוּ. Rudolph
       suggests here that it is an Aramaizing usage
       (compare 3:9), but 3:9 is part of a late passage where
       such usage is not surprising, while the present
       passage is genuine to Jrm. Furthermore the lack of
       yod here is hardly a slip of the pen if the same form
       occurs in 19:5. One can only conclude that Jrm
       intended a frequentative use here; the usage in
       37:15 is comparable ("they kept beating him"). For
       possible word-play here see Interpretation.
b—b   Both *G* and *T* read "a high place" (singular) for
       the plural of *M*. If the verb is frequentative (see a—
       a), then the plural is probably correct. On the other
       hand, there may actually have been only one high
       place at the location, and Jrm may have been
       exaggerating for effect, so that the singular would
       simply be a correction for "accuracy."
c—c   The name תֹפֶת has been given the Masoretic
       vocalization תֹּפֶת on the analogy of בֹּשֶׁת "shame" or
       of תֹּפֶת "spitting" (Job 17:6). The *G* spelling ταφεθ
       suggests an original vocalization like תָּפֶת: the word

pit,[c] which is in the Valley of Ben-Hinnom,
to burn their sons and daughters with fire,
something which I did not command,[d] nor
did it come to my mind. 32/ Therefore the
time is surely coming—oracle of Yahweh
—when it will no longer be said, "The
Fire-pit," or "Valley of Ben-Hinnom," but
rather "Valley of Murder"; and they shall
bury at a fire-pit, without a "place." 33/
And the corpses of this people shall
become food for the birds of the heavens
and for the beasts of the earth, with none
to frighten them off. 34/ And I shall
silence from the cities of Judah and from
the streets of Jerusalem the voice of joy
and[a] the voice of gladness, the voice of
the bridegroom and the voice of the
bride, for [b]the land[b] shall become a ruin.

appears to be cognate with the Aramaic תְּפָיָא
"fireplace, cookstove." See Interpretation.

d   A few MSS., G, and S read צִוִּיתִים "command
them" (like v 22) for M צִוִּיתִי. The parallelism with
"come to my mind" suggests that M is preferable.

34a   A few MSS. omit this occurrence of וְ "and."

b—b   A few MSS., and G and S, read כָּל־הָאָרֶץ "all the
land" here; "all" is doubtless an expansionist gloss
(compare Janzen, pp. 65, 68).

Structure

For the place of division within vv 21–34, see vv 21–28,
Structure and Form; and for the related shift of "And
you shall say to them" from the beginning of v 28 to the
beginning of v 29, see v 28, Text note a. For the placement of vv 21–28 and 29–34 with respect to each other,
see again vv 21–28, Structure and Form. For the
necessity of separating vv 29–34 from 8:1–3, see 8:1–3,
Structure, Form, Setting.

Given the late setting proposed for vv 21–28 (594),
one must envisage the present passage as originally
having followed directly on vv 16–20 in the second
scroll; Yahweh's direct address to Jrm will thus have
continued from vv 16–20 to vv 29–34. (There is an
analogy in the connection between 11:14, in which Jrm is
prohibited from praying for the people, and the poem in
11:15–16; see the discussion in 11:1–17, Structure.)
This connection will offer continuity in the word "place"
(vv 20, 32), a continuity already established from earlier
in the chapter (vv 3, 7, 12, 14).

In the framework of large-scale structure in the second
scroll, it is possible that the present passage, with "bride"
(כַּלָּה) in v 34, formed an inclusio with 2:2, "bridal days"
(כְּלוּלֹתָיִךְ), and 2:32, "bride" (כַּלָּה).

The basic movement within this passage is from the
specificity of the atrocities committed at the temple (v
30) and at the Valley of Ben-Hinnom (v 31), to the
generalizations: in time to come there will be no proper
funerals (v 33) or weddings (v 34). This structure is close
to that in 16:5–9, which it closely resembles (see there).

Form

Verse 29 is a call to lament, one of the traditional tasks of
the prophet. For the form see 4:8. It is to be noted that
Mic 1:16 is comparable in form, and may be in content
(on this see further Interpretation on v 29).

Though v 29b may be the prophet's statement of the
ground for the lament ("for Yahweh has rejected . . . ," so
the current English translations), it is better to take it as
the content of the lament itself (compare the same form
in 4:8 and 6:26).

The grounding for the lament then comes in vv 30–
31, the reasons for Yahweh's judgment: abominations in
the temple (v 30), child sacrifice at the Valley of Ben-
Hinnom (v 31). Verses 32–34, introduced by "therefore"
(לָכֵן), are Yahweh's announcement of judgment, his
intervention: he will change the name of the Valley of
Ben-Hinnom to something far worse (v 32), and there
shall neither be funerals (v 33) nor weddings (v 34).
Crucial in Yahweh's intervention will be his renaming of
the Valley of Ben-Hinnom (v 32);[1] the announcement of
renaming is related to the more general announcement
of a change in speech-pattern (for which see 3:17).

Setting

The diction of vv 31–33a is very close to that of 19:5–7.
Those verses in chapter 19 are widely thought to be
secondary there, but the analysis given in the present
study indicates, to the contrary, that they are intrinsic to
that chapter (see 19:1—20:6, Preliminary Observations).
One must conclude that 19:1–15 is a narrative version of
the speech of the present passage, like the relation of

---

1   Otto Eissfeldt, "Renaming in the Old Testament,"
*Words and Meanings, Essays Presented to David Winton
Thomas on His Retirement from the Regius Professorship of*
Hebrew in the University of Cambridge, 1968 (ed. Peter
R. Ackroyd and Barnabas Lindars; Cambridge:
Cambridge University, 1968) 69–80, esp. 72.

chap. 26 to 7:1–12 (so, first, Abraham Kuenen; see again 19:1—20:6, Preliminary Observations). It follows that one must find the same setting for both the present passage and for 19:1—20:6.

There is no reason to doubt the authenticity of this parallel material. There is a commanding authoritativeness about the announcement of the change of name of the Valley of Ben-Hinnom (compare 20:1–6; 23:1–6) that is hardly conceivable to a redactor. The curious phrase "without a 'place'" (מֵאֵין מָקוֹם, v 32), with the possibility of multiple meanings, also points to the prophet.

The parallel in chapter 19 indicates that the words were part of a symbolic action offered at the Potsherd Gate overlooking the Valley of Ben-Hinnom. If the temple sermon, vv 1–12, paralleled in chapter 26, was the public discourse par excellence that offered to the people an appeal for repentance characteristic of the period of the first scroll, then this discourse, and its accompanying action, was the public declaration par excellence that the judgment of Yahweh was now inevitable. Some of the diction here (in vv 33–34) is paralleled in 16:4–9, part of the call to celibacy, another public gesture signifying the inevitability of disaster. Both the call to celibacy and the declaration at the Potsherd Gate belong to the period of the second scroll (600 or thereafter): by the proposal of the present study the passage under discussion was one of those added in the dictation of the second scroll. Given the assumption that the call to celibacy came early in 600 (see 16:1–9, Setting), and given the shared diction with the present passage, one must understand the present passage likewise to have been made public in 600 or soon thereafter.

Interpretation

■ **29** The people are addressed in the feminine singular, as they are often in chapters 2—6 (6:26, for example). The verb גזז means "shear" and is normally used of sheep; it is used of a man's head of hair in Job 1:20, and of a woman's head of hair only otherwise in Mic 1:16, a verse which is likewise a call to lament. The action of cutting the hair off is thus a gesture of mourning (compare 16:6). But the object of the verb is נֵזֶר, normally "consecration [of a priest or Nazirite]," here by extension "the head of hair which is consecrated." It is possible then that

the people are addressed as a woman who has taken the vow of a Nazirite (which women as well as men could take, Num 6:2): one of the obligations of that vow is not to cut the hair. The *NEB* paraphrases "O Jerusalem, cut off your hair, the symbol of your dedication."

It is not clear how the metaphor of lamenting and/or Naziriteship should be construed. Is the addressee the wife of the deceased, called here "the community of his rage," or is the deceased understood to be the children of the addressee, like Rachel lamenting her children (31:15) (so Duhm)? In that case the woman is perhaps not a Nazirite, and the object "consecration" is not intended literally; the diction of Mic 1:16 would then be comparable. It is of interest that *T* interprets the object נֵזֶר as "your princes," moving out from the meaning of that word as "crown, headband" in many passages (e.g., 2 Sam 1:10), and Rashi follows this interpretation ("regal power"). Or is the woman really a Nazirite? So Symmachus, who renders "the holy hair of your Naziriteship." In this case the metaphor suggests that the woman who is consecrated has inadvertently touched a corpse, and so must shave her head and begin her vow again (Num 6:9–12), with the implication that the people are for the moment unconsecrated to Yahweh (Calvin). Commentaries through the nineteenth century have divided on the issue, and more recent studies have not clarified the matter.

The verb "throw away" (שלך hip'il) was used in v 15. For the image of lamenting on the caravan-tracks see 3:21.

For Yahweh's rejecting (מאס) his people see 6:30. "Forsake" (נטש) appears here for the first time in the book. It appears of the people's forsaking Yahweh (15:6), and appears elsewhere three times of Yahweh's forsaking his people (12:7; 23:33, 39); Isa 2:6 is a good antecedent, the only other occurrence in the prophets.

"Community" (דּוֹר) occurred in 2:31, but the phrase "community of [Yahweh's] rage" (דּוֹר עֶבְרָתוֹ) is found only here in the OT; a parallel, however, is "people of [Yahweh's] rage" (עַם עֶבְרָתִי) in Isa 10:6, referring likewise to Judah.

■ **30** The phrase "children of Judah" (בְּנֵי יְהוּדָה) is striking: it is found in the eighth-century prophets only in Hos 2:2, in Jer otherwise only in 32:30–32 (a passage imitative of the present one) and 50:4, 33; in the sixth-century prophets only in Obadiah 12. Jrm wishes to underline the fact that this sin is something that only the people of Judah have committed. The phrase "do evil in [Yahweh's] eyes" is common in the Deuteronomic literature (e.g., Deut 17:2; 1 Kgs 11:6);[2] it may well be part of the conventional prose of the seventh century.

For "vile things" (שִׁקּוּצִים), meaning idolatrous images, see 4:1. For the phrase "house which bears my name" see 7:10, 11. For "defile" (טמא) see 2:7.

If the passage is genuine to Jrm (see Setting), and if the present study has dated it correctly, then it is prime evidence for the renewed practice of pagan rites in the temple area during the reign of Jehoiakim (see further on v 31). Ezek 5:11 uses the same vocabulary, though there the term "vile things," lacking in *G*, seems to be a secondary addition.[3] Such a reversion must have been appalling to Jrm.

■ **31** The verb "they keep building" (וּבָנוּ) is here accepted as correct (see Text note a—a). Jrm seems to wish to underline the constant activity of building "high places" (בָּמוֹת, see below) at this location, whether that perception is exaggerated or not. One notes the word-play of the verb with "Ben(-Hinnom)" and "their sons" (בְּנֵיהֶם).

The noun בָּמָה is conventionally translated "high place," but in spite of intensive research the precise denotation of the term remains imprecise in our understanding. The conventional view is well set forth in the handbooks.[4] By this view the word essentially means "back (of the body of an animal)," "ridge," then "high place," referring to a cult place, particularly a pagan one. William F. Albright made the suggestion in 1956 that the term referred to a "tomb-shrine,"[5] but this view has

not found acceptance.[6] It is clear in any event that the identification of the term to specific archeological remains continues to be uncertain.[7] The descriptions in the OT are meager: there was an altar, there was an "Asherah" (evidently a symbolic wooden pole, 2 Kgs 21:3) and a "Massebah" (an upright stone or stone pillar, 2 Kgs 23:13–14) or more than one; there was evidently a building for sacrificial meals (1 Sam 9:19, 22) and perhaps for cult prostitution (compare Ezek 16:16). But one must conclude that the text communicates more distaste than specific information, and archeological data are up to now unhelpful on the matter.

The word here translated "The Fire-pit," conventionally transliterated "Topheth" (הַתֹּפֶת), appears in four passages: 2 Kgs 23:10; Isa 30:33; here in Jer 7:31–32; and 19:6–14. In Isa 30:34 the noun, without article (but with possessive pronoun?—see *BHS*), seems to be generalized, "funeral-pyre" or the like, but in the other three passages it has reference to a specific location "which is in the Valley of Ben- (or Bene-)Hinnom." The Aramaic cognate of the word means "fireplace, cook-stove," and the Hebrew word doubtless originally carried different vowels (see Text note c—c). This was the designation given to a place outside the walls of Jerusalem where child sacrifice took place: 2 Kgs 23:10 states that that sacrifice was "to Molech," understood to be a pagan god, but there is evidence from Punic sources that that phrase may originally have meant "as a votive offering," and the interpretation "to Molech" was a secondary development.[8] In short, the OT was by no means clear on the details of "The Topheth," under-

---

2   For a partial listing see Weinfeld, *Deuteronomy*, 339.

3   See Zimmerli, *Ezekiel 1*, 151.

4   See particularly G. Henton Davies, "High place, Sanctuary," *IDB* 2:602–4, with bibliography, and Klaus-Dietrich Schunck, "בָּמָה," *TDOT* 2:139–45, with bibliography.

5   William F. Albright, "The High Place in Ancient Palestine," *Volume du Congrès* (VTSup 4; Leiden: Brill, 1957) 242–58.

6   W. Boyd Barrick, "The Funerary Character of 'High Places' in Ancient Israel: A Reassessment," *VT* 25 (1975) 565–95.

7   Patrick H. Vaughan, *The Meaning of 'Bāmâ' in the Old Testament: A Study of Etymological, Textual and Archaeological Evidence* (SOTSMS 3; Cambridge: Cambridge University, 1974); Menahem Haran, "Temples and Cultic Open Areas as Reflected in the Bible," *Temples and High Places in Biblical Times* (ed. Avraham Biran; Jerusalem: The Nelson Glueck School of Biblical Archaeology of Hebrew Union College—Jewish Institute of Religion, 1981) 31–37; W. Boyd Barrick, "What Do We Really Know About 'High-Places'?" *SEÅ* 45 (1980) 50–57; Mervyn D. Fowler, "The Israelite *bāmâ*: A Question of Interpretation," *ZAW* 94 (1982) 203–13.

8   Otto Eissfeldt, *Molk als Opferbegriff im Punischen und Hebräischen und das Ende des Gottes Moloch* (Halle [Saale]: Niemeyer, 1935); compare John Gray, "Molech, Moloch," *IDB* 3:422–23.

standably, given the horror with which the practices were held by orthodox Yahwists. Given that it appears here (and elsewhere) with the definite article, it seems best to try to translate it rather than simply transliterating it.

The name of the valley is variously given as The Valley of Hinnom, The Valley of Ben- [= the Son of] Hinnom, or The Valley of Bene- [= the Sons of] Hinnom. Most authorities, following Gustaf Dalman, identify the valley with *wādi ar-rabābi*, the "Western Valley" which runs north-south, west of the Old City of Jerusalem, and then cuts east, meeting the Valley of Kidron.[9] But other identifications have been proposed: Hugo Gressmann suggests *wādi an-nār*, the valley south of the junction between the Western Valley and the Valley of Kidron[10] (and one notes that the Arabic name means "Valley of Hell"); and recently A. Douglas Tushingham has argued persuasively for the Tyropoean Valley, that is, the "Central Valley" running south from the southwest corner of the temple mount.[11] Given the areas of occupation of Jerusalem in preexilic times, the Tyropoean Valley seems the best candidate.

The setting proposed for the present passage in this study is early in 600 or soon thereafter (see Setting). Now according to 2 Kgs 23:10, King Josiah had destroyed the installation at "Topheth" so that "no one might burn his son or his daughter as an offering to Molech." If that notice is trustworthy, then Jrm is here testifying that the practice was reinstated, overtly or covertly, during the kingship of Jehoiakim. The reference to "your way in the Valley" in 2:23 is doubtless a reference to child sacrifice (see there). Such sacrifice is recorded as having been resorted to by both Ahaz (2 Kgs 16:3) and Manasseh (2 Kgs 21:6), though the record does not say in what circumstances. Since Ahaz saw the fall of Samaria to Assyria, and Manasseh was king during the long period of vassalage of Assyria, one can imagine the political and psychological pressures under which these kings acted. But what the pressures were under which

common citizens resorted to child sacrifice we cannot imagine. Political-military emergencies like the capture of Ashkelon by Nebuchadrezzar in December 604? The drought that evidently prevailed by autumn 601? (See "A Chronology of Jeremiah's Career.") Or various private fears, motivating parents to superstitious action, now impossible to document? There is an extensive literature on human sacrifice in Israel, a topic which has wide ramifications; one must take account of the practices of non-Israelite peoples, of texts like Exod 13:1–2 and 22:29, concerned with the "consecration" of firstborn sons, and of irregular, perhaps syncretistic acts of various sorts in Israel (see Bibliography).

Two observations should be made about the closing phrases, "something which I did not command, nor did it come into my mind." The first is that it indicates that the sacrifice of children was offered to Yahweh (albeit a Canaanized Yahweh): if the sacrifice had been to Baal (or the presumed "Molech"), the phraseology would have been different[12]—Mic 6:7 suggests the same phenomenon. The second is that "which I did not command" attracts comparison with the same phrase in v 22, used there with reference to burnt offerings and sacrifices. The phrase suggests in both instances that Jrm is trying to correct a false understanding that people might gain from legal tradition (compare Interpretation on v 22). The Covenant Code offers laws about burnt offerings and sacrifices (Exod 20:24; 23:18), and the same code states, "The first-born of your sons you shall give to me" (Exod 22:30). Later tradition obviously interpreted that law otherwise than as a demand for child sacrifice, but clearly the law might have been taken as a demand for such sacrifice.[13] The same prohibition against child sacrifice is found explicitly in Deut 18:10.

■ 32 The phrase "the time is surely coming" (הִנֵּה יָמִים בָּאִים, literally "behold, days are coming") is a stock phrase in Jer (fifteen times), though it appears in earlier material (Amos 4:2; 8:11; for example). It refers to the transformation of present conditions by the events of a

9 Gustaf Dalman, *Jerusalem und sein Gelände* (Gütersloh: Bertelsmann, 1930) 199–208. See further Georges A. Barrois, "Hinnom," *IDB* 2:606; Kathleen M. Kenyon, *Jerusalem, 3000 Years of History* (New York: McGraw-Hill, 1967) 13.

10 Hugo Gressmann, *Der Messias* (Göttingen: Vandenhoeck & Ruprecht, 1929) 116 n. 1.

11 Denis Baly and A. Douglas Tushingham, *Atlas of the Biblical World* (New York: World Publishing, 1971) 158. For a topographical map of Jerusalem see there, 159.

12 Compare Rudolph, p. 59.

13 Compare Bright, p. 57.

new era—not that it is eschatological, but simply that there will be a profound reversal in the near future.[14]

In the first half-verse Jrm announces a change of name of the Valley of Ben-Hinnom, and such a procedure elsewhere suggests that we have here some kind of play on words or meaning (see, for example, Jrm's change of the name of Pashhur in 20:1–6). But commentators have as yet made no suggestions as to what Jrm saw in *gê' ben-hinnôm* "Valley of Ben-Hinnom" to link to the new name, *gê' hahărēgâ* "Valley of Murder." Jastrow[15] cites a talmudic association with *ḥinnām* (חִנָּם, "gratuitous act, vanity": see *b. 'Erub.* 19a), but this is rabbinic homiletics rather than a clue to Jrm's mentality—h and ḥ do not substitute for each other at that period. Baumgartner[16] connects *hinnôm* with the Arabic *hanna* "whisper," with hesitation; but it is not clear whether this derivation is suggested as a true one for the proper name *hinnôm*, or as a "folk etymology" in Jrm's mind, or as both; but that root is (otherwise) unattested in Hebrew and appears dubious to the present situation.

I would tentatively propose another solution. It is clear that the pronunciation of the original name may undergo some distortion. Thus in the instance of Pashhur, the name of the priest, *pašḥûr*, a name no doubt of Egyptian origin, was evidently distorted by Jrm into *pāš-sĕḥôr*, an Aramaic phrase, in order for the change of name to take on meaning (see again 20:3). In the present instance the new name has the definite article before *hărēgâ* "murder" —"the murder," suggesting then that the old name was distorted into a noun with the definite article, *hannôm*. This suggests the root נום "sleep": the verb occurs in the OT, as do two related nouns נוּמָה and תְּנוּמָה. In Arabic the noun *nawm* "sleep" occurs; the equivalent of that masculine form in Hebrew would be **nôm* (נוֹם), just as the Arabic *yawm* "day" is the Hebrew *yôm* (יוֹם). The word "sleep" is an understandable euphemism for death: Ps 76:6 uses the verb in a way suggesting the death of warriors in battle. Is it possible, then, that the noun existed in Hebrew, and that **ben-hannôm* was a way of speaking of "someone destined for sleep" just as *ben-māwet* (בֶּן־מָוֶת, 2 Sam 12:5) denotes "someone deserving death"? If such a euphemism was employed by parents sacrificing their children, or if Jrm suggests for the sake

of the word-play that such a euphemism was employed, then his change of name gives the lie to the euphemism: it is not what Yahweh demands, it is murder. (Aside from the parallel to the present passage in 19:6 Jrm uses the word "murder" once otherwise, in 12:3.) One other thought: the mysterious term "Valley of Vision" (גֵּיא חִזָּיוֹן) in Isa 22:1, 5 may point in the same direction. It is generally assumed by scholars that that designation in Isaiah refers to the Valley of Ben-Hinnom,[17] but the phrase has never been satisfactorily explained. One notes that the word in the plural, "visions," is parallel with "dreams" in Job 7:14. Is Isaiah in his designation somehow using a similar euphemism, or referring to it with similar irony? Does Isaiah's use of "Valley of Vision," with a possible implication of "dreams," suggest a similar sally on Jrm's part implying "sleep"?

The last clause in the verse is puzzling. It is clear that some kind of punishment or reversal is designated for "Topheth" (here vocalized without a definite article), but the meaning of מֵאֵין מָקוֹם, literally "without a place," is mysterious. Aside from the occurrence of the phrase in the parallel in 19:11, there is no other instance of its use in the OT. Of the twenty-four occurrences of מֵאֵין ("without") in the OT, fifteen are in Jer. One can reject Duhm's judgment that v 32b is an insertion. Commentators and translators have assumed that the phrase either means "because there is no room (elsewhere)" (Qimḥi, Calvin, Cornill, Condamin, Rudolph) or "until there is no more room (there)" (Bright). True, there is a phrase in the prophets for "until there is no more room," עַד אֶפֶס מָקוֹם, Isa 5:8, but the phrase in Jer may not have the same meaning as that in Isaiah.

I suspect that the clue lies in the meaning of מָקוֹם as "special place, cultic place." This is the meaning in 7:3, 7, and 12, and in 7:20. Jrm has in mind the principle of "let the punishment fit the crime." If Yahweh has withdrawn his support from the people, then he will reverse Deut 12:5—there will be no more "place" that Yahweh has chosen. (For the association with vv 21–28, which reverse Deut 12:6, see vv 21–28, Structure and Form.) If the "place," assumed to be the temple, will no longer be a "place," then it is the end for the people, and they shall simply bury bodies—and at the Fire-pit in the Valley of

14 Gerhard von Rad, "ἡμέρα," *TDNT* 2:946.
15 Jastrow, p. 358a.
16 *HALAT*, 242b.

17 Wildberger, *Jesaja*, 813.

Ben-Hinnom, or at any fire-pit (if the lack of definite article here is correct); why not?—since all is lost.

This is not to suggest that the other meanings proposed for "without a place" are not present also; Jrm is accomplished in offering multiple meanings. But what it presented here is primarily a picture of the horrible future, when all that betokened Yahweh's presence with his people is withdrawn, a future which the people themselves have helped to shape by their crimes and misdeeds.

■ **33–34** The sequence of thought of these verses is comparable to that in 16:5–9.

■ **33** It was a conventional curse that a corpse remain unburied (compare 1 Sam 17:43–46).[18] It is an appalling thing to witness vultures or jackals tearing at the corpse of a fallen cow, the scavengers too bloated to escape too far; it is far worse to imagine the corpses of folk who have been part of one's community prey to such scavengers, and to know that no one will be present to prevent the scavenging.[19] "Corpses" and "birds" are collective singulars (נְבֵלָה and עוֹף), and "beasts" is here singular as well (בְּהֵמָה): the verse offers the scene of a typical corpse, a typical bird, a typical beast, capturing in a nutshell the repeated scenes of the fate of the fallen.

The last phrase, "with none to frighten them off" (וְאֵין מַחֲרִיד) is again a conventional expression, found, for example, in Nah 2:12. Deut 28:26 resembles the present verse closely, and it is likely that that verse is dependent on the present one.[20]

■ **34** The verb here translated "silent" (שבת hipʿil) means literally "bring to a stop."

The pair "joy" (שָׂשׂוֹן) and "gladness" (שִׂמְחָה) occur in the poetry of 15:16, and "joy" is paired with the cognate verb "give gladness" (שׂמח) in 31:13; beyond this the full fourfold set of phrases "voice of joy," "voice of gladness,"

"voice of the bridegroom," and "voice of the bride" is found in 16:9; 25:10; and 33:11. "Joy" and its cognates are frequently used in wedding contexts (Ps 45:8; Isa 62:5; compare Ps 19:6, where יָשִׂישׂ is poised between "bridegroom" and "warrior"). Its parallel "gladness" is a more general term. The parallel of the two words in 15:16 likewise implies the metaphor of marriage, since "I am called by your name" is a self-designation of a bride (compare Isa 4:1; see Interpretation of 15:16). The totality of the four parallel phrases here then speaks of wedding festivities; it is even possible that specific wedding-songs are referred to.[21] Weddings will be taken away from the whole land, just as it was said there will be no proper funeral or burial (v 33). The fate that there will be no more weddings, a cessation of joy in the land, is a conventional curse like the curse that there will be no more proper burial.[22] The whole land is to become a חׇרְבָּה, a place of rubble and ruin (this is the same word as the Arabic ḥirbah in present-day names of ruined sites).

Aim

The people have set up foul images in the temple area and are constantly improving the facilities for child sacrifice in the Valley of Ben-Hinnom. Yahweh decrees therefore that there will be a cessation of the continuity of the community: no temple, no one left to bury, no one left to marry. To persuade the people that this is not simply a threat, that he intends to go through with it, Yahweh paints the picture dark indeed, and his declaration that there will be no more funerals and weddings is reinforced by his prohibition to Jrm against attending either (16:5–9).

18   Hillers, *Treaty-Curses*, 68–69.
19   For the Israel outlook on burial see Pedersen, III/IV, 478–80.
20   Weippert, *Prosareden*, 184 and n. 350; Mayes, *Deuteronomy*, 350–51.
21   Jean-Paul Audet, "Le Sens du Cantique des Cantiques," *RB* 62 (1955) 213–14.
22   Hillers, *Treaty-Curses*, 57–58.

Bibliography
Cogan, Morton
  "A Note on Disinterment in Jeremiah," *Gratz
  College, Anniversary Volume* (ed. Isidore D. Passow
  and Samuel T. Lachs; Philadelphia, 1971) 29–34.

8

1　**At that time—oracle of Yahweh—**[a] **they
shall bring out**[a] **the bones of the kings of
Judah, and the bones of its officials, and
the bones of the priests, and the bones of
the prophets, and the bones of the inhabitants of Jerusalem, from their graves; 2/
and they shall spread them out for the sun
and for the moon and for all the host of
heaven, which they loved, and which they
served, and after which they walked, and
which they sought, and which they
worshiped; they shall not be gathered or
buried—dung on the face of the ground
they shall become. 3/ And death will be
preferred to life by all the remnant which
remain from this wicked clan, in all the
places [which remain]**[a] **where I have
scattered them—oracle of Yahweh of
hosts.**

Text

1a—a　Read with qere' and many MSS. יוֹצִיאוּ in
preference to the ketib וְיֹצִיאוּ, which could only be
וְיֹצִיאוּ "then let them bring out."

3a　This word (הַנִּשְׁאָרִים) is omitted by one MS. and
by *G* and *S*; it is dittographic from the previous
phrase.

Structure, Form, Setting

The style of these three verses is not that of chapter 7.
They are separate from 7:29–34, introduced by the
connecting phrase "at that time."[1]

The stylistic peculiarities include the fivefold repetition of "the bones of" (עַצְמוֹת) in v 1 and the fivefold
repetition of "which" (אֲשֶׁר) in v 2, and the tautological
"which remain" (הַנִּשְׁאָרִים) modifying "the remnant"
(הַשְּׁאֵרִית) in v 3. Phrases and motifs from Jrm's diction
have been employed: "kings, officials, priests, prophets"
(compare 4:9); "dung on the face of the ground" (compare 16:4). If the passage is secondary to Jrm, it must be
placed in the exilic period. The linking of "sun," "moon,"
and "host of heaven" is found otherwise only in Deut
4:19; 17:3; and 2 Kgs 23:5, and all of these verses are
suspected of being exilic insertions into their surrounding material.[2] The passage is a judgment on the astral
cult, clearly a temptation for Jews in exile (as well as at
other times). It seems to reflect a neo-Assyrian (and

Babylonian?) practice of disinterment of corpses as a
desecration and curse when a vassal was judged to have
broken covenant[3] (see Interpretation).

The position of the passage, after 7:29–34, is logical:
both passages deal with the reversal of normal burial.

The passage is in form a judgment oracle.

Interpretation

The desecration of graves has been a familiar feature in
both Egypt and Mesopotamia: graves were constantly
robbed for their treasure. Sometimes the motive was not
greed so much as a ritual of dishonoring. Thus Ashur-
banipal records his action during a campaign against
Susa, the Elamite capital: "The tombs of their former
and latter kings, (who had) not revered Ashur and Ishtar,
my lords, (who had) harassed my royal ancestors, I
(Ashurbanipal) ravaged, tore down and laid open to the
sun. Their bones I carried off to Assyria, thus imposing
restlessness upon their spirits, and depriving them of

1　See Wildberger, *Jesaja*, 681, regarding Isa 18:7.
2　Mayes, *Deuteronomy*, 148, 266; Gray, *Kings*, 732.
3　Wildberger dates Isa 34:1–4, which offers a similar

motif, to the beginning of the sixth century: *Jesaja*,
1341.

food offerings and libations."[4]

Such desecration of graves would have been an occasion of horror to any people who suffered it; it was certainly an occasion of horror to the Israelites (see 7:33, Interpretation). Josiah had desecrated the tombs at the northern sanctuary of Bethel and had exposed the bones (2 Kgs 23:16).

The present passage announces that such would be the fate of tombs in Judah as well, a punishment for their devotion to the cults of sun and moon and stars, cults current in the period of vassalage to Assyria (2 Kgs 21:5; Zeph 1:5) and a temptation in the period of Babylonian exile. The phrase "host of heaven" denotes the celestial army made up of the heavenly bodies, animated by divine spirits and in control of human destiny.[5] How ironic that the bones of the devotees of astral bodies be exposed permanently to the same bodies that they had worshiped!

For the phrase "become dung on the face of the ground" see 9:21, Interpretation.

There are a few expressions elsewhere in the OT comparable to the phrase "death will be preferred to life" (v 3): Lam 4:9, "Happier were the victims of the sword than the victims of hunger, who pined away, stricken by want of the fruits of the field," and Jonah 4:3, 8, "It is better for me to die than to live." Jer 22:10, "Do not weep for him who is dead, . . . do weep for him who is gone," is not exactly the same affirmation, but plays ironically with conventional views. For "clan" (מִשְׁפָּחָה, often translated "tribe"), see 1:15.

Aim

The hatred of pagan worship by orthodox Yahwists is a steady thread through the OT; it was always a temptation for Jews to give way to astrological beliefs of one sort or another. The prophet who is responsible for this brief passage was convinced that the punishment would fit the crime, and that the bones of those who had been devoted to the astronomical bodies should be permanently exposed to those bodies. The thought is macabre but effective. That death should be preferable to life is a thought that flits through the mind of many people from time to time, but that a whole population should succumb to the thought would spell the end of solidarity between the covenant people and Yahweh, the God of the living. That such nihilism was not unknown in the early exilic period is indicated by Lam 4:9, but that Yahweh should sponsor it is appalling.

---

4   Rassam Cylinder 6.70–76. See Maximilian Streck, *Assurbanipal und die letzten assyrischen Könige bis zum Untergange Nineveh's* (Vorderasiatische Bibliothek 7; Leipzig: Hinrichs, 1916) 54–57, and the discussion in Morton Cogan, "A Note on Disinterment in Jeremiah," *Gratz College, Anniversary Volume* (ed. Isidore D. Possaw and Samuel T. Lachs; Philadelphia, 1971) 30.

5   Bernhard W. Anderson, "Hosts, host of heaven," *IDB* 2:655a.

Not Only Will the Enemy Destroy: Even the Order of Creation Will Fall

Bibliography

Aberbach, D.
  "*w'tn lhm y'brwm* (Jeremiah viii 13): The Problem and its Solution," *VT* 27 (1977) 99–101.

Berridge
  pp. 171–73.

De Roche, Michael
  "Contra Creation, Covenant and Conquest (Jer. viii 13)," *VT* 30 (1980) 280–90.

Hyatt, J. Philip
  "Torah in the Book of Jeremiah," *JBL* 60 (1941) 382–84.

Lindblom
  "Wisdom in the Old Testament Prophets," 195–96.

McKane
  Prophets and Wise Men, 102–7.

Overholt
  Falsehood, 81–82.

Whybray, Roger N.
  The Intellectual Tradition in the Old Testament (BZAW 135; Berlin: de Gruyter, 1974) 22–24.

8

4 And you shall say to them, Thus 《 this people 》[a] has said,
    "Will they fall and not rise (again)?
      [b] Will he turn (away)[b] and not turn (back)?"
5   Why then [a] has [. . .] Jerusalem

Text

4a Inserting הָעָם הַזֶּה here from v 5 (see note a—a there), instead of the *M* reading "Yahweh." For the reasons for this reconstruction see Structure, and Form and Setting. One may assume that the words dropped out by haplography with the he of הֲיִפְּלוּ, were written in the margin, and reinserted wrongly before יְרוּשָׁלַם, and that then יהוה was inserted to "correct" a defective text. (Compare the reconstruction given in this study for 32:36, 42, where evidence is given that "Yahweh" is likewise secondary.) It is conceivable that the original text read, "And you shall say to them, Thus Yahweh has said, Thus this people has said . . . ," but the present reconstruction is the most economical.

b—b The Oriental MS. tradition reads a qere' here, a plural in this word (יָשׁוּבוּ, "they turn") for the singular reading in *M*. This reading is reflected in the interpretation of Qimḥi on the passage, but symmetry suggests the variation is secondary. See Interpretation.

5a—a The verb (or adjective) שׁוֹבְבָה is feminine, agreeing with "Jerusalem," but not with the masculine "this people" which adjoins the verb (or adjective). The commentators deal with the matter in various ways. Thus Michaelis and Cornill suggested that the verb is transitive and that "this people" is object, thus "Why then has Jerusalem turned this people in permanent turning?"; but "this people" and "Jerusalem" are identified in similar passages (4:10, 11). Volz proposes that שׁוֹבְבָה (to be vocalized שׁוֹבְבָה) is substantival ("Why does the

turned[a] a permanent turning?
They have clung to deception,
   refused to return.

6   I have paid attention and listened,
   they speak what is not right;
no one is regretful of his evil,
   saying, "What have I done?"
Everyone[a] stays turned in his course[b]
   like a horse charging into battle.

7   Even the stork in the heavens knows her
      season,[a]
   the turtle-dove and the swift[b] [(and}[d]
      the bulbul(?)}]c keep the time of
      their coming;
     but my people do not know the order
      of Yahweh.

8   How can you say, "We are wise,
   and the law of Yahweh is with us?"
    No, look: the lie of the scribes has
      made the pen into a lie!

9   The "wise" have stood shamed,
   aghast and ensnared;
    look: they have rejected the word of
      Yahweh,
    so what wisdom do they have?

10 Therefore I shall give their wives to
      others,
   their fields to new owners;
[for from the least of them to the greatest
     each is getting his own cut,
   and from prophet to priest each
     practices falsehood;

11 and they have treated the fracture of my
    fair people offhandedly,
   saying "Peace, peace,"
    when there is no peace.

12 They have behaved shamefully when
    committing abomination,
   yet they were not at all ashamed,
    nor did they know how to be
     humiliated;
therefore they shall fall among the fallen:
   at the time when they are dealt with
    they shall stumble,
             Yahweh has said.][a]

apostate, this people Jerusalem, the faithless one, cling to deception . . . ?"). Rudolph suggests that the he of שׁוֹבְבָה is dittographic with the he of הָעָם, so that the verb (or adjective) is masculine (so also Janzen, p. 174). *G* reads "my people" for "this people" and omits "Jerusalem" altogether; it is thus forced to construe the verb (or adjective) as if masculine. Most commentators follow *G* and assume that "Jerusalem" is a gloss, but one wonders why a gloss would be necessary on such an obvious phrase. Bright suggests that *M* is a conflate text, one tradition reading the masculine with "this people" (compare *G*) and the other reading the feminine with "Jerusalem." This is a good solution, but "this people" fits admirably in v 4, hence the solution proposed here. The vocalization of שׁוֹבְבָה has been disputed (see above) but is altogether satisfactory as a polel perfect feminine (see further Interpretation).

6a   *M* spells כָּלֹה with final he, though some MSS. offer a qere' with final waw (compare 2:21). The meaning is unaffected.

b   Read qere' בִּמְרוּצָתָם, literally "in their course," rather than the ketib בִּמְרוּצוֹתָם "when they are determined" (infinitive construct of רצה), though *S* and *T* follow the latter interpretation. The comparison is with the horse in the next colon; note further that the second meaning, "in their extortion," demands the qere'. See Interpretation.

7a   Read the singular מוֹעֲדָהּ with a few MSS. and all Versions instead of *M* מוֹעֲדֶיהָ "her seasons."

b   Reading the qere' וְסִיס for the ketib וְסוּס, which could mean "and (the) horse," though the ketib spelling may be correct for the bird as well; note the same uncertainty in Isa 38:14. See further Interpretation.

c   The word עָגוּר is of uncertain meaning; it is evidently the designation of a bird, and the word here is either a gloss or evidence of a conflate text; if a gloss, it is perhaps here to protect the preceding word from being taken to mean "and (the) horse." A similar textual problem is found in Isa 38:14. See further Interpretation.

d   The copula is missing in *G*; it was evidently added later to smooth the text.

10–12a   These verses are omitted in *G* and are a doublet of 6:13–15; they are rightly judged secondary by Duhm, Cornill, Giesebrecht, and Rudolph (so also Janzen, pp. 95–96). Condamin asserts that an author has a right to repeat himself; but it is better to trust *G* here. The two texts differ as follows. (1) Differences of wording: 6:13 מִקְּטַנָּם, 8:10 גְּדוֹלָם, גָּדוֹל מִקָּטֹן (but θ' and *S* follow 6:13 here); 6:13 וּמִנָּבִיא, 8:10 מִנָּבִיא (but many MSS. and *S* agree with 6:13 here); 6:15 גַּם־הַכְלִים, 8:12 וְהִכְלָם; 6:15 פְּקַדְתִּים, 8:12 פְּקַדְתָּם; (2) differences of spelling: 6:13, כָּלֹּה twice with final waw, 8:10 כָּלֹה twice with final he; 6:13 בּוֹצֵעַ with waw, 8:10 בֹּצֵעַ without; 6:14 וַיְרַפְּאוּ with 'alep, 8:11 וַיְרַפּוּ without (but a few MSS. agree with 6:14 here); 6:15 הֹבִישׁוּ with yod, 8:12

13 ᵃ I shall gather up their Ingathering:ᵃ
oracle of Yahweh,
there are no grapes on the vine,
there are no figs on the fig-trees,
and the foliage has withered;
and I have given them ᵇ(what)
they pass over for them.ᵇ

הֻבְשׁוּ without; 6:15 יֵבוֹשׁוּ with medial waw, 8:15 יֵבֹשׁוּ without.

13a—a The consonantal text of this line, I submit, is sound, but the vocalization is uncertain for three reasons: (1) there is uncertainty as to the extent to which Jrm is playing on the diction of Zeph 1:2–3, and as to the vocalization of those phrases; (2) there is uncertainty as to the range of vocalizations of the verb אסף; and (3) there is uncertainty to what extent Jrm intends here double meanings with סוף hip'il and/or the noun אָסִיף. See Interpretation.

b—b This difficult verb (יַעַבְרוּם) has given rise to several MS. variations. Several MSS. read יַעַבְדוּם "they shall (or, let them) serve them"; one MS. reads וְעַבְדוּם "and they shall serve them," and one reads וְעָבְרוּם "and they shall transgress them" (or whatever other translation this verb calls forth). The verb is evidently intended to carry multiple meanings (see Interpretation), so that emendations such as that of Condamin (יַעֲבִרוּם, "they shall carry them off") or of D. Aberbach (יַעַר עָרוּם, "a forest stripped bare": see Bibliography) are unnecessary.

Structure

These verses offer many interlocking problems in regard to the text, the extent of the unit, the identification of the group(s) addressed, and the setting. In addition the passage appears to offer several expressions open to multiple meanings, and the connotation of some of the phrases is uncertain.

Extent of Unit. The material from 8:4 through 9:8 is difficult to subdivide into constituent units: it offers diction similar to that in 4:5—6:30 and appears to have evolved within a limited period of time. Commentators differ in their solutions. Thus (to stay within the compass of chap. 8) Rudolph subdivides the material into vv 4–7, 8–9, 10–12, 13–17, and 18–23, while Bright takes vv 4–12 as a unit and then separates 13–17 and 18–23. On the other hand Hyatt and Weiser make a major break between vv 13 and 14, and this is undoubtedly correct. The link between vv 13 and 14 (the verb "gather" [אסף]) is a catchword link here: v 14a is a variation on 4:5, which itself marked a new beginning. Verses 14–15 are clearly spoken by the people. Verse 13, by contrast, concludes Yahweh's announcement of judgment which begins in v 10 (with "therefore").

The question whether there is a break in units between v 7 and v 8 is a difficult one to resolve, depending as it does on one's understanding of who speaks and who is addressed in these verses, and in particular on the specific setting of the "scribes" and the "wise" in vv 8–9 (for these issues see in more detail Form and Interpretation). Thus Rudolph asserts that vv 4–7 are to be separated from vv 8–9, since the subject of the former is the people, while v 8 addresses "the wise." In contrast Martin A. Klopfenstein observes (correctly, in the view of the present study) that the expression "order of Yahweh" (מִשְׁפַּט יהוה) in v 7 is parallel to "law of Yahweh" (תּוֹרַת יהוה) in v 8.[1] (It may be noted that מִשְׁפָּט [normally translated "justice"] and תּוֹרָה ["law"] are parallel in Isa 42:4; 51:4; and Hab 1:4.) Form-critically vv 4–7 are an accusation speech, while vv 8–9 continue Yahweh's accusation and v 10 begins his judgment speech (see further Form). Admittedly this consideration is not crucial, for accusation speeches and judgment speeches may be interwoven (for example, in 6:16–21), but it is at least suggestive. It may also be noted that the questions "How can you say?" (v 8) and "What have I done?" (v 6) resemble the diction within 2:23, where "How can you

1   Martin A. Klopfenstein, *Die Lüge nach dem Alten Testament* (Zurich: Gotthelf, 1964) 133.

say?" and "Know what you have done" both appear. Furthermore both vv 4–7 and vv 8–13 appear to have the same setting, namely the autumn of 601 (for the details see Setting). It would be prudent, then, to take vv 4–13 as a unit.

Placement of Unit. Conceivably this unit begins a series that is arranged chronologically—there is no way to be sure. But since the passage seems to have a setting close to that of 5:1–9; 5:10–17; and 6:9–15, its placement here, after the sequence of prose in chapter 7, may suggest that Jrm had in mind an inclusio with 4:1–2 (the double phrase using "[re]turn" [שׁוּב], 4:1; 8:4).[2] Indeed it may be significant that the present passage, in which v 4 resembles 4:1, is followed by v 14, which resembles 4:5.

Internal Structure. Excluding the introductory words in v 4, the passage breaks into two halves, vv 4–7 and 8–13 (compare the discussion above, *Extext of Unit!*); if the judgment to exclude vv 10aβ–12 is correct, there are fourteen cola in each half-section. Verse 8 must be analyzed (against Rudolph) as a tricolon; the two particles here translated "no, look" (אָכֵן הִנֵּה) stand outside the metrical scheme,[3] and the remaining words cannot be divided into two cola (for the syntax see Interpretation). The verse then consists of two cola of Yahweh's quotation of the people and one colon of his counterstatement; it will be argued below (see Form) that vv 4aβ–5a are parallel in this respect. Each half-section likewise ends in parallel fashion: v 7 is a tricolon and v 13 is evidently a pentacolon, the middle three cola of which are tightly parallel. These beginnings and endings enclose bicola, four in vv 5b–6 and three in vv 9–10aα. There are smaller unities within the passage. Thus verse 7 is united by "know" in both the first and last cola, and vv 5b–6 are perhaps united by "(re)turn" (שׁוּב qal: infinitive in the last colon of v 5, perfect in the next-to-last colon of v 6). One notes further the parallel of "no one" (אֵין אִישׁ) and "everyone" (כֻּלֹּה) in v 6, and the assonance of "her season" (מוֹעֲדָהּ) with "know" (ידע) in v 7, and of "charging" (שׁוֹטֵף) with "order of" (מִשְׁפַּט) in vv 6–7. Then the first two cola of v 8 ("wise," "law of Yahweh") are chiastically arranged with respect to the last two cola of v 9 ("word of Yahweh," "wisdom"). Finally "I shall give" (אֶתֵּן) in the first colon of v 10 seems

to be united with "and I have given" (וְאֶתֵּן) in the last colon of v 13 (but on this question see further Interpretation on v 13).

Form

The first order of business is the identification of the speaker or speakers in these verses, and the best procedure is to work backward. It is clear that v 10aα + 13 is an announcement of judgment, spoken by Yahweh. By the same token vv 8–9 are spoken by Yahweh, in spite of the third-person reference in v 9: the phrase "How can you say?" introduces the argument of the plaintiff in legal confrontation (for the details see Form on 2:23). Indeed the presentation of the accusation in these verses follows to some degree the presentation of 2:26–28: the affirmation of the "shame" of the defendants (v 9, compare 2:26), the rhetorical question "What wisdom do they have?" (v 10, compare 2:28), and the speaker in 2:26–28 is Yahweh (see 2:27).

In vv 4–7, however, no audience is named, and it is unclear from the context whether the speaker is to be understood as Jrm or Yahweh. It is an old problem: Qimḥi states that the subject of the verbs in v 6 is Jrm, while Calvin and Michaelis assume that God is. Volz, Rudolph, and Bright all argue that Jrm speaks through the whole passage, and they therefore excise the introductory words "Thus Yahweh has said" in *M*.[4] The decision must be based on grounds other than this rubric (or the third-person reference to Yahweh at the end of v 7: compare 2:3). One further datum in favor of Jrm's speaking at least v 5b would be that fact that "they refused to return" is assigned to Jrm in 5:3.

Berridge proposes an ingenious interpretation of v 4: that Israel is the subject of "fall" and "rise," and that Yahweh is the subject of the two occurrences of "turn";[5] the questions then have a specific connotation and not an abstract one (on both these points see further Interpretation). Berridge goes on then to propose that Jrm is the speaker in v 4, that Yahweh is the speaker in v 5, and that Jrm resumes speaking in vv 6–7. One datum in favor of Berridge's proposal that the speaker shifts to Yahweh in v 5 is that there is evidently a parallel shift of speaker to Yahweh for the third question in the threefold

---

2   Holladay, *Architecture*, 97–99.
3   See O'Connor, *Structure*, 300, 305–6.
4   So also Janzen, p. 134.

5   Berridge, pp. 171–72.

question form in v 19 (see further below, and see Interpretation there).

But the matter is not so simple. There are a series of parallels between the diction of v 6 here and the material about the false prophets in chapter 23. Thus "what is not right" (לוֹא־כֵן) and the ambiguous "course/oppression" (מְרוּצָה) are found in 23:10, where Yahweh is the speaker (see there). Further "and I have listened" (וָאֶשְׁמָע) corresponds to "I have heard" (שָׁמַעְתִּי) in 23:25, where again Yahweh is the speaker, and what Yahweh has heard in 23:25 is the word of the false prophets, "I have dreamed, I have dreamed." I propose then that what Yahweh has paid attention to and listened to in the present passage (v 6) is the two questions of v 4: that Berridge is correct, the speaker shifting to Yahweh in v 5, but that the questions in v 4 are not spoken by Jrm but are a quotation of what the people are saying, perhaps specifically what the false prophets are saying, cited by Yahweh. (This surmise may be reinforced by the word "course" in v 6, which suggests the activity of the false prophets: compare 23:21. See further Interpretation.) If this reasoning is correct, then the phrase "this people," which does not belong in v 5, has a place in the opening of v 4 (see Text). In this way the diction is parallel to that of v 19: v 19aα refers to the voice of the people, v 19aβ cites the double question of the people, and v 19b is Yahweh's counterquestion, introduced by "why, then?" (מַדּוּעַ).

One concludes that the entire passage is spoken by Yahweh.

Verse 4 begins with an instruction to Jrm (note that the same instruction "And you shall say to them" is found in *M* in 7:28; in the present study on that passage it is transferred to the beginning of 7:29). No one is addressed in vv 4–7: what Jrm is to communicate is thus a kind of divine soliloquy, but the intent of the passage is an accusation speech (as in 23:10 and 23:25–27, which share diction with these verses). The form of threefold question is used to raise the issue why the people are so adamant in refusing to change.

The question "What have I done?" (v 6) implies a legal context. The related question, "What have you done?" or "What are you doing?" is a reproach formula (see 2:23, and compare also Judg 8:1; Eccl 8:4); so "What have I

done?" may be either an appeasement formula, rhetorically suggesting the answer, "Nothing" (1 Sam 17:29; 26:18), or else meant sincerely, as here, an embarrassed acknowledgment of guilt.[6]

In v 7 Yahweh uses an analogy from nature (as in 5:22) to contrast the behavior of birds with the behavior of the people: such discourse draws on the conventions of wisdom teaching (compare the references to birds in Prov 7:23; 26:2; 27:8).

And, as already noted, vv 8–9 continue the accusation speech, as Yahweh addresses his audience with the question "How can you say?" appropriate to legal speech, and vv 10aα + 13 make up the announcement of judgment. This announcement begins with "therefore" (לָכֵן): compare 5:14. The diction in v 10aα is very close to that of 6:12, with its implication of the carrying out of a curse against Israel, a curse which ends with the implication of the reversal of creation (v 13). Verse 10aα describes defeat in battle, while v 13 describes drought; in this way the announcement of judgment offers the twin themes of 14:1—15:9 (see there).

Setting

Both the first half (vv 4–7) and the second half (vv 8–13) of the passage point to a setting in the autumn of 601 (compare Structure, *Extent of Unit*), more specifically to September/October of that year, when the feast of booths was celebrated. Thus v 13 strongly implies the onset of the great drought, dated in the present study to 601–600 (see "A Chronology of Jeremiah's Career"); the word-play on "Ingathering" in v 13 implies the celebration of the feast of booths (= ingathering) (see Interpretation); the mention of "law of Yahweh," "scribes," and "pen" in v 8, and perhaps "order of Yahweh" in v 7, at least implies the recitation of the law of Deuteronomy, and the autumn of 601 was one such occasion (see again "A Chronology of Jeremiah's Career"). There are parallels in diction to 5:1–9 ("they refused to return," 5:3 and v 5 here) and 5:20–29 (the analogy from nature), and to 23:10 and 23:25–27 (see Form); those passages likewise seem to have their setting in the autumn of 601, when the conflict with the optimistic prophets was evidently already under way (see

---

6   Irene Lande, *Formelhafte Wendungen des Umgangssprache im Alten Testament* (Leiden: Brill, 1949) 99–101; Hans Jochen Boecker, *Redeformen des Rechtslebens im Alten Testament* (WMANT 14; Neukirchen: Neukirchener, 1964) 33.

4:5—10:25, Preliminary Observations, *Settings*, and see Setting for 23:10 and for 23:25–32).

At may be added that Hab 3:17, which closely resembles v 13 here, may have had the same setting (see 14:1—15:9, Setting).

Interpretation

■ **4** For the clause "Thus this people has said," see below on the poetic lines, and see further Text, and Form and Setting.

Verses 4–6 contain six instances of the root "(re)turn" (שוב).[7] Commentators have generally understood the two lines of poetry to be offering general truths of human nature: "Do people fall and not rise again? Does one turn away and not turn back?"[8] It is true that both third plural and third singular are used for the impersonal "one",[9] but the shift from plural to singular is odd for an expression like this, if the intended subject is "one" for both cola: Volz suggests that the text might have become corrupted, pointing to G and V, both of which read a singular in both cola. But the shift from singular to plural would hardly arise spontaneously, so the difficulty may be in the conventional interpretation.

Both Rashi and Qimḥi take the second colon as other than a general truth; according to them the first verb applies to Israel and the second to God, and both refer to positive "turning": "Does Israel turn to God and God not turn to them?"—though Rashi mentions another, the interpretation of *T*, by which the colon means "Does Israel turn back but not turn back sincerely?"

Though these Jewish interpretations identify the subjects wrongly, they are correct, I believe, that the passage applies to Israel and Yahweh rather than to a general truth. Berridge argues persuasively that the plurals in the first colon refer to Israel and the singulars in the second to Yahweh.[10] Beyond the present passage the verbs "fall" (נפל) and "rise" (קום) are paired in the prophetic literature in Isa 24:20; 26:18–19; Jer 25:27; Amos 5:2; 8:14; and Mic 7:8; in all those passages the

action is the result of Yahweh's will and in most if not all of them the subject of the verbs is Israel. Particularly apposite are Amos 5:2, "Fallen, no more to rise is virgin Israel" (נָפְלָה לֹא־תוֹסִיף קוּם בְּתוּלַת יִשְׂרָאֵל) and 8:14, "they [who swear by pagan gods] shall fall and never rise again" (וְנָפְלוּ וְלֹא־יָקוּמוּ עוֹד).

It is less obvious that Yahweh is to be understood as the subject of the two occurrences of "turn" in the next colon. Given the opposing pair "fall" and "rise," the two occurrences of "turn" must be understood to carry negative and positive meanings respectively. There is only one other instance in which Yahweh is the subject of שוב qal in a covenantal context with the meaning "turn away" without an appropriate prepositional phrase— Josh 24:20: in two other instances a prepositional phrase is present (Deut 23:15; Jer 32:40). And there is no other such instance, with Yahweh as subject, meaning "turn back," without prepositional phrase (three late passages offer the meaning with prepositional phrase, Zech 1:3; Mal 3:7; 2 Chr 30:6).[11] Nevertheless I submit that the interpretation is plausible in the present context.

Data given above (see Form and Setting) indicate that these two cola are Yahweh's quotation of the optimistic prophets. "If Israel falls, she will rise again, will she not? And if Yahweh turns away from us, he will turn back to us, will he not?" If this interpretation is sound, the irony is appalling: Yahweh has in brighter days indicated that the people can turn toward him as easily as away from him (4:1); now, when it is clear that the people have no intention of turning back to him (v 5), the optimistic prophets continue to trust that Yahweh will come to the rescue. The fatuity of these questions is matched by those in v 19a.

■ **5** Now comes Yahweh's crucial question, "Why, then . . . ?" (For the threefold form of question see 2:14.) The verb in v 5a is most simply taken to be the polel perfect third singular feminine of שוב. The few other instances of the polel of this verb appear to be transitive,[12] but in any event the noun translated here

---

7   See the treatment in Holladay, *Šûbh*, 1–2.
8   So Duhm, Cornill, Giesebrecht, Volz, Condamin, Rudolph, Bright, and Thompson; see particularly the comments of Rudolph and Thompson.
9   GKC, sec. 144d, f.
10   See n. 4.
11   For these data see Holladay, *Šûbh*, 81.
12   Ibid., 106–7.

"turning" (מְשׁוּבָה) may be taken as a cognate accusative (so this noun also in the interpretation of 3:12 in the present study). Alternatively the verb may be taken intransitively and the noun adverbially (so most commentators usually emend the verb: see Text). The meaning in any case is clear: the verb carries a negative meaning, "turn away," as it does in Isa 47:10; Ezek 38:4; 39:2; and in Jer 50:6 qere'. Since the verb may also carry a positive meaning (five instances in the OT), any potential ambiguity is resolved in v 5b.

"Permanent" translates the niphal participle of נצח: this stem of the verb appears only here in the OT, but the related noun נֶצַח (3:5) means "perpetuity," and the meaning is clear. Though people may theoretically change in their relationship with Yahweh (4:1), and though the optimistic prophets may believe that Yahweh may change his attitude in the relationship with his covenant people (v 4), in actuality Israel is locked into a permanent estrangement from Yahweh. Why?

The question is reinforced by v 5b. For "cling" (חזק hip'il) see 6:23–24 (translated there "grip"). "Deception" (תַּרְמִית) may be quite general (Zeph 3:13), but it may have a particular reference here. Rudolph proposes that it refers to false gods.[13] But it is noteworthy that in both 14:14 and 23:26 the noun occurs in the context of false prophets, those who say, "I [Yahweh] will give you assured peace in this place" (14:13). The deception then may well be the conviction that the political situation and the nature of the relationship to Yahweh is not in serious trouble.[14] For the clause "they have refused to return" see 5:3.

■ 6 If one concludes that Yahweh is the subject of the verbs in v 6aα (see Form and Setting), to whom has he paid attention and listened? To the false prophets, who speak the words of v 4aβb (see there).

In the second colon the expression לוֹא־כֵן is open to two interpretations. The word כֵּן might mean "thus"— "no such word do they speak": this is the understanding of G, and Bright understands it so. The other possibility is that כֵּן is the substantive "(what is) right, true," as in 2 Kgs 17:9, דְּבָרִים אֲשֶׁר לֹא־כֵן "things which are not right." Given the parallel between לוֹא־כֵן and "evil" in 23:10, a similar text, the latter interpretation is surely correct.

"No one is regretful of his evil": this phrase appears to be a play on the old creed of Exod 34:6–7. The phrase appears in Joel 2:13 and Jonah 4:2 in a reuse of that creed, and the phrase occurs five times in Jer alone with Yahweh as subject. The model is then Yahweh, who is regretful of the evil (= disaster) that he has intended to do to his people; but ironically no one among the people is regretful of the (moral) evil that he has done against Yahweh.

"What have I done?" To come to terms with this question is a steady concern of Jrm (compare 2:23, "Know what you have done"; see further Form).

The colon here translated "Everyone stays turned in his course" (כֻּלֹה שָׁב בִּמְרוּצָתָם, assuming the text is correct) has raised many questions. What kind of "turning" is implied here, a turning away or a turning back? The preposition "in" (בְּ) is puzzling. I propose that the participle here must be interpreted in the light of the parallel colon, "No one is regretful of his evil," where another participle occurs (נִחָם); by this clause the people are set in their evil ways. The present clause must mean something similar: the participle שָׁב must mean, not "is turning away," but "having turned away, continues so"— compare the participle מֵת, which means not only "dying" (rarely, for example, Gen 48:21) but "dead" (the usual meaning). With this meaning, assured by the context, the preposition "in" becomes understandable. The people have turned a permanent turning (v 5).

The word translated "course" (מְרוּצָה) indeed means "course, running" (root רוץ)—is there an association here with the "running" of the false prophets (23:21)?—but there is a homonym מְרוּצָה "oppression, extortion" (root רצץ), which occurs in 22:17. Jrm declares not only that the people are determined to run the course they have chosen for themselves, but that they are confirmed in injustice and oppression with each other (for the thought compare 6:6; 9:5).

The meaning of the participle שׁוֹטֵף in the last colon has caused difficulty. The verb שׁטף is normally used of rivers, "overflow" (47:2). As Volz points out, the verb involves the sudden overflowing of watercourses in wadis; it is the impulsiveness of the war-horse that is referred to here, like our idea of the fire-horse that

---

13 Rudolph, p. 61.
14 Compare Overholt, *Falsehood*, 67.

strains to go when the fire-bell sounds. The translation "charging" is from *JB*. This explanation is more likely than that of Mowinckel, that the horse is "whipped."[15] The point of the simile is that the horse himself struggles to plunge into battle; the imagery is thus close to that of the female wild ass that cannot be held back from the pursuit of her mate (2:24).

■ 7 The identity of the birds mentioned in v 7a has given varying degrees of difficulty. The first (חֲסִידָה) is transliterated in *G* and translated "kite" in *V*, but *S*, *T*, and Rashi translate "stork": it is an unclean bird (Lev 11:19; Deut 14:18) that builds its nest on high (Ps 104:17). Driver has recently suggested the word refers to the heron as well,[16] but since both the stork and the heron are of the same family Ciconiidae, the same term was doubtless applicable to both.[17]

About the second bird (תּוֹר), there is no doubt: it is the turtledove.

Regarding the bird or birds mentioned after the turtledove there is uncertainty. Before an identification is made, one needs to take account of the following data. (1) *M* and the Versions all reflect two birds. These two birds appear in *M* only in the present passage and in Isa 38:14; in both passages they appear in the same order. (2) In the *M* of both the present passage and Isa 38:14 the first of them reads סוס in the ketib and סִים in the qere': the ketib could be misunderstood as "horse" (compare the last colon of v 6 in the present passage!), though the spelling nevertheless might reflect a valid homonym. This bird is traditionally translated "swallow" (so *G* and *V*: for the other Versions see [4] below). (3) The second bird (עָגוּר) is variously rendered, being transliterated in *G* and translated "stork" in *V*. (4) Given the translations of (2) and (3), the renderings of *S* and *T* appear to be reversed: both have "crane and swallow." (5)

The second bird overloads the meter[18] and appears at least in the *M* of Isa 38:14 to be a gloss. Given this datum and datum (4), it is likely that the word is a gloss in both passages to guarantee that the previous word not be misunderstood as "horse."[19] (See Text notes c and d.)

Though the traditional translation for סוס/סִים is "swallow" (see [2] and [4] above), there are two considerations that suggest the translation should be "swift." First, Henry Tristram pointed out a century ago that the swallow is only a partial migrant in Palestine, many of them remaining in the winter, while the swift is migratory.[20] Second, Alice Parmelee has pointed out that Isa 38:14 suggests that the cry of the bird is like a human scream: this description fits much more the swift than the swallow, which twitters and warbles.[21] Driver likewise proposes "swift," noting that the Arabic *sîs* carries this meaning,[22] and Baumgartner agrees.[23]

The identification of the bird intended in the presumed gloss (עָגוּר) is more difficult. If it is indeed a gloss, then it is not likely to be a bird of far larger size like "crane" (see above). Many suggestions have been made; Baumgartner lists three, the bulbul, the tower swallow, and the wryneck.[24] Of these perhaps the bulbul, *Pycnonotus Reichenovi*, is the best candidate, since its Arabic name, *ta'jarī*, seems to be cognate.[25]

The stork in the air knows her season: that word (מוֹעֵד) is used of an appointment, of both time and place. The migratory bird appears on time. It must be stressed that Jrm is not referring here to the "laws of nature"; rather it is that the birds obey Yahweh's will, while the covenant people do not.[26] (For the same thought compare Isa 1:2, regarding the ox and ass.) On the other hand, it must be admitted that Jrm had a keen eye out for the regularities of nature (compare his observation on the behavior of animals in 2:23–24 and of the sea in 5:22). Yahweh's

15 Sigmund Mowinckel, "Drive and/or Ride in O.T.," *VT* 12 (1962) 287.
16 Godfrey R. Driver, "Birds in the Old Testament—I," *PEQ* 87 (1955) 17.
17 So Zorell, p. 257a.
18 The colon would exceed M. O'Connor's constriction of five units: see O'Connor, *Structure*, 75.
19 Wildberger, *Jesaja*, 1443.
20 Henry B. Tristram, *Natural History of the Bible* (London: Society for Promoting Christian Knowledge, 1868) 205.
21 Alice Parmelee, *All the Birds of the Bible* (New York:

Harper, 1959) 174.
22 Godfrey R. Driver, "Birds in the Old Testament—II," *PEQ* 87 (1955) 131.
23 *HALAT*, 710a.
24 Ibid., 740b.
25 Ludwig Köhler, "Hebräische Vokabeln I," *ZAW* 54 (1936) 288–89.
26 Berridge, pp. 171–72.

people do not know his "order" (מִשְׁפָּט); again, comparable passages are Isa 1:3 and Jer 4:22 and 5:4, especially the last, where the same noun appears. But in 5:4 the association of the noun is with the "way" of Yahweh, that way which enjoins right dealings with one's neighbor. Here, however, the association of the word is with the orderly habits of the birds; it refers then to the orderliness of Yahweh's will in the world. In passing one may note how frequent bird imagery is in Jrm's utterances: beyond the present passage see 4:25; 5:27; 12:9; 17:11.

■ 8 For the phrase "How can you say?" see Form, and compare 2:23. The total colon is close to Isa 19:11, "How can you say . . . 'I am a son of the wise'?" (אֵךְ תֹּאמְרוּ . . . בֶּן־חֲכָמִים אָנִי). But it would be difficult to prove any dependence in either direction. (It may be noted, with regard to Isa 19:1–15, that Hans Wildberger comes to the conclusion the passage may be genuine.)[27]

Though the two clauses in the quotation are joined by "and," they are not quite correlative: since they are balanced chiastically by the last two cola of v 9 (see Structure), Bright is correct in seeing the second clause here as the occasion for the boasting in the first clause. Jrm has elsewhere denied that the people have dealt rightly with Yahweh's law (2:8; 6:19); this verse is consistent with those passages. It is a deadly complacency against which the prophet is struggling.

The meaning of the second half of the verse is notoriously difficult; the difficulties are partly syntactic and partly a matter of interpretation of the connotations of the words used. The Versions are no help. G renders "In vain has a false pen come to be [ἐγενήθη] for the scribes," V "Indeed the lying pen of the scribes has worked falsehood," S "Truly a lying reed is made useful to the scribe for falsehood," and T "In vain has the scribe made a pen of falsehood to do forgery [זוּף pa'el]." That is, given the last three words of the verse (עֵט שֶׁקֶר סֹפְרִים), G and S have taken "pen of falsehood" as the subject and "scribes" as a kind of indirect object, while T has taken "scribes" as subject and "pen of falsehood" as object, and V has taken the three words as a triple construct chain functioning as subject. The interpretation of the words as a triple construct chain was accepted by Qimḥi, but he

treated לְשֶׁקֶר (here "into a lie") more carefully than did V: "The pen of the scribes has been to no purpose." Calvin either paraphrases or reassesses the syntax: "Surely, behold in vain hath the writer prepared his pen, in vain are the scribes!" All commentators in the modern period (Michaelis, Naegelsbach, Duhm, Cornill, Giesebrecht, Condamin, Rudolph, Bright) have assumed a triple construct chain; the verb עָשָׂה is either declared to be used absolutely, with "law of Yahweh" understood as the unexpressed object (Michaelis, Naegelsbach, Giesebrecht, Volz, Condamin), or else the verb is reconceived as עָשָׂה "made it [feminine object, that is, 'the law']" (Duhm and Cornill suggest this possibility, and Rudolph accepts it). These syntactic assumptions assume further that the "law of Yahweh" (תּוֹרַת יהוה) referred to in the second colon and presumably assumed in the last two cola is the written content of the scroll that came to light in Josiah's time, doubtless some form of the Book of Deuteronomy.[28] Indeed Cornill was convinced this verse is the sole evidence of Jrm's attitude toward the Deuteronomic reform. More recently, scholars have backed away from this sole identification and have seen the verse as Jrm's polemic against any written torah (Rudolph, Hyatt, Bright): these scholars believe that the contrast is between the (written) torah of Yahweh and the (prophetic) word of Yahweh (v 9). This whole set of questions needs reexamination, however.

There is no warrant for the assumption that there is a contrast between the torah of Yahweh and the word of Yahweh. In 6:19 "my torah" and "my words" are in parallelism, and the verb "reject" (מאס) appears there, as in v 9 here; similarly in Isa 1:10 the parallelism is between "the torah of Yahweh" and "the word of our God." The word tôrâ (תּוֹרָה) in Jrm's poetry has a positive connotation (not only in 6:19, but 2:8 as well; and see further Structure on the relation between vv 8 and 9). The contrast here is between the "law of Yahweh" and the "lie of the scribes" (שֶׁקֶר סֹפְרִים): both these phrases are two-unit construct chains, content plus source in both instances. Just as the subject in the second colon is "the law of Yahweh," so I propose that in the third colon "the lie of the scribes" is the subject of the verb (עָשָׂה). In 9:2 I understand "the lie" (שֶׁקֶר) as the bow which shoots the

27   Wildberger, *Jesaja*, 707 ("Es liegt nahe, dass . . .").
28   For this view see Julius Wellhausen, *Prolegomena to the History of Ancient Israel* (Edinburgh: A. & C. Black, 1885, rep. New York: Meridian, 1957) 403 n. 2; so also Duhm, Cornill, Giesebrecht.

tongue out as if it were an arrow: indeed in 9:7 the tongue is referred to as an arrow. Jrm evidently understands "the lie" as a quasi personification in that passage, and the same usage, it seems, is present here. This leaves "the pen" (עֵט) free to be object of the verb (just as Calvin understood it). (It may be remarked that when the word order verb-object-subject occurs, the morphemes usually make the identification of subject and object clear, e.g., Hab 3:3ba; Ps 34:22a; but not always—see Job 11:19b.)

The "pen" (עֵט) was doubtless made from a reed.[29]

Who were the "scribes" (סֹפְרִים)? The term was applied in this period to court officials who were record-keepers, whether of legal documents (32:12–15) or of finance (2 Kgs 22:3). There were undoubtedly scribal schools connected with the court,[30] and there is now indication that Jrm's scribe Baruch had been a royal scribe before becoming attached to Jrm.[31] Now whatever be the group addressed by Jrm (see below), it is clear that the scribes were a group to which the terms "wise" and "wisdom" could cling.[32] Given the likely setting of the present passage at the time of a recitation of the Deuteronomic law (see Setting), the references here to "scribes" and "pen" doubtless refer in some way to that recitation. The scribes referred to here would then be priestly scribes, but one must not assume any separation between priestly scribes and royal ones (compare 36:10 and 12): it was under royal patronage that the scroll of the law which had come to light in Josiah's time has been copied and then expounded.

And one must not assume (with Cornill and others) that this verse sets forth Jrm's attitude toward the Deuteronomic reform: if the setting proposed in the present study is correct, the onset of that reform was a full generation past. And it is certainly not the case that Jrm is saying, "The written code kills, but the Spirit gives life" (2 Cor 3:6). It is not that writing laws is bad; writing is often a good thing—after all, Jrm dictates to Baruch. What is bad is the lying spirit of the scribes that motivates their work: they manage to produce written results that are a crystalization of "falsehood" (שֶׁקֶר). These scribes then are not much different from the priests referred to in 2:8—those who deal with torah do not know Yahweh.

Who then is the audience addressed in the first half of the verse? Who is the "we" who claims wisdom? Verses 8 and 9 clearly raise a complicated set of issues: whether a specific class of "wise men" is addressed, whether the class of "scribes" is addressed, and what relation the law of Deuteronomy has to either or both. Scholars have offered a variety of solutions, but they are essentially three. (1) The audience is the class of "the wise" such as is referred to in 18:18.[33] (2) The audience is the "scribes," or the priests, or both.[34] (3) The audience is the people in general.[35]

If one assumes a unity between vv 4–7 and vv 8–13 (see Structure), then the implications of vv 4–7 are relevant for the question of the present verse. In v 5 the reference is to "Jerusalem," and in v 7 to "my people"; the impression left by vv 4–7 is that it was by the optimism of the false prophets that the people had been led into complacency (see Form, and also Interpretation on v 4). Certainly many optimistic prophets were attached to the temple (26:7; 28:1; compare 29:24–32), and their words would have reinforced the conviction of priestly circles that loyal adherence to the law of Deuteronomy would guarantee their protection by Yahweh. If the setting proposed here is correct, namely the feast of booths celebrated in September or October 601, then it is relevant to recall the treatment which Jrm's first scroll received in December 601: it was inspected by one scribe after another. It was first read in the temple, in the

29   Ronald J. Williams, "Pen," *IDB* 3:711. For depictions see James Pritchard, *The Ancient Near East in Pictures Relating to the Old Testament* (Princeton: Princeton University, 1954) 73–74, figures 231–35.

30   James Muilenburg, "Baruch the Scribe," *Proclamation and Presence, Old Testament Essays in Honour of Gwynne Henton Davies* (ed. John I. Durham and J. Roy Porter; Richmond: John Knox, 1970) 215–38.

31   Nahman Avigad, "Baruch the Scribe and Jerahmeel the King's Son," *IEJ* 28 (1978) 52–56, adapted in *BA* 42 (1979) 114–18.

32   Whybray, *Intellectual Tradition*, 22–24.

33   Henri Cazelles, "A Propos d'une phrase de H. H. Rowley," *Wisdom in Israel and in the Ancient Near East* (VTSup 3; Leiden: Brill, 1955) 29 and n. 1.

34   Duhm; Volz; Rudolph; Lindblom, "Wisdom in the OT Prophets," 195–96; McKane, *Prophets and Wise Men*, 102–3.

35   Bright; Whybray, *Intellectual Tradition*, 22–23.

chamber of a scribal family (36:10), then a member of that family sent word to the palace, to the chamber of the scribe there, and the palace scribe was present as well as the son of the temple scribe (36:12); and after its reading and after news of it was sent to the king, it was stored in the chamber of the palace scribe (36:20–21). One pictures Jrm's scroll—in his perception the only way to rediscover Moses—becoming the pawn of bureaucrats: this in spite of the fact that several scribes urged the king (unsuccessfully) not to burn it (36:25). It would seem, then, that the audience in this verse is what Jrm in 5:5 calls "the leaders," those whose perception shapes that of the whole people. Their mood, as Deuteronomy is recited, is one of confidence; the thought if not the words of Deut 4:6 is their conviction: "Keep [the statutes and ordinances] and do them; for that will be your wisdom and your understanding in the sight of the peoples, who, when they hear all these statutes, will say, 'Surely this great nation is a wise and understanding people.'"[36]

"To the contrary," Jrm hears Yahweh say (for אָכֵן as a particle of contradiction see the discussion in 3:23—note that the expression לַשֶּׁקֶר is prominent in that verse as well). Jrm's first scroll was a fresh attempt (with a scribe!) to publish instruction from Yahweh which would suffer a better fate than the scroll which had been read to Josiah: the fate of engendering a complacent spirit, indeed a lying spirit.[37]

■ **9** The verb here translated "have stood shamed" (בוש hip'il) seems in 2:26 and 6:15 to carry a meaning distinct to the hip'il stem (see those passages), but there appears here to be no discernible contrast with the meaning of the qal stem (Giesebrecht, however, says the hip'il here denotes the outward appearance of shame, as it does in 2:26). For the verb חתת qal (here "[be] aghast") see the remarks on the nip'al of this verb in 1:17; the meanings of the two stems are indistinguishable. Though the verb לכד normally means "catch, capture" (6:11), the meaning here is metaphorical, "be ensnared" (NAB) or "caught out" (JB). All three verbs are either perfects or waw-consecutive imperfects; Giesebrecht and Rudolph call them "prophetic perfects"—that is, their action is understood as about to be accomplished in Yahweh's

intention—but Volz, perhaps more accurately, calls them perfects of certainty.[38] That is: whether they know it or not, they are caught out.

For "reject" (מאס), where the object is the word of Yahweh, compare 6:19.

Volz and Rudolph wish to emend the last colon from וְחָכְמַת מֶה־לָהֶם to וְחָכְמָתָם מָה־לָהֶם, "and their wisdom, what (does it help) to them?" and Bright mentions the emendation as a possibility. But an interrogative pronoun may be construed in the genitive after a construct: for another example with מָה see Num 23:3, דְּבַר מָה, literally "word of what?" The question is not "What good does their wisdom do them?" but "What wisdom do they really have, anyway?"

■ **10a**α These two cola are reminiscent of 6:12a and stimulated the M doublet text of vv 10aβ–12. For the general pattern of thought on the curse that wives and fields be given over to others, see 6:12. "New owners" (יוֹרְשִׁים) is literally "those who dispossess" (compare Deut 12:2); the rendering here is that of the NEB. "Conquerors" (RSV) is not right; they may not be military conquerors but simply those taking over one's property for any reason at all.

■ **10a**β**-12** See Text, and see 6:13–15.

■ **13** The first and last cola of this verb are very difficult to interpret, and any understanding of them must be tentative; much of the difficulty, it seems, revolves around the multiple meanings which the words carry.

The first colon is rendered periphrastically by G, "and they shall gather their fruits": since in G that clause is a continuation of v 10aα, it is assumed that conquerors shall gather Israel's fruits (for that sequence of thought compare Isa 65:21–22). But there is no reason to doubt the first-person singular verb in M, and the other Versions agree, V translating the equivalent of "I shall surely gather them" and S and T the equivalents of "I shall surely destroy/consume them." These Versions reassure us of the consonantal text but are of little aid in establishing the meaning precisely.

It is clear that in some way Jrm is referring here to

---

36   Whybray, *Intellectual Tradition*, 23.
37   On the nature of "the lie" in this passage see further
       Overholt, *Falsehood*, 81–82, and, more generally,

McKane, *Prophets and Wise Men*, 102–12, and the literature cited there.
38   GKC, sec. 106i.

Zeph 1:2–3;[39] in v 2 there *M* offers אֹסֵף אָסֵף. (One notes in passing that 12:4 seems also to be built on Zeph 1:2–3.) As vocalized, the first word of that combination is the infinitive absolute of אסף. If the second word is the qal imperfect first singular of the same verb, one would expect אֶאֱסֹף (Mic 2:12) or possibly אֹסֵף (compare Ps 104:29); Arvid S. Kapelrud suggests the former,[40] Karl Elliger the latter.[41] But some have thought that Zephaniah intended a combination of two different verbs, אסף for the infinitive absolute and סוף hip'il "bring to an end" for the imperfect (called here a hip'il jussive);[42] but such a combination of verbs is unlikely. Liudiger Sabottka ingeniously suggests "I shall again [אֹסֵף, יסף hip'il] sweep away (or gather) [אסף]":[43] for יסף hip'il followed by a finite verb compare Hos 1:6. In any event it is clear that in Zeph 1:2–3 the action is denoted by אסף, a verb meaning "gather up, remove," often used of contexts of death ("gather someone to his fathers," 2 Kgs 22:20). But one is left in some uncertainty what the precise denotation is of Zephaniah's expression, and this compounds one's uncertainty in regard to Jrm's expression.

The colon here, as vocalized, reads אָסֹף אֲסִיפֵם. The first word, again as vocalized, can be nothing but the infinitive absolute of אסף qal. The second word is odd; with the vocalization given one assumes the hip'il of סוף, but the hip'il of that verb is attested in no other passage of the OT. The meaning would then be "I shall make an end of them," but the combination with the infinitive absolute of another verb is dubious (as it is in the Zephaniah passage), unless the Masoretes intended by this vocalization to preserve a double tradition of some sort. One suggestion is to revocalize to אֹסֵף אֹסְפֵם (אסף qal), "I shall surely gather them" (so BDB). But a more likely suggestion is that of Charles François Houbigant in the eighteenth century, to read the second word as *G* does, as an accusative noun (*G*: "their fruits")—אֲסִיפֵם "their harvest, their Ingathering"; this reading is accepted by Duhm, Cornill, Giesebrecht, Volz, and Rudolph. All these commentators read the first word as the first

singular imperfect of אסף qal, אֶאֱסֹף or אֹסֵף.[44] The exegesis given below will indicate that "I shall gather their Ingathering" is close to the center of Jrm's intention. The noun "Ingathering" (אָסִיף) appears in Exod 23:16; 34:22 as the JE equivalent of the feast of booths (Sukkoth, סֻכּוֹת), the term in D, P and later material (see further Setting).

A related question is the poetic relation of v 13 to v 10aα. This is essentially a problem of structure, but it can be dealt with only on the basis of an exegesis of the diction of the passage. The question is a double one. (1) Is v 13 a continuation of the thought of v 10aα without interruption? (2) If so, does one understand vv 10aα + 13 as a sequence of two tricola plus a closing colon, or as a bicolon (v 10aα) followed by a pentacolon (v 13) which is arranged in an inclusio, the opening and closing cola surrounding the inner three parallel cola?

As to the first question, it is attractive to see "I shall give" (אֶתֵּן) in v 10aα balanced by "and I have given" (וְאֶתֵּן) in the last colon of v 13. The verb in v 13 may be understood to refer to the good gifts Yahweh has given to Israel (see below); there is then an ironic contrast between the gracious gifts of Yahweh to Israel (v 13) and his "gift" of Israel's wives and fields to the foe (v 10aα). Given the tissue of multiple meanings which seem intended in v 13, this contrast appears deliberate. It is also clear that Jrm intends the first word in v 13, the verb "gather" (אסף) to be an antonym to the verb "give" (נתן). Of course the normal antonym of "give" is "take" (לקח: Job 1:21 and often), but that verb would not offer the range of meanings which "gather" offers. One can pair passages, however, in which "give" and "gather" are opposites, e.g., Jer 23:40, "bring [נתן] reproach (upon you)," and Isa 4:1, "take away [אסף] reproach (from us)." Jrm is well aware of Yahweh's reversals (45:4); so what Yahweh has given (v 13, last colon) he will gather up (v 13, first colon) and give to others (v 10aα). If one understands v 13 as following directly upon v 10aα, however, this brings motifs of the reversal of creation

39   De Roche, "Contra Creation," 281; compare his "Zephaniah i 2–3: The 'Sweeping' of Creation," *VT* 30 (1980) 104–9.

40   Arvid S. Kapelrud, *The Message of the Prophet Zephaniah* (Oslo: Universitetsforlaget, 1975) 21–22.

41   See *BHS*.

42   J. M. Powis Smith, *A Critical and Exegetical Commentary on the Books of Micah, Zephaniah and Nahum* (ICC;

New York: Scribner's, 1911) 191; Bauer-Leander, p. 279 n. 1.

43   Liudger Sabottka, *Zephanja, Versuch einer Neuübersetzung mit philologischem Kommentar* (BibOr 25; Rome: Biblical Institute, 1972) 6–7.

44   It should be stated that Duhm also suggests the possibility of a masculine singular imperative, אֱסֹף.

directly into association with motifs of conquest by the foe. That this is possible in Jrm's mentality is shown by the collocation of 4:19–21 and 4:23–28, which are structurally integrated (see on those passages). One may conclude, therefore, that Jrm was convinced that for Yahweh to reverse the conquest of Canaan (which is the burden of v 10aα and similar passages elsewhere) is equivalent to reversing creation. It makes sense, then, to understand v 10aα as having been followed by v 13 without a break.

The second question, the poetic organization of vv 10aα + 13, is more difficult to answer; De Roche analyzes v 13 as a pentacolon, and this analysis seems safer than the alternative.

The specificity of the second, third, and fourth cola of v 13 indicates the theological reach of the passage. "There are no grapes on the vine, there are no figs on the fig trees": conceivably this could be the result of the plunder of the enemy, who take wives and fields; after all, the enemy will "eat up your vines and your fig trees" (5:17). But "the foliage is withered"! This is not the action of the enemy, but the withdrawal of fertility (compare the similar diction, "Its foliage does not wither," Ps 1:3). There is a match between what Yahweh does through enemy pillage and what Yahweh does directly by the withdrawal of fertility. The lack of grapes and figs is here not simply an unfortunate loss in war. The vine and fig tree are evidences of Yahweh's presence and favor (see 1 Kgs 4:25 and Mic 7:1); now this presence and favor will be withdrawn.

Once more, then, the first colon of the verse: "I shall gather up their Ingathering." Yahweh will take back all the blessing represented in the feast of booths—while the people hope for a harvest, Yahweh will make his own permanent harvest so that the gifts of creation are no longer available. In Hos 4:3 one learns that the land mourns, and all who dwell in it languish (this latter verb serves elsewhere as a parallel for "be withered" [נבל], the verb occurring in the fourth colon of the present verse: see Isa 24:4), also the beast of the field and the birds of the air, and even the fish of the sea are taken away (= gathered, אסף nip'al). So the first colon is not simply modeled on Zeph 1:2–3; it is modeled rather on a whole

set of utterances having to do with the reversal of creation.[45] Once, at the beginning, Israel was the first fruits of Yahweh's harvest (2:3), so that all the foes who ate from Israel would be punished; now Yahweh will gather up his harvest, and in the process the foe will take over.

Both in syntax and meaning the last colon is difficult. If the text is correct, the parataxis of the last verb can be understood only as a relative clause, the object of the preceding verb.[46]

The meaning of the last colon seems purposely nonspecific: whom or what is Yahweh giving to whom? On the face of it, Yahweh has given everything to humankind, beginning with Gen 1:29, "Behold, I have given you every plant yielding seed which is upon the face of all the earth, and every tree with seed in its fruit; you shall have them for food." And his lavish activity has continued specifically for Israel as he gave the people the law (Deut 11:32) and the land (Deut 1:8)—especially the vine and fig tree, gifts that were thought by many in Hosea's time to have been given by the Baals (Hos 2:14). But Yahweh's gift may not always be benevolent: it may be that he is given the enemy to Israel (so Naegelsbach). Again, perhaps Yahweh is giving something to the enemy: in v 10aα one hears that Yahweh will give to the enemy Israel's wives and fields. This clause trembles between blessing and curse.

But the last verb offers no hint of blessing, however that verb be understood; and it can be understood at least four ways, each of which has been proposed by some exegetical tradition or other. (1) "And I have given to them that which they [Israel] have been transgressing (= the commandments)." This is the interpretation of *T* and Rashi; Volz accepts it. Here the suffix must be accusative, and the imperfect verb suggests habitual or repetitive action. What Yahweh gives is then the commandments of the law. The diction is very close to that of Ps 148:6, "He [Yahweh] fixed a limit/gave a statute, and it shall not pass away/he [Israel] shall not transgress (it)" (חָק־נָתַן וְלֹא יַעֲבוֹר). Jrm played with this psalm verse in 5:22 (see there) and appears to do the same here. But this time Israel does transgress: the verb in Ps 148:6 is imperfect for the impossibility of transgression, while

---

45   See again De Roche, "Contra Creation."
46   So Rudolph; see GKC, sec. 155n.

here the verb is imperfect for a way of life. (2) "And I have given to them that [the land, the gifts] which shall pass in ownership to them [the enemy]." This is the interpretation of Qimḥi. Here the suffix is dative. The verb (עבר) carries the technical meaning "pass to new ownership" in Num 27:7, 8, and the announcement has already been made in v 10aα. This nuance strongly emphasizes the reversal of the conquest of Canaan. (3) "And I have given to them those (= the enemy) who shall overrun, violate them (= Israel)." This is the interpretation of Hermann Venema, Naegelsbach, and Cornill. This nuance of the verb is found in Isa 51:23, where the land is personified as a woman and where the implication is both of invasion and of sexual violation; it underlines the parallel of "wives" and "fields" in v 10aα. (4) "And I have given to them that [the land, the gifts] which shall pass away, disappear in their [Israel's] regard." This is the interpretation of V. This meaning of the verb is found in 5:22 (see there) as well as 13:24. The suffix would be a dative of disadvantage; one finds such a dative suffix in M of Ps 36:12; 38:5 with the verb בוא.

Jrm in this verse links the canceling by Yahweh of the conquest and of creation, and by the vibration of these multiple denotations and connotations brings an impact that plain speaking could never achieve.

Aim

This passage is heavy with ambiguities and double meanings, at the beginning (v 4), in the middle (v 6b), and at the end (v 13). On first hearing the questions about falling and rising, of turning away and turning back (v 4), are words of common sense. Of course they will rise again! Of course he will turn back once more! But if the people assume a flexibility to Yahweh's turning, Yahweh accuses the people, by the same verb, of inflexibility (v 5), whether that inflexibility involves staying in a running course or in violent oppression (v 6). The tension of these ambiguities and double meanings dramatize the uncertainty of the situation. Will the people change their ways before it is too late? Calvin nicely parallels Jesus' words to the Pharisees and Sadducees in Matt 16:1–3: "When it is evening, you say, 'It will be fair weather; for the sky is red.' And in the morning, 'It will be stormy today, for the sky is red and threatening.' You know how to interpret the appearance of the sky, but you cannot interpret the signs of the times." Jesus' opponents understood the weather but not the necessity for repentance. According to Jrm the birds understand Yahweh's will better than his covenant people do; the people, seduced into complacency by the scribes' complacent misinterpretation of the instruction of Yahweh, fall into a consequent pride that is utterly misguided.

The punishment for all this will be appalling: not only will the enemy overrun Israel's territory and take over its womenfolk, but the very order of creation will pass away. Does the punishment fit the crime? If the hearers do not think so, then they have no awareness of what is at stake in listening to the instruction of Yahweh. Proverbs teaches that "When pride comes, then comes disgrace; but with the humble is wisdom" (Prov 11:2). This is a lesson the scribes have not learned, nor the people who listen to them. St. Paul much later would teach that "God chose what is foolish in the world to shame the wise" (1 Cor 1:27).

**The Coming Destruction of the
People Brings Jeremiah to Weep**

Bibliography

Berridge
  p. 170.
Dahood, Mitchell
  "Hebrew-Ugaritic Lexicography II," *Bib* 45 (1964)
  393–412, esp. 402–3.
Gevirtz, Stanley
  "The Ugaritic Parallel to Jeremiah 8:23," *JNES* 20
  (1961) 41–46.
Holladay
  "Deuteronomic Gloss."
Holladay
  "Style," 48–49.
Jongeling, Bastiaan
  "L'expression *my ytn* dans l'Ancien Testament," *VT*
  24 (1974) 32–40.
Loretz, Oswald
  "Jer 8,23 und KTU 1.16 I 26–28," *Mélanges
  bibliques et orientaux en l'honneur de M. Henri Cazelles*
  (ed. André Caquot and Matthias Delcor; AOAT
  212; Neukirchen-Vluyn: Neukirchener, 1981)
  297–99.
McKane, William
  "Poison, trial by ordeal and the cup of wrath," *VT*
  30 (1980) 474–92.
Reventlow
  Liturgie, 189–96.

8

14 people: **Why are we sitting?**
   **Gather and let us get in to the fortified
      cities—**
   and meet our doom there!
for [Yahweh][a] our God has doomed us
   and given us poisoned water to drink:
   **how we have sinned against
      Yahweh!**
15 Jeremiah: **To think of longing for well-being when
      there is no good,**
   for a time of healing[a] when look: terror!
16 Yahweh: **From Dan [a]is heard[a] the snorting of his
      horses;**
   **from the sound of the neighing of his
      steeds the whole land quakes;**
   **they have come and devoured the land and
      what fills it,**
   the city and its inhabitants.
17   **Indeed I am going to send among you
      poisonous snakes**
   against which there is no charm,
   and they shall bite you,
            [a]oracle of Yahweh.[a]
18 Jeremiah: [a] ⟨**To think my pleasures have flown,**⟩[a]

Text

14a   For *M* "Yahweh our God" *G* reads simply "God."
Read "our God": I suspect that between this
expression and "Yahweh" in the last colon one has
the break-up of a stereotyped phrase: compare the
parallelism of "Yahweh" and "her king" in v 19, and
compare further the treatment of a similar situation
in 3:25. Janzen (p. 81) also suggests the possibility of
an expansion here.

15a   The accepted *M* spelling here is מרפה, but many
MSS. read מרפא. The difference in no way affects
the meaning.

16a—a   *M* נִשְׁמָע may be construed either as nip'al
perfect, "is heard" (so *V, S*), or as a qal imperfect "we
shall hear" (so *G*). The context indicates that the
former is correct (compare Structure and Form,
where it is established that Yahweh speaks in v 16).

17a—a   This expression is omitted by *G*, assuming it to
be a secondary alteration, given the interpretation
of the first word of v 18 (see note a—a).

18a—a   The text of this sequence needs remedying. For
the first word in *M*, מַבְלִיגִיתִי, material from the
Cairo Genizah and some MSS. read two words, מבלי
גיתי, presumably construing גיתי as an infinitive from
גהה; the two words would then mean "without
healing." *G* follows the latter interpretation and,
having omitted "oracle of Yahweh" at the end of v

torment is upon me,
my heart is sick.

19   Listen—[the voice of][a] the outcry of
my fair people from the land
far and wide:

people: "Is Yahweh not in Zion?
Is her King not in her? . . ."

Yahweh: Why then have they offended me with
their idols,
with alien nothings?

20 people: "The harvest is past,
the summer is gone,
but we have not been saved."

21 Jeremiah: By the shattering of my fair people [a]I am
shattered,[a]
I am in mourning, horror has gripped me.

22 Yahweh: Is there no balm in Gilead?
Is there no healer there?

Jeremiah: Yes!—why then has there not arisen
new flesh for my fair people?

23 [9:1]   O that my head were water
and my eye[a] a fountain of tears,
so that I might weep day and night
for[b] the slain of my fair people!

17, links the expression with what precedes, thus "They shall bite you incurably"; θ' similarly. Volz, Rudolph, and Bright follow this lead, emending the second word, however, to גהת. But it is likely that a substantive from the root בלג is present here after all; I suggest the vocalization מַבְלִיגוֹתִי, from a noun *מַבְלֵגָה, formed analogously to the noun מַגֵּפָה (Bauer-Leander, p. 492, sec. 61s). This proposal would conform to Rashi's suggested translation "my diversions, recreations." The identity of the second word (עָלַי) likewise offers difficulty, and that difficulty is reinforced by the placing of the Masoretic 'atnaḥ with the third word יָגוֹן ("grief"). Once the verse is seen as a tricolon (see Structure and Form), the present word becomes the verb (root עלה) with the previous noun as subject, rather than a preposition (= עַל) with יָגוֹן which follows. If מַבְלִיגוֹתִי is correct, the consonantal text of the verb is wrong for a finite form. I would propose the infinitive absolute עָלֹה (= עָלוֹ): compare the suggestion of David Noel Freedman, cited in Lundbom, *Jeremiah*, 85. For the spelling compare עָשׂוֹ for עָשׂה in 4:18. For the rendering "to think" compare v 15.

19a   Omitting קוֹל with Janzen (p. 11); the noun here is evidence of a conflate text (compare Ps 18:7, where קוֹל and שַׁוְעָה are in parallelism).

21a—a   Both *G* and *S* omit הִשְׁבָּרְתִּי. One can defend the *G* text as more concise and explain *M* as dittographic, or defend *M* and explain *G* as haplographic. *M* appears preferable.

23a   *M* reads a singular (עֵינִי), while a few MSS. and the Versions read "my eyes" (עֵינַי). Obviously either reading is satisfactory, but the singular is probably the *lectio difficilior* and preferable with the singular "fountain."

b   *M* offers אֵת (the sign of the accusative) here (thus literally "bewail . . . the slain"), but a few MSS. read עַל (literally "weep . . . over the slain"), and *T* suggests עַל also (*S* is not definitive). The meaning is unaffected.

Structure and Form

Extent of Unit; Placement of Unit. Because the material from 8:4 though 9:8 appears to have a common setting, it is difficult to determine the boundaries of the component units. The present study concludes that there is a break between vv 13 and 14 (see 8:4–13, Structure). There are two considerations that lead one to propose another break, between 8:23 and 9:1. (1) The sequence 8:14–23 offers shifts of speaker (see below). By contrast it appears that Yahweh speaks consistently within 9:1–8;

Rudolph and Bright assume that Jrm speaks in vv 1–3, but they must alter the text for consistency (for this whole matter see 9:1–8, Form). (2) Each component appears to have its own unity of imagery. Thus 9:1–8 is united by the image of the deceitful tongue (9:2, 4, 7) which is an arrow (9:2, 7) against the neighbor (9:4–7). On the other hand 8:14–23, which would seem to break into two subsections (vv 14–17 and 18–23: see below), offers a unity between those two subsections in several respects. Thus one finds "healing" (מַרְפֵּה) in v 15 and

288

"healer" (רֹפֵא) in v 22. More prominently there is מֵי־רֹאשׁ in v 14, literally "waters of poison" but perhaps also "waters of the head = tears" (see Interpretation), and רֹאשִׁי מַיִם (literally "my head waters") in v 23. This unity may be reinforced by the imagery of "weeping"—in 23 and perhaps in v 14 as well (one meaning of דמם: see again Interpretation). Finally if there is an infinitive absolute in the first colon of v 18, that infinitive absolute echoes the one in v 15. If this analysis is correct, it follows that the expression מִי־יִתֵּן (literally "who will give?") at the beginning of both 8:23 and 9:1 does not unite two sections of a single discourse but rather serves as a catch-word linking two adjoining units: the present study indeed concludes that Jrm is the speaker in 8:23, while Yahweh is the speaker in 9:1. This catch-word link functions just as "gather" (אסף) does between 8:13 and 14: these are the links that join 8:4–13; 8:14–23; and 9:1–8.

Now is there justification for subdividing 8:14–23?—Rudolph and Bright make a division between vv 17 and 18. It is true that vv 14–17 center on the military emergency, while vv 18–23 center on Jrm's shattered emotions, but on balance, given the unifying features within vv 14–23 already cited, it is better to take the sequence as a single unit.

Identification of Speakers. The structure of vv 14–23 is shaped by the shifts of speaker, but the specification of speaker is not in every instance easy. It is clear that Yahweh speaks in vv 16–17 (first-person singular in v 17, and in general the giving of war news: compare 4:6–7, 13a, 15–16, and often). Yahweh likewise speaks in the interruption in v 19b. It is equally clear that the people speak in v 19aβ and v 20.

Verse 23 is spoken by Jrm; it is closely comparable to 14:17–18, which shares the same setting with the present passage, and Jrm speaks those verses (note 14:18!). It might be objected that, by Jrm's perception, Yahweh also weeps over the territory of his covenant people (9:9–10); but the setting of that passage is not altogether certain

(see there), and the close similarity of 14:17–18 takes precedence. By the same token Jrm is the speaker in v 21.

But v 22 needs care. The questions of v 22a are appropriate in the mouth of Yahweh: self-evident rhetorical questions are his stock in trade (notably in Job 38—39,[1] but compare also 1 Sam 16:1 and Jer 30:15). I would propose then that v 22a is spoken by Yahweh, but v 22b by Jrm: the conjunction כִּי (here translated "yes") at the beginning of v 22b, which is so curious that some MSS. omit it, would then mark the shift of speaker, as it does also in 4:31, according to my analysis. By this proposal both threefold question sequences, in v 19 and v 22, offer interruptions that shift the speaker. Unity of emotion then suggests that Jrm likewise speaks vv 18–19aα.

Who speaks v 14? The diction is congruous with that in 4:5bβ: there the command was given to the people to shout "Gather and let us go in to the fortified cities," and here the command is carried out; one concludes therefore that v 14 is the voice of the people, and consistency of diction with v 20 (first-person plural) would lead to the same conclusion. But there is a problem here: the phrase "We have sinned against Yahweh" duplicates a phrase in 3:25, and it was determined that the phrasing there represents Yahweh's scenario for genuine repentance. Have the people here suddenly come to their senses? Reventlow believes so.[2] Or is Jrm speaking on behalf of the people, ironically picking up the wording of 4:5 to tell them that he and they are moving into a trap, and then explaining why? This is Berridge's suggestion.[3] Certainty is impossible, but I would suggest that v 14 is the people's voice heard in Jrm's imagination (see below on form).

Who speaks in v 15? One assumes Jrm does: it is the distanced contemplation of the current situation similar to that in 4:18, where there seems likewise to be an infinitive absolute.

Internal Structure. The passage thus breaks into two

---

1   See Gerhard von Rad, "Job xxxviii and Ancient Egyptian Wisdom," *The Problem of the Hexateuch and Other Essays* (New York: McGraw-Hill, 1966) 281–91 = "Hiob xxxviii und die altägyptische Weisheit," *Wisdom in Israel and the Ancient Near East, Presented to Professor Harold Henry Rowley* (ed. Martin Noth and D. Winton Thomas; VTSup 3; Leiden: Brill, 1955), 293–301 = *Gesammelte Studien zum Alten Testament*

(TBü 8; Munich: Kaiser, 1958) 262–71.
2   Reventlow, *Liturgie*, 191.
3   Berridge, p. 98 n. 144.

sections, a shorter one (vv 14–17) in which the three voices each speak once, and a longer one (vv 18–23) in which they speak in a more complex fashion. The shorter section hints, both at the beginning and the end, at a parity between the foe ("fortified cities," v 14a, and the description in v 16) and nature (poisoned water, v 14a, and poisonous snakes, v 17, though the terminology for "poison" is not the same). The longer section in turn divides into two subsections (vv 18–20, 21–23), each centered in an interrupted threefold question (vv 19, 22); and that section is united by the four occurrences of "my fair people" (בַּת־עַמִּי, vv 19, 21, 22, 23).

Verse 14 is best analyzed as two tricola, united by the two stems of "doom" (דמם) in the third and fourth cola. Verse 15 can only be a bicolon (הִנֵּה, here "look," with its following noun, cannot be a complete colon).[4]

Verse 16 is made up of four cola. (This analysis is against that of Rudolph, who analyzes the verse as six cola, four in v 16a; but a subject cannot be separated from its verb in the first clause, and symmetry suggests two cola, not three for that half verse.)[5] Verse 17 is a tricolon (against Rudolph: the object cannot be separated from its verb).[6]

The text of v 18 is difficult, but there seem to be three cola within the verse. It is possible that the first colon of v 19 makes a tetracolon with v 18. The words of the people in v 19aβ make up a bicolon. Yahweh supplies the third question in the sequence (v 19b), another bicolon. The closing words of the people (v 20) are a tricolon. Verse 21 is again a bicolon; v 22, another triple question, is a tricolon. And finally v 23 is a tetracolon.

Form. One's understanding of the form of the passage depends completely on the identification of the succession of speakers (see above). The core of the passage is perhaps Yahweh's announcement of judgment (vv 16–17), but clustered around that announcement is Jrm's lament that his people are destined to be slain.

There are no introductory clues to v 14 by which to understand how the words are to be perceived; it is

possible that such clues originally existed but have been lost. As it stands, v 14a is the response to the commands of 4:5abα: the people utter an appeal to flight, flight which is, however, doomed to failure in the face of Yahweh's punishment. The appeal to flight has its origin in the diction of holy war (see Form for 4:5–6 and 6:1). It is suggested here, however, that this ironic and self-defeating appeal to flight, which ends with the people's admission of guilt (v 14bβ), is only hypothetical in Jrm's mind (see above on identification of speakers); for a parallel admission of guilt see 3:25aβ. If v 15 is spoken by Jrm, it seems to be a summary appraisal (compare 4:18; 7:28).[7] The structure of the expression is close to that of Isa 5:7b ("He hoped for X, when, look, Y") and even closer to that of Hag 1:9a, even to the infinitive absolute at the beginning), so one may have here a conventional mode of expression for an outcome contrary to expectations.

In vv 16–17 Yahweh directly announces the judgment coming both through the enemy (v 16, compare 4:13, 15; 5:15; 6:22–23) and through nature (v 17).

Verses 18, 21, 22b, and 23 are expressions from Jrm himself of his reaction to the news of the coming judgment; vv 22b and 23 offer rhetorical questions which add to the emotional pitch (in v 23, "O that my head were water" is literally "Who will give [מִי־יִתֵּן] my head water?"). These phrases are reminiscent of those in 4:19–21 (see Form there) and are expressions of personal lament (compare Psalm 55: note there also מִי־יִתֵּן, v 7). In vv 19–20 Jrm quotes the people's puzzled questions, questions based on the expectations traditional for Israel; the rhetoric is appropriate to a communal lament (compare Psalm 80). For the double questions in v 19a ("Is Yahweh not in Zion? Is her King not in her?") Mic 3:11 is a good parallel. Yahweh's interruption at the end of v 19 poses the real question, the question of the idolatry of the people. The words of v 20a may represent a popular proverb (so already Qimḥi, and so also Volz); see Interpretation. Verse 22a is here assigned to Yahweh

---

4   O'Connor, *Structure*, 305, 314–16.

5   It is to be noted that ‑כָּל, here "the whole," is not a "unit," so that the length of the colon does not violate O'Connor's constraints; see O'Connor, *Structure*, 266, on Ps 78:14b.

6   The pronoun "you" (אֶתְכֶם) counts as a "unit" in the last colon; compare the treatment of 3:14b, and see 2:1—4:4, n. 16.

7   See Childs, *Isaiah and the Assyrian Crisis*, 128–36.

(for the form see above on identification of speakers). As in similar passages elsewhere Jrm manages by constantly shifting rhetorical devices to ring the changes on the divine announcement of doom.

Setting

Several data suggest that this passage took shape in the autumn of 601, just before the king burned Jrm's scroll. (1) Verse 23 offers diction similar to that of 14:17, part of the liturgy on the drought, to be dated to that period. (2) Though the expression "The harvest is past, the summer is gone" may be understood metaphorically or even proverbially (see Structure and Form), there is no reason not to understand it as actualized in the drought (see Interpretation). The rhetorical questions of Yahweh (vv 19b, 22a) and Jrm (v 22b) perhaps suggest a time before Jrm became convinced of the irrevocability of Yahweh's punishment of the people.

Interpretation

■ **14** The words that commanded the people (4:5) are now spoken, but they become the vehicle for the darkest irony (see Structure and Form): words which were intended to move the people to safety now move them into the deathtrap of the city (third colon), an experience traced to twin causes: Yahweh's punishment and the people's sin.

The wording of the verse is remarkably undergirded by the ambiguity of two expressions—the verb דמם, which appears in the qal stem in the third colon and in the hiphil in the fourth, translated here "meet our doom," "doomed us," evidently can mean both "perish" and "weep"; and the expression "poisoned water" (מֵי רֹאשׁ, literally "water of poison") may well mean "water of the head = tears" as well. The irony that the call to seek safety within the walled city will result in tragedy is underlined because one of the crucial matters in the defense of a city under siege is ready access to a secure water supply;[8] but now the water that Yahweh will

supply will be—what? poisoned water? or simply the tears of the refugees? All this must now be examined in detail.

There is a close parallel to the first colon (עַל־מָה אֲנַחְנוּ יֹשְׁבִים) in 2 Kgs 7:3, "Why should we sit here waiting till we die?" (מָה אֲנַחְנוּ יֹשְׁבִים פֹּה עַד־מָתְנוּ). The implication of the present passage is the same—Why are we sitting still? What are we waiting for? There is no time to lose!

For the wording of the second colon see 4:5. It may be noted in passing that 4:5 has a cohortative, וְנָבוֹאָה, while the present verse has the simple imperfect וְנָבוֹא; there is no discernible difference in meaning (compare GKC, sec. 107n).

The verb דמם, which occurs in the third and fourth cola, has the basic meaning of "be/become still, silent" (See Job 31:34). The form in the third colon can be analyzed as a cohortative of either the qal or nip'al stem (GKC, sec. 67dd). When a form of this verb which is demonstrably nip'al occurs (25:37), it means "be rendered silent, destroyed." But the existence of a second root דמם "weep" is now confirmed by Ugaritic evidence;[9] the third colon may thus be understood as "and weep there," and the fourth colon as "for our God has made us weep" as well (see Structure and Form).

The perception that ambiguity is intended is deepened when the phrase "poisoned water" (מֵי־רֹאשׁ) is encountered. The noun רֹאשׁ is the common word for "head," but a homonym refers to some poisonous plant (the Versions: "gall") and then to poison in general.[10] All the Versions and commentators here assume that the phrase means "poisoned water"; indeed the mention of poisonous snakes in v 17 reinforces the image (see Structure and Form), and the phrase in its other occurrences in Jer (9:14 and 23:15) must mean nothing but "poisoned water." The idea that Yahweh gives the people poisoned water to drink reminds Rudolph of the ordeal set forth in Numbers 5 which a woman accused of adultery must undergo (note particularly the phrase מֵי הַמָּרִים, Num 5:18, understood as "water of bitterness"). But the possibility exists that the phrase here also implies "water

---

8   See Yadin, *Warfare*, 24, and more specifically R. W. Hamilton, "Water-works," *IDB* 4:815–16.

9   Ug. 16.25–26; see Dahood, "Hebrew-Ugaritic Lexicography II," 402–3.

10   The matter is discussed extensively in McKane, "Poison," 479–82; see more briefly John C. Trever, "Gall (herb)," *IDB* 2:350.

of the head = tears," given the variation in v 23, and the ambiguity of דמם. For the image of drinking one's own tears see Ps 80:6.[11]

It remains to be pointed out that the nuance of the cohortative in the third colon is result: "Let us get into the fortified cities so as to meet our doom/weep there."[12] The fourth colon then explains why: it happens to us because Yahweh intends it so.

For "how" (כִּי) in the last colon see 3:25.

■ **15** For the translation "to think" to introduce the infinitive absolute see 3:1; 4:18; 4:18 is likewise a summary appraisal. For a discussion of this matter, and of the parallels in Isa 5:7b and Hag 1:9a, see Structure and Form.

The verb קוה pi'el is normally translated "hope," but it has nuances much more in the direction of "wait with longing."[13] For "well-being" (שָׁלוֹם, often translated "peace") see 4:10.

The noun מַרְפֵּא/מַרְפֵּה is open to two interpretations, and both of them fit here. The first is "healing" (root רפא), and in view of the mention of poisonous snakes which cannot be charmed (v 17) and of "balm" and a "healer" in v 22, this meaning is appropriate. But some passages containing the word suggest a derivation from the root רפה "relax," thus "calmness, softness,"[14] and this is an appropriate contrast to the last word ("terror"). That word (בְּעָתָה) appears in the OT only here and in the doublet passage in 14:19, but the meaning of the related verb is clear ("startle, terrify"). How pathetic, but how natural that people should hope for the best when the events of history come tumbling in on them!

■ **16** For "Dan" see 4:15–16a; for the demoralizing effect of horses see 4:13.

Though the word נַחְרַת (construct of a presumed נַחְרָה) occurs only here in the OT, a related noun נַחַר occurs in Job 39:20, and their meaning ("snorting") is not in doubt. The "snorting" is a nice parallel to the "neighing" in the next colon (the latter noun is related to the verb which appears in 5:8). The noun to which the "neighing"

refers is אַבִּירָיו, literally "his mighty ones"; it is used of men (Isa 46:12) and of bulls (Ps 22:13) as well as of horses (once otherwise in parallelism with the common word for "horse," as here—Judg 5:22; twice otherwise with the clear implication of "horses"—Jer 47:3; 50:11). For "quake" (רעש) see 4:24. For the image of "devouring" (אכל, "eating") the land and its contents see 2:3, and especially 5:17.

■ **17** For the sequence כִּי הִנְנִי compare the discussion on 1:15.

Yahweh will send poisonous snakes. Are the snakes to be understood as a metaphor for the invading army, or as real snakes? The lion, wolf, and leopard in 5:6 are probably to be understood metaphorically. The snakes here are understood to be a figure for the enemy in *T*, an interpretation approved by Qimḥi, and this interpretation has continued into the present century (Duhm, Cornill, Giesebrecht, and evidently Rudolph), a cogent one if "bite" in v 17 is connected to "devour" in v 16. On the other hand, if Yahweh can give poisoned water to drink (v 14), he can send poisonous snakes, and Volz insists that real snakes are intended, as does Delbert R. Hillers;[15] compare in particular Num 21:6. A נָחָשׁ is any sort of snake; a צִפְעֹנִי is some kind of poisonous snake, perhaps the Palestinian viper.[16] The presence of both substantives suggests that we might have a double text, or that צִפְעֹנִים is a gloss (so Giesebrecht), but there is no Versional support for such a suggestion. The belief that snakes can be charmed is widespread—see Ps 58:5–6 and Eccl 10:11; Calvin cites Virgil, *Eclogues* 8, 71, likewise.

■ **18** For Jrm's description of physical symptoms here and in v 23, see the discussion in 4:19–20.

If the text is correctly understood (see Text), there is a nice contrast between the first and second cola: Jrm's joys have gone up and away, while grief has come down upon him, yet the two directions are both expressed by the consonantal sequence על[17] (for a similar ironic contrast between "up" and "down" see 14:2, and for the ironic contrast using the same words עלה "go up" and עַל

11   For the ambiguities of this verse see again Dahood, "Hebrew-Ugaritic Lexicography II," 402.
12   Joüon, *Gramm.*, sec. 115a.
13   Compare Walther Zimmerli, *Man and His Hope in the Old Testament* (SBT 2d Series 20; Naperville, IL: Allenson, 1971) 7–8.
14   The word is cited in both Zorell and *HALAT* for Prov 14:30; 15:4; and Eccl 10:4.
15   Hillers, *Treaty-Curses*, 55.
16   Bodenheimer, "Fauna," 254.
17   On the contrast see Lundbom, *Jeremiah*, 85.

"upon" see Isa 14:8, 13, 14).

The reconstructed noun "my pleasures" (מַבְלִיגוֹתִי) would be related to the root בלג "smile"; its verb "have flown," here assumed to be an infinitive absolute עָלוֹ, literally means "go up"; it is similarly used of the disappearance of dew in Exod 16:14.

The noun translated "torment" (יָגוֹן) denotes a profound affliction of the emotions.[18] One notes its occurrence in Gen 44:31, to express how Jacob will feel if he does not see Benjamin again; the related verb in the hip'il stem clearly means "torment" in Isa 51:23.

For "heart" see 4:4. The adjective דַּוָּי occurs only three times in the OT, always as a description of "heart"—its root reflects "the mental effects of weakness."[19]

■ **19** The noun שַׁוְעָה is a "cry for help." For "my fair people" see 4:11. The phrase "land far and wide" (אֶרֶץ מֶרְחַקִּים) is literally "land of distances"; the same expression is found in Isa 33:17. The people on every hand cry out.

For the form of the threefold question with הֲ, אִם, מַדּוּעַ, see 2:14. The question "Is Yahweh not in Zion?" and its parallel is on one level a natural question for the people to raise, given such affirmations as those in Pss 46:6; 84:8; or 99:2; Yahweh surely resides in Zion (compare 7:3).[20] Given such assumptions, the final question (with "why?") that is expected would doubtless be "Why has he struck us down?" (compare 14:19) or "Why has he not hastened to save us?" But in the mouth of Jrm these questions become the expression of fatuous complacency (for the resemblance to a similar question in Mic 3:11, see Form). The people do not know the signs of the times. So Yahweh interrupts with the apposite question of his own: "Why have they offended me with their idols . . . ?" This interruption is not a Deuteronomic gloss, as Giesebrecht, Volz, Hyatt, and Rudolph have assumed (and evidently Bright as well, who brackets the question), but is a deliberate rhetorical effect.[21] This question from Yahweh of course embodies a traditional concern: wording close to it is found in Deut 32:21 and is

then reflected in Huldah's speech, 2 Kgs 22:17.[22] For the matter of offending Yahweh by idolatry see 7:18–19; one notes especially the occurrence there of the same verb כעס. The word here for "idol" (פָּסִיל) designates something hewn or carved;[23] the parallel "nothings" (הַבְלֵי, non-gods) is the plural of the same word that occurs in 2:5 (הֶבֶל, see there), and for "alien" (נֵכָר) see 5:19, where the word appears in a similar context.

■ **20** After the interruption of Yahweh, the people's utterance seems reduced to a pathetic mutter!—it is getting late, and Yahweh has not saved us yet. (For a similar word of distress from the people involving lateness of time see 6:4b.) It has been traditional to see the opening words here as a proverbial expression (see Structure and Form); but it is altogether likely that the reference here is to the great drought under way (see Setting), or else Jrm is using a popular proverbial expression in its literal meaning. Note that "we" is emphatic in the last colon, suggesting a contrast (hence "but"); for the same idiom see 5:4.

■ **21** For "shattering" (שֶׁבֶר) see 4:6. The verb "shatter" is cognate in Hebrew as well; for other forms of the verb see 2:13, 20. "I am in mourning" is literally "I have become dark" (verb קדר, as in 4:28); the extended meaning evidently comes about through the mourner's neglecting to wash his or her person and clothes (there is a glimpse of such a practice in 2 Sam 19:25). The noun שַׁמָּה may mean "a place of horror" (2:15), a "horrible thing" (5:30), or, as here, "(the emotion of) horror." For the use of "grip" (חזק hip'il) with an emotion see 6:24.

■ **22** For the proposal that Yahweh speaks the first two cola see Structure and Form. Yahweh raises the question why the people have not availed themselves of a cure for their sickness.

Gilead is a mountainous area east of the Jordan, roughly east of Samaria. Baly defines it as a triangular area bounded on the west by the Jordan, on the north by a line beginning roughly where the Yarmuk River enters the Jordan and proceeding east-southeast to the present

18 Josef Scharbert, *Der Schmerz im Alten Testament* (BBB 8; Bonn: Hanstein, 1955) 35.

19 Wolff, *Anthropology*, 143.

20 On the Zion theology see von Rad, *Old Testament Theology 2*, 155–69. For God as king see Matitiahu Tsevat, "King, God as," *IDBSup*, 515–16.

21 Holladay, "Deuteronomic Gloss."

22 For a possible connection between the two cited

passages see Jack Lundbom, "The Lawbook of the Josianic Reform," *CBQ* 38 (1976) 293–302.

23 William L. Reed, "Graven images," *IDB* 2:471.

village of Mafraq, on the south by a line from Mafraq proceeding south-southwest to the point where the River Zerqa Maʻin enters the Dead Sea. The territory within that area is uniformly mountainous or at least hilly, broken only by the deep canyon of the Jabbok.[24]

The identity of the specific "balm" (צֳרִי) in Gilead is uncertain. It is mentioned again as from Gilead in 46:11, but that reference may simply be a reflex of the phraseology here; and as part of the goods of a Gileadite caravan in Gen 37:25. It was sent by Jacob to Joseph in Egypt (Gen 43:11) and exported from Israel to Tyre (Ezek 27:17). The only other occurrence in the OT, Jer 51:8, adds nothing to our knowledge. *G* renders the word by ῥητίνη and *V* by *resina* (both "resin," without greater specificity). *T* is periphrastic, while *S* offers "wax" (šĕʻûtāʼ) in the present passage and other renderings elsewhere. It is clear that the word refers to a resinous exudation, probably aromatic, from some tree or shrub. There are three main candidates for the identity: the storax (or styrax), *Styrax officinalis* (so Hyatt, Rudolph); the balsam, *Balsamodendron* (or *Commiphora*) *opobalsamum*; and the mastic, *Pistacia mutica* (or *lentiscus*). Opinion now seems to favor the mastic.[25] Such resins were widely used in healing in ancient times;[26] they were not only soothing, but their pleasant aromas counteracted the smell of putrefying wounds.[27]

If Yahweh's interruption of the people in v 19 brought an altogether different question than that which the people would have asked, Jrm's interruption of Yahweh here brings much the same question Yahweh would have asked: why do the people not avail themselves of a cure?

Such a cure, in the OT understanding, would have consisted of the rising of "new flesh" (אֲרֻכָה) at the wounded spot (that is, under the scab).

■ **23** The expression here translated "O that . . . were" (מִי־יִתֵּן, literally, "who will give?") is a common idiom for a contrary-to-fact wish.[28] The poetic vocabulary, with "head," "fountain" and "tears," may well be traditional: a Ugaritic passage is very close.[29]

The vocalization of וְאֶבְכֶּה, with simple וֹ, suggests that the verb must be understood as a virtual cohortative, like its parallel in 9:1 (see further Judg 9:26); verbs of the form III-he cannot mark the cohortative (GKC, sec. 75l; compare 4:21). The sequence must therefore be understood as a final clause ("so that I might weep").[30] Jrm expresses here in classic form his empathy with his people. The psalmist might say that "My tears have been my food day and night" (Ps 42:4), but while the psalmist wishes for the presence of God for himself, Jrm, identifying with his people and yet forbidden (or about to be forbidden) to pray for them (7:16: compare Setting there and here), wishes he could weep for them unceasingly. Jesus would later weep over Jerusalem (Luke 19:41). Volz notes this: "In this sympathy [that is, Jrm's] he has come closest of all the great predecessors of Jesus."[31]

The noun "slain of" (חַלְלֵי) means literally "those pierced of" and is a fairly common expression for those violently killed (Num 19:16). But the genitive construction here is ambiguous, not only "the slain of my fair people" (compare the use in 51:49) but also "those slain by my fair people" (compare "those slain by the sword," 14:18, and "those slain by Yahweh," 25:33). Given the

24   Baly, *Geography*, 219–21; see further Magne Ottosson, *Gilead, Tradition and History* (ConB, OT Series 3; Lund: Gleerup, 1969).

25   Ludwig Köhler, "Hebräische Vokabeln III," *ZAW* 58 (1940–41) 232–34, in a detailed examination of linguistic, classical, and Arabic evidence; Kurt Galling, "Harz," *Biblisches Reallexikon* (ed. Kurt Galling; HAT; Erste Reihe 1; Tübingen: Mohr, 1977) 138; Roland K. Harrison, "Balm," *IDB* 1:344.

26   See, for example, Henry E. Sigerist, *A History of Medicine, I: Primitive and Archaic Medicine* (New York: Oxford University, 1951) 340.

27   Guido Maino, *The Healing Hand* (Cambridge: Harvard University, 1976) 216–17.

28   Bastiaan Jongeling, "L'expression *my ytn* dàns l'Ancien Testament," *VT* 24 (1974) 32–40, esp. 35.

29   Ug. 16.1.26–28. See Stanley Gevirtz, "The Ugaritic

Parallel to Jeremiah 8:23," *JNES* 20 (1961) 41–46; Yitshak Avishur, "Should a Ugaritic Text be Corrected on the Basis of a Biblical Text?" *VT* 31 (1981) 218–20; Stanley Gevirtz, "Should a Ugaritic Text be Corrected on the Basis of a Biblical Text?— A Response," *VT* 33 (1983) 330–34.

30   Joüon, *Gramm.*, sec. 116c.

31   Volz, p. 112: *In diesem Mitleid ist er unter allen grossen Vorgängern Jesus am nächsten gekommen.*

context of fraternal treachery in 9:1–5, the second possibility looms large.

Aim

This passage and 14:17 are the source for our designation of Jrm as "the weeping prophet." The sentence of death is near to being passed by Yahweh: the nation is to be destroyed. Jrm sees the people trapped within their fortified cities (v 14) as the enemy approaches with his horses (v 16), yet oblivious to what looms ahead and puzzled that Yahweh is delayed in rescuing them (vv 19–20). Yahweh is at the end of his patience (vv 19b, 22a). Jrm for his part is stunned by the collision course on which Yahweh and the people are bent; tears are the only appropriate response. Was such a discourse as this really offered publicly as a warning of judgment ahead?

Sins of the Tongue

Bibliography

Berridge
  pp. 173–76.
Overholt
  Falsehood, 82–83.
Soggin, Alberto
  "*le'ĕmûnāh* (Jeremiah 9,2): Emphatic *Lamed*?" *Old Testament and Oriental Studies* (BibOr 29; Rome: Biblical Institute, 1975) 221–22 = "Nota, Le'ĕmûnâ (Gen. 9,2): *lamed 'enfatico'*?" *BeO* 7 (1965) 282–83.

9

1 [2]
O that I had in the wilderness [a] a wayfarers' lodging,[a]
  so that I might abandon my people
    and walk away from them!—
  for they are all adulterers,
    an assembly of traitors;

2 [3]
⟨And they have drawn⟩[a] their tongue,
  [b] their bow is falsehood,
    and not for honesty have they been
      valorous[b] in the land,

Text

1a—a For *M* מְלוֹן אֹרְחִים *G* reads "a lodging most remote," evidently reading the phrase as מְלוֹן אַחֲרוֹן. This is not an implausible reading, and Giesebrecht accepts it, comparing a similar expression in 2 Kgs 19:23. But no other Version supports it, and it is better to stay with *M*, given the diction of 14:8 (see Interpretation).

2a Vocalize the verb as a qal (וַיִּדְרְכוּ) instead of the *M* hip'il (וַיַּדְרְכוּ): the form of the hip'il is exceptional, lacking the yod (=î) after the resh (see GKC, sec. 53n). The lexica propose that the hip'il would have the same meaning as that assigned to the qal, but it would be a unique usage of the hip'il, and the qal stem offers parallels (see Interpretation).

b—b This sequence of words has caused confusion for the Versions and the commentators and has called forth many emendations, but *M* is sound (even to the zaqep qaṭon over שֶׁקֶר). The basic confusion has been to assume that the tongue is compared to a bow that shoots out lies; to the contrary, the tongue is the "arrow" (see v 7) that is shot out by the lie, which is the "bow." The earliest evidence of the confusion is *G*: "They bent their tongue like a bow; falsehood and not faithfulness have prevailed on the earth." *S* follows the first half but stays closer to *M* in the second half: "They have bent their tongue like their bow; with falsehood and treachery have they been great in the land." *V* ignores the suffix on "bow": "They have extended their tongue like a bow of falsehood and not truth; they are strong in the land." (*T* is periphrastic.) The assumption that the tongue is compared to a bow has followed everyone: Rashi, Luther, *KJV*, down to the present century. Duhm solves the problem by omitting "They have drawn their tongue, their bow," calling this "an unlovely image" (*Ein unschönes Bild*); Condamin rearranges the text. Volz, Rudolph, and Bright follow *G*, a procedure that entails omitting the mem in קַשְׁתָּם (or reading קֶשֶׁת with an enclitic mem), omitting the ל in לֶאֱמוּנָה (with one MS.—as does

but from evil to evil have advanced,
and me they do not know,
    ^coracle of Yahweh.^c

3 [4]   ^aLet^a each of you ^awatch out^a for his
        neighbor,
    and put no trust in a[ny]^b brother,
        for every brother acts like a Jacob,
        and every neighbor is a slanderer.

4 [5]   Each cheats his neighbor,
        they never speak the truth,
        they teach their tongue to speak
            falsehood,
            ^a ⟪ they act perverse, ⟫ ⟨are too tired
            5 [6]/ to return;
    oppression upon⟩^a oppression,
        fraud upon fraud!—
        they refuse to know me,
            ^boracle of Yahweh.^b

6 [7]   Therefore thus Yahweh of hosts has said:
    I am going to refine them and assay
        them;
        for ^a⟪ a calamity ⟫ I shall make ⟨in my
            fury,⟩
        ⟪ the ruin of ⟫^a my people.

Michaelis), or assuming it to be the emphatic lamed
(so Friedrich Nötscher, "Zum emphatischen
Lamed," *VT* 3 (1953) 380, and J. Alberto Soggin,
"*Le'ĕmûnāh* (Jeremiah 9,2): Emphatic *Lamed*?" *Old
Testament and Oriental Studies* [BibOr 29; Rome:
Biblical Institute, 1975] 221–22) and emending גִּבְרוּ
to גִּבְרָה. This set of misunderstandings misses the
metaphor and ignores the poetic pattern (see
Structure and Interpretation).

c—c   *G* omits, and this omission is accepted by Volz,
Rudolph, and Bright, who assume that Jrm is
speaking and therefore that וְאֹתִי must stand for an
abbreviation, 'וְאֶת־י, i.e., "Yahweh they do not
know." But Yahweh is speaking, and the rubric is
doubtless original (compare 8:17).

3a—a   For the *M* imperative הִשָּׁמְרוּ there are MSS.
which read תִּשָּׁמְרוּ (second plural imperfect) or יִשָּׁמְרוּ
(third plural jussive). The meaning is virtually
identical in any instance.

b   Omitting כָּל־ with *G*; it spoils the symmetry of רֵעַ,
כָּל־רֵעַ, כָּל־אָח, אָח (Janzen, p. 65).

4–5a—a   Following *G*; *M* is impossible ("To commit
iniquity they weary themselves. Your sitting [is] in
the midst of . . ."). The emendation of most (since
Michaelis) in the fourth colon of v 4 is to הֶעֱווּ נִלְאוּ
שָׁב and in the first colon of v 5 to תֹּךְ "oppression."
One notes the association of תּוֹךְ "oppression" with
מִרְמָה "fraud" in Pss 10:7 and 55:12, and with ארב
"ambush" in Ps 10:7 as well.

b—b   This rubric is lacking in *G* (compare 8:17; 9:2).

6a—a   The text in *M* for v 6b is dubious and must be
dealt with as a whole; for further discussion of both
the difficulties of the present text and of the solution
offered here see Interpretation. *S* takes the words
literally, presumably as a question, "For how will I
do from the presence of the daughter of my
people?" *V* paraphrases: "For what else shall I do
before the daughter of my people?" *G* appears to
ignore "how" and to read (or assume) "the evil of"
before "daughter of my people": "For I shall do
from the presence of the evil of the daughter of my
people"; *T* reads "how" but also reads "evils of":
"For how shall I do from the presence of the evils of
the assembly of my people?" The agreement of *G*
and *T* in reading "evil(s)" is striking, and Duhm,
Giesebrecht, and Condamin therefore emend the
text by inserting רָעַת before בַּת־עַמִּי, while Volz,
Rudolph, and (with hesitation) Bright read רָעָתָם
instead of בַּת־עַמִּי. But it seems unlikely that such a
common word as רָעַת would have dropped out of
the text, and I suspect that *G* and *T* have separately
tried to remedy a defective text. I follow Michaelis's
suggestion to read אֵיד "calamity" (see 18:17) for אֵיךְ;
one notes that dalet and final kap are very close in
the Aramaic script of the fourth century B.C.E. (see
Frank M. Cross, "The Development of the Jewish
Scripts," *The Bible and the Ancient Near East* [ed. G.
Ernest Wright; New York: Doubleday, 1961] 137,
line 1). I further revocalize מִפְּנֵי to מִפָּנַי "my

7 [8]	A sharpened[a] arrow is their tongue,

7 [8]   A sharpened[a] arrow is their tongue,
        deceitful is the speaking 《 in their
              mouth: 》[b]
           he speaks peace with his neighbor,
             but in his inner self he sets up his
                ambush.

8 [9]   With these (folk) shall I not deal by those
            (punishments)?
                        oracle of Yahweh—
         upon[a] a nation like this shall my soul
            not gain satisfaction?

presence," with the nuance of "my fury." I propose further to emend בַּת "daughter of" to בְּתָת "ruin of" (the construct of בָּתָה, Isa 5:6).

7a   The ketib reads שׁוֹחֵט, literally "slaughtering," therefore "deadly"; 4QJer[a] suggests the same reading (חט[, Janzen, p. 175), and this reading is followed by G and V. The qere' and many MSS. read שָׁחוּט, literally "beaten," therefore "sharpened," and this is followed by S and T. Either reading gives sense.

b   Reading בְּפִימוֹ or בְּפִיהֶם with G and T for M בְּפִיו "in his mouth," so Duhm, Giesebrecht, and Condamin. The symmetry of the verse is thereby improved (compare the symmetry of v 3 with respect to "brother" and "neighbor"). Given "their tongue" in vv 2 and 4, this is a better solution that the correction of Volz and Rudolph to "his tongue" in the first colon.

8a   Some MSS. read וְאִם, thus prefixing an "and" to the colon (compare 5:29).

Structure and Form

For the demarcation between 8:23 and 9:1 and for the position of the present passage see 8:14–23, Structure and Form. The present passage has a unity of message, a form-critical unity, and ends, as does 5:1–9 and 5:20–29, with the same refrain.

In contrast to 8:14–23, in which there are several shifts of speaker, in the present passage Yahweh is the only speaker. Commentators have assumed otherwise: Volz, Rudolph, and Bright emend v 2bβ so that Jrm speaks, assuming he spoke v 1a as well (see Text). But the diction of v 1a is appropriate to Yahweh, in contrast to that of 8:23 (see Interpretation), and there is no warrant to emend the text.

Form-critically the passage is centered in the announcement of judgment (v 6); around it are two sequences of accusation speeches, vv 1b–5 and v 7 (see further below). There is nothing implausible in this structure, so that there is no reason for Volz to omit v 7 or for Rudolph to relocate the verse between vv 3 and 4. Both accusation speeches center on the "tongue" (vv 2, 4, 7) that is an arrow (v 7, and by implication v 2: see Interpretation), shot out by falsehood (vv 2, 4) when someone speaks (vv 4, 7) to his neighbor (vv 3, 4, 7). Verse 7 thus is a compressed recapitulation of vv 2–4. Preceding the first accusation speech is a contrary-to-fact wish of Yahweh's (v 1a: see again below).

Verses 1–5 break into two subsections (vv 1–2, 3–5). Each subsection ends with the phrase "know me," preceded in each case by the structure X–preposition–X

("evil to evil," v 2; "oppression upon oppression, deceit upon deceit," v 5). (Each subsection also closes with the rubric "oracle of Yahweh," but that datum is not the crucial one.)

Verses 1 and 2 are each made up of a tricolon (vv 1a, 2a) followed by a bicolon introduced by כִּי (vv 1b, 2b); the two tricola are united by "in the wilderness" in the first colon of v 1a and "in the land" in the third colon of v 2a (compare the collocation of "wilderness" and "land" in 2:6–7). Verses 3–5 are more complicated; they must be analyzed as two tetracola and a tricolon. Verse 3, the first tetracolon, is chiastic ("neighbor," "brother," "brother," "neighbor"). Then the first colon of v 4 is generated from the diction of v 3 (אִישׁ בְּרֵעֵהוּ matching אִישׁ מֵרֵעֵהוּ— "each . . . his neighbor"). But though there is the hint of chiasmus in v 4 ("falsehood" and "truth" in the second and third cola), the scheme is not carried through. Verse 4 in fact not only reflects v 3 (the first colon of each: see above) but rings the changes on phrases and themes from vv 1–2 as well ("tongue" and "falsehood," the scheme of X–preposition–X, the phrase "know me"). This sub-section is also united by reminiscences of the Jacob narrative in Genesis, not only the pun on "Jacob" in v 3, but also "cheats" in v 4 (compare Gen 31:7) and "fraud" in v 5 (compare Gen 27:35; 34:13): for the details see Interpretation.

The introductory first clause of v 6 stands outside the poetic structure. The balance of v 6 (as the text is here reconstructed) is a tricolon.

Verse 7 is a tetracolon like v 4: the first two cola are

nominal clauses, the second two verbal, and the second and third cola share the root "speak." It is better to include the expression "in their mouth" with the second colon (compare *G*) rather than (as the atnaḥ in *M* suggests) with the third colon; in this way each colon contains three units (so most commentators). For v 8 see 5:9.

Verse 1a is a fantasy of Yahweh's (see Interpretation); it is a negative fantasy, comparable to the positive fantasy heard in 3:19, and strikingly both passages deal with the land: Yahweh's dream was to be a covenant God to the people in the land, but now the covenant is so broken that his dream is to walk away from the land and its people. Verse 1b, the beginning of the first accusation speech, is introduced by the conjunction כִּי: the motivation for Yahweh's wish to be rid of his people is that of which the people stand accused. The accusations in vv 2 and 4–5 center on sins of the tongue; the accusation in v 3 is in the form of a rhetorical warning, "Do not trust anyone!" Such diction can be found among moralists everywhere: a parallel is to be seen in the Egyptian "Instruction of King Amen-em-het" (twentieth century B.C.E.): "Hold thyself apart from those subordinate to (thee), lest that should happen to whose terrors no attention has been given. Approach them not in thy loneliness. Fill not thy heart with a brother, nor know a friend. Create not for thyself intimates—there is no fulfillment thereby. (Even) when thou sleepest, guard thy heart thyself, because no man has adherents on the day of distress."[1] But that Egyptian warning is a piece of wisdom for the royal court, while the present passage is an indictment of the whole community. Verse 6, introduced by the messenger formula, brings the announcement of judgment. Verse 7 is a recapitulation of accusation, and v 8 concludes the passage with a refrain embodying a rhetorical question of self-justification.

Setting

There are no direct clues in this passage for its setting, but several phrases are identical with or reminiscent of phrases in passages elsewhere to which a setting can be assigned. Thus "me they do not know" (v 2) is found in

4:22, and the comparable "me do they not fear?" in 5:22, with emphatic object pronoun; "they refuse to know me" (v 5) is comparable to "they refuse to return" in 5:3 and 8:5. And of course the refrain in 9:8 is identical with that in 5:9 and 5:29. As with the 8:4–13 and 8:14–23 which immediately precede, this passage is best assigned to the autumn of 601, at the time when the drought was well under way. Both the position of the passage in the book and the addition of "by those (punishments)" in v 9 suggest a setting somewhat later than that of 5:20–29.

Interpretation

■ **1** In spite of the diction of vv 2 and 5 ("know me [i.e. Yahweh]"), Volz, Rudolph and (with hesitation) Bright have assumed that Jrm speaks in v 1 and have therefore emended those phrases in vv 2 and 5. But this procedure is unwarranted. Jrm speaks the contrary-to-fact wish in 8:23 out of grief for his people, while Yahweh speaks the parallel contrary-to-fact wish in the present verse out of rejection of his people. The same association of ideas as that in v 1 is found in 14:8, a passage from the same period—"wayfarer" (אֹרֵחַ), the root "lodge" (לוּן); in that passage the people are puzzled why Yahweh should act like a wanderer who can find no shelter for the night. For the idiom for a contrary-to-fact wish (literally "who will give?") see 8:23. The verbal suffix is dative (GKC, sec. 117x, ff). The wilderness (מִדְבָּר) is conventionally thought to be at the edge of Yahweh's touch (on this matter see 2:6); that Yahweh should prefer to stay in the wilderness to being in companionship with his people in the land of Canaan is grotesque—he should be at home in Zion (8:19)! The mood and some of the vocabulary (בַּמִּדְבָּר, מִי־יִתֵּן) is similar to that in Ps 55:7–9, and again one thinks of Elijah's flight to the wilderness where he lodged (1 Kgs 19:4–9); but the psalmist's wish to flee, and Elijah's flight, are one thing, while the notion of Yahweh's fleeing is quite another.

There is division among commentators whether the verbs in v 1aβγ are subordinate to (as translated here) or correlative with the verb in the first colon (in the latter case the translation would read "O that I had in the wilderness a wayfarers' lodging! O that I might abandon my people . . ."). Giesebrecht, Volz, and Rudolph hold

---

1   *ANET*, 418b.

the latter position (for earlier commentators holding the view the verbs are subordinate, see Volz), but there is scarcely any difference in meaning. For uses of "abandon" (עזב) in which the people abandon Yahweh see 2:13, 17, 19; 5:7, 19; this is the first occurrence of the verb in Jer in which Yahweh abandons the people (see further 12:7). The idiom "walk away from" (הלך מֵאֵת) is used in 3:1 of wife leaving husband; here again the metaphor is reversed from what is expected. Yahweh wishes to leave his covenant people.

The reason comes in v 1b: "they are all adulterers" (מְנָאֲפִים), "an assembly of traitors" (עֲצֶרֶת בֹּגְדִים); for the verbs נאף pi'el and בגד see 3:8. The same phrase "they are all adulterers" is found in Hos 7:4: Jrm is here quoting and adding the parallel phrase. The word "assembly" (עֲצָרָה) is normally used of a cultic assembly, one gathered either for Yahweh (Lev 23:36) or for Baal (2 Kgs 10:20); the phrase here suggests the organization of treachery.

■ 2 Verse 2a has been steadily misunderstood; both *G* and the rabbinic tradition have assumed that the tongue is here compared to a bow that shoots out lies (see specifically Rudolph), and this assumption has deformed any attempt to understand the text. The text is clear. Verse 7 indicates that the tongue is likened to an arrow (compare the metaphors in Ps 57:5), not to a bow. The verb דרך is used of an arrow as well as of a bow (Ps 58:8, though there the text is in disarray; 64:4). The verb דרך normally means "tread down," as of tramping warriors (see 4:11) or of those treading grapes; but it has the meaning "exert force" (on a bow or arrow), as here. "Falsehood" (שֶׁקֶר, the "lie") is their bow: Jrm has here assumed almost a hypostasis for falsehood as the motivating center for the tongues of the people which shoot out to damage the common life. Is this use of "falsehood" suggestive of Baal?—compare 5:31; 13:25; 23:14. Overholt remarks, "The term *šeqer* implies the operation of a destructive power, and is thus peculiarly applicable to the social, political, and religious situation in which the prophet worked."[2]

The third colon continues the military image: the people march valorously (גבר, "be victorious"), but not for "honesty" (אֱמוּנָה, "faithfulness"), which is that on which Yahweh has his eye (5:3).

The conjunction כִּי at the beginning of v 2b is usually taken as "for," like the one in v 1b, but is better taken as "but" after the negative in the previous colon. The verb "advance" (יצא, literally "go out") is doubtless military or cultic, and the colon may be Jrm's parody of Ps 84:8, "They go [הלך] from strength to strength [or, from bulwark to bulwark]," part of a pilgrim psalm.[3] These people march on from one wickedness to another. For the last colon see 4:22.

The question may be raised, why the emphasis on words and tongue? The problem of "unclean lips" had been central to Isaiah's call (Isa 6:5, 7), and that prophet spoke sternly against those who call something by its opposite (Isa 5:20). The OT tradition held that one's speech is an extension of oneself and that one's speech betrays one's basic character.[4] The tongue is a major expression of a person's psychic nature.[5]

■ 3 Not only have the people made common cause in treachery (v 1); there is now total breakdown of community solidarity in speech—it is brother against brother. What Isaiah had predicted of the Egyptians (Isa 19:2) has now come to pass in Israel.[6] Similar laments are heard elsewhere (Mic 7:5; Ps 12:3), but the phraseology here is certainly pointed. Do not trust any fellow citizens! Everyone is now living up to the heritage embodied in the name "Jacob" (יַעֲקֹב), who according to the word-play in Gen 25:26 and 27:36 "deceived" (עקב) his brother Esau: the clause here means literally "every brother surely deceives." Here Jrm derives a judgment oracle from the name Jacob just as Hosea had done (Hos 12:3–5).

For the phrase "go about as a slanderer" (הלך רָכִיל) see 6:26. In this passage it is conceivable that Jrm had in mind a sequence of laws like Lev 19:16–18: "You shall

---

2   Overholt, *Falsehood*, 101. See also Martin A. Klopfenstein, *Die Lüge nach dem Alten Testament* (Zurich: Gotthelf, 1964) 98–99, who points out the phrase "lying spirit in the mouth of the prophets" in 1 Kgs 22:23, and a similar semipersonification in Isa 57:4. Ultimately the devil would be called the "father of lies," John 8:44.

3   For the suggestion see Overholt, *Falsehood*, 83 n. 24,

who attributes it to Gösta Ahlström.
4   Pedersen, I/II, 167–68.
5   Johnson, *Vitality of the Individual*, 47–48.
6   On the breakdown of solidarity in urban centers see Pedersen, I/II, 264.

not go about as a slanderer [תֵּלֵךְ רָכִיל] among your people, and you shall not stand forth against the life of your neighbor: I am the Lord. You shall not hate your brother in your heart, but you shall reason with your neighbor, lest you bear sin because of him. You shall not take vengeance or bear any grudge against the children of your people, but you shall love your neighbor as yourself: I am the Lord." How far the people have traveled from this standard! And as Rudolph reminds us, this judgment on the breakdown of community solidarity was not simply a general one; Jrm himself experienced it personally (11:19; 12:6; 20:10).

■ **4** Synonymous accusations continue. The verb יַהְתֵּלוּ is a curious formation, the hip'il of תלל with the he retained in the imperfect (GKC, sec. 53q). The verb means "cheat": Jacob accuses Laban of having "cheated" him (Gen 31:7), and it is thus likely that if Jrm in v 3 reminds the hearer that Jacob deceived Esau, he reminds one here that Laban cheated Jacob. For "truth" (אֱמֶת) see 4:2. It is striking that people must "teach" their tongue to speak falsehood: it is not something that comes naturally but takes planning and effort (compare similar statements in 4:22, "they are wise in doing ill," and 6:7, "[the city] keeps fresh her evil"). If one reads the text for "act perverse" correctly, it will be the only instance in the OT of the intransitive of this verb (for a transitive occurrence see 3:21). For the expression "they are too tired to return [to Yahweh]" (נִלְאוּ שָׁב) compare 6:11, "I am tired of holding it in" (נִלְאֵיתִי הָכִיל); *NEB* here translates, "They cannot retrace their steps."

■ **5** For "return" (שׁוּב) without modifier, meaning "repent," here reconstructed in the text, see 3:22. "Oppression" (תֹּךְ, likewise reconstructed in the text) does not appear elsewhere in *M* of Jer, though in the present study it is similarly reconstructed in 17:1. It is, however, parallel with "fraud" (מִרְמָה) in Pss 10:7 and 55:12.

If in v 3 there is a reminiscence of the meaning of "Jacob" in Genesis and a further reminiscence of the Jacob narratives in v 4 ("cheats"), then in the present verse there is evidently another, with "fraud" (מִרְמָה): this word appears twice in Genesis and not again in the OT until 2 Kings—Isaac sadly reports to Esau that Jacob had

taken his brother's blessing "by fraud," "deceitfully" (בְּמִרְמָה, Gen 27:35), to which Esau replies with a word-play on "Jacob" (v 36); and then it is said that the sons of Jacob answered Shechem and his father "deceitfully" (בְּמִרְמָה), because Shechem had defiled Dinah (Gen 34:13). It would appear that Jrm is consistently using the diction of Genesis to underline the heritage of Jacob which Israel carries. For the last colon compare "they refuse to return," 5:3 and 8:3, and "me they do not know" in v 2 and 4:22.

■ **6** For the messenger formula compare 5:14. For "refine" see 6:27, and for "assay" see 6:29. In 6:27–30 Jrm was deputized by Yahweh to refine and assay the people; here one finds the more conventional metaphor: Yahweh is himself the refiner and assayer (11:20; 12:3; 17:10; 20:12; and often in other books).

The text of v 6b is dubious. If correct, the clause is either a question or an exclamation. If a question, it would have to mean "How shall I act/manage in the presence of my fair people?"—for אֵיךְ אֶעֱשֶׂה compare אֵיךְ תַּעֲשֶׂה "How will you manage?" in 12:5. But 12:5 is part of Yahweh's rhetorical question to Jrm, while the present passage is part of Yahweh's announcement of judgment, and such a question, even a rhetorical question, is not appropriate. If an exclamation, it must mean "How (terribly) I shall act in the presence of my fair people!"—3:19 offers such an exclamatory "how," and this is the explanation of the present passage in BDB.[7] Hos 10:15a seems to reflect similar diction, though that text too needs some correction (see the commentaries). But an exclamation seems out of place in an announcement of judgment. Further the expression "from the presence of" (מִפְּנֵי, literally "from the face of") seems strange here; it does occur in Hos 10:15, but one would expect it to be followed by an expression like "the evil of," which the Hosea passage has (so the reading of *G* and *T* in the present passage!—see Text). Without something like "the evil of," the expression seems out of place in an announcement of judgment: it is Yahweh's presence, not that of the people, which is at issue. Finally one may raise the question whether "my fair people" (בַּת־עַמִּי, literally "daughter of my people") is appropriate here: all occurrences of the expression except this one (and 4:11, where

---

7   BDB, 32b.

the identity of the speaker is not clear [see Interpretation there], and 8:11, where the text is dubious) are in the mouth of Jrm (6:26; 8:19, 21, 22, 23; 14:17).

The emended text offered here may not be correct, but it emends only one consonant (a suggestion of Michaelis: איד for איך) and assumes a haplography of one other consonant (בתת for בת); the resultant expression is at least consistent with an announcement of judgment. "Calamity" (אֵיד) occurs in 18:17 in a similar context; one notes also its occurrence in Deut 32:35, a passage which may have stimulated Jrm. "In my fury" is literally "from my face." The same nuance of "fury" for "[Yahweh's] face" may be found in 4:26 and 5:22; it is suggested by Dahood for several passages in the Psalms.[8] "Ruin of" (בְּתַת) would be the construct of בָּתָה, which occurs in Isa 5:6, a passage form-critically similar to the present one; though this noun occurs only there in *M* and has occasioned doubt, the context makes the meaning plausible there, and commentators now accept it.[9]

■ 7 In this recapitulation the tongue is once more a destructive arrow (compare v 2). Words can kill (compare the array of seven things that Yahweh hates, Prov 6:16–19).

There is no reason to emend "speaking" (דִּבֶּר): the word, with the same vocalization, seems to occur in 5:13. For "deceit" (מִרְמָה) see v 5. For the thought expressed in the last two cola compare 12:2; Ps 28:3. For "peace" (שָׁלוֹם) see 6:14, and note also its occurrence in 8:15. For "inner self" (קֶרֶב) see 4:14; the word is a synonym for "heart," indicating the mind. The noun "ambush" (אֹרֶב) is rare (the only other instance, Hos 7:6, is textually

dubious), but the related verb is used in a similar context in Mic 7:2.[10]

■ 8 For the verse in general see 5:9. *M* of this verse differs from 5:9 and 29 by the addition of בָּם (here "by those [punishments]") after the verb in the first colon, an addition, however, which occurs in some MSS. of 5:9 and 29 as well. For the question of text and for the meaning of the addition see the discussion in 5:9.

Aim

Yahweh wishes he could walk out on his people! Why?—are they murderers, torturers? Hardly; at least that is not the center of this indictment. Rather they are indicted for sins of the tongue: they speak lies, they are dishonest, they slander, their speech is hypocritical. Jrm would not understand our modern depreciation of "mere words." Words are crucial. Cursing a deaf person is as harmful as putting a stumbling-block before someone who is blind (Lev 19:14); words tear down a community as thoroughly as does civil war. The community has ceased to be Yahweh's covenant people, the destiny of those named "Israel": instead every member has the character traits of "Jacob." Such a noncommunity Yahweh has no choice but to destroy.

---

8 See Dahood, *Psalms I*, 133–34, on Ps 21:10, where the meaning fits admirably; and see the index of each volume of his *Psalms* under *pānîm* for further suggested instances.

9 See Wildberger, *Jesaja*, 164, and particularly Godfrey R. Driver, "Linguistic and Textual Problems: Isaiah i—xxxix," *JTS* 38 (1937) 38, who connects the word with the Akkadian *batū* "ruin."

10 It is possible that Mic 7:1–7 is in part dependent on the present passage: see James L. Mays, *Micah* (Philadelphia: Westminster, 1976) 150, and compare Hans Walter Wolff, *Micha* (BKAT 14/4; Neukirchen: Neukirchener, 1982) 177–78.

**Even Yahweh Will Weep
Over What Is Lost**

Bibliography
Castellino
"Observations," 403–4.

9

9 [10] For the mountains ᵃI shall lift upᵃ weeping and wailing,
   and for the pastures of the wilderness a
      lamentation:
"Oh, ⟪ they are desolate ⟫ᵇ without a man
   [passing by,]ᶜ
      they have heard no sound of cattle;
         from birds of the heavens to beasts
            they have fled, have gone."
10 [11] And I shall make Jerusalem into stone-
heaps,
   a lair of jackals,
      and the cities of Judah I shall make a
         desolation, withoutᵃ
            inhabitant.

Text

9a—a For M (and 4QJerᵃ) אֶשָּׂא G and S read a plural
imperative, thus שְׂאוּ. Given the form-critical
difficulty of M, Cornill, Condamin, Volz, and
Rudolph prefer G. But M, the *lectio difficilior*, is
preferable (so Duhm, Giesebrecht, Bright); for a full
discussion see Structure, Form, Setting.

b For M נִצְּתוּ "be burned" (יצת nip'al) a few MSS.
read נִתְּצוּ "are destroyed" (נתץ nip'al); on the other
hand G, S, and T all read "are deserted, desolate,"
suggesting a form of נצה, and the verb in v 11
likewise presupposes נצה. These three roots are
virtually synonymous, and Jrm varies them in similar
contexts (compare 2:15; 4:7, 26); the Versions show
much confusion as to which is which. The best
guidance here is context: the adjoining phrases all
bespeak desolation, so that if M cannot imply "be
desolate," the verb should be emended to (נצה) נִצּוּ
nip'al: so Duhm, Giesebrecht, Rudolph, and so KB
and *HALAT*). The taw in M would then be a
copyist's error from v 11. For further discussion of
the meaning of the verb see Interpretation.

c Omitting עֹבֵר with G as a gloss, overloading the
line (see Janzen, p. 38). Verse 11 has מִבְּלִי עֹבֵר,
evidently the source for the gloss here. The phraseology of Zeph 3:6 also suggests that the word is
superfluous here (so again Janzen).

10a For M מִבְּלִי many MSS. read the synonymous
מֵאֵין, and a few the synonymous בְּלִי. Either מִבְּלִי or
מֵאֵין is possible here (contrast 2:15 and 4:7 on this
phraseology, and see again Zeph 3:6).

Structure, Form, Setting

The crucial question here is the verb in the first colon of
v 9. It is clear that Yahweh speaks in v 10. The first-
person singular verb in v 9 presents us with three alternatives. (1) M is correct, and the two verses are two
fragments not originally a unit: then Jrm speaks in v 9,
and Yahweh in v 10 (so Duhm, Bright). Giesebrecht
believes that Yahweh takes up the rhetoric which Jrm
began; Karl Budde makes the same suggestion but
proposes that Yahweh's speech begins with v 9b.[1] (2)
The two verses are a unity, and since one assumes that
Yahweh cannot initiate a lament, one must adopt the G
reading (so Cornill, Condamin, Volz, Rudolph; *RSV, JB,
NAB*). (3) Yahweh initiates a lament: this is the alternative adopted here.

With regard first to the choice between M and G, it is
obvious that M offers the *lectio difficilior*; G appears to be
an accommodation to the jussives in v 17, where similar
vocabulary occurs. With regard, second, to the question
of the unity between the verses, there is no reason to
doubt it. Verse 9 speaks of rural destruction, v 10 of
urban destruction, and they are nicely parallel in the two

---

1 Karl Budde, "Das hebräische Klagelied," *ZAW* 2
   (1882) 22–23.

expressions with "without" (מִבְּלִי), "without a man" in v 9 and "without inhabitant" in v 10. Of course there is no way to insist on unity, but given the sequence of the two verses, unity is more than likely.

Since there is another instance of Yahweh's lament over his heritage in 12:7–13 (so also Rudolph), one is led to propose that Yahweh here also laments;[2] see further Interpretation.

If the setting for this short passage is somewhat later than that for 8:14–23; 9:1–8; and 9:16–21, then the placement of this passage here may be due simply to its being put after "weep" in 8:23 and before "wailing" in 9:17, 18, 19: one might surmise that at the time of the insertion of the present passage 8:14–23 and 9:1–8 were already perceived to be an indivisible pair united by מִי יִתֵּן (literally "who will give?") in 8:23 and 9:1. This explanation is more economical than the more elaborate one which I have proposed earlier.[3]

The genre of v 10 is a announcement of judgment (like 4:7); the content of v 9αβb (the section beginning with כִּי) is a lamentation (for this function of כִּי compare 4:8; 6:26). Yet (unless the two verses are unrelated: see above) the content of v 9αβb is just as much a judgment as is that of v 10, while v 10 might well continue to embody the content of the lamentation begun in v 9; as already noted, the images of v 9 are rural, those of v 10 urban. Verse 9αα is thus Yahweh's announcement of his lament. In sum: if the passage is understood rightly, it is both a lament and a judgment speech in the mind of Yahweh: here is a passage in which divine pathos and judgment are blended.

Verse 9αα is a bicolon; the rest of the verse (beginning with כִּי) is best analyzed as a tricolon (third plural verbs in each colon). Verse 10 is likewise a tricolon (for the place of the phrase "without inhabitant" in the analysis of cola see the discussion in 2:15, Structure).

There is no reason to doubt the genuineness of this short passage: the diction is Jrm's, and the notion that Yahweh raises a lament is a striking one, worthy of Jrm.

But clues for a more specific setting are slim. The diction of v 9 suggests the drought here dated to 601–600 (compare the loss of "beasts and birds" in 12:4 and the mention of "pastures of the wilderness" in 23:10). Form-critically the passage is closest to 12:7–13. One can imagine that once Jehoiakim had burned Jrm's scroll in December 601, and Jrm became convinced that Yahweh's punishment of the people was inevitable, Jrm might perceive Yahweh to lament the inevitability of that punishment: the winter of 600 is therefore a plausible setting.

Interpretation

■ 9 For the conclusion that Yahweh is the speaker in this verse as well as in v 10, see Structure, Form, Setting. In 8:23 Jrm wishes to weep for his people; here Yahweh, it appears, wishes to weep, not so much for his people as for the territory given to the people (a note also struck in 12:7–13, another lament by Yahweh). The preposition עַל is ambiguous here: it may be "on the mountains," "on the pastures"; but since one weeps "on" or "over" a dead body, the preposition is used regularly for the object of the lament and is surely so intended here (see the discussion of Volz). For the phrase "lift up" with the object an expression of lamentation compare Amos 5:1. The word "wailing" (נְהִי) is not a common one, but it does occur several times in Jrm's poetry (see 17–19; 31:15).

One must bear in mind that "wilderness" (מִדְבָּר) does not necessarily denote the sandy desert but is often (as here) associated with pasturage (Exod 3:1); it refers to "agriculturally unexploited areas, mainly in the foothills of southern Palestine, which serve as the grazing land par excellence for the flocks."[4] The phrase "pastures of the wilderness" is a set phrase, appearing also in 23:10; Ps 65:13; and three times in Joel (1:19, 20; 2:22). Later Ezekiel would develop further the image of the curse on mountains and pastures (Ezek 36:1–14).

For the understanding of כִּי to introduce the content of the lament see Structure, Form, Setting, and compare

2   So also Berend J. Oosterhoff, "Ein Detail aus der Weisheitslehre (Jer. 9,11ff.)," *Travels in the World of the Old Testament, Studies Presented to Professor M. A. Beek on the Occasion of his 65th Birthday* (ed. M. S. H. G. Heerma van Voss et al.; Assen: Van Gorcum, 1974) 197.

3   Holladay, *Architecture*, 113–16.

4   Shemaryahu Talmon, "The 'Desert Motif' in the

Bible and in Qumran Literature," *Biblical Motifs: Origins and Transformations* (ed. Alexander Altmann; Cambridge: Harvard University, 1966) 40.

4:8 and 6:26.

The identity of the verb which immediately follows כִּי is a puzzle (see Text); if *M* were correct, it would be odd that "they are burned" is applied to mountains and pastures. Giesebrecht is impelled to insist that the image is not that of a prairie fire but is simply a vivid way of depicting devastation, but the tradition in the Versions, "they are desolate," is doubtless correct: no people, no cattle, no birds or beasts. There is a hint here of the absence of both domestic creatures and wild ones: "without a man" suggests inhabitants, and "cattle" (מִקְנֶה) are owned by someone, while "birds of the heavens" and "beasts" are a standard pair beginning with Gen 2:19. For the image of the disappearance of birds see 4:25. The disappearance of both birds and beasts here suggests that the covenant with Noah is now abrogated (Gen 9:10). For the abrogation of the covenant with Abraham and Jacob see 20:1–6.

■ **10** The mention of Jerusalem comes on abruptly, but it is the city par excellence in contrast to the rural scene of v 9. Does the notion that Yahweh belongs in Zion (8:19) play a part here? It is not only modern artillery and bombs that reduce a city to rubble: ancient warfare accomplished the same result (Job 15:28)—compare Jesus' words regarding the temple buildings in Jerusalem in his day (Mark 13:2). The jackal (*Canis aureus*) haunts waste places far from human habitation (Isa 34:13–14): that they should howl in the edifices of Jerusalem is horrifying (compare similar words about Babylon in Isa 13:22). For the last colon compare 2:15; 4:7.

Aim

If the passage is here understood rightly, it takes us into the inner musing of God. This was the case with 3:19 and 9:1 and will be the case with 12:7–13, but the present passage is unique in setting forth God's impulse to weep over what he has lost. The NT found the focal point for this insight in the weeping of the man who revealed God (Luke 19:41–44), but the OT was not afraid to affirm the weeping of God himself. "God's pain and disappointment ring throughout the book of Jeremiah. . . . The heart of melancholy beats in God's words."[5]

---

5   Heschel, *The Prophets*, 109–10; see further 110–12, 221–25.

An Explanation for Misery

Bibliography

Long
"Schemata," 129–39.
McKane
"Poison."
Oosterhoff
"Detail."

9

11 [12] **Who is the wise man? Let him understand this, and let him to whom the mouth of the LORD has spoken declare it! Why is the land ruined and desolate like the wilderness without a passer-by? 12 [13]/ And the LORD said, "Because they have abandoned my law which I set before them, and did not obey my voice [nor walk in it,]ª 13 [14]/ and walked after the stubbornness of their heartª and after the Baals of which their fathers taught them." 14 [15]/ Therefore thus the LORD of hosts, the God of Israel, has said, "I am going to feed them [this people]ª wormwood and give them poisonedᵇ water to drink; 15 [16]/ and I shall scatter them among nations whom neither they nor their fathers have known,ª and I shall send after them the sword until I have destroyed them."**

Text

12a   "In it" refers to "my law"; the expression is distant from its reference and the whole clause "nor walk in it" is lacking in *G*. The clause is an expansionist gloss based upon a passage like 26:4 (Janzen, p. 38).

13a   A few MSS., *G*, and *S* add הָרָע after לִבָּם, that is, "their evil heart." This is an expansion from 3:17 and 7:24.

14a   *M* has אֶת־הָעָם הַזֶּה as well as the object suffix on the participle; *G* does not have the phrase, and it is clearly a gloss or an evidence of a conflate text (compare Janzen, p. 11).

b   Instead of the normal reading רֹאשׁ some MSS. read the alternate spelling רוֹשׁ.

15a   A few MSS. read יְדָעוּם instead of יְדָעוּ. The suffix is unnecessary to reinforce the relative אֲשֶׁר; the meaning is unaffected.

Structure, Form, Setting

The passage is here primarily because v 11 reflects v 9, secondarily because v 14 reflects 8:14. The passage has two subsections (vv 11–13, 14–15). The first raises the question, "Why [עַל־מָה] is the land ruined . . . ?" and answers it, "Because they have abandoned [עַל־עָזְבָם] . . ."; this is the kind of question-and-answer schema found in 5:19 and elsewhere, a form coming out of the milieu of wisdom. Long discusses the passage briefly[1] and concludes that though related to his "Type B," for which compare 5:19, the form has been elaborated by Deuteronomistic influence. The second section here, vv 14–15, is a judgment speech beginning with the messenger formula.[2]

The closest form-critical parallel with v 11 is Hos

14:10 and Ps 107:43. It is clear from this trio of passages that we have to do here with commentary on the fixed wording of a text (whether that text is oral or written is immaterial).[3] The stress on the ruin of the land suggests the origin of this material at least in the exilic if not in the postexilic period.

To the question raised by the interpreter of the tradition, "Why has all this happened?" the answer comes as a divine word couched in Jeremianic phrases (for the details see Interpretation). Therefore by definition the material conveys to the audience Jeremianic tradition, though one may doubt whether that tradition has any independent validity.

From the point of view both of the phraseology of the passage and of its form criticism the passage must be

---

1   Long, "Schemata," 134, 138, 139.
2   Oosterhoff, "Detail," 198.
3   Wolff, *Hosea*, 239.

judged late. Many of the phrases are of course those used by Jrm, but they appear to be used derivatively; in general the phraseology of the passage is quite mixed (for the details see Interpretation). As for form criticism, the messenger formula (v 14) is the normal transition between an accusation and the announcement of judgment (compare, for example, 8:4–13).[4] But vv 12–13 are not an accusation in the first instance; they are the explanation for the question posed in v 11. Either of two conclusions is possible: either the wisdom passage in vv 11–13 arose, perhaps in the exilic period, and vv 14–15 were added still later, or else the whole sequence was devised at a time when the awareness of the form of the announcement of judgment had faded. The indications are that that time was well into the postexilic period.[5]

Interpretation

■ **11** The syntax of the verse gives difficulty. Is "To whom has the mouth of the Lord spoken?" parallel with "Who is the wise man?" so that there is a parallel between divine revelation and human wisdom? Bright groups the words this way, and this is the presentation of several recent translations (*RSV*: "Who is the man so wise that he can understand this? To whom has the mouth of the Lord spoken, that he may declare it?"— and similarly *JB* and *NJV*). Then some of these translations begin a new question with "Why is the land ruined?" (Bright, *RSV*), while some take "Why is the land ruined?" as anticipated by the suffix ("it") in the previous question (*JB*: "Who has been charged by Yahweh's own mouth to tell why the land lies in ruins . . . ?"). None of this seems rightly to reflect וַאֲשֶׁר; if the clauses were truly parallel one would expect וְאֶל־מִי (1 Sam 6:20) instead of וַאֲשֶׁר. The next difficulty is the relation between the opening clause "Who is the wise man?" and the clause which follows; is the second clause a subordinate result clause (so most, e.g., *NAB*: "Who is so wise that he can understand this?"),[6] or is the first clause a relative clause depending on a following jussive (Luther: "Whoever is

wise, let him understand this"),[7] or are the two clauses separate, an independent question followed by a jussive (so the translation here)? It is clear that we are dealing with a form-critical pattern; Hos 14:10 is very close (מִי חָכָם וְיָבֵן אֵלֶּה), and similarly Ps 107:43. Berend J. Oosterhoff argues convincingly that after a clause introduced by מִי מִי or מָה a result clause is introduced by כִּי (Exod 3:11, "Who am I that I should go to Pharaoh?").[8] Similarly the "whoever" construction exists in Hebrew but appears to be expressed by a question followed by a jussive unconnected by וּ (Exod 24:14, מִי־בַעַל דְּבָרִים יִגַּשׁ אֲלֵהֶם).[9] It is therefore safer to follow Oosterhoff in translating the present passage (and Hos 14:10 and Ps 107:43) by two independent clauses.

Rudolph and Bright propose that the verb וְיָבֵן is hip'il and that it therefore means "explain" rather than "understand." But in the imperfect the qal and hip'il of בִּין are identical, and in any case the hip'il of this verb can mean either "understand" (Isa 29:16) or "teach, explain" (Job 6:24). One must therefore be guided by the form-critical parallels: in Hos 14:10 the verb is parallel to "let him know them," and in Ps 107:43 the verb that follows is "let him observe." Clearly "understand" is the meaning.

The point of the first half of the verse then is that anyone to whom wisdom is attributed will have such wisdom because of God's revelatory activity and should put his talent to grasping the words of Jer. It should be noted that "the mouth of the Lord has spoken" is a phrase not otherwise found in Jer, though it is in the Isaianic corpus and in Micah (Isa 1:20; 40:5; 58:14; Mic 4:4).

The second half of the verse is a paraphrase of v 9 (compare Structure, Form, Setting).

■ **12–13** God's answer ensues. The phrase "my law which I set before them" is also found in 26:4, but curiously enough "abandon" (עזב) with "law" is found nowhere else in Jer (usually the object is God himself; "covenant" occurs in 22:9); the phrase occurs only three times otherwise (Ps 89:31; Prov 4:2; 2 Chr 12:1). The phrase

---

4   See further Westermann, *Basic Forms*, 174–75.
5   See Wolff, *Hosea*, 239, on the setting for Hos 14:10.
6   So GKC, sec. 166a.
7   So Carl Brockelmann, *Hebräische Syntax* (Neukirchen: Erziehungsverein, 1956) sec. 157, on the parallel Hos 14:10.
8   Oosterhoff, "Detail," 199.

9   So also Judg 7:3; Isa 50:8b; 54:15; Prov 9:4a = 16a; Ezra 1:3.

"did not obey my voice" occurs in Jrm's poetry in 3:13 and 22:21 and often in prose (e.g., 7:28). The phrase "walk after the stubbornness of one's heart" occurs in 23:17 and often in prose (e.g., 7:24). "Walk after the Baals" is adapted from 2:23, but the phrase "Baals of which their fathers taught them" is unique in the OT; the nearest is "they taught my people to swear by Baal" in 12:16. God's answer sounds stereotyped and is close to the diction of a passage like 7:24 but by no means slavishly imitates any sequence elsewhere. It expresses the conviction that the land is ruined because the people left the expressions of God's will and followed instead spurious impulses of their own.

■ **14–15** The judgment speech begins with the messenger formula and continues with phrases derived from 23:15. "Give them poisoned water to drink" is found in 8:14, but its parallel "feed them wormwood" is found only here and in 23:15. "Wormwood" (לַעֲנָה), *Artemisia herba-alba* or *A. absinthium* is a low shrub with extremely bitter leaves and fruit used in folk medicine.[10] "Scatter them among nations" is similar to a phrase in 30:11. "Nations whom they/you have not known" is found only otherwise in Ezek 32:9, though the same phrase, using "land,"

is found five times in Jer, e.g., 16:13. The phraseology of the last half of the verse is found otherwise only in 49:37, in the oracle against Elam. God states, then, that he will poison the people, exile them, and kill them in battle.

Aim

The misery to which the Jews were reduced only began with the exile in 587; it continued through the Persian period (and beyond). Thus it is clear from archeological evidence that the population of Palestine was far lower in the Persian period than at the end of the monarchy: for example, Magen Broshi has estimated the population of Jerusalem at 20,000 in Josiah's time, and at 4,800 in the period just before Alexander the Great.[11] In view of the high destiny for Israel which the tradition had taught, that misery continued to call for explanation; and when the misery was anticipated by words of judgment from Jer, the old words stimulated the framing of question-and-answer material which served to give some perspective to the life of a community convinced it was forgotten in the events of the Persian period.

---

10   Michael Zohary, "Flora," *IDB* 2:297b.
11   Magen Broshi, "La population de l'ancienne Jérusalem," *RB* 82 (1975) 13; compare his "Esti-mating the Population of Ancient Jerusalem," *BAR* 4/2 (June 1978) 12–13.

Death Has Entered Our Citadels

Bibliography

Paul, Shalom M.

"Cuneiform Light on Jer 9,20," *Bib* 49 (1968) 373–76.

9

16 [17]   [Thus Yahweh of hosts has said:]ª
ᵇ **Make inquiry and call the dirge-
women and let them come,**
and for the skilled women send《 and
let them hurry 》《 and pour (it)
forth, 》

17 [18]   [. . .]ᵇ **and let them raise over us a**
wailing,
that our eyes may run down with
tears
and our pupils flow with water:

18 [19]   "Oh, the sound of wailing is heard ª from
Zion:ª

Text

16a   Omit as an erroneous messenger formula; Jrm speaks (see v 17, and the discussion in Structure and Form). *G* here has simply λέγει κύριος, but this may reflect a text tradition which had נְאֻם־יהוה at the end of v 15.

16–17b—b   The texts of *M* and *G* contrast in v 16aβb and the first word of v 17. *G* is shorter and offers an acceptable reading: "Call the dirge-women and let them come, and for the skilled women send and let them speak out, [(17) and let them raise over us . . .]." There are thus three contrasts. (1) *G* omits הִתְבּוֹנְנוּ וְ (as does *S* as well), and the expression is therefore omitted by Cornill, Giesebrecht, Volz, and Bright. But there is no need to omit it; the verb is associated with שִׁלְחוּ elsewhere (2:10) and is here in assonance with לַמְקוֹנְנוֹת and וּתְבוֹאֶינָה. I propose that in the poetic structure two imperatives and one jussive in this colon balance one imperative and two jussives in the following colon (see [3] below, and see Structure and Form); *M* should thus be retained here. (2) In the second colon *M* reads "and for the skilled women send so they may come [וְתָבוֹאנָה]": thus the second colon ends with the same verb with which the first ended, and, assuming a dittography, Cornill and Giesebrecht omit the second occurrence, while Rudolph omits the first occurrence. But for the second "so they may come" *G* reads καὶ φθεγξάσθωσαν "and let them speak out"; this verb (φθέγγεσθαι) translates נבע hip'il in Pss 78:2 and 94:4, a circumstance suggesting the reading proposed here, וְתַבַּעְנָה. Thus both verbs may stand. (3) *G* omits "so they may hurry" (וּתְמַהֵרְנָה) which in *M* is the first word of v 17. But the word is not a gloss and surely belongs, and one can conclude that with "let them pour (it) forth" it balances the two imperatives in the previous colon (see [1] above). But semantically it balances "so they may come"; I therefore propose that if it was omitted by haplography in the text tradition which produced *G*, in the text tradition which produced *M* it was written in the margin and reintroduced into the text at the wrong spot, after "so they may pour (it) forth" instead of before it.

18a—a   A few MSS. and *G* read בְּצִיּוֹן "in Zion"; either reading will do, but מִן is doubtless preferable, given

'How ruined, how deeply shamed we
are!'"
"Oh, we have left the land!"
^b and "Oh,^b 《 we are thrown 》^c from
our tabernacle!"

19 [20] "Hear, you women, the word of Yahweh,
and let your ear take up the word of his
mouth,
and teach your daughters a wailing,
and each her neighbor a dirge:

20 [21] 'Oh, Death has climbed through our
windows,
has entered our citadels,
to cut off the children from the
streets,
the youth from the squares,

21 [22] [Speak, thus (is the) oracle of Yahweh:]^a
so that corpses of people fall
like dung on the face of the field,^b
and like grain-stalks behind the
reaper,
and no one gathering.'"

my suggestion that it does double duty in the last
colon (see note c below).

b—b For *M* כִּי many MSS. read וְכִי, and *G* and *S* read וְ;
וְכִי is to be preferred (see Structure and Form).

c *M* reads הִשְׁלִיכוּ, thus "They have cast [or, thrown
away] our dwellings," presumably meaning "They
have cast down our dwellings," and *V* and *T* take this
as an impersonal "Our dwellings are cast down." But
this use of שׁלך hip'il is odd and gives poor parallelism. *G* ἀπερρίψαμεν "we have abandoned" gives
warrant to presume a text השלכנו. But an active
verb gives difficulty: in the meaning "reject" this
verb takes objects which are repellant (unacceptable
meat, Exod 22:30; cords of bondage, Ps 2:3). It is
dubious to presume the verb used by the people here of
their own homes (or Yahweh's dwelling: see Interpretation) in a lament. The proposal that Rudolph
makes hesitantly is best, to read a hop'al, הָשְׁלַכְנוּ: it
employs the consonants presupposed by *G* and gives
good parallelism. Note that שׁלך hop'al in 22:28
appears in a very similar context. I further propose
that מִן in the first colon does double duty here.

21a The words are missing in *G* and are out of
context; indeed the phraseology is completely odd.
Since θ' translates by θανάτῳ "with death," one may
assume that the phrase began as a marginal gloss
דֶּבֶר "pestilence" as an explanation of מָוֶת "death,"
inasmuch as מָוֶת specifically means "pestilence" in
15:2; 18:21; and 43:11. If דֶּבֶר were written and
then revocalized as דַּבֵּר "speak," the present text
might have emerged.

b For *M* הַשָּׂדֶה some MSS. and *G* read הָאֲדָמָה "the
ground." The latter word appears consistently in the
prose passages (8:2; 16:4; 25:26, 33; 28:16; 35:7)
and is here clearly an accommodation to them. Read
M.

Structure and Form

All commentaries agree that vv 16–21 make up a unit,
though the passage does break into two halves, vv 16–18
and 19–21 (compare Condamin). But unless the conjunction כִּי at the beginning of v 19 is unoriginal, v 19 must
in some way offer a continuation (see below). The
passage is part of the basic stratum of this section of Jrm's
second scroll, alongside 8:14–23; 9:1–8; 10:17–25; and
perhaps 9:9–10. It shares with 8:14–23 and 9:9–10 the
theme of weeping and wailing (8:23; 9:9), and with 8:14–
23 and 10:17–25 the verb "gather" (אסף, v 21 here, see
8:14 and 10:17); these associations doubtless dictated the
placement of the passage here.

Basic to the organization of the passage is the remarkable series of five occurrences of כִּי (v 18, three times; v
19, v 20): the conventional translations of "for" and
"because" (as in *RSV*) may not do the situation justice.
And involved with one's understanding of the function

of the successive occurrences of כִּי is an understanding of
the boundaries and levels of the quotational material in
the passage. Many translations and commentators do not
try to mark the material with quotation marks; those that
do come to various solutions. Most see in the material in
v 18 after "from Zion" as a single lament, the content of
the sound of wailing (thus Bright: "How ruined are we,
How covered with shame! For we must leave the land, be
hurled from our homes!"; so Volz, Condamin, Rudolph,
JB). But commentators and translations differ on their
treatment of vv 19–21: thus Condamin and Bright see no
quotational material here, introducing v 20 with the
conventional "for." *JB* to the contrary assumes that vv
20–21 are the content of a single lament which the
women are to teach each other (v 19), while Volz
similarly sees vv 20–21 as quotational material, but as
two laments, v 20 and v 21, and Rudolph sees v 19b as
the beginning of the "word of Yahweh" (referred to in v

19a) and implies (by a colon at the end of v 19) that vv 20–21 are a single subquotation. Clearly the matter needs careful examination.

It is best to begin with vv 19–21. Rudolph's division of v 19 is implausible, and he must omit "and" before "teach" to begin a quotation with v 19b. By the same token Volz's analysis of vv 20–21 into two laments is forced; the actions described in v 21 are consequent on those in v 20. It seems clear then that vv 20–21 is the content of the lament enjoined in v 19; the lament is introduced by כִּי as the laments are in 4:8 and 6:26.

The women addressed in v 19 are to be identified with the "dirge-women" and "skilled women" summoned in v 16. Those told in v 16 to summon the women are expected to address them, but the speech they are to give to the women is deferred till v 19. That speech to the women is thus a quotation, one introduced by כִּי. Verses 19–21 are therefore to be set off with quotation marks, and vv 20–21 by subordinate quotation marks.

Within v 18 it is clear that אֵיךְ שֻׁדַּדְנוּ בֹּשְׁנוּ מְאֹד "How ruined, deeply shamed we are!" is (at least part of) a lament: one may compare כִּי שֻׁדָּדְנוּ in 4:13, which would seem to have the same value. Several considerations suggest that the first colon of v 18 is itself a lament, parallel to two other laments in the third and fourth cola of the verse. (1) The first and third cola begin with כִּי, and (in the text preferred here) the fourth colon begins with וְכִי; this suggests the possibility of parity in the first, third, and fourth cola. (2) There is the possibility that מִן "from [Zion]" in the first colon does double duty in the fourth ("from our tabernacle"): see Interpretation. (3) The diction of imperatives in v 19 moves to perfect verbs in the subquotation in v 20; so the diction of imperatives in v 16 (and of their associated jussives in v 17) moves to perfect verbs in v 18. These considerations suggest that the first, third, and fourth cola in v 18 are parallel expressions, each introduced by כִּי, of the "wailing" mentioned in v 17, and that the second colon, introduced by אֵיךְ, is the expression of the "wailing" referred

to in the first colon. By this understanding none of the occurrences of כִּי is to be understood to mean "for" or the like.

The passage (as already affirmed) breaks into two subsections, vv 16–18 and 19–21; vv 16–17 embody a summons, and v 18 a series of laments; v 19 is again a summons, and vv 20–21 embody a lament. Is there a hint of chiasmus in the two sequences of lament?—one hears of "the land" and then "our tabernacle" (or in an alternative translation "our dwellings") in v 18, while v 20 offers urban images and then v 21 rural ones.

Verses 19, 20, and 21 are each tetracola.[1] Verse 19 contains the imperatives to the women to lament, and vv 20–21 are the content of that lament. There is a nice contrast between the "climbing" (עלה) of Death in the first colon of v 20 and the "falling" (נפל) of the corpses in the first colon of v 21 (the same antonymous parallelism is found in Isa 14:12–13). Verse 18 is likewise a tetracolon (compare the discussion above on the quotations in that verse). This leaves vv 16–17, which are best understood as a pentacolon: the first two cola (in v 16) are tightly parallel, two imperatives and one jussive in the first colon, an imperative and two jussives in the second. The third colon (which begins v 17) offers a further jussive parallel to the last jussive of the second colon (which ends v 16), and the last two cola are dependent on the third. Question: Given the parallelism between "climb" in v 20 and "fall" in v 21, is there an analogous parallel between "raise" (נשא) and "run down" (ירד) in v 17?

Jrm summoned the people to lament in 4:8; similarly Jrm is the speaker here (note the first-person plural suffixes in v 17).

The summons to lament in the OT is often a simple call to the community to lament the death of an individual, but sometimes it is concerned with communal tragedy, and the community is summoned to lament in the context of public fasting, prayer, and repentance: Joel 1:5–14 is a prime example.[2] The prophet used the

---

1 For וְאֵין as a verb substitute in the last colon of v 21 see O'Connor, *Structure*, 304, and, for example, 197 on Deut 32:12b.

2 See the analysis of this form in Hans Walter Wolff, "Der Aufruf zur Volksklage," *ZAW* 76 (1964) 48–56 = his *Gesammelte Studien zum Alten Testament* (Munich: Kaiser, 1973) 392–401, and a summary in his *Joel and Amos*, 21–22.

summons to lament, blending both settings, in what must have been ad hoc appeals to the community to lament over fallen Israel,[3] but until this time in Jrm's career such appeals appear to be couched in contexts where repentance is at least a theoretical possibility. But in the present passage one may surmise that Jrm is appealing to the traditional mourning women to lament the death of the community exactly as they would be summoned to lament the death of a fallen hero. There is here no implication of a call to repentance, not even an indirect one (compare Setting, and compare the contexts of 4:8 and 6:26 and their settings); rather one hears the death knell of the people.

There is another possibility, and that is that Jrm is here mocking the women who lament the dead Baal. There is precedent in Elijah's mocking of the prophets of Baal: Elijah characterized the god as sleeping or otherwise unavailable (1 Kgs 18:27). Specifically there seems to be in the present passage a reminiscence of Jezebel, who had sponsored the prophets of Baal in Elijah's day (v 21). But the various indications that the passage is Jrm's mockery of the women who lament the dead Baal are not obvious: they are discussed in detail in Interpretation, vv 16–17, 19, 20–21.

The laments share the marks of that form, being introduced by כִּי (vv 18, 20: compare 4:8; 6:26) or אֵיךְ (v 18, compare 2 Sam 1:25, 27; Lam 1:1; 2:1; 4:1); the verb "ruin" (שדד) is employed (v 18, compare 4:13). And in the lament of vv 20–21 a mythological image is used which lends cosmic resonance to the tragedy (see Interpretation on "Death" in v 20).

Out of this passage will come the laments of the Book of Lamentations when other poets are aroused by the historical event of the fall of Jerusalem itself.

Setting

There are several small indications that point toward a setting for this passage. (1) "To cut off the children from the streets, the youth from the squares" is close to "Pour (it) out on the children in the streets, and on the circle of youths as well" in 6:11; the setting assigned to that passage in the present study is December 601 or early 600 (see there). (2) If the reconstruction of שלך hopʿal in

v 18 is correct, the occurrence of that same form in 22:28 is comparable; there Jehoiachin and his offspring "are thrown out" of their land, and the setting of that passage is therefore early in 597. (3) If the passages forming the basic stratum of this section of the book were added to the second scroll chronologically, as is altogether possible, and 10:17–25 is to be dated to the first siege of Jerusalem (December 598 to March 597), then the date of the present passage is previous to that siege. (4) One cannot be certain how much the passage presupposes a setting during the drought (see Interpretation, vv 16–17, 19, 20–21), nor can it be determined how long the drought might have persisted, but the passage seems to imply the continuation of the drought. All these considerations suggest that a setting early in 600 is not unlikely, with the possibility open that it might have been uttered several months later.

Interpretation

■ 16–17 For בִּין (הִתְבּוֹנְנוּ hitpoʿlel) see 2:10. There the verb means "take a good look and draw your conclusions," but here it is not so clear; it may mean "keep alert, pay attention" (so Rudolph, and compare the nuance of Ps 37:10), or it may mean "behave with understanding," that is "be prudent" (so HALAT, compare the nuance of Ps 119:100).

The word translated here "dirge-women" is a unique feminine participle מְקוֹנְנוֹת. The verb is evidently a denominative; the participle then means "one who chants a קִינָה (dirge)," the Irish "keener." The parallel here is חֲכָמוֹת, literally "wise women." This is the only reference in the OT to professional mourning women, but Jerome remarks in the fourth century, "This custom continues everywhere in Judea today; women scatter their hair and bare their breasts and then adjust their voice to rouse everyone to weeping." Missionaries and travelers in the Near East in the nineteenth century found the same custom among the Muslims; typical is the following description from the Damascus area: "At funerals, and over graves in which relatives and friends have recently been buried, manifestations of grief are often boisterous and extravagant; but many of the mourners are hired for the occasion, and weep, lament, beat their breasts, and

---

3   See the discussion in Eissfeldt, *Introduction*, 95–96.

tear their hair, according to custom and contract."[4] But more may be involved here than a reference to village women mourning the dead: it is possible that Jrm here is summoning those women who mourn the death of Baal and is mocking them.[5] The only OT passage bearing on the question is Ezek 8:14, "And he brought me to the entrance of the gate of the house of Yahweh, which lies toward the north, and behold, there were women who were sitting down and weeping for Tammuz." Though Tammuz was a Babylonian deity, identified with Adonis (= Baal) only (as far as one is aware) by Origen and Jerome, both in Babylonia and in Syria-Palestine the same customs of lamenting the dying and rising god seem to have prevailed.[6] If Jrm is mocking those who mourn the dying Baal, is the great drought under way (compare Setting)? Clearly the metaphors here are of the production of water, implied by "pour (it) forth" in v 16 and by the expressions in v 17 (for the details see below)—as those in v 21 are of manure and grain stalks.

The verb "pour forth" (נבע hip'il), an emendation at the end of v 16, occurs several times in the metaphor of pouring forth speech (e.g., Ps 19:3), but the base meaning is of pouring forth water (a related noun, מַבּוּעַ, is a "spring," Isa 35:7; 49:10); if the reading is here correct, and if the context presupposes the drought, the word contributes to the irony: Jrm is telling the women to "start bubbling forth."

The drumbeat of feminine plural nouns and verbs makes a striking impression here; the verbs particularly are long, wĕtābō'énā, ûtĕmahērnā, wĕtiśśénā, whose sound ironically contrasts with the wish for the women to

hurry: does one imagine stiff, elderly women struggling to assemble for their task? For the assonance of the verbs in v 16, see Text, note b—b; the effect of the sound of the whole passage, then, must be deliberate.

The vocabulary of v 17 is similar to that in v 1. The parallel to "eyes," עַפְעַפַּיִם, has been widely misunderstood: it is not "eyelids" (so G, V, and most translations) or "eyelashes" (Volz, Rudolph, Bright) but simply a poetic synonym for the eye itself, thus "pupil" (S) or "eyeball" (T). In a Ugaritic text the 'p'pm of the maiden Ḥuray are described as "bowls of onyx"[7] (note also Prov 4:25, where the עַפְעַפִּים "look straight ahead").[8] Its verb, "flow" (נזל), is normally used of water or clouds (18:14).

■ **18** The mention of "Zion" here is surprising and raises the question whether the noun in the last colon, מִשְׁכְּנוֹתֵינוּ, does not balance it and mean "our tabernacle" (see below). Zion is central to Jrm's concern; the funeral women are to prepare a dirge for the death of a whole people and a whole land, and their center is Zion.

For "we are ruined" see 4:13; for "be shamed" see 2:26. The people lament that they have been forced to "leave" (עזב) the land; similarly in 4:29 it was the cities that were abandoned. All that is central and dear to the people must be left.

Though מִשְׁכְּנוֹתֵינוּ here is universally translated "our homes" or "our dwellings," it is used (in the plural) of Yahweh's dwelling on Zion (Ezek 37:27; Pss 43:3; 84:2; 132:5, 7); the expression here seems deliberately ambiguous.

■ **19** The feminine plural imperatives continue; the two occurrences here of the suffix כֶם with feminine refer-

4 William M. Thomson, *The Land and the Book* (New York: Harper, 1880–85) 3:401–2. For general discussion and further bibliography see Edmond Jacob, "Mourning," *IDB* 3:453–54.

5 The suggestion that the women are Baal mourners is found in Elmer A. Leslie, *Old Testament Religion in the Light of its Canaanite Background* (New York: Abingdon, 1936) 212; I owe this reference, and the further suggestion that Jrm is mocking the women, to my former student the Rev. Mr. James A. Tilbe.

6 For a convenient presentation of a text of Ishtar's lament for Tammuz, see *ANET,* 109a; for a short recent treatment of Tammuz and Adonis, with recent bibliography, see Zimmerli, *Ezekiel 1,* 242–43, and for an older treatment, with more details, see George A. Cooke, *A Critical and Exegetical Commentary on the Book of Ezekiel* (ICC; New York:

Scribner's, 1936) 96–99.

7 Ug. 14.147–48, 295.

8 See Harold Louis Ginsberg, *The Legend of King Keret* (*BASOR* Supplementary Studies 2–3; New Haven: American Schools of Oriental Research, 1946) 39; Christianus H. W. Brekelmans, review of Joseph Aistleitner, *Wörterbuch der ugaritischen Sprache,* in *BO* 23 (1966) 308; Dahood, *Psalms I,* 70, on Ps 11:4, and *Psalms III,* 244, on Ps 132:4.

ence are curious.[9] One is accustomed to hear the command "hear the word of Yahweh" in the masculine plural, but this is the only instance of that phrase in the feminine plural in the OT. How ironic that the masculine address is so frequently a summons to hear an appeal to repentance (e.g., 2:4), while the only feminine address is to help bury the covenant people; how horrible that those who are supporters of life are asked to deal with wholesale death![10] And having heard the word, the women are to pass it on to others. Though the profession of dirge-women was no doubt hereditary,[11] the word "daughters" here simply stands in parallel with "neighbors" (compare the rhetorical use of "daughters" in 2 Sam 1:24). Or is this a parody of Deut 11:19, where the words of Yahweh's covenant are to be taught to the "children" or "sons" (בָּנִים)?

■ **20–21** This lament begins with a personification of Death (מָוֶת). Since there was a god Mōt who functioned in the Ugaritic pantheon as the archenemy of Baal,[12] there has been widespread discussion of the relation between the present passage and the Ugaritic texts. Thus it was suggested by Umberto Cassuto[13] that when Baal does not want to put a window in his palace,[14] it is because he wants to prevent Mōt from kidnaping his daughters; and several later scholars picked up the idea.[15] Linked with this suggestion is the proposal that "our citadels" (אַרְמְנוֹתֵינוּ) in v 20 should be emended to "our lattices" (אֲרֻבּוֹתֵינוּ) on the basis of the Ugaritic text.[16] These proposals, however, are not justified (for the soundness of the expression "our citadels" see below); a far closer parallel is offered by Babylonian texts

contemporaneous with Jrm which refer to a demon Lamaštu, who enters through windows and climbs over walls to prey on infants and young people.[17] In any event if Jrm's image of Death was based on Canaanite patterns, he may well be suggesting ironically that if the people resort to Baal, it is Baal's enemy that will respond. "Death" implies pestilence (see Text, v 21, note a), carrying off children; the infant mortality rate in those times must have been tragically high (compare Isa 65:20).[18] The Canaanite mythological background is responsible not only for the personification of Death here but elsewhere (Hos 13:14; Ps 49:15; Job 18:14: see the standard commentaries). Many cultures have personified death;[19] but this passage was the specific stimulus for rabbinic speculation on the angel of death,[20] and, stimulated by the image of the fourth horseman in Rev 6:8, it passed into Christian symbolism[21] as the "Reaper" (compare Volz), particularly after the time of the Black Death in the fourteenth century.[22]

The impression of Canaanite background for the figure of Death increases with the mention of "windows," given the evidence of a literary motif of the harlot peering through the window (see on 4:30), and of ivory plaques surviving from Nimrud which evidently represent Astarte peering through a window.[23]

For "citadels" see 6:5. The parallelism of "windows" with "citadels" is odd (see above), but the same association of ideas is found with different terminology in Joel 2:9; the point is that there is no hiding place, not in one's home, not even in the ultimate citadel of the city.

The insistence of Volz and Rudolph that the infinitive

9 For a discussion see König, *Syntax*, sec. 9.
10 This last suggestion I owe to my former student the Rev. Ms. Suzanne Burris.
11 So Jacob, "Mourning," 453b.
12 Marvin H. Pope, "Mot," *IDBSup* 607–8.
13 Umberto Cassuto, "Il palazzo di Ba'al nella tavola II AB di Ras Shamra," *Or* 7 (1938) 265–90, esp. 285–86 = "The Palace of Baal in Tablet II AB of Ras Shamra," *Biblical and Oriental Studies II* (Jerusalem: Hebrew University, 1975) 113–39, esp. 134; see also his "The Palace of Baal," *JBL* 61 (1942) 51–56.
14 Ug. 4.5.123–27.
15 So Alfred Pohl, "Miszellen, 3) Jeremias 9,20," *Bib* 22 (1941) 36–37; Harold Louis Ginsberg, "The Ugaritic Texts and Textual Criticism," *JBL* 62 (1943) 113–14; and see notably Hyatt, p. 893.
16 So Ginsberg (see n. 15).
17 Shalom M. Paul, "Cuneiform Light on Jer 9,20," *Bib* 49 (1968) 374–76.
18 Compare Edward Neufeld, "Hygiene Conditions in Ancient Israel (Iron Age)," *BA* 34 (1971) 42–66, esp. the remarks on infant mortality, 49–50.
19 A. Closs, "Death (Primitive Concepts of)," *New Catholic Encyclopedia* (New York: McGraw-Hill, 1967) 4:686–87 with bibliography; for classical Greek personifications, see Rudolf Bultmann, "θάνατος, κτλ.," *TDNT* 3:8, n. 2.
20 Dov Noy, "Angel of Death," *EncJud* (New York: Macmillan, 1971–72) 2:951–56, with bibliography.
21 Compare Montague R. James, *The Apocalypse in Art* (London: Oxford University, 1931) passim, e.g., 57.
22 Barbara Tuchman, *A Distant Mirror* (New York: Ballantine, 1979) 124–25.
23 Barnett, *Nimrud Ivories*, 145–51.

"to cut off" (לְהַכְרִית) does not express purpose but rather attendant circumstance (see GKC, sec. 114o) is unnecessary: the expression of purpose here renders the image all the more horrifying. For "children" and "young men" see 6:11; for "streets" and "squares" see 5:11. The assonance of 6:11 is increased here—*miḥûṣ, baḥûrîm, mĕrĕḥōbôt*, with precise reversal of the consonants of the two last-mentioned words.

For the form of וְנָפְלָה (waw-consecutive perfect after an infinitive), see Joüon, *Gramm.*, sec. 119o. For "corpses" (נְבֵלָה) see 7:33; the assonance between *wĕnāpĕlâ* and *niblat* is noteworthy.

Many commentators have omitted "like dung" (כְּדֹמֶן) as an alien image introduced from 8:2 (Cornill, Duhm, Giesebrecht, Volz, Rudolph): according to this proposal, Death is thought of as a reaper, the sheaves ready to fall, and the image of a field scattered with dung (8:2) does not belong (Volz). They are encouraged in this proposal by the fact that G here reads "for an example" (εἰς παράδειγμα) for "like dung." The simile was no doubt offensive to the G translations: the same translation in G is given in 8:2 and 16:4, so they doubtless read the word as כְּדָמְיֹן (see Ps 17:12). But there is no need to excise the word; in 8:2 the dung is lying on the surface of the ground, but here it is dropping. The only earlier use of the word in the OT is the striking one in 2 Kgs 9:37 in which Elijah is quoted as saying that the corpse (נְבֵלָה) of Jezebel shall be like dung on the open field (כְּדֹמֶן עַל־פְּנֵי הַשָּׂדֶה): Jrm is suggesting that the people are all comparable to Jezebel.[24] Indeed is the parallel with Jezebel not reinforced by the reference to "windows" in v 20?—Jezebel looked out her window before she was assassinated, and was doubtless thrown to her death through her window (2 Kgs 9:30, 32): compare the theme of the harlot peering through the window, already referred to

(4:30).[25] Jrm makes Elijah's rude simile for Jezebel even ruder by speaking of the "falling" of dung. "The prophet here denotes stench and a deformed sight by the comparison of dung: yet we know with what pride the people were then filled. This threatening then was to them very disagreeable; but as they flattered themselves in their vices, it was the more necessary to treat them roughly" (Calvin). Indeed Jrm is speaker here of more than the covenant people: it is "humanity, people" (הָאָדָם); he is here generalizing beyond Israel as he did in 4:23–28 (see Aim).

The word עָמִיר should not be translated "sheaves," as most do; the latter are tied bundles of grain stalks, while the word simply means the stalks once cut: the Versions render by words for "grass" or "hay" (in Mic 4:12 the word is used for grain stalks gathered on the threshing floor). It is understandable how hearers should assume that the reaper is Death (see above), but the image is simply of the steady fall of grain stalks, like the fall of dung. Grain stalks that are not gathered up are wasted. The corpses of the population will be wasted.

Aim

Jrm's lyricism is here at its height for the darkest of messages: the passage ranks with 4:23–28 in this respect. In the passage in chapter 4 Jrm sees the universe again in the state in which it had been before Yahweh began his work; here the old pagan god Mōt, the god of death, is at work once more, destroying the people. And more than the people of the covenant: it is the corpses of "humanity" that shall fall. The drumbeat of these laments has the power even today to awe the hearer; the words must have chilled the blood of Jrm's hearers.

---

24   Holladay, "Prototype," 359.
25   See n. 23.

Let One's Boast
Be in Knowing Yahweh

Bibliography

Brueggemann, Walter A.
  "The Epistemological Crisis of Israel's Two
  Histories (Jer 9:22–23)," *Israelite Wisdom,
  Theological and Literary Essays in Honor of Samuel
  Terrien* (ed. John G. Gammie et al.; Missoula, MT:
  Scholars, 1978) 85–105.
Kutsch, Ernst
  "Weisheitsspruch und Prophetenwort, Zur
  Traditionsgeschichte des Spruches Jer 9,22–23,"
  BZ NF 25 (1981) 161–79.
Schreiner, Josef
  "Jeremia 9,22–23 als Hintergrund des
  paulinischen 'Sich-Rühmen,'" *Neues Testament und
  Kirche, Für Rudolf Schnackenburg* (ed. Joachim
  Gnilka; Freiburg: Herder, 1974) 530–42.

9

22 [23]   **Thus Yahweh has said,**
Let not the wise man boast of his wis-
dom,
    and let not the strong man boast of his
    strength,
      and[a] let not the rich man boast of his
      riches;
23 [24]   **but let him who boasts boast in**
      this:
to have the sense to know me—
  that I am Yahweh who show love,
   [a] (who do) justice[a] and righteousness
   on earth,
    for in these I take pleasure,
        oracle of Yahweh.

Text

22a   Following many MSS. and all Versions; *M* omits
"and."

23a—a   The qere' of Oriental MSS. and all Versions
read "and justice"; *M* reads simply "justice" ("who
do" being implied). One's judgment on this reading
depends to some degree upon the analysis of
Structure (which see).

Structure

There is no way to be sure why this unit is placed here. Is
it because "wise man" (חָכָם) is associated with "the wise
women" (הַחֲכָמוֹת) in v 16?[1] Or is there a more intricate
scheme?—v 20 offers "children," "streets," and "youth," v
23 here offers "take pleasure" (חפץ), and vv 24–25 offer
"uncircumcised" (ערל), a sequence found in reverse
order in 6:10–11, "uncircumcised" (ערל), "take pleasure"
(חפץ), and "children," "streets" and "youth."[2] If both the
present passage and vv 24–25 were inserted here at the
same time, the latter alternative is attractive.

The inner structure of the passage is to a great extent
obvious. After the messenger formula there are in v 22
three closely parallel cola. The first colon of v 23 points
both backward (in its use of "boast") and forward (in the
pronoun "this"). But the phrase "for in these" (כִּי־בְאֵלֶּה)
in the last colon of v 23 is parallel to "but in this" (כִּי־אִם
בְּזֹאת): one is therefore moved to analyze the passage as
two tetracola. There is lingering uncertainty, however,
how to divide the material from "that I am Yahweh" to
"on earth." The second colon may be complete with "that
I am Yahweh," and the *M* accent zaqep qaton so marks it.

---

1   Compare Brueggemann, "Crisis," 89–90.
2   Holladay, *Architecture*, 123–24.

But this leaves the third colon unexpectedly long. "Justice" and "righteousness" are a standard pair. There are instances of parallelism between "love" (חֶסֶד) and "justice" (Hos 12:7; Mic 6:8) and between "love" and "righteousness" (Hos 10:12), but the full triplet is not found elsewhere. One is led therefore to divide the cola after "love" (so also Condamin, Rudolph, Bright). This division makes less likely the reading of "and" before "justice" (see Text, v 23, a—a).

Form and Setting

This short passage has characteristics of "wisdom" style, so that earlier commentators tended to reject its authenticity. Thus Volz judged it to be "theological" and abstract in contrast to Jrm's practical interest elsewhere. But opinion has now shifted; though Hyatt remarked that it, "being somewhat proverbial in nature, . . . differs from [Jrm's] usual style,"[3] he did not wish to deny it to the prophet, and Rudolph has affirmed that "its genuineness should not be objected to"[4] (similarly Bright). And recently Walter A. Brueggemann has gone beyond a passive acceptance of its authenticity: he views the passage as a specific expression of Jrm's prophetic message[5] (see below).

Though this passage comes out of a wisdom milieu in its listing of categories of people whose boasting is beside the mark (compare the listings in Prov 30:11–31), there is no parallel in Proverbs for such negative jussives with categories of people. Imperatives, of course, are found in Proverbs, particularly in the latter part of Proverbs 22 and in 23—24; but it is not easy to find parallels in Proverbs for the message and structure of the present passage (Prov 27:1–2 is perhaps closest). The passage offers a critique of the misuse of wisdom as much as of the misuse of power and riches: in content Prov 9:10 is

close.[6] It may be noted further that the form "let not X boast" is at home in traditional wisdom (see 1 Kgs 20:11).[7]

The present passage is not, however, simply a reflection of folk wisdom; it is a prophetic oracle, offering the self-designation "I am Yahweh." (It might be added that the passage is further marked as an oracle by the messenger formula at the beginning and the rubric "oracle of Yahweh" at the end, but these might have been added secondarily.)[8] There are other passages in the prophetic corpus that summarize a theocentric orientation in a way not far from wisdom modes of expression: one thinks of Mic 6:8 at the end of a torah-liturgy (Mic 6:6–8), though that passage offers its own difficulties in dating.[9] But the present passage is a critique of the royal ideology in Jrm's day, quintessentially prophetic (see further Interpretation).[10]

Interpretation

One hears here of three traditional human pursuits: "wisdom" (חָכְמָה), a term which ranges across theoretical and practical knowledge, intelligence, and experience;[11] "strength" (גְּבוּרָה), which includes not only physical valor (Judg 8:21) but military and political power as well (1 Kgs 15:23; Isa 11:2); and "riches" (עֹשֶׁר). These are three preoccupations of wisdom literature as well: wisdom itself of course (e.g., Prov 1:2; 2:6), strength (e.g., Prov 20:29), and riches (e.g. Prov 11:4); Qoheleth tries to work out the relation, or nonrelation, among them (Eccl 9:11, 16). And they are the preoccupations of Israel's royal history: "Jeremiah disposes in one stroke of all the sources of security and well-being upon which the royal establishment is built."[12] But these are not to be one's ultimate concern, Jrm says; one is not to "exult" or

---

3   Hyatt, p. 894.
4   Rudolph, p. 69.
5   Brueggemann, "Crisis."
6   See the remarks on the limits of wisdom in von Rad, *Wisdom*, 97–110; for the present passage see 102–3.
7   Carole R. Fontaine, *Traditional Sayings in the Old Testament* (Sheffield: Almond, 1982) 127–38.
8   Brueggemann, "Crisis," 91.
9   Mays, *Micah*, 138, separates Mic 6:1–5 and 6–8; the latter passage he assigns to "a prophet of a later period." Delbert R. Hillers, *Micah* (Hermeneia; Philadelphia: Fortress, 1984), takes Mic 6:1–8 as a

unit; as to setting, he is more cautious, saying it "is not impossible in Hezekiah's reign," 79. Wolff, *Micha*, 144–45, does not find any sure clues for a precise date.
10   Brueggemann, "Crisis."
11   See the discussion in von Rad, *Wisdom*, 12–14.
12   Brueggemann, "Crisis," 93.

"boast" regarding any of them (for the verb הלל hitpoʻlel see 4:2).

One's boast must be centered in Yahweh: it is he that must excite the people, he about whom one is to be proudest, he about whom one cannot refrain from telling our neighbor. The phrase הַשְׂכֵּל וְיָדֹעַ אוֹתִי is imprecise and open to a variety of translations. The verb שׂכל hipʻil itself ranges widely: "consider," "have insight," "act prudently," "have success." And so do the nuances of "knowing" God (see 4:22). Finally the relation between the two verbs is uncertain. They may be parallel (Volz, Condamin, Rudolph)—"that he has sense and knows me." If so, it is not likely that the object pronoun is shared by both verbs (as *RSV* implies, "that he understands and knows me"): in the instances where שׂכל hipʻil takes an accusative, it is either a vague "this" (Deut 32:29) or phrases like "[God's] wonderful works" (Ps 106:7; Job 34:27). On the other hand, the first verb may be understood to govern the second (Bright: "that he has the wisdom to know me"; *NAB*: "in his prudence he knows me"), or else the two verbs may be taken as a hendiadys (*NJV*: "his earnest devotion to me"). The translation offered here is thus only one possibility. The first כִּי in the second tetracolon hardly introduces a reason, as Condamin and many translations assume ("for I am Yahweh"), but rather expands the content of knowing Yahweh ("that": so Giesebrecht, Volz, Rudolph, Bright).

It is Yahweh who practices covenant love (חֶסֶד: see the discussion on 2:2), and justice and righteousness (for these correlates see 4:2): but the verb עשׂה here means not only "practice" but "create." And Yahweh creates them not only "in the land" of Israel but everywhere "on earth": the unrestricted milieu of the passage justifies the latter translation of בָּאָרֶץ.

And what is the reference for "in these" in the last colon?—is it to love and justice and righteousness, or is it to those people who know Yahweh? It can be either, as Michaelis noted (so, recently, Bright). Commentators and translators who have not left the reference ambiguous have come down on one side or the other: Jerome assumed it was neuter, Calvin insisted it was masculine; in this century Cornill, Giesebrecht, Volz, and Rudolph declare the pronoun masculine, Condamin takes it as neuter. For "take pleasure" (חפץ) see 6:10.

Aim

This passage has become a classic expression of the call of the faithful to a theocentric orientation. One finds an echo of it in the Aramaic version of Aḥiqar: "Let not the rich man say, 'In my riches I am glorious.'"[13] Paul quoted it twice (1 Cor 1:31; 2 Cor 10:17) and used its vocabulary for his long passage on "boasting" in 2 Cor 11:1—12:10. The Epistle of James also had it in mind ("Let the lowly brother boast in his exaltation and the rich in his humiliation," James 1:9–10), and *1 Clem.* 13.1 quotes almost all of it. True glory resides in God.

---

13   *ANET*, 430b.

9

24 [25] The time is surely coming, oracle of
Yahweh, when I will deal with everyone
who is physically circumcised, **25 [26]**/
with Egypt, and with Judah, and with
Edom, and with the Ammonites, and with
Moab, and with all (whose hair is) shaven
at the temple, living in the wilderness; for
all the nations are (really) uncircumcised,[a] while the house of Israel is
uncircumcised in heart.

Text

25a   *G*, *S*, and *T* all add "in (their) flesh" here, and the
agreement of *G* and *T* is striking. Such a reading
would make a good parallel to "uncircumcised in
heart" at the end of the verse, but it contradicts
what seems to be the meaning of the passage, and it
thus probably an interpretative tradition which
stressed the contrast between Israelites and non-
Israelites.

Structure, Form, Setting, Interpretation

For the placement of this passage here see the suggestion
in 9:22–23, Structure.

The phrase at the end of v 24, "physically circumcised," is literally "circumcised in foreskin," and the
phrase in v 25, "all (whose hair) is shaven at the temple,"
is literally "all those cut at the side": both translations are
interpretative.

As to the meaning of the passage, one hardly knows
whether it is badly framed and/or badly preserved, or
whether it is making a subtle and ironic point, or both.
Certainly what has been transmitted is far from easy to
follow.

As to the facts of circumcision, the practice was widespread outside of Israel, as the passage affirms. The
Egyptians practiced circumcision, but the practice was
evidently not universal there, being perhaps confined to
the priests or upper classes, and there is evidence that the
Egyptian operation was a slightly different one.[1] The
evidence for Edom, Ammon, and Moab is indirect,
though Ezek 32:29, by distinguishing Edom from "the
uncircumcised," that is, the Philistines, suggests that
Edom practiced the custom. If the phrase "all those cut at
the side" does mean "all whose hair is shaven at the
temple" (see above; note that the same phrase is found in
25:23 and 49:32), it evidently refers to various Arab
tribes "living in the wilderness"; Herodotus mentions the
hair-cutting custom among them.[2] Circumcision among
the Arabs is implied by the narrative of the circumcision
of Ishmael (Gen 17:25), on which Josephus expands,
stating that the Arabs circumcise at the age of thirty
years.[3] The Qurʾān does not mention it, but it is universal among Muslims. The *NEB* proposes another
interpretation of "those cut at the side, living in the
desert," namely "(those) who haunt the fringes of the
desert," but this is dubious, especially given the fact that
"those cut" (קְצוּצֵי) is a passive participle.

The most remarkable single feature of the passage is
the listing of Judah second, after Egypt and before
Edom. This curiosity led the main uncials of *G* to read
ἰδουμαίαν "Idumea" for ἰουδαίαν "Judah" here, thus
leading to two references to Edom. There is no conceivable way this series could have arisen in the period
after Jrm's time (compare the rhetoric of Isa 19:23–25, a
postexilic universalistic passage): the present passage
points to a particular political situation at the end of the
Judean monarchy when a purely political listing could be
offered in a geographic series—Egypt, then Judah, then
the trans-Jordanian states, then Arab tribes. Rudolph is
undoubtedly correct in his proposal that one has here
evidence of an anti-Babylonian coalition led by Egypt,
even though the evidence for such a coalition is otherwise lacking. One can imagine the slogan "The circumcised against the uncircumcised!" (so again Rudolph)

---

1   The fullest literary evidence for the Egyptian custom
is in Herodotus 2.36, 37, and 104, and Diodorus
Siculus 1.28. The best discussion, with material up to
the end of the nineteenth century, is to be found in
Emil Schürer, *Geschichte des jüdischen Volkes* (Leipzig:
Hinrichs, 1901) 1:675–76; Schürer cites in Greek or
Latin the full texts not only of Herodotus and
Diodorus Siculus but of other ancient authors as well.

   For a recent treatment, with archeological evidence,
see Jack M. Sasson, "Circumcision in the Ancient
Near East," *JBL* 85 (1966) 473–76.

2   Herodotus 3.8.

3   Josephus *Ant.* 1.12.2.

with the inherent assumption that divine favor was on the side of all circumcised nations.

The point of the passage is that Yahweh will punish everyone in the coalition, pagans and Jews alike: neither group has a leg to stand on. Pagans, though they circumcise, do not do it with any sense of belonging to God; it is a purely ethnic custom. Jews, though they circumcise with the understanding that they belong to Yahweh, are not circumcised in heart (compare 4:4; 6:10). It is tempting to follow Volz's interpretation, that the passage indicates Israel is the "most uncircumcised people," but he emends the text to rid it of the naming of other states. The point of the passage is that Yahweh's judgment falls equally (though for different reasons) on pagan and Jew. Equally to be rejected is Rudolph's emendation from עֲרֵלִים to הָאֵלֶּה, so reading v 25b, "for all these nations and all the house of Israel are uncircumcised in heart"; the emendation is unlikely and the argument is spoiled. Now we see why both the term "Judah" and the term "house of Israel" are used: the first is a political term, the second a covenantal one.

If this interpretation is sound, the passage is so ironic a judgment speech that it can only be genuine to Jrm. Perhaps one can hope some day for extrabiblical evidence for the setting out of which the passage comes.

It is noteworthy that alongside the designation "Edom" and "Moab" the OT almost always refers to Ammon as

בְּנֵי־עַמּוֹן (literally "children of Ammon"); the origin of this distinction is somewhat obscure[4] but reflects the Ammonites' own self-designation: recently discovered Ammonite inscriptional material offers several occurrences of the phrase "children of Ammon"[5]—compare 27:3.

Aim

This passage joins others in which Jrm points to the ultimate purpose of circumcision and Judah's inability to achieve that purpose (compare 4:4; 6:10); in contrast to those other texts, however, this one appears to have a specific political setting. Though the setting became lost, the phraseology here entered into the tradition as spokesmen struggled with the problem of the relation of Jews and pagans: Ezekiel speaks in God's name that the uncircumcised are to be excluded from the temple (Ezek 44:7, 9), while Trito-Isaiah just as surely speaks in God's name to welcome foreigners there (Isa 56:6–7). In the first century Jesus sees in a Roman centurion a faith superior to that of any in Israel (Matt 8:10; Luke 7:9), and then Stephen and Paul are impelled to reiterate the ultimate meaning of circumcision and uncircumcision (Acts 7:51; Rom 2:25–29; and often).

---

4   George M. Landes, "Ammon," *IDB* 1:109a.
5   Siegfried H. Horn, "Ammon, Ammonites," *IDBSup*, 20. In addition to the bibliography in that article see now Felice Israel, "L'inscrizione di Tell Siran e la Bibbia: la titolatura del sovrano ammonita," *BeO* 22 (1980) 283–87.

The Folly of Idols

Bibliography

On the motifs and forms exemplified by the passage:

Crüsemann, Frank
  Studien zur Formgeschichte von Hymnus und Danklied in Israel (WMANT 32; Neukirchen: Neukirchener, 1969) esp. 111–14.
Labuschagne, C. J.
  The Incomparability of Yahweh in the Old Testament (Leiden: Brill, 1966) esp. 67–70.
Preuss, Horst Dietrich
  Verspottung fremder Religionen im Alten Testament (BWANT 92; Stuttgart: Kohlhammer, 1971) esp. 166–70.

On the passage in general:

Ackroyd, Peter R.
  "Jeremiah x. 1–16," *JTS* NS 14 (1963) 385–90.
Andrew, Maurice E.
  "The Authorship of Jer 10_{1-16}," *ZAW* 94 (1982) 128–30.
Bogaert, Pierre-Maurice
  "Les mécanismes rédactionnels en Jér 10,1–16 (LXX et TM) et la signification des suppléments," *Le Livre de Jérémie, Le prophète et son milieu, Les oracles et leur transmission* (ed. Pierre-Maurice Bogaert; BETL 54; Leuven: Leuven University, 1981) 222–38.
Davidson, Robert
  "Jer 10:1–16," *Glasgow University Oriental Society Transactions* 25 (1973–74, published 1976) 41–58.
Krašovec, Jože
  Antithetic Structure in Biblical Hebrew Poetry (VTSup 35; Leiden: Brill, 1984) 76–85.
Margaliot, M.
  "Jeremiah x 1–16: A re-examination," *VT* 30 (1980) 295–308.
Overholt, Thomas W.
  "The Falsehood of Idolatry: An Interpretation of Jer. x. 1–16," *JTS* NS 16 (1965) 1–12.
Wambacq, Bernard N.
  "Jérémie X, 1–16," *RB* 81 (1974) 57–62.

On specific verses and phrases:

Carmignac, Jean
  "Le texte de Jérémie 10,13 (ou 51,16), et celui de 2 Samuel 23,7 améliorés par Qumran," *RevQ* 7 (1969–71) 287–90.
Dahood, Mitchell
  "The Emphatic Double Negative *m'yn* in Jer 10:6–7," *CBQ* 37 (1975) 458–59.
Deist, Ferdinand E.
  "Jer 10:5: 'Palmboom' of 'Voëlverskrikker'?" *Nederduitse Gereformeerde Teologiese Tydskrif* 13 (1972) 115–18.

Deist, Ferdinand E.
"Zu כְּתֹמֶר מִקְשָׁה in Jer 10₅," *ZAW* 85 (1973), 225–26.

Driver, Samuel R.
"Grammatical Notes: 2. On מֵאֵין כָּמוֹךָ (Jer. x, 6, 8)," *Hebraica* (= *AJSL*) 2 (1885–86) 34–37.

Kissane, Edward J.
"'Who Maketh Lightnings for the Rain,'" *JTS* NS 3 (1952) 214–16.

10

1   [Hear the word which Yahweh has
             spoken to[b] you, house of Israel:
2   Thus Yahweh has spoken:][a]
     The manner of the nations do not [c]start
             learning,[c]
         nor by the omens of the sky be panicked;
         yes, the nations are panicked by them,
3   but the customs[a] of the peoples are
             a nothing!
     For he cuts it from a tree in the forest,
         the work of the hands of the craftsman
             with an adze;
4   with silver and gold he decorates[a] it,
             [b] with nails and hammers[b] they
                 fasten them [c]so that it cannot
                 wobble!

Text

1–2a These introductory words contradict the hymnic address to Yahweh in vv 6–7; if those verses are genuine, these words must have been added secondarily. Compare the secondary additions of such formulas in 9:16, 21.

b The preposition עַל־ means basically "concerning," "over," or "against." But it is occasionally the equivalent of אֶל־ "to"; so, evidently, here. *G* has ἐπί "over" or "against"; *V* "over."

c—c The translation is an effort to catch the nuance of the curious use of אֶל־ with למד "learn." There is no parallel for the combination. Volz wishes to delete the preposition with *S*, but one cannot be sure the preposition was missing from the text used by *S*. Similarly Rudolph wishes to emend the preposition to אֶת־, citing the usage of 12:16. But אֶל־ is surely the *lectio difficilior*, and *G* has κατά, so there is validation of the preposition in that text tradition as well. The proposal of Mitchell Dahood, "Hebrew-Ugaritic Lexicography IV," *Bib* 47 (1966) 410, to vocalize the consonants as אֵל "God" with "Yahweh" just preceding, is fanciful; these introductory words do not use אֵל.

3a חֻקּוֹת normally means "statutes," then, more generally, "customs." The word is unexpected in this context, particularly as a plural followed immediately by the singular pronoun reference הוּא. But this may simply be the first instance of the deliberate shifts between singular and plural appropriate to this genre (see Preliminary Observations). The emendation of Giesebrecht, adopted also by Rudolph, to read חֲתַת "Terror" here (compare Gen 35:5) is attractive but probably to be rejected, given the likelihood of parallelism between חֻקּוֹת and דֶּרֶךְ "manner" in v 2.

4–5a Both *S* and *T* here read "covers," presupposing יְצַפֵּהוּ (צפה pi'el), a plausible reading.

b—b Both 4QJer[b] and *G* reverse these terms, "with hammers and nails." *M* is doubtless the *lectio difficilior*.

c—c For the enclosed material *G* reads: "They will set them up, and they will not move; it is chased silver, they will not walk, it is applied silver from Tarshish, gold will come from Mophaz, and the hand of goldsmiths, all (of them) the works of craftsmen, (with) hyacinth [blue?] and purple they shall clothe them." It will be seen that *G* offers an expansion of the last colon of v 4, that it has taken כְּתֹמֶר מִקְשָׁה "like a scarecrow in a cucumber-field" differently, reading perhaps כְּתֶם מִקְשָׁה "gold of turned work,"

5   They are like a scarecrow in a cucumber-
field and cannot speak;[c]
    [d] they must even be carried,[d] for they
cannot walk!
        Do not fear them, for they cannot do
harm,
            though doing good is not ⟨in them⟩[e]
either.

6   ⟨Whence⟩[a] is any like you, Yahweh?
    Great you are,
        and great your name in strength.

7   Who shall not fear you,
    King of the nations?
        for it befits you;—
    for in all [a]the wise men[a] of the nations
and in all their dominion[b]
        ⟨whence⟩[c] is any like you?

8   Let them burn as well as be foolish;
        the instruction of nothings is wood!

9   Beaten silver is brought from Tarshish,
    and gold from Uphaz,[a]
        the work of a craftsman and the
handiwork of a smith,
            blue and purple are their clothes,
                all of them the work of wise men.

10   But Yahweh is God, he is reality,
    the living God and the everlasting King;
    with his fury the earth quakes,
        the nations cannot endure his rage.

11   [a] *Thus[b] shall you say[b] to them:[b]*
    *"The gods by whom the heavens and the
earth are not made—*
        *these shall perish [c]from the earth[c] and
from under the heavens!"[a]*

12   《Yahweh》[a] is the maker of the earth by
his power,
    the establisher of the world by his
wisdom,
        and by his understanding he
stretched out the heavens.

and that it then inserts v 9 (omitting "the work of a craftsman"); thereafter it reads the balance of v 5 and goes directly to v 11, omitting altogether vv 6–8 and 10. Some of this can be retrojected into Hebrew, but not all of it with any confidence; the data are not sufficient at present to display in Hebrew a "shorter recension." It should be added, however, that the scrap of 4QJer[b] for the passage reflects the *G* form of text. See further Preliminary Observations and Setting.

d—d   *M* reads the imperfect verb with metathesis of consonants, ינשוא, but some MSS. read correctly ינשאו.

e   *M* reads the accusative pronoun אוֹתָם; many MSS. read the word without waw, allowing the vocalization אִתָּם, the prepositional expression required by the syntax. These forms are often confused in the MSS.

6a   *M* מֵאֵין in vv 6 and 7b is puzzling. Literally it would mean "without (any)" [like you]; מֵאֵין = "without" is common (e.g., 4:7), but the expression hardly constitutes a clause (which would require אֵין). König, *Syntax*, sec. 352x, suggests a double negative here, reading the mem as מֵ־; Mitchell Dahood, "The Emphatic Double Negative *m'yn* in Jer 10:6–7," *CBQ* 37 (1975) 458–59, likewise suggests a double negative, reading מֵה־. Rudolph suggests perhaps omitting the mem as dittographic. But given the question in v 7a and the question מֵאֵין כָּמוֹהוּ "whence is any like it?" in 30:7, it is better to read מֵאֵין here as well (so BDB). But compare v 7, note c.

7a—a A few MSS. read "kings"; that is the *lectio facilior* and perhaps dittographic from "king" just above.

b   *θ'* reads "kings."

c   *M* מֵאֵין here, as in v 6, should be vocalized as מֵאֵין. One MS. reads אֵין "there is not (any)."

9a   If the text is correct, the place is unknown. The same name appears in *M* of Dan 10:5, but that occurrence may be based on the present one (Cornill). Both *S* and *T* read "Ophir" here, which is probably correct (so Cornill, Giesebrecht); it is possible that reš and zayin were confused in the old Aramaic script. *G* reads "Mophaz."

11a—a The entire verse is in Aramaic, hence the typography here with italics. See Preliminary Observations, Interpretation.

b   MSS. vary in their spelling: for כדנה some read כדנא, for תאמרון some read תימרון, for להום some read להון.

c—c 4QJer[b] reads the correct Aramaic מן ארעא for the Hebraizing *M* מֵאַרְעָא.

12a   Reading with *G* and *S*; *M* lacks "Yahweh," so that one must read simply "the maker of the earth by his power," an unsatisfactory first colon. An alternative is to revocalize עֹשֵׂה "maker of" as עָשָׂה "he made" (so, evidently, *NJV*). But since all the other sections of the poem dealing with Yahweh name him, the proposed reading is preferable.

13	《At his voice is poured out》[a] an uproar of waters in the heavens, and he has made mists rise from the ends of [b]the earth,[b] lightning-bolts for the rain he has made, and has brought forth the wind from his storehouses.
14	Every person is too stupid to know, every smith is put to shame by (his) idol, for [a]his (molten) image is[a] falsehood, there is no breath in them.
15	They are a nothing, a work of mockery, at the time [a]of their punishment[a] they shall perish.
16	Not like these is the portion of Jacob, [a] for he forms everything, and Israel is the tribe of his possession,[a] Yahweh [b]of hosts[b] is his name.

13a   M לְקוֹל תִּתּוֹ gives no sense ("at the voice of his giving forth"?), and G omits the words here, but in the duplicate text of 51:16 G reproduces something like this (G 28:16), εἰς φωνὴν ἔθετο, "at a voice he placed." Volz offers an ingenious set of emendations, but they are too hypothetical for consideration here. Bright is perhaps correct in suggesting that after these words several words have dropped out, so that "an uproar of waters (is) in the heavens" would make up a full colon in itself. I have adopted Duhm's suggestion, accepted by Rudolph, of reading לְקוֹלוֹ נִתַּךְ (נתך) nip'al); for לְקוֹל compare 11:16; for נִתַּךְ compare 2 Sam 21:10.

b—b   Ketib אֶרֶץ without article, qere' הָאָרֶץ with article: either reading is possible.

14a—a   For נְסְכּוֹ G reads נָסַךְ "he has poured out."

15a—a   For פְּקֻדָּתָם 4QJer[b] reads פְּקַדְתִּים "when I punish them"; compare 6:15, Text note b—b.

16a—a   M is literally "the one who forms everything (is) he, and Israel is the tribe of his possession"; G omits "and Israel is the tribe of," reconstruing the words as "the one who forms everything, he (is) his [i.e., Jacob's] possession."

b—b   This expression is omitted by G; compare Janzen, p. 79.

Preliminary Observations

This passage offers interlocking problems of text, structure, form, and setting which are difficult to resolve. Any solution must take account of the following data. (1) The passage was evidently added secondarily into the basic stratum of Jeremianic material in chapters 8—10 (see 9:16–21, Structure and Form). (2) Both style and content are divergent from what we know of Jrm's style and concerns elsewhere; the passage bears a resemblance to passages mocking idols found in Deutero-Isaiah, notably Isa 44:9–20. (3) Verse 11, in contrast to what lies before and after, is in Aramaic. (4) G offers a contrasting recension, preserving the passage in the order vv 1–4, (5aα?), 9, 5aβb, 11–16, omitting vv 6–8 and 10; and there are other minor variations. Both recensions are old: 4QJer[a] reflects M (small portions of vv 9–14 survive, and v 9 is followed by v 10), while 4QJer[b] reflects G in its placement of v 9 before v 5.[1] Furthermore there is a doublet of 10:12–16 (but not what precedes) in 51:15–19; and though G for the latter passage (that is, G 28:15–19) differs in small respects from G in 10:12–16, they are both translations of the same Hebrew archetype. (5) The text and style, both as to syntax and parallelism, seem ragged.

The general scholarly consensus has been that the passage is unoriginal to Jrm (see, for example, Rudolph and Bright), a late addition to the book, that v 11 is a curious Aramaic gloss—Duhm stated that that verse is evidence of the uncriticalness of copyists and redactors—and that in general the passage gives indication of careless transmission. The present study would like to propose another approach (compare Ackroyd, Overholt, Margaliot: see the Bibliography).

The first question to be dealt with is that of the maligned "Aramaic gloss" in v 11: since the eighteenth century scholars have considered the verse to be a late taunt, originally written in the margin, incorporated into the text but interrupting the flow of the poem (so Houbigant and Venema, according to Naegelsbach, and so the commentators of this century: see for example Rudolph). Baumgartner judges it to be a fifth-century product on the basis of the alternation of the two spellings of "earth" (ארקא and ארעא) side by side.[2] It is true that this variation in spelling is characteristic of the fifth century (see Interpretation on the verse), but it is equally true that a spelling lapse need not date the origin

1   Janzen, pp. 181–82; Frank M. Cross, *The Ancient Library of Qumran and Modern Biblical Studies* (Garden City, NY: Doubleday, 1961) 187 n. 38.

2   Walter Baumgartner, "Das Aramäische im Buche Daniel," *ZAW* 45 (1927) 101.

of the passage in question. It is also assumed by all commentators that the passage is in prose. But the verse, after the introductory words, is chiastically arranged: *'ĕlāhayyā', šĕmayyā', 'arqā', 'ăbadû; yē'badû, 'ar'ā', šĕmayyā', 'ēlleh.* If it is not poetry, it is at least carefully framed. There is a pun on the verbs "make" (עבד) and "perish" (אבד) which is exact: 'ayin and 'alep were not distinguished at least in the Aramaic of Mesopotamia[3] (compare Setting); the pun could not in any case be transferred to Hebrew, where עבד has a different range of meanings. In the century previous to Jrm there was knowledge of Aramaic at least among the officials of Judah (2 Kgs 18:26), and Jrm himself evidently employed an Aramaic pun on at least one other occasion (see Interpretation of 20:3–6). In 8:19 and perhaps in 22 "interruptions" form climaxes in the sequence (see there); one is therefore led to the possibility that the ironic saying in Aramaic was part of the poem from the beginning, indeed from its placement might be the climax of the poem.

The next question to be dealt with is that of the "raggedness" of the poem as a whole. There is no question that the passage gives an impression of carelessness. Thus there is a baffling shift between singular and plural in reference both to the idols and to the idolmakers: for example, v 4 offers "he decorates it" and "they fasten them" in adjoining cola. Other prophetic passages offer such inconcinnities, but there seems to be more here than normal. But the same trait is noticeable in Isa 44:9–20, the passage most comparable to the present one: one notes Isa 44:15, with הָיָה (singular), מֵהֶם (plural), עָשָׂהוּ (singular), and the shift from singular to plural in reference to the idol-makers in v 18 of that passage. One might conclude, as the commentators have, that this is an example of late carelessness in drafting and transmitting such passages. But there is another possibility: the impression of "raggedness" may be part of the literary genre—a sloppy shift from singular to plural and back again may betoken a mockery of whether the gods

are one or many, a kind of "devil-may-care" attitude on the part of the poet.

The same may be said of raggedness in the poetic structure. There has been uncertainty whether Isa 44:9–20 is prose or poetry (compare the typography of that passage by Rudolf Kittel in *BHK* and by Thomas in *BHS*); and while the passage before us has been taken as poetry, the parallelism is rough enough to raise doubts (see in detail Structure). The judgment of Christopher North about Isa 44:9–20 is applicable to the present passage as well: "Parallelism is discernible throughout but it is not great poetry. It was not intended to be; it is a kind of 'Skeltonical' doggerel that suits its theme admirably."[4] His reference is to the poetry of John Skelton (c. 1460–1529) which consists of short irregular lines with frequent running on of the same rime. There is thus the possibility that the literary form of mockery of idols demanded a sort of doggerel that was intended to spoof its subject. The way is therefore open to the possibility of authenticity to the time of Jrm. Nevertheless the lack of firm poetic structure and the abundance of rare vocabulary does not facilitate the establishment of a sound text.

The existence of a long recension in *M* and a shorter one in *G* for vv 1–16 and the existence of vv 12–16 in a doublet poses keenly the problem of choice for a basic text. The separate existence of vv 12–16 suggests to some that it was a later addition to vv 1–11.[5] The alternation of material mocking idols and material praising Yahweh, as well as the existence of the shorter recension in *G* in which v 9 is inserted in the middle of v 5, has stimulated commentators to several reconstructions of the original text. Thus Volz proposes vv 1–5, 10, 12–16, omitting vv 6–9 and 11 as supplementary fragments, while Rudolph proposes vv 1–3, 4a, 9, 4b, 5, 8, 10, 12–16, omitting vv 6–7 and 11 as supplementary fragments. But these reconstructions are based on no existing recension; they are subjective proposals which would "tighten" the phraseology.[6] On the other hand,

---

3 See Sabatino Moscati et al., *Introduction to the Comparative Grammar of the Semitic Languages* (Wiesbaden: Harrassowitz, 1964) secs. 8.54, 8.56.

4 Christopher R. North, *The Second Isaiah* (Oxford: Oxford University, 1964) 139.

5 Preuss, *Verspottung*, 169.

6 Overholt, "Idolatry," 2.

Horst Dietrich Preuss is convinced that the "idol" verses may be genuine to Jrm while the "Yahweh" verses are secondary additions.[7] But all this is arbitrary. Verses 12–16 offer an alternation between "idol" and "Yahweh" sequences; the recension of G offers such an alternation, and so does the fuller recension of M. Since there is no other example in the OT of a passage alternating the mockery of idols with hymnic praise of Yahweh, or to Yahweh, one is led to the conclusion that the alternation was intrinsic to the passage from the beginning. Verses 6–7 should not be excised simply because they offer second-person address to Yahweh while the other hymnic sections are in third-person form; hymns elsewhere in the OT offer the same shift (see Form). If they are to be excised, it should be simply on the basis that G omits them, but then one must stay with the recension of G unless it is demonstrably wrong; this, however, one is unable to do.[8] Given no indication for the superiority of either recension, one is moved to stay with M, in the order of its verses. (For a possible explanation of the origin of the two recensions see Setting.)

A word must now be offered on the relation of this passage to similar material in Deutero-Isaiah and on the general problem of the authenticity of such a passage as this to Jrm. It is widely assumed that if a passage in Jer resembles a passage in Deutero-Isaiah, then the passage in Jer must be secondary, added to the corpus under the stimulus of the poetic material in Deutero-Isaiah (see the discussion in Giesebrecht and Hyatt on 30:10–11). But obviously this argument can cut the other way: the passage may be genuine to Jrm, and then Deutero-Isaiah might have imitated the style of that genre. Such an approach is relevant here. If the present passage were authentic to Jrm, then it might have stimulated Deutero-Isaiah himself to offer sequences mocking idols. The question can scarcely be answered by asking whether there is anything else in Jer like the present passage—there is not (though see the remarks on 16:19–21 in Setting on the present passage). The question is whether

the passage offers clues in vocabulary, theme and word-play which could plausibly be attributed to Jrm so that this passage, unique as it is, may have a claim to authenticity. The genre of mockery of idols is old (compare Form), and Jrm himself mocks idols in other passages that are demonstrably authentic to him (notably 2:27–28). Further, there are likenesses of vocabulary that make authenticity plausible (for details see Setting).

It is possible, then, that general critical work on this passage has been beside the mark.

Structure
One suspects that the passage was added secondarily to a preexistent stratum of material (specifically between 9:16–21 and 10:17–25) on the basis of either or both of the following catch-words: למד qal "learn" in v 2 with למד pi'el "teach" in 9:19, and בער nip'al "be stupefied" in v 14 (compare the same or a homonymous verb in the qal stem in v 8) with the same verb in v 21.

As already noted, the passage consists of an alternation of descriptions of idols and mockery of them with descriptions of Yahweh (or, in one instance, vv 6–7, if the text is correct, an address to Yahweh): vv 2–5, idols; vv 6–7, address to Yahweh; vv 8–9, idols; v 10, Yahweh; v 11, climactic mockery of idols in Aramaic; vv 12–13, Yahweh; vv 14–15, idols; v 16, Yahweh.[9] The length of these successive sections shortens to the climax at v 11; the next section (vv 12–13) begins fairly long once more, shortening again to the last section (v 16).[10]

The first idols section is in vv 2–5; on analysis it turns out to be composed of three tetracola. At first glance the material in v 2 (after the secondary messenger formula) appears to be a tricolon, "manner of the nations" in the first colon being parallel to "omens of the sky" in the second, and "be panicked" occurring in both the second and third cola. But closer inspection reveals that the first colon of v 3 makes a fourth colon in a tetracolon, beginning with an asseverative כי parallel to the one at the beginning of the third colon, and offering "customs of

---

7   Preuss, *Verspottung*, 168.
8   Compare ibid., 167 n. 259.
9   For an examination of this scheme of alternation see Overholt, "Idolatry," and Jože Krašovec, *Antithetic Structure in Biblical Hebrew Poetry* (VTSup 35; Leiden: Brill, 1984) 80–84.
10 Compare my remarks on the tension between chiastic

structure and sequentiality in Holladay, "Recovery," 410, 411, 432–33.

the peoples" in parallel with "manner of the nations" in the first colon, more closely parallel than "omens of the sky" in the second colon is to "manner of the nations": the tetracolon thus is to some degree chiastic. A new thought begins with the second colon of v 3, the handiwork of craftsmen. Verses 3b–4 thus make up a second tetracolon: the first two cola deal with cutting the tree and shaping it with an adze, the second two with the accessories, "silver and gold" being parallel to "nails and hammers"; it is to be noted that the phrase "so that it cannot wobble" (וְלוֹא יָפִיק) cannot make up a colon by itself. Verse 5 is likewise a tetracolon bound closely to v 4: one notes that "and cannot speak" (וְלֹא יְדַבֵּרוּ) and "for they cannot walk" (כִּי לֹא יִצְעָדוּ) parallel "it cannot wobble" at the end of v 4. Further the position of "for they cannot walk" (כִּי לֹא יִצְעָדוּ) at the end of the second colon of the verse suggests that the closely similar "for they cannot do harm" (כִּי־לֹא יָרֵעוּ) is in the same position at the end of the third colon, and the fourth colon of course is closely parallel with the third. Finally one may note that this first section (vv 2–5) is bound together by the inclusio of the two prohibitions "do not start learning" and "do not be panicked" at the beginning of the poem in v 2 and the prohibition synonymous with "do not be panicked," namely "do not fear," at the beginning of v 5b.

The first Yahweh section (vv 6–7) offers a similar inclusio, the two occurrences of "Whence is any like you?"; and vv 2–5 and 6–7 are tied together by the noun "nations" (vv 2, 7) and the verb "fear" (vv 5, 7). Verses 6–7 are composed of three tricola.[11] The first tricolon (v 6) offers in its second and third cola the repetition of "great" (גָּדוֹל), and the third tricolon (v 7b) in parallel fashion offers in its first and second cola a repetition of "in all" (בְּכָל־). The middle tricolon (v 7a) begins, as the first tricolon begins and the last tricolon ends, with a rhetorical question. The last colon of v 7a, kî lĕkā yā'ātâ ("for it befits you"), is in close assonance with kāmôkā ("like you") in vv 6 and 7b and 'attâ ("you [are]") in v 6.

The next idols section (vv 8–9) echoes the first idols section at two points: "wood" (v 8) is a variant translation of עֵץ, translated "tree" in v 3; and "the work of a craftsman and handiwork of a smith" (v 9) echoes "the work of the hands of a craftsman" in v 3. It also echoes the first Yahweh section in its use of "wise men" (vv 9, 7). Within itself the new section offers an inclusio, between "be foolish" (סכל) in the first colon of v 8 and "wise men" (חֲכָמִים) in the last colon of v 9. The section, if the text is correct, consists of a bicolon (v 8) and a pentacolon (v 9). The bicolon (v 8) offers the ironic parallel (see Interpretation) between "burn" and "wood," and between "foolish" and "instruction." The first four cola of the pentacolon (v 9) are grouped in two pairs: "silver" is parallel with "gold" in the first two, and the second two each offer inner parallelism ("the work of a craftsman and the handiwork of a smith" and "blue and purple"). This leaves the last colon a single summarizing one, but it echoes "the work of" from the third colon and "be foolish" from v 8 (see above on the inclusio).

Verse 10 is a short Yahweh section composed of two bicola; the words "King" and "nations" echo those words in v 7.

The Aramaic verse (v 11), after the introductory words, offers a remarkable chiasmus of eight elements (see Preliminary Observations).

The next Yahweh section (vv 12–13) consists of a tricolon (v 12) followed by a tetracolon (v 13)—unless the text is defective (see Text, v 13 note a). The arrangement of "the earth" and "the heavens" is noteworthy: these two expressions have appeared in two pairs arranged chiastically in v 11; they appear again in two pairs in vv 12 and 13a, again arranged chiastically, but in the reverse order of that in v 11. "The earth" and "the heavens" are joined by a third term, "the world," in the tricolon of v 12; those cola also contain "by his power," "by his wisdom," and "by his understanding" for tight synonymous parallelism. The tetracolon of v 14 offers similar synonymous parallelism, with four manifestations of weather. Yahweh's "wisdom" (v 12) stands in contrast to the foolishness of idols (v 8) and to the spurious "wise men" (vv 7, 9) who make idols.

The last idol section is vv 14–15. Verse 14 is a tetracolon. The first two cola are closely parallel, not only in the subjects and verbs but in the prepositional phrases

---

11   With regard to v 7b, note that "all" (כָּל־) is one "unit" in O'Connor's analysis of cola: see O'Connor, *Structure*, 318, no. 30, Judg 5:31a.

מִדַּעַת (literally "from knowing") and מִפֶּסֶל (literally "from [his] idol"); it is better to analyze the verse as a tetracolon than as two bicola if "his image" (נִסְכּוֹ) in the third colon reflects "from (his) idol" (מִפֶּסֶל) in the second. Verse 15 is evidently a tricolon, "a nothing" (הֶבֶל) echoing "nothings" (הֲבָלִים) in v 8, "work of" echoing the same expression in vv 3 and 9, and "they shall perish" (יֹאבֵדוּ) echoing its Aramaic cognate in v 11 (יֵאבַדוּ).

Finally v 16 returns to Yahweh in a strong tetracolon. For the first time "Jacob" and its parallel "Israel" appear, in the first and third cola, and the participle "he forms" (יוֹצֵר) in the second colon parallels the participles of creation in the first two cola of v 12.

Form

The total format of this passage is unique in the OT: the alternation of expressions of contempt for pagan gods and their idols with hymnic descriptions of Yahweh (see Structure). Whether or not the hymnic sections were added secondarily, this alternation defines the form of the present text, and this is true whether one is dealing with the recension of *M*, the recension of *G*, or simply the truncated section vv 12–16 found likewise in 51:15–19 (see Preliminary Observations). The alternation sets forth in the most vivid way possible the contrast between the gods and their idols, which are unreal, and Yahweh, who is incomparable. The same contrast is implied by the placement of passages in Deutero-Isaiah which mock the idols: thus Isa 44:9–20 is placed between two divine admonitions, reflections of the genre of a trial-speech, one a self-description (44:6–8) and the other an assurance of salvation (44:21–22).[12] But the present passage is unique in achieving this contrast by the technique of alternation.

Verses 2–5, 8–9, 11, and 14–15 are concerned with idols, and these verses use a variety of genres: parenetic appeal ("the manner of the nations do not start learning," v 2) and reassurance ("do not be afraid," v 5); mocking descriptions of the manner by which idols are constructed (vv 3, 9) and affirmations that they are without power (vv 4–5), of no value to their makers (v 14), or even that they are unreal (vv 3, 5, 8, 14–15); predictions of their demise or maledictions for their demise (vv 8, 11, 15). It may be noted here that the Aramaic v 11 may be interpreted either as an announcement of judgment (if the main verb is taken as an indicative: compare Ps 82:7) or as a curse formula (if the main verb is taken as a jussive: compare Ps 109:12–13); see in detail Interpretation.

Mockery of pagan gods and idols is traditional in Israel (one notes, for example, Deut 32:37–38, dated by Albright and Otto Eissfeldt to the eleventh century;[13] this passage was evidently imitated by Jrm himself in 2:27–28), and such mockery in all periods employed a variety of specific genres.[14] It should be stressed that the mockery here, as elsewhere, identifies the deities themselves with the idols representing them, whether this identification is deliberate or casual.[15]

The hymnic sections, devoted to Yahweh, share characteristics with hymns elsewhere, especially in the Book of Psalms. The material here is both in the second person (vv 6–7) and third person (vv 10, 12–13, 16), but this is a general feature of hymns (see, for example, Exod 15:1–18; Psalm 145). The sections stress Yahweh's incomparability, both in affirmations and in rhetorical questions,[16] and his mastery over both nature (vv 10 and 13) and history (by implication vv 10 and 16). The passages dealing with his mastery over nature suggest the language of theophany.[17] The last line of the passage is the hymnic refrain "Yahweh [of hosts] is his name."

12   See recent commentaries, for example Westermann, *Isaiah 40—66*, 138–44; Elliger, *Deuterojesaja*, 398–400, 443.

13   William F. Albright, "Some Remarks on the Song of Moses in Deuteronomy xxxii," *VT* 9 (1959) 339–46; Eissfeldt, *Introduction*, 227; but it should be said that not all scholars accept such an early date: compare Mayes, *Deuteronomy*, 381–82.

14   Preuss, *Verspottung*, 269.

15   For a discussion of this identification see Yehezkel Kaufmann, *The Religion of Israel, From Its Beginnings to the Babylonian Exile* (Chicago: University of Chicago, 1960) 7–20.

16   C. J. Labuschagne, *The Incomparability of Yahweh in the Old Testament* (Leiden: Brill, 1966); for rhetorical questions in this regard see there, 16–28, esp. 27 for this passage.

17   See Jörg Jeremias, *Theophanie, Die Geschichte einer alttestamentlichen Gattung* (WMANT 10, 2d ed.; Neukirchen: Neukirchener, 1977) 19–21.

Setting

Under the circumstances there is no way unequivocally to prove or disprove the authenticity of this passage to Jrm, but the remarks in Preliminary Observations have set the stage for a cautious marshaling of evidence for authenticity.

The very oddity of the Aramaic verse (v 11) can suggest authenticity as much as it suggests that it is a late gloss: as already noted (Preliminary Observations), Jrm made use of Aramaic elsewhere (see 20:3–6), the verse offers a carefully constructed chiasmus of eight members, it ironically suspends the identity of the subject ("God" or "the gods"?) until the middle of the verse, and the middle two words, the verbs, offer a word-play. It might well fit Jrm's talent to frame a clever curse-form shaped in the language of the idolaters among whom his audience found themselves (see below). Rudolph thinks that if the setting were the exiles in Babylon and v 11 were genuine, the words "thus shall you say to them" would not be in Aramaic;[18] but this is to be overlogical—one could without difficulty imagine a comedian interrupting his English material to say, "On peut dire, 'Vive l'amour!'"

The diction of the verses specifically concerned for idols (vv 2–5, 8–9, 11, 14–15) finds more parallel with demonstrably Jeremianic language than does the diction of the verses concerned with Yahweh.[19] Thus "nothing(s)" (singular הֶבֶל, vv 3, 15; plural הֲבָלִים, v 8) in reference to idols is a favorite of Jrm elsewhere (singular 2:5, plural 8:19 and 14:22); the word does not appear in Deutero-Isaiah with reference to idols. The phrase "time of their punishment" (עֵת פְּקֻדָּתָם, v 15) and its variants is a favorite with Jrm (6:15 [compare 8:12]; 11:23, 23:12; four times further in the oracles against foreign nations—46:21; 48:44; 50:27; 51:18); the phrase is not found at all in Deutero-Isaiah, and the phraseology of Isa 10:3 and Hos 9:7 is slightly different. The parallelism of "do good, do harm" (יטב hip'il and רעע hip'il, v 5) is found in 2:33 (corrected text), 4:22, and 13:23; it appears once in the context of idols in Isa 41:23 (and one may note also its use in Zeph 1:12, spoken by those who doubt Yahweh's sovereignty). All this suggests at the least a poet whose mentality is shaped by Jrm's diction, and it

renders authenticity to Jrm plausible.

And beyond the wit of the Aramaic verse one senses in the diction of these verses word-plays, ambiguities, and shifts of meaning appropriate to Jrm's style. Thus "(so that) it cannot wobble" (וְלוֹא יָפִיק, v 4) appears at first to be a final clause completing "with nails and hammers they fasten them," but then it appears to be in structural parallelism with "and cannot speak" (וְלֹא יְדַבֵּרוּ, v 5: compare Structure): but the hearer must assume that "so that it cannot wobble" is an advantage, and "and cannot speak" is a disadvantage. There is the ambiguity of the meaning of בער in v 8, "burn" and "be stupid"; an evident shift of function of the preposition מִן־ in the first two cola of v 14; and a possible ambiguity in the meaning of "mockery" in v 15. True, not all these details may be valid—the text is difficult to interpret; but the impression left by these lines is that of Jrm, with his penchant for irony.

The material in the verses concerned with Yahweh (vv 6–7, 10, 12–13, 16) are harder to assess. Jrm himself could quote the Psalms (10:25), but this proves nothing. The phrase "living God" (אֱלֹהִים חַיִּים) reminds one of the "spring of running [= living] water" in 2:13, but the phrase here is a traditional liturgical one. The most one can say is that these verses, by their vocabulary, both in identity and contrast, appear to be integrated into the sequence. Thus one is not to fear the idols (v 5) but to fear Yahweh (v 7); the "nations" have their idols (v 2), but Yahweh is King over the nations (vv 7, 10); Yahweh establishes the world by his wisdom (v 12), while the wisdom of the wise is spurious (vv 7, 9); Yahweh is the only real God (v 10), while the idols are falsehood (v 14): on these connections compare Structure. One notes in passing the resemblance of the first colon of v 12 to 27:5.

It is possible that this passage, if authentic to Jrm, is a product of his meditation on the incident of the Assyrian siege of Jerusalem in the eighth century, when the officer of the Assyrian king, the Rabshakeh, made light of the city and its God (2 Kings 18—19): it is likely that Jrm had that incident in mind in the words of 4:10 (see Interpretation there). The Rabshakeh belittled the power of the gods of the nations (2 Kgs 18:33–35); Hezekiah complained that the Rabshakeh had come to

18 Rudolph, pp. 71–72.
19 Compare Preuss, *Verspottung*, 168.

mock the living God (2 Kgs 19:4), and, according to the narrative, Hezekiah prayed to Yahweh, noting that the kings of Assyria had laid waste the nations and had "cast their gods into the fire; for they were no gods, but the work of men's hands, wood and stone; therefore they were destroyed" (2 Kgs 19:18). And above all, of course, that incident on the walls of Jerusalem involved the confrontation of the Hebrew and Aramaic languages (2 Kgs 18:26–28). My proposal is that Jrm picked up themes from that earlier incident and sent mockery of Mesopotamian pretensions back from Jerusalem to the east, making sure to include in the mockery a few words of Aramaic.

This proposal, that the passage is authentic to Jrm, is strengthened slightly by one's assessment of 16:19–21. That passage, too, concerns the worthlessness of the idols of the nations; it offers, however, diction which strikes one as more like the diction of Jrm found elsewhere. The two passages are, however, in a sense mirror images of each other: the present passage says, "Do not adopt the ways of the nations," while 16:19–21 says, "The nations are about to adopt the worship of Yahweh." The authenticity of 16:19–21, which is argued on its own merits in the present study, reinforces to a degree the proposal that the present passage is likewise authentic.

There are two other passages in which Jrm mocks the powerlessness of idols, 14:22, which in the present study is dated to 601, and 2:26–28, which in the present study is dated to 594. It is conceivable that Jrm sent the present passage to those who were exiled in the first deportation to Babylon: chapter 29 records a letter Jrm sent to the exiles, doubtless in that year, and it is recorded in 51:59–64 that he sent a collection of words against Babylon by the hand of Seraiah, the brother of his scribe to Baruch, in 594/593. One might even wonder whether the two recensions in *M* and *G* represent his words in 594 and again in 587 at the time he was taken to Egypt.[20] But given the uniqueness of the passage, such suggestions are no more than speculation.

Interpretation

■ **2–3aα** The verb "learn" (למד) is curious here, for the context both here and in v 5 leads one to expect a verb for "fear"; but the identity of the verb is secure (compare Structure on the placement of this passage). In no other occurrence of this verb is it accompanied by the preposition אֶל־; there is doubtless a special nuance of the verb here, perhaps "resort to" or "become involved with learning" (hence the rendering here, "start learning").

The parallelism of "manner" (דֶּרֶךְ, literally "way") with "customs" (חֻקּוֹת) is also unique to this passage. The noun דֶּרֶךְ is used by Jrm in 2:23 with the implication of Canaanite religious practices, so both words clearly mean "religious practices": Lev 18:3 is close (and compare the Greek ἡ ὁδός "the way" for the Christian religion in Acts 9:2). The vague and perhaps euphemistic terms "manner" and "customs" give way to specifics in the second colon, however: Jews are not to pay any attention to the "omens [literally 'signs'] of the sky" (אֹתוֹת הַשָּׁמַיִם) which so panic the pagans. This combination, again, is not found elsewhere in the OT. The omens referred to here are not only unexpected phenomena like comets and meteors but predictable astronomical phenomena; one recalls from Gen 1:14 that the sun and moon themselves are intended to be "signs" (אֹתֹת). These omens make up the whole lore of astrology that preoccupied Mesopotamia.[21] Astrological omens may terrorize pagans, but they are really הֶבֶל "emptiness, nothing" (on this word see 2:5). The precise function of כִּי at the beginning of the third and fourth cola is not altogether clear. One is

---

20 Janzen assumes the passage is not authentic, but his summary of Cross's view on the provenience of *M* and *G* (a Palestinian text-type and an Egyptian text-type respectively) are relevant here: see Janzen, pp. 127–32.

21 The literature is extensive. For a description of the fear which so gripped its devotees see G. Ernest Wright, *The Old Testament Against Its Environment* (SBT 2; Chicago: Regnery, 1950) 78–81; the source for his quotations, a standard work in English, is Reginald Campbell Thompson, *The Reports of the Magicians and Astrologers of Nineveh and Babylon in the*

British Museum (London: Luzac, 1900). For a convenient description of astrological omen texts, see A. Leo Oppenheim, "Assyria and Babylonia," *IDB* 1:284–87; for examples of correspondence from royal astrologers, see his *Letters from Mesopotamia* (Chicago: University of Chicago, 1967) 160–62.

tempted to understand "even though the nations are panicked by them" (so Rudolph, Bright). Rudolph explains it as "I say (do not be panicked), because the nations are panicked" (compare *RSV*). If one translates the first כִּי as either "though" or "because," then the second כִּי, which begins v 3, can be "for" (so all the commentators); but this colon is in such strong contrast to the one preceding it that "but" is a plausible rendering. Since the following colon, "He cuts it from a tree in the forest," likewise begins with כִּי, it is clear that the poet intends ironically to highlight the variety of perspectives hovering around the spectacle of idolatry.

■ **3aβb-4** Abruptly the reference shifts from the omens of the sky to the cutting of a tree for an idol. How easy it is for a superstitious population to be awestruck by some celestial phenomenon; but really it has no more significance than a tree felled by a woodsman in the forest— what a stunning *reductio ad absurdum*! And the reduction is reinforced by the word "hands" in the next colon: an idol is a human creation, an expression of human imagination. The misplaced faith of pagans is nothing but a set of do-it-yourself tasks in a workshop. The subject of "he cuts" is not stated (compare GKC, sec. 144d).

The חָרָשׁ is any kind of craftsman, whether in wood, stone, or metal; here it is clearly a carpenter or wood-carver that is intended. It is uncertain what kind of tool a מַעֲצָד is; the word appears only here and in Isa 44:12 in a similar passage. But the word *mʿṣd* appears several times in lists of agricultural implements in Ugaritic texts;[22] C. H. Gordon suggests the meaning "scythe,"[23] while the Arabic cognate *miʿḍad* is a bill-hook, an implement for pruning trees. The latter meaning is appropriate if the action described is trimming a piece of timber, but if a trimmed log is being carved into shape (which is more likely), then "adze" is the meaning, as it is in postbiblical Hebrew. One notes the assonance of *ʿēṣ, maʿăśēh*, and *maʿăṣād* in this sequence, and its continuation with *yiṣʿādû* in v 5.

The wooden core of the idol is then decorated (or possibly "overlaid": see Text, vv 4–5, note a) with silver and gold. But what is meant by the "fastening" in the last colon? The colon ends with the clause "so that it cannot wobble" (וְלוֹא יָפִיק), implying that the image is fastened to a base (so also the implication of Isa 40:20; 41:7) or perhaps to the ground, so that it cannot be tipped over or stolen. Though the verb פוק hipʿil appears only here in the OT, the meaning "wobble" is fairly certain: the qal stem appears in Isa 28:7 meaning "stagger." But one wonders whether there is not an ambiguity here, since in postbiblical Hebrew פוק hipʿil may mean "utter" (words), and the first colon in v 5, in parallel fashion, ends with וְלֹא יְדַבֵּרוּ "and (they) cannot speak." Does the expression then also mean "and it cannot utter (anything)"?

■ **5** The word "scarecrow" (תֹּמֶר) appears only here in the OT and was misunderstood by the Versions (G omits; V and S assume the vocalization תָּמָר "palm-tree"), but Ep Jer 69 "like a scarecrow (προβασκάνιον) in a cucumber-field" secures the meaning.[24] In aniconic Israel the only public images were scarecrows, ridiculous images to frighten off birds. As the signs of the sky are reduced to an idol, idols are here reduced to scarecrows; religious images that awe the populace are no different from a pole in a garden hung with rags waving in the wind. Scarecrows cannot speak; idols cannot speak. And more than not speaking, they even have to be picked up and carried, since they cannot walk.

The description of the way idols are made makes it crystal clear that there is nothing in them to inspire fear; they cannot do any harm—but of course they cannot do any good either. (Compare Zeph 1:12, where the doubters are portrayed as saying the same thing about Yahweh.)

Yehezkel Kaufmann has pointed out how curious it is that the prophetic mockery of idolatry never mocked any of the myths of the gods, myths which would have offered a fertile treasure-store for satire.[25] But it is true that the pagans made no clear distinction between the heavenly bodies and the gods manifested in those

---

22   Ug. 2048, 2053.
23   *UT*, 460, no. 1904.
24   *V* here likewise has "scarecrow" (*formido*: the reference is Bar 6:69). This evidence speaks against the proposal of Deist (see bibliography).
25   Yehezkel Kaufmann, *The Religion of Israel, From Its Beginnings to the Babylonian Exile* (Chicago: University of Chicago, 1960) 7–17.

heavenly bodies, and between the gods and the idol-images in which the gods were made manifest; and this confusion allowed the prophet to make the dizzying reduction from an alarming portent in the sky to the contemptible scarecrow in a few short verses, demythologizing the whole pagan religious system by attacking it at its weakest point.[26]

■ **6–7** For the theme of the incomparability of Yahweh see Form. One moves from the ridiculous to the sublime: Yahweh is worthy to be feared; the nations should by rights fear their true King, who has placed the signs in the heavens (compare again Gen 1:14). The verb "befit" (יאה) appears only here in the OT; its cognate is common in Aramaic and Syriac, but this is no necessary indication that the usage here is an Aramaism or that its use bespeaks the lateness of the passage (against BDB). The word "wise men of" (חַכְמֵי) in v 7b is unexpected, and it is no wonder that a few MSS. read "kings of," reflecting the second colon of v 7 (see Text). But if "kings of" is correct, "their dominion" (מַלְכוּתָם) can hardly be correct. "Wise men of" is evidently correct, an anticipation of the "wise" craftsmen in v 9: among all those clever people who construct idols, there is no one comparable to Yahweh, who makes everything. "Their dominion" (or "kingship") is the kingship of the nations; and this word, suggesting power, moves one's attention back to the "strength" (גְּבוּרָה) of Yahweh's name affirmed in v 6: גְּבוּרָה and מַלְכוּת are parallel in 1 Chr 29:30.

■ **8** Though it is clear that this verse begins a new section mocking idols, the thought of the verse is far from clear, especially that of the second colon, where the Greek traditions offer a different text. Thus θ' reads the verse, "For at once the hearts of the foolish shall be burned up and be weak; it is wood": that recension thus reads "the instruction of nothings" as "the hearts of the foolish." And some G MSS. that reflect Hexaplaric and Lucianic recensions offer "the heart of vanities is wood" for the second colon. The persistent reading "heart" is thus either an interpretation of מוּסָר or perhaps represents a reading מוֹסָד or מוּסָד "foundation." Furthermore Rudolph suggests emending "wood" (עֵץ) to מֵעֵצָה "without counsel," and it may be that this root did appear in the original line. All in all, however, it is better to stay

with M.

If the text is sound, the verse offers two peculiarities not dealt with in the translations. (1) The introductory expression וּבְאַחַת "and at the same time" is emphatic and comports poorly with two verbs taken as close synonyms, בער "be stupid" and כסל "be foolish." (2) The connective ו suggests that the imperfect verbs are to be taken as jussives. If the first line means "they are both stupid and foolish" (RSV), the most natural way it would be expressed is גַּם־בֹּעֲרִים גַּם־כְּסִילִים הֵמָּה or the like (compare Ps 94:8). I propose that the verse is highly ironic, and that even though the two verbs in the first colon are heard in the first instance as the synonyms "be stupid" and "be foolish," the presence of "at the same time" at the beginning of the verse and "wood" at the end leads the hearer to understand בער as the homonym "burn" (so θ': see above). The verb בער does mean "be stupid" in v 14 (there the stem is nip'al), but the primary meaning here must be "burn": in Isa 44:15, 16, and 19 the prophet insists that the same tree from the forest that is used for an idol is used to kindle a fire. Idols are made of wood (v 3 here) and so deserve to burn, just as their lack of wisdom offers nothing of instruction or discipline (מוּסָר). Understood so, the suggestion that the idols will be burned anticipates the destruction of the gods set forth in v 11.

■ **9** This verse is closely modeled on vv 3aβb–4. The silver here is described as מְרֻקָּע "hammered, beaten, flattened"; one assumes that the silver was imported in plates. And one hears the sources for the silver and gold, Tarshish and Uphaz.

Tarshish is a distant port hardly to be located specifically. Silver, iron, tin, and lead were available there (Ezek 27:12). The implication of Jonah 1:3 and other texts is that it is a port in the western Mediterranean, but the problem is complicated by the fact that the phrase "ships of Tarshish" referred to any seagoing vessel (e.g., Isa 23:1), so that Solomon could send such a fleet (1 Kgs 10:22) in a direction almost surely along the Red Sea toward India. The name is not to be identified with Tarsus in Cilicia (against Josephus);[27] cuneiform texts render the two names differently.[28] There is strong likelihood that it is Tartessus, a trading colony at the

26 William L. Holladay, *Isaiah, Scroll of a Prophetic Heritage* (Grand Rapids: Eerdmans, 1978) 139–47.

27 Josephus *Ant.* 9.10.2.

28 Hans Walter Wolff, *Obadja und Jona* (BKAT 14/3; Neukirchen: Neukirchener, 1977) 78.

mouth of the Guadalquivir River in Spain, outside Gibraltar; it was a Greek colony and had evidently been a Phoenician colony earlier.[29] This identification was made in the seventeenth century,[30] evidently having been anticipated by Eusebius; it would fit the list of minerals in Ezek 27:12. Recently, reading "Tarshish" in the Phoenician inscription from Nora in Sardinia, Albright has suggested a location in Sardinia for the name and further suggests that the name was originally a common noun, "refinery."[31] This proposal has not been accepted, but the name may well have been attached to more than one port.[32] Recently Gordon has suggested that the word simply meant "the open sea," which was (in Homer's phrase) "wine-dark," related then to תִּירוֹשׁ "wine."[33] But there is no consensus on the question.[34]

The location of "Uphaz" is unknown. The text is open to doubt (see Text, note a). If the text should read "Ophir," then the location may well be in present-day Somaliland.[35] Whatever the identity of the name, the poet may well have wished to suggest in the sources for silver and gold the extremes of west and east respectively (compare Cyprus and Kedar in 2:10).

The syntax of the third colon is unclear. The phrase is literally "the work of a craftsman and the hands of a smith." Most translations take the last section as a triple construct chain ("the work of a craftsman and of the hands of a smith," so *RSV*, *JB*, *NJV*), but the pairing of "blue" and "purple" in the following colon suggests a balance here (compare Structure), so that "hands" may suggest "handiwork" (the singular "hand" appears in this meaning in Exod 14:31); this is the understanding of *NAB*.

A "smith" (צוֹרֵף) is literally a "smelter, refiner"; for the verb see 6:29. The term refers without differentiation to a silver- or a goldsmith.

"Their clothes" are of course the clothes of the idols. There is no way to distinguish the two dyes named, תְּכֵלֶת and אַרְגָּמָן, though they doubtless refer to slightly different colors and/or processes; the two words usually occur side by side in the OT. The word 'argmn occurs in Ugaritic[36] but in a context meaning "tribute" which does not aid in identification. Tyrian purple was extracted from a number of mollusks, *Murex brandaris, M. trunculus, Helix ianthina*, and *Purpura haemastoma*.[37] It is assumed today that the two words refer not to contrasting species but to contrasting processes in extraction which resulted in different colors;[38] but ancient color words are notoriously inexact,[39] and the Versions give no real guidance in identification (the *G* renderings ὑάκινθον and πορφύραν are just as difficult to interpret).

The closing line summarizes. The word "wise" is ironic; meaning "skilled," it does refer to artisans (Exod 28:3), as it seems to have in v 7, but these "wise men" are making things that are essentially foolish (v 8).

■ **10** It is difficult to determine the syntax of the first colon. Analogy with the position of הוּא in vv 3 and 8 suggests that the pronoun here closes the colon (against the *M* accent zaqep qaton): the idols may be "a nothing," or wood, but Yahweh is "reality" (אֱמֶת)—so Graf. Most commentators, however, read אֱמֶת adverbially, as in 23:28 and Ps 132:11: "Yahweh is truly God." Dahood construes a mem enclitic, אֱלֹהִי־ם אֱמֶת, "[Yahweh is] the true God," comparing אֱלֹהֵי אֱמֶת in 2 Chr 15:3.[40]

The phrase "living God" (אֱלֹהִים חַיִּים) occurs in this form in four other passages (23:36; Deut 5:23; 1 Sam 17:26, 36). The phrase is no doubt liturgical here, but it functions to reinforce "reality" (אֱמֶת) in contrasting Yahweh with the gods who are nothing but immobile

29 Donald Harden, *The Phoenicians* (London: Thames and Hudson, 1963) 159–60.
30 By Samuel Bochart in 1651: see W. Max Müller, "Tarshish," *Dictionary of the Bible* (ed. James Hastings; New York: Scribner's, 1902) 4:684.
31 William F. Albright, "New Light on the Early History of Phoenician Colonization," *BASOR* 83 (October 1941) 21–22.
32 Speiser, *Genesis*, 66.
33 Cyrus H. Gordon, "The Wine-Dark Sea," *JNES* 37 (1978) 51–52; compare Sidney B. Hoenig, "Tarshish," *JQR* 69 (1978–79) 181–82.

34 For recent general discussion on the matter see Westermann, *Genesis 1*, 678; Wildberger, *Jesaja*, 110–11; Hans Walter Wolff, *Obadja und Jona* (BKAT 14/3; Neukirchen: Neukirchener, 1977) 78–79.
35 Gus W. Van Beek, "Ophir," *IDB* 3:605–6.
36 Ug. 2.1.37.
37 Lloyd B. Jensen, "Royal Purple of Tyre," *JNES* 22 (1963) 104–18.
38 Friedrich S. Bodenheimer, "Fauna," *IDB* 2:246–56, esp. 255–56.
39 Richard W. Corney, "Colors," *IDB* 1:657.
40 Dahood, *Psalms III*, 69.

scarecrows.[41]

The phrase "everlasting King" (מֶלֶךְ עוֹלָם) does not occur otherwise, but analogous phrases for "everlasting God" do, אֵל עוֹלָם in Gen 21:33 (J) and אֱלֹהֵי עוֹלָם in Isa 40:28. The expression means not so much "everlasting King" as "King over the whole expanse of time filled with history."[42]

The expressions in v 10a are all noun phrases and tempt one therefore to hear them as static descriptions; the temptation is dispelled by the violent verbal clauses that follow. The synonyms "fury" (קֶצֶף) and "rage" (וַעַם) appear in parallel in Ps 102:11 as well as here. Both terms are used in the OT overwhelmingly of God's wrath rather than of human wrath (for both words, twenty-six out of twenty-eight instances). Here his wrath causes earthquakes (so also Isa 29:6), and the nations of the world cannot sustain his wrath (compare 6:11, where, with the same verb, Jrm cannot sustain Yahweh's wrath).[43] The verse affirms that Yahweh, by the very fact of who he is, the only valid God, shapes both nature and history.

■ 11 For the climactic role played in the passage by this Aramaic verse see Preliminary Observations. The verse opens with the Aramaic version of the formulaic instruction to the hearers to carry a message (for the Hebrew equivalent see 27:4) "to them"—as it turns out, to the nations and their idol makers.

As already noted (see Form), the main verb of the message may be taken either as indicative ("they shall perish") or jussive ("let them perish"). Both G and V take the verb as jussive; recent translations divide on the question (indicative: RSV, JB, NEB; jussive: NAB, NJV). The verb is poised between the jussive of v 8a and the indicative of the Hebrew cognate יאבדו in v 15.

The word order is ironic: the main verb seems to be

delayed, though the word order subject + verb may have been normal in the Mesopotamian Aramaic of this period, as it was in Akkadian.[44] In any event, the deferment of the verb allows for the ambiguity in the initial words, since אֱלָהַיָּא, like the Hebrew הָאֱלֹהִים, could evidently mean either "God" or "the gods";[45] so one hears "God/the gods who the heavens and the earth" before the identity of the subject is made known by the negative לָא and the plural verb עֲבַדוּ. And right on the heels of this identification comes the verb "they shall perish" (יֵאבַדוּ), a word-play on the verb just preceding ('ayin and 'alep were evidently not distinguished in pronunciation: see Preliminary Observations).

The initial words of the verse remind one of liturgical formulas for the God of creation (compare "God Most High, maker of heaven and earth," אֵל עֶלְיוֹן קֹנֵה שָׁמַיִם וָאָרֶץ, Gen 14:19,[46] and "Yahweh maker of heaven and earth" and variations, Pss 121:2; 124:8; 134:3; 146:6); but of course the deferring of the verb defers the negative as well, so that this formulation turns the normal form upside-down.

The shift from אַרְקָא to אַרְעָא within short compass is curious. The spelling with qop is earlier (in the Zenjirli and Sefire inscriptions of the ninth/eighth centuries); the Elephantine papyri of the fifth century uses both spellings, and later Aramaic used the spelling with 'ayin,[47] so that one must simply assume the carelessness of a copyist—the shift plays no part in the rhetoric of the passage.

The word "under" (תְּחוֹת) is not necessary for the symmetry of the passage, so its presence must be deliberate. The pagan gods are not heavenly beings at all, but are earthbound!

Earlier commentators assumed that the last word of the verse, אֵלֶּה, is Hebrew;[48] but recently uncovered

41 For treatments of the phrase see Johnson, *Vitality of the Individual*, 105–7; Helmer Ringgren, *Israelite Religion* (Philadelphia: Fortress, 1966) 87.

42 See Ernst S. Jenni, "Das Wort 'ōlām im Alten Testament," *ZAW* 64 (1952) 197–248; 65 (1953) 1–35.

43 For the theology of the wrath of God see conveniently Johannes Fichtner, "ὀργή κτλ.," *TDNT* 5:395–409.

44 Compare the remarks in Hans Bauer and Pontus Leander, *Grammatik des Biblisch-Aramäischen* (Halle-Saale: Niemeyer, 1927) sec. 99a, on Dan 4:16.

45 The word takes a singular verb in the Aramaic Aḥiqar, line 126, in Arthur E. Cowley, *Aramaic Papyri of the Fifth Century B.C.* (Oxford: Clarendon, 1923).

46 See Westermann, *Genesis 1*, 243.

47 See in detail *DISO*, 25, and conveniently Jonas C. Greenfield, "Aramaic," *IDBSup*, 39–40, John C. L. Gibson, "Inscriptions, Semitic," *IDBSup*, 433–34, and Michael C. Astour, "Ya'udi," *IDBSup*, 975.

48 Emil F. Kautzsch, *Grammatik des Biblisch-Aramäischen* (Leipzig: Vogel, 1884) 22; Cornill.

documents make it clear that it is good Aramaic for the period.[49] Its syntax is ambiguous. *G, S,* and *T* construe the word with "heavens": "They shall perish from the earth and from under these heavens" (so *KJV, NEB, NAB, NJV*). *V* surprisingly stretches the Aramaic to translate "Let them perish from the earth and from those (places) which are under the heavens." But others have construed the word to modify "the gods" (so Calvin, and so also Condamin), and, given the chiastic arrangement (see Preliminary Observations) and the initial ambiguity of אֱלָהַיָּא ("God" or "the gods": see above), this construction is doubtless correct: the word would be a final emphasis on the plurality of the gods.

The whole verse is heavy with sarcasm: these gods depicted by the idols had no part in the creation of heaven and earth and do not belong upon the earth or under the heavens. They must disappear.

■ 12 Having aborted the expected liturgical formula "maker of heaven and earth" in v 11, the poet offers the valid formula now, expanding the two terms "heaven" and "earth" into three by adding "world" (תֵּבֵל) and expanding "strength" (גְּבוּרָה, v 6) into the triad "power" (כֹּחַ), "wisdom" (חָכְמָה), and "understanding" (תְּבוּנָה). Since אֶרֶץ (normally "earth") in some texts has the nuance "underworld,"[50] Dahood has suggested that one has here (and in Ps 77:19) a tripartite division of the universe into underworld, earth, and heavens;[51] this is possible, since Ps 89:12 offers the same triad. The language of the verse is similar to that of many passages in the Psalms describing the creative activity of Yahweh (for example, Ps 65:7).

■ 13 The creative word of Yahweh is now made more specific in four manifestations of the storm: the roaring of rainwater, mists, lightning bolts, and wind.[52] For "uproar" (הֲמוֹן) see 3:23; it is used of the sound of rain in 1 Kgs 18:41. One notes the assonance of *hămôn mayim baššāmayim.* The last three cola of the verse are found in Ps 125:7, but it would be difficult to prove dependence in either direction. Question: Is "mists" (נְשִׂאִים) a word-

play on "they must even be carried" (נָשׂוֹא יִנָּשֵׂאוּ) in v 5? The third colon is ambiguous, either "lightning-bolts for the rain he has made" or "lightning-bolts into rain he has made" (for עשה לְ in this meaning see 37:15). *T* may have retained an awareness of the ambiguity with its paraphrase, "lightning-bolts in the time of rain he has made" (so Cornill). The concept of the "storehouses of Yahweh" for rain, hail, or snow is found more than once (see Deut 28:12; Ps 33:7; and Job 38:22). Those manifestations of the storm that were attributed by the Canaanites to Baal and by various Mesopotamian peoples to Adad[53] are affirmed to be under the direction of Yahweh.

■ 14 Verse 14a is far from clear. The two cola are closely parallel in structure, but do the two instances of מִן carry parallel or contrasting meanings? Who is "every person" (כָּל־אָדָם)?—it is an odd phrase to place in parallel with "every smith." Isa 44:11 affirms that the craftsmen are simply men; so here, these craftsmen who are supposedly shaping gods are themselves nothing but human beings. The verb בער nip'al means "become stupid," like cattle (בְּעִיר); this verb is hinted at in v 8, though the proposal offered in this study is that the verb there means primarily "burn." The phrase מִדַּעַת (literally "from knowledge") has elicited many interpretations. Jerome assumed that it was God's knowledge that is referred to: "Every person (no matter how wise) is stupid in comparison to the knowledge of God." It is clear, however, that the "knowledge" is human. The general consensus of commentators (Volz, Rudolph) and translations is that מִן is privative: "Everyone is stupid, without knowledge." But this interpretation makes מִדַּעַת the functional synonym of the verb "is stupid" (נִבְעַר), and since the prepositional phrase in the second colon is not a synonym of the verb in its colon, synonymity seems dubious here. Calvin interprets the line as "every craftsman is foolish through (his own presumed) knowledge," where מִן is understood as cause; this interpretation has the advantage (so Cornill) of matching the function of מִן in the second colon. Another possibility is the one offered here,

49 *DISO,* 78; Ernst Vogt, *Lexicon Linguae Aramaicae Veteris Testamenti Documentis Antiquis Illustratum* (Rome: Pontifical Biblical Institute, 1971) 8.
50 *HALAT,* 88a.
51 Dahood, *Psalms II,* 232.
52 For a description of thunderstorms in Palestine see Baly, *Geography,* 49.
53 See John Gray, "Baal," *IDB* 1:328–29; A. Leo

Oppenheim, *Ancient Mesopotamia, Portrait of a Dead Civilization* (Chicago: University of Chicago, 1964) 196.

by which מִן expresses negative consequence; the phrase would be exactly parallel to Gen 27:1, וַתִּכְהֶיןָ עֵינָיו מֵרְאֹת "and his eyes became too dim to see," thus "every person is too stupid to know." But the colon may be deliberately ambiguous (see below).

In the second colon every smith is put to shame, stands ashamed, because of what he has built: not that "he is ashamed of his idol," not that he is conscious of the foolishness of what he has done, but rather that he is ultimately humiliated (*NEB*: "discredited") by the nature of his work, since the very nature of the enterprise is folly. And now we see the irony of "knowledge" in the first colon, whether it be taken as "every person is made a fool through his own presumed knowledge" or "every person is too stupid to have any real knowledge": how can "knowledge" be identified with an idol?—and the syntax of the two cola makes them parallel!

This irony is reinforced by v 14b. A נֶסֶךְ is properly something poured, a molten image, but it is used here simply in parallelism with an "idol" (פֶּסֶל). And it is "falsehood," "a lie" (שֶׁקֶר), beings without "breath" (רוּחַ), in contrast to Yahweh who brings forth the wind (רוּחַ, v 13).

■ **15** They are a nothing, a zero (הֶבֶל; this has already been heard, vv 3, 8). They are "a work of mockery" in two senses: idols are worthy only to be mocked as one would mock a scarecrow (so the Versions), but further the idols mock their worshipers in their very powerlessness (so Cornill, Giesebrecht). Except for this passage (and the parallel in 51:18) all other occurrences of "in the time/year of their punishment" refer to the punishing of ungodly men (11:23; 23:12; 46:21; 48:44; 50:27; compare Isa 10:3; Hos 9:7; and compare Jer 6:15; 49:8; 50:31); this passage then implies that Yahweh will treat the gods and their images as he treats people who disobey him (compare Ps 82:6–7): they shall perish (compare v 11).

■ **16** This verse finally brings a mention of the covenant people. Yahweh is here designated "portion (or possession) of Jacob" (חֵלֶק יַעֲקֹב). This phrase is unique to this passage (and the parallel 51:19), but Yahweh is called "portion" (חֵלֶק) elsewhere (Num 18:20; Pss 16:5; 53:26; 119:57; 142:6; Lam 3:24). It is an astonishing

metaphor, doubtless derived from land apportionment: the Levites had no allocation of land, so Yahweh was their allocation (Num 18:20), and the metaphor was then generalized in liturgical contexts, thus the Psalms passages.[54] The participle of the verb "forms" or "shapes" (יוֹצֵר) also means a "potter" (18:2–6); the verb is central in the J-narrative of creation (Gen 2:7, 8, 19). The expression "everything" (הַכֹּל) virtually means "the universe" (compare Pss 103:19; 119:91). The third colon is the obverse of the first: if Yahweh is the portion of Jacob, then Israel is the tribe of Yahweh's possession. Yahweh and Israel belong indissolubly to each other, and these expressions involving the covenant enclose an affirmation of Yahweh as creator of the whole universe. "Possession" (נַחֲלָה) is a traditional term for Israel: see 12:7. The verse concludes with the refrain typical of hymns, "Yahweh of hosts is his name" (see Form).

Aim

The tension within this passage brought about by the contrast between the flippant contempt the poet expresses for the pagan gods and their images on the one hand and the awe he expresses for Yahweh is almost unbearable. Yahweh is unique, and great, and worthy of fear, the master of earthquakes and the Lord of history; the idols, by contrast, are nothing but scarecrows, dolled up with bits and pieces of decoration, worthy only to frighten passing birds intent on a meal. Yahweh and the idols—they are hardly in the same universe of discourse at all, yet the poet shifts repeatedly from the one to the other, giving the hearer a kind of vertigo in awareness. The idols are mocked in a kind of doggerel poetry, laughed to scorn; Yahweh is addressed and hymned in the solemn language of liturgy. Deutero-Isaiah would manage the same shift, but in large literary units (Isa 44:6–22); the poet in the present passage manages to shift the hearer from the ridiculous to the sublime, back and forth, dizzyingly, and as a climax, as a bonus, he tosses in a word to say to the idolaters and the idol makers in their own tongue, a joke that spells the doom of their whole elaborate religious system with the plurality of their gods: "these"—the isolated plural pronoun—must ultimately perish, perish because

---

54   For a discussion of the metaphor see von Rad, *OT Theology 1*, 403–5.

Yahweh will ultimately deal with them. What a word from a defeated population lost among all the populations in the vast Babylonian Empire!—what a word, that Yahweh of hosts, who is the portion (almost the "possession") of Jacob, will see to the destruction of the idols of that empire! If the idols are doomed, can Babylon's doom be far behind? The stage is set for the ringing faith of Deutero-Isaiah.

Get Ready for Exile!

Bibliography

Berridge
  pp. 176, 194–97.
Kumaki
McKane
  Prophets and Wise Men, 90–91.
Reventlow
  Liturgie, 196–205.

10

17 Jeremiah: **Gather up from the land your bundle,**
             (you who are) enthroned[a] under siege!
18   **For thus Yahweh has said:**
   Yahweh: **I am going to sling out the inhabitants of**
             the land ⟪ in rage, ⟫[a]
             and I will make (it) too narrow for them
             so ⟪ they will be squeezed dry. ⟫[b]
19 people: **Woe is me for my fracture,**
             my wound is unhealable;
             I for my part had thought,
             "This is just ⟨my sickness,⟩[a] and I
             must bear it."
20   **My tent is devastated,**
             and all my tent-cords snapped;
             my children have gone out from me
             and are no more,
             no one any longer spreading my
             tent
             and setting up my curtains.
21 Jeremiah: **Indeed, the shepherds are stupid,**
             they have not consulted Yahweh;
             that is why they have failed,
             and all their pasturage is scattered.
22 Yahweh: **The sound of rumor—listen!—is coming,**
             and a great commotion from the land of
             the north,
             to make the cities of Judah a desolation,
             a lair of jackals.
23 people: **I know, Yahweh,**
             that a person's way is not his (to
             choose),
             nor[a] is it for a man to walk
             [b] and make firm[b] his step.
24   **Correct me, but in moderation,**
             not in your anger, or you reduce me (to
             nothing).
25   **Pour out your wrath on the nations who**
             do not know you,
             and on tribes[a] who do not call on your
             name;
             for they have devoured Jacob [and

Text

17a   Reading qere' יֹשֶׁבֶת; ketib ישבתי is equivalent—see GKC, sec. 90n.

18a   Reading בְּזַעַם (compare Hab 3:12). *M* בָּעֵם הַזֹּאת "at this time" overloads the colon (six "units": see O'Connor, *Structure*, 138), and "at this time" is an unlikely colon of its own (against Rudolph). In *G* "this" modifies "land," and there is no equivalent of "at the time," a datum suggesting that "this" is a floating word, perhaps introduced secondarily in the margin. *M* בָּעֵם is textually distinctive but does not seem to make sense on its own; my suggestion at least conforms to the genre, and pe and zayin could easily have been confused in the early Aramaic script (compare Frank M. Cross, "The Development of the Jewish Scripts," *The Bible and the Ancient Near East* [ed. G. Ernest Wright; New York: Doubleday, 1961] 133–202, esp. 137). See further Interpretation.

b   This passage needs remedy; *M* יִמְצָאוּ "they may find" is impossible. But the consonantal sequence is old: *G* and *V* read a passive, "they may be found," thus יִמָּצְאוּ, nip'al. The emendation accepted here, with reservation, is that of Driver, יִמָּצּוּ (מצה nip'al), which is also adopted by Bright and *NEB*: see Driver, "Jeremiah," 107. Another possibility, given the occurrence of יצא in v 20, is to see a form of that verb here (thus a hop'al, יוּצְאוּ, "they may be brought out," compare 38:22).

19a   Reading חָלְיִי = חָלִי with *V, S, T* (compare *G*) for *M* חֳלִי "a sickness" (so also Giesebrecht and Volz). For the defective spelling compare the qere' and ketib of Zeph 2:9b; for the preferable syntax of the emendation see GKC, sec. 126y.

23a   Reading וְלֹא with many MSS. and with the Versions instead of *M* לֹא.

b—b   One MS. omits "and," and this reading is followed by Rudolph and Bright; but the grammatical difficulty may be solved without resorting to the omission (see Interpretation).

25a   Some MSS. of the Hebrew as well as some MSS. of *G*, and *T*, and the parallel in Ps 79:6, read מַמְלָכוֹת "kingdoms" (and *V* reads "provinces" here). Both words are found in the conflate text of *M* in 1:16 and are clearly old alternatives, but מִשְׁפָּחוֹת is doubtless more original.

devoured him]^b and destroyed him,
and devastated his sheepfold.

b　וַאֲכָלֻהוּ is probably dittographic; it is omitted by a
few MSS. and by *G*. The parallel in Ps 79:7 omits
not only this verb but וַיְכַלֻּהוּ "and destroyed him"
which follows. It is possible that "devour" and
"destroy" themselves represent a conflate text and
that *M* represents a still later expansion (Janzen, p.
11). On the other hand, Mitchell Dahood, "The
Word-pair *'ākal//kālāh* in Jeremiah xxx 16," *VT* 27
(1977) 482 n. 2, defends the repetition of "devour"
here, proposing a tricolon.

Structure, Form, and Setting

Extent and Integrity of the Unit; Identification of Speakers.
Verses 1–16 make up an intact unit, and 11:1 begins a
prose section; what intervenes appears miscellaneous,
and most commentators see these verses as multiple. All
of them reject v 25 as a secondary insertion from Ps
79:6–7, and several see vv 23–24 as unconnected with
what precedes (Volz, Rudolph). Verses 23–24 have
received the most varied treatment: they are a prayer
uttered by Jrm on behalf of the people (Cornill,
Rudolph), or on behalf of himself (Hyatt, Bright), or of
the people on behalf of themselves (Condamin); or else
they (with v 25) are a late, unauthentic addition (Duhm,
Giesebrecht, Volz). Volz furthermore is convinced that v
22 does not belong with vv 17–21, and he indeed sees vv
17–21 as a series of disconnected fragments, namely vv
17 + 18b, v 18a, vv 19–20, v 21.

One cannot demonstrate a unity to the passage, but I
propose that it is indeed a unity and consists of two cycles
of a sequence of speakers, Jrm, Yahweh, and the people.
The first cycle is clear. Yahweh speaks after the opening
rubric of v 18, and there is no reason to doubt the
originality of the rubric, the existence of which implies
that Jrm speaks in v 17 (compare the shifts in 5:12–14).
The text of *M* in vv 19–20 demands that the people be
the speaker (for the diction see 4:20), but it should be
noted that *G* uses "your" instead of "my" in some of the
cola—one assumes this is a secondary shift. It is to be
noted further that "but I myself had thought" (וַאֲנִי
אָמַרְתִּי) in v 19b does not mark a shift of speaker (any
more than it does in 5:4).

Verses 21–25 give difficulty. As Volz noticed, there is
a shift in diction from v 20 to v 21: v 20 is a complaint of
the people, and v 21a is some kind of judgment. Verse
21 has parallels to 5:5–6: the judgment on the leader-

ship, the expression "that is why" (עַל־כֵּן), and those
verses are part of a sequence spoken by Jrm; it is appropriate then to assign v 21 to Jrm (so also Condamin,
Rudolph). But, as Volz likewise noticed, there is another
shift between v 21 and v 22 (against Condamin and
Rudolph): v 22 offers the war news, and such announcements have been assigned to Yahweh from chapter 4
onward: to stay only with references to the coming of the
enemy from "the north" compare 4:6; 6:1, 22. But there
is a problem: form-critically the verse is an audition
report, and such reports are normally offered by the
prophet (see *Form* below). If the verse is assigned to
Yahweh (as both content and symmetry suggest), then it
evidently offers an ironic reuse of the form.

Verses 23–25 are united in being citations of or
expansions of scripture: v 23 is adapted from Prov 16:9
and 20:24; v 24 is an expansion of Ps 6:2, and v 25 is a
citation of Ps 79:6–7. Since Jrm has on other occasions
offered citations of or allusions to scripture (notably 4:3–
4), one cannot reject any of these verses out of hand. The
pattern of shifts of speaker in this sequence suggests that
they are spoken by the people: just as the mood of vv 19–
20 is self-pity, so in these verses, I propose, Jrm is
quoting the people's citation of traditional material to
justify their irresponsibility (see Interpretation). This
analysis is strengthened slightly by the occurrence of אַךְ
in both vv 19 and 24. Thus what other commentators
have assumed to be fragmentary or anticlimactic
emerges, to the contrary, as a climax: the people will
never learn.[1]

Of course one could analyze the passage without vv
23–25: by such an analysis the lament of the people (vv
19–20) would be the central portion of vv 17–22. But
given the sequence that has come down to us, the analysis
offered here is reasonable, and again the precedent of

1　For this analysis of vv 21–25 see Holladay, *Architecture*, 117–21.

4:3–4 should make one hesitate to reject any of vv 23–25. Indeed might the two passages be seen as bracketing the material on the foe from the north?

Placement of the Unit; Setting. This passage, which mentions the foe from the north (v 22), belongs to the "basic stratum" of the material added by Jrm in the second scroll, along with 8:4–13, 14–23; 9:1–8, and 16–21; the catchword "gather" (אסף) links several of these passages (8:13, 14; 9:21; 10:17). Material that intervenes within this sequence seems to have been added later, or secondarily (see the various passages). If, as is altogether likely, the succession of the passages in the basic stratum is chronological in the order in which they were delivered, then the present passage, in which the city is envisaged to be under siege (v 17)—though the invading army is not yet in sight (v 22)—is to be dated after 8:4–13 (proposed date: autumn of 601) and before the next substantial passage, 11:1ff (proposed date: 594—see there). One is then led to a setting just before the siege of Jerusalem which began in December 598.

Internal Structure of the Passage. For the basic structure of the passage, the symmetry of the two cycles of speakers, see above. There is minimal parallelism at the beginning of the passage, more regular parallelism later on, but whether this is an intentional effect or is the consequence of textual difficulties in vv 17–18 would be difficult to say.

Jrm's speech in v 17 would seem to be a bicolon without parallelism.[2] Yahweh's speech in v 18 would again have to be a bicolon, the two first-person verbal expressions being in parallelism. The people's speech in vv 19–20 breaks into two halves, v 19 (diction on the theme of "wound"), and v 20 (diction on the theme of "tent"). Verse 19 must be a tetracolon, bound together by "my fracture," "my wound," and "my sickness" in the first, second, and fourth cola. "But I myself had thought" (וַאֲנִי אָמַרְתִּי) must be taken as a separate colon (compare 3:19 and 5:4: so the Masoretic accent zaqep qaṭon, against Rudolph here). Verse 20 is a pentacolon with a

close network of parallelism, a lovely expansion of the bicolon in 4:20b: the cola with "my tent," "my tent-cords," "my tent," and "my curtains" surrounds the central colon which speaks of loss of children. Jrm's second speech (v 21) is a tetracolon shaped by the first and fourth cola ("the shepherds," "their pasturage"): note that the phrase with כֵּן counts as a "unit" in the third colon (as also in the fourth colon of 12:8).[3] Yahweh's second speech (v 22) is two bicola, the first a variation on 6:22, the second a variation on 9:10. The closing speech of the people is divided into three subsections, each a citation of or an allusion to scripture (see above)—a tetracolon (v 23), a bicolon (v 24), and two bicola (v 25, against Rudolph, who divides v 25a into four cola).

Form. If the present passage is a rhetorical unity, as is here argued, it is at the same time a sequence in which there is not only variation in speaker but a great variety of genres as well, as if Jrm wishes to communicate the very brokenness of the covenantal relation (compare שֶׁבֶר "brokenness, fracture," v 19).

Verse 17 is a battle-call, not a call to alarm (as 4:5–6 and 6:1 are) but a call to march out among the prisoners; it is phrased in such a way, however, that there is a hint of a taunt (יֹשֶׁבֶת "enthroned": see Interpretation). Verse 18 is an announcement of judgment. The people offer a lament in vv 19–20, embedded in which (v 19b) is their own summary appraisal ("this is just my sickness").[4]

Verse 21 is Jrm's report that the leaders have not learned their lesson; this "report" form is derived from a wisdom setting.[5] But is this not also in fact another summary appraisal, Jrm's attempt to clarify ("that is why," עַל־כֵּן) what the people cannot clarify? Verse 22 is an audition report, a form normally employed by the prophet (compare a form of audition report in 4:19–20).[6] Here, however, it it evidently employed by Yahweh (see above, *Identification of Speakers*): is this an ironic reuse of the form, indicating that Yahweh is as stunned by what is coming as the population would be?

Verses 23–25, if the present analysis is correct, are the

---

2   For O'Connor's similar analysis of Zeph 2:3 see his *Structure*, 249. Isa 14:12 offers the same pattern of vocative in second colon (and fourth colon).

3   See ibid., 302 for כֵּן, and, for an example, 230, on Judg 5:31a.

4   Childs, *Isaiah and the Assyrian Crisis*, 128–36.

5   McKane, *Prophets and Wise Men*, 90–91.

6   For a brief survey of the audition report see Lindblom, *Prophecy*, 135–37.

people's use (or rather abuse) of traditional words in Proverbs and Psalms which justify their irresponsibility: it is no wonder that Jrm has said that "the shepherds are stupid" (v 21)!

Interpretation

■ **17–18** Exact meanings in these two verses are difficult to determine, because of what seems to be a web of word-plays and double meanings. These ambiguities puzzled the Versions and have left modern commentators in doubt about the text, so that many emendations have been proposed. Though no certainty can be gained about the dependability of the text, it is better to err on the side of conservatism, making what one can of the present text, than to give way to subjective reconstruction.

Jrm addresses the hearer in the feminine singular; she is the city personified (compare such personifications in chaps. 2—3).

The verb ישׁב means both "sit" and "dwell," and current translations all use "live" or "dwell" here, and this is surely implied: "you who dwell under siege" (*RSV*). "Sitting," however, may be involved too (compare ישׁב "sit" in 8:14), particularly if the image is of a refugee woman sitting among her belongings. But most particularly the participle יֹשֶׁבֶת is an ironic epithet for Jerusalem enthroned on Zion (compare further 21:13; 22:23; 46:19). Given the liturgical description of Yahweh as יֹשֵׁב הַכְּרֻבִים "enthroned on the cherubim" (1 Sam 4:4) and the contemptuous address to Egypt in 46:19, one must hear יֹשֶׁבֶת as a sarcastic address to the capital city which has considered herself regal in prerogatives. But what good are royal pretensions when the city is not הַמִּבְצָר "fortified" (4:5; 8:14) but rather בַּמָּצוֹר "under siege"?— for that word is surely an ironic variation on the word which appears in those earlier passages. Question: Was the word vocalized without the article, בְּמָצוֹר (compare 19:9), so that it might also be heard as "in Egypt" (compare 2 Kgs 19:24; Isa 19:6; Mic 7:12), addressed to a city counting on Egyptian support (2 Kgs 24:7), this in the context of a word-play on "Canaan" (see below)?

As for the first three words, the personified city is told to "gather up" or "tie up" her כנעה. That noun is a *hapax*

legomenon in the OT, and the Versions divide: V and S assume a derivation from כנע "be humble" (V: "confusion"; S: "degradation"), while G translates "your substance," implying perhaps "your riches," and s' and T "your wares." It is likely that Jrm had in mind some kind of word-play on כְּנַעַן "Canaan" or כְּנַעֲנִי "Canaanite" (so also a suggestion of Volz), since Hos 12:8 offers such a word-play with כְּנַעַן: "Canaan" came to mean the land of "traders, merchants," everything by which Phoenicia lived, the very opposite of the ethic of the covenant[7]— compare Zeph 1:11 and in general the lexica under כְּנַעַן and כְּנַעֲנִי. Given the parallel of 46:19, it is likely that כִּנְעָתֵךְ here means either "your wares" or "your bundle." S. R. Driver, with hesitation, connected the meaning "bundle" with the Arabic root *kana'a* "be contracted," (of an eagle) "fold (wings)," thus "something done up tightly." But in any event the connotation of the illegitimate ethic of profit hangs over the passage: אסף means "get rid of" as well as "gather up" (compare 8:13), and "get rid of the life-style of profit" is a strong implication here. And what of מֵאָרֶץ (here "from the land")? If it is a question of the life style of profit making, then "from the land" is implied. Question: Is there a hint here of "from Sheol," as if profit making is part of the realm of Death?—compare the remarks on 14:18. On the other hand, if it is a question of the bundle of the refugee woman, then "from the ground" is the right rendering. But since the people are about to go into exile (v 18, compare again 46:19), "from the land" is right once more.[8]

For the messenger formula at the beginning of v 18a, in the midst of a unit, see 5:14 (and see the discussion in Structure, Form, Setting). The verb Yahweh uses for his action, קלע, is a drastic one, "sling out": it is the normal one for hurling a slingstone (compare the use of synonyms in Isa 22:17–18). Yahweh's speech then picks up two words from Jrm's speech, יוֹשְׁבֵי "inhabitants of" (יֹשֶׁבֶת "enthroned") and "land."

For the problems with M "this time" (בַּפַּעַם הַזֹּאת) see Text, v 18a: the suggestion "in rage" (בְּזַעַם) is a plausible match to the extreme diction of "sling out."

The text continues to offer difficulty in v 18b. Given the fact that the beginning of Yahweh's speech in v 18a

---

7   See Wolff, *Hosea*, 207, note n, and 214.
8   For depictions of prisoners being marched off with their bundles, see Yadin, *Warfare*, 433, 437.

has mimicked Jrm's speech, one is not surprised that it continues, with וַהֲצִרוֹתִי as a play on מָצוֹר "siege." If the verb is correctly vocalized and understood, it is צרר hip'il; the verb in general means "bring distress on" (so most translations) but more particularly "make narrow." It is proposed here then that with לָהֶם "for them" the verb means not so much "bring distress on them" as "make (the land) too narrow for them": it is likely that Isa 49:19–20 is commentary on this phrase. But one wonders: given the fact that many hip'il verbs are denominative (GKC, sec. 53g), and given the context, does the noun צְרוֹר "bundle, pouch" not stand somewhere behind this verb? The last clause is incomprehensible in M (see Text, v 18b). One can be sure that the verb continues the word-play on מָצוֹר (v 17); the suggestion adopted here at least appears to fit the metaphor, but the matter remains uncertain.

■ **19** The people speak (see Structure, Form, Setting). For "woe is me" compare 4:13, 31. The noun שֶׁבֶר, as elsewhere, is broader than any English counterpart (for the range of meanings see 4:6): here the accompanying vocabulary is medical, so that "fracture" is the primary meaning, but since the personification is that of the whole people, it is the people's collapse that is meant. The nouns "wound" (מַכָּה) and "sickness" (חֳלִי) are also associated in 6:7. The attribute נַחְלָה (חלה nip'al participle: for the vocalization see GKC, sec. 63c) is (almost) always associated with מַכָּה (beyond the present instance, 14:17; 30:12; Nah 3:19; the word is alone only in Isa 17:11, where the text may be damaged). The context of 30:13 and Nah 3:19 indicates that "incurable" is a justified translation.

For the meaning "think" for אמר see 3:19; for a parallel to the sequence וַאֲנִי אָמַרְתִּי אַךְ see 5:4. Earlier commentators and translations have assumed that the people here admit their guilt and are determined to bear their punishment stoically, and *RSV* reflects this interpretation: "But I said, 'Truly this is an affliction, and I must bear it'" (so Cornill and Giesebrecht, and so also *NEB* and *NJV*). But it is perhaps better to understand that the people assume the hardship is not serious and therefore easily to be borne (so Rudolph, Bright, and so *JB*, and less specifically, *NAB*). As presently vocalized,

וְאֶשָּׂאֶנּוּ must be construed as a jussive, so that "and I must bear it" or "so let me bear it" is the rendering. But the vocalization of the conjunction might be וְ־ (compare *G*), in which case the self-quotation would end with "my sickness," and the verb would be translated "and I had borne it"; in this case the verb would be parallel with "but I myself had thought."

■ **20** The diction of this verse is very close to that of 4:20 (which see); there, however, if the rhetoric is correctly understood, Jrm hears the shouts of the people in his mind, while here the people are quoted directly. I accept the suggestion of Kumaki (see Bibliography) that the diction here, as in 4:20, refers to the loss of the temple in Jerusalem; it is possible that the tabernacle was actually erected in the holy of holies.[9] The two parallel words of 4:20, "tent(s)" and "curtains," are joined here by "tent-cords" (מֵיתָרִים); this word, like the other two, is part of the diction in P for the tabernacle (e.g., Exod 35:18), and the three words come together again in Isa 54:2 to suggest the temple. Since "shepherds" in v 21 refers to the civil rulers (see there), the reference to "children" here is to the citizens, but on a deeper level the diction is profoundly emotional and domestic: compare the phraseology of 31:15, where Rachel weeps for her children. Noteworthy is the dative suffix in יְצָאֻנִי "have gone out from me,"[10] but one may also explain the suffix as an accusative of separation (compare Gen 44:4).

■ **21** Jrm speaks (see Structure, Form, Setting).

The verb בער nip'al "be stupid," literally "become like cattle," appeared in v 14 (see there). "The shepherds" (הָרֹעִים) are the civil rulers (see 2:8) who have not measured up to the needs of their office; it is appalling that they, of all people, should have become brutish. The phrase דרש יהוה is not quite "seek Yahweh," though it is often translated this way (see the translations of Amos 5:4, 6), but rather "consult Yahweh." Claus Westermann points out that the phrase in this context means "turn to God through a prophet";[11] compare its use in 21:2, 37:2, where Jrm is asked to be intermediary. Yahweh has no place in their plans.

The predicate לֹא הִשְׂכִּילוּ covers a large semantic field and is difficult to pinpoint here. "Have not prospered" is true enough (*JB*, *NEB*, *NJV*), but that is hardly the issue

---

9   See 4:5–31, n. 65.
10   Compare GKC, sec. 117x; Dahood, *Psalms III*, 377–78.
11   Claus Westermann, "Die Begriffe für Fragen und Suchen im Alten Testament," *KD* 6 (1960) 16–22.

when the circumstances are the death throes of the nation. "Are unsuccessful" is equally true but sounds like a shocking understatement. William McKane links the second and third cola together and renders this colon, "Consequently they have no grasp (of the situation)," no insight, precisely because they have neglected the source of insight, namely Yahweh;[12] and this is plausible, given the assonantal and semantic link between the first and fourth cola (see Structure, Form, Setting). The only other relevant occurrence of this verb with the negative is in a very strong context (20:11: "They will be greatly shamed . . . their eternal dishonor will never be forgotten"), thus the translation offered here, "That is why they have failed."

The noun translated "pasturage" (מַרְעִית) is curious here; it ordinarily means "place of pasture" (25:36), but it is used here by metonymy for the sheep, doubtless in part because of assonance with "shepherds."

The diction of wisdom here, as in 4:22, is in strong contrast to the emotional level of the surrounding verses. The people and their leaders have not measured up: it is as simple as that.

■ **22** Yahweh speaks (see Structure, Form, Setting). The meaning of קוֹל שְׁמוּעָה is by no means clear. The second noun ordinarily means "news, rumor," but the parallel רַעַשׁ גָּדוֹל "great shaking" suggests a noise, not news. Evidently both the news and the noise of battle are approaching. Traditionally קוֹל in this and similar contexts has been taken not as "noise of" but as an interjection, "hark!" (so GKC, sec. 146b); one might take it here as an inner parallel with הִנֵּה (here "listen!"). But the examples of the presumed interjection have in many cases been explained otherwise,[13] and it seems safer to take the whole of the first colon as a participial clause interrupted by הִנֵּה.

In a culture largely preliterate, word of mouth was the medium for news; but when that news is news of an army on the march from a distant land, then it is rumor, with all the panic rumor always engenders. A רַעַשׁ is first of all an earthquake (Amos 1:1), then any shaking of the earth by the march of warriors (Isa 9:4) or by war-chariots (Jer 47:3). The rumor of the coming army comes no faster than the foreign troops themselves! For "land of the north" see 6:22, for "make the cities of Judah a desolation" compare 4:7; 6:8; 9:10; and for "lair of jackals" see likewise 9:10.

■ **23–25** For the authenticity of these verses as an integral part in the passage, and their character as the people's insensitive citations of scripture, see Structure, Form, Setting. All these verses are scripture texts or variations of them: v 23 is an expansion of Prov 16:9 and 20:24, v 24 is an expansion of Ps 6:2 (compare Ps 38:2), and v 25 is a citation of Ps 79:6–7. In 4:3–4 Jrm cites material from Hosea and Deuteronomy which he enjoins the people to take seriously. The present sequence is spoken by the people, but it is Jrm's quotation of the people: this is scripture, he says, which people prefer to cite, pious self-exculpation, whining, revenge.

There is no need (with Cornill and Rudolph) to emend "I know" in v 23 to "you know." The people are confident of their own knowledge. The second colon is literally "that not to a person is his path." The Hebrew of v 23b appears odd, with הֹלֵךְ (a participle, modifying "a man," literally "walking") seeming to be parallel with וְהָכִין (an infinitive, literally "and to make firm"). Most commentators omit "and," and Bright, for example, translates "a man walking" as "a living man." But this is to misunderstand the construction; Preben Wernberg-Møller has assembled a number of passages in which the infinitive and participle resemble each other in function, even in which they are in parallelism, as here—1 Sam 4:19 is a good parallel.[14] It is to be noted that V also understood the passage so. Prov 16:9 says, "the heart (= mind) of a person plans his way, but Yahweh makes firm his step." How can Yahweh expect people, they wonder, to "make good" their "ways and doings" (7:3) if their ways are not really under their own control?—how can Yahweh really hold people responsible? This fatuous expression of irresponsibility by the use of scripture is devastating. King Ahaz did the same thing once, using scripture to justify irresponsibility (Isa 7:12, where the king used Deut 6:16).

Verse 24 expands on Ps 6:2, "Yahweh, do not rebuke me in your anger (אַל־בְּאַפְּךָ), nor in your wrath correct me (תְיַסְּרֵנִי)." The first personal singular is used here at least partly because that is the diction of the Psalm verse;

12 McKane, *Prophets and Wise Men*, 90–91.

13 See Westermann, *Genesis 1*, 385, on Gen 4:10, and Elliger, *Deuterojesaja*, 2 and 3, on Isa 40:3, 6.

14 Preben Wernberg-Møller, "Observations on the Hebrew Participle," *ZAW* 71 (1959) 66.

G understood the context of the present verse, however, in its shift to first plural ("correct us," "reduce us"). The verb יסר pi'el is related to the noun מוּסָר "discipline, chastisement" and helps to present the mood of wisdom and the schoolroom begun in v 23. The word בְּמִשְׁפָּט, here translated "in moderation" (*JB*: "gently"), is a deft touch. The expression literally means "in justice," of course, but "justice" implies a sobriety and a fairness to which the speaker appeals (compare, among many such passages, the picture of the man who conducts his affairs בְּמִשְׁפָּט, Ps 112:5, who is generous and gracious).[15] Beyond that is the suggestion that the Judge of all the earth should do justice, as Abraham long ago reminded Yahweh (Gen 18:25). And the particle אַךְ!—"just" in moderation, "only" in moderation; it is perhaps an echo of v 19, where the people thought the crisis was "only" a bearable illness (see Structure, Form, Setting). Of course the "anger" (אַף) is from Yahweh too, but it may do no harm to appeal to his "justice" in contrast to his "anger." And the final link in the argument: if Yahweh's anger is too wild, the people will be reduced to annihilation. This is the same argument Job uses against God: you have created me, so now why do you want to destroy me (Job 10:8)?—the time may come when you will wish for your creature once more (Job 14:15). In the present passage the threat of reduction is the opposite of the promise of increase of the population given to Abraham and Jacob in Gen 17:6, 20; 35:11: note the contrast of the verb רבה "become many" and מעט "become few" in Jer 29:6 and 30:19, and note also the use Jrm made elsewhere of the promise to the patriarchs to be fruitful (in the Pashhur incident, 20:1–6). One has the impression here, then, both in the use of "in justice" and in the verb "reduce me" (תַּמְעִטֵנִי), that the people are referring indirectly to patriarchal tradition in a desperate effort to sway Yahweh's decision. Deutero-Isaiah evidently understood the sequence in this way: one notes in Isa 54:2–3 the movement from "tent," "curtains," "cords" to the reaffirmation of the promise to Jacob made in Gen 28:14.

And then in v 25 the people quote Ps 79:6–7: if you wish to exercise your wrath, Yahweh, do it on other nations, not on us, for they do not know you or call upon your name, as we do (by implication, v 23: "I know, Yahweh"). Instead of reinforcing what the other nations have done in their devouring of Jacob, you should punish them for what they have done; it is our liturgical tradition.

It is appalling to see traditional words used to justify irresponsibility, but there is no doubt that such words were used in this way in Jrm's day, and his weaving together of these texts is an ironic way to give resonance to Yahweh's determination to punish.

Aim

This passage joins others in the series depicting the coming defeat by the foe from the north, the reaction of the people, and the theological meaning of that defeat (compare 8:14–23; 9:1–8, 16–21). Jrm uses here both irregular and regular poetic structures, a variety of speakers and a variety of emotional levels (compare vv 21 and 22) to communicate the brokenness of covenant and the people's situation within the broken covenant, and he climaxes the passage with the horrifying sequence of scripture quotations to which the people resort in order to justify themselves and to urge light punishment for themselves and heavy punishment for their enemies. The people have heard nothing and learned nothing; that they should quote traditional wisdom and liturgy and thereby convict themselves of invincible ignorance is a shocking climax to Jrm's second scroll as it existed in 597. Whether or not it is true that "The devil can cite Scripture for his purpose" (Shakespeare, *Merchant of Venice* I, 3), Jrm was convinced that the people could and that their purpose was irredeemably wrong.

---

15   See Edmond Jacob, *Theology of the Old Testament* (New York: Harper, 1958) 100–101, on this colon; for a different suggestion see Berridge, pp. 194–96.

**There Is Conspiracy
Against Yahweh**

Bibliography

Selected literature on covenant and בְּרִית:
Kutsch, Ernst
 *Verheissung und Gesetz, Untersuchungen zum
 sogenannten "Bund" im Alten Testament* (BZAW 131;
 Berlin: de Gruyter, 1973).
McCarthy, Dennis J.
 Treaty and Covenant (AnBib 21A; Rome: Biblical
 Institute, 1978).
Mendenhall, George E.
 "Covenant," *IDB* 1:714–23.
Quell, Gottfried
 "διαθήκη," *TDNT* 2:106–24.
Riemann, Paul A.
 "Covenant, Mosaic," *IDBSup*, 192–97.
Weinfeld, Moshe
 "בְּרִית," *TDOT* 2:253–79.
Weinfeld, Moshe
 "Covenant, Davidic," *IDBSup*, 188–92.

**On the passage in general, and on Jeremiah
and Deuteronomy:**
Cazelles, Henri
 "Jérémie et le Deutéronome," *RSR* 38 (1951) 5–
 36.
Granild, Sigurd
 "Jeremia und das Deuteronomium," *ST* 16 (1962)
 135–54.
Puukko, Antti F.
 "Jeremias Stellung zum Deuteronomium," *Alttesta-
 mentliche Studien Rudolf Kittel zum 60. Geburtstag
 dargebracht* (Beiträge zur Wissenschaft vom Alten
 Testament 13; Leipzig: Hinrichs, 1913) 126–53.
Robert, André
 "Jérémie et la réforme deutéronomique, d'après
 Jér. xi, 1–14," *Science Religieuse, Travaux et
 Recherches* [*RSR*] 31 (1943) 5–16.
Rowley, Harold H.
 "The Prophet Jeremiah and the Book of Deuter-
 onomy," *Studies in Old Testament Prophecy* (ed.
 Harold H. Rowley; Edinburgh: Clark, 1950) 157–
 74.
Schofield, John N.
 "The Significance of the Prophets for Dating
 Deuteronomy," *Studies in History and Religion* (ed.
 Ernest A. Payne; London: Lutterworth, 1942) 44–
 60.

On specific verses and problems:
Hyatt, J. Philip
 "The Original Text of Jeremiah 11:15–16," *JBL*
 60 (1941) 57–60.
Levy, Abraham J.
 "Jeremiah 11,15," *JAOS* 49 (1929) 363.

Wilhelmi, Gerhard
"Weg mit den vielen Altären! (Jeremia xi 15)," *VT*
25 (1975) 119–21.

11

1/ The word which came to Jeremiah from Yahweh, as follows: 2/ ᵃ [Hear the words of this covenant;] ⟪ "Speak" ⟫ᵃ to the men of Judah ᵇ and toᵇ the inhabitants of Jerusalem, 3/ and say to them:
 'Thus Yahweh the God of Israel has said, "Cursed is the man who does not hear the words of this covenant, 4/ which I commanded your fathers on the day when I brought them out of the land of Egypt, from the iron furnace, as follows, 'Obey my voice, and do [them]ᵃ according to everything I shall command you, and you shall be a people to me, while I shall be God to you,' 5/ in order to perform the oath which I swore to your fathers, to give themᵃ a land flowing with milk and honey, as at this day"; and I answered and said, "So be it, Yahweh."'
6/ 'And Yahweh said to me, "Call out allᵃ these words in the cities of Judah and the streets of Jerusalem, as follows: 'Hear the words of this covenant and do them, 7/ ᵃ for I really have admonished your fathers from the day I brought them

Text

2a—a   *M* of this section of v 2 is impossible; it reads literally, "Hear [imperative plural] the words of this covenant, and you shall speak [plural, with most MSS., or 'you shall speak (singular) them (i.e., the words),' with the Leningrad Codex, taken as the basis of *BHK* and *BHS*]." Verse 3 begins with a singular verb "and you shall say." This mixture of number is followed by *V* and *T*. In *G* the reference shifts from imperative plural in the first verb of v 2 to second singular in the second verb (but without accusative suffix). However, the Catena-group of *G* MSS. and *S* read two singular imperatives in v 2. In regard to the vowels of ודברתם, the Leningrad Codex is clearly wrong. But on the larger problem two possible solutions present themselves. (1) The words "hear the words of this covenant" in v 2 are secondary, borrowed from v 6; in this case one must follow the *G* Catena MSS. and *S* and read the verb "speak" in v 2 as an imperative, without "and," thus דַּבֵּר. This is the solution of Volz and Bright. In this case the shift to a plural perfect for "speak" in v 2 is a late effort at harmony with "hear." (2) Excise all of v 2 and the initial words of v 3, "and you shall say to them," as expansionist. This is the solution of Rudolph. In this case the *G* Catena MSS. and *S* offer a secondary revision to the singular because the plurals in v 2 do not fit the context. Solution (1) is adopted here as more economical (and compare Janzen, p. 133).

b—b   Instead of *M* וְעַל־ read with some MSS. וְאֶל־, matching the previous אֶל־. *T* reflects a contrast in the prepositions, so the contrast is old, but it is clearly secondary.

4a   Omitting אוֹתָם with *G* and *V*; *T* reads the word as אַתֶּם "you" (plural, subject). The word is evidently a gloss from a similar sequence in v 6.

5a   Two MSS. and *S* read לָכֶם "to you" (plural) for *M* לָהֶם.

6a   A few MSS. and *G* omit "all." It is difficult to say whether its inclusion or omission is more original (compare Janzen, p. 65).

7–8a—a   *G* omits all the enclosed material, v 7 and most of v 8; and since v 2 gives evidence of expansionist tendencies, and since the contents of vv 7–8 replicate to some degree those of vv 4–5, one can argue that *G* represents a more authentic text tradition, while *M* has expanded the text secondarily. On the other hand, the contents of vv 7–8 have a different reference from those of vv 4–5: vv 4–5 are conup from the land of Egypt, until[b] this day—early and constantly—as follows: "Obey my voice!"' 8/ But they have not heard, nor turned their ear, but each of them has walked in the stubbornness of their own evil heart, so I have brought over them all the words of this covenant which I commanded them (to do)[a] but they did not."'

9/ 'And Yahweh said to me, "There is a conspiracy to be found among the men of Judah and the inhabitants of Jerusalem: 10/ they have returned to the iniquities of their earlier fathers who refused to listen to my words—they for their part have walked after other gods, to serve them; the house of Israel and the house of Judah have broken my covenant which I made with their fathers."'

11/ 'Therefore thus Yahweh has said, "I am going to bring upon[a] them disaster which they cannot escape: they shall cry out to me, [b] but I will not[b] listen to them. 12/ Then the cities of Judah and the inhabitants of Jerusalem will go and cry out to the gods to whom they burn offerings, but they will in no way save them in the time of their disaster. 13/ [Indeed as many as your cities are your gods, O Judah, and as many as the streets of Jerusalem {you have put up altars to Shame}[b] are the altars to burn offerings to Baal.][a] 14/ As for you, do not pray for this people, do not lift up for them cry or prayer; I will not listen at the time when 《 you call 》[a] to me, [b] at the time of[b] their disaster."''

15   What 《 have your kettles to do with me? 》[a] in my house 《 you have done 》[b] 〈these schemes!〉[c]
《 Have 》[d] 《 the fatlings 》[e] and meat of 〈my sanctuary〉[f] 《 been (so) pleasing 》[d]

cerned with the oath sworn to the fathers, while vv 7–8 deal with the persistent stubbornness of the Israelites since that time; one concludes that *G* is damaged by haplography. See the careful analysis of the question by Janzen, pp. 39–40.

b   Many MSS. read עַד for *M* וְעַד. The meaning is unaffected.

11a   Preferring some MSS. which read עֲלֵיהֶם for *M* אֲלֵיהֶם; the meaning and usage of the two are scarcely to be distinguished.

b—b   The Oriental tradition reads וְאַל here for *M* וְלֹא; that reading would imply "but let me not" (compare GKC, sec. 107p) but is undoubtedly a mistake.

13a   A secondary gloss from 2:28 (so Volz, Rudolph); see Interpretation.

b   *M* reads a conflate text: the words מִזְבְּחוֹת לַבֹּשֶׁת "altars to Shame" are omitted in *G* and are simply a variant of the following words (Janzen, p. 12).

14a   Reading קְרָאֲךָ with *T* (compare 7:16) for *M* קְרָאָם "they call."

b—b   Reading with many MSS. and with *G*, *V*, *S*, and *T* בְּעֵת for *M* בְּעַד "for (the benefit of)"; the latter reading emerged under the stimulus of בְּעַד and בַּעֲדָם earlier in the verse.

15–16a   Reading with Rudolph לִידִידִי בְּ for *M* לִידִידֶיךָ "has my beloved (to do) in." The word יְדִיד "beloved" does not fit here either in gender or in diction (see Interpretation). The kap was misread as bet.

b   Reading with Rudolph (and with *S*!) עֲשִׂית for *M* עֲשׂוֹתָהּ "her doing"; one notes that *G* and *V* read a third singular perfect verb here. The infinitive developed after the reading לִידִידִי developed and a nominal form became necessary.

c   The present *M* הַמְזִמָּתָה is read as accented on the penult and has traditionally been explained like לַיְלָה (GKC, sec. 90a), but the text is corrupt. Read a plural הַמְזִמּוֹת with *V*, and carry the final he to the next word as interrogative he (see note e).

d   Read the verb as עָרְבוּ for *M* יַעֲבֹרוּ; the *M* read has been construed either as a qal ("pass away," so Calvin, *KJV*), or as a hip'il without yod (GKC, sec. 53n, "take away," so the Versions and many commentators). I propose that the yod is the suffix on the previous word (see note f). The verb proposed here occurs in 6:20 in a similar context; for the proposal of a similar metathesis of עבר and ערב see 5:28. See Interpretation.

e   Reading הַהֲבָרִים with Driver, "Jeremiah," 109, J. Philip Hyatt, "The Original Text of Jeremiah 11:15–16," *JBL* 60 (1941) 58, and Rudolph, for *M* הָרַבִּים, understood as "the many." The word in *M* cannot be construed with the context: its masculine plural cannot modify the previous noun, which is feminine, whether singular or plural, and traditionally it has been translated "with many" (Calvin, *KJV*). See Interpretation.

f   Reading קָדְשִׁי, taking the yod from the following word (see note d), for *M* קֹדֶשׁ "holiness," the phrase

《 to you 》[g]
  that 《 from your evils 》[g] 《 I would
    cleanse you, 》[h]
    《 with the sound of a great crowd 》[i]
    you would exult?

16   "A green olive-tree,
    《 most lovely 》[j] in form,"
    Yahweh named you;
    [. . . .][i]
    he has set fire to 《 its leaves, 》[k]
    and its branches 《 shall burn. 》[l]
  17/ [And it is Yahweh of hosts, he who
    planted you, who has spoken disaster
    against you because of the evil of the
    house of Israel and the house of Judah
    which they have done for themselves, to
    offend me, to burn offerings to Baal.][a]

g   Reading עָלֶיךָ and מֵרָעֹתֶיךָ ("from your evils," plural), or מֵרָעָתֶךָ ("from your evil," singular: see below) for *M* מֵעָלַיִךְ and רָעָתֵכִי respectively; perhaps a mem fell out of the text and was wrongly reinserted, or perhaps the mem was deliberately shifted when the remainder of the text was in process of being misconstrued. As to *M* מֵעָלַיִךְ, it is perhaps significant that de Rossi lists two MSS. which omit the mem. And as to *M* רָעָתֵכִי, one notes that *G* and *V* read "your evils," plural; this reading is preferable as a parallel to the plural "schemes." Whether the yod in *M* was misplaced from before the kap, or has another origin, would be difficult to say.

h   As they stand, the sequence of the last two words of v 15 in *M* are impossible, אָז תַּעֲלֹזִי, "then you exult." "Then" (אָז) is an emphatic word and would have to come directly after כִּי. For אָז I suggest the beginning of a verb, a variation of Rudolph's suggestion; I read אָזְכֵּךְ זכך hip'il; two kaps could very well have been misconstrued as a taw (see Cross, "Scripts," 137) and then omitted by haplography with the taw of תַּעֲלֹזִי. See Interpretation.

i   I follow Volz and Rudolph in shifting this phrase from the middle of v 16 to v 15, but I insert it at a slightly early position.

j   Following the suggestion of Duhm, accepted by Cornill, Giesebrecht, Volz, and Rudolph, reading יְפֵיפָה, a reduplicated form of יָפֶה (compare the same reconstructed word in 46:20), for *M* יְפֵה פְרִי "fair of fruit." The *M* phrase does not fit תֹּאַר "form," and "fruit" is missing in *G* (though the translation there is somewhat periphrastic).

k   *M* עָלֶיהָ "upon her" has the wrong gender; read then with Volz, Rudolph, and Bright עָלֵהוּ (with or without the prefix בְּ): the noun is עָלֶה.

l   Reading וּבָעֲרוּ with *V* for *M* וְרֵעוּ "shall be evil" (רעע I) or "shall break" (רעע II).

17a   This verse is a secondary insertion to accommodate v 16 to v 15 and both to vv 1–14 (so Giesebrecht, Volz, Rudolph). See Interpretation.

Structure, Form, Setting

Hierarchy of Quotations. The first matter to establish is the hierarchy of quotations. It is clear that the following are parallel: "Thus Yahweh the God of Israel has said" (v 3), "and Yahweh said to me" (v 6), "and Yahweh said to me" (v 9), and "Therefore thus Yahweh has said" (v 11); these are variations of the messenger formula and introduce messages that Jrm is bidden by Yahweh to speak to the people. If the text is correctly set forth here for vv 2–3, those parallel formulas are governed by "speak . . . and

say to them" in vv 2–3, and the words of v 1 serve therefore as a general title for the passage.

In v 4 the quotation that begins "obey my voice" ends with the close of v 4, since "in order to perform the oath" (v 5) is an action of Yahweh, not of the people: that infinitive depends upon "which I commanded your fathers" at the beginning of v 4.

Given the parallel of Deut 27:15–26, it is clear that "and I answered and said, 'So be it, Yahweh'" (v 5) is equivalent to Jrm's saying, "Yes, that man is cursed"; thus "and I answered" is coordinate with "Thus Yahweh the God of Israel has said" in v 3.

In v 6 the quotation "Hear the words . . ." begins a sequence of second-person plurals; this continues through the end of v 7. Verse 8 shifts to third plural, so the quotation "Hear the words . . ." closes with the end of v 7; v 8 is a report of Yahweh to Jrm. The rest of the material is straightforward.

Extent of Unit; Unity of the Passage. The material of vv 1–14 can be understood (with the exception of the bracketed phrases) as an integrated discourse: four utterances of Yahweh, each introduced by the messenger formula, vv 3–5, 6–8, 9–10, 11–14 (for the unity of these utterances, see *Form* below). But vv 15–16 suddenly shift to poetic material which seems to offer no link with what precedes (but see below). Verse 17, finally, appears to be a secondary pastiche to accommodate vv 15 and 16 to vv 1–14. Verse 18 begins the sequence of Jrm's "confessions": a new unit begins at that point.

The two verses of poetry do not seem to be integrated with each other, and furthermore there is no verbal link between the poetry and the prose that precedes. Thus Volz assumes three separate units here, vv 1–14, v 15 (plus the phrase "at the sound of a great crowd" and a parallel phrase he reconstructs from *G*) and v 16; Rudolph assumes two units, vv 1–14 and vv 15–16. It is always possible, of course, that this material has come together in some random way, or in some way whose purpose cannot now be reconstructed. But there is evidence that points to the unity of vv 1–16.

One turns first to vv 15–16. Ps 52:10 offers the phrase "green olive-tree in the house of God": if vv 15 and 16 are a unity, as is here assumed, then the Psalm verse is a plausible key to the train of thought within the two verses.

Verses 3–10 are closely parallel to 7:22–26; v 14 is closely parallel to 7:16; vv 15–16 resemble 7:29 at least to the degree that both short poems address the people in the feminine singular, but v 15 is similar to 7:21 in that both deal in an ironic mood with the pleasure of eating sacrificial meat. It is proposed in the present study that the original setting for both 7:16–20 and 7:29–34 was directly after the king burned the scroll in late 601 or early 600, and that the setting for 7:21–28 was 594; 7:21–28 then may have been inserted in the sequence of 7:16–20 + 29–34 at the time the present passage took

shape. And there is another possible parallel. If the verb ערב "be pleasing" is correctly reconstructed for v 15, it is the same verb which appears in 6:20 in a similar context. And since 6:19 has "I am going to bring disaster on this people," the same phrase as "I am going to bring upon them disaster" in v 11 of the present passage, one is led to believe that vv 1–14 and 15–16 do belong together (see further *Form*).

Internal Structure. The prose of vv 3–14 clearly breaks into four subsections, each introduced by "Yahweh said." The poetry (vv 15–16) is so difficult to reconstruct as to make any analysis uncertain; I have suggested a bicolon and tricolon, followed by a tricolon and bicolon.

Authenticity. Every commentator gives an extensive treatment of vv 1–14, because it has appeared to offer clues to the attitude of Jrm toward Deuteronomy and/or the Deuteronomic reform, or at least clues to the attitude of later Jeremianic tradition toward those matters. Thus it has seemed plausible to many to view the phrase "this covenant" (vv [2,] 3, 6, 8) as a reference to the covenant concluded by Josiah at the time of the reform stimulated by the discovery of Deuteronomy in 622 (so most, including Duhm, Cornill, Giesebrecht, Condamin, Eissfeldt, and Bright); on the other hand, a minority (including Volz and Rudolph) have seen linguistic objections to this (in v 3 the phrase appears to refer to what follows) and have insisted that the phrase refers simply to the one Sinai covenant (compare v 4). These considerations have been complicated by the presence here of rhetoric reminiscent of Deuteronomy: some scholars have held that Jrm was deliberately using phrases reminiscent of Deuteronomy (for example, Weiser), while others assume that the passage is the product of Deuteronomistic revision of the book and can credit it with minimal authenticity (Rudolph tends to this view). All of this is complicated by the fact that the majority of scholars hold to a higher chronology, by which Jrm would have begun his prophetic career in 627, so that one expects some kind of reaction from him to the events of 622. But the present study holds to a lower chronology, and since the crucial resemblances to Deuteronomy in the present passage are confined to vv 3–5 (see below) and since much of the diction is close to authentic words of Jrm elsewhere, the interlocking questions bearing on the setting of the passage deserve a fresh examination, and I shall not submit a thorough survey of critical opinion (for such opinion see Rudolph, and the Bibliography offered here).

It is not enough to say that this material contains "Deuteronomistic" phraseology. Verses 3–5 do, as will be shown, but for a specific reason; vv 6–14 do not, at least to the same degree.

Verses 3–5 are a deliberate variation on the pattern of Deut 27:15–26, where a series of verses begins with "cursed" (אָרוּר) and ends with "so be it" (אָמֵן, "Amen"). It will be suggested below that this variation is deliberate on Jrm's part: one may note in passing that the only other relevant use of "so be it" (אָמֵן) in the prophets is in 28:6, in Jrm's response to Hananiah. The material intervening in vv 3–5 appears to draw most heavily on Deut 4:20, "Yahweh . . . has brought you out of the iron furnace, out of Egypt . . . as at this day"; 7:8, "(because Yahweh loves you) and is keeping (שמר) the oath (שְׁבוּעָה) which he swore to your fathers"; 8:18, "that he may confirm his covenant (לְמַעַן הָקִים אֶת־בְּרִיתוֹ) which he swore to your fathers, as at this day"; 26:8–9, "and Yahweh brought us out of Egypt . . . and gave us this land, a land flowing with milk and honey,"; and 31:20, "When I have brought them into the land flowing with milk and honey, which I swore to give to their fathers." There are of course many other passages with some parallels to this sequence, but these are the key ones. One must examine the details.

The phrase "iron furnace" (כּוּר הַבַּרְזֶל, v 4) presents a special problem. Beyond the present passage it occurs only in Deut 4:20 and 1 Kgs 8:51. In the last-named passage it is clearly late, part of the second Deuteron-omistic redactor;[1] for the question whether 11:4 or Deut 4:20 is prior, see below, *Setting of vv 1–16*. Ezek 22:18–22 is evidently an expansion of the phrase.

"Perform the oath" (הָקִים הַשְּׁבוּעָה) is not found in Deuteronomy. The noun does not occur elsewhere in Jer; it does appear once in Deuteronomy, as the object of "keep" (שמר 7:8, see above), while the verb in this context also appears once (8:18, see above), following

לְמַעַן. The combination of the verb and noun appear only once otherwise in the OT (Gen 26:3 [J], God's reassurance to Isaac).

The phrase "which I swore to your fathers, to give them a land flowing with milk and honey" (or variations for changes of person) occurs once otherwise in the prose of Jer (32:22, a prayer in the context of the purchase of the field at Anathoth), and five times outside Jer: Exod 13:5 (D);[2] Deut 11:9 (part of a homily); 26:15 (part of the formula spoken by the layman as he presents his tithe); 31:20 (part of the introduction to the Song of Moses, reminiscent of E);[3] and Josh 5:6 (part of Deuteronomistic editorial work).[4] The components are of course more common: thus "the land flowing with milk and honey" is found in J (Exod 8:3, 17),[5] often in D, and in Ezek 20:6 and 15.

One notes that Jer 2:5–7 offers in poetic form much the same kind of material ("fathers," "bring up from the land of Egypt," "plentiful land"). On the basis of vv 3–5 here one may believe Jrm was reshaping the phraseology of Deuteronomy for his own purposes.

But the material in vv 6–14 gives a different impression. As for vv 6–8, one finds that the verb "admonish" (עוד hip'il, v 7) is used with that meaning in Deut 8:19, but nowhere else in Deuteronomy; and one finds further that the occurrence in Deut 8:19 does not offer an infinitive absolute. On the other hand, the verb occurs with that meaning in Jrm's poetry (8:10). The infinite absolute הַשְׁכֵּם (translated "early and constantly," v 7) in not found at all in Deuteronomy but is a feature of Jer (compare its occurrence in 7:25; it is redactional in 7:13). The parallelism of "hear" with "turn the ear" (נטה hip'il + אֹזֶן, v 8) does not occur in Deuteronomy. The phrase "stubbornness of the heart" (v 8) is found once in Deuteronomy (Deut 29:18), but in a passage considered to be late:[6] is the phraseology there secondary to Jer?[7] The phrase בוא hip'il + דְּבָרִים "bring (over someone) the words" (v 8) is odd, in spite of the commonness of its components: the only parallels in the OT are 25:13 and

1   Gray, *Kings*, 214.
2   Martin Noth, *Exodus* (Philadelphia: Westminster, 1962) 93; Childs, *Exodus*, 184.
3   Eissfeldt, *Introduction*, 227.
4   Soggin, *Joshua*, 68.
5   Childs, *Exodus*, 52.
6   Eissfeldt, *Introduction*, 231; Mayes, *Deuteronomy*, 359.
7   For its occurrence in the prose of Jrm, see, for example, 7:24.

2 Kgs 22:16, part of the prophetess Huldah's reply to the emissaries of Josiah. If the present passage is authentic to Jrm, then, the parallel suggests not only that Jrm is reinforcing Huldah's pronouncement, but that he has identified "this covenant" with Huldah's "the book which the king of Judah has read"—a not unimportant finding. (One more parallel to the phrase, a more distant one, might be cited, Josh 23:15, but this verse is part of the exilic Deuteronomistic redaction of that book.)[8]

In vv 9–10 the word קֶשֶׁר "conspiracy" (v 9) occurs only here in Jer and not at all in Deuteronomy. The closest parallel, with "find" (מצא), is 2 Kgs 17:4 (there in the qal stem): the king of Assyria finds conspiracy in Hoshea of Israel, a prelude to the fall of Samaria. The use of הָרִאשֹׁנִים (v 10), literally "the first," modifying "fathers," is unparalleled in the OT (see Interpretation). The verb פרר hip'il "break," with "covenant" (v 10), is found elsewhere in Jer (14:21; 31:32; 33:20); it is found in Deuteronomy only in 31:16, 20, part of the introduction to the Song of Moses, which resembles E.[9]

There is nothing Deuteronomistic in vv 11–12 and 14. The phrase "I am going to bring disaster on" (הִנְנִי מֵבִיא רָעָה עַל, v 11) is not found in Deuteronomy at all; nothing like it is there, but it is phraseology common in Jrm's poetry (5:15; 6:19; compare 4:6; 31:8; 49:5). The phraseology with יצא in the meaning "escape" (v 11) is striking; again there is nothing like it in Deuteronomy, and the only parallels are scattered (perhaps 48:9, though the text is difficult; Judg 16:20; 1 Sam 14:41; 2 Kgs 13:5; Ezek 15:7; and perhaps a few others). The verb "cry out" (זעק, vv 11, 12) is not common in Jer and is not found at all in Deuteronomy; one wonders if the diction here is not the reversal of Deut 26:7, where the by-form צעק appears, the only relevant use of that verb in Deuteronomy. And v 14 is a close parallel of 7:16, again without matching material in Deuteronomy.

Both 7:1–12 and 11:1–14 have been thought by commentators to be parade examples of Deuteronomistic diction, so that it is worth comparing the diction of the two passages. There are important differences between them; in 7:1–12 one finds irony and several striking syntactical constructions, while here the diction seems more conventional. But the message of 7:1–12 centers around an appeal to change (7:3, 5–6), while here the appeal to obedience is only indirect (vv 3, 4, 6–7); it would seem that the time for irony is now past and that traditional covenantal forms are what the present situation demands. It must be emphasized, however, that there are several surprising turns of phrase here: the mimicking of the form of Deut 27:15–26; the phrase "bring (over someone) the words" in v 8 which reminds the hearer of Huldah's words to Josiah's emissaries; the word "conspiracy" in v 9 which reminds the hearer of the situation of King Hoshea in the face of Assyria. And most notably there is the puzzling phrase "this covenant" (vv 3–8). That phrase is not found elsewhere in Jer; it does occur in Deuteronomy, but only three times—5:3; 29:8, 13—and chapter 29 is evidently part of a secondary addition to Deuteronomy,[10] so that the only valid parallel is Deut 5:3, part of the introduction to the Decalogue there.

Enough data are at hand to conclude that vv 1–14 are authentic to Jrm. And in spite of the difficulties in reconstructing the text of vv 15–16, there is no reason to question the authenticity of those two verses.

Setting. Jrm here offers to the people a word of judgment after the pattern of material in Deuteronomy. Since the first part of the passage is so closely modeled after Deuteronomy, a plausible setting would be the context of a recitation of Deuteronomy (compare the setting proposed for 7:21–28, a passage closely analogous to the present one; and compare further the settings proposed for 2:1–3 and 8:4–13). This proposal gains slightly in plausibility because of the presence of the verb "call out" (קרא, v 6), which occurs also in 2:2, there likewise in the context of material with parallels to Deuteronomy. One might even propose the specific year. In the late spring or early summer of 594 there occurred the anti-Babylonian conference in Jerusalem narrated in chapter 27 (the date in 27:1 is erroneous and must be corrected from 28:1, as all commentators agree: see there). Though "conspiracy" (קֶשֶׁר) does not occur in that narrative, its occurrence here in v 9 is so appropriate to that circumstance that one can propose the festival of booths in September/October 594, when Deuteronomy was recited, as the occasion for the present passage.

8   Soggin, *Joshua*, 218–19.
9   See n. 3.
10 See n. 6.

At this point one's attention is called to the phrase "iron furnace" in v 4, for in his encounter with Hananiah in July/August 594, Jrm envisages the "iron yoke" that Nebuchadrezzar would impose on all nations (28:14). Now it appears that Jrm saw the nation tragically moving from the iron furnace of Egypt to the iron yoke of Babylon. Indeed it is possible that Jrm originated the phrase "iron furnace" and that it entered Deuteronomy secondarily, since Deut 4:1–40 was evidently added secondarily.[11]

In conclusion, "this covenant" refers not to Josiah's covenant but to the covenant given at Sinai and summarized by Deuteronomy.

A Possible Prehistory for Verse 9. I would like to set forth the possibility that v 9 had a prehistory, that it served as a backdrop for Jrm's "confession" in vv 18–20. There are two considerations here, perhaps three. (1) Verse 18 comes on without introduction, and there is no antecedent reference for "their deeds" at the end of the verse. (2) Verses 18–20 describe a "conspiracy" against Jrm. (3) If קֶשֶׁר in v 9 does mean "conspiracy," then vv 10–13 do not appear to follow v 9 with absolute smoothness. It is possible that v 9 had been a private revelation to Jrm at the time when vv 18–20 took shape (see Setting for 11:18—12:6), and that "conspiracy" then gained fresh meaning when the rest of vv 1–16 took shape in Jrm's mind and was publicly proclaimed in 594 (see further Interpretation on v 9).

Placement of Unit. It is proposed in the present study that the "confessions" of Jrm, which begin with 11:18, were proclaimed publicly only after the death of Hananiah, in September/October 594: see 28:17). If the setting of the present passage was at the time of the recitation of the Deuteronomic law in that month, then the present passage may well have served as an introduction to the "confessions," or at least have been inserted chronologically after 10:17–25, the setting for which is 597 (see there), and before the "confessions." This suggestion gains slightly in plausibility if v 9 had served as a backdrop to vv 18–20 when those verses first took shape (see above, *A Possible Prehistory for Verse 9*).

Form. Verses 1–14, like 7:1–12, are a covenant speech offered by Jrm, who functions as a covenant mediator.

Though it is vv 3–5 that are heavy with phraseological reminiscences of Deuteronomy (see *Setting*), the whole passage is couched in the repetitive homiletical style which is that of Deuteronomy as well. The passage differs from 7:1–12, however, in that that passage was parenesis, appeal to obedience, while in the present passage the appeal to obey is virtually *pro forma*. It begins, ominously, with "cursed is the man who does not hear," and vv 3–5 otherwise describe the stipulations given to the fathers. Verse 6 is indeed parenesis, but then vv 7–8 go on to describe Yahweh's constant warning and the people's constant unwillingness to obey which characterizes the time since the fathers. Verses 9–10 strikingly state that there is a "conspiracy" among the people to turn their back on all the covenantal appeal of Yahweh; vv 11–12 describe the punishment that is coming as a consequence, and v 14 contains a prohibition to Jrm himself not to try to intercede for the people, words almost identical to those in 7:16.

Two matters are noteworthy here: first, that the speeches of Yahweh involve Jrm directly—not only the command to "speak" (v 2) but more particularly Jrm's "Amen" in v 5, the word vouchsafed to Jrm about a conspiracy (v 9), and the prohibition against intercession in v 14; and second, that the covenant speech is so heavy with divine judgment.

Beyond vv 3–5, where the style is directly imitative of Deuteronomy, the rhetoric of the rest of the prose of the passage resembles that of Deuteronomy. This is doubtless because both Deuteronomy and the prose of the present passage represent the style of solemn discourse in the late seventh century; William O. E. Oesterley and Theodore H. Robinson noted long ago, "It may at once be admitted that the style is Deuteronomic, but, as we have observed more than once, this is no more than the rhetorical prose of the period, which begins about the time of Jeremiah and extends probably till after the Return."[12] But the style evidently had its origins in very early times: comparable are Exod 19:3–6 (E?),[13] Joshua 24 and 1 Samuel 12, any or all of which may well have undergone Deuteronomistic editing but which surely preserve early memories.[14]

At the heart of vv 1–14 is the pronouncement of

11 Mayes, *Deuteronomy*, 148.
12 William O. E. Oesterley and Theodore H. Robinson, *An Introduction to the Books of the Old Testament* (New York: Macmillan, 1934) 304.
13 Childs, *Exodus*, 344–51.
14 Muilenburg, "Covenantal Formulations"; Klaus

curse: it is not simply the phrase "cursed is the man" in v 3, though that is a primary clue; it is that the whole passage is the pronouncement of a curse—"disaster which they cannot escape" (v 11) because of the disobedience of the people. The curse is the negative side of the covenant bond, as the oath (v 5) is the positive side.[15]

The form of vv 1–14 is not altogether comparable to anything else because of the specificities that Jrm understood: Yahweh was about to carry out a thoroughgoing curse upon the people such as had only been threatened at earlier historical junctures.

The poem in vv 15–16 offers ironic questions (v 15) followed by a word of judgment, a sequence found elsewhere (compare 7:19–20 and 8:8–10a, 13).

The presentation here after the form of Deuteronomy (vv 1–14) seems to demand being rounded off by a poem. One wonders whether Jrm's presentation is modeled after a recitation of Deuteronomy which concluded by the poem of Deuteronomy 32: that poem also offers rhetorical questions about sacrifice (Deut 32:37–38).

Interpretation

■ **1–2** For the idiom "the word which came to . . . from Yahweh" see 1:2. For "men of Judah and inhabitants of Jerusalem," see 4:4.

■ **3–5** Commentators and translations differ whether to render אָרוּר הָאִישׁ as "cursed be the man" (Condamin, Bright) or "cursed is the man" (Volz, Rudolph). The present passage imitates the diction of Deut 27:15–26 (see Structure, Form, Setting), and one assumes that the words in Deuteronomy are to be understood as divine words stating an accomplished fact, not words expressing a wish; the passage before us must therefore be heard in the same way, so that "is" is preferable.[16]

To "hear" the words of this covenant implies "obeying" them (see on 3:13). The phrase "this covenant" refers to the covenant at Sinai (see v 4) set forth in the recitation of Deuteronomy (see Structure, Form, Setting). Except

for the phrase "ark of the covenant" in 3:16, this passage marks the first occurrences of the word "covenant" (בְּרִית) in Jer. The term refers to a central feature of OT faith.[17] It encompasses the specific agreement Israel understood Yahweh to have made with her, obligating Yahweh to uphold and bless her, and obligating Israel to be obedient. (For some of the implications of covenantal expression in Jrm's proclamations, see particularly Interpretation for 2:1—4:4.) The word "covenant" itself is common in Deuteronomy (twenty-seven times) and P but is uncommon in the preexilic prophets.[18]

The phrase "when I brought them out of the land of Egypt" occurs elsewhere in the prose of Jer (7:22, 34:13), and, with the alternate verb "bring up" (עלה hip'il), in v 7 below. The phrase "iron furnace" is a striking one (see Structure, Form, Setting). A furnace for smelting iron is a furnace that must achieve a far higher temperature than is necessary for other metals; thus copper ore can be smelted at about 800 degrees C., while iron melts only at 1535 degrees C.[19] This metaphor for a severe ordeal was later expanded in Ezek 22:18–22. The phrase "everything I command you" is a commonplace in D and P but appears to be integrated into Jrm's call in 1:7 as well. For the covenant formula "you shall be a people to me, while I shall be God to you," see 7:23 and the Bibliography cited there.

For the occurrence of the phrase "perform the oath" see Structure, Form, Setting. An oath (שְׁבוּעָה) is a solemn promise, Yahweh's act of obligating himself in the covenant.[20]

For the occurrences of the phrase "which I swore to your fathers, to give them a land flowing with milk and honey," see Structure, Form, Setting; its components are part of traditional cultic material.[21] The expression "as at this day" (כַּיּוֹם הַזֶּה, twenty-one times in the OT) is common both in Deuteronomy (six occurrences) and in the prose of Jer (five occurrences);[22] it emphasizes here the continuity of Yahweh's promise from the time of Sinai to Jrm's present. And Jrm's response is to affirm for

Baltzer, *The Covenant Formulary in Old Testament, Jewish, and Early Christian Writings* (Philadelphia: Fortress, 1971).

15 For bibliography on "curse," see Josef Scharbert, "ארר," *TDOT* 1:405–18, esp. 405–6.

16 On the question see ibid., 408.

17 Compare Eichrodt, *Theology*.

18 On this matter see Lindblom, *Prophecy*, 329–31. For

the literature on "covenant" in general see Bibliography.

19 Forbes, "Extracting, Smelting, and Alloying," 572, 573–76, 577, 593.

20 Moshe Weinfeld, "בְּרִית," *TDOT* 2:256.

21 Von Rad, *Old Testament Theology 1*, esp. 297–98.

22 For the use of the phrase see Weinfeld, *Deuteronomy*, 174–75; compare Simon J. De Vries, *Yesterday, Today*

himself the curse that Yahweh has pronounced.

These verses thus remind the hearer of the basic obligation that Israel has had laid upon her as a covenant people—the bare bones of the agreement, so to speak.

■ **6–8** For the verb "call," used of prophetic proclamation, see 2:2 (and compare Structure, Form, Setting). For "admonish" (עוד hipʻil) compare 6:10: Jrm is at pains to insist on the reiteration of Yahweh's warnings to Israel— the diction is parallel to that in 7:25, where "early and constantly" (הַשְׁכֵּם) likewise appears. For the parallelism of "listen" and "turn one's ear," and for "walk in the stubbornness of their own evil heart," see 7:24. For the striking phrase "bring over them all the words of this covenant" see Structure, Form, Setting: the phrase suggests the diction of the prophetess Huldah to the emissaries of Josiah, 2 Kgs 22:16 (see also 25:13). The implication of "their earlier fathers" in v 10 (see below) makes it likely that the focus in the expression "your fathers" in v 7 is on Josiah and his generation (so Volz). These verses then shift from Sinai to the recent past, to Yahweh's efforts to remind people in more recent generations of their obligations.

■ **9–10** The noun "conspiracy" (קֶשֶׁר) is related to קשר "tie": there is a plot among the people to rebel against Yahweh, just as Hoshea of Israel plotted against the king of Assyria (2 Kgs 17:4). In the context of 594, the conspiracy against Nebuchadrezzar is a conspiracy against Yahweh. But if there is a prehistory to v 9, then at the time vv 18–20 first took shape, a conspiracy against Jrm was a conspiracy against Yahweh (for all these specific matters see Structure, Form, Setting). The expression אֲבוֹתָם הָרִאשֹׁנִים (v 10) can only mean "their earlier fathers," in contrast to the "fathers" of Josiah's generation (v 7) who were admonished: more recently the people have reverted ("returned," שָׁבוּ, v 10) to the evils of the previous generation (so Volz). Does the parallel of "house of Israel" and "house of Judah" here suggest that the same fate that overtook the northern kingdom is now about to overtake the south? If one understands these verses correctly, Jrm is accusing those in the period after Josiah's death of backsliding into the ways of the time before that king's reform. (See the similar comparison of generations in 7:26.)

■ **11–14** For the phrase "I am going to bring upon them disaster" compare 4:6; 5:15. The use of יצא מן for "escape" is unusual; see Structure, Form, Setting. The use of "cry" (זעק) may suggest a deliberate reversal of Deut 26:7, where the by-form צעק appears—the Sinai covenant will at last be overturned (see again Structure, Form, Setting). There are no other relevant instances of this phraseology in comparable material, though Isa 1:15 offers the same thought. For the motifs of v 12, see 2:27–28. Verse 13 is a secondary insertion from 2:28 (including two cola missing there in *M* but supplied from *G*): the shift from third-person (vv 11–12) to second-person plural in reference to the people in this verse is impossible, given the second singular address to Jrm in v 14 (so Volz, Rudolph). For the contents of v 14 see 7:16. There is no hope for the people, given their invincible loyalty to paganism (v 10): Yahweh will not listen to their cry for help, and the pagan gods to whom they cry for help will not respond; further, Yahweh forbids Jrm to intercede on their behalf.

■ **15–16** The text of these verses is exceedingly corrupt, and no reconstruction can be anything but tentative. The proposal offered here takes account of the basic imagery of the verse and the general patterns of Jrm's diction and seeks a text with minimum change of the consonants of *M*. The Versions are of little help; the text was evidently damaged at an early date.

Verse 15 is evidently about "meat" (בָּשָׂר) offered at the temple (compare 7:21). The word "to my beloved" (לִידִידִי) is impossible here; such diction is found in 12:7, but the genre of that passage is different from that of the sarcastic word of judgment here, and furthermore the masculine word does not fit with later feminine references (so also Volz, Rudolph). The suggestion of Rudolph to read לִי דוּדַיִךְ "to me your kettles" (not, as Rudolph suggests, "baskets": see below) is brilliant and undoubtedly correct; "kettles" are mentioned in both early and late narratives as part of the equipment at the sanctuary for cooking the meat which is offered (1 Sam 2:14; 2 Chr 35:13). The kap at the end of דוּדַיִךְ would then have been read as a bet; the word בֵּיתִי itself can mean "in my house."

The word הָרַבִּים does not fit; *G* rightly reads an

and Tomorrow: Time and History in the Old Testament (Grand Rapids: Eerdmans, 1975) 52n.

interrogative here, but its reading "vows" (נְדָרִים) is needlessly far from both context and the consonantal text. The suggestion of Driver and Hyatt (see Text, note e), accepted by Rudolph, is excellent, to read הַבְּרִים "fatlings" (with he interrogative), though I would read הַבְּרִים with definite article (to match "the meat of my sanctuary," see below), using the he of the previous word as the he interrogative. And instead of reading בְּשַׂר־קֹדֶשׁ as "holy meat" I would use the yod following קֹדֶשׁ to read בְּשַׂר־קָדְשִׁי "meat of my sanctuary," understanding "my sanctuary" as parallel to "my house."

The verb is not right as a form of עבר either; the reading which commends itself, I propose, is ערב III "be to one's tastes"—that verb occurs in 6:20 in a similar context, and that occurrence lends some plausibility to the reconstruction here (see Structure, Form, Setting, on the relation of vv 15–16 to vv 1–14). This verb takes the preposition עַל (Ezek 16:37; Ps 104:34).

The כִּי which follows introduces a clause dependent on the he interrogative: for the same construction see 18:20. The verb "cleanse" (זכך hip'il) is guesswork, but at least the word is in the semantic field of the verse: the same stem is used in Job 9:30 of cleaning one's hands, and the related adjective זַךְ is used of "pure" frank-incense in Exod 30:34 (P) and Lev 24:7 (H).

The meaning of הַמוּלָה has recently been clarified by the Ugaritic hmlt: the word means "multitude, crowd" (see for example the context of Ug. 3.3.25, where the parallel is nšm "mankind"). The larger phrase then cannot mean "with mighty thunder clap" (the conventional view, so Condamin and Bright) but must mean "at the sound of a great crowd," a phrase which does not fit the context of v 16: it must be shifted to somewhere at the end of v 15 (so Volz, Rudolph).

The verb "exult" (עלז) is appropriate in the context of psalms (see for example Ps 149:5).

The verb יצת hip'il "set (fire) to" otherwise takes the preposition בְּ either with the word "fire" or with the object burned; one is left uncertain whether a בְּ has dropped out from one or the other term, or whether poetic diction allows the phrase without preposition.

The diction of the first colon of v 15 is very close to that of Isa 1:11, לָמָּה־לִּי רֹב־זִבְחֵיכֶם "What has the multitude of your sacrifices to do with me?" The noun דּוּד, if correctly restored here, means "kettle" (it occurs in 24:1 meaning "basket"). Rudolph, who suggested the

emendation, believes that the word here means "baskets" and refers to the offering of first fruits (Deut 26:2); by this interpretation both grain offerings and animal offerings are referred to. But the word for "basket" in Deut 26:2 is another word (טֶנֶא), and in the meantime דוד in the meaning "kettle" appears in sacrificial contexts (see above). If that is the meaning here, then the imagery of the whole verse centers on meat (see above).

It is not clear what it is to which the phrase "you have done these schemes" refers: does "schemes" refer to "plots" against Yahweh, like "conspiracy" in v 9, or does it refer to the arrangements for animal sacrifice? The definite article with "schemes" suggests a demonstrative, and a demonstrative suggests a connection with sacrifice (7:22 carries the same meaning negatively). But the word is also used of destructive schemes in general (Ps 37:7). Perhaps "your evil" and "sound of a great crowd" are equally ambiguous (see below).

The word בְּרִיא, if correctly reconstructed here, is not the normal word for "fatling," which is מְרִיא (Isa 1:11); passages in which the word appears suggest that the word is the "secular" word for "fat" (Judg 3:17; Ezek 34:3)—Jrm may have intended to shock by avoiding the liturgical word. The phrase "holy meat," the translation of M, appears in Hag 2:12, but I propose "meat of my sanctuary" instead (compare the discussion of 23:9).

The verb ערב "be pleasing," if correctly reconstructed here, was evidently a technical cultic term—a sacrifice was to be pleasing to Yahweh (6:20, compare Mal 3:4); but here Jrm is speaking of the sacrificial meat as being pleasing to the worshipers (Hos 9:4 offers a similar accusation).

To what does "your evil" refer? It might be either "the evil you commit," a meaning suggested by "these schemes" above, or it might be "the disaster which you will undergo" (compare "at the time of their disaster [רָעָתָם]," v 12). Possibly the phrase is deliberately ambiguous: you seek to be cleansed from the evil that you do by the multiplicity of your sacrifices, and seek as well to evade the punishment that is coming (compare 7:10, which in different words carries much the same message).

To what does "the sound of a great crowd" refer (assuming that the phrase belongs in this location)? Is it the noise of the crowd of worshipers at festival time, like the "trampling of Yahweh's courts" or "solemn assembly"

(Isa 1:12, 13), or is it the noise of the enemy army at the gates, "shouting against the cities of Judah" (4:16)? Again it might be either, but in either event, the sacrificial system gives no protection.

The imagery of Israel as a "green olive-tree" is dependent on Hos 14:7, וִיהִי כַזַּיִת הוֹדוֹ, "And let his [Israel's] beauty be like the olive-tree." One can do no better than to cite, as Wolff does,[23] Dalman's description of the olive-tree in Palestine: "The rich abundance of its tender branches, and the crisp foliage growing above its strong trunk are a picture of the highly satisfied life."[24] The other relevant passage is Ps 52:10, where "green olive-tree" is a description of the psalmist in the temple (see Structure, Form, Setting). The tender comparison to an olive-tree reminds one of 6:2, "You are like the most delicate pasture, fair Zion" (reconstructed text): in that passage, too, the tender comparison is followed by an announcement of destruction.

"Set fire to" (יצת hip'il + אֵשׁ) is common in the prophets (for example, Amos 1:14; Jer 21:14); for the image of destruction, compare the destruction of the vineyard Israel in Isa 5:5–6; Jer 5:10; 6:9.

■ 17 The first part of this verse is peculiar. It is evidently an attempt by a redactor to relate vv 15–16 (the "green olive-tree") to vv 1–14 ("house of Israel and house of Judah," v 10; "burn offerings," v 12); so Volz, Rudolph. There may be a conscious attempt as well to make a bridge with v 18, since both verses begin with the subject "and Yahweh" (וַיהוה). For the metaphor of "planting" Israel see 2:21.

Though on first hearing the phrase "speak disaster" (רָעָה pi'el + דבר) seems unremarkable, it happens that the combination occurs only six times in the OT beyond the present passage (all with Yahweh as the subject: five times in Jer, 16:10; 26:19; 35:17; 36:31; 40:2; 1 Kgs 22:23).

The preposition בִּגְלַל "because of" occurs otherwise in the book only in 15:4, there, too, evidently in secondary material.[25] The rest of the verse uses diction found elsewhere in secondary material (thus "burn offerings to Baal" in v 13).

Aim

Judgment is decreed: Yahweh will allow his covenant people to be destroyed, because they prefer the Baals. The Baals cannot save—and Yahweh will not save. There was a chance to be saved, earlier, when Yahweh's warnings came in Josiah's generation, but the people have lost it by reverting to the way they have been pursuing before Josiah's time. Those who prefer the Baals of course read history differently (44:15–19), and between these two understandings of events there is no middle ground. Ultimately history would offer reinforcement of Jrm's analysis, but in the short run one can only listen to the claims of the two sides and choose.

The proclamation of judgment ends suddenly with a poem offering some of the tenderness and irony of the material in the first scroll: one thinks of the rhetorical questions in chapter 2 as one listens to v 15 here, but the message of "burning" associated with inevitable judgment is here nevertheless (v 16). It is a pity that a passage so characteristic of Jrm's outlook should have been so damaged textually.

If the verb "be pleasing" (ערב) is to be read in v 15, the people stand accused of satisfying not only their consciences but their stomachs by the meat offered in sacrifice. Centuries later Paul would accuse the church at Corinth of using the celebration of the Lord's Supper to satisfy their hunger, and he, too, would raise rhetorical questions about the circumstances of those whom he was addressing (1 Cor 11:20–22).

Beyond the details of the behavior of Judah are deeper issues: their assumption that the sacrificial system offers sanctuary against the coming disaster, the expectation of Yahweh as he contemplates the rebellion of his people. The only solution, it appears, is burning.

23   Wolff, *Hosea*, 236.
24   Gustaf Dalman, *Arbeit und Sitte in Palästina* 4 (Gütersloh: Bertelsmann, 1935) 164.
25   Volz, p. 161 n. 1.

Bibliography

Ahuis, Ferdinand
Der klagende Gerichtsprophet, Studien zur Klage in der Überlieferung von den alttestamentlichen Gerichts-propheten (Stuttgart: Calwer, 1982).

Baumgartner, Walter
Die Klagegedichte des Jeremia (BZAW 32; Giessen: Töpelmann, 1917).

Behler, Gebhard-Maria
Les confessions de Jérémie (Tournai: Casterman, 1959).

Berridge
pp. 114–83.

Blank, Sheldon H.
"The Confessions of Jeremiah and the Meaning of Prayer," *HUCA* 21 (1948) 331–54.

Blank, Sheldon H.
"The Prophet as Paradigm," *Essays in Old Testament Ethics, J. Philip Hyatt in Memoriam* (ed. James L. Crenshaw and John T. Willis; New York: Ktav, 1974) 111–30 = Sheldon H. Blank, *Prophetic Thought, Essays and Addresses* (Cincinnati, Hebrew Union College, 1977) 23–34.

Boer, Pieter A. H. de
Jeremia's Twijfel (Leiden: Brill, 1957).

Bright, John
"Jeremiah's Complaints—Liturgy or Expressions of Personal Distress?" *Proclamation and Presence, Old Testament Essays in Honour of Gwynne Henton Davies* (ed. John I. Durham and J. Roy Porter; Richmond: John Knox, 1970) 189–214.

Harvey, Julien
"The Prayer of Jeremias," *The Way* 3 (1963) 165–73.

Hubmann, Franz D.
"Stationen einer Berufung, Die 'Konfessionen' Jeremias," *TPQ* 132 (1984) 25–39.

Hubmann
Untersuchungen.

Ittmann, Norbert
Die Konfessionen Jeremias: Ihre Bedeutung für die Verkündigung des Propheten (WMANT 54; Neu-kirchen: Neukirchner, 1981).

Lamparter, Helmut
Dein Wort war zu mir mächtig. Die Bekentnisse des Propheten Jeremia (Metzingen/Württ.: Franz, 1965).

Leclercq, J.
"Les 'Confessions' de Jérémie," *Etudes sur les prophètes d'Israël* (ed. Ph. Béguerie, J. Leclercq and J. Steinmann; LD 14; Paris: Cerf, 1954) 111–45.

Mihelic, Joseph L.
"Dialogue with God: A Study of Some of Jere-miah's Confessions," *Int* 14 (1960) 43–50.

Rad, Gerhard von
"The Confessions of Jeremiah," *A Prophet to the*

Nations, Essays in Jeremiah Studies (ed. Leo G. Perdue and Brian Kovacs; Winona Lake, IN: Eisenbrauns, 1984) 339–47 = "Die Konfessionen Jeremias," *EvT* 3 (1936) 265–76 = Gerhard von Rad, *Gesammelte Studien 2* (TBAT 48; Munich: Kaiser, 1973) 224–35.

Reventlow
  Liturgie, 205–57.

Wang, Martin Cheng-Chang
  "A Theology of Frustration—An Interpretation of Jeremiah's Confessions," *South East Asia Journal of Theology* 15/2 (1974) 36–42.

Welten, Peter
  "Leiden und Leidenserfahrung im Buch Jeremia," *ZTK* 74 (1977) 123–50, esp. 137–45.

Jeremiah's Confessions: Introduction

At 11:18 there begins a series of deeply personal laments offered by Jrm to Yahweh. These have come to be called Jrm's "confessions"; the term is not entirely appropriate —a better term would be "complaints"—but the traditional designation will be retained here. Some of these confessions have matching responses from Yahweh recorded, while others do not. The series is completed at 20:18.

The lists of what is included in the confessions vary. By common consent the following are included: 11:18–12:6; 15:10–12, 15–21; 17:9–10, 14–18; 18:18–23; 20:7–12, 14–18. Aage Bentzen suggested expanding the list to include 4:19–21; 8:18–23; 10:19–23; 13:17; 14:17–18; and 23:9.[1] Most of these suggested additions are passages in which Jrm weeps or otherwise expresses emotion over the fate of his people, but even though there are expressions of dismay by Jrm over the fate of his people in the confessions proper (for example, 12:4), the category should be restricted to laments or complaints offered to Yahweh centering on the problem of Jrm's status before the people, the problem of Jrm's call, and his existence as a valid messenger from Yahweh. Bentzen's suggestion of the inclusion of 10:19–23 is to be rejected: by the analysis offered here at least vv 19–20 and 23 are spoken by the people. Similarly Hyatt suggests that 10:23–24 be included,[2] but this suggestion has not won general acceptance: Condamin rightly sees the passage as a prayer by the people for themselves (see there).

On the other hand, with Franz D. Hubmann I add 15:13–14 to Yahweh's response in 15:12. And there are four other units which, I submit, are related to the confessions. The first is 17:5–8: both rhetoric and content suggest its inclusion.[3] The passage, it is true, is not a lament or complaint; it is, I suggest, Jrm's act of repentance in response to the word from Yahweh in 15:19. And 20:13, though seemingly alien to the context, surely belongs in the sequence from v 7 to v 18 of that chapter. Then 16:1–9, though form-critically no part of the series (it is not a complaint but a supplementary call from Yahweh), is from a rhetorical or structural point of view closely related to the series: it is clear that it was included from an early stage in the growing collection of confessional material and may be useful in helping to interpret that material. The confessions emerge out of Jrm's struggle with the meaning of his vocation, so that this passage, concerned with Yahweh's call, is relevant. Finally the complex on the drought and threatened invasion, 14:1—15:9, is embedded in the confessional sequence and is rhetorically and structurally integrated with it; it too has a part to play in interpreting the confessions.

It may also be mentioned that Joseph L. Mihelic includes Jrm's initial call narrative, 1:4–19, among the confessions;[4] this is not useful except as a reminder of the close link between the confessions and the prophet's call. It might be said that Jrm's confessions to Yahweh are his response to Yahweh's call in the light of his living out that call.

Jer is unique among the prophetic books in preserving such a series of prayers, which appear to give extraordinary insight into the inner life of the prophet. The historical value of the passages for our knowledge of the man Jrm has been challenged (see below), but the fact remains that no other prophetic book has such a series of complaints.

It is useful, however, to search for what is comparable within the OT. Form-critically the relevant body of material is of course the individual laments among the

---

1   Aage Bentzen, *Introduction to the Old Testament,* 2, 121.
2   Hyatt, pp. 782, 902–3.
3   Holladay, *Spokesman,* 98–99; *Architecture,* 152–54.
4   Joseph L. Mihelic, "Dialogue with God: A Study of Some of Jeremiah's Confessions," *Int* 14 (1960) 43.

Psalms (see below), but so far as our knowledge goes these are anonymous. The tradition about Moses preserves the memory that when he was confronted by the "murmuring" of the people, he cried to Yahweh, "What shall I do with this people? They are almost ready to stone me" (Exod 17:4; the literary source of this verse is disputed).[5] When Samuel received word from Yahweh that Yahweh had rejected Saul, Samuel, we are told, was angry and cried to Yahweh all night (1 Sam 15:11), but we are not given the content of his cry. The closest comparable material is the word of Elijah to Yahweh from the cave at Horeb: "I have been very jealous for Yahweh, the God of hosts; for the people of Israel have forsaken your covenant, thrown down your altars, and slain your prophets with the sword; and I, even I only, am left; and they seek my life, to take it away" (1 Kgs 19:10). One might also mention the single phrase from the narrative of Isaiah's call: "Then I said, 'How long, O Lord?'" (Isa 6:11).

There are three bodies of material in the OT whose motifs derive from Jrm's confessions, and each has a contrasting motif. The poem of the book of Job has democratized the experience of the prophet: now the experience of agony in a world governed by a God who is seemingly unjust is not that of God's prophet, but simply of a just man; and Job's words are words of cursing the day he was born (Job 3) and of legal argumentation with God (Job 9 and often) which are derived from Jer 20:14–18 and 12:1 respectively.[6] The figure of the Servant of God in Deutero-Isaiah (Isa 53:6–8), obedient even in his suffering, is described in phrases derived from Jer 11:19; 15:11; and 15:15. And the Book of Jonah presents one with the picture of a rebellious prophet who argues with God about his fate and wishes he could die (see esp. Jonah 4): here the prophet is ironically portrayed as one disobeying God and then obeying him unenthusiastically.

There are other motifs in the prophets that are related to the confessional material but are not strictly comparable. Thus one of the functions of a prophet was to intercede with God on behalf of the people (compare the discussion on 7:16), so that one finds passages like Amos 7:1–9. One also finds passages in which the prophet expresses emotion over the fate of his people (Isa 22:4). And there are many passages beyond the prophetic books which narrate someone's discussion or argument with God—one thinks of Abraham's bargaining with God over the number of righteous men it would take to save Sodom (Gen 18:23–32). But none of these is directly comparable to the prayers in which Jrm struggles with Yahweh.

As a reaction to earlier scholarship that saw the confessions as a direct window into Jrm's psychology and personal feelings, typified by the study of John Skinner in 1922,[7] Reventlow in 1963 published a study which insisted that Jrm was the holder of a cultic office and that the "I" of Jrm's words was simply a way to say "we" on behalf of the people.[8] That is to say, the individual laments in the psalms had their setting in the cult, so that one must understand Jrm's confessions likewise as having their setting in the cult. This extreme view has been refuted by Bright[9] and Berridge:[10] Jrm is an individual prophet with a unique voice. But Reventlow's study is a reminder that the confessions were preserved not because of any biographical concern for Jrm's psychology but because Jrm spoke for his people in their corporate agony (particularly in the exile) and because Jrm's words became useful in the people's worship of God. And there was evidently a more particular reason for Jrm to publish them: to affirm God's validation of his prophetic office (on all these matters see below).

It has already been suggested that Jrm's confessions grew naturally out of his call. He hesitated in his call (1:6), and he perceived, once he had accepted the call, that Yahweh reassured him of protection (1:8, 17–19). Then when opposition came and he saw no evidence of Yahweh's protection, he became convinced that Yahweh was breaking his promise. Jrm therefore sought his vindication and used the same forensic terminology

---

5   Childs, *Exodus*, 306.
6   Holladay, "Lawsuit," 285–86.
7   Skinner.
8   Reventlow, *Liturgie*.
9   John Bright, "Jeremiah's Complaints—Liturgy or Expressions of Personal Distress?" *Proclamation and Presence, Old Testament Essays in Honour of Gwynne Henton Davies* (ed. John I. Durham and J. Roy Porter;

Richmond: John Knox, 1970) 189–214.
10   Berridge: see esp. pp. 210–20.

against Yahweh that Yahweh had been using through Jrm against the people.

In his complaints to Yahweh he avails himself of the genre of individual laments; we find in the confessions, then, the same characteristics as are to be found in that genre: addresses to Yahweh, expressions of confidence in him, the details of his complaints—the words of his opponents, Yahweh's neglect of him—and his pleas that Yahweh vindicate him and destroy his opponents. In taking over the genre of the individual lament Jrm has cut that genre loose from its place in the cult. Here, as in so many other ways, Jrm shows himself an innovator in making fresh use of earlier genres.

It has been stated already that Jrm's basic problem with Yahweh is that Yahweh did not seem to be keeping his promise to Jrm to protect him when opposition came. This may be part of the matter but is evidently by no means the whole story. Evidence will be given in the present study that this opposition to Jrm came quite specifically from the optimistic prophets and that the confessions arose during the times when the optimistic prophets pressed hard on Jrm, specifically in the autumn and winter of 601–600 and in the summer and autumn of 594. Thus there are data that this is the identity of the "guilty" (רְשָׁעִים) in 12:1 and the "merrymakers" (מְשַׂחֲקִים) in 15:17; they are people who ask about the fulfillment of the word of Yahweh (17:15) and themselves use Yahweh's name (12:2), indeed they "proclaim" Jrm's own divine words (20:10) in order to entrap him. Jrm, after the king burned his scroll in December 601 (36:22–23), proclaimed inevitable disaster for the people (36:31), a disaster which was evidently foreshadowed by the drought and by Jrm's conviction that the Babylonians still represented a military threat (see 14:1—15:9, Setting). When that disaster was not immediately forthcoming, the optimistic prophets must have renewed their persecution of Jrm; and his plea in 18:21–22a is evidently not so much a prayer that Yahweh punish his enemies as that Yahweh complete the disaster of the people in such a way that the word he proclaimed would be vindicated (see there). It may also be the explanation of the original setting of 11:22.

This deposit of prayers for retribution (11:20 = 20:12; 15:15) and for the death of segments of the population (11:22; 18:21–22a) leaves a bad taste in the mouth of the modern reader: Jrm is in no way the Suffering Servant described by Deutero-Isaiah. But it must be borne in mind that he is not reacting out of personal pique against personal enemies: he is reacting in bewilderment to God who is not protecting the divine word given him to proclaim as was his expectation. If Jrm's enemies are mocking him and planning to kill him, then those enemies are guilty of lese majesty, and Yahweh needs to manifest himself as God to these mockers, else Jrm's understanding of his mission is threatened at the foundation.

Part of the horror of these complaints is the irony that Jrm's enemies are attempting to do to him what Jrm is convinced Yahweh has already done. Thus his enemies try to cut him off from the land of the living, so that his name may no longer be remembered (11:19), but remembrance is carried on by sons, whom Yahweh has denied to Jrm (16:1–4). His enemies seek to "deceive" him and "overpower" him (20:10), but Jrm accuses Yahweh of having already "deceived" and "overpowered" him (20:7). Jrm thus endures the nightmare that his enemies might be doing the will of God.

In his rhetoric of struggle with Yahweh Jrm edges close to what more timid souls would deem blasphemy. Thus he sues Yahweh for breach of contract (12:1); his accusation to Yahweh of deception suggests seduction (20:7); he announces that the day he was born is cursed (20:14), an announcement tantamount to declaring his call from Yahweh to be cursed (compare 1:5). One has the impression that these words, hammered out on the anvil of Jrm's personal agony, raise theological issues hardly touched to such a degree elsewhere in the OT.

But if Jrm's complaints are startling, they are at least consistent: "Why is my pain unceasing?" (15:18)—the pain of the enemies' attacks and the pain of Yahweh's inaction on his behalf. On the other hand, Yahweh's answers are startling, and they are at the same time disturbing in their variety. (1) I shall protect you (15:20–21) and punish your enemies (11:21–23). (2) If you think your situation is bad now, it will get worse (12:5); indeed it has got worse (12:6). (3) I intend for you to be persecuted; I know exactly what I am doing (15:12). (4) Your despair is a sign that you need to repent (15:19). (5) You will suffer, but your enemies will suffer more (15:13–14). The analysis offered in the present study suggests that there is wording in 11:21 and 23, as well as 12:6; 15:13–14; and 15:20–21 which represent expansions of original answers, so that these various answers doubtless came to Jrm over a period of time. But their variety only makes more difficult the riddle of Jrm's undeserved suffering which he underwent. And of course one must go on to observe that though these answers from Yahweh are various, they are at least answers; but the prophet's complaints in 17:14–18; 18:18–23; 20:7–12; and 20:14–18 receive no recorded answers (20:13 is at best Jrm's response to Yahweh's response: see below); Yahweh's silence is thus even more agonizing.

There has been much speculation about the mode by which these private transactions between Jrm and Yahweh became part of the public testimony of the book. Scholars have differed whether Jrm ever proclaimed the words publicly. Thus Eissfeldt and Bright think it unlikely that he would have done so,[11] while Berridge firmly assumes it,[12] noting that those confessions that are recorded as evoking an answer from Yahweh are especially relevant to the public, in that some of the answers mention the fate of the prophet's opponents as well (11:21–23; 15:13–14; and, by implication, 15:20–21).

In material offering so few clues to setting any reconstruction is fraught with difficulty. But it does appear that the material in the basic stratum of the second scroll from chapter 8 onward was added chronologically. The collection of confessions begins directly after 11:1–17, dated here to the festival of booths in 594. A notable event of that festival must have been the death of the optimistic prophet Hananiah (28:17). Since a false prophet, by the Deuteronomic law recited at that festival, must die (Deut 18:20), the death of Hananiah must have been the most dramatic possible demonstration that Yahweh had validated the prophetic office of Jrm. I propose that this is the meaning of that curious verse, 20:13: Jrm rejoices that Yahweh has answered his prayers. By this proposal that verse will have closed a cycle of confessions which offers an inclusio (11:20 = 20:12): that cycle of confessions will then be offered publicly as Jrm's testimony of Yahweh's validation of him. It follows that 20:14–18 is an appendix, a reflection of a later crisis.

There is evidence of more than one recension within this cycle of confessions, however: to stay only within 11:18—12:6, Hubmann has shown that 11:21, the phrase "to the men of Anathoth" in 11:23, and 12:6 are all later additions (see there), I propose by Jrm himself. There are a few clues that some of the confessions took shape at the time of the drought (12:4; 15:18; compare 17:8); as already noted, that was also a period in which Jrm was opposed by the optimistic prophets (14:13–16), so that it is plausible to see some of the confessions as having taken shape at that time, in a collection not made public. Whether any of the material took shape still earlier in his life is difficult to assess. The details will be dealt with in the individual passages.

If these complaints emerged out of Jrm's own agony, it nevertheless remains true that Jrm represented the people in their agony to come, so that his life became a paradigm to the people of Yahweh's action; in this task the confessions became a subtle kind of symbolic action, except that that action was not so much a striking gesture as a protracted experience of endurance and of suffering.[13] The old assumptions that God rewards the innocent and punishes the guilty were breaking down at an ever-increasing rate at the time of the fall of Jerusalem and the consequent exile, and the agony of Jrm spoke to the people's condition. Jrm's confessions in this way broke new ground in mapping the relation between Yahweh and his people.

---

11   Eissfeldt, *Introduction*, 357; John Bright, "The Book of Jeremiah, Its Structure, Its Problems, and Their Significance for the Interpreter," *Int* 9 (1955) 265.
12   Berridge, pp. 157–58.
13   See particularly Stoebe, "Seelsorge"; Berridge, pp. 157–58; Sheldon H. Blank, "The Prophet as Paradigm," *Essays in Old Testament Ethics, J. Philip Hyatt in Memoriam* (ed. James L. Crenshaw and John T. Willis; New York: Ktav, 1974) 111–30 = Sheldon H. Blank, *Prophetic Thought, Essays and Addresses* (Cincinnati: Hebrew Union College, 1977) 23–34; Hubmann, *Untersuchungen*, 316–17.

**Jeremiah Struggles
with the Meaning of Threats
to His Life**

Bibliography

Hubmann
  Untersuchungen.
Reventlow
  Liturgie, 240–57.
Rowley, Harold H.
  "The Text and Interpretation of Jer. 11:18—
  12:6," *AJSL* 42 (1925/26) 217–27.
Schreiner, Josef
  "Unter der Last des Auftrags: Aus der Verkün-
  digung des Propheten Jeremia, Jer 11,18—12:6,"
  BibLeb 7 (1966) 180–92.

On 11:18–23:

Berridge
  pp. 166–68.
Burkitt, Francis C.
  "Justin Martyr and Jeremiah xi 19," *JTS* 33 (1931–
  32) 371–73.
Dahood, Mitchell
  "Hebrew-Ugaritic Lexicography IV," *Bib* 47
  (1966) 409.
Dahood, Mitchell
  "Ugaritic Studies and the Bible," *Greg* 43 (1962)
  66.
Houberg, R.
  "Note sur Jérémie xi 19," *VT* 25 (1975) 676–77.

On 12:1–6:

Berridge
  pp. 160–66.
Driver, Godfrey R.
  "Difficult Words in the Hebrew Prophets," *Studies
  in Old Testament Prophecy, Presented to Theodore H.
  Robinson* (ed. Harold H. Rowley; Edinburgh:
  Clark, 1950) 59–61.
Driver, Godfrey R.
  "Jeremiah xii, 6," *JJS* 5 (1954) 177–78.
Ehrman, Albert
  "A Note on בוטח in Jer. xii. 5," *JSS* 5 (1960) 153–
  55.
Holladay
  "Lawsuit."
Holladay
  "Style," 49–51.
McKane, William
  "The Interpretation of Jeremiah xii. 1–5," *Glasgow
  University Oriental Society Transactions* 20 (1963–64)
  38–48.
Stummert, Friedrich
  "Bemerkungen zu Jer. 12, 1–6," *Miscellanea Biblica
  et Orientalia Athanasio Miller oblata* (ed. Adalbert
  Metzinger; Studia Anselmiana 27–28; Rome:
  Pontifical Institute S. Anselm, 1951) 264–75.

18 ᵃ "O Yahweh, ⟨inform me⟩ᵃ ⟨so I can know
        it!"⟩ᵇ
     That was when ᶜ you showed meᶜ
        what they are doing:

19 I for my part had been like a trusting lamb
        (who) is led to slaughter;
     I had not known that against me they
        made plans:
     "Let us destroy the tree ⟨through his
        opponent,⟩ᵃ
        and let us cut him off from the land of
           the living,
        and his name shall be remembered
           no more."

20 So, O Yahweh of hosts, righteous judge,
     you who test the mind and the heart,
        let me see your retribution on them,
        for ⟪ to me you have revealed my
           adversaries. ⟫ᵃ

Text

18a—a Reading וְיהוה with *G* and *S* as a vocative, and
vocalizing the verb as הוֹדִיעֵנִי, imperative, for *M*
הוֹדִיעַנִי "[Yahweh] has informed me." See Preliminary Observations, Form.

b Vocalizing וְאֵדָעָה, cohortative; see Interpretation.
M vocalizes וָאֵדָעָה, following the previous verb: "and
I knew." The suffix in that vocalization is acceptable
(GKC, sec. 49e), but the emended vocalization is
preferable (see Interpretation).

c—c *G* reads a qal, רָאִיתִי "I saw"; this reading is
accepted by Giesebrecht, Cornill, and Volz. But if
one reads גִּלִּיתָ "you revealed" in v 20 (see there),
then *M* is preferable here. The transition to the
second colon is abrupt in *M*, but Duhm's suggestion,
followed by Rudolph, that a vocative יהוה "Yahweh"
dropped out of the second colon, becomes unnecessary by the proposal here to read יהוה as a vocative
in the first colon.

19a Reading בְּלַחְמוֹ (compare Ps 35:1) for *M* בְּלַחְמוֹ "in
(or 'with') his bread." The traditional text is a well-
known crux. *G* and *V* keep עֵץ "tree, wood" and
"bread" and read "let us put wood in his bread";
thus they read the verb as נָשִׂיכָה or נַשְׁלִיכָה, נִשְׁלְחָה.
T reads the verb similarly and renders "let us put
deadly poison in his bread"; this is logical but
evidently only a guess. There have been three
proposals to solve the puzzle. (1) It is suggested that
לֶחֶם means "pulp of a tree" (Guillaume, *Prophecy and
Divination*, 343, and n. 2). (2) Emend בְּלַחְמוֹ to בְּלֵחוֹ
"in its freshness, sap" (compare Deut 34:7; so
Duhm—and, according to him, Ferdinand Hitzig
before him; so Giesebrecht, Cornill, Condamin,
Rudolph). A variation on this suggestion is to see in
the word an enclitic mem, vocalizing בְּלַחְמוֹ or the
like, with the same meaning (so Dahood, Bright). (3)
Accept the verb in *G* and *V*, נָשִׂיתָה, and redivide to
עֵצֶב לַחְמוֹ, "let us make trouble his bread" (Francis
C. Burkitt, R. Houberg). For the present suggestion
see Interpretation.

20a Reading אֵלֶיךָ גִּלִּיתִי אֶת־רִיבִי for *M* אֵלַי גִּלִּיתָ יְרִיבִי
"to you I have revealed my (legal) case." The verb "I
have revealed" does not fit the object, and most
commentators have accepted the revocalization
proposed by Hitzig, to read גַּלּוֹתִי (גלל) qal) "I have
entrusted" (compare Pss 22:9; 37:5): so also Duhm,
Cornill, Volz, Condamin, Rudolph, and (with
hesitation) Bright. This is an attractive possibility,
but unity of diction makes the present proposal
preferable (see Interpretation). The rare word יְרִיבִי
"my adversaries" occurs in 18:19; one notes that
there *G* reads רִיבִי. In Ps 35:1 יְרִיבִי stands in parallelism with לֹחֲמָי (see v 19, note a). The sign of the
accusative אֵת in *M* is either misplaced or secondary.
The kap of אֵלֶיךָ was a false correction once the
object was understood as רִיבִי; note that in 2:19 אֵלַי
is to be restored from *M* אֵלַיִךְ.

21 Yahweh: **Therefore thus Yahweh has said, [Concerning the men of Anathoth who seek your[b] life and say, "You shall not prophesy in the name of Yahweh, or you will die by our hand";[c]][a]**

22 **[therefore thus Yahweh of hosts has said,][a]**
I am going to deal with them:
the young men shall die by the sword,
their sons [and their daughters][b] shall die by famine,

23 **and they shall have no remnant;**
for I shall bring disaster [to[b] the men of Anathoth,][a]

12

the year of their visitation.

1 Jeremiah: **You will be innocent, Yahweh,**
when I dispute with you;
nevertheless I will speak judgments upon you.
Why has the way of the guilty succeeded,
(why) can the betrayers be secure?

2 **You have planted them: they take root as well;**
they grow: they bring forth fruit as well;
"You are near" is in their mouth
but is far from their mind.

3 **But you, Yahweh, (who) have known me, (who) see me,**
and (who) have tested whether my heart is with you,
separate them like sheep for slaughter,
and dedicate them for the day of killing.

4 **How long must the land be dry,**
and the grass of every field wither,
because of the evil of those who dwell in it?
⟨You have swept away⟩[a] beast[b] and bird,
for they have said, "He will not see where we end!"

5 Yahweh: **When you have run with foot-soldiers and they tire you,**
how will you compete[a] with horses?
So it is in prosperous land that you trust!—
how will you do in the thicket of the Jordan?

6 **[Yes, even your brothers and your father's house,**
even they have betrayed you,
even they have called behind you, "Drunk!"
Do not believe them
when they speak fine words to you.][a]

21a These words are redactional, contradicting the context of conspiracy in vv 18–20: see the detailed discussion in Hubmann, *Untersuchungen*, 68–95, and see Structure, Setting, and Interpretation.

b *G* reads "my life" here, and this reading is preferred by Condamin and Rudolph. But the redactor evidently intends "Concerning the men of Anathoth" to begin the quotation of Yahweh's words, while *G*, understanding "concerning the men of Anathoth" to continue the messenger formula, has secondarily corrected the reference.

c Many MSS., and *G, V, S,* and *T* read בְּיָדֵינוּ "by our hands" (plural).

22a The words are missing in *G*; since the messenger formula has already appeared in v 21, it is dittographic here. Or *M* may represent a conflate text, if there was a text tradition in which the messenger formula was missing at the beginning of v 21.

b This expression breaks the poetic pattern: בְּנֵיהֶם "their sons" should be understood as "their children," since בָּנִים is a standard parallel to בַּחוּרִים "young men" (6:11; 9:20). The expression was doubtless added when 16:1–9 was added to the complex (see Structure there). This solution seems preferable to that of Volz and Rudolph, that הַבְּחוּרִים "the young men" is dittographic from בַּחֶרֶב "by the sword" and יָמֻתוּ "shall die," thus reading "their sons shall die by sword, and their daughters shall die by famine": the gender of the second יָמֻתוּ would be difficult, and how, really, could such a dittography have arisen?

23a These words are redactional; they could well have been added by Jrm himself, however, when v 21 and 12:6 were added. See Setting.

b A few MSS. read עַל־ for *M* אֶל־. The corresponding preposition in v 21 is עַל־. The meaning is hardly affected.

12:4a Vocalizing with J. D. Michaelis סָפְתָה for *M* third singular feminine סָפְתָה (presumably "are swept away"). See Interpretation.

b Read with a few MSS. and *V* and *T* בְּהֵמָה for *M* plural בְּהֵמוֹת "beasts."

5a I propose the word be vocalized תִּתְחָרֶה (see Text on 22:15). The meaning is unaffected.

6a This verse has been added secondarily (see Preliminary Observations, Structure), but, I propose, by Jrm himself (see Setting).

Preliminary Observations

These twelve verses present a set of problems of great complexity, and one can gain only moderate certainty on details of text, redaction, structure, form, and setting. As elsewhere, these specific problems interact, so that one's decision on one has consequences for the others.

As the text now stands, 11:18—12:6 forms a unit made up of a complaint of Jrm (11:18–20), an answer from Yahweh (11:21–23), a complaint of Jrm (12:1–4) and an answer from Yahweh (12:5–6). There are thematic and catchword links within the material. But there are strong reasons to believe that the unity of the passage has been achieved secondarily and that in their original form 11:18–23 and 12:1–6 were separate units (see below).

As for 11:18–23, most critics in the last several decades have assumed dislocations of the text. Thus Cornill assumed that the third colon of 12:1 must be inserted in 11:22 after "Therefore thus Yahweh of hosts has said." The schemes have been elaborated; Hubmann lists fourteen, of various commentators.[1] The most widely accepted suggestions are that 12:6 belongs in the middle of 11:18 and that 12:3 belongs in the middle of 11:20. Thus Rudolph proposes 11:18; 12:6; 11:19, 20a; 12:3; 11:20b, 21–23; 12:1–2, 4bβ–5 (by his analysis 12:4abα is redactional). Bright offers a simpler scheme, simply reversing the order of the halves (12:1–6; 11:18–23) but admits that the "dislocation of the text seems to be somewhat more complicated than this."[2] These reconstructions attempt to bring coherence into the sequence of thought; but if they are valid, then one must assume either accidental displacement (the circumstances for which are difficult to imagine) or deliberate re-editing (but redaction by expansion is in general more likely than redaction by rearrangement). There are real problems in understanding this material, but the solution to the problems should be sought for in other ways than large-scale displacement of cola or whole verses.

Hubmann's literary-critical and structural analysis of the passage[3] demonstrates that in the earliest stage the confessional material in chapter 11 was separate from that in chapter 12, and that the original form of the material in chapter 11 was vv 18–20, 22–23 (without the phrase "to the men of Anathoth" in v 23), and that in chapter 12 excluded v 6; Hubmann maintains that 11:21, the phrase "to the men of Anathoth" in v 23, and 12:6 were added redactionally when the two units were brought together (see in detail Structure). Thus a theory of displacement of verses is unwarranted.

Two interlocking problems call forth the solution of displacement of verses. (1) Verse 18 seems to begin *in medias res*—vv 18–20 do not seem coherent. (2) The specific circumstances of the danger in which Jrm found himself are not clear. Commentators who bring 12:6 into the context of 11:18 assume that 12:6 is the content of Yahweh's revelation to Jrm. But the intention of 12:6 is to heighten the threat of Jrm's fellow villagers: 12:5 speaks of a heightening, and 12:6 explains that heightening (the particle גַּם "even" occurs three times). Thus 12:6 belongs where it is. Again 12:3 shares phraseology with 11:20, but 12:3 is not necessary to explain 11:20.

The M vocalization of v 18a, "And Yahweh informed me, so that I knew," demands a most awkward shift from the third person there to the second person in v 18b ("that was when you showed me their deeds"). Since וַיהוָה in v 20 is vocative ("O Yahweh"), one is led to take the same expression in v 18a as a parallel vocative, as *G* and *S* do: "O Yahweh, inform me so I can know." In this way "Yahweh" is second person in both cola of v 18. But there is still a surprising shift from imperative in v 18a to historical past in v 18b, a shift marked by the emphatic "then" (אָז, here rendered "that was when"). The solution proposed here is to understand v 18a as a prayer and v 18b as a testimony of the fulfillment of that prayer: in short, to understand v 18a as a self-quotation (see further Form). The proposal gains somewhat in plausibility when this passage is compared with 20:7–13, with which it has much in common (including the virtual duplication of v 20 in 20:12); there, too, Jrm quotes himself (20:8 and 9) and then quotes his opponents (20:10, compare v 19 here).

The passage becomes even clearer if the diction of Ps 35:1 is restored to vv 19 and 20 ("his opponent," "my adversaries"). The sequence of thought in vv 18–20 is now seen to involve three steps. (1) There is talk against

---

1   See the discussion, Hubmann, *Untersuchungen*, 30–41, and the table, 42.

2   Bright, p. 90.

3   Hubmann, *Untersuchungen*, 57–108.

Jrm, and the prophet wants to know what it involves (v 18a). (2) Yahweh reveals to him that it is more than talk, it is action—specific plans to have Jrm killed (vv 18b–19). Jrm's enemies (the optimistic prophets, as Hubmann proposes, a proposal accepted here—see Setting) suggest making common cause with an established opponent of Jrm's (Pashhur?—20:1–6) in order to rid themselves of him. (3) Jrm then asks Yahweh to do more than reveal the substance of the plot: he asks him to take action himself against the plotters (v 20).

The sequence of thought becomes even clearer if, as is proposed in the present study, 11:9 is prefixed to v 18 (see 11:1–17, Structure, Form, Setting, *A Possible Prehistory for Verse 9*). By this understanding Yahweh has revealed to Jrm the existence of a conspiracy, and v 18 is his response to that revelation.

Structure

The Basic Stratum of 11:18—15:21. Portions of 11:18–23; 12:1–6; 14:1—15:9; and 15:10–21 formed a unit at an early stage of the collecting process. That is to say, some at least of the confessional material in chapters 11, 12, and 15 is associated with the drought-battle liturgy in 14:1—15:9. For the details see 14:1—15:9, Preliminary Observations.

Extent of Unit. Confessional material begins at 11:18 and closes at 12:6; 12:7 begins a lament by Yahweh himself over his lost possession, a passage perhaps linked with what precedes by the catchword "house." Though it will become clear that 11:18–23 and 12:1–6 were originally separate units (see below, *Unity or Disunity in the Sequence*), the two are parallel and existed side by side in the earliest redaction. It is therefore economical to consider them together.

Position of Unit. It is the proposal of the present study that the confessional collection (through 20:13) was proclaimed publicly after Hananiah's death in September/October 594 (see above, Jeremiah's Confessions: Introduction, and in particular see Interpretation of 20:13); the material of 11:1–17 shares the same setting. And in particular if both 11:9 and 18 were associated in Jrm's mind at an earlier period, then it is altogether appropriate that 11:18—12:6 follows 11:1–17.

Basic Pattern of the Sequence; Unity or Disunity in the Sequence. The pattern of the sequence, as it now stands, is a simple one: (1) first section—(a) complaint of Jrm, 11:18–20; (b) reply of Yahweh, 11:21–23; (2) second section—(a) complaint of Jrm, 12:1–4; (b) reply of Yahweh, 12:5–6.

The first section, as it now stands, sets forth a conspiracy by the "men of Anathoth" (vv 21, 23) to kill Jrm; then in 12:5 Yahweh implies to Jrm by his metaphorical counterquestions that the prophet's situation will become even worse, and in 12:6 that heightening is revealed to be the treachery of Jrm's own family (the threefold "even"). On the face of it, then, the sequence is a unity.

There are convincing reasons, however, to believe that that unity is secondary, and that the two sections were originally separate.[4] These reasons have to do with both content and structure.

There are four considerations of content. (1) There is no vocabulary in 11:21 appropriate either to the context or to Jrm's poetry in general.[5] (2) The last verse, 12:6, offers only one vocabulary link with vv 1–4 ("betray," בגד, v 1) and none with v 5; it simply offers a heightening over 11:21.[6] (3) From a practical point of view, there can be no "heightening" of a plot to murder Jrm:[7] 12:6 can offer nothing more dangerous. This circumstance is a motive for many commentators to shift the position of 12:6 (see Preliminary Observations). (4) There is a contrast of content between 11:19 and 21: the first offers hidden plans for murder, the second offers open threats.[8]

As to structure, both 11:18–23 and 12:1–5 have respective internal congruences that affirm the internal unity of each section (see below), but three conclusions must be underlined. (1) The material of 11:21 and the phrase "to the men of Anathoth" in v 23 do not participate in the internal structure of 11:18–23. (2) There is no participation of 12:6 in the internal structure of 12:1–5. (3) The links between 11:18–23 and 12:1–6 are, at the most, catchword links.[9] It is true, of course, that "men of Anathoth" appears in both 11:21 and 23 as a kind of inclusio, that that inclusio overlays the inclusio of פקד "deal with, visit(ation)" in vv 22 and 23. And there is of course the link between the two sections provided by the citing of the "men of Anathoth" and the members of

---

4   Ibid., 68–95.
5   Ibid., 65.
6   Ibid., 71.

7   So already Cornill, p. 154; see Hubmann, *Untersuchungen*, 68.
8   Hubmann, *Untersuchungen*, 69.

Jrm's family in 12:6, but this link, it is proposed, is secondary, a redactional attempt to unite the two sections (see further Setting and Interpretation).

Even when the redactional nature of 11:21, the phrase "to the men of Anathoth" in v 23, and 12:6 is recognized and they are removed, there remains no intrinsic unity between the 11:18–20 + 22–23 and 12:1–5. Thus the first sequence is about a plot to kill Jrm, and Yahweh's answer in vv 22–23 is reassuring to the prophet; Jrm continues to function within the framework of Deuteronomic theology, by which innocent people are rewarded and guilty people are punished. By contrast the second sequence is about theodicy, and Yahweh's answer is not at all reassuring; Jrm's assumption about Deuteronomic theology has collapsed. (On this contrast see further Setting.)

Structure of 11:18–23. Hubmann demonstrates[10] a nice congruence between Jrm's complaint (vv 18–20) and Yahweh's response (vv 22–23). Both have at their midpoint a tricolon whose first two cola are closely synonymous and positive and whose third colon is less closely synonymous and is negative:

Let us destroy the tree through his opponent,
> and let us cut him off from the land of the living,
>> and his name shall be remembered no more.
>>> (v 19bβ)

The young men shall die by the sword,
> their sons shall die by famine,
>> and they shall have no remnant. (vv 22b–23a)

This congruence goes so far that the third colon of each tricolon offers the subject before the negative verb. And the congruence of structure is matched by congruence of content: the plotters plot to do away with Jrm so that he will have no sons to carry on his name (see Interpretation), and Yahweh intends to do away with the plotters so that they will have no sons to carry on their name.[11]

There is another link between the two sections: the root פקד in vv 22 and 23 answers נקם in Jrm's prayer (v 20)—these two roots are in synonymous parallelism in

5:9 (= 5:29; 9:8) and in 15:15.

The structure of vv 18–20 is as follows:[12]

(a) section beginning with וַיהוה, offering a form of the verb ראה, closing with כִּי עָלַי . . . (vv 18–19ba);

(b) tricolon, the quotation of the plotters (v 19bβ);

(a') section beginning with וַיהוה, offering a form of the verb ראה, closing with כִּי אֵלֶיךָ . . . (v 20). If the reconstruction of the last colon is correct, there is an inclusio between v 18 and the end of v 20 in references to Yahweh's revelation (see Interpretation on v 20).

The original form of Yahweh's response, vv 22–23 (without "to the men of Anathoth") is too short to have an elaborate form, but notice has already been taken of the midpoint, the tricolon with two positive cola and one negative one, and it must be added that this tricolon is framed by the two occurrences of the root פקד "deal with, visit."[13]

Structure of 12:1–5. Verses 1–4 are a complaint of Jrm, while v 5 contains Yahweh's response. The basic parallelism between the two sections is the two questions of Jrm, "why?" (v 1) and "how long?" (v 4), and the two counterquestions of Yahweh ("how?" twice). Each of Jrm's questions is structured chiastically, in the opposite way ("why?": subject, verb, verb, subject; "how long?": verb, subject, subject, verb); and each of Yahweh's counterquestions is also structured chiastically, but in the same way (first question: prepositional phrase, verbs, "how?" + verb, prepositional phrase; second question: prepositional phrase, verb, "how?" + verb, prepositional phrase).[14] There appears to be no close link between Jrm's first question and Yahweh's first counterquestion, and the repetition of "land" in Jrm's second question and Yahweh's second counterquestion is a small matter.[15]

Hubmann analyzes vv 1–4 in two parts:[16]
vv 1–2:
v 1a: address to Yahweh (with אַתָּה)
v 1b: question (chiastic)
v 2a: elucidation
v 2b: return to the relation with Yahweh;

9   Ibid., 75–95, correctly against Holladay, *Architecture*, 141–42.

10   Hubmann, *Untersuchungen*, 79–81.

11   Ibid., 80–81.

12   This analysis is adapted from ibid., 77–79.

13   Ibid., 79–82.

14   Ibid., 85–87.

15   Though it is noted by ibid., 87.

16   Ibid., 82.

vv 3–4:

v 3: address to Yahweh (with אַתָּה)
v 4a: question (chiastic)
v 4b: elucidation
v 4c: (כִּי-clause) return to the relation with Yahweh.

This analysis may be helpful, but the distribution of cola, it appears, suggests a slightly different analysis.

Verse 4 can hardly be construed as other than five cola. In spite of the *M* accent 'atnaḥ at the end of the second colon, I propose that the real break comes at the end of the third colon (see Interpretation): the first two cola and the fourth refer to the drought, while the third and fifth cola refer to "their" evil. Similarly v 1 must be construed as five cola; there are three on Jrm's relation with Yahweh, and two on the "guilty" (רְשָׁעִים). Verses 2–3 are made up of four bicola. Thus the two sequences of five cola begin and end Jrm's complaint: v 1—three cola, then the question in two cola; v 4—the question in three cola, then two cola. Formally this analysis appears valid, but in content other patterns are apparent. Thus v 1a begins with צַדִּיק אַתָּה and v 2b with קָרוֹב אַתָּה: these seem to be related (see Interpretation). Then v 3, with a hymnic address to Yahweh and a prayer, is the central point of the utterance.[17] And there is the subtle contrast between the vocabulary of fertility in v 2a and of drought in v 4, and between the way the "guilty" speak in v 2a and the last colon of v 4. Finally, if the emendation "you have swept away" in v 4 is correct, there may be a contrast with "you have planted them" in v 2.

For the structure of v 5, see above.

Structure of 12:6. There is no reason to display this verse as prose, as Rudolph does (*BHS*). The three occurrences of "even" (גַּם) unite the first three cola; the second colon is parallel with the fourth (the theme of "trust"), and the third colon is parallel with the fifth (theme of "speaking").

Form

For general remarks on the form of the confessions see above, Jeremiah's Confessions: Introduction.

Jrm's utterance in 11:18–20 is in the form of an individual lament. The prayer "inform me" is found in individual laments in the Psalms (Pss 39:5; 143:8). The

emphatic אָז "then," here rendered "that was when," marks the testimony of answer to prayer (compare Ps 6:10 for a similar acknowledgment of divine response, though it is to be noted that אָז is used in the Psalms in such contexts only in an affirmation of future response, as in 56:10). Verse 19 then embodies the complaint. The simile "like a trusting lamb" reminds one of other similes for helplessness in laments in the Psalms (compare Ps 22:15–16, "I am poured out like water," "my heart is like wax," "my strength is dried up like a potsherd," and 102:4–12). For the complaint of "plans" against Jrm, compare Ps 56:6. Laments in the Psalms often quote the words of the enemy; there are no comparable cohortatives there, but the wording of Ps 71:11 is close to the quotation here (see further Pss 13:5; 22:9; 35:21, 25; 59:8 [?]; 70:4). And outside the Psalms, Prov 1:11 offers comparable cohortatives.

Verse 20 then brings a closing invocation with hymnic elements, followed by Jrm's plea: similar diction is found in Ps 59:6 and 144:1–2.

Verses 22–23 embody Yahweh's response. It is a word of judgment on Jrm's enemies (or perhaps on the people in general: see Interpretation); in form it is no different from 5:15–17 or any other oracle of judgment. Close parallels are to be found in Amos 7:17, where similar diction is used for a personal word of judgment against Amaziah,[18] and in Jer 20:4–6, the judgment against Pashhur (similarly with הִנְנִי, 20:4).

The tone in 12:1–4 is set by Jrm's use, at the very beginning of the complaint, of forensic terminology[19] (compare Interpretation). This use is quite free, and the tone ironic: the emotional level is comparable to that in 2:35, where Yahweh accuses Israel in spite of her protestations of innocence. The frustration Jrm feels, that Yahweh will turn out to be innocent, is similar to the frustration Job expresses in Job 9:12–20, though in that passage Job is formally addressing his friends and refers to God in the third person.

Jrm's complaint in vv 1b–2 is similar to the laments in Hab 1:3 and Ps 10:1–4. The question "why?" (v 1b) is frequent in laments (Hab 1:3; Pss 10:1; 22:2; 43:2; and often), but the word in those passages is לָמָּה, while here it is Jrm's preferred word מַדּוּעַ (of sixty-one occurrences

---

17   So also ibid., 86.
18   Berridge, pp. 167–68.
19   Ibid., 161–62.

of the word in the OT, sixteen are in Jer). The word may carry a reproachful tone.[20] The material in vv 1b–2 is essentially an accusation to Yahweh of not adhering to his covenant promises; Jrm makes use of material from Psalm 1 in v 2a to set forth his accusation.

The climax of the lament comes in v 3, which closely resembles 11:20; here again we have the address to Yahweh with hymnic elements, followed by Jrm's plea (for similar diction in the Psalms see on 11:20 above).

The question (v 4) "how long?" like the question "why?" is found more than once in the Psalms, particularly in laments (see Interpretation), but its use in the context of the drought suggests a specific adaptation of the form by Jrm (see Setting). The closing cola of v 4 are a reference to Yahweh's judgment on those who are contemptuous of him (compare 5:12–13; Zeph 1:12): the last colon is comparable to one in Ps 10:4 (a psalm which, as has already been noted, offers diction much like the whole complaint of Jrm's).

Yahweh's answer in v 5, by means of counterquestions, is in the form of the "how much more" argument (see Form on 3:1).[21] It is precisely the mode of God's answer to Job in Job 38—41; the material in Job is derivative from Jrm's confessions in other respects as well (see on v 1 above, and compare the remarks in Jeremiah's Confessions: Introduction).[22]

The supplemental material in v 6 is a warning offered by Yahweh to Jrm; Yahweh offers a similar warning to Israel in 9:3. The warning to Jrm is revelational instruction much like the reassurance to Jrm in 1:17 regarding enemies.

Setting

The determination of settings for the units of confessional material is a precarious task; the material uses conventional forms and offers few historical clues, and such prayers can always be reused in fresh contexts.

I have already proposed that the confessional collection was made public at the time of Hananiah's death in the autumn of 594 (see above, Jeremiah's Confessions: Introduction). Because the collection of confessions gives evidence of stages of redaction, one assumes there were earlier settings for these prayers in the course in Jrm's career; the task here is to determine these, so far as possible.

It has already been shown that 11:18–20 + 22–23 (less "to the men of Anathoth" in v 23) is a separate unit from 12:1–5 (see Structure, *Unity or Disunity in the Sequence*). The task then is to locate the occasion when 11:18–20 + 22–23 (less "to the men of Anathoth") first took shape for Jrm, the occasion when 12:1–5 first took shape, and then the occasion for the expansions.

The reply of Yahweh in 11:22–23 offers a few clues. Thus the parallelism of "sons/children" (בָּנִים) and "young men" (בַּחוּרִים) is found also in 6:11 and 9:20, and "year of their visitation" (שְׁנַת פְּקֻדָּתָם) reminds one of "at the time I deal with them" (בְּעֵת־פְּקַדְתִּים) in 6:15; those passages, 6:9–15 and 9:16–21, have been dated in the present study to December 601 or early in 600. The parallelism of "sword" and "famine" is found in 5:12 and six times in 14:1—15:9, the drought and battle liturgy (14:12–18; 15:2); both that liturgy and 5:10–17 are here dated at the time the king burned the scroll or soon thereafter. On the other hand, Jrm portrays himself here as naive: he is initially unaware of any plot around him, and his response accepts the conventional Deuteronomic theology (see Structure, *Unity or Disunity in the Sequence*). If 12:1–5 is to be assigned to the same general period (see below), then one is led to allow some time-lapse between the two complaints.

Can the plot be identified? Much depends upon one's interpretation of the data in chapter 36. If 36:5 is associated with the fast declared by the king (36:9), then there is already opposition to Jrm at the temple (v 5), and 36:10–19 suggests that opposition developed at the palace as well, opposition which culminated in the king's decision to arrest him (36:26). All of this could well be a background for a plot against Jrm. But one has no

20 Alfred Jepsen, "Warum? Eine lexikalische und theologische Studie," *Das ferne und nahe Wort, Festschrift Leonhard Rost* (ed. Fritz Maass; BZAW 105; Berlin: Töpelmann, 1967) 106–13.
21 For Bibliography see 2:1—4:4, n. 26.
22 Compare Samuel Terrien, "Introduction to Job," *IB* 3:888–89.

further information. For example, there is no way to identify Jrm's "opponent" (11:19), assuming that the vocalization of the text offered here is correct. A connection has often been made between Jrm's exclusion from the temple (36:5) and the incident with Pashhur (20:1–6),[23] but it is proposed here that 20:1–6 is connected with chapter 19, a setting for which would have to be after the king burned the scroll (see there). But Pashhur may have been an "opponent" before Jrm was locked in the stocks. If the setting assigned in the present study for 8:4–13 is correct (the festival of booths in September/October 601), one has the impression that Jrm had access to the temple area on that occasion (see 8:8). Was his being excluded from the temple area (36:5) the result of that oracle? In any event it must be stressed that within this tissue of probabilities and possibilities there is no way to be sure. There may have been earlier occasions for a plot against Jrm; thus there was an attempt to kill Jrm as early as the occasion of the temple sermon in the autumn of 609 (26:8), and there may have been further trouble for him in 605, the year of the battle of Carchemish (why should he have resorted to the dictation of a scroll in that year?—36:1–2).

The setting of 12:1–5 must be placed somewhat later: Jrm knows his opponents and wishes Yahweh to treat them (12:3) as the plotters had earlier wished to treat Jrm (11:19).

Who are these opponents, the "guilty" (רְשָׁעִים), if one excludes the identification of them with "the men of Anathoth" (see above)? Many suggestions have been made, including the whole people of Judah.[24] They are set in contrast to Jrm in v 3a. Their conduct toward Jrm forces him to accuse Yahweh of breaking the promise (v 1a) made to him at the time of his call, to protect him (1:8). Since the name of Yahweh is on their lips (v 2), it is altogether likely that they are Jrm's prophetic opponents, the optimistic prophets: this is the proposal of Hans W. Hertzberg and Hubmann.[25] The last colon of v 4 is form-critically comparable to the quotations in 5:12

and 23:17, and 5:12–13 and 23:16–17 deal with the optimistic prophets; these parallels reinforce the likelihood of the identification of the "guilty" here with the optimistic prophets. Jrm may say that he wants to know why the guilty in general thrive, but it is the particular guilty people who oppose him who are the problem.

Verse 4 describes a drought, and it is likely that that drought is identical to the one which gave rise to the material in 14:1—15:9, material which deals substantially with the optimistic prophets (14:13–15). Since it is the proposal of the present study that it was the drought which was the occasion of the fast declared by the king (see 14:1—15:9, Setting), one is led to a setting after the king burned the scroll, when the optimistic prophets would have been in ascendancy. Jrm expresses surprise, anger, and a sense of betrayal, so the complaint must have been uttered soon after the king burned the scroll. A date late in December 601 thus suggests itself. Since 11:18–20 + 22–23 exhibits the conventional Deuteronomic theology and 12:1–5 questions that theology, one can gain some idea (assuming the settings arrived at here are sound) how overwhelming to Jrm's thinking the king's burning of the scroll must have been.

Can a setting be located for the addition of 11:21, of the phrase "to the men of Anathoth" in 11:23, and of 12:6? There is a likeness between the words of the men of Anathoth in 11:21 and the words of the religious authorities and people of Jerusalem in 26:8–9, but whether this is deliberate or is the traditional form to depict opponents of a prophet (compare Isa 30:10–11), is difficult to say. Hubmann holds that all three additions are a later theological construct, the addition of a redactor.[26] Arguing against the historicity of the enmity of the "men of Anathoth," he notes that there is no evidence elsewhere for any prophetic activity by Jrm in Anathoth, no evidence for the enmity of the inhabitants of Anathoth, and that there is furthermore positive evidence for Jrm's good relations with family and associates (32:6–15; 37:12).[27] On the other hand, the

---

23 See, for example, Rudolph, p. 233; Bright, p. 179.

24 For these suggestions see Hubmann, *Untersuchungen*, 133 n. 1.

25 Hans W. Hertzberg, *Prophet und Gott, Eine Studie zur Religiosität des vorexilischen Prophetentums* (BFCT 28/3; Gütersloh: Bertelsmann, 1923) 218; Hubmann, *Untersuchungen*, 136.

26 Hubmann, *Untersuchungen*, 169–72.

27 Ibid., 169.

very specificity of 11:21 and 12:6 is unlikely to be the sort of thing a redactor would draft for himself (Cornill makes this point on 11:21).[28] Furthermore the phraseology of 12:6 is unusual: one notes the threefold "even" (□ֵגַ) and the shout of family members (see Interpretation). This is not the stuff of redactional prose. Furthermore, given the lack of evidence elsewhere for enmity from fellow villagers and family members, the argument can work in the other direction: a redactor would hardly be moved to depict family enmity, given the tradition of 32:6–15 and 37:12, unless it were true. The phraseology of 16:5–9 (the abstention from funerals and weddings) at least suggests a continued contact between Jrm and his village. It would be surprising indeed if there were no opposition to him from those with whom he grew up, particularly in the light of his abstaining from community occasions (see below).

Conceivably the addition of 11:21 and the phrase "to the men of Anathoth" could have been added to 11:18–23 at a time prior to the addition of 12:6 to 12:1–5, but it is unlikely: the existence of Yahweh's answer in 12:5, that there will be an intensification of opposition to Jrm, suggests that the situation in Anathoth was imposed upon the whole sequence at a single time.

There is no way of course to determine a setting, but again one may suggest some possibilities. The only other confessional material that mentions family members is Jrm's apostrophe to his mother in 15:10 and his mention of his mother and father in 20:14–18, and both these passages mention his mother in the same way ("who bore me"); these passages then may have a setting in common with 11:21 and 12:6. Indeed 12:6, in the mention of Jrm's "father," and 15:10, in his mention of his "mother," nicely bracket 14:1—15:9, and complement the joint mention of both parents in 20:14–18.[29] One must assume that 20:14–18, coming after Yahweh's answering of Jrm's prayer (20:13, evidently in September/October 594: see Jeremiah's Confessions: Introduction), is an indication of continued opposition to Jrm, perhaps from family members. On the other side, if the interpretation of 15:12 offered in the present study is correct, 15:10–12 also has a setting in the opposition to Jrm from Hananiah in the summer of 594 (see Setting on that

passage). Hananiah was from Gibeon (28:1), not far from Anathoth. And outside 1:1, Jrm is identified as from Anathoth only in 29:27, a narrative which again comes out of the context of 594. What evidence there is points to opposition in Anathoth during the crisis in Jrm's life in that summer.

As already indicated, Jrm was reconciled to (at least one member of) his family at the time he purchased the field from his cousin (chap. 32), evidently in the summer of 588. Was the buying of the field in the first instance a gesture of reconciliation by Jrm? (for the date, and the discussion of the reconciliation, see there). One concludes that as far as the limited data indicate, there was opposition to Jrm in Anathoth in the summer of 594, and opposition from his family that continued after Hananiah's death. But of course such opposition from his fellow villagers could have emerged earlier (compare the remarks above on Jrm's abstention from funerals and weddings, and see the treatment of 16:5–9).

Interpretation

■ **11:18** There are two difficulties in the first colon. (1) The words appear to lack context: Jrm is referring to Yahweh's informing him about what? (2) There are two contrasting vocalizations in the tradition: *M* reads "Yahweh informed me, so I knew," and *G* reads "O Yahweh, inform me and I shall know." The first difficulty is solved if a proposal of the present study is accepted, that v 18 was in the first instance a continuation of v 9 (see 11:1–17, Structure, Form, Setting, *A Possible Prehistory for Verse 9*). What Yahweh is asked to make known then is a conspiracy against Jrm. By this proposal Rudolph's suggestion is unnecessary, to read an indefinite (feminine) suffix on the second verb ("so I knew it"). Form-critically the vocalization of *G* is preferable (see Form). The sequence of ידע hip'il ("inform") followed by ידע qal ("know") is not common, but there is a close parallel in Ps 39:5, where the address is likewise to Yahweh and the verb forms are identical, and there, too, the qal verb may be construed as a final clause.[30] But the use of two verb stems in a double expression is a usage with a long tradition in both Ugaritic and the OT.[31] It is

28   Cornill, p. 152.
29   This is the burden of the analysis in Holladay, *Architecture*, 126–37, though I have revised the

conclusions reached in that study.
30   Kraus, *Psalmen*, 299–300.
31   See 1:4–19, n. 95.

favored by Jrm;[32] for other instances within the confessions see 15:19; 17:14; 20:7.

The emphatic "that was when" (אָז literally "then") begins the second colon, introducing the verb which declares that the prayer has been fulfilled (see Form). The hip'il of ידע ("inform") in the first colon is answered by the hip'il of ראה ("show") here; the two verbs in the qal stem are linked in 12:3 and often elsewhere (see the citations in the discussion of 2:19). The expression "what they are doing" is literally "their deeds." The noun (מַעֲלָלִים) is generally used in a bad sense in Jer (compare 4:4, 18), and even when neutral (7:3, 5) the word has a bad odor. What they are doing is bad news for Jrm.

■ **11:19** The main verbs in this verse refer to Jrm's innocence, so they must be translated with pluperfects (so also Rudolph, Bright). The verb begins with an emphatic וַאֲנִי "I for my part": as far as Jrm was concerned, he had known nothing of what the conspirators were doing. The emphasis is reinforced by the position of "against me" (עָלַי) in the third colon.

A כֶּבֶשׂ is a lamb. Cornill points out that of the 116 occurrences of the word in the OT all but 5 are instances in which the lamb is for sacrifice. This fact may have encouraged G, V, and T to translate the second colon as "led to sacrifice," even though the verb in M in that colon is not the normal verb for sacrifice (זבח) but the one that ordinarily refers to domestic slaughter (טבח). Jrm may then be hinting that he thinks of himself as a potential sacrificial victim. The attribute "trusting" (אַלּוּף) occurs in 3:4 (there "companion"): Jrm had no reason not to trust his associates. The symbolism of Jrm as a lamb led to slaughter entered into the symbolism of Deutero-Isaiah in Isa 53:7 (though the word for lamb there is different—שֶׂה)[33] and ultimately into the Johannine metaphor of Christ as the Lamb of God (John 1:29, 36; 27 times in Revelation).[34]

The verb יוּבַל is construed as יבל hop'al "be led, conducted." In the second half of the verse one has the metaphor of Jrm as a tree, as one has also in 12:2 and

17:8. Both those latter verses are strongly shaped by Ps 1:3 (see there), and it is therefore worth noting that 17:8 offers the related noun יוּבַל "stream," parallel with "water," and that Ps 1:3 has יִבּוֹל "wither," נבל qal (and what about תֶּאֱבָל "dry up" in 12:4?). This kind of word-play is evidence that Jrm had his head ringing with Ps 1:3 (which must therefore have been in existence by this period),[35] and that in this confession it is a source for his Deuteronomic theology.

The third colon picks up the verb "know" from v 18a: what Jrm had not known, Yahweh revealed to him. "Against me" is in an emphatic position, as "I for my part" is in the first colon. The noun מַחֲשָׁבוֹת is "schemes, plans"; the linking of the verb חשׁב and its cognate accusative occurs elsewhere in Jer as well (18:11, 18; 49:30).

Now one hears Jrm's enemies speak: the implication is that the quotation is revealed to him by Yahweh. The cohortative "let us destroy" (נַשְׁחִיתָה, שׁחת hip'il) is intended to offer assonance with "made plans" (חָשְׁבוּ מַחֲשָׁבוֹת) just preceding: 18:18 offers a variation on the same word-play. The background of the quotation is evidently the law in Deut 20:19 forbidding the destroying (שׁחת hip'il) of a fruit-bearing tree belonging to a besieged city by cutting it down (כרת). That passage also, curiously enough, asks whether fruit trees are like human beings, that they should be cut down. Jrm, in understanding himself to be a fruit-bearing tree (compare 12:2; 17:8), has the law in Deuteronomy in mind when he conceives of the conflict waged against him by his adversaries to be like the felling of a tree. Since in that verse in Deuteronomy the verb לחם (in the common nip'al stem) appears, it is plausible to find that root in the present text in the word vocalized in M as "in his bread." The proposal offered here fits the consonantal text and gives good sense: the use of בְּ with a person to express agency can be paralleled by an expression like עַל־כֵּן חָצַבְתִּי בַּנְּבִיאִים "therefore I have hewn by the prophets" (Hos 6:5). By this understanding Jrm's adversaries turn

---

32   Holladay, "Style," 46.
33   See Baumgartner, *Klagegedichte*, 31; Christopher R. North, *The Suffering Servant in Deutero-Isaiah* (London: Oxford University, 1956) 192; and for a general discussion of the "Servant" passages in the light of Jrm's confessions see Walther Zimmerli, "παῖς θεοῦ," *TDNT* 5:670–72.
34   See conveniently Raymond E. Brown, *The Gospel*

According to John (i—xii) (AB 29; Garden City, NY: Doubleday, 1966) 60–61.
35   See my treatment of the matter in Holladay, *Architecture*, 152–53; see further the discussion on 17:5–8, Preliminary Observations.

to someone already identified as an opponent of Jrm for help in getting rid of him; for speculation who that opponent might have been see Setting. The (reconstructed) word לֹחֲמוֹ "his opponent" then balances (the reconstructed) יְרִיבַי "my adversaries" (v 20): compare the parallelism in Ps 35:1.

The penultimate colon continues the figure of the tree by the use of "cut (off)" (כרת). The phrase "land of the living" occurs only here in Jer but occurs thirteen times elsewhere in the OT: the phraseology in Ps 52:7 is particularly close, since God will uproot (שׁרשׁ) the evil person from the land of the living (one notes the enrooting [שׁרשׁ] of the guilty in 12:2). "Land of the living" is no doubt in contrast to the land of the dead; elsewhere Jrm sees his opponents the prophets and priests going off to "the Land," that is, the land of the dead (14:18: see there). One other noteworthy occurrence of "the land of the living" is Isa 53:8: given the derivation of Isa 53:7 from the simile of the lamb led to slaughter here, it is clear that "he was cut off out of the land of the living" in Isa 53:8 continues the indebtedness to the present passage (though the verb "cut off" is different).[36]

The diction of the last two cola is very close to Ps 83:5, where Israel's enemies say, "Come, let us wipe them out (כחד hipʿil) from (being a) nation, that the name of Israel may be remembered no more." Pedersen has written definitively on the meaning of the forgetting of someone's name: "The extermination of the name is so dreadful, because it implies complete annihilation. In the name lies the whole substance of the man's soul; if it is killed, then there is only absolute emptiness. . . . Nothing has such an effect in Israel as the danger that the name may be exterminated."[37] Since one's name is "remembered" by sons (compare the poignant negative instances in Isa 56:5), it is ironic that Yahweh himself is perceived to accomplish in Jrm what Jrm's human enemies wish to do, for he calls Jrm to abstain from marriage and children (16:2). This irony, that Yahweh anticipates in his own plans the plans of Jrm's enemies against him, will reach a horrifying peak in a climactic confession, 20:7–10 (see there).

■ **11:20** The first half of the verse is made up of two cola of vocatives to Yahweh, nominal descriptions of him in doxological elaboration (see Form). These vocatives match the vocative at the beginning of v 17 (as here understood).

The phrase שֹׁפֵט צֶדֶק offers both textual and semantic ambiguity. It means "judge of righteousness" with the implication of "righteous judge." But the parallel instance of this sequence in 20:12 has בֹּחֵן צַדִּיק, which can be either "righteous tester" or "tester of the righteous (man)": this leaves the possibility open that the phrase in the present passage should be understood as שֹׁפֵט צַדִּיק, perhaps written defectively. It is perhaps significant that the two models in the Psalms offer the two alternatives: one finds שׁוֹפֵט צַדִּיק in Ps 7:12 and שׁוֹפֵט צֶדֶק in Ps 9:5. The phrase שֹׁפֵט צַדִּיק would likewise mean "righteous judge" but could also be construed to mean "judge of the righteous (man)," in this case Jrm.

That possibility is reinforced by a parallel question raised by the diction of the second colon: whose mind and heart is Yahweh testing? The parallel in 12:3 states that Yahweh tests Jrm's heart, and if the phrase in the first colon implies "judge of the righteous (man)," then the second colon surely implies that Yahweh tests Jrm's mind and heart. On the other hand, 12:1 imputes to Yahweh the description of צַדִּיק, "You will be innocent, Yahweh"; and the occurrence of "on them" (מֵהֶם) in the third colon of the present verse suggests that Yahweh is to test the mind and heart of Jrm's enemies, and the implication that Yahweh is the judge of the righteous (man) and the tester of Jrm's mind and heart fades away. One concludes simply that there is the possibility of ambiguity here.

For בֹּחֵן "tester, assayer" see 6:27: there Jrm is appointed to be the tester, while here Yahweh is affirmed to be the tester. The כְּלָיוֹת are literally the "kidneys"; as the protected, inmost organ, the kidneys signify the deepest aspects of the character: "Indeed the reins form so vital and so sensitive a part of the body that in a measure it is here, concealed from one's fellow creatures if not from God, that the real sentiments of the elusive *ego* (אָנֹכִי or אֲנִי) find their expression."[38] "Mind" is thus a justifiable translation. The word is parallel with "heart" (לֵב) not only in the parallel in 20:12 but also in a similar

---

36   The other passages in which the phrase occurs are Isa 38:11; Ezek 26:20; 32:23–32; Pss 27:13; 142:6; and Job 28:13.

37   Pedersen, I/II, 255–56.

38   Johnson, *Vitality of the Individual*, 76; compare Pedersen, I/II, 173–74, and Wolff, *Anthropology*, 65.

passage in 17:10, and in Pss 7:10 and 26:2. Indeed, given the phrase "righteous judge" in Ps 7:12, one may conclude that Ps 7:10–12 is the background of the phraseology here. But the linking of "kidneys" and "heart" is found already in Ugaritic (Ug. 1001.1.3 [= *PRU* II.1.3]).

The third colon is the prayer for Yahweh's action: "Let me see your retribution on them." It has been assumed that נְקָמָה (root נקם) is "vengeance," and this is the standard translation here;[39] but Mendenhall has recently shown that this root refers to the exercise of sovereignty: "It is a command that the sovereign authority of Yahweh should be placed in action in order to punish/redress an action that is incompatible with the sovereignty of that same ultimate authority."[40] Jrm never speaks of "my נְקָמָה" but rather of Yahweh's נְקָמָה; the conspirators have challenged the legitimacy of Yahweh's messenger, so the messenger is asking that Yahweh exercise his sovereignty upon them. Thus "retribution" or "vindication" is the right nuance for the word (compare the semipagan use of the word by Jrm's enemies in 20:10). The preposition מִן is the idiom with this root (compare 20:10).

The last colon is a puzzle. The reading of *M* is "for to you I have revealed my cause [or lawsuit]," but this can scarcely be right; if Jrm is Yahweh's messenger, his "cause" (רִיב) cannot be unknown to Yahweh until Jrm reveals it. To the contrary, it is Yahweh who has revealed to Jrm the nature of his predicament (v 18). The suggestion of Hitzig, to read גִּלּוֹתִי "I have committed, entrusted" (גלל qal), has been adopted by most commentators and translations (see Text) and is very attractive: Pss 22:9 and 37:5 have such diction with that verb, though only the latter passage offers an object for the verb, and it is דַּרְכֶּךָ "your way," not a form of רִיב "cause." If this emendation is correct, then Jrm is saying, in effect, "Yahweh, I have committed my life completely to you so that my enemies are your enemies as well: therefore take the steps necessary to manifest yourself to them, so that they know who is in control."

But there are several considerations leading to the suspicion that this is not the correct reading. (1) Other than the presumed use here and in the parallel 20:12, Jrm does not use רִיב "cause" for his own predicament.

The third colon of 12:1 does not mean "I would plead my case before you" (*RSV*, *NEB*) but something else altogether, and the idiom does not use רִיב in any case. Jrm speaks of "bearing reproach" (15:15) or "seeing toil and sorrow" (20:18), but he does not speak of his רִיב "cause." He is an אִישׁ רִיב, one who is a center of contention (15:10), but otherwise the word appears (a) twice in the oracles against Babylon as a cognate accusative (50:34; 51:36)—in both cases Yahweh conducts or pursues Israel's case, and (b) once in 25:31, where Yahweh has a legal case against the nations. That is not to say that the use of רִיב "cause" is impossible here, but there are no good parallels. (2) One cannot make too much of an argument from word-order, but the appearance of אֵלֶיךָ "to you" in the emphatic position is odd: "For you are the one to whom I have committed my cause" is not what one would expect—one would respond "pray, to whom else?" given the normal affirmation that Yahweh pursues the cause of the righteous (Pss 43:1; 55:10; 119:154). The emphasis in the passage has been on the first-person singular ("I for my part," "against me," v 19), so one might have expected כִּי רִיבִי גִּלּוֹתִי אֵלֶיךָ.

Given the emphasis on the first-person singular and given the fact that Yahweh has already revealed to Jrm the existence of the conspiracy against him, the possibility is open that the verb גלה pi'el "reveal" is correct after all, but that אֵלֶיךָ is a mistake for אֵלַי "to me." If this is the case, then the object that fits the context is יְרִיבִי "my adversaries," a noun which then balances the reconstructed "his opponent" (לֹחֲמוֹ) proposed for v 19 (compare again Ps 35:1): one notes that יְרִיבִי "my adversaries" occurs in 18:19 (where *G* reads רִיבִי "my cause"!). For the sequence of thought, see Preliminary Observations: there is here an inclusio with v 18 on the action of revelation (see Structure).

■ **11:21** The entire verse is redactional (see Structure, Setting): it speaks of those who challenge Jrm openly, in contradiction to the situation assumed in vv 18–20, where there is a conspiracy hidden from Jrm. For a suggested historical context for the opposition of the men of Anathoth, see Setting. For "seek one's life" see 4:30. The phrase "prophesy in the name of Yahweh"

---

39   See, for example, the treatment of vengeance in Pedersen, I/II, 388–90.

40   Mendenhall, *Tenth Generation*, 91. His whole essay, "The 'Vengeance' of Yahweh," 69–104, deals with the root; for his treatment of the present passage see 97.

appears in Jer only otherwise in 26:9 and 20, though the phrase "prophesy in my name" appears several times to designate the activity of the false prophets (14:14, 15; 23:25; 29:9, 21). But here (as in chap. 26) true prophecy is rejected. It certainly puts the Jrm's role in sharp relief.[41]

The prohibition spoken here, "You shall not prophesy," is the apodictic prohibition (with לֹא). This is astonishing. When Yahweh speaks to Jrm, his prohibition against praying for the people uses the vetitive אַל־ (7:16; 11:14); the apodictic prohibition occurs when Yahweh prohibits Jrm from marrying (16:2). But here the men of Anathoth use לֹא: "Never prophesy in the name of Yahweh!" It sounds like the prohibition uttered by Amaziah against Amos at Bethel (Amos 7:13, 16)— indeed that passage, preceding Amos 7:17, might have encouraged the drafting of v 21 here. Bright observes of the present passage and analogous ones, "Always the issuing of an apodictic prohibition presupposes that he who does so has the authority or power—or believes that he has—to make his command stick, whether through divine or civil sanctions, or moral suasion, or naked force."[42]

The occurrence of וְלֹא before the last verb in this verse is curious; it is not parallel with the previous לֹא, as it might appear, but signals a negative final clause: "so that you will not die" = "or otherwise you will die."[43]

■ **11:22–23** The verb "deal with" (פקד) answers Jrm's prayer for "retribution" in v 20 (on this see Structure); for the nuances of "deal with" (פקד), see 5:9.

The three cola of the tricolon are synonymous. For the parallelism of "young men" (בַּחוּרִים) and "sons, children" (בָּנִים) see 6:11; for the parallel of "sword" (חֶרֶב) and "famine" (רָעָב) see 5:12. The word-play of בַּחוּרִים and חֶרֶב is worth noting. The phraseology of such punishment is applied to the whole people in 6:11; in 18:12, where it recurs, it likewise (by the proposal offered there) applies to the whole people. By this understanding the opposition to Jrm from the optimistic

prophets came because the final destruction of the nation, proclaimed by Jrm, was delayed. It is likely that this is the nuance here: Yahweh is assuring Jrm that his prophetic opponents will be destroyed in the context of the destruction of the whole people. This argument is reinforced by the likeness of v 23b here to 23:12b (see 23:9–12, Interpretation).

"Remnant" (שְׁאֵרִית) occurs in 6:9, likewise referring to Israel as a whole (see above). For "bring disaster" see 4:6. For a discussion of the context in which "to the men of Anathoth" was added here, see Setting. The last phrase is ordinarily translated "in the year of their visitation"; but structural analysis suggests that the phrase is in parallelism with "disaster" (רָעָה) in the previous line; by this understanding "year" is a parallel object of "bring."[44]

■ **12:1** The first three cola offer forensic vocabulary. The first colon, it is true, is ambiguous, since צַדִּיק means both "righteous" and "innocent." Applied to God, the phrase צַדִּיק אַתָּה at first hearing is assumed to mean "you are righteous"—that is the correct understanding of the phrase in Ps 119:137. But the phrase is evidently also the formula for the declaration of acquittal pronounced in a law court (compare Prov 24:24 and the more informal context of 2 Kgs 10:9).[45] On hearing the phrases of the second and third cola, then, one reconceives the first colon in a forensic context. But to pronounce an acquittal on Yahweh is to be bitterly ironic (compare the similar diction and similar tone in Job's words about God in Job 9:14–22).

The verb ריב in the second colon is more wide-ranging than any single English word; it covers both public quarreling (Gen 26:20) and formal legal suits (1 Sam 24:16). The idiom here, with אֶל־, is found in 2:29: there Jrm announces that Israel has no case against Yahweh, while here Jrm declares that he has a case against Yahweh. The line means "when I make a case against you," "when I dispute with you"—*NJV* has "when I present charges against you." Yahweh is here conceived not primarily as a judge before whom Jrm is pleading his

41 Compare Hubmann, *Untersuchungen*, 168.

42 Bright, "Apodictic Prohibition," 197.

43 GKC, sec. 109g.

44 Cornill suggests the possibility but rejects it for the common interpretation. See recently Hubmann, *Untersuchungen*, 49, 54.

45 See Ramsey, "Speech-Forms," 52.

case (as *NEB* has it); he is in Jrm's mind a defendant against whom Jrm has a quarrel (though Yahweh will doubtless find a loophole and turn out innocent).

The particle כִּי which begins the second colon has elicited comment. Berridge believes it means "whenever" here;[46] Theodorus C. Vriezen believes it is emphatic ("even if now I have to dispute with you").[47] Rudolph believes that the verb is a potential imperfect and translates, "if I wished to dispute with you." One has the impression that though any of these options are possible, they are offered in part because of the theological threat that a real quarrel would raise. "When" or "if" is quite adequate here (GKC, sec. 164d).

The third colon is introduced by אַךְ, which is restrictive or adversative:[48] "yet," "even so," "nevertheless." The particle is used in a similar context of arguing with God in Gen 18:32, "Let me speak just this once (more)," so here there may be a nuance of "but just let me. . . ." For the idiom דבר pi'el + מִשְׁפָּטִים אֶת־ see the discussion in 1:16. The phrase in every case means "pronounce judgments on"; in 39:5 = 52:9 the implication is also "pass sentence on." There is no warrant to posit a different translation for this one instance, such as "discuss a legal case with" (as Volz and Rudolph do).[49] Jrm insists on his own integrity, insists on his right to pronounce judgment on Yahweh just as Yahweh has pronounced judgment on Israel (1:16).

Both Jerome and Calvin, in their respective commentaries on Jer, refer to Psalm 73 at this juncture, as a comparable complaint that the despisers of God should prosper. Calvin points out that this psalm begins with the particle אַךְ, just as the third colon of the present verse does. But the passages are not directly comparable: in Ps 73:1 the phrasing means "nevertheless God is good to Israel," while the present phrasing means "nevertheless, Yahweh, I pronounce you unfair to me." The psalm is a moving expression of submission to God; the present passage is an equally moving insistence by the prophet that he have with God his day in court.

In the last two cola of the verse Jrm's complaint begins. The two adjectives צַדִּיק "innocent" and רָשָׁע "guilty" are correlative (Gen 18:23 and often). Yahweh may turn out to be "innocent," but why has the way of the "guilty" succeeded? The next-to-last colon is clearly a variation of Psalm 1 (as is v 2a here as well). Ps 1:1 says, "Blessed is the man who walks not in the counsel of the wicked/guilty [רְשָׁעִים], nor stands in the way [דֶּרֶךְ, the word here] of sinners," and Ps 1:3 says, "(in) all that he does, he has success" [צלח hip'il: the word here is qal]. Why is the affirmation of Psalm 1 no longer valid? For "why?" in laments, see Form.

Who are the "guilty" here specifically? Evidence has been given that they are to be identified with the optimistic prophets (see Setting). The verb צלח, when used of the spirit of Yahweh, means "be powerful, effective"; here it means "succeed, prosper." Such success is assumed to be the consequence of Yahweh's blessing (compare its use in the good wishes to the king at his wedding, Ps 45:5):[50] but how can the "guilty" receive blessing? The word is turned upside down.

And the last colon is synonymous. For "betray" (בגד) see 3:20; but only here (and in the grotesquely expanded diction of Isa 24:16) is the verb linked with the cognate noun. The participle is parallel with "wicked, guilty" (רְשָׁעִים) in Prov 2:22 as well; and it appears twice in individual laments in the psalms (Pss 25:3; 59:6). The verb שלה means "be at ease, have peace and quiet." Ideally it is what the faithful pilgrim experiences (Ps 122:6); but Job testifies that he lacks it (Job 3:26) while robbers enjoy it (Job 12:6)—indeed in the topsy-turvy world after the fall of Jerusalem Judah's enemies enjoy it (Lam 1:5).

■ **12:2** The variation on Psalm 1 continues. In Ps 1:3 the innocent man is compared to a tree "planted" (שָׁתוּל) by water. Here the synonymous verb נטע is used, but it is specifically said that Yahweh has planted the "guilty": it is not by Yahweh's absent-mindedness that the guilty thrive; rather, Jrm insists, Yahweh deliberately plants

46   Berridge, p. 161 n. 253.
47   Theodorus C. Vriezen, "Einige Notizen zur Übersetzung des Bindeworts *ki*," *Von Ugarit nach Qumran, Beiträge zur alttestamentlichen und altorientalischen Forschung* (ed. Johannes Hempel; BZAW 77; Berlin: Töpelmann, 1958) 272.
48   Norman H. Snaith, "The Meaning of the Hebrew אַךְ," *VT* 14 (1964) 221–25.
49   See Holladay, "Style," 49–51, and "Lawsuit," 280–87; and see further Berridge, pp. 161–62, and John Bright, "A Prophet's Lament and Its Answer," *Int* 28 (1974) 66 n. 10.
50   Pedersen, I/II, 196.

them so they thrive. He plants them, and they take root (שרש), a detail not found in Ps 1:3, though implied. They grow (הלך). This is an odd meaning for that verb, which ordinarily means "go, walk," but it is substantiated by Hos 14:7. They bring forth fruit, a detail likewise found in Ps 1:3 (though with a synonymous verb). And the "why?" of v 1 continues to echo through these lines.

The third colon makes a subtle point not noticed by the translations. With "but far from their mind" one expects "you are near to their mouth" (with the preposition אֶל or לְ), and that is what G and V render; such an expression for hypocrisy is part of the message here (see below) but by no means the whole of it. The presence of 23:23–24 in the midst of the collection against the false prophets (23:9–40), even though these two verses make no overt reference to Jrm's controversy with those prophets, suggests that the two verses embody the argumentation of that controversy. "Am I a God nearby [הַאֱלֹהִים קָרֹב אָנִי: for the easy revocalization see Text there] and not a God far off?" Jrm's opponents have been addressing Yahweh with "you are near" (קָרוֹב אַתָּה). In the present passage one hears Jrm's quotation of his opponents, "'You are near' is in their mouth": for "in their mouth" as a designation for someone's speech see Deut 30:14; 2 Sam 17:5; 18:25; 1 Kgs 17:24. Jrm might be paraphrasing such an affirmation as Deut 4:7; but if he is not paraphrasing, then there is one instance of קָרוֹב אַתָּה in the OT beyond the present passage, Ps 119:151. It becomes possible then that Jrm is quoting Ps 119:137 in the first colon of v 1 and v 151 of that psalm here; if so, he is giving a special twist to each phrase: "You will be innocent" even when I declare you guilty; my opponents say "you are near" even when they are unjustified in doing so.[51] If Jrm is citing Psalm 1 in the first half of the verse, it is plausible that he is citing Psalm 119 here.

But if Jrm's opponents speak as if Yahweh were intimate with them or with the people, the prophet insists that the reality is the opposite (again compare 23:23). If the third colon contains a quotation, then the fourth

must mean that that quotation is far from their mind (literally, "from their kidneys": see 11:20). But semantically this affirmation is hardly different from affirming that Yahweh himself is far from their mind. There are proverbial expressions in the background of this half-verse, such as Prov 15:28–29: "The mind of the righteous [לֵב צַדִּיק] ponders how to answer, but the mouth of the wicked [פִּי רְשָׁעִים] pours out evil things. Yahweh is far from the wicked [רְשָׁעִים], but he hears the prayer of the righteous [צַדִּיקִים]." A similar indictment of the people was made in 9:7, but the content of this bicolon probably owes more to Isa 29:13 or to Ps 28:3, part of a lament: the latter verse says of the רְשָׁעִים, "They speak peace with the neighbors, while mischief is in their hearts [לְבָב]."

In the NT the concept of a "hypocrite" was common currency, but the OT conventionally took it for granted that a person's ideas and words and impulses are a continuum,[52] so that expressions like this one represent a profound dislocation of the expected order of things. These guilty ones to whom Jrm is referring thus speak Yahweh's name but do not understand his will. Jesus' word is similar: "Not every one who says to me, 'Lord, Lord,' shall enter the kingdom of heaven, but he who does the will of my Father who is in heaven" (Matt 7:21).

■ **12:3** The analogy of 11:20 and form-critical parallels suggest that the first two cola of this verse do not embody independent predications but subordinate descriptions of the God upon whom Jrm calls for help (see Form), hence the parenthetical "who" is the translation. The address "but you, O Yahweh" (וְאַתָּה יהוה) points in the same direction (compare Ps 59:6). The diction "you have known me," "you see me" suggests Ps 129:1–2; here is the same collocation of "know" and "see" which occurs in 11:18 and elsewhere. The alternation of perfect ("have known," "have tested") with imperfect forms ("see") is stylistic, as often in poetry (see the remarks on 5:6). The verb "you have known me" (יְדַעְתָּנִי) answers "I knew you" (יְדַעְתִּיךָ) in 1:5: Jrm is simply affirming the cornerstone of his life, his vocation.[53]

---

51 If Jrm is citing Psalm 119, then one cannot accept a postexilic date for it; see Kraus, *Psalmen*, 820–23. In this case Dahood's judgment, that the psalm comes out of the time of the Deuteronomic reform, would be substantiated; see Dahood, *Psalms III*, 173. Certainly Lamentations demonstrates that acrostics were a feature of the period.

52 See Pedersen, I/II, 166–68.

53 So also Hubmann, *Untersuchungen*, 137.

For "test the heart" see 11:20. But "with yourself" (אִתָּךְ) is puzzling: what does "test someone's heart with oneself" mean? A close analogy may be Gen 40:14, כִּי אִם־זְכַרְתַּנִי אִתְּךָ כַּאֲשֶׁר יִיטַב לָךְ, which Ephraim A. Speiser translates "so if you still remember that I was here with you, when all is well with you again."[54] Thus one must understand "have tested whether my heart is with you"[55] (most commentators propose more distant circumlocutions: Rudolph—"you test my heart, how it is inclined toward you"; and Bright—"[Thou] dost examine my thoughts toward thyself"). On another occasion Jrm says that the heart of the faithless man departs from Yahweh (17:5); so here Jrm affirms that his heart is "with" Yahweh.

The verb נתק hip'il means "segregate, single out, separate." Jrm in 11:19 was like an innocent lamb led to slaughter; here he asks Yahweh to single out the specific רְשָׁעִים to whom he has been referring, like sheep for slaughter. Is there a contrast of age intended here between Jrm and his opponents, when "lamb" is used for himself and "sheep" is used for his opponents? Another query: Is the verb form here, הַתִּקֵם, intended as a word-play on נִקְמָתְךָ "your retribution" (11:20) or הִנָּקֶם "bring down retribution" (15:15), key words at the corresponding point in other confessions?

The parallel verb in the last colon (הַקְדִּשֵׁם) is also hip'il and is in assonance with the previous verb. The only other occurrence of this verb in the hip'il stem is in 1:5, and the usage here must be heard in the light of that occurrence in Jrm's call (see there); the usage here is thus highly ironic. Since the verb is also used of consecrating the firstborn of herd and flock (Deut 15:19) and even, symbolically, of men (Num 3:13, P), Jrm appears to be saying, "You consecrated me to yourself when you called me, but you have treated me like a lamb consecrated for sacrifice; instead you should exercise your consecrating power upon my opponents—let them be dedicated to your purpose." It must be stressed, however, that "slaughter" (טִבְחָה) suggests domestic purpose, not cultic sacrifice (compare 11:19), and that "killing" (הֲרֵגָה) is equally untouched by cultic associations. Jrm is thus pressing the notion of dedication of consecration in a practical direction: "God, get rid of them." This prayer

of Jrm's is not so much an expression of his own vengeance as his wish that Yahweh exercise his sovereignty over those who challenge that sovereignty (see the comments on the matter in 11:20).

■ **12:4** The first four cola of this verse appear so much to be a non sequitur that most commentators have excised them (first Hitzig; then Cornill, Volz, Rudolph, Hyatt ["probably"], Bright; Giesebrecht omits the last colon as well); among the major commentators only Condamin assumes their authenticity. Hubmann's structural analysis, however, indicates that the material belongs (see Structure). The contents have their own inner logic and historical context (see Setting), but the train of thought may have been reinforced by Amos 9:4–5, which has the same sequence of הרג "kill" and אבל understood as "mourn" as vv 3–4 offer here; one notes also that in Amos 9:5 the subject of "mourn" is "those who dwell in it" (יוֹשְׁבֵי בָהּ), a phrase occurring in the third colon of the present verse.

The verb אבל means both "mourn" and "be(come) dry." It is uncertain whether there are two homonymous verbs or a single verb denoting both physical and psycho-logical manifestations (see 4:28), but the context here demands the meaning "be dry": the parallel יבש is "wither." The phrase "grass of the field" is traditional: the present phrase appears to be a variation of "every grass of the field" in Gen 2:5; Jrm may here be sug-gesting that the situation in the land is analogous to pre-creation chaos, when "Yahweh God had not caused it to rain upon the earth" (the context of Gen 2:5). The mind-set of this passage is thus close to that of 4:23–28, not only in the use of the verb "mourn/be dry" but in the background of the creation narrative.

A pretty problem is whether the third colon is to be heard with the first and second or with the fourth and fifth cola. The *M* accent 'atnaḥ divides the verb after the second colon. On the other hand, the third colon appears also in Ps 107:34 (see below), and in that passage the expression ends its clause. On balance, given the struc-ture of the verse, the colon is better construed with what precedes.

As just noted, that colon is also to be found in Ps 107:34. Verses 34–43 of that psalm make up a hymnic

54   Speiser, *Genesis*, 306.
55   So also Hubmann, *Untersuchungen*, 50.

section that is considered by most commentators to be a later addition to the psalm proper,[56] but recently Dahood has defended the unity of the psalm.[57] Verses 33–34 there describe Yahweh's ability to turn the fruitful land into a desert. One wonders whether Jrm was not familiar with these words: the unique expression "fruitful land" (אֶרֶץ פְּרִי) in Ps 107:34 reminds one of the synonymous אֶרֶץ הַכַּרְמֶל in Jer 2:7, collocated with "desert" (מִדְבָּר) in 2:6. Nah 1:5 may also be a relevant parallel to the present passage (and to Jer 4:24, part of a passage resembling this one). It is ironic that Yahweh originally brought the people out of a desert that had no inhabitants (2:6) into a land they could inhabit, but now, because of the evil of those inhabitants, the land is turned into a desert.

The verb ספה appears only here in Jer. For the revocalization to a transitive, "you have swept away," see Text. This usage brings the passage into parallel with Zeph 1:3, which undoubtedly stands in the background of Jrm's diction here (whatever may be the verb[s] in the Zephaniah passage: on this see the discussion in 8:13)—that passage, too, includes "beast" and "birds of the air." Though this verb appears only here in Jer, the theme of the disappearance of bird and beast is found elsewhere (9:9, with the verb נדד).

The verse closes with a כִּי-clause explaining the circumstances of the drought: the inhabitants say, "He will not see where we end." There is textual evidence for the identification of the subject of the verb as Yahweh: G has "God" in this clause, and 4QJer[a] has yh[wh "Yahweh" just after the verb.[58] One or the other of these readings could represent the original text; or they could be glosses to identify the subject, whether they arose independently or together. In any event, the identification is undoubtedly correct, although there have always been scholars who have explained the subject as Jrm (either "he will never [live to] see . . ." or "he cannot foresee . . .")—so Michaelis, Naegelsbach, and Condamin. The noun אַחֲרִית here means "one's final situation": the line seems imitative of Deut 32:20, אֶרְאֶה מָה אַחֲרִיתָם, "(And he [Yahweh] said, 'I will hide my face from them,) I will see what their end (will be)." The doubters whom Jrm quotes reject the affirmation in Deuteronomy 32. A less likely reading is

that of G, which offers the Greek equivalent of אָרְחוֹתֵינוּ, "(He will not see) our paths." In either case the people are contemptuous of Yahweh's superintending of their lives (compare 5:12; Zeph 1:12).

■ 12:5 Yahweh's answer to Jrm comes in the form of two synonymous counterquestions, both of which indicate that Jrm's situation will become worse (see Form). The first question offers no difficulty of interpretation, but one wonders whether the particular terms used have specific reference to Jrm's career. The verb רוץ refers specifically to a messenger's "running" (51:31); in 23:21 the reference is to the "running" of the (false) prophets. Is the "running" in that passage simply a symbolic reference to the task of the prophet as a messenger, or is it a concrete reference to prophetic behavior? (See Interpretation on that verse.) If the latter, then the "running" here has a double reference, both to Jrm's function as a messenger of Yahweh, and to his effort to compete with others manifesting prophetic behavior. The רַגְלִים are those on foot (Exod 12:37), especially foot soldiers (1 Kgs 20:29). A runner ordinarily has no difficulty competing with those on foot, who presumably walk: if he does, he has lost his function as a messenger.[59] And Jrm does. Yahweh is suggesting that if Jrm is wearied by the "guilty" (רְשָׁעִים), then he should not be—worse is yet to come, for horses are well known for their galloping (Amos 6:12). That competition will surely be hopeless: or will it?—is there a hint here of Elijah's running in front of Ahab's chariot (1 Kgs 18:46)? Yahweh's answer implies that Jrm's call has given him a superiority over the "guilty," that Yahweh has higher expectations for him than Jrm has realized, and that Yahweh knows exactly what he is doing. The answer is analogous to that in 15:11–12.[60]

The second question depends for its understanding of the meaning of the verb בטח, which normally means "trust." The second and fourth cola are closely parallel, so that one expects the third colon to be parallel with the first, and the normal translation, "and if you trust in easy country" (or the like), suggests success, not defeat. The problem was felt early; alongside "trust" in G appears "do not trust" in G[B] and G[88], and Volz accepts that reading. The alternative is to posit a homonymous verb meaning

56 Kraus, *Psalmen*, 736.
57 Dahood, *Psalms III*, 89.
58 Janzen, p. 176.

59 Hubmann, *Untersuchungen*, 151.
60 Ibid.

379

"fall down," cited in Arabic. This solution was already proposed in the tenth century by David ben Abraham al-Fāsī (perhaps stimulated by the rendering of *T*, see below) and has been revived in modern times;[61] the proposed meaning for the verb appears to fit other passages as well, particularly Prov 14:16. *T* translates "feel secure and fall down," and if the second verb is not a guess from the context, then this Version offers both meanings.

But there are difficulties with this suggestion. First, the Arabic *baṭaḥa* is transitive, "prostrate (someone)"; the intransitive meaning is found in two derived forms *tabaṭṭaḥa* and *inbaṭaḥa*. Second, "trust" is a well-known meaning for בטח; it should be used if possible, and it is possible in the present passage. The "trust" here implies trust in Yahweh (compare 17:7). The "easy country" (אֶרֶץ שָׁלוֹם) is a reference to v 4, land suffering from drought (see below), so that the implication is, "If it takes a land without drought for you to exhibit trust (in me), then what will you do in the thicket of the Jordan?" It is to be noted that the line offers a participle, not a perfect verb as the first colon does. The clause speaks of a permanent attitude of Jrm's, not a specific action.

There is no exact parallel to the phrase אֶרֶץ שָׁלוֹם, literally "land of peace"; but the phrase נְוֵה שָׁלוֹם occurs in Isa 32:18, and the context immediately preceding is that of fertility as well as safety. The contrast here with "thicket of the Jordan" (see below) suggests open country —*NEB* has "easy country"; but the repetition of "land" from v 4 suggests strongly that the contrast is also with the drought-ridden land (see above), so that "prosperous land" is perhaps the best.

The "thicket [literally 'pride'] of the Jordan" is a phrase that appears four times in the OT (elsewhere: 49:19 = 50:44; Zech 11:3). The noun גָּאוֹן is essentially "height"; the reference here is to the area which the Jordan may overflow and to its thicket of reeds, bushes and trees, a lair for lions.[62]

Given the pairing of "sword" and "famine" in 11:22

and in the drought-battle liturgy (14:13, 15, 16, 18), one wonders whether the reference to "foot-soldiers" and "horses" in v 5a, and the reference to a land without drought in v 5b, do not reflect that pairing. In general the verse presupposes diction suggestive of holy war adapted for the life of Jrm. Yahweh's righteousness is secure; Jrm has not understood the circumstances into which he will fall!

■ **12:6** This verse, like 11:21, was added secondarily (see Preliminary Observations, Structure), but, it is here argued, by Jrm himself (see Setting) to offer a fresh interpretation of the worsened circumstances predicted in v 5: not only are his fellow villagers plotting against him, but even the members of his own family are betraying him. The verse is an ironic development of 9:3–4: in 9:3 it is said that one must not trust one's brother, and in 9:4 that no one speaks the truth (אֱמֶת, root אמן); so here, given "trust" in v 5, it is said that Jrm's brothers are betraying him, that they are not to be believed (אמן) when they speak.

The thrice-repeated גַּם־ does not mean "both . . . and . . . and" as in Gen 32:20 and elsewhere, but refers three times to the same subject, "even they"; in this meaning it appears twice in Nah 3:11, but an appearance three times is highly unusual and indicates extreme emphasis.

There is no way to distinguish carefully between "brothers" and "father's house": both terms suggest "family, kinsmen" in the wider sense,[63] so that it is best to see the colon as a hendiadys; if anything, "brothers" is the more extensive term, while "father's house" suggests a restriction to one's own household. But in the context both expressions are taken together (גַּם־הֵמָּה twice) and are in contrast to the "men of Anathoth" in 11:21 and 23. "Betray" (בגד) is picked up from v 1: not only are the "guilty" (רְשָׁעִים) betrayers, but even your household participates in betrayal.

The expression קָרְאוּ אַחֲרֶיךָ מָלֵא, literally "they have cried after you full [masculine singular]," has elicited much discussion. All the Versions are interpretative and

---

61 Solomon L. Skoss, "The Root בטח in Jeremiah 12.5, Psalms 22.10, Proverbs 14.16, and Job 40.23," *Jewish Studies in Memory of George A. Kohut, 1874–1933* (ed. Salo W. Baron and Alexander Marx; New York: Alexander Kohut Memorial Foundation, 1935) 549–53; Driver, "Jeremiah," 111–12.

62 Menashe Har-El, "The Pride of the Jordan, The Jungle of the Jordan," *BA* 41 (1978) 65–75.

63 Pedersen, I/II, 51–59.

among them offer three understandings. *G* reads καὶ αὐτοὶ ἐβόησαν, ἐκ τῶν ὀπίσω σου ἐπισυνήχθησαν, "And they themselves have cried out, among those behind you they are gathered": here מָלֵא suggests "they are gathered," similar to מַלְאוּ in 4:5 (see there). Rashi has a similar interpretation, stating that מָלֵא means "a gathering of men," and Qimḥi concurs (so *KJV*). Recently Thomas has pressed for this solution, stating that מלא means "gather," as he proposes it does in 4:5.[64] *S* and *T* evidently construe מלא as מִלָּה "word": *S* renders "Even they have spoken words about you," presumably hostile words, and *T* makes it explicit, "Even they have spoken bad words against you," contrasting these with the "good words" in the last colon. *V* translates, "They have called behind you in full voice," and this interpretation has been preferred by many (Duhm, Cornill, Giesebrecht, Condamin, Bright), even though this meaning hardly fits the impression of conspiracy and hypocrisy that the rest of the verse gives. Volz has proposed an emendation, קָשְׁרוּ אַחֲרֶיךָ כֻלָּם "all of them have conspired behind you," and Rudolph accepts this proposal.

The conclusion to which Hubmann has come, accepted here, is to see the word מָלֵא as a single-word quotation; the other examples in the OT of קָרָא אַחֲרֵי are followed by a quotation (1 Sam 20:37, 38; 24:9). The proposal is not new; it appears to have been anticipated by Luther, who translated, "und schreien zeter! über dich" ("and cry murder! over you")—if one assumes that "zeter!" is a quotation. Sebastian Schmidt, in 1685, suggested it explicitly,[65] and he was followed by Chr. B. Michaelis (eighteenth century), C. F. Schnurrer (1793), and E. F. C. Rosemüller (1826), after which the notion seems to have been dropped until recently.[66] In our century G. R. Driver has proposed that the word is a cry for help: "Even they have called after thee 'Help, everyone!'";[67] and Hubmann has explored the matter at length.[68] If the quotation is some kind of hostile utterance, it makes a perfect balance to the reference to "fine words" in the last colon (compare the remark on *T*

above).

But if מָלֵא is a quotation, it is not easy to establish its meaning; there is no parallel for such an expression in the OT. Sebastian Schmidt and those who followed him believed that the expression was short for מְלֵא יָמִים "full of days" (6:11), that is, that he was of an age ripe for killing. But the phrase in 6:11 evidently means "aged" (see there), hardly an appropriate word for Jrm. Several lines of evidence, on the other hand, favor the interpretation suggested here, "drunk." (1) On another occasion Jrm describes himself as being "like a drunken man, like a fellow overcome by wine" (23:9). (2) Twice Jrm uses the verb מלא to speak of himself as "filled" with Yahweh's wrath (6:11; 15:17). One may conclude that Jrm describes himself as "filled" with Yahweh's words and that on occasion he feels (or acts) drunken. (3) The passage 13:12–14 uses מָלֵא and the verb מלא in connection with wine and drunkenness, and it is altogether likely that that passage was associated with 12:6 on the basis of shared words (on this see 12:7–13, Structure, *Placement of Unit*). If that association exists, it would tend to support the proposal here that מָלֵא implies "drunk." (4) Other men and women in the OT and NT who manifest religious emotion are assumed by bystanders to be drunk: Hannah (1 Sam 1:12–15), and those who received the Holy Spirit at Pentecost (Acts 2:13) of whom the bystanders said, "They are filled with new wine." (5) Many languages use words for "full" or "loaded" to refer to drunkenness; thus the Arabic *wāzin*, literally "of full weight," may mean "drunk," and the French *plein* and the German *voll* and Dutch *vol*, all meaning "full," are slang for drunk; so similarly in Norwegian and Swedish. None of these considerations is conclusive, but they are all suggestive. By implication Jrm was called "a madman" (מְשֻׁגָּע, 29:26), and centuries later Jesus' family would try to take him away, because, they said, he was out of his mind (Mark 3:21): evidently similar behavior evokes a similar response.

The verb אמן hip'il + בְּ means "believe (someone)";

---

64   Thomas, "מלאו," 49.
65   See his statement in Hubmann, *Untersuchungen*, 101–2.
66   See the details in ibid., 102.
67   Godfrey R. Driver, "Jeremiah xii, 6," *JJS* 5 (1954) 177–78.
68   Hubmann, *Untersuchungen*, 97–106.

Prov 26:25 has a similar expression, "When he speaks graciously, do not believe him." The prepositional expression בָּם underlines the parallel of this colon with "even they have betrayed you" above: אַל־תַּאֲמֵן בָּם parallels גַּם־הֵמָּה בָּגְדוּ בָךְ. This parallelism reinforces the suggestion made above that "Even they have called behind you, 'Drunk!'" is parallel to "when they speak fine words to you": the prepositional expressions are contrastive—what is said אַחֲרֶיךָ "behind your back" is in contrast to what is said אֵלֶיךָ "to your face." It has been pointed out that דבר pi'el + טוֹבָה/טוֹבוֹת occurs several times in covenantal contexts (1 Sam 25:30; 2 Sam 7:28; 1 Kgs 12:7; 2 Kgs 25:28), as does טוֹב more widely;[69] here the nuance is the manifestation of good relations within the family.

Aim

There are many levels of aim in these passages: the aim of Jrm, turning his attention from announcing Yahweh's word to his people to struggling with Yahweh as to the meaning of the threats to his life; the aim of Jrm in sharing the struggles with his fellow men, Baruch no doubt (compare 45:3), but ultimately his fellow citizens as well; and the aim of the community in taking these words to heart as a reflection of its corporate and individual agony in the decades that followed the fall of Jerusalem. And overarching these related aims is the putative aim of God in exposing his own messenger to the danger of death, that aim with which Jrm himself seeks to come to terms. Why does God not hurry to validate his promises to his faithful servants? Sometimes, it appears, he assures us that the promise is sure, even if the time is postponed (11:23); at other times, it appears, he suggests that opposition is intrinsic to the prophetic vocation. The conundrum of theodicy, so pressing for Jrm, would become before long the urgent problem of the whole people, and would continue to be so, as is attested by such varying literary deposits as Job, 2 Esdras, the passion narratives of Jesus, and the Holocaust literature.

69   Michael Fox, "Ṭôḇ as Covenant Terminology," *BASOR* 209 (February 1973) 41–42.

Yahweh's Love, Sorrow, and Anger Over His People

Bibliography

Emerton, John A.
"Notes on Jeremiah 12₉ and on some suggestions of J. S. Michaelis about the Hebrew words *naḥā*, *ʿaebrā*, and *jadaʿ*," *ZAW* 81 (1969) 182–88.

Müller, Hans-Peter
"'Der bunte Vogel' von Jer 12₉," *ZAW* 79 (1967) 225–28.

Soggin, J. Alberto
"Jeremias xii 10a: Eine Parallelstelle zu Deut. xxxii 8/LXX?" *VT* 8 (1958) 304–5.

12

7 I have abandoned my house,
    deserted my possession,
        given the beloved of my soul
            into the grasp of her enemies.

8 My possession has become for me
    like a lion in the thicket,
        she has raised her voice against me:
            that is why I hate her.

9 Does the hyena《 look greedily 》[a] on my
    possession for me?
    Are birds of prey around her?
        Go 《 gather, 》[b] all you beasts of the
        field,
            come[c] ⟨to devour her!⟩[d]

10 Many shepherds have destroyed my
    vineyard,
        trampled my portion,[a]
            turned my precious portion
                into a desert of desolation.

11 ⟨They have made her⟩[a] into a ⟨dried-up⟩[b]
    desolation,

Text

9a Reading הַעַיִט (עיט qal). The meaning here is attested in Sir 14:10 and fits in Sir 31:16. *M* reads הַעַיִט; with the word צָבוּעַ (which is here translated "hyena" but traditionally understood as "speckled") the line has been translated "My possession is to me a speckled bird of prey." The word would have been miscopied because of הַעַיִט at the beginning of the second colon. See Interpretation.

b Reading the nipʿal (intransitive) הֵאָסְפוּ with *V* for the qal אִסְפוּ, "gather (the beasts . . .)"; this brings the verb into consistency with the imperative in the fourth colon (see note c). No audience has been suggested for the transitive imperative. So Volz, Condamin, Rudolph.

c Reading with three MSS. and *V* אֵתָיוּ (qal) for the *M* הֵתָיוּ "bring (them)" (hipʿil); so Cornill, Volz, Condamin, Rudolph. Note that *G* reads "let them come." Compare note b.

d Vocalizing לְאָכְלָה for *M* לְאָכְלָה; the latter has been construed either as an alternative infinitive construct without personal suffix (BDB) or as a noun, "for eating" (Zorell; *HALAT*).

10a Some MSS. read נַחֲלָתִי "my possession," as in vv 7, 8, and 9, and Volz and Rudolph follow this reading. But no Version reflects it, and *M* חֶלְקָתִי is to be preferred; the occurrence of חֶלְקַת in the third colon no more argues against the reading than the three occurrences of נַחֲלָה in vv 7–9. The poem is heavy with repetitions; see Interpretation, vv 7–13. Soggin argues for *M* on other grounds.

11a Reading with all commentators שָׂמָהּ with *V*, *S*, and *T* for *M* שָׂמָהּ "he has made her."

b Poetic considerations suggest that the *M* accent zaqep qaton is wrongly placed in v 11a so as to produce two words in the first colon and three in the second, traditionally "he has made her [see note a] a desolation; it mourns unto me, desolate" (compare Volz). The word אבלה needs to be construed with what precedes, leaving the next two words for the second colon. Vocalize אֲבֵלָה here

on my account ⟨she has become
        desolate,⟩[c]
    the whole land is desolated,
    《and》[d] no one pays attention.
12 On all the caravan-tracks in the desert
    devastators have come,
    for the sword of Yahweh devours
        from one end of the land to the other;
        no flesh has peace.
13 [They have sown wheat,
        but thorns they have reaped;
    they wear themselves out to[b] no avail,
    and are ashamed of 《their harvests,》[c]
        because of the hot anger of
        Yahweh.][a]

with Rudolph; this adjective is used of "roads" in
Lam 1:4. For the meaning "dried-up" see Interpretation.

c   Instead of the adjective שְׁמֵמָה the word needs to
be vocalized as a verb, thus שָׁמְמָה; see Interpretation.

d   Reading וְ with Duhm, Cornill, Rudolph for M כִּי
"for"; the phrase with וְ appears in Isa 57:1. See
Interpretation.

13a   This verse is an addition: see Structure, Setting,
Interpretation.

b   Many MSS., and V and S, insert וְ "and" (here =
'but') before "not" and the verb. It is a possible
reading but by no means a necessary one.

c   Reading מִתְּבוּאֹתֵיהֶם for M מִתְּבוּאֹתֵיכֶם "your
harvests."

Structure

Extent of Unit. Though v 14 shares "possession" (נַחֲלָה)
with vv 7, 8, and 9, in the earlier verses that noun implies
both people and territory, while it implies only territory
in v 14. Further, the message of v 14, that those among
whom Judah is exiled will be punished, is different from
vv 7–13, Yahweh's lament over his own possession.

Verse 13 presents a more difficult problem. Duhm was
rightly troubled about the shift of subject in the verbs
from the devastators (vv 7–12) to the Judean farmers (v
13), and in general about the shift from military devastation to a drought; he thus judged v 13 to be the
reflection of a reader. On the other hand, Cornill and
Condamin judge the verse to be genuine to Jrm but an
isolated utterance: Condamin was convinced the passage
breaks nicely into two symmetrical halves, vv 7–9 and
10–12 (see below). Duhm was also influenced by the fact
that in v 13 "Yahweh" is referred to in the third person;
he avoids the same problem in v 12 by excising the words
"the sword of Yahweh devours" there. All these observations have merit, but the situation is less clear-cut than
any given commentator has seen.

The first point to be made is that commentators must
become less uneasy about odd totals of cola in a group.
Thus all commentators who display the material in poetic
form assume that "they have sown wheat, but thorns they
have reaped" in v 13 makes up a single colon, while

commentators on Hosea all display Hos 8:7, "for they
sow the wind, but they shall reap the whirlwind," as a
bicolon.[1] What each group of commentators has done is
to try to preserve bicola by holding to four cola in v 13
and to six cola in Hos 8:7. But the last colon of v 13,
"because of the hot anger of Yahweh," makes the third
colon in a tricolon in 51:45, and similar phraseology
stands outside the close parallelism of 4:26 and 25:37.

Verse 12 (at least in its present form) has five cola.
Duhm, as already noted, excised "for the sword of
Yahweh devours," and in this he is followed by Rudolph.
Volz omits all of v 12b ("for the sword . . . peace"). Bright
omits "from one end of the land to the other." What
judgment may be made? The phrase "sword of Yahweh"
(חֶרֶב לַיהוה) occurs in a genuine passage of the prophet in
47:6, and the third-person mention of "Yahweh" in a
speech of Yahweh's is not a difficulty (see 2:3). The
phrase "from one end of the land/earth to the other" has
been considered a Deuteronomistic one.[2] But it occurs
only four times in the OT: in Deut 13:8, in Deut 28:64,
where it is part of a late stratum of the book,[3] in the
present passage, and in 25:33. In 25:30–37 one finds
what is evidently a genuine oracle of Jrm's which uses
diction from Amos and Hosea and from the prophet's
oracles elsewhere to extend the usual judgment against
Judah into a judgment that begins with Judah and
extends to all nations (see there). The phrase in question

---

1   See typically *BHS*.
2   Weinfeld, *Deuteronomy*, 358.
3   Mayes, *Deuteronomy*, 349, 357.

means "from one end of the earth to the other" in that passage and seems integral to that passage, and there is no reason why it cannot be authentic to the present passage in the meaning "from one end of the land to the other." (The phrase is somewhat ambiguous in Deut 13:8.) The phrase in the present verse can, after all, balance the first colon, which likewise is an adverbial phrase of location. The five cola of the verse then appear authentic.

Verse 13 (or at least its first four cola) would appear to shift the diction radically (Duhm is correct), and one must thus judge those lines to be a secondary addition (but likely by Jrm himself: see Setting). There can be no certainty about the last colon, however. Conceivably it was part of vv 7-12, thus originally following "no flesh has peace," but it is simpler to see the totality of v 13 as an addition. One small datum in favor of that judgment is that in 25:30-37, a poem with similar diction (see above), the conjunction כִּי three times introduces a tricolon (25:30, 31, 36b-37), a circumstance suggesting that in v 12 here כִּי introduces three cola that close the poem.

Placement of Unit. I propose that 12:7-12; 13:1-12aα; and 13:12aβ-14 were added as a group into the corpus of Jeremianic material, and that the catchword links are with successive verses of 12:4-6. By this proposal the present passage is linked to 12:4 by the root אבל "dry up," which appears in v 11; 13:1-12aα is linked to 12:5 by the word גְּאוֹן, literally "pride of," which appears twice in 13:9; and 13:12aβ-14 is linked to 12:6 by the root מלא "fill" (13:12, 13) and by "brothers" and "fathers" (13:14).

Internal Structure. Verses 7-12 by the present analysis have twenty-five cola, vv 7-11 having four each and v 12 having five. In most instances the tetracola offer close parallelism in the first three cola and something less close in the fourth. This is true of v 7. In a way it is true of v 8: the first two cola are not parallel but form a totality, but the third colon reflects both the first two ("raised her voice" implies the roar of a lion—compare Amos 1:2; 3:4—and "for me" is lightly balanced by "against me"), and the fourth colon is separate. Verse 10 is close in structure and meaning to v 7: "my vineyard" parallels

"my house" (compare Isa 65:21), "my portion" parallels "my possession," and "my precious portion" parallels "the beloved of my soul"; furthermore, the verbs of the third colon of each verse are perfects of נתן qal, and the fourth cola of each verse are a prepositional phrase. Verse 11 offers a variety of forms of the root שׁמם in the first three cola, while attention shifts to "no one" in the fourth (though the verb in that colon, שָׂם, balances an occurrence of that verb in the first colon). One notes also that the last colon in v 12 offers the negative אֵין as the last colon of v 11 does.

The close match between vv 7 and 10 raises the question whether one does not have two matching halves here, vv 7-9 and 10-12. One may affirm that "my possession," thrice repeated, holds vv 7-9 together, and that an inclusio of "desert" in the last colon of v 10 and the first colon of v 12 holds vv 10-12 together (so Condamin); but there is little else to support the proposal (עָלַי in vv 8 and 11 might match, but this appears less than substantial). It might be said that "many shepherds" in v 10 is matched by "devastators" in v 12, but it is perhaps better simply to see the poem as breaking into two halves of twelve and thirteen cola respectively.

Form

One may affirm that the passage is a lament by Yahweh over his own people,[4] but it must be admitted that the passage does not carry any of the traditional vocabulary of a lament ("weep," "lament," and the like) as 9:9-10 does; the only possible exception is the use of "caravan-tracks" (שְׁפָיִם, v 12), a word associated with "weeping" in 3:21. The problem is that Yahweh is responsible for the end of his people, so that he causes his own loss. The lament is thus at the same time a judgment oracle (see particularly v 12 and the last colon of v 13). The result is an expression of deep ambivalence on the part of Yahweh—he expresses both love (vv 7, 10: "beloved of my soul," "precious portion") and hate (v 8).

In spite of the close-knit structure the passage exhibits a variety of rhetorical forms: simile and metaphor (vv 8, 9), rhetorical questions (v 9, if the text is rightly understood), phraseology appropriate to wisdom (the added material in v 13: see Interpretation). Most of the diction,

---

4   Westermann, *Basic Forms*, 202-3.

however, is a simple statement of fact couched in the perfect tense: Yahweh states that he has abandoned his people (v 7), that foreign invaders have taken over (vv 10–12). The emotional impact of the passage comes from the tension between the matter-of-factness of these statements on the one hand and the genre of lament on the other.

Setting

The focus of vv 7–12 is the devastation of the land by military invasion; the added cola of v 13 focus on a drought. There is no reason to doubt the authenticity of the original form of the passage, and there is no reason to doubt the authenticity of v 13 (for resemblances to poetic passages elsewhere see the Interpretation on specific verses). Indeed there is no reason to doubt that Jrm himself extended vv 7–12 by the addition of v 13.

There are only indirect indications for a setting for this passage, but several considerations point to a time in 605 or just thereafter. (1) The mention of the "hyena" and "beasts of the field" in v 9 reminds one of such expressions in 4:7 and 5:6, part of sequences of that period; and the combination סָבִיב עָלֶיהָ (literally "around against her") in that verse is found in 4:17 and 6:3, again from that period. In v 10 the phrase חֶלְקַת חֶמְדָּתִי (literally "portion of my preciousness," that is, "my precious portion") appears, and in 3:19 the phrase אֶרֶץ חֶמְדָה (literally "land of preciousness") appears; that verse is assigned in the present study to the early recension to the north. (2) If the present passage was associated with 13:1–11 and 13:12–14 in being introduced into the Jeremianic corpus (see Structure, *Placement of Unit*), then the settings of those passages may be relevant for the establishing of a setting for the present passage, and evidence on other grounds leads to a setting of 605, or perhaps just before, for 13:1–11, and of that general period for 13:12–14 (see those passages). (3) If v 13 reflects the drought of 601–600, then one is led to the conclusion that vv 7–12 took shape earlier.

The other divine lament (9:9–10) has been given a date in the context of the burning of the scroll (601–600: see on that passage). A contrast of date between that passage and the present one may explain the contrast of

mood: in the later 9:9 Yahweh weeps, whereas in the earlier present passage Yahweh is ambivalent, both hating (v 8) and loving (vv 7, 10) his possession (compare Form).

Cornill and Volz believe that the passage is the description of an actual invasion, while Rudolph leaves open the question whether the description is actual or envisioned. What data are available suggests the invasion is still envisioned.

Interpretation

■ **7–13** The poem offers a high incidence of word-play and assonance. Thus one may note the repetition of "my possession" (נַחֲלָתִי) in vv 7, 8, and 9, and parallel to these (still with *na-*) the forms of נתן—נְתַתִּי in v 7, נָתְנָה in v 8, and נָתְנוּ in v 10; the repetition of feminine suffixes in אֹיְבֶיהָ (v 7), שֹׁנְאַתִיהָ (v 8), and עָלֶיהָ (v 9); the play on צָבוּעַ, סָבִיב, and בֹּסְסוּ in vv 9 and 10, and then a form of אסף (*M* אֹסְפוּ, emended here to הֶאֱסֹפוּ) in v 9 and וּבֹשׁוּ in v 13; the play on the root עיט in v 9 (which evidently confused a copyist); the plays on שָׁמָּה (twice), שְׁמֵמָה, and נָשַׁמָּה in vv 10–11, and then the assonantal שָׂמָהּ (emended from *M* שָׂמָהּ) and שָׁם. There is more, but this is a long enough list to indicate a poem of intricate repetitions.

The focus of the poem begins on the people (vv 7–9), but by v 10 the focus is on the land which the people inhabit.

■ **7** Yahweh speaks. "My house" is here not the temple, as elsewhere in Jer (11:15; 23:11), but, as its parallels here indicate, a term for Israel.

The noun נַחֲלָה "possession" occurs in vv 7, 8, and 9. As in 10:16, it refers metaphorically to Israel. The word means "possession, property" which comes by inheritance, usually land or buildings but occasionally other goods as well. It is striking that both the first and second cola here use metaphors of property for Israel. The noun, as a metaphor for Israel, is found in the Deuteronomic literature[5] but is certainly earlier (1 Sam 10:1, Early Source); Israel's alienation from the land in the exile, however, encouraged its use.[6] Now the unthinkable is happening: Yahweh is deserting his own inalienable possession.

The emotion of the poem is deepened even more by

5   Weinfeld, *Deuteronomy*, 328.
6   Harold O. Forshey, "The Construct Chain *naḥalat*

YHWH/'elōhîm," *BASOR* 220 (December 1975) 51–53.

the phrase "beloved of my soul" (יְדִדוּת נַפְשִׁי): for the combination compare שֶׁאָהֲבָה נַפְשִׁי in Cant 1:7; 3:1, 2, 3, 4. The love expressed here to be laid alongside "hate" (שׂנא) in v 8. Yahweh is compelled to let her enemies take Israel over.

■ 8 Yahweh's "possession" has become to him like a lion in the thicket: in what sense? The lion normally represents Yahweh himself (Amos 1:2) or the enemy that threatens Israel (4:7; 5:6)—indeed Amos 1:2 states that Yahweh "raises his voice" in Jerusalem. But here Israel has raised her voice against Yahweh: Israel has taken on the prerogatives of Yahweh against Yahweh, and this Yahweh cannot accept. In passing it is to be noted that in the present phrase קוֹל "voice" is preceded by the preposition בְּ, a usage found also in Ps 46:7; there is no way to determine what nuance, if any, is expressed by the preposition, which is not normally present in the phrase. The last colon is appalling in its directness: "That is why I hate her" (עַל־כֵּן שְׂנֵאתִיהָ); a very similar and equally abrupt line is found in Hos 9:15, כִּי־שָׁם שְׂנֵאתִים, "Indeed there (and then) I (began to) hate them."

■ 9 This verse offers several textual difficulties. As it stands, M offers הַעַיִט at the beginning of both the first and second cola; the noun means "bird(s) of prey" and is construed here either with the interrogative הֲ (the traditional interpretation) or as the definite article (so, for example, Rudolph, for the second occurrence of the word). Given the assumption of two occurrences of "bird(s) of prey," the second word of the first colon, צָבוּעַ, has been interpreted as the passive participle of a root צבע "dye" occurring in the noun צֶבַע "dyed stuffs," Judg 5:30, thus the traditional "speckled bird of prey" in the first colon, and the explanation that birds will attack another bird of unfamiliar plumage, or else that the first bird of prey is "stained" with blood (so Rashi and other traditional commentators).

But another line of interpretation is more likely. The word צָבוּעַ is well attested as "hyena" in Sir 13:18[7] and in the Talmud;[8] and G translates the word in this passage as "hyena." The word עַיִט in its second occurrence is doubtless the noun "bird(s) of prey" as a parallel to "hyena," but the first word in the verse is evidently a verb, the root עיט. The difficulty comes in clarifying the

form and meaning here of this uncommon verb. The he prefixed to the root suggests either a hip'il stem or the he interrogative; the he prefixed to the noun עַיִט in the second colon suggests either the definite article or the he interrogative. The word "hyena" does not have the definite article, so that it is unlikely that "birds of prey" carries it. A he interrogative in the second colon is unlikely without a corresponding question in the first line; further, the hip'il of the verb עיט is not attested (the occurrence in Ps 55:4 conjectured by Ludwig Koehler in KB is dubious). The he is better understood as a he interrogative: two parallel he interrogatives are known elsewhere (Eccl 3:21 in the vocalization following the Versions and almost all commentators). This suggests in turn that the form of the verb here is a qal, doubtless an imperfect יָעִיט. The meaning is not easy to establish. There are two possible Arabic cognates, 'ayyaṭa "yell, scream," and taḡayyaẓa "become angry"; the Syriac 'aytā' "anger" is no doubt cognate with the latter Arabic verb. In 1 Sam 25:14 either meaning would do, but the former ("yell") is more likely (BDB, HALAT). Both 1 Sam 14:32 qere' and 15:19 carry the same meaning, a meaning closely related to the noun עַיִט "bird(s) of prey," whether the verb is here denominative (so BDB) or simply carries a derived meaning: BDB suggests "dart greedily (upon the spoil)," HALAT "swoop down with shrieks (upon the spoil)." There are also two occurrences in Sirach: Sir 14:10 says "an evil eye looks greedily [תָעִיט; G 'is envious'] upon bread." In Sir 31:16 the verb evidently means "be greedy." The instance in Sir 14:10 fits the context of the present passage admirably; there the preposition before "bread" is עַל, and I would propose that עַל be understood here, the עָלֶיהָ in the next colon doing double duty. The metaphor here then is that Yahweh's "possession" is envisaged as a corpse and the hyena as a scavenger ready to pounce;[9] and this is at Yahweh's behest (so the nuance of לִי, "for me": compare 4:12).

The parallel to the hyena is the "bird(s) of prey" in the second colon; both Isa 18:6 and Ezek 39:4 link the latter noun with wild animals, and, with other vocabulary, the

7   It is v 17 in Israel Lévi, *The Hebrew Text of the Book of Ecclesiasticus, Edited with Brief Notes and a Selected Glossary* (SSS 3; Leiden: Brill, 1904).

8   See Jastrow.

9   See W. Stewart McCullough, "Hyena," *IDB* 2:666–67.

pairing is very common (15:3; 16:4).[10] For the phrase סָבִיב עָלֶיהָ, literally "around against her," compare 4:17 and 6:3.

The last half of the verse is a summons to the beasts to gather for the feast; again the diction resembles that of 4:16–17 and 6:3.

■ **10** For "shepherds" for foreign rulers see 6:3. For "destroy" (שׁחת pi'el) see 5:10; that passage likewise offers the vineyard metaphor, a metaphor going back to Isa 5:1–7, and found in Jer 6:9 as well as in 5:10. This is the only occurrence in Jer of "trample" (בוס po'lel), but for a similar image see 4:11. For the double text tradition in the second colon, "possession" (נַחֲלָה) and "portion" (חֶלְקָה), see Text. The nouns are virtual synonyms; חֶלְקָה is, strictly speaking, the portion of common land allotted to someone. Soggin believes that the usage here goes back to the belief in the apportionment of the boundaries of the nations, each with its guardian angelic beings.[11] The last two cola similarly play on the pattern of v 7b: "my precious portion" matches "beloved of my soul," and the identical verb construction, נתן ל, carries two meanings "give (something) to (someone)" in v 7b and "turn (something) into (something else)" here. For חֶמְדָּה, literally "preciousness," see 3:19; indeed that earlier verse contains diction much like the present verse. For "desolation" (שְׁמָמָה) see 4:22; 6:8; 9:10; 10:22.

■ **11** This verse rings the changes on the root of שָׁמֵם "desolation" (see above, vv 7–13). The vocalization of the first two cola is askew in *M* because of a wrong division between the two cola: אבלה must be an adjective, and שממה at the end of the second colon must be a verb (see Text). The verb אבל may mean either "mourn" or "dry up" (see v 4), and perhaps both; though the adjective אָבֵל is normally translated "mourning," the rendering "dried-up" is also appropriate (see, for example, Lam 1:4, where the word is linked to the root שׁמם). The word עָלַי is to be construed not with the verb אבל, as the traditional interpretation has it, but with the verb שׁמם; it means "on my account, because of me"—a good parallel is Ps 44:23, where again the prepositional expression stands before the verb. *M* opens the last colon with כִּי, which would make it read "for no one pays attention." But the movement of thought here is far from stating any reason for

the desolation; the line needs to be a part of a description of it. The emendation to "and" (see Text) is thus justified—exactly the same clause is found in Isa 57:1. The phrase שָׂם עַל־לֵב is literally "lay on the heart"; its parallel in Isa 57:1 is בין hip'il "discern," in Isa 42:25 ידע "know, understand," and in Isa 47:7 זכר "remember." It is appalling when the whole land is desolate and no one takes notice.

■ **12** For "caravan-tracks" in the desert see 3:2; 4:11; for the association of the word with lamentation see 3:21. For the occurrence of "devastator" (שֹׁדֵד) see 6:26.

For parallels to "from one end of the land to the other" see Structure. The verb אכל "eat, devour" is here repeated from v 9; for its use with "sword" see 2:30. The phrase "sword of Yahweh" is found in the book otherwise only in 47:6, part of Jrm's oracle over the Philistines, but its occurrence in a battle shout in Judg 7:20 suggests that it is a old phrase. The expression אֵין שָׁלוֹם, literally "there is no peace," is reminiscent of 6:14. The phrase "all flesh" suggests "all humankind" (Isa 40:6), and with the association of "from one end of the land/earth to the other" that meaning was surely uppermost in Jrm's mind (compare the association of the two phrases in 25:31, 33); but the phrases here appear to give a larger-than-life connotation to the population of Judah.

■ **13** The first two cola, with the parallelism of "sow" and "reap," sound sapiential (compare Form), but other occurrences in the OT use the verbs metaphorically (Hos 8:7; Prov 11:18; 22:8; Job 4:8); here, by contrast, real sowing and reaping are intended. The anti-harvest, the harvest of thorns, may be compared to the inadequate harvests described in Isa 5:10 or Deut 28:38, where the result is likewise due to the withdrawal of Yahweh's blessing. "Wheat" (חִטִּים) is *Triticum aestivum* or *durum*, a grain with a complicated genetic history in ancient times.[12] For "thorns" (קֹצִים) see 4:3.

The verb נֶחְלוּ (חלה nip'al) means literally "become exhausted, be taken ill"; "wear themselves out" tilling the soil is what is implied here. The form is a word-play on נַחֲלָה "possession" in vv 7, 8, and 9; indeed the consonants can be vocalized נָחֲלוּ "they have inherited" and are so translated in *G* and *V*. The last phrase of the colon, לֹא יוֹעִלוּ, "to no avail," is literally "they do not profit"; the

10 Note the drawing on a late pre-dynastic Egyptian palette in Othmar Keel, *The Symbolism of the Biblical World* (New York: Seabury, 1978) 104, no. 135.

11 So *G* in Deut 38:2; see J. Alberto Soggin, "Jeremias xii 10a: Eine Parallelstelle zu Deut. xxxii 8/LXX?" *VT* 8 (1958) 304–5.

phrase occurs in 2:8 and 11 to refer to the Baals, and thus the phrase here carries all the innuendos of the false search for fertility that brought on all the trouble which the people now undergo.

The verb in the fourth colon, בֹּשׁוּ "they are ashamed," occurs often in Jer (first in the hip'il in 2:26, first in the qal in 2:36) but now stands in assonances with בֹּסְסוּ "they have trampled" in v 10. For its use in the context of drought see the discussion in 14:3-4. For "harvest" (תְּבוּעָה) see 2:3.

The last colon is a set phrase (see 51:45); the meaning is the same as the similar phraseology at the end of 4:26, which see.

Aim

This poem offers to an extraordinary degree an expression of the love, sorrow, and anger of Yahweh over his people. "God's sorrow rises again and again to unconcealed heights of expression"[13]—we are at the furthest remove here from the notion, insisted upon by the later church fathers influenced by Aristotle, of the impassibility of God. One looks at the words here to describe the people: "my house," "my possession," "the beloved of my soul," "my vineyard," "my portion," "my precious portion"—all that Yahweh has held dear, all that has been considered inalienable to him, he is casting off, deserting, all because "she has raised her voice against me." Emotionally and theologically the passage has much in common with Isa 5:1-7; there, too, the destructive work of Yahweh is laid alongside his devoted constructive work of earlier years. And it is the finality of the project that is so terrible to contemplate: we who from our almost-twenty-six-hundred-year-later vantage point assume ourselves to be part of Yahweh's house find it hard to listen to the passage with the assumption of finality that it originally carried. The heritage of Yahweh would disappear, and "no one would ever notice" (v 11).

12   See conveniently John C. Trever, "Wheat," *IDB* 4:839-40, and, with botanical detail, Jane M. Renfrew, *Palaeoethnobotany, The Prehistoric Food Plants* of the Near East and Europe (New York: Columbia University, 1973) 40-67.

13   Heschel, *The Prophets*, 111.

Fresh Glimpses of the Future

Bibliography
McKane, William
"Relations between Poetry and Prose in the Book
of Jeremiah with Special Reference to Jeremiah iii
6–11 and xii 14–17," *Congress Volume, Vienna, 1980*
(VTSup 32; Leiden: Brill, 1981) 220–37.

12

14 Thus Yahweh has said: Concerning all my
evil neighbors who touch the possession
which I have given to my people Israel to
possess:
I am going to uproot them from their soil,
and the house of Judah I shall uproot
from their midst.
15/ And then after I have uprooted them, I
shall once more show mercy on them,
and I shall bring them back, each to his
possession and each to his land. 16/ And
if they really learn the 《 way 》ª of my
people, to swear in my name, "As
Yahweh lives," just as they taught my
people to swear by Baal, then they shall
be built up in the midst of my people. 17/
But if they do not obey, then I shall
uproot that nation, uproot and destroy—
oracle of Yahweh.

Text
16a   Reading דֶּרֶךְ, singular, with *G*, for *M* דַּרְכֵי "ways"
(compare 10:2).

Structure, Form, Setting

Commentators have differed whether any of these verses
are genuine to Jrm and whether there is integrity in the
passage. Duhm and Volz reject the whole passage as late,
while Friedrich Nötscher[1] and Weiser[2] defend the
authenticity of the passage as a whole. Rudolph accepts
only v 14, seeing in vv 15–17 a secondary addition. His
division between v 14 and v 15 is convincing for two
reasons. Verse 14b has the concision of poetry and a
chiastic inversion of object and verb in the second colon;
vv 15–17, however, are prose. Verse 14b announces the
shift of punishment from Judah to the people among
whom Judah is exiled; vv 15–17, however, announce
Yahweh's mercy both to Judah and her neighbors.

The verses are here because of the occurrences of
"possession" (נַחֲלָה) in vv 14 and 15 and the related verb
נחל hipʻil in v 14, linked to the occurrences of the noun
in vv 7, 8, and 9.

Verse 14 opens with the familiar messenger formula

and announces the topic; v 14b is a bicolon, both a
judgment oracle on Judah's neighbors and a salvation
oracle to Judah. Verse 15 promises a return from exile
both for Judah and her neighbors, and vv 16–17 offer
two covenantal requirements (compare 7:9, 13, which
also have the verbs "swear" and "listen" nearby).

Verse 14b thus offers an application of the verb
"uproot," one of the two negative verbs in Jrm's call in
1:10, and vv 15–17 expand on the bicolon by offering an
application of one of the positive verbs in his call, "build"
(v 16). All three verses show the parity of Judah and her
neighbors: Judah shall be "uprooted" from the "midst" of
the nations (v 14), but the nations shall be "built up" in
the "midst" of Judah (v 16).

It has already been intimated that v 14 can be accepted
as genuine to Jrm: there is certainly nothing in the verse
to suggest lack of authenticity. The verse announces that
what Judah now suffers shall be visited upon her captors;
the same message is found in 30:16. The unique refer-

1   Friedrich Nötscher, *Das Buch Jeremias* (Die Heilige
Schrift des Alten Testaments 7, 2; Bonn: Hanstein,
1934) 117.

2   Weiser, p. 107.

ence by Yahweh to "my neighbors" suggests the words are intended to be heard alongside "my house" and the rest in vv 7–10. One could suggest a setting with confidence if one knew who these "neighbors" were understood to be. One wonders whether it is a reference to the raids of the Arameans, Moabites, and Ammonites in 600/599 or 599/598 (2 Kgs 24:2; compare Jer 35:11?).[3] In 594 Jrm is convinced that all the nations of the earth must serve Nebuchadrezzar (27:7) for a long time; it is possible, then, that this verse emerged in the prophet's mind at some point after 598.

Verses 15–17, however, also give evidence of being authentic. The reference to "that nation" in v 17, and the general perspective of all nations responding to Yahweh's command, is reminiscent of 18:1–12, a passage judged in the present study to be genuine to Jrm and having a setting early in his career (see there). The phrase "learn the way of my people" in v 16 is reminiscent of "learn the way of the nations" in 10:2, and 10:1–16 is likely, by the conclusion of the present study, to be authentic, perhaps part of Jrm's communication to the exiles in Babylon in 594 (see on that passage); these are the only two passages in the OT in which "way" is the object of "learn." The notion that Yahweh will show mercy to Judah's neighbors as well as to Judah (v 15, compare v 16) is astonishing; one thinks of the word to the exiles in Babylon to pray for their captors (29:7), a word again associated with 594. A plausible conclusion then would be that Jrm announced the words of v 14 in the time just after the defeat of 598 and the words of vv 15–17 in the period around 594. But no certainty is possible.

Interpretation

■ **14** The syntax of v 14a is uncertain. The present text can be made to yield sense if the quotation is begun with "concerning all my evil neighbors," as is done here. But Rudolph omits עַל "concerning": this makes "all my evil neighbors" the anticipated object of "uproot," but this is still awkward. *G* and *T* read not "my evil neighbors" but "the evil neighbors" (a reading chosen by Volz), but it is likely that these Versions secondarily softened the anthropomorphism of "my evil neighbors" (see below)

rather than offering a better text.

There is no parallel elsewhere for the expression "my neighbors" in the mouth of Yahweh. The expression, however, is consistent with Jrm's diction elsewhere: Yahweh is conceived of as looking for shelter for the night (14:8) or willing to go into exile in the desert (9:10), or, in happier times, being willing to reside in Canaan (7:3, 7 as here vocalized; the same root שׁכן is used in those verses as in "neighbors" here).

The implication of "touch" (נגע) is of course "harm." For "possession" see v 7; it is to be noted, however, that in that passage the word was applied to the people as well as to the territory, while here it applies to the land. Here it is the cognate accusative of the verb נחל, which here means "grant as a permanent possession."

For the message of v 14b, and the possible identity of the "evil neighbors," see Structure, Form, Setting.

■ **15–17** This passage offers an astonishing message of "universal" restoration: both Judah, cast among pagan nations, and those nations themselves can receive Yahweh's mercy, living a life of integrity if they are willing to adopt Judah's religion. Only if they reject that religion will they be uprooted and destroyed. The passage expresses the parity of the pagan nations with Judah by matching "build" and "in the midst of my people" in v 16 with "uproot" and "from their midst" in v 14 (see Structure, Form, Setting). The expression "each to his possession and each to his land" reflects some awareness that Babylon had deported many peoples besides the Jews, and "they taught my people to swear by Baal" surely suggests the Canaanites, unless the diction is inexact.

The "way of my people" (v 16) is an expression for the Jewish religion (compare "way of the nations" in 10:2). Swearing "As Yahweh lives" or swearing by Baal is a touchstone of the direction of a people's religious loyalty (5:2, 7); for "As Yahweh lives" see 4:2. The verb "be built up" (בנה nip'al) is curious, and its meaning is not altogether clear; it may mean "prosper," as it seems to in Mal 3:15, or it may mean "live on by gaining children" (compare Gen 16:2). The two infinitive absolutes following a finite form of the first verb is striking.[4]

---

3   Bright, *History*, 327.
4   See Joüon, *Gramm.*, sec. 123m, and, less clearly, GKC, sec. 113s.

Aim

Verse 14 softens the condemnation against Judah implied in vv 7–13 (see especially v 8), and vv 15–17 expand on v 14. The question of Yahweh's purpose for Judah's neighbors was a perennial one and was particularly acute when Judah was led off to exile; Jrm here offers fresh glimpses of the future.

The Linen Loincloth

Bibliography

On symbolic acts in general:

Fohrer, Georg
"Die Gattung der Berichte über symbolische Handlungen der Propheten," *ZAW* 64 (1952) 101–20 = Georg Fohrer, *Studien zur alttestamentlichen Prophetie (1949–1965)* (BZAW 99; Berlin: Töpelmann, 1967) 92–112.

Fohrer, Georg
Die symbolischen Handlungen der Propheten (2d ed.; ATANT 54; Zurich: Zwingli, 1968).

On this passage specifically:

Balla, Emil
"Jeremia xiii, 1–11," *In Deo omnia unum, Eine Sammlung von Aufsätzen Friedrich Heiler zum 50. Geburtstage dargebracht* (ed. Christel M. Schröder; Munich: Reinhardt, 1942) 83–110.

Baumann, Eberhard
"Die linnene Schurz Jer. 13₁₋₁₁," *ZAW* 65 (1953) 77–81.

Birch, W. F.
"Hiding Places in Canaan. I.—Jeremiah's Girdle and Farah," *PEFQS*, 1880, 235–36.

Bondt, Aart de
"De linnen gordel uit Jer. 13:1–11," *Gereformeerd Theologisch Tijdschrift* 50 (1950) 17–39.

Southwood, C. H.
"The spoiling of Jeremiah's girdle (Jer. xiii 1–11)," *VT* 29 (1979) 231–37.

13

1 **Thus Yahweh said to me: Go buy yourself a linen loincloth and put it around your waist, but do not soak it in water. 2/ So I bought the loincloth, according to the word of Yahweh, and put it on. 3/ And the word of Yahweh came to me a second time, as follows: 4/ Take the loincloth which you bought and which is around your waist and go at once ⟨to Parah,⟩[a] and hide it there in the crevice of a rock. 5/ So I [went and][b] hid it ⟪ at Parah, ⟫[a] as Yahweh had commanded me. 6/ And after a long time Yahweh said to me, Go at once ⟨to Parah,⟩[a] and take from there the loincloth which I commanded you to hide there. 7/ So I went ⟨to Parah⟩[a] and dug, and I took the loincloth from the place where I had hidden it: but it [*M*: the loincloth][c] was ruined, of[d] no use for anything.**

8/ And the word of Yahweh came to me, as follows: 9–10/ Thus Yahweh has

Text

4–7a Vocalizing פָּרָתָה in vv 4, 6, and 7 for *M* פְּרָתָה "to Perath = the Euphrates"; it is to be noted that α' in v 4 likewise read εἰς φαραν. Jrm evidently goes to Parah, a village near Anathoth, but that location symbolized for him the Euphrates. In v 5 *M* בִּפְרָת "at Perath = the Euphrates" must be emended to בִּפְרָתָה. It is noteworthy that 4QJer[a] reads בפרתה here (Janzen, p. 177); a place-name with a preposition may appear with the he *locale* (compare מִבָּבֶלָה, 27:16, and see GKC, sec. 90e), so that if this reading is not a secondary accommodation to the spelling in vv 4, 6, and 7 but rather the original text, then the consonants need only be vocalized to בִּפְרָתָה as in the other three instances, and *M* would represent a secondary correction. For Parah and the Euphrates see Interpretation, vv 1–12aα.

b The expression is lacking in *G* and is an expansion in *M* (see Janzen, p. 40), no doubt from v 4.

c The word is lacking in *G* and is an expansion in *M* (see Janzen, p. 40), no doubt from v 7a.

d Many MSS. and *S* add וֹ "and" here before the

said, So also I will ruin [a] the great, [. . .] evil pride of ⟪ this people ⟫ [Judah] and of Jerusalem,[a] who refuse to hear my words, [who walk in the stubbornness of their heart,][b] [and they walked after other gods to serve them and worship them,][c] and let it be like this loincloth, which is of no use for anything; 11/ for just as the loincloth clings to someone's waist, so I caused the whole house of Israel and the whole house of Judah to cling to me— oracle of Yahweh—to become to me a people, and for a name, praise and honor; but they would not hear. 12aα/ And you shall say to them this word.

negative.

9–10a—a   The text of the end of v 9 and the beginning of v 10 has been damaged. I propose to read אֶת־גְּאוֹן הָעָם הַזֶּה הָרָע. The reading יְהוּדָה "Judah" will have arisen as a variant reading for "this people"; this is the reading of G. G will also have suffered the loss of הָרָע by haplography. M is evidently a conflate text with both "this people" and "Judah," but "this people" was at one time a marginal addition and was inserted at the wrong position, leaving the curious expression הָעָם הַזֶּה הָרָע. (See further Interpretation, vv 1–12aα.)

b   The phrase is lacking in G; it is an expansion in M (see Janzen, p. 40); one notes that the following verb is also הלך. The phrase is borrowed from 7:24; 11:8; or 23:17.

c   The bracketed words are Deuteronomistic and interrupt the continuity of the comparison; see Interpretation, vv 1–12aα.

Structure and Form

Extent of Unit. Though the unit is ordinarily assumed to end with v 11, there are reasons to include v 12aα as well. (1) The setuma (closed paragraph) division of M divides the material so. (2) There are only two instances of the clause "And you shall say to them this word" (וְאָמַרְתָּ אֲלֵיהֶם אֶת־הַדָּבָר הַזֶּה) in Jer—here and in 14:17. In the latter passage it is clear from rhetorical data that the clause refers to what precedes. Here in v 12 it is the first of two rubrics, the second of which obviously refers to what follows. Rudolph, Bright, and Janzen[1] attempt to solve the problem of the double rubric by following G, which has only one. But if the clause in question refers to what precedes, then G must be an erroneous secondary adaptation.

Placement of Unit. The passage evidently formed a collection alongside 12:7–13 and 13:12aβ–14; the collection was inserted after 12:6 on the basis of catch-word associations with 12:4–6 (for the details see 12:7–13, Structure). The catchword in question here is גְּאוֹן "pride of" (compare 12:5).

Form and Internal Structure. The passage is the report of a symbolic action told in the first person (not a vision report: see Interpretation, vv 1–12aα). The structure is:
(1) First command of Yahweh (v 1)
   Report of execution of command (v 2)
(2) Second command of Yahweh (vv 3–4)

   Report of execution of command (v 5)
(3) Third command of Yahweh (v 6)
   Report of execution of command and discovery (v 7)
(4) Meaning of the symbolic act revealed by Yahweh (vv 8–11)
(5) Fifth command of Yahweh, to proclaim the action and its meaning publicly (v 12aα).

Georg Fohrer has offered the basic studies of symbolic actions.[2] There are other reports of symbolic actions both within Jer and in the books of other prophets, but it is difficult to make useful comparisons with similar reports elsewhere, because the differences are sometimes as many as the likenesses. There are three other first-person reports of symbolic acts in Jer: the visit to the potter's workshop (18:1–12), the wearing of thongs and yoke-pegs (27:2–11), and the buying of the field at Anathoth (chap. 32). But none of these offers multiple commands from Yahweh; all of them have a single command. The narrative in 27:2–11 contains no report of the execution of the command; chapter 32 contains a report of the execution of the command (vv 9ff) without the command itself—the text is evidently in disarray, and "buy it for yourself" (v 8) needs to be reinserted at the end of v 7 (see there). The visit to the potter's house (18:1–12) is the closest parallel in Jer; the passages are not only form-critically parallel but share the verb "be ruined" (שחת nip'al, 13:7; 18:4).

---

1   Janzen, p. 85.
2   See bibliography; for the present passage see Georg Fohrer, *Die symbolische Handlungen der Propheten* (2d

ed.; ATANT 54; Zurich: Zwingli, 1968) 33–35, 78–80, 99.

The smashing of the flask (19:1–13) does not at the beginning declare for a format in the first person or the third person in *M* (*G* does in 19:1—first person—but this may be a secondary correction); *M* does declare for the third person in 19:14. But that symbolic action offers no report of the execution of the command, and the report of the command is accompanied by extended speeches which (in spite of critical opinion: see Preliminary Observations there) appear to be part of the original narrative. That passage is thus not comparable to the present one.

There are two other reports of symbolic actions in Jer which are in the third person. The first is the burial of the stone at Tahpanhes (43:8–13), but here too a report of the execution of the command is missing. The other is the sinking of the scroll in the Euphrates (51:59–64), but this action was to be carried out not by Jrm himself but by others at his behest. The sequence in 16:1–9 is in a way a series of commands to execute symbolic actions (abstention from marriage, from funerals, from weddings), but form-critically it is better understood as a series of supplementary calls to Jrm comparable to the material in chapter 1. There is also the narrative of a set of symbolic actions in the confrontation between Hananiah and Jrm in chapter 28, but the only symbolic action proper is that of Hananiah against Jrm and his proclamation of the meaning of that action (28:10–11).

Outside the Book of Jer are the following first-person narratives: Hosea 3; Isa 8:1–4 (containing two commands of Yahweh each followed by a prophetic report); a whole series in Ezekiel—Ezek 12:1–11; 12:17–20; 21:23–29; 24:1–14; 24:15–24; 37:15–28; and the sign of temporary dumbness narrated in 3:22–27; 24:25–27; and 33:21–22; and Zech 6:9–15.

It is clear that this genre is related to call narratives on the one hand (see above, on 16:1–9) and to vision reports on the other; indeed it is an open question whether theologically there is a difference between an inner vision through which Yahweh reveals himself and an outer action through which he likewise reveals himself (compare Ezek 37:1–14 with 15–28). This uncertain boundary has encouraged some commentators to understand the present narrative as that of a vision (see Interpretation, vv 1–12aα).

With regard to the details of the present passage, the first and third commands of Yahweh are introduced by the expression "Yahweh said to me," while the second command and the revelation of the meaning of the incident are introduced by the expression "and the word of Yahweh came to me as follows." Both forms are common in such commands.[3] The verbs used for the commands proper are an infinitive absolute followed by a perfect consecutive in the first command (v 1, compare 19:1) and imperatives in the second and third. The report of the execution of the command follows the wording of the respective command in each case. It is noteworthy that there are no witnesses to the action; it is more common to report witnesses either in the command of Yahweh (19:1; 27:3; 43:9) or in the report of the execution of the command (32:9–13). If v 12aα is included in the passage (see above, *Extent of Unit*), it is the command to proclaim the action; it is surprising that that command is deferred to the end (compare 19:3–9, 11–13; 27:4–11; 43:10–13). The relation between the action and the meaning of the action is expressed in v 9 by כָּכָה "so" (compare 19:11; 51:64; and, of Hananiah's symbolic actions, 28:11) and in v 11 by כַּאֲשֶׁר "just as" and כֵּן "so" (compare 19:11–12).

Jrm is here told to perform an action with a piece of his clothing; one thinks of the narrative of Ahijah, who tore his garment into twelve pieces (1 Kgs 11:29–39), and of Elijah's throwing his garment on Elisha (1 Kgs 19:19–21). So many of the symbolic actions of the prophets are destructive ones: Jrm was to break the flask (19:10); Hananiah broke Jrm's yoke-pegs (28:10). Only occasionally are they constructive ones: Jrm watched the potter rework the clay (18:4).

For the specific symbolism involved in the action with the loincloth, see Interpretation, vv 1–12aα. For the theology of symbolic actions, see Excursus.

Setting
The wording of the report of Jrm's action associates it with 4:29 and 47:2 (see Interpretation, vv 1–12aα); the former is in this study assigned a setting in the period of Carchemish, and the best setting for the latter is in the summer or autumn of 604, when the Babylonian army

---

3   Fohrer, "Gattung der Berichte über symbolische Handlungen" = *Studien*, 104–5.

invaded Philistia. The wording of the present passage is much like that in 18:1–12: not only are both analogical experiences of Jrm's, but both center on the word "ruined" (נִשְׁחַת, v 7 here, compare v 9; and 18:4). The dating given in the present study for that passage is between 609 and 601 (see Setting there), probably earlier within that span because of likeness between 18:11 and 7:3, 5 in the temple sermon. And if the reconstruction of the text of v 9 offered here is correct, the parallelism of "this people" and "Jerusalem" is reminiscent of that same parallelism in 4:10 and 11. All this evidence points toward a setting around the time of the battle of Carchemish (May/June 605). This dating is in line with the dates offered for 12:7–13 and 13:12aβ–14, adjoining passages that evidently were added as a collection to the corpus of Jeremianic material at the same time (see Structure and Form, *Placement of Unit*).

Interpretation

■ **1–12a**α This passage, with its picturesque narrative, has occasioned much discussion.

The most basic question is geographical. Is one to understand the location mentioned in vv 4, 5, 6, and 7 to be "the Euphrates" (so the text) or a local alternative? And related to this: Is one to understand the narrative as a series of actions actually carried out, or as a vision or parable? The unlikelihood of two round trips to the Euphrates—several hundred kilometers in either direction—is obvious. To Calvin it was self-evidently a vision. "[Jeremiah] was, we know, continually engaged in his office of a teacher among his own people. Had he undertaken so long a journey, and that twice, it would have taken him some months." Beyond the matter of distance is a further datum: the vicinity of the Euphrates offers no rocks in which to hide a garment; one would

have to go north of Carchemish to find such rocks—a long way from the center of Babylonia. But against the notion of a vision is the absence of any verb for "see" (compare 1:11–13; 24:1–3).

The search for a local alternative began early. Samuel Bochart (1646), followed by Venema (1765) and Hitzig (1841), suggested reading אפרתה, that is, "Ephrathah," identified with Bethlehem (Mic 5:1), but the 'alep is a problem and the solution has rightly been rejected.[4] The solution of Parah (Josh 18:23) first occurred in modern times to a German (C. Schick)[5] and an Englishman (W. F. Birch),[6] but the translation of α' offers it, perhaps inadvertently (see Text, vv 4–7a), and it was likewise anticipated by the Jewish lexicographer al-Fāsī in the eleventh century.[7] The suggestion was taken up by George A. Smith[8] and is accepted by Bright.

Parah, the present-day ḥirbet fārah near 'ain fārah (Atlas of Israel grid 177–137), lies eight kilometers northeast of biblical Jerusalem and four kilometers northeast of Anathoth. Here, certainly, are rocks to hide a loincloth.[9] But if Jrm walked to Parah to hide the loincloth, it is nevertheless clear that to him Parah represented the Euphrates and therefore the power of Babylon (see below), so that the present text of *M* is correct on the level of symbolism if not on the level of Jrm's historical act. It should be noted that the contrast between "to Parah" and "to the Euphrates" may have been less in Jrm's ear than the Masoretic vocalization would have it (pārātā and pĕrātā respectively), and that even in the form in which the name appears in v 5 there is uncertainty how the contrast would have been heard by Jrm: thus one may ask whether 4QJer^a offers a more accurate text (see Text, 4–7a), or indeed whether the village of Parah carried an alternative form of name with -t.[10]

4   For citations to these early commentaries see Condamin.

5   "Mittheilungen von Baurath C. Schick in Jerusalem," bearbeitet von Karl Marti, *ZDPV* 3 (1880) 11.

6   W. F. Birch, "Hiding Places in Canaan. I.—Jeremiah's Girdle and Farah," *PEFQS*, 1880, 235–36.

7   Godfrey R. Driver, review of *The Hebrew-Arabic Dictionary of the Bible known as Kitāb Yāmiʿ al-Alfaẓ (Agron) or David ben Abraham al-Fāsī*, in *The Society for Old Testament Study Book List, 1947*, 42.

8   George A. Smith, *Jeremiah, Being the Baird Lecture for*

1922 (4th ed.; Garden City, NY: Doubleday, Doran, 1929) 184.

9   See the illustration in William H. Morton, "Parah," *IDB* 3:657; compare Baly, *Geography*, 179.

10 Compare the remarks on sufformatives of names in Yohanan Aharoni, *The Land of the Bible, A Historical Geography* (Philadelphia: Westminster, 1967) 109.

Verses 9–11 appear to raise issues of text and redaction, but commentators differ in their analyses. Nicholson, for example, takes both verses as editorial expansion,[11] while Hyatt takes v 11 as an addition. But the matter is not simple.

Something is amiss with the text at the end of v 9 and the beginning of v 10. *M* reads literally "the pride of Judah and the pride of Jerusalem, the great [masc.], this people, the evil one, who refuse. . . ." The word order of "this people, the evil one" (הָעָם הַזֶּה הָרָע), with the descriptive adjective after the demonstrative, is dubious, but even with the adjectives reversed the phrase "this evil people" does not occur otherwise in the OT. *G* reads "the pride of Judah and the pride of Jerusalem, this great pride, who refuse . . . ," omitting "this evil people." I propose that *G* has omitted "the evil" by haplography, that "this people" was the original counterpart of "Jerusalem" here (compare 4:10, 11) and that "Judah" is a variant reading, that *M* is a conflate text containing both variants, and that "this people," having fallen out of *M*, has been reinserted at the wrong spot (see Text). One argument in favor of reading "this people" is that "this loincloth" (v 10) and "people" (v 11) may echo it. Now "this people" and "Jerusalem" (v 9) are balanced by "the whole house of Israel and the whole house of Judah" (v 11).

The phrase "who refuse to hear my words" (with participle, הַמֵּאֲנִים לִשְׁמֹעַ אֶת־דְּבָרַי) appears only here in Jer; with the corresponding finite verb the phrase appears in 11:10. These two occurrences have no real parallels; "refuse to hear" (but without an object) appears otherwise in the OT only in Neh 9:17. There is no reason then to judge the phrase redactional; it appears to be balanced by the phrase "but they would not hear" at the end of v 11. Verse 10a*β* "and they walked after other gods to serve them and worship them" is certainly a Deuteronomistic cliché[12] and interrupts the flow of the rhetoric (compare Volz). The remainder of the verse is appropriate to the authentic portion of the passage. As

for the phrase "for a name, praise and honor" in v 11, there is no reason to judge it redactional simply because it also occurs in Deut 26:19: that one occurrence in Deuteronomy hardly makes it "Deuteronomistic phraseology."[13] I suggest two data which suggest that the phrase is original. First, "honor" (תִּפְאֶרֶת) may offer a word-play on פָּרָתָה "to Parah"; second, 13:18–19 and 13:20–27 appear to be placed here because of the catchword תִּפְאֶרֶת (see 13:18–19, Structure), suggesting that the word was here early.

An אֵזוֹר is a loincloth (see further below on v 1), the most intimate garment, as close to the wearer as Yahweh intended Israel to be to him (v 11). W. Robertson Smith cites an Arabic proverb which is peculiarly appropriate (and which carries the cognate of the Hebrew word): *huwa minnī ma'qida 'l-izār* "He is with respect to me in the place where the *izār* is knotted," that is, very near to me.[14] Verse 11 uses דבק "cling" twice, once in the qal and once in the hip'il; the choice of verb reminds one of Gen 2:24, "A man leaves his father and his mother and clings to his wife." Yahweh intended Israel to be as close to him as wife to husband, as close as the loincloth to Jrm. Is it possible that because Jrm did not take a wife (16:2) as Hosea did, the analogue of the loincloth was appropriate to him?

The loincloth was of linen, but nothing in the narrative itself indicates whether the material itself carried any symbolic value. Since, however, priests wore linen garments (Exod 28:39), one thinks immediately of the vocation of the people to be a kingdom of priests and a holy nation (Exod 19:6); the fact that earlier in Exodus 28 the garments for Aaron are intended to be "for honor" (v 2 there), the same expression found here in v 11, may reinforce this interpretation.[15] On the other hand Koehler suggests that the material is simply cooler,[16] while Hyatt notes sensibly that in the context of the symbolic act linen will rot easily while leather will not (compare 2 Kgs 1:8).[17]

It was to be worn by Jrm but not to be soaked in water

11 Nicholson, *Jer. 1—25*, 122.
12 Weinfeld, *Deuteronomy*, 320, 321.
13 As assumed in ibid., 328, no. 8.
14 W. Robertson Smith, "Notes on Hebrew Words, I," *JQR* 4 (1891–92) 290.
15 So Naegelsbach, p. 139.
16 *HALAT*, 26b.
17 Hyatt, p. 923.

(v 1)—"[not] to wash it," as Rashi commented, "so that it may rot more quickly when it is full of sweat." But if the hiding place at Parah represents the Euphrates, then Parah will be the "water" that will do its work on the loincloth, rather than any water which Jrm might have used (see below).

The second and third commands are to take the loincloth and go to Parah and hide it in the crevice of a rock (see below, on v 4), and then after a time to retrieve it. The symbolism here has been clarified by C. H. Southwood.[18] There are two other occurrences of "crevice" (נְקִיק) in the OT, both in the same construct phrase "crevice(s) of the rock(s)," 16:16 and Isa 7:19, and both passages are relevant for the interpretation of Jrm's action. In 16:16 the rock crevices are hiding places for Judah, but they will be of no avail against the foe sent by Yahweh. The passage in Isaiah also depicts hiding places for Judah, and this passage is a key to the passage before us. Isa 7:18–19 reads in part (excluding in particular the gloss adding Egypt):[19] "Yahweh will whistle . . . for the bee which is in the land of Assyria. And they will all come and settle in the steep ravines, and in the clefts of the rocks, and on all the thorn-bushes." That is to say, the enemy will come from Mesopotamia in a swarm and will overwhelm Judah. This passage in Isaiah is followed soon after by a passage depicting the sweep of the "River" (= the Euphrates) over Judah, Isa 8:7–8 (again excluding glosses): "Yahweh is bringing up against them the waters of the River, mighty and many . . . and it will rise over all its channels and go over all its banks; and it will sweep on into Judah, it will overflow and pass on, reaching even to the neck."

Jrm's symbolic action appears then to be a working out of these two passages of Isaiah in combination. Jrm uses both images separately elsewhere, both the "hiding places in the rocks" and the "overflowing river." For the first, we have not only 16:16 (see above) but also 4:29, part of a poem on the foe from the north: "From the shout 'Horseman and archer!' every region is fleeing; they have gone into the caves, and have hidden in the thickets, and into the rocks have gone up. . . ." For the second, we have 47:2, part of an oracle over the Philistines: "Behold, waters are rising out of the north and shall become an overflowing torrent; they shall overflow the land and all that fills it, the city and those who dwell in it."

The act symbolizes the threat of the Euphrates to inundate Judah even though Judah might want to wish to hide. Now it is clear what the word-play between Parah and the Euphrates represents: not simply that the local village is a convenient symbol for the Euphrates, a place closer to home so that Jrm will not have to walk to the actual Euphrates and back: no, Parah represents the Euphrates on Judah's soil, the symbolic fulfillment of Isaiah's words in Isa 8:7–8. Rudolph is correct, then, when he maintains that the symbolic act has nothing to do with Judah's exile in Babylon; one may note that there is no phraseology to suggest exile in vv 9–11. The symbolic act must be laid alongside other declarations regarding the foe from the north.

Finally Yahweh says that the Euphrates, that is, the invading army of Babylon, will ruin the "pride" (גָּאוֹן) of Judah and Jerusalem. And here there is one more passage in Isaiah which is relevant, Isa 2:6–22: there we are told that Judah is to "enter the rock and hide in the dust from before the terror of Yahweh and from the glory of his majesty [גָּאוֹן]. . . . For Yahweh of hosts has a day against all that is proud [גֵּאֶה] and lofty . . ." (Isa 2:10, 12). This passage goes on to repeat the phrase of Yahweh's majesty (2:19, 21) and says (v 21) that men shall "enter the caves of the rocks and the clefts of the cliffs" (הַסְּלָעִים, plural of the word used in v 4 of the present passage). The present passage is thus a kind of midrash on that passage in Isaiah which contains so many synonyms for and examples of "pride": Yahweh, through the Euphrates, will finally ruin that pride of Judah which has taken refuge in the crevices of rocks.

Excursus: The Theology of Symbolic Actions

Both prophetic visions and the symbolic actions of the prophets share the Israelite sense that Yahweh may reveal himself through ordinary human experience: the prophet is enabled to experience ordinary events as revelatory of Yahweh's power and intention. Since דָּבָר means both "word" and "thing," and since the name of

---

18   C. H. Southwood, "The spoiling of Jeremiah's girdle (Jer. xiii 1–11)," *VT* 29 (1979) 233–34.

19   Wildberger, *Jesaja*, 301, 303–4.

a person or place may contain insight into Yahweh's purposes, it is clear that Yahweh may bring to bear upon the event in which the prophet participates a meaning that transcends the event itself.

This is particularly the case with a complex symbolic act like the burying of the loincloth: the word-play between "Parah" and "Euphrates," the various details of the action, all of these participate in the perceived set of meanings in Jrm's mind.

Let two authorities speak on the matter. "The 'symbolic acts,' of which we hear so often, mean that the prophets personally pass through the entire fate they behold in their vision. . . . The feeling that he was filled with the spirit of Yahweh gave to the prophet a high-strung selfconsciousness. Through him Yahweh says 'I'. His speech is not his own, it comes from the depths where all power is concentrated."[20] "As a divine word, the word uttered by a prophet had an effective power. The same is true of the visible word, the so-called symbolic action. Such an action served not only to represent and make evident a particular fact, but also to make this fact a reality. In this respect the prophetic actions were akin to . . . magical actions. . . . But there are significant differences. . . . The power of the magical action was dependent on the inner power connected with them and their performance in accordance with definite magical laws; the power of the prophetic actions like the power of the prophetic word was derived from Yahweh's will."[21]

■ **1** For the idiom with the infinitive absolute הָלוֹךְ followed by a perfect consecutive see 2:2. The verb קָנָה means in general "acquire," but usually "buy" in the specific sense (either by barter or by weighed silver: compare 32:7–10).

Ancient depictions of the "loincloth" (אֵזוֹר) show two types. One is a simple wrapper which does not pass between the legs;[22] the other is a garment made up of narrow strips of overlapping cloth which does pass between the legs.[23] There is no way to know which is intended here (G translates περίζωμα, a term used for both the undergarment of a soldier and for the apron worn by a smith or cook).

The loincloth is to be of linen (see above, vv 1–12aα).[24]

■ **4** For the translation "the crevice of a rock," with definite article followed by indefinite article, see GKC, sec. 127e.

■ **6** The phrase מִקֵּץ יָמִים רַבִּים is literally "at the end of many days"; compare מִקֵּץ יָמִים in Gen 4:3 and the frequent phrase יָמִים רַבִּים (for example, 37:16).

■ **7** The verb שׁחת nip'al covers a wide semantic range; in 18:4 it is used of the clay vessel in the hands of the potter which "turned out badly" or "was spoiled," while here it clearly means "rotted." For צלח see 12:1: here it means "be useful" (as in Ezek 15:4).

■ **9–10** For the questions these verses raise of text and recension see vv 1–12aα. If the solution offered here is correct, both הרב and הרע were intended to modify "pride," and it is to be assumed that it is the pride both of Judah (or, as restored here, "of this people") and of Jerusalem which is described, rather than of Jerusalem only (against Bright).

The subject of "let it be" (v 10b) is "pride" (so also Bright).

■ **11** "A name, praise and honor": to become such is to become an object of praise and renown for Yahweh. The same phrase (with "name" and "praise" reversed) is found in Deut 26:19. Commentators often note the suggestion that Deut 26:17–19 may embody the formula of the covenant concluded by Josiah with the people after the discovery of Deuteronomy,[25] so that Jrm may have had the passage in mind, and that setting.

■ **12aα** The rubric at the beginning of this verse belongs with what precedes (see Structure, *Extent of Unit*), as does the same rubric at the beginning of 14:17 (see there). It is an instruction to Jrm to make public the private revelation of the symbolic act and its meaning. There may be a touch of irony here; v 10 describes the people as "refusing to hear my words," and v 11 ends with "but they would not hear"—so this clause should perhaps be introduced by "so" rather than "and": "So you shall say to

---

20   Pedersen, III/IV, 112, 113.

21   Lindblom, *Prophecy*, 171.

22   See the depiction of a Canaanite warrior in *BHH*, 963, illustration 1, 1.

23   See the Egyptian painting of Syrians in *ANEP*, 3, no. 6.

24   For the details of preparation of linen see Jacob M. Myers, "Linen," *IDB* 3:134–35; for an Egyptian

model of the preparation of linen see *ANEP*, 42, no. 142.

25   Alfred Bertholet, *Deuteronomium erklärt* (Freiburg: Mohr, 1899) 82; so also Gerhard von Rad, *Deuteronomy* (Philadelphia: Westminster, 1966) 162, and Mayes, *Deuteronomy*, 338.

them this word," the implication being that the refusal to hear the positive words of Yahweh brings on this negative word.

Aim

The symbolic act carried out by Jrm elicited the revelation of the potential destruction of the people by the foe from the north. It was a message which Jrm would deliver again and again to the people, until the foe became real in the sieges of 597 and 587. The one symbolic act concentrated several prophecies of Isaiah (see Interpretation, vv 1–12aα). If Dante was right to place pride first among the capital sins (and he followed Thomas Aquinas in this),[26] then it is noteworthy that Jrm perceived Yahweh's answer to Judah's pride to be the symbolic inundation of the Euphrates, the military power of Babylon, the central tragedy of the OT.

---

26 *Summa Theologica* II, ii, quaest. 162, artt. 5–8.

**Eat and Drink,
but Tomorrow You Will Die**

Bibliography
McKane, William
  "Jeremiah 13:12–14: A Problematic Proverb,"
  *Israelite Wisdom, Theological and Literary Essays in
  Honor of Samuel Terrien* (ed. John G. Gammie et al.;
  Missoula, MT: Scholars, 1978) 107–20.
Long
  "Schemata."

13

**12aβb/ Thus Yahweh, the God of Israel,
has said: "Every jug should be filled with
wine." And《if》[a] they say to you, "Don't
we know that every jug should be filled
with wine?" 13/ then you shall say to
them, Thus Yahweh has said, I am going
to fill all the inhabitants of [a] this land [—
[b]and especially[b] the kings who sit on
David's throne, the priests, the prophets
and all the inhabitants of Jerusalem—][a]
with drunkenness. 14/ [And I shall smash
them, each against his brother, fathers and
sons together, oracle of Yahweh. I shall
not pity or spare or have compassion when
I destroy them.][a]**

Text

12a   Reading with *G*; *M* omits, evidently by haplography with the following 'alep-mem.

13a—a   The sequence is evidently an expanded text.
One may either assume that the bracketed words
are a gloss like the gloss in 2:26 (so Giesebrecht and
Volz)—one may note that *G* has "and Judah" after
"the prophets," thus evidently offering a continuation of the glossing process (so Janzen, p. 63), or
else that the original text read "fill all the inhabitants of Judah and all the inhabitants of Jerusalem"
and that *M*, offering "of this land" as a variant for
"of Judah," added at a later stage the specific listing
which the tradition of *G* thereupon borrowed
(compare Cornill).

b—b   The ן "and" here is either to be omitted (Rudolph)
or understood as the waw *explicativum* (GKC, sec.
154a [1b]).

14a   This verse, though authentic, was evidently added
by Jrm after vv 12aβ–13 had been proclaimed: see
Setting.

Structure

This short passage offers its share of puzzles. Though
both vv 12aβ–13 (except for a redactional expansion, see
Text, v 13a) and v 14 give evidence of being authentic to
Jrm, the two parts evidently took shape in separate stages
(see Setting and Interpretation).

Placement of Unit. It has already been proposed that this
unit, along with 12:7–13 and 13:1–12aα, were as a
collection integrated into the collection of Jeremianic
material on the basis of successive catchwords in 12:4–6
(see 12:7–13, Structure, *Placement of Unit*). By this
proposal the present passage is linked with 12:6 on the
basis of the root מלא (nip'al, "be filled," v 12, and pi'el,
"fill," v 13) which occurs as the adjective מָלֵא in 12:6, and
on the basis of "brother" and "fathers" in v 14 and

"brothers" and "father" in 12:6. If the link between vv
12–13 and 12:6 is valid, it reinforces slightly the interpretation given to the adjective "full" in 12:6 (see there).
And if the link between v 14 and 12:6 reinforces that
between vv 12–13 and 12:6, it is a datum that suggests
the authenticity of v 14 to Jrm, whether or not that verse
was added by him some years after vv 12–13 had been
proclaimed (see below, Setting).

Form

Long classifies the passage as a specimen of his "Type B"
schema of question and answer, couched as a word of
Yahweh to the prophet (like 5:19), consisting of (1) the
setting (v 12aβ–ba), (2) the question (v 12bβ), and (3) the
answer (vv 13–14).[1] But the passage varies from the

---

1   Long, "Schemata," 134–35.

other passages belonging to this type which he cites in that in the others the question is an information question, not a yes-or-no question. The parallel he cites in which the question is for clarification of a previous saying (15:2) offers "and when they ask you, 'Where shall we go?'"—but the question in the present passage is not "How should every jug be filled with wine?" or "Why do you say, 'Every jug should be filled with wine'?" The sequence here then does not quite fit the general form, and the answer that comes in v 13 does not quite fit the question in v 12; a missing term, understood between v 12 and v 13, might be something like, "No, you do not; not in the sense that Yahweh intends it; for thus Yahweh has said. . . ." The saying itself, "Every jug should be filled with wine," sounds like a conventional *māshāl* (proverbial saying),[2] but there is no way to be sure. For the rhetorical use made of the *māshāl* see Interpretation. But the ultimate form of both v 13 and v 14 is the judgment oracle.

Setting

Evidently v 14 is a later addition to vv 12aβ–13: the images of "drunkenness" and "smashing" are difficult to bring together (see in detail Interpretation). But v 14 is authentic to Jrm: the phrase "fathers and sons together" appears in 6:21, and the phraseology of v 14b is similar to that in 4:28b. Both 6:21 and 4:28 are part of passages dated in the present study to early in 600, and without further data this must be the tentative date for this verse.

There are no data for a setting for vv 12aβ–13: one can easily imagine a vintage festival or a cultic festival (for the latter see Volz, Hyatt, Weiser), but this is only to assume the obvious. As for a dating, if one assumes that v 14 was a later addition by Jrm to vv 12aβ–13 (see Interpretation), then one has to propose an earlier date than for v 14. One is drawn to 25:15–17, 27–29, where the same imagery prevails; it is tentatively suggested in the present study that the setting for 25:15–17 was between the battle of Carchemish in the early summer of 605 and December 604 when the Babylonian army sacked Ashkelon. If that is a valid suggestion, the same period is plausible for the present passage.

Interpretation

■ **12aβ–14** There has been uncertainty since ancient times regarding the meaning of נֵבֶל here, whether "wineskin" or "(earthen) jar." Thus Jerome notes that G translates ἀσκός "wineskin," that a' in his first edition translated (in Latin, *laguncula*, presumably) ὑδρία "flask," then in his second edition simply transliterated *nebel* (to play it safe, one wonders?!), that s' translated (in Latin, *crater*, presumably) κρατήρ "mixing bowl," and that θ' translated (in Latin, *vas*, presumably) κεράμιον "vessel." Jerome himself used "flask" but offered "wineskin" in his commentary as an alternative. One may add that both S and T render with a word that can mean either. Lexicographers have always offered both,[3] and so, recently, BDB and Zorell; but KB and *HALAT* only offer "jar." The context here is not definitive; if the symbolic reference is to the bellies of the drinkers, then "wineskin" is appropriate; if v 14 is relevant, then "smash" must imply "jar." McKane surveys all the problematic passages in the OT which contain the word and concludes that "there is no usage of *nēbel* in biblical Hebrew for which the sense 'skin' is certainly established."[4] As to pottery type, the נֵבֶל is a storage jar.[5] But jars existed in smaller sizes than the large storage jars, and the rendering *laguncula* by the Vulgate and the equivalent in a' suggest an individual drinking flask. The translation "jug" is appropriate in its association with wine-drinking and in not specifying a size (so Bright, *JB*; *NAB* has "wineflask").

It is worth noting that Michaelis raises the question whether there is wordplay here on נָבָל "fool." Could Jrm have employed a standard proverb but substituted "fool" for "flask"? There is no trace of this in the Versions, but he uses נָבָל elsewhere (17:11) and uses synonyms for "fool" to describe the people (4:22); it remains then an interesting possibility.

---

2   For the *māshāl* see conveniently Sheldon H. Blank, "Proverb," *IDB* 3:934–36, and James L. Crenshaw, "Wisdom," *Old Testament Form Criticism* (ed. John H. Hayes; San Antonio: Trinity University, 1974) 229–39, and the bibliographies in those works.
3   McKane, "Jeremiah 13:12–14," 107–9.
4   Ibid., 110.
5   Kelso, "Pottery," 851, and James L. Kelso, *The Ceramic Vocabulary of the Old Testament (BASOR* Supplementary Studies 5–6; New Haven: American School of Oriental Research, 1948) 25–26; A. M. Honeyman, "The Pottery Vessels of the Old Testament," *PEQ*, 1939, 84–85.

Commentators and translators have used a variety of modal auxiliaries to translate יִמָּלֵא: "must be filled" (Moffatt), "should be filled" (Bright, *NJV*), and rephrasings bring other nuances: *JB*, "Any jug can be filled with wine"; *NEB*, "Wine jars should be filled with wine," and the similar *NAB*, "Every wineflask is meant to be filled with wine." So what is the accent here? Is it a kind of glorified mutual encouragement at a festival or drinking bout, "Fill 'em up!"? Or, more philosophically, "Let wine jugs fulfill their function"? Or is it a quiet criticism of drinking bouts, "It is not very hard to fill wine jugs" (thus the understanding of *JB*)—something like "A fool and his money are soon parted"?

And, more generally, did Jrm devise the proverb ad hoc? Or is he quoting a current proverb? If he is quoting it, is it quoted ironically? Commentators remark widely that the saying is banal (Calvin, Duhm, Giesebrecht, Volz, Rudolph). Calvin's comments, quoted by McKane, are worth repeating: "The general introduction might have appeared to be of no weight, for what instruction does this contain. 'Every bottle shall be filled with wine.' It is as if one were to say that a tankard is made to carry wine and that bowls are made for drinking; this is well known even to children. And then it might have been said that this was unworthy of a prophet: 'What do you say? You say that bottles are the receptacles of wine, even as a hat is made to cover the head, or clothes to keep off the cold—you seem to mock us with childish trifles." But this is not the only occasion in which a prophet appears to make ironic use of banal material: Isa 28:23–29 is probably of the same sort.[6]

To these uncertainties another is added: one senses a disjunction between the image of drunkenness in v 13 and "smashing" in v 14. Both are derivable from v 12, but they fit with difficulty. Duhm puts it well: "What is meant by filling the people with drunkenness is not immediately clear; and if the Israelites are jars, then they can shatter against each other without being filled with wine."[7] McKane explores the matter and concludes that

v 14 has been added secondarily to vv 12–13, the primary proverbial unit; v 14 introduces the idea of "shattering," which does not integrate well with vv 12–13.[8]

The first task then is to try to discern the meaning of vv 12aβb–13; again McKane has surveyed the possibilities thoroughly. Essentially three explanations have been offered. (1) The proverb is expressive of popular complacency: every jug will be filled with wine, and Yahweh will always reward us. Jrm applies the proverb in a contrary way: every jug should be filled with wine, so every inhabitant of Judah will be filled with the wine of Yahweh's wrath and become "drunken" (so Leonard E. Elliott-Binns and Norman C. Habel).[9] (2) The proverb means something like "everything has its use"; the people interpret this as a warrant for a drinking bout—it is a toper's jest—but Jrm intends it as a word of Yahweh's judgment (so many older commentators: Robert Lowth, Blayney, Graf, Hitzig, Karl Friedrich Keil; recently Bright). (3) This view is similar to (2) but emphasizes the banality of the proverb. Jrm deliberately uses a phrase which appears to be noncommunication in order to jolt his hearers into asking, "What is the point of his saying that?" He is deliberately being banal in order to penetrate the inattentiveness of his audience (so most recent commentators: see particularly Volz). McKane believes (3) is the most likely understanding of the verses.[10]

This interpretation is encouraged by the striking syntax of the people's response in v 12, a *he* interrogative followed by the infinitive absolute, a negative, and the finite verb; I have found no parallel for this sequence elsewhere in the OT. The closest parallel is the sequence of the same verbs in the same forms, without the negative, in Gen 43:7: "They replied, 'The man questioned us carefully about ourselves and our kindred, saying, "Is your father still alive? Have you another brother?" What we told him was in answer to these questions; הֲיָדוֹעַ נֵדַע כִּי יֹאמַר הוֹרִידוּ אֶת־אֲחִיכֶם—could we in any way know that he would say, "Bring your brother down"?'" That question

---

6 Edwin M. Good, *Irony in the Old Testament* (London: SPCK, 1965) 126–27.

7 Duhm, p. 122.

8 McKane, "Jeremiah 13:12–14," 117.

9 Leonard E. Elliott-Binns, *The Book of the Prophet Jeremiah* (Westminster Commentaries; London: Methuen, 1919) 117; Norman C. Habel, *Jeremiah, Lamentations* (Concordia Commentary; St. Louis:

Concordia, 1968) 130.

10 McKane, "Jeremiah 13:12–14," 113–15.

implies a negative answer; the question in the present passage implies a positive one, "Don't we know (very well) that . . . ?"

The judgment expressed in v 13, "I am going to fill all the inhabitants of this land with drunkenness," is somewhat puzzling. Does it suggest that Yahweh is sending upon the people a sense of delusion, a condition of dazedness, of stupor, so that they are unable to make responsible decisions? The diction of 51:39 and 57, regarding the leaders of Babylon, point in this direction. Or is one to understand by this judgment the image of the "cup of wrath" which Yahweh sends upon the people in his anger? Volz suggests that it is both. The latter image is widespread in the OT, both in the prophetic literature (25:15, 17, 28; 49:12; Hab 2:15–16; Obadiah 16; Ezek 23:31–34; Isa 51:17, 22; Zech 12:2) and outside it (Pss 60:5; 75:9; Lam 4:21). It is evidently derived from the institution of the ordeal, Num 5:16–28.[11] In Israel it was used both of Yahweh's action against Israel (Ps 60:5) and against his enemies (Ps 75:9); the present passage is one of the earliest instances of its use in the prophets, certainly of a prophetic use of the image in speaking of Yahweh's wrath against Israel.[12]

The listing of specific segments of the population in v 13 is undoubtedly a glossator's expansion; the phrase "the kings who sit on David's throne" is derived from 22:4. For a gloss like this compare 2:26.

If v 13 explicated the potential of "be filled" and "wine," v 14 explicates the potential of "jug" and therefore moves the symbolism in a new direction to some degree in conflict with that in v 13 (see above). The verb נפץ means "smash"; it is used repeatedly of action with a war-club in 51:20–23. But what does "smash" symbolize here, particularly with "each against his brother, fathers and sons together"? The phrase אִישׁ אֶל־אָחִיו, particularly

without the balancing אִישׁ אֶל־רֵעֵהוּ (31:34) may mean a bit more than "against each other." At one point Jrm evidently had his own experience with his brothers (12:6). He was concerned about the relation of brother with brother (9:3), and his word in chapter 34 about bad faith in taking back freed slaves uses the phrase in question three times (34:9, 14, 17). What he foresaw was a total breakdown of the solidarity of the community; it was to some degree self-induced (9:3 once more) but ultimately would be brought about by Yahweh, who would smash every individual in the community (and 51:20–23 is once more relevant).

The negative verbs are all synonymous, piled up for effect. The verb חמל qal and חוס qal are not common in Jer, and this is their first appearance in the book; רחם pi'el has appeared before (6:23; 12:15). They may be chosen here partly for the repetition of ḥ in all three and ḥ-m in two of them. The diction, however, is very close to that of 4:28 (see Setting). There will be no turning back.

Aim

"Let us eat and drink, for tomorrow we die" (Isa 22:13)—it is an age-old notion. Samuel N. Kramer cites a Sumerian proverb, "We are doomed to die, let us spend; we will live long, let us save."[13] One find the same mood reflected in Ecclesiastes, for example, Eccl 5:17; "Behold, what I have seen to be good and to be fitting is to eat and drink and find enjoyment in all the toil with which one toils under the sun the few days of his life which God has given him, for this is his lot."

Jrm takes this mood of merriment and turns it into nightmare: "Yes, eat and drink, but tomorrow you will die." It is not a time for jollity, it is a time of crisis; business as usual will not do, for Yahweh is about to intervene, and there will be no second chance.

---

11   See on this Richard Press, "Das Ordal im alten Israel, I," *ZAW* 51 (1933) 126–29, and his discussion there of earlier literature, particularly the investigations of Hugo Gressmann.

12   On the meaning of "drunkenness" here see further McKane, "Jeremiah 13:12–14," 111–12.

13   Samuel N. Kramer, *History Begins at Sumer* (Garden City, NY: Doubleday, 1959) 121.

13

15 Hear and give ear, don't be haughty,
   for Yahweh has spoken;
16 give to Yahweh your God glory
      before he brings darkness
      and before your feet trip
         on the mountains of twilight;
   and you will long for light,
      but he will make it deep darkness
      ªand bringª a thick cloud.
17 But if «in rebellion»ª you do not hear it,
      my soul will weep in the presence of
         pride,
      [. . .]ᵇ
      and my eye will run down with tears,
      «yes, indeed shed tears,»ᵇ
         for Yahweh's flock «will be
            broken.»ᶜ

Text

16a–a The qere' reads וְשִׂית, that is, "and" followed by an infinitive absolute functioning as a finite verb (as in 14:5; see König, *Syntax*, sec. 218b); the ketib reads יָשִׂית "he will bring." Either reading will do; Rudolph elects the qere'.

17a   Reading בְּמִסְרָדִים, the proposed noun *מִסְרָדִים being derived from סרד "be rebellious," rather than *M* בְּמִסְתָּרִים "in hiding places": the emendation is that of Rudolph, adopted by *NAB*. The traditional interpretation of the sequence in *M* (which would be translated "but if you do not hear it in hiding places") is to understand "in hiding places" to modify the clause in the second colon (thus "my soul will weep in secret"). Duhm and Cornill try to explain the expression from 36:26, the narrative of Yahweh's hiding Jrm and Baruch at the time of the burning of the scroll, but there are several difficulties with this explanation. Rudolph asks how Jrm could have made the word available to the public if he speaks of himself in hiding. More substantially, "but if you do not hear it" cannot make up a colon of its own. Furthermore the setting proposed here for the passage makes that explanation doubtful.

b   The bracketed words are lacking in *G*, and Rudolph omits them. But they are unlikely to be dittographic: the verb is a *hapax legomenon* in the OT. I propose that they originally stood as the fourth colon of the verse rather than the third, that they dropped out of the text by haplography (a stage represented by *G*), and that they were reinserted at the wrong spot.

c   Reading נִשְׁבַּר with *G* for the *M* נִשְׁבָּה "will be taken captive." *M* gives a plausible reading, and no commentator, to my knowledge, prefers *G* here. But Jrm's diction elsewhere and considerations of unity of imagery here render the reading of *G* preferable; see Interpretation.

Structure

This is the first of three passages which make up the balance of chapter 13 (vv 15–17, 18–19, 20–27). These three passages share vocabulary in common which suggests that catchwords have united them in a small collection: ירד (v 17, "run down"; v 18, "come down"); תִּפְאֶרֶת "honor" (vv 18, 20); עֵדֶר "flock" (vv 18, 20). This

collection will then have been inserted after the collection of 12:7–13; 13:1–12aα; and 13:12aβb–14 on the basis of the link with תִּפְאֶרֶת "honor" in v 11. In addition there may be a link between גֵּוָה "pride" (v 17) and גָּאוֹן "pride" in v 11: lexicographers refer both nouns to the root גאה.[1] But the settings of the three passages appear to be various, so that their incorporation into the

---

1   Holladay, *Architecture*, 148.

growing collection of Jeremianic material may not have been immediate.

On first hearing the first colon of v 16 is parallel to the first colon of v 15: "give Yahweh glory" matches "don't be haughty." But the two cola in v 16 beginning with "before" are dependent on the first colon, so that v 16a forms a tetracolon alongside v 15, a bicolon. Verse 16b, a tricolon, is parallel to both v 15 and v 16a: the first colon of each has a subject in the second-person plural, and the material after the first colon shifts to the activity of Yahweh. Verse 17 forms an inclusio with v 15: the first colon of each offers "hear" in the second-person plural, and the last colon of each is a כִּי clause involving Yahweh. The intervening cola in v 17 (three, if the text is correctly analyzed) moves surprisingly to Jrm's emotions. And one wonders whether the five cola of v 17 fill out the three of v 16b to offer a satisfying total of eight.

Form
Jrm speaks (v 17, compare 8:23; 14:17); Yahweh's expression of weeping (9:9) is more subdued and with a different range of images. The passage is thus an appeal to repentance mediated by the prophet (compare 3:14, 22; 4:14; 6:8). Verse 15 is a summons to attention: it offers diction reminiscent of Isa 1:2, but the summons there to the heavens and the earth is a summons to witnesses in a cosmic lawsuit (so also Jer 2:12; 6:19), whereas here the imperatives are simply a summons to receive instruction, like those in Hos 5:1.[2] The motivation to their attention, as usual, is given by a כִּי clause (compare 8:14).

The imperatives of the first cola of vv 15 and 16 are commands to serve Yahweh and are followed by the "before" clauses, which threaten the hearers with the dire alternative: this same form is found in Zeph 2:1–2, though there are text problems there. The description of the judgment awaiting those who do not serve Yahweh continues to the end of v 16.

Verse 17 begins with a typical protasis of refusal ("if you do not . . ."), and one expects the apodosis to express Yahweh's punishment (compare 12:17). Instead it expresses Jrm's helpless reaction of grief over the people;

and the closing line gives the ultimate fate of the people and thus the ultimate motivation for Jrm's grief.

Setting
The M reading of the last colon of v 17, "will be taken captive," has led some to think of a date just before 597, and the association of this passage with the word about Jehoiachin (vv 18–19), with its word of exile, reinforces that impression (so Weiser). But the threat of captivity was always valid, and that threat is therefore not a sufficient datum to establish a setting. And this consideration is irrelevant if the original text is reflected in G, as proposed here (see further Interpretation).

The passage assumes the possibility of repentance and service to Yahweh, so by the assumption of the present study it must have a setting before the king burned the scroll in December 601. The diction of v 17 is so close to that of 14:17, part of the liturgy associated with the drought, dated in the present study to December 601 (see 14:1—15:9, Setting), that the most appropriate setting is late autumn of 601; by this understanding it is a last-ditch appeal by the prophet for repentance.

Interpretation
■ **15–17** This impressive poem develops images of height ("be haughty," v 15; "give glory," v 16; "pride," v 17) and movement downward ("run down," v 17), and of light and darkness (v 16). The mood of urgency in v 15 is deepened in v 16 and culminates in the grief of v 17. The word "glory" (כָּבוֹד) at the beginning of v 16 controls the symbolism. In its nuance "honor, dignity," it suggests eminence, so that one can come down from glory (compare 48:18). It is appropriate then that the people not be too haughty, that is, not try to be too high (v 15: the root גבה is identical with that seen in "high" in 2:20): the people are caught in "pride" (v 17). On the other hand, in its nuance meaning "shininess," "glory" begets the words for darkness and light here (for the "shininess" of כָּבוֹד see for example Ezek 43:2).

■ **16** Curiously, the expression "give glory to Yahweh" (and the like) is not common in the OT: the only comparable passages are 1 Sam 6:5, where the Philistines are told to give glory to Yahweh in order that Yahweh's

---

2   Compare Wolff, *Hosea*, 95–97.

hand be lightened in the land, Mal 2:2, part of a speech of Yahweh's, and possibly Ps 115:1, where the people urge Yahweh to give glory to himself (Ps 29:1 might be added, though the verb is not נתן but the synonymous הָבוּ). Though חשׁך is the common root for "be dark" in Hebrew, the verb in the second colon (חשׁך hipʻil) is the only occurrence of any word of this root in Jer. The verb in the third colon (נגף hitpaʻel) occurs only here in the OT, but the qal stem means "hit," as of one's foot against a stone (Ps 91:12), so that the hitpaʻel stem must mean "stumble repeatedly" or "stumble against each other." And "twilight" (נֶשֶׁף) occurs only here in Jer; the word may be used of the half-light either of morning or (as here) of evening. The poem is heavy with assonance: נֶשֶׁף picks up the combination n-p from the verb of the previous colon, and all three of its consonants are picked up again in נַפְשִׁי "my soul" in the second colon of v 17.

"Light" in the first colon of v 16b is of course the standard antonym for "darkness"; for "deep darkness" (צַלְמָוֶת) see 2:6. The noun עֲרָפֶל in the last colon has turned up in a Ugaritic text with the meaning "storm-cloud";[3] Zeph 1:15 offers a good contemporaneous text.

The "mountains of twilight" and the reference to the flock in v 17 inevitably remind the hearer of Ps 23:4. Sheep must be brought to the fold before darkness falls; by the same token, the people are to give glory to Yahweh before it is too late.

■ **17** The reconstructed noun "rebellion" in the first colon is cognate with the verb סרר which occurs in 5:23 and 6:28 (see there). The object suffix "it" with the verb "hear" refers to the general message; for the same suffix see 5:20. The metaphor of the people as Yahweh's flock is common in Psalms (see Pss 80:2; 95:7; 100:3).

The verbs translated "will run down" and "shed tears" must be understood either as nonconsecutive imperfects or as jussives ("so that my eye might run down").

The *G* reading "will be broken" is to be preferred in the last colon, given the association elsewhere of Jrm's weeping with the root שׁבר "break" in reference to the people: it is to be seen in 14:17, "Let my eye run tears night and day, and let them not stop: (with) what a great fracture [שֶׁבֶר] is broken [נִשְׁבְּרָה] my poor virgin people," and it is to be seen in 8:21–23, "By the shattering [שֶׁבֶר] of my poor people I am shattered [הָשְׁבָּרְתִּי]. . . . O that my head were water and my eye a fountain of tears, so that I might weep day and night for the slain of my poor people!" One may note further 10:19, in which the people themselves cry out over their brokenness (שֶׁבֶר), and Jrm responds with imagery of shepherds and pasturage (10:21). These considerations render the *G* reading preferable. It may be argued, furthermore, that in the darkness sheep are likely to fall and be broken but are hardly likely to be captured. It must be admitted, however, that the image of the "scattering" of the sheep became the dominant one during the exile (23:1; Ezek 34:11–16), so that the *M* reading in the present text became a plausible one.

Aim

The sense of Yahweh's steady expectations, the awareness of the onset of the final darkness of the national life of Judah, and of Jrm's crushing grief over the prospect, all come together in this poem; it is simple, and it is devastating. Jrm extends the call to the people to hear and respond, but the compelling images of the poem are of gathering gloom, so that his call to respond is swallowed up by the vision of what is ahead. Doom is not inevitable—one has here no apocalyptic timetable; but the time is short.

---

3   The spelling is *ġrpl*, Ug. 5.8.8, 9, 12, 19; see conveniently Dahood, *Psalms I*, 107.

The King's Head
Does Not Wear the Crown
for Long

Bibliography

Dahood, Mitchell
    "Two Textual Notes on Jeremia," *CBQ* 23 (1961)
    462–64, esp. 462.
Hermisson, Hans-Jürgen
    "Jeremias Wort über Jojachin," *Werden und Wirken
    des Alten Testaments, Festschrift für Claus Westermann
    zum 70. Geburtstag* (ed. Rainer Albertz et al.;
    Göttingen: Vandenhoeck & Ruprecht;
    Neukirchen: Neukirchener, 1980) 266–68.

13

18   Say to the king and to the queen-mother:
         Take a lower seat,
           for there comes down ⟨from your
                heads⟩[a] your splendid crown;

19   The [a] store cities[a] are shut,
         with none to open:
           [b] Judah ⟪is⟫ all ⟪exiled a total exile.⟫[b]

Text

18a   *M* מראשותיכם is vocalized by the Masoretes as
מַרְאֲשׁוֹתֵיכֶם, understood as "your head-pieces" or
"your head-ornaments": the noun would be subject
and the verb irregularly singular. But *G*, *V*, and *S*
read "from your head," and all commentators have
thus emended the text to מֵרָאשֵׁיכֶם. Dahood,
however, has recently pointed out that Ugaritic has
a plural *rašt* of the word "head" as well as *rašm*: that
is to say, given that evidence the present text might
be vocalized to מֵרָאשׁוֹתֵיכֶם.

19a—a   Explaining הנגב as a noun from a root נגב
"provision (an army)" with Mitchell Dahood,
Ugaritic-Hebrew Philology (BibOr 17; Rome: Pontifical
Biblical Institute, 1965) 66. The meaning is affirmed
by Gordon (UT, 441, no. 1605a) and is cited by
Charles Virolleaud for a Mari text (Joseph
Aistleitner, *Wörterbuch der ugaritischen Sprache* [4th
ed.; Berlin: Akademie, 1974]). The meaning fits the
present context (see Interpretation) and, as Dahood
points out, would fit Isa 30:6 as well. The vocalization of the noun is uncertain.

b—b   Though the meaning is tolerably clear, the text
here appears to have been damaged. "Judah" is here
feminine (כָּלֹה); its verb הָגְלָת is treated as an older
form (GKC, sec. 75m), but one expects הָגְלְתָה (Esth
2:6); furthermore *G*, *V*, and *S* take the last two
words of the verse as a cognate accusative, as Amos
1:6 has it, גָּלוּת שְׁלֵמָה, probably rightly, so that a he
may have fallen out of the text of the verb and been
replaced before the accusative. Certainly the form
שְׁלוֹמִים here is dubious (see the lexica and commentators).

Structure

For the placement of the passage see 13:15–17, Structure.

One is left in some uncertainty how to divide up the cola. Verse 18b (the כִּי clause) must be a single colon (against Rudolph): the subject cannot be separated from the predicate. Since v 19a offers the parallels "shut" and "open," this sequence presumably makes up two cola. This circumstance suggests in turn that v 18a makes up two cola[1] and that v 19b is a single colon (see Text, Interpretation). If this analysis is correct, one has two tricola, each consisting of two short cola and one long colon.

Form

There is divergence regarding the imperative in the first colon of v 18: *M* has a singular, while *G* and *S* have a plural. The plural would suggest a command to the people (Rudolph accepts this reading), while a singular would assume a command to Jrm. On balance it is better to stay with *M*.

There is no way to determine whether the quotation ends with v 18 (so Rudolph, Bright, and the translations that mark quotations) or continues in v 19 as well.

The remainder of v 18 uses the motif of the king coming down from his throne. It is an old motif, found in Ugaritic of El's descent from the throne when he mourns the death of Baal;[2] it is found in taunts over the enemy (48:18; Isa 47:1) and in dirges over one's ally (Ezek 26:15–18). How the motif functions here depends on one's understanding of the first colon (see above). If Jrm speaks, the tone must be analogous to his other pronouncements over Jehoiachin (see Setting), namely 22:24–27 and 28–30. It is thus hardly a taunt, and it is unlikely to be a dirge if understood as a word from Yahweh. It is best left in the general category of a judgment speech, and v 19 confirms that characterization.

Setting

The king and queen-mother must be Jehoiachin and his mother Nehushta (2 Kgs 24:8, 12, 15), and the passage must be set on the eve of the fall of Jerusalem, early in 597: the king ruled three months (2 Kgs 24:8), and the city fell on March 16.[3]

Interpretation

■ **18** For the difference of opinion on the imperative in the first colon see Form.

The queen-mother (גְּבִירָה) is mentioned along with Jehoiachin as having been taken into exile (2 Kgs 24:12, 15; Jer 29:2). The office was one of high rank with official prerogatives,[4] but it would be especially so for the mother of an eighteen-year-old king.

The second colon is literally "come lower, sit down" (see GKC, sec. 120g). The sense of height is deep-grained in a hierarchical society (compare Prov 25:6–7; Luke 14:7–10); a king who is to sit in a lower position is no longer king.

The mixture of plural ("heads") and singular ("crown") is curious but understandable, given the plural address in the imperatives in the second colon over against the tendency to use the singular when each person possesses one of something (the Hebrew in 14:3, 4 is literally "their head"). The "crown" in Judah was probably a golden diadem, perhaps worn over a turban (compare Ps 21:4; Ezek 21:26).[5]

■ **19** The subject of the first colon, עָרֵי הַנֶּגֶב, has traditionally been understood as "cities of the Negeb," that is, of the south. Given this translation, one must assume that the Chaldean army or its clients had already cut off the cities to the south from Jerusalem, or that those cities had closed their gates against the enemy. There is evidence that the cities in the Negeb were threatened by Edomites at this period, acting either on their own or at the instigation of the Babylonians: an ostracon found at Arad mentioning the threat of Edomite attack is particularly vivid.[6] The general situation for the period is

---

1 Compare the treatment of Exod 15:9a and b in O'Connor, *Structure*, 182.
2 Ug. 5.6.11–14.
3 Bright, *History*, 327.
4 See de Vaux, *Ancient Israel*, 117–19, and in more detail Niels-Erik A. Andreasen, "The Role of the Queen Mother in Israelite Society," *CBQ* 45 (1983) 179–94, esp. 192.

5 For descriptions and illustrations of royal crowns in the ancient Near East see Lawrence E. Toombs, "Crown," *IDB* 1:745–46.
6 Yohanan Aharoni, "Arad: Its Inscriptions and Temple," *BA* 31 (1968) 17–18; Jacob M. Myers, "Edom and Judah in the Sixth-Fifth Centuries B.C.," *Near Eastern Studies in Honor of William Foxwell Albright* (ed. Hans Goedicke; Baltimore: Johns

indicated by 2 Kgs 24:2.

On the other hand, from the standpoint of poetic style the mention of the Negeb here is odd. One would expect some kind of parallelism to the idea expressed by "cities of the Negeb" (it is to be noted that "Judah" is hardly the parallel here: the Negeb is part of Judah, Josh 15:20–32). In Obadiah 19 "Negeb" is paralleled by "Shephelah" (as in Josh 15:21 and 33), and in Isa 21:1 the word seems to be parallel with "desert."[7] Why, one wonders, single out the cities of the Negeb if Jehoiachin's rule is coming to an end?—surely armies would surround him on every side. Dahood's suggestion of "store cities," then, is persuasive (see Text). The king's supplies are cut off, and his days as king are numbered. (Or, one wonders: Did Jrm intend a double meaning here?) For a simple description of a besieged city see Josh 6:1.

Verse 19b stresses the totality of the coming exile. The exile of 597 did not turn out to be total; as Rudolph points out, either Jrm is using poetic license, or else he did not know, when the oracle was proclaimed, that Nebuchadrezzar would be less severe than had been thought.[8] The number of those exiled at that time is given in 52:28 as 3,023, though there are difficulties in accommodating this datum with that given in 2 Kgs 24:12–16 (see the discussion on 52:28).

Aim

The new king scarcely had time to wear his crown when he had to take it off: Nebuchadrezzar was at his gates, and he must lead his people to exile, he and his mother, to a land they had never seen (22:26–27, 28). The poem is short, as the king's reign is short.

Hopkins, 1971) 390–91.

7   Dahood believes he has found a parallel for "Negeb" in Ps 126:4, a mention of "sand" in v 1 there (*Psalms* *III*, 220).

8   Rudolph, p. 96.

Is It Really Possible
for the People to Change?

Bibliography
Skweres
"Strafgrunderfragung," esp. 195–96.
Williamson, H. A.
"Jeremiah 13:21," *ExpTim* 36 (1924/25) 45.

13

20 ᵃ Lift up,ᵃ 《 Zion, 》ᵇ 《 your eyes, 》ᶜ
and seeᵃ those who come in from the
north!
Where is the flock which was given you,
your splendid sheep?

21 What will you say when 《 your lambs 》ᵃ
《 are missing? 》ᵇ —
and it was you who trained them! —
⟨your sucklings,⟩ᶜ 《 as if trained 》ᵈ ⟨by
the poor man.⟩ᵉ
Will not pangs seize you
like a woman giving birth?

22 And when you say to yourself,
"Why have these (things) happened to
me?"
for your great guilt your skirt is exposed,
your body ravished.

23 Does the Ethiopian ever change his skin,
or the leopard his spots? —
(then) you too can do good
who are trained to do ill!

24 And I shall scatter themᵃ like stubble
vanishing
on the desert wind.

25 Such is your lot,
your measured portion ⟨I have given a
hundredfold⟩ᵃ —oracle of
Yahweh;

Text

20a—a Reading the ketib of both imperatives as
feminine singulars with many MSS. and *G*; the qere'
(followed by *V*, *S*, and *T*) reads masculine plurals.
But all Versions agree on feminine singular address
beginning in v 20b and continuing for the rest of
the poem. The masculine plural would have arisen
after the vocative dropped out of the first colon (see
b), under the influence of vv 18–19.

b *G* reads "Jerusalem" at this point (and this reading
is accepted by Cornill, Volz, and Bright), but
Rudolph's conjecture of "Zion" (צִיּוֹן), though lacking
textual support, is more likely; the omission would
have arisen by haplography with עֵינַיִךְ (compare the
textual confusion of 'ayin and ṣade in the qere' and
ketib of 2 Kgs 20:4). But either vocative will do; it
will balance the vocative "Jerusalem" in v 27.

c Reading עֵינַיִךְ with *G*; *M* in reading the masculine
plural suffix is simply consistent with the qere' (see
a—a).

21a Emending עָלַיִךְ "over you" to מְלָאיִךְ on the basis
of the diction in Isa 40:11; see Interpretation.

b *M* reads יִפְקֹד "he appoints"; *G* reads the verb as
יִפָּקְדוּ, plural. *G* evidently read the correct consonantal text; vocalize as יִפָּקְדוּ, nip'al—see Interpretation.

c Vocalizing עָלַיִךְ "over you" as עֻלַיִךְ on the basis of
the diction in Isa 40:11; see Interpretation.

d *M* אַלֻּפִים needs the preposition כְּ (compare כְּמוֹ in
v 21b), which has fallen out by haplography; see
Interpretation.

e *M* לְרֹאשׁ "for a head" (or the like) is to be
revocalized as לְרָאשׁ or לָרָאשׁ (2 Sam 12:1–4); see
Interpretation.

24a The shift from second to third person is awkward,
and Rudolph emends the verb from וַאֲפִיצֵם to
וַאֲפִיצְכֶם "and I shall scatter you [masculine plural]";
perhaps there was a copyist's confusion, given the
following kap. On the other hand, perhaps the verb
is deliberately framed as a quotation (Gen 49:7?) or
there is some other reason for the form.

25a *M* מֵאִתִּי "from (with) me" is hardly correct.
Vocalize מֵאֵתִי pi'el of a denominative verb מאה from
מֵאָה "hundred" (compare the proposal for 2:36–37).
This verb is proposed by Dahood for Pss 22:26
(*Psalms I*, 42); 66:20 (*Psalms II*, 125); and 109:20

	as often as you have forgotten me,
----	have trusted in the Lie.
26	And I too have pulled off your skirt [. . . ,]ᵃ
	and your shame is to be seen.
27	《 In my presence 》ᵃ are your adulteries and
	your neighings,
	the infamy of your whoring:
	On hillsᵇ and in the field
	I have seen your vileness;
	Woe to you, Jerusalem, (that) you are not
	clean!—
	⟨other (partners) you designate.⟩ᶜ

(*Psalms III*, 107). For a justification of this proposal
see Interpretation. It makes unnecessary the
proposal of Volz and Rudolph to read מֶרְיֵךְ "(the
portion of) your obstinacy" with *G* for *M* מִדַּיִךְ "your
measure."

26–27a *M* עַל־פָּנָיִךְ, which occurs after "your skirt," both
overloads the colon and is unnecessary for the
image. It is evidently misplaced and should be read
as עַל־פָּנַי "in my face = in my presence" at the
beginning of v 27, supplying the predicate for the
noun phrases in the first two cola of v 27 (so also
Volz). The expression, reinserted at the beginning
of v 27, then supplies a balance with the phrase with
עַל in the third colon and with "I have seen" in the
fourth colon.

b Reading a וֹ with *G*; the two expressions in this
third colon thus balance "your adulteries" and "your
neighings" in the first colon.

c The expression in the last colon, אַחֲרֵי מָתַי עֹד
(literally "after when still?") is impossible. Revocalize
to אֲחֵרִים תִּיעֲדִי (יעד qal); or, if the textual tradition
of וַתּוּכָל in 3:5 is correct for a closing second
singular feminine, the verb here may be תִּיעָד and
the consonantal text thus sound (see GKC, sec. 145t,
and the discussion in 3:5, Interpretation). The
expression here has reference to Exod 21:8–10; see
Interpretation.

Structure

For the placement of this unit see 13:15–17, Structure.

Some commentators have assumed that this passage is
not unified. Thus Volz believes that vv 20–22 + 25–27
made up an original unit, and that into this passage two
additions have been inserted, v 23 and v 24; Rudolph
believes that there are three fragments, vv 20–22, 23–
24, and 25–27. Rudolph points out that in vv 20–22 the
punishment is stressed (vv 20–21) more than the guilt (v
22), whereas in vv 25–27 the guilt is stressed (vv 25, 27)
more than the punishment (v 26). Volz reaches his
conclusions because of the shift of personal reference:
second singular feminine for Jerusalem in vv 20–22 and
25–27, second plural masculine in v 23, and third plural
masculine in v 24.

These observaions are acute but are not such as to
destroy the unity of the passage; Jrm elsewhere uses the
technique of temporary deferment of like material for
esthetic effect (compare the placement of "that I may
pardon her" and "how can I pardon you" in 5:1, 7). The
shift from feminine singular to masculine plural in v 23 is
surprising, but it may have been accompanied by a

change of rhythm or gesture in the presentation which
we do not understand. For the shift to third person in v
24 see Text.

If one assumes a unity to the passage, one may find
links in vocabulary between material in vv 23–24 and
what comes before and after: למד pi'el "teach, train" in
vv 21 and 23, and perhaps the formal parallel of "you
too" (גַּם־אַתֶּם) in v 23 and "and I too" (וְגַם־אֲנִי) in v 26.

The passage begins and ends with vocatives (if the
reconstructed text in v 20 is correct). Verses 20–22, as
here set forth, have thirteen cola, and vv 25–27 have
twelve; given the match of second singular feminine
references in these two sections, one must assume they
are parallel, enclosing a shorter central section of six
cola. The parallel between vv 20–22 and 25–27 is
reinforced by the repetition of "your skirt" (שׁוּלַיִךְ) in
both v 22 and 26, though a question has been raised
about the word in v 22 (see Interpretation on that verse).

Form

The material in vv 20–22 and 25–27 (see Structure) is a
mixture of accusation (vv 22, 25b, 27) and announce-

ment of judgment (vv 20–21, 25a, 26); there is no orderly separation of the two, and the mixture may betoken heightened emotion. The diction of v 20 resembles that of 3:2, but whereas the appeal to "look" in 3:2 is a call to view the evidence of guilt, here it is a call to view the evidence of the coming judgment. The rhetorical question "Where is the flock . . . ?" mocks the situation of Jerusalem, suffering the judgment of Yahweh, bereft of her population; a similar mocking question is found in Nah 2:12, and in Jer 2:28 with regard to pagan deities. Verse 21a carries another rhetorical question, "What will you say when . . . ?"—for a similar question see 5:31, "What will you do when . . . ?" And v 21b carries a rhetorical question of the inevitability of punishment much like that of 5:9, "With these folk shall I not deal . . . ?"

Verse 22 offers the question-and-answer schema which Long has analyzed.[1] The present passage is more like his Type A (the scheme used by people to try to explain their own predicament, as opposed to Type B, instruction to the prophet about what to tell people when they pose the question to the prophet); but his examples of Type A (e.g., 22:8–9) use the third person to refer to the people raising the question, whereas the scheme here employs the second person, "When you say to yourself. . . ."

Verse 23a uses proverbial material, a depiction of the impossibility of change. Gemser cites an Egyptian parallel with the same theme, "There is no Negro who lays off his skin."[2] Verse 23 in general then is a mocking assessment by Yahweh of the chance Jerusalem will change her ways. Verse 24 is a brief judgment announcement.

Verse 25a is what Childs calls the "summary appraisal";[3] the diction here resembles that in Isa 17:14b (see Jer 7:28 and compare 4:18); v 25b, a motivation clause, suggests that the punishment fits the crime (an implication of 4:18 also): for v 25 compare 22:21b.

Setting

The passage offers imagery and phraseology that resemble material already assigned in the present study to the first scroll, notably 2:10–25, 29–37 (see the analysis in 2:1—4:4, Preliminary Observations), to be

dated therefore in the period up to 604. Thus the mocking rhetorical questions in vv 20–21 find parallels in the latter part of chapter 2; "do good" and "trained to do ill" (v 23) are comparable to 2:33; the expression of Yahweh's punishment with a denominative verb from "hundred" (v 25) corresponds to the expression in 2:36–37 of the changes of Jerusalem's loyalty, using the same verb, if these reconstructions are correct; "forget Yahweh" (v 25) is comparable to 2:32; "on hills and in the field" (v 27) is comparable to 2:20; the accusation by Yahweh that Jerusalem is not clean (v 27) is comparable to his citation of Israel's claim that she is not unclean (2:23); the reference to "other" sexual partners (v 27), if that reconstruction is correct, is comparable to 2:25. The metaphor of foreign invaders and shepherds coming in (vv 20–21) is comparable to 6:3, part of a sequence likewise assigned to the first scroll (see Setting there). There are a few parallels suggesting a slightly later period: thus the verbs "commit adultery" (נאף) and "neigh" (צהל) in v 27 are comparable to 5:7–8, part of material evidently added in the second scroll, but there are indications that 5:1–9 took shape in the autumn of 601 (see Setting there). All in all a setting in 605 or a year or two thereafter is most plausible.

Interpretation

■ **20** For the parallel "lift up your eyes" and "see" see 3:2. For the invaders "from the north" compare 1:15; 4:16; 6:3, 22; 8:16. For "flock" (עֵדֶר) as a designation of the people of Judah see v 17. The phrase נִתַּן־לָךְ "(which was) given you" has no parallel in Jer: the flock is the population which has been entrusted to the city. The noun תִּפְאֶרֶת (here "splendid"), used here to describe the sheep, was used to describe the king's crown in v 18.

■ **21** The first half of the verse is impossible in *M* and needs emendation at several points. The text now reads "What will you say when he punishes you [or, when he appoints (someone) over you], and it was you who taught [or trained] them, over you chiefs [or confidants] for a head." Since v 20b says "Where is your flock which is given to you?" and v 21b says "Will not pangs seize you like a woman giving birth?" the most plausible meaning for v 21a is something like "Your sheep will be taken

---

1   Long, "Schemata."
2   Berend Gemser, "The Instructions of 'Onchsheshonqy and Biblical Wisdom Literature,"

Congress Volume, Oxford 1959 (VTSup 7; Leiden: Brill, 1960) 126.
3   Childs, *Isaiah and the Assyrian Crisis*, 128–36.

from you." Since the nip'al of פקד means "be missing," that reading of the verb in the first colon is a plausible one; it is to be noted that in 23:4, in the context of the restoration of shepherds, it is stated that none of "my sheep" "will be missing." This suggests that the first עָלַיִךְ, which follows the verb, represents the subject of the verb; indeed the second עָלַיִךְ, toward the end of the half-verse, no doubt represents a word carrying the same function, though the subjects are likely to be synonyms and not the identical word. The vocabulary of Isa 40:11 supplies the vocabulary; that passage, too, speaks about Yahweh as a shepherd restoring his flock (עֶדֶר). The word for "lambs" there is טְלָאִים, so I propose טְלָאַיִךְ, though the form of the word in Aramaic suggests that a possible plural was טְלָיַיִךְ, which may be the form here. In any event, ṭet and 'ayin were very close in early scripts (compare the confusion of מִטַּל with מֵעַל or מַעַל in the MSS. and Versions of Deut 33:13). The second colon needs no emendation: למד pi'el is used of "training" a calf in 31:18. The third colon brings עָלַיִךְ once more. Isa 40:11 offers, as a parallel to טְלָאִים "lambs," עָלוֹת "those (ewes) giving suck"; I propose here עֹלָיַיִךְ "your sucklings." It is true, this noun is found otherwise only of human infants (Isa 49:15; 65:20), but given the feminine participle of the related verb in Isa 40:11, the proposal here is a plausible one: it fits the semantic field and the parallel in Isa 40:11, it makes a nice assonantal and semantic pair with טְלָאַיִךְ, and it needs a shift of only one vowel in M. It also fits the imagery of 1 Sam 12:1–4 (see again below). The word אַלּוּף not only means "chief" or "confidant"; it is an adjective meaning "trusting" or "tame" and is so used by Jrm in 11:19. This usage suggests we are still on the right track with our reconstruction. Finally I suggest that לְרֹאשׁ "for a head" (or the like) must be read as לְרָאשׁ (or לְרֵשׁ, or לְרָשׁ or לְרָאשׁ): this noun, "poor man," appears in Nathan's parable of the ewe lamb in 2 Sam 12:1–4. That poor man fed his ewe and gave her drink in his bosom. If the reference here is to that parable, one needs "like" (כְּ) before אַלּוּפִים (see Text). The poor man in the parable had his ewe lamb taken away from him; so the lambs of Jerusalem will be taken away. "Like those tamed" would then be an expression for "tamed like the one tamed": כְּ may be used for hypothetical comparisons, "as if" (Lam 2:22). The לְ before "poor man" is to some degree parallel with "(to) you" in v 20b: the ewe lamb had the same relation

to the poor man as the flock has to Jerusalem; or, perhaps better, it expresses the agent (GKC, sec. 121f).

The imagery of "sucklings" proposed for the third colon leads to the imagery of birth pangs in v 21b and that of rape in v 22: the reverse chronological sequence is analogous to that in Hos 9:11 ("no childbirth, no fruitful womb, no conception"). The loss of the sheep will bring on pangs as keen as those of childbirth. The form לֵדָה is a valid infinitive construct (so again Hos 9:11), but one might have expected the participle יֹלֵדָה (as in Hos 13:13, so Volz).

■ 22 The first colon is literally "And when you say in your heart"; for the expression see 5:24. For a prose equivalent of "Why have these things happened to me?" see 5:19. It is conceivable that "these (things)" (אֵלֶּה) should be revocalized to "a curse" (אָלָה, compare 2:34; 4:12; 5:25; 14:22), but there is no diction for drought in the vicinity (unless it be the "desert wind" in v 24), and the revocalization is thus risky. The first phrase in the third colon is literally "for the greatness of your guilt"; for similar expressions see 5:6; 14:7; and 30:15. The noun שׁוּל means "skirt" (Isa 6:1; "his skirts filled the temple"); here it is evidently a euphemism for the genitals. Since שׁוּלַיִךְ is repeated in v 26, it is tempting here to read שׁוֹקַיִךְ "your thigh" following the diction in Isa 47:2 (so Rudolph): it must be admitted that "your skirt" fits the verb in v 26 better than the verb here, and that "your thigh" here would fit the parallelism with עֲקֵבַיִךְ better (see below), but G gives the identical (euphemistic) translation both here and in v 26, so that it is safer to stay with M. The noun עָקֵב is literally "heel," but again "your heels" is clearly euphemistic, like "feet" in Isa 6:2 and elsewhere. This is the only instance of חמס nip'al "suffer violence" in the OT; the related noun occurs in 6:7. Here again it is clearly sexual violence that is meant: the imagery has shifted from the loss of the flock to ravishment, an image for invasion (compare "those who come in" in v 20, which may have a sexual connotation—compare the remarks on 6:3); the image will be resumed in v 26.

■ 23 Verse 23a offers two rhetorical questions which come out of the sphere of wisdom: "Does the Ethiopian change his skin, or the leopard his spots?" (for parallels see Form). The verb הפך only rarely means "change"; it is used of a diseased spot changing color in Lev 13:55. Jrm uses it of "perverting" the words of God (23:36). The

414

כּוּשִׁי (here "Ethiopian") is the inhabitant of Cush, the term for the region south of Egypt corresponding to the present-day Sudan and beyond.[4] The description of the Cushites in Isa 18:2 ("lanky and shiny") suggests members of Nilotic tribes such as inhabit southern Sudan today.[5] The traditional translation "Ethiopian," which began with G and V, is today somewhat misleading, but it may be noted that S and T use "Indian" here! The German commentators, following Luther, use "Moor."

For "leopard" (נָמֵר) see 5:6. The noun חֲבַרְבְּרֹת occurs only here in the OT; though the Versions render it by various general words for "variegated pattern," if the animal is correctly identified, it must mean "spots" (so already Rashi).

Though the English translations are accustomed to translating the first as well as the third colon with "can" ("Can the Ethiopian change his skin?"), the verb יכל appears only in the third colon, so that it is better to save the nuance of ability for that expression. The sequence of הֲ interrogative followed by גַּם ("[you] also") is, so far as I am aware, without parallel. The הֲ is the functional equivalent of "if":[6] "If the Ethiopian ever changes his skin. . . ." There are elicitation questions in the OT that are the functional equivalent of "if"-clauses ("who?" Hos 14:10; Ps 107:43; "why?" Job 3:11–13), and an instance in the Greek NT of a yes-or-no question that so functions (Jas 5:13), but this is evidently the only such instance in the OT. The particle גַּם introduces apodoses elsewhere following "if"-clauses: Gen 13:16, "If someone could count the dust of the earth, your offspring also (גַּם־זַרְעֲךָ) would be counted" (so also Jer 31:36, 37; 33:21, 26).[7]

The address in v 23b is masculine plural (see Structure). The diction is particularly close to that in 2:33 ("do good," "do ill," למד pi'el); compare also 4:22. For Christians who search the OT for evidence of the bondage of the will to sin this is a prime text. Thus Alexander MacLaren matches this text with 2 Cor 5:17 and Rev 21:5 to proclaim "An Impossibility made Possible,"[8] affirming that this text sets forth "the

unchangeableness of character, especially of faults." But Calvin carefully insists that the passage does not deny free will: "Learned men in our age do not wisely refer to this passage when they seek to prove that there is no free-will in man; for it is not simply the nature of man that is spoken of here, but the habit that is contracted by long practice." Eichrodt remarks,

> Jeremiah is the one who ponders most over the riddle of the hypnotic force with which men are attracted to evil, and indeed cannot go on living without the narcotic of sinful pleasure. He compares the enslaving power which leaves his people no more free will to the irresistible force of the mating drive in animals in season, the zeal in safeguarding the cosseting injustice to the water stored cool in the cisterns, the evil habitus which has become second nature to them, and which is impervious to all exhortation, to the colour of the Ethiopian or the markings of the leopard.[9]

Helga Weippert remarks perceptively that Jrm offers real alternatives to the people but expects them to make their decision in a particular direction.[10]

■ **24** For the shift from "you" to "them" see Text. The verb "scatter" is the same as that in 9:15.

The noun קַשׁ is "stubble," the base of the stalks left in the field after reaping. Three nouns—קַשׁ "stubble," תֶּבֶן "straw," and מֹץ "chaff"—are all waste products of the harvest, but they must be carefully distinguished,[11] as they were in postbiblical Hebrew: in *Gen. Rab.* 83 there is a parable about the straw, the stubble, and the chaff which once argued with each other, each saying, "For me the field is sown." The parable ends when the chaff is carried away by the wind, the straw is thrown on the ground, and the stubble is burned. In the OT all three may be carried away by the wind (compare Ps 1:4; Job 21:18). But קַשׁ was sought for when תֶּבֶן was forbidden in making bricks (Exod 5:12), and in contrast to the others קַשׁ is spoken of as inflammable (e.g., Isa 5:24): evidently

4   Thomas O. Lambdin, "Ethiopia," *IDB* 2:176–77.
5   See Wildberger, *Jesaja*, 689.
6   Joüon, *Gramm.*, sec. 167m.
7   König, *Syntax*, sec. 415γ.
8   Alexander MacLaren, *Expositions of Holy Scripture*, 8: *Isaiah Chapters XLIX to LXVI; Jeremiah* (New York: Hodder & Stoughton, 1906) 274–81.
9   Eichrodt, *Theology* 2, 389.
10   Weippert, *Prosareden*, 62.
11   Against H. Neil Richardson, "Chaff," *IDB* 1:549.

fields were often deliberately burned after the harvest.[12] If not burned, the stubble in a field soon dries up and is scattered by the wind (so here).[13]

The participle עוֹבֵר "passing by, vanishing" is used of chaff in Isa 29:5. The preposition לְ expresses the agent of the action (GKC, sec. 121f), as it may in v 21. For the desert wind (sirocco) see 4:11–12.

■ 25 The diction of the second colon in *M* is odd, literally "the portion of your measure from with me." "Portion" is a good parallel to "lot" (compare Ps 16:5, where מְנָת is parallel with חֵלֶק, a word standing in parallel with גּוֹרָל in Isa 17:14), but "from with me" injects an alien note.

I therefore propose to read מֵאֵתִי, literally "I have done (something) a hundredfold" (see Text); this verb is also proposed in 2:36–37 and is proposed by Dahood for three passages in the Psalms. I do not assume that all his proposals are acceptable, but the context here suggests that an expression of numeration is appropriate. Thus there is the word מִדַּיִךְ "your measure." Further the diction of the third colon, "you have forgotten me," is reminiscent of "my people have forgotten me days without number" in 2:32. As here understood, the verse suggests that far from being a punishment out of proportion to the crime (compare 10:24), the punishment leveled by Yahweh is appropriate to the instances in which the people forgot him. (Question: Should this verb also be restored in Isa 54:17?)

The pronoun "this" (זֶה) at the beginning of the verse is a little harsh but perhaps appropriate to the genre (see Form). In such expressions of enumeration כֵּן "thus" might have been expected (compare 33:22, and see below); it is noteworthy that a corrected reading in *G*[B] gives οὕτως "thus" for οὗτος "this," but this is perhaps an inner Greek shift which is coincidental.

This is the only occurrence in Jer of גּוֹרָל "lot": the term means specifically the lot cast for the division of land, and then more generally it is used for recompense or retribution (Isa 17:14). The phrase "measured portion" is synonymous.

The conjunction אֲשֶׁר, which at first seems unexpected, is appropriate to an expression of numeration (compare 33:22); it functions something like the English "inasmuch as." For "you have forgotten me" compare 2:32; for

"have trusted in the Lie" compare "trust in deceptive words [literally, words of a lie]" in 7:4. Bright suggests that שֶׁקֶר "lie" is probably a designation for Baal (compare 5:31 and 23:14); this is plausible.[14]

■ 26 Though formally the emphatic וְגַם־אֲנִי "and I too" balances גַּם־אַתֶּם "you too" in v 23, the thought goes back to v 22: the invaders (v 20) humiliate Jerusalem, but Yahweh does it too. The verb חשׂף is used of stripping the bark off trees. *M* appears to say "pulled up your skirt over your face," but "over your face" overloads the colon and spoils the image: it is not that Jerusalem is deprived of sight but that her private parts are exposed. The expression with "face" belongs at the beginning of v 27 (so Volz: see Text). For "skirt" see v 22. The noun קָלוֹן "shame" is used of the condition of disgrace (Hos 4:7 and often), but once otherwise it is used, as here, of the female pudenda (Nah 3:5).

■ 27 For the reconstruced text עַל־פָּנַי compare 6:7. This is the only occurrence of the noun נִאֻפִים in Jer (and the only other occurrence at all, Ezek 23:43, is in a difficult text); but the related verb נאף occurs frequently (qal: 3:9; 5:7; 7:9; 23:14). For "neighings" (מִצְהֲלוֹת) in a literal meaning see 8:16, and as a sign of sexual excitation see 5:8. The noun זִמָּה may mean a "plan" in general but became a technical term in cultic law for indecent conduct, especially of sexual misdeeds (Judg 20:6); this is the only occurrence in Jer. For זְנוּת "whoring" see 3:2, 9.

"On hills and in the field" is a variation on the phrase "on every high hill and under every leafy tree" (2:20). "I have seen" resonates with the passive "is to be seen" in v 26: there one expects "I have seen" after "I have pulled off your skirt," but this expression is deferred till now. For שִׁקּוּצִים "vileness" compare the same word in 4:1 and 7:30: there it refers to pagan idols, while here it refers more abstractly to Jerusalem's foul behavior with those pagan deities. (One notes also that in 4:1 the people are asked to remove their vile things מִפָּנַי "from my presence," another clue that the reconstruction at the beginning of this verse is correct.)

The phrase "woe to you," with an expression for the second person, is not common in the OT: beyond the present passage it appears in 48:46, which is a reflex of Num 21:29, and in Ezek 16:23, where it seems to be

12   Wildberger, *Jesaja*, 196.
13   For the process of reaping, threshing, and winnowing among present-day Palestinian peasants see Lucian

Turkowski, "Peasant Agriculture in the Judaean Hills," *PEQ* 101 (1969) 105–8.
14   See further Overholt, *Falsehood*, 67.

secondary (see the commentaries): it is an exclamation of distress over the situation.

"You are not clean" cannot stand alone in a colon; it must therefore be construed with "woe to you, Jerusalem" as a dependent clause (so *G* and *S*, which translate as if the clause were introduced by כִּי). The verb טהר "be (ritually) clean" is the opposite of טמא "be (ritually) unclean" (2:23, where the people say, "I am not defiled").[15] Jerusalem has made herself ritually (and morally) unclean by her whorings. Rudolph notes that the verb may also be vocalized תִּטְהֲרִי "you (do not) purify yourself," a plausible reading.

The reading of *M* in the last colon is impossible, אַחֲרֵי מָתַי עֹד, literally "after when still?" The preposition עַד "until" is often used with "when?" to mean "how long?" but there is no parallel for the expression here, nor is "when" ever followed by "still" elsewhere. One expects a verbal clause which either continues to depict the whoring of Jerusalem or which depicts Yahweh's punishment on her. If אַחֵרִים "others, strangers" is present, then we have the possibility of an imperfect verb prefixed with taw. The consonantal text yields יעד תִּיעֲדִי, תִּיעֵד or qal (see Text), and the expression evidently has reference to the collection of laws in Exod 21:8–10. There the verb יעד is a technical term: the head of a household "designates" or "makes disposition of" an Israelite slave-girl as concubine. The syntax of Exod 21:8 is by no means clear,[16] but the general meaning of the verb in question is clear enough; Exod 21:8–9 deals with cases in which the head of family considers the designation of a slave-girl, and then Exod 21:10 goes on to speak of what

happens if the head of household takes another slave-girl (אַחֶרֶת). Jrm is here suggesting a monstrous situation: Jerusalem, personified as a female, has made her designation of various sexual partners (אַחֵרִים) in a way appropriate in patriarchal Israel only to the male head of household (compare the use of זָרִים "strangers" in 2:25). If the yod was missing at the end of the verb (see again Text), it is no wonder the verb was misunderstood: who expects a feminine form? Jrm uses imagery resulting from a reversal of sex roles elsewhere as well: see 3:1; 30:6; and 31:21–22.[17]

Aim

This poem is a kaleidoscope of various kinds of words from Yahweh to the people: warnings of the coming judgment mixed with accusations, rhetorical questions that hurt and mock, references to the tender love of the city to her inhabitants and to the shocking harlotry which that city commits, harlotry which merits her public stripping and ravishment. If such words as these cannot communicate, nothing can communicate; and Yahweh is virtually convinced that the people will not change (v 23). Yahweh no doubt hopes for change, but his hope is waning fast, for the evidence he sees is without exception shameful (v 27).

---

15 See Lawrence E. Toombs, "Clean and unclean," *IDB* 1:641–48.

16 Jacob Hoftijzer, "Ex. xxi 8," *VT* 7 (1957) 388–91.

17 The reconstructed text here may be compared to my reconstruction of the last colon of Isa 1:4b, נָזֹרוּ אָחֹר "they have dedicated themselves to another (god)": see William L. Holladay, "A New Suggestion for the Crux in Isaiah i 4b," *VT* 33 (1983) 235–37.

**A Counter-Liturgy
for Drought and Battle**

Bibliography

On 14:1—17:27:
Olmo Lete, Gregorio del
"La unidad literaria de Jer 14—17," *EstBib* 30
(1971) 3–46.

On 14:1—15:9:
Beuken, W. A. M., and H. W. M. van Grol
"Jeremiah 14,1—15,9: A Situation of Distress and
Its Hermeneutics, Unity and Diversity of Form—
Dramatic Development," *Le Livre de Jérémie, Le
prophète et son milieu, Les oracles et leur transmission*
(ed. Pierre-Maurice Bogaert; BETL 54; Leuven:
Leuven University, 1981) 297–342.
Castellino
"Observations," 406–7.
Fohrer, Georg
"Abgewiesene Klage und untersagte Fürbitte in Jer
14,2—15,2," *Künder des Wortes: Beiträge zur
Theologie der Propheten; Josef Schreiner zum 60.
Geburtstag* (ed. Lothar Ruppert et al.; Würzburg:
Echter, 1982) 77–86.
Kessler, Martin
"From Drought to Exile: A Morphological Study
of Jer. 14:1—15:4," *Amsterdamse cahiers voor exegese
en Bijbelse theologie* 2 (Kampen: Kok, 1981) 68–85.
Reventlow
Liturgie, 149–88.

On 14:1–6:
Holladay
"Style," 51–52.
Marenof, Shlomo A.
"A Note on Jer 14:4," *AJSL* 55 (1938) 198–200.

On 14:10–16:
Meyer
Jeremia, 47–65.
Weippert
Prosareden, 79–80.

On 14:17–18:
Thomas, D. Winton
"A Note on ולא ידעו in Jeremiah xiv 18," *JTS* 39
(1938) 273–74.

On 14:19–22:
Dahood, Mitchell
"Emphatic *lamedh* in Jer 14:21 and Ezek 34:19,"
CBQ 37 (1975) 341–42.

On 15:5–9:
Berridge
  pp. 176–79.
Christensen
  Transformations, 192–93.

14

1   This has come as the word of Yahweh to
        Jeremiah concerning the drought:
2   Judah has dried up,
        and her gates languish,
            they are dark to the ground,
                and the outcry of Jerusalem rises.
3   And《 her nobles 》[a] send [b] their menials[b]
        for water:
        they go to the cisterns
            but[c] find no water;
                their vessels come back empty.
    They are ashamed and humiliated
        and cover their heads.
4   〈In her yield the soil〉[a] is dismayed,
        since there has been no rain on the
            land;
        the farmhands are ashamed
            and[b] cover their heads.
5   Yes, even the doe calves in the field and
        abandons,
        since there has been no grass,
6   and the wild asses stand on the caravan-
        tracks,
        they gasp for breath like the crocodile,
            their eyes fade,
                since there is no pasture.
7   (Even) if our iniquities have testified
        against us, Yahweh,
        act, for your name's sake.
    So many are our turnings,
        we have (so) sinned against you!
8   O hope of Israel, [a]O Yahweh,[a]
        her savior in time of distress,
    why are you like a stranger in the land,
        and like a traveler stopping for the night?
9   Why are you like a helpless man,
        like a champion who cannot save?
    You are indeed in our midst, Yahweh,
        and we bear your name: do not leave
            us!
10 Thus Yahweh has said to this people:
        So have they loved to wander,
            they have not spared their feet;
    But Yahweh has not approved them:
        now he shall remember their iniquity
            and deal with their sin.
11/ And Yahweh said to me, Do not pray
    for this people for (their) good: 12/ even if
    they fast, I will not listen to their cry, and
    even if they offer up a burnt offering or a
    cereal offering, I will not approve them;
    for by sword, famine and pestilence I am
    destroying them.
13/ But I said, "Ah Lord Yahweh, look, the
    prophets are saying to them,
    You shall not see sword,

Text

14:3a   Reading וְאַדִּרֵיהָ with *G* for *M* וְאַדִּרֵיהֶם "and their
        nobles." *M* is not impossible, but two -*hem* suffixes in
        the same colon are heavy, and "her gates" in v 2
        gives warrant for reading "her nobles" here. *M* will
        have arisen by dittography.

b—b   Reading צְעִירֵיהֶם with the qere' for the ketib
        צעוריהם, which seems to be simply a mistake. But
        48:4 has an identical qere'-ketib issue with the same
        noun: is this simply a coincidence?

c   Read וְ with many MSS. and *G*, *S*, and *T*; *M* lacks
        the conjunction.

4a   *M* in this colon is dubious ("because of the soil
        [which] is dismayed"); the simplest emendation,
        adopted here, is a suggestion of Michaelis, building
        on Houbigant (1753): בַּעֲבוּרָה אֲדָמָה (for עָבוּר "yield"
        see Josh 5:11, 12); see Condamin. For discussion see
        Interpretation.

b   Reading וְ with many MSS. and *S*; *M* omits the
        conjunction, but it is present in the same wording of
        v 3.

8a—a *M* lacks "O Yahweh," but some MSS. have it, *G*
        has it, and 17:13 has it.

nor famine shall you have,
but ªtrustworthy peaceª I shall give
you in this place.
14/ But Yahweh said to me, It is a lie which
the prophets prophesy in my name: I did
not send them, nor command them, nor
speak to them; it is a lying vision, ª worthless divination,ª the deceptionᵇ of their
mind that they prophesy to you. **15/**
Therefore thus Yahweh has said concerning the prophets who prophesy [in
my name,ᵇ though I did not send them,
yet they say,]ª "Sword and famine shall
not occur in this land": By sword and by
famine those prophets shall perish. **16/**
And the people to whom they prophesy
shall remain cast out in the streets of
Jerusalem because of famine and sword,
and there shall be no one to bury them—
[they, their wives and their sons and
daughters;]ª I shall pour out upon them
their wickedness. **17/** And you shall say
to them this word.

Let my eyes run down with tears,
  night and day [and]ª let them not stop;
(with) what a great fracture is broken my
    fair [maiden]ᵇ people,
  (with what) a very sore wound!

18   If I should go out to the field,
      look: those slain by sword!
      And if I should go into the city,
        look: diseases of famine!
    For both prophet and priest peddle (their
      wares),
      to the Land (where)ª they have no
      knowledge.

19   Have you really rejected Judah?
      Does your heart abhor Zion?
        Why, then, have you struck us down,
        and we have no healing?
    [To think of longing for well-being when
      there is no good,
    andᵇ for a time of healing when look:
      terror!]ª

20   We know, Yahweh, our guilt,
      the iniquity of our fathers,
      how we have sinned against you!

21   Do not spurn, for your name's sake,
      doª not disdain your glorious throne;
      remember, do not break, your
      covenant with us.

22   Are there among the non-gods of the
      nations any rain-bringers?
      Can the heavens ever give showers?
    Is it not you, Yahweh,
      our God,ª for whom we long?ª
        Indeed it is you who have made the
        whole ⟨curse.⟩ᵇ

15

1/ And Yahweh said to me: Even if Moses
or Samuel were to stand before me, I
would have no heart for this people:
ªsend them outª from my presence so that
they may go away. **2/** And when they say
to you, "Where are we going?" you shall
say to them, Thus Yahweh has said:

13a—a   *M* reads שְׁלוֹם אֱמֶת, literally "peace of trust-
    worthiness," but a few MSS. and *S* read שָׁלוֹם וֶאֱמֶת
    "peace and trustworthiness," as does 33:6; further-
    more *G* reads the two terms, linked by "and," in
    reverse order. If the reading with "and" is correct,
    the expression is an hendiadys, so that the meaning
    is clear.

14a—a   Literally "divination and worthlessness,"
    another hendiadys. The ketib reading for "worth-
    lessness" is אֱלוּל, doubtless a spelling error for qere'
    אֱליל.

b   Reading qere' תַּרְמִית; ketib תַּרְמוּת is doubtless a
    spelling error.

15–16a   For these two glosses see Interpretation.

b   *G* adds "lies" = שֶׁקֶר here, compare v 14 and
    23:25; the reading may be correct.

17a   "Let them not stop" cannot stand alone in a colon,
    so that "night and day" belongs with it: the "and" is
    evidently dittographic.

b   Omit with *G*; the word overloads the colon.

18a   Omitting וֹ "and" with many MSS., with *G*, *V*, and
    *T*ᶠ. The reading preferred is a stronger text, open to
    multiple meanings (see Interpretation).

19a   These words are a duplicate of 8:15. In that
    passage they are understood as Jrm's word (see
    there); they fit poorly here in the context of words
    of the people. Further, one suspects that the
    duplication of "healing" in this verse is not accept-
    able style (so also Berridge, p. 104, against Rudolph,
    who judges the words to be original here and
    unoriginal in 8:15, and against Bright, who accepts
    the words in both passages).

b   Many MSS. and *G* and *T* omit "and" as in 8:15.

21a   Many MSS. and *V* and *S* prefix "and" to this colon.

22a—a   *M* reads וֹ "and" after "God"; in that case "our
    God" is to be read with the preceding colon, and
    this colon translated "and we long for you." But it is
    better to omit "and" with one MS. of *G* and with *V*
    (so also Volz, Rudolph).

b   Vocalizing אֵלֶה for *M* אֵלֶּה "these" ("Indeed it is
    you who have made all these"); see Interpretation.

15:1a—a   For *M* שַׁלַּח "send out" (without object) read
    שַׁלְּחֵם with *V* and *S*; the mem evidently dropped out
    by haplography.

Those (marked) for Death, to Death,
  those (marked) for the sword, to the
    sword,
    those (marked) for famine, to famine,
    [and those (marked) for exile, to
      exile.]ᵃ
3/And I shall appoint over them four sorts
  (of destroyers)—oracle of Yahweh: the
  sword to slay, the dogs to drag off, and
  the birds of the heavens and the beasts
  of the earth to devour and destroy. 4/
  And I shall make them a terrorᵃ to all the
  kingdoms of the earth, [on account of
  Manasseh, son of Hezekiah, king of
  Judah, because of ᶜall thatᶜ he did in
  Jerusalem.]ᵇ

5 So who will pity you, Jerusalem,
     who will grieve for you,
       and who will turn aside to ask
         about your well-being?

6 It is you who have forsaken me,
                    oracle of Yahweh,
     you have walked away from me;
   and I have stretched out my hand over
       you and destroyed you:
     I am tired of retracting.ᵃ

7 I have winnowed them with a pitchfork
     at the gates of the Land;
       I have made my people childless,
         wiped them out
           from their ways of no return.

8 ᵃ Their widowsᵃ have become for me
       more
       than the sand of the seas;
     I have brought in [to them]ᵇ upon the
       mother of young men the devas-
         tator at noon,
     I have thrown down ᶜupon herᶜ sud-
       denly agitation and terror.

9 She languishes who has borne seven,
     her breath gasps out its life,
       her sun ᵃis setᵃ while yet day,
         she is ashamed and abashed:
   and their remnant I shall give to the sword
     before their enemies
                    oracle of Yahweh.

2a   The words are a secondary addition (see Inter-
      pretation); captivity is not a death.
4a   On the four occasions when this word appears in
      Jer (here; 24:9; 29:18; 34:17) the ketib is זועה,
      evidently זֲעָה (Isa 38:19), and the qere' is זֲוָעָה. The
      form preserved here in the qere' is also the sole
      form in Ezek 23:46 and 2 Chr 29:8. Since the root
      is זוע, the original form is doubtless זֲוָעָה.
b   The bracketed material is secondary (see Inter-
      pretation).
c—c   Read with a few MSS. and G, V, and S (and
      evidently T as well, which paraphrases) כָּל־אֲשֶׁר for
      M אֲשֶׁר.
6a   For M הִנָּחֵם (נחם nip'al) G and S have הַנִּחָם
      "letting them go" (נוח II hip'il). This is a very
      attractive possibility, given the use of that verb in
      14:9: the statement would then be Yahweh's ironic
      granting of the earlier request. See Interpretation.
8a—a M אלמנתו must be construed as an aberrant
      spelling of "his widows" (V); but read אַלְמְנֹתָם
      (compare GKC, sec. 91n) with G, S, and T; the mem
      evidently dropped out by haplography.
b   Omit with G; the word overloads the colon and
      adds nothing (so also Duhm, Cornill, Giesebrecht,
      Condamin, Bright); it may be dittographic from
      עַל־אֵם.
c—c   A few MSS. and S and T read אֲלֵיהֶם "upon them"
      for עָלֶיהָ, a reading to be rejected: the word is
      parallel to "upon the mother."
9a—a "Sun" may be either masculine or feminine: the
      ketib is a feminine verb and the qere' masculine.
      Gen 19:23 has a similar contrast between the
      Samaritan text and M.

Preliminary Observations

In dealing with 14:1—15:9 questions of structure, form, and setting are mutually dependent, and commentators have taken a variety of options in the approach to this section.

Some have simply assumed a collection of disparate pieces, "a mixed collection of oracles."[1] Any order or unity perceived here will then be a secondary one. This is the approach of Duhm, Skinner, John W. Miller,[2] and Bright.

Others have been impressed by the rubric "You shall say to them this word" at the beginning of 14:17 and have seen 14:1–16 and 14:17ff as two separate units: there is in each case a word of desolation (the drought,

---

1   Skinner, p. 128.
2   John W. Miller, *Das Verhältnis Jeremias und Hesekiels   sprachlich und theologisch untersucht* (Assen: Van Gorcum, 1955) 51.

14:2–6; Jrm's lament over the desolation of the land, 14:17–18), followed by a lament of the people (14:7–9; 14:19–22), followed in turn by Yahweh's prohibition to Jrm against interceding (14:11–12) and his word that he will accept no intercession from anyone (15:1): Yahweh's word to Jrm is rounded off by 14:16 and 15:4. This is the conclusion of Weiser.[3]

But the very parallels between 14:2–16 and 14:17—15:4 have led most commentators to assume a unity for the two sections (Volz, Rudolph, Eissfeldt[4]).

Others have seen no reason to exclude 15:5–9 from the sequence and have therefore seen it to comprise 14:1—15:9 (so Giesebrecht, Reventlow,[5] and recently Beuken and van Grol[6]). This will be the option taken in the present study, on the basis of fresh data.

Commentators likewise diverge as to what the purpose of this material was. Many assume that Jrm here functions as a cult prophet, composing a liturgy for the people at a time of national emergency.[7] In this way the passage would function as Joel 1—2 doubtless did. But the word of Yahweh in the Book of Joel is a word of good news (Joel 2;18–27, whether that material is primary or added secondarily),[8] whereas the word from Yahweh in this sequence is a word of bad news. One is then faced with the possibility here that the sequence is to be understood as an imitation liturgy, a counter-liturgy as a vehicle for the judgment of Yahweh (Eissfeldt considers this option,[9] and it is the conclusion of Rudolph).

Much depends upon the extent to which the sequence offers an internal structure. Though form-critically 14:2–6; 14:17–18; and 15:5–9 offer different speakers (Jrm speaks in 14:17–18, Yahweh speaks in 15:5–9, or at least in 15:6–9, the speaker is undeclared in 14:2–6), these three passages function identically in the sequence, to declare the nature of the emergency. The emergency in 14:2–6 is the drought; in 15:5–9 it is a military catastrophe in which widows increase in number and mothers are bereft of their soldier sons. But drought implies famine (thus the implication of 14:4), and 14:17–

18, the central section, speaks of the emergency as both sword and famine. This central section thus binds 14:2–6 and 15:5–9 together. Both the outer two have references, it would appear, to the gates of Sheol (14:2 by implication; 15:7 specifically, and perhaps several others in that section: for the details see Interpretation), and 14:18 also seems to have a reference to Sheol. There is a strong probability, then, that these three passages must be understood together; it would seem, in fact, that 18:21 is an outline for the three.

Both laments of the people likewise share phraseology: "we have sinned against you" (14:7, חָטָאנוּ לְךָ; 14:20, חָטָאנוּ לָךְ), the use of the root "long for" (קוה: 14:8, מִקְוֵה; 14:22, וּנְקַוֶּה).

And there is not only a parallelism of substance between 14:11–12 and 15:1 (no intercession) but a parallelism of diction as well: אֵינֶנִּי שֹׁמֵעַ אֶל־רִנָּתָם (14:12) and אֵין נַפְשִׁי אֶל־הָעָם הַזֶּה (15:1).

Given these structural features, the most plausible solution is to view the whole complex, 14:1—15:9, as a unity drafted at one time for a specific setting, a counter-liturgy as an expression of the judgment of Yahweh (for the details see Setting).

The unity proposed here for 14:1—15:9 then raises the question about the relation of this complex to 11:18—12:6 and 15:10–21, the confessional material which precedes and follows it. Thus the link between 15:10 ("my mother") and 12:6 ("your father") is so apt that it is difficult to believe it to be other than intentional. On the other hand, one can assume that 15:10 is linked to 15:8 and 9 ("mother," ילד "give birth"), a link first proposed by Hitzig and more recently by Rudolph,[10] and the description of the drought in 14:2–6 can be linked just as easily to 12:4, with its brief description of the drought. One may note also that both 15:1 and 15:19 offer the phrase עמד לִפְנֵי "stand before (Yahweh) [as messenger]": in 15:1 Moses and Samuel are referred to as standing before Yahweh, while in 15:19 it is Jrm who is to stand before him. Thus both models are available:

3   Weiser, p. 121.
4   Eissfeldt, *Introduction*, 355–56.
5   Reventlow, *Liturgie*, 150–53.
6   Beuken and van Grol.
7   So Aage Bentzen, *Introduction to the Old Testament* (Copenhagen: Gad, 1952) I, 164; Reventlow, esp. p. 186; Eissfeldt, *Introduction*, 356; Weiser.
8   On this problem see Wolff, *Joel and Amos*, 57–59.

9   Eissfeldt, *Introduction*, 356.
10   Compare the discussion in Hubmann, *Untersuchungen*, 302–4.

that which sees the two collections of the confessions as having had an independent unity, and that which understands the present complex—a liturgy of drought and battle—as being linked with the preceding and following confessional collections from the beginning; on balance the second alternative is better—to see both the confessional collections and the intervening liturgy as having been brought together in the same editorial process.

Structure

General Structure. For the extent of the sequence and its link with the confessional material before and after it, see Preliminary Observations, where some of the structure of the sequence is also set forth. That structure is as follows:

(1a) description of the drought (14:2–6);

(1b) lament of the people (14:7–9);

(1c) Yahweh's judgment on the people (14:10), his prohibition to Jrm against intercession (14:11–12), Jrm's puzzlement about the false prophets (14:13), and Yahweh's judgment on the false prophets (14:14–16), all in prose;

(2a) Jrm's lament over the people regarding sword and famine (14:17–18);

(2b) lament of the people (14:19–22);

(2c) Yahweh's refusal to accept intercession (15:1), and Yahweh's judgment on the people (15:2–4), all in prose;

(3) Yahweh's judgment on the people by sword (15:5–9).

As is indicated in Preliminary Observations, there are close ties between (1a), (2a), and (3); between (1b) and (2b); and between (1c) and (2c).

The sequence manifests not only this symmetry but a sense of heightening as one moves from 14:2–16 to 14:17—15:4;[11] thus one moves from the drought itself (14:2–6) to both sword and famine (14:17–18), from a concern for the prophets alone (14:13–16) to prophet and priest (14:18), from an acknowledgment of the sins of the present generation (14:7) to an acknowledgment of the sins of the fathers as well (14:20), from a simple prohibition to Jrm not to intercede for the people (14:11–12) to an insistence that even Moses and Samuel

would not turn Yahweh's head now (15:1); and finally to a horrifying description of the loss to be sustained from a battle, a description that includes not just one hint of Sheol (as in 14:2; 14:18), but several scattered all the way through the final passage (15:5–9).

Structure of 14:2–6. These five verses make up a poem of great compactness and intensity. The general structure is: v 2, four cola of a description of Judah and Jerusalem; v 3, six cola describing the shame of the nobles; v 4, four cola describing the shame of the farmhands; and vv 5–6, six cola describing the death of the animals. The last two cola of v 3 are widely thought to be secondary, since *G* omits them and they are largely duplicated in v 4; but the symmetry just outlined encourages a confidence in *M* at this point. The two central sections (vv 3–4) are thus united by the two cola describing the shame of the nobles and of the farmhands (v 3bβ, v 4b). The last two sections are bound together by the three ‫כי‬ clauses in vv 4, 5, and 6 which offer steady compression of expression ("since there has been no rain on the land," "since there has been no grass," "since there is no pasture": see vv 5–6, Interpretation).

The parallelisms within each verse are so many that in some instances it is difficult to be sure which cola are parallel to which. Thus in v 2 the two proper names "Judah" and "Jerusalem" are parallel, leaving "her gates" the subject in the second colon and therefore doubtless the third as well (see Interpretation). But at the same time "has dried up" is in parallel with "languish" in the first and second cola, and "to the land" suggests a contrast to "rises." (There is no warrant to the proposal of Duhm and Cornill to shift the fourth colon to the first position!) And in v 3 the first and third cola are parallel in offering "water," and the second and third in offering the verbs "go" and "come back." But the assymetry of subjects—"nobles" in the first colon, "menials" in the second and third, leads to a perception of a similar shift in the fourth colon, where "vessels" is the subject (see Interpretation). The first and sixth cola stand apart, and, as already noted, are tied closely to the last two cola of v 4.

In v 4, the last two cola are in close parallelism, but "ashamed" in the third colon is balanced by "is dismayed" in the first colon, the subject of which is "the soil." This leaves the second colon, the כִּי clause, more independent, anticipating similar cola in vv 5 and 6 (see above).

Verses 5 and 6 round off the poem by descriptions of the doe and the wild asses; the first colon of v 5 and first three cola of v 6 describe the unexpected behavior of the animals in parallelisms that bring mounting horror.

Structure of 14:7–9. Structurally this is a simpler poem, in six bicola. The main rhetorical feature that binds the passage together are the vocatives, "Yahweh." There is a vocative in v 7a: Rudolph (*BHS*) has it begin the second colon; but this seems dubious—in Ps 109:21a the vocative is clearly in the first colon, and the second colon begins with the imperative עֲשֵׂה, a colon very similar to the second one here. Then there is a vocative "Yahweh" at the end of the third colon of v 9, balancing the first vocative. And it is plausible to supply a third vocative at the end of the first colon of v 8 (see Text). Beyond these binding vocatives the structure is defined more by content and the consequent form-critical subdivisions. Verse 7a outlines the two foci of the poem—the acknowledgment of sin (the first colon) and the appeal for help to Yahweh (the second). Verse 7b then embodies the acknowledgment of sin as a central affirmation. The rest of the poem is an elaborate appeal for help (vv 8–9), the central feature of which is four cola of similes for Yahweh's lack of prowess, introduced by the twofold "why?" (vv 8b–9a). See further Form.

Structure of 14:10. The first clause of the verse is evidently not a rubric standing outside the structure but is integral to the structure. The poem will then consist of two tricola, linked by "Yahweh" in the first colon of each. The quotation takes up the second and third cola of v 10a. The second tricolon (v 10b) is a quotation of the middle portion of Hos 8:13, so it, too, in a sense, is a quotation of Yahweh's. (*G* omits the last colon, but there is no need to reject it: "iniquity" and "sin" are picked up from v 7.)

Structure of 14:11–12, 13, 14. The word from Yahweh to Jrm (vv 11–12) is hardly long enough to offer a structure of its own (see Form). Jrm's protest to Yahweh (v 13) is likewise short, though his quotation of the prophets gives the suggestion of a tricolon. Yahweh's answer to Jrm (v 14) offers a hint of chiasmus, the two

participles of נבא (nip'al and hitpa'el) bracketing a triad of negative verbs and what appears to be a triad of designations of empty words ("lying vision . . .").

Structure of 14:15–16. These verses offer a balance to each other when the glosses are removed (see Interpretation): the two occurrences of the participle נִבְּאִים "(who) prophesy" at the beginning of each verse, the balance of "sword and famine" in v 15 and "famine and sword" in v 16; the possibility of a balance between "this land" (v 15) and "those prophets" (v 16).[12]

Structure of 14:17–18. For v 17aα see Interpretation. The emotional poem that follows offers its share of difficulty in structure. "Let them not stop" counts only as a single word, so that "night and day" must precede it to make up the second colon: one can only assume that "and" before אַל is a copyist's error (see Text). Verse 17 will then consist of two bicola (so also Rudolph). Verse 18a is clearly a tetracolon. The analysis of v 18b depends to some degree on exegesis of the words. The compound subject and the verb must stay together in one colon (against Rudolph); for the last colon see Interpretation.

Structure of 14:19–22. This poem appears symmetrical. Thus both v 20 and v 21 are tricola (v 20: "guilt," "iniquity," "sin"; v 21, three prohibitions). If one excises v 19b (see Text), what is left in v 19a is four cola offering the threefold question form הֲ, אִם, מַדּוּעַ (compare 2:14, 19; 8:19, 22; 22:28; 49:1). The last colon of v 20 and the last colon of v 22 are introduced by כִּי, and v 22 offers הֲ and אִם in its first two cola to balance the first two cola of v 19: in short, the poem breaks into two halves, vv 19–20 and vv 21–22.

Structure of 15:1–4. This section, like 14:11–16, is in prose, though there is the obvious triple parallelism in the saying of v 2. And, one wonders: Did Jrm have in mind the parallelism of "three plus four" in vv 2–3 such as is found in Amos 1:3 and its parallels through Amos 2:6, and in Prov 30:15, 18, 21, 29?

Structure of 15:5–9. The structure of the final section is not easy to set forth. Verses 5–6 embody two groups of four cola with an address to Jerusalem in the second-person singular feminine; this address does not recur in the rest of the poem. (There is no reason to see two poems here, however.)[13] Verses 7–8aα offer six cola of

---

12 Compare Weippert, *Prosareden*, 79.
13 Compare Berridge, p. 176 n. 334.

reference to "them," third-person plural masculine, and this reference recurs in the last two cola of v 9. Sandwiched between are six cola (vv 8aβb–9a) where the reference is to the parallel "mother" and "she who has borne seven." These parallel feminine singular subjects come in the first colon of v 8aβb and the first colon of v 9a, and this fact renders misguided the attempt of several commentators to rearrange cola in these verses (see Interpretation). With respect to content rather than structure the reference to "their widows" in v 8aα leads into the reference to "the mother of young men" in v 8aβb, so that in a sense the two images are parallel. The poem is not symmetrical: the center of gravity is strongly toward the end, giving an emotional climax to the sequence; in this way the poem matches the one in 14:2–6.

Form

This study understands the passage to embody a counter-liturgy, Jrm's imitation of the official liturgy of the people in time of need (see Preliminary Observations); compare in this regard Jrm's imitations of Deuteronomic recitation in 7:21–29 and 11:1–17. For the occasion of this counter-liturgy see Setting.

Form of 14:2–6. This description of the drought does not specify a speaker. It could be the people: disaster reports often take up much of the content of communal laments (Joel 1:4–12; Ps 74:4–9; Lam 5:2–18; and often). It could be Jrm himself (so most commentators; see, for example, Rudolph). But if the symmetry analyzed in Preliminary Observations is sound, this passage should match 15:5–9. In that section Yahweh is the speaker, so he is likely to be the speaker here. The match of "she is ashamed" in 15:9 with "they are ashamed," said of both the nobles and the farmhands here (vv 3, 4), reinforces that likelihood.

Form of 14:7–9. The essential genre here is a communal plea for help, appropriate to communal laments. There is one surprise here, however: the first colon of v 7 is an admission of sin, and the last two cola of that verse are a confession of sin; such confessions are sometimes found in individual laments (Ps 51:7) but are hardly to be found in the communal laments of the Psalms. Thus Lam

4:13 contains an admission of sin, but one is more likely to find a declaration of innocence in communal laments, and a salvation oracle (*Heilsorakel*) is usually expected. Leopold Sabourin remarks, "Gradually the Israelites learned to interpret even divine punishment as medicinal and the *Heilsorakel* was entirely replaced by the confession of sins and a begging for forgiveness (cf. Ezr 9:5ff; Dn 9:5f)."[14] The second colon of v 7 and the last phrase of v 9 are petitions for help. Verse 8a and v 9b (until the last phrase) offer vocative appellations of Yahweh, hymnic elements such as are found in laments (compare Ps 17:7, where "savior" likewise appears). Verses 8b–9a offer an elaborate set of "why?" questions, frequent in laments (Ps 44:24–25, part of a communal lament, offers a similar pair). The similes in these questions, however, are almost without parallel: the only comparable passage which I can locate is Job 19:22, in which Job compares his friends to God: "Why do you, like God, pursue me? Why are you not satisfied with my flesh?"

Form of 14:10. The general context of this poem is juridical: the second and third cola are an accusation, the fourth is a verdict of rejection by Yahweh, and the last two are the announcement of punishment.[15] The fact that the last three cola are a quotation from Hos 8:13 lends resonance to the passage: an old verdict and an old declaration of punishment have now been reactivated.

Form of 14:11–12. The passage is a message from Yahweh to Jrm in the form of a prohibition against his exercising one of the functions of his prophetic office, namely intercession. The prohibition (v 11) opens the passage, and it closes with the announcement of judgment introduced by כִּי (v 12b: "for by sword . . ."). These bracket two parallel pairs of protasis-apodosis clauses ("when," "then") that are modeled after covenantal conditions ("if/when you do this, I shall do that"); for the form compare Exod 22:22, 26.[16] But these formulations have negative apodoses ("I will not listen to their cry"; "I will not approve them"); the covenantal relationship has been broken, and the formulations have become judgmental instruction. Exactly the same form is to be found in Isa 1:15.

Form of 14:13–16. Jrm's word to Yahweh (v 13) begins with the expression of dismay, "Ah, Lord Yahweh,"

---

14   Leopold Sabourin, *The Psalms, Their Origin and Meaning* (New York: Alba House, 1974) 296.

15   See Wolff, *Hosea*, 136, 145.

16   See in general Muilenburg, "Covenantal Formulations," 351–55.

which appears in 1:6 and 4:10. This verse is not exactly
an intercession, as Reventlow and Berridge claim it is;[17]
Jrm has just been forbidden to intercede (v 11). But Jrm
does raise the issue how the people can be held responsible when they are receiving contradictory words from
those claiming to speak a valid word from Yahweh; it is a
kind of plea for extension (compare 4:10, Form). Verse
14 embodies Yahweh's assessment of these false
prophets: he denies having authorized them to speak. It
is almost a declaration of innocence (compare 7:22;
23:21); for Jrm's declarations of innocence see 15:17a;
17:16a. In vv 15–16 there is a divine judgment speech
concerning the false prophets and the people who listen
to them.

Form of 14:17–18. These verses make up a lament
spoken by Jrm; the diction of v 17 is paralleled in Lam
2:18 and 3:49. The lament employs what might be called
the "motif of alternative deaths" in v 18a. This motif no
doubt has its origin in real-life situations (2 Kgs 7:4) but
is shaped by folk wisdom (the pre-Deuteronomic curse, 1
Kgs 14:11; 16:4; 21:24).[18] The motif is similar to that of
"alternative meetings with Yahweh" found in Amos 9:2–
4 and Ps 139:8–12: those passages, like the present one,
offer אִם "if" for the conditions; and one may note Jesus'
parable of the Children in the Marketplace (Matt 11:16–
17 = Luke 7:31–32)—neither alternative is satisfactory.
In v 18b the כִּי clause introduces what sounds like a
divine indictment but in the context of Jrm's lament can
only be an admission of corporate guilt.

Form of 14:19–22. Like 14:7–9, this passage is a
communal lament.[19] The first two cola of v 19 are
reproachful questions to Yahweh. Similar diction is to be
found in Lam 5:22, though the syntax there is difficult,
and it is by no means certain that that verse embodies a
question, as *RSV* has it.[20] For the question "why?" in
laments, compare the treatment of Form for 12:1 and
14:7–8. Verse 20 is an admission of sin, for which see
above, on the first colon of v 7. Verse 21 is a petition for
help (compare the second colon of v 7 and the last

portion of v 9); the vetitive ("do not . . .") phrases are
similar to that found in Ps 79:8, another communal
lament, and the request to "remember" the bond
between Yahweh and Israel is reminiscent of Ps 25:6–7,
an individual lament. Verse 22a brings rhetorical
questions about the ability of pagan gods to bring rain,
questions which expect the answer no. One can find
rhetorical questions elsewhere that underline the unique
work of God (for example, Eccl 7:13), and many affirmations that Yahweh is the bringer of rain (5:24) and
that he brings fertility while the Baals do not (Hos 2:7,
10); but there are no rhetorical questions elsewhere
comparable to these. Verse 22b closes the lament with
hymnic affirmations similar to those in v 9b; the phrase
אַתָּה־הוּא "it is you" is found in Ps 44:5, part of a communal lament.

Form of 15:1–4. Yahweh's reply to the communal
lament is refusal (v 1a), taking the form of a concessive
contrary-to-fact protasis and negative apodosis ("Even if
X were to happen, I would not do Y"): parallel instances,
with a human subject in the apodosis, are Num 22:18
and 1 Kgs 13:8, and with divine subject in a positive
apodosis, Amos 9:2–4. Verse 1b is a judgment on the
people couched in the form of a command to Jrm to
carry out the punishment (compare 6:9, 11). Verse 2
takes the form of the question-and-answer scheme
already seen in 5:19 and 13:12–14:[21] the question-and-
answer scheme is cast as part of a speech of Yahweh
directed to the prophet, with (1) a setting ("And when
they say to you"), (2) the question ("Where are we
going?"), and (3) the answer (the balance of the verse).
The answer is of course part of a pronouncement of
judgment, a pronouncement which continues through vv
3–4a. Verse 4b is a secondary explanation for the
judgment.

Form of 15:5–9. It is clear that the passage ends in
judgment (at least vv 7–9), whether the words are taken
as an announcement of judgment to come (in which case
the verbs are "prophetic perfects"),[22] or whether they are

17 Reventlow, *Liturgie*, 123; Berridge, pp. 110–11 n.
   210.
18 See von Rad, *Studies in Deuteronomy*, 82–83;
   Weinfeld, *Deuteronomy*, 131–32.
19 Berridge, p. 168.
20 For a thorough discussion of the syntax of that verse
   see Delbert R. Hillers, *Lamentations* (AB 7A; Garden
   City, NY: Doubleday, 1972) 100–101.
21 Long, "Schemata," 134–38.
22 GKC, sec. 106n.

taken as judgment in process (as Beuken and van Grol believe).[23] But vv 5–6 have taken diction from other genres.

The first question is the identity of the speaker. Verse 5 appears to be in lament (qinah) meter, so Berridge believes that Jrm is uttering a lament in that verse and that Yahweh replies in vv 6–9.[24] But there is no reason to divide the poem by speaker: neither 14:2–6 nor 14:17–18 shifts speaker, and there are good reasons to assume that 15:5–9 was conceived to balance those two passages (see Structure).

Yahweh may indeed offer a sincere lament over Jerusalem: such a genre is found in 9:9–10 and 12:7–13. But what is here seems to be a bit different. The closest parallels to the rhetorical questions in v 5 are found in Isa 51:19 and Nah 3:7. Beuken and van Grol, noting the use of the verbs "condole" and "comfort" in those parallel passages, speak of a genre of condolence here;[25] but Nah 3:7 is surely Yahweh's mockery over Nineveh, and Isa 51:19 is a retrospective look at what Jerusalem underwent: Yahweh is there either quoting the city's lament over itself[26] or quoting the enemy's mockery over the city. Whether sincere condolence lies ultimately behind this form of words or not, it seems clear that Yahweh is mocking Jerusalem, particularly if there is a pun on Sheol (see Interpretation). Yahweh can use lament meter for a mocking lament or condolence as well as for a sincere one.

Verse 6a expresses Yahweh's indictment, as so often in chapters 2—6 (compare the indictment, also with emphatic אַתְּ, in 3:1). The balance of the poem, as already noted, consists of a long proclamation of judgment, mostly with first-person singular verbs, but the long toll of those verbs is broken by verbs whose subject is the people or a portion of them (vv 8a, 9a) describing their decimation and humiliation.

Setting

I propose that the date of the emergency that gave rise to this counter-liturgy was November/December 601. Several interlocking bits of evidence contribute to the hypothesis.

(1) The only instances in which "fasting" is mentioned in Jer are in 14:12 and in 36:6 and 9. Rudolph points out[27] that there were evidently no regular days of fasting in Judah until the time of the exile, when such days were established to remember the tragedy of the fall of Jerusalem (Zech 7:3, 5; 8:19); the day of atonement in the form in which it is described in Leviticus 16 was evidently a development of the postexilic period,[28] and in any case "afflict oneself" (Lev 16:29) does not specify fasting, even though it was eventually assumed to imply it. Passages elsewhere similar to 14:12 in which Yahweh states that he will not pay attention to the people in spite of their cultic observances (7:16; Isa 1:15) do not mention fasting; one is thus left with the impression that the reference in 14:12 is to a memorable public event associated with a crisis (compare Joel 1:14, on the occasion of a locust plague). It is plausible then to associate 14:12 with 36:6, 9, even though the nature of the emergency that gave rise to the fast narrated in chapter 36 is not specified and even though the association of 14:12 with the drought described in 14:2–6 is only contextual.

(2) The fast (36:9) was declared in the ninth month (thus Chislev = November/December) of either the fifth year of Jehoiakim (M: the year would be 604) or the eighth year of Jehoiakim (G: 601). In the Mishna (m. Ta'an. 1:5) it is stated, "If the first of Chislev was come and no rain had fallen, the court enjoins on the congregation three days of fasting." It is plausible then to suggest that a drought was a motivation for that fast.

(3) Lohfink argues persuasively that the reading of G is correct in 36:9.[29] In November/December 604 there was a military emergency in Judah. The Babylonian Chronicle reports that Nebuchadrezzar had mustered his army in Sivan (May/June) of that year and marched west, sacking Ashkelon in Chislev of 604 and destroying

---

23   Beuken and van Grol, p. 320.
24   Berridge, p. 177.
25   Beuken and van Grol, pp. 316–17.
26   Westermann, *Isaiah 40—66*, 245.
27   Rudolph, p. 233.
28   J. Coert Rylaarsdam, "Atonement, Day of," *IDB* 1:314; see further Kraus, *Worship*, 68–70.
29   Norbert Lohfink, "Die Gattung der 'Historischen

Kurzgeschichte' in den letzten Jahren von Juda und in der Zeit des Babylonischen Exils," *ZAW* 90 (1978) 324–28.

it.[30] It is conceivable, if *M* is correct in 36:9, that Jehoiakim declared the fast because of the immediate threat of the Babylonian army to his west; this is the view of Abraham Malamat.[31] One might conclude that Jehoiakim would declare a fast for such a military emergency, but it would be hard to imagine even so insensitive a king as Jehoiakim burning Jrm's scroll on such an occasion, given the fact that the scroll undoubtedly carried Yahweh's warnings about the foe from the north. On the other hand, in Chislev of 601 the Babylonian army, by then fighting in the Egyptian delta, was dealt a defeat by the Egyptian forces and withdrew to Babylon.[32] If the Babylonian army was perceived by the king and his optimistic advisors to be a "paper tiger," then one has a motivation for his burning Jrm's scroll.

This historical circumstance makes persuasive the date of *G* in 36:9 rather than that of *M*. "Fifth" (החמשית) resembles "eighth" (השמנית) to some degree, and given "fourth year" in 36:1, "eighth" is clearly the *lectio difficilior*.

(4) The wording of 8:4–13 implies both a drought (v 13) and a recitation of Deuteronomy (vv 8–9); if the law of Deuteronomy was recited every seventh year (Deut 31:10–11), and if the initial promulgation of Deuteronomy was in 622, there would have been a reading in the autumn of 601. This datum suggests the drought described in 14:2–6 was already under way in that year (see 8:4–13, Setting).

(5) The only two occurrences in the OT of the combination of an imperfect of היה and the hop'al participle of שלך are in 14:16 and 36:30: in the latter passage the king's corpse will stay lying in the street, and in the former passage the people's corpses will stay lying in the street. The word of judgment on Jehoiakim after he burned the scroll was evidently generalized to all the people in the counter-liturgy on the drought.

(6) If the analysis offered in Preliminary Observations is correct, the present sequence is structured around two descriptions, that of a drought (14:2–6) and a military disaster (15:5–9). This double focus is reflected in the combination "sword" and "famine" (14:13–18). It is proposed here that the sequence in its totality assumes both. Thus beyond 14:2–6 the word מִקְוֵה in 14:8 is a pun that involves water imagery (see Interpretation there), and 14:22 is certainly concerned with a drought. On the other hand 14:9 suggests a deity who cannot bring military victory (see again Interpretation there).

There is a similar parity in several other passages in Jer. Thus in 12:7–13 Yahweh declares that he has abandoned his people and affirms that foreign armies will ravage the land (vv 10–12 there), and to this declaration have been added lines describing a drought; there is no reason to doubt the authenticity of either segment (see Setting there). Again in 5:12 the people affirm that neither "sword" nor "famine" will come upon them, and there is the structural parallel of 4:9–10 ("sword") and 4:11–12 (the hot wind, implying desiccation), and the parallel of 4:19–22 (a battle emergency) and 4:23–28 (a vision growing out of a drought—note the parallel verbs of 4:28a and of 14:2).

It is pointed out in Interpretation of 14:11–12 that the specific pairing of "sword" and "famine" is not to be found in pre-Jeremianic material. Since this pairing is found repeatedly in Jer, and the triad "sword, famine, pestilence" repeated in Jer and Ezekiel, the most plausible explanation is a specific historical context. It is proposed here, then, that it was a combination of the real drought and Jrm's perception that the Babylonian army was a real threat which called forth the present sequence.

The fast declared by the king would have been accompanied by an official liturgy (compare Joel 1—2 in the context of the emergency of the locust plague, and note Joel 1:14, the declaration of a fast), but the present sequence is not that official liturgy (for this matter see Preliminary Observations). Instead it is a counter-liturgy (see Form). It assumes that Yahweh will not hear the prayers of the people or the prayers of the prophet on their behalf (14:11–12; 15:1–4). The content and

30   Wiseman, *Chronicles*, 68–69; the reference is B. M. 21946, Obv. lines 15–20.

31   Abraham Malamat, "A New Record of Nebuchadrezzar's Palestinian Campaigns," *IEJ* 6 (1956) 251–52; "The Twilight of Judah," *Congress Volume, Edinburgh 1974* (VTSup 28; Leiden: Brill, 1975) 123–45, esp. 130.

32   Wiseman, *Chronicles*, 70–71; the reference is B. M. 21946, Rev. lines 5–7.

diction of these verses assume Jrm's attitude after the king burned the scroll, and the vocabulary has many links with the material elsewhere added in the second scroll (4:9–12, 19–28, and 5:12 mentioned above; 7:16–20 and 11:14).

Jrm was evidently in hiding when the fast was declared in November/December 601 (so the implication of 36:10, 19, 26: see there). It is better then to assume that the present liturgy was not delivered publicly by Jrm but is a private revelation from Yahweh to Jrm, Yahweh's answer to the prophet's question whether the word he has proclaimed is a valid word. This setting would explain the position of the liturgy between two sequences of confessions.

One must assume, then, that the drought continued past the time when the king burned the scroll, and that the present liturgy is a reflection in Jrm's mind of the official efforts made to beg the help of Yahweh. A date in December 601 or early in the winter of 601/600 fits these data.

It may be added that Baruch Margulis has associated the words of Hab 3:17 (and of his reconstruction of v 16) with a drought and an associated public lament.[33] The critical questions of Habakkuk 3 and its relation to Habakkuk 1—2 are too complex to enter into here, but it is at least possible that those words reflect the same setting as that of the present sequence: note the resemblance of Hab 3:17 to Jer 8:13.[34]

Interpretation

■ **14:1** The verse offers a fresh superscription, introducing the sequence on the drought and battle. The syntax of the expression is odd but is not a copyist's error; the same structure appears in 46:1; 47:1; and 49:34; and probably 1:2.[35] This superscription may govern a short passage (49:34) as well as a long one; it is likely that it governs here the whole counter-liturgy (compare Structure). The word "drought" here is בַּצָּרוֹת; there is some uncertainty how to analyze the word. A related

word "drought" is בַּצֹרֶת, of which the word in the present passage may be a plural of intensity (GKC, sec. 124e), but there also exists a singular בְּצָרָה (Pss 9:10; 10:1), a word which, however, has been understood as "in distress" (צָרָה) following G. On the other hand, the present word may not be correctly vocalized: an abstract singular בַּצָּרוּת has been proposed on the analogy of the Syriac beṣîrût "lack (of rain)." In any event the meaning of the word here is clear.

■ **14:2** This verse is compact and the vehicle for multiple meanings. The first word sets the stage, the verb אבל, which means both "mourn" and "dry up," whether to be considered as one verb with two foci of meaning or as two homonymous verbs (see the discussion in 4:28). The verb in the third colon, קדר, "be dark," parallel with this one, suggests that אבל must be understood as "mourn" (so the same parallelism in 4:28; note also that קדר in 8:21 implies being in mourning). On the other hand, the whole context of the poem is drought; one must conclude that אבל carries both meanings equally.

The immediate parallel of "Judah" is "her gates." The term is metonymy for "her cities" (compare 1 Kgs 8:37 and often), as Rashi already noted. Its verb is אמל pu'lal "waste away, wither," a frequent parallel with אבל (so Hos 4:3, a likely model for the present passage). But a verb meaning "be dry," "be no longer able to bear children" (so the verb in 15:9) creates a striking image with "her gates" (so likewise Lam 2:8).

The verb in the third colon, קדר, meaning "be dark," implies the wearing of mourning clothes (see above). Who wears mourning? Since "Judah" and "Jerusalem," both proper names, seem to be parallel, one is led to assume that the "gates" wear mourning; there is no purpose in softening the harsh image by inserting "people" or "men" with several recent translations (RSV, NEB, NAB, NJV). What does לָאָרֶץ "to the ground, to the earth" mean? It is clear that the expression points the hearer downward in a balance to "rise" (עלה) in the last colon; there is the same contrast between לָאָרֶץ and עלה

---

33 Baruch Margulis, "The Psalm of Habakkuk: A Reconstruction and Interpretation," *ZAW* 82 (1970) 438.

34 For the association of the drought in Jer 14 and Habakkuk 3 I am indebted to my former student Kathrene Duhon.

35 See GKC, sec. 138e, note.

in Isa 14:12, 13. One has the impression first of gates draped in black from top to bottom; next of a population gathered at the gates bowed down in mourning (compare the association of קדר "be dark" with שחח "be bowed down" in Pss 35:14; 38:7); Isa 3:26 offers a similar image with similar wording, and that verse may be a model for the present colon—and one notes also "her gates have sunk into the ground" in Lam 2:9. But there is another possibility raised by the meaning of לָאָרֶץ in Isa 14:12, because it is clear from Isa 14:15 that לָאָרֶץ there means Sheol, as אֶרֶץ often does (see on 10:12).[36] The occurrence in v 18 and in 15:5–9 of other expressions implying Sheol (see Structure and Interpretation of those passages) suggests that the present colon may imply "(her gates) are dark to Sheol" or even "(her gates) are dark in Sheol" (compare Hos 5:1 for לְ "at, in" a locality). Sheol, too, has gates (Ps 9:14), which are evidently implied in 15:7, and that the gates of Jerusalem might merge in this poem with the gates of Sheol, or remind the hearer of the gates of Sheol, is horrifying: one notes that Ps 9:14–15 contrasts the gates of Sheol with the gates of Zion. There is one more datum suggesting the אֶרֶץ means "Sheol" here. There is a companion piece to this verse, 4:28, shaped during the same period of time (see Setting there); and there, in the parallel to the verb אבל, it is the "heavens" that "are dark [קדר] above [מִמַּעַל]." Since the parallel to the present colon has "rise" (עלה), one is led to wonder whether Jrm's mind did not at this point go from heaven to Sheol (compare not only Isa 14:12–15 but also Amos 9:2).

Finally, in the closing colon, one has the proper name parallel with Judah: Jerusalem. There arises the צְוחַת, the outcry of Jerusalem. Is this an outcry from the living city of Jerusalem? Or is it an outcry of Jerusalem from Sheol?—Isa 29:4 describes the voice of "Ariel" (evidently Jerusalem) arising from Sheol, and the present phrase may reflect that image. And does Isa 5:13–14 stand in the background, with its images of drought and of the multitude of Jerusalem in Sheol?

One has, in short, a verse which compresses images of desiccation and of mourning, of Palestine and Sheol, into nine words.

■ **14:3** The scene shifts from a general description to that of the nobility: the subject precedes the verb, suggesting a shift of attention. The word אַדִּיר is essentially an adjective meaning "majestic, glorious"; it was a traditional term for those in authority, chiefs and the like (Judg 5:13), like the "lords" of the feudal period. One cannot help having the impression, however, that the term is here used ironically, since the nobles have no advantage over the farmhands (v 4): neither group has water. The correlative צָעִיר is likewise an adjective, "little, insignificant." The word here can refer either to people who are young or people who are lower in social class: in a feudal society servants are often both young and subservient ("menials" is the rendering of the Chicago Translation).[37] This is the only instance in the OT where this adjective is employed for "servants," so that it is likely that the word here is used in an ad hoc fashion as a counterpoise to the term for nobles. Knox translates, "Master sends man to fetch water."

The context makes it clear that the subject shifts in the second and third cola: it is of course the menials who go to the cisterns only to find no water. The noun גֵּב occurs otherwise only in 2 Kgs 3:16 but occurs extensively in postbiblical Hebrew, and there is an Aramaic cognate, so that there is no doubt of its meaning, "catchment pool" (2 Kgs 3:16), "cistern."

There have been three interpretations of the last colon. *G* and *V* translate שׁוב qal transitively as if hip'il, "bring back" or "carry back," and this understanding has carried into the Reformation (so Luther). Others assume that "their menials" is the subject of שׁוב intransitive and "their vessels empty" is an accusative of manner: *KJV* has "with their vessels empty," and most commentators follow this; it is the interpretation that Brian Walton's Polyglot gives for the rendering of *S* and *T* (Brian Walton, *Biblia Sacra Polyglotta* [London, 1657]). But the more natural reading of those Versions, which render *M* exactly, is the third alternative, which is that the subject of the verb is "their vessels." Of translations and commentators which I have consulted, only Freedman and Knox offer it (Knox: "back go the pails empty"). The phraseology is then similar to that of Isa 55:11, "[My word] shall not return to me empty." The poetic structure of the verse encourages this interpretation: if there

---

36   Note further Magnus Ottosson, "אֶרֶץ," *TDOT* 1:399–400, and Dahood, *Psalms I*, 106.

37   J. M. Powis Smith et al., and Edgar J. Goodspeed, *The*   *Complete Bible: An American Translation* (Chicago: University of Chicago, 1939).

is a shift of subject between the first and second cola, one expects another shift between the third and fourth. The progression "nobles," "menials," "vessels" reinforces the desolate impression of the poem. There is no need, then, to emend רֵיקָם, the adverb "empty," to רֵיקִים, the adjective "empty" (plural), with Duhm. One is led to conclude that it is the nobles' vessels that are meant, not those of the menials, though the point is a small one.

It does, however, lead to a more important one: that the subject of the three verbs in the last two cola of the verse is the nobles: it is the nobles that are humiliated and cover their heads. The question has not had much critical attention because most scholars have omitted the last two cola with G as dittographic from v 4 (Hitzig, Duhm, Cornill, Volz, Rudolph); but the two cola belong—the verb וְהָכְלְמוּ, a rare form, is not in v 4 and helps assure the genuineness of this portion of the verse (Giesebrecht), and the overall poetic structure likewise suggests that the cola are genuine (see Structure). But there have been commentators of earlier centuries who suggested that it is the nobles that are being described in these lines: Thomas Gataker (seventeenth century), Venema (1765).[38] The point of the duplication of these verbs in vv 3 and 4 is that both high and low among the population respond the same way: the nobles are no different from the farmhands.

The reaction of shame strikes one as curious: our own reaction might be frustration, or panic, or rage. But different cultures react to emergencies in different ways, and it will not do to try to search for some meaning other than "be ashamed" for בוש and its synonyms here. King David was not lacking in courage, yet as he fled Jerusalem at the time of Absalom's revolt, he wept with his head covered, and the people who followed him did likewise (2 Sam 15:30). To cover one's head then is a gesture of shame, and וְהָכְלְמוּ (כלם hop'al) is synonymous, "and they have been humiliated." The shame of the nobles arises from their sense of weakness, from the withdrawal of Yahweh's blessing, from the devastation which the disaster works on the community. The drought has brought all life to a stop, and the reaction of the nobles is to withdraw from a world that no longer offers life.[39]

■ 14:4 There is widespread doubt about the text of the first colon, which reads literally "because of the soil (which) is dismayed." The verb חתת "be dismayed" is otherwise used only of persons and is normally in parallelism with בוש "be ashamed" (as in 8:9). Further G reads a different text ("and the labors of the land failed"), suggesting that some form of the root עבד was read for the first word instead of a form of עבר. These uncertainties have led to universal emendation of the text (various suggestions have been made by Duhm, Cornill, Giesebrecht, Volz, Condamin, Rudolph, and Bright). The verb is assuredly odd, but no more so that the personification of the gates in v 2. The nearness of בוש (vv 3, 4) makes dubious the suggestion of Shlomo A. Marenof[40] to see here a cognate of the Ethiopic ḥatawa "burn." Houbigant (1753) suggested that the line contains the noun עָבוּר "produce, yield" (Josh 5:11, 12), and Michaelis (1793) offered, among others, the suggestion adopted here (compare Condamin as well), to accept that noun and to see in the article of אֲדָמָה "soil" the suffix on "yield." The soil, then, is embarrassed because of its small yield, leading the farmhands to be ashamed in their turn—just as the empty return of the water vessels led the nobles to be ashamed in v 3. For "rain" (גֶּשֶׁם) compare 5:24.

The word אִכָּר is an Akkadian loanword; in Akkadian *ikkaru* means "hired farm laborer," "a small farmer (often dependent on a larger organization)." It is a word that evidently came into use in Hebrew to refer to farm workers on royal estates (2 Chr 26:10).[41] These are not then local peasants with their own freehold; they are at the bottom of the social scale, but their reactions are identical with those of the leading citizens (v 3). (Note that the "farmhands" and vinedressers have the same emotional reactions in Joel 1:11 to the locust plague.) If

---

38 See the note of John Owen in John Calvin, *Commentaries on the Book of the Prophet Jeremiah and the Lamentations* (Calvin Translation Society, 1850–55, rep. Grand Rapids: Eerdmans, 1950) II, 206.

39 See Pedersen, I/II, 240–41.

40 Shlomo A. Marenof, "A Note on Jer 14:4," *AJSL* 55 (1938) 198–200.

41 Harmut Gese, "Kleine Beiträge zum Verständnis des Amosbuches," *VT* 12 (1962) 432–33.

the farmhands find no water, there is no bread, and the result is famine (vv 13, 15, 16, 18).

■ **14:5–6** The כִּי which opens v 5 is exclamatory and governs both verses: both animals act against their normal behavior. The אַיֶּלֶת is the female deer, probably the red deer, *Cervus elaphus*.[42] She normally calves far from human observation (Job 39:1), deep in the woods, but now the lack of fodder in her natural habitat drives her into the open field even for calving. And then she leaves her young!—the doe was well known in ancient times for her tender maternal affection (Qimḥi notes the trait), so this behavior is unprecedented. (For the infinitive absolute עָזוֹב see GKC, sec. 113z.)

The wild asses are accustomed to the desert (2:24) and can find grass anywhere (Job 39:5–8). But even they now give up: instead of ranging the mountains (Job 39:8) they stand still on the desert paths, dying. (For "caravan-tracks" see 3:2.) To what are they compared in the second colon of v 6? The word תַּנִּים means "jackals" (9:10; 10:22); but twice (Ezek 29:3; 32:2) the word appears as an aberrant spelling for the singular תַּנִּין "sea-monster, crocodile."[43] The meaning here depends to an extent on one's understanding of the verb associated with the animal. It can mean "pant": it is used of the quick sniffing of the female wild ass in heat (2:24) and is used of the sun in Eccl 1:5, perhaps as a man doing heavy labor[44] or as driving a chariot pulled by panting horses,[45] and jackals, like other canines, pant in the heat. On the other hand, the verb is used of the breathing of a woman in travail (Isa 42:14), where "gasp" is more appropriate. In the present instance the wild asses are dying, and the verb appears to refer to the labored breathing of a dying creature. The crocodile spends many minutes under water and then rises to breathe in a great inhalation, so that this description could well fit the gasping here referred to (so also Condamin). The use of "eyes" with "fail" (כלה qal) occurs in seven other passages (Pss 69:4; 119:82, 123; Job 11:20; 17:5; Lam 2:11; 4:17); in Lam 4:17 and in the Psalms passages the

expression is used of the eyes' fading, waiting for help that never comes, and in Lam 2:11 the eyes are used up from constant weeping. In the Job passages the expression is used for a general curse (the eyes of the wicked, or of the children, will fail). The present passage is the only one where the eyes become lifeless as death comes, but the nuance of hopelessness may be present as well here.

The three כִּי clauses in vv 4, 5, and 6 make a striking succession of steady compression: v 4, כִּי לֹא־הָיָה גֶשֶׁם בָּאָרֶץ; v 5, כִּי לֹא־הָיָה דֶשֶׁא; v 6, כִּי־אֵין עֵשֶׂב—"since there has been no rain on the land"; "since there has been no grass"; "since there is no pasture"—in the pronunciation of Jrm's day, seven syllables, five, and three respectively (segolates were monosyllabic). There is no consensus on the denotation of דֶשֶׁא ("grass") and עֵשֶׂב (translated here "pasture"): some think that עֵשֶׂב, which includes grass, green vegetation, and cereals, is contrasted with דֶשֶׁא "grass," while others think that דֶשֶׁא is an inclusive term which comprises עֵשֶׂב and עֵץ "trees."[46] The question is of no consequence here where the intention is clear.

■ **14:7–9** The question whether these verses offer Jrm's expression for sincere repentance on behalf of the people in which he is equally sincere, or whether they offer Jrm's ironic quoting of the people's appeal, a quoting which is a rejection by Yahweh of the possibility of repentance, can be solved only in an examination of the wider context of these verses: see Form, Setting.

■ **14:7** The flow of thought in this verse is by no means clear. Whatever the first colon means, the second is a call to Yahweh for help. The third and fourth cola are an acknowledgment by the people of their sins, introduced by כִּי normally translated "for." But "act, for we have sinned against you" cannot be right. Thus כִּי must be "so" here, as it does in Gen 18:20 (כִּי רָבָּה, "so great," *NAB* and *NJV*) and Isa 59:12.[47] The third and fourth cola are not an explanation but a full-bodied admission. Then the conjunction אִם introducing the first colon cannot be "if," as if the question were open, but concessive, "even if": the conjunction with a perfect verb is concessive in Job

---

42   Bodenheimer, "Fauna," 251a.
43   See Walther Zimmerli, *Ezekiel 2* (Hermeneia; Philadelphia: Fortress, 1983) 106, 154.
44   Aare Lauha, *Kohelet* (BKAT 19; Neukirchen: Neukirchener, 1978) 34.
45   George A. Barton, *A Critical and Exegetical Commentary on the Book of Ecclesiastes* (ICC; Edinburgh: Clark, 1908) 71.
46   For the literature see *HALAT*, 224b.
47   See ibid., 448b, I, 1.a.

9:15 as well (GKC, sec. 160a).

The idiom עָנָה בְּ means "testify against": two instances that are comparable to the present passage are 2 Sam 1:16, "Your own mouth has testified against you," and Job 15:6, "Your own lips testify against you." For עשׂה used absolutely, "act," see 9:6; an almost identical colon is found in Ps 109:2. For כִּי "how" see 3:25. For מְשׁוּבֹת "turnings = acts of apostasy" see 3:22: a bicolon very much like v 7b is to be found in 5:6, where מְשׁוּבֹת also occurs.

■ **14:8** The expression מִקְוֵה יִשְׂרָאֵל is a striking double-entendre. There is no doubt that מִקְוֵה can mean "hope" (Ezra 10:2), and in 1 Chr 29:15 it seems to mean "security";[48] compare the verb קוה in v 22. But it can also mean "pool" (Exod 7:19): in 17:13 the same vocative to Yahweh is set in the context of "the spring of running water" (מְקוֹר מַיִם־חַיִּים), and that parallel is reinforced by the parallelism of מָקוֹר and מִקְוֵה in 1QS 11:6 and 1QH 12:29.[49] It is appropriate to address Yahweh as the source of hope for Israel,[50] but it is particularly appropriate in the context of a drought to address Yahweh as the true pool of water for Israel. There is of course no way to render the double meaning into English.

The designation of "savior" (מוֹשִׁיעַ) for Yahweh is traditional (Hos 13:4) and became common in the salvation oracles of Deutero-Isaiah (Isa 43:3 and often). An attempt has recently been made to understand the word in a forensic context, "advocate" or the like,[51] but it is better to stay with the context of battle, "defender, liberator."[52]

The expression עֵת צָרָה "time of distress" is very close to עִתּוֹת בַּצָּרָה in Pss 9:10; 10:1, an expression which can be translated either "times of drought" or (by assuming a prepositional expression in a construct chain[53] or emending the text from בְּ to הָ[54]) "times of distress." Given the double meaning in the first colon, one wonders whether we do not have a forgotten double meaning here in the second.

For גֵּר "stranger, resident alien" see 7:6. The expres-

sion כְּאֹרֵחַ נָטָה לָלוּן, literally "like a traveler (who) has turned aside to lodge for the night," is very close to מְלוֹן אֹרְחִים "lodging for travelers" in 9:1. In that passage (see Interpretation there) Yahweh declares he would rather find temporary shelter in the wilderness than stay any longer with his people; here the people ask why he acts as helpless as a traveler looking for a place to stop. Does he not know his way around his own land? Or is the land so identified with Sheol (vv 2, 18; 15:7) that Yahweh is thereby a stranger?

■ **14:9** The "why?" questions continue: "Why are you like a helpless man?" The nip'al participle נִדְהָם appears only here in the OT; G evidently read נִרְדָּם "asleep," a reading which commended itself to Giesebrecht and was adopted by Cornill. But the verb דהם has turned up in a recently discovered letter of the seventh century at Yavneh-Yam and must mean "be helpless."[55]

There is no need in the second colon to emend גִּבּוֹר to גֶּבֶר "man, fellow" following the implication of the rendering in G, as Rudolph does; Zeph 3:17 refers to Yahweh as גִּבּוֹר יוֹשִׁיעַ "a champion who saves," and the words just preceding in that passage have "Yahweh is in your midst," a phrase like that in the third colon here. But of course a "champion" by definition can "save"; why is Yahweh's behavior a contradiction in terms? The third and fourth cola shift from questions to a reaffirmation of Yahweh's presence. The third colon is introduced by וְ: the context indicates that this "and" is strongly contrastive, however it is to be translated (Rudolph: "even so you are in our midst, Yahweh").[56] That affirmation, that "Yahweh is in our midst," is likewise found in Mic 3:11: it was an affirmation that no doubt originally indicated Yahweh's presence in the temple (Ps 46:6)[57] but could easily be transferred in the crisis of the drought to an affirmation of Yahweh's sure presence with her people. This affirmation is reinforced by the statement in the last colon, "We bear your name." The temple bears Yahweh's name (7:10 and often), and Jrm affirms that he bears Yahweh's name (15:16). But only rarely in the OT

---

48 Pieter A. H. de Boer, "Etude sur le sens de la racine QWH," *OTS* 10 (ed. Pieter A. H. de Boer; Leiden: Brill, 1954) 239–40.

49 See Mitchell Dahood, "The Metaphor in Jeremiah 17,13," *Bib* 48 (1967) 109–10; "Hebrew-Ugaritic Lexicography V," *Bib* 48 (1967) 430.

50 Zimmerli, *Hope*, 112.

51 John Sawyer, "What was a mošiaʻ?" *VT* 15 (1965)

475–86.

52 Elliger, *Deuterojesaja*, 296–97.

53 Dahood, *Psalms I*, 52.

54 Kraus, *Psalmen*, 76.

55 Joseph Naveh, "A Hebrew Letter from the Seventh Century B.C.," *IEJ* 10 (1960) 131, line 14; 134–35.

56 "Aber du bist doch in unserer Mitte, Jahwe."

57 van der Woude, *Micha*, 119–20.

is it said that the people bear Yahweh's name (beyond the present passage: Deut 28:10; Dan 9:19; 2 Chr 7:14; and compare Isa 63:19). The people are desperate. And they voice their pathetic appeals, אַל־תַּנִּחֵנוּ, "Do not desert us!" The verb נוח II hipʿil here means "abandon, desert": a close parallel is Ps 119:121, בַּל־תַּנִּיחֵנִי לְעֹשְׁקָי, "Do not abandon me to my oppressors."

■ **14:10** The preposition לְ normally means "to," so that the first colon would be most naturally understood as "Thus Yahweh has said to this people." What follows, however, refers to the people in the third person. One must therefore either understand the preposition to mean "about" (Gen 20:13), or a mistake for עַל, or else one must imagine Yahweh speaking to the people but referring to them in the third person as if they were no longer conversational partners; there is no way to be sure.

The adverb כֵּן "thus, so" normally points to what has just been said; one must understand then that the word refers to vv 7–9 or even to vv 2–9. For כֵּן אָהֲבוּ "so have they loved" compare אָהֲבוּ כֵן, 5:21. The verb נוע is used of oscillating motion—of the swaying of trees in the wind (Judg 9:9), of the staggering of drunkards (Isa 29:9). Here it evidently means "wander a considerable distance [compare the third colon], drifting this way and that" (Rudolph: "stagger here and there"). There may be a word-play between לָנוּעַ here and לָלוּן "spend the night" in v 8, but certainly there is a resemblance of theme: the people there accused Yahweh of being a helpless wanderer, but now one hears that it is the people that have done the wandering. The reference is not only to Israel's freedom to walk away from Yahweh (2:31) but to her going off first to Egypt, then to Mesopotamia for help (2:18). The verb חשׂך means "restrain, spare"; a similar idea with different vocabulary is found in 2:24.

If the second and third cola are a direct quotation, v 10b is another kind of quotation—from Hos 8:13; and it picks up "iniquity" and "sin" from v 7. Since the people are determined to wander off from Yahweh, he has no choice but to set in motion a judgment announced long since. "Remember" implies taking action (2:2), as "deal with" (פקד) indicates (compare 5:9). Years later Jrm will announce the reversal of this terrible judgment in the new covenant (31:34).

■ **14:11–12** Yahweh's word to Jrm begins with the prohibition also found in 7:16 and 11:14, with the explanatory addition here of the expression לְטוֹבָה "for good, benefit"; most translations paraphrase with "Do not pray for the welfare of this people." See further 7:16.

Verse 12 begins with כִּי. It is clear that the people are indeed fasting (see below). The conjunction can therefore mean either "when," "although," or "even if":[58] from the verse alone it is difficult to be sure of the nuance. But the corresponding expression 15:1, which begins with אִם, can only mean "even if," so that the same translation is appropriate here. This is the only occurrence in Jer of the verb צום "fast," and the related noun צוֹם is found only in 36:6, 9; there is strong reason, then, to connect the two passages (see Setting). The phrase "I will not listen to their cry" is again an adaptation from 7:16 and 11:14, for those passages speak of "lifting up a cry" and affirm that "I will not listen to you." For the "burnt offering" (עֹלָה) see 6:20. The מִנְחָה, literally "gift," was originally a general term for any offering, whether involving the sacrifice of blood or not (Judg 6:18–21), but by this period referred to offerings other than meat, which could include grain, fruits, oil, and wine. The contrast here, then, is between animal offerings and nonanimal offerings.[59] The phrase "I will not approve them" (אֵינֶנִּי רֹצָם) picks up "has not approved them" (לֹא רָצָם) in v 10 and suggests, as does the parallel "I will not listen to their cry," that the object "them" refers to the people, not to their offerings only.

The triad "sword, famine, pestilence" is a fixed combination appearing thirteen times in Jer; this is its first occurrence. Though the triad is found within the present complex in 15:2 as well, these instances are essentially expansions of the pair "sword, famine," which not only appears in vv 13, 15, 16 (in reverse order!), and 18, but which appears to regulate the structure of the whole passage (see Preliminary Observations). The history of the triad is complex.[60] There are many early expressions, either positive or negative, which refer to the curse of these three and others like them, or the blessing of the lack of them (Deut 7:12–16; 32:23–25). It is possible, then, that the triad existed in oral tradition

58 Joüon, *Gramm.*, sec. 171b.
59 Kraus, *Worship*, 114–15.
60 See the careful study in Weippert, *Prosareden*, 148–91.

long before Jrm's time. On the other hand, though the pairs "pestilence, sword" and "famine, pestilence" appear in pre-Jeremianic passages (Exod 5:3 [JE]; 2 Sam 24:13; Amos 4:10), there is no occurrence before Jer of the pair "sword, famine." Its repeated occurrence in the present passage, and in comparable passages like 5:12 and 11:22, suggests that a specific historical crisis stimulated the pair at this time (see Setting) and stimulated the use of the triad repeatedly in Jer and Ezekiel. Miller remarks, concerning the repeated use of the triad in Jer and Ezekiel, "It must not be forgotten that during this time these words were slogans which were accepted and rejected by many people."[61] One question arises: Does the use of the definite article with "sword, famine, pestilence" here and elsewhere indicate a prose style, or does it suggest "the sword" and "the famine" that precipitated the crisis at the time?

■ **14:13** The verse begins with the same phrase of dismay, "Ah Lord Yahweh, look," with which 1:6 begins (and compare 4:10). Jrm evidently offers a plea of extenuation for the people (see Form), since it is hardly their fault if they have been receiving contradictory instruction from other prophets; for their same rejection of "sword" and "famine" see 5:12. The expression "trustworthy peace" (שָׁלוֹם אֱמֶת) is suspect; all other expressions in the OT in which the construct of שָׁלוֹם occurs are followed by a designation of persons, groups, or the like ("the peace of Jerusalem," Ps 122:6); the alternative reading, with "and," expressing a hendiadys, is probably correct (see Text). These prophets continue to preach an assurance of security when Jrm is convinced there will none (compare שָׁלוֹם שָׁלוֹם, "all is well, all is well," 6:14, and Setting there).

■ **14:14** Yahweh replies that what these prophets are uttering is שֶׁקֶר "a lie, falsehood." It had been said before in Israel (Mic 2:11) but becomes particularly apposite now: the prophets who speak this way are deceiving the people.[62] The synonyms pile up: Yahweh did not send them, command them, speak to them; he did send,

command Jrm (1:7). What they preach Yahweh typifies by an array of synonyms for emptiness. It is a חֲזוֹן שֶׁקֶר, a lying vision; חֲזוֹן often refers to visionary revelation (it is in parallel with "dream" in Isa 29:7), but may just as often refer to an auditory revelation (Ezek 12:21–28; 13:16).[63] Jrm, however, uses it only here and in 23:16, both times of false revelation. Then there occurs the only instance of קֶסֶם "divination" in Jer. Though the word appears once in a good sense, "oracle" or the like (Prov 16:10), this word and its cognate are otherwise used only in reference to forbidden religious practices (Deut 18:10; 2 Kgs 17:17): Ezek 21:26 describes the king of Babylon engaging in these by shaking arrows, consulting the teraphim, and looking at the liver. The designation is reinforced by אֱלִיל "worthlessness," a word that in other contexts is used to refer to pagan gods (Ps 96:5), so that the phrase here suggests that what the prophets preach is no better than pagan hocus-pocus. For "deception" (תַּרְמִית) see 8:5. "Mind" is literally "heart" (see 4:4)—the "deception of their mind" is what they devise from their own imagination.

Two stems of the verb "prophesy" (נבא) occur here, the nip'al at the beginning of the verse and the hitpa'el at the end. Is there any difference? The hitpa'el stem originally described characteristic prophetic behavior, which sometimes included ecstatic or trance behavior, though this was not always the case. The nip'al stem designated characteristic prophetic speech, but more and more the hitpa'el was used for the same purpose, until the two became synonymous.[64] It would be easy to conclude that the verbs are synonymous here, but it may well be that Jrm perceived Yahweh deliberately shifting the form to suggest aberrant behavior. After all, in early texts the hitpa'el stem of the verb can mean "rave" (1 Sam 18:10) and have nothing directly to do with prophesying; the shift may thus be deliberately derogatory.

The pronoun לָכֶם "to you (plural)" at the end of the verse is unexpected and many MSS. read לָהֶם "to them." Rudolph suggests that its occurrence here indicates that

61   John W. Miller, *Das Verhältnis Jeremias und Hesekiels sprachlich und theologisch untersucht* (Assen: Van Gorcum, 1955) 86.

62   See Overholt, *Falsehood.*

63   See B. Davie Napier, "Vision," *IDB* 4:791.

64   Robert R. Wilson, "Prophecy and Ecstasy: A Reexamination," *JBL* 98 (1979) 329–36, esp. 336.

Jrm himself was for a time influenced by the optimistic oracles of the competing prophets.[65] It is possible that for a time he did not believe the drought would last (does 12:4 suggest this?). On the other hand the use of the pronoun here may mean little more than "in the hearing both of you and of the rest of the people."

■ **14:15–16** In their present state these verses arouse uneasiness; Giesebrecht judged them secondary because they express a viewpoint of *lex talionis* alien to the sequence. But the viewpoint is not quite that of *lex talionis* (see below), even though the verses leave an impression of an interruption. Surrounding prose verses are couched in rhythmic prose (*Kunstprosa*)—vv 11–12, 14; 15:1–4; the style of the present verses seems by comparison diffuse and verbose. On the other hand within these verses are found striking expressions that give every evidence of being genuine. The solution, it appears to me, is to excise the two bracketed phrases; what remains gives good structure. Thus the phrase "in my name, though I did not send them" is adapted from v 14, and the listing in v 16 is similar to that in 2:26.

There is distinctive language in what remains. Thus one notes the parallel of "(who) prophesy" (הַנִּבְּאִים) at the beginning of vv 15 and 16 and the reversal of order of "sword and famine" between vv 15 and 16. Further the verb form יִתַּמּוּ "they shall perish" is not common; it does, however, recur in 44:12, where Jrm is reported to have said, "By sword and famine they shall perish." The verb שלך hop'al "be cast out" is used twice otherwise by Jrm, once for Jehoiachin (22:28) and once, in phrasing very close to that found here, with reference to Jehoiakim at just this period (36:30). Again the phrase "no one to bury" (אֵין מְקַבֵּר) is found nowhere else in the OT; the equivalent אֵין קוֹבֵר is found twice, in Ps 79:3, a passage that must have offered a model to Jrm in such diction, and in 2 Kgs 9:10, part of Elijah's oracle over Jezebel. Since equivalent words over Jezebel (2 Kgs 9:37) find a place in one of Jrm's pronouncements over the people (9:21: see Interpretation there), one is led to conclude

that the expression is genuine to Jrm. In general, then, the verses, excluding the glosses, belong in the sequence.

The quotation of the prophets, "Sword and famine shall not occur in this land," is a paraphrase of the expression in v 13. The verb "perish" (תמם) occurs earlier in the book in a slightly different meaning ("be used up," 1:3; 6:29).

In v 16 the expression יִהְיוּ מֻשְׁלָכִים gives at first the impression of the kind of periphrastic usage typical of late Hebrew,[66] but the same expression is found in 36:30, and the context both there and here indicates that the phrase means "shall remain unburied."[67]

Lack of proper burial was considered a great tragedy (7:33; 8:2; Deut 21:23; 2 Sam 21:10).[68] The lexica indicate that the qal stem of קבר simply means "bury," while the pi'el stem (found here) implies mass burial;[69] if so, Jrm is heightening the horror communicated by the expression in Ps 79:3 and 2 Kgs 9:10.

For "pour out upon them their wickedness" compare the similar diction of 6:11. This is the only instance in the OT where this verb is used with this object; but a similar expression is found in 2:19, where it is the wickedness of Judah that will chasten her.

These verses do not so much express the *lex talionis* as they reassure Jrm that his own message is valid. The prophets may say that sword and famine will not prevail, but they are wrong; and the people, alas, who have believed their false news will die and remain unburied, victims of Yahweh's judgment which begins with the king (36:30–31).

■ **14:17** This verse begins with the instruction, "And you shall say to them this word." But it makes no sense for Yahweh to instruct Jrm to repeat to the people the prophet's words of weeping over them (particularly after v 11); the weeping is Jrm's own initiative, indeed his initiative over against Yahweh (see 8:23—9:1, Interpretation). The instruction refers to the preceding word of judgment that had been vouchsafed privately to Jrm (v 14) and is now to be published (compare Volz); note that

65   Rudolph, p. 101; so also Berridge, pp. 110–11.
66   Joüon, *Gramm.*, sec. 121e, note 2.
67   Ibid., sec. 121e.
68   William L. Reed, "Burial," *IDB* 1:476.
69   The one occurrence of a seeming pu'al, Gen 25:10, is probably a qal passive (Zorell; *HALAT*); if so, this interpretation of the pi'el is strengthened.

the similar instruction in 13:12 has the same function (see there).

Several commentators have translated the first verbs of the poem "My eyes run tears . . . and cannot [or must not] stop" (Duhm, Cornill, Volz, Rudolph). The first verb can of course be indicative rather than jussive, and it is true that אַל may be used occasionally not for the negative of the jussive but with the nuance of "cannot": in 46:6, for example, the verb surely means "cannot flee."[70] But it is probably better to stay with the jussive translation "Let . . . ," since the parallel in 8:23 expresses a wish rather than a fact.

The passage is then a striking expansion of 8:23. It is amusing that G and S have "day and night" rather than the reverse, but surely "night and day" is correct, given the opportunity to vary 8:23.

Michaelis suggested that instead of תִּדְמֶינָה (דמה "stop") the vocalization should be תִּדָּמֶינָה (דמם "be still, silent"). The parallel in Lam 2:18 has דמם, and the one in Lam 3:49 has דמה. Indeed there is no discernible pattern among the Versions in these three passages. G reflects M in the present passage and Lam 2:18, but reads דמם in Lam 3:49. V and T read דמם in all three passages. S reads דמם in the present passage; its understanding of the two passages in Lamentations is uncertain. Given the contrast of M in the two passages of Lamentations, the vocalization in the present passage can be either; one may as well then accept the vocalization of M here.

For "great fracture" (שֶׁבֶר גָּדוֹל) see 4:6; 6:1; for a form of the verb שבר with שֶׁבֶר see 8:21. The conjunction כִּי here can of course mean "for," as it does in 4:6 and 6:1, but in the context of lament it is appropriate to understand it as exclamatory (see 4:8, 13, and often). For "wound" (מַכָּה) with "sore" (נַחְלָה) see 10:19.

Jrm is impelled to continuous weeping for the total demise of his people.

■ **14:18** Given the hint in v 16 that Jrm is adapting words of Elijah about Jezebel (see there), one wonders whether the "alternative death" motif in the first four cola here is not stimulated by the old curse-form found in 1 Kgs 14:11; 16:4; 21:24; and there is further the pattern "cursed shall you be in the city, and curse shall you be in the field" in Deut 28:16 (see Form). For the nuance of "should" for the Hebrew perfect in conditions compare 2 Kgs 7:4, where much the same diction is to be found.[71] For חַלְלֵי "slain of" see 8:23; here, however, the Hebrew genitive expresses the agent ("by the sword"). The metonymy of "diseases of famine" for "those ill from famine" is striking; Dahood has collected examples in the Psalms.[72] For the phraseology of "look" found here compare 4:23–26 and 8:15.

The phrase "for both prophet and priest" is to be found in 23:11 as well. But what is the predicate of "prophet and priest" here?—its meaning has given much difficulty. Beyond the present passage the verb סחר qal appears about fifteen times in the OT in the participial form סֹחֵר, where the meaning is "merchant," and in finite forms three times—Gen 34:10, 21, and 42:34. The meaning of the Genesis passages is disputed. Given the participle, many assume it means "trade" (RSV); Cyrus Gordon, Albright, and de Vaux have recently affirmed this.[73] On the other hand, Speiser defends strongly the meaning "journey (in a circuit)," insisting that the meaning of the participle is a later secondary development;[74] and HALAT and Westermann[75] have accepted that definition. One could propose in the present instance a rendering like "make their rounds," but the parallel passage in which "both prophet and priest" occurs, 23:11, has a strongly pejorative verb, חנף "be godless, pollute," and "make their rounds" hardly has a similar impact. I therefore suggest here "peddle," whatever the meaning of the rest of the predicate may be.

What can אֶל־אֶרֶץ, literally "to the/a land," mean? Given the images of death earlier in the verse and the suspicion that אֶרֶץ refers to Sheol in v 2 and 15:7, one is led to conclude that the word here likewise refers to Sheol; and the diction of 23:11–12a makes it virtually

70 Joüon, Gramm., sec. 114k.
71 See GKC, sec. 106p.
72 Dahood, Psalms III, 412.
73 Cyrus H. Gordon, "Abraham and the Merchants of Ura," JNES 17 (1958) 29; William F. Albright, "Abram the Hebrew, A New Archaeological Interpretation," BASOR 163 (October 1961) 44; Roland de Vaux, "Les patriarches hébreux et

l'histoire," RB 72 (1965) 17.
74 Ephraim A. Speiser, "The Word SHR in Genesis and Early Hebrew Movements," BASOR 164 (December 1961) 23–28.
75 Westermann, Genesis II, 651.

certain (see there). The preposition אֶל occurs elsewhere with אֶרֶץ signifying Sheol (Job 10:21), so that the expression is a plausible one. The prophets and priests will peddle their wares all the way to the grave. Does the incident of 20:1–6 lie behind his indictment of the priests?

The last clause is also difficult. If וֹ stands at the beginning, then the clause means simply "and they have no understanding." But if the text lacks וֹ (see Text), then the clause may be construed as subordinate (without אֲשֶׁר) modifying "land." And that subordinate clause can be understood in several ways. It can be "the land which they do not know," since they are not yet in the grave. Or it can be "land where there is no knowledge"—Sheol is described in Ps 88:13 as the אֶרֶץ נְשִׁיָּה "land of forgetfulness," where it may be asked, "Are your [Yahweh's] wonderful works known [ידע nip'al]?" One must conclude that these multiple meanings are part of the text (compare 8:13), lending resonance to the affirmation that neither prophet nor priest has a clue what is happening in their midst.

These considerations lend cogency to the division of the two cola proposed here (against Rudolph, who separates the compound subject from the verb: compare Structure).

■ **14:19** The parallel of "Judah" is usually "Jerusalem" (v 2 and often), occasionally "Israel" (5:11) or "Jacob" (5:20); this is the only occurrence in Jer of a parallel with "Zion." If "Zion" has a parallel, it is usually "Jerusalem" (Isa 2:3; Mic 3:10). The impression left here then is that the people are concerned for political integrity ("Judah") and hope to retain it through faith in the cult ("Zion"); see below on v 21. One hears in 6:20 that Yahweh has rejected Judah. There is of course no way to know whether this rhetorical question is predicated on Jrm's prior proclamation of 6:30, but whether it is or not, the questions with הֲ and אִם in the threefold question form imply a negative answer (compare 2:19, 31; 22:28; those with a negative imply a positive answer—8:19, 22): compare the rhetorical questions below in v 22. The people cannot believe that the sentence has already been pronounced, and the infinitive absolute in the first colon reinforces the disbelief ("really?"). The verb in the second colon, גָּעַל "abhor," is found only here in the book, but a similar expression is found in the threat in 6:8 (verb: יקע): in both, the נֶפֶשׁ of Yahweh (his self, his

"soul") is represented as turning away from his people in loathing. For Yahweh's striking down (נכה hip'il) the people see 2:30; 5:3; for the "healing" for which the people hope in vain see 8:15.

For v 19b see 8:15.

■ **14:20** The admission of guilt in this verse offers diction very similar to that in 3:25; see the discussion there. For כִּי = "how" in a confession of sin compare v 7 and see 3:25.

■ **14:21** The phrase "do not spurn" (נאץ qal) is based on Deut 32:19, "Yahweh saw it [the way by which the people forgot him] and spurned them" (for other reminiscences of Deuteronomy 32, see especially 2:27–28); Ps 107:11 admits that in times past some Israelites had spurned the counsel of the Most High, but now they ask Yahweh to show mercy. There has always been the tendency to assume that the first colon means "do not spurn us" (so V, T; so RSV, JB, NAB, NJV), but it is clear from the poetry that the verbs of both the first and second cola carry as their object "the throne of your glory." The parallel verb in the second colon, נבל pi'el, has a similar meaning. The only other occurrence in the OT in which Yahweh is subject is Nah 3:6, where the object is Nineveh; the background passage is again evidently in Deuteronomy 32, this time v 15 there, where "Jeshurun" (= Israel) showed disdain for the Rock (= Yahweh). Again Yahweh is asked to abstain from doing to Israel what Israel has done to him.

There is no parallel for the phrase "the throne of your glory" in the OT, though in Ps 47:9 it is affirmed that Yahweh sits on "the throne of his holiness." In both instances the phrases mean "your glorious throne," "his holy throne." The closest passage in general diction to the present one is Lam 5:18–21; there, too, Yahweh's throne is in the context of "Zion" (vv 18–19 there). One notes also Isa 66:1, where Yahweh's throne is affirmed to be heaven, so that it is unnecessary to build a house for him. These texts make it clear that the reference here is to the temple and its cult; and the mention of Yahweh's name in the first line subtly reinforces this reference (the temple is the house which bears Yahweh's name, 7:10). The appeal in the third colon may be fatuous: if the people have broken the covenant with Yahweh (11:10), how can they expect Yahweh not to break the covenant with them?—and here the hopeless hope is similar to that in the first two cola of v 19; but the appeal to the temple cult is a kind of last redoubt of hope, that sense of final safety in the temple against which Jrm struggles in 7:1–12.

■ **14:22** The first two cola offer rhetorical questions the expected answer to which is no, and these questions form a nice counterpoise to the first two cola of v 19. If the questions about the pagan gods expect the answer no, then surely the questions about Yahweh can expect the answer no as well. For the phrase "non-gods of the nations" (הַבְלֵי הַגּוֹיִם) compare "alien non-gods" (הַבְלֵי נֵכָר) in 8:19. The hip'il plural participle מַגְשִׁמִים "rain-bringers" is unique, and Jrm may have devised it for the occasion: its very plurality is a contradiction in terms—how could there be a multiplicity of divine rain-bringers? The parallel to that participle is a bit more surprising in our day—we are so accustomed to looking to the sky for signs of rain: but of course the second colon carries the same question the first does. The "heavens" are a part of creation, created by Yahweh as much as the earth is, and the heavens do not produce rain of themselves; note that they are personified as cosmic witnesses in 2:12 (compare Isa 1:2). For "showers" (רְבִבִים) see 3:3; Ps 65:11 affirms that Yahweh brings them. The verb "long for" (קוה pi'el) subtly picks up the reference to Yahweh as the "hope/pool" (מִקְוֵה) of Israel in v 8.

M of the last colon says "Indeed it is you who have made all these." If this is the correct text, then "these" (אֵלֶּה) refers to the "showers." But it is noteworthy that 5:25 in M has "these" in the context of "rain" (גֶּשֶׁם, 5:24) and that in 23:10, where M has "curse" (אָלָה), a few MSS. and G and S have "these"—this in a verse concerned with drought. Given such evidence the present study has emended "these" (אֵלֶּה) to "curse" (אָלָה) in 2:34; 4:12; and 5:25 and does so here as well. There is no question but that "curse" may be used in the context of drought (Isa 24:6 is another instance—compare v 4 there): it is the notion of a kind of positive malevolent force that gains power over the land. On the other hand 30:15, where there is similar diction (Yahweh as subject, the verb "do," and the controverted substantive as object), is not to be emended, not at least if the original setting of that verse is long before the great drought. Therefore I propose that Jrm used "curse" here but that it is an ironic variation on normal diction which would have "these," and the vocalization of M slipped back to the expected word. The colon here, thus understood, gives a strong close to the verse and to the lament. If Yahweh can bring the drought, then he can bring rain.

■ **15:1** The opening rubric, "And Yahweh said to me," governs all of vv 1–4. The conjunction אִם here means "even if" (compare 14:12); but in contrast to the real condition in 14:12, the condition here is contrary to fact.[76] This shift heightens the rhetorical effect: they do fast, but it does no good; even if Moses were here, it would do no good. Though the Hebrew says literally "Moses and Samuel," the conjunction doubtless has alternative force, as often (Gen 26:11); and the singular verb reinforces that impression. Both Moses and Samuel were great intercessors in the past (Moses: Exod 32:11–13, 20–34; Num 14:13–19; Samuel: 1 Sam 7:9; 12:19–25); Ps 99:6 mentions Moses, Aaron, and Samuel. The mention of these earlier intercessors is striking: Moses is mentioned only four times otherwise in the prophets (Isa 63:11, 12; Mic 6:4; Mal 3:22) and Samuel not at all otherwise (compare the discussion before, on v 9). These men were not only intercessors but covenant mediators: for Samuel see 1 Samuel 12.[77] The mediation of these giants would do no good; nothing will change Yahweh's determination to carry out his sentence on the people. The phrase "stand before" (עמד לְפָנַי) with Yahweh carries a variety of connotations in the OT. It connotes "presenting oneself for worship" (7:10). It occurs four times, used by Elijah and Elisha, in the set phrase "As Yahweh (God of Israel/of hosts) lives, before whom I stand" (1 Kgs 17:1; 18:15; 2 Kgs 3:14; 5:16), so that it suggests the activity of a prophet or mediator. It also occurs with a king, of "attending" him, as a servant does (1 Kgs 1:2). The phrase אֵין נַפְשִׁי אֶל־הָעָם הַזֶּה is literally "my soul is not to this people": it is a unique construction in the OT (there is no other example of נֶפֶשׁ with אֵין, though it occurs with the positive יֵשׁ in Job 16:4). It is functionally equivalent to אֵינֶנִּי with the participle in 7:16; 11:14; and 14:12.

The imperative שׁלח pi'el "send (them) out" is richly ironic here, because this imperative is the watchword of the exodus from Egypt: "let my people go" (Exod 5:1;

---

76 Joüon, *Gramm.*, sec. 167f.
77 Muilenburg, "Covenantal Formulations," 360–64.

7:16, 26; 8:16; 9:1, 13; 10:3). Moses' task was to get the people out of Egypt; Jrm's task is to get the people out of Yahweh's presence. And the verb יצא "go out, away" is equally a verb of the exodus. The final verb may equally well be translated "and let them go away."[78]

■ **15:2** The question אָנָה נֵצֵא is not one demanding decision of the people ("Where shall we go?"—compare 2 Sam 2:1) but implies "Where are we being taken?"—compare Deut 1:28.

The answer comes in parallel cola. There are two reasons to take the last colon as a secondary addition. (1) The parallel in 14:12 has "sword, famine and pestilence," and it is clear that "death" here is a poetic synonym for "pestilence" (see below). (2) The first three are all alternative forms of death, a preoccupation continued in v 3, while "exile" is obviously not of this sort. The line is an exilic mitigation, stimulated by the similar diction of 43:11;[79] and perhaps the addition of a fourth term was further stimulated by the "four" in v 3 (Naegelsbach tried to insist that the sword in v 3 works on the living, while the other three destroyers work on the dead). The compressed phraseology with אֲשֶׁר "he who, those who," is found elsewhere in striking or proverbial expressions (Num 22:6; 2 Kgs 6:16).

The use of מָוֶת, literally "death," for "pestilence" is confined in the OT to this passage, to 18:21 and to 43:11, but it survives as θάνατος = "pestilence" in Rev 2:23; 6:8; and 18:8. The usage is found elsewhere in northwest Semitic;[80] the expression "Black Death" in the Middle Ages carries the same meaning (compare the remarks about personified Death in 9:20).

■ **15:3** The meaning of פקד qal, "appoint," is identical with that of the hip'il in 1:10. The use of מִשְׁפָּחוֹת here, literally "clans," for "sorts" of destroyers is unique in the OT, though the word means "species (of animals)" in Gen 8:19. Is there a play on the diction of 1:15, where Yahweh calls forth the clans of the earth against Judah? (so Giesebrecht, Volz).

G and *V* translate the verb סחב, the activity of the

dogs, as "tear," and this meaning has survived in *KJV* and *RSV*. But 2 Sam 17:13 confirms the meaning "drag off," which is found in the translation of *S* and *T* here (so also Rashi and Qimḥi). One has the impression that there is a sequence of actions here, "slay, drag off, devour, destroy," but the attempt by earlier commentators to identify which of the two last-named destroyers devours, and which destroys (Duhm, followed by Cornill, emends to "birds of the heavens to devour and the beasts of the earth to destroy") is ill-advised: both devour, and both destroy.[81]

■ **15:4** The diction of v 4a has many parallels in Jer.[82] The pattern is found in Mic 6:16, a passage no doubt genuine to that prophet. The phrase is duplicated in Deut 28:25b, but the priority must belong to Jrm.[83] The meaning of זְוָעָה is determined by the verb זוע "tremble" (in fear, as before a superior, Esth 5:9; see also the use of the noun in Isa 28:19).

Verse 4b is an alien addition to the words of Jrm. The punishment that is to be visited upon the people was due to their own sins as well as to those of the "fathers" (14:20); to specify Manasseh is a diversion from Jrm's message, though Manasseh's sins were a concern to the exilic redactor of Kings (2 Kgs 23:26; 24:3;[84] there may also be redactional expansion in 2 Kgs 21:2–17[85]). One may also note that the other occurrence in Jer of the preposition בִּגְלַל "on account of," namely 11:17, also seems to introduce secondary material.

■ **15:5–9** This extraordinary poem depends for its impact on several expressions hinting of Sheol, beginning with לִשְׁאֹל in v 5, which means both "to ask" and "to Sheol" (see below on v 5). It is difficult to be sure how many others there are, given our uncertainty about expressions for Sheol, but there are at least three others, and perhaps an additional one or two. Given the use of אֶרֶץ "land" to indicate or imply Sheol in 14:2 and 18, the references to Sheol here provide strong indication that the passage belongs in the sequence which begins in 14:1 (see Structure).

78 See Alonso Schökel, "Jeremías como anti-Moisés," 251.
79 See on this Holladay, "Prototype," 362.
80 See *DISO*, 146, entry מות II.
81 Compare the traditional curse-form, the unburied corpse, prey to bird and beast, in Hillers, *Treaty-Curses*, 68–69.

82 For a thorough survey see Weippert, *Prosareden*, 187–91.
83 Ibid., 191; von Rad, *Deuteronomy*, 175; Mayes, *Deuteronomy*, 350–51.
84 Gray, *Kings*, 745–46, 757–58.
85 Ibid., 707–9.

■ **15:5** The conjunction כִּי with which the verse begins is omitted by *G* and *S*, but there as no reason to delete it (as Volz and Rudolph do); judgment speeches of Yahweh elsewhere begin with the word (4:15), and one may take it as an emphatic particle. For "pity" (חמל) compare 13:14. The verb נוד has already appeared in 4:1 in the meaning "wander." The basic meaning of the word is "oscillate," and it is used of rocking motions of the head or body as a stylized manifestation of condolence (Job 2:11) or grief; it occurs in parallelism with "weep" in 22:10. The verb סור means "turn aside" (from an appointed path); compare 5:23. In referring to the שָׁלוֹם (literally "peace") of Jerusalem, Jrm evidently has Ps 122:6–8 in mind.[86]

There is no doubt that לִשְׁאֹל carries a double meaning, both "to ask" and "to Sheol." The phrase "ask about your well-being," literally "ask about peace for you," is equivalent to "greet" (that is, "ask 'How are you?'"), as in 2 Sam 8:10—that parallel also has the infinitive construct לִשְׁאֹל. This is the interpretation of the phrase followed by all commentators and translations. But it is equally true that סור is used with לְ and designations of place (Judg 20:8) and that לִשְׁאֹל may mean "to Sheol" (Pss 16:10; 31:18; 49:15; 88:4: the last-named passage is particularly close in diction to the present one). Given the likelihood that the "gates of the land" in v 7 refer to the gates of Sheol (see there), the double meaning here is particularly striking. (A similar pun of "ask" and "Sheol" is clearly to be seen in Isa 7:11: compare the Versions there.)

The ironic questions imply a negative answer: No one.

■ **15:6** The first colon of the verse begins with an emphatic subject pronoun. The verb נטש has appeared in 12:7: there Yahweh has "forsaken" his people. The reference here evidently is linked to 14:21, and both passages are linked to a parallelism in Deut 32:15. That is to say, in Deut 32:15 Yahweh says that Jeshurun (= Israel) forsook (נטש) God and disdained (נבל pi'el) the Rock (= God); in 14:21 the people beg God not to disdain (נבל pi'el) his glorious throne, so now Yahweh replies that it was the people who began the process of forsaking.

The second colon is literally "you have walked backward." There are no parallels in the OT to הלך with אָחוֹר, so that it is difficult to be certain of the imagery. The verb שׁוּב "return" does, however, occur with אָחוֹר, three times: in two instances the subject is the enemy who retreats (Pss 9:4; 56:10), and in the other instance (Lam 1:8) the subject is Jerusalem, who turns away (by implication: from Yahweh). In 7:24 there is an expression for apostasy (הָיָה לְאָחוֹר) evidently equivalent to that found here (and compare the image in 2:27), so that "walk away from me" cannot be far from the thought.

For "stretch out my hand over (the people)" see 6:12.

For לאה nip'al "be tired of, too tired to" see 6:11 and 9:4. The last verb in the verse gives textual uncertainty. the reading of *M*, הִנָּחֵם, gives excellent sense: Yahweh has stated in 4:28 that he will not "relent."[87] But the reading of *G* and *S*, הַנֵּחַ "letting them go," would reflect the verb in 14:9, and, if correct, would be Yahweh's ironic answer to the people: in 14:9 they said, "Do not leave us!" (that is, help us). Yahweh's answer would be, "I am tired of leaving you" (to your own impulses)—in short, Yahweh will answer the people's prayer, but not in the way they expect. The only argument against this reading is the shift from "you" to "them": it is better to save the shift until the beginning of v 7 (see Structure on 15:5–9).

■ **15:7** For זרה "winnow" see 4:11. The מִזְרֶה is the tool for winnowing, a winnowing-fork. In Palestine it is still made of wood, shaped like a pitchfork but with thicker tines.[88] After the grain has been threshed, it is winnowed with the winnowing-fork, and then the last of the chaff is removed with the winnowing-shovel (Isa 30:24).[89] The process here is a metaphor for judgment and defeat (compare Isa 41:15–16).

"At the gates of the land" has been a steady puzzle, and the *G* rendering, "at the gates of my people," has not

86 Berridge, p. 178.
87 See 4:28 and n. 101 there.
88 For drawings of winnowing-forks of present-day Palestinian peasants see Lucian Turkowski, "Peasant Agriculture in the Judaean Hills," *PEQ* 101 (1969) 107.
89 See H. Neil Richardson, "Winnowing," *IDB* 4:852,

and, in more detail, Wildberger, *Jesaja*, 1202, with further bibliography.

aided exegetical certitude. Some have thought the phrase to refer to the gates of the cities of the land, while others have translated הָאָרֶץ as "the earth" and assumed that "in the gates of the earth" referred to the coming exile of the people in various cities of the earth (*T*, Qimḥi). It is now clear that אֶרֶץ here refers to Sheol: Sheol has gates (Isa 38:10; Sir 51:9; compare Job 38:17).[90] Yahweh, then, has winnowed them, scattered them at the gates of Sheol. (Given this fresh understanding, it is uncanny to read Jerome's paraphrase in his commentary: "I have scattered them as with a winnowing-fork, so that I may purify my threshing-floor; and I have scattered them at the gates of the earth, so that they may tread, in a certain manner, the thresholds of the nether-world.")

The verb שׁכל pi'el means "make (someone) childless, deprive of children"; this is the only occurrence of the verb in Jer. There may here be a reminiscence of Deut 32:25, where the sword will deprive of children, given the use of "sword" in v 9 and given the fact that that verse in Deuteronomy speaks of בָּחוּר "young men," a word which occurs here in v 8 (compare the possible reference to Deut 32:15 in v 6). The verb אבד pi'el "wipe out" has already occurred in 12:17.

The last colon, מִדַּרְכֵיהֶם לוֹא־שָׁבוּ, is open to multiple interpretations. It is conceivable that it may be taken as an independent clause, "From their ways they did not turn": there is the repeated pattern in the prose of Jer, "turn, each from his evil way."[91] H. Conrad von Orelli took this option,[92] as do all recent translations; it is assumed by such a translation, given the parallels in the prose, that the "ways" are the wicked ways of the people, but Orelli assumed that it is the paths of war and exile from which the people will not return. Other commentators see the other syntactical possibility, that מִדַּרְכֵיהֶם modifies the verbs in the previous colon and that לוֹא־שָׁבוּ is a subordinate clause modifying מִדַּרְכֵיהֶם; but here the options are many. One may understand the expression as "because of their ways from which they have not turned":

G has taken this tack, understanding the preposition to express cause, when it paraphrases "because of their evil," omitting the verb. But the preposition can be taken as expressing comparison: the second colon of v 8, parallel with the present colon, carries such a meaning. One would then translate "I have wiped them out to a greater number than their ways from which they do not return": 2:36 refers to the people's "changing" their way, and 2:28 refers to the number of the people's gods and altars to Baal; further 5:6 and 14:7 refer to the number of the people's transgressions. Given the fact that a clear-cut מִן of comparison occurs in v 8, this is not a strong possibility, but it hovers in the background. But there is one more, a hint of Sheol: Sheol is the place from which one does not return (Job 7:10; 10:21). Since "in the way of all the earth" is a euphemism for dying (Josh 23:14; 2 Kgs 2:2), and since מִן sometimes carries the nuance of "in" as much as "from" (9:18; 18:22), the phrase here can well mean "I have wiped them out in the paths from which they cannot return." This possibility is increased slightly by the parallel structure in 14:18, "the land in which they have no knowledge" (see Interpretation there).

■ **15:8** For עצם "be(come) (more) numerous" see 5:6. It is a terrible reversal of the great promise to Abraham and Jacob (Gen 22:17; 32:13) that the number of their offspring should be more in number than the sand of the sea: how appalling that more should be less. (Compare the same implication in 10:24 and 20:1–6.) There is no need to shift these lines elsewhere (Condamin, Rudolph); the lines fit the structure where they are (see Structure).

The rest of the verse shares diction with 6:26: "devastator" (שֹׁדֵד), "come upon" (בוֹא עַל), "suddenly" (פִּתְאֹם). The third colon is odd and "to them" must be excised (see Text), but there is no need for elaborate emendations proposed by Volz and Rudolph: "mother" balances "she who has borne seven" in v 9 (see Structure), and the link between "mother" here and "my mother" in v 10 seems secure. The בָּחוּר is the "young man" in his prime,

---

90   See Dahood, *Psalms I*, 57, 106.

91   For a discussion of the pattern see Holladay, "Prototype," 355, and, in much more detail, Weippert, *Prosareden*, 137–48: see 137–39 for the present passage.

92   H. Conrad von Orelli, *Die Propheten Jesaja und Jeremia* (Kurzgefasster Kommentar zu den heiligen

Schriften Alten und Neuen Testaments; Nördlingen: Beck, 1887) 268.

of the age for soldiering (11:22); here it is the mother of such young men who are crushed by the battle—the expression is in parallelism with "widows" earlier in the verse. Why "noon"? It is the time of greatest security (see on 6:4), the time of surprise attacks. Weiser's suggestion, that it is the "noontime" of the lives of the young men, is not impossible but lies in the background.

The first word of the last colon, עִיר, is open to multiple meanings. All commentators agree that the primary meaning is "agitation," that is, that the word is עִיר II, a noun formed from עוּר "rouse oneself"; this is doubtless true, given the parallel בֶּהָלוֹת "terror." But of course the common word עִיר I "city" lies in the background ("Jerusalem" is named in v 5): if נפל hip'il can be used of throwing down a wall in 2 Sam 20:15, it can be used of throwing down a city here. But beyond that is the possibility that "city" here implies Sheol: "Sheol" and "terror" would make a good pair. There is the possibility that a phrase in Job 24:12 must be read עִיר מֵתִים "city of the dead," a reference to Sheol, and that the text of Ps 73:20 contains such a reference.[93] It is certain that the synonymous *qrt* in Ugaritic may be used of Sheol.[94] And after all, "gates" (v 7) implies a city.

■ **15:9** For "she languishes" (אֻמְלְלָה) compare 14:2, where the verb is used of Judah's gates. Now it is the mother of seven who is no longer able to bear. The colon here is a reference to 1 Sam 2:5b, part of Hannah's song: "The barren has borne seven, but she who has many children languishes." That is to say, Yahweh "brings low, but he also exalts" (1 Sam 2:7). But the verse just preceding in her song makes the point specific: "Yahweh kills and brings to life; he brings down to Sheol and raises up." Here again is a reference to Sheol: Yahweh is busy with the maleficent aspect of his work. The expression "mother of seven" is a proverbial one for the fulfilled mother (Ruth 4:15); one recalls the narrative in 2 Macc 7:1—42 of the mother who was deprived of her sons, one after the other.

It is an interesting question whether one of the motifs

of vv 5–9 is a reference to Samuel (given his mention in v 1). One has not only the reminiscence of the Song of Hannah here, but a possible reminiscence in v 7 to Samuel's word to Agag before he slew him ("As your sword has made women childless [שׁכל pi'el], so shall your mother be childless among women" [or, "be more childless than (other) women"][95]—1 Sam 15:33) and Saul's consulting Samuel by having him summoned from Sheol (1 Samuel 28). For Jrm's possible connection with the traditions of Shiloh see 1:1, Interpretation.

In the second colon it is a pretty question whether נַפְשָׁה "her life, breath" is the subject of the verb ("her breath gasps") or adverbial ("she gasps out her life/her breath"). Since נֶפֶשׁ can be a synonym for the person himself or herself, either construction is possible. Since the fourth colon ("she is ashamed and abashed") offers "she" as subject, and the third colon has "her sun" as subject, a chiastic structure suggests that נַפְשָׁה is the subject here. For this subject with the verb "gasp" (נפח), compare the subject רוּחַ in Ezek 37:9; the passive participle of this verb occurs in 1:13 ("being fanned").

The expression in the third colon, "her sun is set while yet day," clearly balances the reference to the devastator at noon in v 8. Question: Is there any hint here that the sun "sets" (literally "goes in") into the underworld at night? This is the Egyptian belief;[96] in any event, it is clear that the concept of darkness was associated with Sheol (Ps 56:14). A very similar expression is found in Amos 8:9–10.

Her reaction is the same as that of the nobles and the farmhands in 14:3–4: she is ashamed; the parallel חפר pi'el is synonymous and almost always in parallelism with בושׁ "be ashamed."

For the destruction of the remnant compare 6:9.

Aim

If the reconstruction of the setting of this liturgy is correct, two traditional scourges, famine and sword, become real for Judah. The sword was at the moment

---

93   For these passages see the discussion in Dahood, *Psalms II*, 193–94.

94   Ug. 4.8.11.

95   BDB, 1013b.

96   See conveniently Henri Frankfort, *Ancient Egyptian Religion* (New York: Columbia University, 1948; rep. Harper, 1961) 106.

only potential: it had been real in Ashkelon in 604 and would become real again in Jerusalem in 598. But famine loomed. And in all this Jrm saw the hand of Yahweh, and he could not grasp why the people would continue to ignore the deeds of Yahweh (5:12; 6:14), indeed why the prophets should continue to assure the people that the evidence was illusory (14:13). The king declared a fast, and an official liturgy was offered by the authorities. But when the king burned Jrm's scroll, the prophet perceived that Yahweh had determined on his course and would not turn from it. The result was Jrm's own version of a liturgy for the emergency, a liturgy which would demonstrate the fruitlessness of any attempt by the community to turn Yahweh's hand from them. Though rains doubtless came, and though Babylon stayed its hand in the short run, Jrm continued to insist the army would return. Even after the first conquest of Jerusalem in 598 there were those who insisted there were better days ahead (28:3–4), but Jrm continued to preach the doom of his nation. When, fourteen years later, his word was vindicated, the twin scourges of sword and famine struck again (Lam 4:9), so that those two, and the third that follows—pestilence—became a constantly repeated slogan, helping to shape the apocalyptic mind-set in the centuries that followed (Mark 13:7–8).

Bibliography

(See also "The Confessions of Jeremiah" before
11:18)

Behler, Gebhard-Maria
"Vocation menacée et renouvelée, Jr 15,10–11.
15–21," *VSpir* 120 (1969) 539–67.

Bright, John
"A Prophet's Lament and Its Answer: Jeremiah
15:10–21," *Int* 28 (1974) 59–74.

Gerstenberger, Erhard
"Jeremiah's Complaints: Observations on Jer
15₁₀₋₂₁," *JBL* 82 (1963) 393–403.

Hubmann
Untersuchungen.

Reventlow
Liturgie, 210–29.

On vv 10–14:

Smith, G. V.
"The use of quotations in Jeremiah xv 11–14," *VT*
29 (1979) 229–31.

On vv 15–21:

Berridge
pp. 114–37, 158–60, 208–9.

Bracke, John M.
"Jeremiah 15:15–21," *Int* 37 (1983) 174–78.

Jüngling, Hans-Winfried
"Ich mache dich zu ehernen Mauer,
Literarkritische Überlegungen zum Verhältnis von
Jer 1,18–19 zu Jer 15,20–21," *Bib* 54 (1973) 1–24.

15

10

Woe is me, mother, that you (ever) bore
  me,
  a man of lawsuit and strife[a] for the
    whole land!
I have not lent, nor have they lent to me,
  (yet) ⟨all of them have treated me with
    contempt.⟩[b]

Text

10a   Omitting with a few MSS. and *G* a second
occurrence of אִישׁ ("a man of lawsuit and man of
strife"). The word overloads the colon. The linking
of a noun in the construct state with two coordi-
nated nouns in the absolute state is possible (König,
Syntax, sec. 276b) but is largely confined to older
portions of the OT, so the inserted word is an
understandable gloss.

b   *M* reads כֻּלֹּה "each one" followed by the consonantal text מקללוני, read by the ketib מְקַלְלוּנִי, by the
qere' and by a few MSS. מְקַלְלֵנִי, and by the qere' of
a few MSS. מְקַלְלַנִי. Though the spelling of כֻּלֹּה,
with a he, is odd, it is cited elsewhere in Jer (2:21;
8:6; 20:7). But the verb, no matter how pronounced, is certainly an impossible form. A singular
participle could conceivably have a pronoun suffix
appropriate for verbs, but one would expect מְקַלְלֵנִי
(GKC, sec. 116f); the ketib form, however, a
participle with a perfect plural ending, is surely an
error. All commentators have followed the suggestion of Michaelis to revocalize the two words as

[Yahweh has said:]ᵃ
I swear ᵇI have armored youᵇ well,

כְּלִמָּם קִלְלוּנִי, which is plausible, though it should be stressed that כְּלִמָּם is not otherwise attested (the nearest is the pausal form כְּלִמָּה, 2 Sam 23:6). One wonders if we do not have a conflate text before us of two traditions, כְּלֹה קִלְלַנִי "each one has treated me with contempt" (compare the singular in 20:7), and כְּלָם קִלְלוּנִי "all of them have treated me with contempt," with both he and mem written. In any event the meaning of the colon is clear.

11a   *M* "Yahweh has said" is odd; the only parallel in the prophets of such a rubric (without כה "thus") is 46:25, where the rubric is more elaborate. Giesebrecht points out that *G* reads ἡ ἰσχύς μου = כֹּחִי at the beginning of the last colon of v 10, so he suggests that the Hebrew prototype of *G* may in this way have preserved a misplaced and misread כה. Further a few MSS. of the Hebrew do read "Thus Yahweh has said" (so de Rossi). But how could so common a phrase ever have been misread? The Hebrew text being dubious, all commentators (and *RSV, JB, NAB*) follow *G* here, γένοιτο δέσποτα, reading אָמֵן יהוה, "so be it, Yahweh," assuming that Jrm continues to speak in v 11. But the present study, to the contrary, proposes that Yahweh speaks (see Preliminary Observations, Interpretation), so that the indication of *M* is correct. Given the full rubric in 15:19, "Therefore thus Yahweh has said," one must either assume that in some mysterious way a similar rubric here was mutilated, or one has the insertion of a secondary (but correct) indication of shift of speaker; the second possibility is more likely.

b—b   The consonantal text, שׁורתך, has been given many interpretations. The ketib has traditionally been read as שֵׁרוּתֶךָ, understood as a contracted form of שְׁאֵרוּתֶךָ "your remnant." The qere' and some MSS. read שֵׁרִיתֶךָ, שׁרה pi'el, understood as "I have loosened you," "I have set you free," but the only cited form of this verb (Job 37:3) is in the qal stem, not the pi'el. MSS. differ for the ketib: there are many reading שׁרותיך, and scattered ones reading an 'alep after the šin, שׁארותך, שׁארותיך, שׁאריתך, שׁאריתיך. The reading with the 'alep indicates an understanding of the word as שְׁאֵרִיתֶךָ "your remainder" (so, already *V, a', s', T*); Rashi explained this as the equivalent of הִשְׁאַרְתִּיךָ "I have left you." Most recent commentators (Volz, Condamin, Rudolph, Bright) read שֵׁרַתִּיךָ, שׁרת pi'el, "I have served you," a reading based on the assumption that Jrm continues to speak (compare note a and Preliminary Observations). Another suggestion was originally that of Hitzig, to assume the verb שׁרר qal, the root implicit in the word שֹׁרְרִי "my enemies" in the Psalms (e.g., Ps 5:9): Hitzig assumed an anomalous qal infinitive, thus שְׁרוֹתֶךָ, while Naegelsbach proposed the finite verb שֵׁרוֹתִיךָ (compare Holladay, *Spokesman*, 96). But the difficulty is that the verb means "defame," as indicated by the Amarna glosses (Dahood, *Psalms II*, 25), a meaning that does not fit the present context. I read the qere' שֵׁרִיתִךָ as a denominative piel (שׁרה)

I swear I have intervened with you
  in a time of disaster
    and in a time of distress
    [that is, the enemy.]ᶜ

12 Can ᵃ he breakᵃ iron,
  iron from the north, and bronze?

13 Your power and your treasures as loot I
    shall give away, for no payment—
    butᵃ not for any of your sins or any of
      your boundariesᵇ either!

14 And I shall transferᵃ your enemies
  to a land ᵇyou do not know,ᵇ
  for fire ᶜhas broken outᶜ in my anger,
   ᵈ over you allᵈ it is kindled.

15 You know, Yahweh:
  remember me and deal with me
    and gain satisfaction for me from my
      persecutors;
    do not, because of your ⟨slowness⟩ᵃ
      of anger, take me away,
      consider how I have borne disgrace
      on your account.

16 Your words were found, and I ate them,
  and ᵃyour wordᵃ became for me a joy
    and the delight of my heart,
  for I bear your name,
    Yahweh, God of hosts.

17 I have not sat in the circle of the merry-
    makers,
    nor exulted, because of your hand;
  I have sat alone,
    for you have filled me with male-
      diction.

18 Why has my pain become endless,
  my wound incurable,
    refusing to be healed?
  You really are becoming for me, as it
    were, a deception,
    untrustworthy waters!

19 Therefore thus Yahweh has said:
  If you come back and I take you back,
    (then) in my presence you shall stand;
      and if you utter what is precious
        rather than rubbish,
      (then) my mouth you shall be, as it
      were;
  they are the ones to come back to you,
    not you to go back to them.

20 [And I shall make you to this people
    into a fortified bronze wall;
  though they shall fight against you,
    they shall not overcome you,
  for I am with you
    to save you and rescue you,
          oracle of Yahweh;

21 and I shall rescue you from the hand of
    the wicked,
  and ransom you from the grasp of the
    violent.]ᵃ

from שִׁרְיוֹן "armor" (so Franz Hubmann, by personal communication); see Interpretation.

c   By the exegesis given here, אֶת־הָאֹיֵב must be taken as a gloss, like אֶת־יהוה in 17:13 (see there), and like "the king of Assyria" in Isa 7:17 (see Wildberger, *Jesaja*, 268); compare "spirit of Yahweh" in Mic 3:8 (on which see Wolff, *Micha*, 61). See Interpretation.

12a–a   *M* reads הֲיָרֹעַ, רעע II qal "break"; this is no doubt correct (see Interpretation). But a few MSS. read הֲיֵדַע, thus "Can one know iron?" and *G* and θ' read the equivalent, "Can iron be known?" And s' reads הֲיָרַע, "Does iron go bad?" (רעע I), and a' and *V* read הֲיֵרַע (defectively) "Shall iron be allied with . . . ?" (רעה). But one may accept *M* (see Interpretation).

13a   Two MSS. and *G* and *V* omit the conjunction ו; the general lack of understanding of the syntax has led to confusion here and elsewhere in this verse. The conjunction belongs.

b   Many MSS. read גְּבוּלְךָ "your boundary" (for *M* ⟨גְּבוּלֶיךָ⟩); the meaning is scarcely affected.

14a   Many MSS. (and evidently *T*) read וְהַעֲבַדְתִּי "and I shall make . . . serve," and a few MSS. and *G* and *S* read וְהַעֲבַדְתִּיךָ "and I shall make you serve" with 17:4. *M* is correct, a deliberate variant from 17:4; see Interpretation.

b—b   Many MSS. insert the conjunction אֲשֶׁר before the verb phrase: the meaning is unaffected, but the addition is prosaicizing. The few MSS. read the verb here as יְדַעְתֶּם (second plural) rather than the singular יָדַעְתָּ of *M*; *T* reads this verb as plural along with its plural reading of the verb in the first colon as "and you shall serve": that tradition of interpretation assumes wrongly that the address is to the people.

c—c   A few MSS. follow 17:4 in reading קְדַחְתֶּם "you [plural] have kindled."

d—d   The Hebrew here is עֲלֵיכֶם "over you [plural]": the shift to plural here indicates both Jrm and his enemies (see Interpretation). Some MSS. read עַד־עוֹלָם "for ever" with 17:4; a few read a mixed text, עַד־עֲלֵיכֶם or עֲלֵיכֶם עַד־עוֹלָם.

15a   The *M* vocalization אֶרֶךְ "slow" is based on the phrase in Exod 34:6, "slow of anger"; but the vocalization here must surely be that of the noun אֹרֶךְ (Volz, Rudolph).

16a–a   Read, with many MSS. and the qere' and with *G* and *V*, דְּבָרְךָ (singular) instead of the ketib דְּבָרֶיךָ "your words" (so Volz, Rudolph). The verb is singular, and the wording of *G* and *V* indicates that the shift from the plural in the first colon to the singular here is old; it is certainly the *lectio difficilior*, and the parallel phraseology of 20:8 offers the singular. The solution of Duhm, Giesebrecht, and Bright, to omit "your word" as a gloss (Bright: "and it is was my joy . . . to bear your name"), is scarcely preferable.

20—21a   These verses are a secondary addition, by Jrm himself, when vv 15–19 were combined with vv 10–14; see Interpretation.

Preliminary Observations

Verses 10–21 comprise a sequence of confessional material analogous to that in 11:18—12:6. This sequence appears to break into two units, vv 10–14 and 15–21. But whereas the cores of the two units in 11:18—12:6 seem to have had settings near in time to each other, and therefore to have analogous structures (see there), the two units here seem to have had different settings, vv 15–19 in the winter of 601–600 (like that of the core of the two units in 11:18—12:6), vv 10–14 in the summer of 594, when also vv 20–21 were appended to vv 15–19 (see Setting). It would therefore be possible in the present study to consider vv 10–14 separately from vv 15–21. They are considered together as a matter of convenience, and to bring vv 20–21 into the context of vv 10–14. (There may in addition be some matching in structure between the two: see further Structure.)

The exegesis of vv 15–21 can proceed with little difficulty, but vv 11–14 bristle with interrelated problems, few of which can be solved with finality. The data for the conclusions reached in the present study are offered in the appropriate sections below, but some preliminary account must be given here.

(1) How should one understand vv 13–14? These verses are a variation of 17:3–4. In both passages Yahweh is the speaker, but the words are addressed to Judah in 17:3–4 and appear to be addressed to Jrm here. Because v 12 here mentions "iron" and that word appears also in 17:1, Volz and Rudolph judge vv 13–14 to be a damaged variant of 17:3–4; this judgment has been accepted so widely that *NEB* omits the verses. (Indeed Rudolph believes v 12 is likewise a corruption from 17:1–2, and Bright omits vv 12–14, stating that "its text is much disturbed," and *NAB* does likewise.) Of course there is no way in this circumstance to prove that vv 13–14 are not a careless variation of 17:3–4, but there are contrasts in wording which appear to be due to something other than carelessness (thus v 13: לֹא בִמְחִיר; 17:3: בָּמֹתֶיךָ: for a complete comparison see Interpretation), and therefore the option is worth pursuing that the contrasts in wording between the two passages are deliberate, that vv 13–14 are an ironic variant of 17:3–4,

an adaptation of that passage as an address to Jrm (so Hubmann).[1]

(2) It is clear that Jrm speaks in v 10 and Yahweh speaks in vv 13–14, but who speaks in vv 11–12? The wording of both verses is difficult (see below), and the rubric at the beginning of v 11 in *M* ("Yahweh has said") is dubious. Commentators have therefore concluded that *G* is here correct ("So be it, Yahweh") and consequently that Jrm continues to speak in vv 11–12. But exegesis of v 11 suggests that Yahweh speaks (see Interpretation, particularly on the verb הִפְגַּעְתִּי). The conclusion reached here is that the rubric is correct[2] but that it may have been a secondary addition (see Text).

(3) The meaning of v 11 is puzzling, but that of v 12 is opaque: what is the subject?—what is the object? The solution taken here, following Rudolph, is that "iron," "iron from the north," and "bronze" are parallel objects, but in contrast to Rudolph (and the translations that follow him, *RSV* and *JB*), I believe that the subject of "break" is not the impersonal "one" ("does one break iron . . . ?" but rather "he," that is, Hananiah, the context being 28:13 (for the details see Setting, Interpretation).

(4) Do vv 11–12 offer good news or bad news? Evidently Yahweh's answers to Jrm's laments may be of either kind. Thus 11:22–23 is reassuring, while 12:5 implies that worse is yet to come; 15:19 suggests that Jrm's task is more costly than he had understood it to be, while vv 20–21 are reassuring. The conclusion reached in this study is that vv 11–12 (and vv 13–14 as well) offer both good news and bad news, and that this mixed news is expressed by ambiguity and irony (see Interpretation on the verses). If that is the case, it is no wonder that exegesis of the verses has proved difficult.

(5) What is the meaning and place of "you know" at the beginning of v 15? The expression is missing in *G*. Rudolph believes it is original but belongs at the end of v 11 (he assumes that vv 12–14 are an insertion). If the expression belongs where it now stands, it could either close off v 14, Yahweh's speech to Jrm, or begin v 15, Jrm's fresh speech to Yahweh (so Hubmann).[3] Given the similar expression at the beginning of 18:23, the latter alternative is accepted here.

If these preliminary observations are correct, then the

---

1   Hubmann, *Untersuchungen*, 233.
2   So ibid., 206.
3   Ibid., 272–73.

structure of this sequence is identical with that of 11:18—12:6: a lament of Jrm (v 10), an answer from Yahweh (vv 11–14), a second lament of Jrm (vv 15–18), an answer from Yahweh (vv 19–21); see further Structure.

Structure

This confessional sequence appears to have been collected and placed in the second scroll along with 11:18—12:6: both collections consist of a pair of laments from Jrm and their answer from Yahweh (see Preliminary Observations), and there is the match of "your father" in 12:6 with "my mother" in v 10 here.[4] It is also likely that these two confessional sequences were collected along with the liturgy on the drought and battle (see 14:1—15:9, Preliminary Observations): there may be a link between the description of the drought in 12:4 and that in 14:2–6, and between 15:8–9 (15:8, "mother," and 15:9, "give birth" [ילד]) and 15:10 ("my mother" and "give birth" [ילד]).[5] It is also conceivable that the sequence was perceived to form an inclusio with chapter 1: v 10 here with 1:5, and vv 20–21 with 1:18–19.

There may be a parallelism between vv 10–14 and vv 15–21: v 11 has אם־לא twice, and v 19 has אם twice;[6] but given the contrast of meaning between the two expressions and the contrast of settings of the two passages, this parallel may be less than compelling.

Structure of vv 10–14. There are, on the other hand, structural connections between the lament in v 10 and Yahweh's answer in vv 11–12. Thus "I have not lent, nor have they lent to me" (v 10b) balances "I swear I have armored you . . . I swear I have intervened with you" (v 11aβbα), parallel clauses each introduced by לא, the second verb in each instance complemented by בְּ and suffix, בִי in v 10, בְךָ in v 11. And one could draw a parallel between "a man of lawsuit and strife" in v 10 and "in a time of disaster and in a time of distress" in v 11; the parallel is even closer if "man of" is to be repeated before "strife" (compare Text).

There is no structural connection between vv 10–12 and vv 13–14, and, given that fact and given also the fact that vv 13–14 are a variant of 17:3–4, one must conclude that vv 13–14 were added secondarily to vv 10–

12[7] (see further Setting).

Verse 10 is best analyzed as two bicola. The fourth colon balances both the first colon (קִלְלָנִי [or whatever], "abused me"; יְלִדְתָּנִי, "you bore me") and the second (both contain כֹּל), and the second and third balance in that each has a double expression ("man of lawsuit and strife," "I have not lent nor have they lent to me"). One assumes v 11 is a tetracolon. Verse 12 is a puzzle; if it is a bicolon it cannot be divided except between "iron" and "iron from the north."

One assumes that the material in vv 13 and 14 can be divided into cola. In v 13 "your strength" and "your treasures" are parallel objects of "I shall give away," and the division of cola cannot separate an object from its verb; one has, then, a colon with internal parallelism, so that "for all your sins" and "for all your boundaries," matching them, must likewise be a parallel within a single colon. In v 14 "to a land you do not know" must make up a separate colon in the way it does in 14:18 (and compare the last colon of 15:7). Both verses, then, are bicola.

Structure of vv 15–21. There are no structural connections between vv 15–19 and vv 20–21;[8] one must therefore conclude that the latter were added secondarily (see Setting).

There are two points in vv 15–21 where there is uncertainty of division into cola, in v 16 and v 17. The difficulty in v 16 is how to divide v 16aβ ("and your word . . . my heart"). The Masoretic punctuation pauses after "for me"; but 6:10 has a colon which must consist of "Look: the word of Yahweh has become for them a reproach," so that by this pattern the division here must come after "a joy" (so also Rudolph). Then in v 17 the Masoretic punctuation suggests a tricolon, the divisions occurring after "nor exulted" and "sat alone." This is possible, but the arrangement of a tetracolon offered here, with the three first-person verbs in separate cola, seems preferable. (Duhm and Cornill emend or rearrange the text; Condamin assumes words are missing after "nor exulted," and Rudolph mechanically combines the five cola of v 16 with three cola in v 17 to make eight, without regard to parallelism.)

In v 15 each colon after the introductory one has an

---

4   Holladay, *Architecture*, 138–40.
5   Ibid., 146.
6   Hubmann, *Untersuchungen*, 254–57.
7   Ibid., 257.
8   Ibid., 250–51, 290–93.

imperative to Yahweh (or, in the third colon, a prohibition). And v 16a is a tight tricolon, with "your words" and "your word" in the first and second colon, "joy" and "delight" in the second and third, and "my heart" in the third to match the image of the mouth in the first. Verse 17 is similarly a tight tetracolon, with "I have sat" in the first and third cola, "circle" and "alone" in the first and third, "merrymakers" and "exulted" in the first and second, and the hint of chiasmus in the second and fourth in the arrangement of Yahweh's actions and Jrm's. The first three cola of v 18 form as tight a tricolon as the one in v 16a. In fact vv 15–16 match vv 17–18 in the sequence of tetracolon, tricolon, and bicolon: and is the hearer to perceive that the two bicola both deal with the identity of Yahweh? At the same time form-critically v 15 is tied to v 18, and vv 16 and 17 belong with each other: v 15 is a plea for action from Yahweh, and v 18 is the plaintive question why there has been no action, while v 16 is Jrm's reminder to Yahweh of their initial companionship and v 17 is a declaration of the prophet's innocence, both verses concluding with כִּי clauses of motive (see Form). In this way the whole discourse forms a kind of chiasmus.

Verse 19 embodies the original response from Yahweh (see Setting and Interpretation, vv 20–21). It is a poem in six cola that is again tightly organized. The first four cola (v 19a) consist of two pairs of protasis ("if" clause) and apodosis ("then" clause). The second and fourth cola are thus parallel, leading one to interpret the first by the third (see Interpretation). Verse 19b (the last two cola) are parallel with each other, both offering an occurrence of "return" (שׁוב qal), these occurrences balancing the occurrences of the two stems of שׁוב (qal: "come back"; hip'il, "take back") in the first colon. Verse 19a on first hearing appears to refer to the relationship between Jrm and Yahweh, and v 19b to the relationship between Jrm and his enemies; but if these enemies are the false prophets (see Interpretation), then the second and fourth cola have at least indirect reference to the false prophets, who have not stood in the council of Yahweh (23:22) and who do not function as Yahweh's mouth (23:31).

Verses 20–21 have a structure closely resembling that of 1:18–19, of which this is a variant; see there.

Form

Verse 10 embodies a lament of Jrm's analogous to those in 11:18–20 and 12:1–4. It opens with an apostrophe to the prophet's mother; this is, of course, a rhetorical device—Jrm's mother need no longer be living, any more than Jonathan was in David's apostrophe to him (2 Sam 1:26), or Absalom (2 Sam 19:1). The expression "woe is me" is typical in this book for the introduction to laments (4:13, 31; 6:4; 10:19; 45:3); the כִּי which follows introduces the basis for the lament. For the motif "Why was I born?" compare 1 Macc 2:7 and 2 Esdr 5:35, though the expression in these texts may have been shaped to some degree by the present passage. The second half of the verse embodies an assertion of innocence such as is found in individual laments in the Psalms (Ps 35:7, 19, "without cause").[9] It is couched in a form which may be proverbial ("I have not lent, nor have they lent to me"), but there is no way to be certain (see Interpretation).

Yahweh's response begins in v 11 by two clauses each introduced by the oath-particle אִם־לֹא, translated here "I swear," though the sense of a divine oath may be attenuated here (see Interpretation). If the interpretation here of the first verb is correct ("I have armored you"), one has an expression of Yahweh's equipping Jrm as a warrior for a holy war against Judah.[10] The second verb, here translated "I have intervened with you" (הִפְגַּעְתִּי בְךָ), seems close to one of the verbs of Jrm's call, "I have appointed you" (הִפְקַדְתִּיךָ): coming after Jrm's reference to his birth in v 10, the diction suggests that Yahweh is still very much in control of Jrm's calling. The general tone of v 11 is then a reassurance analogous to that found in the oracle of salvation (compare on 1:17–19).

Verse 12 offers a rhetorical question to Jrm parallel to the rhetorical questions in 12:5; the question here implies a negative answer and thus Jrm's success in his struggle.

Verses 13–14 must be understood as an expansion of Yahweh's answer to Jrm: they are an adaptation of words which Jrm has previously addressed to the people (17:3–4).[11] If the present study has understood the text correctly, the verses combine many genres: an announcement to Jrm of Yahweh's judgment on his enemies (v

---

9   Hermann Gunkel, *Einleitung in die Psalmen* (Göttingen: Vandenhoeck & Ruprecht, 1933, 1966) 238–40.

10   For the theme see Berridge, p. 200.

11   See n. 1.

14a) which is moderate reassurance to Jrm; an announcement of the suffering that the prophet is undergoing (v 13a) which is still moderate reassurance to him (v 13b); and a summary statement about the coming destruction, introduced by כִּי, which acknowledges the suffering that both Jrm and his enemies are destined to undergo (v 14b).

The form of the second lament has already been given in outline (see Structure). It begins with pleas to Yahweh (v 15; compare 11:20; 12:3); the parallel of "remember me" and "deal with me" is duplicated in Ps 106:4, and one may also note Samson's prayer which begins, "Yahweh, remember me" (Judg 16:28). Verse 17 is a declaration of innocence (see below), but v 16 is not quite that: it is more nearly a recitation of the positive joy which the prophet received in the first instance from his calling. It is possible that the shift of thought from "remember me" in v 15 to "joy" in v 16 may stem from the same shift in Psalm 106 from v 4 to v 5 there. In any event the testimony of "joy" belongs more to the category of a hymn than of a lament (note the language of Ps 119:111). Verse 17, as already stated, is a declaration of innocence—very similar language is found in Ps 26:4–5. Verse 18 closes the lament with a question "why?" (compare 123:1)—the language is similar to that in Ps 42:10–11, and with an accusation (compare the language of 2:31 and 14:9!).

The response of Yahweh to that lament (v 19) opens with a parallel pair of covenant conditions analogous to the covenant condition in Exod 19:5–6: "If you will obey my voice . . . you shall be my own possession among all peoples. . . ."[12] The analogy of the form of these conditions to the covenant condition found in Exod 19:5–6 and elsewhere reinforces the phraseological parallel here between the word from Yahweh to Jrm, "Repent!" and the same word from Yahweh to Israel in chapter 3, "Repent!" The contrast between the content of the two cola in v 19b is best understood as an adaptation of a presentation of covenant choice, such as "Behold, I set before you this day a blessing and a curse" (Deut 11:26), or "If you be unwilling to serve Yahweh, choose this day whom you will serve" (Josh 14:15).[13]

Verses 20–21 are a salvation oracle; for the details see the discussion in Form for 1:18–19, of which the present verses are a variant.

Setting

Evidence suggests that there are two strata of vv 10–21: (1) a lament of Jrm (vv 15–18) and Yahweh's reply (v 19); and (2) a supplement to that early lament (vv 20–21: see Structure) which took shape at the same time as a second lament of Jrm (v 10) and Yahweh's reply (vv 11–12 + 13–14: see again Structure). This proposal for an identical setting for both vv 10–14 and vv 20–21 becomes more likely in view of the fact that 17:14–18 shares diction found in both 15:11 and 1:17, and 1:17–19 is itself a doublet of 15:20–21 (see 17:14–18, Setting).

The only datum within vv 15–19 for a setting is the hint in v 18 of diction suggesting a drought. Of course such diction need not specify a setting at the time of the drought, but it is at least appropriate for that period. More substantial is the setting of 17:5–8. It is suggested in the present study that that passage is Jrm's act of repentance in response to Yahweh's call to the prophet for repentance in v 19 here (see 17:5–8, Setting). If that interpretation is sound, then the phrase "year of drought" (17:8), though metaphorical, may offer a literal datum pointing toward the time of the drought as well. It will be suggested that the "merrymakers" (v 17) are the optimistic prophets, like the "guilty" of 12:1 (see Interpretation). It is altogether plausible, then, to propose the same setting for vv 15–19 as for 11:18–20 + 22–23 and 12:1–5, that is, at the time just after the king burned the scroll, in December of 601 or early in 600.

Verses 20–21 were added to v 19 at the same time that the similar 1:18–19 was added to the call. Central to this material is the image of Jrm as a fortified bronze wall (v 20). The most likely surmise would be to associate that image with "bronze" in v 12, and "bronze" in v 12 is associated in turn with "iron" and "iron from the north" there, and those phrases lead one to the confrontation with Hananiah in the summer of 594 (chap. 28): one may suspect that "iron from the north" is a figure for Nebuchadrezzar (28:14) and that "iron" represents the yoke-pegs of iron that figure in Yahweh's word to Jrm on that

---

12   Muilenburg, "Covenantal Formulations," 352–55.
13   Ibid., 358.

occasion (28:13). Indeed one may suspect that the image of "iron" was a preoccupation of Jrm at that time (see 11:1–17, Setting). One is led, then, to the tentative conclusion that vv 10–12 had a setting in that specific confrontation; one wonders whether Jrm's retreat from Hananiah narrated in 28:12 was not the occasion for vv 10–12 here. And one must understand vv 20–21 to have been added to vv 15–19 in the same period of time.

There is no way to establish a setting for vv 13–14. These verses are a variation on 17:3–4, and one suspects that those verses originated in a preoccupation with the plunder by Nebuchadrezzar of Jerusalem in 598 (note "strength, military power" [חַיִל] in 2 Kgs 24:14 and "treasures" [אוֹצְרוֹת] in 2 Kgs 24:13), a preoccupation which was still very much in the minds of people in 594 (note the priorities in 28:3–4, 6!). One must conclude that not too long after vv 10–12 took shape, they were extended by vv 13–14.

Interpretation

■ 10 Though the vocative is "my mother," it is a figure of speech: his mother may not even be living (compare Form). Jrm's cry concerns his call, which was from the womb (1:5); he will use similar language in greater despair in 20:14–18. Since his cry concerns his call, it is directed by implication to Yahweh, who answers in vv 11–12. For "woe is me" compare 4:31; for the conjunction כִּי "that" compare that passage and 45:3.

Jrm describes himself as a "man of lawsuit and strife." The two nouns רִיב and מָדוֹן are virtual synonyms, as are their related verbs רִיב and דִין: both refer to public argumentation that often results in formal lawsuits, but both are used as well for quarreling and argumentation that does not come to law, and מָדוֹן is never used forensically (compare the "quarrelsome woman," אֵשֶׁת מִדְיָנִים, in Prov 21:9; 25:24; 27:15). One therefore assumes at first that the words are objective genitives, that is, that Jrm is the victim rather than the instigator of quarrels. This assumption is borne out by the last colon, "All of them treat me with contempt."[14] But רִיב is also specifically Yahweh's covenant lawsuit against "the whole land" which Jrm mediates (compare the verb in 2:9), so that in a curious way the first genitive at least is also subjective: Gemser remarks that Jrm is the 'îš rîb par excellence.[15] Jrm is thus both the victim of people's quarrels and the mediator of Yahweh's quarrel with the people, and in both these contexts, "All of them treat me with contempt."

"I have been neither a lender nor a borrower"—this statement has a proverbial ring about it (Cornill), for it is folk wisdom that borrowing and lending are a fertile source of quarrels; Job 6:22 reflects a similar mentality, and the English-speaking person thinks of Polonius's advice to Laertes, "Neither a borrower, nor a lender be; / For loan oft loses both itself and friend."[16]

This is the only occasion in the book for קלל pi'el, here translated "treat with contempt." The verb is normally translated "curse," but its usage is different from that of ארר (11:3): Herbert C. Brichto demonstrates[17] that the meaning of the verb ranges from physical abuse (Gen 8:21) to denunciation (Prov 30:10) and general verbal abuse (Eccl 7:21–22). The verb carries the general meaning "be light, swift"; it is clear that the use of the related noun קְלָלָה to refer to scattered refugees (24:9) and the rubble of cities (25:18) cannot mean "an object of cursing" so much as "an object of contempt or ridicule" (see on 24:9). In a culture in which honor and shame are important categories[18] such an attitude is as devastating as cursing. In the present passage it is difficult to be precise about the nature of the activity directed against Jrm: Brichto remarks in the present context that Jrm felt like a lamb led to the slaughter (11:19) and that he might welcome purely verbal abuse,[19] so that physical abuse might be indicated. On the other hand, Jrm certainly perceived his opponents, in opposing him, to be opposing Yahweh, so that he may have understood his opponents' action as the expression of malediction. *NEB* translates here "abuse";

14 For the vocabulary see Isaac L. Seeligmann, "Zur Terminologie für das Gerichtsverfahren im Wortschatz des biblischen Hebräisch," *Hebräische Wortforschung, Festschrift zum 80. Geburtstag von Walter Baumgartner* (VTSup 16; Leiden: Brill, 1967) 256–57.

15 Gemser, pp. 131, 133–35.

16 Shakespeare, *Hamlet*, act 1, scene 3, lines 75–76.

17 Herbert C. Brichto, *The Problem of "Curse" in the* Hebrew Bible (*JBL* Monograph Series 13; Philadelphia: Society of Biblical Literature and Exegesis, 1963) 120–77.

18 Pedersen, I/II, 213–44.

19 Herbert C. Brichto, *The Problem of "Curse" in the Hebrew Bible* (*JBL* Monograph Series 13; Philadelphia: Society of Biblical Literature and Exegesis, 1963) 123.

"treat with contempt" is perhaps the safest rendering.

■ 11 The difficulties of this verse have evoked a long array of solutions, only a few of which can be referred to here.[20] Critical work in this century has tended to make two linked assumptions: first, that the G reading "So be it, Yahweh" (אָמֵן יהוה) is preferable to the M reading "Yahweh said" (אָמַר יהוה), so that v 11 continues Jrm's lament; and second, that the verb שֵׁרוּתִךָ (the ketib) is to be read as שֵׁרַתִּיךָ "I have served you" and its parallel הִפְגַּעְתִּי בָךְ to be translated "I have entreated you for": on this understanding Jrm is affirming his intercessory prayers to Yahweh on behalf of his enemies (reading "I have served you": Volz, Condamin, Rudolph, Bright; following G at the beginning of the verse: all those named, and Duhm and Cornill as well). But behind the commentators' work in this century lies a long history of difficulty with the verse, beginning with the Versions; it should be noted that G differs from M not only in the first word but more generally in the verse. It is unnecessary to review the whole tangled tale, because it is the proposal here to follow M as it stands.

On the assumption, then, that vv 11–12 embody a response from Yahweh, the analysis here begins with the expression הִפְגַּעְתִּי בָךְ (פגע hip'il), conventionally translated "I have entreated you." The rendering "entreat" fits this verb in 36:25, but the basic meaning in that verse is evidently "intervene," as Isa 53:12 and 59:16 demonstrate. But that meaning is not valid for Isa 53:6, and it is that passage that offers the same particles as those here, the preposition בְּ and the sign of the accusative אֶת־ (with הָאֹיֵב "the enemy"). Isa 53:6 has to mean something like "he imposed on him the iniquity of us all"; by that model the present passage must be taken to mean, "I have imposed on you in a time of disaster and a time of distress the enemy." By this understanding Yahweh is giving Jrm bad news (as he did in 12:5): in effect, "Jeremiah, I know exactly what I am doing, and I am deliberately bringing your enemy upon you as part of your vocation." One would then search for a parallel verb for bad news in the puzzling שֵׁרוּתִךָ. I assumed some years ago that it could be read שֵׁרוֹתִךָ, qal of שׁרר (the verb was proposed by Hitzig, the finite form by Naegelsbach; my proposal was then accepted by Hubmann);[21] but the verb

essentially means "defame," a dubious meaning here (for the details see Text).

A suggestion of Hubmann's to read the puzzling verb as a piel denominative, שֵׁרִיתִיךָ, "I have armored you," from שִׁרְיוֹן, is most attractive. The vowels are those of the qere'. The diction forms a link with "iron" and "bronze" in v 12, so that the wording of that verse does not come unprepared for. But if this is a correct solution, then Yahweh is announcing good news to Jrm, and the interpretation just offered for הִפְגַּעְתִּי בָךְ is off the mark: it must mean "I have intervened with you" after all. But this leaves the expression "the enemy" a puzzle.

I propose that אֶת־הָאֹיֵב is a gloss. (1) The word order is unusual: if it is construed as a direct object, it is strangely far from its verb, with the parallel expression "in a time of disaster and a time of distress" intervening. The word order is not impossible, but is open to question. So far as I can see, it renders the verse incapable of division into cola. (2) The diction is odd. Nowhere else in the confessional material (except in v 14, part of material evidently adapted from 17:3–4) are Jrm's opponents called "the enemy": they are his "persecutors" (17:18; 20:11) or whatever, but "enemy" is reserved in the poetic material for national enemies. And in those passages the word is either a plural, with a suffix, or a singular without article. The singular, with article, is unparalleled. (3) There is another instance of what seems to be the same phenomenon in 17:13, at the end of two rather puzzling verses: both Rudolph and Bright hold that אֶת־יהוה there is a gloss (see on that passage). An analogous instance is Isa 7:17, again at the end of a puzzling verse, where "king of Assyria" seems clearly to be a gloss.

I suspect that Yahweh's reply in both vv 11–12 and 13–14 is to be heard as both good news and bad news. I further suspect that the two occurrences of פגע hip'il in Isaiah 53 represent an early midrash on the present passage (note that Isa 53:7 seems to develop Jer 11:19), v 6 there offering bad news, and v 12 there good news. (Compare Interpretation for 1:5, which points out that the two meanings possible for the first verb are found in Isa 49:1 and 5 respectively.) By this understanding the verb here will mean both "I have intervened with you" and "I have imposed on you," and "the enemy" will be a

---

20   See in more detail Hubmann, *Untersuchungen*, 206–8, 262–63.

21   See Holladay, *Spokesman*, 96; Hubmann, *Untersuchungen*, 262.

gloss inserted in an attempt to clarify an ambiguous text. As a matter of fact, even "I have armored you" can be ambiguous, because it is not clear whether Jrm is armored adequately enough to be victor in his combat.

Both verbs are introduced by the particle אִם־לֹא. In origin this is an introduction to oaths, "I swear that . . ."; so in the mouth of Yahweh, with the verb "swear," in Isa 14:24, and perhaps originally Isa 5:9, though if so, the text there is damaged. The oath form is probably implied in the present passage, but the particle is in many contexts simply one of asseveration (1 Kgs 20:23), so that it is difficult to be sure.[22] Yahweh is certainly emphasizing his affirmation here.

The expression לְטוֹב, literally "for good," is unclear. Does it mean "for Jrm's good," or "for the general public good," or does it have some idiomatic connotation like "intentionally" or "thoroughly"? The closest parallel is Mic 1:12, כִּי־חָלָה לְטוֹב יוֹשֶׁבֶת מָרוֹת כִּי יָרַד רָע מֵאֵת יהוה, literally, "How she writhes for good, the inhabitant of Maroth [or, Maroth enthroned], for disaster comes down from Yahweh." Because "for good" seems to clash with "writhe," Wellhausen's emendation to יָחֵלָה "she waits, hopes" is usually chosen;[23] but van der Woude wishes to preserve M[24] by accepting Robert Gordis's suggestion regarding both Mic 1:12 and Jer 15:11, to translate לְטוֹב as "greatly," parallel to such a meaning in the Aramaic טוּבָא "very much."[25] The proposed meaning exactly fits the passage here, whatever be the translation of the accompanying verb.

The two phrases "in a time of disaster" and "in a time of distress" are obviously parallel. "In a time of distress" is found twice elsewhere in the book (14:8; 30:7); the occurrence in 30:7 is particularly noteworthy—the military emergency is a "time of distress" for Jacob. And one finds "in a day of disaster" in another confession (17:17).

■ 12 Exegesis of this verse has given great difficulty, given the uncertainty regarding the syntactic function of the nouns, the metaphorical reference of these nouns, and even the identity of the verb (for which see Text). Duhm

called the verse "clear nonsense," and Volz described it as "quite obscure." Rudolph regards it as a corruption of 17:1, and Bright, suspecting this judgment to be correct, calls it textually uncertain and omits it along with vv 13–14. But I propose that a solution is within reach.

If "I have armored you" is correct in v 11, the diction of this verse is prepared for.

The verb is evidently רעע II "break." If this is the case, in the background of the verse lies Ps 2:9, תְּרֹעֵם בְּשֵׁבֶט בַּרְזֶל, "You will break them with a rod of iron." The occurrence in Ps 2:7 of יְלִדְתִּיךָ, "I have given birth to you," a form resembling יְלִדְתַּנִי, "You have given birth to me," found in the present passage in v 10, reinforces the parallel (see below). Given the fact that the verb in Psalm 2 is transitive, one concludes that it is transitive here; the choice then (already set forth in Calvin) is between "Can iron break iron from the north and bronze?" (compare Luther, KJV, NEB, NJV) and "Can (someone) break iron, iron from the north, and bronze?" (compare Rudolph, RSV, JB). And as to the signification of the metals, Rashi pointed out that "iron" here may symbolize either Jrm, made into a metaphorical iron pillar and bronze wall (1:18), or the refractory people, called "bronze and iron" (6:28). There has been diverse opinion, too, about the reference of "iron from the north." Some have assumed the phrase to mean high-quality iron or even steel: both Greeks and Romans refer to the tribe of Chalybes, a caste of smiths on the Black Sea, famous for their steel;[26] others assume that the phrase refers to the military might of the Babylonians (so already T, as well as the medieval Jewish exegetes, and Calvin, and so recently Reventlow[27]).

Certainty is ruled out, but one argument against the interpretation "Can iron break iron from the north and bronze?" is that the verse cannot be divided into cola. Of course one could assume a single colon here, or else assume that a colon has been lost by haplography, but it is safer to stay with the text as it is. But the alternative "Can (someone) break iron, iron from the north, and

22   Compare GKC, sec. 149.
23   So Wolff, *Micha*, 13; Mays, *Micah*, 49.
24   Van der Woude, *Micha*, 50.
25   Robert Gordis, "A Note on טוב," *JTS* 35 (1934) 187.
26   Thus Aeschylus, *Prometheus Bound*, 715; Vergil, *Georgics*, I, 58. For more references see the older commentaries such as Michaelis or Naegelsbach.
27   Reventlow, *Liturgie*, 215.

bronze?" is equally odd. The discourse up to this point is clear in personal reference, and the indefinite subject ("can one break?") is unsatisfactory.

I propose, then, that the verse has a specific setting in the encounter with Hananiah (chap. 28). Jrm had a set of wooden yoke-pegs around his neck as a symbol of the necessity of submission to the yoke of Nebuchadrezzar (27:2; 28:10), and he had evidently given duplicate sets to the emissaries to Zedekiah's Jerusalem conference (27:3). Hananiah had broken the pegs on Jrm's neck (28:10), whereupon Yahweh suggested to Jrm that they would be replaced by iron pegs (28:13), since Nebuchadrezzar would impose an iron yoke of servitude on the nations (28:14). My suggestion, then, is that the subject of the verb in the present verse is Hananiah: "Can he break iron [that is, the theoretical iron pegs], iron from the north [that is, the yoke of Nebuchadrezzar], and bronze [that is, the fortified wall of bronze into which Yahweh had made Jrm, 15:20]?" This setting gives unified meaning to the verse (and to v 11 as well). If it is correct, the very specificity of its setting, once lost, would have rendered the phraseology puzzling to later centuries.

A word must be said about Jrm's use here of Ps 2:9 (see above). Jrm had a keen sense that though he was born physically from his mother, his true nurture came from Yahweh; Ps 22:10–12 must have been very much on his mind.[28] Therefore a word like that of Ps 2:7 could well have been taken by Jrm as a personal word; for such a use of royal ideology compare the parallels to royal self-designations in 1:4–10, Form. The question raised by Yahweh in this verse therefore continues to deal with Jrm's understanding of his call and thus rounds off the expression at the beginning of v 10.

■ **13–14** Because the text of these verses is very close to that of 17:3–4, and since 17:3–4 is addressed to the people and the present verses appear to do likewise, thus seeming to interrupt the sequence of confessions, almost all commentators since Hitzig have excised them here as alien, perhaps triggered by v 12, which has "iron," as 17:1 does (so Rudolph). Since the present study follows Hubmann in affirming the integrity of the present *M*, the rightness of these verses in their present position, and

their applicability to Jrm, not to the nation,[29] an examination of the matter is in order.

Though in certain MSS. there is contamination with the text of 17:3–4, the majority text of *M* in these verses maintains significant contrasts with that in chapter 17; in this respect the situation is different from that which prevails in the doublet of 6:13–15 and 8:10b–12, for example. Laying aside small matters of phraseology and spelling, the differences are these: (1) 15:13 לֹא בִמְחִיר "for no payment," 17:3 בָּמֹתֶיךָ "your high places"; (2) a clause at the beginning of 17:4, "and you will loosen your hand (?) from your inheritance which I have given you," which is not present in 15:14; (3) 15:14 וְהַעֲבַרְתִּי (hip'il), literally "and I shall make . . . cross over," here translated "and I shall transfer," 17:4 וְהַעֲבַדְתִּיךָ (hip'il), "and I shall make you serve"; (4) 15:14 עֲלֵיכֶם "over you" (plural, a shift from previous singulars), 17:4 עַד־עוֹלָם "for ever." These differences are so appreciable that one must conclude either that copyists have been extraordinarily careless, or else that the differences are deliberate. One might explain (3) as carelessness—mutual misreadings of reš and dalet are legion—but (1) is striking and hardly explicable except as a deliberate shift.

On the other hand the nouns here, "strength," "treasures," "sins," "boundaries," all identified with the second-person singular possessor, are nouns which point to a reference to the people. They are indeed addressed to the people in 17:3–4, but the proposal here is that the present passage is an adaptation of the reference of the nouns in 17:3–4 to an address to Jrm. Whether "the enemy" in v 11 is part of the original text or a gloss making explicit what is only implied, and whether vv 10–12 fit the encounter with Hananiah or not (see on v 12), Jrm has certainly been preoccupied with his opponents, the optimistic prophets. And the sudden shift from singular address in v 14 to plural address in "over you" suggests that the reference in that expression is to both Jrm and his enemies[30] (see below). Again in 17:4 the phrase is "And I shall make you serve your enemies in a land you do not know"; given 22:28 "Why are he [Jehoiachin] and his children hurled and cast into a land they do not know?" one sees 17:4 as a word of judgment

28   Holladay, "Background."
29   See n. 1.
30   Hubmann, *Untersuchungen*, 271.

on the people, who must become servants of the (national) enemies. But the present passage, by the text of *M*, shifts "your enemies" from outer to inner object, reading, "I shall make your enemies cross over to a land you do not know": the judgment is now on "your enemies," and if these are Jrm's enemies, then the passage offers itself as a continuation of Yahweh's reply to Jrm begun in vv 11–12.

I suggest that the clue to understanding v 13 is the curious use of לֹא before בִּמְחִיר, literally "not for payment." It has not been noticed, but I suggest that לֹא governs all three phrases that follow to the end of the verse: all of them offer a בְּ of price (see below), so that they are all parallel. (Dahood has collected examples of double-duty לֹא,[31] but the phenomenon is generally acknowledged;[32] Job 28:17 is a good parallel, or indeed v 17 in the present chapter, where *G* and *S*, not understanding the construction, are content with periphrases.) The two occurrences of כָּל־ in the last two phrases, combined with the implied negative, is to be construed as "not . . . any," as in 2:24 and 9:3.[33]

Thus Yahweh addresses Jrm in v 13, "Your strength and your treasures I will give away, with no recompense: but at least this loot will not be recompense for your sins, as is the case with the people, nor to buy territorial integrity, as is the case with the monarchy." The ironic phrase in current English, "Be glad for small favors," matches the thrust of this verse. Its mood is then very close to that of 45:5, the divine word to Baruch, "Do you seek great things for yourself? Do not seek them . . . but I will at least grant you your life. . . ."

The question arises what חֵילְךָ and אוֹצְרוֹתֶיךָ, literally "your power" and "your treasures," can mean in this context. The surface meaning refers to military power, and to public treasure: this is a meaning appropriate for 17:3. (The interpretation for that passage points out that these terms are found in 2 Kgs 14:13–14, the narrative of Nebuchadrezzar's looting of Jerusalem in 598: see there, and compare Setting on the present passage.) These words seem ill-suited to Jrm. It is true that he was able to produce seventeen shekels of silver when called upon to purchase the field at Anathoth (32:9), but we are not told otherwise of any "holdings" of Jrm. It is possible

that the connotation of the words makes them ironic here: "Your own 'power' and your own 'treasures,' such as they are, I will give away as loot, without any compensation. . . ."

But there is another possibility, which, if valid, may lie only in the background: the words may refer to Jrm's sexual "power." The word חֵילְךָ "your power" in Prov 31:3 is sexual, and that passage has the same verb "give" as here: "Do not give your 'strength' to women." (For the possibility of the same double meaning in 17:1–4, see there.) The proximity of 16:1–4, in which Jrm is called to abstain from marriage as a sign of the end, lends some plausibility to the suggestion. There is no direct information for a date for 16:1–4; but if 17:5–8 serves as Jrm's response to 15:19 in the winter of 601/600 (see Setting for 17:5–8), then the possibility is open to understand 16:1–4 as a later insertion, perhaps in 594. And there is the nearer proximity of 15:16, with its hint that Jrm's vocation as prophet is a substitute for marriage (see on that verse). If the suggestion is valid, one could see a connection between vv 10–12 and these two verses, since v 10 deals with birth, as 16:1–4 does. But given the paucity of data, the suggestion can be no more than an interesting possibility.

For "loot" (בַּז) see 2:14. The noun מְחִיר is "payment, compensation"—that which is normally given in barter or purchase (1 Kgs 21:2). Here, in contrast, there is no compensation; the same expression, לֹא בִמְחִיר, is found in a happier context, a word of restoration, in Isa 45:13 (compare Isa 55:1).

Verse 14b, introduced by כִּי, gives the explanation for the dislocations: fire has broken out, is kindled, in Yahweh's anger. This passage joins others in which Yahweh's judgment is described in terms of fire (5:14; 7:20; 11:16), but the phrase "for fire has broken out in my anger" is a quotation from Deut 32:22 (for another reminiscence of Deuteronomy 32 compare 2:28).

The surprise here, however, is the shift from second-person singular to second-person plural: the intention is evidently to include both Jrm and his enemies in the description of the effect of Yahweh's anger. The shift underlines what is already clear: both Jrm and his enemies will suffer. There is no way Jrm can be exempt

31 Dahood, *Psalms III*, 438.
32 GKC, sec. 152z.
33 Ibid., 152b.

from the tragedy that is coming. This awareness that innocent suffer along with the guilty is reflected in Habakkuk 1 and is stated precisely in Job 9:22: "It is all one; therefore I say, he destroys both the blameless and the wicked." The present verses are more subtle: both will suffer, but in different ways.

Though the exegesis of these verses assumes they are part of Yahweh's response to Jrm, the fact remains that they move in a different direction from that of vv 11–12. Yahweh's response in 12:5 was a pair of rhetorical questions, and it is therefore likely that v 12 ended Yahweh's response to Jrm's lament in v 10. In vv 11–12 Jrm's enemies are exerting their will upon him, while in vv 13–14 they are depicted as suffering exile. Since vv 20–21 (which likewise move in a different direction from v 19) are a variation of 1:18–19, and since vv 13–14 are a variation of 17:3–4, the best solution[34] is to see both vv 13–14 and vv 20–21 as later extensions of Yahweh's answers when vv 10–12 was combined with vv 15–19 (see Structure, Setting, and Interpretation of vv 19–21). In this way the verses not only clarify the fate of Jrm and his enemies but serve subtly to introduce v 15 ("your wealth . . . I shall give away [נתן]," v 14; "do not . . . take me away [לקח]," v 15). But vv 13–14 may not have been added too long after vv 10–12 took shape (see again Setting).

■ **15** The first two words of the verse, אַתָּה יָדַעְתָּ, are missing in *G*; if they are correct, they begin the fresh lament to Yahweh (compare the diction of 18:23). But they fit poorly with the imperative דַּע "know" (translated here "consider") later in the verse, so they remain something of a mystery (see Preliminary Observations).

Both "remember" (זכר) and "deal with" (פקד) indicate an active intervention in the status quo; the verbs are parallel in 14:10, where Yahweh will intervene to punish sin; here Jrm is appealing to Yahweh for action on his behalf—the parallelism is very close to that in Ps 106:4.[35] For the connotation of "remember" see 2:2. The instances of "deal with" (פקד) so far in the book all

carry a negative meaning (with the preposition עַל, for example 11:22), but the verb carries a positive meaning elsewhere too (32:5).

The Hebrew of the second colon is far more concise than in English (three words). The general meaning of נקם nip'al is "excise sovereignty" (see 11:20). This is the only instance in the OT where the phrase using this verb expresses both the adversary and the beneficiary. Jrm is asking Yahweh to exert his authority in such a way that he, Jrm, will be vindicated and his opponents justifiably discomfited.[36]

The diction of the third colon, אַל־לְאֶרֶךְ אַפְּךָ תִּקָּחֵנִי "do not, because of your slowness of anger, take me away," with the wide separation of the negative אַל from the verb (GKC, sec. 152h), is based upon the pattern in Ps 6:2, אַל־בְּאַפְּךָ תוֹכִיחֵנִי "do not in your anger rebuke me" (compare Ps 38:2); the same sequence of אַל־בְּאַפְּךָ is found in 10:24, although there the verb has already appeared. Jrm has reference here to the formulation of Exod 34:6, where Yahweh is described as אֶרֶךְ אַפַּיִם "slow to anger";[37] here, then, on the basis of the traditional creed, is the witty opposite of the phrase in the Psalms: not, "Do not in your anger let me die," but rather, "Do not in the postponement of your anger let me die":[38] the form "take me away" (תִּקָּחֵנִי) appears to be a deliberate variation of תוֹכִיחֵנִי in Ps 6:2 (see above). The verb לקח occasionally has the nuance, with God as subject, of "take (a person) away (to death)," as it does here: see Job 1:21, "Yahweh has given, Yahweh has taken away"; and the qal passive לֻקַּח "he was taken away" in Isa 53:8 may be an echo of the present passage.

The last colon (like the second) is far more concise in Hebrew than in English: it is literally "know my bearing upon your disgrace." The imperative דַּע, literally "know," echoes "remember" in the first colon. The rest of the phrase is a citation from Ps 69:8, כִּי־עָלֶיךָ נָשָׂאתִי חֶרְפָּה, "For on your account I have borne disgrace"; a similar line helps define עָלֶיךָ, literally "upon you"—Ps 44:23, כִּי־עָלֶיךָ הֹרַגְנוּ כָל־הַיּוֹם, "For on your account we

---

34   Hubmann, *Untersuchungen*, 254–58.

35   Baumgartner, *Klagegedichte*, 35; Reventlow, *Liturgie*, 219.

36   For the phrase in this passage see Mendenhall, *Tenth Generation*, 97.

37   Stoebe, "Seelsorge," 124; Reventlow, *Liturgie*, 219; Berridge, p. 115.

38   Compare Berridge, p. 215.

are killed all the day." For "disgrace" (חֶרְפָּה) see 6:10; the word may refer either to the insult of an enemy (51:51) or the resulting disgrace which rests upon someone (31:19). Here it can be either or both, but since 31:19, like the present passage, has the verb "bear" (נשׂא), it is doubtless more the latter than the former.

■ 16 The expression "your words were found" is curious enough that several commentators earlier in this century have followed the different text of *G* (Duhm, Cornill),[39] but opinion has more recently swung to *M*.[40] The reading of *M* is certainly reinforced by the use by Ezek 2:8—3:3 of the phrase "and I ate them" (see below); one notes particularly the diction of Ezek 3:1, "what you find [מצא], eat [אכל]."

Rudolph stresses a parallel with Lam 2:9, "and her prophets find no vision from Yahweh"; but the verb in the present passage is the nip'al stem, not the qal. Giesebrecht called the phrase "a somewhat drastic expression": more is at stake here than what Weiser assumes, Jrm's "reception of revelation." Berridge writes, "It has traditionally been held that Jeremiah testifies to his ready reception of revelations received at an earlier time. We would suggest instead that Jeremiah here makes reference to such literary works as Judah possessed at this time, including, in particular, earlier prophetic words."[41] But Berridge criticizes[42] my proposal that the expression is an echo of the finding of the Deuteronomic scroll in 622:[43] since "and I ate them" is evidently a reference to Yahweh's putting his words into Jrm's mouth (1:9—see below), the proposal implies that the finding of the scroll predates Jrm's acceptance of his call, a proposal necessitating a lower chronology, which he rejects. But since the present study accepts a lower chronology on the basis of other data, the evidence of this verse may play its part.

There are three occurrences of דָּבָר or דְּבָרִים as the subject of a finite form of "be found" (מצא nip'al), 1 Kgs 14:13; 2 Chr 19:3; 36:8; in all of these the noun means "thing(s)," so that these passages are irrelevant to the present discussion. There remain two instances in which an expression with דְּבָרִים is modified by the nip'al participle of מצא: דִּבְרֵי הַסֵּפֶר הַנִּמְצָא "words of the book which was found," 2 Kgs 22:13, and דִּבְרֵי סֵפֶר הַבְּרִית הַנִּמְצָא "words of the book of the covenant which was found," 2 Kgs 23:2; both of these refer to the Deuteronomic scroll. Jrm evidently understood himself to be the "prophet like Moses" (Deut 18:18: see 1:4–10, Form). In that self-understanding the finding of the Deuteronomic scroll, identified as words of Moses, was a signal event; Jrm later produced a scroll of his own (chap. 36), and the narrator of that event was aware that the prophet was following a precedent (compare 36:24 with 2 Kgs 22:11, and see Interpretation of chap. 36). It would not be surprising, then, if the phrase "your words were found" is a reference to that earlier event in 622; that scroll would certainly be prominent among "such literary works as Judah possessed at this time" (Berridge once more).

As already mentioned, "and I ate them" is a reference to Yahweh's putting his words into Jrm's mouth (1:9); the phrase then refers to Jrm's acceptance of his call—he made them part of himself. The association of food and Yahweh's word is found elsewhere. It is found in Deut 8:3, "Man does not live by bread alone, but . . . by everything that proceeds out of the mouth of Yahweh," and it is found in Isa 55:1–11. And Ezekiel would later take the specific phrase in the present passage and expand it into a (visionary?) narrative of eating a scroll (Ezek 2:8—3:3).

For the word-pair "joy" (שָׂשׂוֹן) and "delight" (שִׂמְחָה) see 7:34. In that passage (and in 16:9) the words are associated with "bridegroom" and "bride," and elsewhere, too, the association of these words is with weddings (note particularly שִׂמְחַת לִבּוֹ, "delight of his heart," parallel with "his wedding" in Cant 3:11). Though that association is not paramount here, the phrase "for I bear your name" may subtly reinforce it, since a wife bears her husband's name (compare Isa 4:1). Jrm was called to

---

39   For an extensive list see Hubmann, *Untersuchungen*, 275 n. 65.

40   See particularly Reventlow, *Liturgie*, 219–20; Berridge, pp. 118–21; Hubmann, *Untersuchungen*, 275–76.

41   Berridge, p. 119.

42   Ibid., p. 119 n. 33.

43   Holladay, "Jeremiah and Moses, Further Observations," 21–24.

remain celibate (16:2), so the implication here is that Jrm's acceptance of the call to be a messenger of Yahweh's word gave him the delight analogous to that in marriage; his word of accusation to Yahweh in 20:7 carries a sexual connotation to suggest that the metaphorical "marriage" was a deception. The parallel between וַיְהִי דְבָרְךָ לִי לְשָׂשׂוֹן "and your word became for me a joy" here and כִּי־הָיָה דְבַר־יהוה לִי לְחֶרְפָּה "for the word of Yahweh become for me a (source of) disgrace" in 20:8, and the presence of "disgrace" (חֶרְפָּה) here in v 15 as well, suggests that the two are contrasted in Jrm's mind: a source of joy to the prophet in his relation to Yahweh, particularly at the outset of his prophetic work, a source of disgrace to him in his relation to his opponents, particularly as opposition grew (20:7–12 is undoubtedly later than the present passage: compare the diction of 20:7a with that of 15:18b).

For "bear Yahweh's name" as an expression of being owned, see 7:10; the connotation of the phrase is of course primarily religious, as it is for the temple that bears Yahweh's name in 7:10, but it may here continue the marriage metaphor as well (see above). The phrase "Yahweh, God of hosts" is construed by all commentators as a vocative, but it is conceivable that it is an inner quotation, the appositional naming of the name: "for I bear your name, 'Yahweh of hosts'."

■ **17** The "circle" (סוֹד) is described by Ludwig Köhler:[44] it is the circle of men of standing in the community who share a common discourse—who discuss the affairs of the community, and gossip, and make decisions, and who carry on the traditions of the community. It is basic to village life in the eastern Mediterranean and beyond. It is more difficult to determine what group is meant by the "merrymakers" (מְשַׂחֲקִים). The verb שׂחק pi'el is used for the carrying out of a tournament (2 Sam 2:14), of singing that mocks (1 Sam 18:7), of deceptive joking (Prov 26:19), of children's play (Zech 8:5), of general merriment when Israel is restored (30:19; 31:9). The word is then broader than we are comfortable with, covering joking, high spirits, and laughter whether cruel or innocent. The parallel here, "exult" (עלז), does not help much in the determination of meaning: that verb is used of exulting in victory (50:11) or exulting in Yahweh (Ps

28:7). But the fact that in 50:11 (and in Zeph 3:14) that verb is in parallel with the root שׂמח "delight" suggests that the train of Jrm's thought is moving ironically from the wholehearted delight (שִׂמְחָה) that he finds in Yahweh's word (v 16) to a merrymaking from which he is here excluded. It is further to be noted that he complains to Yahweh of having become a "laughingstock" (שְׂחוֹק, 20:7), a word related to "merrymakers" here. One senses then that the merrymakers were not making merry in general but were making merry at Jrm's expense, or at the expense of his message. The contrast to the merrymakers is found in the last colon of the verse: Yahweh has filled Jrm with זַעַם. That word stands elsewhere in parallel with Yahweh's wrath (Ps 69:25), but the traditional translation "indignation, fury" (so BDB) is not quite accurate; Hos 7:16 demonstrates that the word means "word of execration, curse."[45] Yahweh has filled Jrm with words of judgment that will do damage to the people (compare 5:14). It is this burden of negative words that keeps Jrm at a distance from the merrymakers. Since the verse is part of Jrm's declaration of innocence (see Form), the circle of merrymakers must be those who are guilty before Yahweh (compare the phraseology of Ps 26:4–5, "I have not sat . . ."); otherwise the declaration of innocence makes no sense. One is thus led to the conclusion that the "merrymakers" are the false prophets, the purveyors of good news.[46] This conclusion is not new: it was proposed by Isaac Abrabanel (fifteenth century) and then by Sebastian Schmidt (seventeenth century).[47] By this understanding, then, the verse is not so much a complaint of Jrm that he is excluded from the pleasures of normal social gatherings, though that is involved, as it is a declaration by Jrm that he could not count himself among the company of those whose hearts were cheered by good news for the future of the people.

The expression "because of your hand" (מִפְּנֵי יָדְךָ) needs clarification. This is the only passage in Jer where "hand of Yahweh" is used with respect to prophetic experience; there are three instances before Jrm's time, 1 Kgs 18:46 (Elijah), 2 Kgs 3:15 (Elisha), and Isa 8:11, and then seven occurrences in Ezekiel (Ezek 1:3; 3:14, 22; 8:1; 33:22; 37:1; 40:1). Zimmerli has stressed the fact

---

44   Ludwig Köhler, *Hebrew Man* (London: SCM, 1956; Nashville: Abingdon, 1957) 102–7.
45   See Wildberger, *Jesaja*, 395.
46   So Hubmann, *Untersuchungen*, 279–80.
47   Ibid., 281.

that the phrase "the hand of Yahweh came/fell over me" introduces all five of Ezekiel's visions, and that the phrase and the visions lead back from Ezekiel to the manner of expression and the world of ideas of pre-classical prophecy;[48] the expression has deep roots in Israel's tradition. With regard to Isa 8:11, Zimmerli remarks that it is "a text which clearly shows in its formulation . . . something of the fearful strength of the divine grip which shook the prophet."[49] Then with regard to the present passage he notes, "Most of all the direct physical pain of isolation from other men under the hand of Yahweh is given expression in the confessions of Jeremiah (Jer 15:17). At the same time it is clear that what it meant for a person to be held 'by the hand of Yahweh' lay in the receipt of Yahweh's word (cf. Jer 15:16), which, because it was a message of judgement, prohibited any spontaneous freedom of conversation with other persons. . . ."[50] J. J. M. Roberts points out that the phrase, and equivalent expressions in the languages of other cultures in the ancient Near East, was associated with disease; and he points out how close the phraseology of the present passage is to that of Ps 38:3–4: "For your arrows have descended into me; your hand has come down upon me. There is no soundness in my flesh because of your curse [מִפְּנֵי זַעְמֶךָ]; there is no well-being in my bones because of my sin."[51] Robert Wilson cautions against concluding that the phrase in question is a description of ecstasy or a trance state.[52] In summary: Jrm is using here a traditional expression that indicates the power and authority of Yahweh's grasp of his life under which he functions; it may also suggest a crippling of normal behavior that would cause him to be shunned.

"Alone" (בָּדָד) occurs with "sit, dwell" (ישׁב) in three other passages. Two of them are in Lamentations: the phrase is used of the city itself in Lam 1:1, and of the behavior of someone prostrate for his sins (Lam 3:28); in both these instances the phrase may be dependent on the present passage. The third instance is in Lev 13:46: "He [who has 'leprosy'] shall remain unclean as long as he has the disease; he is unclean; he shall dwell alone in a habitation outside the camp." It is difficult to avoid the conclusion that Jrm is here indicating that he is considered a social "leper."[53] In this way Jrm continues the vocabulary of illness hinted at in "your hand," which will continue in v 18. The action here is more permanent than "sitting," then; "dwelling" is implied. *JB* covers both with "I held myself aloof."

One more possibility hovers at the edge, but no proof is possible, given the present paucity of data, and that is that marriage imagery continues here. Was there a custom that the bride was left alone in the bridal chamber on the wedding night to await the arrival of the bridegroom? I have in mind the custom among the Arabs of the *duḥla* (literally "entering"), which Edward W. Lane has described;[54] my daughter has remarked from her observations in El Fasher, western Sudan, on the loneliness of the bride in the bridal chamber while the bridegroom's party try on horseback to force an entry of the courtyard of the bride's family.[55] It is a long way back to the Israelite customs of the preexilic period, but such a practice may have been in existence there as well. The "merrymakers" would then suggest the rest of the wedding party.

There may be a nice contrast between the last colon here, "You have filled me with malediction," and 12:6, with its statement that the members of Jrm's family called him "full [= drunk?]" behind his back; yes, says Jrm, I am full, but not with wine. (Compare the similar diction of 20:9.)

■ **18** Jrm resorts more than once to medical terminology: frequently for the sickness of the people (6:7; 8:21–22; 20:12, 15) and for the sympathetic symptoms he manifests because of his people's plight (4:19; 8:21), and here for his own disability in the face of persecution. The word "pain" (כְּאֵב) occurs here for the only instance in Jer; the related verb is used in Gen 34:25 of the pain experienced by the Shechemites the third day after their circumcision—that is, the word may refer to purely

---

48 Walther Zimmerli, "The Special Form- and Traditio-Historical Character of Ezekiel's Prophecy," *VT* 15 (1965) 516.

49 Zimmerli, *Ezekiel 1*, 117–18.

50 Ibid., 118.

51 J. J. M. Roberts, "The hand of Yahweh," *VT* 21 (1971) 244–51; compare Reventlow, *Liturgie*, 224.

52 Robert R. Wilson, "Prophecy and Ecstasy: A Reexamination," *JBL* 98 (1979) 321–37.

53 So also Reventlow, *Liturgie*, 224, against Berridge, pp. 124–25.

54 Edward W. Lane, *Manners and Customs of the Modern Egyptians* (New York: Dutton, 1908), 174, 177 (original title: *An Account of the Manners and Customs of the Modern Egyptians*; 5th ed., 1860).

55 Catherine Holladay, personal communication.

physical pain as well as psychic pain. "Endless" (נֶצַח)
occurs in 3:5 in the expression "for ever" (לָנֶצַח); the
parallel "incurable" (אָנוּשׁ) occurs with "wound" (מַכָּה) in
Mic 1:9 and with "pain" (כְּאֵב) in Isa 17:11. The opening
tricolon thus rings the changes on the vocabulary of
illness: Jrm is prostrated by the sense not only that he
suffers public opposition but also abandonment by
Yahweh. "Why?" is the question, as it was in 12:1 (with a
different but synonymous interrogative) and will be in
20:18.

The infinitive absolute before the finite verb תִהְיֶה
"you are becoming" underlines the affirmation of the
verb against an assumed denial—"You are, are you not?"
It is bold and bitter language to level at Yahweh, without
phraseological parallel in the OT: what Yahweh rhetorically has asked of Israel ("Have I become a wilderness to
Israel?" 2:31) Jrm now turns back affirmatively onto him
with regard to their own relationship. The language is so
bold that both *G* and *V* construe תִהְיֶה as third-person singular feminine, a predicate of "my wound," and *T* simply
paraphrases ("Let your word not be to me like . . ."); but
the words are addressed to Yahweh, as Rashi already
affirmed. It has been suggested that the "why?" of the
first part of the verse should carry over to the last part
(Naegelsbach); while this might seem to soften the
language, the construction with the infinitive absolute
after "why?" is dubious (Josh 7:7 is textually difficult).
Volz and Rudolph emend the infinitive absolute (הָיוֹ) to
הוֹי "woe!" but there is no warrant for this emendation.
The rhetorical question posed by Yahweh in 2:31 (see
above) is related there to the metaphorical identity of
Yahweh in his dispute with Israel: he is the spring of
running water (2:13): see 2:31, Interpretation. Now Jrm
accuses Yahweh of being to him what he had assured
Israel Yahweh would never be—untrustworthy waters.
The כְּמוֹ (= כְּ) "like" is curious: neither 2:13 nor 2:31
have "like," nor is there any such qualifier when Jrm
accuses Yahweh of deception in 20:7. Here one can only
conclude that, in spite of the affirmation betokened by
the infinitive absolute, Jrm holds back a bit, at this time,
from a blatant accusation of deception. The "like"
functions then in the same way as do the repeated
occurrences of "like" in Ezekiel's bold description of the
throne-chariot of Yahweh (Ezek 1:4 and often in that
chap.)—it is best translated "as it were." It will be picked
up by כְּפִי "as it were, my mouth" in v 19. There is some

uncertainty whether אַכְזָב has the more general meaning
"(something) deceptive," or whether the word specifically
applies to a watercourse that dries in the heat of summer:
it is a word which appears only here and in Mic 1:14, and
in the latter passage the context does not solve the
question. In any event, the image is clear from the last
colon: the disappointment which a dried-up stream bed
occasions for the thirsty traveler. The same image is
elaborated in Job 6:15–20 (and compare the reference in
Job 24:19); it is a common experience in Palestine. So
Jrm wishes to have recourse to the ever-running spring
that is Yahweh, only to be disappointed by dry sand.

Question: Given the association of drought with battle
emergency in 14:1—15:9, does the accusation that
Yahweh is like deception, like untrustworthy waters here
(and, by implication, in 17:5–8), match the accusation in
20:7 that Yahweh has "overpowered" Jrm, as if they were
in combat together?—compare 20:11, where Yahweh is
called a "terrifying warrior."

■ **19** This verse brings Yahweh's reply. After the introductory rubric comes a compact poem of six cola which
offers several problems of interpretation. The first two
cola balance the second two, in that each pair offers a
protasis ("if"-clause) and an apodosis ("then"-clause); and
the first colon, with its two forms of שׁוּב "return,"
balances the last two cola, with two more occurrences of
the same verb. The syntax of the first colon has called
forth several interpretations, and the connotations of
"return" in this verse need exploration. Since the second
and fourth cola are parallel in meaning, it is better to
defer a discussion of the first and second cola and begin
with the third and fourth.

In the third cola the adjectives are clear: יָקָר means
"precious"—it is used several times in connection with
precious stones (1 Kgs 10:2), and the related verb is used
in connection with gold (Isa 13:12); and זוֹלֵל means
"worthless." But what does the verb יצא hip'il (literally
"bring out") imply here? *G* simply offers a literal translation; but *V* and *S* assume the verb means "produce
(what is precious from what is worthless)" (*S*), or, indeed,
"separate (what is precious from what is worthless)" (*V*). *T*
takes the phrase to mean "produce righteous people out
of wicked people," an interpretation followed by Rashi
and Qimḥi: "separate the worthy man from the wicked
one to restore him to the good," an interpretation which

continued into the Reformation period.[56] Given the association of יָקָר with precious stones and gold, another interpretation of "separate" arose in the seventeenth century, the metaphor of separating precious metals from bad.[57] This metaphor may lie in the background but is evidently not the central one, which is that of "bringing forth words"—the verb means "utter" in many passages (thus Job 15:13 and Eccl 5:1, passages which offer diction close to what is found here: so Rudolph). In this case מִן (literally "from") must be understood as "rather than" (Hos 6:6; Hab 2:16; compare the suggestion in 6:27).

The phraseology that evidently lies behind the verb here is Deut 8:3, "Man does not live by bread alone, כִּי עַל־כָּל־מוֹצָא פִי־יהוה = but by everything which is brought forth from (uttered by) the mouth of Yahweh." (Compare the remarks on that parallel in the discussion of "and I ate them," v 16.) Similar diction is found in 17:16, מוֹצָא שְׂפָתַי "what is brought forth from (uttered by) my lips." Given "my (= Yahweh's) mouth" in the fourth colon of the present poem, one may reject the metallurgical metaphor and accept "utter" here. It must be assumed, then, that "what is precious" implies what Yahweh gives Jrm to proclaim, and "what is worthless, rubbish" implies what Jrm has just affirmed about Yahweh; the content of "what is worthless" will be spelled out in the last two cola of the verse.

The fourth colon, כְּפִי תִהְיֶה, has some curious features. Yahweh had stated in 1:9 that he had put his words in Jrm's mouth; here that task is reaffirmed in "you shall be like my mouth." Why is the כְּ "like" present? In Exod 4:6 Aaron becomes Moses' mouth (הוּא יִהְיֶה לְךָ לְפֶה), and the preposition there is לְ; in the correlative passage in v 16 the preposition is likewise לְ (לְשָׁוֹן, etc.). One can only conclude that the כְּ here is an echo of כְּמוֹ "like" in v 18—that Yahweh is paralleling the tentativeness of Jrm's accusation to Yahweh by similar diction here: "my mouth you shall be, as it were." There is another possibility, however—that כְּפִי means "according to my command"

(1 Chr 12:24); perhaps a double meaning is intended. Though other prophets made use of phrases involving Yahweh's mouth ("the mouth of Yahweh has spoken," Isa 1:20; Mic 4:4), Jrm was particularly remembered as the one "who spoke from the mouth of Yahweh" (2 Chr 36:12). There is in this confession and Yahweh's reply a series of expressions involving identities: at the beginning Yahweh's word became for Jrm a matter of delight (v 16), while now Yahweh really does seem like a deception to Jrm (v 18)—to which Yahweh replies that if Jrm will only utter what is of value instead of rubbish, then he can be (once more) the mouth of Yahweh. All these expressions involve היה "be, become," just as a corresponding series of true and false identities is presented in chapter 2 involving the relation of Yahweh with Israel (see especially on 2:31).

Now one turns to the first and second cola. Here the qal (simple) stem of שׁוּב "return" is followed by the hip'il (causative) stem—אִם־תָּשׁוּב וַאֲשִׁיבְךָ, but the syntactical relations between those verbs, and with the next clause, are not clear. The most common traditional translation is that of G, V, and S, to construe וַאֲשִׁיבְךָ as the beginning of the apodosis ("then I shall take you back": for the syntax of G compare BDF, sec. 442 [7]) and the second colon as a coordinate apodosis—one must assume a connective "and" ("and in my presence you shall stand": so Luther, KJV, RSV, NEB, NJV). It is true that וַאֲשִׁיבְךָ could be construed as an apodosis, particularly if it were understood as a virtual cohortative (Gen 13:9).[58] But the lack of וְ "and" at the beginning of the second colon is a problem, and the parallelisms of poetic structure in the verse are against this solution (see below). The other interpretation is to take "in my presence you shall stand" as the apodosis ("then in my presence . . .") and all that precedes as protasis. There are two alternative possibilities here. One is to take וַאֲשִׁיבְךָ as a final clause ("If you come back so that I may take you back, then in my presence . . ."); simple וְ plus imperfect may carry that force (Jon 1:11),[59] and that is the solution of NAB. The

56   Cornelius a Lapide, 1689 (so Hubmann, Untersuchungen, 286).
57   So, first, Sebastian Schmidt, Commentarii in Librum Prophetiorum Jeremiae (Frankfurt am Main, 1706) (so Hubmann, Untersuchungen, 286); in the present century, Annesley W. Streane, The Book of the Prophet Jeremiah, Together with the Lamentations (Cambridge Bible for Schools and Colleges; Cambridge:

Cambridge University, 1881) 120; Condamin; Gebhard-Maria Behler, Les confessions de Jérémie (Tournai: Casterman, 1959) 40.
58   Joüon, Gramm., sec. 176k.
59   Ibid., 116h.

other is to take וַאֲשִׁיבְךָ as a coordinate protasis ("If you come back and [if] I take you back, then in my presence . . ."); אִם "if" may carry over in a double protasis (Job 16:6),[60] and this is the solution of Harry Freedman and of Hubmann[61] and the one accepted here (see below). There is one other proposal which should be mentioned, since it is the prevailing critical view (Cornill, Giesebrecht, Volz, Condamin, Rudolph, and Bright): to take וַאֲשִׁיבְךָ as carrying an adverbial meaning with the following clause ("If you come back, then I shall again let you stand in my presence"); but even though the qal stem of שוב may carry this meaning, it is not cited elsewhere for the hip'il.

The interpretation of parallel protases in the first colon is confirmed by several considerations. The two occurrences of שוב qal in the last two cola of the verse are parallel. Again the third colon contains a parallel protasis, while its apodosis comes in the fourth colon, and since the fourth and second cola are closely parallel, it is likely that the third colon is to be taken as parallel with the first. Again two verbs in a single colon are best taken as coordinate—one notes the two parallel verbs in the first colon of Jrm's lament in v 15. (For two stems of the same root compare 1:4–19, n. 95, and 11:18.)

But if the two verbs are parallel, they hang marvelously in tension between synonymity and antonymity. They are in a sense synonyms because both suggest the reestablishment of a relation between the prophet and Yahweh. But the structure of the rest of the poem suggests a strong tension between the two. Thus when תָּשׁוּב occurs again, it is in the sixth colon, carrying a negative, in contrast to the balancing positive verb in the fifth colon. And the parallel protasis in the third colon carries internal antonyms, "what is precious," "rubbish."

This collocation of the qal and hip'il stems of the verb "return" raises the question of the relation between the actions. How is Jrm's "coming back, returning" related to Yahweh's "taking back, accepting the return" of Jrm? (A similar question arises with the same stems of the verb in 30:18.)

There is another passage in which אִם־תָּשׁוּב appears, 4:1: Yahweh is addressing Israel, and the expression is completed by אֵלַי תָּשׁוּב—"if you turn . . . to me you

should turn." Since the occurrences of שוב qal in the fifth and sixth cola each are completed by אֶל with a suffix, one may conclude that a plausible expression in the first colon would have been אִם־תָּשׁוּב אֵלַי "if you come back to me." The hip'il verb וַאֲשִׁיבְךָ is then in some sense a substitute for "to me," but it does not carry at all the same meaning. It is not a question of Jrm's simply returning to Yahweh: his return is parallel to Yahweh's reaching out to him.

But even if Yahweh's reaching out is coordinate with Jrm's return, how are the actions related? Specifically, what is the relation between Jrm's freedom, his initiative, and Yahweh's sovereignty? The hip'il of שוב carries a variety of nuances of the extent of control of the subject over the object, depending on the sort of object in a given instance. Thus if the object of the verb is inanimate, the control of the subject is complete: Yahweh will "bring back" the temple treasures (28:3). And when the object is animals, the control of the subject is moderate: the Israelites are to "lead back" or "take back" some calves (1 Sam 6:7). Again when the object is human beings and they are booty, the control of the subject is complete: David "brought back" sons, daughters, and spoil (1 Sam 30:19). But if human beings are both subject and object, then the object may well have some control, depending on the circumstances: Abraham's servant can "lead/guide/take" Isaac back to the homeland (Gen 24:5). And what if a restoration of relation is involved?— when the Levite went to speak kindly to his concubine to "bring her back" (Judg 19:3), it surely involved "accepting her back" as well as "taking her back."[62] So what is one to say here with regard to the sovereignty of Yahweh over Jrm's calling and with regard to Jrm's initiative in returning to faithful service? Further, are the parallel protases two separate conditions ("if you come back to me and then if I take you back"), or is the second action the equivalent of the first action from Yahweh's viewpoint rather than Jrm's ("if you come back to me, an action which is at the same time my acceptance of you")? The text, obviously, does not say; this is the difficulty. But if, as already affirmed, the two actions are in some sense opposite, then one must understand that Jrm is to move toward Yahweh and that Yahweh is to move

---

60 Ibid., 167p.
61 Hubmann, *Untersuchungen*, 204.

62 For a survey of שוב hip'il with these distinctions in mind see Holladay, *Šûbh*, 87–105.

toward Jrm in taking him to himself. Both must choose. Yahweh is over against Jrm; Yahweh is in no sense some kind of projection of Jrm's craving for security.

The mode of expression in the third and fourth cola is not quite what the reader today expects, and the unexpected mode of expression in those cola throws additional light on the meaning of the two verbs in the first colon. What one would expect in the third and four cola is, אִם־בְּפִיךָ אֶתֵּן דְּבָרִי לָמָּה תוֹצִיא זוֹלֵל, "If in your mouth I put my word [compare 1:9], why do you utter rubbish?" The contrast between this hypothetical pair of cola and what is actually in the text underlines the surprising responsibility Jrm has been given. Yahweh is not an actor in the third and fourth cola. Jrm is responsible, and his functioning as Yahweh's mouth depends upon the nature of what he says. He is on his own: whether he is in fact a messenger of Yahweh is his own decision. The colon is not אִם־תָּשׁוּב אֵלַי "if you come back to me": that has been established. But the colon is not אִם־אֲשִׁיבְךָ וְאִם־תָּשׁוּב "if I take you back and if you come back" either. Yahweh's action is necessary in Jrm's action of returning, but not primary. The impression that one gains here of Yahweh's "low profile" is in strong contrast to the sovereignty of Yahweh in Jrm's call (1:7—10), to Yahweh's action through Jrm to the people (5:14), and to Jrm's perception of Yahweh's overriding power in his life in another confession (20:7, 9). (For another hint of the condescension of Yahweh in the process of mutual return, compare "would he return to her?" in 3:1, and see Interpretation there.)

Jrm, then, must return. The prophet has had many occasions to voice Yahweh's appeal to Israel to "come back, return" (esp. in 3:1—4:4). Now Yahweh addresses the same word to Jrm himself: "If you return." Israel has treated Yahweh as a dubious source of fertility (2:31), and now Jrm has treated Yahweh in the same way (v 18); so the word which Israel has needed to hear, Jrm now needs to hear: "return, come back to Yahweh." If, Jrm, you come back, and if in the mystery of my sovereignty I take you back, then our relationship will prevail, as I have intended it to. This is a surprise: who ever heard of a prophet of Yahweh who needs to repent?

If you repent, then you shall stand in my presence.

There is a nice parallel here between "in my presence," literally "to my face," and "like my mouth" in the fourth colon. For the phrase "stand in Yahweh's presence" see 15:1. If the expression here is in close parallelism with the fourth colon, then it is a phrase that connotes the attendance of a messenger upon a sovereign to receive the word that is to be proclaimed (compare also "stand in the council of Yahweh," 23:22).

The scene shifts in the last two cola from the relation between Jrm and Yahweh to the relation between Jrm and "them," a shift marked by the emphatic subject pronouns "they" (הֵמָּה) and "you" (אַתָּה). "They" are to be identified with the "merrymakers" of v 17, who, by the analysis presented there, are the false prophets (so Duhm, Cornill), not with "this people" in v 20 (for which see vv 20–21). The presence of תָּשׁוּב in the sixth colon, as it was in the first, suggests that the meaning of שׁוּב "return" here is analogous to its meaning in the first colon. For Jrm, to "return" to Yahweh is a right sort of return, but to "return" to them—that is, to the false prophets—is a wrong sort of return. "Return" in the first colon indicates a return to a previous relationship of loyalty and obedience and dependence. But in what way is the relation of the false prophets to Jrm analogous to Jrm's relation to Yahweh? Clearly the false prophets are to resort to Jrm, in that for them Jrm is the source of dependence on Yahweh; Jrm is for them the channel for the word from Yahweh which they need. He is to utter what is precious and thus serve as Yahweh's mouth. This action is in contrast to Jrm's illicit return to them: Jrm has been doubting the effectiveness and even the validity of Yahweh's promises in the same way as the false prophets had been doing, in effect if not in theory, and this he must not do. They may claim to speak for Yahweh (14:14; 28:2), but they challenge the judgment Yahweh has announced and thus doubt the validity of Yahweh's word as thoroughly as Jrm had.[63]

That these occurrences of שׁוּב "return" carry a strong element of trust is demonstrated by the use of "trust" (בטח) in 17:5, 7, part of a passage which, I propose, is consequent upon the present one. There Jrm affirms that the man who trusts in Yahweh is blessed, while the man who trusts in human beings is cursed.

63　For a similar analysis see Hubmann, *Untersuchungen*, 287–90.

■ **20–21** These two verses are not an original part of Yahweh's answer in v 19. There is no shared vocabulary with v 19. In contrast to v 19, in which Jrm carried the responsibility, Yahweh is here the actor. In v 19 Jrm's status is dependent on the condition of his obedience, while here Yahweh's promises are unconditional. In general the focus of these verses is different: a promise of rescue rather than a challenge to fidelity.[64]

The opposition here to Jrm is explicitly "this people," a generalization of the opposition of which v 19 speaks, the "they" who are the "merrymakers" of v 17, that is, the false prophets (see on those verses); by v 20, then, the scope of v 19 is enlarged.

The opposition here of "this people" is the same opposition assumed for vv 13–14. And these two verses resemble vv 13–14 in another respect, since they are an adaptation of 1:18–19 in the same way as vv 13–14 are an adaptation of 17:3–4: the two expansions effect a bridge between vv 10–12 and vv 15–19. Thus "bronze" in v 20 is linked to "bronze" in v 12.

Most of the phrases here have been dealt with in 1:18–19 (see there); only brief notices are necessary here. The first verb in v 20, וּנְתַתִּיךָ, is a waw-consecutive perfect, while the corresponding expression in 1:18 is הִנֵּה נְתַתִּיךָ, a perfect without waw; if the analysis of our grammars is correct, one must understand the word in 1:18 as a statement by Yahweh of what he has done, and understand the word here as a promise, a reassurance to Jrm that Yahweh will renew the prophet's strength. In 1:18 Jrm is made into a "fortified city, an iron bolt and a bronze wall"; here this designation is compressed into a "fortified bronze wall," the two words for "fortified" being not identical but related (1:18, מִבְצָר; here בְּצוּרָה). But if that designation is here compressed, the last element in 1:19 ("to rescue you") is here expanded by preceding it with "to save you" and by adding the two cola of v 21 to explicate "to rescue you." For "the wicked" (רָעִים) compare 6:29. The verb "ransom, redeem" (פדה) occurs in Jer only here and in 31:11;

though the basic meaning of the word is "pay a ransom to effect the freeing of" someone, it tends to be simply a synonym for "rescue." The adjective "violent" (עָרִיץ) occurs in Jer only here and in 20:11: there it is an attribute of Yahweh, "dread (warrior)," while here it is an attribute of Jrm's enemies.

Yahweh thus promises to stand by Jrm and guarantee his safety from all attacks from his people.

Aim

What is said in 11:18—12:6, Aim, is valid for the present passage as well. But the present sequence probes more deeply than that one did: Yahweh implies that though he continues to direct Jrm's life, the course of that life involves pain (vv 11–12). Jrm not only asks "why?" (v 18), as he did in 12:1, but accuses Yahweh of deception (v 18); and Yahweh suggests that Jrm needs to repent (v 19). In the first sequence the relationship of Jrm and Yahweh is under strain; here the relation continues but is ruptured by Jrm's accusation that Yahweh is unfaithful and by Yahweh's counterproposal that Jrm must mend the relation which he, Jrm, has ruptured by his accusation. The successive complaints of Jrm may not be in chronological sequence, but they are in a sequence of steadily increasing tension between the prophet and Yahweh. One senses here many layers of meaning: a prophet charged with proclaiming Yahweh's word, rejecting the fidelity of Yahweh, and then affirming by the recording of the interchange that, paradoxically, Jrm's pain, his accusation to Yahweh, and Yahweh's call to the prophet to repent, are integral to Yahweh's word to Jrm's generation. It is a paradox not far from that which Paul proclaimed: "Christ was innocent of sin, and yet for our sake God made him one with the sinfulness of men, so that in him we might be made one with the goodness of God himself" (2 Cor 5:21, *NEB*).

---

64   On these contrasts see ibid., 290–91.

**The Call to Celibacy
and to Abstention from
Funerals and Weddings**

Bibliography

On the passage in general:
Cañellas, Gabriel
    "El celibato en el Antiguo Testamento," *Biblia y Fe*
    5 (1979) 241–53, esp. 248–49.
Goldman, M. D.
    "Was Jeremiah Married?" *AusBR* 2 (1952) 42–47.
Holladay
    "Recovery," 412–20.

On מַרְזֵחַ and v 5:
Barstad, Hans M.
    *The Religious Polemics of Amos, Studies in the
    Preaching of Am 2, 7b–8; 4,1–13; 5,1–27; 6,4–7;
    8,14* (VTSup 34; Leiden: Brill, 1984) 127–42.
Eissfeldt, Otto
    "מַרְזֵחַ und מַרְזְחָא 'Kultgenossenschaft' im spät-
    jüdischen Schrifttum," *Kleine Schriften V*
    (Tübingen: Mohr [Siebeck], 1973) 136–42.
Friedman, Richard E.
    "The *MRZḤ* Tablet from Ugarit," *Maarav* 2
    (1979/80) 187–206.
Loretz, Oswald
    "Ugaritisch-biblisch mrzḥ 'Kultmahl, Kultverein'
    in Jer 16,5 und Am 6,7," *Künder des Wortes:
    Beiträge zur Theologie der Propheten* (ed. Lothar
    Ruppert et al.; Würzburg: Echter, 1982) 87–93,
    esp. 88–90.
Margalit, Baruch
    "The Ugaritic Tale of the Drunken Gods: Another
    Look at RS 24.258 (*KTU* 1.114)," *Maarav* 2
    (1979/80) 65–120.
Miller, Patrick D., Jr.
    "The *Mrzḥ* Text," *The Claremont Ras Shamra Tablets*
    (ed. Loren R. Fisher; AnOr 48; Rome: Pontifical
    Biblical Institute, 1971) 37–48.
Pope, Marvin H.
    "A Divine Banquet at Ugarit," *The Use of the Old
    Testament in the New and Other Essays, Studies in
    Honor of William Franklin Stinespring* (ed. James M.
    Efird; Durham, NC: Duke University, 1972) 170–
    203, esp. 190–94.
Pope
    Song of Songs, 220–29.
Porten, Bezalel
    *Archives from Elephantine, The Life of an Ancient
    Jewish Military Colony* (Berkeley and Los Angeles:
    University of California, 1968) 179–86.
Tarragon, Jean-Michel
    *Le culte à Ugarit: D'après les textes de la pratique en
    cunéiformes alphabétiques* (Cahiers de la Revue
    Biblique 19; Paris: Gabalda, 1980) 144–47.

1 The word of Yahweh came to me as follows: 2/ You shall never take for yourself a wife, nor shall you ever have sons or daughters in this place; 3/ for thus Yahweh has said about the sons and daughters born in this place, and about their mothers, who bear them, and their fathers, who beget them, in this land: 4/ Terrible deaths they shall die; they shall not be lamented, nor shall they be buried; they shall become dung on the surface of the ground; by sword and famine they shall perish, and their corpses shall become food for the birds of the heavens and the beasts of the earth.

5 Thus[a] Yahweh has said: Do not enter the house of funeral feasting, nor go to lament, nor grieve for them; for I have taken my peace away from this people— oracle of Yahweh, (my) favor and compassion. 6/ Great and small shall die in this land; ⟨one shall not bury,⟩[a] nor lament for them, nor slash oneself, nor shave one's head for them; 7/ one shall not break bread[a] for ⟨the mourner,⟩[b] to condole him for the deceased, and one shall not give ⟪him⟫[c] the cup of condolence to drink for his father or his mother. 8/ And the house of feasting [a]do not[a] enter, to sit [b]with them[b] to eat and drink. 9/ For thus Yahweh [a]of hosts,[a] the God of Israel has said: I am going to silence, from this place, before your eyes and in your days, the voice of joy and the voice of delight, and the voice of the bridegroom and the voice of the bride.

Text

5a Omitting the prefixed כִּי with *G*; see Structure and Form.

6a For *M* יִקָּבְרוּ "they shall not be buried," one must read יִקְבְּרוּ, literally "they shall not bury," in parallel with the expressions in this verse and v 7 (compare the two passive expressions in v 4).

7a Read לָחֶם with a few MSS., *G* and *V* for *M* לָהֶם "for them" (so all commentators).

b Read אֵבֶל with *V* for *M* אָבֵל "mourning."

c Read אֹתוֹ with *G* for *M* אֹתָם "them."

8a—a Read אַל, the negative of immediate prohibition, for *M* לֹא, the negative of permanent prohibition ("never"). The negatives in v 5 are אַל, with which the present verse is parallel. The negatives in v 2 are לֹא.

b—b Read with some MSS. אִתָּם for *M* אוֹתָם "them" (accusative).

9a—a One MS., *G*, and *S* omit.

Structure and Form

Many commentators take vv 1–13 as a unit (Volz, Rudolph, Bright); but it is better to separate vv 1–9 from vv 10–13. There is no shared vocabulary between the two sections, and whereas vv 1–9 are rhythmic prose (*Kunstprosa*), vv 10–13 are not. Verses 10–13 belong with vv 1–9 in the same way 9:11–15 belongs to 9:9–10.

The question may be raised whether vv 1–4 and 5–9 are separate units; vv 1–4 are a permanent prohibition against the prophet's marrying and having children, while vv 5–9 are a prohibition against the prophet's attending funerals (and perhaps weddings) (see Interpretation, vv 5–9, v 8, and v 9). The negatives with the prohibitions in vv 5–9 are immediate (at least in v 5: see Text on v 8). But the prohibitions in vv 5–9 have the same purpose as those in vv 1–4, and they share vocabulary (see below); the phraseology may simply signify, "Do not ever marry, and do not even attend funerals." It is

thus better to take the sequence as a single unit (see further Setting).

There are many possible scenarios by which the present passage may have been placed here. (1) If 17:5–8 is Jrm's act of repentance in response to Yahweh's challenge in 15:19 (see 17:5–8), and if 15:19 and 17:5–8 were at one time linked, then the present intervening sequence would have been added later. (2) It may have followed 15:19 from the beginning, explicating by vv 1–4 the metaphor of marriage in 15:16 and the phrase "I sat alone" in 15:17, and picking up "joy" and "delight" in 15:16 here in v 9. (3) It may have rounded off the first collection of confessions, 11:18—12:6 and 15:10–21, picking up "father" (12:6) and "mother" (15:10) by the diction of v 3 here; indeed, in offering a supplementary call (see Form) it may have served as an inclusio with the call in chapter 1. There is a striking assonantal link between קָרוֹב "near" and רָחוֹק "far" in 12:2 on the one hand and *יְקַבְּרוּ "bury" (M יִקְבְּרוּ) and יִקְרַח "shave one's head" in v 6 here, a bit of word-play which is hard to credit to coincidence.[1] Whatever the reason for the placement of the unit here, it must have been integrated into the confessional material early.

Attempts have been made to analyze the passage as poetry (Condamin, all nine verses;[2] Volz, vv 4 and 8–9). But I believe these attempts are ill-conceived: the material is rhythmic prose (*Kunstprosa*); one senses a multitude of parallelisms, but any structures that one attempts to discern fade away.

There is structure in the passage, however, both in subject matter and in form-critical patterns. Thus vv 1–4 contain a prohibition to Jrm not to marry, while vv 5–9 contain prohibitions against his attending funerals (and perhaps weddings), and the negatives of the two sections are contrastive (on all this see above). Verses 5–9 seem to divide in two: vv 5–7, the prohibition against entering the בֵּית מַרְזֵחַ, "house of funeral feasting," v 5, and vv 8–9, the prohibition against entering the בֵּית מִשְׁתֶּה, "house of feasting," v 8. At the same time there appears to be an inclusio in the whole passage: v 9, with its references to "bridegroom" and "bride," is reminiscent of the prohibition to marry in v 2.

Each word to Jrm (vv 2, 5a, 8) is followed by a motivation introduced by כִּי (vv 3–4, 5b–7, 9). The first and last motivations are introduced by "for thus Yahweh has said," the first and second motivations are linked by the verbs "bury" and "lament" (vv 4, 6), and all the motivations contain one or two of the phrases "in this place," "in this land," and "from this place" (vv 3, 6, 9).

The passage is essentially a supplementary call from Yahweh, but the rubric in v 1 and the second-person plural suffixes in the expression "before your eyes and in your days" in v 9 suggest that, once received, that call was then proclaimed publicly as a word of judgment on the people. Verse 2 is couched like an apodictic prohibition in the Decalogue; it is the reverse of the phraseology of the call to Hosea, "Take for yourself a wife. . . ." It is a call from Yahweh not to do something, analogous in genre to the positive calls to Jrm to "go" and "speak" (1:7). The motivational כִּי clause which follows is an elaborate one (vv 3–4); its terrible repetitions ("sons,"

"daughters," "mothers," "fathers") are appropriate to the astonishing prohibition in v 2. The motivation includes the citation of a word of judgment from Yahweh (v 4) that contains traditional curse forms.[3]

The M text of v 5 begins as does v 3, "for thus Yahweh has said." But v 5a is not a motivation as are vv 3–4; v 5a is an independent set of prohibitions parallel to the prohibition in v 8, and therefore vv 5–9 are on the same rhetorical level as are vv 1–4 (see above). Volz and Rudolph translate כִּי here as "further," but given the pattern of motivation clauses in vv 3, 5b, and 9, and the evident lack of כִּי in the text used by G (see Text), it is better to omit it as a dittographic error.

The prohibitions here (and the one in v 8, if the proposed emendation is correct) are those of immediate application analogous to those in 7:16 prohibiting Jrm from praying for the people. These prohibitions, against participating in funerals, are again followed by a motivation clause (vv 5b–7), one almost as elaborate as that in v 4, a veritable catalogue of funeral customs. The prohibition in v 8 is more compact than those in v 5a; its motivation clause (v 9) is heavy with parallelisms.

It may be noted that the verbs "bury" and "lament" in v 6 are in reverse order in comparison to those verbs in v 4, and that "father" and "mother" in v 7 are in reverse order in comparison with "mothers" and "fathers" in v 3. These reversals are not likely to be accidental.

Setting

By the assumptions of the present study Jrm became convinced, after Jehoiakim burned his scroll (November/December 601), that Yahweh would not be swayed from his determination to bring disaster on his people (36:31). This assumption governed the material that was added in the second scroll (36:32), and the most dramatic possible presentation of this decision by Yahweh would be Jrm's public declaration of celibacy as a sign of the end of the people (vv 1–4 here). The most plausible context for vv 1–4, then, is just after the burning of the first scroll, in December 601 or early in 600. The mention of "dung on the surface of the ground" and "sword" and "famine" in v 4 reinforces that suggestion. The first phrase reflects the usage of 9:21,

---

1   For some of these links see Holladay, *Architecture*, 129–30, 138–45.

2   So my recent attempt, Holladay, "Recovery," 412–

20.

3   Hillers, *Treaty-Curses*, 68–69.

the proposed setting for which in the present study is early in 600; and the association of "sword" and "famine" occurs often in the liturgy on drought and battle in 14:1—15:9, the setting for which is December 601. By the reckoning of the present study Jrm was twenty-six or twenty-seven years old. It is possible that the declaration of celibacy stimulated persecution by Jrm's own family (12:6). If the reversals of "lament" and "bury" (vv 4, 6) and "mother(s)" and "father(s)" (vv 2, 7) are deliberate, it suggests either that vv 5–9 were conceived as part of a single unit, vv 1–9, or else that they were a supplement to vv 1–4. Since the message communicated by vv 5–9 is in any case analogous to that in vv 1–4, one must assume a time not far from that proposed for vv 1–4; the wording of v 5b at least hints at the drought (the words "peace" and "compassion" may point in that direction: see Interpretation on v 5).

Interpretation

■ **1** For this rubric see 1:4.

■ **2** For the parallel of this prohibition to the call of Hosea see Structure and Form. Skinner has noted, "What Hosea had learned through the bitter experiences of his home life led Jeremiah early to renounce the hope of marriage, because he felt himself to be like his predecessor the prophet of a nation's dying agony."[4] If one believes that Hosea deliberately married a harlot, then one can go further: Hosea married a harlot to demonstrate the corruption of Israel's relation to Yahweh, while Jrm married no one at all to demonstrate the end of Yahweh's relation to Israel. Celibacy was virtually unknown in Israel; Köhler notes that the Arabs still call the bachelor *'azab*, "forsaken, lonely," and that the OT has no word for this at all, so unusual is the idea.[5] One has to move past the OT period to find any evidence of celibacy: for Qumran the evidence is mixed;[6] for the NT see Matt 19:12; 1 Cor 7:8, 26, 32–34, and commentaries on those passages. Childlessness, furthermore, suggests worthlessness (22:30). Indeed marriage is a part of the

order of creation (Gen 1:27–28; 2:21–24), and the sense of being part of a chain between past and future was so strong that one must understand Jrm to be called to extinction as an act symbolic of Yahweh's decision for the nation (compare Isa 56:5 for an expression of the poignancy of childlessness). Stanley Frost has suggested that a motivation for the collection of biographical material about Jrm (to be attributed to Baruch?) is the fact that Jrm had no sons to carry on his name;[7] see further 11:19. The poignancy of Jrm's sacrifice appears to have been particularly keen, given the number of references to bride and bridegroom (2:32; 7:34; 25:10). But Jrm's sense of having been Yahweh's man from birth (1:5) made it appropriate that by his life he should symbolize the death of his people.

It may be noted that in the precritical period there was speculation whether Jeremiah was or was not celibate; Calvin mentions the question but lays it aside as pure speculation. But 37:12 reads, "Jeremiah set out . . . to receive his share of property there among the people," which *T* translates, "Jeremiah went out . . . to divide (his) inheritance there in the midst of the people," and there have been editions of *T* which, after "inheritance there," add "with his sons and his brothers."[8] The Roman Catholic commentator Casp. Sanctius (Leiden, 1618) denied this proposal, assuming the prophet's celibacy; Sebastian Schmidt (Strasbourg, 1706) states that of course Jrm might have had a wife previously who had died, and even sons and daughters, and thus the divine command would refer to a second marriage.[9] M. D. Goldman has recently suggested that Jrm was simply forbidden to marry "in this place," that is, Anathoth. All this is pure speculation; one must stay with the text as it is.

"In this place" (here and in v 3) is synonymous with "in this land" (v 3); but the nuance of מָקוֹם as a cultic place (7:3) is doubtless present: the land is a special place, heretofore the recipient of Yahweh's blessing, but now that blessing has been withdrawn.

---

4 Skinner, p. 22.

5 Ludwig Köhler, *Hebrew Man* (London: SCM, 1956; Nashville: Abingdon, 1957) 89.

6 See conveniently Geza Vermes, "Dead Sea Scrolls," *IDBSup*, 114–15; Helmer Ringgren, *The Faith of Qumran, Theology of the Dead Sea Scrolls* (Philadelphia: Fortress, 1963) 139–40.

7 Stanley Brice Frost, "The Memorial of a Childless

Man, A Study in Hebrew Thought on Immortality," *Int* 26 (1972) 446–47.

8 Thus Alexander Sperber, ed., *The Bible in Aramaic, Based on Old Manuscripts and Printed Texts, III* (Leiden: Brill, 1962) 223, cites this reading for the Antwerp Polyglot Bible, 1569/73.

9 For Sanctius, and for Schmidt's counterargumentation, see Sebastian Schmidt, I, 649.

■ **3** The motivation clause (see Structure and Form) mentions specifically every member of the family. All alike will die.

■ **4** The first clause is heavy with alliteration and redundancy: מְמוֹתֵי תַחֲלֻאִים יָמֻתוּ, literally "(with) deaths of pain/diseases they shall die." The noun תַחֲלֻאִים is assumed to mean "diseases" (Deut 29:21; Ps 103:3), but doubtless the plural can be a collective (2 Chr 21:19). Here the expression does not refer to various diseases each of which has a distinct diagnosis, but in general to suffering and pain, the horror of mass death.

Burial was an imperative duty in Israel: "to be left unburied, a prey to the birds and the wild beasts, was the worst of all curses"[10] (compare the remarks on 8:1–3, on the desecration of graves); and the absence of lamentation over the dead was as terrible a misfortune as lack of burial.[11] One can imagine a situation in which there are so many corpses that burial is impossible (14:16), but none left to lament?—then no one is left alive! For "dung on the surface of the ground" see 9:21; for "sword" and "famine" see 14:12–18; for "their corpses shall become food for the birds of the heavens and the beasts of the earth" see 7:33.

■ **5–9** A basic question is whether Jrm is prohibited from attending weddings (vv 8–9) as well as funerals, or whether there is only one prohibition here, against attending funerals. When commentators deal with the issue at all, they are largely content to leave the matter unsolved, referring simply to "joyous festivals" for vv 8–9 (compare Volz, Rudolph); Thompson does refer to weddings.[12] The evidence largely revolves around the meaning of the two terms בֵּית מַרְזֵחַ (v 5), here translated "house of funeral feasting," for which cognate Semitic evidence, particularly that from Ugaritic, is crucial; and בֵּית מִשְׁתֶּה (v 8), "house of feasting"; for the evidence see below on the respective verses. But two contrary observations are in order here. (1) The expression בֵּית־מִשְׁתֶּה comes first in v 8, before the verb, suggesting a shift of subject; and v 9 appears to be a fresh motivation clause,

parallel with the motivation clause in vv 5b–8. These data suggest a separate prohibition against attending weddings. On the other hand, (2) it is perhaps significant that in the tractate *Semaḥot* ("Mourning," literally "Rejoicings," a euphemism) the deceased man or woman is referred to in two paragraphs as "groom" and "bride";[13] one must further note that in two additional paragraphs between these references the regulations seem to concern literal brides and grooms.[14] Now it is true that in citing Ugaritic data and rabbinic data on this passage one is dealing with evidence from a millennium before and a millennium after the passage; but funeral customs are notoriously conservative. It is clear that vv 5–9 stress funerals: if weddings are referred to, they are an afterthought. A paraphrase might be, "Do not attend funeral feasts. As a matter of fact, do not attend any communal feasts at all." But the question must remain open.

■ **5** The prohibitions here are not of the permanent variety, as they are in v 2; the assumption may be that on previous occasions Jrm has attended funerals (compare the remarks on the prohibition not to pray for the people, 7:16).[15] "Do not enter the house of *marzēaḥ*." This term appears only once otherwise in the OT (Amos 6:7), but its meaning has been clarified in recent years, particularly by its appearance in Ugaritic texts. Bezalel Porten has brought into convenient compass all the extrabiblical texts[16]—those from Ugaritic, the Aramaic texts from Elephantine, Punic, Nabatean, and Palmyrene inscriptions, and the Talmudic tradition. In general in northwest Semitic culture the *marzēaḥ* was a religious association, usually for funerary purposes, often maintaining a banquet hall. These funerary banquets were marked by an excess of drinking and often by licentious behavior.[17] Pope assumes that these were characteristics of the Israelite *marzēaḥ*,[18] but one must use care in applying the array of non-Israelite data to the biblical situation. What is clear is that Amos 6:7 suggests a context of revelry,[19] and that the present passage

---

10 De Vaux, *Ancient Israel*, 56.
11 Edmond Jacob, "Mourning," *IDB* 3:452–54, esp. 452.
12 Thompson, p. 406.
13 *Sem.* 8.2, 7.
14 *Ibid.*, 8.3–4. For a discussion of all this see Dov Zlotnick, *The Tractate "Mourning"* (Yale Judaica Series 17; New Haven, CT: Yale University, 1966) 14–17.
15 Bright, "Apodictic Prohibition," 185–204, esp. 194.
16 Porten, *Elephantine*, 179–86.
17 Ibid.
18 Pope, *Song of Songs*, 210–29.
19 Wolff, *Joel and Amos*, 277–78.

describes a funerary situation. Whatever the customs were, Jrm is forbidden to participate in them. One must not, by the way, assume that the "house" refers to a specific building set aside for the purpose; it probably refers to any house where a death has taken place.

Recent scholarly work on the meaning of house of *marzēaḥ* in this verse has assumed that the phrase is synonymous with "house of feasting" in v 8;[20] this is possible but by no means assured (see on v 8).

For נוד "grieve," literally "rock in grief," see 15:5.

Jrm's abstention from attendance at funerals would have been almost as shocking to his people as his abstention from marriage. Both abstentions signify a breach in the social network of the covenant community. If the time will come when normal funeral customs will no longer be observed, then Jrm signals the beginning of the process in his own action. Many years later Ezekiel will abstain from the normal mourning rites for his own wife, in a similar gesture (Ezek 24:15–27).

The motivation for the prohibition comes in vv 5b–7. Yahweh, we hear, has taken away his *šālôm*—his peace and blessing. Yahweh's removal of his *šālôm* may suggest the drought: one thinks of the usage of the word in 12:5 (see there). The false prophets had assumed that Yahweh was giving his secure peace (14:13), when at this time the reverse was the case. In this context Yahweh's *šālôm* is reinforced by mention of *ḥesed*, his covenant love or favor, and his "compassion" (רַחֲמִים) (these two are also linked positively in Hos 2:21). What a terrible thing it is to hear that Yahweh's steady blessing is now to be withdrawn; it is "the suspension of the covenant community and the delivering up of the people to death."[21] It will be many decades before a trustworthy spokesman for Yahweh assures his people that his *šālôm* and *ḥesed* will not depart (Isa 54:10). Question: does "compassion" (רַחֲמִים) here imply "rain"?[22]

■ **6** In 6:13 one hears that from small to great everyone is greedy; here one hears that great and small will die— every rank of society. The verb גדד hitpolal is "slash oneself" (1 Kgs 18:23); it occurs in 5:7 in the context of the frenzy of Baal worship (see there), while here it is a funerary practice. Again קרח nipʿal means "make oneself bald (by shaving)," another mourning custom. Both these customs are forbidden in the legal tradition (Lev 19:28; 21:5; Deut 14:1); the question then arises what their status was. In any event the word to Jrm is not "Do not do these because they are pagan and forbidden," but "Do not do these because you are forbidden to participate in funeral customs." It is possible that the prohibition implies "Do not participate in any customs, whether licit or illicit." Is there any significance in the fact that the verbs "bury" and "lament" are plural, while "slash oneself" and "shave one's head" are singular? Both singular and plural may indicate an indefinite subject (GKC, sec. 144d, f), but one wonders whether the singulars here indicate that one person practiced these customs as representative for the community.

■ **7** This verse speaks both of "bread" and "cup." For the bread compare 2 Sam 3:35 (David on the death of Absalom). De Vaux points out that the house of the deceased was unclean, so that food had to be prepared elsewhere and brought in.[23] The root נחם carries what seems to be a wide range of meanings; basically it may have meant "breathe deeply," but in any event the meanings appear to be united by the idea of bringing relief to one's emotions. The nipʿal is used in 4:28 and 15:6 to mean "regret, be sorry for (a decision)," and the piʿel is used here of sharing sorrow, "condole," and thus also the related תַּנְחוּמִים "condolence" in the next phrase. The mention of "his father" and "his mother" here is particularly poignant, given the less-specific מֵת "deceased" just above. Of the custom of this meal, Jerome remarks, "It was usual to carry provisions to the mourners and to prepare a feast which the Greeks call περίδειπνα and which we commonly call *parentalia*, since the ceremonies are carried out for parents."

■ **8** The verse begins with the expression "the house of feasting." Given the fact that the same expression, בֵּית מִשְׁתֶּה, occurs in Eccl 7:2 in contrast to the בֵּית אֵבֶל "house of mourning," and given the reference to "bridegroom" and "bride" in v 9, one might assume that, in contrast to vv 5–7, the reference here is to the place where weddings are celebrated. The word מִשְׁתֶּה "feast" is associated with a wedding elsewhere as well (Judg 14:10, 19). But the matter is not clear (see above, on vv 5–9). Jrm may be content simply to leave the matter

20   Porten, *Elephantine*, 181; Pope, *Song of Songs*, 216.
21   Eichrodt, *Theology* 1, 237.
22   Gary Rendsburg, "Hebrew *rḥm* = 'rain,'" *VT* 33

(1983) 357–62.
23   De Vaux, *Ancient Israel*, 59–60.

ambiguous, wishing by the expressions in v 9 to bring an inclusio to v 2 (see Structure and Form). The whole emphasis in the passage is on death, not life.

"To sit" is not parallel with "to eat and drink": the latter verbs are subordinate to it (compare Gen 37:25; Esth 3:15). One has the impression both from the present passage and from Esth 3:15 that "sitting" carries a more formal, ceremonial content than the English implies (commentators point out the effective contrast between the "sitting" of the king and Haman and the perplexity of the surrounding city).[24]

■ 9 The motivation is no different from those in vv 3–4 and vv 5b–7. Now it is the sound of wedding festivities that will be heard in the land no more. For the diction compare 7:34 and the comment there. The expression "before your eyes and in your days," for which I can find no parallel, means something like "here and now"; the phrase embodies an address in the second plural, the only such address in the whole passage.

Aim

What would be the reactions of those who heard this announcement? Some would doubtless take it as demented (compare 12:6; 29:26), but some must have taken it seriously, and for them it was the solemn death knell of the nation.

No response from Jrm is recorded for this call, no "Ah, Lord Yahweh, look, how long?" (compare 1:6; Isa 6:11). It was a prohibition that Jrm simply accepted dumbly. He was willing to fit his action to his word, to become a public curiosity, a permanent offense to all sensibilities: no wife and children, no participation even in the last rites of the people close to him. Jesus told a parable about petulant children who refused to play either "wedding" or "funeral" (Matt 11:16–17 = Luke 7:31–32), but Jrm was not playing, and he was not petulant: it was God's will for the people of which he was to be a permanent demonstration. Paul would abstain from marriage because of the shortness of time before the end

(1 Cor 7:7, 26, 32–34), but that abstention was not a sign of the end, it was a matter of prudence; and in any event Paul's view of the end time was one of glory (1 Cor 15:51–57). For Jrm it was a different matter.

There is no way from this distance to assess to cost of such discipleship. Let a poem of Dietrich Bonhoeffer's, written about himself, suffice, for Bonhoeffer loved Jeremiah:[25]

Who Am I?

Who am I? They often tell me
I would step from my cell's confinement
calmly, cheerfully, firmly,
like a squire from his country-house.

Who am I? They often tell me
I would talk to my warders
freely and friendly and clearly,
as though it were mine to command.

Who am I? They also tell me
I would bear the days of misfortune
equably, smilingly, proudly,
like one accustomed to win.

Am I then really all that which other men tell of?
Or am I only what I know of myself,
restless and longing and sick, like a bird in a cage,
struggling for breath, as though hands were compres-
    sing my throat,
yearning for colours, for flowers, for the voices of
    birds,
thirsting for words of kindness, for neighbourliness,
trembling with anger at despotisms and petty humili-
    ation,
tossing in expectation of great events,
powerlessly trembling for friends at an infinite
    distance,
weary and empty at praying, at thinking, at making,

---

24   Lewis B. Paton, *A Critical and Exegetical Commentary on the Book of Esther* (ICC; New York: Scribner's, 1908) 211; Carey A. Moore, *Esther* (AB 7B; Garden City, NY: Doubleday, 1971) 42.

25   Dietrich Bonhoeffer, *The Cost of Discipleship* (New York: Macmillan, 1959) 15, and *Letters and Papers from Prison* (New York: Macmillan, 1971) 347–48.

faint, and ready to say farewell to it all?

Who am I? This or the other?
Am I one person today, and tomorrow another?
Am I both at once? A hypocrite before others,
and before myself a contemptibly woebegone weakling?

Or is something within me still like a beaten army,
fleeing in disorder from victory already achieved?

Who am I? They mock me, these lonely questions of mine.
Whoever I am, thou knowest, O God, I am thine.

You Will Serve Foreign Gods in a Foreign Land

Bibliography

Long
"Schemata," esp. 134–38.
Skweres
"Strafgrunderfragung."

16

10/ And when you tell this people all these words, and they say to you, "Why has Yahweh spoken against us all this great disaster? What is our offense?—what is the sin which we have committed against Yahweh our God?" **11/** then you shall say to them, "Because your fathers abandoned me"—oracle of Yahweh—"and walked after other gods, and served them and worshiped them, but abandoned me and did not keep my law. **12/** As for you, you have done worse than your fathers: here you are, each walking after the stubbornness of his evil heart, so as not to obey me; **13/** so I shall hurl you off this land onto a land which neither you nor your fathers have known, and you will serve other gods there, day and night, ᵃ who ⟪ will show ⟫ᵃ you no mercy."

Text

13a—a   Reading יִתְּנוּ with *G* and *V* for *M* אֶתֵּן, presumably "since I shall show." *T* offers, "You will serve there peoples who serve idols day and night, who will show you no mercy." That is to say, *T* had a text which ended "who will show you no mercy" and avoided the implication that pagan gods have power by a periphrasis that made "peoples" the antecedent. *M*, then, is a second attempt to avoid implying that idols have power.

Structure

For a separation of vv 10–13 from vv 1–9, see vv 1–9, Structure and Form. Verses 14–15 duplicate 23:7–8 and were inserted here secondarily. The passage, like 5:19, appears after words of harsh judgment.

Form

The passage is an instance of the question-and-answer schema analyzed by Burke Long, his Type B,[1] wherein the word is addressed to the prophet about a future question from the people (compare 5:19; 13:12–14; 15:1–4). For an extrabiblical parallel see 5:19, Form.

Setting

Though Rudolph assumes that this passage is the product of later redaction, several data should give one pause. The verb טול hip'il "hurl" (v 13) occurs in Jer only here and in 22:26 (and the hop'al in 22:28); in chapter 22 the verb is used specifically of Jehoiachin and his

mother. It was thus not a conventional term of later redaction but appears to have a specific historical setting. Again there is the irony of pagan gods who "will show you no mercy." Jrm would of course insist that they do not show anything, either mercy or judgment (2:11; compare 10:5), but that is not the point here. Jrm elsewhere challenged the pagan gods to bestir themselves to rescue (2:28), and this passage suggests the same mentality. And the expression was alarming enough that later piety shifted the text in two different ways (*M* and *T*: see Text). Further the comparison "you have done worse than your fathers" is identical with that in 7:26, a passage judged in the present study to be authentic.

The passage is closely related to 5:19, not only in form but in content, for that verse hints at what is explicit here, namely that the people will serve foreign gods; 5:19 offers diction of its own suggesting that it is authentic to Jrm (see there). One may conclude that the present passage is likewise authentic. Since the key verb here is

---

1   Long, "Schemata," 134–38.

associated with the exile of Jehoiachin (see above), an appropriate date is in 598 or soon thereafter. One must envision a span of two or three years, then, between the announcement contained in vv 1–9 and that embodied here.

Interpretation

Most of the expressions in this passage are conventional in Jrm's discourse and have been met repeatedly in previous chapters. The reinforcement of the people's question in a parallelistic fashion ("why? what? what?") lends poignancy and insistence to the problem. Given all that Jrm has proclaimed in the context of the drought (note particularly 14:7, 20), the people's raising the question at this point suggests their utter inability to hear, understand, and obey (v 12).

Yahweh's answer to the people's question is twofold: the punishment is coming because your fathers abandoned me (2:5, 13; compare 11:10; 14:20), and because your yourselves have done no better, indeed have done worse (so also 7:26). Why worse? The present passage does not say clearly, but Jrm's discourse elsewhere suggests that it is because the present generation has not heeded the prophets (7:25). For the diction of v 11 compare 1:16; 9:12; for the diction of v 12 compare 7:24; 9:13.

Yahweh's punishment is set forth in v 13. The verb טול hip'il "hurl" is used of throwing a spear (1 Sam 18:11; 20:33); it is as violent a term as קלע "sling out" (10:18), likewise used of the inhabitants of the land on their way to exile. For "a land you do not know" see 15:14. For serving other gods in exile compare the implication of the double meaning in 5:19. The noun "mercy" (חֲנִינָה) appears only here in the OT. It is ironic that the people will be destined to worship nonentities; the punishment will most terribly fit the crime (see Setting).

Aim

The punishment will fit the crime: having worshiped alien gods in the homeland, they are sentenced to worship them in exile, gods who are nonentities. The true God has withdrawn his blessing, and the people are given no assurance that they will any longer have access to him on foreign soil. How terrible to be allowed to worship only ghosts!

A Short Passage on Restoration

16

Bibliography
Weinfeld
"Metamorphosis," 40–43.

14   Therefore the days are surely coming—
oracle of Yahweh, when [a] it shall[a] no
longer [a]be said,[a] "As Yahweh lives, who
brought up the children of Israel from the
land of Egypt," 15/ but rather, "As
Yahweh lives, who [a] brought up the
children of[a] Israel from the land of the
north,[b] and from all the lands where[c] [d] he
has chased them";[d] [e] and I shall settle
them[e] on their own soil [f] which I gave to
their fathers.[f]

Text

14a—a   For יֵאָמֵר G, T, and 23:7 read יֹאמְרוּ "they shall
say"; either reading is appropriate.

15a—a   G reads "brought up the house [of]"; 23:8 reads
"brought in the offspring of the house of."

b   For צָפוֹן 23:8 reads צָפוֹנָה; there is no difference in
meaning.

c   For אֲשֶׁר . . . שָׁמָּה 23:8 reads שָׁם . . . אֲשֶׁר; there is
no difference in meaning, but the present text is
more acceptable.

d—d   For הִדִּיחָם a few MSS., V, S, and T read הִדַּחְתִּים "I
have chased them."

e—e   For וַהֲשִׁבֹתִים 23:8 reads וְיָשְׁבוּ "and they shall
dwell"; either reading is appropriate.

f—f   These words are omitted in 23:8.

Commentary

With minor variations this passage is duplicated in 23:7–
8 (see Text). The passage is appropriate in the context of
other restoration material in 23:1–6; here, by contrast, it
appears to have been inserted secondarily (so other
commentators), though restoration material was conventionally added to judgment material such as vv 1–13

here represent. The passage will be dealt with in detail in
23:7–8.

**The People Will Be Caught
by Fishermen and Hunters**

Bibliography

Aalders, Gerhard C.
"The Fishers and the Hunters," *EvQ* 30 (1958)
133–39.

16

16   I am going to send for many fishermen[a] —
oracle of Yahweh, and they shall fish
them out; and afterward I shall send for
hunters, many of them, and they shall
hunt them out from every mountain, and
every hill, and from the crevices of the
rocks. 17/ For my eyes are on all their
ways: [a] they are not hidden[a] from my
presence, nor is their iniquity sheltered
from before my eyes. 18/ So I shall [first][a]
recompense them double for their
iniquity and their sin, because they have
profaned my land: with the corpses of
their vile things and their abominations
they have filled my heritage.

Text

16a   The ketib reads דַּוָּגִים and the qere' reads דַּיָּגִים;
the former spelling appears in Ezek 47:10 and the
latter in Isa 19:8, so that either is evidently valid. It
is דייגים that occurs at Qumran (1QH 5.8).

17a—a   Some MSS. and *G* and *S* insert "and" before the
negative.

18a   Omitting this word with *G*; it is a redactional gloss
(see Interpretation).

Structure

Extent of Unit. Form-critically vv 19–20 are separate from
vv 16–18: vv 19–20 offer diction in which the prophet
speaks in the first person, phraseology not unlike that in
the confessions. Verses 16–18 form a separate unit.

Position of Unit. Commentators are accustomed to
assuming that the passage deals with deportation (Volz,
Rudolph): by this understanding the fishermen and
hunters catch the population in order to exile them. But
the passage does not speak of deportation, and one
wonders if that interpretation would be current if the
passage were not in its position after v 13, to which it is
connected by these commentators. I propose instead an
association with vv 1–9 on the basis of a secondary
connection. The only pre-Jeremianic occurrence of
"fishermen" (דַּיָּגִים or דַּוָּגִים) is in Isa 19:8 (see Interpretation), and there it is stated that the fishermen will
"lament and mourn [אָבְלוּ]"; this verb may have
prompted a redactor to place the unit after vv 1–9,

where mourning customs are mentioned (note *אָבֵל in v
7);[1] compare the similar suggestion on the placement of
18:13–17. If this surmise is correct, it reinforces the
proposal that the "fishermen" here are to be identified
with the Egyptians, the identity in Isa 19:5–10 (see
Interpretation).

Internal Structure. The only question here is whether v
18 is an original part of vv 16–17. Verse 17 is introduced
by כִּי explaining the circumstance, and v 18 sounds
resumptive or summarizing of v 16. It is conceivable,
therefore, that Jrm himself added v 18 at the time the
material was recorded; there is no evidence that the
verse is the product of a later glossator (compare
Setting).

Form

The passage is an oracle of judgment: v 16 announces
the punishment, and the first clause of v 18 summarizes
the punishment. Verse 17 (introduced by כִּי) explains the

---

1   For this suggestion see Holladay, *Architecture*, 150.

circumstance. Verse 18aα resumes the announcement of punishment, and the balance of v 18 justifies the punishment by naming the offense. For the possibility that v 18 is a later addition see Structure and Setting.

Setting

There are three clues that place vv 16–17 in the period from 609 to 605. The first is the "fishermen" and "hunters" in v 16: evidence is given in Interpretation to identify the "fishermen" with Egypt and the "hunters" with Babylon. Since the utterance assumes that neither power is as yet perceived to be a threat, the period just mentioned is appropriate. A setting identical with others in Jrm in which Egypt and Mesopotamia are balanced (2:14–19, 33–37) is indicated. During the period 609–605 Judah was a vassal to Egypt. Jehoiakim claimed the rights of primogeniture over Jehoahaz and was backed by Egypt in his ascending the throne (2 Kgs 23:34);[2] the king doubtless looked upon Egypt as a loyal sponsor rather than a potential enemy, and the battle of Carchemish (early 605) was still ahead, the battle which crushed Egypt and opened the way to Babylonian hegemony over Judah. The second clue is the phrase "crevices of the rocks" (נְקִיקֵי הַסְּלָעִים, v 16), which is reminiscent of the "crevice of the rock" (נְקִיק הַסָּלַע) in which Jrm is to hide his linen loincloth (13:4): these two passages are the only ones in which נְקִיק occurs in Jer. And the date established in the present study for 13:1–12aα is the period of the battle of Carchemish. The third clue is the curious parallelism of "their ways" and "their iniquity" in v 17: this is the same parallelism as that found in 3:13, and the diction there, it was proposed, suggests that "their ways" means "their strength, wealth," offered first to Egypt and then to Babylon (see v 17, Interpretation, and see 2:1—4:4, Preliminary Observations, on 3:13).

Verse 18 appears somewhat odd in the context (see Structure, Form), but there is nothing in the diction which suggests that it is unauthentic to Jrm. It is possible that it is Jrm's reflection on the sieges of 598 and 587 (see Interpretation on vv 16–18 and v 18), so it might have been added by him in the context of the second siege. It is altogether likely that Isa 40:2 is a reflection of

this verse, though the expression for "double" is different; in this case one must assume that the verse was a secure part of the lore to which Deutero-Isaiah had access.

Interpretation

■ **16–18** Critical opinion on these verses has shared several assumptions which, by the analysis presented here, are erroneous. Several scholars have seen in the two groups mentioned, the "fishermen" and the "hunters," and in the word "double" in v 18, reference to the two deportations in 598 and 587 (Duhm, Cornill), or at least that vv 16–17 here refer to deportation (Volz, Rudolph). By hindsight these two deportations were the twin tragedies that brought national life to an end, but there is no assumption of deportation here at all: that idea comes from the association of these verses with vv 10–13. The evidence offered here indicates that the verses are here by association with vv 1–9 (see Structure) and that vv 10–13 were added subsequently. Again Rudolph and Hyatt presume that v 18 is of Deuteronomistic origin; but there is in the passage no phraseology typical of that material: the verse may have been a later expansion of vv 16–17 but gives every evidence of being genuine to Jrm himself.

■ **16** The symmetry of word order here is evidently deliberate: רַבִּים "many" follows "fishermen" (the normal order) but precedes "hunters"; the latter order is highly unusual (in spite of GKC, sec. 132b). One must therefore reject the emendation of Condamin, who would reverse "hunters" and "many."

The rarity of the term "fishermen" (דַּיָּגִים or דַּוָּגִים) in the prophets may allow one to identify the reference: the only pre-Jeremianic passage is Isa 19:8 (compare Structure). The passage in Isaiah (Isa 19:5–10) mentions the "Nile" repeatedly, suggesting that the metaphor in the present passage represents the Egyptians. The term "hunters" (צַיָּדִים) by itself has no particular national association, but the depiction here, of hunters who will hunt them out "from the crevices of the rocks," is strongly reminiscent of the "crevice of the rock" in which Jrm had been commanded to bury his linen loincloth (see Setting), and that crevice of the rock is of course in the context of the village which represents the Euphrates, a

2   Malamat, "Twilight of Judah," 126–27.

circumstance suggesting that the metaphor represents the Babylonians. (Compare Lam 4:18–19, where the identification of "hunters" [צָיָדִים] is clear.) Jrm thus proclaims that an incursion of the fishermen will be followed by an incursion of the hunters ("afterwards," אַחֲרֵי־כֵן); Jerome notes that in his day the Jews interpret the "fishermen" as the Chaldeans and the "hunters" as the Romans, "who have hunted an unhappy population from the mountains and hills and the caves of rocks": that is, it is clear that it is a succession of two different invaders that is intended. The interpretation of v 17 reinforces this understanding.

The verb "catch (fish)" (דיג) appears only here in the OT, and it is uncertain whether the form (וְדִיגוּם) is an unusual qal (so *HALAT*), a hip'il (compare BDB), or whether the form should be revocalized to a pi'el וְדִיגּוּם (Zorell).[3]

■ 17 The parallelism of "their ways" and "their iniquity" here is identical with that found in 3:13: "their ways" suggests the scattering of their treasure, first to Egypt, then to Babylon (compare also the references to the "way" to the Nile and the "way" to the Euphrates in 2:18). These ways and this iniquity is open to the scrutiny of Yahweh (for the preference which Yahweh's eyes have, see 5:3).

■ 18 The word "double" (מִשְׁנֶה) occurs elsewhere in Jrm's words (17:18); here one must understand it to refer to the visitation of the "fishermen" and then the "hunters." The term "vile things" (שִׁקּוּצִים) is a derogatory term for idols (4:1; 7:30): but the witty notion that the land is piled up with the corpses of idols appears nowhere else in Jrm. One does find it reflected, however, in Lev 26:30 (with a different word for "corpse"), but it is difficult to establish the priority of the two passages. The material at the end of Leviticus 26 clearly reflects the specificities of

the tragedies of 598 and 587,[4] and therefore it is plausible that the Jer passage has the priority. The notion here reflects the same mentality as that in v 13: the pagan gods cannot do anyone any good; here one learns that the idols are dead (whether they were ever alive is another question!).

One is left uncertain whether to divide the last part of the verse as *M* has done, with the atnaḥ accent at "my land," the division reflected in the translation here, or whether the division should be at "their sin," so that the last part of the verse is balanced between "they have profaned my land with the corpses of their vile things" and "with their abominations they have filled my heritage" (so Rudolph): the word choice favors the latter analysis, but the syntax (infinitive followed later by finite verb) favors the former.

The word "first" (רִאשׁוֹנָה) does not really fit the context and is missing in *G*. It is evidently a gloss inserted after vv 14–15 were in place, to explain the sequence of events.

Aim

If the historical setting proposed for this passage is correct, Jrm is giving early warning that the two great powers, successively, would catch the people of Judah. He could hardly have been aware of how his "fishermen" and "hunters" would be reinterpreted in the repeated tragedies of the ensuing centuries (compare Jerome's report on the Jewish interpretation in his day: see Interpretation on v 16). One assumes that Jesus gave a positive interpretation of the "fishermen" in his remark about making his disciples "fishers of men" (Mark 1:17; Matt 4:19):[5] but perhaps Jesus' saying was not intended to be altogether benevolent![6]

3   Compare Bauer-Leander, sec. 56w.
4   Compare Martin Noth, *Leviticus* (Philadelphia: Westminster, 1965) 199–200; Eissfeldt, *Introduction*, 237–38.
5   Compare, for example, Vincent Taylor, *The Gospel According to St. Mark* (New York: St. Martin's, 1952) 169.
6   For a thorough exploration of Jesus' intention see

Wilhelm H. Wuellner, *The Meaning of "Fishers of Men"* (Philadelphia: Westminster, 1967).

16   In the End the Nations Will Turn to Yahweh

19	Yahweh, my strength and my protection,
	  my refuge in the day of trouble,
	to you the nations shall come
	  from the ends of the earth to say:
	"A mere sham our fathers inherited,
	  a nothing, something profitless.

20	Can a human being make himself
	  gods? —
	  but they are non-gods!"

21	"Therefore I am going to make known to
	  them,
	  once and for all I shall make known to
	  them my hand and my might,
	  and they shall know that ª my name
	  isª Yahweh."

Text

21a—a   A few MSS. read אֲנִי "I am" for *M* שְׁמִי. The alternative reading seems to be an accommodation to the repeated phraseology of Ezekiel (Ezek 6:7 and often).

Structure

The passage has doubtless been placed here because of the references to "vile things" (= idols) in v 18.

   The passage offers four cola of the prophet's affirmation, four cola of his quotation of the speech of the nations, and three cola of Yahweh's promise. The nouns "strength" (עֹז, v 19) and "power" (גְּבוּרָה, v 21) stand elsewhere in parallelism (Ps 21:14): they thus help to bind the passage together. By the same token the nations are represented as affirming the nonexistence of idols while Yahweh assures the listeners that they will know the true God: in this way the speech of the nations and the reply of Yahweh are bound together.

Form

The first two cola offer phrasing typical of both personal laments (Ps 28:8) and of thanksgivings (2 Sam 22:3, 33); Jrm uses vocabulary like this in his confessions (17:17). But the vocatives to Yahweh are followed by an affirmation of the conversion of the nations; this shift suggests that the model is Psalm 22, in which lament (vv 2–22 there) is followed by thanksgiving (vv 23–32 there) with strong hymnic elements: and the conversion of the nations is affirmed (vv 28–29 there). The quotation of the nations is similar to that found in Isa 2:3 = Mic 4:2. The passage closes (v 21) with a solemn asseveration by Yahweh himself: "Therefore I am going to make it known to them. . . ." It is the kind of prediction of self-revelation which one finds in Deutero-Isaiah (Isa 45:6; 49:26). The last colon, "and they shall know that my name is Yahweh," is analogous to the repeated formula in Ezekiel, "you/they will know that I am Yahweh," and "I am Yahweh" in the Holiness Code. In the self-revelation the speaker introduces himself and implies the recognition of the hearer.[1]

Setting

Commentators are divided on the authenticity of this passage to Jrm. Volz admits that Jrm may have expected the conversion of the nations (compare 4:2b), but he is convinced that the poem lacks coherence and is the product simply of a glossator who has mined phrases of Jrm's. Rudolph likewise rejects any authenticity, stressing the likeness of the passage to material in Deutero-Isaiah and Ezekiel. Weiser, on the other hand, believes that the central affirmation of the conversion of the nations belongs to ancient covenant traditions[2] and is therefore plausible for Jrm's affirmation (so also, cautiously, Bright).

   A solution can be reached only by an appeal to diction and literary technique; that is to say, a likeness to Deutero-Isaiah might mean that material influenced by Deutero-Isaiah might have been inserted in the corpus of Jrm's material, but it might also mean that Deutero-

---

1   For this formula see the discussion in Zimmerli, *Ezekiel 1*, 37–38, and the bibliography in n. 194 there.

2   Artur Weiser, *The Psalms* (Philadelphia: Westminster, 1962) 37.

Isaiah was influenced by a genuine word from Jrm.

The parallels to Jrm's diction are clear. Verse 19a is reminiscent of 17:17, the words for noneffectiveness in v 19b (שֶׁקֶר, here translated "a mere sham"; הֶבֶל, translated "a nothing"; the negative of יעל hip'il, translated "something profitless") are found with similar nuances in 2:5, 8, 11, and 13:25, and the colon וְהֵמָּה לֹא אֱלֹהִים, v 20b, is likewise found in 2:11. The question is: How are these words and phrases used? The answer must be: They are used in fresh ways. The last phrase of v 19, אֵין־בָּם מוֹעִיל, is a fresh expression; the parallel elsewhere is לֹא־יוֹעִלוּ, לוֹא יוֹעִיל (2:8, 11). Again the phrase וְהֵמָּה לֹא אֱלֹהִים in v 20b may be duplicated in 2:11, but it has a fresh use here: 2:11 means something like "Has any other nation been so disloyal as to forswear their gods, even though we know those gods are non-existent?" while here the expression means something like "Can a human being create a deity?—of course not, and anyway we understand now that there is no purpose in it, since such deities do not exist." That is to say, 2:11 is Yahweh's affirmation, while the passage here is the affirmation of the pagans. The parallel between v 19a and 17:17 is one of creative variation of synonyms. In short, one would accept the present passage as a genuine poetic sequence of Jrm's if it were not for the subject matter. But one is not far from the present subject matter in the expressions of 2:11 and 4:2b, and one must therefore take seriously the possibility that the passage is genuine to the prophet.

The passage is not so incoherent as Volz thought (compare Structure). The expression in v 19a is appropriate not only to individual laments but to thanksgivings as well (see Form), and in any event Psalm 22 gives a good model for a lament that culminates in an affirmation of the conversion of the nations. Verses 19b–20 use terms elsewhere employed by or about Judah ("our fathers" in 3:24; 14:20; the words for "worthlessness") in a fresh way to express the affirmation made by the nations; but the affirmation is not so propagandistic as one might have expected (the nations do not name Yahweh's name: it is left to Yahweh to do that himself)—the diction thus carries a note of realism and even empathy. It is not alien to the mode of argumentation in

27:5, where one hears Jrm mediating Yahweh's word to foreign kings (see there).

Jrm draws on Psalm 22 elsewhere as a model;[3] if that psalm stands behind the present passage (see Form), then that fact increases slightly the likelihood the passage is authentic to the prophet.

Given all these data, one must conclude that the passage is authentic to Jrm; this has consequences for one's assessment of 10:1–16 (see Setting there).

There are no internal clues by which one might determine a date or historical context for the passage; but the basic message ("the nations shall see that their religious orientation is folly") is the mirror image of that of 10:1–16 ("you must not learn the ways of the nations"), and if a setting in the period after 598 is appropriate for that passage, then the same setting is appropriate here. The two passages share vocabulary (הֶבֶל, 10:3, 8, 15; שֶׁקֶר, 10:14; "Yahweh is my/his name," 10:16) and approach.

Interpretation

The nouns עֹז "strength" and מָעֹז "protection" (v 19) sound as if they are cognate, but the lexica assure us that the former is from the root עזז and the latter from the root עוז, the respective Arabic cognates of which have different dentals; nevertheless the words are close enough in sound in Hebrew to have been associated elsewhere (Ps 28:8) as well as in the present passage. Indeed the two make up a hendiadys here, "my strong protection." Neither word is common in Jer (nor is מָנוֹס "refuge"). Nevertheless the second colon of 17:17 uses synonyms which result in a similar expression.

Is one to understand the speaker here as speaking for himself or as speaking on behalf of the nation? There is no clue in the passage itself, and form-critically the expression could represent either option.

The idea of the nations coming from every part of the earth to learn the law became a convention in the exilic and postexilic period (compare 3:17, and Isa 2:3 = Mic 4:2), but there are contrasts between the affirmation in this passage and comparable ones elsewhere. There is here no centrality of Jerusalem or Zion. There is a quotation of the people's affirmation of the emptiness of

3   Holladay, "Background," esp. 159.

idols: in no other passage do the converts make such an affirmation. And the quotation is startlingly realistic: there is no mention of the name of Yahweh (that is left for Yahweh himself to proclaim), simply the negative statement that their heritage is worthless.

The vocabulary of noneffectiveness here is paralleled elsewhere in Jer: שֶׁקֶר "shame," literally "a lie," compare 10:14 (= 51:17) and 13:25; הֶבֶל "emptiness," compare 2:5 and 10:15 (= 51:18); אֵין־בָּם מוֹעִיל "something profitless," literally "there is not in them anything profitable," compare 2:8, 11.

The question in the first colon of v 20 is an ironic reversal of Gen 1:26, וַיֹּאמֶר אֱלֹהִים נַעֲשֶׂה אָדָם, "And God said, 'Let us make a human being.'" Here one has הֲיַעֲשֶׂה־ לּוֹ אָדָם אֱלֹהִים "Can a human being make himself God/a god/gods?" The ambiguity is deliberate (compare the same ambiguity in 10:11): it is blasphemous to conceive of a human being creating God, but for a human being to create a plurality of gods is simply misguided, since "they"—the clarifying pronoun comes first in the second colon—are not divinities at all. (Compare Interpretation on 2:11.)

The self-affirmation of Yahweh in v 21 is held together by the threefold use of "know" (ידע), the hip'il stem in the first two cola and the qal in the last colon: the peoples of the earth will learn Yahweh's name. But of course to "know" Yahweh's name is to acknowledge or confess it (see Form). The phrase בַּפַּעַם הַזֹּאת has its expected meaning "this time" in 10:18, but in the present passage is better translated "once and for all" (*NJV*). The two nouns "hand" and "might," in reference to Yahweh's power, are associated elsewhere as well (Deut 3:24).

Aim

The extent of Yahweh's sway over all the nations of the world will ultimately be acknowledged by those nations themselves. It was an old dream, but it came with new cogency in Jrm's day, when the nation with whom Yahweh had covenanted was being swallowed up by those nations of the world. Jrm would offer no eschatological version of the dream, in which all nations would stream to Zion to hear the law: here is a version soberer and trimmer, in which the nations would be pressed, by the evidence of Yahweh's hand in the events of the day, to acknowledge that the heritage they had learned from their ancestors was but dust and ashes. And not a dream, but a solemn announcement: it is about to happen, here and now, once and for all!

Others who came after Jrm would make similar solemn announcements (Isa 40:1–5; Mark 1:15). Such announcements become cornerstones of the faith of the communities that respond to them, but subsequent generations must continue to find ways to fit them into their perception of the workaday world.

**Judah Rebels in the
Depth of the Heart and at
the Altar of the Temple**

Bibliography

Allen, Leslie C.
"More Cuckoos in the Textual Nest: At 2 Kings
xxiii.5; Jeremiah xvii.3,4; Micah iii.3; vi.16 (LXX);
2 Chronicles xx.25 (LXX)," *JTS* NS 24 (1973) 70–
71.
Couroyer, Bernard
"La tablette du coeur," *RB* 90 (1983) 416–34, esp.
429–33.
Hubmann, Franz D.
"Textgraphik und Textkritik am Beispiel von Jer
17,1–2," *Biblische Notizen* 14 (1981) 30–36.
Lattey, Cuthbert
"The Text of Jeremiah 17:1–2," *ExpTim* 60
(1948/49) 52–53.

17

1
The sin of Judah is written with an iron
pen,
with an emery point incised on the
tablet of their heart,
and at the horns of 《 the altar is their
oppression. 》[a]

2
As . . . remembered 《 . . . . .
. . . 》[a] their children 《 . . . 》[a] their altars
and their Asherahs:
[on leafy trees, on high hills][b]

3
[a] ⟨the mountain of strife⟩ 《 is
devastated. 》[a]
Your power and[b] your treasures as loot I
shall give away,
your high places for sin in[c] all your
boundaries;[d]

4
and you shall drop 《 your hand 》[a]
from your inheritance which I have
given you,
[b] I shall make you serve your enemies[b]
in a land[c] you do not know,
for a fire 《 I have kindled against you 》[d] in
my anger
forever burning.

Text

1a Reading מִזְבֵּחַ תֹּכָם for *M* מִזְבְּחוֹתֵיכֶם "your [plural]
altars." The second-plural suffix is clearly wrong
(compare the second-singular suffixes in vv 3–4),
and the plural of "altars" is wrong (see
Interpretation). Many MSS., *V*, and *S* read "their
altars," an effort to bring the word into congruence
with *M* "their children" at the beginning of v 2.

2a It is proposed here that the text has suffered the
omission of parts of two cola by haplography; for a
possible reconstruction see Preliminary Observations.

b The bracketed words are a variation of phraseology in 2:20; the form of the words is careless (עַל
"on" with עֵץ "tree": see Holladay, "On Every High
Hill," 174), and they appear to be a gloss extending
the mention of "mountain" at the beginning of v 3
(compare Giesebrecht, Volz, Rudolph).

3a—a Reading הַר רִיב שָׁדוּד for the impossible *M* הֲרָרִי
בַּשָּׂדֶה "O my mountain in the field" (or the like); see
Preliminary Observations.

b With many MSS., *V*, *S*, and *T* (and with 15:13); *M*
omits "and."

c Many MSS. omit בְּ "in."

d Many MSS. read גְּבוּלְךְ "your boundary" for the
plural of *M*.

4a Reading יָדְךְ with Michaelis (so Duhm and Cornill,
though they judge the whole clause to be a
secondary addition; Giesebrecht, Volz, Condamin,
Rudolph, Bright); the *M* וּבְךְ "[and you shall drop
(something)] and in/with you" is impossible.

b—b A few MSS., influenced by 15:14, read the verb as
וְהַעֲבַרְתִּי "transfer (your enemies)."

c The relative אֲשֶׁר is omitted in 15:14 and may be
a prosaic addition here.

d Emend to קְדַחְתָּךְ (with dative suffix). Alternatively
one may read with a few MSS., *G^L* and *G^O*, and *T*

קְדְחָה "(a fire) is kindled" with 15:14, but that reading is probably a secondary correction by analogy. The *M* reading קְדַחְתֶּם "you [plural] have kindled" is impossible. *V* has seen the difficulty and has changed the second-person plural verb to second-person singular. For a discussion of the problem see Preliminary Observations.

Preliminary Observations

There are grave textual difficulties in the passage, and the fact that *G* omits the whole passage has not raised confidence in what is before us. As to the omission in *G*, Cornill suggests, probably correctly, that it was the result of haplography between "Yahweh," the last word in 16:21, and "Yahweh" in the rubric of 17:5; the omission is therefore not germane to the validity of the passage. As for the difficulties of text, it is true that one can get some kind of sense out of the text of *M*, but it is clear that much has gone wrong with it.[1] It is unnecessary to examine all the proposals offered by the commentators, because my own proposal, though tentative, differs greatly from any heretofore published; it has been greatly stimulated by personal communication with Franz Hubmann.

At the outset I make two assumptions and one suggestion. My first assumption is that *M* preserves what it has been able to of a damaged text, so that my aim is to emend the consonants of *M* as little as possible; and my second is that there is a single train of thought and to some degree at least a common fund of diction through the poem (in which case Volz is wrong to divide vv 1–2 from vv 3–4). My suggestion is that v 2 has suffered from a large haplography; whatever unity of diction there is in the poem may be an aid in restoring the text.

One can begin to unlock the difficulties at the end of v 1. "Your altars," with a second-person plural suffix, is clearly wrong, given "their children" in v 2 and the second-person singular forms in vv 3–4. I propose that the word conceals תֹּכָּם "their oppression": the word תֹּךְ is likewise concealed in 9:5 (see there). "Oppression" rounds off the verse as "sin" begins it. The verse then deals with one altar, the altar in Jerusalem, not altars, plural.

I propose that כִּזְבֹּר at the beginning of v 2, an expression which seems so wrong, is in fact correct. In two other passages of accusation (2:26; 6:7) one finds כְּ "as" with an infinitive construct, followed in the next colon by

כֵּן "so" and a finite verb. The possibility is open, then, that the passage originally read, "As A remembered X, so their children have remembered their altars and their Asherahs." If that is so, the agent in the first colon will have to be אֲבוֹתָם "their fathers" (compare 2:5, 9; 6:21): "As their fathers remembered X, so their children have remembered their altars and their Asherahs."

What would the former generation have remembered analogous to the remembrance by the current generation of their altars and their Asherahs? The clue may lie in the reconstructed last colon of v 1, "and at the horns of the altar is their oppression." The incidents that immediately come to mind are Benaiah's killing of both Adonijah and Joab, each of whom had fled to catch hold of the horns of the altar (1 Kgs 1:50; 2:19–25; 2:28–35); these incidents, of course, are "remembered" at least by having entered into the material in 1 Kings. (This would not be the only instance in which Jrm draws on material from the early monarchy: compare his reminiscence of Jezebel in 9:21.) If Jrm is referring to Benaiah's violence here, then it is in keeping with his description of the temple as a "robbers' cave" (really a "den of brigands," 7:11). What would be the noun to describe Benaiah's killing? I propose יָד "hand": in 1 Kgs 2:25 Solomon "sent by the hand of [= by means of] Benaiah . . . and he struck him [Adonijah] down, and he died." (If that reconstruction here is correct, and if the reconstruction of "your hand" is correct in the first colon of v 4, then there is a pleasing link in the poem between the generation of the fathers and the present generation.)

Benaiah's own name is not likely to appear in a poetic colon unless his patronymic were to appear in a parallel colon (compare Num 23:18; 2 Sam 20:1); if he is mentioned once, as I assume here, he is likely to be designated by his patronymic alone (compare Isa 11:1). I propose, then, that the two cola of v 2 read: כִּזְבֹּר אֲבוֹתָם יַד בֶּן־יְהוֹיָדָע / כֵּן זָכְרוּ בְנֵיהֶם מִזְבְּחוֹתָם וַאֲשֵׁרֵיהֶם, "As their fathers remembered the hand of the son of Jehoiada, so their children have remembered their altars

1   Compare Bright, pp. 117–18.

and their Asherahs." If that reconstruction is correct, the word "son of" (בֶּן) resonates with "their children" (בְּנֵיהֶם) in the second colon, and the name "Jehoiada" (יְהוֹיָדָע) with "Judah" (יְהוּדָה), with "hand of" (יַד) earlier in the colon (and perhaps in v 4), and with "know" (יָדְעָתָּ) in v 4.

The first two words in v 3 in *M*, הֲרָרִי בַּשָּׂדֶה, are a mystery. The traditional translation, "O my mountain in the field" (*KJV*), makes no sense, and the reading of θ', הָרָרֵי, "mountains (in the field)" is possible from the point of view of morphology and syntax but still dubious (what, really, is being referred to?). I propose that the words mask the expression הַר רִיב, "mountain of strife" (compare Jrm's designation of himself as an אִישׁ רִיב, "man of lawsuit," 15:10). The expression could be completed by שָׁדוּד, the participle "devastated" (compare 4:29); the sequence waw-dalet could be mistaken for he in the early Aramaic alphabet.[2] This participle would match the participles in v 1.

One more textual difficulty must be discussed here, the verb associated with "fire" in the next-to-last colon of v 4. The second-person plural verb קְדַחְתֶּם is clearly wrong, and most commentators read the verb as it appears in the parallel in 15:14, namely the intransitive "(a fire) is kindled," but this does not explain the strange form in *M*. I would propose a first-singular verb to match the previous verbs in vv 3–4, but to read קְדַחְתִּי is not satisfactory: yod and mem are dissimilar at all periods, and one must explain the fact that *M* has shifted from verbs ending in -*tî*. A likely proposal is קְדַחְתְּךָ, with confusion of kap and mem (compare 2 Kgs 22:4, where the *M* reading וְיַתֵּם is almost surely to be וְיַתֵּךְ with the Versions and v 9 there: see commentaries on that passage), assuming a dative suffix (GKC, sec. 117x) of disadvantage.[3] On this understanding, when the suffix became puzzling it encouraged the misreading to mem and the construing of a second-plural verb. It is to be noted that other passages in which the "fire" image occurs likewise speak of Yahweh's initiative (compare 4:4; 5:14).

Structure and Form

There is no doubt that this unit extends through four verses: vv 1–2 embody an accusation of Judah's wrong-

doing, and vv 3–4 Yahweh's word of judgment. Volz separated vv 1–2 from vv 3–4 on the basis of their seeming disparity; but my tentative reconstruction of the text suggests that the two sections belong together (see Preliminary Observations).

There can be no certainty why the passage has its position here. But it must be borne in mind that the various units in 16:10–21 were probably inserted in their position after 17:1–8 were in place, so that one must imagine 17:1–8 coming directly after 15:10–21 or at the least after 16:1–9.

As to the specific reason for the position of the passage here, there would seem to be two possibilities. (1) If 15:10–12 (without 15:13–14) was inserted before 15:15–19, and if the reconstruction of הַר רִיב ("mountain of strife") in v 3 is valid, then that phrase may supply the clue: this unusual expression suggests an association with אִישׁ רִיב ("man of lawsuit") in 15:10. If 17:5–8 is associated with 15:15–19, as the present study proposes, then the prefixing of the present passage before 17:5–8 could well have been related to the prefixing of 15:10–12 before 15:15–19. (2) If 15:13–14 were integrated with 15:10–12 before their incorporation in the corpus of Jeremianic material, then the resemblance of 15:13–14 to vv 3–4 here would supply an even more cogent reason for its insertion.

If the reconstruction of the text offered here has validity, vv 1–3aα offer two tricola, in a common pattern: each tricolon has two long cola closely parallel and a shorter third colon less closely parallel. Verses 3aβb–4 are made up of four bicola of a more conventional sort. The division between the two halves thus evidently corresponds to the form-critical division between accusation and announcement of judgment: the colon "the mountain of strife is devastated" at the beginning of v 3, if correctly reconstructed, would then belong to the accusation rather than the announcement of judgment.

Setting

The reference to the "horns of the altar" suggests a setting at an observance of the day of atonement, an occasion when sacrificial blood was smeared on the horns of the altar (Lev 16:18): this is the suggestion of Volz.

---

2   Compare Cross, "Scripts," 137.
3   See further Dahood, *Psalms III*, 377–78, and compare his vocalization of Ps 44:16 in *Psalms I*, 266.

But of course other sacrifices involved the smearing of blood of the victim on the horns of the altar (see for example Lev 4:7), so that that specific setting is not required. The mention of "your power" (חֵילֶךָ) and "all your treasures" (כָּל־אוֹצְרוֹתֶיךָ) in v 3 reminds one of the actions of Nebuchadrezzar after the siege of Jerusalem in 598: 2 Kgs 24:13 speaks of "all the treasures [כָּל־אוֹצְרוֹת] of the house of Yahweh and the treasures of the house of the king" which Nebuchadrezzar took, and 2 Kgs 24:14 of the "mighty men of valor" (גִּבּוֹרֵי הַחַיִל) who were exiled at that time. If, as is likely, 15:13–14 took shape in the summer of 594, and those verses are an adaptation of vv 3–4 here, then the date is narrowed to the period 598–595. But of course Jrm might have anticipated Nebuchadrezzar's policy and anticipated the siege of the city.

Interpretation

Exegesis must be based on a convincing text, and there is no way to be sure of the text of at least some of this passage; the interpretation must therefore be tentative.

What is the "heart" of Judah (v 1)? It is first of all, of course, an expression for the will of the nation (4:4, 14); in that sense the sin of Judah is deeply incised into the heart, into the will of the nation. The diction in the new covenant passage (31:33) is a counterpoise to the expression here: there it is Yahweh's torah which will be written, not on tablets, but on the "heart" of the people; here it is not Yahweh's torah that is written on outer tablets but rather the sin of Judah which is written on an inner tablet, the "tablet of their heart."

But the implication of the new covenant passage and of 4:14 suggests that "heart" here carries a second meaning, that of the geographical center of the nation, the center of attention of the nation. That center is of course Jerusalem, and, by the phrasing of the passage, the center of Jerusalem is the altar, and at the altar the horns (see further below). At the very center of the life of the people, then, is oppression. That sin is incised in

their heart, as it were, by an iron tool, a tool that should touch no altar (Deut 27:5; compare Exod 20:25). It is a terrible accusation to level at the center of priestly orthopraxy.

For עֵט "pen" see 8:8. The parallel צִפֹּרֶן appears only once otherwise in the OT, in Deut 21:12, where it means "fingernail"; but it is clear that it means here an engraving tool. The material שָׁמִיר is difficult to identify. The conventional translation "diamond" is surely wrong except as a "dynamic equivalent" for an exceptionally hard substance: the earliest references to diamonds that are clearly such are to those found in India by the army of Alexander the Great. The word here is rendered by *V* with the Greek derivative *adamantinus*: this was an all-purpose term for various substances of great hardness—it was applied by Theophrastus to the hardest gem then known, the emery-stone of Naxos.[4] This emery-stone, a variety of corundum (aluminum oxide, Al_2O_3), was widely used in engraving gems.[5] The verb חרש means both "engrave, incise" and "plow" (see below). The context reminds the hearer of Exod 32:16, "And the tablets were the work of God, and the writing was the writing of God, incised [חרת, a verb evidently related to חרש] upon the tablets." But the writing in the present passage, by contrast, is ungodly writing.

If the restoration of the end of v 1, תֹּכָם "their oppression," is correct (see Preliminary Observations), it is a word which picks up "sin" in the first colon and points ahead to the description of oppression in v 2. But תֹּכָם has another meaning, "their middle, their center"; the horns of the altar are at their very center, and in this way points back to "heart." One thinks of the phrase בְּתוֹךְ לִבִּי "in the center of my heart" in Ps 40:11; does one have in the present passage the break-up of a stereotyped phrase?[6] If the word is correctly restored, the double meaning would be an example of what Cyrus Gordon has called "Janus parallelism."[7]

The horns of the altar were projections above the altar on the four corners;[8] they were the most sacred part of

---

4   See the *Oxford English Dictionary* under "adamant."

5   For the possible meanings of שָׁמִיר see the articles by William Ridgeway in Thomas K. Cheyne and J. Sutherland Black, *Encyclopaedia Biblica, A Critical Dictionary of the Literary, Political, and Religious History, the Archaeology, Geography, and Natural History of the Bible* (New York: Macmillan, 1899–1903), "Adamant," cols. 63–64; "Diamond," cols. 1097–98.

6   See 2:1—4:4, n. 79.

7   Cyrus H. Gordon, "New Directions, I. Janus Parallelism," *BASP* 15 (1978) 59–60; see further Gary Rendsburg, "Janus Parallelism in Gen 49:26," *JBL* 99 (1980) 291–93, and David T. Tsumura, "Janus Parallelism in Nah 1:8," *JBL* 102 (1983) 109–11.

8   For a photograph of a horned incense altar from

the altar (compare Lev 16:18; Amos 3:14), the place of sanctuary (1 Kgs 1:50).[9]

The reconstruction of a text involving Benaiah's violence (see Preliminary Observations) is obviously only a suggestion, but if it has validity, it suggests that Jrm saw Judah's sin to be centered at the altar of sacrifice from the time of beginning of Solomon's kingship. What a terrible event to remember!

By contrast, the current generation remembers its "altars" and "Asherahs." One must assume that Jrm here has reference to the altars and Asherahs which Josiah destroyed at the time of the Deuteronomic reform (2 Kgs 23:6, 12, 15). Jrm, who as a young man was a supporter of Josiah's reform program,[10] here levels an accusation against those still loyal to the pre-Josianic patterns. We have no detailed knowledge what an Asherah was; it was evidently an upright wooden symbol of some sort which represented a fertility goddess[11] (compare the discussion on 2:27).

If the reconstruction "the mountain of strife is devastated" in v 3 is correct, and if that colon is part of the accusation (see Structure and Form), then this is a striking statement (the verb שדד otherwise appears in announcements of judgment or analogous utterances): the sin of Judah has brought its own religious devastation to the temple area (compare 2:19; 4:18).

"Your power" (חֵילְךָ) and "your treasures" (אוֹצְרוֹתֶיךָ) refer to the losses to Nebuchadrezzar in 598 (2 Kgs 24:13–14; see Setting): חַיִל is "military power" and אוֹצְרוֹת refers to the gold and other treasures looted from the palace and temple. The phrase then deals with Yahweh's punishment of the people by the loss of their power and wealth to Babylonian looting. "Your high places" is evidently again a reference to Josiah's action in defiling or destroying these sites (2 Kgs 23:8, 13, 15, 19); the coupling here of "your high places" with "your power" and "your treasures" is an ironic comment on Judah's ultimate devotion.

If the restoration of "your hand" is correct in v 4, it suggests "your power"; if the restoration of "hand" is correct in v 2 (see Preliminary Observations), it picks up the mention of Benaiah's power. There is an ironic contrast between "your inheritance" which Yahweh had "given to you" in the beginning of Israel's history, and "your power" and "your treasures" which Yahweh is now "giving away" to the national enemies.

There is another set of possibilities of interpretation of these verses, however: I suggest that behind the religious and political vocabulary here is a texture of sexual innuendo. I suggest that just as Jrm (like Hosea before him) perceives Yahweh to have accused Israel of harlotry, so he perceives Yahweh to be accusing Judah of a preoccupation with male sexuality; Judah continues to live out the behavior of the eponymous ancestor Judah in his intercourse with Tamar (Genesis 38). Edwin Good suggested some years ago that the difficult expression in the blessing of Jacob on Judah, Gen 49:10, should be read, "The scepter shall not depart from Judah, nor his 'staff' from between his 'feet,' until Shelah comes,"[12] that is, that that passage is a witty comment on Judah's intercourse with Tamar. The present passage may be another such: if Jrm could play on the Jacob narrative (9:3), he may be playing on the Judah narrative here.

Thus "iron pen" and "emery point" may be phallic images. The participle "incised" (חֲרוּשָׁה) may also mean "plowed"; in that meaning the verb (חרש) is used for sexual intercourse in postbiblical Hebrew,[13] as is the cognate ḥaraṭa in Arabic;[14] indeed the imagery is almost inevitable anywhere.[15] By this understanding a preoccupation with male sexuality is at the heart of Judah's being. Indeed the very "horns of the altar" are part of the phallic imagery.

The altars and Asherahs that Josiah destroyed were deeply associated with sexuality (2 Kgs 23:5–7); though destroyed, the present generation remembers them with longing. One wonders whether the verb "remember" (זכר) conceals a double meaning with a word related to "male" (זָכָר): Isa 57:8, with זִכָּרוֹן, seems to have such a

Megiddo see Kurt Galling, "Incense altar," *IDB* 2:699 or *BA* 37 (1974) 1; for a photograph of the reconstruction of a horned altar from Beer-sheba see Yohanan Aharoni, "The Horned Altar of Beer-Sheba," *BA* 37 (1974) 3.

9   Montgomery, *Kings*, 80.
10   Lohfink, "Der junge Jeremia."
11   William L. Reed, "Asherah," *IDB* 1:250–52.

12   Edwin M. Good, "The 'Blessing' on Judah, Gen 49₈₋₁₂," *JBL* 82 (1963) 429–30.
13   See Jastrow.
14   See the imagery in *Qur'ān*, 2:223.
15   Compare the phrasing in Shakespeare, *Antony and Cleopatra*, act 2, scene 2, line 236.

meaning.[16]

"Your power" (חֵילֶךָ) in Prov 31:3 is sexual, and it is there accompanied by the same verb "give" found here: "Do not give your 'power' to women." If "your power" here suggests "your penis," then "your treasures" might suggest "your testicles": "jewels" has been a jocular and vulgar expression for testicles in English since as early as 1450.[17] If "your power" and "your treasures" suggests sexuality, it is no wonder that "your high places" is parallel with them in the poem.

If the restoration of "hand" in v 4 is correct, that word, too, is a euphemism for "penis" from beginning to end in Hebrew: it occurs in Ugaritic,[18] it evidently does in Isa 57:8 and 10 and perhaps in the imagery of Cant 5:4,[19] and it carries that meaning in the Qumran material.[20] Judah must finally relinquish it!

Finally, the expression "and I shall make you serve your enemies in a land you do not know" would seem unequivocal enough, but I propose here also a second possibility. The verb "serve" (עבד) may be used specifically of "tilling" the soil (Gen 2:5 with an object, Deut 15:19 without). Given the connotations of "plowed" in the participle "incised" in v 1, I propose that וְהַעֲבַדְתִּיךָ here may also mean "and I shall make you till." In this case אֶת־ would be construed not as the sign of the accusative (as in the first interpretation) but as the preposition "with": "and I shall make you till with your enemies" (the synonymous preposition עִם is so used with עבד qal in Gen 29:25). And the preposition בְּ with "land" would not be "in a land" but "for a land," the בְּ of price (that nuance of בְּ is found with "Rachel" in Gen 29:25,

already cited). Thus: Your misguided efforts at fertility here at home will merit you the labor for the fertility of an alien land beyond your ken.

Though these implications of sexuality cannot be proven, they may lie in the background. By this understanding Judah's punishment will fit his crime: he will be emasculated by the Babylonians. (For the possibility that the adaptation of vv 3–4 to Jrm's own situation, 15:13–14, carries over the implication of sexuality, see Interpretation on those verses.)

Question: Are the difficulties of text in the passage due to their having been censored, consciously or unconsciously?[21]

Aim

Jrm elsewhere mediates Yahweh's accusation against the cultic observances at the temple (7:21–28; 11:15–16); here, however, one hears that it is not simply the observances that are against Yahweh's will: Judah's rebellion against Yahweh is at the core of her being, both in her will and at the altar of Jerusalem, rebellion that involves violence and impure worship.

And beyond violence and impure worship it seems to be implied here that Judah's rebellion involves a preoccupation with male sexuality: the concerns of Baal have taken over Judah's heart. The words must have brought shock to Jrm's hearers: was this what they were to hear on the day of atonement? If the passage carries these implications, it is no wonder Jrm's ribald phrases were quickly lost in the piety of later generations.

---

16 For a similar suggestion see Pope, *Song of Songs*, 226.
17 See the *Oxford English Dictionary*.
18 Ug. 23.33, 34, 35.
19 Pope, *Song of Songs*, 517–18.
20 1QS 7.13.
21 For possible "censorship" elsewhere in the OT, compare the suggestion of that possibility in Isa 65:3 in Paul D. Hanson, *The Dawn of Apocalyptic* (Phila-

delphia: Fortress, 1975) 140–41, note e, and references there. One also wonders whether the difficulties of the text in Isa 57:7–8 are not the result of conscious deformation.

**Trust in Yahweh Avails
Even in a Time of Dryness**

Bibliography

On 17:5–13:
Alonso Schökel, Luis
"'Tú eres la esperanza de Israel' (Jer 17,5–13),"
*Künder des Wortes, Beiträge zur Theologie der
Propheten* (ed. Lothar Ruppert et al.; Würzburg:
Echter, 1982) 95–104.

On 17:5–8:
Davidson, Robert
"The Interpretation of Jeremiah xvii 5–8," *VT* 9
(1959) 202–5.
Holladay
"Style," 52.
Lindblom
"Wisdom in the OT Prophets," 199–200.

17

5   [Thus Yahweh has said:][a]
Cursed is the man who trusts in human
      beings,
    and makes flesh his arm,
      and whose heart turns from Yahweh;
6   He shall be like a juniper in the desert,
    and shall not see when bounty comes,
      but shall dwell in the stony fields of
       the wilderness,
       [a]a salty and uninhabited land.[a]
7   Blessed is the man who trusts in Yah-
      weh,
    so that Yahweh becomes his trust;
8   he shall be like a tree transplanted by
      water,[a]
    which puts out its roots by a canal;
    it shall not fear[b] when heat comes,
    and its leaves shall be green;
      it shall not be anxious in a year of
       drought,
      nor fail to give fruit.

Text

5a   Omit with rubric with *G* (so other commentators).
It is not an oracle (Bright), and it is proposed here
that the passage is an utterance from Jrm in
response to Yahweh's word in 15:19 (see Preliminary Observations).

6a—a   Some MSS. read בְּאֶרֶץ "in a land" for *M* אֶרֶץ "a
land," and many MSS. omit "and" before לֹא תֵשֵׁב
"uninhabited."

8a   Some MSS. add פַּלְגֵי "channels of" before
"water," following Ps 1:3.

b   Reading the ketib יְרָא with *G*, *V*, and *S*; the qere'
and *T* read יִרְאֶה with v 6. See Interpretation.

Preliminary Observations

It is universally recognized that there is a close relationship between this passage and Psalm 1. Criticism has
been hampered, however, by two assumptions which (I
propose) are erroneous: first, that Psalm 1 is late, and
second, that the psalm is dependent on the present
passage.[1] These assumptions have tended to classify both
passages as wisdom poems, and commentators on Jer
have therefore separated this passage from the message
of Jrm (Volz, Rudolph, Bright). This approach needs to
be questioned.

    Some scholars have pulled back from a late dating of
Psalm 1.[2] Beyond that matter it is clear that Jrm plays in
12:1–2 with themes and expressions found in Psalm 1

---

1   For both these assumptions see Rudolf Kittel, *Die
Psalmen* (Leipzig: Deichert, 1914) 6, and William O.
E. Oesterley, *The Psalms* (London: SPCK, 1953)

119–20; and for a late dating of Psalm 1 see Kraus,
Psalmen, 2–3.

2   Thus Eissfeldt, *Introduction*, 359.

(see Interpretation there): he reverses the affirmation of the psalm by saying it is the "guilty [or wicked]" whose way prospers, who send forth roots and bear fruit, rather than the "innocent [or righteous]." But in the present passage there are also differences from Psalm 1: here the order of the presentation of the good and the bad is reversed, and, more subtly, both the good and the bad experience lack of water—the bad man is likened to a desert shrub, corresponding to the chaff in Psalm 1, but the good man is likened to a tree planted by water that experiences "heat" in a "year of drought." This shift makes the present passage dynamic, in contrast to the static categories of Psalm 1. Since both 12:1–2 and the present passage shift the categories of Psalm 1 in different ways, the conclusion is likely that Psalm 1 is prior and 12:1–2 and the present passage are variations by Jrm of that psalm.

But if Jrm draws on the model of Psalm 1 here, he also draws on Ps 40:4–5: the play on "see" (ראה) and "fear" (ירא), the phrases about trusting in Yahweh.

Just as 12:1–2 has a specific locus within the confessional material, so, I propose, one must see the present passage, with its talk of a drought, of the lack of life-giving water, to be Jrm's response to the diction of 15:18 and 19: in 15:18 Jrm accuses Yahweh of being waters that fail, and in 15:19 Yahweh challenges Jrm to repent and stop his concern for what his persecutors do. Thus Jrm here contrasts the person who is dependent on other human beings with the person who is dependent on Yahweh: the latter brings forth leaves when heat comes, brings forth fruit when drought comes.

The assumption that the passage is authentic to Jrm gains support from the use made of the word-play between "see" and "fear" (a word-play that confused the copyist at some point): though Jrm drew on the diction of Ps 40:4 (see above), the way the word-play is integrated into the structure of the poem is distinctive.[3]

If the interpretation of the passage offered here is sound, it explains the position of the unit here after 15:15–21 and 16:1–9, material that must immediately have preceded it as the present passage was gathered into the growing corpus of material. One can imagine the process in two different ways. (1) The *hapax legomenon*

יוּבָל "canal" in v 8 might echo its homonym יוּבַל "led" (יבל hop'al) in 11:19. This link is reinforced by the word that follows in 11:19, לְטְבּוֹחַ "to slaughter," a word which itself is likely to be linked to its assonantal partner בֹּטֵחַ "trusting" in 12:5. The present passage likewise offers the verb יִבְטַח "trusts" in vv 5 and 7. These links suggest simply that the present passage could serve to round off the collection of "confessions" and the liturgy of drought and battle in chapters 11, 12, 14—15, closed by 16:1–9. (2) There may be an inclusio between the present passage and 20:14–18, not only the use of "cursed" and "blessed" (בָּרוּךְ, אָרוּר) in both passages, but the striking word-play of בָּשָׂר "flesh" in 17:5 and בִּשַּׂר "brought good news" in 20:15 (compare the same word-play, בָּשָׂר "flesh" and מְבַשֵּׂרֶת "bringer of good news" in Isa 40:5, 6, 9). By this datum the present passage, along with the confessional material in chapters 17, 18, and 20, might have been added in a block to the confessional material which ends with 16:1–9.[4] Perhaps both linkages played a part in the process by which the material was brought into the collection. In any event, this analysis suggests the conclusion that the present passage is not an orphan wisdom poem lodged here casually.

Structure

If Psalm 1 is the model for the present passage, the passage is confined to these four verses. For its placement here see Preliminary Observations.

The passage breaks neatly into the curse of vv 5–6 and the blessing of vv 7–8 in a way similar to that of the model passage, Psalm 1 (compare Preliminary Observations). The parity between the two sections is close: the first colon of v 5 matches the two cola of v 7 ("cursed/ blessed is the man who trusts in . . ."), the first colon of v 6 matches the first colon of v 8 ("he is like [a sort of plant or tree]"), and above all there is the word-play between "shall not see [יִרְאָה] rain come" in v 6 and "shall not fear [יִרָא] when heat comes." But the number of cola do not match: Jrm has deliberately given a skewed poem, indicating the disparity between someone who puts trust in a fellow human being and someone who puts trust in Yahweh. Thus the simile of the cursed man is four cola (v 6), and the simile of the blessed man is six (v 8). By way

---

3   Holladay, "Style," 52.
4   Holladay, *Architecture*, 132, 151–58.

of compensation the curse formula in v 5 is three cola and the blessing formula in v 7 is two.

Form

If the proposal in Preliminary Observations is sound, this passage is not a general wisdom poem but Jrm's affirmation of faith in response to Yahweh's suggestion that the prophet repent (15:19). This affirmation is couched in the form of a matching curse formula and blessing formula. Such formulas are found both elsewhere in the OT and in inscriptional material as well:[5] compare the curse formula in 11:4–5. There is an Egyptian parallel to Psalm 1 and the present passage, the Instruction of Amen-em-opet, fourth chapter: it contrasts the "hot man," who is like a tree growing in the open, with the "silent man," who is like a tree growing in a garden.[6]

Setting

The suggestion in Preliminary Observations, that the present passage is Jrm's response to 15:19, immediately suggests a historical setting for the passage, early in 600. The passage speaks of a "year of drought," and while that reference need not indicate that the verses took shape during the great drought described in 14:1–6 and dated here to the summer and autumn of 601 and beyond, nevertheless it would not be implausible if it did.

Interpretation

■ **5–8** It is a pretty question whether the curse and blessing formulas here are the expression of a wish ("cursed/blessed be the man," so *KJV*, and so the implication of *JB* and *NEB*), or a statement of the existing situation ("cursed/blessed is the man," so *RSV, NAB, NJV*). The genre of these formulas elsewhere indicates that both the wish and the statement may be conveyed by them.[7] The matching passage in the confessions, 20:14–18, is normally translated as a series of wishes, but data in the present study suggest that it is in fact a series of statements (see Preliminary Observations, Form, and Inter-

pretation there). And Psalm 1 intends its expressions to be statements of permanent truths. Given these parallels, one must opt for statements of the existing situation here as well.

The word גֶּבֶר (vv 5, 7) sometimes carries overtones of a "man" who is young and powerful (Prov 30:19), but since it appears in the Psalms in wisdom statements (אַשְׁרֵי הַגֶּבֶר, "happy/blessed is the man," Pss 34:9; 40:5; 94:12; 127:5), one must assume here that it is simply a poetic synonym for הָאִישׁ (Ps 1:1: compare 20:15). The subordinating particle אֲשֶׁר "who," vv 5, 7, normally thought of as inappropriate to poetry, seems to belong here, again on the model of Psalm 1. The expression בטח בּ (vv 5, 7) is the normal way to say "trust in": in 5:17 the reference is to those who trust in military preparedness. Here the contrast is between those who trust in אָדָם "human beings" and those who trust in Yahweh. For vv 5 and 7 two parallels come to mind. The first is Ps 118:8, טוֹב לַחֲסוֹת בַּיהוה מִבְּטֹחַ בָּאָדָם, "It is better to take refuge in Yahweh than to trust in human beings." The other is the contrast between אָדָם "human beings" and אֵל "God" found in Isa 31:3. The Isaiah passage antedates the passage under discussion, but it would be difficult to assign priority between Psalm 118 and the present passage. As for vv 6 and 8, the expression וְהָיָה כְּ "(and) he shall be like" is found elsewhere in the genre of the curse or blessing formula (20:16; compare Ps 1:3).

The word-play on ראה "see" and ירא "fear" is found elsewhere in the OT (Pss 40:4; 52:8; and, after Jrm, Isa 41:5), but those are simple collocations, while Jrm has managed to place the two verbs in parallel patterns in the two halves of the passage (see Structure).

■ **5–6** If the analysis proposed here is sound (see Preliminary Observations), Yahweh has abruptly jarred Jrm loose from his preoccupation with his own loneliness and lack of support from his fellow citizens: there are larger issues at stake, as the people try to put their trust in alliances and military support from one great power or another. (Compare Isa 31:3, already referred to: "The

5   For both OT and inscriptional material see, on "curse," Scharbert, "ארר," 408–12, 413, and on "blessing," Josef Scharbert, "ברך," *TDOT* 2:284–87, 300. For a recent inscription that appears to have both a blessing formula and a curse formula see William G. Dever, "Iron Age Epigraphic Material from the Area of Khirbet el-Kôm," *HUCA* 40/41 (1969–70) 159–65.

6   *ANET*, 422.

7   Scharbert, "ארר," 408; "ברך," *TDOT* 2:284–86.

Egyptians are men, and not God; and their horses are flesh, and not spirit.") There must always have been those in the court who hoped for help from Egypt as Babylon came and went. But what is true for the nation is also true for Jrm personally: he cannot count on flesh and blood for his help. Question: Does בָּשָׂר "flesh" here carry an innuendo of Jrm's sexuality? The word means "penis" in Lev 15:2, 3, 7; Ezek 16:26; 23:20. Given the motif of aloneness in 15:17 and the call to abstain from marriage in 16:1–4 (to say nothing of the suggestions of sexuality in 17:1–4), "who makes 'flesh' his arm" may bear this specific personal meaning for Jrm.

For "heart" = "mind" or "will" see 4:4.

The עַרְעָר is evidently the juniper, *Juniperus oxycedrus*, still called *'ar'ar* in Arabic;[8] it is usually a low shrub. There is a nice word-play with the location, בָּעֲרָבָה, "in the Arabah," the area of the Jordan rift valley from the river valley proper south to the Gulf of Aqaba.[9] The desert plant is Jrm's simile for the man without a trust in Yahweh, his equivalent of the dry chaff (Ps 1:4).

The word טוֹב is the most general word for "good." In the social context of Jrm's day it implied deliverance (8:15). Dahood insists that in the present passage it means "rain,"[10] the same meaning he suggests for 5:25 (see there). "Good" here is in opposition of חֹם "heat" in v 8, and "rain" is an appropriate translation in the context of a tree; there is no doubt that this is a major nuance of the word (compare טוֹב "good" in Deut 28:12). But given more than one level of imagery in the present passage, it is better to stay with the more general word (here "bounty").

The word חֲרֵרִים occurs only here in the OT. It is doubtless connected with the verb חרר "burn," hence an area burned by the sun, but there is uncertainty how specific the designation is. The Arabic cognate *ḥarra* means "stony area, lava field." The Arabic nuances of the word fit the volcanic, stony areas in Bashan[11] (where the juniper grows):[12] either the Jebel Druze or, as Eissfeldt has suggested, the region of aṣ-Ṣafā, east of the Jebel Druze.[13] On the other hand, "salty" suggests the Dead Sea area. The presence of salt in soil was a curse.[14] The verb ישׁב carries the meaning "be inhabited" here; for the theme of the uninhabited land see 2:6; 4:29.

■ 7–8 Verse 7 is a variation on Ps 40:5a. Giesebrecht and Rudolph omit v 7b: Rudolph calls it a "weak repetition." But it would seem it is neither weak nor a repetition: the subject of וְהָיָה is "Yahweh," not "his trust."[15] The subject therefore shifts from the bad man or the good man who is the subject of וְהָיָה in vv 6 and 8 and emphasizes Yahweh's participation in the process of trust (compare the diction of the first colon of 15:19).

The first colon of v 8 is a shortened version of the first colon of Ps 1:3 (without פַּלְגֵי "channels of"; but see Text). The verb שׁתל properly means "transplant" rather than simply "plant."[16] A reference to "roots" is lacking in Psalm 1 but is found in Jrm's other use of that psalm, 12:2. The noun יוּבַל occurs only here in the OT, though it occurs twice in the Qumran material in phrases imitative of this one;[17] the word in its context implies an irrigation canal,[18] Jrm's synonym for the omitted word פַּלְגֵי. (He doubtless also chose it because of לֹא־יִבּוֹל "does not wither" [נבל qal] in Ps 1:3. For the word-play with

8   George E. Post, *Flora of Syria, Palestine and Sinai* (Beirut: American, 1932–33) II, 801.

9   Simon Cohen, "Arabah," *IDB* 1:177–79.

10   Dahood, "Hebrew-Ugaritic Lexicography II," 411; *Psalms I*, 25.

11   Baly, *Geography*, 216–17.

12   Post, *Flora*, II, 802.

13   Otto Eissfeldt, "Das Alte Testament im Lichte der safatenischen Inschriften," *ZDMG* 104 (1954) 100; for map see Baly, *Geography*, 214.

14   Compare the discussions in A. M. Honeyman, "The Salting of Shechem," *VT* 3 (1953) 192–95, and Frank Charles Fensham, "Salt as Curse in the Old Testament and the Ancient Near East," *BA* 25 (1962) 48–50.

15   The diction is unique, so far as I am aware: וְהָיָה יהוה appears in only four other passages in the OT—in

two "Yahweh is with [עִם]" someone (Judg 2:18; 2 Kgs 18:7), and in the other two "Yahweh becomes [לְ היה]" judge or king (1 Sam 24:16; Zech 14:9).

16   Charles A. Briggs and Emilie G. Briggs, *A Critical and Exegetical Commentary on the Book of Psalms* (ICC; New York: Scribner's, 1906–7) I, 6, 9; Dahood, *Psalms I*, 3.

17   1QH 8.7, 10.

18   Philippe Reymond, *L'eau, sa vie, et sa signification dans l'Ancien Testament* (VTSup 6; Leiden: Brill, 1958) 70, 129–30.

Psalm 1 and perhaps with 11:19 see Preliminary Observations.)

The חֹם is the heat of summer (compare Gen 8:22; Job 24:19); it is parallel to "year of drought" below. For עָלֶה "leaves" see 8:13; the word here reflects its use in Ps 1:3. For רַעֲנָן "green" see 2:20. For בַּצֹּרֶת "drought" see 14:1; "in a year of drought" here subtly reflects בְּעִתּוֹ "in its season" in Ps 1:3. "Fruit" likewise occurs in Ps 1:3 as well. The difference between v 8 here and Ps 1:3 is that the psalm verse describes a tree that is watered, but Jrm is describing a tree that expects water, does not get it, yet because of deep rootage manages some leaves and fruit even when water is lacking (see Preliminary Observations).

Aim

Jrm had accused Yahweh of being something other than the spring of running water (2:13), that he was, in fact, untrustworthy waters (15:18). Now, sobered by Yahweh's instruction to repent, he offers his own version of Psalm 1: those who depend on human resources become as dried up as a desert shrub which produces no fruit whatever, but those who continue to depend on Yahweh can expect to stand firm and produce fruit even in a dry year. It is a moving testament to faith when all the props of faith seem to have gone. It is not a fair world: the signs and rewards of faith are motives for our gratitude when they are present, but we cannot always count on them. It still makes a difference, Jrm says, whether one has a trust in Yahweh or not, even though those who trust and those who do not trust may both lack water. This paradox will be Job's struggle ("he destroys both the blameless and the wicked," Job 9:22), and Jesus will give it a positive turn ("he makes his sun rise on the evil and on the good, and sends rain on the just and on the unjust," Matt 5:45). Jrm makes his affirmation of faith, but there is no recorded response from Yahweh, and that silence dramatizes Jrm's sense that he is alone.

17 The Heart Is Devious

9 Jeremiah: **The mind is devious above all else,**
 perverse it is:
 who can understand it?

10 Yahweh: **I am Yahweh who search the mind**
 and[a] **test the heart,**
 [b] **and so give**[b] **to everyone according to his**
 way,[c]
 and[d] **according to the fruit of his deeds.**

Text

10a Reading "and" with many MSS. and *G*, *V*, and *S*; *M* lacks "and."

b—b *M* וְלָתֵת is literally "and to give." Many MSS. and *G* lack "and." But the sequence may idiomatically be translated as given here (Joüon, *Gramm.*, sec. 124p), and the omission is unnecessary. Note that *V* translates *qui do*, "(I) who give."

c Read with the ketib, 4QJer[a] (Janzen, p. 178) and *V* "way" (singular). The qere', many MSS., *G*, *S*, and *T* read "ways." Compare the Text note on 4:18.

d Read with many MSS., *G*, *V*, and *S* "and"; *M* and 4QJer[a] (Janzen, p. 178) lack "and."

Structure

This little exchange between Jrm and Yahweh was not part of vv 5–8, which have their own structure (see there). The verse about the partridge (v 11) is also separate. Verses 9–10 thus make up a unit of their own.

If the passage is considered analogous to the confessions, and if the passage is next after vv 5–8 to take shape in Jrm's mind, then no further justification for its position here is necessary. But in addition there may be structural links with the confessional material before and after. Thus there may be a link between "fruit" here in v 10 and the same word in v 8. More substantially, one may note in v 10 the combination of לֵב (literally "heart," here translated "mind"), כְּלָיוֹת (literally "kidneys," here translated "heart") and בחן "test": the same combination is found in 11:20. And אָנֻשׁ "perverse, incurable" (v 9) is also found in 15:18 and 17:16.

Jrm's word (v 9) is so slight it is hard to know its structure. Is it prose? If it is poetry, is it a tricolon? Yahweh's answer (v 10) is a simple pair of bicola.

Form

Verse 9 is an expression spoken by Jrm, and v 10 is a response from Yahweh; though they match in word—both are concerned about the לֵב ("mind," literally "heart")—they hardly match in mood (see Interpretation). Jrm's observation is couched in wisdom style (for "who knows/understands" compare Prov 24:22; for generalizations about the "heart" compare Prov 14:10), though his conclusions stem directly from his own experience. Verse 10 is a self-asseveration (self-designation) of Yahweh, again with wisdom orientation: compare the self-designation in 9:23, which again uses wisdom diction. Here Yahweh describes himself by a formula used by Israel in hymnic affirmation of Yahweh (Pss 7:10; 17:3)—"who try the mind and test the heart," and similar phraseology is used by Yahweh in an announcement of judgment in 9:6. The phrases of v 10b seem to be original in Jrm's diction.

Setting

Though Volz, assuming the passage to be a wisdom saying, doubted its authenticity to Jrm, recent scholarship has not questioned it (so Rudolph, Bright). Verse 10a is in keeping with Jrm's vocabulary (11:20), and once the sequence is seen to be part of the dialogue between Jrm and Yahweh, its genuineness is assured.

There are no clues by which to date it, however, except to assume that it took shape sometime after vv 5–8, for which the present study proposes a date of 600 or soon thereafter (see Setting there). This date is reinforced slightly if the resemblances of phraseology between this passage and 9:3 and 6 suggest some contemporaneity; the dating for 9:1–8 suggested here is in the autumn of 601 or thereabouts.

Interpretation

■ **9** Though the general semantic range of all the words in this musing of Jrm's is clear, it is far from easy to translate the verse. The לֵב is the "heart," the "mind," the "will," that central faculty within the person (v 5) and the community (v 1) which makes decisions: for a discussion of the word, with bibliography, see 4:4. This is the only instance in the OT in which the word appears with the definite article: that article signals Jrm's leap of generalization. In Proverbs it is usually a particular לֵב that is characterized—the לֵב of a wise man (Prov 16:23) or of kings (Prov 25:3), but occasionally there it is anyone's

לֵב—in Prov 16:9 it is the לֵב of a human being in contrast to God, and in Prov 14:10 it is simply לֵב (without the article) in an expression of the isolation of someone's לֵב. But here it is הַלֵּב "the heart," the summation of the character of any heart, which is the topic.

And that לֵב is עָקֹב. This adjective is found in M of Hos 6:8, but that text must be emended (see the commentaries); it appears only otherwise in Isa 40:4, where it describes the opposite of מִישׁוֹר "level ground." It is thus uneven, bumpy ground (Zorell; HALAT), or steep, hilly ground (BDB). The word also appears in Sir 6:20,[1] but the context does not help. G seems to have read עָמֹק "deep," which is a plausible reading: this is the description of the לֵב in Ps 64:7, and some scholars have accepted that reading here (Duhm, with hesitation; Condamin). On the other hand one can argue that Jrm was playing with the diction of Ps 64:7 and substituting a word reminiscent of יַעֲקֹב "Jacob"; compare the pun in 9:3. V uses pravum, "crooked, deformed"; Jerome cites at this point in his commentary[2] Gen 6:5, "Yahweh saw that the wickedness of man was great in the earth, and that every imagination of the thoughts of his heart was only evil continually." It is not impossible that Jrm had this passage in mind himself. T uses "crafty" here. If מִישׁוֹר is the opposite of the adjective in question in Isa 40:4, then its cognate יָשָׁר is used in the context of the לֵב (or the synonymous לֵבָב) in Deut 9:5; 1 Kgs 9:4; Ps 119:7; and Job 33:3; the word suggests "uprightness, steadiness, dependability." The adjective in question, then, suggests by contrast "devious, difficult." NAB uses "tortuous": this is excellent, considering Isa 40:4. JB and NJV use "deceitful," which is probably as close as one can get.

The second adjective is אָנֻשׁ. This word appears in seven other passages in the OT: 15:18; 17:16; 30:12, 15; Isa 17:11; Mic 1:9; and Job 34:6. In six passages the context is medical, and the adjective modifies words for "pain," "fracture," "wound." In Jer 17:16 it modifies "day," and here לֵב. The meaning "incurable" seems well established for the medical contexts (see on 15:18). Is one to assume that Jrm considers the לֵב a medical problem?—NAB here renders "beyond remedy." V, taking a clue from "who can understand it?" gives here a general rendering inscrutabile "inscrutable." One is a bit

nervous about using "incurable," with its suggestion of original sin, so that "perverse" is perhaps best (compare Aim).

The expression מִכֹּל in a comparison is rare: Dan 11:2 has גָּדוֹל מִכֹּל "greater than all (the others)"; but the expression here, general in the extreme, is striking.

The question מִי יֵדָעֶנּוּ "who can understand it?" is hardly a request for information: it is much more a rhetorical question. The לֵב is beyond understanding. Though Jrm is voicing an observation of extreme generality, his experience with the לֵב of his people is what has driven him to his despairing conclusion: it is a לֵב which needs washing (4:14), which is stubborn and rebellious (5:23), a לֵב on whose tablet the sin of Judah is deeply incised (17:1). Who could grasp such a situation?

Yet it may be that Jrm has his own לֵב in mind as much as he does that of his people. Yahweh's answer it that he, Yahweh, searches the לֵב (v 10); the other occasions in which that phraseology is used (11:20; 12:3) are occasions in which Jrm's לֵב is under scrutiny (especially 12:3). Again the confessional section following in this chapter (vv 14–18) begins with "Heal me, Yahweh, and I shall be healed"—this thought may well be linked to the "incurable" לֵב in this verse. Thus Jrm is struggling to understand his own reactions as much as he is those of his fellows.

■ 10 There is an answer from Yahweh, but it is an answer whose assurance comes from the standard assumptions of Israel. Yahweh is the tester of the "mind" and the "heart": one hears this in the Psalms (Pss 7:10; 17:3). He will give everyone his due (Isa 3:10–11). There is no way to measure the reaction that Jrm would have after hearing this response from Yahweh: it might reassure him, or it might not. But one cannot avoid the impression that Jrm and Yahweh are in a dialogue of the deaf: here, in a nutshell, is the disjunction between Job and his friends.

For the pairing of לֵב and כְּלָיוֹת (here "mind" and "heart") see 11:20. This is the only occurrence in Jer of חקר "search": it is used in a very similar context in Ps 139:1, 23, parallel to ידע "know, understand," and (in v 23 there) to בחן "test," as here. For the pairing of "way"

---

1   In the edition of Lévi it is 6:19.
2   (S.) Hieronymi Presbyteri in Hieremiam Prophetam, Libri

Sex (ed. Siegfried Reiter; CChr, Series Latina 74; Turnhout: Brepols, 1960).

and "deeds" see 4:18. The expression "fruit of one's deeds" seems to be dependent on Isa 3:10.[3]

Aim

Jrm was driven by his own experience to a desperate conclusion: the human heart is devious past all accounting. It is a conclusion he expressed elsewhere in other ways ("Can the Ethiopian change his skin or the leopard his spots?" 13:23), but the word here is stripped of all particularity: not the heart of Judah, not the heart today, but the heart, the mind, anywhere, any time: devious above all else, of any sort.

It is a conclusion that resonates profoundly with the experience of the Christian community. Only the rather different rendering of v 9 in *G* could have prevented its

use in the NT, for it reflects Paul's perceptions admirably (Rom 7:14–25). In this context Stanley Hopper quotes Blaise Pascal: "We are only falsehood, duplicity, contradiction; we both conceal and disguise ourselves from ourselves."[4]

Yahweh's answer, in v 10, is an attempt to match Jrm's conclusion, though whether in Jrm's context it did or not one cannot be sure (see Interpretation). But the assurance that God understands the heart created in the NT community a Greek coinage, $\kappa\alpha\rho\delta\iota\sigma\gamma\nu\dot{\omega}\sigma\tau\eta\varsigma$, "the One who knows the heart" (Acts 1:24; 15:8).

---

3   Compare Holladay, "Prototype," 355–56.
4   Stanley R. Hopper, "Exposition of Jeremiah," *IB*

5:952; the quotation is from Blaise Pascal, *Pensées*, no. 377.

The Partridge Cannot Protect Her Eggs

Bibliography
Sawyer, John F. A.
  "A Note on the Brooding Partridge in Jeremiah xvii 11," *VT* 28 (1978) 324–29.
Woods, Francis H.
  "Note on Jeremiah xvii. 11," *ExpTim* 20 (1908/09) 375–76.

17

11

(Like) the partridge (that) broods but does not hatch
(is) he (who) makes riches, but not with justice:
midway in his days[a] he will abandon them,
and at his end he will be a fool.

Text

11a   Reading יָמָיו with the qere' and *G, V, S*, and *T*; ketib ימו "his day."

Structure

The verse is a unit by itself, but its presence here is puzzling. Qimḥi (and Hyatt after him) assumed that the verse is an illustration of v 10a, but this connection is doubtless too general to be a satisfactory solution. Alonso Schökel proposes that all of vv 5–13 have a unity of theme, the contrast between false confidence (here, in riches; in vv 5–8, in human resources) and true confidence in Yahweh,[1] and this may be the answer. But the answer may lie in another direction. The only other occurrence in the OT of the verb "brood" (דגר) is Isa 34:15; there that verb follows the verb "split, hatch" (בקע). A striking word with the reverse order of consonants occurs here in v 9, "devious" (עָקֹב); it is conceivable that such an association brought the verse here (so the association between 18:13–17 and 18:1–12: see Structure on 18:13–17). But this is only a suggestion; the true explanation may be far more arbitrary.

The verse is a tetracolon with a complicated structure: the third and fourth cola are parallel, and the second shares with the third and fourth a reference to a man who is the object of the comparison, while the second colon is structurally parallel to the first (repetition of "but not," וְלֹא).

Form

This proverbial comparison is of the simplest sort: the identity of the partridge and the man who gains riches unjustly is expressed by the bare collocation of the two, without any grammatical tags for comparison (so Prov 25:11–12).[2] The comparison is intended as a taunt, like the saying in 13:23.[3]

Setting

Several commentators have suggested that the target of this saying was Jehoiakim (Rudolph, Weiser), and this is probable: the verse uses the phrase וְלֹא בְמִשְׁפָּט, and 22:13, part of an oracle against that king, offers בְּלֹא מִשְׁפָּט, both expressions indicating "unjustly," and the continuation of that oracle, 22:17, speaks of the king's hunger for dishonest gain. Jehoiakim reigned from 609 to 598. The phrases of the the third and fourth cola suggest a time early in his reign, if the oracle does refer to Jehoiakim; but no greater certainty is possible.

Interpretation

The identity of the bird קֹרֵא is hardly in doubt. The noun occurs once otherwise (1 Sam 26:20); in both passages *V* gives *perdix* ("partridge") and *S* ḥaglā' (again "partridge," cognate with the Arabic ḥijlā with the same meaning), and in the present passage *G* likewise gives πέρδιξ. (In 1 Sam 26:20 *G* has a different translation, naming a bird difficult to identify; and *T* in both passages gives a cognate of the Hebrew term.)

---

1   Alonso Schökel, "Esperanza," 98–99.
2   See the acute remarks on this form in von Rad, *Wisdom*, 119.
3   See on this R. B. Y. Scott, *Proverbs, Ecclesiastes* (AB 18; Garden City, NY: Doubleday, 1965) 6.

Commentators and translations have offered a variety of interpretation of the two verbs in the first colon, דגר and ילד: "the partridge gathers what it has not laid" (*G*, *T*; *RSV*, *NEB*), "the partridge hatches what it has not laid" (*V*; Duhm, Giesebrecht, Cornill, Condamin, Rudolph, Weiser, Bright; *JB*, *NAB*, *NJV*), or "the partridge broods but does not hatch" (Qimḥi, Volz, Luther; *KJV*). (A fourth interpretation, "the partridge calls those it has not laid," *S* and Rashi, is a midrashic interpretation of קֹרֵא "partridge" understood as "one calling" and can be laid aside.)

The question has been clarified by the study of John F. A. Sawyer,[4] though the matter is not so clear-cut as he maintains. The verb דגר appears once otherwise in the OT, in Isa 34:15. If the verb does mean "brood," as *HALAT* and Sawyer affirm, then it is unfortunate that the four verbs in Isa 34:15 seem to be out of order: "nest, lay, hatch, brood"; but perhaps the verb there implies keeping hatched chicks warm as well as keeping eggs warm. Both the Talmud (*b. Ḥul.* 140b) and Qimḥi agree on the meaning "brood": the Talmud uses the noun דְּגִירָה on both the Isaiah and Jeremiah passages with the meaning "brood," and Qimḥi defines the verb here as "sits on the eggs and keeps them warm." The meaning "gathers" for this verb, found in both *G* and *T* appears to derive from the meaning of the Aramaic דגר, which does mean "gather."

The verb ילד is of course well known in the meaning "give birth." One could imagine the verb here as meaning either "lay eggs" or "bring forth young." The difficulty with the former meaning is a simple grammatical one: one expects two verbs connected by ו to express consecutive events; if the line means "hatches what it has not laid," in which the second action is prior to the first, then one would surely expect אֲשֶׁר instead of ו. (I fail to find any example in the OT of the pattern "he reaps what he has not sown" or the like: I suspect the pattern is that simply found in Jesus' parable, Matt 25:24, 26 = Luke 19:21–22.) The OT expression is consecutive, so far as I can tell: in Isa 65:22 the Hebrew reads, "They shall not build and another inhabit," where today one is likely to say, "They shall not inhabit what they have not built."

The situation is complicated by the fact that both verbs are masculine. The verb ילד is rarely masculine in the qal stem (the exceptions: twenty-two times in the genealogies of J, for example Gen 4:18; in metaphorical contexts like Ps 2:7, of Yahweh's relation to the king). In the physiological meaning it is a contradiction in terms (30:6!). But it was noticed by Aristotle and Pliny that the female partridge may lay two broods of eggs, one of which is incubated by her, the other by the male.[5] If ילד here means "bring forth young," then the masculine is appropriate.

The situation is also complicated by the fact that commentators have repeated the statement that the partridge robs the nests of other birds for her eggs. But Jerome is wrong when he states that this habit is noted by the ancient natural historians; as Bochart already noted in 1663, that habit is referred to only in commentaries on the present verse and literature dependent on them.[6] This understanding of the verse is produced both by the tradition that דגר means "gather" and by the presence in the second colon of the phrase "but not with justice." If the rich man amasses his riches unjustly, then the partridge must have gathered what does not belong to it. But if the first colon is to be translated "The partridge broods but does not hatch," then the point of the passage is not so much that the rich man has gathered his riches unjustly, but rather that, having gathered his riches unjustly, the punishment will fit the crime, and he will lose what he has amassed, so that he should not count on holding on to what he has gained.

The point of the verse, by this analysis, is identical with the English proverb, "Don't count your chickens before they're hatched." The comparison focuses not so much on ill-gotten gains as on complacency. Jerome already cites the parable which Jesus told, perfectly parallel here, of the rich man to whom God said, "Fool! This night your soul is required of you, and the things you have prepared, whose will they be?" (Luke 12:20). Jesus may well have had the present verse in mind.

The partridge once more: it is well known that the bird lays her eggs in shallow nests, on exposed ground, and that the eggs are vulnerable, then, to being crushed, stolen, or eaten by predators; her only defense is the

---

4 Sawyer, "Partridge," 324–29.

5 Ibid., 326, and n. 6 to ancient and modern authorities.

6 Ibid., 327, and references.

great number of eggs she lays. The expression "cower like a partridge" occurs more than once in Greek poetry.[7] The partridge lays her eggs, she (and her mate) both brood upon them, but they cannot be sure of hatching all of them.[8]

So with the rich man. He makes riches, עֹשֶׂה עֹשֶׁר—it must have been a tongue twister in Hebrew—but "unjustly": the expression here is reminiscent of בְּלֹא מִשְׁפָּט "unjustly" in 22:13 (see Setting). The riches have been gotten in a way contrary to the way Yahweh expects of his people (compare בְּמִשְׁפָּט "with justice" in 4:2). Midway in his career the rich man and his riches will part ways. But will he abandon his riches, or will his riches abandon him? Grammatically it could be either, but the fact that "he" is the subject of the verb in the last colon suggests that it is he that abandons his riches; Jrm may have had in mind the fate of exile for the king. (So V, T, Condamin, JB, NEB, against G, Bright, RSV, NAB, NJV; S is ambiguous, and the German commentators leave their translations ambiguous.)

For אַחֲרִית "end" see 5:31. This is the only occurrence of נָבָל "fool" in Jer. In this context it reflects the nuance of "but not with justice." Isa 32:6 is a good commentary on this verse: "The fool speaks folly, and his mind plots iniquity . . . to leave the craving of the hungry unsatisfied, and to deprive the thirsty of drink." Pedersen comments, "The sinner is a *fool*, because he cannot devise plans which are worth anything. The fool belongs together with the perpetrator of violence . . . , with him whose soul lacks health. . . . His counsel lacks firmness and must collapse."[9]

Aim

It is humiliating to be compared to a poor bird that cannot protect her eggs: the more so if one happens to be king.

---

7   For example, Archilocus, 95.
8   Sawyer, "Partridge," 327.
9   Pedersen, I/II, 429.

Yahweh's Ways Are Higher than Their Ways

Bibliography

On 17:12-18:
Berridge
    pp. 137-51, 160.
Reventlow
    Liturgie, 229-40.

On 17:12-13:
Dahood
    "Jeremiah 17,13."
Schwartz, O.
    "Jer. 17,13 als möglicher alttestamentlicher
    Hintergrund zu Jo. 8,6. 8," *Von Kanaan bis Kerala,
    Festschrift für Prof. Mag. Dr. Dr. J. P. M. van der
    Ploeg, O.P.* (ed. W. C. Delsman et al.; AOAT 211;
    Neukirchen: Neukirchener, 1982) 239-56.

17

12   The throne of glory is on high,
          from the beginning is the place of our
              sanctuary;
13   O pool of Israel, O Yahweh,
          may all who abandon you ⟨wither,⟩[a]
          《 and may those who turn from you 》[b] be
              enrolled in the Land,[b]
          for they have abandoned the spring of
              running water,
          [Yahweh.][c]

Text

13a   Reading יָבֹשׁוּ (יבשׁ qal) with Dahood for *M* יֵבֹשׁוּ
       "be ashamed." The vocabulary of water demands it,
       though Jrm's hearers may have expected "be
       ashamed." See Interpretation.
b—b   The qere' and many MSS. read וְסוּרַי "and those
       who turn from me"; the ketib יְסוּרַי is presumably to
       be understood as "those chastised by me" (יסר
       passive participle). Read וְסוּרֶיךָ אֶרֶץ, substituting kap
       for bet (Rudolph).
c   The expression is a gloss, not part of the poetic
       sequence (Rudolph, Bright).

Preliminary Observations

Verses 12-13 form a separate unit; evidence is given
both below and in Structure.

These two verses offer difficulty in interpretation, in
part because the passage is so short. The conventional
interpretation, based on the Masoretic punctuation and
the Versions, is to view v 12 as a separate rhetorical unit,
grouping the first four words (v 12a) together, and the
last two (v 12b) together, making of it a nominal sentence: "A glorious throne set on high from the beginning
is the place of our sanctuary" (*RSV*). The difficulty with
this is that it is so trite. This is diction referring to the
temple, one assumes, and the people are speaking. But
why does such diction figure in an oracle of Jrm's? The
second colon of v 13 reads "all who abandon you shall be
ashamed" (or, as revocalized here, "shall wither": see
below). Such a colon is appropriate to Jrm's diction. So
what is the purpose of the words of v 12: is he quoting
the temple liturgy ironically? Where is the prophetic
cutting edge?

Uneasy with this solution, several commentators and
translations have proposed that v 12 is a series of vocatives[1] (Condamin, Weiser; *NEB, NJV*). It is clear that the
first colon in v 13 is vocative (so the same sequence in
14:8); and communal laments may offer such a series of
vocatives (Ps 80:2; Jer 14:8). Thus *NJV* translates, "O
Throne of Glory exalted from of old, Our Sacred Shrine!
O hope of Israel! O Lord!" But how is one to understand
"throne" (כִּסֵּא) and "place of" (מְקוֹם) in v 12? Does one
have some vocatives addressing the temple, and then a

---

1   First Karl H. Graf, *Der Prophet Jeremia erklärt* (Leip-
     zig: Weigel, 1862) 246; so also Baumgartner,
     Klagegedichte, 41-42, and Berridge, pp. 149-50.

vocative to Yahweh? Or is one to understand "throne" and "place of" as metonymy for God himself? There are no parallels for this; "glory," yes (2:11); "sanctuary," yes (Ezek 11:16), but not "throne" or "place."

But more basic than syntax is the problem of locating the unity of the discourse, seeing the train of thought that binds the passage together. The key is the phrase that has given much difficulty, בְּאֶרֶץ יִכָּתֵבוּ (or, as proposed here, אֶרֶץ יִכָּתֵבוּ). Given the likeness of diction between the present passage and that of 14:8, 21–22, part of a long sequence in which references to Sheol play a prominent part (see 14:1—15:9, Preliminary Observations), the suggestion of Baumgartner,[2] adopted by Dahood and considered by others,[3] must be correct, to see in אֶרֶץ here a reference to Sheol; the phrase then means "shall be enrolled in Sheol," that is, be destined for death.

If אֶרֶץ means "Sheol," then the way is open to see מָרוֹם "height" as a balancing contrast: מָרוֹם is in opposition to אֶרֶץ in Isa 24:18 and 21, and probably in v 4 there as well (see commentators on that passage). If the predicate of the difficult phrase in v 13 means "shall be enrolled in Sheol," then one expects a predicate in v 12 to balance it: "The throne of glory is in the height." That is to say, vocatives are ruled out in v 12 (though Jrm may have intended a nominal clause by mimicking vocatives: see Form and Interpretation).

Now how shall the words be grouped? One can group the six words in v 12 in three pairs: "The throne of glory is (in) the height from the beginning, the place of our sanctuary"; in this case the last pair echoes the subject of the nominal clause. But one can also take two groups of three words (so Condamin, though he understands vocatives): "The throne of glory is (in) the height, from the beginning is the place of our sanctuary." This is undoubtedly correct: one has a chiasmus of adverbial predicates in the central two words surrounded by nominal clause subjects. Now, too, one has a double-duty preposition in מֵראשׁוֹן "from the beginning": מִמָּרוֹם means

"on high" (Isa 24:18).[4]

The purpose of these affirmations is now clear: the true throne of Yahweh, the true place of his sanctuary, is heaven, not the temple. This affirmation is consistent with 23:23–24 (as well as other prophetic statements like Isa 66:1). If the setting in these verses is comparable to that of 14:1—15:9 (see Setting below), then Jrm is casting doubt that those who center their attention on the temple are sufficiently loyal to Yahweh.

If the preceding analysis is correct, the syntactical structure is clear: v 12 is a bicolon; the first colon of v 13 is a vocative; this is followed by a bicolon with verbal clauses and is closed by a line introduced by כִּי which stands by itself and thus answers to the first colon of the verse: both carry water imagery.

Structure

There has been a recent opinion that vv 12–18 form a unit.[5] But the shift from first-person plural ("our sanctuary," v 12) to singular ("heal me," v 14) should bring caution. One must assume that the architecture of the chapters immediately before and after the present passage is built around the confessions, of which at least vv 14–18 form one. If vv 5–8 (plus perhaps vv 9–10) are part of the original sequence associated with the confessions, and if vv 14–18 form another unit of the confessions, then one is moved to see both v 11 and vv 12–13 as later additions to that sequence. This is the assumption of the present study for v 11 (see Structure there), and I propose that vv 12–13 are to be treated in the same fashion. Alonso Schökel sees vv 12–13 as another illustration of false confidence (in the temple, in the present instance) in contrast to true confidence in Yahweh.[6] But if one concludes that the present passage was inserted here secondarily, one is then faced by the question why it was placed here. One possibility is that it is based on the sequence in 14:21, where "disdain" (נבל pi'el) is followed immediately by "your glorious throne" (כִּסֵּא כְבוֹדֶךָ): v 11 here has "fool" (נָבָל), and v 12 here has "throne of glory"

2   Baumgartner, *Klagegedichte*, 40.
3   Mitchell Dahood, "The Value of Ugaritic for Textual Criticism," *Bib* 40 (1959) 164–66, "Jeremiah 17,13," and *Psalms I*, 106. The suggestion is cited as a possibility by Bright and is approved by Berridge, pp. 149–50.
4   See conveniently Dahood, *Psalms III*, 435–37.
5   Baumgartner, *Klagegedichte*, 40–42; Reventlow,

6   *Liturgie*, 229–40; Berridge, pp. 137–51, 160.
    Alonso Schökel, "Esperanza," 99–100.

(כִּסֵּא כָבוֹד).

For the internal structure of the passage see Preliminary Observations.

Form

The noun phrases of v 12 ("throne of glory," "place of our sanctuary") are reminiscent of hymnic affirmations in the Psalms (Pss 24:3; 26:8; 78:69; 89:15) regarding the temple, but Jrm is using them to affirm that Yahweh's true habitation is far higher and older than the temple (see Preliminary Observations, Interpretation). The vocative in v 13 is likewise appropriate to a lament (so in 14:8). The third-person verbs in v 13 may be understood either as jussives or indicatives (see Interpretation); given the implications of the genre, it is better to take them as jussives, a prayer that Yahweh see to the demise of those unfaithful to him. The first-person plural in v 12 is then not so much Jrm's expression of solidarity with the people as it is his use of corporate liturgical expressions to suggest that the common liturgical forms mislead.

Setting

There is a close connection between this passage and 14:1—15:9: the phrase "throne of glory" is close to that found in 14:21, and the Hebrew of "O pool of Israel, O Yahweh" is identical with that found in 14:8; further, the reference to Sheol in v 13 is characteristic of that longer passage. The setting for that passage in the present study is the period of the fast declared by Jehoiakim in November/December 601 because of the great drought (see Setting there). The water imagery of the present passage suggests that this passage, too, reflects the experience of drought. But in 14:1—15:9 the nation has already been committed to Sheol (14:2, 18; 15:5–9); here, by contrast, Jrm either makes a general statement that this is what happens to people who abandon Yahweh, or, more likely, is voicing a wish that the nation be committed to Sheol (see Interpretation). The present passage implies that attention to the temple liturgy is not sufficient. All this makes the passage appropriate to a time just before that of 14:1—15:9, perhaps an anticipation of that liturgical sequence. For Jrm the fast declared by the king is not enough. Soon, when the king burns the scroll, Jrm

will become convinced that the fate of the nation is sealed.

Interpretation

■ 12 For a discussion of "throne of glory," both in the context of the temple cult and of Yahweh's throne, see 14:21. The word מָרוֹם means "height"; it is often a synonym for "heaven," or a term descriptive of heaven, particularly in the Psalms (see Ps 102:20). Here מִמָּרוֹם "on high" is implied (see Preliminary Observations).

The expression מֵרֹאשׁוֹן "from the beginning" is a striking parallel to מָרוֹם "(on) high"—there is no other instance of this parallelism in the OT. Yahweh's habitation extends through time and space: it is not historically contingent. For the nuance of מָקוֹם, a holy place, see 7:3. The noun מִקְדָּשׁ "sanctuary" appears in Jer only otherwise in 51:51; it refers to pagan sanctuaries, to old Israelite sanctuaries, and especially to the Jerusalem temple and its precincts (often in Ezekiel and P). There are one or two passages in the Psalms, however, where the noun may refer to the heavenly sanctuary: Ps 68:36 would be one instance (compare שְׁחָקִים "clouds" in v 35 there), and Ps 73:17 may be another.[7]

The diction which others may use for the temple precincts Jrm declares is appropriate only for Yahweh's heavenly sanctuary.

■ 13 The expression מִקְוֵה יִשְׂרָאֵל means both "hope of Israel" and "pool of Israel" (see the discussion on 14:8). Here the translation must lay emphasis on the imagery of water, hence "pool." The parallelism of מִקְוֵה "pool" and מָקוֹר "spring" is also found in Sir 10:13 (see NAB).

A major question is whether the main verbs in the second and third cola are to be translated as jussives, "may they . . . ," or as indicatives, "they shall . . ." (see Form). G takes the first option, and V the second. Given the genre of lament in which the first colon here functions where it appears in 14:8, and given the general impression of liturgical language in the passage, the jussive option is preferable.

For "abandon [עזב] Yahweh" see 1:16. The phrasing here is reminiscent of "they have abandoned me, the spring of running water" in 2:13. The main verb in this colon in M is יֵבֹשׁוּ "shall be ashamed," and that verb is

---

7   See Dahood, *Psalms II*, 192.

appropriate both to the diction of chapter 2 (see 2:36) and to that of 14:1—15:9 (see 14:3, 4; 15:9). But Dahood has suggested the revocalization here to יָבֵשׁוּ "shall wither," a verb appropriate to the context of water and drought. Jrm's hearers doubtless expected to hear "shall be ashamed," so that if the suggestion is correct, the shift would have created a striking effect. If it is correct, it is the only instance in the OT of this verb with a personal subject—though it is found elsewhere with subjects which are parts of the body denoting psychological entities ("my heart," Ps 102:5). Jrm has used the verb (with "grass" as subject) in an utterance from the drought setting (12:4). But most significantly the verb is used in the context of reference to Sheol ("my strength is dried up [יבש] like a potsherd, and my tongue cleaves to my jaws; thou dost lay me in the dust of death," Ps 22:16). Belief was widespread in the ancient Near East that the abode of the dead is a place of thirst;[8] Dahood gives several OT references to the theme,[9] and although not all are equally convincing, Ps 143:6 is a good candidate.[10]

The text reconstructed as וְסוּרֶיךָ "and those who turn from you" is difficult, but the general meaning is not in doubt; compare 6:28. For an initial discussion of יִכָּתֵבוּ אֶרֶץ "be enrolled in Sheol" see Preliminary Observations; the theme is exactly comparable to נֶחְשַׁבְתִּי עִם־יוֹרְדֵי בוֹר "I am reckoned among those going down to the Pit" in Ps

88:5, and to the Ugaritic "be counted with them that go down into the 'earth'."[11] It is to be noted further that the verb כתב carries the meaning "enrolled" in a similar context in Ps 69:29, "Let them be blotted out of the book of the living; let them not be enrolled among the righteous." For a discussion of אֶרֶץ "land" = Sheol see 10:12 and 14:2.

For the phraseology in the last colon see 2:13. The contrast between the realm of the dead and the word חַיִּים "living" = "running (water)" is nice.

Aim

In a time of drought Jrm knew that the only hope was to adhere to Yahweh, the spring of running water, but there were those whose loyalty to Yahweh was expressed in the specificities of the temple cult. To these folk Jrm insisted that "your God is too small"[12]—as he reported Yahweh saying on another occasion, "Am I a God at hand and not a God afar off? . . . Do I not fill heaven and earth?" (23:23–24). Deutero-Isaiah would proclaim the same in a time pregnant with new beginnings: "For as the heavens are higher than the earth, so are my ways higher than your ways" (Isa 55:9).

---

8   See Theodor H. Gaster, *Thespis* (Garden City, NY: Doubleday, 1961) 204–5.

9   Dahood, "Jeremiah 17,13," 110 n. 5.

10   Dahood, *Psalms III*, 324.

11   Ug. 4.8.9.

12   John Bertram Phillips, *Your God Is Too Small* (New York: Macmillan, 1954).

**Jeremiah Prays for Help
from Yahweh**

Bibliography

Althann, Robert
  "Consonantal *ym*: Ending or Noun in Isa 3,13; Jer
  17,16; 1 Sam 6,19," *Bib* 63 (1982) 560–65.
Hauret, Charles
  "Note d'exégèse: Jérémie xvii, 14: Sana me,
  Domine, et sanabor," *RevScRel* 36 (1962) 174–84.

17

14 Heal me, Yahweh, so that I may be
  healed,
  save me, so that I may be saved,
   for you are my (only) 《hope. 》ᵃ

15 Look, they keep saying to me,
  "Where is the word of Yahweh?—let it
   come!"

16 But I have not been eager ⟨to be "best
  man"⟩ᵃ behind you,
  nor have I longed for the day of collapse:
  it is you who know the utterance of my
   lips,
  it has been right in front of you.

17 Do not become a terror to me,
  you are my refuge in the day of
   distress.ᵃ

18 Let my persecutors be ashamed, not I,
  let them be panicked, not I:
  bring on them the day of disaster,
  and shatter them with double
   shattering!

Text

14a Emending *M* תְּהִלָּתִי "my praise" to תׄחַלְתִּי with
Duhm, Giesebrecht, Volz, Rudolph. The reading of
M is normal diction (Ps 71:6), but then so is the
emendation (Ps 39:8), and the latter is more
appropriate to the context.

16a Vocalizing מֵרֹעֶה, pi'el participle of the denominative verb רעה II "serve as 'best man'" (Judg
14:20): this is the suggestion of Hubmann, by
personal communication. This rendering is the
implication of *G*; see further Interpretation.

17a Reading with four MSS. and *T* צָרָה for *M* רָעָה.
The expression יוֹם רָעָה appears in v 18; one expects
parallelism rather than repetition between the two
expressions, and in 15:11 one finds בְּעֵת־רָעָה וּבְעֵת
צָרָה.

Structure

Verses 14–18 form a unit distinct from vv 12–13 (see
Structure there). The passage is one of the confessions
and as such forms part of the original deposit of material
in this section of Jer, having been added to vv 5–8 (and
perhaps 9–10): one notes the collocation of אָנוּשׁ in both
v 9 (there translated "perverse") and v 16 (here translated "of collapse").

 There is an A—B—A' form to the passage, vv 15–16
being the central section. That central section is held
together by the subject pronouns "they" (הֵמָּה) in v 15
and "I" (אֲנִי) and "you" (אַתָּה) in v 16 in clauses offering a
description with the participle (v 15) and declarations
with perfect verbs (v 16). The outer sections (v 14 and vv
17–18) balance in offering imperatives (vv 14a, 18b), a
prohibition (v 17a) and jussives (v 18a), and in offering
double expressions from the same verb root (vv 14a,
18aα and β). The two identities ("you are my hope," v

14b, and "you are my refuge," v 17b) likewise balance.
The six cola of the final section (vv 17–18) are united by
the parallelism "day of distress" and "day of disaster" in
the second and fifth cola; the central two cola are the
strong climax (verb contrasts implying "they, not I"), and
that climax at the same time picks up the pronouns
"they" and "I" from vv 15 and 16a.

Form

This confession, like the others, offers phrasing characteristic of personal laments. Verse 14a is a plea for help.
For "heal me, Yahweh," see Ps 6:3, and for "save me" see
Ps 6:5; the latter imperative occurs in ten other passages
in the Psalms. The linking of two stems of a verb (here
active and passive) is likewise found in the Psalms: Ps
69:15 is a good example in a lament.[1] For "you are my
hope," v 14b, compare Ps 39:8; for the *M* reading "you
are my praise" compare Ps 71:6. In either case the phrase

is an affirmation of confidence.

Verse 15 is a description of suffering: for הֵמָּה אֹמְרִים "they keep saying" compare רַבִּים אֹמְרִים "many are saying" in Pss 3:3 and 4:7, but even closer is the phrase with an infinitive, "while they say to me, 'Where is your God?'" in Ps 42:4, 11.

Verse 16a is a declaration of innocence like 15:17; v 16b is an affirmation of confidence (compare Ps 40:10).

Verse 17a is a plea once more, and v 17b an affirmation of confidence (for the latter compare Ps 71:7). Verse 18 embodies wishes against the enemies of the prophet: Ps 31:18 is very close to v 18a here.

Setting

This passage may be dated by reference to parallel vocabulary in other passages. Thus the double use of חתת "be panicked" in v 18 is reminiscent of a similar double use of that verb by the prophet in reference to himself in 1:17, and data there suggest a setting in the crisis in Jrm's life in the summer of 594. The doublet of 1:17–19, namely 15:20–21, evidently has the same setting, and one notes the parallel between Jrm's plea "save me" in the present passage, v 14, and Yahweh's word to Jrm "to save you" in 15:20. Similarly the parallelism of יוֹם צָרָה "day of distress" (v 17, if that is the correct reading) and יוֹם רָעָה "day of disaster" (v 18) is comparable to בְּעֵת־רָעָה וּבְעֵת צָרָה in 15:11, part of confessional material dated to 594. Finally הֵמָּה אֹמְרִים "they keep saying" (v 15) is found in a similar context in 2:27, and the present study proposes that 2:26–28 was added to chapter 2 in 594. The evidence thus suggests that date for this passage as well.

Interpretation

■ **14** For the double expression of two stems of a verb root see in the confessions 11:18. It is curious that the fourth verb in the verse, וְאִוָּשֵׁעָה ("so that I may be saved") is cohortative, but the corresponding second verb וְאֵרָפֵא ("so that I may be healed") is not; conceivably a he has dropped out by haplography, but in any event the verbs are parallel and must be understood as expressing purpose (GKC, sec. 108d).

"Heal me, so that I may be healed" must be understood in the context of "Why has my pain become endless, my wound incurable, refusing to be healed?" (15:18). That question in chapter 15 is followed immediately by Jrm's accusation to Yahweh that he has become like water that fails. Yahweh thereupon tells him to repent (15:19), and according to the present study Jrm makes an affirmation of repentance (17:5–8). Given that affirmation, Jrm prays that Yahweh bring him healing. For Jrm's word "save me" compare Yahweh's word "to save you" in 15:20.

Jrm is desperate: his prayer to Yahweh here takes the form of phrases long familiar in the laments of the Psalms (see Form), that he find healing and rescue from his bleak situation. The last colon of the verse is again psalm-terminology (whichever reading one accepts); see again Form. Yahweh is Jrm's only hope.[2]

■ **15** The participial clause הֵמָּה אֹמְרִים is best rendered by the frequentative "they keep saying" (for the same phrase see 2:27; compare 7:8). Jrm's scoffers doubt his descriptions of the doom to come (compare 5:12), and he cites their words in phrasing very similar to that of Isa 5:19—complacency is not something that began with Jrm's generation. "Word of Yahweh" of course implies "action of Yahweh" as well (see 1:1).

■ **16** The meaning of the first colon has never been certain; the crucial word (מרעה) has been given a variety of vowels and a variety of interpretations. The text of M (מֵרֹעֶה) would seem to mean literally, "But I did not hurry from a shepherd after you." There have been recent efforts to find an acceptable understanding from this vocalization. Thus Wernberg-Møller has suggested that some participles (of which "shepherd" is one) may signify abstract actions as well, action for which one would expect an infinitive; he suggests the colon means, "I have not hurried from shepherding after you."[3] But Rudolph calls the suggestion very improbable. But it should be pointed out that "from" (מִן) may mean "from being a": thus 48:2, מִגּוֹי "from being a nation"; 48:42, מֵעָם "from

---

1   See Held, "Action-Result," and Dahood, *Psalms III*, 414.

2   For a brief discussion of תֹּחֶלֶת "hope," and the related verb יחל, see Zimmerli, *Hope*, 6–9.

3   Preben Wernberg-Møller, "Observations on the Hebrew Participle," *ZAW* 71 (1959) 64.

being a people";[4] this is Weiser's understanding of the colon. Berridge presses the point that Jrm could have designated himself a "shepherd."[5] But all in all, the expression so understood is awkward at best, and a solution may better be found elsewhere.

The Versions scatter. *G* reads "I was not weary following [κατακολουθῶν] after you," a rendering which will become the basis for the reading proposed here. *V* seems to offer a periphrasis combining both the *M* and *G* traditions ("I am not troubled following you [as my] shepherd"). Both *a'* and *s'* read מֵרָעָה "from evil," and *S* reads בְּרָעָה "in evil." Most commentators have read "evil" with one preposition or another. Thus Michaelis favored either (1) מֵרָעָה (thus "I have not shrunk by fear of evil from following you") or (2) בְּרָעָה ("I have not shrunk in adversity from you"); Duhm and Giesebrecht favor (1), Volz favors (2) or possibly (3) לְרָעָה, and Rudolph (3), this last implying "I have not pressed you to send evil" or the like.

Given the tradition of *M*, followed also by *a'* and *s'*, by which the mem is interpreted as מִן "from," it is remarkable that *G* does not use "from" here but understands the word in question as a participle, and therefore as the pi'el or hip'il of whatever verb is involved. There is only one candidate among verbs cited in the OT, the pi'el of רעה II "be 'best man' (at a wedding)" (Judg 14:20), a verb which is apparently a denominative from רֵעַ "friend, neighbor."[6] Though the precise wedding imagery (about which see below) was evidently not in the mind of the *G* translator, the translation (implying "be a follower") points in the direction of the proposal here.

The verb אוץ does not mean "be weary," as *G* has it, but "be in a hurry" (Josh 10:13; Prov 28:20). The clause then evidently means, "I was in no hurry to be your 'best man'." This diction ties the passage into the implied imagery of marriage in 15:16 and into Jrm's hesitation in remaining a prophet implied in Yahweh's response in 15:19. On the other hand, one may be pressing the idiom too far by proposing a wedding context: the expression may simply mean "be a ceremonial supporter," a meaning appropriate to the second colon, which seems to imply "the day of Yahweh's judgment." (The Greek παράνυμφος means "best man," but as that

word was borrowed into English [*paranymph*], it was used in the seventeenth century for "spokesman, supporter," and the same meaning applies in Dutch [*paranimf*] for the ceremonial supporter for a doctoral candidate at the public examination.)

In the second colon Jrm is mimicking Amos 5:18, "Woe to those who long for the day of Yahweh: why would you have the day of Yahweh?" Amos insisted that day would be darkness, not light. So here the יוֹם אָנוּשׁ is the "incurable day," the "day from which there shall be no recovery."[7] The day is incurable for a people whose "heart" or "mind" is incurable (v 9). Jrm suggests here that it was not his idea to proclaim that day, it was Yahweh's command; so again Jrm did not rush into the task of being a prophet. The words he spoke were Yahweh's words: Yahweh has known them (the third colon) and therefore owns them. The "utterance of my lips" (מוֹצָא שְׂפָתַי) is closely related to "if you utter what is precious . . . my mouth you shall be" in 15:19; indeed "it has been right in front of you" (נֹכַח פָּנֶיךָ הָיָה) may suggest the parallel in 15:19, "in my presence you shall stand" (לְפָנַי תַּעֲמֹד).

If Yahweh got Jrm into his present predicament, he should rescue him from it.

■ 17 The verb in the first colon is a unique form, אַל־תִּהְיֵה, where one would expect אַל־תְּהִי (see GKC, sec. 75hh). The noun "terror" (מְחִתָּה) is related to the verb חתת "be panicked" in the second colon of v 18; the verb is discussed in 1:17, and the noun of course implies "source of terror." The contrast, "refuge" (מַחְסֶה), is used eleven times in the Psalms to refer to Yahweh (notably in Ps 46:2). The "day of distress" (or "disaster") is Jrm's personal experience of desolation, not the doom of the nation (the implication of "day of collapse" in v 16); compare 15:11.

■ 18 The participle רֹדְפִים "persecutors" has already appeared in 15:15. For בוש "be ashamed" see 2:26; for חתת "be panicked" see 1:17. The opposition between "they" (הֵמָּה) and "I" (אֲנִי) is analogous to the contrast between 12:3 and 11:19 (the thought is expressed in the English idiom "turnabout is fair play").

The imperative form הָבִיא is irregular; one expects הָבֵא (see GKC, secs. 53m, 72y). The "day of disaster"

---

4 See BDB, 583, 7.b (b).
5 Berridge, p. 140.
6 See George F. Moore, *A Critical and Exegetical*

Commentary on Judges (ICC; Edinburgh: Clark, 1895) 339–40.
7 Berridge, p. 141.

must be understood not as the doom of the nation but as the time of discomfiture of Jrm's persecutors, who are presumably the false prophets (compare the discussion in 12:1). For the repetition of the root "shatter" (שבר) compare 8:21.

Aim

One must understand that Jrm has made an attempt to repent (vv 5–8), has puzzled over the intricate nature of the human heart and mind, his own and others' (vv 9–10), and now once more he raises a prayer to Yahweh for help. He reminds Yahweh that his prophetic activity is not at his own initiative (v 16); Jrm knows that Yahweh knows it (15:11, 19), but he cannot help himself. The prayer tumbles out; traditional phraseology from the Psalms comes to his lips. But now, for the first time, there is no matching answer from Yahweh. What is one to conclude?—that not only is no immediate help forthcoming from Yahweh, but no further reassurance either? Where is he?

The Community Must Not Forget the Sabbath

Bibliography

Andreasen, Niels-Erik A.
The Old Testament Sabbath (SBLDS 7; Society of Biblical Literature, 1972) 31–34, with literature.
Barnes, W. Emery
"Prophecy and the Sabbath (A Note on the Teaching of Jeremiah)," *JTS* 29 (1927–28) 386–90.
Fishbane
"Revelation and Tradition," 348–49.

17

19 Thus Yahweh has said to me: Go and stand in the Gate of the Sons of [a] the People,[a] through which the kings of Judah go in and out, and in all the gates of Jerusalem, 20/ and say to them, Listen to the word of Yahweh, you kings of Judah, [a] and all Judah,[a] and all you inhabitants of Jerusalem, who enter these gates: 21/ Thus Yahweh has said, For the sake of your lives beware that you do not carry any burden on the sabbath day, nor bring it in through the gates of Jerusalem; 22/ never bring out a burden from your houses on the sabbath day, nor ever do any work (then): keep the sabbath day holy, as I commanded your fathers. 23/ Yet they did not listen or turn their ears, but stiffened their neck so as not to listen[a] or accept discipline. 24/ And so if you do listen to me—oracle of Yahweh—so as not to bring a burden in through the gates of this city on the sabbath day, and keep the sabbath day holy, so as not to do [a] on it[a] any work, 25/ then there shall come in through the gates of this city kings [and officials][a] who sit on the throne of David, mounted on chariots and horses, they and their officials, the men of Judah and the inhabitants of Jerusalem, and this city shall be inhabited for ever. 26/ And (people) shall come from the cities of Judah, from the region about Jerusalem, from the land of Benjamin, from the Shephelah, from the hill country, from the Negeb, bringing burnt offerings and sacrifices, cereal offerings and frankincense [and those bringing thank-offerings][a] to the house of Yahweh. 27/ But if you do not listen to me, to keep the sabbath day holy and not carry a burden nor 《bring》[a] it through the gates of Jerusalem on the sabbath day, then I shall light a fire in her gates, and it will devour the strongholds of Jerusalem and not go out.

Text

19a—a Reading with the qere'; the ketib omits "the."

20a—a A few MSS. of the Hebrew (and a few of *G*) omit these words, but the omission is haplographic.

23a Reading שֹׁמֵעַ with the qere'; the ketib שׁומֵע is hardly to be vocalized and is evidently a slip of the pen.

24a—a Reading בּוֹ with the qere'; the ketib may be read either as בֹּה or as בָּה (feminine), in which case it must be understood as "in it" (the city).

25a This expression must be a dittographic addition: שָׂרִים do not sit on the throne of David, and they are mentioned later in the verse.

26a The bracketed words do not fit the syntax, and the category of "thank-offerings" does not fit the listing of types of sacrifice by material (see Interpretation). The words are an insertion from 33:11 (Duhm, Rudolph).

27a Emending וּבֹא "nor come in" to וְהָבֵא to match v 21; "coming in" through the gates is not forbidden (compare Rudolph).

Structure

The most likely reason for the insertion of this passage here is that "day" (of the sabbath) appears seven times (vv 21 once, 22 twice, 24 twice, 27 twice): it would have been associated with vv 14–18, in which "day" occurs three times (vv 16, 17, 18). But there may be other possibilities. For example, "word of Yahweh" appears in Isa 1:10, and "sabbath" in Isa 1:13; this might have given warrant for placing a passage about the "sabbath" after a passage in which people are said to ask, "Where is the word of Yahweh?" (v 15)—compare the reason suggested for the insertion of 18:13–17 after 18:1–12.

For the internal structure of the passage see Form.

Form

This is a covenant speech analogous to 7:1–12 or 11:1–14. In it Jrm is perceived to function as the covenant mediator (vv 19–20), reminding the hearers of their covenant obligations. The parenetic appeal is found in vv 20–23: imperatives (vv 20–21) and prohibitions (v 22), followed by the citation of the negative example of the "fathers" (v 23), analogous to 11:7–8. The remainder of the passage is taken up by covenant conditions, both a positive one (vv 24–26), repeating the stipulations about the sabbath from vv 21–22 and offering an apodosis of promise (vv 25–26), and then a negative one (v 27) which again offers an apodosis, this time of judgment. For extended discussion of the genre of covenant speech see Form for both 7:1–15 and 11:1–17 and the literature cited there.

Setting

Though the genre is one appropriate to Jrm (see Form), neither the diction nor the subject matter can be identified with anything authentic to him. There is here none of the striking rhetoric found in 7:1–12 or 11:1–17 (see there), but instead repetitious diction such as must be attributed to a later source. The urgency about carrying burdens in and out of Jerusalem on the sabbath exactly matches that in Neh 13:15–22. The description in v 25 of kings riding with chariots and horses is one that bespeaks a time of dreams of restoration of the monarchy.

Other commentators are more cautious. Those who adhere to a belief in a Deuteronomistic editing of the book associate this passage with that edition, for example, Rudolph,[1] and Bright says, "Contrary to the opinion of some, the passage is not, either in style or content, necessarily very late. Moreover (cf. Rudolph), there is every likelihood that it does develop actual words of Jeremiah on the subject."[2] Of course there is no way to demonstrate that Jrm could not have had an interest in the sabbath, nor any way to demonstrate that the passage is not a memory of something Jrm said. But it must be stressed that there is no hint elsewhere in Jer of any interest by the prophet or attributed to the prophet in the matter of sabbath, nor of any interest in "kings of Judah," plural, such as one finds in vv 19, 20, 25 (the reference in 1:18 is in the context of a listing of groups in society). When Jrm preaches the temple sermon (7:1–12), he mentions several items of the Decalogue, but sabbath observance is not among them. It is far more likely that this passage was developed as a specific supplement making good that omission; 7:1–12, like the present passage, portrays Jrm as standing in a gate preaching to those entering. The present passage then functions in a way analogous to the way Amos 2:4–5 functions alongside Amos 2:6–8: when "Israel" in the latter passage was assumed to refer to the northern kingdom only, a redactor developed a fresh passage referring to Judah. (For a parallel between this passage and Amos 2:5 see Interpretation on v 27.)

There is no way to date the present passage except within wide limits. The suggestion of Andreasen, "not . . . later than the middle of the sixth century B.C.,"[3] may well be based more on his concern for the sabbath than intrinsic plausibility: if the "Gate of the Sons of the People" (v 19) is a temple gate, which is likely, then one must assume a time when the temple was functioning. There was a concern late in the sixth century for sabbath observance (Isa 56:2, 4, 6), but the wording here is so close to that of Neh 13:15–22 as to make that period, in the last half of the fifth century, the most likely date. Material attributable to Jrm reinforcing Nehemiah's concern would have been heard gratefully by those who shared that concern.

1   Rudolph, pp. 119–21.
2   Bright, p. 120.
3   Niels-Erik A. Andreasen, *The Old Testament Sabbath*
        (SBLDS 7; Society of Biblical Literature, 1972) 34.

Interpretation

■ 19 The "Gate of the Sons of the People" is otherwise unknown; the name is odd enough that Volz emends בְּנֵי הָעָם to בִּנְיָמִן "Benjamin," the name of a city gate (37:13; 38:7), and that emendation has been adopted by *RSV*, *NEB*, and *NAB*. It is an attractive emendation but one for which there is no textual warrant; it is better to leave the text as it is. There is reason to believe, in fact, that a temple gate rather than a city gate is referred to. Graf, followed by Naegelsbach and Giesebrecht, pointed out that the order "go in" and "go out" is appropriate to a temple gate (compare the diction of 2 Chr 23:8, regarding access to the temple on the sabbath), while the reverse would be appropriate to a city gate. The expression בְּנֵי הָעָם "sons of the people" is used for the laity by the Chronicler (2 Chr 35:5, 12, 13), and if the passage is to be dated in the fifth century (see Setting), then that usage would suggest a temple gate. True, the same expression was used in Jrm's time for "commoners," as opposed to the upper classes (26:23), but to speak of a (city) gate for "commoners," through which the kings of Judah went in and out would be very odd; better to understand the "kings" as "laity" (as opposed to priests). Again, if the present passage is modeled on 7:1–12 (see Setting), then it is no doubt a temple gate, as the reference is in 7:2.

Why "kings" should be mentioned here at all is unclear, except that the writer had kings on his mind (v 20 and esp. v 25): it is the restoration of the monarchy that is the issue (see Setting). According to the instruction, the prophet is portrayed as told to stand in the particular named gate and in general in all the city gates of Jerusalem.

■ 21–22 The expression בְּנַפְשׁוֹתֵיכֶם means "for the sake of your lives" or even "at the peril of your lives,"[4] an instance of the בְּ of price. Sabbath observance is made the basis for the survival of the people. For the nip'al imperative הִשָּׁמְרוּ "beware" see 9:3. Curiously the expression נשָׂא מַשָּׂא "carry a burden," with cognate accusative, seems to occur in the OT only here, but "burden" (מַשָּׂא) occurs in similar contexts in Neh 13:15, 19. The emphasis here on carrying burdens is curious, since the formulation in the Decalogue is against doing any work

(Exod 20:10; Deut 5:14), and that prohibition is found here (vv 22, 24), but it is consistently subordinated to the specific work of carrying burdens, the concern of Nehemiah (Neh 13:15–22; see Setting). The phrase "do not do work" and "keep the sabbath day holy" (vv 22, 24, 27) is identical with that in the Decalogue. For "I commanded your fathers" compare 11:4.

■ 23 "But they did not listen or turn their ears, but stiffened their neck": see 7:26. "Not to listen or accept discipline": see 7:28. The reference to the "fathers" is found in 7:22, 25–26, and 11:10.

■ 25 The climax of Yahweh's promise, if the people keep the sabbath, is the coming of kings through the gates, kings who are seated on thrones and mounted on chariots and horses;[5] the emphasis here is a snapshot of the yearnings of the period in which the passage was shaped (compare the remarks above on v 19).

■ 26 The listing of six regions occurs also in 32:44 and 33:13; the analysis in 32:44 indicates that the first three are primary, and the last three are a gloss on the third (see 32:1–44, Preliminary Observations): the occurrence of the listing of all six in 32:44 doubtless gave rise to the listing here. As for the first three, "Benjamin" and "Judah" together are the tribal territories making up the kingdom of Judah (see on 6:1), and the mention of "Benjamin" in 32:44 was doubtless a reflection of the purchase of the field in Anathoth, part of Benjamin (1:1). On the other hand, "Judah" and "Jerusalem" are a standard pair in Jer (as in v 25). Thus the סְבִיבוֹת are not only the "surroundings of" (*RSV* "places round about") Jerusalem, but include Jerusalem itself (thus Volz and Rudolph, *Bezirk*, "district [of]"). The last three—the Shephelah, the hill country, and the Negeb—are listed in Josh 10:40: the hill country is immediately to the north of Jerusalem and to the south (the heights of Hebron); the Shephelah is to the west, the area of lowlands which begins just to the east of the Philistine plain, cut by wadis running east and west, and which continues up to the hill country; and the Negeb is to the south, the arid desert land of Beersheba and beyond.[6]

For "burnt offerings" and "sacrifices" see 6:20; for "cereal offering" (along with "burnt offering") see 14:12; and for "frankincense" see again 6:20. These four are in

---

4   BDB, 90a.

5   W. Boyd Barrick, "The Meaning and Usage of RKB in Biblical Hebrew," *JBL* 101 (1982) 481–503, esp.

491–92 and n. 65 there.

6   For a description of these regions see Baly, *Geography*, 140–43, 177–90; William H. Morton,

general the main sacrifices: "burnt offerings" and "sacrifices" were both of animals, the former burned completely, the latter shared with the worshiper (Leviticus 1 and 3 respectively), the "cereal offering" (Leviticus 2) was of grains, and "frankincense" was associated with the cereal offering (Lev 2:1, 2, 15, 16). A תּוֹדָה "thank-offering," part of a phrase here inserted later, is hardly parallel with these: in Lev 7:12–15 the provision is made for a worshiper who wished his "peace-offering" (which is a זֶבַח "sacrifice," Lev 3:1) to be a "thank-offering," then he adds to the זֶבַח "sacrifice" various kinds of cakes, in short, a kind of מִנְחָה "cereal offering" (compare Lev 7:12 with 2:4); that is, the "thank-offering" is a term for a classification of purpose, not of material.

■ **27** For "light a fire" see 11:16. For "strongholds" see 6:5; "it will devour the strongholds of Jerusalem" is a phrase found exactly in this form in Amos 2:5—that passage may have been the source for the phrase here. For "and not go out" see 7:20.

Aim

The survival of the community depends upon the observance of the sabbath. It is not, we conclude, a word from Jrm, but it is a word that helped to shape the outlook of the postexilic community. It is a word that reminds us of Nehemiah's humorless zeal, but that zeal helped to assure the survival of the community. In a very real sense, then, the sermon is true: generation in, generation out, the Jews have adhered to the law of the sabbath and thereby maintained their integrity as a people.

"Shephelah," *IDB* 4:324–25; Simon Cohen, "Negeb," *IDB* 3:531–32; and further references in these works.

Yahweh the Potter

Bibliography

Brekelmans, Christian
"Jeremiah 18,1–12 and Its Redaction," *Le Livre de Jérémie, Le prophète et son milieu, les oracles et leur transmission* (ed. Pierre-Maurice Bogaert; BETL 54; Leuven: Leuven University, 1981) 343–50.

Johnston, Robert H.
"The Biblical Potter," *BA* 37 (1974) 86–106.

Mize, Roger
"The Patient God," *Lexington Theological Quarterly* 7 (1972) 86–92.

Moss, R. Waddy
"A Study of Jeremiah's Use (xviii. 1–17) of the Figure of the Potter," *ExpTim* 2 (1890/91) 274–75.

Wanke, Gunther
"Jeremias Besuch beim Töpfer, Eine motiv-kritische Untersuchung zu Jer 18," *Prophecy, Essays presented to Georg Fohrer on his sixty-fifth birthday, 6 September 1980* (ed. John A. Emerton; BZAW 150; Berlin: de Gruyter, 1980) 151–62.

Weippert
Prosareden, 48–62, 191–209.

18

1 The word which came to Jeremiah from Yahweh, as follows: 2/ Go down at once to the potter's house, and there I shall announce my word to you. 3/ So I went down to the potter's house, [a] and there he was,[a] doing his work at the wheel. 4/ And whenever the vessel which he was making was spoiled, [a] as happens with clay[a] in the hand of the potter, then he 《 would remake 》[b] it into another vessel, as ⟨seemed right⟩[c] in the eyes of the potter to make. 5/ And the word of Yahweh came to me as follows: 6/ Am I not able to do with you, house of Israel, like this potter?—oracle of Yahweh— look, like clay in the hand of the potter, so are you in my hand, house of Israel. 7/ Suddenly when I speak concerning a nation or a kingdom to uproot and demol- ish [and destroy,][a] 8/ but that nation turns from its evil [against whom I have spoken,][a] I retract my decision about the

Text

3a—a Read with the qere' וְהִנֵּה הוּא; the synonymous ketib וְהִנֵּהוּ is otherwise unattested (the form is הִנּוֹ, three times, e.g., Num 23:17).

4a—a So some MSS.; many MSS. and *a'* and *θ'* read בַּחֹמֶר "in clay," but this results in a tautology, "And when the vessel was spoiled which he was making in clay in the hand of the potter." See Interpretation.

b Emending to וְשָׁב וְעָשָׂהוּ; *M* reads וְשָׁב וַיַּעֲשֵׂהוּ. The waw-consecutive perfect of שׁוב almost certainly implies a waw-consecutive perfect in the second verb (Mal 3:18; Dan 11:13); this would parallel the much commoner pattern with waw-consecutive imperfects of both verbs (Gen 26:18; Num 11:4; and often). The sequence in Eccl 4:1 = 7 is evidently careless usage. Compare Joüon, *Gramm.*, sec. 118n.

c Revocalizing the perfect יָשַׁר to the imperfect יִשַׁר (Volz, Rudolph); compare b.

7a This verb, וּלְהַאֲבִיד, is a gloss, like the third verb in *M* of 1:10 (see Text there). This single additional verb here corresponds to the single additional verb in *G* of 1:10. It is noteworthy that *S* and two printed editions of *M* insert, before וּלְהַאֲבִיד here, the fourth verb in *M* of 1:10, וְלַהֲרוֹס. The texts and Versions of 1:10 and the present passage thus illustrate stages of expansion of the original four verbs.

8a This phrase is at a distance from the noun to

disaster which I have intended to do to them; 9/ and suddenly, when I speak concerning a nation or a kingdom to build and to plant, 10/ but it does ᵃwhat is badᵃ in my eyes, not to listen to my voice, I retract my decision about the good which I have thought to do to them. 11/ So now, just say to the men of Judah and to the inhabitants of Jerusalem, as follows: Thus Yahweh has said: I am going to shape against you disaster and intend against you a plan; just turn, each of you, from your evil way, and make good your ways and your doings.

12/ [But they kept saying, "We don't care!—we will follow our own plans, and each of us will exercise the stubbornness of his heart."]ᵃ

which it refers ("that nation") and is missing in *G* and *S*; it is doubtless a gloss (compare Rudolph).

10a—a   Reading the qere' הָרַע; the ketib הָרָעָה is similar in meaning and is influenced by הַטּוֹבָה "the good" later in the verse. But הָרַע is the form found with "in the eyes of."

12a   The verse is an authentic addition by Jrm at a later date: see Interpretation.

Structure

It is not apparent why this passage has its present position here. Since 17:19–27 is likely to be dated late (see Setting there), one must assume that when the present passage was placed here it came directly after 17:14–18. If so, there are at least two possibilities. (1) Given the cogency of the explanation of vv 13–17 after the present passage on the basis of the sequence of "potter" and "Lebanon" in Isa 29:16 and 17 respectively (see vv 13–17, Structure), it is possible that the occurrence of "lips" in both Isa 29:13 and Jer 17:16 triggered the insertion of both the present passage and vv 13–17 at the same time: this is the only occurrence of "lips" in Jer (but there are other occurrences of "lips" in passages of Isaiah likely to be available to a redactor of Jer). (2) The present passage closely resembles 13:1–11 both in form and in their use of the verb "be spoiled" (שחת nip'al, 13:7 [compare 9] and v 4 here). In 13:1–11 what was spoiled was "pride" (גָּאוֹן), and that link with 12:5 explains the position of 13:1–11 (see Structure there). What is spoiled in the present passage is a "vessel" (כְּלִי, v 9), and given the association of "their vessels," "they are ashamed" (בֹּשׁוּ) and "is dismayed" (חַתָּה) in 14:3, the occurrence of forms of the two last-cited words in 17:18 and "vessel" in the present passage may have brought the passage here; it is to be noted that v 4 and v 9, in which "vessel" appears, are the only two occurrences in Jer until 19:11. If, on the other hand, 17:19–27 was in place before 18:1–12 was added, the association may be the phrase "do work" (עשׂה מְלָאכָה), 17:22, 24, and v 3 here; the phrase does

not appear again until 48:10.

For the internal structure of the passage see Form.

Form

Though this is not, strictly speaking, a narrative of a symbolic action (Jrm does nothing except observe and listen to Yahweh), the diction is very close to that of 13:1–11 (see Structure, Setting); one might call the passage then the narrative of a symbolic event. The narration proper is in the first person (vv 3, 5), so the rubric in v 1, identical with 7:1 and 11:1, must have been added at a later stage (compare the first-person form of 13:1, and the contrast between 32:1 [third person] and 32:6 [first person]). Verse 2 is the command of Yahweh; vv 3–4 are the report of the execution of that command, including the details of what Jrm saw when he followed the command. Verses 5–6 outline the meaning of the event as Yahweh revealed it; Yahweh couches v 6a as a rhetorical question, and both 6a and 6b offer comparisons. The passage is striking in that the event of revelation is anticipated in the command (v 2b). Though vv 7–11 have been thought by some commentators to be a secondary expansion, there is no warrant for this judgment (see Setting); these verses simply explicate v 6. The presentation of alternatives is certainly found in prophetic material elsewhere (Isa 1:19–20). These verses suggest priestly instruction, but this genre was made to serve prophetic purposes (compare Ezek 18:5–20, where a series of legal clauses spells out the combinations of righteous and wicked father and son). Verse 11, introduced by the formula וְעַתָּה "so now," is the concluding command to Jrm, to announce Yahweh's word, a word of judgment introduced by הִנְנִי and the participle (1:15; 5:15; and often), a participle identical with "potter" in vv 2–6; the word of judgment closes with a parenetic appeal to repentance (3:12, 22; 7:3), an indication that the word of judgment is one of potential judgment only.

Verse 12 offers difficulty; it is proposed here that it is a report added by Jrm at a later time, recording his experience in communicating the message of the event (see Interpretation).

Setting

Many scholars have denied some or all of this passage to Jrm. Thus Duhm called the whole passage "a very childish haggadah,"[1] and Mowinckel concurred.[2] Others who see original material in vv 1–6 believe that vv 7–11 (12) are the product of a Deuteronomistic editor.[3] Rudolph believes that the whole passage comes from "Source C" (that is, a Deuteronomistic editor) but that the redactor had access to the testimony of Jrm. Bright and Weiser, on the other hand, have accepted it as genuine.

Recently Weippert has subjected the passage to close scrutiny[4] and concludes that there is no justification for calling the passage or a portion of it Deuteronomistic;[5] her investigation of the matter appears definitive. Thus she points out that the climax of the passage is the use of the word יוֹצֵר "potter" (vv 2, 3, 4, 6) as the participle יוֹצֵר "am shaping" in v 11; there is thus no way to separate vv 7–11 from vv 1–6.[6] Again the use of רֶגַע "suddenly" in vv 7 and 9 is not a Deuteronomistic usage, but the word does appear in 4:20,[7] and the reuse of the verbs that appear in Jrm's call (1:10) here in vv 7 and 9 is not Deuteronomistic.[8] It may be added that there is irony in the use of נחם nip'al "regret" with "the good" in v 10, irony characteristic of Jrm and not of a redactor (see Interpretation on vv 7–10).

Nevertheless it is clear that form-critically the passage is complete with v 6, and it is equally clear that one senses a rhetorical shift with the onset of v 7. Verses 7–11 contain many phrases that are part of prose vocabulary elsewhere in the book. Thus "make good your ways and your doings" (v 11) is found in the temple sermon (7:3, 5), and what precedes that phrase in v 11 is close to the wording of 36:3—here in v 11 we find "I am going to shape against you disaster [רָעָה] and intend [חשב] against you a plan; just turn, each of you, from your evil way [שׁוּבוּ נָא אִישׁ מִדַּרְכּוֹ הָרָעָה]," and in 36:3, "It may be that the house of Judah will hear all the disaster [רָעָה] which I intend [חשב] to do to them, so that each may turn from his evil way [וְיָשׁוּבוּ אִישׁ מִדַּרְכּוֹ הָרָעָה]." Is there a clue in the contrast here between "house of Israel" (twice in v 6) and "men of Judah and inhabitants of Jerusalem" in v 11? There is at least the possibility that "house of Israel" referred originally to the northern kingdom (compare 2:4), as is the hypothesis of the present study for the original form of 1:11–16; 2:4–9; 2:12–15; and portions of chapters 30—31: in this way 18:1–6 would have been an early recension of the passage, and it would have extended by vv 7–11 sometime between the time of the temple sermon (the autumn of 609) and the time of the dictation of the first scroll (605/604). If the passage took shape at once, then the setting must be that proposed above for vv 7–11, namely 609–605/604.

It is proposed here that v 12 is an authentic report by Jrm, added at a later time, recording his experience in communicating the message of the event (see Interpretation); the reaction is appropriate to the time of the second scroll.

Interpretation

■ 1–11 Commentators have differed on the basic meaning of this narrative. Some have thought it a message of hope: the potter will not accept spoiled vessels but will remake them to his satisfaction; thus Yahweh will not accept defeat, but will accomplish good with his people (Cornill).[9] Others have thought it a message of doom:

1   Duhm, p. 153.
2   His "Source C": Sigmund Mowinckel, *Zur Komposition des Buches Jeremia* (Kristiania: Dybwad, 1914) 31.
3   Thus Siegfried Herrmann, *Die prophetische Heilserwartungen im Alten Testament* (BWANT 5; Stuttgart: Kohlhammer, 1965) 162–65; Thiel, *Jer. 1—25*, 210–17; Nicholson, *Jer. 1—25*, 155.
4   Weippert, *Prosareden*, 48–62, 191–209.

5   Ibid., 60.
6   Ibid., 55.
7   Ibid., 58.
8   Ibid., 191–209.
9   So also Skinner, 162–64.

this is the point of v 11 (Giesebrecht). Those who have held that vv 7–11 are secondary have assumed that an optimistic message has been overlaid by a darker one.[10]

Two things must be emphasized. First, the clay is not altogether passive. Any potter will affirm that because of the centrifugal force developed on the wheel the clay presses against the hands of the potter.[11] The process of shaping pottery is therefore an extraordinarily apt analogy for the work of Yahweh with his people: though he is sovereign, the people have a will of their own which they exert against him. Second, Yahweh can change his mind if the decision of his people warrants it: this is the point of both v 6 and vv 7–10. Verse 11 is not really pessimistic. Yahweh has a "plan" (מַחֲשָׁבָה) which he "intends" (חשׁב); but whether he puts it into operation or not depends upon whether or not the people turn from their evil way: if they will, he will not. Yahweh is capable of both uprooting and demolishing on the one hand, and of building and planting on the other. He may intend the one, but if the response of the people demands it, he will do the other. This is the lesson of the potter. Some pots turn out fine the first time. Some do not, so the potter changes his tactics. It is a striking presentation of divine sovereignty and human freedom (compare the exegesis of רֶגַע "in an instant" in vv 7 and 9).

■ **1** For the wording of the introductory verse see 7:1; 11:1.

■ **2** The opening words are literally, "Arise and go down to the potter's house"; the imperative "arise" lends urgency to the command (compare 13:6). "Go down": Annesley W. Streane was of the opinion that this verb suggests Jrm was on the temple mount (compare 36:10, 12),[12] but doubtless the verb simply means that the potter's workshop was at a lower part of the city:[13] he would need a water supply.

The word "potter" is simply the participle יוֹצֵר "shaper." Since the verb is used often of Yahweh's creative ability (Gen 2:7, 8, and often in the Psalms, for example Ps 94:9), the analogy easily suggested itself:

indeed the same analogy was offered by Isaiah (Isa 29:16).

Earlier commentators make a great deal of the question whether the sequence of the command here must be taken literally, or whether Jrm, in a visit to the potter's workshop, gained a lesson of divine activity and thus became convinced that Yahweh had sent him there (Cornill).[14] That such a "humanistic" explanation is possible no one doubts; but the sense of divine compulsion under which the prophets worked might have produced the event much as this verse says it did.

■ **3** Earlier commentators and translators were puzzled by the term for "wheel," אָבְנָיִם, a dual; the word resembles "stone," and G thus translates here "stones." S and T both thought of something hard, heavy, and immovable: T uses סְדָנָא which is normally a "block" (S uses the same word, but it means "anvil" in Syriac); Rashi (and thus Calvin) assumed "moulds." V correctly translates "wheel." Jrm's potter would not be using the tournette (slow wheel), which may have been assumed by T, but the fast wheel, and the dual for the word is appropriate. The lower wheel functions like a flywheel, is made of stone, and is turned by the feet. The upper platform, which was probably of wood, was the base on which the clay was shaped. Both turned together by a vertical shaft.[15] Compare Sir 38:29: "So too is the potter sitting at his work and turning the wheel with his feet."

■ **4** The verbs in this verse are waw-consecutive perfects. Because these verbs are in the context of past narrative, they must be taken as frequentatives (Volz, Rudolph, Bright); thus the translation "whenever" here (and thus also the slight emendation of "would remake" and "seemed right": see Text). For שׁחת nip'al "be spoiled, ruined," see 13:7.

The (slightly emended) expression כַּחֹמֶר, literally "like clay," is a compressed expression for "as clay does" or "as happens with clay"; compare "like this potter" in v 6, which of course means "as this potter does to the clay."[16] The implication here is that the clay deliberately thwarts

10 Ibid., 163.

11 Roger Mize, "The Patient God," *Lexington Theological Quarterly* 7 (1972) 88.

12 Annesley W. Streane, *The Book of the Prophet Jeremiah, Together with the Lamentations* (Cambridge Bible for Schools and Colleges; Cambridge: Cambridge University, 1881) 133.

13 Freedman, p. 125.

14 So also Skinner, 162.

15 For a photograph of a similar village potter's wheel today see Robert H. Johnston, "The Biblical Potter," *BA* 37 (1974) 100; the article cited, 86–106, discusses the whole matter in detail.

16 See more generally König, *Syntax*, sec. 319g.

the purpose of the potter: for the pressure of the clay against the hand of the potter due to centrifugal force, see the comment above under vv 1–11.

The verb שׁוב "(re)turn," followed in the verbal expression by a parallel verb, frequently means "again"; here "return and make" means "remake."[17] The verb עשׂה "make" in this instance takes two accusatives, thus "make (something into something)." The verb ישׁר with בְּעֵינֵי "in the eyes of" means "it pleased (the potter)."

The potter is not thwarted by any perversity of the clay; the potter is able to change his intention in order to accomplish his ultimate goal, the making of an acceptable vessel.

■ **5** This rubric fulfills the same function here as it does in 13:8; see further 1:4, 11; 2:1; 16:1.

■ **6** This is the only instance of the interrogative הַ with the preposition כְּ in Jer; the phraseology is reminiscent of Amos 9:7, הֲלוֹא כִבְנֵי כֻשִׁים אַתֶּם לִי "Are you not like the Ethiopians to me?" For "like this potter" see above, v 4. Both halves of the verse express the analogy: the potter is to the clay as Yahweh is to Israel.

■ **7–10** The first two verses set forth one possibility, the second two the opposite one; either may happen. Two understandings are possible for the double expression וְרֶגַע . . . רֶגַע at the beginning of vv 7 and 9. One is that found in T, which reads וּזְמַן . . . זְמַן "one time . . . another time"; all lexica and twentieth-century commentators agree on this meaning, though רֶגַע does not occur correlatively in any other passage in the OT. The other is that found in V, where the adverb in both instances is given its meaning "suddenly" (*repente*, v 7; *subito*, v 9), the same meaning it carries in 4:20; this is the meaning, I submit, which it also carries here. The point of the passage is clearly not that Yahweh makes a judgment for some nations and against others, almost as if it were a matter of whim; the point is that whatever decision Yahweh has made about a nation, he is able "quickly" or "suddenly" to reverse the decision if the conduct of that nation merits it. That is to say, רֶגַע "suddenly" modifies the apodosis of each expression, not the protasis (as Naegelsbach pointed out). The fact that the syntax is paratactic, with protases and apodoses only implied, makes the expression easier. Verses 7–8 are literally:

"Suddenly I shall speak concerning a nation to uproot and smash . . . , and that nation turns from its evil . . . and I shall retract my decision concerning the evil which I have intended to do to it." Indeed the "suddenly" may refer to the nation's change of heart as much as to Yahweh's change of plan, but the main emphasis is on Yahweh's sudden change. So with vv 9–10. The phenomenon by which רֶגַע logically modifies only the last clause (here the apodosis) is analogous to the same phenomenon with the negative לֹא, with פֶּן "lest," with an introductory causal word or with an interrogative word.[18]

The preposition עַל cannot mean "against" (v 7) but must mean "concerning" (see v 9). The pairing of "nation" and "kingdom" is a reflex of those words in 1:10, given the use of the series of verbs of that verse here also. For those verbs, "uproot," "demolish," "build," and "plant," see 1:10. For נחם nip'al "retract one's decision" see 4:28.[19] Zorell points out[20] that the use of the verb here in v 10 is ironic: Yahweh is not retracting a punishment but rather a gracious gesture. For חשׁב "plan, intend" see 11:19.

■ **11** The verse opens with one of the two instances in Jer where Yahweh commands Jrm with אֱמֹר "say" (the other being 13:18), and the only instance of אֱמָר־נָא (the modal particle added): the frequent pattern is וְאָמַרְתָּ (8:4 and often). The occurrence again of the particle נָא after שׁוּבוּ "turn" here (the phraseology of 25:5 and 35:15 is imitative) suggests an emotional urgency to both commands: it is so easy, if they only would!

For "men of Judah and inhabitants of Jerusalem" see 4:3; and in a prose context 11:2 (and often). The participle of יצר "shaper," having been used for "potter" in vv 2, 3, 4, and 6, is used here as part of the judgment declaration. It is important to note, however, that יצר means not only to "shape" but also to "frame" or "plan" something; thus in Isa 22:11 וְיֹצְרָהּ מֵרָחוֹק "and he planned it long ago" (compare also Isa 37:26). Thus the verb has the implication of "plan" even aside from its parallelism here to חשׁב "intend." Again, to revert to the analogy of the clay: the potter "shapes" the clay just as he "intends"; but if the clay surprises the potter, the potter will change his plan. Yahweh here has a "shape," a "plan"

---

17 See Holladay, *Šûbh*, 66–72.
18 For these see Joüon, *Gramm.*, secs. 176t, 168h, 170m, and 161k respectively.
19 See further the reference in 4:5–31, n. 101.
20 Zorell, p. 510b.

for Judah's future, and that "shape," that "plan" is for רָעָה "disaster"; but if they respond to his appeal and surprise him by turning from their own רָעָה "evil," then Yahweh will be delighted to change his mind (v 8). The participle with הִנֵּה gives a sense of immediacy: Yahweh is about to do it, but what he is about to do is not yet action, it is the carrying out of a "plan" that may still be shifted by the reaction of Judah. It is an astonishing balance between Yahweh's sovereignty and human freedom.

■ **12** This verse offers difficulties of interpretation. On the face of it, it begins with a waw-consecutive perfect and so means "and/but they will say." The other occurrence of נוֹאָשׁ "I/we don't care!" is in 2:25; there it is preceded by וַתֹּאמְרִי, a waw-consecutive imperfect, Yahweh's accusation against Israel of what she has said (and thus of her being caught in a contradiction): see Interpretation there. The other occurrence of נוֹאָשׁ in the OT is Isa 57:10, where it is preceded by לֹא אָמָרְתְּ, a perfect. Both parallels thus are narratives of past events, and it is therefore a temptation to emend וְאָמְרוּ to וַיֹּאמְרוּ "but they said." Such a translation is given by all the Versions, but whether they had a text with a yod or whether they simply so interpreted the verb in *M* is uncertain. Nevertheless earlier verbs in the passage are waw-consecutive perfects (וְשָׁב, וְנִשְׁחַת, v 4), so that one should not be hasty either in emending the text or in interpreting *M* to mean "and they said."

Since the verse in some way contradicts the hope of v 11, the question arises, Who is understood to be speaking? It is hardly possible to understand Yahweh as the speaker: such a verse would make a mockery of the hope of v 11. Is it a marginal note (so Volz)? Hardly; the expression נוֹאָשׁ appears otherwise only in prophetic discourse proper and is unlikely diction for a glossator. Is it Jrm himself, then? If the opening verb means "but they said," then one can imagine it as some kind of report to Yahweh (like 6:28). But if the opening verb means "but they will say," then it must be understood as an objection leveled by Jrm against the appeal from Yahweh. There are several considerations that speak against understanding the verse as an objection, however. For one thing, one would expect an introductory word וָאֹמַר "but

I said," or even the more extended וָאֹמַר אֲהָהּ אֲדֹנָי יהוה "but I said, 'Ah, Lord Yahweh!'" as in 1:6; 4:10; 14:13. In fact 14:13 has an objection much like what might be envisioned here, but the basis of the objection is a participial clause; so that the objection one might expect here would have הֵמָּה אֹמְרִים (compare also 2:27; 17:15). More fundamentally, such an objection would exhibit a Jrm more pessimistic about the people than Yahweh is, whereas all the evidence elsewhere is that Jrm understands himself to be more hopeful than Yahweh (4:29 against 4:30–31; 5:1 against 5:4; and the repeated prohibition from Yahweh that Jrm not pray for the people, 7:16; 11:14; 15:1). All these considerations lead to a tentative conclusion: the verse is an authentic observation from Jrm, added some time later on the basis of his experience of attempting to communicate the message of vv 1–11; the opening represents a frequentative past. In this way the opening verb subtly reflects the frequentatives in v 4.

For נוֹאָשׁ "we don't care!" see 2:25. The following כִּי implies "to the contrary": see again 2:25. The likeness to 2:25 continues with the verbal phrase הלך אַחֲרֵי "walk after, follow." The "plans" of the people are in contrast to Yahweh's "plan" of v 11; is there in the plural "plans" a hint of divided loyalties, even of polytheism?—note the plural with "go after" in a similar sequence in 2:8. The phrase "stubbornness of one's heart" is found frequently in Jer (see 3:17), but this is the only occasion when it is the object of עשה "do," here "exercise"; it is not a Deuteronomic phrase.[21]

Aim

In the early years of his career Jrm saw in the work of the potter an apt analogy to the work of Yahweh with his people. The potter can change his plans when the tug of the clay demands it, and so Yahweh can change his plans with his own people: he has the resource to meet any response his people may offer him. Indeed Yahweh may balance his plan for ill for one nation with his plan for good for another; but either nation may surprise him by an unexpected response, so that his work for ill may become a work for good, and his work for good may become a work for ill. Specifically for Judah, we hear,

---

21   Weippert, *Prosareden*, 60.

Yahweh has plans for ill. Can the nation change its ways so that he may transform his plans to good? By the understanding of v 12 adopted here, the answer to the question became no, a circumstance that implies that the plans for ill must go forward.

In the next century another prophetic voice declared that Yahweh's plans for ill were to be executed against Babylon, and the stubborn of heart of his own people were to be rescued (Isa 46:8–13). Each generation then is forced to discern the plan God has in mind and respond.

The balance always is between God's plans and human decision making: both are here affirmed. So one might hear the appeal to turn about couched in terms of the terrible plans of God (as John the Baptist voiced it, for example, in Luke 3:7–9). The balance has not always been kept between an awareness of God's will and an awareness of the difference that human response can make; but it has rarely been so nicely expressed as in this analogy with the work of the potter.

The Faithless People Are
Condemned to Endless Walking

Bibliography

Albright, William F.
"A Catalogue of Early Hebrew Lyric Poems (Psalm
LXVIII)," *HUCA* 23 (1950/51) part 1, 23–24.
Dahood, Mitchell
"Philological Notes on Jer 18,14–15," *ZAW* 74
(1962) 207–9.
Driver, Godfrey R.
"Things Old and New in the Old Testament,"
MUSJ 45 (1969) 467–69.
Gordis, Robert
"The Biblical Root ŠDY-ŠD: Notes on 2 Sam. i. 21;
Jer. xviii. 14; Ps. xci. 6; Job v. 21; Isa. xiii. 6," *JTS*
41 (1940) 37–39.
Loretz, Oswald
"Jeremia 18,14: Stichometrie und Parallelismus
Membrorum," *UF* 4 (1972) 170–71.

18

13 Therefore thus Yahweh has said:
Just ask among the nations,
Who has heard of such ⟨a curse?⟩[a]
Something quite horrible
maiden Israel[b] **has done.**
14 **⟨Is⟩**[a] **a field ⟨forsaken⟩**[a] **⟨by flints,⟩**[b]
Lebanon by snow?
Or are ⟪cities⟫[c] **uprooted by the waters,**
⟨the capital⟩[d] **⟨by floods?⟩**[e]
15 **But my people have forgotten me,**
have sacrificed to Nullity,
⟨so that they have tripped them⟩[a] **in their**
ways,
in endless tracks,
to walk ⟪aimless⟫[b] **paths,**
a way ungraded,
16 **to make their land a desolation,**
an endless hissing,[a]
so that everyone passing is horrified at it
and shakes his head.
17 [a] **As with**[a] **the east wind I shall scatter**
them
before the enemy:
my back and not my face[b] **I shall show**
them[b]
on the day of their calamity.

Text

13a Reading אֵלֶּה for *M* אֵלָּה "these." The noun אָלָה
"curse" is associated with the desert wind here (v 17)
as it is in 4:11–12 (as reconstructed: see Text note
12a there).

b A few MSS. and *G*[A] read "Jerusalem" instead.

14a Reading the nip'al הֲיֵעָזֵב for the *M* qal הֲיַעֲזֹב "does
one forsake?" See Interpretation.

b Reading with Albright מִצּוֹר for *M* מִצּוּר "from
(the) rock."

c Reading עָרִים for *M* זָרִים "strangers." The text has
been influenced by מַיִם זָרִים in 2 Kgs 19:24. See
Interpretation.

d Reading קִרְיָה for the first three consonants of *M*
קָרִים "cool," masculine plural. See Interpretation.

e Reading the preposition מִן, the last consonant of
M קָרִים, with נוֹזְלִים. See Interpretation.

15a Reading וַיַּכְשִׁלוּם for *M* וַיַּכְשִׁלוּם "and they have
tripped them." See Preliminary Observations, Interpretation.

b Inserting תֹּהוּ with Rudolph; the word would have
dropped out by haplography. See Interpretation.

16a The ketib is שְׁרוּקַת; the qere' is שְׁרִיקוֹת, which
would be an intensive plural. The meaning is similar
in either case.

17a—a Many MSS. read בְּרוּחַ "with the (east) wind" for
the *M* כְּרוּחַ; see Interpretation.

b—b Vocalizing the hip'il with the Oriental tradition
and *G, V, S,* and *T,* אַרְאֵם; *M* read the qal אֶרְאֵם "I
shall see them."

Preliminary Observations

The whole passage raises a web of problems, both textual and form-critical, and many of these are interrelated. The text difficulties of v 14 are notorious, though they may be soluble with less emendation of the consonantal text than has been thought: the proposal of the present study demands the change of only one consonant and the insertion of a he (see Interpretation). But whatever the meaning of v 14, it is rhetorically isolated from the rest of the poem: it is clear that the verse raises rhetorical questions intended to set in relief the accusation of v 15a, "But my people have forgotten me, have sacrificed to Nullity."

The key question is what to do with, how to understand, the verb in v 15b which in M is וַיַּכְשִׁלוּם. By any reading the verb involved is "stumble, trip" (כשל), and the context of "ways," "paths" substantiates this. The first portion of the poem which clearly must express a declaration of judgment is v 17. But "stumble" (כשל) belongs to declarations of judgment in 6:15 and 6:21; "make someone's land a desolation" belongs to declarations of judgment in 4:7 and 10:22 (though a similar phrase is part of an accusation speech in 2:7), and the diction of v 16b is very close to that of 19:8, which is part of a declaration of judgment. In short, the diction of the passage suggests strongly that the judgment speech begins with v 15b and the verb וַיַּכְשִׁלוּם.

But if this is the case, one expects a first-person singular verb to match the first singular of v 17; to this end Volz and Rudolph emend the verb to "I shall trip them" (אַכְשִׁלֵם), and in addition Volz suggests moving the "therefore" from the beginning of v 13 to a position before this emended verb. This makes a plausible sequence, but there is no textual warrant for it. The Versions do read the verb differently but not in a way that would imply this emendation (see below).

The text of M is odd: who is the "they" in "they have tripped them"? Abravanel in the fifteenth century ingeniously proposed the "endless tracks," since that

word is not marked with "in" (so Sebastian Schmidt),[1] and Gerhard Lisowsky assumes the same in our day;[2] but this will not do: the "endless tracks" are parallel with "in their ways." Other solutions less tied to the text have been proposed (Qimḥi: "the false prophets"), but the only solution that may be supplied from the text is "idols": the singular "Nullity" implies the plural of "idols," and a parallel may be the plural "useless things" in 2:8, which becomes the singular "useless thing" in 2:11.

The difficulty of this verb is signaled by the reading of G, V, and S, a qal without suffix, "and they stumbled" (וַיִּכָּשְׁלוּ), and this reading is accepted by Duhm, Giesebrecht, Condamin, Bright, and Dahood,[3] and by RSV, JB, NEB, and NAB. The final mem in the text of M is a problem; Dahood proposes that it is a mem-enclitic.[4] But that solution of the mem strikes one as ad hoc, and it is clear that between the reading of M and that of G, V, and S the M offers the lectio difficilior and therefore lays its claim upon us. (The reading of G and V is encouraged by their understanding of לַשָּׁוְא in v 15a as "in vain": the "idols" thus disappear. See Interpretation.) The waw-consecutive vocalization of M seems dubious in the context, but the revocalization to וְיַכְשִׁלוּם, thus a final clause,[5] is easy and would bring the verb into parallel with the verbs in v 16a. (It is to be noted that Volz proposes such a nonconsecutive ו to prefix his amended verb if the transfer of "therefore" is to be rejected, and Rudolph accepts the nonconsecutive ו on the amended verb; see above.)

One is left, then, with the choice of the difficult verb "so that they have tripped them," which is the reading of the consonantal text, with the implication that vv 15b–16 embody a continuation of the accusation speech, in spite of the diction of these cola that suggests a declaration of judgment; or else an emended verb to render vv 15b–16 part of the declaration of judgment, as the diction suggests. Given the fact that there is no textual warrant for the emendation to the first-person singular, and that one may exegete the consonantal text as it stands, it is

---

1   Sebastian Schmidt, I, 763.
2   Gerhard Lisowsky, *Konkordanz zum hebräischen Alten Testament, nach dem von Paul Kohle in der Biblia Hebraica edidit Rudolf Kittel besorgten Masoretischen Text* (Stuttgart: Württembergische Bibelanstalt, 1958) 704a.
3   Dahood, "Jer 18,14–15," 207.
4   Ibid.
5   GKC, sec. 165a.

better to stay with it.

One's uncertainty whether vv 15b–16 close the accusation speech or begin the declaration of judgment is matched by other uncertainties in the text (see below), so that it may well be that the poem is deliberately "fuzzy" on the details: did Jrm wish to suggest that it hardly matters whether the people's "tripping" in their ways is part of the current state of infidelity to Yahweh or part of the ultimate punishment of the people? The identification of the two is the implication of 2:17 and 19a. And the fact that the second line of v 15 may be translated "have sacrificed in vain" as well as "have sacrificed to Nullity" (see Interpretation) points in the same direction.

There are two other sources of uneasiness in vv 15b–16. One is the implication of the two infinitives, "to walk" (לָלֶכֶת, v 15b) and "to make" (לָשׂוּם, v 16). Are they parallel or not? Who is assumed to be the subject of these actions? Clearly it is the people who "walk," but is it the people who "make their land a desolation"? They make Yahweh's heritage loathsome in 2:7, but the closer parallels in 4:7 and 10:22 imply the agency of Yahweh. If one reads "I have tripped them" in v 15b, then it is possible that the agency of "make their land a desolation" here is also Yahweh; but if one stays with the consonantal text with "they have tripped them," and if the subject of that verb is "idols," then it is conceivable that "idols" becomes the agent of "make their land a desolation": in either of these cases the infinitives would be nonparallel. If one follows the consonantal text with "they have tripped them," then the second infinitive hovers between two agents, the people and the idols. The diction of 2:5 is perhaps a clue: there it is said that the people went after a "nothing" and thereby shared in "nothingness," and the implication that the people take on the characteristics of the idols they worship may lie in the background of the ambiguity in v 16a.

The other source of uneasiness is the nature of the "ways, tracks, paths" in v 15b. "Their ways" may either be the good ways prescribed by Yahweh or the bad ways in which the people walk in their infidelity. The diction of 6:16, "paths of old" (נְתִבוֹת עוֹלָם), stands in the background: that phrase denotes the paths laid out by Yahweh for covenantal obedience. In the present passage one has "their ways," an ambiguous expression, and שְׁבִילֵי עוֹלָם, which could well be translated "tracks of old" like 6:16 (so Bright). But עוֹלָם occurs also here in v 16, in

"endless hissing," a description of the terrible state into which the land is coming; this leads one to translate the phrase in v 15b as "endless tracks," part of the nightmare. "A way ungraded" is thus also part of the nightmare, and these parallels make attractive the emendation of the colon just preceding "to walk aimless paths" (see Text). "Their ways" are thus unfaithful ways (so Condamin) and the first colon of v 15b cannot mean, as *KJV* and Bright have it, "They have tripped them from their ways."

To sum up: if one is to trust the consonantal text of the verb in the first colon of v 15b, the action of Yahweh does not enter until v 17: it is there that the declaration of judgment is to be found. Verses 13–16 thus make up the accusation speech. It is curious that there is no rhetorical marker for the beginning of the declaration of judgment, so that Volz's suggestion that the word "therefore" at the beginning of v 13 is misplaced may be correct, but if so, then by the exegesis presented here the word (or the whole clause, "Therefore thus Yahweh has said") belongs at the beginning of v 17 and not at the beginning of v 15b, as Volz suggested. On the other hand, the diction of vv 15b–16, by the evidence of the consonantal text part of the accusation speech, is characteristic of declarations of judgment elsewhere, so that one can only conclude that there is a deliberate fuzzing of these two sections of the form. That conclusion is reinforced by other reasons for uneasiness in this passage. Thus who is responsible for the actions of vv 15b–16, if not Yahweh: the idols or the people?—as if there is no longer any clear-cut responsibility for the events of the day. The people have become like the idols they worship; the idols who are really inoperative (2:28) are suddenly busy destroying through their devotees, and behind it all stands Yahweh.

Structure
This passage is placed after the passage about the "potter" (vv 1–12) because of a secondary association with Isa 29:16–17: in the first of those verses "potter"

appears, and in the second "Lebanon."[6] (In the Isaiah sequence the two verses, which belong to separate oracles, are united by the verb "be regarded" [יֵחָשֵׁב], so that the collocation of "potter" and "Lebanon" there is fortuitous.) This explanation then suggests that the rubric at the beginning of v 13 does not relate to vv 1–12, whether it is present secondarily or not (see Preliminary Observations, Interpretation).

The poem is united by the association of "curse" (v 13), if that is a correct reconstruction, with "east wind" (v 17), both of which are prefixed by כְּ "such a," "as with," and by the association of "horrible thing" (שַׁעֲרוּרִת, v 13) and "desolation" (שַׁמָּה, v 16); for these associations see Interpretation.

One must assume that the poem breaks into two sections on the basis of the form-critical contrast between the accusation speech and the declaration of judgment. Where the break comes depends on one's understanding of the verb at the beginning of v 15b (see Preliminary Observations). Volz and Rudolph, who emend the verb, begin the declaration of judgment at v 15b, but if the consonantal text is trustworthy, as is here affirmed, then that second section will consist only of v 17. By this reading the accusation speech is by far the longer of the two sections; the accusation proper may be presumed to be in vv 15–16, and vv 13–14 are anticipatory rhetoric. Nevertheless the poem is held tightly together not only by the unifying associations of words (see above) but by the parallel between v 13b and v 15a ("virgin Israel," "my people," and the parallel predicates) and the movement from what is inconceivable in the natural world (v 14) to what is inconceivable and yet true between Israel and Yahweh (v 15a).

Within these sections the smaller parallelisms are clear: the double set of rhetorical questions in v 14, the pair of infinitive phrases in vv 15b–16a (though these may not be parallel: see Preliminary Observations), and the expected parallelisms within the bicola.

Form

For the general division of the passage into an accusation speech (vv 13–16) and a declaration of judgment (v 17) see both Preliminary Observations and Structure.

The inquiry among foreign peoples and the rhetorical question of precedents (v 13a) are found in 2:10–11, and the accusation against Israel is found in similar wording in 2:13. The rhetorical questions (expecting a no answer) in v 14, followed by the accusation that "my people have forgotten me" are found in the same pattern in 2:32. The infinitive phrases in vv 15b and 16a are closely comparable to the infinitive phrase in 10:22, but there the phrase is part of a judgment speech; that datum casts some doubt on the analysis of the present passage (see again Preliminary Observations).

Setting

The parallels of this passage are overwhelmingly with the diction of chapter 2 associated in the present study with the first scroll. Thus v 13a resembles 2:10–11, v 13b resembles 2:13, and vv 14–15a parallel 2:32. One may note that "my people have forgotten me" (v 15) is found not only in 2:32 but in 13:24–25, and that "I shall scatter them" (v 17) is likewise comparable to 13:24–27; 13:20–27 is assigned here to the period in 605 or soon thereafter (see Setting there). The present passage may tentatively be assigned to the same period, 605 or soon thereafter.

There are only two bits of evidence suggesting a later period: "back and not face" in v 17 resembles that phrase in 2:27, part of a passage here assigned to the second scroll; and there is a slim possibility that the mention of the "east wind" in v 17 (and the "snows of Lebanon" in v 14?) point to the time of the great drought, dated here to the autumn and winter of 601/600.

On balance, however, the evidence suggests a date early rather than late in the period 605–601.

Interpretation

■ 13 The rubric at the head of the passage, "Therefore thus Yahweh has said," appears twenty-six times in Jrm (for example, 5:14) but does not fit here: form-critically it introduces a declaration of judgment.[7] The rubric would fit without "therefore," and the "therefore" is commonly judged by commentators to be a secondary addition linking the passage with vv 1–12 (so Volz, Rudolph, Bright). But Volz suggests the word may have

---

6   Holladay, *Architecture,* 159.
7   Westermann, *Basic Forms,* 174–75.

strayed from the beginning of v 15b; the present study would have to say "may have strayed from the beginning of v 17" (see v 17, and see Preliminary Observations).

For the particle נָא with imperatives of inquiry compare 5:1; for inquiry among the nations compare 2:10–11. The plural כָּאֵלֶּה "like these" is peculiar; the word has no reference to a plural noun (contrast 5:9; 9:23), and one would expect כָּזֹאת for an indefinite reference (compare 2:10 once more). In four previous passages אָלָה "curse" has been proposed for אֵלֶּה "these" (2:34; 4:12; 5:25; 14:22). In one of those passages (4:12) the word is in the context of the desert wind, as it is here (v 17). The two expressions both use the preposition כְּ. But there is evidence from another direction. In 42:18 one finds the phrase וִהְיִיתֶם לְאָלָה וּלְשַׁמָּה "and you shall become a curse and a desolation," and in 44:12 the same phrase occurs with a third-person plural verb, and in still other passages there is diction linking לְשַׁמָּה "(for) a desolation" to לִשְׁרֵקָה "(for) a whistling/hissing" (19:8; 25:9, 18; 29:18): in short, there is a pattern in the prose linking "curse," "horror," and "whistling," and such prose patterns more than once reflect patterns in the poetry.[8] Given "desolation" (שַׁמָּה) and "hissing" (שְׁרִיקַת) in v 16, the proposal of "curse" becomes plausible. For כְּ "such" compare 38:4, כַּדְּבָרִים הָאֵלֶּה "such words as these." If אָלָה "curse" is linked to "east wind" in v 17, שַׁעֲרֻרִת "horrible thing" (v 13) is linked to שַׁמָּה "desolation" in v 16: compare the linking of שַׁמָּה "desolation" with שַׁעֲרוּרָה "horrible thing" in 5:30. If "ask among the nations" reminds one of 2:10–11, the second half-verse reminds one of 2:13.

■ 14 The M text of this verse is impossible (KJV!), and any reconstruction must proceed with care. Suggestions have been various, some quite ingenious, but except for that of Dahood they are far from the consonantal text. It is unnecessary to review all the proposals which have been made—they are available in the commentaries; but the present state of the question can be judged by the five textual proposals made by Rudolph in BHS. The recon-struction offered here assumes damage to only one consonant (I suggest reading עָרִים for זָרִים) and the omission of a final he; but in contrast to the proposal of Dahood, I propose nothing that is out of keeping with what we know of diction of the period of Jrm.

Commentators divide as to whether they see in v 14a a single clause or two. The traditional view is of one clause (so already V: "Shall the snow of Lebanon fail from the rock of the field?"), but because עזב qal "forsake" does not otherwise take the preposition מִן "from" (Rudolph), a whole array of emendations of either the verb or the nouns has been proposed. The other option is to see two clauses (Volz, Albright, Dahood): Volz translates, "Does soil disappear from rocks, snow from Lebanon?" assuming a second מִן "from" with "Lebanon" with G: but שָׂדַי hardly means "soil," and Rudolph is right, עזב "forsake" does not otherwise take "from." Albright therefore omits the מִן before (his emended) צוּר, and Dahood takes it as a mem-enclitic with the verb. In the meantime Albright correctly saw in צור the word צוּר "flint." But מִן is not a problem if the verb is vocalized as a nip'al, as the parallel verb is in v 14b: עזב nip'al is accompanied by מִן in Lev 26:43 in the meaning "be forsaken by." The first half-verse then reads, "Is a field forsaken by flints, Lebanon by snow?" The מִן thus does double duty (compare Interpretation on 3:23).[9] For שָׂדַי see 4:17.

There are fields of flint in Transjordan,[10] but the parallelism with the snow in Lebanon suggests that Mount Hermon, and the flint fields nearby, are the basis of the comparison. Actually snow does leave Mount Hermon in June,[11] as it does the highest mountain in Lebanon, Qurnat as-Sawdā', in late August,[12] but these peaks are indeed snow-capped for a greater part of the year. As for flint, there are fields of it southwest of the present-day town of rāšayyā, just west of Mount Hermon, and evidence there too of Stone Age flint industry.[13]

Given the analysis presented here for two clauses in v 14a, one must assume two parallel clauses in v 14b. The material is more difficult to sort out. Given M מַיִם

---

8   Holladay, "Prototype"; on this particular association of words see Weippert, Prosareden, 187–91.
9   See further Dahood, Psalms III, 437.
10   Baly, Geography, 31.
11   Robert Boulanger, The Middle East (Paris: Hachette, 1966) 253.
12   Ibid., 203.
13   My family and I have collected many hand axes and partially flaked flints there.

"water," the verb יִנָּתְשׁוּ "are uprooted" is out of place, and Johannes Cocceius in the seventeenth century (so Duhm) and Michaelis in the eighteenth proposed reading יִנָּשְׁתוּ "are dried up," a proposal which has won such universal acceptance that KB lists the verb here under נשת "with metathesis"[14] (though *HALAT* offers it simply as a conjecture). Dahood, on the other hand, suggests a derivation from נשה "forget" with a *t*-infix, given שכח "forget" in v 15a. It is true, there is evidence of verbs with *t*-infix in northwest Semitic,[15] but to my mind this in an unnecessary suggestion.

Given the preposition מִן in the first colon, it would be plausible to read the second word in the third colon as a parallel word with מִן, thus מַיִם (יָם "sea"); Cornill so understood the word, though the rest of his reconstruction is different. But there are two considerations against this reading. First, נוֹזְלִים "streams, floods," the last word in the verse, which (I submit) is correct there, is in parallelism with מַיִם "waters" and תְּהֹמֹת "deeps" in Exod 15:8. Second, I shall propose to read the mem just before נוֹזְלִים as the preposition מִן; the symmetries of poetry suggest that if מִן is correct for the first and the eighth nouns in the sequence, then one must understand a double-duty מִן with נוֹזְלִים which governs מַיִם as well.

The verb in the third colon is nip'al, as I have proposed for the verb in the first colon; one can then assume the normal meaning of this verb: "Or are . . . uprooted by the waters?" a rhetorical question standing in parallelism with the question in the first colon.

The noun זָרִים would then be wrong; "Or are strangers uprooted by the waters?" will not do, nor any revocalization of the word. It is likely that this sequence has been influenced by מַיִם זָרִים "strange waters" in 2 Kgs 19:24 (and the parallel in Isa 37:25?). The fact that עָרִים "cities" is the object of נתש qal in Ps 9:7 may be the needed clue: there it is affirmed that Yahweh uproots cities. (One may note further that the nip'al of the same verb, with Jerusalem as subject, occurs in Jer 31:40: "Jerusalem shall not be uprooted.") "Cities," then, by the present reconstruction, are not uprooted by the waters —only Yahweh does this; the primeval waters have been put in their place by Yahweh (5:22 and often).

The fourth colon, the last two words, are equally

impossible: נוֹזְלִים "streams, floods" is acceptable (see above, on the parallelism of this word with מַיִם "waters"), but if קָרִים is an adjective "cold" (so the usual understanding), the words are in the wrong order. If, however, the suggestion of עָרִים in the third colon is correct, then one may see קִרְיָה "city" in the first word, and the preposition מִן once more in the last consonant of that word. The noun קִרְיָה is often used for Jerusalem (for example, Isa 1:21, 26), and (if this is the right solution) the capital city is doubtless referred to here (as also in Lam 2:11); in this case עָרִים "cities," the suggestion in the third colon, would refer to the cities of Judah (compare the references in 2:28 as reconstructed). By this suggestion, then, the two pairs of nouns in v 14b are chiastically arranged: "Or are cities uprooted by the waters, the capital by floods?"

As already indicated, the "waters" and "floods" are references to the myth of combat with the sea.[16]

By this reading "uproot" is correct after all. Verse 14, then, is not about abandoning and forgetting but about events that never happen. The rhetorical questions and the verb form of the verse, with הֲ, אִם, and the כִּי with which v 15 begins, are completely comparable to Amos 6:12, in which likewise rhetorical questions are posed about events that never happen; and one thinks also of Jer 2:32, which likewise offers rhetorical questions about events that never happen.

■ 15 From the tone of the rhetorical questions in v 14 one would think that the people could never forget Yahweh, but they have; the diction is particularly close to 2:32, where "my people have forgotten me" is likewise preceded (as already noted) by a pair of rhetorical questions; but for "forgetting Yahweh" compare also 3:21 and 13:25.

The second colon is ambiguous; it can be taken as "have sacrificed in vain" (so *G, V, T*: compare the expression in 2:30; 4:30; 6:29), but לַשָּׁוְא, literally "to vanity," may better be understood as an expression for "to Baal," which appears with the same verb "sacrifice" (קטר pi'el) in 7:9; 11:13, 17: for this verb see 1:16. For the euphemism compare "a nothing" (הֶבֶל) in 2:5, "lie" (שֶׁקֶר) in 5:31 and 13:25, and "shame" (בֹּשֶׁת) in 3:24 and 11:13.

For the vocalization of the verb "so that they have

---

14   KB, 641a.
15   Dahood, "Jer 18,14–15," 207, note b.
16   See for example, Brevard S. Childs, "A Traditio-

Historical Study of the Reed Sea Tradition," *VT* 20 (1970) 412–13.

tripped them" (וַיַּכְשִׁלוּם) see Preliminary Observations. If the text is correct, this is the only occurrence of this verb in the hip'il stem in Jer; for the qal and nip'al stems of the verb see 6:15, 21. It is implied that the idols make the people trip in their ways; see again Preliminary Observations.

The four cola of v 15b each contain a word for "path"; in Preliminary Observations it was established that all these references are to bad paths: though the designation עוֹלָם was positive in 6:16 ("paths of old"), that word occurs here not only with "tracks" in this verse but with "hissing" in v 16, so it must here be translated "endless" with a negative connotation. The word "tracks" (שְׁבִילֵי) is known otherwise only in Ps 77:20, but there its meaning "paths, tracks" is well established, so that there is no reason to find a fresh meaning in the present passage (as Dahood does, reading the MS. variant שְׁבוּלֵי and proposing "nomads"). The last colon of the verse offers another pejorative description of a path, לֹא סְלוּלָה, a road "not built up, not constructed," as a well-traveled road would be. Thus the third, fourth, and sixth cola of the verse contain elements indicating a destructive situation: "trip them," "endless," "not built up." This leaves the fifth colon, which in the present text reads "to walk paths" (לָלֶכֶת נְתִיבוֹת). In Judg 5:6 the phrase הֹלְכֵי נְתִיבוֹת means simply "travelers"; the phrase in the present passage is surely incomplete. The solution of Naegelsbach and Giesebrecht is to construe נְתִיבוֹת as construct, thus "to walk paths of a way ungraded," which is not impossible, but דֶּרֶךְ as the genitive of such a phrase would seem an odd choice of words. Rudolph has made the happy suggestion that "formlessness" (תֹּהוּ) has dropped out by haplography after נְתִיבוֹת, and that suggestion is adopted here. Given the assonance of שְׁבִילֵי and סְלוּלָה, and the repetition of עוֹלָם and דֶּרֶךְ, this addition would give good assonance and good sense. But it is more than an arbitrary guess. In Deut 32:10 תֹּהוּ is in parallelism with אֶרֶץ מִדְבָּר "desert land," the region which is here implied by such paths; and in Isa 59:4 תֹּהוּ is in parallelism with שָׁוְא "emptiness," a word occurring here in v 15a.[17] There are two other associations of תֹּהוּ which are relevant here: in 1 Sam 12:21 the word is used for idols "which do not profit" (לֹא־יוֹעִילוּ), the same

description given to the Baals in Jer 2:8 (the implication here of שָׁוְא, it is proposed); and תֹּהוּ is associated with "the sea" in Job 26:7, 12. It may be noted further that תֹּהוּ is elsewhere part of Jrm's vocabulary (4:23).

It appears then that the phrase of נְתִיבוֹת עוֹלָם "paths of old" (6:16), a description of the ways laid out by Yahweh for covenant obedience, assumed by Bright to be relevant for the present passage, is a false one (compare Preliminary Observations), unless it is in ironic contrast to that phrase. All these synonyms are those of endless walking without pattern or goal—the endlessness of walking is indicated by the repetition of parallels, and this repetition is reminiscent of the repeated parallels in the nightmare description of the desert in 2:6.

■ 16 For "to make their land a desolation" see 4:7.

The second and fourth cola of this verse offer two parallel human responses to the desolation of the land, though it is not clear whether the response is one of contempt or of a superstitious effort to ward off the demons of destruction.

The precise vocalization of the noun translated "hissing" is uncertain, since both שְׁרֵיקָה and שְׁרִיקָה are attested, but the root is not in doubt. Again the precise sound is uncertain: both "whistling" and "hissing" are proposed for the word, and both G σύριγμα and V sibilus, the renderings here, may be used for either "piping, whistling" or the "hissing" of a snake. The matter is complicated by the fact that some cultures do not "whistle" tunes or signals (that is, with pursed lips) but "hiss" them (that is, by a particular shape of tongue). The word is used for signaling in Isa 5:26; 7:18; in the present passage, as already noted, the action may be either one of contempt or an effort to ward off demons.[18] The action is referred to elsewhere (Lam 2:15–16), and the phraseology here is imitated in Deuteronomistic passages (1 Kgs 9:8). The reference here is of course to the land as an object of or occasion for hissing.

The nonconsecutive וְ in the verb of the last colon indicates that the verbs of both the third and fourth cola are final clauses expressing result;[19] whether the two clauses are subordinate to the infinitive in the first colon, or coordinate with it, scarcely matters. The verb יָשֹׁם "is

17   Compare the description of these two words as synonyms in Pedersen, I/II, 413.

18   For the latter possibility see Richard Lasch, "Das

Pfeifen und seine Beziehung zu Dämonenglauben und Zauberei," ARW 18 (1915) 589–92.

19   GKC, sec. 165a; Joüon, Gramm., sec. 116e.

horrified" is cognate with שַׁמָּה "desolation" in the first colon, and the two make a fine assonantal sequence with לְשׁוּם "to make." For the meaning of the verb שׁמם see 2:12.

The qal of נוד appears in 15:5 (which see); here the verb is hipʿil (transitive), "shake the head." The same context (with the parallel "hissing") appears in Lam 2:15 with the hipʿil of נוע, so that one may conclude that both verbs indicate the same action, an oscillation of the head; though what the precise gesture is here, and precisely what emotional tone it indicates (contempt, horror, dread) is to some degree uncertain.

■ 17 Many MSS. read בְרוּחַ "with the (east) wind" here, and this is a plausible reading (compare 13:24, with לְ); but if there is a subtle parallel with (the reconstructed) אָלָה "curse" in v 13, which is introduced by כְּ (see Structure), then כְּ (as perhaps the *lectio difficilior*) is preferable. The noun קָדִים, either alone or with רוּחַ, means "east wind," that is, the scorching sirocco (רוּחַ צַח "scorching wind," 4:11; רוּחַ מִדְבָּר "desert wind," 13:24). For אֲפִיצֵם "I shall scatter them" see 13:24. The expression לִפְנֵי "before" with "the enemy" is literally "to the face of," so that there is a nice play with "my back and not my face I shall show them" in the next colon. That colon is Yahweh's answer to the stance of the people in 2:27, "they have turned their back to me and not their face"; see the discussion there. The noun אֵיד appears

four times in chapters 46—49, but this is the only other occurrence in the book; it refers to both national and personal calamity. For the phraseology compare "day of trouble" (יוֹם צָרָה), 16:19; "day of disaster" (יוֹם רָעָה), 17:17; "time of trouble" (עֵת צָרָה), 14:8; and "time of disaster" (עֵת רָעָה), 2:28; 11:12, 14; 15:11.

Aim

Jrm perceives Yahweh as never being able altogether to believe that Israel would forget him: it is inconceivable, yet it is true. The punishment will fit the crime, and Israel is condemned to endless walking away from her land, the land a ruin; the people will be face to face with the enemy and will find Yahweh walking off. There are many passages like this in Jer, and many passages like it elsewhere in the OT, but few with the sense of scope of this one: high, distant Lebanon; the cosmic sea; desert paths stretching off without aim or end. The rescue from Egypt had been described in cosmic terms (Exod 15:4–10); it was Jrm's task to use cosmic terms in depicting the disobedience and consequent demise of the people.

**Jeremiah Looks for the People's
Doom As a Sign
of the Word from Yahweh**

Bibliography

Hubmann, Franz D.
"Jer 18,18–23 im Zusammenhang der Konfessionen," *Le Livre de Jérémie, Le prophète et son milieu, les oracles et leur transmission* (ed. Pierre-Maurice Bogaert; BETL 54; Leuven: Leuven University, 1981) 271–96.

18

18 And they said, "Come, let us make plans
against Jeremiah, for the law will not fail
from the priest, nor counsel from the
wise man, nor the word from the
prophet; come, let us strike him down
⟨with his tongue,⟩[a] let us [not][b] pay
attention to all his words."

19 Pay attention, Yahweh, to me,
 and listen to the voice of my adversaries:
  "Is evil a recompense for good?"—
  yes, they have dug a pit for my life.
 Remember my standing before you
  to speak good regarding them,
   to turn back your wrath from them.

21 In this circumstance give their children to
famine,
 and deliver them into the hands of the
  sword;
 let their wives become childless and
  widowed,
  their husbands slain by pestilence,
   and their youths struck down by
   sword in battle.

22 Let a cry be heard from their houses,
 when you suddenly bring troops upon
  them!—
 yes, they have dug a plot[a] to catch me,
 and snares they have laid for my feet.

23 But you, Yahweh, know:
 all[a] their plans are against me for
  death;
 do not cover their iniquity,
  and their sin do not [b] blot out[b] from your
  presence;
   《may》[d] 《their offense》[c] 《be》[d]
   before you,
    at the time of your anger take action
    on them.

Text

18a Reading with *S* בִּלְשׁוֹנוֹ for *M* בְּלָשׁוֹן "with the tongue" (so Volz, Rudolph). The word is followed in *M* by וְ "and," which may be the remains of the suffix (though *S* has "and" as well). Otherwise the suffix was lost by haplography. See Interpretation.

b Omit *M* אַל with *G* (so Duhm, Giesebrecht, Cornill, Volz, Rudolph); for another secondary אַל see 5:10. For the superiority of the *G* reading see Interpretation.

22a It is difficult to be sure of the identity and meaning of this noun. The qere' and many MSS. read שׁוּחָה "pit" identically with the noun in the second colon of v 20; the ketib is שִׁיחה or שִׂיחה, a word which can be vocalized as שִׁיחָה with an identical meaning, a form appearing in Pss 57:7 and 119:85. But a purely assonantal variation carries little poetic effect. *G* for both v 20 and here read "word(s)" (v 20: ῥήματα; here λόγον), suggesting that *G* read both words as שִׂיחָה "concern, occupation of thought" (Ps 119:97, 99; Job 15:4), and the ketib suggests the presence of that word in this passage. Jrm is dealing in the two cola with both the idea of a physical trap ("snare" in the following colon) and verbal plots ("voice of my opponents," v 19; "counsel against me for death," v 23), and such a pun on "pit" would explain the seeming repetition of phraseology in v 20 and here. Compare 17:6 and 8 for a similar confusion of tradition regarding a pun, and see further Interpretation.

23a Verse 23aα must be divided into two cola, since five "units" (roughly, words) is the maximum for a colon (O'Connor, *Structure*, 138). Delete אֶת־, the *nota accusativa*, before "all."

b—b The form תֶּמְחִי (מחה hip'il) is strange for a second-person singular masculine (see GKC, sec. 75ii), and תֶּמַח may have been intended.

c Reading with *G* מִכְשֹׁלָם (Rudolph).

d If one reads a singular subject (see note c), then both *M* readings are irrelevant (ketib וְהָיוּ, qere' וְיִהְיוּ), since both are plural. Read יְהִי with *G* (Rudolph).

Preliminary Observations

In spite of the relatively sound text of this passage, there are two questions that affect its total meaning. (1) Is v 18 original to the passage, or was it attached later to vv 19–23 on the basis of the catchword association of קשׁב hip'il "pay attention" (v 18, 19)? And in either case have we established a sound text?—the choice for or against *M* in the two contested expressions of the verse (see Text) has consequences for one's understanding of the movement of thought. (2) The prayer for "their" destruction in vv 21–22a moves beyond the diction of the rest of the passage and of the rest of Jrm's confessions. If one assumes, as all commentators have, that the reference in these lines is to Jrm's opponents, then the words of that section seem excessive alongside simpler prayers that Yahweh exert retribution on the prophet's opponents (11:20 = 20:12), that he pull them out like sheep for slaughter (12:3), that he bring upon them the day of evil (17:16). Thus after the overwhelming prayer for destruction here, what could "do not forgive their iniquity" (v 23) mean? And one could see a reference to the opponents' children and wives, but what would their "husbands" mean, or their "youths"? No wonder Duhm and Cornill concluded that vv 21–23 are a secondary addition. More recent commentators have backed away from this extreme position and have explained the excessive language of the section as Jrm's giving way to human weakness, but in so doing they have not dealt carefully with the inconsistencies mentioned here.

The crucial clue for a solution of the second question, as pointed out by Hubmann,[1] is to understand the first colon of v 20 as a quotation of Jrm's opponents: this is, after all, what *M* implies by the second colon of v 19. Current critical opinion has not followed this direction because Giesebrecht, Volz, and Rudolph have followed *G* in the second colon of v 19 and read רִיבִי "my (legal) case" instead of יְרִיבָי "my opponents." But in another of the occurrences of יָרִיב (Isa 49:25) *G* has likewise read רִיב; only in the remaining occurrence of the word (Ps 35:1) has *G* rightly understood it. There is no reason to doubt *M* here.

It must be admitted that all the rhetorical cues lead the hearer to assume that the question in v 20 is raised by Jrm rather than by his opponents. Thus the phraseology of רָעָה תַּחַת תוֹבָה "evil instead of good" with שׁלם "repay" is found in Pss 35:12 and 38:21 as part of the complaint of the psalmist regarding his enemies; and the fourth colon of v 20, in which Jrm refers to the "good" which he has tried to do for his opponents, reinforces that assumption. But the diction is playing tricks on the hearer, and Jrm here is deliberately taking the old phrase and putting it to new use in the mouths of his opponents (see below, and see further Interpretation on v 20).

If the colon in v 20 is a question posed by Jrm's enemies, then the question is whether "evil" (רָעָה, specifically national disaster) is to be a recompense for the "good" which they perceive themselves to have done. What they challenge is whether Jrm's word that disaster is inevitable is a valid word. One is led then to the conclusion to which we have arrived in the confessions already dealt with, that is that Jrm's opponents were the optimistic prophets (see 12:1 and 15:17, and further 4:10; 5:12).

We return now to vv 21–22a. These verses have their closest parallel in 6:11aβ–12, where Yahweh instructs Jrm to pour out the divine wrath on all the population groups; that passage is part of material added in the second scroll, the purpose of which is to proclaim that doom is sure. The words of vv 21–22a then refer to the whole population, not simply to Jrm's opponents: one notes the same categories ("children," "wives," "husbands," "youths," houses") here as in 6:11–12. Jrm is then not asking for revenge on his opponents but rather asking Yahweh to finish off in deed what he has assured his prophet in words was to take place, so that Jrm's prophetic word would be validated. Verses 21–22a then refer to the time of the second scroll, and v 20b refers to the time of the first scroll, when Jrm was still attempting to warn people to change their ways so that the disaster might be averted. One must therefore conclude that the third-person plural reference shifts from Jrm's opponents to the general population in v 20b (for a similar shift see 5:14).

The passage thus depends for its effect on shifts of reference that are puzzling to the modern reader; but the shift in v 20 from "the people think they do good to

1   Franz D. Hubmann, "Jer 18,18–23 in Zusammenhang der Konfessionen," *Le Livre de Jérémie, Le prophète et son milieu, les oracles et leur transmission* (ed.   Pierre-Maurice Bogaert; BETL 54; Leuven: Leuven University, 1981) 284.

Yahweh" to "I do good to the people" parallels the shift from "my opponents pay attention to me" to "Yahweh, you pay attention to me" (vv 18–19) in a completely symmetrical fashion, and this circumstance suggests in turn that v 18 is not associated secondarily with vv 19–23 but was integrated with it from the beginning, and that *G* is correct in v 18: the "not" is secondary (see Text). Thus the first basic question of the passage may be resolved.

Structure

These verses form one of the confessions of Jrm and as such were part of the basic stratum of the material of chapters 11—20. But it should be noted that if the setting offered here for the passage is correct (late in 601 or early in 600), and that offered for 17:14–18 is correct (594), the confession in chapter 17 took shape at a later date than the present one, and therefore the order of the confessions in these chapters is not chronological but was based on considerations that are now obscure.

The question whether v 18 belongs with vv 19–23 has been answered in the affirmative (see Preliminary Observations).

Though v 18 is displayed as prose, it offers symmetry: the quotation opens and closes with לְכוּ "come" and with cohortatives ("let us make plans," "let us strike him down," "let us pay attention") and enclosing the threefold parallelism of priest, wise man, and prophet.

Verses 19–23 have a central section (vv 20b–22a) referring to the people in general, a prayer for the fulfillment of the words of judgment on the nation (see Preliminary Observations). This central section consists of a tricolon, a bicolon, a tricolon, and a bicolon, ten cola in all. It is held together by the two occurrences of עֲלֵיהֶם "regarding/upon them" in vv 20 and 22. The first half has singular imperatives ("remember," "give," "deliver") and the second has jussives ("let their wives become . . . ," etc.). The population groups appear to be arranged chiastically ("children," "wives," "husbands," "youths") in comparison to the order in 6:11; these terms appear in the central bicolon and tricolon of the section. The term "houses" in v 22 stands apart from the population groups and formally balances the first tricolon in v 20.

This central section is surrounded by four cola in vv 19–20a and eight in vv 22b–23. The last four cola of v 23 are best analyzed as a tetracolon: the first three cola are closely parallel. Similarly vv 19–20a are best taken as

a tetracolon, since the first three cola interlock ("pay attention," "listen"; "voice of my opponents"; and the quotation, on which see Preliminary Observations). At the same time "for they have dug a pit for my life," which closes off the introductory section, parallels "for they have dug a plot to catch me," which begins the closing section.

It is to be noted that vv 19–23 open with a vocative "Yahweh" and with "pay attention" (קשׁב hip'il, v 19) and close with a vocative "Yahweh" and "counsel" (עֵצָה, v 23): both "pay attention" and "counsel" occur in v 18.

Form

Verse 18 is the citation of the words of Jrm's opponents, first a general summons, "Come, let us make plans against Jeremiah," followed by the כִּי clause of motivation, and closing with the more specific summons, "Come, let us strike him down." For a parallel for such a summons compare Gen 37:20.

Verses 19–23 embody Jrm's word to Yahweh, a confession which as such takes the form of a personal lament. The invocation and plea in v 19 is similar to some in the Psalms (Pss 5:3; 17:1; 55:3; 61:2; 142:7); for "listen to the voice [קוֹל] of my opponents" compare Ps 74:23, "do not forget the clamor [קוֹל] of your foes."

In Preliminary Observations it is proposed that the first colon of v 20 is to be understood as a quotation of Jrm's opponents, part of his description of his predicament, and as such is comparable to such quotations in the Psalms (Ps 42:4, 11). The description of the trap set by the enemy is a convention of laments (Pss 57:7; 140:6; 142:4). Verse 20b is essentially a plea of innocence like 15:17 and 17:16; it is a reminder to Yahweh of Jrm's earlier efforts on behalf of the people and is thus comparable to Neh 13:14, 22.

Verses 21–22a are not a prayer for the punishment of Jrm's opponents, as commentators have assumed, but a prayer that Yahweh carry out on the whole population the word of disaster which he has vouchsafed to Jrm (see Preliminary Observations), a plea, in short, that Yahweh keep his promise (compare Ps 119:49); the prayer is thus a curse form.[2] Verse 22b resumes the complaint of v 20 that his opponents have set a trap for him.

Verse 23a by its vocative to Yahweh reaffirms faith in him; for confidence in Yahweh's knowledge of his predicament compare Ps 69:20. The passage ends with a prayer that Yahweh not forgive Jrm's opponents, a striking expression (compare Neh 3:37), but such a prayer is parallel to the plea to "listen to the voice of my opponents" in v 19. Similar wording is found in Ps 74:23 and Neh 13:29.

Setting

The considerations in Preliminary Observations suggest that the passage has its setting in the period after the king burned Jrm's first scroll (December 601). In v 20b Yahweh is asked to "remember" the period before the king burned the scroll, when Jrm assumed Yahweh still hoped for repentance. In vv 21–22a Jrm asks Yahweh to validate by action the prediction of inevitable disaster for the people. If the close likeness between vv 21–22a and 6:11–12 suggests the same date, then a time at the end of 601 or early in 600 is appropriate. This conclusion is reinforced by likenesses of phraseology in this passage to phraseology in 14:1—15:9, dated to the same period. Thus the parallel of "famine" and "sword," with or without "pestilence," in v 21 is reminiscent of that parallelism in 14:12, 13, 15, 16, 18; 15:2; the expressions "childless" and "widowed" in v 21 find parallels in 15:5–8; and the imperative עֲשֵׂה to Yahweh, "act, take action" in v 23 is also found in 14:7.

Interpretation

■ **18** Here is the voice of Jrm's enemies. For "make plans" = "plot" see 11:19. They plot against him because they are complacently convinced that life will continue to go on as before, and that the religious leadership will continue to function rightly. The expected pairing of "priest" and "prophet" (2:8; 5:30; and often) is enlarged by a third, the "wise man" (8:8–9; in that passage, however, the "wise" are associated with "the law"). For the association of "law" with "priest" see 2:8. It is not clear what group is here referred to by "wise man"; R. B. Y. Scott suggests that Jrm may be referring simply to royal councilors who offer political advice.[3] But one has a similar triad in Ezek 7:26: "(In vain) they seek a vision-oracle [חָזוֹן] from the prophet, but law [תּוֹרָה] fails from the priest, and counsel [עֵצָה] from the elders," so that it is clear that more than prudential advice is referred to in our passage: "Wisdom was considered to be a source of divine authority alongside the other two."[4]

The M reading "let us strike him down with the tongue" suggests "slander him" (so T); but it is clear that Jrm's enemies intend to kill him (v 23), and that one of their means to that end is the use of Jrm's own words against him, so the S reading "with his tongue" is to be preferred. It is ironic that elsewhere Jrm concluded that the people were not able to pay attention to him (6:10), but here some of the people are urging each other to pay attention to him in order to do away with him.

The conclusion given in Preliminary Observations is that this verse is integral to vv 19–23; and since in that discussion it was determined that Jrm's opponents are the optimistic prophets, one must conclude that "they" here are that group, who continue to speak of Yahweh's care for the people and thus wish to do away with Jrm by the weapon of his own words.

■ **19** The word יָרִיב "adversary" occurs in the OT only otherwise in Isa 49:25 and Ps 35:1, but there is no warrant to follow G here (see Preliminary Observations); in Ps 35:1 it has the same form as here (יְרִיבַי) and is there parallel with לֹחֲמַי, a reading proposed for 11:19 (see there). Question: Might there be a double meaning here of קוֹל, not only "voice" but "levity, abuse"?—the word occurs in 3:9 and is related to the verb קלל "abuse, make light of" which occurs in 15:10, part of a confession: "All of them [my opponents] abuse me." It is possible. It is noteworthy that a variation of the formula "evil for good" (v 20) is found in 2 Sam 16:12, טוֹבָה תַּחַת קְלָלָה "good for curse."

■ **20** The formula "repay evil for good" is found (with the verb used here, שׁלם hip'il/hop'al) in Gen 44:4; Pss 35:12; and 38:21; and with synonymous verbs in 1 Sam 25:21 and Prov 17:13 (שׁוב hip'il) and Ps 109:5 (שׂים). In all these passages the subject of "repay" is a human being: in the Psalms passages it is the psalmist speaking of his enemies who have repaid him evil for good, in Gen 44:4

---

2   Hillers, *Treaty-Curses*.
3   R. B. Y. Scott, "Priesthood, Prophecy, Wisdom, and the Knowledge of God," *JBL* 80 (1961) 3.
4   Ibid., 1–15; von Rad, *Wisdom*, 21.

it is Joseph speaking of what his brothers had done to him, in 1 Sam 25:21 it is David speaking of what Nabal had done to him, and in Prov 17:13 it is a general statement about someone who repays evil for good. Only in 2 Sam 16:12 (referred to at the end of the remarks on v 19) is it hoped that Yahweh will repay with good the "curse" of Shimei. The phraseological parallels are all such as would lead the hearer to assume that Jrm asks Yahweh why his opponents should return evil for the good he, Jrm, had done them; most particularly the form-critical parallels in the Psalms encourage this understanding (see Form). Nevertheless taking the question as a quotation of Jrm's opponents (see Preliminary Observations) takes at face value the wording of v 19b and solves the problem of the seeming harshness of vv 21–22a. In this instance the "evil" (רָעָה) is not that which the opponents inflict on Jrm but the "disaster" that Yahweh has revealed to Jrm he will inflict upon the people. The word occurs repeatedly in this meaning in Jer; one notes it particularly in the context of the optimistic prophets, 5:12 and 23:17 (compare 4:10). Similarly the "good" (טוֹבָה) is not the good that Jrm has done on behalf of the people (contrast the meaning of that word in the fourth colon), but rather the good that the optimistic prophets assume the people have done to fulfill their obligation to Yahweh (compare דֶּרֶךְ הַטּוֹב, 6:16; for טוֹבָה in this usage see Neh 2:18b). The "good" which the people had done is doubtless a reference to the fulfillment of the Deuteronomic prescriptions under Josiah (compare אָז טוֹב "then it was well," 22:16), though there is no way to be sure.

Giesebrecht and Rudolph omit "for they have dug a pit for my life," assuming that it is dittographic from v 22; and in doing so they produce four cola in v 20. There is no reason, however, to excise the colon: it here ends with "for my life," and in v 22 "to catch me," and structural analysis indicates that the two cola bracket the prayer that Yahweh destroy the people (see Preliminary Observations, Structure). But I propose that two different objects occur in the respective cola, "pit" here and "plot" in v 22 (see Text, and see Interpretation on v 23).

Jrm's opponents are trying to entrap him; the כִּי that introduces the second colon may not mean so much "for"

as be a particle of asseveration. The entrapment expressed here is consonant with the expressions in v 18 and the mocking doubt the opponents express regarding Jrm's testimony which is implied in the question cited in the first colon. The word שׁוּחָה "pit" occurs in 2:6 as a description of the wilderness; though it may appear again in the parallel colon in v 22, it is proposed there that another word is there instead. A similar phrase to that found here, with the variant שִׁיחָה "pit" but the same verb, is found in a lament in the Psalms (Ps 57:7).

The use of the imperative "remember" with Yahweh is reminiscent of 15:15; for "stand before Yahweh" see 15:19. The last two cola clearly refer to Jrm's activity in interceding for the people before Yahweh (compare 7:16; 11:14; 14:11; 15:1), an activity which he undertook as part of his task in the period covered by the first scroll (see Setting). Jrm's "standing before Yahweh" is thus part of that intercessory activity as well, as 15:19 indicates (the phrase there is parallel with "be Yahweh's mouth"). Thus the reference of the third-person plural pronouns here has shifted in the last three cola of the verse from Jrm's opponents to the people in general (see Preliminary Observations).

■ **21–22a** The phrases here are similar to those found in 6:11–12 (see Setting), but whereas there they are part of Yahweh's statement of divine judgment, here they are part of Jrm's plea to Yahweh. The contrast between the reminiscence of the period of hope in v 20b and the present period, in which Jrm perceives hope to have vanished, makes the translation "therefore" for לָכֵן inappropriate. Pedersen points out that this conjunction is often best translated "under these circumstances."[5] The same function of לָכֵן is found in 30:16, where an oracle of judgment is transformed by fresh material offering hope.

The particular type of death reserved for each portion of the population is not to be taken literally: it is a way of saying "everyone will die from a variety of causes" (compare 6:11–12; 15:2). For the linking of "famine" and "sword" see 14:13–16, 18 (compare Setting). The phrase נגר hip'il + עַל־יְדֵי חֶרֶב is puzzling; it appears only otherwise in Ezek 35:5 and Ps 63:11, and one may surmise that Jrm here is referring specifically to

---

5   Pedersen, I/II, 116–17.

the idiom in Ps 63:11. The verb in the hipʿil means "pour down" (Ps 75:9) or "hurl down" (Mic 1:6) in its other occurrences, and the hopʿal in Mic 1:4 means "be poured down," but "pour them onto the hands of the sword" is opaque. Dahood's suggestion, "smite them with the edges of the sword,"[6] is unsatisfactory: there is no evidence that "hands" of the sword means "edges," and his analysis of the verb is unconvincing. I suggest with some hesitation that the phrase in Ps 63:11 may have arisen as a conscious variant of the idiom מָלֵא piʿel + יַד or יְדֵי "fill the hand(s) of," meaning "consecrate," usually with reference to a priest but once with reference to an altar (Ezek 43:26). "Pour (the enemy) onto the hands of the sword" would then be a way of saying "consecrate the sword for battle." One notes that Jrm played elsewhere with the idiom "fill the hands of" (5:31, by the suggestion offered there), and that קדש "consecrate" is parallel with נתן "give = appoint" in 1:5. Whether the suggestion has merit or not, the metaphor has faded; the traditional translation "deliver them" is sufficiently close in parallelism to the first colon to be satisfactory, and the translation "hands of," whether it means "power of" or not, is a reminder that a metaphorical expression lies behind the line.

For שַׁכֻּלוֹת "childless" compare the root שכל piʿel in the same context in 15:7, and for אַלְמָנוֹת "widows = widowed" see 15:8. The "periphrastic" verbal expression יִהְיוּ הֲרֻגֵי מָוֶת is awkward to translate; both the nipʿal and qal passive of this verb occur in the OT (once each), but the qal passive participle also occurs (seven times before this instance in various forms), and the parallelism here encourages such an expression—"become slain" is a close approximation. For מָוֶת "death = pestilence" see 15:2. The repetition of "sword" within the verse is curious, but the meaning is obviously that the children are to die by violence, and the "youths," that is, young men of an age for soldiering, are to die in battle.

The noun זְעָקָה "cry" is related to the verb זעק (11:11, 12: see Setting and Interpretation there); it is a cry of distress, a cry for help. The mention of "houses" seems unexpected, but the same association of thought occurs in 6:11–12. The noun גְּדוּד "troops" occurs only here in Jer; the word means a "raiding party" or "contingent of

troops." The adverb פִּתְאֹם "suddenly" is characteristic of Jrm's description of battle disaster; compare 4:20; 6:26; and 15:8, all of which evidently come from the same period.

■ **22b** The last half of the verse reverts to the diction of v 20a (see there, and see Preliminary Observations and Structure). The כִּי is again evidently a particle of asseveration, as it is in v 20. One may guess that Jrm offers word-play between the objects in the cola parallel in v 20 and here and that instead of the identical word שׁוּחָה which the qereʾ preserves here a similar word is to be found, but one is left uncertain precisely what that word is. There are two semantic fields involved here, that of plots, trapping, and killing, and that of words as weapons. These two fields are adumbrated in v 18 ("let us strike him down with his tongue") and are clearly evident in vv 19–20a, where we find "voice of my opponents" and "they have dug a pit for my life." But the translation "word(s)" in G in both the colon in v 20 and here (see Text) suggests that the tradition was aware of that second semantic field in these lines, and the phraseology of Prov 16:27, אִישׁ בְּלִיַּעַל כֹּרֶה רָעָה, literally "a worthless man digs evil," that is, digs a pit = plots mischief, suggests that the combination of these two semantic fields is an old one. Given then the variation from the colon in v 20 in the ketib of the present passage, שׁיחה or שׂיחה, one may propose שִׂיחָה as the most economical solution. This noun occurs three times in the OT, Ps 119:97, 99, and Job 15:4, and means "thought, meditation." All three occurrences are in the context of godly thinking, and if that is the connotation of the word and if it occurs here, then it would be ironically employed; Jrm's opponents are "meditating" on ways to kill him. The word "plot" is used here in the translation as a way to suggest a word-play on "pit." For לכד "catch" see 5:26. The פַּח "snare" is essentially a bird-trap.[7] The verb טמן, here translated "laid," is literally "hidden" (13:4–7).

■ **23** The syntax of v 23aα is puzzling; the clause literally reads "But you, Yahweh, know all their plans against me for death." The predicate is heavy, and seven words are too many for a colon.[8] The easiest solution is to see the first three words as a separate colon (so the same three words, in a different order, in Ps 40:10b; compare Jer

---

6 Dahood, *Psalms II*, 101.

7 Lawrence E. Toombs, "Traps and snares," *IDB* 4:687–88.

8 By O'Connor's analysis, כֹּל- is a "unit" (that is, a word): see O'Connor, *Structure*, 317, constellation no. 15 (Exod 15:15c); and five units is the outer limit

15:15a) and to delete the sign of the accusative אֶת as an erroneous secondary addition (see Text).

For confidence in Yahweh's knowledge of the situation compare 17:16. The repetition of עֵצָה "counsel, plans" here after its occurrence in v 18 is ironic: here is counsel against Yahweh's prophet. The prayer that Yahweh not forgive the sins of one's opponents is not unparalleled in the OT, but it is rare; the best parallel, Neh 3:37, may have been based on the present passage. The verb כפר pi'el, which occurs only here in Jer, implies "forgive," but in the overwhelming majority of its occurrences in the OT the subject is a person who effects atonement for someone's sins—particularly in P, the Holiness Code, and Ezekiel, where the subject is the priest. In only seven or eight instances beyond the present passage (of ninety-two in the OT) is the subject God,[9] and it is best, therefore, not to translate "forgive" but to stay with the basic denotation "cover."[10] Such a translation fits well with the parallel מחה "blot out." For עשה "act, take action," see 14:7.

expressing his frustration to Yahweh both for the plots of the optimistic prophets against him and for the lack of fulfillment by Yahweh of the word of inevitable judgment which has been vouchsafed to the prophet, and the central prayer (vv 21–22a) is that that judgment be carried out in order that Jrm's standing as a true prophet of Yahweh might be validated. The psychic cost of such a prayer must have been overwhelming: on other occasions during this same period he expresses deep emotion that his people must suffer (4:19–21; 8:21–23), but now he prays that the blow will fall. Such an emotional shift must have been elicited at least in part by the continued prestige of the optimistic prophets and their plots against him and because of his consequent doubt, perhaps subconscious, whether his word from Yahweh was indeed valid. That doubt will later emerge into the light of day (20:7).

It is a terrible time for Jrm. The die is cast, but when, oh when, will Yahweh's decision be manifest? At this point there is no answer from Yahweh.

Aim

If the interpretation presented here is sound, Jrm is

for a colon (see Text).

9 Deut 21:8; 32:43; Ezek 16:63; Pss 65:4; 78:38; 79:9; 2 Chr 30:18; and perhaps Dan 9:24.

10 For the verb see Pedersen, III/IV, 359–62; Eichrodt, *Theology* 2, 443–48, and, most recently, Jacob Milgrom, "Atonement in the OT," *IDBSup*, 78–82.

The Breaking of the Flask,
and a Night in the Stocks

Bibliography

Wanke, Gunther
Untersuchungen zur sogenannten Baruchschrift
(BZAW 122; Berlin: de Gruyter, 1971) 6–19, 74–
77.

On 20:1–6:

Christensen, Duane L.
"'Terror on Every Side' in Jeremiah," *JBL* 92
(1973) 498–502.
Holladay
"Jer 20:1–6."
Honeyman, A. M.
"*Māgôr mis-sābîb* and Jeremiah's Pun," *VT* 4 (1954)
424–26.
Nestle, Eberhard
"Ein aramäisch-hebräisches Wortspiel des
Jeremia," *ZDMG* 61 (1907) 196–97.
Nestle, Eberhard
"Pashhur = Magor-missabib," *ExpTim* 18
(1906/07) 382.
Wächter, Ludwig
"Überlieferungen zur Umnennung von Pašḥūr in
Māgôr Missābîb in Jeremia 20,3," *ZAW* 74 (1962)
57–62.

19

1 **Thus Yahweh said: Go and buy yourself a
flask ⟨shaped⟩**[a] **of earthenware, and
⟪take with you⟫**[b] **some of the elders of
the people and some of the elders of the
priests, 2/ and go out to the Valley of
Ben-Hinnom, which is at the Potsherd**[a]
Gate, and call out there [b] **the words**[b]
**which I shall speak to you, 3/ and say,
Hear the word of Yahweh, you kings of
Judah and inhabitants of Jerusalem: Thus
Yahweh of hosts, the God of Israel has
said, I am going to bring disaster on this
place such that** [a] **the ears**[a] **of everyone
who hears it will ring;**[b] **4/ because they
have abandoned me and have made this
place alien and have sacrificed in it to
other gods whom neither they nor their
fathers had known,** [a] **and because the
kings of Judah ⟪have filled⟫**[a] **this place
with the blood of innocents 5/** [a] **and have
kept building**[a] **high places of Baal, to burn
their children with fire, [burnt offerings to
Baal,]**[b] **something which I did not
command**[c] **[nor speak]**[d] **nor did it come to
my mind, 6/ therefore the time is surely
coming—oracle of Yahweh—when this
place will no longer be called "The Fire-
pit," or "Valley of Ben-Hinnom," but
rather "Valley of Murder." 7/ And I shall**

Text

19:1a   Reading יְצוּר with *G* for *M* יוֹצֵר (so Duhm).

b   Adding after וְ לָקַחְתָּ אִתְּךָ with *S* and *T*; *G* has the
verb "lead" but not "with you." So Condamin,
Rudolph, Bright.

2a   The qere' (חַרְסִית) is undoubtedly correct (*G*
χαρσιθ); the ketib חרסות must be read either as a by-
form חַרְסוּת or as a plural חֲרָסוֹת.

b—b   For הַדְּבָרִים a few MSS. and *G*[B] read הָאֵלֶּה הַדְּבָרִים
"these words."

3a—a   For אָזְנָיו a few MSS., and a few MSS. of *G*, read
שְׁתֵּי אָזְנָיו "both ears."

b   For תִּצַּלְנָה for the expected תְּצִלֶּינָה see GKC, sec.
67g.

4a—a   For *M* וּמָלְאוּ read מָלְאוּ with *G*. The text of *M*
forces a regrouping of the phrases: ". . . whom
neither they nor their fathers nor the kings of Judah
had known, and keep filling. . . ." So Rudolph and
Bright.

5a—a   So one must understand וּבָנוּ; see 7:31, Text.

b   The phrase is lacking in *G* and in the parallel in
7:31 and must be secondary.

c   A few MSS. read צִוִּיתִים "command them" (compare 7:31, Text).

d   The phrase is lacking in *G* and in the parallel in
7:31 and must be secondary.

annul the plans of Judah and Jerusalem in this place, and I shall make them fall by the sword and by the hand of those who seek their lives; and I shall give their corpses to be food for the birds of the heavens and for the beasts of the earth. 8/ And I shall make this city a desolation and a hissing so that everyone passing shall be horrified at it and hiss at [a]all her[a] blows. 9/ And I shall feed them the flesh of their sons and the flesh of their daughters, and they shall eat each other's flesh, in the siege and hardship which their enemies [and those who seek their lives][a] shall inflict upon them.

10 And you shall break the flask in the sight of the men walking [a]with you.[a] 11/ And you shall say to them, Thus Yahweh of hosts has said, So shall I break this people and this city as one breaks a potter's vessel which cannot [a]be repaired[a] again; and they shall bury at a fire-pit, without a "place" to bury. 12/ Thus will I do to this place—oracle of Yahweh—and to its inhabitants, [a]to make[a] this city like the Fire-pit. 13/ And the houses of Jerusalem and the houses of the kings of Judah shall be 《defiled》[a] like the place of the Fire-pit—all the houses upon whose roofs they have sacrificed to all the hosts of heaven and poured out libations to other gods.

14 And Jeremiah went in from the Fire-pit where Yahweh had sent him to prophesy, and he stood in the court of the house of Yahweh and said to all the people: 15/ Thus Yahweh of hosts, the God of Israel has said: I am going to bring upon this city, and all her (daughter-) cities, all the disaster which I have spoken against her, for they have stiffened their neck so as not to hear my words.

20

1 Pashhur, the son of Immer, the priest, who was chief officer of the house of Yahweh, heard Jeremiah prophesying these things; 2/ so [a]he [M: Pashhur] ⟨struck him⟩ [M: struck Jeremiah the prophet][a] and put him in the stocks which were at the Upper Benjamin Gate in the house of Yahweh. 3/ But when Pashhur the next day took Jeremiah out of the stocks, Jeremiah said to him, Yahweh has not called you Pashhur, but Magor-missabib! 4/ For thus Yahweh has said,

I am going to make you a *māgôr* [to yourself and][a]
to all your friends;
they shall fall by the sword [b]of their enemies[b]
while your eyes look on;
[and I shall give all Judah into the hand of the king of Babylon, and he shall exile them to Babylon and strike

8a—a One MS. and *G* and *V* read the singular כָּל־מַכָּתָה, "all her wound," "all her misery."

9a Omit with *G;* see Janzen, p. 41 (b').

10a—a For אוֹתָךְ a few MSS. read the more expected form אִתָּךְ, though the substitution is known elsewhere (see 2:35).

11a—a Many MSS. give an alternate spelling, לְהֵרָפֵא.

12a—a Omitting וְ before לָתֵת with *G.*

13a Reading מְטֻמָּאִים with *S; G* likewise gives evidence of having a text with mem, understood there as the preposition מִן. The *M* reading הַטְּמֵאִים "those unclean" is awkward syntactically. So Volz, Rudolph; compare Bright.

20:2a—a *G* reads simply "and he struck him"; omit "Pashhur" and "Jeremiah the prophet" as secondary omissions (compare Janzen, pp. 69–75). The verb in *M* has a peculiar form, וַיַּכֶּה instead of the expected וַיַּךְ (discussed in GKC, sec. 76c); I propose that this may be a remnant of וַיַּכֵּהוּ (with haplography with the following וַיִּתֵּן).

4a These words are lacking in *G* and are dittographic: the meaning of the first two cola of the poem is confused by them. See Interpretation.

b—b A few MSS. read "of the hand of their enemies"; the addition is dittographic from v 5.

them down with the sword. 5/ And
I shall give all the wealth of this
city, and all its earnings, and all its
valuables, and all the treasures of
the kings of Judah {I shall give}[d]
into the hand of their enemies; and
I shall plunder them and take them
and bring them to Babylon;][c]

6 and you [Pashhur][a] and [all][b] the residents of your household shall go
into captivity:
into Babylon you shall enter,
and there you shall die,
and there you shall be buried,
you and all your friends,
to whom you have prophesied
falsely.

4–5c   Verses 4b–5 are a prose expansion generalizing
the words to all Judah.

5d   This verb is lacking in *G* and is an unnecessary
resumption.

6a   Lacking in *G*; his name has been "changed" for
purposes of the poem. See Interpretation on the last
colon of the verse.

b   Omit כל, which overloads the colon: subject
cannot be separated from predicate (O'Connor,
Structure, passim, against Holladay, "Jer. 20:1–6,"
308, and Christensen, "Terror," 502). For the place
of כל in O'Connor's analysis, see 18:18–23, n. 7.
For the frequency of the addition of כל in the text
see Janzen, pp. 65–67; for the omission here compare Christensen, "Terror," 502.

Preliminary Observations

Two questions need discussion, whether chapter 19 and
20:1–6 are connected, and the nature of chapter 19
itself. I shall deal with them in reverse order.

Chapter 19 has stimulated critics to propose a variety
of hypotheses, because the command to buy a flask (v 1)
is separated from the command to break the flask (v 10)
by a long speech (vv 3–9) and because vv 5–7 appear to
be a doublet of 7:31–33. Abraham Kuenen suggested
that this chapter has the same relation to 7:30–34 as
chapter 26 does to 7:1–15: that is, it is a narrative
account parallel to the simple text of the speech.[1] Duhm
concluded that the whole chapter is secondary.

With regard to vv 1–13, a consensus is to be found
among almost all commentators, beginning with Cornill
and Giesebrecht: that within these verses only vv 1–2a
and 10–11a are original; thus by this view vv 2b–9 and
11b–13 are secondary (beyond Cornill and Giesebrecht:
Volz, Rudolph, Bright).[2] It should be noted that Cornill
includes part of v 12a as well in what is original, and that
Giesebrecht includes v 2a as well in what is original.
(Cornill and Volz go on to propose that vv 7–9 are
tertiary additions.)

This consensus is satisfying to the theory of a Deuteronomistic redaction, since the material proposed as
secondary appears to conform to that style.[3] It is also
satisfying to the form critic, who sees v 10 in this way

brought next to vv 1–2a, so that the presumed original
passage offers commands for a symbolic act which match
the form of 13:1–11.[4]

The principal difficulty with this proposal is that it
relegates to a redactor the word-play between בַּקְבֻּק
"flask" (vv 1, 10) and וּבַקֹּתִי "and I shall annul" in v 7.
Volz is uneasy about the matter: he admits that the word-
play may be original but reassures himself that the
redactor here has given a variation on Isa 19:3 (which
contains both the verb בקק and עֵצָה "counsel"). But this
will not do: it is unlikely that a redactor would shape a
word-play, and the word-play seems built into the
narrative. There are two parallel associations of thought
which dominate the narrative: the vessel which Jrm takes
is specifically called a vessel made of "earthenware" (חֶרֶשׂ,
v 1), so that he performs his symbolic act at the "Potsherd" Gate (הַחַרְסִית, v 2); at the same time it is a "flask"
(בַּקְבֻּק, vv 1, 10) which he takes, so that Yahweh will
"annul" (וּבַקֹּתִי, v 7) the plans of Judah and Jerusalem.
Both word associations are intrinsic to the passage. A
"Potsherd" Gate is otherwise unmentioned in the OT
(see Interpretation), but there is no reason to doubt the
existence of a gate of that name overlooking the Valley
of Ben-Hinnom. Thus if Jrm were led to choose the
"Potsherd" Gate to make potsherds of his flask, and if
that gate overlooked the Valley of Ben-Hinnom, then
symbolic words to accompany the symbolic act would be

---

1   Abraham Kuenen, *Historisch-Critisch Onderzoek naar
het Ontstaan en de Verzameling van de Boeken des Ouden
Verbonds* II (Leiden: Engels, 1863) 187–88.

2   So also Wanke, *Baruchschrift*, 16.

3   See in particular Weinfeld, *Deuteronomy*, 348–49,
nos. 21, 22, 23; 350, nos. 5, 6; 353, nos. 7, 8; and
356–57, nos. 4, 14.

4   Wanke, *Baruchschrift*, 16.

appropriate. One is thus led back to the proposal of Kuenen already cited, that the present passage is a narrative version of 7:30–34.

The word-play between "flask" and "annul" is only the chief difficulty with the assumption that vv 2b–9 and 11b–13 are redactional. Though some of the diction could be characterized as "Deuteronomistic," some of it is distinctive. Thus "ears . . . will ring" in v 3 is found only here in Jer; it seems to be dependent on the narrative of the boy Samuel in 1 Sam 3:11, and the occurrence in 2 Kgs 21:12 seems dependent on the present passage. The denominative meaning "make alien" in v 4 for נכר pi'el is found only here in the OT, and seems dependent on Jrm's phrases אֱלֹהֵי נֵכָר (5:19) and הַבְלֵי נֵכָר (8:19) for the pagan gods. In v 8 the phrase "everyone passing shall be horrified at it and hiss at all her blows" is a variation on phrasing in 18:16, and the duplication in 1 Kgs 9:8 may be dependent on the present passage. The prediction of cannibalism in v 9 is not duplicated by anything else in Jer, and the close parallel in Deut 28:53 is probably dependent on the present passage. (For the details of all these observations, see the respective verses in Interpretation.)

Reference has already been made to the suggestion that chapter 19 bears the same relation to 7:30–34 as chapter 26 does to 7:1–15. That parallel is reinforced by a small detail hitherto overlooked, namely that the introductory words in both 19:1 and 26:1 lack personal references, and in both instances the lack was remedied by one or more Versions: in 19:1 *M* has "Thus Yahweh said," and *G* and *S* have added "to me," while in 26:1 *M* has " . . . this word came from Yahweh," and *L* and *S* have inserted "to Jeremiah" after "came." But it is proposed here that this lack betrays a common narrative pattern, and further that this lack suggests the work of Baruch, who was closely associated with Jrm. This datum then reinforces the contention of those commentators who have attributed both passages to Baruch.[5] Chapter 26 narrates Jrm's public appeal for repentance, the purpose of the first scroll (36:2–3), while the present chapter narrates Jrm's public declaration that hope is no longer possible, the purpose of the second scroll (36:30–32).

This conclusion moves one to an answer to the first question raised here, namely the possible connection between chapter 19 and 20:1–6. For if chapter 26 narrates the conflict with the authorities which Jrm underwent as a consequence of the temple sermon, one is moved to include 20:1–6 with chapter 19 as a single narrative. That is to say, chapter 19 "needs" 20:1–6: both chapter 26 and 19:1—20:6 narrate an initial statement by Jrm, then his arrest, then a statement after his arrest. With this understanding, the expression "these things" in 20:1 refers to the words (and actions) in chapter 19. And is there any parallel between Jehoiakim's "striking" (נכה hip'il) Uriah (26:23) and Pashhur's "striking" (נכה hip'il) Jrm (20:2)?

Structure

Considerations emerging from parallels with chapter 26 (see Preliminary Observations) lead to the conclusion that 19:1—20:6 form a single narrative (so also Rudolph, Bright, and compare Volz).[6]

It is difficult to establish why this passage is placed here. The easiest assumption is that it is because of the association of the phrase "terror on every side," 20:3–6 and 20:10; but if the confessions form the basic stratum of this section of the Jeremianic corpus, an assumption of the present study, then one might have expected the present passage to be inserted after 20:7–13, not before it (compare other secondary additions). But perhaps the present passage, which narrates a crucial event in Jrm's career, is itself part of the basic stratum, placed here chronologically after 18:18–23; in this event the association of "terror on every side" might nevertheless be valid, 20:7–13 (which by the conclusions of the present study is dated later) occurring after the present passage but in association with it.

The passage breaks in two at the chapter division: chapter 19 gives Jrm's action and proclamation, and 20:1–6 gives the consequence: Pashhur's punishment of Jrm, and Jrm's word to Pashhur. Both involve a change of name (19:6; 20:3). The last two verses of chapter 19 are a transition in the narrative, moving Jrm from the place of his proclamation to the temple area. The structure of 19:1–13 is defined by the drumbeat of second

---

5   Compare ibid., with full bibliography.
6   See in detail ibid., 6–19.

singular waw-consecutive perfects, הָלוֹךְ וְקָנִיתָ "go and buy," the reconstructed וְלָקַחְתָּ "and take" (v 1), וְיָצָאתָ "and go out," וְקָרָאתָ "and call out" (v 2), וְאָמַרְתָּ "and say" (v 3), וְשָׁבַרְתָּ "and break" (v 10), וְאָמַרְתָּ "and say" (v 11). There is thus the alternation of action (vv 1–2), words (vv 3–9), action (v 10) and words (vv 11–13), an alternation that has brought forth the critical view that the words are a secondary addition (see Preliminary Observations). The structure of the two speeches is best analyzed under Form (which see).

In chapter 20 vv 1–3 are narrative prose, but vv 4–6 contain a poem: the parallelism is clear in what is set out here in v 6 as the second through the fifth cola, and the first colon ("and you and the residents of your household") and the sixth ("you and all your friends") likewise balance. (It may be noted in passing that G, after "in[to] Babylon," omits "you shall enter, and there": conceivably M is an expansion, but there is no reason to doubt the words, and it is thus better to assume a haplography in G.)[7] This moves one to see poetry in v 4a as well: the structure there is on the basis of personal references ("you," "all your friends," "they," "your eyes") and the overall structure of the poem turns out to be the successive meanings of מָגוֹר (see Interpretation) as "terror" (v 4aα), "attack" (v 4aβ), and "sojourning" (v 6) respectively, and "you" and "for all your friends" in v 4a balances the fifth colon of v 6. The last colon of v 6 is then a summary of the meanings of the name change (see again Interpretation). The prose insertion (vv 4b–5) interrupts the structure of the poem.[8]

Form

When the entire passage is taken as a unit (see Preliminary Observations), it must be understood as a unit of prophetic biography just as chapter 26 is.[9]

If 19:14–15 and 20:1–6 are taken as integral to 19:1–13, then it is a third-person narrative (just as chap. 26 is). The first thirteen verses of chapter 19 relate Yahweh's commands, commands marked by second-person verbs

in vv 1, 2, 3, 10, and 11 (see Structure). The command to "hear," followed by the vocative, followed by the messenger formula at the beginning of v 3, parallels the introductory material in 2:4–5. Verse 3b contains a summary pronouncement of judgment introduced by הִנְנִי and the participle (compare 1:15; 5:14). This is followed by the specific accusation giving the basis for judgment, introduced by יַעַן אֲשֶׁר (compare again 5:14): the specific accusation is contained in vv 4–5. The pronouncement of judgment begins again in v 6 and continues through v 9. Verse 6 contains a prediction of a change of name of the site, and v 7 a word-play on the "flask" which is the object of the symbolic act. Verses 8–9 offer more general judgments against the city.

Verse 10 resumes with a command to effect the symbolic act, and v 11 is a command parallel to that in v 3 to speak Yahweh's words. Again one hears the messenger formula, followed by the words of comparison כָּכָה "so" and כַּאֲשֶׁר "as" (v 11), and כֵּן "thus" at the beginning of v 12 (for this sequence compare 13:9, 11). These words of comparison communicate a further declaration of judgment (vv 11–13). There is no declaration of the performance of these commands; if 20:1–6 narrates the consequence, a declaration of performance is unnecessary.

Verses 14–15 embody narrative that was only hinted at in v 1; v 15 closes with a word of divine judgment.

For further material on symbolic actions see 13:1–11, Structure and Form.

The narrative is continued in 20:1–6 with Jrm's announcement to Pashhur, the priest who had arrested him, that Yahweh had changed his name; on the matter of renaming see 7:30–34, Form, on the incident narrated in 19:6.[10] The meaning of the new name is explicated in a judgment speech to the priest, beginning with the messenger formula and continuing with the announcement of judgment.[11] The judgment speech to Pashhur has been generalized secondarily to "all Judah" by the prose insertion in vv 4b–5.

7   So also Janzen, p. 119.
8   See in general Holladay, "Jer 20:1–6," 308–9, and Christensen, "Terror," 501–2.
9   See March, "Prophecy," 174–75.
10   See in particular Otto Eissfeldt, "Renaming in the Old Testament," *Words and Meanings, Essays Presented to David Winton Thomas on his Retirement from the Regius Professorship of Hebrew in the University of Cambridge, 1968* (ed. Peter R. Ackroyd and Barnabas Lindars; Cambridge: Cambridge University, 1968) 69–80, esp. 73–74.
11   Compare Westermann, *Basic Forms*, 129–63, esp. 146–47.

Setting

For the authenticity of chapter 19 to the memory of Jrm see Preliminary Observations; there is no reason either to doubt the authenticity of 20:1–6, a vivid and specific narrative of a particular incident with a named priest.

It is suggested in Preliminary Observations that the present passage is to be attributed to Baruch (so likewise chap. 26: see Preliminary Observations there). That is, the present passage is a narrative version of 7:30–34, just as chapter 26 is a narrative version of 7:1–15; and both passages begin curiously with introductory words about the revelation of Yahweh's word but without a specification of recipient ("to me" or "to Jeremiah"). Chapter 26 gives the narrative of Jrm's public appeal to repent, appropriate to the period of the first scroll, while the present passage appears to be a corresponding narrative of Jrm's public declaration that there is no longer any hope, characteristic of the period of the second scroll.

The implication of 36:26 is that Jrm and Baruch were out of the public eye for some time after the king burned the scroll. If the reasoning offered here is sound, however, the prophet was soon back in the public eye again and was arrested for his words and action; the date, then, must have been at the end of December 601 or early in 600.

A determination of an approximate date for this passage is a key to the dating of 6:25 and 46:5 as well as 20:10, passages that have generalized the use of the phrase "terror on every side": see Setting for the respective passages in which those verses occur.

The mention in the gloss in 20:4b–5 of the "treasures of the kings of Judah," and of its parallels, leads one to the suspicion that it was the events in 597 which stimulated those words: 2 Kgs 24:13 mentions "treasures of the king's house"; though of course one cannot exclude the possibility that the words come from 587 instead.

Interpretation

■ **19:1** For the opening words, "Thus Yahweh said to me"

and "go and buy," see 13:1. The noun בַּקְבֻּק "flask" appears only here and in v 10, and in 1 Kgs 14:3; in the last passage it is a container for honey, but it is clear that it is a general term for a container for water. Rashi equates it with the צְלוֹחִית; both were evidently wide-bellied bottles with a narrow neck—the name is onomatopoeic, from the gurgling sound made when pouring water.[12] James Kelso remarks that the narrow neck and consequent gurgling of the water helps to aerate it as it is poured,[13] and that its use by Jrm "was doubly significant since it had the narrowest neck of all the pitchers, and therefore could never be mended."[14] The phrase "shaped of earthenware" is not necessarily a tautological addition—there were doubtless similar vessels of metal: but the phrase really points to the association with the "Potsherd" Gate (v 2).

"Elders of the people": analogous leaders figured in the narrative of the temple sermon, an event of several years before (26:17). They represent the laity here, the people at large. "Elders of the priests": G omits "elders of" and reads simply "some of the priests"; though the phrase "elders of the priests" (= "senior priests") does exist (2 Kgs 19:2), referring to those with access to the court, the reading of G may be correct—Cornill, Volz, and Rudolph elect it,[15] for Rudolph is convinced that Jrm could not have had access to the senior priests. But there were those within the court who could protect Jrm (26:24; 39:14), and haplography is as likely an explanation for G as dittography would be for M. Jrm seems to have wished to have representatives from both laity and the priesthood, and symmetry might well have led to the event as remembered by M.

■ **19:2** For the location of the Valley of Ben-Hinnom see 7:31. The location of the Potsherd Gate (שַׁעַר הַחַרְסִית), mentioned only here, is unknown. The normal identification with the Dung Gate (Neh 2:13; 3:13–14; 12:31), made by T, may be correct:[16] both "dung" and "potsherds" may signify a gate through which trash was thrown into the valley. But since the location of the

---

12　For photographs see Kelso, "Pottery," 857, plate 63, no. 7e, and, in more detail, the "decanters" in Ruth Amiran, *Ancient Pottery of the Holy Land* (New Brunswick, NJ: Rutgers University, 1970) 262–63, photographs 258–61.

13　Kelso, "Pottery," 851.

14　James L. Kelso, *The Ceramic Vocabulary of the Old Testament* (BASOR Supplementary Series 5–6; New

Haven: American School of Oriental Research, 1948) 17.

15　So also Janzen, p. 41.

16　For example, *HALAT*, 341b.

Dung Gate is likewise uncertain,[17] the identification is both uncertain and unhelpful.

Jrm is not only to perform a symbolic act but to accompany it with symbolic words (compare Preliminary Observations); on the close association of word and act see 1:1.

■ **19:3** The vocative "kings of Judah" is unexpected here but is appropriate in the context of a judgment about the blood of innocents (Manasseh—2 Kgs 21:16; 24:4) and about child sacrifice (Ahaz—2 Kgs 16:3; Manasseh—2 Kgs 21:6); see vv 4–5. For הִנְנִי מֵבִיא רָעָה "I am going to bring disaster" see 11:11. The word "place" here suggests, as often, a cultic place; for the use of the term to refer to the temple area see 7:3, and for its association with the Valley of Ben-Hinnom see the implications of "without a 'place'" in v 11 and the discussion of that phrase in 7:32.

The phrase תִּצַּלְנָה or תְּצַלֶּינָה with אָזְנָיו "his ears ring" is found only here in Jer, and only otherwise in 1 Sam 3:11 and 2 Kgs 21:12; since both the latter passages include the word "both" in the phrase, that reading may be correct (see Text). The passage in Kings is part of the exilic Deuteronomistic redaction[18] and thus doubtless dependent on the present passage. But the occurrence in 1 Sam 3:11 is part of the instruction of Yahweh to the boy Samuel and might well be a stimulus for Jrm's words here: as Samuel was to proclaim judgment on the priesthood of his day, so Jrm is to proclaim judgment on the cult of his day. (For another reference to Samuel see 15:1, and see the remarks about Anathoth in 1:1.) The verb צלל is used once of the lips "quivering" (Hab 3:16); "ring" is the appropriate word for ears.

■ **19:4** "They have abandoned me" is conventional diction in such a context (1:16; 2:13; and often). By contrast "they have made this place alien" (נכר pi'el) is a striking and unique phrase. The verb is here a denominative, given the phraseology of אֱלֹהֵי נֵכָר "alien gods" in 5:19 and הַבְלֵי נֵכָר "alien nothings" in 8:19: by sacrificing to "other gods" the people have "alienified" the place. For "sacrifice to other gods" see 1:16; for "other gods whom you have not known" see 7:9; for "you and your fathers" see 7:14.

The accusation of kings of Judah who "have filled this

place with the blood of innocents" is a specific reference to the acts of Manasseh (2 Kgs 21:16; 24:4) and Jehoiakim (22:17). The phrase in 2 Kgs 21:16 and in Jer 22:17 uses שׁפך "shed"; the Kings passage is the product of the first Deuteronomistic editor,[19] and it is possible that Jrm in 22:17 is dependent on that account of Manasseh (see the discussion there). But the present passage, and 2 Kgs 24:4, uses מלא "fill"—in Kings "filled Jerusalem," here "filled this place," and since 2 Kgs 24:4 is attributed to the exilic Deuteronomistic editor,[20] it is probable that the Kings passage is dependent on the present one. For "innocent blood" see 2:34.

■ **19:5–6** See 7:31–32; the variations of wording are trivial.

■ **19:7** The verb וּבַקֹּתִי "and I shall annul" is a play on בַּקְבֻּק "flask" (see Preliminary Observations). For עֵצָה "counsel, plans" compare 18:23. The translation "I shall make them fall by the sword and by the hand of those who seek their lives" is the consensus of commentators and translations, but it should be noted that the preposition בְּ means both "by (means of)" and "in, on." Thus נפל qal + בְּיַד means "fall into the hand (= power) of" in Judg 15:18 and Lam 1:7, and "fall by the hand (= agency) of" in 2 Sam 21:22 = 1 Chr 20:8; the expression is ambiguous in 2 Sam 24:14 = 1 Chr 21:13 and 1 Chr 5:10. One may assume that the hip'il verb may participate in the same ambiguity, and this ambiguity in turn suggests that the first phrase may mean "fall into the sword" as well. For v 7b compare 7:33a.

■ **19:8** For "make . . . a desolation and a hissing, so that everyone passing shall be horrified at it" see 18:16. The parallel to "shall be horrified at it" here is "and hiss at . . . ," so that the verbs correspond to the objects expressed in the first half of the verse (contrast 18:16). The duplication in 1 Kgs 9:8 may be dependent on the present passage.[21]

■ **19:9** Cannibalism was a historical reality in times of famine (2 Kgs 6:24–31 of Samaria in the ninth century, Lam 4:10 of Jerusalem in the sixth). Beyond this fact, "eating the flesh of one's children" was a traditional curse form.[22] As a potential threat the theme is found beyond the present passage in Lev 26:29; Deut 28:53; Isa 9:19 (Versions); Isa 49:26; and Zech 11:9. Of these passages

---

17 Millar Burrows, "Jerusalem," *IDB* 2:854–55; Jacob M. Myers, *Ezra, Nehemiah* (AB 14; Garden City, NY: Doubleday, 1965) 114, 116.

18 Gray, *Kings*, 705.
19 Ibid., 704–5.
20 Ibid., 757.

Deut 28:53 is particularly close, having not only "eat the flesh of your sons and your daughters" but also "in the siege and hardship which your enemies shall inflict upon you." Deut 28:45–57 is evidently a late expansion:[23] the best solution then is that Deut 28:53 is dependent on the present passage.[24]

One notes the word-play of מָצוֹר "siege" and מָצוֹק "hardship," and of the latter word with the related verb צוק hipʿil "distress"; the second-named word-play is found only here and in the imitations in Deut 28:53, 55, 57.

■ **19:10** Here, finally, is the instruction for the symbolic act (compare the excursus "The Theology of Symbolic Actions" in the course of Interpretation on 13:1–12aα). The breaking of a pottery vessel as a symbol of the destruction of a people is widespread (compare the expression in Ps 2:9); specifically one thinks of the Egyptian ritual of coronation and jubilee festivals, wherein the king smashes pottery vessels on which the names of his enemies have been inscribed.[25]

■ **19:11–13** Here is the explanation of the symbolic act. The phraseology is similar to that in 13:9–11; but whereas there Yahweh would spoil the pride of Judah and Jerusalem, here Yahweh will break the people and the city so that it cannot be put together again. For the irreparability of the flask, compare the remarks on v 1. For v 11b see 7:32b. In vv 12–13 Jrm deliberately identifies the illicit activities in the "Fire-pit" at the Valley of Ben-Hinnom (v 6) with the destiny of the city. In v 13 the kings of Judah are mentioned once more. In 7:30 the people put up idols in the temple to "defile" it (טמא); here the houses of the city (including the palaces!) will be "defiled" (טמא).

Verse 13b, and a passage dependent on it, 32:29, mention sacrifice to pagan gods on the roofs of houses; 2 Kgs 23:12 and Zeph 1:5 reflect the same practice (in the latter passage likewise to the "host of heaven"). In the Gilgamesh epic Ninsun evidently ascends the roof to offer incense to Shamash, the sun-god,[26] and the same practice seems to be referred to in the Keret epic at Ugarit.[27] For "host of heaven" see 8:2; for "pour out libations to other gods" see 7:18.

It is curious that vv 1–13 are instructions for performing a symbolic action (and to speak out symbolic words) but that there is no narrative of the carrying out of the instructions (compare 13:2, 5, 7). One can only speculate whether the text ever carried a brief notice like "And Jeremiah did as Yahweh had said" which subsequently dropped out (compare, however, the problem of 25:17 in the context of 25:15–29 (see on that passage Structure, Form, Setting).

■ **19:14–15** The חָצֵר is a courtyard, the walled-in enclosure around a building. The walls around Solomon's temple are not known archeologically, but there have been attempts to depict the courtyard for the Herodian temple.[28] The use of "her cities" (עָרֶיהָ) after "this city" is odd but understandable, since "cities of Judah" is a standard expression (2:28). G shifts here from τὴν πόλιν ταύτην "this city" to τὰς κώμας αὐτῆς "her towns," which catches the connotation of subservience, but the daughter cities were evidently walled. Dahood's suggestion, that עָרֶיהָ means "her protectors" (cognate with a Ugaritic verb ġyr "protect," that is, "her pagan gods,"[29] is unnecessary (compare again 2:28).

■ **20:1** "Pashhur" is a name borne by several men mentioned in this period and thereafter: indeed 21:1 mentions another Pashhur, the son of Malchiah. The name is also found on a Hebrew seal of the last half of the seventh century[30] and on an ostracon found in the Arad sanctuary, thus perhaps the name of a priest (late eighth or early seventh century).[31] It is clear that Jrm in his

21 Eissfeldt, *Introduction*, 301.
22 Hillers, *Treaty-Curses*, 62–63.
23 Von Rad, *Deuteronomy*, 175–76; Mayes, *Deuteronomy*, 356.
24 For another discussion of the curse form in relation to Deuteronomy 28, but with the conviction that the Jer passage is Deuteronomistic, see Weinfeld, *Deuteronomy*, 126–28.
25 See the "Execration of Asiatic Princes," *ANET*, 328–29.
26 Tablet III, Assyrian Version, ii 8; see *ANET*, 81b.
27 Ug. 14.80, compare line 76. It should be noted that

Ug. 35.50 is too fragmentary for evidence.
28 See Meir Ben-Dov, "Temple of Herod," *IDBSup*, 870, fig. 2.
29 Dahood, *Psalms I*, 55–56.
30 Adolf Reifenberg, *Ancient Hebrew Seals* (London: East and West Library, 1950) 38, no. 24 = Herr, *Scripts*, 98, no. 36.
31 Yohanan Aharoni, "The Israelite Sanctuary at Arad," *New Directions in Biblical Archaeology* (ed. David Noel Freedman and Jonas C. Greenfield; Garden City, NY: Doubleday, 1971) 36 and fig. 54; Yohanan Aharoni, *Arad Inscriptions* (Judean Desert Studies;

name change of "Pashhur" is indulging in word-play (see v 4) and that his twisting of the name is an ad hoc insult and not to be taken seriously as the actual derivation of the name. The name appears to be Egyptian in origin, meaning "son of Horus."[32] The priest's patronymic Immer is the name of a priest or priestly house first listed as a contemporary of David in 1 Chr 24:14, and this priestly line is represented among the priests returned from Babylon (1 Chr 9:12; Ezra 1:37).[33] S records the name as "Amariah," likewise the name of several priests,[34] but there is no need to question M.

The priest's office is given as פָּקִיד נָגִיד. It has been suggested that נָגִיד is a gloss (Cornill), but recently both titles have turned up in parallelism in Old Aramaic in one of the Sefire treaties (mid-eighth century).[35] The second term may still be a gloss, but the Aramaic evidence indicates that the titles are valid for the period. G translates both terms, and one doubtless has here a double title (Eduard König compares the German "prince-bishop").[36] The noun פָּקִיד in general means "overseer"; it may be used in military contexts (52:25) as well as in contexts of the priesthood, as here. The passage in 29:26 is a good explanation of the present passage (though M there has an erroneous plural פְּקִדִים); a priest was appointed פָּקִיד in the house of Yahweh "for any madman who plays the prophet, by putting him into the stocks and collar." The noun נָגִיד is a general word for "leader, chief," used as a euphemism for "king" in reference to Saul (1 Sam 9:16) and as a term for "leader" among the priests (2 Chr 31:13), but whether Pashhur filled two offices, or whether a single official was called "chief overseer," or whether the two terms are interchangeable, is uncertain. What is clear from his action is that he functioned to keep order in the temple area in a way like that of the beadle in an English church. Given the action and words recorded in chapter 19, it would be easy to judge Jrm another "madman."

■ 20:2 The words "so Pashhur struck Jeremiah the prophet" greatly troubled the commentators of the Reformation period: Calvin remarks, "This was unworthy of his station, and contrary to the rights of sacred fellowship; for if the cause of Jeremiah was bad, yet a priest ought to have pursued a milder course . . . ," and so on, for a full page. Hugo Grotius and Houbigant translated "arrested him" or "had him seized" (so Condamin). Volz and Rudolph translate "Pashhur had Jeremiah the prophet beaten," Rudolph remarking that the passage does not mean that Pashhur did the beating himself. But this seems like modern overscrupulousness: none of the ancient Versions had any difficulty with the notion. Bright notes, "No doubt 'had him beaten'; but the meaning could be that he 'struck Jeremiah.'" It is better to stay with the literal meaning.

The meaning of מַהְפֶּכֶת, translated here "stocks," is uncertain; it occurs only in this and the following verse, in 29:26, and in 2 Chr 16:10 in the phrase בֵּית הַמַּהְפֶּכֶת, "house of stocks [or whatever]" for a sort of place of confinement. It has been assumed that its root הפך "turn" suggests a device which confines the body in a stooped position, but this is by no means sure. The Versions vary. G gives καταρράκτης, which evidently means "trap-door" (2 Kgs 7:2) and therefore "dungeon"; s' renders ποδοστράβη, which is an instrument of torture for twisting the feet. V uses *nervus*, a general term which can mean "fetter," specifically foot-fetters of iron— Jerome remarks that he chooses the word because he has in mind the confinement of Paul and Silas in Philippi (Acts 16:24): the ξύλον there may have been "stocks" for confinement or an instrument of torture.[37] S simply translates "circle" (ḥādartā'), guessing from the verbal root. T gives כֻּפְתָא; unfortunately, however, this word has two ranges of meaning (or there are two homonymous words): "vault," therefore "prison," and some kind of wooden "collar" for confinement, thus also a muzzle with feeding bag for animals. One cannot therefore know what T understands (unless ambiguity!). In 29:26 the noun is paired with צִינֹק, normally translated as another restraining device, "collar": but in that passage G

Jerusalem: Israel Exploration Society, 1981) 86, no. 54.

32 For a recent discussion see S. Aḥituv, "Pashhur," *IEJ* 20 (1970) 95–96; see further Manfred Görg, "Pašḥur and Pišanḥuru," *Biblische Notizen* 20 (1983) 29–33.

33 Bruce T. Dahlberg, "Immer," *IDB* 2:688 (1).

34 Frederick T. Schumacher, "Amariah," *IDB* 1:102–3.

35 Sefire III 10; see Joseph A. Fitzmyer, *The Aramaic*

Documents of Sefire (BibOr 19; Rome: Pontifical Biblical Institute, 1967) 98–99.

36 König, *Syntax*, sec. 333s.

37 See Johannes Schneider, "ξύλον," *TDNT* 5:37, 39; Frederick F. Bruce, *The Acts of the Apostles* (London: Tyndale, 1952) 318, with a citation from Eusebius.

translates the two words with ἀπόκλεισμα ("guardhouse") and καταρράκτη ("dungeon"), but in reverse order; V translates with *nervus* (as here) and *carcer* ("prison"), S (like G) translates both words by synonyms for prison, and T translates the word in question again with the ambiguous כְּפְתָא and the second word by its own cognate צִינוֹקָא traditionally interpreted as "narrow prison" (Jastrow). In short, the Versions give no specific help. Qimḥi lays out both interpretations, "prison" and "stocks"—the latter he defines as a device made of two pieces of wood enclosing the neck of the prisoner. Modern interpreters have not gone beyond these suggestions. The conclusion must be that there is no question of torture here, though doubtless submitting to the מַהְפֶּכֶת was not comfortable; that the meaning "prison" is doubtful, because on those occasions when Jrm was confined in a way analogous to a prison the circumstances are specifically described (37:15–16; 38:6–13), and because the pairing of two words in 29:26 suggests two devices (the rendition of various words for "prison" in the Versions is thus simply guesswork); and that therefore we are dealing here after all with a device to immobilize a prisoner. But the nature of the device must remain uncertain: every age seems to be able to devise its own devices to render prisoners immobile and helpless. "Stocks" will have to do.

There was a city gate called the "Benjamin Gate" (37:13; 38:7), doubtless on the north or northeast side of the city, since that is the direction in which the territory of Benjamin lay (compare the present-day "Damascus Gate"); but the present context suggests a gate of the temple courtyard; is one to understand that the "Upper" Benjamin Gate was a temple gate, whereas the (lower) Benjamin Gate was a city gate, the temple area being of higher elevation?[38]

■ **20:3–6** Jrm renamed Pashhur "Magor-missabib": this phrase is normally translated "terror on every side," but the possibility of multiple meanings (see below) is such that it is preferable to leave it untranslated. The new

name must be assumed to have some relation to the old name, but the relation is here not self-evident, and a great range of suggestions have been made.[39] Basic to the interpretation of the renaming is the point first made (to my knowledge) by Johann Michaelis, that Jrm's use (or deformation) of "Pashhur" need have no relation to the actual derivation of the name: "Fresh etymologies with proper names are allowable in insult, provided they fit the nature of the language."[40] It is clear, too, from the existence of מִסָּבִיב "on every side" in the new name, that the Aramaic סָחוֹר "surrounding" is part of Jrm's deformation of "Pashhur"; this is implied by the rendering here in T, מִסָּחוֹר סָחוֹר, and it figures among Rashi's suggestions, though not clearly; it is found clearly in the Jewish exegete J. H. Altschul(er) in the seventeenth century[41] and is assumed by Michaelis. (Compare the translation סָחוֹר for סָבִיב in 4QTgLev 2.2, second century B.C.E.)[42]

The set phrase מָגוֹר מִסָּבִיב appears, beyond the present passage, in 6:25; 20:10; 46:5; 49:29; and Ps 31:14; all of these passages (with the possible exception of Ps 31:14) are dependent upon the present one; they offer no independent data for establishing meaning. With regard to מָגוֹר the Versions vary in their renderings. G has μέτοικος "emigrant, alien," and S *tawtābā'* "newcomer, foreigner"; these two translations thus identify the word with the verb גור "sojourn." V here has *pavor* "terror"; T paraphrases with "they shall gather against you who kill with the sword." It appears, then, that V connects the word with the verb גור "dread," while T connects it with the verb גור "show enmity, attack" (these verbs are listed in both BDB and *HALAT* as I, III, and II respectively). It is difficult to state the evidence for the possibility that there are three homonyms of the noun מָגוֹר corresponding to the three homonymous verbs. But it is clear that there is a noun מָגוֹר "sojourning," cited eleven times in the plural in the OT (for example, Gen 17:8) and in the singular at Qumran (1QH 5.8), and that מָגוֹר "terror" occurs in Isa 31:9 (parallel there with "flee in

---

38   See Millar Burrows, "Jerusalem," *IDB* 2:853.
39   For a number of these suggestions see Holladay, "Jer 20:1–6," 305–6 n. 1.
40   "Licitae sunt convicio nominum propriorum novae etymologiae, modo ingenio linguae conveniant": Johann D. Michaelis, *Supplementa ad Lexica Hebraica* (Göttingen: Rosenbusch, 1784–92) no. 2089.
41   In מקראות גדולות (Warsaw: 1874–77) ad locum.

42   The text reads *sḥ[wr*, and the reference is to Lev 16:18. See Roland de Vaux and Jozef T. Milik, *Qumran Grotte 4, II* (DJD 6; Oxford: Oxford University, 1977) 86–89 = 4Q 156.

panic"), so there is no theoretical reason why a מָגוֹר "enmity" should not exist.

My proposal is that Jrm offers three denotations of מָגוֹר here and then explicates them one by one in the poem of vv 4a + 6. It is clearest that v 6 refers to "sojourning"; the verb גור "sojourn" is used eight times in chapters 42—44 (for example, 42:15) of staying in Egypt to avoid Babylonian power, so the noun is used here of Pashhur's future forced stay in Babylon. The third and fourth cola of the poem in v 4 describe the experience undergone by Pashhur's friends as מָגוֹר "enmity, attack": one notes the resemblance between the words there, "they shall fall by the sword of their enemies while your eyes are watching," and the rendering in *T* of מָגוֹר in v 3, already cited, "they shall gather against you who kill with the sword." This leaves the first two cola of the poem in v 4 to be an explication of מָגוֹר "terror": the diction of "I am going to make you a מָגוֹר to all your friends" is close to such phraseology as וּנְתַתִּים לְזַוְעָה "and I shall make them a horror" (to all the kingdoms of the earth, 15:4). Thus Jrm is saying, "You will be a מָגוֹר = 'terror' to all your friends; your friends will be an occasion of מָגוֹר = 'attack' to you by falling by the sword of the enemy, and you and they will be an occasion of מָגוֹר = 'sojourning' by exile in Babylon."

Now the connotations of מִסָּבִיב become clear: it is not only spatial, "on every side," but notional, "from every point of view"—מָגוֹר with every nuance." The related verb סבב carries such a metaphorical meaning: in 2 Sam 14:20 one finds לְבַעֲבוּר סַבֵּב אֶת־פְּנֵי הַדָּבָר "in order to change the course of affairs" (*RSV*), "to give a new turn to this affair" (*NEB*). Jrm offers here a little series of dictionary entries on the word (or, to be fairer to his mind-set, offers a set of images generated by the vocable). Now one sees why מִסָּבִיב does not occur in the lines of the poem in vv 4–6 but is necessary in the new name: Rudolph and Janzen[43] are wrong to delete it at the end of v 3.

As already stated, the second part of Pashhur's name was deformed by Jrm into the Aramaic סְחוֹר "surrounding." It is not surprising that Jrm would use Aramaic: it had become the *lingua franca* of Mesopotamia and would be particularly appropriate for Pashhur, whose days would end in Babylon (compare the remarks on 10:11, if that Aramaic pun is to be credited to Jrm). Jrm's play on the first part of Pashhur's name must likewise be Aramaic. The obvious solution is פָּשׁ, participle of פוש "be fruitful." (This solution was proposed over two centuries ago by Christian Benedikt Michaelis but has not to my knowledge been taken up since.)[44] The verb was regularly used in *T* as a translation of the Hebrew פרה: one notes particularly פּוּשׁוּ וּסְגוֹ "be fruitful and multiply," the phrase in *T* in Gen 1:22, 28; 9:1, 7. By deforming Pashhur's name as פָּשׁ־סְחוֹר "fruitful all around" Jrm assumes a positive meaning in the name; his new name, in contradistinction, will carry a triple negative meaning. As I have pointed out,[45] the verb פרה "be fruitful" appears repeatedly in Genesis in the narratives (in the P tradition) of the covenants with Abraham and Jacob, and in particular it is associated with the renaming of Abram as Abraham (Gen 17:5, 20) and of Jacob as Israel (Gen 35:10, 11); and in the reprise of the covenant to Jacob in Gen 48:4 one has הִנְנִי מַפְרְךָ "I am going to make you fruitful," quite analogous to the diction here, הִנְנִי נֹתֶנְךָ לְמָגוֹר "I am going to make you a *māgôr*." (For the availability of the P tradition to Jrm, see the remarks on 4:23–26.) One may conclude that the use here of the Targumic equivalent of "be fruitful" in the context of a name change makes it apparent that Jrm in this incident was announcing a reversal of Yahweh's covenant with the patriarchs. (Compare the word in 15:8, "Their widows have become for me more than the sand of the seas.")

It must be stressed that Jrm is not indulging in a private insult; he is announcing a fresh word from Yahweh that Pashhur's name is no longer valid, and as such the new name becomes a vehicle for Yahweh's judgment on Pashhur and his associates. It is as yet a judgment on Pashhur and his associates alone—its application to the nation would come somewhat later (6:25, and compare the prose addition here in vv 4b–5).

Who are כָּל־אֹהֲבֶיךָ "all your friends," literally "all those who love you"? Curiously enough there is no other occurrence of this participle in the context of "colleagues" or "subordinates," the nuance which seems to be implied here (unless Haman's "friends" are such, Esth 5:10, 14). The finite verb אהב is used of Saul's "loving"

---

43   Janzen, p. 73.
44   See n. 40.
45   Holladay, "Jer 20:1–6," 316.

David (1 Sam 16:21) and of David's "loving" Jonathan (1 Sam 18:1, 3; 20:17). It must be reiterated that "love" has in the OT a strong basis in covenantal ties (see 2:2), so that Jrm here appears to have reference to all the priests with whom Pashhur had dealings (and/or over whom he had supervision).

The meaning is not at all clear in the first two cola of the poem in v 4. The words can theoretically mean "I am going to give you to מָגוֹר . . . ," but given the context and the parallels of "I am going to make them a horror" and the like with the verb נתן (see above), "give" is effectively ruled out; the phrase must mean, "I am going to make you מָגוֹר, to yourself and to all your friends." However, since "to yourself and" is missing in G, it is likely to be dittographic. If מָגוֹר really has three successive meanings in the poem (see above), then v 6 says that Pashhur and all his friends (next-to-last colon) are to be an example of "sojourning" in foreign lands, the third and fourth cola of v 4 say that Pashhur's friends are to be exemplars of "attack" while Pashhur looks on, so that symmetry suggests that the first and second cola of v 4 indicate that Pashhur is to be an exemplar of "terror" to his friends. This symmetry suggests in turn that the words "to yourself and" are indeed secondary (see Text).

There is no need to be puzzled why Pashhur's friends both "fall by the sword" (v 4) and "are buried in Babylon" (v 6): the cola of the poem explicate three scenarios for מָגוֹר and are not to be taken in logical sequence.

Pashhur and his household are to "sojourn" in Babylon and die and be buried there: they are reversing the story of Abraham and his descendants, who "sojourned" in Canaan and who died and were buried there—one thinks of passages like Gen 35:27–28, "And Jacob came to his father Isaac at Mamre, or Kiriath-arba (that is, Hebron), where Abraham and Isaac had sojourned. Now the days of Isaac were a hundred and eighty years. And Isaac breathed his last; and he died and was gathered to his people, old and full of days; and his sons Esau and Jacob buried him."

The mention of "Babylon" in v 6 is striking: it is the only mention in Jrm's poetry of the land of exile outside chapters 50—51 (compare his use of "Assyria" in 2:18, 36). By this period it was clear to everyone who the

"foe" is.

The last colon of the poem is curious, since we had no indication that Pashhur was a prophet. It is naive, I believe, to assume that Pashhur exercised what we assume to be prophetic functions (Volz speaks of oracular devices, augury, and the like); Jrm, when he states that Pashhur has prophesied falsely, is summing up his poem on the name change, and one must conclude that what is meant here is that by his very bearing the name "Pashhur," understood as פַּשׁ־סָחוֹר "fruitful all around," the priest is making a false statement which Yahweh has now reversed.[46] (Compare the rather different implication of "prophesy falsely [= by the Lie]" in 5:31.)

The long prose insertion of vv 4b–5 generalizes the personal word addressed to Pashhur, making it relevant to "all Judah." Verse 4b gives the prose equivalent of vv 6 and 4aβ respectively. Verse 5 piles up the synonyms for "treasure": for the last noun in the series here, אוֹצָרוֹת, translated "treasure," compare 15:13; 17:3; for the second, יְגִיעַ, translated "earnings," see 3:24. The third, יְקָר, translated "valuables," occurs in a different context in 15:19, and the first, חֹסֶן, "wealth," occurs in Jer only here. Given the later insertion of vv 4b–5, it was necessary to insert "Pashhur" in v 6 to move the reference from "all Judah" back to the priest.

Aim

Jrm is commanded to combine word and act in public proclamation of the inevitable doom of the nation. His vantage point will have the city behind him and the Valley of Ben-Hinnom ahead; he is to give a new symbolic name to the valley appropriate to its function, and to identify the grisly activity of child sacrifice in the valley with the fate of the city to his rear (19:12). He is deliberately to address the long line of kings of Judah (19:3), thus combining the actions of the past with those of the present: the past, one must understand, is relevant to Yahweh's judgment on the present just as the activity in the valley is relevant to Yahweh's judgment on the city. There is no way now to avoid the consequences of atrocities for which the hearers would rather avoid responsibility. The city and its people are to be broken,

---

46   Compare Christensen, "Terror," 502.

irreparably (19:10).

Jrm is punished by the chief of the temple police, but the prophet has the last word: if the valley is to get a new name, so is the arresting priest, a name suggesting not fertility but a curse. And Jrm names the enemy through which the curse will come: it is Babylon.

Jeremiah Accuses Yahweh
of Deceiving Him

Bibliography

On 20:7–18:
Clines, David J. A., and David M. Gunn
  "Form, Occasion and Redaction in Jeremiah 20,"
  ZAW 88 (1976) 390–409.
Janzen, J. Gerald
  "Jeremiah 20:7–18," *Int* 37 (1983) 178–83.

On 20:7–13:
Berridge
  pp. 151–55, 160.
Clines, David J. A., and David M. Gunn
  "'You Tried to Persuade Me' and 'Violence!
  Outrage!' in Jeremiah xx 7–8," *VT* 28 (1978) 20–
  27.
Fishbane, Michael A.
  "'A Wretched Thing of Shame, A Mere Belly': An
  Interpretation of Jeremiah 20:7–12, *The Biblical
  Mosaic, Changing Perspectives* (ed. Robert M. Polzin
  and Eugene Rothman; Philadelphia: Fortress; and
  Chico, CA: Scholars, 1982) 169–83.
Fishbane, Michael A.
  Text and Texture (New York: Schocken, 1979) 91–
  102.
Hartman, Geoffrey
  "Jeremiah 20:7–12: A Literary Response," *The
  Biblical Mosaic, Changing Perspectives* (ed. Robert M.
  Polzin and Eugene Rothman; Philadelphia:
  Fortress; and Chico, CA: Scholars, 1982) 184–95.
Holladay
  "Style," 52–53.
Hubmann, Franz D.
  "Anders als er wollte: Jer 20,7–13," *BLit* 54 (1981)
  179–88.
Levenson, Jon D.
  "Some Unnoticed Connotations in Jeremiah 20:9,"
  CBQ 46 (1984) 223–25.
Marrow, Stanley B.
  "Ḥāmās ("violentia") in Jer 20,8," *VD* 43 (1965)
  241–55.
Von Rad
  OT Theology 2, 203–6.

20

7 You have deceived me, Yahweh, and I let
      myself be deceived,
    you are stronger than I and have over-
        powered me.
   I have become a laughingstock the whole
      day,
    the whole of it mocks me.
8 Every time I speak,

cry out "Violence!"
and "Destruction!" shout,
(then) the word of Yahweh becomes for
me a reproach
and derision the whole day;

9   and (every time) I think, "I shall not
remember it
or speak any more in his name,"
(then) it is in my heart,
(it is) like burning fire,
⟨(like) pressure⟩ᵃ in my bones,
and I am tired of holding (it) in,
and cannot overpower (it).

10   For I have heard the defamation of the
crowd,
"'Terror on every side!' —
announce, yes, let us announce it!"
All humankind is ⟨my recompense,⟩ᵃ
the watchmen of my rib:
"Perhaps he will be deceived, and we
can overpower him,
and take our retribution on him."

11   O Yahweh, ⟪I have desired you,⟫ᵃ O
terrifying warrior,
that is how my persecutors might
stumble, might not overpower:
they should be utterly discredited that
they have no insight;
the everlasting disgrace will never be
forgotten.

12   O Yahweh of hosts, righteous tester,
you who see the mind and the heart,
let me see your retribution on them,
for ⟪to me you have revealed my
adversaries. ⟫ᵃ
- - - - - -

13   Sing to Yahweh!
Praise Yahweh!
for he has saved the life of the poor man
from the hand of evildoers!

Text

9a   Reading עָצֵר (Ernst Kutsch, "Die Wurzel עצר im Hebräischen," *VT* 2 [1952] 58) for the *M* masculine passive participle עָצֻר "shut up." "Fire" is feminine, and the masculine is odd (though not impossible: see GKC, sec. 132d), but if the participle were intended, it would more likely be written עָצוּר. See Interpretation.

10a Reading שְׁלוֹמִי for *M* שְׁלֹמִי, part of a phrase understood as "(every man of) my peace," that is, "every one of my familiar friends." See Interpretation.

11a For *M* כִּ אוֹתִי "(But Yahweh is) with me [assuming the expression = אִתִּי like," reading אַוִּתִיךָ. Though the Versions and all translations and commentaries accept *M*, there are cogent contextual and form-critical reasons against the reading: see Preliminary Observations, Structure, Form, and Interpretation.

12a See 11:20.

Preliminary Observations, Structure, Form

There are two or three points in this passage where the text appears to need a fresh interpretation. In v 10 these reinterpretations do not have large consequences beyond the verse in question, so that discussion of them will be offered in Interpretation on the verse. But the reinterpretation in v 11 has structural and form-critical consequences and must therefore be dealt with here (see below).

Extent of Unit. Verses 7–18 make up a sequence of confessional material; it is not self-evident whether the sequence is single or multiple, and, if multiple, where the divisions are; structural and form-critical data are determinative.

Form-critically vv 14–18 embody a cursing by Jrm of

his life, tantamount to a cursing of his call; there is none of this in vv 7–13. Further vv 14–18 exhibit a structure suggesting that the five verses make up a unit of their own: the motifs of birth in vv 14–15 and 17–18 form an inclusio. The five verses share no significant diction with vv 7–13 (only "day," vv 7, 8, 14, 18; "forever" [עוֹלָם], vv 11, 17; and "be discredited, ashamed" [בוש], vv 11, 18). One suspects that vv 14–18 form a closure to the whole confessional collection: "my mother" (v 14) and "my father" (v 15) pick up "your father" (12:6) and "my mother" (15:10), as well as the mention of "mothers" and "fathers" in 16:3.[1]

Verses 7–13 have received varied treatment. The most common division is between vv 9–10 (so first Baumgartner,[2] so Volz and Berridge[3]). It is clear that

---

1   Holladay, *Architecture*, 130–34.
2   Baumgartner, *Klagegedichte*, 65–66.
3   Berridge, p. 114 n. 1.

Jrm's quarrel is with Yahweh in vv 7–9, and he does not mention his persecutors (this is especially the case by the interpretation offered here of כָּלֹה, that it refers to the "day," not to a vague group of people); by contrast in vv 10–13 he seeks help from Yahweh against his persecutors. Baumgartner insisted that only vv 10–13 are a personal lament, whereas vv 7–9 is a connected narrative. But surely a "connected narrative of difficulties undergone is part of the genre of personal laments."[4] I conclude on form-critical grounds that there is no justification for dividing the passage between vv 9 and 10. Condamin, on the other hand, divides the passage between vv 10 and 11. Indeed he counts vv 4–6 as one strophe, vv 7–10 as a second strophe, and vv 11–13 as a third: he sees inclusios in each of his first two strophes, "you and all your friends" in vv 4 and 6, and the verbs "deceive" and "overpower" in vv 7 and 10; but by the analysis of the present study a combination of vv 4–6 and vv 7ff in a single sequence is impossible. It is arbitrary to separate v 11 from vv 7–10, given the fourth occurrence here of "overpower" (יכל).

Earlier critical commentators of this century judged vv 12 and 13 to be secondary (Duhm, Cornill, Giesebrecht, Volz); Duhm notes, "Verse 12 is identical with 11:20 and not from Jeremiah himself, but added by a reader as a quotation, the more so because v 11 makes a good closing. . . . Verse 13 is a psalm-verse which does not belong to the context and apparently was written in the margin." On the other hand recent commentators have taken both verses to be genuine (both Rudolph and Bright regarding v 13, Rudolph regarding v 12; Bright is uncertain about v 12).

Nature of v 13. The diction of v 13 suggests that it is genuine to Jrm (see Interpretation). Form-critically it is a hymnic song of thanksgiving; such a hymnic song may close a lament. This is notably the case with Psalm 22: vv 2–22 in that psalm form the lament proper, and vv 23–32 a hymn. Since this psalm may have shaped Jrm's self-understanding,[5] the addition of v 13 here may have been encouraged by the structure of that psalm. On the other hand, the verse shares no phraseology with vv 7–12; I propose that it was added after vv 7–12 took shape, indeed I propose a specific setting for the verse (see

Setting).

Meaning of v 11. All the Versions, commentaries, and translations translate the first colon of v 11, "But Yahweh is with me as a terrifying warrior." By this understanding the colon (and what follows) is an affirmation of confidence: such an affirmation is found elsewhere in laments (Pss 5:5–7; 31:4), and a third-person affirmation, followed by the conjunction עַל־כֵּן and a word about the enemies, is found likewise in Ps 25:8. But several considerations should give one pause. (1) There is no other instance in Jrm's confessions of such a third-person affirmation of confidence. (2) The expression וַיהוה at the beginning of a colon is a vocative in v 12 (= 11:20) and is taken as a vocative in the vocalization of 11:18 in *G*, the reading accepted in the present study; there are no other comparable instances in Jer. (3) In particular, given the vocative in v 12, one is moved to understand the sequence in v 11 as a parallel vocative. Of course if v 12 is added secondarily, this datum is irrelevant; but it has not been proved that v 12 is added secondarily—it is only an assumption, given the fact that v 12 is a variation of 11:20. But given Jrm's self-quotations in v 8 (compare v 10, where he seems to cite his enemies, who are quoting Jrm), one may see v 12 as a final self-quotation by Jrm. (4) If v 11 is an affirmation of confidence, and if the second colon of the verse means "therefore my persecutors will stumble, they will not overcome me," or the like, then v 12, a prayer for help, comes on curiously; though again, as with (3), if v 12 is added secondarily, the matter is irrelevant. But עַל־כֵּן, the conjunction at the beginning of the second colon, usually means something like "that is why," and it is normally followed by perfect verbs (5:6; 27–28; 10:21; 12:8; 30:20); given the genre of affirmation of confidence, the imperfects here do attract attention. (5) The spelling of אוֹתִי likewise attracts attention. Of course one may interpret the word as the equivalent of אִתִּי (compare 2:35), but it may be noted that in 8:8 an expression similar to that assumed to be here is written without waw.

I propose that the sequence of consonants be read אִוִּיתִךָ. "Yahweh" will then be a vocative, like v 12, and the colon will read, "O Yahweh, I have desired you, O terrifying warrior." A similar phrase appears in Isa 26:9,

---

4   David J. A. Clines and David M. Gunn, "Form, Occasion and Redaction in Jeremiah 20," *ZAW* 88 (1976) 394.

5   Compare Holladay, "Background."

נַפְשִׁי אִוִּיתִיךָ בַּלַּיְלָה, "My soul has desired you [= Yahweh] in the night." The related noun אַוּת appears in 2:24 of sexual desire; if the vocalization here is correct, and if that nuance is suggested, it picks up the sexual nuance of "seduced" in v 7 (see Interpretation, and compare further the marriage image in 15:16); in this way as well as in the repetition of "overpower" the verse is a reprise of v 7. By this understanding the verse is not so much Jrm's affirmation of confidence as his affirmation of a deep desire for Yahweh and for his help. The imperfects of the second colon are then not a prediction of the fall of the persecutors but a statement of the hoped-for result of Yahweh's help (see further Interpretation).

Nature of v 12. Though v 12 is a virtual repetition of 11:20, it is integrated here, especially if the understanding just offered of v 11 is valid. (1) The "retribution" of Yahweh (v 12) answers the hoped-for "retribution" of Jrm's opponents (v 10). (2) The verse 11:19 ends with "shall be remembered no more" and v 11 here ends with "will never be forgotten." One may conclude that Jrm himself intended to close vv 7–11 by v 12.

Placement of the Unit. It is usually assumed that the passage is here because of the repetition of "terror on every side" (vv 3, 10: so Bright);[6] indeed Condamin held that vv 7–13 continue the words to Pashhur in vv 4–6 (see above). But the matter is not necessarily so simple. If the confessions are the basic stratum of this section of Jer, then 19:1—20:6 would have been inserted after the present passage was in place. On the other hand, 19:1—20:6 may also have been a part of the basic stratum (see Structure on that passage); in that case the association of "terror on every side" may indeed unite the two passages. Of course if the passage is to be dated at the end of 601 or early in 600, then it may represent Jrm's utterance directly after the incident with Pashhur, as the crowd takes up the phrase "terror on every side" (v 10). But the passage is tentatively assigned a setting in 594 (see Setting), so that one must conclude after all that it is simply the verbal repetition of "terror on every side" that brings it here.

Internal Structure. The structure of vv 7–12 is not easy at every point to discern, especially in the matter of division into cola in vv 8–9 (see Interpretation on those verses).

There is a major rhetorical break between vv 9 and 10 (see above under *Extent of Unit*). Verses 7–9 embody a complaint to Yahweh in which Jrm does not refer to his opponents; vv 10–11, by contrast, make up a complaint about the words and actions of his opponents. The two portions are united by the two verbs "deceive" (פתה) and "overpower" (יכל) (vv 7, 10, 11), and more subtly by the fact that in the first half Jrm quotes himself (vv 8, 9) and in the second half Jrm quotes his enemies (who are quoting Jrm!) (v 10). And it is conceivable that v 12 was understood as a further quotation by Jrm of himself (see above, *Extent of Unit*).

Verse 7 is made up of two bicola: in the first there are verbs of Yahweh's relation to Jrm, and in the second there are the parallel expressions "the whole day" and "the whole of it," and "laughingstock" and "mocks." By contrast v 8a seems to be a tricolon, if "every time" (מִדֵּי) governs all three verbs (see Interpretation); v 8b, however, can only be a bicolon, a long colon (compare cola with the same phraseology in 6:10b and 15:16a) followed by a short one: conceivably, then, v 8a is in parallel fashion to be construed as a bicolon, a long colon followed by a short one. Verse 9 must be analyzed as a bicolon, a tricolon, and a bicolon: the tricolon (v 9aβ) has "in my heart" and "in my bones" in the two outside lines, and "like burning fire" in the center—this analysis holds good whether the word עצר is revocalized (see Text) or not. In sum, v 7 functions in two ways: (1) it "outlines" vv 8–9 (in reverse order) in that v 7b (mockery) anticipates v 8 and v 7a anticipates the diction of v 9, but (2) that diction comes in v 9b ("overpower") in such a way that vv 7a and 9b really form an inclusio. Verses 8 and 9 then set up the two situations, what happens when Jrm does speak (v 8) and what happens when he does not (v 9).

Verse 10 takes a quantum jump, in that now Jrm's opponents quote phrases of that "word of Yahweh" which Jrm has been proclaiming; and that quantum jump is signaled structurally by a verse of seven cola, the first, fourth, and fifth embodying words of Jrm to Yahweh, the remaining cola embodying words of the opponents—the second and third cola involving Jrm's own phrase, and the sixth and seventh cola expressing the plotting of

---

6   Bright, p. 134.

the opponents. In a sense, then, the seven cola extend the theme of vv 8 and 9 (word of Yahweh) and the structure of v 9 (seven cola). Verse 11 embodies four cola; given the shift from imperfect to perfect verbs between the second and third colon, it is better to take them as two bicola. If v 10 balances vv 8 and 9, v 11 balances v 7 ("deceive," "overpower").

Verse 12 is made up of two bicola (like 11:20); v 13 is likewise a pair of bicola.

Form. This confession, like others in the series, belongs to the genre of individual laments.

Verses 7–10 embody a complaint to Yahweh, in which Jrm describes his suffering. Verse 7a is unique, an accusation of deception leveled at Yahweh. There are many complaints in the Psalms that Yahweh has taken the psalmist to the gates of Sheol or the like (for example, Ps 88:7), but there is no parallel for this accusation; the closest is perhaps the well-known question, "My God, my God, why have you forsaken me?" (Ps 22:2). Verse 7b is a more conventional statement, the complaint that the suppliant is the cause of derision (Pss 22:8; 44:14–15; 79:4); but vv 8–9 connect that derision with the word of Yahweh, and that is new. Verse 10 continues the complaint by a description of the enemies, including a quotation of the words used by the enemies (compare Pss 22:9; 71:11);[7] but some of these words were originally Jrm's own, given him by Yahweh!

Verse 11, by the reading of *M*, is an affirmation of confidence, but by the revocalization offered here v 11 joins v 12: both of them are invocations with hymnic elements, v 11 an affirmation of desire for Yahweh and his help (see above), and v 12 a renewed plea for help (see on 11:20).

For v 13 see above.

Setting

There are no clues within vv 7–12 that could specify a time when this lament was uttered; one must proceed indirectly. For v 13, however, I propose a specific setting. The diction of v 13b, "for he has saved the life of the poor from the hand of evildoers," is close to that of 15:21, "I will save you from the hand of the wicked, and ransom you from the grasp of the violent." The setting

for 15:20–21 in the present study is the summer of 594; v 13, then, is likely to be from the same period. I may go further, however, and propose that it was uttered at time of the death of Hananiah in September/October 594 (28:17), indeed that Jrm's vindication as a true prophet by Hananiah's death was the occasion for the publication of the confessions (see Jeremiah's Confessions: Introduction, before 11:18).

As to vv 7–12, one is uncertain whether they are to be assigned to the first crisis that Jrm underwent because of the opposition of the optimistic prophets (end of 601 or 600) or the second (summer of 594). In favor of the former option is the repetition of "terror on every side" (v 10); if the phrase here is a quotation by the crowd (see Interpretation), then it is plausible to assume a setting directly after the incident with Pashhur (see Setting on 19:1—20:6). In favor of the latter option, however, are the following considerations. (1) Jrm's outlook on Yahweh is far darker than that in 15:16, assigned to the period of the end of 601 or 600: in 15:16 the metaphor of marriage is current for him while in the present passage the metaphor is of Yahweh's seduction of him (v 7); in 15:16 he says, "Your word became for me a joy and the delight of my heart," whereas here in v 8 he says, "The word of Yahweh becomes for me a reproach and derision the whole day." (2) Jrm uses the striking word "terrifying" (עָרִיץ) of Yahweh in v 11, and of his opponents in 15:21, and 15:20–21 is assigned to the summer of 594 (see above). (3) There is a close similarity between v 11 and 17:18: the two verses contain the only instances in the confessions of the expression "my persecutors" (רֹדְפַי), and both verses likewise contain the verb בוש "be ashamed, discredited." In the present study 17:14–18 is assigned by other data to the summer of 594. (4) If v 12 is a self-quotation (of 11:20), then it is plausible to understand it as a repetition from his prayer in an earlier crisis. (5) Verse 13 becomes a conclusion to a sequence uttered in the same period.

None of these considerations is utterly persuasive, but it is likely that the summer of 594 is the setting for the whole passage, crowned by v 13 at the end of the summer.

---

7   For an analysis of the wicked work of the tongue of one's enemies in the Psalms see Pedersen, I/II, 447–50.

Interpretation

■ **7** The verb that occurs twice in the first colon (פתה, pi'el and nip'al) has been understood as leveling a very strong accusation against Yahweh. Two notable uses of the verb in the pi'el in the OT come into discussion. The first is Exod 22:15, where it is used of "seducing" a virgin; this semantic range, of the relation between man and woman, is found elsewhere—of Yahweh's "alluring" Israel (Hos 2:16), of a wife "tricking" her husband by her wiles (Judg 14:15; 16:5). The other is of Yahweh's "deceiving" a prophet, notably in the episode of Micaiah ben Imlah (1 Kgs 22:20, 21, 22; compare also Ezek 14:9). Both ranges of meaning have been proposed for the present passage.

The Versions reflect one or both of these semantic fields. G and S each use the same verb here which is used in both Exod 22:15 and 1 Kgs 22:20–22 (ἀπατάω and *šdl* pa'el respectively). V and T both use verbs here with a sexual connotation (V *seduxisti me*; T שַׁבֶּשְׁתַּנִי); V likewise uses *seduco* in Exod 22:15.

The language here, if this understanding is correct, raises grave theological issues. Calvin wrote, "Some think that these words were not spoken through the prophetic Spirit, but that Jeremiah had uttered them inconsiderately through the influence of a hasty impulse. . . . Others give even a harsher explanation—that the Prophet had been deceived, according to what is said elsewhere, 'I the Lord have deceived that Prophet.' (Ezek xiv. 9.) But there is no doubt but that his language is ironical, where he says that he was *deceived*. He assumes the character of his enemies, who boasted that he presumptuously prophesied of the calamity and ruin of the city, as no such thing would take place. . . ."

Recently David J. A. Clines and David M. Gunn have argued[8] that the verb does not mean "seduce," "deceive," but rather "try to persuade": that in the case of Exod 22:15 the connotation is "entice, cajole," and that in the case of 1 Kgs 22:20–22 the connotation is "urge"—they point out that v 22 there ends with וְגַם־תּוּכָל "and you will succeed." But their analysis is not convincing. Though one could always make out a case for "attempt to persuade" (it would be difficult to disprove in a given instance), 2 Sam 3:25 can hardly be anything else than "deceive." The goals of the "persuasion" in Exod 22:15

and in 1 Kgs 22:20–22 are clearly destructive (given the assumptions of the culture). It is clear that in the present passage Jrm is engaged in a bitter complaint to Yahweh, that Yahweh led him into a situation of misery and danger. The metaphor of marriage is implied in another confession (15:16), so the nuance of "seduce" here is not too strong. It is possible that the image of seduction is carried forward in the verb חזק "overcome" in the second colon (so Bright);[9] see below.

But the nuance of Yahweh's deception of his prophet is equally present. The incident with Micaiah ben Imlah in 1 Kings 22 was a classic instance of prophet against prophet: the four hundred court prophets said yes to the proposed battle for Ramoth-gilead, while Micaiah said no. Micaiah's explanation of the contrast was that the four hundred were indeed from Yahweh, but that Yahweh had "deceived" (פתה pi'el) Ahab by putting a "lying spirit" (רוּחַ שֶׁקֶר) in the mouths of the four hundred. Jrm interpreted the contrast between the prophets of his own day who proclaimed good news and his own proclamation of bad news in the same way: Yahweh had "deceived" this people and Jerusalem (נשא hip'il, 4:10). Now, however, faced with opposition and without the validation which would come from the ultimate collapse of the nation, Jrm questions the effectiveness of Yahweh's word and accuses Yahweh of misleading him (compare the "deceitful brook," 15:18).

The matching of two stems of a verb is a favorite device of Jrm's: compare 11:18; 15:19; and 17:14 at the beginning of confessional utterances. Both 11:18 and 17:14 are uttered by Jrm in the context of faith, either a testimony of Yahweh's help (11:18) or a prayer for help (17:14); here, by contrast, is an accusation of Yahweh's false dealing. The form פִּתִּיתַנִי "you have deceived me" is likewise comparable to יְדַעְתָּנִי "you have known me" (12:3): Yahweh is accused of having broken the relation which he had initiated with Jrm. The choice of the nip'al stem rather than the pu'al for the second occurrence of the verb may suggest more "I let myself be deceived" than simply "I was deceived" (see Bright).[10]

The companion verb חֲזַקְתַּנִי is curious: the form without suffix, חָזַקְתָּ, means "you have become strong, are strong"; the suffix for this intransitive verb is thus

---

8 David J. A. Clines and David M. Gunn, "'You Tried to Persuade Me' and 'Violence! Outrage!' in Jeremiah xx 7–8," *VT* 28 (1978) 21–23.

9 So also Berridge, p. 152.

10 Compare Joüon, *Gramm.*, sec. 51c.

"dative," expressing comparison.[11] *V* has understood the verb in the same way (*fortior me fuisti*); *G* has ignored the suffix. Ehrlich's emendation to הֶחֱזַקְתַּנִי "you have seized me" is thus unnecessary. It is conceivable that this verb, like those in the first colon, can carry a sexual connotation: חזק qal does in 2 Sam 13:14 (וַיֶּחֱזַק מִמֶּנָּה, "and he was stronger than she"), and the hip'il of חזק does in Deut 22:25, a law analogous to that in Exod 22:15. Berridge points out[12] that two verses later in Deuteronomy 22 (Deut 22:27) the young woman in question is said to have cried out for help in vain: "cry out" there is צעק, evidently a by-form of זעק, the verb found here in v 8 ("cry out"). Further von Rad has suggested[13] that חָמָס ("violence," v 8) may have been the standard cry by someone suffering a grave injustice (compare Hab 1:2; Job 19:7), and Berridge goes on to suggest[14] that that may have been the cry that the violated woman referred to in Deut 22:27 was expected to use. All this is less than an airtight argument, but the probability is strong that the verb "you are stronger than I" continues the semantic field of sexual violence with which the verse began. Since these verbs are used in laws against sexual violence, the implication is that Yahweh has broken his own torah in his treatment of Jrm.[15]

Of course on the more literal level the accusation is truistic: Yahweh is stronger than Jrm, *ex hypothesi*. But Jrm is not offering a theological affirmation, he is angry: "You won, you are victorious over me!" And וַתּוּכָל "and overpowered (me)" is synonymous; the same form appears in Gen 32:29, regarding Jacob's "prevailing" over God and men.

Verse 7a thus embodies an outburst that is deeply rebellious, not to say blasphemous: Jrm understands Yahweh as brute force, as deceptive, beyond any conventional norm. Having earlier thought that Yahweh called him into a relation of mutual trust and responsibility (15:16), he now perceives Yahweh to have tricked him, made sport of him beyond all comprehension.

The nuance of "sport" continues in v 7b; Jrm has

become שְׂחוֹק "a laughingstock" (a nice word-play on חזק, the first verb in the second colon of the verse). This root appears in 15:17 ("merrymakers"): see the treatment there. Jrm did not sit in the company of the merrymakers, who were not only those with a cheerful outlook on the future but those who made fun of Jrm. Now the hint is that Yahweh is behind the process by which Jrm is mocked. The word שְׂחוֹק, properly an infinitive, means "laughter," and then (as here) "an object of laughter." Though the modern reader might tend to overlook it, the phrase "the whole day" (כָּל־הַיּוֹם) appears in Jer only twice, here and in v 8; the phrase then carries an important burden. Of the forty-three instances in the OT, it appears in the Psalms twenty-six times, particularly in laments; the phrase here denotes the steady misery to which Jrm is subjected. And the phrase is reinforced by the last colon כֻּלֹּה לֹעֵג לִי. The word כֻּלֹּה evidently does not mean, as all commentaries and translations assume, a vague "all of them" (referring to his enemies): there is no other reference to enemies in vv 7–9, Jrm depicting himself simply standing in isolation with Yahweh, an object of derision from unidentified sources. The expression instead picks up "the whole day" (כָּל־הַיּוֹם) in the previous colon, in a pattern identical to that in 4:27 (as reconstructed). The whole day mocks Jrm. The metaphor is no more surprising than that Jrm should curse the day of his birth (v 14); "day" is half-personified in other passages (Job 3:3; Prov 27:1). And, using the verb found here, one hears of an eye which "mocks a father" (לֹעֵג לְ, Prov 30:17). The expression here is very close to that in 15:10, where Jrm accuses everyone of abusing him: there the expression with כָּל־ refers structurally if not morphologically back to "the whole land." This is the only occurrence of לעג in Jer; it is found elsewhere as a parallel of שׂחק (Prov 1:26).

■ **8–9** The syntax of these verses, in which successive cola are introduced by כִּי and וְ, is not self-evident. Since מִדֵּי means "as often as" or "whenever," and since "violence and destruction" (חָמָס וָשֹׁד) is a fixed pair (6:7), the

---

11 See König, *Syntax*, sec. 22; Pierre-Maurice Bogaert, "Les suffixes verbaux non accusatifs dans le sémitique nord-occidental et particulièrement en hébreu," *Bib* 45 (1964) 242–43. Bogaert cites Isa 65:5 and Ezek 16:52 as other examples of the same phenomenon, And Dahood proposes a revocalization in Ps 77:14 which would result in another example: see his *Psalms II*, 230.

12 Berridge, pp. 153–54.
13 Gerhard von Rad, *Genesis* (Philadelphia: Westminster, 1961) 206.
14 Berridge, pp. 153–54.
15 Ibid., 216.

consensus for v 8a is a translation like, "For whenever I speak, I cry out, I shout 'Violence and destruction!'" (*RSV*). But Hab 1:2 offers the phrase זָעַק חָמָס "cry out 'Violence!'" (as does Job 19:7 with the equivalent verb צעק), and *V* pairs each noun chiastically ("I cry out 'Violence!' and 'Destruction!' shout"); poetically this is a more likely grouping of the words (compare the separation of the same pair in Isa 60:18 and Hab 2:17) and suggests then a tricolon for this half-verse.

Now the question arises how far the jurisdiction extends of the expression מִדֵּי (translated here "every time"). The analysis of 31:20 indicates that this conjunction governs two synonymous predicates (see there). In the present passage *S* alone of the Versions allows it to extend for two verbs ("for every time I speak and cry out, 'Violence and destruction!' I must shout"). But if, as has just been suggested, the nouns "Violence!" and "Destruction!" are to be divided between the second and third verbs as *V* does, then one must conclude that מִדֵּי governs all three times; they are after all virtually synonymous. In that case the apodosis begins in v 8b.

But the repetition of "speak" (דבר pi'el) at the beginning of v 9 after its occurrence in v 8 suggests in turn that כִּי . . . מִדֵּי must be understood to govern this verse as well: "And (every time) I think, 'I shall not remember it or speak any more in his name,' then it is in my heart. . . ."

Now the phrases must be examined in detail. The implication of shouting "Violence and destruction!" (or "Violence!" and "Destruction!") is ambiguous. Rudolph and Berridge[16] list three possibilities which have been proposed. (1) Jrm is proclaiming the coming punishment on the nation: Yahweh will bring "violence and destruction" upon them.[17] (2) Jrm is denouncing the people's sin: the people have continued to commit "violence and destruction" (compare 6:7).[18] (3) Jrm is complaining to Yahweh of the "violence and destruction" by which his opponents abuse him.[19] But there is a fourth possibility, that Jrm is complaining of the "violence and destruction"

which Yahweh has done to him; this is implied by the second colon of v 7.[20] Given the general density of imagery in the passage, all four possibilities may compete for the hearer's attention.

The close match between v 8b and v 7b suggests that if Jrm became a source of derision to the people, then likewise the word of Yahweh which Jrm preached became a source of derision to the people. Jrm had identified himself so much with the task of proclaiming the word of Yahweh that derision for one was derision for the other. Both Rashi and Qimḥi insist that this is the meaning of the passage; Rashi says, "They have spoken reproach to me, for they are reviling me." But analogies elsewhere suggest another possibility. In 6:10 one has דְּבַר־יהוה הָיָה לָהֶם לְחֶרְפָּה "the word of Yahweh has become for them a reproach," that is, "They held the word of Yahweh in contempt." In 15:16 one has וַיְהִי דְבָרְךָ לִי לְשָׂשׂוֹן, "Your word became to me a joy." Thus given the phrase לִי לְחֶרְפָּה, the implication is, "the word of Yahweh has become contemptible to me": since Yahweh seems to have acted irresponsibly toward Jrm (v 7a), Jrm now treats the word of Yahweh, which he is obligated to proclaim, with contempt and derision.

For the meaning of חֶרְפָּה "reproach" see 6:10. Its parallel קֶלֶם is found only here in Jer; it is paired with לַעַג in its other two occurrences, Pss 44:14 and 79:4, and that noun is cognate with the verb לעג occurring in v 7b. That connection confirms the close match between vv 7b and 8b.

For אמר = "think" in v 9 see 3:19. The waw-consecutive perfect וְאָמַרְתִּי is iterative (GKC, sec. 112kk). There is the widespread conviction that זכר (normally "remember") here means "mention, name," like the Arabic *ḏakara*;[21] compare 23:36. The hip'il can carry this meaning, and it is possible that the instance here and in 23:36 must be vocalized as hip'ils. On the other hand it is possible that "not remember" simply means "forget" (Gen 40:23): that, "I would prefer to forget about him," or, more likely, "I would prefer to forget about it" (the

16   Ibid., 153.
17   So, for example, Gerhard von Rad, "The Confessions of Jeremiah," *A Prophet to the Nations, Essays in Jeremiah Studies* (ed. Leo G. Perdue and Brian Kovacs; Winona Lake, IN: Eisenbrauns, 1984) 343 = "Die Konfessionen Jeremias," *EvT* 3 (1936) 271, with hesitation; Sheldon H. Blank, "The Confessions of Jeremiah and the Meaning of Prayer," *HUCA* 21

(1948) 346–47.
18   Nötscher, p. 158.
19   Baumgartner, *Klagegedichte*, 64.
20   Berridge, pp. 153–54.
21   Josua Blau, "Reste des i-Imperfekts von *zkr* qal," *VT* 11 (1961) 81–83; Pieter A. H. de Boer, *Gedenken und Gedächtnis in der Welt des Alten Testaments* (Stuttgart: Kohlhammer, 1962) 13–14.

word of Yahweh: compare Rudolph), inasmuch as the subject of וְהָיָה in the third colon is doubtless the same (Bright). The adverb עוֹד "any more" doubtless does double-duty for both cola (so again Rudolph). The "speaking in his name" reflects "speak" in v 8. This phrase occurs twelve times in the OT, notably in Exod 5:23 (J; referring to Moses) and Deut 18:19–22 (four times);[22] the occurrences suggest that the stimulus for the phrase here is the tradition regarding Moses in Exod 5:23 and in the context of the "prophet like Moses" (Deut 18:18) regarding true prophecy.

"In my heart" and "in my bones" are parallel (compare 23:9; Prov 15:30); this circumstance suggests that the central phrase, "like a burning fire," is the second colon in a tricolon. The subject of וְהָיָה is doubtless "the word of Yahweh" (v 8b: compare the remarks above on the identity of the object of "remember" in the first colon of the verse)—so KJV against RSV, and so NEB and NJV against JB; the alternative here rejected is to take the clause to mean "a burning fire is, as it were, in my heart. . . ." The word עצר is vocalized in M as עָצֻר "shut up." This passive participle is then parallel with the participle בֹּעֶרֶת "burning." But a masculine participle so close to the feminine בֹּעֶרֶת is odd (though see GKC, sec. 132d), and it is likewise to be noted that if a masculine participle it is nevertheless written defectively, without waw. It is thus better to accept Kutsch's revocalization to עֹצֶר "pressure" (Isa 53:8), a reading which is not at all an anticlimax (as Rudolph claims). The כְּ "like" with "fire" then does double-duty. The poetic structure is as well served by a parallel to "fire" as a parallel to "burning." For the comparison of the word of Yahweh to fire see 5:14 and 23:29. The description here of the compulsion of the word of Yahweh on Jrm's psyche is a classic one, but he gives a parallel description in 23:9; compare also Amos 3:8.

The phrase וְנִלְאֵיתִי כַּלְכֵל "and I am tired of holding (it) in" is almost identical to נִלְאֵיתִי הָכִיל in 6:11: the two stems (pilpel and hip'il) appear to be interchangeable. For the phrase see 6:11—there it was the "wrath of Yahweh" which Jrm could not hold in (parallel there to "word of Yahweh"), here it is the "word of Yahweh" itself. The parallel וְלֹא אוּכָל "and cannot overpower (it)"

forms an inclusio with וַתּוּכָל in v 7a: there Jrm accuses Yahweh of overpowering him, while here, correlatively, Jrm admits that he cannot overpower Yahweh's word. Jrm's sense of powerlessness over against the pressure of Yahweh in his time of bitterness matches Jrm's inability to sustain an objection to Yahweh's call at the beginning (1:7).

Jon Levenson has pointed out[23] that behind these last two cola is another semantic range: וְנִלְאֵיתִי כַּלְכֵל may also mean "I am tired of nourishing (it)" (for כול pilpel in that meaning see 1 Kgs 18:4, 13), and that "I cannot eat" would be וְלֹא אֹכַל, a vocalization not far from what is given. Levenson does not insist on a double meaning here but suggests that the semantic field of feeding lies at the edge of the expression.

■ **10** The noun דִּבָּה is not (as the traditional translation has it) specifically "whispering," but deliberate talk calculated to hurt someone's reputation, whether true (Gen 37:2) or false (Prov 10:18).[24] Sometimes, then, it means "bad report," sometimes "slander," but "defamation," though a heavy word, is perhaps the best rendering here. The רַבִּים (literally "many") are not identified: the denotation is doubtless the specific group of prophets who plot against Jrm (see the remarks on 11:18). But, if the fourth colon is here correctly understood, the "many" expand there to "all humankind," so the translation "the crowd" (so also NJV) is appropriate.

The next four cola need careful treatment: it is proposed here that several matters have been misunderstood. The third colon, containing the pair of verbs הַגִּידוּ וְנַגִּידֶנּוּ, is clearly a quotation, and several commentators have suggested that the second colon, "Terror on every side," is likewise a quotation, words of Jrm's that his enemies are throwing back at him (Condamin, Rudolph, Bright). These two cola, words of Jrm's opponents, then balance the last two cola of the verse, likewise words of his opponents. The double occurrence of the same verb in the same stem is remarkable, but 35:11 contains an identical sequence, so the phenomenon is not unique (and compare the last colon of 20:15 as here revocalized).

The RSV has inserted an erroneous "say" after the third colon; the action of "saying" is implicit rather in the

---

22   The other passages, beyond the present one: Jer 26:16; 29:43; 44:16; Zech 13:3; Dan 9:6; 1 Chr 21:19.

23   Jon D. Levenson, "Some Unnoticed Connotations in Jeremiah 20:9," CBQ 46 (1984) 223–25.

24   Heinz-Josef Fabry, "דִּבָּה," TDOT 3:76–79.

"defamation" of the third colon. Further, the repeated verb in the third colon does not imply hostility, as has been thought (Cornill: "band together"; *RSV*: "denounce him"), a notion going back to *G* ("conspire") and *V* ("pursue"); rather the verb is simply "announce," and the suffix on the second occurrence is not "him" (that is, Jrm), but "it," the word "Terror on every side!" just as "remember it" in v 9 refers to the word of Yahweh. The verb "announce" is a standard introduction of a prophetic judgment (so 4:5; 5:20; 46:14; 48:20; 50:2), so that one can imagine Jrm's opponents either giving a mock proclamation of their own or mimicking Jrm's proclamation.

One must now ask what the intention is of the use that Jrm's enemies make of his phrase; it is evidently more than the mockery that Bright suggests. The motive would seem to be that expressed in the last two cola of the verse: "perhaps he will be deceived, and we can overpower him. . . ." They were trying to provoke him, playing the role of *agents provocateurs,* insincerely spreading his word, trying to "fool" him into trusting them, hoping he would utter words by which he might be accused. One is then led back to inimical prophetic circles such as are here identified as Jrm's opponents in the case of 11:18—12:5 and 15:15–19.

Something is amiss, I suggest, in *M* of the next two cola. The words have always been understood as "all my familiar friends are watching for my stumbling," or the like, but this is odd enough to raise questions. (1) The idiom "all my familiar friends" elsewhere (38:22; Obadiah 7; Ps 41:10) suggests that what one would expect here is either כָּל־אַנְשֵׁי שְׁלוֹמִי or כָּל־אִישׁ שְׁלוֹמִי; the word אֱנוֹשׁ which appears here is not a poetic equivalent אִישׁ but a collective for "humanity." This is not to say that Jrm could not have used the word here, but it is odd. (2) The cola before and after the presumed phrase here are short: a colon with four units is of course possible but is not in keeping with the two-unit cola nearby.

I propose that the sequence makes up two parallel cola. The first will be כָּל־אֱנוֹשׁ שְׁלֹמִי "all humankind is my recompense." The noun שָׁלוֹם occurs with the parallel נָקָם "retribution" in Isa 34:8 (compare Deut 32:35, with the same roots), and the related נְקָמָה "retribution"

occurs in the last colon of the present verse. If this vocalization is correct, then Jrm is suggesting both that the crowd is Yahweh's "recompense" to Jrm, which he is convinced he does not deserve, and also more loosely that the crowd is attempting to exact its recompense on Jrm, a notion that anticipates the thought of the last colon; this double vision of Yahweh's enmity and the enmity of the crowd is reflected generally in vv 7–10. The noun שָׁלוֹם (Isa 34:8; Hos 9:7) denotes the compensation which restores balance and harmony;[25] Jrm's problem is that he does not see any justice in his situation. It may be added that if this vocalization is correct, Jrm doubtless had the common idiom "my familiar friends" in mind and was playing on it here: it is ironic, then, that the vocalization was lost.

The noun at the end of the colon, צַלְעִי, is ambiguous, either "my rib" (צֵלָע) or "my stumbling" (צֶלַע), and both are evidently intended. The meaning "rib" is employed in *V* ("my side") and *θ'*, and evidently also by *s'* and implied by *a'* (both cited in the Syro-Hexapla); both Rashi and Qimḥi, on the other hand, interpret the word as "stumbling," as do all modern commentators (Rudolph notes that the word cannot mean "side," because with persons the word means "rib," an observation that might stimulate the response, Why not, then, "rib"?). If one takes the meaning "stumbling," the connotation is clearly hostile (compare Pss 35:15, וּבְצַלְעִי שָׂמְחוּ וְנֶאֱסָפוּ "and at my stumbling they gathered in glee", and further 56:7, הֵמָּה עֲקֵבַי יִשְׁמֹרוּ "they watch my footprints," and 71:10, וְשֹׁמְרֵי נַפְשִׁי "those who watch for my life"). If one takes the meaning "rib," the connotation may likewise be hostile, but not necessarily; or rather, Jrm may be using a phrase that under other circumstances may have had a benevolent meaning and turning it to hostile purposes. Johann Friedrich Schleusner in the eighteenth century cites the phrase in the Qur'ān, 4:40, *aṣ-ṣābihu bil-janbi* "the companion of one's side" = "traveling companion,"[26] and one thinks of phraseology such as is found in Ps 121:5, יהוה שֹׁמְרֶךָ יהוה צִלְּךָ עַל־יַד יְמִינֶךָ "Yahweh is your watcher, Yahweh is your shade on your right hand." Thus the plurality of שֹׁמְרֵי here (like Ps 71:10), in contrast to the singularity of Yahweh, who is one's true keeper, may suggest hostility, a hostility that is under-

---

25 Compare, on the whole concept, Pedersen, I/II, 392–95.

26 Johann Friedrich Schleusner (editor) in Michaelis (1793) 172.

lined by the homonymous "my stumbling."

The fifth colon ironically repeats verbs from the first two cola of v 7. The first, יְפֻתֶּה, is puʻal, corresponding to the piʻel "you have deceived me" in v 7; the passive in v 7 is nipʻal, not puʻal (see there). What Jrm's enemies hope for, Jrm has already accused Yahweh of having accomplished: Jrm has already let himself be deceived by Yahweh, Yahweh has overpowered Jrm (v 7), Jrm cannot overpower Yahweh's word planted within him (v 9). The opponents say "perhaps" when it is already done! This irony is parallel to that found in 11:19; there the opponents hope that Jrm's name will be remembered no more, a hope that was already fulfilled by Yahweh's call to Jrm to remain celibate (see there). The deception that Jrm's enemies anticipate is evidently to be accomplished by their using his words (see above, on the second and third cola), and the overpowering as well.

The last colon is an expression of the enemies' hope that they can take their נְקָמָה on Jrm, whereas what one must expect from the solidarity of the covenant is that Yahweh take his נְקָמָה on Jrm's enemies (v 12 = 11:20). For a general explication of this noun see 11:20; the word refers to the "retribution" or "vindication" that is characteristic of the sovereign. The horror of the present clause is that Jrm's enemies undertake to act on behalf of Yahweh against Jrm, Yahweh's man.[27]

The material in vv 7–10 gives the impression that Jrm is in a hall of mirrors: that Yahweh is his enemy (v 7) and that his enemies pretend to be his friends (v 10); that his enemies hope to do what Yahweh has already done— deceive him and best him (vv 7, 10); that he feels trapped, without any possibility of escape (v 9). Rarely have the ambiguities of life with God been so starkly portrayed, and the ambiguities with which these lines are filled aids in the effect.

■ 11 For the justification for a revocalization in the first colon of this verse, see Preliminary Observations, Structure, Form, *Meaning of v 11*. If the revocalization is correct, "Yahweh" is vocative here (as it is in v 12). The suggested verb, אִוִּיתִךָ, is אוה piʻel, "want, crave, desire." It normally appears with נֶפֶשׁ as subject, suggesting the context of appetite, and a related noun אַוָּה is used of sexual appetite in 2:24. The verb appears with Yahweh

as object in Isa 26:9. If correct, it is a poignant expression of Jrm's willingness to accept the companionship of Yahweh in his life (compare the sexual implication of the verbs in the first colon of v 7).

In 14:9 the people compare Yahweh to an impotent גִּבּוֹר "warrior"; here, by contrast, Jrm understands him as a "violent, terrifying" גִּבּוֹר. Jrm uses the same adjective (עָרִיץ) in 15:21 of his own enemies; by his description here he evidently trusts that Yahweh will fight fire with fire. It is striking that this is the only instance in the OT where this adjective is applied to Yahweh; it is used otherwise of foreign nations and of the wicked in general. With regard to the comparison of Yahweh to a warrior, one wonders whether Jrm had in mind here Ps 78:65, "Then Yahweh awoke as from sleep, like a warrior (כְּגִבּוֹר) shouting from wine," especially since the next verse in that psalm (78:66) states that Yahweh put his adversaries to "everlasting shame" (חֶרְפַּת עוֹלָם)— compare "everlasting disgrace" (כְּלִמַּת עוֹלָם) here.

For עַל־כֵּן "that is how" see 5:27. But in that passage (as is normal) the conjunction is followed by perfect verbs; here, by contrast, they are imperfects, suggesting that these verbs express a hypothetical result, the result of Jrm's unfulfilled hopes.

There are two previous passages with diction resembling the present one. The first is 6:15, where "stumble" (כשל) and "be ashamed, discredited" (בוש) are likewise found. There the subject is the people in general, but evidently with the accent on those who preach good news instead of bad, including prophets (6:13, 14). The other parallel is 17:18, another confession: there one finds both "be ashamed" (בוש) and "my persecutors" (רֹדְפַי) (compare Setting).

Neither "be ashamed" nor "succeed" is quite right here for בשׁו qal and שׂכל hipʻil respectively. The verb בוש appears in a similar context in Mic 3:7, of an invalid word; prophets with an invalid word will be "discredited." Similarly שׂכל hipʻil is here "have insight" (compare 9:23). The phrasing in 10:21 may be relevant here: there it is said that the shepherds (= the kings) have not inquired of Yahweh, and "that is why [עַל־כֵּן] they have failed [לֹא הִשְׂכִּילוּ]," that is, have no insight. What has happened to the kings must happen to those who

27   Mendenhall, *Tenth Generation*, 97.

encourage them, the optimistic prophets.

The verb "overpower" (יכל) occurs here for the fourth time in the passage. The whole passage turns out to ring the changes on power: Yahweh is stronger than Jrm; Jrm is not stronger than Yahweh's word; Jrm's enemies assume they are stronger than Jrm; Jrm's enemies, if Yahweh will work as he should, will not ultimately be strong. The noun חֶרְפָּה (here "disgrace") reaches back to its occurrence in v 8, where it was the word of Yahweh that was a "disgrace," a source of "reproach." The phrase "will never be forgotten" here is an echo of "I shall not remember it" in v 9: Jrm wants to forget Yahweh's word, but he does not want the offense of his enemies to be forgotten. The verb here further echoes "and his name shall be remembered no more" in 11:19 (the phrase here leads into v 12, a variation of 11:20): Jrm's enemies wish his name not to be remembered, but Jrm wishes the offense of his enemies not to be forgotten (for all this see Preliminary Observations, Structure, Form).

■ 12 This verse is almost identical with 11:20; the only difference is that 11:20 reads שֹׁפֵט צֶדֶק בֹּחֵן "O righteous judge, O you who test [the mind and the heart]," while the present verse reads בֹּחֵן צַדִּיק רֹאֶה "O tester of the righteous/O righteous tester, O you who see [the mind and the heart]." The textual differences do not significantly change the meaning; the expression שֹׁפֵט צֶדֶק in 11:20 is ambiguous, and בֹּחֵן צַדִּיק here is similarly so: for a discussion of the ambiguities and of the verse in general see 11:20. The third colon here, "let me see your retribution on them," balances the last colon in v 10, "and take our retribution on him": Jrm asks that Yahweh counter the intention of his enemies.

The diction of v 10 suggests that Jrm only gradually became aware of the maleficent motives of those who were quoting his words: in that way the diction of the emendation of the last colon of the verse ("to me you revealed my adversaries") is relevant in the situation of the present passage as much as the phrase was in the situation of 11:18–20.

■ 13 As already noted (see Preliminary Observations, Structure, Form), this verse has often been considered secondary. Word usage suggests, however, that it is genuine.[28] Thus Jrm uses אֶבְיוֹן "the poor" in poetic

oracles elsewhere—5:28 ("the needy") and 22:16 (in 2:34 the word is evidently a gloss). The phrase יַד or יְדֵי + מְרֵעִים "hand(s) of evildoers" appears otherwise only in 23:14 and Job 8:20. The phrase נצל hip'il + מִיַּד "save from the hand of," though common in the OT, appears in 15:21, "save from the hand of the wicked," part of another confessional passage. These data do not prove the passage to be genuine, but they do indicate that the diction is not alien to Jrm. (One may note further that if "evildoers" [מְרֵעִים] is correctly restored in 23:10, the word there is associated with [unfaithful] priests and prophets; this suggests in turn that "evildoers" here is a term for those persecuting Jrm, thus enhancing the possible authenticity and appropriateness of the present verse.)

Form-critically the verse, an acknowledgment of Yahweh's help, may round off a lament (see Form). There is therefore no need to resort to an assumption of irony or sarcasm.[29]

Curiously the parallel of שִׁיר qal "sing" and הלל pi'el "praise" occurs only once otherwise in the OT (Ps 149:1). The two verbs are found near each other in Ps 104:33, 35, but the parallel is by no means a standard one.

If the verse is authentic to Jrm, it is striking that he uses the term "poor man" to refer to himself.

Aim

Jrm here effects a complicated set of testimonies about his perception of his life as Yahweh's prophet. Initially he expresses his bitter accusation to Yahweh that Yahweh has deceived him, seduced him, tricked him; in blasphemous daring this accusation is unmatched in the Bible. Job would be portrayed as accusing God of overpowering him (Job 9:16–19), the psalmist had accused God of abandoning him (Ps 22:2), but an accusation of deception presses God into a diabolic frame which is unique. The evidence Jrm brings to bear for this deception is his experience as proclaimer of Yahweh's word: he is "damned if he does and damned if he doesn't" speak out that word (vv 8–9).

Yet that accusation leaves Jrm with no one else to turn to; the hint in the cry "Violence!" and "Destruction!" that he is asking for help from an unfeeling universe for the

---

28   See Holladay, "Style," 52–53, though the data there are stated somewhat inaccurately.

29   Against my tentative suggestion in Holladay, "Style,"

53; compare Eissfeldt, *Introduction*, 117.

violence that Yahweh has done to him (see on v 8) is only that: a hint. Though he may cry that Yahweh has deceived him, there is no one to turn to but Yahweh, and that conclusion is signaled first by his very complaint to Yahweh of ill treatment, and then by the word of v 11 (whether taken as an affirmation of confidence with *M* or as an affirmation of desire by the revocalization suggested here). If Jrm has been bitter toward Yahweh, he does not abandon his relation with him, as one might today.[30]

But if Jrm has expressed his ambivalence toward Yahweh in his shift from bitter accusation to positive trust, he is at the same time expressing other ambiguities. His enemies are said to be planning the overpowering of Jrm in the way the prophet accuses Yahweh of having done (v 10 against v 7); this is a theme met in an earlier confession (11:19). The enemies themselves are not what they seem: not only do they plan secretly to kill Jrm (so again 11:19), but they openly use Jrm's own words against him (v 10). And underlying this sense that Jrm expresses of being trapped in a hall of mirrors (see on v 10) is a steady web of ambiguity in vv 7–10, multiple meanings and multiple possibilities of interpretation that cannot be accidental: the force of the cries "Violence!" and "Destruction!" in v 8a, the uncertainty whether in v 8b the word of Yahweh attracts laughter from Jrm's enemies or from Jrm himself, the pun of "my rib" and "my stumbling" in v 10. By these means the prophet lends complexity to the expression he gives of his predicament.

In this confession, as in others in the series, Jrm gives

classic form to the love-hate relation he has with Yahweh, with whom he is bound through thick and thin. And Jrm's shift from accusation to trust is surprisingly crowned by his affirmation that Yahweh has after all saved him from his enemies (v 13).

The sense Jrm has given in this passage of being existentially trapped is analogous to that expressed by Paul many centuries later: "In my inmost self I delight in the law of God, but I perceive that there is in my bodily members a different law, fighting against the law that my reason approves and making me a prisoner under the law that is in my members, the law of sin. Miserable creature that I am, who is there to rescue me out of this body doomed to death?" (Rom 7:22–24, *NEB*). Paul's answer, "God alone, through Jesus Christ our Lord! Thanks be to God!" (v 25a there) is analogous to the affirmation of Jrm's in v 13 here. And if Jesus in the ordeal of his crucifixion gave voice to the psalmist's cry of abandonment ("My God, my God, why have you forsaken me?" Ps 22:2; Mark 15:34 = Matt 27:46), Christian tradition has matched that cry with another cry of Jesus, likewise from a psalm of lament, but this time an utterance of confidence ("Father, into your hands I commend my spirit," Ps 31:6; Luke 23:46).

---

30   Terrien makes the same point about Job; see Samuel Terrien, "Introduction to Job," *IB* 3:898–99.

Why Was I Born?

Bibliography
Prijs, Leo
"Jeremia xx 14 ff.: Versuch einer neuen Deutung,"
VT 14 (1964) 104–8.

20

14   **Cursed is the day on which I was born,**
    the day when my mother bore me—
      how could it be blessed?

15   **Cursed is the man about whom my father**
    ⟨**was brought news**⟩:[a]
    "A son is born to you!"
    a male (who) did delight him.

16   **He [that man][a] shall be like the cities**
    which Yahweh overthrew
    《**in anger**》[b] **and without pity,**
    and he shall hear an outcry in the
      morning
    and an alarm at [c] time of[c] noon:

17   **(a time) when ⟨pregnant⟩[a] 《she did not kill**
    me,》[b]
    so that my mother would have been for
      me my grave,
    ⟨**(my) loving-mother**⟩[c] **forever with**
      child!

18   **Why from the womb did I come forth**
    to see hardship and torment
    and my days end in shame?

Text

15a   Vocalizing בֻּשַּׂר, pu'al, for *M* בִּשַּׂר, by which the clause would read "who brought news to my father." See Interpretation, vv 14–18.

16a   Omit as a gloss; the two words overload the colon. The "cities" should be defined by the restrictive relative clause within a single colon, and five "words" constitute the maximum for a colon (O'Connor, *Structure*, 138). It may be noted that Giesebrecht also deleted the words as a gloss, although he substituted אָרוּר "cursed" for them. See further Interpretation, vv 14–18.

b   Inserting בְּאַף (or בְּחֵמָה) with *G* (ἐν θυμῷ), against Janzen, p. 64, who assumes that the expression is an addition in *G* from Deut 29:22. See Structure.

c—c   Two MSS. and *G* and *S* omit "time of."

17a   Reading the consonants as a substantive parallel with "mother," the same word as evidently occurs in Isa 49:15a (Dahood, *Psalms I*, 49; "Denominative *riḥḥam* 'to conceive, enwomb,'" *Bib* 44 [1963] 204). Dahood vocalizes the word as a pi'el participle, מְרַחֵם, but this is by no means certain. See Interpretation, vv 14–18.

b   Reading the verb as מוֹתְתַתְנִי third-person singular feminine (compare וּמְמֹתְתֵהוּ, Ezek 31:4), for *M* מוֹתְתַנִי, masculine: see Interpretation, vv 14–18.

c   *M* רַחְמָה is traditionally understood as a by-form of רַחְמָהּ "her womb." But "womb" is masculine and the adjective הָרַת "pregnant" is here feminine. Further there is no other passage in which the adjective הָרָה modifies "womb"; always otherwise it modifies a "woman." Parallelism here demands a term for "my mother" (thus the suggestion of Meir Wallenstein, "Some Aspects of the Vocabulary and Morphology of the Hymns of the Judean Scrolls," *VT* 7 [1957] 213). One must assume either a pi'el participle מְרַחֲמָה without mem or else a feminine noun or adjective for רחמה with uncertain vocalization.

Interpretation

■ **14–18** It is clear that Jrm is here using extreme language, but disturbing questions are raised by the traditional understanding of the passage, beginning with what *M* seems to have and with what *G* and *V* have, and continuing to the present day (represented well enough by the *RSV*). The first necessity, then, is to investigate the meaning of the passage as a whole.

Duhm has laid out the difficulties with admirable clarity. One might understand that Jrm would curse the day he was born (v 14). But then his leveling a curse against the man who had brought to Jrm's father the news of the birth of the baby boy (v 15) is remarkable. One assumes that if one is forbidden to curse one's mother or father (Deut 27:16), then this man becomes the object of Jrm's cursing: one tends to punish the messenger who brings bad news! But the preoccupation with the messenger continues in v 16, where he becomes the central figure, and one wonders, why should this messenger be treated like Sodom and Gomorrah of old? The problem becomes even more severe in v 17, where one understands the messenger to be the subject of "kill": it is hard to credit the notion of the messenger's killing the unborn child. Accordingly Cornill, Volz, and Rudolph emend "that man" in v 16 to "that day," although there is no textual warrant for this change. Two other emendations have also been made: in the text of *M* in v 16 the two main verbs are "indicative" ("shall be," "shall hear"), not jussive ("let him be," "let him hear"), as one might expect them to be if the curse clauses continue: indeed the *G* and *V* do render them as if jussives. Accordingly Volz emends וְהָיָה to יְהִי, and Rudolph and Bright emend both וְהָיָה and וְשָׁמַע to יְהִי and יִשְׁמַע respectively. But this whole tissue of assumptions and emendations needs to be challenged.

Leo Prijs meets half the problem of the nature of the curse[1] by proposing that v 15 is not the expression of a wish but the declaration of a fact:[2] by this understanding the two main verbs in v 16 are indicative after all. Prijs

suggests that Jrm is not cursing the messenger, rather he is pitying him because he is cursed—the messenger, by announcing Jrm's birth, announces his own downfall, since Jrm has become the prophet of the destruction of the people. By this understanding the messenger is simply an anonymous representative of Jerusalem, the city that will fall like Sodom and Gomorrah (v 16).

But if v 15 is to be translated "cursed is the man," what about v 14? Understanding of that verse is shaped by the negative jussive in the last colon, אַל־יְהִי בָרוּךְ, which appears to mean "let it not be blessed": by that understanding the first colon must likewise carry a jussive meaning and be rendered "cursed be the day." But it is proposed here that this verse, too, is the declaration of a fact, parallel with vv 15–16, and not the expression of a wish: the first colon is to be translated "cursed is the day."[3] I submit that the negative jussive in the last colon of the verse is explicated by a similar sequence in Obadiah 12—14. There one finds a whole series of prohibitions with אַל, but they all refer to the past, not the present: "you should not have gloated," rather than "do not gloat," and so on; Julius A. Bewer remarks, "They do not refer to the fut. but to the past which the vivid imagination of the prophet conjures up."[4] This usage was understood by *KJV* ("thou shouldest not have looked on") and is understood by recent translations (*NJV*: "How could you gloat. . . ?"). The usage of the present passage differs from that sequence in Obadiah 12—14 only in having a subject in the third person instead of the second. It is possible therefore to translate here "How could it be blessed?" rather than "Let it not be blessed!"

By this understanding Jrm is expressing dismay rather than anger toward Yahweh, emotion appropriate for laments (see Form). And by this understanding, too, the passage conforms to the interpretation in the present study of 11:3 and 17:5, where likewise the translation is "cursed is . . ." rather than "cursed be. . . ."

The next problem to be faced is the question of the subject of "kill" in v 17. Rashi assumed it to be the angel

1   Leo Prijs, "Jeremia xx 14 ff.: Versuch einer neuen Deutung," *VT* 14 (1964) 104–8.
2   For the distinction see Scharbert, "ארר," 408.
3   Franz D. Hubmann, by personal communication, against Scharbert, "ארר," 408.
4   Julius A. Bewer, *A Critical and Exegetical Commentary on the Books of Obadiah and Joel* (ICC; New York: Scribner's, 1911) 27; similarly König, *Syntax*, sec. 190b.

of death, omitted by ellipsis. The difficulty of assuming it is the messenger who brought the news to Jrm's father has already been stated, but emending "man" to "day" in v 16 is not called for.

One possibility would be to understand the subject as God: it is God who shapes the fetus in the womb (Ps 139:13), it is God who takes the infant from his mother's womb (Ps 22:10),[5] above all it is Yahweh who called Jrm to be a prophet before he came forth from the womb (1:5), so it is plausible to propose Yahweh as the subject of the verb here. One could vocalize the consonants of the verb as second-person singular (מוֹתַתְנִי) rather than third-person singular: this is what Luther seems to have done ("dass du mich doch nicht getötet hast").

The difficulty with this solution, however, is that by this reading this clause would be the only instance of direct address in the passage; further, the confessional sequence most like this one, 15:10–11, does not contain an address to Yahweh. A preferable solution, I propose, is to understand Jrm's mother to be the subject of the verb: a third-person singular feminine verb would have a sequence of three taws (see Text), leading almost inevitably to a simplification to two taws. This reading makes the subject of this verb identical with the subjects of the verbs in the other two cola of the verse; the word מרחם, read in M as "from the womb," is here taken as subject (see Text, and see further Interpretation of v 17). By this understanding the verb offers a nice balance with the verb in the second colon of v 14: מוֹתְתַתְנִי will balance יְלָדְתְנִי; and, more subtly, "the day when" in v 14 is balanced by "(a time) when," the interpretation to be proposed for אֲשֶׁר in v 17.

Interpreters have assumed that the messenger of whom v 14 appears to speak is still the center of vv 15 and 16. One might assume, as Prijs does, that the nation is doomed and that the messenger is an exemplar of that nation, doomed to be destroyed (v 16), but it is a strange preoccupation in the poem; after all, the climactic question is not "When, O Yahweh, will you destroy the nation?" but rather "Why was I born?" (v 18). Even more troublesome is the very idea of a male messenger to deliver the news to Jrm's father (v 15): one would expect the midwife, or a servant girl, to bring the news, unless

indeed Hilkiah was in Jerusalem (see on 1:1). One can explain the phrases of the text in M one way or another, but one cannot avoid the sense that the flow of thought is puzzling.

I propose that there is no messenger at all; I propose that the pi'el verb בִּשַּׂר "brought news to" in v 15 be revocalized as a pu'al (passive) בֻּשַּׂר "was brought news" —in this way the "man" in vv 15 and 16 is understood to be Jrm himself. The following data are relevant. (1) The construction of the sign of the accusative אֶת־ with the formal subject is normal for a passive (GKC, sec. 121a). (2) A pu'al in the first colon of v 15 after אֲשֶׁר would parallel a pu'al (or passive qal) יֻלַּדְתִּי after אֲשֶׁר in the first colon of v 14. (3) More substantially, Jrm refers to himself as "man" (אִישׁ) in 15:10, a passage dated to the same period as that to which I arrive for the present passage (see Setting). Indeed 15:10a has diction closely comparable to that of the present passage: "Woe is me, mother, that you (ever) bore me, a man of lawsuit and strife for the whole land." (4) Whether "that man" in v 16 is a gloss or not (see Text, see below, and see Structure), if one construes the actions of the main verbs in that verse to be actions of Jrm, they state that Jrm will be overthrown like Sodom and Gomorrah. By comparison, 15:13–14, part of Yahweh's answer to Jrm's word in 15:10, is likewise concerned with Jrm's suffering when the nation collapses. And in 4:19 Jrm hears in his mind's ear the "alarm [תְּרוּעָה] of war," just as the subject of the verb in v 16b of the present passage will hear "an alarm [תְּרוּעָה] at time of noon." (5) I propose a parallel between "hear an outcry . . . and an alarm" in v 16 and "to see hardship and torment" in v 18; in v 18, of course, Jrm is the subject. (6) It might be objected that Jrm's sense that he is as doomed as the cities of old contradicts Yahweh's promise to him to make him a "fortified bronze wall" (15:20). But that promise was specifically to arm Jrm against those who oppose him among the people, especially the optimistic prophets. This affirmation cuts deeper: in 20:7 Jrm accuses Yahweh of bad faith in the prophetic vocation; so here, by implication, Jrm affirms that his whole life is for nought. (It may be noted in passing that if this conclusion is sound, it would be difficult to find a passage where interpretation shifts so

---

5   Holladay, "Background."

markedly on the basis of a single vowel!)

The passage, by this understanding, may be paraphrased as follows. "Doom hangs over the day of my birth; indeed doom has hung over me from the very time of my birth. I will be destroyed as thoroughly as Sodom and Gomorrah were destroyed, but that destruction of old was done by Yahweh in his anger and in broad daylight, whereas in my own case Yahweh called me from birth to be his prophet, had his positive purpose for me. If my life is for nought, why was I not killed in the dark, before I was born? Why did I come into the world at all?" This movement of thought is focused and is coherent with that of the other confessions.

It must be stressed that if one reads the verb בשר in v 15 as a pu'al and understands the "man" to be Jrm, then one cannot read the verb מותתני in v 17 as it is ordinarily read, having as subject the "man," inasmuch as the object of the verb (first-person singular) is obviously Jrm. But it must also be admitted that if the contention of the present study is correct, that the subject of מותתני is other than the "man," then the relative conjunction אֲשֶׁר at the beginning of v 17 becomes a problem: it cannot refer to the subject of מותתני, as the verse is ordinarily understood.

These considerations lead to an examination of the five occurrences of אֲשֶׁר in the passage: I am unsure about whether they are original to the text. Cross and Freedman and their students delete this particle in preexilic poetry as an insertion appropriate to prose but not to the poetry of that period.[6] But one could conceive that the occurrences are original to the poem and help not only to clarify the syntax of the various dependent clauses but help to give structure to the poem as a whole. On the other hand, the occurrence of the particle at the very beginning of v 17 is notably awkward, as already stated, particularly if the verb is to be construed as feminine: if the particle is original, it is best translated "when," referring to "time of noon." In this way it will be a counterpoise to "(the day) when my mother bore me"

in v 14 (see above). But my own judgment is that it is better omitted, and therefore the other occurrences of the conjunction are also likely to be secondary.

I also propose that "that man" in v 16 is a gloss. If the first colon of v 16 includes "which Yahweh overthrew," as would seem necessary to define "like the cities," then the colon as it stands contains six "words," one too many for O'Connor's constraints on length of colon (see Text). The phrase may offer a correct reference for the subject of the verbs, but it still appears to be a prosaic addition, added after the verb at the beginning of v 15 was read as a pi'el; see further Structure.

And then there is the word לֵאמֹר (literally, "saying") at the end of the first colon of v 15; that word seems necessary in 6:14 but does not add much to the present poem. It is likely, then, that the original poem was somewhat more concise than the text before us.

For Interpretation on the individual verses, see after Setting.

Structure

Verses 14–18 form a separate unit of confessional material (see vv 7–13, Preliminary Observations, Structure, Form, *Extent of Unit*). Its position here suggests that it was the last of the confessions to be recorded (see Setting). But its position here also serves as an inclusio to round off the confessions ("my mother," v 14, compare 15:10; "my father," v 15, compare "your father," 12:6, and further "mothers" and "fathers" in 16:3), indeed as an inclusio to the whole collection of material that begins with the call in chapter 1: v 18 here is comparable to "before you came forth from the womb I dedicated you" in 1:5.[7]

The internal structure of the passage may be set forth in a variety of ways. In general the poem ends as it began, with the theme of Jrm's birth. Similarly the passage begins with "the day" (twice in v 14), shifts to "the morning" and "the time of noon" in v 16, and reverts to "my days" in v 18.

6   Contrast the remarks in Frank M. Cross and David N. Freedman, *Studies in Ancient Yahwistic Poetry* (SBLDS 21; Missoula, MT: Scholars, 1975) 28, concerning that conjunction in "authentic old Hebrew poetry," and the deletion of the conjunction in 20:6 in Christensen, "Terror," 502.

7   For these and further suggestions regarding the way the passage offers an inclusio within the confessions

see Holladay, *Architecture*, 129–34; for the inclusio with 1:5 see Lundbom, *Jeremiah*, 28.

Rudolph displays v 14 as four cola (see *BHS*), but in v 14b the subject cannot be separated from its verb, and "day" in v 14a needs its restrictive relative clause ("on which I was born") to be included within its colon; I therefore take the verse to be a bicolon. The verse offers a nice chiasmus (cursed/blessed, was born/bore). Rudolph is also in error in displaying v 15 as four cola: v 15aα cannot be broken up; the verse is a tricolon (although in contrast to *M* I separate בֵּן from its parallel זָכָר: see Interpretation on v 15). Verse 15 offers at least some parallel to v 14 ("cursed is the day," "cursed is the man," followed in both instances by אֲשֶׁר). If the first colon of v 14 includes the restrictive relative clause (see above), then the first colon of v 16 evidently must be analyzed analogously. This leaves "without pity" (literally "and was not sorry") too short to make up a colon; the *G* text supplies the needed expression (see Text). Verse 16 then emerges as a tetracolon. Verses 17–18 are two tricola. The length of successive verses becomes great from v 14 to v 16 (bicolon, tricolon, tetracolon); now the poem tightens as it moves to the end (tricolon, tricolon).

Form

The comparable phrases in Job 3:1–26 embody a self-curse; that genre is an extension of the curse against one's enemy.[8] But if the analysis already made is correct (see Interpretation, vv 14–18), Jrm is not here leveling a curse against the day of his birth, he is not expressing a wish, rather is simply stating a fact, affirming that the day of his birth is already cursed. For the pronouncement of the curse see Form for both 11:1–17 and 17:5–8. One does not find any similar affirmation of a curse in other laments, but there are laments in the Psalms that review the speaker's life from birth (Pss 22:7–11; 71:6), and Ps 51:7 affirms the speaker's tendency to iniquity from the time of birth. Jrm affirms that his purpose in life, to be Yahweh's prophet, has come to nought, because he is not heard. It is that tension that brings him agony (v 17). This affirmation of the curse on Jrm's life includes the reuse of other forms. Thus "A son is born to you" (v 15) is evidently the set formula to declare a birth (see Interpretation on that verse); in v 16 one hears an echo of an announcement of judgment. Then in v 18 Jrm

offers rhetoric normally associated with the lament: לָמָּה "why?" (compare 15:18, and often in the Psalms); עָמָל "hardship" (Pss 10:1; 22:2; 42:10; 43:2; 88:15); יָגוֹן "torment" (Pss 13:3; 31:11; 116:3); "my days end" (Pss 31:11; 102:4); "in shame" (Pss 44:16; 69:20).

Setting

The diction of this confession offers no clues for a setting. But the mention by Jrm of his parents is comparable to their mention elsewhere in the confessions (12:6; 15:10); those verses in the present study have a setting in the summer of 594, and there is no reason not to suggest the same general period for the present passage. If v 13 is a reflection of the death of Hananiah in September/October 594 (see on that verse), then one assumes the present passage to have taken shape afterward, from renewed hardship. Even if the death of Hananiah lent a legitimation to Jrm's vocation, did opposition from the prophet's immediate family continue, even increase?

Interpretation

■ **14** For the translations "cursed is the day" and "how could it be blessed?" see above, Interpretation, vv 14–18.
■ **15** For the exegesis of the verse that excludes consideration of a messenger and understands "the man" to refer to Jrm see above, Interpretation, vv 14–18. The birth of a son is eagerly awaited (compare the phrasing of 31:9 and Prov 4:30); the verb בשר pi'el is normally used of bringing good news, and the double use of שמח "rejoice" reinforces the impression. All this makes shocking Jrm's declaration of a curse on the event.

The phrase "a son is born to you" appears to be the standard form of declaration at such an event: a Ugaritic phrase suggests that standard form,[9] and Isa 9:5 and Ruth 4:17 offer parallels. If that is the standard form, then the following word, "a male" (זָכָר), which is included in the phrase if the Masoretic accentuation is to be followed, is tautological. I therefore assume that "a male" begins the next colon.
■ **16** For the exegesis of the verse that understands the subject of the main verbs to be Jrm, and for the exclusion of the phrase "that man" as a gloss, see above, Interpretation, vv 14–18.

---

8   Friedrich Horst, *Hiob 1—19* (BKAT 16/1; Neukirchen: Neukirchener, 1968) 40–41.
9   Ug. 17.2.14.

"The cities which Yahweh overthrew [הפך]" are of course Sodom and Gomorrah; the same verb is used in the narrative of the overthrow of those cities in Gen 19:21, 25, 29. Jrm refers by name to Sodom and Gomorrah in 23:14; they had been referred to repeatedly in prophetic oracles earlier than Jrm (Amos 4:11; Isa 1:9, 10; 3:9; Zeph 2:9). Jrm, like everyone else in the nation, will experience the same fate as did those ancient cities: that is the curse (see above, Interpretation, vv 14–18).

For "in anger," a phrase supplied from G, compare 21:5, where three synonymous expressions appear. The expression וְלֹא נָחָם "without pity," literally "and was not sorry," is not otherwise applied to the overthrow of Sodom and Gomorrah, but Jrm uses it to describe Yahweh's determination to destroy his covenant people (4:28), and in this he was imitated by later prophets (Ezek 24:14; Zech 8:14). The diction of "outcry in the morning" and "alarm at noon" likewise reminds one of Jrm's scenario for the fall of Jerusalem (6:4–5). The word זְעָקָה "outcry" is used in the description of Sodom and Gomorrah in Gen 18:20, but there it refers to the cry of those in the city who had suffered oppression while the city was intact;[10] here, by contrast, it refers to the "outcry" of citizens who suffer when the city is overthrown (compare 18:22). The תְּרוּעָה "alarm" is likewise a war signal (4:19).

■ 17 For the vocalization "she did not kill me" see above, Interpretation, vv 14–18. The verb "kill," מות polel, in contrast to the hip'il stem or to הרג qal, which might have been used (see 4:31), evidently carries a particular nuance. Aside from its occurrence here (the only one in Jrm) and two occurrences in the Psalms (Pss 34:22; 109:16), the only occurrences are five in Judges and Samuel (Judg 9:54; 1 Sam 17:51; 2 Sam 1:9, 10, 16)—of the armor-bearer killing Abimelech, of David's killing the Philistine after striking him with the stone, of the Amalekite killing Saul. The meaning appears to be "despatch, put someone out of his misery," and that is precisely the nuance that fits here: Jrm wishes he had been the victim of mercy killing.

The reading of M at the end of the first colon, מֵרֶחֶם, literally "from the womb," is troublesome; G and S read it as if בְּרֶחֶם "in the womb." The solution, to read the word as a substantive in parallel with "my mother," is substan-

tiated by the diction of Isa 49:15a (see Text). Indeed given the three occurrences in M of רֶחֶם "womb" in vv 17–18, a revocalization of the first two instances, reconceiving them as cognate words, is preferable from the point of view of poetic technique.

The syntax of the verb in the second colon is uncertain. The waw-consecutive imperfect וַתְּהִי may be construed either as a result (so the translation here, "so that [my mother] would have been"), here not a real result but a contrary-to-fact result (compare GKC, sec. 111l), or else as a simple consecutive, with the negative of the previous colon doing double-duty, "and (so) (my mother) was (not)."[11]

Jrm knows well the pride of a mother in her son and her desolation if that son has died (6:26, compare again Prov 4:3). That he should pronounce such desolation upon his own mother is a measure of the meaninglessness of his life in his perception.

■ 18 The enclitic זֶ, added to לָמָּה "why?" lends emphasis or urgency to the question (GKC, sec. 136c); compare the same expression in 6:20 and an analogous one in 6:16.

For a discussion of the import of the question voiced in this verse see above, Interpretation, vv 14–18.

It is to be noted that the expression מֵרֶחֶם יָצָאתִי "from the womb did I come forth" here exactly matches תֵּצֵא מֵרֶחֶם "you came forth from the womb" in 1:5 (see Structure).

This is the only occurrence in Jrm of עָמָל "hardship"; for יָגוֹן "torment" see 8:18 (it occurs further in 31:13; 45:3). The connotations of עָמָל cover "hard work" and "trouble": "hardship" is perhaps the best English equivalent. This is the only OT passage where these two words are linked.

There are two interpretations of the last clause in v 18, with the waw-consecutive imperfect וַיִּכְלוּ: most take it as dependent on the previous infinitive, "[to see hardship and torment,] to end my days in shame" (Volz, Condamin, Rudolph, Bright; see GKC, sec. 114r); but it is perhaps simpler to see the verb as coordinate with the perfect יָצָאתִי in the first colon (so Giesebrecht, and so here).

---

10 Westermann, *Genesis*, II, 353.
11 Compare Dahood, *Psalms III*, 438.

Aim

Biblical faith is so life-affirming that actual suicide is exceedingly rare. In the record one finds: Abimelech, by requesting his armor-bearer to kill him, Judg 9:54; Samson, by bringing the hall down upon himself and the crowd, Judg 16:26–30; Saul and his armor-bearer, according to 1 Sam 31:4–5; Ahithophel, 2 Sam 17:23; Zimri, 1 Kgs 16:18; Judas, Matt 27:5. Most of these instances are matters of honor in war.[12]

Here, by contrast, is the expression of one who was convinced he was a prophet, one whom the biblical tradition has affirmed to be a prophet. He is not contemplating suicide, but he is affirming that his life has no value, and in doing so he offers diction which would later be used in Job's rejection of his life (Job 3:1–26). Even more, Jrm is affirming that Yahweh's vocation for his life has no value, and in so doing he comes close to following the action recommended by Job's wife to Job ("Curse God, and die," Job 2:9).

It is the affirmation that Yahweh's life with him has no value that is the ultimate horror of this utterance. It is a theme that others would take up later on. It is the implication of Jesus' story of the prodigal son: by asking his father for his share of the property (Luke 15:12), the son indicates that he wants his father to die, the father who in the story represents God.[13] To affirm that a curse hangs over the day of one's birth, the day when one's vocation with God comes to light; to wish God's own death—these are correlative efforts to remove the appalling tension created when God's people perceive that the demands laid on them by God are unendurable.

Yet such utterances, preserved in Scripture, form part of the paradox of God's work with his people, that even an affirmation that a vocation initiated by God is meaningless is encompassed by his sovereign concern for his people and his world.

---

12   For postbiblical Jewish thinking on suicide see G. Margoliouth, "Suicide (Jewish)," *Encyclopaedia of Religion and Ethics* (ed. James Hastings; New York: Scribner's, 1920–30) 12, 37–38; Haim H. Cohn, "Suicide," *EncJud*, 15, 490–91.

13   Kenneth E. Bailey, *Poet and Peasant, A Literary-Cultural Approach to the Parables in Luke* (Grand Rapids: Eerdmans, 1976) 161–62.

Zedekiah Begs Jeremiah
for a Hopeful Word

Bibliography

On 21:1–14:
McKane, William
  "The Construction of Jeremiah Chapter xxi," *VT*
  32 (1982) 59–73.

On 21:1–10:
Pohlmann, Karl-Friedrich
  *Studien zum Jeremiabuch, Ein Beitrag zur Frage nach
  der Entstehung des Jeremiabuches* (FRLANT 118;
  Göttingen: Vandenhoeck & Ruprecht, 1978) 31–
  47.

On 21:1–7:
Overholt, Thomas W.
  "King Nebuchadnezzar in the Jeremiah Tra-
  dition," *CBQ* 30 (1968) 39–48.
Reventlow
  Liturgie, 143–49.
Selms, Adriaan van
  "The Name Nebuchadnezzar," *Travels in the World
  of the Old Testament, Studies Presented to Professor M.
  A. Beek on the Occasion of his 65th Birthday* (ed. M. S.
  H. G. Heerma van Voss et al.; Assen: Van Gorcum,
  1974) 223–29.
Weippert, Helga
  "Jahwekrieg und Bundesfluch in Jer 21, 1–7,"
  ZAW 82 (1970) 396–409.
Weippert
  Prosareden, 67–86.

21

1 The word which came to Jeremiah from
Yahweh, when King Zedekiah sent to
him Pashhur the son of Malchiah, and
Zephaniah the son of Maaseiah the
priest, to say, 2/ "Please inquire of
Yahweh on our behalf, for [Nebuchad-
rezzar][a] the king of Babylon is fighting
against us; perhaps Yahweh will act
[with us][b] according to all his marvelous
deeds by making (him) withdraw from
us." 3/ But Jeremiah said to them, "Thus
shall you say to Zedekiah, 4/ Thus
Yahweh [God of Israel][a] has said, I am
going to turn the weapons around—
which are in your hand, with which you
are fighting [the king of Babylon and][b]
the Chaldeans besieging you—from the
outside of the wall [and I shall gather
them][c] toward the center of the city. 5/
And I myself shall fight against you with
outstretched hand and mighty arm, in
anger, wrath and great rage. 6/ And I
shall strike down the inhabitants of this
city, both man and beast: with great

Text

2a   Lacking in *G*; the addition of the name "Nebuchadrezzar" is typical of the expansionist tendency
of *M* in the prose of Jer. See Janzen, pp. 69–70, 72.

b   Lacking in *G*, doubtless an expansionist gloss. *M*
אוֹתָנוּ must be understood as אִתָּנוּ, as often in Jer
(compare 2:35).

4a   Lacking in *G*; see Janzen, pp. 75–76.

b   Lacking in *G*; it is an expansion probably on the
basis on v 2. See Janzen, p. 43, no. 43.

c   Lacking in *G*; the words are evidently a secondary
expansion in *M*. See again Janzen, p. 43, no. 43.

pestilence they shall die. 7/ And afterward—oracle of Yahweh—I shall give
Zedekiah king of Judah, and his servants,
and the people left[a] in this city from
pestilence and[b] sword and famine [into
the hand of Nebuchadrezzar king of
Babylon and][c] into the hand of their
enemies [and into the hand of those][d]
seeking their lives; and ⟨they shall strike
them down⟩[e] by the edge of the sword; ⟪I
shall not spare⟫[f] them or ⟪pity⟫[f] or ⟪have
mercy.⟫⟫[f]

7a Reading with a few MSS. and *G*, *S*, and *T*; *M*
inserts וְאֶת־, so that the passage reads "and the
people and those left. . . ."

b Reading with many MSS. and *G*, *V*, and *T*; *M*
omits "and."

c Lacking in *G*; that omission may be due to
haplography, but it is more likely an expansionist
gloss. See Janzen, p. 41, c'.

d Lacking in *G*; an expansionist gloss (compare
19:7). See Janzen, p. 41, c'.

e Reading וְהִכּוּם with *G* for *M* וְהִכָּם "and he shall
strike them down." *M* has evidently shifted the
attention to Nebuchadrezzar (compare c, f).

f Reading אָחוּס, אַחְמֹל, and אֲרַחֵם; *G* reads only the
first and last verbs, having evidently omitted the
second by haplography or an effort at concision, but
the two verbs in *G* are first-person singular. *M* reads
יַחְמֹל, יָחוּס, and יְרַחֵם "he shall not spare them," etc.
M has shifted the action to Nebuchadrezzar
(compare e). The only other occasion for these three
verbs in Jer is in 13:14, and there Yahweh is the
subject. Theologically the readings in *G* represent
the *lectio difficilior*; it is easier to imagine a shift of the
subject of these verbs from Yahweh to Nebuchadrezzar than the reverse.

Structure

Extent of Unit; Placement of Unit. Some commentators have
treated 21:1—23:8 as a literary unit (Nötscher: "Jeremiah and the Royal House"; Hyatt: "Oracles Concerning
Kings of Judah"; compare also Condamin). Others (by
the view of the present study, correctly) separate 21:1–
10 from 21:11—23:8 (Rudolph, Weiser).

The collection of 23:9–40 is a self-enclosed one with a
title of its own, "Concerning the prophets." The question
here, then, is that of material which extends no farther
than 23:8.

The core of the material in 21:1—23:8 consists of a
short collection of oracles: (1) an oracle addressed to the
royal house (21:12) attached to 20:14–18 by the catchword "morning" (בֹּקֶר, 20:16—these are the only two
occurrences of בֹּקֶר in Jer) and offering the catchword
"fire" (אֵשׁ) to what follows; (2) two more oracles (21:13–
14; 22:6–7) each containing "fire" (אֵשׁ, 21:14; 22:7),
each concerned with the pride of Jerusalem embodied in
her palace and temple ("forest," 21:14; "Lebanon," 22:6;
"cedars," 22:7), forming an inclusio with a similar oracle,
22:20–23 ("Lebanon," 22:20, 23; "cedars," 22:23)—and
one notes also the expression יֹשֶׁבֶת evidently "en-

throned," in 21:13 and 22:23. The inclusio encloses two
oracles, one on Josiah and Jehoahaz (22:10 + 11–12) and
one on Jehoiakim (22:13–19); the latter likewise has
"cedar" (22:14), and both are concerned with inappropriate death and burial. All these oracles give evidence of
having been delivered before the death of Jehoiakim (see
the respective Settings), and one assumes that the collection took shape soon after, given the attachment to
20:14–18 noted above.

The material about Jehoiachin (22:24–30) and the
oracle about a righteous Branch which offers a play on
the name of Zedekiah (23:1–8, see v 6) will have been
added subsequently to 21:12—22:23, either before or
after the latter was attached to 20:14–18. And although
the material in 21:1–10 deals with Zedekiah's time, there
is no evidence that any of 21:1–10 forms an inclusio with
23:1–8;[1] instead, 21:1–7 (or 21:1–10) appears to have
been inserted at the present point after the attachment of
21:12—22:23 to 20:14–18. It has also been assumed
that 21:1–7 or 21:1–10 are present here because of the
name "Pashhur" (21:1 and 20:1–6: so already Michaelis),
but the two occurrences refer to different men, and the
two occurrences are relatively far from each other. It is

---

1 Against Pohlmann, *Studien*, 42.

more likely that the unit has been placed here because
סבב hip'il "turn around" in v 4 shares the semantic field
with הפך in 20:16: both verbs have to do with over-
turning cities (compare the use of הפך in Hag 2:22 with
סבב hip'il in 1 Chr 10:14).

Now is 21:1–10 to be taken as one unit or two (vv 1–7
and 8–10)? Rudolph understands vv 1–10 to be the
product of the "Deuteronomistic editor" and he therefore considers the ten verses together. The present
study, however, accepts both passages as authentic
material, so that the question remains open. The message of the two passages is congruent—the hopelessness
of continued fighting. And the contents of the two
passages match those in chapter 37 and 38:1–3 (see
there). On the other hand, the introductory verb in v 8,
תֹּאמַר "you shall say" (second person singular), does not
match anything in vv 1–3: the singular verb marks the
contents to be a direct instruction from Yahweh to Jrm,
not a response to the question of a delegation. The two
passages are united not only by general contents but
more particularly by the phrase "the Chaldeans besieging
you" הַכַּשְׂדִּים הַצָּרִים עֲלֵיכֶם, vv 4, 9). That phrase is found
nowhere else in Jer (in 37:5, which appears to offer a
similar phrase, the participle and dependent prepositional phrase were added secondarily: see Text there). It
is better, then, to consider vv 1–7 and 8–10 separately
and to understand "the Chaldeans besieging you" as the
catch phrase by which vv 8–10 were put into position
here.

Internal Structure. The central affirmation of the
passage is that in v 4 the reversal is denoted by the verb
"turn around," which generates the parallelism of "from
outside of the wall toward the center of the city," and the
reversal is also signaled by the exchange of attributes in
the phrase "outstretched hand and mighty arm" in v 5
(see further Setting and Interpretation). Verse 6 likewise
exhibits parallelism. These parallelisms are filled out by
pairs and triplets which are characteristic of structure
prose (*Kunstprosa*).[2]

Form

The passage offers itself as an oracle (הַדָּבָר, "the word," v
1, as in 7:1; 11:1; 18:1), but it is in effect a simple narrative, giving the plea from Zedekiah through his
emissaries as well as the reply from Yahweh through Jrm;
one notes the slight anacoluthon between v 1 and the
introductory words in v 3.

The emissaries ask both for intercession ("on our
behalf," v 2) and for an oracle of reassurance resulting
from that intercession ("inquire").[3]

Jrm's reply is a typical judgment oracle with the
standard phrase הִנְנִי plus participle (v 4: compare 1:15;
6:21; and often); he uses the diction of holy war against
his own people[4] (compare 4:5–31, Form).

Setting

The passage poses both literary and historical questions,
and these are interrelated. A similar narrative is found in
37:3–10, and a similar oracle in 34:1–7. Some have
assumed that the present narrative and that in 37:3–10
refer to the same event.[5] Giesebrecht, however, refuted
this view (and so also Cornill and Volz).

At the same time the historical value of either the
present narrative, or of 37:3–10, or of both, has been
questioned. Thus Duhm thought that 37:3–10 was
legendary midrash and that the present passage was a
free composition by a later editor on the basis of 37:3–10
and 38:1ff. Mowinckel and Rudolph have attributed the
present passage to the "Deuteronomistic editor":
Rudolph points out that v 5a is the traditional description of Yahweh's prowess in battle (on this see below) and
that v 5b is a triad found in 32:37 and Deut 29:27. Since
37:3–10 is precisely dated and the present passage is not,
he concludes that the present passage is a rewriting of
34:1–7 and 37:3–10 without historical value (so also
Hyatt). But this analysis has been challenged by Gunther
Wanke[6] and refuted by Weippert.[7]

As to the literary question, the reversal of the attributes of the phrase in v 5a, "with outstretched hand and

2   For further analysis of the structure of the passage
     see Weippert, *Prosareden*, 75–78.
3   Compare Volz, p. 217.
4   See Pohlmann, *Studien*, 39–40.
5   So Bernhard Stade, "Bemerkungen zum Buche
     Jeremia," *ZAW* 12 (1892) 277–87.
6   Wanke, *Baruchschrift*, 102.
7   Weippert, *Prosareden*, 68–76.

mighty arm," is unique in the OT, and it suggests the reversal by which Yahweh now embarks upon holy war against his own people,[8] a reversal signaled also by the participle מֵסֵב "turn around" (v 4)—the hip'il of סבב does not occur otherwise in Jer, and the singular participle מֵסֵב does not occur otherwise in the OT. The archaic form תֹּאמְרָן (v 3) does not occur otherwise in Jer (compare the normal phrase כֹּה תֹאמְרוּ אֶל־ in 27:4; 37:7); that verbal form occurs only eight times otherwise in the OT, six of them in the expression כֹּה תֹאמְרוּן אֶל־, and all occurrences are in earlier material. The triad "sword," "famine," "pestilence" occurs repeatedly in the book, but it is clearly a combination that may be genuine to Jrm (compare 14:1—15:9, where it is a steady theme). As for the triad "in anger, fury and great wrath" in Deut 29:27, it is clear that that verse is part of supplementary material added to Deuteronomy in the light of the exile ("as at this day," v 28 there),[9] and one could well suppose that the triad there was stimulated by usage which began with Jrm.

Rudolph refers to the "verbosity of expression" in the passage,[10] and Bright describes v 4 as "long and clumsy."[11] But such subjective descriptions are not necessarily valid: the passage exhibits the characteristics of structured prose (*Kunstprosa*),[12] and there is no reason to deny it to Jrm.

Giesebrecht was correct in stating the relation between the event recorded here and that recorded in 37:3–10: the hope expressed in v 2 here is that the Babylonians will "withdraw," while in 37:5 they have withdrawn because of the pressure exerted by the Egyptian army. In the present passage the two emissaries are Pashhur and Zephaniah, while in 37:3 they are Jehucal and Zephaniah: if for some reason the present passage were an adaptation of 37:3–10, it is difficult to imagine how the names of Jehucal and Pashhur could have been confuted. There is nothing implausible in assuming two missions from Zedekiah to Jrm which had a single emissary in common, and the evidence favors it. Temporally the

event described in the present passage must precede that of 37:3–10, since after the event described in the latter passage Jrm was arrested and the subsequent dealings that the king had with Jrm had to be carried on secretly (37:17). The Egyptian invasion took place probably in the course of the summer of 588,[13] so that the date of the event here narrated must be some time early in 588.

The oracle in 34:1–7 has been referred to above (the hypothesis of Rudolph). One must conclude that there is no duplication between the oracle in the present passage and that in 34:1–7: in the present one the fate of the city is central, whereas in 34:1–7 it is the fate of Zedekiah himself that is central; furthermore the present passage assumes a violent death for Zedekiah (v 7), whereas 34:3–5 predicts that he will survive the siege and die peacefully. For the setting of 34:1–7 see there.

The existence of similar material here and in chapters 34 and 37 suggests both that several editors were at work expanding the memoirs of Jrm and that Yahweh's word to Zedekiah during the siege was of central importance to the community.

Interpretation

■ 1 For the phraseology of the introductory words see 7:1. For a possible literary relationship and for the historical relationship between this narrative and those in 34:1–7 and 37:3–10, see Setting.

Pashhur the son of Malchiah is mentioned again in 38:1, and Zephaniah the son of Maaseiah is mentioned again in 29:25 and 37:3 (and compare also 52:24). This Pashhur is one of a group called שָׂרִים "officials" (38:4), so that the two emissaries represent both the civil and the religious advisors to the king, doubtless part of a pro-Egyptian group.[14] For the derivation of the name "Pashhur" see 20:1.

The infinitive לֵאמֹר carries its full meaning "to say"; it does not depend on "the word," as it does in 7:1.
■ 2 For דרש "inquire" see 10:21. For בַּעַד "on behalf of" compare the use of that preposition with "pray" in 7:16.

8   Berridge, pp. 117–18.
9   See Mayes, *Deuteronomy*, 359.
10   "Die Weitschweifigkeit des Ausdrucks," Rudolph, p. 134.
11   Bright, p. 215.
12   See in particular Weippert, *Prosareden*, 75.
13   Bright, *History*, 330.
14   Compare ibid., 327, 329.

The name of the king of Babylon has been inserted in *M*, as often.[15] The name has two main variants in the OT, that with a reš (Nebuchadrezzar) and that with a nun (Nebuchadnezzar), each variant occurring in various spellings in the consonantal text (see the lexica). The form with reš corresponds more closely to the Babylonian form of the name, *Nabū-kudurru-uṣur*; the name means both "May (the god) Nabu protect the boundary (-stone)" and "May Nabu protect the son," evidently by an intentional ambiguity.[16] The spelling with a nun has been explained variously; Adriaan van Selms suggests that it was a scurrilous deformation of his name with the element *kudannu* substituted for *kudurru*: the name would then mean "May Nabu protect the mule."[17] For the contrastive use of the form with reš and the form with nun in Jer see the excursus "Peculiarities of Spelling, 27:1—29:3," before chapter 27.

This is the only occurrence in Jer of נִפְלָאוֹת "marvelous deeds." The word is properly the nip'al participle of פלא; it is used preeminently in the Psalms (twenty-seven times) of the marvelous acts of God, particularly in history.[18] A model like Ps 86:10 would have been in the mind of the king; compare Form.

The verb וְיַעֲלֶה as transmitted (simple וְ with full imperfect) attracts attention. One must understand the simple וְ to indicate that the action is identical with the previous verb, "Yahweh will act."[19] The same sequence of forms in 26:3 suggests that "perhaps" (אוּלַי) attracts this syntax.[20] The commentators and most translations assume that the verb is qal and that one must understand "the king" as subject: "so that (the king) will withdraw from us." The qal of עלה with מֵעַל does mean "withdraw (militarily)" (1 Kgs 15:19; 2 Kgs 12:19), but the verb in its form may just as well be hip'il, and this is the more natural understanding here: "and (thus) Yahweh will make (him) withdraw from us" (so Moffatt, the *American Translation*, and *RSV*, but not more recent translations).

■ 4 The expression with מֵסֵב (סבב hip'il) is unique in the OT. The basic thought is the beginning and the end of the quotation in this verse: "I am going to turn the weapons around from (being directed toward) the outside of the wall toward the center of this city." The verb סבב hip'il is used of turning the face or the eyes in the opposite direction (2 Kgs 20:2), but this is the only instance in which it is used of reversing the direction of weapons. The irony of the pronouncement is heightened by the two אֲשֶׁר clauses defining the weapons, "which are in your hand," "with which you are fighting the Chaldeans besieging you." Thus it is not "the Chaldeans besieging you from the outside of the wall" (*RSV*, *JB*, *NEB*, *NAB*), which in any event would be tautological. The insertion "and I shall gather them" is ambiguous: was it intended to refer to the (kings and the) Chaldeans or to the weapons? *V* and Rashi assume "weapons," and so recently Rudolph; s' and Qimḥi assume "the Chaldeans," and so recently Volz. There is no way to decide.

The word כַּשְׂדִּים "Chaldeans" is the normal designation for the Babylonians in 2 Kings 24—25 and Jer. The term originally referred to tribal groups who lived between the Euphrates and Tigris rivers between the city of Babylon and the Persian Gulf; during the time the Assyrian Empire asserted its authority over the south, these tribes were the center of anti-Assyrian resistance. They therefore initiated a Chaldean dynasty with Nabopolassar, whose son was Nebuchadrezzar. Obviously the Babylonian army included many more nationalities than the Chaldeans (34:1), but the identity of the dynasty determined the biblical designation for the Babylonian power.[21]

■ 5 It is bad enough that the king of Babylon is fighting against the people (v 2), but that Yahweh is not only not going to act according to his marvelous deeds but will actually fight against the people is crushing. And that reversal of Yahweh's role, already anticipated by the reversal of the direction of the weapons (v 4), is the reversal of his role as divine warrior in holy war, and that reversal is rhetorically signaled by the reversal of the attributes of

15   See Janzen, pp. 70, 72.
16   *CAD* 8:497.
17   Adriaan van Selms, "The Name Nebuchadnezzar," *Travels in the World of the Old Testament, Studies Presented to Professor M. A. Beek on the Occasion of his 65th Birthday* (ed. M. S. H. G. Heerma van Voss et al.; Assen: Van Gorcum, 1974) 226.
18   For a general discussion of the OT outlook on the

marvelous deeds of God see Eichrodt, *Theology* 2, 162–67.
19   See Joüon, *Gramm.*, sec. 115a.
20   See König, *Syntax*, sec. 367p.
21   See conveniently A. Leo Oppenheim, "Chaldea," *IDB* 1:549–50.

his hand and arm (see Setting):[22] the normal form of the phrase is "mighty hand and outstretched arm."[23] The formula belongs to the exodus tradition.[24] The triad "in anger, fury and great wrath" also occurs in Deut 29:27, evidently a derivative passage (see Setting); in Jer 32:37 it occurs with personal suffixes.

■ **6–7** The judgment of Yahweh is envisaged as twofold, first pestilence (v 6), then sword (v 7). A siege means a short supply of food (37:21), and malnutrition brings on disease. For "both man and beast" see 7:20. Then when the inevitable surrender comes ("I shall give Zedekiah, and his servants and the people into the hand of their enemies"), the enemies will cut them down with the sword. The king's "servants" are his officials. The triad "sword," "famine," and "pestilence" is a commonplace in Jer (see 14:12; 15:2). The triad "spare," "pity," "have mercy" is found also in 13:14; for the reading in the first-person singular see Text: Yahweh keeps the initiative from the beginning (v 4) to the end.

Aim

This encounter was evidently the first in a series in which Zedekiah begged Jrm for a hopeful word from Yahweh (see Setting, and see the subsequent events in chap. 37). Why would Zedekiah send a delegation to Jrm, of all people? Were there not safer prophets who could be counted on to give a hopeful word? Perhaps the king simply wanted to cover all bases, or perhaps it began to dawn on him and his advisors that in this emergency the "safer" prophets were not of much use: the king of Israel in the ninth century had resorted not only to his four hundred court prophets but to Micaiah ben Imlah (1 Kgs 22: see vv 6–8 there).

But Jrm had no word from Yahweh but the same old word of Yahweh's unyielding judgment that he had been offering for the past twelve years, since Jehoiakim burned his scroll. What is it like for a prophet to extinguish all hope in his hearers?

---

22 See n. 8.
23 Weinfeld, *Deuteronomy*, 329, no. 14.

24 Kurt Galling, *Die Erwählungstraditionen Israel* (Giessen: Töpelmann, 1928) 7 n. 3.

Bibliography
Berridge
pp. 204–5.

21

8   **And to this people you shall say, Thus Yahweh has said, Look, I am setting before you the way of life and the way of death: 9/ he who stays in this city shall die by sword and[a] famine [and pestilence,][b] but he who goes out [and surrenders][c] to the Chaldeans besieging you [d]shall live;[d] he shall at least have his life.[e] 10/ For I have set my face against this city for evil, not for good—oracle of Yahweh; into the hand of the king of Babylon it will be given, and he will burn it with fire.**

Text

9a   Many MSS. omit וְ "and," as does the parallel in 38:2.

b   Omitting וּבַדֶּבֶר with *G*. Obviously the text of *G* could be produced by omission and on the other hand that of *M* could be produced by expansion. Janzen has analyzed all occurrences of this triad, or members of it, in *M* and *G* (Janzen, pp. 43–44, no. 45), and conclude that "the possibility that *G* is original and *M* secondary from the full occurrences is at least as strong, and, in view of the general tendency of the latter tradition, more likely."

c   Omitting וְנָפַל with *S*. The extra verb spoils the symmetry of participle and imperfect verb and appears to be a clarifying gloss.

d—d   The reading of the ketib and many MSS., יִחְיֶה, is preferable to the qere' וְחָיָה, but both are possible. The qere' may have arisen as an accommodation to the inserted וְנָפַל (see c).

e   A few MSS. and *G* add וְחָי "and live" (so the parallel in 38:2); the addition is secondary.

Structure
This passage was evidently added to vv 1–7 because of the obvious association of content between the two passages and because of the catch phrase "the Chaldeans besieging you" (vv 4, 9): see vv 1–7, Structure.

The internal structure is that appropriate to structured prose (*Kunstprosa*), manifested in the opposition between "life" and "death."

Form
The introductory words of v 8 indicate that it is instruction from Yahweh to Jrm, an oracle to be delivered to the people. The oracle adapts in a particular historical circumstance the old covenantal formula that confronted the people with a choice, for life or death: the phrase "I am setting before you the way of life and the way of death" appears otherwise in the OT only in Deut 30:15 and 19 (in the text of *M* in those verses the phrasing is in the second-person singular and without "way"). That

passage seems to have been the conclusion of one edition of Deuteronomy,[1] reflecting early cultic usage.[2] It is, of course, a grotesque adaptation: that surrender to the enemy is life, and fighting for the integrity of Jerusalem is death. Did Jrm have the example of 2 Kgs 7:4 in mind? It may be added that the phrase "he shall at least have his life" (v 9, literally "he shall have his life as booty") may be the remnant of an old soldier's joke (on this see Interpretation, and compare Setting).

Setting
Rudolph assumes that these verses are the product of the "Deuteronomistic editor" and thus without authenticity, as does Weinfeld,[3] who takes the phrase "I set before you life and death" to be due to "Jer. C" (using Mowinckel's designation). But Berridge has refuted this judgment.[4] (1) The use of the phrase found in Deut 30:15, 19 is a fresh use of the idea (see Form). The association of "sword, famine (and pestilence)" is a combination found

---

1   Eissfeldt, *Introduction*, 231; Mayes, *Deuteronomy*, 370.
2   Von Rad, *Deuteronomy*, 184–85; Berridge, p. 205.
3   Weinfeld, *Deuteronomy*, 346, no. 7.
4   Berridge, pp. 204–5.

in the prose of Jer and not in a Deuteronomic work. (3) The expression "he shall at least have his life" (v 9, literally "he shall have his life as booty") is found here and in three other passages (38:2; 39:18; 45:5) and not otherwise in the OT. (4) The phrase by which Yahweh "sets his face against" is typical of Ezekiel and the Holiness Code but is not found in the Deuteronomic writings. There is no reason to doubt the authenticity of the oracle.

The historical setting will have to be within the period of the final siege of Jerusalem, which was from 15 January 588 to 18 July 587[5] (compare 38:1–3), but there is no way to be more specific.

Interpretation

Jrm is commanded to offer to the people in the city a shocking variation on the old covenant formula of Deut 30:15, 19 (see Form). But whereas the old covenant formula indicated that to choose "life" meant to obey Yahweh's will (Deut 30:16), here it is not assumed that Yahweh's will is that the people survive. Yahweh's will is that the city be destroyed (v 10), and if the people wish to survive, it is not in response to an ethical imperative but to simple prudence (v 9). The verb "go out" (יצא) implies surrender in several other passages as well.[6]

The idiom וְהָיְתָה־לּוֹ נַפְשׁוֹ לְשָׁלָל (v 9), literally "and he shall have his life as booty," is a curious one. The expres-

sion appears four times in Jer and nowhere else in the OT (see Setting). Older commentators took the phrase at face value: that one snatches his life from the enemy as one would any other piece of booty (so Rashi, Calvin). But more recently it has become clear that it is an ironic soldier's joke: when a soldier is defeated and escapes, having barely saved his life, he has at least that as "booty."[7] One might say in English, "he shall have his life as a bonus"; the translation given here is that of *NJV*.

The expression of v 10a is that of the hostility of Yahweh against the city (Bright: "I regard this city with hostility, not with favor"); it is an expression favored in Ezekiel and the Holiness Code (see Setting).

Aim

What is life? In the old formulation of Deut 30:15–19 it was obedience to Yahweh's will that secured blessing in the land. Now, the people hear, it is to abandon the city which, they had believed, Yahweh had chosen for his own name (Deut 12:5; 2 Kgs 23:8), and to go out to exile from that land. Can this be life? What kind of life could this be? Or is Jrm simply a traitor (38:4)?

---

5   Malamat, "Twilight of Judah," 145.
6   Jer 38:17, 21; 1 Sam 11:3; 2 Kgs 18:31 = Isa 36:16. All these passages use אֶל rather than עַל, the

preposition in the present passage.
7   So Volz, and compare Bright, pp. 184–85.

The King Must Render Justice

Bibliography
Driver, Godfrey R.
"Jeremiah xxi 12," *VT* 1 (1951) 244.

21

11

[⟨And⟩[b] concerning the house of the king
of Judah.][a]
**Hear the word of Yahweh, 12/ O house of
David! Thus Yahweh has said:**
Render each morning justice,
**and save him who is robbed from the
hand of the oppressor,**
or my wrath will go forth like fire
and burn with none to quench
[from the presence of the evil of [b]your
doings.[b]][a]

Text

11a   This phrase is evidently a superscription parallel
to that in 23:9, intended to refer to the whole
collection 21:11—23:8.

b   "And regarding" is lacking in *G*; "and" is surely an
effort to connect what follows with what precedes
(Rudolph).

12a   The phrase is lacking in *G* and has been supplied
from 4:4 (Rudolph; so also Janzen, p. 44, no. 46).

b—b   Following the qere' many MSS., and *θ'*, *V*, *S*, and
T; the ketib reads מַעַלְלֵיהֶם "their doings," which
must simply be a scribal error.

Structure

Bright takes vv 11–14 as a single poem. But other than
the fact that "fire" (אֵשׁ) appears in both vv 12 and 14, the
poem of v 12 and that of vv 13–14 are not united: thus
the address in v 12 is masculine plural, while that in vv
13–14 is feminine singular; the center of attention in v
12 is on injustice, while that in vv 13–14 is on the pride
of Jerusalem centered in her temple (v 14). The present
passage, vv 11–12, is here because of the catchword
association of "morning" (בֹּקֶר) with that word in 20:16:
see vv 1–7, Structure. The oracle itself is a simple pair of
bicola.

Form and Setting

Verse 12a is admonition comparable to Amos 5:4b, 14–
15; Isa 1:16–17; 56:1a; Ezek 45:9; the form is derived
from priestly torah.[1] Verse 12b is identical with two cola
in 4:4b, an associated threat.

The oracle in 4:4 was addressed to the general population ("men of Judah," "inhabitants of Jerusalem"), so
there is no reason to doubt the address to "house of
David" here, particularly when similar vocabulary is used
in an oracle against Jehoiakim in 22:15–17. The oracle,
like 4:4, must be dated before the burning of the scroll in
601: פֶּן, literally "lest," here translated "or," suggests that
Yahweh still hopes for repentance. The prose version of
the covenant appeal here (22:1–5) is associated with

Jehoiakim (see Setting there) and is dated early in his
reign; here, too, a date in the first year or two of his
reign (that is, 609–608) is indicated (for the details see on
22:1–5).

Interpretation

The preposition לְ in the superscription may be translation "to" as well as "concerning." Is the address "hear
the word of Yahweh, O house of David," ironic, as the
similar address in Isa 7:13 was? Ahaz hardly filled the
shoes of David in Isaiah's day,[2] and Jehoiakim hardly fills
the shoes of David in Jrm's day (compare 22:13–17, and
specifically the mention of Ahaz in the emended text of
22:15). Calvin makes a similar point.

The verb דִּין (translated here "render") takes the
object מִשְׁפָּט "justice" only here in the OT, but the
meaning is clear enough: *NJV* offers "render just ver-
dicts," Bright "execute justice." The modifier לַבֹּקֶר is
unexpected and has no parallelism here. It clearly means
"each morning" (compare Amos 4:4), and does not need
to be emended to לִבְקָרִים (like Ps 73:14, so Rudolph).
But given the parallelism, one wonders whether there
was not a pun here on לַבֹּקֵר "to the herdsman," the self-
designation of Amos (Amos 7:14): since Amos also spoke
about עֹשְׁקוֹת "(female) oppressors" (Amos 4:1), it would

---

1   See 7:21–28, n. 2.
2   Wildberger, *Jesaja*, 275–76.

be appropriate for Jrm to refer here to some incident in which Jehoiakim exploited the herdsmen; it is even possible that this was the original vocalization of the word. But there is no way to verify this; the oracle has "morning" in the tradition that has come to us. And indeed the expression here doubtless suggests "hurrying" to render justice (Bright).

The use of גָּזוּל "him who is robbed" suggests that the diction of Isa 10:2 is in the back of Jrm's mind: there a woe is pronounced against those who "turn aside the needy from justice [דִּין] and rob [גזל] the poor of my people of their right [מִשְׁפָּט]." For עשק "oppress, extort" see 7:6: there is no need to emend the text to "his oppressor" (Volz, Rudolph) with the Versions.

For v 12b see 4:4b.

Aim

There are two foci to the capital, the temple and the palace. The assemblage of people at the temple is addressed in the temple sermon (7:3–12); the court of Jehoiakim is addressed here (and in the prose parallel in 22:1–5). One hopes for justice both at the temple and in the court; one particularly hopes for justice from the king, who sets the drumbeat for the whole kingdom (5:5; compare Ps 72:1–4, 12–14). The fact that Jrm still had hopes for the rendering of justice by Jehoiakim suggests the zenith of the prophet's optimism, but that optimism would soon sour (22:13–19).

21

13   I declare myself against you
who are enthroned over the valley,
a rock over the plain,
oracle of Yahweh;
who say, "Who can come down against
us,
who can enter our habitations?"

14   [But I shall attend to you
according to the fruit of your deeds
oracle of Yahweh;][a]
but I shall set a fire in her forest,
and it shall consume all 《her
thickets.》[b]

Text

14a   The bracketed words are lacking in G; they have
been added here secondarily from 23:2, perhaps
under the stimulus of the similar expansion in v 12
(Janzen, p. 44, no. 47).

b   Reading סְבִכֶיהָ for M סְבִיבֶיהָ "her surroundings."
There is a similar phrase in 46:14, and in that passage סְבִיבָיךְ is translated in G by τὴν σμίλακά σου
"your thicket" (Cornill and Rudolph suggest here
the singular סְבִכָה). Note that סִבְכוֹ occurs in 4:7.

Structure

For the disconnection of this passage from vv 11–12, see
vv 11–12, Structure. The present passage appears to
begin a small collection of oracles ending with 22:20–23,
with which it forms an inclusio (see 21:1–7, Structure).
This collection will then have been attached to vv 11–12
by the catchword אֵשׁ "fire."

Verse 13a is best analyzed as a tricolon, each colon of
which consists of two words: in this way the second and
third cola are in close parallelism, and the figure of
Yahweh in the first colon resonates with "enthroned" and
"rock," words with connotations of the city's self-deification. Verses 13b and 14b are bicola; v 14a is evidently
a secondary insertion (see Text).

Form

The oracle opens with the "formula of encounter" ("I
declare myself against you," literally "behold I am against
you," הִנְנִי אֵלַיִךְ); Humbert calls it a "challenge formula"
(*Herausforderungsformel*), believing it to have originated in
a summons to a duel (compare David to the Philistine in
1 Sam 17:45, though the phrasing is slightly different).[1]
The formula occurs elsewhere in Jer (23:30, 31, 32;
50:31; 51:25), Nahum, and Ezekiel; it clearly introduces
a threat.[2] The vocatives are a parody of traditional
liturgical address to Yahweh (see Interpretation); the
implication is that the city is indulging in self-deification.
Verse 13b offers quotations of the rhetorical questions of
the people which display their complacency (so 49:4);
compare the same use of quotations in 2:23, 35. The
totality of v 13 thus makes up the accusation; the judg-

ment speech proper comes in v 14.

Setting

There are no direct clues within this little piece by which
it might be dated. Volz suggests the possibility of the
period before 588 when there was an effort to rebel
against Nebuchadrezzar (i.e., the period 594/593), but
this is only a guess. Complacency regarding the inviola-
bility of Jerusalem could be manifest at any time. Since
this passage is the opening one in a collection which is
closed off by a similar piece (22:20–23) and which
includes oracles regarding Jehoahaz and Jehoiakim
(22:10–12, 13–19), one suspects that this passage, too,
must be dated to Jehoiakim's reign. The word in v 14
(and in 22:7) that fire will inevitably destroy the city
reminds one of similar words about destruction by fire
which are dated early in 600 or soon thereafter (5:14;
7:20; 11:16; 15:14). If the word צוּר "rock" in v 13
suggests צוֹר "Tyre" (see Interpretation), then one is
reminded of 10:17, in which Jrm likewise suggests the
Canaanizing of the culture, and the latter passage is
again to be dated just before the siege of 598 (see Setting
there). But certainty is impossible.

Interpretation

This little oracle carries ironic multiple meanings; it
implies that Jerusalem has been tempted in her complacency to deify herself, taking on self-descriptions appropriate only to Yahweh.

For הִנְנִי אֵלַיִךְ "I am against you" see Form. The
address is feminine singular, appropriate (as will become

---

1   Paul Humbert, "Die Herausforderungsformel
'hinnenî êlékâ,'" *ZAW* 51 (1933) 101–8.

2   See further Zimmerli, *Ezekiel 1*, 26; and 175 on 5:8–
9.

clear) to Jerusalem.

The phrase יֹשֶׁבֶת הָעֵמֶק is best analyzed as a description of Jerusalem, "enthroned over the valley," exactly analogous to the designation of Yahweh, יֹשֵׁב הַכְּרֻבִים "enthroned on the cherubim," 1 Sam 4:4; 2 Sam 6:2 = 1 Chr 13:6; Pss 80:2; 99:1; this ancient designation of Yahweh originally suggested his presence above the ark, and it doubtless had become deeply associated with the cult tradition of Zion:[3] for the suggestion of parody in this passage see Weiser and Bright. The feminine participle subtly suggests parody, for the rightful attribute is masculine and belongs to Yahweh. Jerusalem has begun to idolize herself.

The word עֵמֶק means "valley," particularly a deep valley. The word was applied to the valleys around Zion (Isa 22:7; Jer 31:40), so that the designation "enthroned over the valley" is appropriate to Zion. On the other hand the word עֵמֶק appears sometimes to carry the meaning "strength, might," as 'mq does in Ugaritic;[4] thus in Job 39:21 עֵמֶק is parallel with כֹּחַ "might."[5] What is deep may thereby be strong, but the use of a word suggesting "strength" here prepares the way for the complacent affirmations of invulnerability in v 13b. Question: Is there any hint here of the wickedness of the Valley of Ben-Hinnom (2:23; 7:31; 19:6)?

The syntax of צוּר הַמִּישֹׁר is ambiguous: is צוּר parallel with יֹשֶׁבֶת, thus "(who are) a rock over the plain," or is the phrase a construct chain parallel with עֵמֶק, thus "over the rock of the plain" (so Bright)? It can be either and was perhaps so intended. The word צוּר indicates a "(large) rock" or "cliff," and although it is not used elsewhere as a designation of Jerusalem, it is an appropriate one. And מִישֹׁר is used of a "plain" (as well as of a plateau) and suggests also comfort and security (Ps 26:12); it is parallel with עֵמֶק in a description of Moab (48:8).

But there are other overtones. Thus צוּר "rock" is an old designation for Yahweh (thirty-three times in the OT, notably sixteen times in the Psalms). That desig-

nation is particularly emphatic in Deuteronomy 32, a poem whose themes Jrm has drawn on, particularly in chapter 2 (see, for example, 2:27–28): the word is used for Yahweh in Deut 32:4, 15, 18, 30, and 31, and for pagan gods in vv 31 and 37 there. Here, then, is a strong background for the innuendo here that Jerusalem has taken upon herself a title appropriate only for Yahweh: and this connotation suggests taking צוּר as a parallel with יֹשֶׁבֶת (see above).

There is another possibility which should not be excluded. G (and a', according to one MS.) vocalize the word as צֹר "Tyre" (for a' compare Jerome's commentary). There is therefore a strong tradition of this interpretation of the word. Ezekiel describes Tyre as being הַיֹּשֶׁבֶת עַל־מְבוֹאֹת יָם "enthroned at the entrances of the sea" (Ezek 27:3) and as taking to herself the role of deity (Ezek 28:2). Is Jrm suggesting that Jerusalem is a "Tyre over the plain," as the Phoenician city is a Tyre over the sea? He has hinted elsewhere that the people has become Canaanized (10:17), so that this is not out of the question.

There is one more possibility: מִישֹׁר means not only "plain" but "equity": it is parallel with צֶדֶק "righteousness" in Isa 11:4. The term צֶדֶק is part of Yahweh's intention for Jerusalem (Isa 1:26), and doubtless מִישֹׁר "equity" is as well. In Mal 2:6 מִישֹׁר "equity" is parallel with שָׁלוֹם "peace"; does one have in the present passage a play on the assumed derivation of "Jerusalem" as implying "peace" (compare the rendering in G εἰρήνη "peace" for שָׁלֵם = "Jerusalem" in Ps 76:3)?

The second half of the verse cites the people's complacent rhetorical questions implying invulnerability. The verb in the first question is odd, יֵחַת "can come down" (נחת qal), so odd in fact that G (and perhaps V) read יְחַת "shall terrify" (חתת hip'il); given the "height" of Zion one would have expected יַעֲלֶה "can come up" (6:4, 5; 2 Kgs 18:25). Does Jrm suggest a bird coming (so Naegelsbach, compare Isa 31:5)? Or does he suggest that the city feels itself invulnerable against Yahweh's coming down

3   Kraus, *Psalmen*, 557.
4   Ug. 17.6.45.
5   See Mitchell Dahood, "The Value of Ugaritic for Textual Criticism," *Bib* 40 (1959) 166–67, on Jer 49:4, and Marvin H. Pope, *Job* (AB 15; Garden City, NY: Doubleday, 1973) 311, on Job 39:21; and compare the discussion in *HALAT*, 803a.

against it (Ps 38:3; compare Isa 31:4)? Or does he suggest that the city is really in residence in Sheol (Job 21:13, compare the steady suggestions in Jer 14:1—15:9)?

The same verb בוא "enter" is to be found in the same sort of rhetorical question suggesting invulnerability in 49:4, spoken there by the Ammonites. The noun מְעוֹנוֹת, like its by-form מָעוֹן, carries two ranges of meaning. The first is the association with Yahweh: Yahweh has his מָעוֹן "habitation" on high (25:30) and his מָעוֹן in the temple (Ps 26:8). Indeed Yahweh is the מָעוֹן (Pss 90:1; 91:9) or מְעוֹנָה (Deut 33:27) for his people (compare the use of the latter form in that sense in the reconstructed text of 3:4). One might note in passing the phrase צוּר מָעוֹן "rock of refuge" as a designation of Yahweh in Ps 71:3: clearly Jrm is playing with liturgical diction here; the question "who can enter our habitations?" suggests that the city is arrogating to herself claims appropriate only for Yahweh, indeed by the plural "habitations" (which on the surface suggests simply the multiplicity of palace and temple buildings, compare "they" [הֵמָּה] in 7:4) is exceeding the prerogatives of Yahweh who needs only a singular "habitation." The other connotation of מָעוֹן or מְעוֹנָה is that of a lair of wild beasts (so מָעוֹן in 9:10 and 10:22, so מְעוֹנָה in Amos 3:4 and often); this nuance prepares the way for "forest" and "thicket" in v 14. Is the suggestion that Yahweh is hunting down the inhabitants in their lairs like wild beasts (compare Nah 2:13–14)?

For the inserted words at the beginning of v 14 see 5:9 for פקד "attend to" and 17:10 for "according to the fruit of one's deeds."

The יַעַר "forest" is an expression for the palace; in 1 Kgs 7:2; 10:17, 21 it is called the בֵּית יַעַר הַלְּבָנוֹן "house of the forest of Lebanon," and in Isa 22:8 בֵּית הַיַּעַר "house of the forest," from the cedar with which it was built (1 Kgs 7:2–12), but the usage here doubtless refers to the temple as well (1 Kgs 6:9–36). The phrase סִבְכֵי הַיַּעַר "thickets of the forest" occurs twice (Isa 9:17; 10:34), the second time referring specifically to the forests of Lebanon: in the parallelism of the present passage we may thus have an example of the break-up of stereotyped phrases.[6] The word יַעַר "forest" is used as the lurking-place of wild beasts (5:6; 12:8) and is therefore appropriate to the imagery of "hiding-place" that is developed in the oracle.

But if יַעַר "forest" has connotations of majesty and of the palace and temple, its parallel *סְבָכִים "thickets" carries only the meaning of a hiding-place for wild beasts. What a pathetic word for the buildings behind which the people of Jerusalem are hiding! A forest fire burns thickets easily (Isa 9:17), and Yahweh will burn the forest Jerusalem has constructed.

Aim

What can be done with a city which presumes herself to be beyond the reach of the enemy, beyond the reach of God even? God has his own solution: what in the minds of Jerusalem is the splendor of Lebanon is in reality only brush-wood, easily kindled. And it came to pass (2 Kgs 25:9).

---

6   See 2:1—4:4, n. 79.

22

**A Prose Version:
The King Must Render Justice**

1 Thus Yahweh has said, Go down to the house of the king of Judah and speak there this word. 2/ And you shall say, Hear the word of Yahweh, O king of Judah, sitting on the throne of David, you and your servants and your people who enter these gates. 3/ Thus Yahweh has said, Do justice and righteousness and save the oppressed from the hand of the oppressor;[a] the sojourner, [b] the orphan[b] and the widow do not exploit and[c] do not treat violently; and innocent blood do not shed in this place. 4/ For if you really do this word, then there shall enter the gates of this house kings who sit for David on his throne, mounted on chariots and on horses, 《 they and their servants and their people. 》[a] 5/ But if you do not obey these words, I have sworn by myself—oracle of Yahweh—that this house shall become a ruin.

Text

3a   The *M* reading עָשׁוֹק is presumed to mean "oppressor" (see the lexica), but the reading should doubtless be עוֹשֵׁק like 21:12. The emendation "his oppressor" (Volz, Rudolph) on the basis of the Versions is unnecessary (compare 21:11–12, Interpretation).

b—b   Some MSS., and *G, V,* and *S* read "and the orphan."

c   Read "and" with many MSS. and *G, V, S,* and *T;* the ו doubtless dropped out of *M* by haplography.

4a   Reading with *G: M* reads "he and his servants and his people" (and compare *V* "they and the servants and their people"). Volz and Rudolph (and Janzen, p. 133) believe that the phrase is an expansionist gloss from v 2: Volz suggests that it was added by a glossator who had the Messiah in mind. I would propose to the contrary that the symmetry of the passage demands parity here with v 2; furthermore the phraseology matches that of 36:31 (on the relation of the present passage to that verse see Setting). The shift of *M* to the singular was doubtless due to messianic concerns.

Structure

If the analysis in 21:1–7 is correct (see Structure there), the present passage was inserted secondarily into the sequence of poems 21:11–12; 21:13–14; and 22:6–7 (and beyond), and it is easy to see that it was on the basis of the phrases "house of David" and "save him who is robbed from the hand of the oppressor" in 21:12, and perhaps the participle "sitting, enthroned" (יֹשֵׁב) in 21:13, that the passage was inserted here. The passage is prose; for its internal structure see Form.

Form

There is here the usual problem of the hierarchy of quotations (compare 11:1–17). The passage is the report of a divine word to Jrm (v 1) commanding him to speak to those in the palace an utterance which begins in v 2. That utterance will include a quotation from Yahweh of divine commands in the plural to those in the palace (v 3): these commands are those of exhortation in a covenant speech, followed in vv 4–5 by the covenant condition, expressed both positively, with divine promise of continued blessing (v 4), and negatively, with divine assurance of destruction (v 5); compare 4:1–2; 7:1–12;

and 11:1–14.[1] And that assurance of destruction is reinforced by an oath formula;[2] for parallels to this oath formula see Setting.

Setting

It is clear that this passage is a prose variant of 21:11–12 (so Duhm and all recent commentators); it has been a parade example of Mowinckel's "Source C" (Rudolph), and those commentators who assume a Deuteronomistic redaction (Rudolph, Weinfeld)[3] not only assign this passage to that redaction but thereby assume it has no independent value.[4] But there are indications against this conclusion.

The verb rendered "exploit" (ינה hip'il v 3) occurs fourteen times in the OT: beyond this passage (its only occurrence in Jer) it occurs once in the Covenant Code (Exod 22:20), three times in the Holiness Code (Lev 19:33; 25:14, 17), once in Deut (23:17), once in Deutero-Isaiah (Isa 49:26), and seven times in Ezekiel (Ezek 18:7, 12, 16; 22:7, 29; 45:8; 46:18). An examination of the passages indicates that it is a verb associated with "sojourner" (and "orphan and widow") in traditional law and that it is at home in priestly circles (thus H and

---

1   For the forms of covenant conditions see Muilenburg, "Covenantal Formulations," 355.
2   See Wolff, *Joel and Amos,* 205.
3   Weinfeld, *Deuteronomy,* 355.
4   Nicholson, *Jer. 1—25,* 181.

Ezekiel).

The expression "I have sworn by myself" (or "you have sworn by yourself") occurs with God as subject five times in the OT: beyond the present passage, in Gen 22:16; Exod 32:13; Isa 45:23; and Jer 49:13. Of these, only Exod 32:13 is considered part of the Deuteronomistic redaction.[5] The Genesis passage is part of a secondary addition to the E-narrative of the attempted sacrifice of Isaac, an addition in the style of J but of uncertain provenience:[6] it would appear to be stimulated by prophetic diction (וְנְאֻם־יהוה). In addition the verb and preposition in question (שבע nip'al + בְּ) appear seven times with noun substitutes for divine self-designation: "I have sworn by my holiness"/"he has sworn by his holiness," Amos 4:2; Ps 89:36; "he has sworn by his soul [בְּנַפְשׁוֹ]," Jer 51:14; Amos 6:8; with similar expressions, Isa 62:8; Jer 44:26; Amos 8:7. The expression is then overwhelmingly an expression of divine intention through prophetic speech; it is unlikely to be a stock in trade of a Deuteronomistic editor.

The wording of v 3 is very close to that of 7:3–7, and the last phrase of v 5 finds parallels in several passages, notably 25:9 (part of the closing statement in the first scroll: see there) and 7:34 (the close of one of the pronouncements of judgment for the second scroll). The word "ruin" (חָרְבָּה) appears beyond these three passages seven times in the book (25:11, 18; 27:17; 44:2, 6, 22; 49:13), fourteen times in Ezekiel, and eighteen times additionally, mostly in the prophetic books, never in Deuteronomy or the Deuteronomistic edition of Kings. Now it is difficult to avoid circular reasoning in assessing the authenticity of these prose passage, but the effort must be made. Both 7:3–12; 7:29–34, and the first and second recensions of 25:1–14 are judged in the present study to offer diction authentic to Jrm. If the judgment on those passages is sound, then one is forced either to conclude that an editor framed the present passage on the model of those others or else that the present passage too is authentic.

The command "go down" (v 1) indicates that Jrm is understood to have received the command at the temple (compare the wording of 26:10; 36:12): this was noted already by Michaelis, who attributes the observation to his father. Thus if the present passage is the work of a redactor, then he has deliberately set the passage as a command received at the temple (so Duhm); otherwise the passage must be authentic.

Not only is the wording of v 3 similar to that of 7:3–7, but the form is identical for both, a covenant speech. But there is a contrast between the form of the two passages as well: 7:3–7 offers only the positive covenant condition, while vv 4–5 here offer both positive and negative conditions: thus it appears that one is in the context of genuine prophetic proclamation, not redaction.

But there is more. The parallel between the present passage and 7:3–7 and 25:5 is based on word-play connected with "dwell"—in 7:3 and 7 שכן "dwell, tabernacle," here and in 25:5 ישׁב "sit, dwell," these two verbs appearing often in parallelism (Isa 18:3). If those in the temple area adhere to the norms of the covenant, then Yahweh will "dwell" ("tabernacle") "in this place," and he will let the people "dwell" in the land (7:3, 7; 25:5); if those in the palace area, it is said here, adhere to the norms of the covenant, then in "this house" the king will "sit" ("dwell") on the throne of David. The present passage then appears to be an exhortation to those in the palace parallel to the temple sermon.

That such an exhortation was made may be inferred from 36:30–31. The end of v 31 there indicates that punishment will come upon the people, punishment which was threatened in 36:3; but the parity in v 31 between the people on the one hand and the king and his court on the other suggests that there was a parallel warning to the king and his court, and the proposal offered here is that the present passage is that warning. Thus one notes the same wording of "sit on the throne of David" in 36:30 and here in vv 2 and 4.

One may conclude that the passage is authentic, but there is no way to be precise about the historical context in which the exhortation was delivered. The wording fits an address to Jehoiakim (compare not only 36:30–31 but vv 13–17 of the present chapter), so the *terminus ad quem* is clearly December 601 (the confrontation narrated in 36:9–31, by the dating given in *G* of 36:9: see there). There is some evidence that Jehoiakim in his palace-building was emulating Egyptian models (see on vv 13–

5   Martin Noth, *Exodus* (Philadelphia: Westminster, 1962) 244; Childs, *Exodus*, 559.
6   Westermann, *Genesis*, II, 434, 445.

17), and such a project best fits the years early in his reign when he was an Egyptian vassal (2 Kgs 23:34–35), that is, before the battle of Carchemish (May/June 605). The positive and negative conditions of the covenant speech here (vv 4–5) suggest that Jrm was more optimistic than his attitude in vv 13–17 indicates; therefore the time for the event narrated here must be early in the reign of Jehoiakim. The parity of the passage with the temple sermon (7:3–12), which is to be dated probably to the autumn of 609 (at the latest March 608), suggests that it was delivered at the same time, but the narrative of the delivery of the temple sermon and its aftermath (chap. 26) hardly suggests that such an event took place precisely at the same time. One is left in some uncertainty, therefore, but a context in the first year or two of Jehoiakim's reign is likely.

Interpretation

Many of the details of the passage are dealt with under Setting (which see).

The whole court is addressed (v 2), not simply the king; there is no reason to doubt (as Duhm does) the genuineness of the words "you and your servants and your people who enter these gates"—the words are repeated with change of person and number in v 4 (see Text), and a similar phrase is found in 36:31. "These gates" are evidently not general city gates but gates belonging to the palace itself (compare v 4); we are not well informed, however, regarding the geographic details of this period. One has the impression of the bustle of officials going in and out of the palace (Thompson): it is they who should hear the appeal to justice.

The phrase "do justice and righteousness" (v 3) is a commonplace (5:1; 7:5): it is an expansion of "render justice" in 21:12, and it is what Josiah had done (v 15) in contrast to the incumbent on the throne. For "save the oppressed from the hand of the oppressor" see 21:12. For the combination "sojourner, orphan and widow" see 7:6: the verb there, however, is "oppress," the same root as that in "oppressor" here (עשׁק), while here the verb is "exploit" (ינה hip'il), which occurs in the Covenant Code (Exod 22:20) and elsewhere. The context of the verb in Lev 25:14; Ezek 18:7; and 46:18 suggests that it centers around the taking of unfair economic advantage of another. Though this is the only occurrence of "treat violently" (חמס qal) in the book, the passive "suffer violence" (the nip'al stem) occurs in 13:22, and the related noun occurs in 6:7 and 20:8. For "shed innocent blood in this place" see 7:6. Verses 4–5 lay out the alternatives: if the royal house is obedient to the covenant, the royal line will continue, but if not, the "house" (both palace and dynasty) will be destroyed. For "mounted" (רכב) see 17:25. For "ruin" (חָרְבָּה) see 7:34.

Aim

See 21:11–12.

22

Bibliography

Soggin, J. Alberto
"The Prophets on Holy War as Judgment against Israel," *Old Testament and Oriental Studies* (BibOr 29; Rome: Pontifical Biblical Institute, 1975) 69–70 = "Der prophetische Gedanke über den heiligen Krieg, als Gericht gegen Israel," *VT* 10 (1960) 81–82.

6   **For thus Yahweh has said concerning the**
         house of the king of Judah:
    (Though) you are Gilead to me,
      the top of Lebanon,
    I swear I shall make you a wilderness,
     ᵃ **uninhabited cities,**ᵃ
7   **and I shall commission destroyers**
         against you,
     each with his tools,
    and they shall cut down your choicest
         cedars
     and throw them onto the fire.

Text

6a—a   All the Versions and the qere' agree on the surprising plural. The ketib places a singular verb ("uninhabited") with the plural "cities," evidently a *lapsus calami*. See further Interpretation.

Structure

This poem is linked to 21:13–14 by the words "cedars" and "fire" in v 7, given "fire in her forest" in 21:14 (see further 21:1–7, Structure).

The poem consists of four bicola in a chiastic pattern: the first and last bicola use the imagery of "forest" as a metaphor for the palace (the second colon, "Lebanon"; the seventh, "cedars"); the second and third bicola offer clauses with first-person singular verbs describing Yahweh's action.

There is no reason to doubt the authenticity of the introductory words, but see further Interpretation.

Form

It is clear that vv 6b–7 make up a judgment speech reinforced by the oath formula אִם־לֹא (compare 15:11), but what precedes (v 6aβ) is not an accusation speech but an expression of comparison for the palace which implies the words of judgment; the difficulty is that the parataxis of the poetry between v 6aβ and 6b leaves one in doubt whether the opening bicolon is an endearing compliment—Lebanon is a symbol of fertility and Yahweh's blessing, for example, in Ps 72:16 (note the chiastic arrangement of that verse)[1]—or whether that opening bicolon already implies the negative tone of the rest of the poem—the trees of Lebanon must be cut down to size in Isa 2:13. Perhaps the closest comparable passage in the prophetic material which offers an oath formula after a preliminary address is Amos 4:1–3; there the oracle opens with an invocation, an appeal to "hear" addressed to the women of Samaria whose misdeeds are then stated. The tone is contrastive with the words of judgment which follow, and the same shift of tone is probable here. See further Interpretation.

Setting

The mention of "fire" suggests that this little judgment oracle is to be dated in the same period as other oracles with "fire" (5:14; 7:20; 11:16; 15:14), that is, early in 600 or soon thereafter (see 21:13–14, Setting). Since the same images are here that are found more explicitly in the poem in vv 20–23, and since the latter poem is in the present study assigned an earlier date, one must assume that the present poem assumes the existence of vv 20–23.

---

1   See Dahood, *Psalms II*, 184.

Interpretation

■ **6** The introductory words are surely correct in their application to the poem that follows, given the designation of the palace of Solomon as the "house of the forest of Lebanon" (1 Kgs 7:2; 10:17, 21), for which see 21:13–14. The linkage between this oracle and 21:13–14 is thus close, and the connective כִּי "for" at the beginning, if original and not added secondarily, must make a link with that earlier passage. The particle may even mean "specifically." The link can hardly be with vv 1–5, since that passage is an invitation to choose, while the present passage is a sure word of judgment.

For the location of Gilead see the discussion in 8:22. The pairing of "Gilead" and "the top of Lebanon" (as in Zech 10:10), given the diction of the rest of the passage, is here a reference to forests.[2] For the designation of the palace of Solomon as a forest see 21:13–14. Magnus Ottosson suggests that the pairing of Gilead and Lebanon here is a way of referring to "east" and "west" respectively,[3] but that seems an unnecessary refinement.

The question of the tone intended by the first bicolon has already been raised (see Form): these phrases are simply joined paratactically to the rest of the poem, and they could be intended either positively (like Ps 72:16) or negatively (like Isa 2:13). The positive tone doubtless prevails; most commentators and translations assume some contrast between the bicolon and the rest of the poem (though Condamin maintains the parataxis). In this connection it should be stressed that this is a metaphor, not a simile: it is not that "you are like Gilead to me," but "you are Gilead to me." There is thus not only the opportunity for an expression of Yahweh's affection, but also the surprise that comes from the comparison of something smaller with something greater. The tone is thus comparable to 15:1, where Jrm is compared to Moses and Samuel.

For the oath particle אִם־לֹא see 15:11. The verb שִׁית, here "make something (into) something," appears in 2:15 in a similar context, but there the second object is introduced by the preposition לְ, while here there are simply two accusatives. If there is a difference, the idiom here expresses even more suddenness than the other; thus "I shall constitute you a wilderness." For the "wilder-

ness" (מִדְבָּר) see the discussions in 2:2 and 9:9; here, clearly, the wilderness is set as the opposite of lush forest.

Why the plural "cities" (the wording of all the Versions as well as M)? One might guess that it is because of the multiple buildings of the palace complex (perhaps on the order of "they" [הֵמָּה] in 7:4 for the temple complex); but more generally it is doubtless an expression commensurate with "Gilead" and "the top of Lebanon"—that is, Yahweh could make a land uninhabitable with the extent of Gilead and all its cities.

■ **7** The verb "commission" is literally "consecrate" (קדשׁ pi'el), the same verb translated "prepare (battle)" in 6:4. Here Yahweh is using holy-war phraseology against his own people: Yahweh's possession has been stressed by "to me" in v 6. For "destroyers" compare 4:7 and 5:26, where the word appears in the singular. Since the word normally occurs in the context of war, and "commission" suggests holy war, there is warrant for the translation "armed host" (*NEB*). "Tools" (כֵּלִים) could just as well be "weapons" (1 Sam 20:40 and often), but since the action is cutting down trees, "tools" is perhaps best (*G* translates "axe" in the second colon). Still the diction of holy war continues (compare the passage on cutting down trees in war in Deut 20:19–20). "Cedars" nicely picks up "Lebanon" in v 6, and "choicest" delicately parallels "top" in that same colon. The verb נפל hip'il here means "throw," but it is also used of "felling" a tree (note the diction of 2 Kgs 3:19).

The wording of the destruction of the palace here is close to the description of the destruction of the temple in Ps 74:4–8, a psalm most commentators date to the time of the Babylonian destruction.[4]

Aim

A royal palace is neutral in Yahweh's sight: it could be a thing of beauty or a challenge to his integrity (see Form, Interpretation). But he does not need it: just as every beast of the forest is his, and the cattle on a thousand hills (Ps 50:10), so every tree of Gilead is his, and the forests of the peaks of Lebanon. Since it is part of what must be destroyed, indeed since it is the center of what must be destroyed, Yahweh will commission his destroyers and they will set to work.

2   For the forests of Gilead see Baly, *Geography*, 221, and Ottosson, *Gilead*, 29.

3   Ottosson, *Gilead*, 244.

4   Compare Kraus, *Psalmen*, 514–15.

Bibliography

Long
  "Schemata."
Skweres
  "Strafgrunderfragung."

22

8 When [many][a] nations shall pass by this city and say to each other, "Why has Yahweh treated this great city like this?" 9/ then they shall say, "Because they have abandoned the covenant of Yahweh [a] their God[a] and worshiped other gods and served them."

Text

8a   Lacking in *G*; it is a gloss from 25:14 (Janzen, p. 44).

9a—a   Some MSS. read אֱלֹהֵי אֲבוֹתָם "the God of their fathers," but there is no Versional support for this reading; it is doubtless an accommodation to general Deuteronomistic diction (compare Judg 2:12).

Structure

This little question-and-answer schema is placed here as a response to both the word of judgment against the city (21:13–14) and the more specific word of judgment against the palace (22:6–7). It is therefore possible that it was placed here before vv 1–5 were inserted in their present position. The structure of the passage itself is simple: the clause in v 8 parallels the clause in v 9, with waw-consecutives with all the verbs, and "say" in each verse; "why?" (עַל־מֶה) matches "because" (עַל־אֲשֶׁר).

Form

This is the only instance in Jer of what Long calls the question-and-answer schema, "Type A";[1] in this type the reference to the one who answers (or the group who answers) is in the third person. His "Type B" (in which the answer is given to the prophet, addressed in the second person) has been met with in 5:19; 9:11–15; 13:12–14; 15:1–4; and 16:10–13. The parallels to this "Type A" are found in Deut 29:22–28 and 1 Kgs 9:8–9 (and thus also in 2 Chr 7:21–22). There is a striking extrabiblical parallel, a narration in the annals of Ashur-banipal, often quoted: "Whenever the inhabitants of Arabia asked each other: 'On account of what have these calamities befallen Arabia?' (they answered themselves:) 'Because we did not keep the solemn oaths (sworn by) Ashur, because we offended the friendliness of Ashur-banipal, the king, beloved by Enlil!'"[2]

Setting

Long is persuasive in his conclusion that the form reflects a peculiar sort of pedagogical historiography that may reflect the rhetorical preaching in exilic situations.[3] It is clear that both parallels, Deut 29:22–28 and 1 Kgs 9:8–9, appear in exilic contexts,[4] and therefore that the same context is likely for the present passage. It is noteworthy that this is the only passage in Jer where the phrase "abandon the covenant" (עזב בְּרִית) occurs; one finds "abandon me [= Yahweh]" in 1:16 and often, one finds "break my covenant" (בְּרִית + hip'il פרר) in 11:10 and 31:32, but the nearest equivalent to the present phrase is "abandon my law" (עזב תּוֹרָתִי) in 9:12, again in one of the question-and-answer schemata. But "abandon the covenant" appears in Deut 29:24. We have then the

---

1   Long, "Schemata," 130–34.
2   Rassam Cylinder 9.68–72. See *ANET*, 300; for the Akkadian text and translation see Maximilian Streck, *Assurbanipal und die letzten assyrischen Könige bis zum Untergange Nineveh's* (Vorderasiatische Bibliothek 7; Leipzig: Hinrichs, 1916) II, 79.
3   Long, "Schemata," 131–34.
4   Mayes, *Deuteronomy*, 359, 367; Gray, *Kings*, 236.

reflection of the community of one and two generations later on the terrible judgment oracles associated with this section of the book.

Interpretation

For perfect consecutives to express protasis and apodosis see GKC, secs. 112kk, 159g. Rudolph insists on translating "many people" here instead of "many nations" because he is convinced in the late period of this passage that גוֹיִם means simply non-Israelites; but this is hardly necessary: Israel was by this time cast adrift among the nations of the world (compare the diction of Deutero- and Trito-Isaiah, for example Isa 52:10; 60:5). For "pass by" see 18:16. The diction "nations say, 'why has Yahweh treated like this'" is found precisely in Deut 29:23 and 1 Kgs 9:8 as well (see Form and Setting), and the latter has "pass by" as well, and (as noted in Setting) the former has "abandon the covenant of Yahweh." For the phraseology of "worship other gods and serve them" compare 1:16; 13:10; and often.

Aim

That precious, that unique city that was the vehicle for both cultic and royal ideology had fallen. One must read a chapter of Lamentations to catch even faintly the mood of shock and disorientation the fall produced. The city had become a permanent warning to the world what Yahweh could do because of what his people had done, and the lesson of the meaning of that warning was repeated to the folk in exile again and again.

**The Captured King
Will Not Return**

Bibliography

On 22:10–12:
Roach, Corwin C.
"Notes and Comments (Jer 22,10–12)," *ATR* 23
(1941) 347–48.

22

10
Do not weep for [a] **him who is dead,** [a]
nor grieve for him:
do weep for him who is gone,
for he shall not return again

Text
a—a The proposal to vocalize with the article, לַמֵּת,
instead of the *M* reading without the article, לְמֵת, is
probably correct, given the *M* reading with the
article, לַהֹלֵךְ, in the third colon; but in the circumstance of poetic diction, vocalizations without the
article are possible for both participles. The evidence from the Versions does not really resolve the
issue (against the commentators).

Structure
The poem is the first of a pair on the kings of Judah (the
other being vv 13–19) placed between two poems using
"Lebanon" as a metaphor for the palace (vv 6–7) or the
city of Jerusalem in general (vv 20–23) in the array of
poems beginning in 21:11–12 (the king) and 21:13–14
(the city): on this arrangement see 21:1–7, Structure.
The two poems here are in chronological order: the
present one, on Jehoahaz (see v 11) precedes the one on
Jehoiakim (vv 13–19). Though for convenience most
commentaries deal with vv 10–12 as a unit, vv 11–12 are
as separate from v 10 as vv 1–5 are from 21:11–12
(which see).

The poem is here set out in five cola. It is true that
Volz, Rudolph, and Bright assume four cola, Volz taking
the fourth and fifth cola as a single colon, and Rudolph
and Bright taking the first and second cola as a single
colon; but these attempts by their contrast suggest simply
a craving on the part of commentators for a poem of
four cola, and most recent translations display five cola,
as here. By this analysis the middle colon resonates both
with the first two (the parallelism of "weep" and "grieve")
and with the last two (Jehoahaz rather than Josiah).

There is also the possibility that "him who is dead" in the
first colon is paralleled by "his birth" in the last colon (see
Interpretation).

Form
The verse is essentially what Westermann calls a "judgment speech without a reason,"[1] as are vv 11–12.
Jehoahaz has not been accused of anything: he simply
suffers in the context of the judgment on the people.
This judgment is an adaptation of a call to communal
lament, for which compare 4:8 and 6:26. The great
example of the genre in the OT, Joel 1:5–14, offers
many parallels.[2] The third colon is of course the appeal
to weep. The parallel admonition not to weep (in the first
two cola) moves out of the milieu of wisdom admonition:
Amos 5:4–5 carries something of the same sort of
prohibition and command[3] (compare the form of 21:12).
The last two cola offer a motivation for the appeal to
weep (introduced by כִּי), narrating what will happen to
the absent king (compare Amos 6:9–10);[4] these lines,
too, carry instruction.

---

1   Westermann, *Basic Forms*, 161.
2   For a discussion see Wolff, *Joel and Amos*, 20–22.
3   See the remarks in ibid., 232.
4   Ibid., 280–81.

Setting

Verses 11–12, present here, identify "him who is dead" as Josiah and "him who is gone" as Jehoahaz and thus set the time of this poem quite precisely, since Josiah was killed at Megiddo, evidently in the month Sivan (May/June) 609,[5] and Jehoahaz reigned three months (2 Kgs 23:31) before he was taken into exile in Egypt (2 Kgs 23:34), thus in August/September of that year. The time of this oracle, then, is the late summer or early autumn of 609.

One can make some assumptions about the audience. There was evidently division in the realm at the time of Josiah's death, as there had been before (compare 2 Kgs 11:20):[6] Jehoahaz was two years younger than Jehoiakim (2 Kgs 23:31 and 36), yet the country gentry managed to place Jehoahaz on the throne (2 Kgs 23:30).[7] Now that Jehoahaz has been taken hostage, Jrm is suggesting that those who had supported him (thus the country gentry) should not maintain a false hope that he would return to take the throne.

It should be noted that this little oracle may have had an ironic reuse twelve years later (compare v 26): Jehoiachin was carried off to exile in Babylon after the first fall of Jerusalem, which by the Babylonian Chronicle took place on 16 March 597.[8] He, like his uncle Jehoahaz, had ruled for just three months (2 Kgs 24:8), so that Jehoiakim his father would have died sometime in December 598. Indeed Qimḥi believes the verse refers simply to Jehoiakim and Jehoiachin. But while Jrm looked at Jehoiachin with the same pathos with which he had looked at Jehoahaz (see vv 28 and 30), the prophet's attitude toward Jehoiakim was altogether different from that toward Josiah (see vv 15–16, and the contrast in tone between vv 18–19 and the present verse). So in the original setting the attitude toward Josiah would have been one of sadness, while in the new setting the attitude toward Jehoiakim would have been one of contempt.

Jerome points out that the verse could also apply to Zedekiah, who went off to exile in 587.

Interpretation

For the identification of "him who is dead" with Josiah, and of "him who is gone" with Jehoahaz, see Setting, and compare v 11. For "grieve" (נוד) see 15:5. For the position of the infinitive absolute after an imperative see GKC, sec. 113r; the nuance of the infinitive absolute here is not intensiveness ("weep bitterly" in *RSV* and *JB*)[9] but is the emphatic contrast with a parallel denial (many recent translations: "weep rather"); 34:17 is a good prose example (compare v 18 there).

Volz and Rudolph assume that וְרָאָה . . . יָשׁוּב is a single verbal idea, "see again" (compare 18:4), but this is evidently false: the adverb "again" (עוֹד) intervenes between the two verbs, the verbs evidently belong to separate cola (see Structure), and the prose parallel in vv 11–12 separates the verbs widely and offers the adverb "again" with each verb.

The word "birth" (מוֹלֶדֶת) could as well mean "kindred" (Gen 12:1), but "birth" is better here, forming an inclusio with "him who is dead" in the first colon; the diction of v 26 also suggests indirectly that "birth" is the nuance.

The use of "go" (הלך) and "return" (שׁוב) is ironic, in that these verbs are used elsewhere of dying: thus in 2 Sam 12:23 David says of his dead child, "I shall go to him, but he will not return to me." The structure of the poem puts in strong contrast Josiah, who is dead, and Jehoahaz, who is alive but has gone into exile; at the same time the diction applying to Jehoahaz suggests strongly that he is as good as dead. It must be remembered that travel away from home is analogous to illness (since both suggest separation from Yahweh): note the wording of David's complaint about being driven from his homeland, 1 Sam 26:19, and the mixture of motifs of distance from Jerusalem and of illness in Pss 42 + 43. (It is perhaps worthy of note that the Arabic greeting *al-ḥamdu lillāh ʿalā as-salāmati* "praised be God for your well-being!" is said both to the traveler returning from a journey and to someone recovered from an illness.) Thus

---

5   Malamat, "Twilight of Judah," 125.
6   Gray, *Kings*, 565–66, 582.
7   See Marvin H. Pope, "ʿAm Haʾarez," *IDB* 1:106, and Malamat, "Twilight of Judah," 126 and n. 6 there.
8   Bright, *History*, 327; Malamat, "Twilight of Judah," 132.
9   See Joüon, *Gramm.*, sec. 123l.

it is not surprising that Jrm uses expressions in describing Jehoahaz's exile suggestive of illness and death.

The resemblance of this verse to 2 Sam 12:23 (see above) is perhaps not fortuitous: Jrm may well have had David and his baby boy in mind when he spoke of Josiah and Jehoahaz; the Deuteronomic assessment of Josiah was that he was a second David (2 Kgs 22:2). It had been ironic that David should weep while his child was alive and should stop weeping when it was dead (2 Sam 12:21); it is a new irony that one should not weep when Josiah had died but should weep when his son is still alive.

Aim
The world is filled with people holding on to lost causes.

Jehoahaz would never come home, nor would Jehoiachin. We do not hear directly of those who held to their hopes for Jehoahaz, but they must have been the first audience for the oracle. We do hear of those who held to their hopes for Jehoiachin (28:4). History does not always give us the fulfillment of the hopes to which we cling (compare Mark 13:21–22).

22

**A Prose Version:
The King Will Not Return**

11   **For thus Yahweh has said of Shallum, son
of Josiah [king of Judah,]ᵃ the ruler suc-
ceeding Josiah his father, who went
away from this place: "He shall not
return there again, 12/ butᵃ in the place
where they have exiled him, there he
shall die, and this land he shall never see
again."**

Text

11a   Lacking in *G* and *S* and clearly a gloss; see Janzen,
pp. 69–75.

12a   For *M* כִּי some MSS. have כִּי־אִם; the meaning is
thereby made less ambiguous but not changed.

Structure

This passage is a prose equivalent of v 10 and therefore
adjoins it, just as vv 1–5 are the prose equivalent of
21:11–12.

Form

See on the last two cola of v 10.

Setting

"Shallum" is an alternative name for Jehoahaz (see 1 Chr
3:15, and further Interpretation); the setting for the
verses is thus assumed to be identical with that of the
original setting for v 10 (which see). It is usually assumed
that these verses are a secondary clarification of v 10
(Rudolph assumes it is to be attributed to Baruch), but
the passage is no different in its nature than are vv 1–5,
and vocabulary analysis of those verses has suggested that
the prose version has its own integrity and its own claim
to authenticity; there is no reason therefore to doubt the
authenticity of these verses to the prophet.

Interpretation

■ **11–12** See in general v 10.

■ **11** Though אָמַר אֶל normally means "say to" (1:7), it may
also mean "say of," as here (and as in v 18).

"Shallum" is the equivalent of Jehoahaz (1 Chr 3:15
and 2 Kgs 23:30). It is an old question (see Naegelsbach)
why the name here should be given as Shallum instead of
Jehoahaz, and what the relation is between the two
names. A. M. Honeyman has proposed[1] that Shallum was
the king's private name and Jehoahaz his regnal name,
and that proposal has been adopted by Rudolph and
Bright, but it is by no means assured, and Wildberger has
since questioned it.[2] One must note that 2 Kgs 23:34 and
24:17 indicate that Jehoiakim and Zedekiah are regnal
names for Eliakim and Mattaniah respectively, but that 1
Chr 3:15 lists Shallum alongside Jehoiakim and Zedekiah, so, if anything, Honeyman's designations should be
reversed. Beyond this question is the puzzle why the
names given in 1 Chr 3:15 should be in the order they
are.[3]

■ **12** For the lack of article with "place" in *M* see Joüon,
Gramm., sec. 129q.

Aim

See v 10.

---

1   A. M. Honeyman, "The Evidence for Regnal Names
     among the Hebrews," *JBL* 67 (1948) 19–20.

2   Hans Wildberger, "Die Thronnamen des Messias,

     Jes. 9,5b," *TZ* 16 (1960) 320–21.

3   Curtis and Madsen, *Chronicles*, 100–101.

The King Who Seeks
His Own Glory
Will Die an Inglorious Death

Bibliography

Dahood
    "Two Textual Notes."
Joüon, Paul
    "Un Parallèle à la 'Sépulture d'un Âne' de Jérémie
    (XXII, 19) en arabe moderne de Palmyre," *RSR* 27
    (1937) 335–36.
Köhler, Ludwig
    "Archäologisches. 9," *ZAW* 34 (1914) 149.

22

13   Woe to him who builds his house with
          unrighteousness,
      and his roof-chambers with injustice,
        and works his fellow without pay
          and his wages does not give him;

14   who says, "Let me build myself a spa-
          cious house
      and wide-open[a] roof-chambers,"
        and enlarges for himself [b] his win-
          dows.[b]
    ⟨Imagine paneling⟩[c] with cedar
      and painting with vermilion;

15   ⟨trying to be king⟩[a] [b] 《 with cedar, 》

Text

14a   The *M* vocalization construes this word as a puʿal participle; the difficulty is that it would be a masculine plural and would not agree with the feminine plural עֲלִיּוֹת "roof-chambers." Given the plural מִדּוֹת in the previous colon, one would expect here a plural noun. Thus Cornill suggests a vocalization מְרֻוָּחִים, so also Rudolph; but one cannot argue from Lev 21:10 to such a vocalization, as Cornill and his predecessors do. For the meaning see Interpretation.

b—b   Reading the waw of the following word with חַלּוֹנַי, with Michaelis and most.

c   Reading סָפוֹן (infinitive absolute) for סָפוּן (passive participle) with Michaelis and most, corresponding to the infinitive מָשׁוֹחַ which follows. For the translation with "imagine" see Interpretation.

15a   Vocalizing a hitpaʿel infinitive absolute הִתְמַלֵּךְ for *M* הֲתִמְלֹךְ "do you reign?" Duhm suggests emending to a hitpaʿel imperfect, הֲתִתְמַלֵּךְ, a suggestion mentioned with approval by Cornill, Condamin, and Rudolph; for the present proposal see Interpretation.

b—b   It is likely that a word is missing after התמלך (here translated "trying to be king"): a single word (that is, "trying to be king") cannot make up a colon (O'Connor, *Structure*, 138). *G* for v 15a reads, "Will you reign, because you are provoked with Ahaz?" Since *G* has translated אֶרֶז "cedar" correctly in v 14, the surprising reading (*lectio difficilior!*) commends itself (compare Volz). Cornill points out that the verb חרה "compete" in 12:5 names the competitor, and the same expectation is likely in the present passage. I propose (1) that Jrm is indulging in word-play here between בָּאֶרֶז "with cedar" (first colon) and בְּאָחָז "with Ahaz," (2) that "with cedar" dropped out of the text (so both *M* and *G*), (3) that it was written in the margin and restored in the wrong spot (so *M*). One wonders if *T* does not have a memory of the text in its translation, "Do you imagine yourself to be like the previous king?" For

as if ⟨competing⟩^c ⟪ with Ahaz! ⟫^b
Your father—did he not eat and drink
and do justice and righteousness?
Then it went well for him.

16   **He pled the pleading of the poor and**
needy:
    then it went well.
    ⟨**Did he not find it fitting**⟩^a **to know**
me?
                oracle of Yahweh.

17   **But your eyes and heart are on nothing**
    but your cut and shedding the blood of
    the innocent
    and extortion and committing
    oppression.

18   **Therefore thus Yahweh has said of**
    Jehoiakim son of Josiah, king of
    Judah:
    ⟪**Woe to this man!**⟫^a
    They shall not lament him,
    "Alas, my brother, and alas, my sister!"
    They shall not ⟪ burn (spices) ⟫^b for him,
    "Alas, lord, and alas, ⟪ lady!" ⟫^c

19   **With the burial of an ass he shall be**
    buried,
    dragged and dumped
    beyond the gates of Jerusalem.

the comparison with Ahaz see Interpretation.

c   Vocalizing the verb as a hitpaʿel, מִתְחָרֶה for M מְתַחֲרֶה: for the identification of the stem of the verb in M, and for a discussion of the question, see Interpretation. A fresh vocalization does not alter the meaning.

16a   M reads "Is this not (to know me)?" The pronoun "it" (הִיא) is feminine, corresponding to the normal gender of the infinitive "to know" (= the noun "knowledge"). But there is a tradition that offers instead the masculine pronoun הוּא, the ketib^{Or} and 4QJer^a; "to know" does seem to be construed as masculine once or twice (see BDB, 395b), or such a variant might be the common ketib/qere' confusion of these pronouns, but I propose that the reading is a *lectio difficilior* that conceals a verb. A verb would be suggested by both the pattern of v 15 and by 9:5, and I propose therefore to read הֲלוֹא־הוֹאָה (+ אֹתִי דַּעַת), a perfect hipʿil of יאה, the qal stem of which occurs in 10:7. See further Interpretation.

18a   Restoring הוֹי עַל־הָאִישׁ הַזֶּה from G (so Cornill, Rudolph, Bright).

b   The repetition of "lament" (יִסְפְּדוּ) here in M is dubious poetically. Read יִשְׂרְפוּ with G here: compare the wording in 34:5 in both M and G. See Interpretation.

c   Reading הֹרָה (literally "she who conceives," participle of הרה I; compare Hos 2:7) for M הֹדֹה "his majesty" with Dahood, "Two Textual Notes" (so also Thompson). G omits "and alas my sister!" and the words following "lord," doubtless because the feminine reference(s) appeared wrong. Symmetry demands two feminine references; see further Interpretation.

Structure

The passage extends through v 19: form-critically vv 13–17 are the accusation speech, and vv 18–19 the announcement of judgment (see Form). The passage is part of the sequence of poems beginning with 21:11–12 and ending with 22:20–23 (see 21:1–7, Structure). There are indications of parallels between the accusation speech of vv 13–17 and the judgment speech of vv 18–19: see below on vv 18–19.

The accusation speech (vv 13–17) falls into three uneven sections: Jehoiakim's actions in building a palace (vv 13–15a), the contrasting actions of Josiah (vv 15b–16), and Jehoiakim's craving for injustice (v 17). The first and third sections are strongly tied together in that both deal with injustice, and the first and second sections are tied together by the words "unrighteousness" and "injustice" (v 13) and "justice" and "righteousness" (v 15), and by the twice-repeated בְּלֹא in v 13 and the twice-

repeated הֲלֹא in vv 15–16. These are even more subtle ties, some of which are only lightly suggested. For example, the word "wide-open" (מְרֻוָּחִים, a word probably cognate with רוּחַ, suggesting a "[cool] breeze") in v 14 is evidently picked up by "competing" in v 15 (vocalized here מִתְחָרֶה, a form connected with חרה "burn with anger"), a word sharing a similar array of consonants but giving an opposite connotation, as if Jehoiakim intended to be "cool" on the roof but instead was "hot" for cedar. Now the same word "compete" is evidently balanced by the noun מְרוּצָה in v 17, given the fact that that word represents two homonyms (as it also does in 8:6: see there): not only "extortion," the translation given here, which is certainly its meaning in the immediate context (thus from the root רצץ), but also "racing" (thus from the root רוץ)—it is to be noted that in 12:5 the verb "compete" is likewise paralleled by "race" (רוץ). On other interconnections in vv 13–17 see below.

There are minor uncertainties of text in the passage, especially in vv 15–16, where G differs in several respects from M and where some commentators have had recourse to G; there are therefore difficulties in the details of the number and grouping of cola in the passage.

Thus Duhm, and after him Cornill and Rudolph, follow G in v 15 and place "then it went well with him" after "Did he not eat and drink?" rather than after "he did justice and righteousness" as M has it; they further omit the parallel "then it went well" in v 16 as dittographic, since G gives no evidence of the clause. But it is likely that "then" (אָז, 'āz) mimics the word "cedar" (אֶרֶז, pronounced in Jrm's day 'arz),[1] and since "cedar" occurs twice within four cola in vv 14–15a, it is plausible to accept a second occurrence of a colon with "then." One could further suggest that in the second occurrence, without "for him" (לוֹ), the meaning may be slightly different (see Interpretation). As to the position of the first of these parallel cola ("then it went well for him"), one could imagine it either after "Did he not eat and drink?" with G or after "he did justice and righteousness" with M; but in the former case the word "and" would have to be moved from before "he did justice and righteousness" to a position before "he upheld the judgment of the poor and needy," and economy of text alteration would suggest staying with M after all.

All this means that the central section (vv 16b–17), concerned with Josiah, consists of six cola; one could set it out as a hexacolon or (as here) as two tricola: the first and the last cola have הֲלֹא "did (he) not?," the third and fifth have "then it went well," and the first, second, and fourth have inner parallelisms ("eat and drink," "justice and righteousness," "poor and needy").

The opening section (vv 13–15a) likewise offers difficulties. The verb in the first colon of both v 13 and v 14 is a participle ("who builds," "who says"), and this fact suggests that the four cola in v 13 are parallel to a group beginning in v 14. The punctuation of M divides v 14 with the 'atnaḥ at "airy roof-chambers," and clearly that is the point at which the quotation ends. But if the verbs "panel," "paint," and "trying to be king" are vocalized as infinitive absolutes, as here proposed, then the colon

beginning with the verb "panel" begins a fresh sequence which ends with the כִּי clause "as if competing," a sequence of four cola. If these are rhetorically distinct, then one must understand a tricolon at the beginning of v 14 from "who says" to "his windows." The tricolon ends rather oddly and abruptly, but this may be a rhetorical device to link the section strongly with v 17 (see below).

Verse 17 is evidently a tricolon, given the constraints of a colon.[2] the last two cola are therefore closely parallel, given the infinitives "shedding" and "committing," and this suggests in turn that there is a parallel between "your cut" and "extortion."

It has already been noted that the tricolon in v 14 ends abruptly. It also ends with a noun with a possessive suffix, "his windows" (if the text is correctly reconstructed). It is possible that the possessed noun may mark a light rhetorical emphasis (implying "he has what he wants"); in this way "his windows" parallels the word in the last colon of v 13, "his wages" (that is, the wages of the king's fellow man): the king gets what he aims for, but the fellow man does not get the wages he deserves. But more, "his windows" may be picked up by "your cut" in the second colon of v 17, which is illegitimate profit. In this way the three cola at the beginning of v 14 may be completed by the three in v 17, so that all that intervenes is a kind of rhetorical aside (see further Form). (For a similar rhetorical "interruption" compare 5:1 and 7.) A subtle innuendo of comparison with "harlotry" in the reference of "window" in v 14 may contribute to the rhetorical rounding-off of the tricolon: on this see Interpretation.

The prose introduction in v 18 does not participate directly in the structure of the passage. If the line "Woe to this man!" is correctly restored, it is parallel to "Alas for him who builds" in v 13. The rest of v 18 consists of two closely parallel bicola. And since "lament" and "bury" are often associated (compare 16:4), the two occurrences of "lament" in v 18 are echoed by "the burial" and "be buried" in v 19. And is there any hint of a parallelism (or partial assonance?) between the infinitive absolutes *סָפוֹן and מָשׁוֹחַ ("panel," "paint") in v 14 and the infinitive absolutes סָחוֹב and הַשְׁלֵךְ ("dragged," "dumped") here? Was Jehoiakim's palace likely "beyond the gates of Jerusalem"?—see Interpretation, vv 13–17.

---

1   Harris, "Linguistic Structure," 145, no. 13.

2   O'Connor, *Structure*, 138.

Form

This passage is an example of a prophetic judgment speech to an individual[3] (compare 20:1–6); vv 13–17 make up the accusation and vv 18–19 the announcement of judgment.

The accusation begins with a "woe"-cry (הוֹי, v 13); the linking of that interjection in v 13 with the same interjection in v 18 (there "alas!") suggests that the "woe"-cry originated in funeral lamentation;[4] that is to say, though "woe" suggests accusation here, it also implies the anticipation of the funeral of the one addressed. The participle is normal with this form.[5] One could guess that the series of infinitive absolutes in vv 14–15a represent a rhetorical flourish appropriate to covenant argumentation (compare the series in 7:9). The reference to Josiah in vv 15b–16 involves rhetorical questions of a search or a precedent by which to compare Jehoiakim's behavior (compare 2:10–11a); v 17 then contrasts the present king's behavior with that of his father (compare 2:11b).

If the colon "Woe to this man!" is correctly restored in v 18, the announcement of judgment begins with a "woe"-cry just as the accusation does. The lack of suitable burial is a traditional curse.[6]

Setting

There are no specific clues within this passage as to when in the reign of Jehoiakim the oracle was delivered, but it is altogether likely that it was early in his reign. (1) Any fresh building project the king undertook for living quarters is likely to have been undertaken early. (2) The notice of the Deuteronomic historian that Jehoiakim taxed the people of the land to raise tribute for Pharaoh (2 Kgs 23:35) clearly took place between 609 and 605 (or 603?), the period of Egyptian vassalage, and the hint in that verse of fiscal pressure matches the indictment of social injustice here. (3) There is the curious circumstance that accusations of social injustice that Jrm levels at the people in chapters 2—6 largely match in the

diction of the accusations which he has leveled at the king in the present passage (see on this Interpretation, vv 13–17); the impression with which one is left is that Jrm saw the general disobedience of the people as contingent on the prior disobedience of the king (compare 5:4–5), so that again one is led toward an early date for the oracle. (4) There is the possibility that the pronouncement of judgment on the king (vv 18–19) is a reflex of the king's action against the prophet Uriah (26:23), which is associated with Jrm's temple sermon in 609: see Interpretation on v 19, the discussion in Setting for chapter 26, and in Interpretation of 26:20–24.

Interpretation

■ **13–17** The poem is of course directed to Jehoiakim (v 18). There is no way to determine for sure whether the reference here is to a renovation and enlargement by Jehoiakim of Solomon's palace, which presumably continued to be the residence for kings in Jerusalem after Solomon's time[7]—inasmuch as "build" may imply "rebuild" (1 Kgs 12:25, compare there *NEB*), or whether the reference here is to an altogether new palace. Though Yohanan Aharoni assumed that it was a new palace which Jehoiakim built, identifying remains at Ramat Raḥel with that enterprise, the identification has been refuted by Yigael Yadin.[8] There is some evidence of "matching" between the wording of the accusation in these verses and that of the judgment speech in vv 18–19 (see on this Structure), and there is evidence elsewhere that Jrm felt that the punishment should fit the crime (compare 17:11 and 20:1–6). In that case the phrase "beyond the gates of Jerusalem" would be plausible though indirect evidence that the building project, too, was beyond the gates of Jerusalem: thus the king's corpse would lie where he wanted to live.

Jrm accuses the king of forcing citizens to work without compensation (v 13), a practice reminiscent of that of Solomon (1 Kgs 5:27–28; 11:28).[9] That accusation is reinforced by general accusations of social injustice (v 17,

---

3 Westermann, *Basic Forms*, 129–63.
4 See Wolff, *Joel and Amos*, 242–45.
5 Ibid.
6 Hillers, *Treaty-Curses*, 68–69.
7 Compare Ovid R. Sellers, "Palace," *IDB* 3:620a.
8 See 6:1–8, nn. 5 and 6.
9 On this matter see Gray, *Kings*, 155–56.

see below); the quiet reminder that the citizens whom Jehoiakim pressed into service were his "fellows" (רֵעַ, v 13) is a nice touch. The Deuteronomic historian records that Jehoiakim had to exact silver and gold from the country gentry in the early years of his reign to pay tribute to Pharaoh (2 Kgs 23:35): his project for more luxurious palace quarters cannot have been popular.

In contrast to the eighth-century prophets there is curiously little emphasis on social injustice in the words of accusation uttered by Jrm; most of the passages that do deal with injustice have phraseological parallels to this passage (compare 5:28, "they have not pled the pleading of the orphan, and the judgment of the needy they have not judged," and v 16 here, "he pled the pleading of the poor and needy": for the details see the individual phrases below). It is almost as if Jrm was convinced that the social injustice of the people stems from the behavior of the king; one gains the same impression from the thought of 5:4–5 (see further Setting).

■ **13–14a** For "woe" see Form. For the poetic negation of the nouns "righteousness" and "justice" by the negative לֹא see 5:7 ("non-gods").

Rhetorically one would expect Jrm to say, "Woe to him who says, 'Let me build myself a spacious house . . .'" and then to follow the quotation with the actuality ("but it is with unrighteousness that he builds his house"). Instead Jrm reverses the parts, putting the negative judgment first and following it with the (by then) fatuous quotation; a similar limp quotation is found in 8:20 after Yahweh's judgment in 8:19b. The word order in the first two cola of v 13 is very close to that in the first two cola of v 14, since the words "with unrighteousness" and "with injustice" in v 13 and the designation of the house as "spacious" and of the roof-chambers as "wide-open" come last in their respective cola.

For the use of "fellow" (רֵעַ) in passages referring to the breakdown of covenant solidarity see 9:3, 4, 7. The verb עבד normally means "serve," but with the preposition בְּ may mean (as here) "keep someone in service" (so 30:8; 34:9, 10). The noun פֹּעַל normally means "work, toil" (25:14 and elsewhere), but may mean "compensation for work" (as here).

The designation of the "house" in v 14a is clear: it is

literally "a house of (striking) extents [בֵּית מִדּוֹת]," thus a house built on large proportions. Unfortunately it is not so clear what the designation of the "roof-chambers" here is. It was often the custom to sleep on the roof of a house (1 Sam 9:25–26), and therefore rooms were sometimes built on the roof to catch the breeze (Judg 3:20, 23; 1 Kgs 17:19, 23; 2 Kgs 4:10–11), thus "roof-chambers." But how are they here described? The vocalization of the word and its precise denotation are uncertain. G translates "airy" (ῥιπιστά) and V by "spacious" (spatiosa). Thus G assumes a connection with רוּחַ "wind," and V with the root רוח "feel relieved" (compare רְוָחָה "respite, relief"). The two centers of meaning may be related ("catch one's breath = "feel relief"), but it is by no means certain.

■ **14b** The verb here translated "enlarge" is literally "tear," usually of tearing garments. The use here of this verb with "windows" is so striking as to have called forth much comment, but the key is evidently the other striking use of the verb in the book, namely in 4:30, where the harlot enlarges her eyes with eye paint. It has already been suggested (see the discussion on 4:30) that windows are associated with harlotry.[10] There are other references to "windows" associated with Canaanite culture: the mother of Sisera peered through the window (Judg 5:28), Jrm speaks of Death climbing through the window (9:20). Given these associations, I suggest that Jrm's word to Jehoiakim, using the same verb by which the harlot enlarges her eyes, hints that the king has metaphorically indulged in harlotry: one notes that after the rhetorical interruptions (see Structure) the address speaks first of the king's eyes (v 17) and moves immediately to his illegitimate profit.

The last two verbs in v 14 (and the first verb in v 15) I take to be a series of infinitive absolutes (see Text). Elsewhere in Jer an isolated infinitive absolute appears to offer a side comment, putting some distance between the speaker and the action (3:1; 4:18; 8:15; 32:33), hence the translation "to think" or "imagine."

Paneling with cedar was to be found in Solomon's palace (1 Kgs 7:7). "Paint" is the verb משׁח, ordinarily translated "anoint." "Vermilion" (שָׁשַׁר) is usually identified with red ocher (hematite),[11] but perhaps it is

---

10   Barnett, *Nimrud Ivories*, 145–51.
11   Chester L. Wickwire, "Vermilion," *IDB* 4:748–49.

minium (lead oxide).[12] The only other occurrence of the word in the OT is in Ezek 23:14 in connection with forbidden paintings.

■ **15** Though *M* for v 15a makes sense ("Do you reign when you are competing in cedar?"), the suggestion of Duhm, favored by Cornill, Condamin, and Rudolph, to read the first verb as a hitpaʿel, makes better sense, and the suggestion given here, to read an infinitive absolute, retains the consonantal text. The hitpaʿel stem of this verb does not otherwise occur, but the meaning of such a verb is clear, "behave like a king," "try to be king"; compare תִּשְׂתָּרֵר, Num 16:13, "set yourself up as prince," "lord it (over us)," from שַׂר "prince, official." The verb does not imply that Jehoiakim is an illegitimate king, as van Selms assumes:[13] it does not necessarily mean "pretend to be king" (while Jehoahaz is the real king), though וַיִּתְהֹלֵל, 1 Sam 21:14, means "pretend to be insane"; it can be said of a legitimate prophet, הַמִּתְנַבֵּא, "who is prophesying," that is, behaving as a prophet does. The point of course is that Jehoiakim is exercising his kingly office by extravagant public works.

For the supplying of "with cedar" after "trying to be king," and the reading of "with Ahaz" with *G* for the *M* reading "with cedar," see Text.

The verb "compete" can also be vocalized (both here and in 12:5) as a hitpaʿel, and for the sake of symmetry with the preceding verb this is a plausible option: there has been difference of opinion whether this verb (in both occurrences) should be vocalized as a tipʿel (so *M*) or as a hitpaʿel.[14] Is it significant that the sequence in 4:30 describing the harlot painting her eyes ends with a hitpaʿel, תִּתְיַפִּי, "try to beautify yourself"?

The mention of Ahaz (if the text is reconstructed correctly) is a surprise. We are not directly informed of Ahaz's construction work in the palace, though an obscure verse, 2 Kgs 16:18, details some building operations which he directed, evidently at the temple, but perhaps concerning the palace as well (compare *NJV* there). But a reference here to Ahaz is not unlikely (the verb "compete" suggests the need to name a competitor: see Text), and the fact that Jrm elsewhere seems to address Jehoiakim as "house of David" (21:12), the same mode of address used by Isaiah to Ahaz (Isa 7:13), reinforces slightly the reading here.

The mention of "your father" (that is, Josiah), is in strong contrast to "you" (the pronoun) in the previous colon; and it is in strong contrast, also, to "Ahaz" (if that is a correct reading)—as if to say, "If you want to pick a predecessor to emulate, try Josiah."

The two verbs "eat" and "drink" form a hendiadys and are therefore joined by a simple copula, not the consecutive waw (compare 1 Kgs 19:6).[15] If the text is here correct (see Structure), the sequence of verbs continues with "do justice . . . ," a verb likewise joined by a simple copula. What is the implication of "eat and drink"? Is it "Josiah lived well and still managed to adhere to the covenant" (Cornill, Bright, Thompson), or is it "Josiah lived simply and was concerned rather to adhere to the covenant" (Duhm, Condamin)? Or is it not rather, as Volz proposed, that there is no opposition between "eating and drinking" and "doing justice": Josiah accepted the responsibility of being the head of his people in both his daily habits and in the royal maintenance of the covenant—this is at least what the syntax implies. The word טוֹב must be construed as a perfect verb, "it went well"; it has the most general application, suggesting not only that life was "pleasing" to Josiah in eating and drinking but that things went well for him as head of the covenant people.

■ **16** The first colon is of course simply an explication of "do justice and righteousness" in v 15. This is the only occurrence of עָנִי "poor" in Jer; it forms a hendiadys with אֶבְיוֹן "needy" (on which see 5:28), and there is no way to distinguish the terms.[16] The colon "then it went well" is not necessarily dittographic (see Structure). Is the fact that "for him" (לוֹ) is missing in this colon an indication that things went well not only for Josiah but for everyone?

12 See KB, 1014a. On the general question of pigments in the ancient Near East see Robert J. Forbes, "Chemical, Culinary, and Cosmetic Arts," *A History of Technology* I (ed. Charles Singer, E. J. Holmyard, and A. R. Hall; Oxford: Claredon, 1954) 238–43.

13 Adriaan van Selms, "Motivated Interrogative Sentences in Biblical Hebrew," *Semitics* 2 (1971/72) 146.

14 For older literature on the question see BDB, 354a.

Electing the tipʿel: *HALAT*, 337b; electing the hitpaʿel: Zorell, p. 267b.

15 And see further Joüon, *Gramm.*, secs. 118k, and 166a, note.

16 C. Umhau Wolf, "Poor," *IDB* 3:843.

The proposal of a verb at the beginning of the last colon of the verse is based on three considerations. (1) The occurrence of "know me" (דַּעַת־אוֹתִי) in 9:5 is preceded by a verb. (2) The earlier occurrence of הֲלֹא in the passage (v 15) is followed by verbs. (3) There is nothing else in the passage of a general wisdom nuance such as the understanding of *M* implies ("Is this not to know me?"). The qal stem of the proposed verb occurs in 10:7, part of a passage attributed to Jrm in the present study. An occurrence of the hip'il stem of this verb would fit the meaning needed in the context and would precisely answer to the consonantal text.

■ **17** The verse opens with כִּי expressing strong opposition, followed by a subordinate כִּי אִם־ with more opposition ("but your eyes . . . are on nothing but . . ."). (For oppositional כִּי after a previous הֲלֹא compare Gen 31:15–16.) For a similar phrase see 5:3 ("Your eyes are on honesty, Yahweh, are they not?"). "Heart" and "eyes" are of course a hendiadys, both representing desire; the two are linked elsewhere (Ps 19:9). For "cut" (בֶּצַע) see 6:13; for "shed the blood of the innocent" see 2:34; for "extortion" (עֹשֶׁק) see 6:6. The word מְרוּצָה may mean either "oppression" or "running": the former is the major emphasis here, but "running" is also implied, in the context of "competing" (v 15); see Structure, and see also 8:6, where the same double meaning is involved.

■ **18** The initial rubric is similar to that in v 11, even to the use of אֶל for "of, concerning." Calvin points out that the rubric, by its mention of Josiah, hints that Jehoiakim had degenerated from the piety of his father.

Although the restored line, "Woe to this man!" may not be altogether necessary, it supplies an antecedent for "him" (לוֹ) in the next colon. The indefinite third-person plural in the repeated "they shall not lament him" is of course the functional equivalent of the passive "he shall be buried" in v 19 (compare 16:6, where the same mixture of forms occurs), but the quotations of the hypothetical laments need an active verb.

The hypothetical laments use הוֹי "woe!" just as v 13 does, and just as the laments do at the end of this verse (here "alas!"). In English this is a strain; one does not feel comfortable with the same interjection for an expression of "woe" and for an expression of lament. It is difficult to

know whether the same sense of stretching the interjection was felt in Hebrew; as it was pointed out in Form, Wolff believes that the "woe"-cry originated in funeral lamentation, but whether any ambiguity was felt is hard to say. It is also difficult to determine whether the "and" links two utterances ("Alas, my brother!" and "Alas, sister!") or is part of a single utterance (so the punctuation here). A decision depends to some degree on how "brother" and "sister" are to be understood, and this question in turn rests upon the question of text.

One would assume that "my brother" refers to the dead king (so evidently 1 Kgs 13:30), but when one is confronted by "sister," one must assume either a more curious sort of parallelism that cannot be taken literally, or that "brother" and "sister" are the address of mourners to each other (Calvin). Perhaps because of the feminine reference here *G* has only the first and third elements: "They shall not lament him, 'Alas, brother!' nor shall they weep for him, 'Ah, lord!'" *V* has four elements, though the second is "brothers" (Jerome in his commentary, however, uses "sister"). *S* has four, but the second repeats the first, and the fourth repeats the third. Clearly, then, *M* in reading "sister" offers a *lectio difficilior* (*difficillima?!*). Dahood has a convincing solution: an emendation of the fourth element, and the background of Phoenician royal inscriptions. As to the fourth element, he emends it to "lady" (הֹרָה, literally "she who conceives"), feminine like the second. He further suggests that "lord" and "lady" here stand for "father" and "mother," and this is doubtless true, but the double meaning by which "lord" may stand for "king" as well as "father" is surely present. (For "lord" = "father" see Ug. 24.33–34, and compare Gen 31:35; for "she who conceives" in parallel with "mother" see Hos 2:7; Cant 3:4.) The key to the diction here, however, is to be found in Phoenician royal inscriptions: in one King Azitawadda states, "Baal made me father and mother [לאב ולאם] to the Dananians,"[17] and in another King Kilamuwa states, "I, however, to some I was a father [אב], and to some I was a mother [אם], and to some I was a brother [אח]."[18] Here, then, is traditional language by which the king is said to fulfill the roles of all family members; and therefore the "and" in the expressions could well be a part of

---

17   Karatepe A 1.3; see *KAI* I, 5, no. 26.
18   Kilamuwa = Zinjirli 1.10–11; see *ANET*, 500, and *KAI* I, 4, no. 24.

the quotation in question, rather than link two separate quotations. One may assume furthermore that the possessive suffix on "brother" does double-duty for "sister" as well.

For the emendation "burn (spices)" see Text. The verb, the ordinary verb for "burn," implies in 34:5 (and here, by the emendation proposed) some funerary rite, but what is burned is not stated. G and V both offer here a verb parallel to lament, but G renders simply κλαίειν "weep, lament," while V offers, curiously, *concrepare* "rattle, sound loudly" (a reference to some other customary behavior in lamentation?). The Talmud states that it was the custom to make a funeral pyre of the bed and other articles as a mark of honor to a deceased king.[19] There is record in 2 Chr 16:14 of such a ceremony for King Asa, which included the burning of spices; the parenthetical inclusion of "spices" in the translation here is therefore appropriate.

■ 19 Verse 18 hints at the pomp and circumstance appropriate for a king's burial; the present verse says that such burial will not occur for Jehoiakim—what will take place instead is the burial of an ass (Bright: "funeral of a donkey"). As the verse implies, a donkey's carcass is simply dragged out of the city and dumped in a field, a prey then to dogs and vultures. It was taken for granted in Israel that all bodies are to be buried (compare 8:1–3; 9:21);[20] it is thus a great curse if one's corpse does not receive burial (Deut 28:26, and see further Form). That a king should be treated like an ass and denied burial is appalling; Jrm evidently used this curse more than once against Jehoiakim (36:30), and it is suggested here that it reflects Jehoiakim's treatment of the prophet Uriah (26:23). Joüon cites an Arabic narrative recorded in Palmyrene dialect: a local chief, having massacred his rivals, swears that they shall not be carried off (for burial) on a bier, and they were dragged off by oxen for burial like dead sheep.[21]

The question of how Jehoiakim finally did die is relevant to the question of the nature of the curse:

Weiser suggests that the verse be taken to mean that "Nebuchadnezzar, at the conquest of Jerusalem, had the grave of his faithless vassal violated."[22] But even though Assyrian and Babylonian kings more than once did disinter the bones of disobedient vassals, disinterment is not at issue here: Jrm speaks of lack of burial.[23]

The question still remains whether the curse came to pass, a question raised as early as Jerome; the historical data are incomplete. One reads in 2 Kgs 24:6 that Jehoiakim "slept with his fathers," but nothing there is said about his burial (compare the notice of the death of Manasseh, "And Manasseh slept with his fathers, and was buried in the garden of his house," 2 Kgs 21:18); one reads in 2 Chr 36:6 that Nebuchadrezzar "bound [Jehoiakim] in fetters to take him to Babylon," but nothing is said there of his death and burial. If the notice in 2 Chronicles is historical, what were the circumstances, given the fact that Jehoiachin reigned three months before the fall of the city (2 Kgs 24:8, 10; 2 Chr 36:9–10)? Graf suggested long ago that "bound him in fetters to take him to Babylon" originally applied to Jehoiachin, and the phrase was transferred to Jehoiakim:[24] could such a transfer have taken place precisely under the influence of the present verse in Jer?—this section of 2 Chronicles is concerned that the word of Yahweh to Jrm be fulfilled (2 Chr 36:21–22). But both textual and historical questions are raised by 2 Chr 36:6 over which one cannot linger here.[25]

In any event the power of the present verse is in its utterance, not in its literal fulfillment.

Aim

Is a king able to use his prerogatives for his own glory and personal satisfaction? Solomon evidently was, so Jehoiakim had good precedent. But Jrm had Nathan for precedent, to affirm to the king that he is not above the law and that in Israel the king is as much responsible for justice and righteousness as any other citizen, indeed has a particular responsibility for justice and righteousness

19   *b. Sanh.* 52b.
20   See William L. Reed, "Burial," *IDB* 1:476.
21   Paul Joüon, "Un parallèle à la 'Sépulture d'un Âne' de Jérémie (XXII, 19) en arabe moderne de Palmyre," *RSR* 17 (1937) 335–36.
22   Weiser, p. 191.
23   Morton Cogan, "A Note on Disinterment in Jeremiah," *Gratz College, Anniversary Volume* (ed.

Isidore D. Passow and Samuel T. Lachs; New York: Ktav, 1971) 32–34.
24   So Naegelsbach, p. 202.
25   See Curtis and Madsen, *Chronicles*, 501.

(compare 2 Sam 12:1–12). Jehoiakim's glory, built up so insubstantially, will merit nothing but degradation when he dies. In David's lament over Abner he asks rhetorically, "Should Abner die as a fool dies?" (2 Sam 3:33); the implied answer is negative. But Jrm affirms most positively that Jehoiakim will die as an ass dies.

Jerusalem Mourns Her Lovers

Bibliography

Daiches, Samuel
"Exegetical Notes, Jer. xxii, 23," *PEFQS* 59 (1927) 163.

22

20
Climb Lebanon and cry out,
  and in Bashan raise your voice,
    《 and wail 》[a] from Abarim:
      for all your lovers have been
        broken.

21
I spoke to you in your complacency;[a]
you said, "I will not listen";
  this is your way from your youth,
    for you have not listened to my
      voice.

22
All your shepherds the wind shall shepherd,
  and your lovers into captivity shall go;
yes, then you shall be shamed and humiliated
    by all 《 your companions. 》[a]

23
You who are enthroned[a] in Lebanon,
  nested[a] in the cedars,
how [b]you have groaned[b] when pangs
  come upon you,
    writhing like a woman in labor!

Text

20a   Reading וְהֵילִילִי for M וְצָעָקִי. It is not appropriate to repeat the identical verb in parallelism, and G renders the two occurrences of the imperative of צעק by different verbs. The verb proposed here is in parallel with צעק in 49:3 and Isa 65:14 (and compare Jer 48:20; Ezek 21:17), and the assonance of the proposed verb with -*lî hallě*- in the first colon makes it appropriate here.

21a   Reading the singular בְּשַׁלְוָתֵךְ with a few MSS. and V and S for the M plural בְּשַׁלְוֹתַיִךְ. Though G understands the meaning of the noun differently, it too assumes a singular.

22a   Reading רַעְתֵךְ or רֵעֹתַיִךְ for M רָעָתֵךְ "your evil" or "your disaster." Though the G reading τῶν φιλούντων σε is ambiguous as to gender, the possibility of a feminine plural is there (compare Rudolph in *BHS*), thus suggesting the proposed reading.

23a   There is a ketib/qere' contrast in these two participles identical with that in 10:17; for a discussion of these forms see GKC, sec. 90n.

b—b   G, V, and S translate this verb as "groan." But this translation has been assumed by scholars to be correct only by reading M נַחַנְתְּ as a metathesis of נֶאֱנַחְתְּ from (אנח נֶאֱנַחְתְּ nip'al), so *HALAT* 68b. The other alternative is to translate "you are to be pitied" (חנן nip'al). Now, however, comes evidence of the root נחן "groan" in a clear context in Ugaritic (Ug. 15.1.7), where it is in parallel with "low" (as of a heifer for her calf): see on this Mitchell Dahood, *Ugaritic-Hebrew Philology* (BibOr 17; Rome: Pontifical Biblical Institute, 1965) 66, no. 1630a (but it must be said that Dahood's citing of a Phoenician example of the verb, Ešmun'azar 12 [*KAI* I, 3, no. 14, 12], is not at all secure: it is usually read as an apocopated form of אנחן "we" [see *ANET*, 505, n. 2], or as חנן nip'al "to be pitied" [*DISO*, 92; Richard S. Tomback, *A Comparative Semitic Lexicon of the Phoenician and Punic Languages* (SBLDS 32; Missoula, MT: Scholars, 1978) 109]). The verb in the present passage is vocalized either as a nip'al or a pi'el, but there is no reason why the consonantal text cannot be vocalized as a qal, and there are no data for a choice.

Structure

These four verses address the city in the feminine singular; the poem is thus set apart from what precedes and what follows. It is part of a sequence of poems on the city and its kings. One notes here "Lebanon" (vv 20, 23) and "cedar(s)" (v 23), associated with "Lebanon" in v 6 and "cedar(s)" in vv 7, 14, 15. One notes also "who are enthroned" (יֹשֶׁבְתְּ and its variant) in v 23 and in 21:13. (For a more extended discussion of the structure of the sequence of poems see 21:1–7, Structure.)

The poem is tightly knit, but its train of thought is not readily apparent. The two occurrences of "Lebanon" form an inclusio in vv 20 and 23, and these occurrences form two associations, that of mountain height in v 20 and that of the cedar forest in v 23. The poem thus unfolds more explicitly the images implied in the poem of vv 6–7 (see vv 6–7, Setting). If behind the wording of v 20 stands the story of Jephthah's daughter (see Interpretation), then the verbs are appropriate to mourning; the balancing image of v 23b is that of childbirth.

Structurally v 21 reflects v 20 (three parallel cola, closed by a כִּי clause), but in form and diction v 21 stands apart (see Form): the burden of the last colon of v 20 (the destruction of lovers) is expanded in v 22, with the evident parallelism of "shepherds," "lovers," and "(female) companions" (if that last word is reconstructed correctly). Verses 22 and 23 are structurally parallel in that the second pair of cola in v 22 are introduced by כִּי (hardly "for" here, better "yes") and the second pair of cola in v 23 are introduced by מַה "how."

Form

Verse 20 is an adaptation of the call to communal lament (compare 4:8);[1] here, however, the address is not masculine plural but feminine singular—the call is to the personified city (compare the diction of Isa 14:31). The verse ends with a statement of motivation, introduced by "for" (כִּי). The first colon of v 21 is Yahweh's recollection to the people of his previous acts of revelation (compare 7:23); the second colon is an accusation of disobedience (compare 2:20a). The third colon is a summary appraisal (compare 4:18; 13:25a),[2] and the fourth colon is again a statement of motivation (exactly like 13:25b), again

introduced by "for" (כִּי). Verse 22 is specifically a judgment speech (compare 13:26). Verse 23a offers two vocative participles that parody the liturgical address to Yahweh (see Interpretation, and see further 21:13). The verse closes with an exclamation over the suffering the city will experience under Yahweh's judgment; but given the mockery of the vocatives in the first half of the verse, this exclamation must likewise be mocking (compare "how" [מַה] with the same tone in Job 26:2–3).

In totality, then, the oracle is a judgment speech.

Setting

There are no clear historical clues by which to date the passage (though a hint may be supplied by "your companions" in v 22—see below). There are, however, many phraseological parallels with passages in chapters 2—6 and with 13:20–27 which (in the hypothesis offered here) were delivered in the period 609–601. Thus "you said, 'I will not listen'" (v 21) is comparable to "and said, 'I will not serve'" (2:20); "from your youth" (v 21) is matched by "my youth" (3:4) and "from our youth" (3:24); "be shamed by your companions" (v 22) is comparable to "be shamed by Egypt as you were shamed by Assyria" (2:36); the colon "writhing like a woman in labor" (v 23) is a duplicate of a colon in 6:24, and the same figure is found in 4:31 and 13:21. Further the summary appraisal formula "this is your way" (v 21) is comparable to such formulae in 4:18 and 13:25.

If "your companions" is correctly reconstructed in v 22, and if that term refers to the other small states in Syria-Palestine (on which see further Interpretation), then it is conceivable that a setting in the summer or autumn of 604, when Nebuchadrezzar's army was marching, would be appropriate: the Babylonian Chronicle records the Babylonian sack of Ashkelon in December 604.[3] But obviously there can be no chance of certainty on the matter.

Interpretation

■ **20** Three mountainous areas are named here, Lebanon in the north, Bashan in the northeast, and Abarim in Moab in the southeast. (G and V offer two variant vocalizations of the word here given as Abarim, but both

---

1   See more generally Wolff, *Joel and Amos*, 21–22.
2   See further Childs, *Isaiah and the Assyrian Crisis*, 128–36.
3   See 14:1—15:9, n. 30.

are to be rejected.)[4] These three mountainous regions surround geographically the personified city of Jerusalem and are therefore three appropriate mountains to climb for mourning. One may take "Lebanon" here either as sharing a double-duty preposition ("in") with "Bashan" or (more likely) as an accusative (like Joel 2:7).

What is the implication of lamenting on the mountains? Is there here a quiet reminiscence of the tragedy of Jephthah's daughter (see Judg 11:37–38)? But what was the significance of "mountains" in the narrative of Jephthah's daughter—is it simply remoteness from community life (compare Jer 3:21)? Or is there some custom existing prior to the incident of Jephthah's daughter of lamenting on the mountains of which we are unaware?—is that part of the significance of "Ramah" (which means "height") in 31:15 (see there)? In any event it is clear that Jrm intends the hearer to be reminded of the tragedies of other women in other times and places. For the reconstruction "wail" see Text; it is clear that the parallelism of these first three cola demands a different verb than the repetition of "cry out" which *M* offers.

The word "lovers" here is the pi'el participle of אהב: only the participle occurs with this stem of the verb. This form occurs five times in Hosea 2 (for example, Hos 2:7) to refer to the fertility deities with whom Israel has prostituted herself;[5] in Ezek 23:5, 9 the word specifically refers to the Assyrians. In Jer the participle appears only here, in v 22 and in 30:14. Since in the two cited passages of Ezekiel the verb used for Israel's action toward her lovers is עגב, and that is the verb which appears for "lovers" in Jer 4:30 (עגבים), the reference is doubtless the same here as in those parallel passages: foreign powers and/or their deities who were expected to control Judah and offer security to her. The verb "have been broken" (שבר nip'al) is surprising with this subject: it is perhaps reminiscent of Isa 8:15 and 28:13, passages depicting the stumbling, the falling, the destruction of the people of Israel. For "your lovers" see further v 22.

■ 21 The content of this verse is reminiscent of many passages earlier in the book (compare Form and Setting) accusing the people of unwillingness to heed Yahweh. The noun here translated "complacency" (שַׁלְוָה) is often rendered "(time of) prosperity" (*RSV*; Bright: "when times were good"), as if the word is parallel with "your (time of) youth" (נְעוּרִים). This is possible, since outer circumstances shape inner attitudes, but it would appear that inner attitude is primary in this word: Ezek 16:49 has שַׁלְוַת הַשְׁקֵט "careless ease" (Zimmerli), "complacent in their prosperity" (*NAB*), and Dan 8:25; 11:21 and 24 have בְּשַׁלְוָה in contexts of attack—"without warning" (*RSV*), "when they least expect it" (*NEB*). The nuance here, then, is complacency.

■ 22 Given the patterns of poetry, there are several uncertainties of text in this verse. *G*[A] omits "all your lovers" in the second colon, and on this basis Duhm deletes the phrase as overloading the line. If this were a sound move, one might well vocalize the first phrase of the verse as "all your partners" (כָּל־רֵעַיִךְ) and view the phrase in the second line as a gloss; one notes that "many partners" (רֵעִים רַבִּים) occurs in 3:1 in a similar context and that some MSS. and Versions read "many shepherds" (רֹעִים רַבִּים) there. In this case the first colon would make a witty triple word-play in Hebrew (כָּל־רֵעַיִךְ תִּרְעֶה־רוּחַ). On the other hand, the canons of Hebrew poetry are hardly secure enough for us confidently to excise a word on the basis of meter, and there are several countervailing considerations. Jrm elsewhere envisages the reversal of occupations (30:16): here, then, the notion is appropriate that shepherds will themselves be shepherded. And this is, after all, the vocalization of *M* and the understanding of the Versions; further, *M* here is sustained if the proposed reconstruction in the fourth colon, a feminine of רֵעִים, is correct. By the reading of *M*, then, the root רעה "shepherd" is doubled; there is assonance with "wind" (רוּחַ), but the impact of the colon is the reversal of the act of shepherding. (Is there an echo of this idea in the diction of Isa 53:6, given the possibility that the shepherds are kings?—compare 52:15.)

Related to these considerations is the question whether one is to take "shepherds" as identical with "lovers" (so Rudolph) or as a separate category. Calvin takes them to be separate, I believe correctly; the shepherds are everywhere the political leaders of Judah (2:8; 3:15; 23:1–4), while the "lovers" are foreign powers giving aid to Judah (see above, on v 20; so also Bright). The judgment that there are two different referents here is

---

4   For the geographical details of Bashan and Abarim see Baly, *Geography*, 216–25.

5   See specifically Wolff, *Hosea*, 35.

reinforced if the reconstruction of "your companions" in the last colon is correct. These companions, by the reconstruction, are feminine; since Judah/Jerusalem is here addressed in the feminine singular, these companions would be other states equally vulnerable to Babylon (see below). The argument offered here is to some degree circular; the reading of *M*, רָעָתֵךְ, which could mean either "your wickedness," "your disaster," or both, would make plausible sense in the context. But *G* suggests a *lectio difficilior* here which the reconstruction meets: such a reconstruction should contain a taw (see Rudolph in *BHS*). The reconstruction is reinforced to some degree by the strong triple parallelism in v 20: "Lebanon," "Bashan," and "Abarim" could well suggest the plausibility of "your shepherds," "your lovers," and "your companions" here.

The image of "all your shepherds the wind shall shepherd" is the same as that in 18:17, where the east wind scatters the people. But the word רוּחַ carries many mutually exclusive connotations: it may be "(God's) spirit," and as such may have revivifying power (Ezek 37:1–9), but it also many mean "(mere) breath," and therefore emptiness (5:13); the varied nuances of both divine power, the destructiveness of the east wind and the emptiness of breath lend disturbing ambiguity to the colon. On the image of the personified wind compare Hos 4:19. "All" does double-duty.[6]

For the parallelism "be shamed" (בוש) and "be humiliated" (כלם) see 6:15. The closest parallel for the present phraseology is 2:36, "by Egypt you shall be shamed as you were shamed by Assyria." But this parallel raises anew the question of the identity of the "shepherds," "lovers," and "companions": one would have expected here "you shall be shamed and disgraced by all your lovers," if Egypt (2:36) could be considered a "lover," and one would have expected "all your shepherds shall go into captivity," if the "shepherds" are a reference to the leaders of Judah (compare 20:6). The only solution, if this understanding of the verse is sound, is that the nouns and actions of the verse are recombined to give a general impression that every stable support will disappear. And if the three nouns are really parallel, then כִּי at the beginning of the third colon cannot mean "for," as

it does at the beginning of the fourth cola in vv 20 and 21, but must be a kind of exclamatory particle, perhaps parallel to "how" (מָה) at the beginning of the third colon of v 24.

Question: Could the "(female) companions" in the last colon be another delicate reminiscence to the narrative of Jephthah's daughter (compare Judg 11:37, 38)? If so, v 22 is linked to v 20 by more than the phrase "all your lovers."

■ **23** For the interpretation of the first participle as "enthroned" see on 21:13: the phraseology is identical. Jerusalem is accused of self-deification, surrounded as she is in both palace and temple by cedar from Lebanon (see v 7). But Lebanon here not only betokens cedars, it betokens height: if Yahweh is enthroned on (the height of) Zion (Ps 9:12), then Jerusalem takes pride in being enthroned on (the height of) Lebanon.[7] The parallel "nested" is lovely, given "in the cedars." The same parallel is found in 48:28, there in derision of refugees.

For "how" as a mocking exclamation compare Job 26:2–3; for "groan" (נחן) see Text. In a similar passage the personified nation is portrayed as "panting" (4:31). The "pangs" occur elsewhere with the figure (13:21; 49:34; Isa 13:8; 26:17); for "writhing like a woman in labor" see 6:24.

Aim

Whom is Jerusalem mourning? What is it like for Jerusalem to mourn when all her companions are gone, both her lovers who could protect her and the maidens who were her confidence? Poor Zion is left like a booth in a vineyard, like a lodge in a cucumber field, like a besieged city (Isa 1:8). What good are her splendid paneled temple and palace buildings if there is no one to help her, even in childbirth? And it is all the judgment of Yahweh, to whom she did not listen.

---

6   Helmer Ringgren, "The omitting of *kol* in Hebrew parallelism," *VT* 32 (1982) 101.

7   Compare the remarks by Dahood on Pss 2:4 and 9:12 in *Psalms I*, 8–9, 57.

**The Young King
Will Be Lost to History**

Bibliography

On 22:24–30:
Hermisson, Hans-Jürgen
    "Jeremias Wort über Jojachin," *Werden und Wirken des Alten Testaments, Festschrift für Claus Westermann zum 70. Geburtstag* (ed. Rainer Albertz et al.; Göttingen: Vandenhoeck & Ruprecht; Neukirchen: Neukirchener, 1980) 253–66.

22

24 As I live, oracle of Yahweh, I swear Coniah son of Jehoiakim, king of Judah, shall never be the signet-ring on my right hand. Yes, from there I would pull you off!—25/ and I will give you into the hand of those who seek your life, [into the hand of those]ᵃ whose presence you fear, [and into the hand of Nebuchadrezzar king of Babylon, and]ᵃ into the hand of the Chaldeans; 26/ and I shall hurl you and your mother, who bore you, to ᵃa[nother]ᵇ landᵃ where ᶜneither of you was born,ᶜ and there ᶜyou both shall die.ᶜ 27/ But to the land where they yearn to return, thereᵃ they shall not return.

Text

25a   Expansions, lacking in *G*; see Janzen, p. 41.

26a—a   Reading אֶרֶץ; the *M* article in הָאָרֶץ is evidently dittographic from v 27 (Rudolph).

b   "Other" is lacking in *G*.

c—c   The verbs of both expressions shift from the previous second-person singular to second-person plural; literally "you were not born" and "you shall die."

27a   *M* has שָׁם שָׁמָּה, literally "there thither." The first word is construed by the Masoretes with the first clause, and the second with the second, but one would expect the first word to be שָׁמָּה as well. Therefore the שָׁמָּה in *M* may be intended for the first clause, in which case שָׁם is dittographic from v 26 (Rudolph).

Structure

This passage is a prose near-equivalent of vv 28–30 and therefore adjoins it, just as vv 11–12 adjoins v 10 and as vv 1–5 are near 21:11–12. The term "near-equivalent" is used here because there may be a slight difference in time between the setting of this passage and of vv 28–30 (see Setting on both passages).

It is possible that the passage is shaped by the shift of personal reference, from third person (v 24a) to second person (vv 24b–26) and to third person again (v 27), but that shift may be less than intentional. The movement from "pull you off (the right hand)" (v 24) to "put you into the hand" (v 25) and perhaps "hurl" (v 26), and the contrasts between both "who bore you" and "neither of you were born" on the one hand and "you shall both die" (v 26) on the other, and between "a land where neither of you was born" (v 26) and "the land where they yearn to return" (v 27), may all play a part in shaping the passage, but there are no structural features strong enough to stand out.

Form

This passage, like v 10 and vv 11–12, is a "judgment-speech without a reason."[1] The diction here has much in common with that of 20:6, but there the judgment against Pashhur is based on an implicit accusation, suggested by 20:2.[2] Here there is no accusation against Jehoiachin, any more than there was against Jehoahaz in vv 10–12; he is simply a king who suffers in the general fate of the covenant people.

1   Westermann, *Basic Forms*, 162.
2   Ibid., 147.

Setting

Rudolph assumes that vv 25–27 are a prose expansion of v 24, but there is no rhetorical break between v 24 and v 25, and in style the two sections are of a piece. This prose has an integrity of its own, as do its prose companions, vv 1–5 and 11–12 (which see), and the passage must be taken as authentic. The striking verb "hurl" (טול hip'il, v 26) is hardly the sign of a redactor (compare Setting on 16:10–13: the same verb occurs also in 16:13), and the nice movement from "pull off (the right hand)" to "put into the hand" to "hurl" (vv 24–26) suggests the mind of Jrm, as do the contrasts between "be born" and "die" and between the two occurrences of "land" (see Structure). The first fall of Jerusalem, according to the Babylonian Chronicle, was on 16 March 597.[3] Though the chronology of the first deportation is in dispute,[4] the fact that Jehoiachin ruled only three months (2 Kgs 24:8) narrows the setting for the passage to the winter of 598/597 (but see further vv 28–30, Setting).

Interpretation

■ **24** This verse offers puzzling syntax. After the initial words "as I live, oracle of Yahweh," comes the conjunction כִּי אִם־, and then after "my right hand" comes another כִּי. How do the conjunctions function, and what is the relation between the two clauses? There appear to be two solutions. One is to see the first clause as a protasis and the second clause as an apodosis: "though Coniah . . . were the signet-ring on my right hand, yet I would tear you off. . . ." This is the rendering of G, V, and S, and of most translations and commentaries. König assumes this, stating that כִּי may come between the protasis and apodosis and that the first כִּי is a כִּי *recitativum*, that is, it functions to introduce direct discourse;[5] and Giesebrecht, Volz, and Rudolph concur. The sequence כִּי אִם־ . . . כִּי in 26:15 appears to reinforce this analysis. But there are difficulties with this solution, so that an alternative is more likely. The verse does not begin with "you know" or the like, as 26:15 does, but rather with "as I

live," an oath form. There are no parallels for "as I live" followed by protasis and apodosis in the twenty-one other instances of "as I live" in the OT; Ezek 14:18 is perhaps the closest, but the clauses are expressed differently there. The oath form suggests that אִם means "that not," "that never": thus in 2 Sam 3:35, after "God do so to me and more also," one finds אִם, literally "if," which has the implication of "I swear I shall never. . . ." The same implication seems to prevail here also. The shift from third person to second person at the end of the verse, after the second כִּי, suggests that that conjunction marks the shift rhetorically (thus "yes" in the translation). This is the solution of Thompson (and of *NEB*) and is adopted here; for further evidence of its correctness see v 25.

It is clear that "Coniah" (כָּנְיָהוּ) refers to Jehoiachin (יְהוֹיָכִין, 2 Kgs 24:8 and often); an extended form of this name is "Jeconiah" (יְכָנְיָהוּ, 24:1). The form "Coniah" appears beyond the present verse only in v 28 and in 37:1. Though it is usual to surmise that "(Je)coniah" was his given name and "Jehoiachin" his throne-name,[6] this is by no means assured; Honeyman simply suggests that the custom of taking a throne-name might play a part in the variations of his name.[7] The two elements of his name are obviously reversed between "(Je)coniah" and "Jehoiachin."[8] So they are also between "Zedekiah" and "Yahweh-ṣidqenu" (23:6), but there is no easy analogy between the two pairs of names.

The word "signet-ring" (חוֹתָם) means a "seal"; these could be either a cylinder-seal worn with a cord around the neck (Gen 38:18)[9] or a stamp-seal as part of a ring, as here. The descriptions in Exod 28:11, 21, 36; 39:6, 14, 30 suggest the skill lavished on such signet rings.[10] The seal was one's signature and therefore represented one's identity; Cant 8:6 suggests the emotional identification with one's seal, and Hag 2:23 suggests how great were the hopes invested in Zerubbabel when it is said that Yahweh will make him like a signet ring. The expression in the present passage, then, is an appalling one: the

3   Malamat, "Twilight of Judah," 132. For the text see Wiseman, *Chronicles*, 72–73: BM 21946, reverse, line 12.
4   Malamat, "Twilight of Judah," 133–34.
5   König, *Syntax*: כִּי intervenes between protasis and apodosis, sec. 415l; the first כִּי introduces direct discourse, sec. 391o. The verse is cited in both sections.

6   Herbert G. May, "Jehoiachin," *IDB* 2:811a.
7   A. M. Honeyman, "The Evidence for Regnal Names among the Hebrews," *JBL* 67 (1948) 16.
8   For a detailed discussion of the etymology see Montgomery, *Kings*, 557.
9   On this passage see Speiser, *Genesis*, 298.
10   For an illustration of an Egyptian example see Olga Tufnell, "Seals and scarabs," *IDB* 4:256, no. 11.

king, Jehoiachin, who should be like Yahweh's signet ring, will not be so treated by Yahweh.[11]

This is the only occurrence of נתק qal "pull off, tear away" in Jer, though the nip'al occurs (6:29; 10:20) as well as the pi'el and hip'il. The suffix -*enkā*, with unassimilated nun energic, is unique;[12] the form may be due to the fact that the word is in pause, but it also may be due to word-play with the first verb in the following verse (which see). Yahweh is utterly rejecting the kingship of Jehoiachin, and the oracle thereby offers no hope at all to those who continue to think of his kingship as the only legitimate one (compare 28:4).

■ **25** The idiom of the first clause is conventional for Yahweh's sending people into exile (21:7 and often), but one cannot help the sense that in this context the idiom carries special irony, since the verb so resembles the last verb in v 24 (*'etteqenkā, ûnetattîkā*): Yahweh will pull Jehoiachin off his right hand and put him into the hand of the enemy. The closeness of the two verbs is reinforced by the shift to second-person singular for the verb in v 24, and the parallelism here reinforces the analysis of the syntax of v 24 given above. For "Chaldeans" see 21:4. The rest of the verse offers conventional diction, as do the expansions in *M*.

■ **26** For "hurl" see 16:13. Jehoiachin's mother, Nehushta (2 Kgs 24:8), was exiled to Babylon along with her son (2 Kgs 24:15); because of the king's youth his mother loomed large in public attention (note 13:18). "Mother, who bore you" is of course tautological, but the intention is to draw a contrast with "where neither of you was born" and "you both shall die." Thus the "land where neither of you was born" is in contrast to "land of one's birth" (v 10). For "there you both shall die" compare 20:6. The words "neither" and "both" are not explicitly in the text but mark the shift of the verbs from singular to plural.

■ **27** "The land where they yearn to return" is in contrast to "a land where neither of you was born" in v 26. "Yearn" is literally "support one's soul" (נשא pi'el + נֶפֶשׁ); the phrase appears in the OT only otherwise in 44:14, a similar context.

Aim

Jehoahaz left no partisans behind him; he must soon have died. But Jehoiachin did have partisans (28:4, and many evidences in Ezekiel),[13] and it must have been painful indeed to hear that the innocent boy-king would be lost to history just as surely as those citizens would be who were more responsible for the misdeeds that brought Yahweh's judgment down. No wonder Habakkuk raised the issue, "the wicked surround the righteous, so justice goes forth perverted" (Hab 1:4).

11 See further Sabatino Moscati, "I sigilli nell'Antico Testamento, Studio Esegetico-Filologico," *Bib* 30 (1949) 319.

12 GKC, sec. 58i; Joüon, *Gramm.*, sec. 61h.

13 See Bright, *History*, 327–28.

**A Poetic Version:
The Young King Will Be Lost
to History**

Bibliography

Berridge
 pp. 179–81.
Herrmann, J.
 "Jer 22,29; 7,4."
Tawil
 "A Lexicographical Note," 408–9.

22

28 Is 《 this man [Coniah] 》[a] a puppet,
 dishonored, smashed, [. . .][a]
 or a vessel no one cares for?
Why then are they hurled [. . .][b] and
 thrown away,
 《 he and his offspring, 》[b]
 to [c]《 a land 》they have not known?[c]
29 Land, land, land,
 hear the word of Yahweh:
30 [Thus Yahweh has said:][a]
 Register this man

Text

28a G omits "this man," and the expression is therefore omitted as a gloss by Duhm, Cornill, Volz,
Rudolph, and Bright. To the contrary, given "this
man" in v 30 and the lack of the specific name of the
king in question in v 10 and in v 13, I suspect that it
is "this man" that is original here and that "Coniah"
is a gloss from v 24, or that "this man" and "Coniah"
represent a conflate text. It is further to be noted
that נִבְזֶה "dishonored" appears to be in assonance
with "this" (הַזֶּה). It is next to be noted that G omits
נָפוּץ "smashed," and Volz and Rudolph therefore
omit the word, assuming it to be a corruption from
חֵפֶץ "pleasure." Giesebrecht, p. xxxvi, assumes
haplography in G (and so Janzen, p. 119); on the
other hand, Volz and Rudolph omit the word,
assuming it to be a corruption from חֵפֶץ (literally
"pleasure," here paraphrased in "no one cares for").
I suspect that נָפוּץ is original to the text, since it
appears to be in assonance with חֵפֶץ. My proposal is
that "this man [Coniah]" was inadvertently omitted
from the text and reinserted wrongly: see in detail
Preliminary Observations.

b G omits "he and his offspring," and Duhm,
Cornill, Giesebrecht, Volz, Rudolph, and Bright
follow G in this omission (and the associated reading
of singular verbs—"is hurled," "is thrown away," "has
known"). Given "this man" and "his offspring" in v
30, and "I shall hurl you and the mother who bore
you" in v 26, it is altogether likely that "hurled" and
"thrown away" offer inner parallelism and that "he
and his offspring" offer a corresponding inner
parallelism in the next colon. If this is the case, one
may presume that the tradition represented by G
saw the words drop out by haplography and the
verbs "corrected" to the singular, and the tradition
represented by M saw the words added in the
margin and restored at the wrong point: see in more
detail Preliminary Observations.

c—c Reading אֶרֶץ with G for הָאָרֶץ "the land" (compare
v 26), and doubtless omitting אֲשֶׁר as well: so Cornill,
Giesebrecht, Volz, Rudolph, Bright.

30a Omit with G: if v 29 is the proper introduction to
v 30 (see Form, Interpretation), then this opening
rubric is extraneous; so Cornill, Giesebrecht, Volz,

《 "dethroned, 》[b] childless,"
  a fellow who shall not succeed in his
                              days,
for no one of his offspring shall succeed
    in sitting on the throne of David
      or in ruling any longer in Judah.

b

Rudolph, Bright (so also Janzen, p. 85).

Supplying מָשְׁלֵךְ, suggested by *G* and *S*; for a full discussion of this reconstruction see Preliminary Observations.

Preliminary Observations

There is little doubt that these three verses make up a unified utterance.[1]

The passage is clear in its general meaning, but *M* and *G* contrast at a sufficient number of points so that the establishment of a secure text has consequences for the structure and form of the passage as well as for its interpretation in detail. Specifically, in v 28 *M* reads: "Is this man Coniah a puppet dishonored, smashed, or a vessel no one cares for? Why are he and his offspring hurled and cast into a land they have not known?" *G* reads: "Jeconiah is dishonored like a vessel in which there is no use, for he is hurled and thrown away to a land which he has not known." In v 29 *M* reads "land" three times, *G* only twice. In v 30 *G* omits "thus Yahweh has said" and "a fellow who shall not succeed in his days." Generally critical opinion since Duhm has tended to accept the shorter *G* text. Bright's decision is typical: "The translation of v 28 follows LXX. MT has a somewhat expanded text that obscures the meter."[2]

I propose, however, that *G* has suffered by haplography or deliberate omission of synonyms, and that *M*, though dislocated, offers in general a more authentic text.

It is clear that the first colon of v 28 in *M*, as it stands, is overloaded: "Is this man Coniah a puppet, dishonored, smashed?" (1) *G* omits "this man" and has only "Jeconiah." But I suspect "Coniah" rather than "this man" is the gloss, for (a) "this man" appears again in v 30, and (b) נִבְזֶה "dishonored" appears to be in assonance with הָאִישׁ הַזֶּה "this man." One may further note that the diction in vv 10 and 13 is equally unspecific. (2) Of the two participles ("dishonored, smashed"), *G* omits "smashed." But I suspect both words belong in the poem; if "dishonored" is in assonance with "this man," "smashed" (נָפוּץ) appears to be in assonance with "pleasure" (חֵפֶץ). There appear to be two solutions. (a) Separate "dishonored" and "smashed," so that "dishonored" modifies "puppet" and "smashed" modifies "vessel." By this reading there would

be three cola: "Is this man a puppet dishonored,/ or a vessel smashed/ which no one cares for?" If that is the original reading, the present text could have arisen by the omission and subsequent reinsertion of "smashed" at the wrong spot. (b) Again there might be three cola, but the pair "dishonored, smashed" would make up the second colon: "Is this man a puppet,/ dishonored, smashed,/ or a vessel no one cares for?" Alternative (b) is preferable: (i) "vessel no one cares for" is a fixed phrase in 48:38 and Hos 8:8; (ii) "vessel no one cares for" will then be paralleled in structure by the last colon of the verse, "land they have not known" (see below); (iii) by evidence given below, the first two cola of v 28b offer inner parallelisms. If that is the original reading, the present text could have arisen by assuming that "this man" and "Coniah" represent a conflate text, and that the phrase "this man," with or without "Coniah," dropped out of the text and was reinserted at the wrong spot.

The words "he and his offspring" in v 28b are omitted in *G* and the three associated verbs there are singular. But given "this man" and "his offspring" in v 30, and "I shall hurl you and the mother who bore you" in v 26, I suspect "he and his offspring" is original here. Likewise "are hurled" and "are thrown away" form an inner parallelism, joined by the simple ו copula, like "eat and drink" in v 15. I propose then that "are hurled and thrown away" is an inner parallelism in the first colon of v 28b, and "he and his offspring" makes up the second colon (for the unusual separation of verbs and compound subject compare Ps 27:2b).[3] The text could have become the sequence of *M* if either וְהֻשְׁלְכוּ "are thrown away" or "he and his offspring" were omitted and reinserted at the wrong spot: the second is the more likely, given the omission of that phrase in *G*.

The reconstruction produces a six-colon verse with pleasing parallelism and assonance.

As already noted, in v 30 *G* omits "a fellow who shall not succeed in his days," and therefore commentators

---

1 Compare Berridge, 179 n. 352.
2 Bright, p. 139, note j.
3 See Dahood, *Psalms I*, 166.

have tended to omit the colon (Bright: "These words are probably not original").[4] This choice may have been due in part to the preference of commentators to four-colon rather than five-colon groups; in any event the colon is assumed to be dittographic. But the word "fellow" (גֶּבֶר) is not a word that a glossator would produce, and it is not to be found elsewhere in the poem: one notes its use in parallelism with "man" (אִישׁ) in 23:9, as it appears to be here. Furthermore the verb "succeed" (צלח) shifts reference (and perhaps connotation) in its second occurrence (see Interpretation). One concludes that G has omitted the colon by haplography.

At this point in the discussion v 30 appears to consist of five cola, two in v 30a and three in v 30b. At the same time v 28, by the reconstruction offered here, will consist of two tricola, the last colon of each of which contains a noun defined by a negative relative clause ("a vessel no one cares for," "a land they have not known"). But since (1) the first colon in v 30a likewise offers "this man," (2) since the second colon in v 30a, "a fellow who shall not succeed in his days," is of the same structure as the third cola of v 28a and v 28b, and (3) since v 30b is a tricolon, one wonders whether an original second colon has not dropped out of v 30a.

M for the first colon reads "register this man childless [אֲרִירִי]." In place of "childless" G reads ἐκκήρυκτον, meaning literally "called out by a herald" but evidently implying "banished" (see LSJ). Since G translates אֲרִירִי as "childless" in its other occurrences (Gen 15:2; Lev 20:20, 21; Sir 16:3), one assumes that it was here translating another word. S has a double reading, mkrz' dl' bnyn. The second element is "without children"; the first, mkrz', is an 'ap'el participle, presumably passive—the verb can mean "renounce, proclaim, excommunicate," so this participle evidently translates the same word reflected in G. If M and G represent variant texts, S could offer a conflate reading, but I propose that the two words make up the missing second colon. The obvious candidate for the missing word is מֻשְׁלָךְ, the hop'al participle of שלך: a finite form of the hop'al of that verb has already appeared in v 28, and the form I suggest would be in assonance with מֹשֵׁל in v 30b. By this reconstruction the second colon of v 30a consists of a pair of words with

inner parallelism, exactly matching the second colon of v 28a and the second colon of v 28b; furthermore, by this proposal the first colon of v 30a, like the first colon of v 28a, ends with הָאִישׁ הַזֶּה "this man."

It has already been stated that the verb "succeed" appears twice, in the last colon of v 30a and the first colon of v 30b. The first occurrence refers to Jehoiachin, and the second to his offspring. Verses 28–30 are thus concerned with Jehoiachin and his offspring just as vv 24–27 are concerned with Jehoiachin and his mother: there is thus a certain parity in the two passages.

Structure
For the unity of these three verses and their inner structure see in detail Preliminary Observations. This poetic oracle, along with its accompanying prose judgment (vv 24–27), were added to the array of passages on the kings and on the city of Jerusalem (see 21:1–7, Structure).

Form
The passage, like its companion vv 24–27, is a judgment speech without a reason (for which see vv 24–27, Form). Verse 29 must be spoken by Jrm, and v 30 must be the content of the "word of Yahweh" spoken of in v 29. Verse 28 cannot be spoken by Jrm: his stance in the poem is one of certainty about the meaning of the event. And the speaker cannot be Yahweh, who is the ultimate cause of the event. The speaker must be the people, who are genuinely puzzled. There continued to be those who were loyal to Jehoiachin (compare 28:4, and see further Aim on vv 24–27), and it is they in whose mouths Jrm places these words; indeed it would appear from v 29 that it is the personified "land" which is understood to be speaking the verse. One notes that the double question with הֲ and אִם normally expects the answer no (2:14, 31; 14:19): the answer yes is expected if there is a negative (8:5, 19, 22). The implication in v 28 is thus that Jehoiachin is not a smashed puppet or vessel no one cares for, but the larger context of the poem corrects that implication.

Verse 29 is a summons to the land to pay attention; Herrmann suggests that the threefold repetition of

4   Bright, p. 139, note 1—1.

"land" is reminiscent of a Babylonian oath form.[5] The words of v 30 are Yahweh's judgment proper. The imperative "register this man 'banished, childless'" suggests the milieu of the census taker (compare Neh 12:22): the plural imperative must be a command to those officials (see further Interpretation.)

Setting

Since Jehoiachin reigned only three months (2 Kgs 24:8), the setting of this passage will be very near to that of vv 24–27 (which see). The question emerges: Does the contrast between imperfect and waw-consecutive perfect verbs in vv 24–27 and the perfect verbs in v 28 suggest that when vv 24–27 was delivered, Jehoiachin had not yet gone into exile, but that when the present passage was delivered he had? The existence of the phenomenon of the "prophetic perfect" (GKC, sec. 106n) warns one not to come to this conclusion too quickly, but it is at least possible. And another question: Given the fact that the prose of 22:1–5 comes after its corresponding poem (21:11–14), and that the prose of vv 11–12 comes after its corresponding poem (v 10), can one conclude, seeing that the prose of vv 24–27 comes before the present passage, not after it, that the poem has a slightly later setting than the prose? In any event, the vividness of the diction here suggests a setting just before, or just after, the king went into exile, thus in the late winter or spring of 597.

Interpretation

■ 28 Verse 28a offers a density of multiple meaning, imagery and sound hardly paralleled in Jer (for the reconstruction of the text offered here, see Preliminary Observations). The sequence '-ṣ-b in "puppet" is picked up by n-p-ṣ in "smashed" and by ḥ-p-ṣ in the phrase here translated "no one cares for," and zeh "this" is picked up by nibzeh "dishonored."

The word עֶצֶב represents two homonyms. The first, the primary referent here, is a *hapax legomenon* in the OT, a noun meaning "a form, creation," related to a verb "to shape": the pi'el occurs once (Job 10:8) in the context of the creation of the individual, and a related noun means "an idol" shaped by man (Isa 48:5); the hip'il of the verb occurs in 44:19 in the context that implies the making of images of the goddess in cakes (see there). Therefore though the noun could well mean "(a pottery) vessel" like the parallel in the third colon (so *V* in both cola, *vas* "vessel"), the medieval Jewish exegetes state that the noun here has to do with shaping: Rashi compares it to the verb "manipulate" or "straighten" (infants),[6] and Qimḥi interprets the word to mean "idol" (so *KJV*). The likelihood then is that we have here a word for a lifeless image, "puppet" (*NEB*) or "figurehead" (Thompson). But the second more common homonym is a noun meaning "pain"; this meaning seems to have been in Luther's mind when he translated "a poor man" (= "a man full of pain"). This cannot be the primary meaning here, but one suspects it hovers in the background, giving rise to the parallel word in the third colon, "no one cares for," literally "there is no pleasure (or desire) in it" (see below). Furthermore in Gen 3:16 it is said that the woman shall give birth to children "in pain" (בְּעֶצֶב), and the tragedy is that Jehoiachin shall see no children of his on the throne (v 30).

The participle נִבְזֶה means "dishonored, despised": it is a description appropriate to Jehoiachin and appears (among other passages) in Isa 53:3, twice, of the servant figure. The participle נָפוּץ means "shattered, smashed," and it is appropriate both for a broken pottery vessel (see above) and for an image made of terra cotta or constructed in some other way. "Coniah" is taken here as a gloss, though it is of course a correct identification; for the name see v 24.

The noun כְּלִי in the third colon may imply not only a pottery vessel but any object made by one's hands: it may be used of an ornament (Gen 24:53) and therefore could imply a signet ring (v 24) (see below on the theological reach of the metaphor here). The phrase כְּלִי אֵין חֵפֶץ בּוֹ is a quotation from Hos 8:8: there "Israel is swallowed up; now they are among the nations as a worthless vessel (or thing)." Now, therefore, Jehoiachin will suffer the same fate as the northern tribes[7] (compare also the same phrase in Jer 48:38). The noun חֵפֶץ means both "pleasure" and "desire." It may be significant that the name of Manasseh's mother was Hephzibah (חֶפְצִי־בָהּ, "my pleasure is in her"), but there is no way to determine

---

5   J. Herrmann, "Jer 22,29; 7,4," 322.
6   *m. Šabb.* 22.6.
7   On the phrase see Wolff, *Hosea*, 132, 142.

whether that earlier royal name resonates here or not.

There is a close parallel between the imagery of v 24 and the imagery here: in v 24 it is denied that Jehoiachin will be Yahweh's signet ring, that is, his representative and most precious possession, while here, too, it is denied (by implication, compare Form) that Jehoiachin will be an intact creation of Yahweh's hands—instead he will be destroyed as junk. In both passages Jehoiachin is a rejected object and will be "hurled" away to another land (vv 26, 28). Here in particular it is implied that Jehoiachin will be like a piece of smashed pottery; the deeper implication is that Yahweh had done the smashing (all the verbs in the verse pertaining to Jehoiachin are passives). But this is irony, for behind the phrases is the word from Ps 2:9: Yahweh there declares to the new king, "You shall break them with a rod of iron, like a potter's vessel smash them [כִּכְלִי יוֹצֵר תְּנַפְּצֵם]." Was this psalm sung at Jehoiachin's coronation? Yahweh's will is ordinarily that the king smash the nations of the earth, but now instead Yahweh will smash the king.[8]

The use of the verb "hurl" (טול hip'il/hop'al) here matches its use in v 26; see the treatment of the verb in 16:13. The verb "throw away" (שלך hip'il/hop'al) here is linked by the simple ו copula (see the discussion of the phenomenon in v 15). The verb appears often in Jer, but its use in v 19 raises the question whether there is not intentional irony here: Jehoiakim was to be "dumped" (הַשְׁלֵךְ) beyond the gates of Jerusalem (v 19), but Jehoiachin and his offspring are to be "thrown away" (הֻשְׁלְכוּ) even farther, to a distant land. If the verb is correctly supplied in v 30, it seems in that instance to mean "dethroned" (see there).

For the expansion of the concern from the king to his offspring as well, see Preliminary Observations. The mention of them makes ironic the word "childless" in v 30. Though there is no way to prove it, there is no reason to doubt that historically one or more of the king's sons did accompany him into exile: seven sons are named in 1 Chr 3:17, and the "wives of the king" are mentioned as going into exile with him (2 Kgs 24:15). A Babylonian document mentions the rations stipulated for five sons of Jehoiachin.[9]

■ **29** The countervailing word to v 28 comes here. The threefold "land" is striking (Volz would omit two of the three!), being matched in the book only in 7:4 (in both these passages G has reduced the three words to two).[10] The repetition communicates impatience or dismay with the naiveté of the sentiment in v 28; there is a resemblance to the diction of 2:31 in the matter of the identity of the community and the appeal to "hear" (or "see") the word of Yahweh, and, beyond that passage, to many others (2:4; 7:2; 44:24, 26): but the present verse is striking in that the vocative precedes the imperative clause. But the threefold repetition may also communicate a formal summons (compare Form).

■ **30** Verse 30a suggests instructions to the census takers (see Form). What does it mean to "register" a king? It is for the king to initiate a census (2 Sam 24:1–32; Josephus *Ant.* 18.1.1; Luke 2:1), so what sort of census is this?—is the king to be registered as one more prisoner of war? The destiny of the king is reversed here fully as much as is implied in v 28.

For the restoration of מֻשְׁלָךְ see Preliminary Observations. The word here is simply the participle "thrown away" (see v 28) but is here translated "dethroned." G translates by an adjective meaning literally "called out by a herald" (see again Preliminary Observations) which Jerome renders by *abdicatum*, implying that the throne is no longer his.

The implication of "childless" is puzzling, since the king had sons (see on v 28). The word עֲרִירִי does mean "childless" (only otherwise in Gen 15:2; Lev 20:20, 21; Sir 16:3), but the point of course is that since he will see no son of his upon the throne of Judah, he is childless in the only way meaningful for a king.

The colon "a fellow who shall not succeed in his days" supplies a parallel not only to "dethroned" but more immediately to "childless": Tawil believes "shall not succeed" carries here the nuance of "is unproductive."[11]

If "succeed" in the third colon implies "succeed in having sons who will continue the dynasty," the verb "succeed" in the fourth colon implies "succeed in functioning as king." The subject of the second occurrence is of course also different: it is "no one [אִישׁ with the

---

8   On this parallel see Berridge, p. 180 n. 354.
9   *ANET* 308b.
10   See Janzen, p. 117.
11   Tawil, "Lexicographical Note," 409.

negative] of his offspring." Since אִישׁ and "fellow" (גֶּבֶר)
are in parallelism elsewhere (23:9) and since the two
verbs are identical, the shift of subject is ironic. The
participles in the last two cola appear to express actions
completing the verb "succeed."[12] Question: Is the adverb
"any longer" (עוֹד) a subtle balance to "in his days" in the
second colon?

Aim
See vv 24–27.

---

12   Joüon, *Gramm.*, sec. 157g.

Yahweh Will Punish the Evil Shepherds and Replace Them with Good Ones

Bibliography

On 23:1–8:
Klein, Ralph W.
  "Jeremiah 23:1–8," *Int* 34 (1980) 167–72.

On 23:1–4:
Holladay
  "Recovery," 420–24.

23

1 Woe to the shepherds who destroy and who scatter the sheep of [a]my pasture![a]— [oracle of Yahweh.][b] **2/** Therefore thus Yahweh God of Israel has said concerning the shepherds who shepherd my people: You for your part have scattered my sheep and chased them and have not tended them: I am going to attend to you for the evil of your doings, [oracle of Yahweh.][b] **3/** And I for my part shall gather the remnant of my sheep [from all the lands where I have chased them,][a] and I shall bring them back to their fold, and they shall be fruitful and multiply. **4/** And I shall appoint over them shepherds who shall shepherd them, and they shall not fear any longer nor be panicked, [a]nor be missing, [a]oracle of Yahweh.

Text

1a–a *G* reads "their pasture" (מַרְעִיתָם); given 10:21 this is an equally plausible reading.

1, 2b These occurrences of נְאֻם־יהוה are lacking in *G* and are probably expansionist glosses here.

3a This is a gloss (compare v 8) which specifies the reality of exile to a greater degree: note that in the bracketed words the exile is Yahweh's work rather than that of the shepherds (see further Interpretation, and compare the emendation of Volz).

4a–a The expression is lacking in *G*; it nevertheless probably belongs here, given the fact that it is a further play on פקד (compare v 2, and see Structure and Form).

Structure and Form

Some commentators deal with vv 1–8 as a unit (Rudolph, Bright, Thompson), but there are surely three units here. Verses 7–8 are a passage duplicated in 16:14–15. Verses 1–4 deal in general with irresponsible shepherds, while vv 5–6 deal with a specific future king whose name is a play on that of Zedekiah; except for the word "I appoint" (וַהֲקִמֹתִי, vv 4 and 5), there is no duplication of vocabulary between the two sequences. There is no way to be sure whether vv 1–4 and 5–6 were added to chapter 22 as a unit or whether they were added separately. If they were added separately, vv 1–4 are appropriately added to the general array in chapter 22 regarding the kings of Judah; in particular the double use of "shepherd" in vv 2 and 4 ("shepherds who shep-

herd") can be linked to the similar double use of the root in 22:22.

The passage is a carefully crafted sequence of structured prose (*Kunstprosa*).[1]

It is a "woe" oracle like 22:13–19: an accusation in the third person introduced by "woe" (הוֹי, v 1, compare 22:13–17), followed by "therefore Yahweh has said concerning" (v 2, compare 22:18). But 21:13–19 is a judgment speech to an individual, while this passage is to a whole group. Westermann points out that "woe" oracles directed to a group resemble more closely the judgment speech to individuals than the judgment speech to the nation.[2] One expects the messenger formula at the beginning of v 2 to be followed directly by the judgment speech (compare 22:18–19), but in this

---

1 Against my proposal that it is poetry: Holladay, "Recovery," 420–24.

2 Westermann, *Basic Forms*, 191–92; compare also

Zimmerli, *Ezekiel 1*, 291, and Wolff, *Joel and Amos*, 243 n. 108, g.

instance something more complicated follows. First one has a repetition of the accusation, not this time in the third person but in direct address, beginning with the emphatic pronoun אַתֶּם (translated here "you for your part"); this accusation picks up the phrase "scatter (my) sheep" from the first accusation. The judgment speech beginning in v 2b moves out from the repetition of the accusation in two parts, v 2b and vv 3–4. (1) Verse 2b offers a play on the nuances of פקד "tend" or "attend": since the shepherds have not "tended" to the sheep, Yahweh is about to "attend" to them for their evil. (2) Verses 3–4 begin with the emphatic pronoun וַאֲנִי (translated here "and I for my part"): if "you" (the shepherds) have scattered my sheep, then "I" (Yahweh) will gather the remnant of my sheep. This word of what Yahweh will do with the scattered sheep is in a way a continuation of the judgment speech to the shepherds, but inasmuch as what he will do with the scattered sheep is to gather them and bring them home again, it is at the same time an announcement of salvation. Verse 3 implies that Yahweh will take over the shepherding from the irresponsible shepherds, but v 4 indicates that he will appoint new shepherds who will shepherd responsibly: again the double use of "shepherds who shepherd," as in v 2. The verse ends with another play on פקד: none of the sheep will "be missing."

Setting

There are those who assume that the passage is "probably from the Deuteronomic authors,"[3] given its presuppositions of the exile. But the play on the nuances of פקד (twice in v 2: "tend," "attend"; once in v 4: "be missing") suggests the mind of Jrm, as does the precise repetition הָרֹעִים הָרֹעִים "shepherds who shepherd" in v 2 (on this repetition see Interpretation). One is therefore directed to the period at the very end of Zedekiah's reign (so also Volz). Jrm had rejected Hananiah's words of restoration in the summer of 594 (28:5–9). It is proposed in the present study that Jrm's words of hope to Judah were proclaimed after the purchase of the field at Anathoth (see Setting for both chaps. 30—31 and chap. 32), evidently in the summer of 588. The period then is an appropriate one for the present passage.

Interpretation

■ **1** For "woe!" see 22:13; for "shepherds" see 10:21. The verb "destroy" (אבד pi'el) can also mean "let perish" (see the lexica on the word in the present passage), but the implication here is that neglect leaves the sheep as dead as if they have been deliberately killed; "scatter" has a similar implication. Both these verbs are normally used with Yahweh as subject (15:7; 18:17). There is irony here: Yahweh may have occasion to punish his people, but it is illegitimate for the kings and officials of the people to do so. "Sheep of (Yahweh's) pasture" is a standard phrase in the Psalms (Pss 74:1; 79:13; 100:3; compare 95:7); for "pasture" (מַרְעִית) see 10:21.

■ **2** The messenger formula is like those in 22:11 and 18, though here the preposition for "concerning" is the more expected עַל instead of אֶל used there. The double expression "shepherds who shepherd," in Hebrew a precise duplication, הָרֹעִים הָרֹעִים, is witty, for it is clear that the assumed syntax is an agent noun followed by a participle with verbal force (see GKC, sec. 116a), analogous to "prophets who prophesy" (הַנְּבִאִים הַנִּבְּאִים) in v 25 (G translates only one word here!).

For the emphatic "you for your part" see Structure and Form. "Scattered my sheep" rephrases the expression of v 1. "Chased" (נדח hip'il) is synonymous; the overwhelming proportion of occurrences of this verb in the OT have Yahweh as subject, so that this verb continues the irony begun in v 1 (see above).

The verb "tend" (פקד) occurs in a wide variety of contexts, and this variety is exploited in the three occurrences in the passage, two in this verse ("tend," "attend") and one at the end of v 4 ("be missing"). "Attend to" is perhaps the nearest general meaning in English: "take care of someone in a particular task" (2 Kgs 9:34), sometimes "muster (troops)" (1 Sam 11:8), almost "number" them; hence to "tend" sheep is to look after them one by one, and this the kings have not done with their people. The result is that Yahweh must "attend to" the kings, that is, punish them (5:9 and often): the punishment will fit the crime. For "evil of their doings" see 4:4.

■ **3** For the emphatic "I for my part" see Structure and Form. The verb "gather" (קבץ pi'el) is the standard term

3   Nicholson, *Jer. 1—25*, 191.

for Yahweh's gathering his dispersed people, and it was doubtless the verb used for regathering scattered sheep.[4] The use of "remnant" is another suggestion of the kings' neglect; Bright translates "what is left of my flock."

The phrase "from all the lands where I have chased them" is an insertion. (1) The verb "I have chased them" contradicts the accusation against the shepherds in v 2 ("you have chased them") and represents the conviction that Yahweh intended the scattering of the exiles; Volz, who retains the expression, emends the verb to "they were chased." (2) The word "lands" is not reflected in the rest of the passage (compare v 8, Interpretation).

The metaphor of "fold" (נָוֶה) is comparable to the use of a related word in 6:2; there the image functions in a judgment oracle—foreign shepherds will take Judah over. Now, by contrast, the rightful sheep will be brought back to their pasture. The feminine plural suffixes in the expressions "them" and "their fold" are curious: "sheep" (צֹאן) is ordinarily feminine, but the word is a singular collective: the feminine plural suggests that the numbering of the sheep is very much at the forefront.

The phrase "be fruitful and multiply" reflects the repeated command to Abraham and Jacob in the P source.[5] Jrm has elsewhere seen the possibility that that command to be fruitful has been reversed in his day (20:1–6, compare 10:24); now he is impelled to proclaim its reestablishment.

■ 4 In times past Yahweh has appointed over the people "watchmen" (6:17); now he is redoing the action of v 2: shepherds have shepherded the people wrongly—now he will appoint over them shepherds who will shepherd rightly. The shift from the participle in v 2 to the waw-consecutive perfect וְרָעוּם here signals that movement: they will really shepherd.

The verb "be panicked" (חתת) is a standard synonym for "fear" (ירא). The passage closes with the last play on "tend" (פקד, see v 2): a final irony, for the verb here clearly means "shall not be missing" (so already V), but it means literally "shall not be mustered" (hence "shall not be lacking"). The shepherds had not "tended" the sheep, so Yahweh must see to it that they are tended, and he will do it in such a way that the sheep will not need "attention" from being missing.

Aim

The fact that the passage is both a judgment oracle and a salvation oracle indicates that it stands at the beginning of a new age for Judah. Behind it stands the imagery of Psalm 23; and one may suspect that the passage became the stimulus for such passages elsewhere: most particularly Ezek 34:1–16,[6] but also Mic 2:12; Isa 40:11; and ultimately John 10:1–18.

In the premonarchical faith of Israel it was understood that Yahweh ruled directly, not through human rulers;[7] Gideon said it: "I will not rule over you, and my son will not rule over you; Yahweh will rule over you" (Judg 8:23). Now in the fresh situation Yahweh must himself take charge before setting human rulers once more over his people.

---

4   Compare the discussion in Mays, *Micah*, 75.
5   Samuel R. Driver, *An Introduction to the Old Testament* (6th ed.; rep. New York: Meridian, 1956) 131, no. 5.
6   Ezek 34:1–16 really follows the outline of the present passage; see Johan Lust, "'Gathering and Return' in Jeremiah and Ezekiel," *Le Livre de Jérémie, Le prophète et son milieu, les oracles et leur transmission* (ed. Pierre-Maurice Bogaert; BETL 54; Leuven: Leuven University, 1981) 139.
7   Mendenhall, *Tenth Generation*, xiii, 13–19.

A Future King Will Carry the Reverse of Zedekiah's Name and Character

Bibliography

Baldwin, Joyce G.
"Ṣemaḥ as a Technical Term in the Prophets," *VT* 16 (1964) 94.

Lipiński, Edouard
"Etudes sur des textes 'messianiques' de l'Ancien Testament," *Semitica* 20 (1970) 53–55.

Swetnam, James
"Some Observations on the Background of צדיק in Jeremias 23,5a," *Bib* 46 (1965) 29–40.

Specifically on the Larnaca Inscription, especially line 11:

Branden, Albertus van den
"L'inscription phénicienne de Larnax Lapethos II," *OrAnt* 3 (1964) 245–61.

Branden, Albertus van den
"Titoli Tolemaici, 'Sâ Râ,' ṣmḥ ṣdq e ἀνατολὴν δικίαν," *BeO* 6 (1964) 60–72.

Cooke
Inscriptions, 82–83, 86–87.

23

5
The days are surely coming,
                    oracle of Yahweh,
when I appoint for David a scion,
    a rightful one who shall reign,
    a king who shall be successful,
    who shall do justice
            and righteousness in the land.
6
In his days Judah shall be rescued,
    and Israel shall dwell securely;
and this is the name ᵃ he shall be
        called:ᵃ
    Yahweh-ṣidqēnû.

Text

6a—a   Literally "one shall call him." A few MSS. vocalize יִקְרְאוּ "they shall call."

Preliminary Observation

There is a parallel to this passage in 33:15–16. That passage is evidently secondary to the present one; for the relation between the two, see there.

Structure

For the place of vv 5–6 within vv 1–8 see vv 1–4, Structure. The placement of this unit after vv 1–4 may be for chronological reasons, if it took shape later, or it may be because of the use of "I appoint" (וַהֲקִמֹתִי), or it may be because by implication Zedekiah, the last king of Judah,

is criticized (see Interpretation on v 6).

The Masoretic punctuation of v 5 leads to a division into four cola: "The days are surely coming (oracle of Yahweh),/ when I appoint for David a rightful scion;/ as a king he shall reign and be successful,/ and shall do justice and righteousness in the land." D. N. Freedman has, however, suggested the division adopted here, into six cola,[1] which is cited as a possibility by Bright and Thompson. (For the syntax, by which ו functions virtually as a relative, compare 1 Kgs 4:7.) Since "rightful scion" is evidently a stereotyped phrase (see Interpre-

---

1   See a paper of David N. Freedman, "Messianic Passages in the Prophets," reported in "Proceedings of the Eighty-eighth Meeting of the Society of Biblical Literature and Exegesis," *JBL* 72 (1953) xx.

tation), with this division one has the break-up of such a phrase.[2] The first colon of v 5 is a standardized phrase in prophetic utterances, but the other five cola are closely parallel. Does "in his days" in v 6 pick up "the days are surely coming" in v 5?

Verse 6 easily divides into two bicola.

Form

The form of this passage is unique in Jer, the announcement of a royal savior; in diction and form it is closely related to Isa 11:1–9, though the specific choice of words is different. It is a plausible form to emerge among any people when political conditions are difficult and one looks for better times; the Egyptian "Prophecy of Nefer-rehu" offers something similar for the first intermediate period in Egypt (22d–21st centuries B.C.E.);[3] there are also fragmentary copies of prophecies from Asshur and Nineveh whose historical context is obscure that speak of rulers to come who will restore prosperity.[4] But the immediate background of the passage is surely Isa 11:1–9.

The climax of the passage is the announcement of the name of the future king, analogous to the announcement in Isa 9:5; the prophecy of Nefer-rehu also names the future king.[5] But behind the announcement of the name is the implication that it is a change, really a reversal of Zedekiah's name (compare the name changes in 7:30–34 and 20:1–6): here Zedekiah himself does not receive a new name, but the name reverses Zedekiah's name with the implication that the reign of the new king will reverse the characteristics of the reign of Zedekiah (see in detail Interpretation).

Setting

Duhm and Volz judge this passage to be late; Cornill, Giesebrecht, Rudolph, and Bright, on the other hand, have taken the passage to be authentic.

The name of the future king involves a play on the name "Zedekiah," and such word-play is characteristic of

Jrm (compare 7:30–34; 20:1–6). There is no reason to question its authenticity. But it is more difficult to make a suggestion when in the reign of Zedekiah the oracle was uttered. Bright says it might have been uttered at the time of the accession of Zedekiah, or just before, and that because of it Zedekiah was given his throne name. Lipiński similarly argues from the G version of the new name, ιωσεδεκ = יְהוֹצָדָק or יְהוֹצָדָק: he believes this is the preferred reading and was an alternative name for Zedekiah (like Coniah = Jehoiachin)—by this understanding the passage was probably the official proclamation of the new king's throne name.[6]

I propose a time at the very end of that king's reign. In 594 Jrm is completely preoccupied with bad news (28:5–16). In vv 1–4 the tone is both positive and negative. But the present passage is completely positive, as is the material in the hopeful scroll embodied in chapters 30—31. There is also here the motif of the reunion of Judah and Israel, a motif likewise found in that hopeful scroll (30:3; 31:27–28; compare 31:6), as if, now that there is parity of doom for Israel and Judah, there can be parity of hope. Since that hopeful scroll seems consequent upon the purchase of the field at Anathoth, probably in the summer of 588, one is pointed for the present passage toward the last few months of the kingdom of Judah, before it fell in July of 587.

Interpretation

■ 5 For the phrase "the days are surely coming" (literally, "behold, days are coming") see 7:32; it occurs repeatedly in prose material, but its occurrence in Amos 4:2 is assurance that it is also at home in a poetic oracle. For "appoint," with Yahweh as subject, compare v 4.

The phrase "rightful scion" (צֶמַח צַדִּיק) is basic to the passage, whether the two words are construed as a united phrase (as in most commentaries and translations) or whether the two words are split in adjoining cola (as here: see Structure). Beyond the doublet in 33:15, the word "scion" (or "branch," צֶמַח) appears in the technical

---

2   See 2:1—4:4, n. 79.
3   *ANET*, 444–46.
4   Ibid., 451–52.
5   Ibid., 445b; the name is in line 58.
6   Edouard Lipiński, "Etudes sur des textes 'messianiques' de l'Ancien Testament," *Semitica* 20 (1970) 53–55.

meaning of a Messiah figure in Zech 3:8 and 6:12. In both the latter passages the reference is evidently to Zerubbabel.[7] Because Zerubbabel's name evidently means "scion of Babylon" in Akkadian,[8] there has been a conviction of some scholars that the use of "scion/branch" in the two passages of Zechariah is the original one and the use of the term in the present passage is secondary (so, for example, Mowinckel).[9] Others who assume the usage in Jer is prior have still taken for granted that the term "scion/branch" was a technical term for a Davidic king to come who would restore the monarchy.[10] That the term became so is undoubted: the present passage and the two in Zechariah stimulated messianic expectations in Judaism.[11] This assumption has been reinforced by the adjective צַדִּיק in the present passage, whose normal meaning is "righteous." The future king, by this interpretation, will be righteous in contrast to Jehoiakim and Zedekiah, who were unrighteous (compare the burden of v 2).

But the phrase must be seen in a larger context, since צמח צדק occurs in a Phoenician inscription of the third century B.C.E.: it is a votive inscription of a Melqart worshiper, found in Lapethos (Lambousa) on Cyprus, evidently to be dated to the year 273/272.[12] In that inscription the phrase clearly means "legitimate scion": the reference is to the legitimate king of the Ptolemaic dynasty. There is no plausible way in which one can assume that the Phoenician phrase somehow stems from a Hebrew phrase having a specific messianic nuance; one must conclude that Jrm is here using a general North-west Semitic term for the legitimate king. Though "branch" (צֶמַח) may have been the normal term, it is clear from Isa 11:1 that the synonymous "shoot" (חֹטֶר) and "sprout" (נֵצֶר) are alternative terms. Behind these nouns is the assumption in Israel that Yahweh "brings the growth" (צמח hip'il) to the Davidic dynasty (2 Sam 23:5 includes both the motif of the everlasting covenant with David and that of Yahweh's bringing forth fresh growth). And now that this meaning of צַדִּיק ("legitimate") is seen to occur in the phrase in Phoenician, one can see it elsewhere in Northwest Semitic: thus in the Ugaritic Keret poem, "his lawful wife" ('aṭṭ ṣdqh),[13] and evidently in the Phoenician phrase bn ṣdq "legitimate heir."[14] This is not to say that the meaning "righteous" is absent from the present passage, but that the nuance of "rightful" is central.

In contrast to Isaiah, Jrm seems to have had little interest in the ideology of the Davidic dynasty as such: he took its existence for granted (21:12) and referred more than once to Davidic monarchs as "those who sit on the throne of David" (22:2, 4, 30). The emphasis in the present passage is not so much on David as on legitimacy. Given the survival in the exile of Jehoiachin and his entourage and the appointment of Zedekiah on the throne in Jerusalem, there must have been steady argument in Judah as to which king was legitimate. Here is Zedekiah, whose name carries the same nuance as the word "legitimate" here, but whose legitimacy is dubious. By contrast Yahweh will in time raise up a legitimate descendant of David; the third colon means practically "who shall reign legitimately." Zedekiah, by contrast, had been a vassal (Bright).

The parallel fourth colon thus means practically "who shall be successful as king," but the verb "be successful" (שכל hip'il) is more wide-ranging (see 9:23), not only "succeed" but "act prudently" and "have insight." This king will then rule ably (Bright) and wisely (NEB) as well as successfully. He shall do justice and righteousness in the land as surely as Josiah did (22:15).

■ 6 The use of "in his days" reminds one of the same

7   David L. Petersen, *Haggai and Zechariah 1—8* (Philadelphia: Westminster, 1984) 273–78.

8   Peter R. Ackroyd, *Exile and Restoration, A Study of Hebrew Thought of the Sixth Century B.C.* (Philadelphia: Westminster, 1968) 174 n. 12.

9   Sigmund Mowinckel, *He That Cometh* (Oxford: Blackwell, 1956) 119–22, 160–65, discusses the Zechariah passages thoroughly.

10 So, for example, Joyce G. Baldwin, "Ṣemaḥ as a Technical Term in the Prophets," *VT* 16 (1964) 93–97.

11 See *T. Judah* 24.4–6, and the discussion in George F. Moore, *Judaism in the First Centuries of the Christian Era, The Age of the Tannaim* (Cambridge: Harvard University, 1950–59) 2:324–25.

12 The expression is in line 11 of the inscription. For an early publication of the inscription see Cooke, *Inscriptions*, 82–83, 86–87; see currently *KAI* I, 10, no. 43; for a recently English translation see Walter Beyerlin, *Near Eastern Religious Texts Relating to the Old Testament* (Philadelphia: Westminster, 1978) 232–34.

13 Ug. 14.1.12.

14 *KAI*, I, 3, no. 16, line 1.

expression in 22:30 with respect to Jehoiachin. The parallelism here of "Judah" and "Israel" suggests that Jrm's old dream of the reunion of north and south (3:18) is still alive, but the reading both of $G^{\aleph}$ and of 33:16 ("Jerusalem" rather than "Israel") suggests that it was easier for a later generation to envisage a restoration of the south alone. Jrm hoped at the beginning of his career that Jerusalem might be "rescued" (ישׁע nip'al, 4:14), but at a particular point it appeared unlikely (30:7). Now comes the word that Yahweh himself will appoint a king who will oversee that rescue. The phrase "dwell securely" (שכן + בֶּטַח or לְבֶטַח) is found several times elsewhere beyond the doublet in 33:16, notably in Deut 33:28, where it is also used of Israel (see further Deut 33:12; Ps 16:9; Prov 1:33); a similar expression, with different vocabulary, is found in 30:10, evidently from the same period. For the people of Yahweh to live quietly and in security, that was the dream (compare the classic formulation in Isa 30:15).

And now the name of the king to come! In G it is given as Josedek ($\iota\omega\sigma\epsilon\delta\epsilon\kappa$ = יֹצְדֶק or יְהֹצְדֶק), which simply reverses the elements of the name Zedekiah (see the discussion in Setting). The reading of M, however, is surely the *lectio difficilior* (see below), Yahweh-ṣidqēnû, literally "Yahweh is our righteousness."

It is clear that a play is intended on the name "Zedekiah" (ṣidqiyyāhû), to be understood in several ways (see again below), but most easily as either "Yahweh is righteousness" or "Yahweh is my righteousness." The implications of the word-play, however, are to some degree obscure. One assumes that Jrm intends the new name to imply some kind of reversal of the old one (compare the play on Pashhur, 20:1–6). Is the opposition simply that the two elements of the name are in reverse order? (Then the text of G will do as well.) But simple reversal of the two elements of royal names are known elsewhere (Coniah = Jehoiachin, for which see 22:24; Jehoahaz = Ahaziah, of Judah in the ninth century, according to 2 Chr 21:17; 22:1) without any overt implication of the reversal of character or fortune. The narrative in 2 Kgs 24:17 states that the king's original name of Mattahiah (מַתַּנְיָה, evidently "gift of Yahweh") and that Nebuchadrezzar changed it to Zedekiah. If the

narrative is trustworthy, it suggests that the Babylonian king, in sponsoring this name change, gives evidence of a respect for Jewish traditions;[15] certainly the name had been current earlier in Israelite history (1 Kgs 22:11). The question then becomes: If "Mattaniah" was understood as "gift of Yahweh," was "Zedekiah" understood as "legitimacy of Yahweh"? That is to say, "Mattaniah" is best understood as a descriptive name, a designation descriptive of the bearer: the man himself is a gift from Yahweh. By analogy then the name "Zedekiah" should be understood descriptively as well: the king himself is the legitimacy of Yahweh. This at least would suit Nebuchadrezzar's purposes. This understanding makes it different from the normal understanding of the name as theophoric, that is, as an affirmation about Yahweh unrelated to the bearer ("Yahweh is [my] righteousness").

In any event, Jrm did not perceive Jehoiachin as legitimate (22:24) and he did not perceive Zedekiah as righteous (compare the judgments in 24:8 and 34:21). The prophet thus proposed a name for the future king which would not only reverse the two elements of Zedekiah's name (so the text of G) but would, by the specificity of the first-person plural suffix, force the hearer to take the name as theophoric, "Yahweh is *our* righteousness." (This emphasis was lost on earlier Christian theologians who, taking this passage as a reference to Jesus Christ, who was one with the Father, insisted the name is descriptive of the bearer: so, notably, Theodoret and Calvin.)[16]

The name is hardly comparable to any other symbolic name. A compound with the full form "Yahweh" (rather than the abbreviated form yō-, as in the text of G) occurs in only a few other instances in the OT. There are names of sacred places: Yahweh-yir'eh, Gen 22:14; Yahweh-šālôm, Judg 6:24; Yahweh-šammâ, Ezek 48:35; and then there is one other, Yahweh-nissî, Exod 17:15, "Yahweh is my banner," which, in having a noun with possessive suffix for the predicate, is most like the present instance—and that is the name of an altar. But there are no other such forms with a first-person plural suffix; the nearest is the symbolic name "Immanuel" ('immānû-'ēl = "God is with us") in Isa 7:14.[17]

The first-person plural moves the attention of the

15   Gray, *Kings*, 762.
16   See the discussion in Rudolph, pp. 146–47.
17   For a general discussion of that name, and various

kinds of parallels, see Wildberger, *Jesaja*, 292–93.

hearer to the people; the future king will embody the faith of the whole people in the realization of righteousness that has its source only in Yahweh.

Aim

Two verses from Jrm which speak of a future king: the prophet could hardly know how much stimulus this short poem would give to future generations. The word "scion/branch" would become a technical designation for the Messiah. Its use was stimulated by Zechariah's application of it to Zerubbabel (Zech 3:8; 6:12). Its occurrence in Isa 4:2 in the more general sense of "what God causes to grow" would be referred in the Targum of that passage to the Messiah.[18] It would be used by the Qumran community to designate the kingly Messiah.[19] It has entered into the Jewish prayer called Shemoneh Esreh (the Eighteen Benedictions): "Cause the Scion of David Thy Servant speedily to sprout, and let his horn be exalted by Thy salvation."[20] G rendered the word "scion/branch" by ἀνατολή, which may mean a "growing" or "sprouting" but in general means "rising" (of the sun or the like); it is uncertain, therefore, whether the usage in Luke 1:78 reflects the present passage, but it is likely.[21] The passage was taken by Christian theologians universally to refer to Christ (see typically Jerome and Calvin). The image of the "branch" has sprouted richly indeed.

18   For the targumic interpretation of the present passage see Samson H. Levey, *The Messiah: An Aramaic Interpretation, The Messianic Exegesis of the Targum* (Monographs of Hebrew Union College 2; Cincinnati: Hebrew Union College, 1974) 69–70.

19   4QFlor 1.11; 4QBless 1.3–4.

20   Cited in George F. Moore, *Judaism in the First Centuries of the Christian Era, The Age of the Tannaim* (Cambridge: Harvard University, 1950–59) 2:325.

21   For recent discussion see Raymond E. Brown, *The Birth of the Messiah, A Commentary on the Infancy Narratives in Matthew and Luke* (Garden City, NY: Doubleday, 1977) 373–74; see further Heinrich Schlier, "ἀνατέλλω, ἀνατολή," *TDNT* 1:352–53, and the literature cited in BAG under ἀνατολή.

23

A New Exodus

Bibliography

Weinfeld
"Metamorphosis," 40–43.

7 Therefore the days are surely coming—oracle of Yahweh—when they shall no longer say, "As Yahweh lives, who brought up the children[a] of Israel from the land of Egypt," 8/ but rather "As Yahweh lives, [who brought up and][a] who brought in [b] the offspring of [the house of] Israel[b] from the land of the north[c] [and from all the lands where[e] ⟪he has chased them⟫[f]]"; [d] [g] and they shall dwell[g] on their own soil.

Text

7a For "children" here and "offspring" in v 8 the tendency is to read "house": so *G* here and so *G* in 16:15, and so in the gloss of *M* in v 8 (see 8b—b).

8a Lacking in *G*; the words are the reading of 16:15, so that *M* here has a conflate text (so Thompson).

b—b "The offspring of Israel" is the original text (see Interpretation), the words in brackets being a gloss or an alternate reading (see 7a and Interpretation) (so Thompson). The Versions vary: *G* "all the offspring of Israel"; *S* "the children of Israel"; *T* in various editions "the offspring of the house of Israel," "the offspring of the children of Israel," or "the children of Israel"; compare 16:15 *M* "the children of Israel," *G* "the house of Israel."

c For *M* צָפוֹנָה 16:15 has צָפוֹן. The meaning is unaffected.

d A gloss: see Interpretation.

e For אֲשֶׁר . . . שָׁם 16:15 has אֲשֶׁר . . . שָׁמָּה. Though the meaning is unaffected, the reading in 16:15 is preferable.

f Reading הִדִּיחָם with *G* and 16:15 for *M* הִדַּחְתִּים "I have chased them."

g—g *G* and 16:15 read וַהֲשִׁבֹתִים "and I shall settle them" for *M* וְיָשְׁבוּ; either reading is appropriate.

Structure

These two verses are found in their present position in *M* but at the end of chapter 23 in *G*. They are also found, with minor variations of wording, at 16:14–15. In chapter 16 both vv 1–13 and 16–18 contain judgment motifs, while in chapter 23 both vv 1–4 and 5–6 are restoration oracles. The present verses thus fit better here; it is plausible to see 16:14–15 as a doublet secondarily added to judgment material to bring hope after judgment (so other commentators). Janzen makes a good case, however, for his proposal that the position of these verses was originally between vv 1–4 and vv 5–6, that they dropped out of their original position by haplography ("the days are surely coming," vv 7 and 5), that they were then written in the margin, perhaps vertically between two columns of the archetype of *M* and *G*; in this way the *G* reading of v 6 can be explained ("and this is the name which the Lord shall call him, Josedek among the prophets"): the phrase "among the prophets" appears in *M* (correctly) as the superscription of v 9.[1]

The passage divides rhetorically into two parallel parts, marked by the verse divisions.

Form

This is a proclamation of salvation (*Heilsankündigung*) in the form of a change of speech pattern of the people: their oath form "As Yahweh lives . . ." will have a different ending, and that oath form will be a steady reminder of the new act of deliverance that Yahweh will accomplish. Similar announcements of a change in speech

---

1   Janzen, pp. 92–93 and n. 17; 220–21.

pattern are found in 3:16 and 31:29–30; such a change of speech pattern is related to changes in names of persons or places (compare form in 7:32 = 19:6 and 20:3).

The oath form "As Yahweh lives" is found in the OT both with and without a further qualifying description of Yahweh, but in only one other instance is the description one having to do with the rescue of Israel—"As Yahweh lives who rescues Israel" (1 Sam 14:39); for the details see Interpretation. The description here, "who brought up the children of Israel from the land of Egypt," is thus (as far as our record goes) an ad hoc formulation suggesting an ideal oath form.

Setting

Most critical commentators have rejected the authenticity of this passage (Duhm, Giesebrecht, Cornill, Volz, Rudolph, Bright); Weiser, Weinfeld,[2] and Thompson defend it. The evidence is against authenticity. It appears to presuppose the exile; this is not a crucial indicator but is suggestive nonetheless. The form (a change of speech pattern) is found twice otherwise, 3:16 and 31:29–30. Of these two, 3:16 is clearly late (probably the Persian period: see Setting for that passage), and 31:29–30, on independent data, is in the present study likewise judged late (see Preliminary Observations on chaps. 30—31). There is one datum that may suggest a date in the fifth century, and that is the occurrence of the phrase "offspring [literally "seed"] of Israel"; this phrase appears also in 31:36 and 37, and outside of Jer in Ps 22:24; Neh 9:2; and 1 Chr 16:13. Jer 31:35–37 is closely associated with vv 38–40 there, and the latter passage is almost surely from Nehemiah's time (fifth century) (see Structure and Setting of chaps. 30—31). And it would appear from the occurrence of "offspring of Israel" in Neh 9:2 and 1 Chr 16:13 that this phrase was congenial to that period. Tentatively, then, one may assign the passage to the fifth century; the fact that the present *M* is a conflate and expansionist text may likewise point in the direction of a late setting.

Interpretation

■ **7** "Therefore" fits better as a connective between the present passage and vv 1–4 (see Structure). "The days

are surely coming" matches that phrase in v 5; that phrase and "it shall no longer be said" are found in 7:32 (see there). For "as Yahweh lives" see 4:2. In most of the occurrences of this phrase in OT "Yahweh" is unqualified. Beyond the two occurrences here, and their doublets in 16:14–15, there are nine instances of a qualification. Four of them are spoken by Elijah or Elisha and are an identical description of their status as a prophet: "before whom I stand" (1 Kgs 17:1; 18:15; 2 Kgs 3:14; 5:16). One is spoken by Solomon and is a description of his status as king: "who has established me and placed me on the throne of David my father, and who has made me a house, as he promised" (1 Kgs 2:24). One is spoken by Zedekiah to Jrm and is a description of the parity of the status of the two of them: "who has given to us the breath of life [נֶפֶשׁ]" (Jer 38:16). Two of them are spoken by David and are an identical testimony of personal rescue that sounds like a set liturgical phrase: "who has ransomed my life from every adversity" (2 Sam 4:9; 1 Kgs 1:29; the phrase "ransom one's life" is found additionally in Pss 34:23; 71:23). Only in the one remaining instance is the qualification one referring to the rescue of Israel; it is spoken by Saul: "who rescues [הַמּוֹשִׁיעַ] Israel" (1 Sam 14:39). The impression with which one is left, then, is that the formulation in the present passage is not a normal formula but an ad hoc formulation, framed by the writer as a striking way of contrasting Yahweh's old rescue with the new one to come.

■ **8** The phrase "land of the north" is found repeatedly in Jer (6:22; 10:22; 31:8; 46:10; 50:9), but here is a nice parallel to "land of Egypt."

The phrase "and from all the lands where he has chased them" breaks the parallelism and injects the alien note that Yahweh will reverse his punishment: the point of the utterance is that there will be a new exodus. The phrase was evidently a conventional phrase reflecting the exile (23:3; 24:9; 27:10, 15; 29:14, 18; 32:27); the origin of the phrase may be its occurrence in 46:28, a variant of 30:11.

"They shall dwell on their own soil" is a reversal of "I am going to uproot them from their soil" (12:14) and is perhaps a reconception of the diction of 25:5b.

2   Weinfeld, "Metamorphosis," 40–43.

Aim

If Israel is to swear by a God of the new exodus, then that new exodus will have to overshadow the old, just as the new covenant (31:31–34) will overshadow the old. The scheme of the new exodus is one which Deutero-Isaiah exploited to the full (see, notably, Isa 43:15–21; 51:9–11).[3]

---

3   Compare the discussion in von Rad, *OT Theology 2*, 243–50.

The Prophets and Priests
Will Go Down to Perdition

Bibliography

On 23:9–40:
Meyer
    Jeremia, 111–40.
Overholt
    Falsehood, 49–71.
See also the general Bibliography on Jeremiah and
the false prophets in *Jeremiah 2*.

On 23:9–12:
Berridge
    pp. 181–83.

23

9	[Concerning the prophets.]ᵃ
	My heart is broken within me,
	all my bones are weak;
	I have become like a man drunk
	and like a fellow overcome by wine,
	because of Yahweh
	and because of his holy words:
10	[. . . .]ᵃ
	Indeed because of the curse
	the land has dried up,
	the pastures of the wilderness have
	withered;
	《 for of adulterers and evildoers
	the land is full, 》ᵃ
	their course has become evil,
	and their might is not right.
11	Indeed both prophet and priest commit
	sacrilege;
	even in my house I have found their
	evil,
	oracle of Yahweh.
12	Therefore their way shall be to them like
	Perdition,
	into Darkness they shall be driven,
	and shall fall into it;
	for I shall bring upon them disaster,
	the year of their visitation,
	oracle of Yahweh.

Text

9a   The superscription is secondary; compare 21:11.

10a   For a discussion of the text of v 10a, and various
solutions, see Interpretation. The solution adopted
here presumes that the words "and evildoers"
(וּמְרֵעִים) dropped out early by haplography, and at a
later stage the remaining words of that bicolon, "for
of adulterers the land is full," dropped out, again by
haplography (hence the text of *G*), and then that
defective clause was restored at the wrong spot
before the cola about the drought (so the present
text of *M*).

Structure

Verse 9 begins a collection of material on the (false)
prophets which ends with v 40; the title of the collection,
"concerning the prophets" (v 9) is analogous to the title
in 21:11. It is more than possible that this collection was
originally appended to the end of the confessions ("my
heart" and "my bones" in v 9 in that case being linked to
the same words in 20:9) and that the intervening
material—the collection in 21:11—23:8 on the kings
and on Jerusalem, and the material earlier in chapter
21—was inserted later, but there is no way to be sure.

Verses 13–15 are closely related to vv 9–12, but they
form a separate unit. Thus vv 9–12 link prophet and
priest, while vv 13–15 compare the prophets of Jerusalem with the prophets of Samaria. Furthermore each
sequence offers an accusation speech followed by an
announcement of judgment. (See further Form and
Interpretation for both passages.)

Form-critically the passage breaks into v 9 (words of
Jrm) and vv 10–12 (words of Yahweh, an accusation

speech, vv 10–11, and the announcement of judgment, v 12). Verse 9 consists of six cola, four parallel cola followed by two cola with parallel phrases dependent on the clauses in the first four cola.[1] The analysis of vv 10–11 depends upon one's solution to the text difficulties of v 10. If the solution proposed here is sound (see Text, Interpretation), v 10 divides into a tricolon and two bicola: the tricolon concerns the drought—its first colon is analogous to the last two cola of v 9 ("because of," מִפְּנֵי). The two bicola concern the evildoers: the second colon ("the land is full," מָלְאָה הָאָרֶץ) matches the second colon of the preceding tricolon ("the land has dried up," אָבְלָה הָאָרֶץ). The tricolon, the first bicolon, and v 11 all begin with כִּי; v 11 is a simple bicolon. Verse 12a is a tricolon (each colon with a verb), and v 12b is a bicolon (compare 11:23b).

Form

In v 9 Jrm speaks, while in vv 11 and 12 Yahweh speaks. Verse 10 is form-critically tied with v 11 (see below). The shift of speaker between v 9 and v 10, and the phrase "his holy words" at the end of v 9, suggests that the conjunction כִּי which begins v 10 (whether in M or in the emended text offered here) is a כִּי *recitativum*, like 4:8b (so Rudolph).[2] Verse 9 embodies Jrm's reaction to the words he must utter and are comparable to 4:19–21 and 8:18 and 23 (for full discussion see both passages, particularly 4:19–21); it is essentially a lamentation comparable to Ps 31:11–13.[3] The words in vv 10–12 make up a judgment oracle; vv 10–11 is the accusation speech and v 12 is the announcement of judgment. For the association of the drought with the evil of the inhabitants see the similar sequence in 12:4.

Setting

This passage offers diction with close parallels with the confessional material in 11:18—12:5, with the sequence on drought and battle (14:1—15:9), and with other material in chapters 4 and 9 which on other evidence has

been assigned to additions in the second scroll. Specifically, with the emotional symptoms in v 9 compare 4:19, 21; 8:18 and 23; with v 9b compare 4:26bβ; with the description of the drought in v 10 compare 9:9; 12:4; and 14:2–6; with "of adulterers the land is full" compare 9:1; with vv 11–12a compare 14:18; and with v 12b compare 11:23b (for the details see Interpretation). These likenesses help to "lock together" and confirm various passages to the same time period, which must be that of the crisis of vocation Jrm underwent when challenged by the optimistic prophets, on the heels of the great drought; by the chronology adopted in this study it is the winter of 600.

Interpretation

■ **9** The words "concerning the prophets" are construed with the colon that follows by *S* and *T* (so also Calvin); *V* understands the expression as a superscription, a preferable understanding (see Structure).

The first four cola of the verse are usually taken as a description of ecstasy,[4] but it must be admitted that Jrm could be describing the impact that the contents of the message has on him rather than the experience through which the message came.[5] One may compare the discussion of 4:19–21; 18:18, 23; and 20:9, where there is similar phraseology.

Since the "heart" is the seat of thinking and planning (see 4:4), Bright's translation and comment are appropriate: "*My reason is staggered.* Literally 'my heart is broken'. . . . But this conveys the wrong impression; Jeremiah is not 'heartbroken,' but extremely disturbed in mind, upset, shocked."[6]

The "bones" of course connote the inmost being of the prophet.[7] The meaning of the verb with "bones" is, however, uncertain; it is a *hapax legomenon* in the OT (רחף qal). The pi'el of רחף appears twice, Gen 1:2 and Deut 32:11, and because of its occurrence in Gen 1:2 this pi'el verb has received much attention. The verb occurs in the Ugaritic texts, and in contexts that match the pi'el

---

1   For a similar analysis, of Zeph 1:2b, see O'Connor, *Structure*, 358–59, sec. 3.5.5.

2   See GKC, sec. 157b.

3   Berridge, pp. 181, 182.

4   Lindblom, *Prophecy*, 194, and see recently Wilson, *Prophecy and Society*, 7–8.

5   Berridge, pp. 182–83.

6   Bright, p. 151.

7   Johnson, *Vitality of the Individual*, 69–70.

occurrences in the OT:[8] the meaning in Ugaritic is clearly "hover, soar," and these meanings are appropriate for Gen 1:2 and Deut 32:11 as well.[9] But it is not at all certain that the qal verb occurring in the present passage is related to the pi'el verb (compare BDB). All four ancient Versions translate the present occurrence by words for "tremble" or "shake." Both Rashi and Qimḥi agree on this meaning, Rashi using a definition which implies that he has Deut 32:11 in mind, and Qimḥi citing Gen 1:2; it is clear that both have the "fluttering" of birds' wings in mind, which suggests that both have used Gen 1:2 and Deut 32:11 in defining the present instance. The question then arises whether the ancient Versions used that route to arrive at their renderings. In short, does their unanimity regarding "shake" have any independent merit, given the prominence of Gen 1:2? Nevertheless most critical opinion accepts "tremble" without question (Giesebrecht, Cornill, Condamin, Rudolph; so *JB* and *NAB*); Volz and *NJV* translate "tremble," but with the notation that the meaning of the verb is uncertain. A second suggestion emerged in the eighteenth century, "have become weak," with the citation in the literature beginning then of a presumed cognate in Arabic, *raḥafa*, with that meaning:[10] Michaelis mentions the possibility, Wilhelm Gesenius gave this meaning for the present passage from 1815 (and so, therefore, BDB), and this meaning has been adopted by Duhm, Bright, and Thompson, and by *NEB*. An argument solely from a presumed Arabic cognate is a weak one, but the proposed meaning gains in cogency by the diction of Ps 22:15, "I am poured out like water, and all my bones are loose [פרד hitpa'el], my heart is like wax, it is melted within my breast." Here "all my bones" and "my heart" are similarly parallel, and this is a particularly appropriate comparison in that Jrm has this psalm in mind elsewhere.[11] "Are weak" is then a preferable choice of translation. (So also Calvin, evidently on the basis of the diction in Ps 22:15.)

Religious emotion is often compared to drunkenness

(1 Sam 1:13, 15; Acts 2:13), so that the third and fourth cola, like the first two, suggest ecstasy; but the association of drunkenness with horror and sorrow in Ezek 23:33 again could suggest that Jrm's experience is the result of the terrible message he has received (see above). The wording of the fourth colon is curious; it is literally "and like a fellow over whom wine has gone": compare the same use of the verb עבר in Ps 38:5.

The double use of "because of" in the last two cola of the verse—with "Yahweh" and a manifestation of Yahweh—finds a nice parallel at the end of 4:26: as "his hot anger" (חֲרוֹן אַפּוֹ) is a manifestation of Yahweh in that passage, so "his holy words" (דִּבְרֵי קָדְשׁוֹ) are the manifestation of Yahweh here. Yet "his holy words" is an odd expression for Jrm to use. In 11:15 the restored phrase בְּשַׂר קָדְשִׁי is translated "meat of my sanctuary" (see there); so here, one wonders whether what is implied is not "words of his sanctuary."[12] If so, there is a nice anticipation of "my house" in v 11. If this is an implication of the phrase, one could go on to ask whether Yahweh's heavenly sanctuary is intended (compare the implication of 22), in contrast to the Jerusalem temple in which the evil of the prophet and priest is to be found (v 11), or whether it is the temple in Jerusalem where Jrm might have received the revelation. There is no way to be sure, but behind the phrase there is at least the possibility of multiple meanings.

■ 10 The text of v 10 is in disarray. *M* begins the verse with the clause "for of adulterers the land is full," while this clause is lacking in *G. M* continues with the two cola about the drought, "indeed because of the curse the land has dried up, the pastures of the wilderness have withered." Then v 10b follows, but in those two lines the antecedent of "their course" and "their power" is not clear. Since the expressions "the land is full" and "the land has dried up" are close (אָבְלָה הָאָרֶץ, מָלְאָה הָאָרֶץ), most commentators have judged the two cola on the drought to be secondary: if they are omitted, v 10b is brought close to "for of adulterers the land is full," and

---

8   *rḥp*: Ug. 18.4.20, 21, 31, 32; 19.1.32.

9   Speiser, *Genesis*, 5; Westermann, *Genesis*, I, 148.

10 The verb is cited in Georg W. Freytag, *Lexicon Arabico-Latinum* (Halle: Schwetschke, 1830–37); it does not appear in Edward W. Lane, *An Arabic-English Lexicon* (London and Edinburgh: Williams & Norgate, 1863–93).

11 Holladay, "Background," 156.

12 Compare the discussion by Dahood on Ps 53:7 and Ps 60:8 in his *Psalms II*, 21 and 79 respectively.

the antecedent of "their course" and "their power" becomes clear. By this assumption, the expression "the land is full" was misunderstood as "the land has dried up" and the diction filled out from the stimulus of 12:4. This is the solution of Duhm, Giesebrecht, Cornill, Volz, Condamin, Rudolph, and, as one alternative possibility, Bright. But it is to be noted that several of these commentators judge 12:4 to be secondary as well (Giesebrecht, Cornill, Volz, Rudolph, Bright). The present study, however, cites evidence that 12:4 is integral to its passage (see there), and the question then arises whether the two cola here on the drought do not belong here as well—the likeness of "the land is full" and "the land has dried up" could be attributed to assonance. The solution adopted here is the other alternative suggested by Bright, namely that the expression "for of adulterers the land is full" is misplaced; by this proposal it would have dropped out of the original text by haplography (כי), thus G, and later restored at the wrong spot, thus M. But in addition I adopt the happy suggestion of Rudolph, that the words "and evildoers" dropped out by haplography (it should be said, Rudolph's suggestion is that "evildoers and" dropped out before "adulterers," but either solution will do: I prefer the word order given here because of assonance and because of the greater chance of a copying error with "indeed because of [the curse]," כִּי־מִפְּנֵי). The verb "commit adultery" (נאף) and "evildoers" (מְרֵעִים) are in parallel cola in v 14, and the present passage as a whole depends upon more than one meaning of "evil" (רָעָה) in vv 10b, 11, 12, a repetition into which the restored word can enter.

The conjunction כִּי before "because of the curse" may simply mark the beginning of Yahweh's speech and so not need translation (see Form). "Curse" (אָלָה) is an expression of Yahweh's wrath which may manifest itself in drought (compare Isa 24:6–7): the word has been restored in the present study by a revocalization of אֵלֶּה "these" in 4:12 and 5:25, where drought conditions are described, and in 2:34 as well; it is noteworthy that in the present passage a few MSS. of the Hebrew text and G and S likewise read "these," so that the possibility of confusion between the two words is demonstrated. There is a nice parallel between "because of" (מִפְּנֵי) in v 9 and the same expression here, suggesting that Jrm has become like a drunken man because of holy words (from Yahweh), while the land has dried up because of the

curse (from Yahweh). For "has dried up" (אבל), which may also mean "mourn," see the discussion in 12:4. For the phrase "pastures of the wilderness" see 9:9; for "wither" (יבש) see 12:4. For the experience of the drought in the context of Jrm's struggle with the optimistic prophets see Setting.

For "adulterers" (נאף pi'el) see 3:8; the word occurs also in 9:1 in a context similar to the present one. It is noteworthy that "evildoers," restored in the present text, occurs also in 20:13 in a context which may likewise refer to those persecuting Jrm (see there). Question: Is the phrase "the land is full" a reminiscence of Gen 6:13?—that passage and Lev 19:29 are the only passages in the OT in which the "land/earth" is "filled" (מלא qal) with something bad.

The noun מְרוּצָה, here translated "course," carries a double meaning here, as, it is suggested, it also does in 8:6 and 22:17 (the diction of 8:6 is close to that of the present passage). The word does mean "course, running," with the implication both of style of life and perhaps more specifically of the "running" of the (false) prophets (which evidently implies "behavior": see v 21 and perhaps 12:5). As such it prepares the way for the occurrence of "their way" in v 12. But there is a homonym meaning "oppression, extortion" (see esp. 22:17), and with that meaning is in parallelism with "power" in the next colon. The images move out in every direction: the land is full of those who are unfaithful to Yahweh, most particularly the prophets and priests, who manifest their unfaithfulness in their specific professional behavior ("running") and in the oppressive ways they lord it over others ("oppression"). The parallel "might" (גְּבוּרָה) is an ironic echo of "fellow" (גֶּבֶר) in v 9. It is normally a reference to the might of a warrior (9:22) or of Yahweh the divine warrior (10:6; 16:21); in the present instance it is not an admirable characteristic of the religious leadership. For "not right" (לֹא־כֵן) compare the discussion in 8:6.

■ 11–12 The sequence "indeed both prophet and priest" (כִּי־גַם נָבִיא גַם־כֹּהֵן) followed by the verb is found also in 14:18b. There the predicate suggests a descent to Sheol (see there); v 12 here implies the same (see below). The two passages are thus products of the same situation (see Setting).

■ 11 Here the prophet and priest both "commit sacrilege" (חנף). The verb is translated "be profaned" in 3:1, but the verb need not have a stative meaning (compare 3:9, where it is transitive); the priests and prophets are doing wrong things (see the second colon), and the verb refers to the realm of that which resists what is sacred,[13] so that the translation here should go beyond the usual "are godless." The word shares some of the same semantic field with "adulterers" in v 10: each verb is associated elsewhere with "be faithless" (בגד: 3:1–2 and 3:20; 9:1), and all three verbs are associated in 3:8–9.

The statement about the prophet and priest is climactic, given the double subject with the double גַּם ("both . . . and") preceding the verb, but the second colon is even more climactic, with the third גַּם (here "even"). One may compare this colon with the expression in 11:15, where Yahweh speaks of what he hates, which takes place "in my house," and with 12:7, "I have abandoned my house." It must stressed that Jrm was not by definition anti-temple (compare the temple sermon, 7:3–12); but he is shocked by what he sees of the wickedness of priests and prophets at the core of Judah's religious life. The verb "find" (מצא) here carries the specific meaning of "discover" or "detect." Curiously there is no obvious parallel for this expression with God as subject and a sin or crime as object;[14] evidently the notion is not common that Yahweh, like a security guard, "discovers" or "detects" crime. The implication is that the discovery is an appalling surprise to him.

■ 12 Behind v 12a lie two other passages. One is Prov 4:19, "The way [דֶּרֶךְ] of the wicked [רְשָׁעִים] is like the darkness [אֲפֵלָה]; they do not know into what they stumble." The implication is that the prophets and priests (v 11) are the "wicked"; compare the occurrence of "way of the wicked" (דֶּרֶךְ רְשָׁעִים) in 12:1 in a context of those persecuting Jrm.

The other is Ps 35:6a, "May their way be Darkness and Perdition" (יְהִי־דַרְכָּם חֹשֶׁךְ וַחֲלַקְלַקּוֹת), together with Ps 35:5b, "(with the angel of Yahweh) driving them on [דּוֹחֶה]." For the capitalization of the nouns and for the translation "Perdition" see below. The wording is so

close as immediately to pose the question which is prior. Jrm evidently made use of other striking expressions of this psalm elsewhere: one notes his use of the rare word "my adversaries" (יְרִיבַי) in 18:19, and its restoration, in the present study, in 11:20 = 20:12, and the restoring of the even rarer synonym "my opponents" (לֹחֲמַי) in 11:19—for both words see Ps 35:1; and note the expression "my stumbling" (= "my rib," צַלְעִי) in 20:10—for the word see Ps 35:15. There can be no doubt, then, that the psalm is the source of Jrm's diction here. Dahood proposes that the two key nouns in Ps 35:6a are terms for Sheol,[15] and given the likeness of v 11a here to Jer 14:18b, and the likelihood that the diction there implies Sheol, this suggestion is to be accepted. The meaning of "Darkness" (אֲפֵלָה) is not in doubt: it is a poetic synonym for חֹשֶׁךְ (Ps 35:6a), confined to the "darkness" sent by Yahweh.[16] But the meaning of חֲלַקְלַקּוֹת is not at all certain. The word occurs (beyond the present passage and Ps 35:6a) in Dan 11:21, 34, where it clearly means "flattery": the root then is חלק "be smooth, slippery." But beyond this root, and a homonymous root חלק "divide, portion," there is evidently a third homonym meaning "perish": its cognate in Ugaritic, ḫlq, clearly has this meaning in Ug. 5.5.10 and parallels, and this verb (in the pi'el, "destroy") is proposed for Lam 4:16[17] and is likely for Ps 17:14.[18] Dahood therefore proposes "Perdition" for the word in Ps 35:6a (and thus for the present passage) instead of the traditional "slippery places" or the like. It is conceivable that the term in these two passages carries a deliberate double meaning, sharing the notion of "slippery mud"[19] and of "perdition." The notion of Dahood that "their way" here is better rendered "their destiny"[20] is unnecessary; the word here is an echo of "their course" in v 10—indeed the word here could well imply "their power" as well (see the discussion of דֶּרֶךְ in 3:13) and thus echo "their might" in v 10.

The verb in the second colon, "shall be driven," mimics the participle in Ps 35:5b (see above) and in

13 Pedersen, III/IV, 271.
14 See the listing in BDB, 593a, 2b; note that in 2:34 the verb should be construed as second-person singular feminine.
15 Dahood, *Psalms I*, 211.
16 Overholt, *Falsehood*, 51–52.
17 So *HALAT*, 310a.
18 So again ibid., and so Dahood, *Psalms I*, 98–99, with

further possible citations.
19 Compare not only Dahood, *Psalms I*, 140, but already Hermann Gunkel, *Die Psalmen* (Göttingen: Vandenhoeck & Ruprecht, 1968) 128.
20 Dahood, *Psalms I*, 211.

addition Prov 14:32a, "The wicked [רָשָׁע] is overthrown [דחה nip'al] through his evil-doing [רָעָתוֹ]." The verb in question evidently has two by-forms, דחה (so Ps 35:5; Prov 14:32) and דחח (so the present passage, if rightly vocalized, יִדַּחוּ, but some MSS. read יִדְחוּ from דחה), but the meaning is identical with either form.

One has heard twice of the "evil" (רָעָה) of the prophets and priests (vv 10b and 11), and the root has appeared a third time if the restoration of "evildoers" (מְרֵעִים) in v 10a is correct. Now one hears of the "evil" (= disaster) which Yahweh will bring upon them as a result. For the general diction of v 12b compare 11:23, and, less closely, 6:15 and its variant 8:12, and 10:15.

Aim

Perhaps the land was not completely full of adulterers, perhaps not all prophets and priests had committed sacrilege, perhaps the temple had not been altogether desecrated, but Jrm was convinced it was; and against a backdrop of the respite which the land had from the pressure of Nebuchadrezzar, a respite which brought momentary optimism to some, Jrm's passion is understandable. Another prophet two hundred fifty years before had had a similar reaction: "I have been very jealous for Yahweh, the God of hosts; for the people of Israel have forsaken thy covenant, thrown down thy altars, and slain thy prophets with the sword; and I, even I only, am left" (1 Kgs 19:10). And in an astonishing way Jrm's pronouncement came true: the prophets and priests of those days went down to Perdition and Forgetfulness, while it is Jrm we remember.

629

Jerusalem Is Worse than Samaria

23

Bibliography
McKane
"Poison."

13   Indeed, in the prophets of Samaria
    I have seen something fatuous:
  they have prophesied by Baal
    and led astray my people Israel.
14   But in the prophets of Jerusalem
    I have seen something horrible:
  imagine committing adultery and
      walking in the Lie!—
  and then they strengthen the hands of
      evildoers,
    so that no one 《 turns 》ᵃ from his evil;
  they have all become to me like Sodom,
    and her inhabitants like Gomorrah.
15   Therefore thus Yahweh of hosts has said
    concerning the prophets:
  I am going to feed them with wormwood,
    and give them poisoned water to drink.
  for from the prophets of Jerusalem
    sacrilege has gone out to the whole
    land.

Text

14a   Reading the infinitive שׁוּב with *G* (and compare also the derivative passage Ezek 13:22) for *M* שָׁבוּ: the perfect is impossible with לְבִלְתִּי (GKC, sec. 152x).

Structure and Form

This passage is distinct from vv 9–12 (see there), and v 16 begins a new unit, so that the present three verses form a single unit: vv 13–14 are an accusation speech, and v 15, beginning with the messenger formula, is the announcement of judgment.

The beginning of v 13 is parallel to the beginning of v 14. One is at first unsure whether v 13a comprises one colon or two, and its parallel in v 14 likewise. The answer comes in v 15b: that sequence is too long to make up a single colon,[1] so that "for from the prophets of Jerusalem" must make up a colon of its own; therefore "in the prophets of Jerusalem" in v 14 makes up a colon, and therefore "in the prophets of Samaria" in v 13 is a single colon. Verse 13 is thus two bicola; its second bicolon is paralleled by the last five cola in v 14, grouped as a tricolon and a bicolon. The speaker in both v 13 and v 14 is Yahweh (v 14b, "to me"). For "I have seen" in an accusation in the mouth of Yahweh compare 13:27. Samaria and Jerusalem are here compared, and the implication is that Jerusalem is worse than Samaria: this implication will be set forth explicitly in Ezek 16:47 and 23:11, and then in Jer 3:11. The accusation ends (v 14b)

with a simile: compare the similes in Jrm's accusation to Yahweh in 15:18b.

Verse 15, the announcement of judgment, offers a description of the punishment only in v 15a; v 15b gives a motivation, really a reversion to accusation, introduced by כִּי; for another example of the interweaving of accusation and judgment see 13:20–27.

Setting

The setting for this passage cannot be other than that for vv 9–12, for the two passages are parallel in theme and wording: one notes the parallel of "adultery" and "evildoers" in v 14 (compare "adulterers" and the reconstructed "evildoers" in v 10), the root "sacrilege" in v 15 (compare v 11); one notes, too, the use of "something horrible" in both v 14 and 5:30: both vv 9–12 and the present passage bear a close resemblance to 5:30–31.

Interpretation

■ **13** There was a tendency in the past to see in the conjunction וְ at the beginning of the verse a scribal error (from the beginning of v 14: so Giesebrecht); but Naegelsbach in the nineteenth century stressed what

---

1   By O'Connor's analysis, in which כָּל־, like more substantial words, is a "unit," no more than five units may make up a colon: see O'Connor, *Structure*, 138,

and for כָּל־ see 317, line type 15.

Rudolph has likewise affirmed, that the two occurrences of ‍ן, here and at the beginning of v 14, stress the correspondence between the prophets of Samaria and the prophets of Jerusalem. Nevertheless it would be difficult to find such a double use of ‍ן elsewhere.

It is not easy to determine the exact meaning of what it is that was seen in the prophets of Samaria: the word is תִּפְלָה. The one other clear instance of the word is Job 1:22, where it is said that Job did not accuse God of תִּפְלָה, evidently "blameworthy" or "wrong" (the instance in Job 24:12 is doubtless to be revocalized). The related word תָּפֵל is used in Job 6:6 of tasteless food which needs salt to be edible, and in Lam 2:14 of unsubstantial prophecies (an instance probably based on the present passage). "Tasteless" is not right here because of the English connotation of bourgeois "good taste"; "unsavory" is too negative. "Fatuous" is the rendering of *V*, and not far from the mark (so Calvin; compare *KJV* "folly"). Renderings like "repulsive" (*NJV*) or "nauseating" (*JB*) are not right, for it is clear that the prophets in Jerusalem are judged more severely (see v 14). The food in Job 6:6 is not nauseating or repulsive, it simply has no character of its own: similarly the prophecies of the prophets in Lam 2:14 lack reality.[2]

"Prophesy" is נבא hitpa'el. For the form of this verb with an assimilated *t* see GKC, sec. 54c. Whether this stem here suggests characteristic prophetic behavior such as ecstasy or trance states is uncertain.[3] For a slightly different formulation of the same phrase, "they have prophesied by Baal," see 2:8: by the hypothesis of the present study that passage likewise was originally part of an accusation against the northern kingdom (see 2:1—4:4, Preliminary Observations). The phrase "lead astray my people," used of the prophets, is found in Mic 3:5, though there it appears to be an indictment against the Jerusalem prophets.[4] There is no warrant for Rudolph to delete "Israel" as a gloss.

■ **14** For the ‍ן at the beginning of the verse see v 13. That a contrast between the prophets of the two capital cities

is intended, and that the comparison is the worse for the prophets of Jerusalem, is indicated by the five cola of description of those in Jerusalem against the two for those in Samaria, and by the more extreme language (so Giesebrecht, Rudolph, and Bright, against Overholt).[5] The word "something horrible" (שַׁעֲרוּרָה) occurs only here and in 5:30 (see there), but the colon is modeled on Hos 6:10, where a by-form of the word appears.

The sudden appearance of the two infinitive absolutes in the third colon (נָאוֹף וְהָלֹךְ) is striking; there is here surely a reminiscence of 7:9, since these two verbs are found in that chain of infinitive absolutes. But while the list in 7:9 was posed as a question—will you continue to do these things?—the present passage is an accusation: the prophets in particular have done these things. How ironical that those charged with religious leadership should be the ones to break the covenant norms! For the translation "imagine" for the infinitive absolutes compare 3:1; 4:18; and particularly 7:9. Given the reminiscence of 7:9 here, one must understand the accusation of adultery to be literal and not metaphorical (so also Bright). What does "walk in the Lie" mean? There are a whole set of intersecting parallels to this phrase. First, Jrm several times uses the phrase "walk in" (הלך בְּ) with the expression "the stubbornness of their evil heart" (note v 17, and the discussion in 3:17 and 7:24); one expects then that the present phrase will be synonymous, that the style of life of the prophets is one based on utter opposition to the way of Yahweh. Second, there is the suspicion elsewhere that "lie" (שֶׁקֶר) is a designation for Baal, notably in 13:25 (see there): the phrase there is "you trusted in the Lie" (כתח בַּשֶּׁקֶר), suggesting a designation for a deity, and the other two passages in which בְּשֶׁקֶר or בַּשֶּׁקֶר appear in Jer are 5:31 and 20:6, "prophesy falsely (or, by the Lie)" (נבא nip'al with the phrase), where there is a similar implication (compare 2:8, "prophesy by Baal," נבא nip'al + בַּבַּעַל). Third, the parallel in 7:9 (see above) uses the frequent expression "walk after other gods" (הלך אַחֲרֵי אֱלֹהִים אֲחֵרִים); here, however, the situation is

---

2   For a full discussion of the word see Samuel R. Driver and George B. Gray, *A Critical and Exegetical Commentary on the Book of Job* (ICC; New York: Scribner's, 1921) I, 10–11.

3   See 14:1—15:9, n. 64.

4   So Mays, *Micah*, 81; Wolff, *Micha*, 71–72.

5   Overholt, *Falsehood*, 52–53.

worse—not "walk behind other gods" but "walk in(side) the Lie," as if worship of Baal had resulted in the prophets' being engulfed by the Lie (compare the implication of 2:5). Ultimately one must assume that though their literal meanings are rather different, the two infinitive absolutes here resonate with each other: if "prophesy by the Lie" implies prophesying by Baal, then "commit adultery" is a metaphor for Baal worship (Hos 4:12–14).

The waw-consecutive perfect in the next colon ("strengthen the hand of evildoers") seems to be analogous to the waw-consecutive perfect in 7:10 after the series of infinitive absolutes; there the implication is "and then you come," so one must assume the same implication here.[6] The expression "strengthen someone's hands" means "encourage" (Judg 9:24; 1 Sam 23:16; Ezek 13:22 is derivative from the present passage; see also Ezra 6:22; Neh 2:18; 6:9). By the syntax accepted here, the prophets live in the spirit of falsity, and the result is that they encourage evildoers. The phrase "so that no one turns from his evil" should be compared with 18:11, "just turn, each of you, from your evil way": 18:11, with its echoes of the temple sermon, is the perfect expression of Jrm's hope for change, but here, by contrast, is the expression of hopelessness.[7]

There is no warrant for Rudolph's emendation of "her inhabitants" on the assumption that only the prophets are referred to; when the prophets fail, the whole people comes under condemnation (9:1–2 describes the whole people in terms similar to those in which the prophets are here accused; compare also the discussion in 18:19–23). The designation "her" then refers to Jerusalem. What is the force of "they have all become to me like Sodom, and her inhabitants like Gomorrah"? The tendency has been to assume that Jrm perceives his fellow citizens to be as

immoral as those cities; that is surely the meaning of Isa 1:10. But Jrm elsewhere in his mention of those cities has their destruction in mind (20:16).[8] Since, however, the judgment speech does not begin till v 15, one must understand these two cola to indicate that the people *deserve* destruction. (Compare 15:18, the simile of Yahweh's disappearance in the perception of Jrm.)

■ **15** The first two cola of the judgment speech are the source for the phrases in 9:14; "wormwood" is discussed there, and "give them poisoned water to drink" is discussed in 8:14, where that phrase appears. It is altogether appropriate that the punishment of prophets, who live by what comes out of their mouth, should be accomplished through what goes into their mouths; this nuance is underlined by "has gone out" in the last colon of the verse (compare the occurrence of the causative of the same verb in 15:19, "if you utter"). What has "gone out" from (the mouth of) the prophets of Jerusalem to the whole land, then, is "sacrilege" (חֲנֻפָּה), a noun from the same root as the verb in v 11 (see there). No wonder the whole land will suffer for what the prophets have done!

Aim

Jrm's fellow citizens must have continued to believe that "where there's life there's hope": that the destruction of Samaria and the continued existence of Jerusalem must demonstrate the moral superiority of Jerusalem. Jrm reverses the judgment and so insists upon the inevitable destruction of Jerusalem, a judgment that would continue to echo through the OT (Ezek 16:47; Jer 3:11). See further vv 9–12.

---

6 So Joüon, *Gramm.*, sec. 119s.
7 On this phrase see Holladay, "Prototype," 255.
8 So Overholt, *Falsehood*, 54–55.

Yahweh's Word Is Bad News,
Not Good

Bibliography

On 23:16–22:
Lipiński, Edouard
"באחרית הימים dans les textes préexiliques," *VT* 20
(1970) 445–50, esp. 448–50.

23

16	[Thus Yahweh of hosts has said:][a] Do not listen to the words of the prophets [who prophesy to you,][b] filling you as they do with nothingness; a vision of their own heart they speak, not from the mouth of Yahweh;
17	they keep saying to ⟨those despising the word of⟩[a] Yahweh, "It shall go well for you!" and (to) everyone walking in the stub- bornness of his heart they say, "Disaster shall not come upon you!"
18	For who has stood in the council of Yahweh ⟨and seen⟩[a] [and ⟨heard,⟩][b] to his word who has paid attention [(to) his word][b, c] and heard?
19	Look!—the gale of Yahweh, (his) wrath has gone forth; [and][a] a gale is whirling, on the head of the wicked it shall swirl.
20	The anger of the Yahweh shall not return until he performs and carries out the decisions of his heart. In time to come you will give it attention [with under- standing.][a]

Text

16a The discussion in Structure and Form suggests that Jrm speaks in vv 16–20; one must conclude that this rubric is secondary.

b Lacking in *G*; omit as a gloss.

17a Vocalizing לִמְנַאֲצֵי דְבַר with *G* for *M* "those despising me, '(Yahweh) has spoken!'" The "me" clashes with the third person "Yahweh" in v 16; the text of *G* makes for better poetic balance within the verse—specifically the phrase "those despising the word of Yahweh" fits better with the parallel "every-one walking in the stubbornness of his heart" (compare 13:10; 16:12).

18a Vocalizing וַיַרְא with *G* for *M* וְיֵרֶא "so that he might see," qal jussive. The jussive evidently emerged when *M* became conflate: see b and c.

b I accept here the suggestion of Janzen (p. 12) that *M* in this verse is conflate ("For who has stood in the council of Yahweh, so that he might see and hear his word? Who has paid attention to his word and heard?"); the text adopted here is that of *G* (though *G* groups the words slightly differently: "For who has stood in the council of Yahweh and seen his word? Who has paid attention and heard?"). It is not possible to designate the steps by which *M* came to its present shape, but at least *G* gives good poetic structure.

c The reading of the qere', "his word," is preferable to that of the ketib, "my word."

19a "And" should be omitted (see the doublet text in 30:23).

20a Omitting the cognate accusative בִּינָה ("with understanding") with *G*, *S*, and 30:24.

Structure

Verse 16 marks a new beginning: though the messenger formula at the beginning of the verse is here taken as secondary (see below), there is a form-critical contrast between vv 15 and 16—v 15 rounds off a judgment speech, while v 16 begins parenetic appeal (see Form).

More difficult is the determination how far the unit extends, since form-critically it is a complicated utterance (see again Form). It is obvious that Yahweh speaks in vv 21–22, but there is no first-person reference in vv 16–20. The third-person references to "Yahweh" in all these verses do not rule out the identification of the speaker as

Yahweh (compare 2:2–3) but they at least make it less likely. Parenetic appeal in v 16 and the vision report in vv 19–20 point to Jrm as the speaker, and this conclusion means both that the messenger formula at the beginning of v 16 is secondary and that vv 21–22 make up a separate unit (against most commentators, and against the study of Edouard Lipiński;[1] but *RSV* and *NJV* rightly separate the two units).

Formally the passage offers an inclusio of second-person plural verbs (vv 16a, 20b). The verse divisions set forth the internal structure of the poem: two verses of four cola each describing the (false) prophets (vv 16–17), a climactic bicolon of rhetorical questions (v 18), and two verses of four cola each embodying the vision report (vv 19–20). Verses 16–17 are held together by verbs for "speaking" (אמר דבר), and vv 19–20 by words for "wrath" (אַף, חֵמָה).

Form

Jrm is the speaker (see Structure) addressing the people (vv 16a, 20b). The prohibition in v 16a is in the form of parenetic appeal (compare 7:4; 10:2). The motivation for the appeal appears in vv 16aβb–17, in effect an accusation speech affirming that the (false) prophets are baseless in their proclamation of salvation. Verse 18 consists of rhetorical questions; they imply the answer, "The (false) prophets have not stood in the council of Yahweh, but rather I, Jeremiah." The closest parallel for such rhetorical questions is 15:5 (likewise מִי . . . כִּי מִי . . . .); those questions are mocking and imply judgment, while these questions, likewise mocking, imply accusation. Verses 19–20 embody a vision report;[2] the closest parallel is perhaps 4:23–26, though here the expression "I looked" (רָאִיתִי) is omitted, doubtless deliberately (see Interpretation). The vision report, offered by Jrm, is in contrast to the "vision of their own heart" (v 16) of the (false) prophets. Though the phrase "It shall happen in time to come" (וְהָיָה בְּאַחֲרִית הַיָּמִים) became a standard introduction for an oracle about the future (Isa 2:2), here the phrase "in time to come" is integrated into the poem. Its closest analogy is perhaps Num 24:14,[3] where it likewise is associated with a reassurance that Yahweh will accomplish his will. The statement about the future

then implies a threat to the people of the inevitable punishment coming (compare 7:14–15).

Setting

The setting of this passage, like that of vv 9–12 and 13–15, must be placed at the time of the crisis of vocation which Jrm underwent early in 600 when confronted by the optimistic prophets: there are many likenesses of diction between this passage and others associated with that period. Thus "vision" (חָזוֹן, v 16) appears in the book only here and in 14:14, in both instances of the vision of the (false) prophets. The saying "It shall go well with you" (שָׁלוֹם יִהְיֶה לָכֶם, v 17) appears in 4:10 and in a similar phrase in 14:13; the saying "disaster [רָעָה] shall not come upon you/us" (v 17) appears in 5:12, and the expression parallel to it in 5:12 ("we/you shall not see sword or famine") appears in 14:13. "Mouth of Yahweh" (v 16) appears in 15:19, and "stand before Yahweh," similar to "stand in the council of Yahweh" (v 18) appears in both 15:19 and 18:20. "Wrath (of Yahweh) shall go forth" (v 19) appears as a threat in 4:4 (= 21:12) and as an actuality in 18:20. The "gale" (v 19) may be comparable to the east wind in 4:11–12, and the description of the decisions of Yahweh in v 20a is comparable to the wording of 4:28b (on both these latter see Interpretation). For "in time to come" (literally "at the end of the days," בְּאַחֲרִית הַיָּמִים) compare "at her end" (בְּאַחֲרִיתָהּ) in 5:31.

Interpretation

■ **16** For the messenger formula, see Structure.

The people are warned against paying any attention to the words of the (false) prophets; the noun with the article implies "these prophets." What they are doing to the people is expressed in the second colon by a participle of הבל hip'il, a *hapax legomenon* in the OT. The qal stem of the verb appears in 2:5: there Israel's ancestors are depicted as pursuing "nothingness" and thereby taking on the characteristic of nothingness. Here, it seems, the (false) prophets bring about the same result among the people. (The rendering of *RSV*, "filling you with vain hopes," is the translation of the *American Translation* and is similar to that of Moffatt; but it is too

---

1 Lipiński, "באחרית הימים."
2 On this form see March, "Prophecy," 170.
3 Lipiński, "באחרית בימים."

specific.) The word order (pronoun after participle) implies something like the translation offered here, "filling you as they do with nothingness." "Vision" (חָזוֹן) appears in the book only here and in 14:14, in both instances of false revelation. For "heart" in the sense of "mind" see 5:21; 7:31. The word from the mouth of Yahweh is a word of death (9:19); it is Jrm, not the (false) prophets, who become his mouth (15:19). These prophets are illegitimate.

■ **17** The infinitive absolute accompanying a participle must follow the participle (GKC, sec. 113r): compare 41:6. The nuance of the infinitive absolute here is not altogether clear, but the parallel "(to) everyone walking" suggests that "keep saying" is not far from the mark. This is the only occurrence in Jer of נאץ pi'el "despise." It is normally used of human beings despising God or his manifestations; perhaps the nearest parallel is Isa 5:24, "they have despised the word of (אִמְרַת) the Holy One of Israel," but Num 14:11, 23 (the people who despise Yahweh will not see the land of Canaan) and Ps 10:3, 13 may also lie behind the wording here. The prophets are feeding with false hopes those who, like them, basically reject Yahweh. For "It shall go well with you!" see 4:10 and compare 14:13. For "walking in the stubbornness of his/their heart" see 7:24, and, with the more common preposition "after," see 3:17. It is unnecessary to emend וְכָל־ to וּלְכָל־ (compare *BHS*): the לְ in the first colon of the verse does double-duty. For "disaster shall not come upon you" see 5:12.

■ **18** Several commentators, assuming vv 16–20 are united to vv 21–22, and seeing in the present verse a contradiction with v 22, excise this verse (so Volz, Condamin, and Rudolph; *JB* places the verse in parentheses). Similarly some wish to add to "who" the expression "of them" (מֵהֶם) in order to assure the answer "no one" and so agree with v 22 (so Weiser; so *RSV* and *NEB*). But if vv 21–22 are separate (see Structure), such emendations are not called for.

The "council" (סוֹד) of Yahweh is the assembly of divine beings assumed to stand in his heavenly court, identical with the "council of the holy ones" in Ps 89:8— and there are still other designations, "assembly [קְהַל] of the holy ones" (Ps 89:6), "divine council" (עֲדַת־אֵל, Ps

82:1). The conception is set forth in lively fashion in 1 Kgs 22:19–22 and Isa 6:1–8.[4] Jrm asserts that a true prophet has stood in that heavenly council before Yahweh; a derived meaning of סוֹד, namely the "plan" vouchsafed to the inner circle around Yahweh, is to be found in Amos 3:7. The verb "stand" with "before (Yahweh)" is used of Jrm in 15:19 and 18:20: the same conception prevails.

If v 18 is the center and climax of the poem (see Structure), then the simplicity and symmetry of the *G* text commends itself and *M* at this point is dittographic or conflate (see Text), and the effort is misguided to rework *M* (for example, reading "so that he may see it," וְיִרְאֵהוּ, because the verb in *S* has a suffix, or reading the second occurrence of "hear" as a hip'il, "so that he may announce [it]," וְיַשְׁמִעַ, as Volz and Rudolph do). For "who" as the second element in a question (the second colon here) compare 2:24.

■ **19–20** Volz and Rudolph wish to excise "wrath" in the second colon of v 19 as a gloss, thus reading three cola in the verse: "Look!—the gale of Yahweh has gone forth,/ a gale swirling,/ on the head of the wicked it shall whirl." But there is no warrant for this change. The only instances in the OT in which the verb "go forth" (יצא) has "wrath" (חֵמָה) as subject are the identical passages 4:4 = 21:12: there those addressed are urged to adhere to the norms of the covenant "lest my [= Yahweh's] wrath go forth"; now it appears that that judgment has become operative. "Wrath" here benefits from the double-duty of "Yahweh" in the first colon:[5] compare "the anger of Yahweh" in the first colon of v 20. The cola in vv 19–20a interlock the two images: one has "the wrath (of Yahweh) has gone forth on the head of the wicked; the anger of Yahweh shall not return . . ." as well as the phrases about the gale. For "return" (שׁוּב qal) with "wrath" compare that verb with synonymous subject in 2:35 and 4:8, and the causative (hip'il) with "wrath" as object in 18:20.

The nouns סַעַר and סְעָרָה are gender-contrastive

---

4   See David Neiman, "Council, Heavenly," *IDBSup*, 187–88; Hans-Joachim Kraus, *Theologie der Psalmen* (BKAT 15/3; Neukirchen: Neukirchener, 1979)

5   58–59.

    Compare the double-duty substantives in Dahood, *Psalms III*, 435.

variants;[6] both denote a violent wind. The terms for strong winds do not seem to be distinguished carefully in Hebrew, and the fact that the synonym סוּפָה (see the parallelism in Isa 29:6) is associated with the east wind in Job 27:19–20 raises the question whether the "gale" in this passage should not be associated with the desert wind described in 4:11–12.[7] In spite of the verbs associated with the "gale" in v 19b, one must not necessarily assume that a whirlwind (that is, a cyclone) is intended; it may indicate only local "dust devils" (compare the wording of Isa 17:13).[8] The verb "whirl" (חול hitpaʻel) occurs only here in the OT, but the related qal stem ("swirl") is again a stylistic variation. The passage is intended to communicate a maximum of emotion by the repetition of sounds. (It may be noted that G omits "the head of," but the assonance, ראשׁ with רְשָׁעִים, speaks for it.) To "perform" (עשׂה) and "carry out" (קוּם hipʻil) are really synonymous; both are used for emphasis (so the diction of 4:28b: "decision" [מְזִמָּה] here is related to "decide" [זמם] there).

Though the phrase "in time to come" (literally "in the future of the days," בְּאַחֲרִית הַיָּמִים) became later a technical term for the eschatological end time (Dan 10:14; 1QSa vi 1; CD iv 4, vi 11), here clearly the phrase

indicates the time in history soon to come when Yahweh will bring his punishment.[9] "Give it attention" (בין hitpaʻel) occurs in 2:10 (the occurrence in 9:16 seems to carry a different nuance). The implication: if you do not follow my advice (v 16) now, the time will soon come when you will know for yourselves that my word is genuine.

Aim

It would be hard to imagine a more telling contrast in messages: those prophets who say "It shall go well for you!" and "Disaster shall not come upon you!"—and Jrm's word of the gale of Yahweh's wrath. Can the ears of the people be closed to the enticing words of the false prophets (v 16)? Some day soon they will learn what the genuine word is from Yahweh (v 20).

But the truth was still not clear six years later, when Jrm confronted Hananiah (chap. 28).

---

6 See Wilfred G. E. Watson, "Gender-Matched Synonymous Parallelism in the Old Testament," *JBL* 99 (1980) 321–41.

7 For a description of various patterns of wind, including the sirocco, see Baly, *Geography*, 64.

8 See again ibid., and R. B. Y. Scott, "Whirlwind," *IDB* 4:841.

9 For the general use of the phrase in the OT see the literature in *HALAT*, 35b, and in Lipiński, "באחרית הימים."

23

21

I did not send the prophets,
but they ran anyway;
I did not speak to them,
but they prophesied anyway.

22

If they had stood in my council,
^a then they would have announced^a my
words to my people,
and brought them back from their evil
way,
and from the evil of their doings.

Text

22a—a *V* reads this verb with the vocalization וַיַּשְׁמִעוּ
and thus translates "and if they had announced,"
and therefore in the next colon "then they would
have brought them back. . . ." This is a plausible
reading (see Interpretation).

Structure

There are both structural and form-critical reasons to
divide vv 16–20 from vv 21–22 (see those sections in the
discussion of vv 16–20). But the present passage is placed
appropriately here not only on the basis of general
subject matter but most particularly because the phrase
"stand in my council" (v 22) is linked with "stand in the
council of Yahweh" (v 18). The present little passage,
concerned with the illegitimacy of the (false) prophets,
must be separated from vv 23–24, which are concerned
with the nature of Yahweh himself. The division
between the two verses divides the two tetracola.

Form

The two verses make up a denial of the legitimacy of the
(false) prophets. Verse 21 is Yahweh's declaration of
nonresponsibility for the behavior, almost a declaration
of innocence (compare 7:22; 14:14), while v 22 is a
contrary-to-fact conditional sentence (see Interpretation)
saying in effect, "They did not stand in my council,
because otherwise the outcome would have been very
different indeed," a conditional sentence that has resemblances to 2:28aβ (see again Interpretation).

Setting

The setting of these two verses must be identical with
that for vv 16–20, since both passages deal identically
with the motif of standing in the council of Yahweh. But
there are further links with passages of the same period:
the insistence on the part of Yahweh that he did not send
the prophets is found also in 14:14, and the motif of the
prophets' "running" is found in 12:5. The phrases of the
last two cola of v 22 are found not in judgment speeches

but in warnings in the earlier, more hopeful period
(18:11; 4:4).

Interpretation

■ **21** The emphatic subject pronouns in the second and
fourth cola express strong contrast (compare Isa 1:2).

What does "run" imply? Normally it has been assumed
that the prophets are simply in a hurry, eager to proclaim
their message (so Qimḥi, so recently Thompson). Against
this interpretation, however, is the evidence that "running" is an activity of Jrm also, at least metaphorically
(12:5); further, nowhere is a verb like "hurry" used for
prophetic activity (unless אוץ "be eager" in 17:16 implies
it). Alternatively, since a king's messengers "run" (51:31;
2 Sam 18:19–26), it is assumed that the verb here
indicates that the prophets understand themselves to be
divine messengers (so Duhm, and so KB and Zorell
under רוץ). But the parallelism in the present verse
between "run" and "prophesy" suggests that "run"
describes prophetic behavior, and the context of the
derived noun "course" (מְרוּצָה) in v 10 points in the same
direction. There is no reason to believe that the verb
suggests prophetic ecstasy, and a connection with the
"limping" of the Baal prophets (1 Kgs 18:26) or of
Elijah's "running" before Ahab's chariot (1 Kgs 18:46)
seems wide of the mark. But could not "course" in v 10
suggest the stylized behavior of the prophets, and "run"
here the unvarying performance of the manifestations of
prophecy (like "I have dreamed, I have dreamed" in v
25)? There is the possibility of a similar usage for the
priests in *Midr. Cant.* 1:17 with the synonymous verb
רהט: the explanation there of the qere' reading וְרִהיטֵנוּ is
clearly a folk etymology, but the usage is still striking—

"the place where the priests ran (at service) [מָקוֹם שֶׁהַכֹּהֲנִים רְהוּטִים] was laid out with cypresses," a reference to 1 Kgs 6:15.[1]

■ **22** As in other passages with protasis and apodosis (4:1–2; 15:19), there is uncertainty where the protasis ends: is the second colon protasis or apodosis? *G* reads the verb in that line as a waw-consecutive qal imperfect (וַיִּשְׁמְעוּ—the expression אֶת־עַמִּי is read otherwise): "and if they had heard my words." And *V* likewise reads that verb as a waw-consecutive hip'il imperfect (וַיַּשְׁמִעוּ): "and if they had announced my words to my people." *M*, to the contrary, reads the verb as a jussive, parallel to the verb in the third colon, "then they would have announced my words to my people." Following the *V* interpretation are *KJV* and *NAB*; most commentators and other translations follow *M*, and the present study will do so.

Equally uncertain is the question whether the conditional expression here is unreal (contrary-to-fact), "If they had stood . . . , they would have announced . . . and brought back . . . ," or real, "If they have stood . . . , let them announce . . . and bring back. . . ." There are clear unreal protases elsewhere which are introduced by אִם "if"—Ps 44:21–22 and Job 9:16.[2] Contrariwise there are

conditional expressions elsewhere that are normally taken as real but which, in the rhetorical context, may just as well be taken as unreal: thus 2:28aβ, perhaps the closest parallel, could be translated, "They would have arisen, if they could save you . . ." as well as "Let them arise, if they can save you. . . ." Electing for a real condition here are Giesebrecht, Condamin, *JB*, *NEB*, and *NJV*; for an unreal condition are Cornill, Volz, Rudolph, Bright, and *RSV* and *NAB*. The decision can be based only on the external consideration of setting: the passage originated in the context of the crisis between Jrm and the (false) prophets in which Jrm perceived Yahweh to have determined irrevocably upon punishment. Hence the expression is unreal.

For "stand in my council" see v 18. For the phrases of the last two lines see 18:11; 4:4.

Aim

"You will know them by their fruits" (Matt 7:16). The false prophets brought about no change in the ways of the people, so they cannot have been sent by Yahweh.

---

1   For the reference see Jastrow, p. 1454a, under רְהַט.
2   See on this König, *Syntax*, sec. 390t.

Is Yahweh Not More Awesome than Anyone Suspects?

Bibliography

Herrmann, Wolfram
"Jeremia 23,23f als Zeugnis der Gotteserfahrung im babylonischen Zeitalter," *BZ* 27 (1983) 155–66.
Lemke, Werner E.
"The Near and the Distant God: A Study of Jer 23:23–24 in Its Biblical Theological Context," *JBL* 100 (1981) 541–55.

23

23 **Am I ⟨a God nearby,⟩**[a]
　　　　　　　oracle of Yahweh,
and not ⟨a God far off?⟩[a]
24 **Can anyone hide in some hole without being seen by me?**
[oracle of Yahweh.][a]
　Are not heaven and earth filled by me?
　　　　　oracle of Yahweh.

Text

23a　Revocalizing אֱלֹהִים קָרֹב and אֱלֹהִים רָחֹק for *M* אֱלֹהֵי מֵרָחֹק and אֱלֹהֵי מִקָּרֹב. The construct before a preposition is theoretically possible (GKC, sec. 130; Joüon, *Gramm.*, sec. 129n), but given the congruence with 12:2b (see Interpretation) the correction is advisable.

24a　The expression is lacking in *G* and is doubtless dittographic here.

Structure

These words have no direct link with what comes before, or what comes after (against Rudolph);[1] it is best therefore to treat it as a short unit of its own (see Form). Nevertheless the connection with 12:2b (see Interpretation) indicates that it is rightly placed here among the utterances dealing with the (false) prophets. Verse 23 is a bicolon, and v 24 is evidently a tricolon: in v 24b the object can hardly be separated from the subject and transitive verb.

Form

Here are three rhetorical questions uttered by Yahweh concerning his own identity; the questions, posed with a negative, expect a positive answer. The closest analogy to these questions of Yahweh's identity in Jer is in 2:31. Both passages display the language of disputation, here with the (false) prophets.

Setting

The connection with 12:2b (see Interpretation) indicates the same setting as that for previous units in this chapter from v 9 onward: the crisis in Jrm's vocation in the face of opposition from the (false) prophets, dated here to a time early in 600.

Interpretation

It is a commonplace of the commentaries on these two verses to state that Yahweh is affirming his transcendence along with his immanence, and this is of course true, but the fact that this little unit is lodged in the collection against the (false) prophets indicates that the argumentation is relevant to the controversy between Jrm and his opponents. The only other passage in the book which contains "near" (קָרֹב) and "far" (רָחֹק) is 12:2b, and the two passages must be seen side by side. (The similarity of the two passages encourages the revocalizations in v 23: see Text.) But the uses of "near" and "far" diverge in the two passages: in 12:2b Jrm affirms that Yahweh is hidden from his opponents, while here Yahweh affirms that no one can be hidden from him. Both passages affirm the sovereignty of Yahweh over any complacent convictions of people, but here "far off" is used with the rather specialized nuance that Yahweh is aware of everything, no matter how remote or obscure.

While 12:2b seems to have its background in conven-

1　Rudolph, p. 153 n. 4.

tional proverbial expressions involving hypocrisy (see there), the background of the present verses is doubtless Psalm 139 and/or Amos 9:2–3, a mocking variation on Psalm 139. Thus Ps 139:2 affirms that Yahweh understands the worshiper's thought "from afar" (מֵרָחוֹק), and vv 7–15 of that psalm name various hiding places which are not at all hiding places from Yahweh. It is perhaps noteworthy that 12:2b associates "far" with "kidneys" (כְּלָיוֹת, here translated "mind"), while in the present passage "far" is associated with hiding places: "kidneys" appears to be parallel with the motif of hiding in Ps 139:13 and 15.[2]

"Some hole" is a free translation (Bright) of "hiding places" (מִסְתָּרִים): the word is used of the ambush in which people (or animals) wait (for example, Ps 10:8); the word is cognate with the verb "hide" here. The emphatic subject pronoun in the second colon of v 24 is best rendered in English by the passive voice with agent expressed; the translation in the last half of v 24 simply reflects the word order of the Hebrew and the parallelism of the subject pronoun.

"Do I not fill heaven and earth?" the literal translation of v 24b, is a unique expression in the OT; the nearest equivalent is Isa 6:3, "Holy, holy, holy is Yahweh God of hosts, the whole earth is full of his glory." (The only reason the expression in the present verse seems familiar is that *1 Clem.* 34.6 has modified Isa 6:3 to "Holy, holy, holy is the Lord of Hosts: all creation is full of his glory," opening the way to the formulation in the Sanctus, for both Eastern and Western churches, "Holy, holy, holy, Lord God of hosts, heaven and earth are full of your glory.") But it is a big jump from Isaiah's formulation to Jrm's, from "the whole earth is full of Yahweh's glory" to "heaven and earth are full of Yahweh." Is there behind Jrm's formulation the phrasing of Gen 1:28; 9:1, wherein humankind is told to "be fruitful and multiply, and fill the earth"? It is in any event a remarkable affirmation against all trivializing of God.

The question surely arises of the relation between the present passage and Deut 30:11–14. The place of that passage of Deuteronomy within the Deuteronomic tradition is difficult,[3] but the passage leaves the impression of being dependent on the present passage of Jer (and perhaps on 12:2b as well)[4] and to be an exilic expression of the nature of the "word" in proto-Deuteronomy.

Aim

A rhetorical flourish may begin as ad hoc argumentation (see Form and Setting) and at the same time end as a confession of faith in the unutterably awesome God. It is the case here. "All [the prophets'] utterances are dominated by *the incomparable greatness of their God*, which lays all human greatness in the dust (Isa. 2.6 ff.), which guides not only Israel but all the nations in their ways (Amos 9.7), and which, filling as it does all heaven and earth, renders futile all human attempts to approach it (Jer. 23.23 f.)."[5]

The NT was impelled to a contrasting emphasis: by God's action the Gentiles had been brought near to him (Eph 2:13).

---

2   On the parallelism of these two psalm verses see Jan Holman, "The Structure of Psalm cxxxix," *VT* 21 (1971) 303–4.

3   Compare von Rad, *Deuteronomy*, 184.
4   See now Mayes, *Deuteronomy*, 367–68.
5   Eichrodt, *Theology* 1, 350–51.

Yahweh's Word Is Fire and Hammer Blows

Bibliography
Holladay
"Recovery," 424–32.
Werblowsky, R. J. Zwi
"Stealing the Word," *VT* 6 (1956) 105–6.

23

25 I have heard what the prophets have said
who prophesy in my name a lie, saying "I
have dreamed, I have dreamed!" 26/
How long? ⟨Can the heart⟩[a] of the prophets ⟨return⟩[a] who prophesy a lie ⟨and who
prophesy⟩[b] the deceit of their own heart,
27/ who intend to make my people forget
my name by the dreams which they tell
each other, just as their fathers forgot my
name for Baal?

28 The prophet who has a dream,
let him tell a dream;
but the one who has my word,
let him speak my truthful word!
What has straw to do with wheat?—
oracle of Yahweh;
《 (with) my word, a dream?

29 Scorching 》[a] is my word like fire,
oracle of Yahweh,
and like a sledgehammer which
smashes a rock!

30 Therefore, I declare myself against the
prophets, oracle of Yahweh, who steal
"my words" from each other; 31/ I
declare myself against the prophets,
oracle of Yahweh, who use their own
tongue to oracle an oracle; 32/ I declare
myself against the prophets of lying
dreams, oracle of Yahweh, who tell them
and lead my people astray by their lies
and by their loose talk: I for my part did
not send them or command them, and
they certainly do not profit this people!—
oracle of Yahweh.

Text

26a *M* offers a text without a subject, "Is there in the heart of the prophets who prophesy a lie . . ." (beginning הֲיֵשׁ בְּלֵב). The grammatical difficulty has always been felt; the Versions offer various periphrases, and precritical commentaries (for example, those of Sebastian Schmidt, 1706, and of Michaelis, 1793) have long discussions of the problem. The suggestion offered here accepts the present consonantal text, proposing a verb and subject, הֲיָשֻׁב לֵב. The verb was proposed (without the interrogative הֲ) by Giesebrecht in his first edition (1894) but then abandoned by him. Duhm thereupon accepted it (with the interrogative הֲ), Cornill called it a "happy solution," and Peake called it "probable." It has not reappeared in recent commentaries, however; the solutions of Volz and Rudolph are far more drastic and thus less plausible. See further Interpretation.

b Revocalizing וְנִבְאֵי with *V*, *S*, and *T* (so also Giesebrecht, Cornill, Rudolph) for *M* וּנְבִיאֵי "and prophets of."

28–29a Inserting דְּבָרִי, assuming this missing word dropped out by haplography ("my word," דְּבָרִי, like "wheat," הַבָּר), and emending *M* "is not thus" (הֲלוֹא כֹה) to two words in separate cola, חֲלֹם and כֹּה. This restoration is an adaptation of the suggestion of Volz, though I assume for simplicity's sake that neither "my word" nor "a dream" carries a preposition, those in the previous colon doing double-duty (compare my proposal for two double-duty prepositions in 3:23a). It must be said, however, that Volz's citation of *G* refers only to *G^L*. It must also be stressed that the proposal to restore "with my word, a dream?" is problematic, while the revocalization to "scorching" is almost certain and is accepted not only by Volz but by Rudolph; so also *HALAT*, and *NEB* and *JB*. Without the reconstructed last colon of v 28 and with the reconstruction in v 29, the latter verse reads, "Is my word not scorching like fire, (is it not) like a sledgehammer which smashes a rock?" See further Structure and Interpretation.

Structure

Verses 25–27 are in structured prose (*Kunstprosa*);[1] vv 28b–29 make up a short poem, whatever the nature of v 28a (see Rudolph, Bright); and vv 30–32 is structured prose once more. The rhetorical question in v 28b attracts comparison with the rhetorical questions in vv 23–24. The question, that is to say, is this: does one have a short poem comparable to vv 23–24 around which prose material was later inserted, or does one have a long prose passage (vv 25–32) in the middle of which is a climactic short poem? Clearly the latter. There is no verbal link between the poem in vv 28–29 and the poem of vv 23–24. On the other hand the poem in vv 28–29 expresses the contrast between the lying prophecy and the true word of Yahweh which both vv 25–27 and vv 30–32 set forth. There is furthermore a symmetry between the two prose sections: "each other" in vv 27 and 30, and probably "their heart" in v 26 and "their tongue" in v 31, and "make my people forget my name by their dreams" in v 27 and "lead my people astray by their lies" in v 32. This analysis is reinforced by form-critical considerations: v 30 begins the judgment speech ("therefore"); it is likely, then, that vv 30–32 has something to precede it. As for vv 33–40, they are likewise in prose, but their subject matter is rather different, and they are rightly taken by all commentators as a separate unit. Verse 28a is set as prose by Rudolph, as poetry by Bright and Thompson. It breaks easily into four symmetrical cola; for וַאֲשֶׁר (and indeed for the general scheme of the cola) compare 15:2. The existence of these four cola makes plausible the reconstruction of a second colon in v 28b with the resultant four cola in vv 28b–29.

Form

Verses 25–27 imply Yahweh's accusation concerning the (false) prophets. Verse 25 is a complaint statement by Yahweh, a complaint that there are prophets claiming unwarrantedly to speak in his name. The opening question in v 26 (if the text is correct: see Interpretation)

is a rhetorical expression which occurs frequently in laments, even, as here, in aposiopesis (that is, as an interjection unattached to a clause: compare Isa 6:11; Hab 2:6; Pss 6:4; 90:13), but it is striking in the mouth of Yahweh. The rest of v 26 and v 27 consists of a long rhetorical question (again if the text is correct) whether the (false) prophets can repent—the expected answer is clearly negative. But in this long question the participial clauses detail the offenses of the prophets to make up the accusation.

The jussives of v 28a indicate Yahweh's challenge to a public trial; compare for this form Isa 41:22 and similar passages. The first colon of v 28b is a short rhetorical question from the milieu of wisdom, though there is no way to know whether it is a traditional proverb (*māšāl*)[2] or only in imitation of one; if there is a second colon of v 28b, as reconstructed here, then it will obviously be on the analogy of the first colon. The simile which Yahweh offers for his word is like the extended simile in Isa 55:10–11; it is a form of divine self-description, a description of his chief means of self-revelation.

Verses 30–32 make up an implied judgment speech by means of the thrice-repeated challenge formula "I declare myself against" (for a discussion see 21:13, Form); v 32b is a declaration of nonresponsibility (see v 21).

Setting

Apart from vv 28–29 this passage is in prose, a circumstance which leads some commentators to assume that the material arose as part of the editing of the exilic period: the occurrence of "I did not send them or command them" in v 32 reinforces this view.[3]

It must be affirmed, however, that the passage contains unusual diction, diction appropriate to Jrm (aside from the poetry in vv 28–29). Thus there is no parallel elsewhere for the expression "I have dreamed" in the mouth of the prophets, and the expression "saying, 'I have dreamed, I have dreamed'" is comparable to

---

1   Weippert, *Prosareden*, 108–21, rightly, against my study, Holladay, "Recovery," 424–32.

2   Eissfeldt, *Introduction*, 82; Carole R. Fontaine, *Traditional Sayings in the Old Testament* (Sheffield: Almond, 1982) 6, 252.

3   So Thiel, *Jer 1—25*, 252–53; compare Nicholson, *Preaching*, 102–3.

"saying, 'peace, peace'" in 6:14. The expressions in vv 25–26 are comparable to those in the poetry of 8:4–7 (for the details see Interpretation) and in the prose of 14:14, and the shape of these expressions here does not seem imitative or secondary. The "challenge formula" is repeated at the beginning of vv 30, 31, and 32 and is found otherwise only in the poetic diction of 21:13. It is unnecessary to affirm the authenticity of vv 28–29, but it might be noted that the diction of v 28a is close to that of 15:2.

In regard to the occurrences here of "prophesy (in my name) a lie," the careful discussion by Weippert[4] indicates the originality of the material in this and similar passages. The conclusion to be drawn is that the passage as a whole is authentic to Jrm.

There is no reason, then, to propose any other setting for the passage than that proposed for the other passages in this sequence, namely early in 600.

Interpretation

■ **25** Given the association of v 26 with 8:5 (see below), the expression "I have heard" may be comparable to 8:6. For "prophesy in my name a lie" see 14:14. This is the only occurrence in Jer of the verb "dream," and four of the six occurrences of the noun "dream" occur in vv 27, 28, and 32. Dreams were a traditional way by which the prophetic word was received (Num 12:6); as is well known, the E source in Genesis maintains a particular interest in revelation through dreams. Deut 13:2–6 is a passage that struggles with the issue of true and false prophecy; the basic stratum of that passage appears to have been a part of proto-Deuteronomy, though expanded by later additions.[5] Whether Jrm had heard something like that passage or not, however, the issue of the validity of prophetic revelation through dreams must have been an urgent one in Jrm's day.[6]

■ **26** Duhm emended the expression "How long?" (עַד־מָתַי) to a third occurrence of "I have dreamed" (חָלָמְתִּי), and this emendation has been adopted by Cornill, Volz, and Rudolph. But the two initial pairs of consonants in no way resemble each other at any period, and the suggestion must be rejected. As an interjection appropriate to individual or corporate laments it is striking in an

utterance of Yahweh's (see Form).

The revocalization to "Can the heart of the prophets return?" commends itself as appropriate to the context (see Text), but it is to be noted in addition that in 8:5 "return" (שׁוּב, without prepositional indicator) is in parallelism with "deceit" (תַּרְמִית), a word occurring near the end of the present verse; the association of the two words in 8:5 thus reinforces the appropriateness of the restoration here.

The rhetorical question "Can the heart of the prophets return?" not only demands a negative answer of itself, but the setting proposed for the passage presumes that Yahweh has decreed destruction for the people and that "return" is out of the question (8:5 once more; and see Setting on the present passage). "Deceit" occurs not only in 8:5 but in the passage regarding false prophets in 14:14; see 8:5.

■ **27** For the meaning of חשׁב with לְ and infinitive, "intend to (do something)" compare 18:8. This is the only occurrence of שׁכח hip'il "make (someone) forget" in the OT. The expression "intend to (do something)" is mostly used of planning harm (1 Sam 18:25; Ps 140:5; Esth 9:24; Neh 6:2, 6); the emotional impact of this accusation is thus considerable—it is not only that the people have forgotten Yahweh (2:32; 3:21; 13:25; 18:15), but that the prophets deliberately plan to make them forget his name. What appalling opposition to the norms of the covenant (Deut 6:12; 8:11–20)! "Tell" (ספר pi'el) is the normal verb for the recounting of dreams (Gen 40:8, 9). The reciprocal "each other" (אִישׁ לְרֵעֵהוּ) has a negative connotation for Jrm (9:3, 4, 19; 31:34): these prophets are not speaking their dreams out to the world but sharing them with each other—it is a mutual admiration society. The association of the "fathers" with Baal is a familiar theme (2:5–8; 9:13; 16:11).

■ **28** The meaning of v 28a is clear, but two details need attention. First, *G* has "let him speak his dream," and Cornill, Rudolph, and Bright accept this reading; certainly a waw could have dropped out of *M* by haplography. On the other hand the symmetry of the four cola suggests that *M* is correct: Jrm may well wish to contrast the one true word of Yahweh with "some dream or other." Second, what is the grammatical place of "truth"

---

4   Weippert, *Prosareden*, 110–14.
5   Mayes, *Deuteronomy*, 230, 232–34.
6   On the general topic of the place of dreams in

prophetic experience see Lindblom, *Prophecy*, 201; on dreams in the OT see Isaac Mendelsohn, "Dream," *IDB* 1:868–69.

(אֱמֶת)? It has always been taken adverbially, "in truth" or "truly" (so the Versions, and so all recent translations). But there are two indications against understanding the word adverbially. First, "truth" seems to be in opposition to "lie" in vv 25 and 26, and that word is the direct object of "prophesy." Second, the parallel to this passage, 14:14, is immediately preceded by a quotation of the false prophets which include the expression "but trustworthy peace [שְׁלוֹם אֱמֶת] I shall give you in this place": there אֱמֶת serves as the second element in a construct chain. The implication then is that one has here a construct chain with intervening suffix, "my word of truth" or "my truthful word."[7]

Yahweh proposes here a test between false prophets and true reminiscent of the contest between the prophets of Baal and Elijah on Mount Carmel, 1 Kings 18.

In v 28b the specific structure of prepositions in the expression "What has straw to do with wheat?" (מַה־לַתֶּבֶן אֶת־הַבָּר) is unique in the OT. This form of expression, with two occurrences of לְ, occurs eleven times, nine times with the two elements linked by "and" (וְ), twice without the conjunction, one of these being the other instance in Jer, 2:18.[8] In spite of the unique אֶת the meaning can hardly be otherwise than the more common idiom, namely "What has X to do with Y?" The *S* paraphrases, "Why mix straw with wheat?" but the figure suggests not the matter of mixing falsehood with truth but rather the absolute distance between falsehood and truth. As Jerome pointed out, John the Baptist is remembered as insisting on such a separation in the last judgment: "His winnowing fork is in his hand, and he will clear his threshing floor and gather his wheat into the granary, but the chaff he will burn with unquenchable fire" (Matt 3:12; compare Luke 3:17). The word "straw" here (תֶּבֶן) is correctly translated (against *KJV* "chaff"), since it is what is used for binder in mud bricks (Exod 5:7–12): for a discussion of the contrasting Hebrew terms for "straw," "stubble," and "chaff" see 13:25. The distinction is rarely crucial, since they are all waste products in winnowing.

If the reconstructed last colon of the verse "With my word, a dream?" is correct, it simply underlines the point of the preceding proverbial saying; but the point is in any case sufficiently clear from the context.

■ **29** The construction "scorching" is almost certainly correct (see Text); it makes a satisfying third constituent in the colon, matching the three in the second colon (compare the reconstruction in 5:13b). Note that if the reconstruction of the second colon of v 28b is not correct, then the present verse must be rendered "Is not my word scorching like fire, and (is it not) like a sledgehammer which smashes a rock?" Whether rhetorical question or affirmation, the message is the same.

The proposed form of "scorching," בֹּוֶה, is a qal participle. This occurrence (and, if correct, the reconstruction in 5:13b) would be the only use of the qal stem of this verb in the OT, but the nip'al occurs twice (Isa 43:2; Prov 6:28), and the qal occurs commonly in postbiblical Hebrew.[9] It may also be noted that the verb occurs in Sir 43:4, but without vocalization its stem is uncertain.[10]

The same pair of similes, the burning and the smashing of rock, occurs for the wrath of God in Nah 1:6. Here Jrm gives the hearer to understand that Yahweh's word for the hour is an utterly destructive one (compare the simile between Yahweh's word and fire in 5:14 and 20:9).

The "sledgehammer" (פַּטִּישׁ) is mentioned twice otherwise (50:23; Isa 41:7); the context here makes it clear that it is the hammer of a smith that is intended. With this word the verb "smashes" (יְפֹצֵץ) makes a nice assonance. It occurs only here in the OT (פצץ polel), though two other stems of the verb each occur once.

■ **30–32** For the "challenge formula," translated here "I declare myself against," see Form and further 21:13.

■ **30** Much attention has been given to the phrase "who steal my words from each other"; R. J. Zwi Werblowsky lays out some of the interpretations which have been offered,[11] but by no means all. Since it is "my words"

---

7   The possibility of such a construction is discussed in general in GKC, secs. 128d, 131r, more examples are suggested by Stanley Gevirtz, *Patterns in the Early Poetry of Israel* (Studies in Ancient Oriental Civilization 32; Chicago: University of Chicago, 1963) 80–81, and see further Dahood, *Psalms III*, 381–82.

8   For all the citations see BDB, 553a: d, (c).

9   See Jastrow, *s.v.*

10   Israel Lévi (*The Hebrew Text of the Book of Ecclesiasticus, Edited with Brief Notes and a Selected Glossary* [SSS 3; Leiden: Brill, 1904]): nip'al or pi'el; Zorell: qal or pi'el.

11   R. J. Zwi Werblowsky, "Stealing the Word," *VT* 6 (1956) 105–6.

which are stolen, Rashi and Qimḥi assert that the false prophets steal Yahweh's word from the true prophets; but the phrase "from each other" will not allow this, as Calvin saw. Calvin, convinced as he was that the false prophets' falsity was deliberate, proposed that they conspired with each other to frame the figments of their imagination, and that this represents "stealing," but such an interpretation of "steal" is surely forced. Condamin believes that the "stealing" consists in usurping the right of speaking in the name of Yahweh, a right which they are denied, but, as Werblowsky points out, גנב does not mean "usurp." Cornill is convinced that the verse (and what follows) cannot be authentic to Jrm, since Jrm himself made use of the words of other prophets and did not consider it theft, and because the only way the phrase makes sense is in assuming that Yahweh's words were stolen from the true prophets, an assumption contradicted by "from each other," as has already been stated.

The verb is גנב pi'el, a form occurring otherwise only in 2 Sam 15:6, of Absalom's "stealing away" the heart (that is, the loyalty) of the people; in contrast to the qal, then, the pie'el may have a more metaphorical meaning ("appropriate to oneself by stealth," so *HALAT*), but such a distinction would be hard to maintain. Werblowsky's suggestion commends itself, that one connect this passage with the use of גנב pu'al in Job 4:12, וְאֵלַי דָּבָר יְגֻנָּב, "to me a word was brought stealthily," since this passage is also concerned with revelation, in this instance by night.

One may presume the following. (1) The false prophets were not deliberately offering false revelation insincerely (against Calvin); they were claiming to speak the words of Yahweh (so Hananiah, 28:2) when it was only the deceit of their own heart (v 26). Since it is not the true words of Yahweh, but only what they claim to be the true words of Yahweh, the expression "my words" must be placed in quotation marks: these words are altogether different from "my truthful word" in vv 28–29. The expression "who steal 'my words' from each other" is highly ironic (as is the corresponding expression in v 31: see below). And is not the plurality of "my words" here a way to underline the irony? (The consonantal text may be revocalized "my word" here, but G

and V agree with M in rendering a plural. S has a plural in vv 28–29 as well as here, and T, as vocalized, has a singular in v 28 and plurals in vv 29 and 30.) (2) Irony is likewise to be found in the fact that the source of the presumed divine words is "each other" and not Yahweh himself: "I did not send them or command them" (v 32), and further in the fact they have to beg, borrow, and "steal" from each other, a dishonest occupation. As Volz points out, Jrm is holding the poverty of the false prophets up to ridicule. (3) The phrase, by using "from each other," attracts attention to the phrase in v 27 which uses "each other," namely "by dreams which they tell each other." And here Werblowsky's suggestion becomes relevant, since dreams come "stealthily" (Job 4:12). A genuine revelation from Yahweh, if coming in a dream, would come "stealthily," as did Eliphaz's nocturnal vision, but since the false prophets do not speak a genuine revelation, they must perforce practice stealth upon each other. Bright sums up the situation succinctly: "This is bitter irony: the prophets, having received no word, repeat what they have heard others say as if this had come to them by direct revelation from Yahweh."[12]

■ **31** The irony continues. The prophets "use their own tongue," literally "take their tongue." They take charge of their own tongue instead of letting Yahweh put his word in their mouth (1:9; 5:14). In 9:4 people are said to "teach their tongue to speak falsehood."

The verb with cognate accusative "oracle an oracle" (וַיִּנְאֲמוּ נְאֻם) is striking; the verb is a *hapax legomenon* in the OT. There is no way to determine on the one hand whether the verb existed in Hebrew already (the Arabic *na'ama* means "to sound, moan"), and Jrm's use of it happens to be its only occurrence, and in this case whether the verb is denominative, derived from the common noun "oracle" (נְאֻם), or on the other hand whether Jrm has here coined a neologism for the sake of irony. There is a verb in postbiblical Hebrew meaning "speak, say," usually נום but occasionally נאם,[13] but it is not certain whether this verb continues the existence of a verb already in existence in Jrm's day, or whether this verb was stimulated by the present passage, or whether in fact it is a "mixed form."[14] The Versions have moved away from what is evidently the specific meaning here: G

---

12   Bright, p. 153.
13   See Jastrow, p. 887b, under נום I.
14   See the notations in *HALAT*, 621b.

has taken the words as verb and cognate accusative of the verb נום "sleep" ("slumber their sleep"), while the other Versions are content to offer a paraphrase (*V*: "and say, 'oracle of Yahweh'")—this paraphrase is justified by a few Hebrew MSS. which substitute for the verb and cognate accusative the normal formula "oracle of Yahweh" (נְאֻם־יהוה), but *M* is surely the *lectio difficilior* and reflects the mentality of Jrm. One must conclude that Jrm used an ironic turn of phrase, whether he devised the verb ad hoc or not. The false prophets use the right formula but the word itself is unreal.

■ **32** The "lying dreams" are presupposed by v 25; "tell them" by v 27. For "lead my people astray" see v 13. "Loose talk" (פַּחֲזוּת) is a *hapax legomenon*, but in Zeph 3:4 the Jerusalem prophets are called פֹּחֲזִים, the participle of the related qal verb: they are "reckless, undisciplined," and that expression may have stimulated Jrm's diction here. For "I did not send them or command them" see 14:14, and in poetry compare 23:21. In 2:8 the Baals are called "those who do not profit"; here the false prophets are similarly described.

Aim
In Jrm's mind there is no comparison between the searing fire and hammer blows of Yahweh's true word and the mirages and specious notions traded by the false prophets. To him it was self-evident: "What has straw to do with wheat?" What can God do but mock their pretensions?—what can he do but consign them to the scrapheap of history?

See further vv 23–24.

You Are Yahweh's Burden!

Bibliography

Boer, Pieter A. H. de
"An Inquiry into the Meaning of the Term משא,"
OTS 5 (Leiden: Brill, 1948) 209–13.

Gehman, Henry S.
"The 'Burden' of the Prophets," *JQR* NS 31
(1940–41) 107–21.

Long
"Schemata," 134–39.

McKane, William
"משא in Jeremiah 23₃₃₋₄₀," *Prophecy, Essays
Presented to Georg Fohrer on His Sixty-fifth Birthday, 6
September 1980* (ed. John A. Emerton; BZAW 150;
Berlin: de Gruyter, 1980) 35–54.

Petersen
Late Prophecy, 27–33.

Walker, Norman
"The Masoretic Pointing of Jeremiah's Pun," *VT* 7
(1957) 413.

Weil, Hermann M.
"Exégèse de Jérémie 23, 33–40 et de Job 34, 28–
33 (Jérémie 44,9)," *RHR* 118 (1938) 201–8.

Wernberg-Møller, Preben
"The Pronoun אתמה and Jeremiah's Pun," *VT* 6
(1956) 315–16.

Zolli, Eugenio
"Note esegetiche all'Antico Testamento, II. Ger.
23,39," *Anton* 31 (1956) 307–9.

23

33 And when this people [or the prophet or priest]ᵃ asks you, "What is the 'burden' of Yahweh?" then you shall say to them, ⟨"You are the burden!"⟩ᵇ —and I shall throw you off!"—oracle of Yahweh.
    [34/ But as for the prophet or the priest or the layman who shall say, "The 'burden' of the LORD," I shall attend to that man and his household. 35/ This is what you are to say to each other, among yourselves: "What has the LORD answered?" or "What has the LORD spoken?" 36/ but "the 'burden' of the LORD" ⟨you are to

Text

33a The bracketed words are a gloss from v 34 (so also Rudolph); see Interpretation. *M* has an article with "prophet" but not with "priest," evidently the result of careless copying; *G* lacks the article with both nouns.

b Revocalizing *M* אֶת־מַה־מַשָּׂא "What burden?" with a virtually inexplicable particle אֶת, to אַתֶּם הַמַּשָּׂא with *G, V,* and all commentators (see GKC, sec. 117m, note, on אֶת and the revocalization). Preben Wernberg-Møller, "The Pronoun אתמה and Jeremiah's Pun," *VT* 6 (1956) 315–16, has ingeniously pointed out that all seventeen instances of אַתֶּם in 1QIsᵃ are spelled אתמה, that is, אַתֶּמָה, and he therefore proposes the same reading here, אַתֶּמָה מַשָּׂא "You are a burden!" But there is no other evidence for this spelling of the pronoun in Jer, and the definite article is appropriate in the answer.

34–40a The bracketed verses are a later midrash (so Volz, Rudolph, and so McKane, "משא," 52–53), though they may have been added in two stages, v 34 and vv 35–40. See Preliminary Observations and

mention)[b] no more; for "the burden" shall pertain to a person's own word, and (using it) you would pervert the words of the living God, the LORD of hosts, our God. 37/ This is what 《you shall say》[b] to the prophet: "What has the LORD answered you?" or "What has the LORD spoken?" 38/ but if you do say, "The 'burden' of the LORD," therefore thus the LORD has said, Because you say this word, "the 'burden' of the LORD," when I sent (word) to you as follows, "You are never to say 'the "burden" of the LORD,'" 39/ therefore look, I shall {surely}[b, c] lift[c] {you}[b] up[c] and throw off you and the city which I gave to you and to your fathers, from my presence, 40/ and I shall put upon you everlasting reproach and everlasting shame, which shall not be forgotten.][a]

Structure, Form, Setting, and Interpretation for the details.

36b Vocalizing with *G* תַּזְכִּרוּ with *G* for *M* תִּזְכְּרוּ "you are to remember."

37b Reading the second-person plural with *G* and *S* (תֹאמְרוּ) for the *M* singular תֹאמַר, which is not in concord with the diction of vv 35, 36, and 38. The alternative is to assume that the second-person singular here is simply a vague "one shall say" (GKC, sec. 144h), but this is less likely.

39b Omitting the infinitive absolute and the first occurrence of "you" with *G*. The position of the infinitive is dubious, and the "you" does not match the compound object of "throw off."

c Reading the verb נשא with a few Hebrew MSS. and *G*, *V*, and *S*. *M* offers a mixture of forms between the finite verb and the infinitive, implying נשה "forget" for the consonantal text of the finite verb and implying נשא "lift" for the consonantal text of the infinitive. *M*, by specifying a šin for both forms, intends "forget" for both. In any event there is much confusion between III-'alep and III-he verbs (see GKC, sec. 75qq); and on the identity of the verb see McKane, "משא," 49–51.

Preliminary Observations and Structure

This passage offers difficulty in translation and understanding—the analysis of McKane[1] is an excellent discussion of the alternatives.

Almost all commentators separate v 33 from vv 34–40. Verse 33 contains an ironic turn on the ambiguous word "burden" (מַשָּׂא), and this utterance is universally attributed to Jrm (see Form, Setting, Interpretation). It is here because "burden" was one traditional designation of a prophetic oracle (see Interpretation) and is therefore appropriate in the collection of material on the false prophets.

Verses 34–40 are a midrashic extension of v 33 from a later period (Duhm, Volz, Rudolph, Bright; McKane[2]). Form-critically and structurally v 34 appears to be separate from vv 35–40: v 34 is a judgment speech, while vv 35–40 offer instruction, appearing to shift to judgment only in vv 38–40 once more. Again v 34 assumes that Yahweh is the speaker ("I shall attend"), while the messenger formula in v 38 suggests that vv 35–40 are conceived as a speech of the prophet (compare Rudolph). Finally vv 35 and 37 seem to be parallel, each the beginning of the two sections of vv 35–40. But the

Hebrew style is so careless in vv 34–40 (see below) that it is impossible to determine whether v 34 and vv 35–40 arose in two stages or whether the lack of integration between the two sequences is further evidence of carelessness.

It is important to stress that the style is both careless and overblown. (1) The use of הָעָם in v 34 to imply "a layman" is unique. (2) The wording "to each other, among yourselves" in v 35 has a place in the diction of 31:34 but is prolix here; and the sequence "the living God, Yahweh of hosts, our God" in v 36 is unique. (3) The difficulties in the second clause of v 36 render that sequence almost incomprehensible; see Interpretation. (4) The shift to the second-person singular in the first verb of v 37 is careless, though this may not be the fault of the writer. (5) The use of "Therefore thus Yahweh has said," normally the introduction to a judgment speech, is remarkable after an "if" clause (v 38; see Form). (6) "From my presence" is awkward in v 39 with "throw off." The passage is clearly not poetry, and one should not look here for any subtlety or irony.

1   McKane, "משא."
2   See ibid.

Form

Verse 33 is a good example of the question-and-answer schema delineated by Long, his "type B."[3] This type is a direct address by Yahweh to the prophet; it consists of a future setting, the question envisioned and formulated, and the answer prescribed (on this form see in detail 5:19, and compare other examples in 13:12–14; 15:1–4; and 16:10–13).

Verse 34 is a curious mixture. Syntactically the first half of the verse is a *casus pendens* which is equivalent to a protasis (see Interpretation). The apodosis in the last half of the verse offers diction appropriate to a divine announcement of judgment (for "I shall attend" compare Amos 3:14; Hos 1:4; 2:15; 4:9), but the announcement of judgment is normally preceded by an accusation, not a protasis. The protasis suggests that what we have here is prophetic torah comparable to that found in Ezek 14:1–11: the origin of that form is sacral-legal; one finds it in a developed form in Haggai and Malachi.

The form of prophetic torah continues in vv 35–40. Verses 35–36 seem to deal with the case where laymen discuss prophetic oracles with each other, while v 37 deals with the comparable case of those inquiring of a prophet. In each case the instruction is to change a speech pattern (compare the changing of a speech pattern announced in vv 7–8). Verse 38 has an explicit protasis analogous to the implicit protasis in v 34a, and it is followed, most remarkably, by the messenger formula "Therefore thus Yahweh has said" to introduce the apodosis as if it were an announcement of judgment: this inconcinnity is hardly smoothed over by translating "therefore" (לָכֵן) as "assuredly" (*NJV*) or "then" (*JB, NAB*, Bright), or omitting it (*NEB*). The "therefore" does properly belong at the beginning of v 39, where it is repeated: v 38, beginning with "Therefore thus . . ." through v 40 is the quotation of a judgment speech, beginning with the messenger formula, continuing with the accusation ("because . . .") and concluding with the announcement of judgment (vv 39–40).

Setting

Verse 33 is authentic to Jrm: the ironic play on the word "burden" is typical (see Interpretation). Long believes that this verse is "the simplest and probably oldest example [of the question-and-answer schema, type B] from the prophets."[4]

Verses 34–40 arose much later; whether v 34 and vv 35–40 arose in two stages (see Preliminary Observations) would be difficult to say. Duhm believed that the passage arose at a very late period, but his argumentation was based in part on a similar late dating for Isaiah 13—23. Nevertheless the insistence that "burden" (מַשָּׂא) shall not be used in reference to a prophetic oracle is curious in the face of the use of that term not only repeatedly in Isaiah 13—23 but also in Zech 9:1; 12:1; and Mal 1:1, material which is to be dated in the late sixth and early fifth centuries.[5] Should one assume an origin for this passage in a circle contemporaneous with Deutero-Zechariah and Malachi but hostile to that material, or an origin later than the time when that material arose?

There are no firm data from within the passage to locate a date, but there are a couple of hints in the confusion in use of diction appropriate to the traditional judgment speech (in vv 34 and 38: see Form) and in many instances of careless or overblown style (see Preliminary Observations); such characteristics again point to a date well into the postexilic period. So perhaps does the gratuitous use of "priest" (v 34).

Finally there is the curious use of "city" in v 39 where one would expect "land" (see Interpretation). The phrase "land which I gave to your fathers" was still appropriate for Ezekiel (36:28); "city" suggests the preoccupations of Nehemiah's time (Neh 2:3, 5: note in the latter passage "send me to Judah, to the city of my fathers' sepulchres, that I may rebuild it"). A date in the middle of the fifth century therefore cannot be wide of the mark for vv 34–40. This is also the conclusion of David L. Petersen, who finds similarities between this passage and 3:16–17.[6]

Interpretation

■ **33** The meaning of this verse is hidden behind a multitude of questions; the matter is made difficult by the fact that the term "burden" or "oracle" (מַשָּׂא) as applied to prophetic utterance appears in Jer only here, in vv 33–

---

3   Long, "Schemata," 134–39.
4   Ibid., 135.
5   Paul D. Hanson, "Zechariah, Book of," *IDBSup*, 983.

6   Petersen, *Late Prophecy*, 32.

40; there are therefore no data elsewhere to indicate how the term functioned in contexts in which Jrm would have had a part. Was the question "What is the 'burden' of Yahweh?" ever posed to Jrm, or is the question offered here only as the vehicle for an ironic answer? How did the term function in Jerusalem?

The noun מַשָּׂא means not only a "burden" (17:21 and often) but is a technical term for a prophetic "oracle" (2 Kgs 9:25), particularly as a title in some of the prophetic books (thus Isa 13:1). There is no clear explanation how the word, which clearly derives from the root נשא "bear," came to carry this technical denotation. The noun in the meaning "burden" and in the meaning "oracle" are listed as homonyms in the lexica, but since a derivation from the same root is given for both words, the warrant for judging them homonyms is not obvious.[7]

There have been two traditional explanations for the turn of meaning. One is that of Jerome, that an oracle is called a "burden" because it is a heavy and menacing prediction laid on the hearer; this view continues in Luther and Calvin and is adopted by Henry S. Gehman.[8] It was refuted by Michaelis, who pointed out correctly that the term is used for oracles that have nothing to do with doom (Zech 12:1) and that the reference is to the "lifting up" of the voice (a view already cited by Qimḥi as the view of his father), thus BDB and *HALAT*; it is the view of most commentators on Jer, but the matter is not settled.[9]

It is noteworthy that the word in the meaning "oracle" does not occur in Jer outside the present passage. It is evidently not a term which this book recorded as applying either to utterances of Jrm or to those of his opponents. Wilson has suggested the possibility that it was a term referring to a particular type of oracle that may have been characteristically Jerusalemite;[10] he believes Jrm represents a specifically Ephraimite tradition,[11] that is, setting forth Moses and the cultic tradition associated with Samuel at Shiloh. And it is true, the term serves as a title of oracles in Isaiah (13:1; 15:1; 17:1; 19:1; 21:1, 11, 13; 22:1; 23:1; 30:6), Nahum (1:1), Habakkuk (1:1), Deutero-Zechariah (Zech 9:1; 12:1) and Malachi (1:1); the only contraindication is 2 Kgs 9:25, part of a northern narrative. An argument from silence is cer-

tainly that the term is absent not only from the material outside the present passage in Jer but from Hosea and from other prophetic material not specifically associated with Jerusalem.

If this understanding of the use of "oracle" (מַשָּׂא) is correct, how is it that anyone would be depicted as asking Jrm, "What is the oracle (= burden) of Yahweh?" Elsewhere Zedekiah is said to have asked Jrm, "Is there any word from Yahweh?" (37:17; the verb "ask" [שָׁאַל] appears there as well), so there is evidence that there were those who sought a prophetic oracle from Jrm, but (to repeat) it is not with this technical term. The context in which this verse appears, namely among utterances against the (false) prophets, suggests that it is a term associated with those prophets (a datum pointing in the same direction as Wilson's suggestion), but if Jrm were perceived as having a point of view different from those optimistic prophets (and the opposition of those prophets, reflected by Jrm's confessions, surely suggests such a perception), then it is hard to imagine anyone with any comprehension of Jrm's point of view who would pose the question in these terms.

The tentative conclusion must be that the diction of the question is not realistic: it is doubtful if many folk asked Jrm "What is the 'burden' of Yahweh?" using this technical term. Yahweh tells Jrm what he is to answer if and when anyone seeks the divine word from Jrm with the assumptions of the Jerusalemite establishment. (Note the use of כִּי "when" in such circumstances in 38:15, where it is better rendered "if.")

The answer plays on the double meaning of the noun and comes in four short Hebrew words: "You are the burden, and I shall throw you off!"—the first and fourth words being the subject and object pronouns "you" respectively.

The precise meaning of the verb translated here "throw off" (נטש) is in dispute. It is clear that the verb is often a synonym of "abandon" (עזב), for example, in 7:29 and 12:7 (see those passages). But both *G* and *V* in the present passage suggest "throw off," and that translation is necessary for Ezek 29:5; 31:12; and 32:4, as Zimmerli recognizes;[12] and that meaning in those passages suggests that the rendering of *G* and *V* in the present passage

---

7 Compare McKane, "משא," 35–40.
8 Henry S. Gehman, "The 'Burden' of the Prophets," *JQR* NS 31 (1940–41) 107–21.
9 See n. 1.
10 Wilson, *Prophecy and Society*, 249.
11 Ibid., 231–51.

is not simply an interpretive translation based upon the meaning "burden."[13]

■ **34** The first half of the verse is a *casus pendens*: for the syntax see GKC, sec. 112mm. The conjunction וְ before "the priest" and "the layman," normally understood as "and," must here clearly be "or" (compare the conjunction in Exod 21:15, 16, 17); one notes that "shall say" is singular. The general term הָעָם, normally "the people," is often used for "common people" (compare 21:7; 22:4); here, in contrast to "the prophet" and "the priest," it implies by exclusion "laymen" (compare 1QS 2.19–21, where it is used in contrast to the "priests" and "the Levites"), indeed quite strikingly here it means (because of the use of the conjunction in the compound subject— see above) "a layman" (so *NEB*, *NJV*). *JB* and *NAB* have "or anyone else"; Bright "or whoever it may be."

Yahweh will "attend to," that is, "punish" (פקד, see 5:9) anyone who uses the phrase "the 'burden' of the LORD"; see Setting.

■ **35** The expressions "to each other" (literally "a man to his neighbor") and "among yourselves" (literally "a man to his brother") are of course synonymous; the sequence is found in 31:34, and one wonders whether such diction, overwrought here, is not imitative of that passage; but Exod 32:27 is comparable, a passage that is probably late.[14] The intention is to deal with the case in which a divine oracle is being discussed by anyone interested, in contrast to the case in which a divine oracle is being sought from a prophet (v 37). Two acceptable forms of question are given (note that here, as in v 34, the conjunction וְ means "or") to supplant the forbidden formula.

■ **36** Verse 36a is clear enough—it is the alternative to v 35. But the first clause of v 36b is almost completely opaque, and a variety of interpretations have been offered; McKane surveys them admirably.[15] The words are literally "for the burden shall be to a man his word." Questions abound. Whose word?—that of a man, or of the LORD? or should the words "to a man his word" be construed as a construct phrase, "to the man of his word" (so *T*)? What in this instance does "the burden" mean?—a genuine word from the LORD, or a human word claimed as a word from the LORD, or the (heavy) punishment which the LORD levels upon those who in some way misuse or misunderstand his word?

V understands the clause as, "For his own (human) word will be 'the burden' for each man," that is, the private thoughts of individual men are given out as if they were "the burden," the genuine word of God.[16] *S*, on the other hand, assumes that "his word" is the divine word; this version evidently implies that the term "burden" should be reserved for Yahweh's word and not used satirically, and this seems to be the understanding of Qimḥi. Rashi, on the other hand, follows *T* (see above), taking "the man of his word" to be the true prophet to whom the LORD vouchsafes his word (as in vv 25–32).

If "shall be" is understood in the future and not as a general description, and if "burden" is understood in the sense of Yahweh's heavy punishment, then the clause becomes a threat: Calvin explains it as "for else to every one of you his word shall be a burden" (so Naegelsbach, Giesebrecht, and others).

Ehrlich[17] suggests revocalizing "the burden" (הַמַּשָּׂא) to understand a he-interrogative (הֲמַשָּׂא): by this suggestion the clause would read "For is his word to be a burden to anyone?" This revocalization has been accepted by Rudolph and Bright. (A second suggestion of Ehrlich's, to emend "his word" to "my [= the LORD's] word," has not been accepted by them.) McKane ultimately accepts this suggestion,[18] convinced that the interpretation of *T*, Rashi, and *NEB* ("You shall never again mention 'the burden of the LORD'; this is reserved for the man to whom he entrusts his message") introduces a preoccupation into the passage which is alien to it (that is, that of vv 25–32).

12   Zimmerli, *Ezekiel 2*, 107, 5a; see further Godfrey R. Driver, "Ezechiel: Linguistic and Technical Problems," *Bib* 35 (1954) 299, 301, and *HALAT*, 657a.
13   On this question see McKane, "משא," 43–44.
14   Childs, *Exodus*, 558, 559.
15   McKane, "משא," 46–49.
16   So recently Arthur S. Peake, *Jeremiah*, I (New Century Bible; New York: Frowde, 1910) 271.
17   Ehrlich, *Randglossen*, 305.
18   McKane, "משא," 49.

In seeking a solution one may note several matters of style and word usage. First, the general style is that of casuistic instruction, not rhetorical argumentation (see Form); the revocalization of Ehrlich is therefore to be rejected. There is no parallel elsewhere in the book for כִּי followed by he-interrogrative. Second, words from God are referred to with baroque elaboration ("the words of the living God, the LORD of hosts, our God"). The writer has used an overelaborate style to speak of the discussion of a prophetic word ("to each other, among yourselves," v 35, with wording that uses "a man" twice). Therefore it is virtually certain that "his word" here refers to a human word, not to a divine one. Third, and related to the observation just made, the construal of a construct chain here ("to the man of his word") is forced; it is far simpler to take "to a man his word" distributively ("to each, his word") like the usage in Gen 40:5 ("each, his dream"). Fourth, given the word order, "his word" is unlikely to be the subject; it is more likely that "the burden," whatever the meaning of that term, is the emphatic subject. Fifth and more generally, given the style of vv 34–40, one is not likely to find subtlety or irony here.

It would appear, then, that the simple solution is to understand היה לְ in its frequent meaning of "belong to" (3:1); there is a contrast, then, between the expression "burden of the LORD" (v 36a) and "the burden" here. To paraphrase: You are to use the term "burden of the LORD" no more—the term "burden" is to be confined to human words, and to use the term to refer to divine words would be to insult the LORD. This is the solution of Volz. It presupposes a suppressed protasis, which is actually found in the first clause of v 38: Volz supplies "therewith" in the last clause of the verse, and a parenthetical "using it" is supplied here.

The meaning of "pervert" (הפך), though not quite paralleled elsewhere, is not in doubt. The verb is used of the leopard's "changing" his skin in 13:23.

The sequence "the LORD of hosts, our God" is unique in the OT (to say nothing of attaching it to the phrase "the living God"); the two segments are in parallelism in Ps 48:9, but never elsewhere in apposition. The usual combination is "Yahweh our God" (3:22 and eighteen

times additionally in Jer). For "living God" see 10:10.

■ **37** The verse is parallel to v 35 (see there). For the curious vocalization of "has answered you" (עָנָךְ) see GKC, sects. 58g, 75ll. For "or" see v 35.

■ **38** For the curious use of "Therefore the LORD has said" following an "if" clause see Form.

■ **39** In spite of the textual confusion the identity of the first verb is not in doubt: it is "lift up" (נשא), a play on "burden" (מַשָּׂא). The second verb repeats the verb at the end of v 33. The expression "from my presence" (מֵעַל פָּנַי) sits uneasily with that verb in the meaning posited in this passage ("lift off"), leading many commentators to question the meaning.[19] The expected verbs with "from my presence" are "dismiss" (שלח pi'el, 15:1), "cast away" (שלך hip'il, 7:15) or "remove" (סור hip'il, 32:31).[20] But the awkwardness of the diction is to be attributed to careless style rather than to a different meaning for the verb.

The verse expands on the judgment of v 33 by the compound object "you and the city." The phrase "which I gave to you and to your fathers" (with variants) is of course common in the book, but "city" here is a unique antecedent; the antecedents otherwise are "land" (אֶרֶץ, 7:7; 30:3), "place" (מָקוֹם, 7:14), "ground" (אֲדָמָה, 16:15; 24:10; 25:5; 35:15) or "inheritance" (נַחֲלָה, 17:4). Indeed the usage is so startling that Volz wishes to emend to "land"! The expression may help in specifying a historical context for the passage; see Setting.

■ **40** The diction here seems to combine the poetic expression "everlasting disgrace will never be forgotten" (כְּלִמַּת עוֹלָם לֹא תִשָּׁכֵחַ, 20:11) with "everlasting shame" (25:9 *G*); "everlasting" is also found with "ruins" (49:13) and "desolation" (25:12; 51:26, 62), but this is the only instance in the book where "everlasting" appears twice in such expressions.

Aim

There is nothing too sacred to be touched by Jrm's irony, not the name of a priest (20:1–6), not the fate of the temple (7:3–12), not the term for a prophetic oracle in the circle of Jerusalem prophets (v 33 here): Yahweh is free to send any human construct, no matter how sincerely intended for the glory of God, into the ashheap

19   Ibid., 49–51.
20   For these phrases and citations beyond Jer see
     Weinfeld, *Deuteronomy*, 347.

of ridicule or contempt; so with the term "burden"!

In the conviction of a later century the word-play has become word-magic: the term "burden" must no longer be used, but other phraseology must be substituted for it. It is an era of solemn piety.

Good Figs and Putrid Ones

Bibliography

Berridge
  pp. 63–72.
Long
  "Reports of Visions," esp. 359.
Niditch
  Symbolic Vision, 53–70.
Pohlmann
  Studien, 20–31.
Raitt, Thomas M.
  "Jeremiah's Deliverance Message to Judah,"
  Rhetorical Criticism, Essays in honor of James Muilen-
  burg (ed. Jared J. Jackson and Martin Kessler;
  Pittsburgh Theological Monograph Series 1; Pitts-
  burgh: Pickwick, 1974) 166–85.
Reventlow
  Liturgie, 87–94.
Thomas, D. Winton
  "A Note on מֻעָדִים in Jeremiah 24,1," *JTS* NS 3
  (1952) 55.

24

1 《Thus》[a] Yahweh showed me: there were
two baskets of figs arranged in front of
the temple of Yahweh [after Nebuchadrezzar king of Babylon exiled Jeconiah
son of Jehoiakim king of Judah, and the
officials of Judah, and the craftsmen and
the smiths, and brought them to
Babylon.][b] 2/ One basket (had) very good
figs, like the early figs, but the other
basket (had) very bad figs, so bad that
they could not be eaten. 3/ And Yahweh
said to me, What do you see, Jeremiah?
And I said, Figs, the good figs very good
ones, but the bad figs so bad that they
cannot be eaten. 4/ And the word of
Yahweh came to me as follows: 5/ [Thus
Yahweh, the God of Israel, has said,][a]
Like these good figs, so I shall consider
the exiles of Judah, [whom I sent away
from this place to the land of the Chaldeans,][b] for good; 6/ and I shall set [a]my
eye[a] upon them for good, and I shall bring
them back onto this land, and I shall build
them and not overthrow, I shall plant them
and not uproot. 7/ And I shall give them a
heart to know me, [that I am Yahweh][a]
and they shall be a people to me, and I
shall be God to them, [for they shall turn
back to me with all their heart.][b] 8/ But
like the bad figs which are so bad that
they cannot be eaten, [for thus Yahweh
has said,][a] so I shall designate Zedekiah
king of Judah, and his officials, and the
remnant of Jerusalem [who remain in

Text

1a   Inserting כֹּה with Duhm on the analogy of Amos
      7:1, 4, 7; 8:1; the word could easily have dropped
      out by haplography with the last word of 23:40. The
      bare verb begins the passage abruptly.
 b   The long historical note is a redactional insertion;
      like 29:2 it is adapted from 2 Kgs 24:15–16 (so also
      Volz, Rudolph, and so Niditch, *Symbolic Vision*, 53,
      54, 56, 60–61); see Interpretation.
5a   Secondary expansion (so also Volz, Rudolph, and
      so also Niditch, *Symbolic Vision*, 53, 57, 59); see Inter-
      pretation.
 b   Omit as a gloss; the clause interrupts the syntactic
      flow: see Niditch, *Symbolic Vision*, 53, 60.
6a—a A few MSS. and *G* and *V* vocalize עֵינַי "my eyes."
7a   Secondary expansion (so also Volz); see Interpre-
      tation.
 b   Secondary expansion; the clause is introduced by
      כִּי and appears elaborative: so Niditch, *Symbolic*
      Vision, 53, 60.
8a   Secondary expansion (so also Volz, Rudolph, and
      so Niditch, *Symbolic Vision*, 53, 57, 59); see Interpre-
      tation.

this land,]b [and those dwelling in the
land of Egypt,]c 《 for evil. 》d 9/ And I shall
make them a terrora [. . .]b to all the
kingdoms of the earth, a reproach and a
byword, a taunt and an object of contempt [in all the places where I shall
chase them.]c 10/ And I shall send
against them sword, famine and pestilence, until they are destroyed off the soil
which I gave to them 〉and to their
fathers.〈a

b   Secondary expansion: so Niditch, *Symbolic Vision*,
    54, 60.
c   Secondary expansion (so also Volz, and so
    Niditch, *Symbolic Vision*, 54, 61); see Interpretation.
d   Transferring this phrase from its present place in
    v 9 to the end of v 8: compare the balancing phrase
    at the end of v 5. The phrase is lacking in *G*. The
    restoration in v 8 is the suggestion of Volz, and
    Rudolph offers it as a possibility.
9a See 15:4, Text.
b   See 8d.
c   Omit the bracketed words with Volz and
    Rudolph; the passage deals with those who stay in
    Jerusalem (v 10). See Interpretation.
10a *G* omits, and Janzen, p. 44, and Niditch, *Symbolic
    Vision*, 54, 59, omit as an expansion; but "you/them
    and your/their fathers" occurs repeatedly in authen-
    tic material (see Interpretation).

Preliminary Observations

This passage has elicited the most varied judgments from commentators. On the one hand stand those like Duhm and Herbert G. May,[1] who place the passage quite late— May compares it with the exclusivism of Ezra—and those like Hyatt and Nicholson, who attribute it wholly to exilic Deuteronomistic redaction (Hyatt: "We must conclude that this chapter is of Deuteronomic origin [ca. 550 B.C.E.] and wholly a literary product, not a true account of a vision experienced by Jeremiah, for it does not represent his own thought").[2] By this view it is a piece of propaganda to uphold the claims of the Baby-lonian exiles. On the other hand stand those like Rudolph who defend its authenticity ("A prophecy after the fact it not at issue here").[3] Bright has a moderate opinion: "[It] may be assumed to derive—with some verbal expansion in the course of transmission—from Jeremiah's own reminiscences."[4] Difficulties with the passage arise on two counts. First, the passage is verbose, and some at least of its wording suggests the kind of redaction attributed to a Deuteronomist. Second, at several points the message seems to diverge from what we know of Jrm's point of view.

The most basic question should be posed first: How likely are we to have a pseudepigraphic vision report in the book? A sermon on the sabbath (17:19–27) or prophetic torah (23:34–40) is one thing, but an autobio-graphical vision report is surely less likely.

It is clear that the passage could have served those in exile and those who came home from exile to encourage that segment of the population, but that obvious fact does not necessarily imply that the passage was a creation *de novo* of that community.

It is true, the passage is verbose, but a careful scrutiny, phrase by phrase, will indicate where expansions have been made (the discernment of Volz is correct, in my opinion, in all but one instance); see Text. If the text has undergone much expansion, that fact in itself is evidence that the passage was an important one to the exilic and postexilic community. When these expansions are trimmed away, however, what remains is structured prose in which vv 5–7 match vv 8–10 with fair exactitude (see Structure and Form). The way is then open to assess the authenticity of the original form of the passage (for which see Setting).

1   Herbert G. May, "Towards an Objective Approach
    to the Book of Jeremiah: The Biographer," *JBL* 61
    (1942) 148–49.
2   Hyatt, p. 998.
3   "Ein vaticinium ex eventu liegt hier keineswegs
    nahe": Rudolph, p. 158.
4   Bright, p. 194.

Structure and Form

It is conceivable that this passage originally followed 22:30. The focus of 22:24–27 is Jehoiachin and his mother, and that of 22:28–30 is Jehoiachin and his sons. This passage, dealing with the ultimate fate of the other members of the first deportation, could logically follow. If this is the case, then 23:1–4; 23:5–6 and the collection on the false prophets in 23:9–40 would have been inserted in such a way as to separate the present passage from its original association.

The internal structure of the passage is a function of its form. It is a more elaborate example of a vision report than either 1:11–12 or 1:13–16. The segments of this form are set forth by Long:[5] (1) the announcement of the vision ("Thus Yahweh showed me"), (2) the transition (וְהִנֵּה), (3) the vision proper—(a) the image ("two baskets of figs arranged in front of the temple of Yahweh," plus all of v 2), (b) the question by Yahweh ("What do you see, Jeremiah?"), (c) the prophet's answer (the rest of v 3), and (d) the oracle of Yahweh (vv 4–10).

The oracle of Yahweh is extensive; since both the good figs and the bad figs need to be explicated, the oracle falls into two halves: after the introduction (v 4) the good figs are explained in vv 5–7 and the bad figs in vv 8–10. The two halves in general correspond: v 5 (ending with "for good") corresponds to v 8 (ending with "for evil" in the reconstructed text).

Setting

It is convenient to examine the arguments of May,[6] which are repeated by Hyatt; they state in the most extreme form the case against the authenticity of the passage to Jrm. He states that it is in the same characteristic style as that of the Sabbath passage (17:19–27) but gives no evidence of this, and as a matter of fact there are no phrases that are shared between them, and only the fact that they are both in prose is a link between them. His labeling of the reference to the Jews in the land of Egypt with "(sic!)" suggests that that inelegant phrase is evidence of late date; but the argumentation of the present study is that that phrase is a late insertion. May contrasts the point of view of the present passage, that Yahweh looks with favor on those who went into exile and looks with disfavor on those who stayed in Jerusalem, with the point of view of Jrm, that all citizens had sinned, both high and low, and there was no honest man, none that did justly (5:1–9). But the message of the present passage is not that the exiles were innocent and those who stay at home were guilty, but rather that Yahweh had positive plans for the exiles, and that those who stay at home should not feel superior; this is the crucial issue (see below). Finally May asserts that the point of view of the present passage toward Zedekiah does not square with Jrm's attitude elsewhere (34:1–5): in the latter passage Jrm says that Zedekiah will fall into the hand of Nebuchadrezzar but die peacefully. Admittedly there is a contrast, but it could be explained by the passage of several years between the time of the present passage and 587. The issue for the king in 587 was whether to surrender (38:18, 21); the promise to Zedekiah in 34:1–5 is predicated on surrender. The issue of the present passage, to repeat, is that those in Jerusalem, including Zedekiah, are not to feel superior to the exiles.

The basic question for authenticity is not whether the present passage could become propaganda for the exiled segment of the community (it most assuredly did) but whether the original form of the passage could have offered to the community at a given time an unconventional prophetic view that cut across popular notions; it is clear that it could. Calvin had the matter straight: "As God had delayed his punishment, they supposed that they had wholly escaped, especially as they had an uncle as a successor to their captive king. Hence, then, was their contempt of threatenings; hence was their greater liberty in sinning: they thought that God had taken vengeance on the exiles, and that they were saved as being the more excellent portion of the community." There are few startling turns of phrase in the passage which might encourage an attribution to Jrm, but the phrasing of vv 9–10, widely imitated in the prose of Jrm, may be distinctive here and thus copied subsequently; this is likely to be the case with the sequence "a reproach and a byword, a taunt and a curse," on which see Interpretation.

Given an attribution to Jrm, it is obviously impossible to establish whether the vision was of externally visible

---

5   Long, "Reports of Visions," 357.
6   See n. 1.

(photographable) baskets of figs or whether the vision was an inner experience of the prophet. Calvin and Naegelsbach assume it was a vision; Calvin: "It may have been that the Prophet was not allowed to move a step from his own house; and the vision may have been presented to him in the night, during thick darkness." Lindblom is convinced that they "were real baskets upon which the eyes of the prophet chanced to fall."[7] Bright concurs: "The present [vision] probably had a physical basis."[8] Rudolph, on the other hand, insists that there were no physical baskets: only the good figs were compared to early figs, and as for the bad figs, why should anyone offer inedible figs for an offering of first fruits? With this judgment the present study agrees; it should only be added that the extreme contrast of the two kinds of figs, and the simplicity of details, strongly suggest dream material.

A date for the passage must obviously fall within the reign of Zedekiah, but only indirect evidence suggests any greater precision. The immediate shock of the exile of Jehoiachin has passed (compare 22:28–30). The point of view on the exiles is the same as that expressed in Jrm's letter to the exiles (29:4–23), the date for which is evidently the summer of 594 (see there). The use of the verb "be destroyed" (תמם) and the expression "off one's soil" (מֵעַל־אֲדָמָה) occur in 27:8 and 10, Jrm's words to foreign kings involved in the conspiracy against Nebuchadrezzar, which again is to be dated to 594. The "bad figs" are mentioned again in 29:17, and if 29:16–20 is an authentic part of Jrm's letter to the exiles, as is argued in the present study (see chap. 29, Preliminary Observations), then again one is led to a setting in 594.

Interpretation

■ **1** For the spelling of דּוּדָאֵי ("baskets of") with an 'alep see GKC, sec. 93x. The participle translated "set down" (מוּעָדִים) is somewhat uncertain in derivation and meaning. Ostensibly it is the hop'al of יעד and so means something like "appointed"; the only other hop'al of this verb, again a participle, is in Ezek 21:21, where it apparently carries a similar meaning.[9] All the Versions here translate "set." Earlier commentators suggested emending the word to עֹמְדִים "standing" or מָעֳמָדִים

"placed." Thomas has proposed that the verb results from a metathesis of מוּדָעִים, hop'al of a verb ידע cognate with the Arabic *wada'a* "put down, deposit." But it seems better to stay with *M*; the translation "arranged" is that of Bright.

There is of course no way to determine whether the two baskets of figs were objectively present or whether one has to do with an inner vision; on this see Setting.

The words from "after Nebuchadrezzar" till the end of the verse interrupt the description of the image and are not only parenthetical but clearly an editorial insertion designed to explain the historical context in which this vision took place. The similar phraseology of 29:2 likewise breaks its context; both appear to be adaptations of 2 Kgs 24:15–16 (see Text).

The spelling here of Jehoiachin's name, "Jeconiah," יְכָנְיָהוּ, is unique in the OT, but the forms of the name vary greatly: beyond "Coniah" (כָּנְיָהוּ) in 22:24, 28, there are three other spellings in the book (see 27:20; 28:4; and 52:31) and further variations elsewhere in the OT.

For "craftsmen" (חָרָשׁ) see 10:3. The noun here (like the following one) is a collective singular, suggesting guilds.[10] The meaning of the companion group, translated here "smiths" (מַסְגֵּר), is uncertain. The Versions try variously to relate it to סגר "shut": *G* "prisoners," *V* "closers" (understood as "setters of gems"?), *T* "doorkeepers" (locksmiths?). By the sixteenth century scholars had suggested "smiths" for the word, matching "carpenters" as a rendering of "craftsmen" (so already Luther). This is likely, given the general semantic field; the Arabic *sajara* "fire up (a stove)" is a likely cognate. Niditch, noting that the group has court status, follows Driver in suggesting "goldsmiths."[11]

■ **2** For the syntax of a noun with article followed by "one" without article see Joüon, *Gramm.*, sec. 142m; for the syntax of a nominal clause the subject of which is the container, and the predicate of which is the thing contained, see Joüon, *Gramm.*, sec. 154e. The "early figs" (בַּכֻּרוֹת) are prized precisely because they appear early in the season. Fig trees bear two crops; the first, on the previous year's branches, appears even before the new leaves sprout, and ripens in late May or early June, while the second, on the new wood, ripens in August or

---

7   Lindblom, *Prophecy*, 140.
8   Bright, p. 140.
9   Zimmerli, *Ezekiel 1*, 431.

10 On this see Montgomery, *Kings*, 557, with bibliography.
11 Niditch, *Symbolic Vision*, 56.

September.[12] For the imagery of figs for Israel compare Hos 9:10, and see Setting on 2:1–3.

■ **5–7** The messenger formula at the beginning of v 5 should be deleted: a messenger formula is inappropriate in a vision report (compare 1:11, 13)—see Text.

By the reconstruction offered here, the phrase "for good" (לְטוֹבָה) is balanced by "for evil" (לְרָעָה) restored at the end of v 8, and the phrase "consider . . . for good" in v 5 is reinforced by "set my eye upon them for good" in v 6. These expressions, "for good" and/or "for evil," are combined elsewhere in the book by a variety of verbal phrases: "set my face" (21:10; 44:11), "bring my words to" (39:16), "watch over" (44:27), "my words shall stand over" (44:29), and the noun "plans" (29:11). Thus it is no surprise to find the verb "consider" (נכר hip'il) in v 5 with "for good," "set my eye upon them" (שַׂמְתִּי עֵינִי עֲלֵיהֶם) in v 6 with "for good," and "designate" (נתן, literally "give") with "for evil" in the restoration of v 8. The idiom is an old one (Gen 50:20, E); the expression here appears to be a deliberate reversal of Amos 9:4, "And I will set my eyes upon them for evil and not for good."[13]

The noun in v 5 translated "exiles" (גָּלוּת) is an abstract noun meaning "deportation," used here (as often) as a collective. (For the vocalization of the construct noun see Bauer-Leander, sec. 76i.)

Though Jrm is clear that the deportation is not accidental, but the will of Yahweh (16:13; 22:24–26), the clause in v 5, "whom I sent away from this place to the land of the Chaldeans," is probably a gloss (see Text).

For "bring back" (שׁוב hip'il) from exile (v 6) compare 23:3.

The four verbs involved in "I shall build them and not overthrow, I shall plant them and not uproot" are a reflection of the original four verbs in the call narrative in 1:10 (see there), with "overthrow" (הרס) substituted for the harsher "demolish" (נתץ). The array of four verbs occurring in the present passage is also to be found in 18:7–9, part of the explanation of the symbolic activity of the potter (the fifth verb there is an expansive intrusion); in 31:28, which is evidently the (genuine) end of the scroll of hope (see there); in 42:10, part of the word to Johanan the son of Kareah; and in 45:4, part of the word to Baruch. In each of these passages the verbs are applied in fresh ways. (In addition the verbs appear in secondary material in 12:15–17.)[14] For the theme of "building" and "planting" on the land see in addition 32:15.

There is no parallel in the OT for the phrase "I shall give [נתן] them a heart to know me" (v 7). The only other instance in Jer of נתן with לְבָב/לֵב as object is 32:39, "I will give them one heart . . . that they may fear me." With God as subject and "one heart" as object, the wording is found in Ezek 11:19; 36:26; and 2 Chr 30:12. The only other comparable passages are 1 Kgs 3:9, 12, part of the narrative of Solomon's dream, "Give your servant an understanding mind to judge [לֵב שֹׁמֵעַ לִשְׁפֹּט] your people," doubtless part of the pre-Deuteronomistic material in the chapter,[15] and Deut 29:3, "Yahweh has not given you a mind to understand [לֵב לָדַעַת]" (without an object for "understand").

The presence of "know me [= Yahweh]" and of the covenantal formula "and they shall be a people to me, and I shall be God to them" here is reminiscent of the same two phrases in the new covenant passage, 31:33–34, and the fact that that passage, which the present study accepts as authentic (see Preliminary Observations, Structure, Setting there), affirms that Yahweh will write his law on the "heart" of the people, suggests in turn that the slightly different phrase here is likely diction appropriate to Jrm. The term "heart," as always, covers a wide range of meaning: *NJV* has "mind," and Bright has "will." Since "knowing" Yahweh involves serving him and doing his will, and the "heart" is the center of decision making, "will" is a good translation.

The bracketed words "that I am Yahweh" are a later addition to the text. The phrase appears otherwise in the book only in 9:23 (there also following "know me"), and that passage, too, is evidently late (see there). The phrase is common in P, H, and Ezekiel. If the "heart to know me" implies the will, then the bracketed phrase moves the diction in a different direction. An argument from silence is furthermore that the phrase is not found in 31:33–34.

The covenantal formula "and they shall be a people to me, and I shall be God to them" and its variations is found seven times in the book: beyond the present pas-

---

12 Post, *Flora*, II, 515.
13 Compare Holladay, "Prototype," 364.
14 Compare ibid., 363–64.

15 Montgomery, *Kings*, 108; Noth, *Könige*, 44–46.

sage and 31:33, it occurs in three further passages here deemed authentic, 7:23; 11:4; and 31:1; in addition it occurs in two passages which are redactional, 30:22 and 32:38. For the background of the expression see 7:23.

The last clause of v 7 must again be bracketed, "for they shall turn back to me with all their heart." This phrase is found in the book only otherwise in 3:10, part of a late midrash; and outside the book only in Deut 30:10, part of the late frame of that book,[16] in 1 Kgs 8:48, part of the exilic Deuteronomistic redaction of that book,[17] and in 2 Kgs 23:25, the judgment on Josiah. Whatever the date of the judgment on Josiah, the generalization to Judah appears late here. (Again, as in the phrase "that I am Yahweh," the clause in question does not resemble anything in 31:33–34.)

■ **8–10** For the parallel of v 8 to v 5, see above on vv 5–7; it was there implied that the verb "designate" (נתן, literally "give") does not otherwise appear with the phrases "for good" or "for evil," but the verb does mean "designate" elsewhere (Num 35:6).

The phrase "for thus Yahweh has said" in v 8 is even less appropriate than is the similar formula in v 5, since it here interrupts the comparison.

Those who were not exiled will not see Yahweh's positive work. The division into the king, his officials, and the remainder of the people is a natural threefold one (compare the diction of 36:31). This consideration leads to the question whether the closing phrase of v 8, "and those dwelling in the land of Egypt," belongs to the original text. Volz deletes it, but Bright defends it on historical grounds—there were doubtless Jews in Egypt who had fled there after Jehoiakim shifted his loyalty from Egypt to Babylon. But that is not the point: the rhetoric here indicates that the phrase is a later expansion (so also Niditch);[18] 44:27 suggests the impulse for its inclusion here.

The material in v 9 is a problem; some if not all of the material is secondary. The last phrase, "in all the places where I shall chase them," is clearly a late insertion (so

Volz and Rudolph): the point of the judgment of those in Jerusalem is that they will have remained in Jerusalem, not be exiled. The phrase is found otherwise in 8:3, a late passage, and in 16:15 = 23:8—in 23:8 the phrase is an insertion, and 16:15 is a secondary reflex of 23:8. Volz, however, further excises "a reproach and a byword, a taunt and an object of contempt," and Niditch[19] excises the whole of v 9. The matter calls for careful examination.

Let us first deal with the listing, "a reproach and a byword, a taunt and an object of contempt." This is the only passage in the book in which the words here translated "byword" (מָשָׁל) and "taunt" (שְׁנִינָה) occur; these two words occur in the same context of obloquy on Judah in three passages outside Jer—Deut 28:37; 1 Kgs 9:7; and 2 Chr 7:20. The Chronicles passage is dependent on the one in Kings. Deut 28:37 is part of the expansion of the curses, not part of the original list, and can be assumed to be exilic;[20] the passage in which 1 Kgs 9:7 is found, namely vv 1–9 there, is Deuteronomic,[21] likely to be part of a second Deuteronomic editing in the exilic period (vv 6–9).[22] One may conclude at this point then either that the words are original to Jrm in this passage, and the other three passages are imitative of it, or else that the words here are part of exilic or postexilic redaction.

Now beyond the use of these two words are ten other passages in the prose of Jer in which two or more words signifying obloquy on Judah are used in diction comparable to the phrase here: 19:8; 25:9, 11, 18; 29:18; 42:18; 44:6, 8, 12, 22; and there are in the prose at least three more passages where a single word appears in such a context: 7:34; 22:5; 26:6. There are two passages in the foreign nations oracles where two or more of such words are used to signify obloquy (on Edom: 43:13, 17); and there are scattered passages in the foreign nations oracles where the single word "desolation" (שַׁמָּה) occurs in such a context. There are two passages of poetry in which "desolation" (שַׁמָּה) is used for Judah (2:15; 4:17),

---

16   Von Rad, *Deuteronomy*, 183; Mayes, *Deuteronomy*, 367, 370.

17   Gray, *Kings*, 226; Noth, *Könige*, 188.

18   Niditch, *Symbolic Vision*, 61.

19   Ibid., 61–62.

20   Von Rad, *Deuteronomy*, 175; Mayes, *Deuteronomy*, 350–51.

21   Gray, *Kings*, 235–36; Noth, *Könige*, 196.

22   See Norman H. Snaith, "Introduction and Exegesis of the First and Second Books of Kings," *IB* 3:91–92.

and two passages in which pairs of words such as those appearing in the listing form appear in parallelism, once regarding Judah (18:16), once regarding Jrm himself (20:8). Outside the Book of Jer the listing of words for obloquy occur (beyond Deut 28:37; 1 Kgs 9:7; and 1 Chr 7:20; already discussed) in several passages: 2 Kgs 22:19 (the word from Huldah the prophetess), Mic 6:16 (evidently redactional),[23] Pss 44:14–15 and 79:4 (hardly datable) and 2 Chr 29:8 (late). One may then conclude that given the stimulus in the Psalms and perhaps the wording of Huldah's oracle, Jrm used such diction in his poetry and could have employed this series of words here. But there is one more step in analysis of the data. In 15:4 one finds "and I shall make them a terror to all the kingdoms of the earth," and that wording occurs also in 34:17; in neither of these passages does the "listing" idiom follow. The "listing" idiom does follow "and I shall make them a terror to all the kingdoms of the earth" here, and it does in 29:18. The vote then is two passages with the listing and two passages without. The cautious approach would then be to accept the words here as authentic and to reject Volz's excision of them.[24] Niditch's rejection of the whole of v 9 appears subjective, and by the analysis here presented is not to be accepted.

For "reproach" (חֶרְפָּה) see 6:10. The term translated "byword" (מָשָׁל) is a term for a proverb or other pithy saying;[25] here of course the meaning is transferred to refer to a people whose ruin will make them "proverbial." "Taunt" (שְׁנִינָה) appears in the OT only in the four passages along with "byword" already cited: it evidently denotes a "sharp" word (שׁנן, "sharpen"). "Object of contempt" (קְלָלָה) is a noun normally translated "curse." But the related verb means "be light, swift," and it is clear here that the issue is not "cursing" a scattered people, or the ruins of cities (25:18): they are the object of ridicule or contempt, an important consideration in a society concerned with honor and shame—*NEB* here translates "a thing of ridicule" (compare the discussion of the related verb in 15:10).

For a discussion of the triad "sword, famine and pestilence" (v 10) see 14:11–12. The triad is the object of "send" (שׁלח pi'el, that is, "send out"), however, only here in the book and in the imitative 29:17, but the verb appears with "famine" (דֶּבֶר) in earlier material (Amos 4:10). There is no parallel in the book for the expression "until they are destroyed [תמם] off the land . . ."; the closest is perhaps 14:15, "by sword and by famine those prophets shall perish [תמם]." For the motif of destruction "off the land [הָאֲדָמָה]" compare 12:14. The theme of "the land which I gave to you and to your fathers" recurs repeatedly: compare "place which I gave to you and your fathers" in 7:7, 14, and "inheritance which I gave to your fathers" in 17:4. The theme likewise appears in poetry ("and I brought you into the garden land," 2:7). "And to their fathers" may be an expansion here, but there is no way to be sure (see Text).

Aim

Yahweh has a future for his people; there will be continuity. But paradoxically that continuity will not be through those who carry on the normal activities of life in Jerusalem: the continuity will be through those whom he has sent out into the unknown to a faraway land. There will be a time when they will return to take up life again on the land as those who stayed behind will be unable to do: but those who return will not simply replicate the past—they will be given a new heart, so that in a basic sense it will be a new start, and in that new start the covenant will be secure.[26] The message thus anticipates that of the new covenant (31:31–34). It also reflects in a wide arena all the transvaluations of conventional assumptions through which God in the biblical record accomplishes his purpose. God was with Abraham, who was sent out to a strange land, and not with Abraham's father's house; and the NT will affirm that God will not be with those who worship either on Mount Gerizim or in Jerusalem (John 4:21) but with those who go and make disciples of all nations (Matt 28:19).

23 See Mays, *Micah*, 148–49; Wolff, *Micha*, 159, 161, 163, 171–72.

24 For further treatments of the "listing" idiom see Weinfeld, *Deuteronomy*, 348–49, nos. 20 and 21; and Weippert, *Prosareden*, 187–89.

25 See in general Sheldon H. Blank, "Proverb," *IDB* 3:934–36, and in more detail Eissfeldt, *Introduction*, 81–87.

26 Von Rad, *Old Testament Theology 2*, 211–12.

Bibliography

On chapter 25 and chapters 46—51:
Rietzschel
    Urrolle, 25–90.

On 25:1–38:
Christensen
    Transformations, 193–203.

On 25:1–14:
On "Nebuchadrezzar my servant":
Lemke, Werner E.
    "'Nebuchadrezzar, my Servant,'" *CBQ* 28 (1966)
    45–50.
Schenker, Adrian
    "Nebukadnezzars Metamorphose—vom Unter-
    jocher zum Gottesknecht," *RB* 89 (1982) 498–529,
    esp. 518–19.
Zevit, Ziony
    "The Use of עֶבֶד as a Diplomatic Term in
    Jeremiah," *JBL* 88 (1969) 74–77.
On "seventy years":
Ackroyd, Peter R.
    "Two Old Testament Historical Problems of the
    Early Persian Period," *JNES* 17 (1958) 23–27.
Borger, Riekele
    "An Additional Remark on P. R. Ackroyd, *JNES*
    XVII, 23–27," *JNES* 18 (1959) 74.
Fishbane
    "Revelation and Tradition," 356–59.
Luckenbill, Daniel D.
    "The Black Stone of Esarhaddon," *AJSL* 41 (1924–
    25) 167.
Orr, Avigdor
    "The Seventy Years of Babylon," *VT* 6 (1956)
    304–6.
Plöger, Otto
    "'Siebzig Jahre,'" *Festschrift, Friedrich Baumgärtel
    zum 70. Geburtstag* (ed. Johannes Hermann;
    Erlangen: Universitätsbund Erlangen, 1959) 124–
    30 = *Aus der Spätzeit des Alten Testaments* (Göt-
    tingen: Vandenhoeck & Ruprecht, 1971) 67–74.
Vogt, Ernst
    "70 anni exsilii," *Bib* 38 (1957) 236.
Whitley, Charles F.
    "The Term Seventy Years Captivity," *VT* 4 (1954)
    60–72.
Whitley, Charles F.
    "The Seventy Years Desolation—A Rejoinder,"
    VT 7 (1957) 416–18.

1 The word which came to Jeremiah concerning all the people of Judah in the fourth year of Jehoiakim son of Josiah, king of Judah, [it was the first year of Nebuchadrezzar king of Babylon,]ᵃ 2/ which he [*M*: Jeremiah the prophet]ᵃ spoke against all the people of Judah and to [all]ᵇ the inhabitants of Jerusalem, as follows: 3/ From the thirteenth year of Josiah son of Amon, king of Judah, to this day—that is, twenty-three years—[the word of Yahweh has come to me,]ᵃ I have spoken to you earlyᵇ and constantly, [but you would not listen,]ᶜ 4/ ᵃ《 and I have sent 》[*M*: and Yahweh has sent]ᵃ to you [all]ᵇ ᶜ《 my servants 》[*M*: his servants]ᶜ the prophets early and constantly, but you have not listened nor turned your ear, [to hear]ᵈ 5/ as follows: "Return, each from his evil way and from the evil of your doings, and remain on the soil which ᵃ《 I have given 》[*M*: Yahweh has given]ᵃ to you and to your fathers, from of old, for ever, 6/ and do not walk after other gods, to serve them and worship them, [and you shall not offend me with the workᵇ of your hands, and I shall do you no hurt]ᵃ 7/ [. . .]ᵃ ᵇ so as not to offend meᵇ with the workᶜ of your hands, to your own hurt, 《 but you have not listened, oracle of Yahweh." 》ᵃ 8/ Therefore thus Yahweh of hosts has said: Because you have not listened to my words, 9/ I am going to send and take [all]ᵃ the tribes of the north, [oracle of Yahweh, and Nebuchadrezzar king of Babylon my servant,]ᵇ and I shall bring them in against this land and against its inhabitants, [and against all these nations around,]ᶜ and shall dedicate them to destruction and shall make them a desolation, a hissing and everlasting

Text

1a Omit with *G*; so Duhm, Giesebrecht, Cornill; so Janzen, p. 100.

2a Omit with *G*; so Duhm, Giesebrecht, Cornill. This gloss evidently arose after the phrase referring to Nebuchadrezzar had been inserted in v 1.

b Omit with *G*; see Janzen, p. 66.

3a Yahweh speaks in the first person in vv 3–5 (so *G*: see Structure and Setting, and Interpretation). This harmonizing gloss is lacking in *G* and is to be omitted; so Duhm, Giesebrecht, Cornill. See the discussion in Janzen, p. 100.

b Reading הַשְׁכֵּם with many MSS. for *M* אַשְׁכִּים, the latter evidently an Aramaizing *lapsus calami* (though Rudolph explains it otherwise).

c Omit with *G*; so Duhm, Giesebrecht, Cornill; so Janzen, p. 44.

4a—a Reading וָאֶשְׁלַח with *G*: Yahweh speaks in the first person; so Janzen, p. 100.

b Omit with *G* as an expansionist gloss (compare note 2b).

c—c Reading עֲבָדַי with *G* (compare note a); so Janzen, p. 100.

d Omit with *G*; so Cornill.

5a—a Reading נָתַתִּי with *G* (compare notes 4a and c); so Janzen, p. 100.

6a *M* of vv 6–7 contains a doublet reading, while *G* contains only a single reading. The reading with "to your own hurt" is the earlier (compare 7:6, and see Interpretation). Thus one should omit in v 6 the *M* reading "and you shall not offend me with the work of your hands, and I shall do you no hurt," and move "but you have not listened, oracle of Yahweh" to the end of v 7 as *G* has it. On the whole matter see Janzen, p. 13.

b *G*, *V*, and *T* read "works"; compare 1:16.

7a—a See 6a.

b—b The *G* reading ὅπως μὴ παροργίζετέ με presupposes either וְלֹא־תַכְעִיסוּ אוֹתִי, the first reading in *M*, understood as a final clause, "so that you do not offend me," or else לְמַעַן תַּכְעִסוּנִי, a variant of the second *M* reading. The *M* qere' is "so as to offend me," and *M* ketib appears to presuppose an aberrant perfect verb (לְמַעַן הִכְעִסוּנִי, presumably "so that they offended me")—but is this an erroneous mixed form? Janzen's explanation is by no means clear (pp. 13 and 194 n. 11). *G* and the two traditions in *M* indicate variant text traditions!

c *G*, *V*, and *T* read "works"; see note 6b.

9a Omit with *G* (compare note 2c).

b Omit with *G*; so Duhm, Giesebrecht, Cornill, Condamin. The phrase "Nebuchadrezzar king of Babylon my servant" is an expansion from the *M* text of 27:6, which see (so also Werner E. Lemke, "'Nebuchadrezzar, my Servant,'" *CBQ* 28 [1966] 45–50). Janzen, p. 44, does not offer the best solution.

c Though the phrase is present in *G* as well as in *M*, it is an expansion based on vv 15–38 and does not

《reproach.》[d] 10/ And I shall extinguish from them the sound of joy and the sound of gladness, the voice of the bridegroom and the voice of the bride, the sound of millstones and the light of the lamp. 11/ And all the [M: this][a] land shall become [a ruin,][b] a desolation; and they shall serve [c]《among the nations》[M: and these nations shall serve the king of Babylon][c] seventy years. [12/ And at the completion of seventy years I shall deal with {the king of Babylon and}[b] that nation, {oracle of Yahweh, their iniquity and the land of the Chaldeans,}[b] and I shall make it[c] an everlasting horror.][a] 13/ [a]And I shall bring[a] upon the [M and G: that][b] land all my words which I have spoken against it, which are written in this book [which Jeremiah prophesied against the nations.][c] [14/ For many nations and great kings shall make slaves of them, and I shall recompense them according to their deed and according to the work[b] of their hands.][a]

belong in a judgment on Judah (v 1) (so Rudolph).

d   Reading with *G* וּלְחׇרְפׇּת for *M* וּלְחׇרְבוֹת; the inhabitants can hardly become rubble. The same three nouns are found in 29:18. So also Duhm, Cornill, Volz, Rudolph, Bright.

11a   Omitting הַזֹּאת with *G*; it is a gloss from v 9. So also Cornill, Rudolph, Bright, and so Janzen, p. 45.

b   Omitting with *G*; so also Cornill, Volz, Rudolph. The two nouns are not linked by "and," and the bracketed noun seems to be a gloss from v 18 (so Janzen, p. 45).

c—c   Reading בַּגּוֹיִם הַגּוֹיִם הׇאֵלֶּה אֶת־מֶלֶךְ with *G* for *M* הַגּוֹיִם הׇאֵלֶּה אֶת־מֶלֶךְ בׇּבֶל. Clearly "among the nations" is a periphrasis for for Babylonian exile (compare 4:16). It is conceivable that *M* arose in several stages: "the king of Babylon" (אֶת־מֶלֶךְ בׇּבֶל) could have been added as a gloss (compare the proposal in 15:11 to understand "the enemy" as a gloss, or compare "king of Assyria" in Isa 7:17). Then "among the nations" (בַּגּוֹיִם) could have been "corrected" or rewritten as "the nations" or "these nations." The latter change of course shifts the reference to all the nations around Judah (v 9).

12a   The whole verse is redactional; v 12a is derived from 29:10, and 12b from 51:26 and 62 (so Duhm, Giesebrecht, Cornill, Volz, Rudolph, Bright). A reference to the punishment of Babylon would not have been germane to the second scroll.

b   These phrases are not in *G* and represent further expansions. Note that "their iniquity" is carelessly introduced by אֶת־.

c   *M* אֹתוֹ presupposes a reference to "that nation"; an emendation to אֹתׇהּ to refer to "land" (so Rudolph) is not called for.

13a—a   The ketib is erroneously written, והבאיתי for והביאתי.

b   Deleting הַהִיא. The problem is analogous to that in v 11 (note a), except that the qualifier is present in *G* as well as *M*, because the shift to a reference to Babylon (the skeleton of v 12) was present in *G*. See Interpretation. (Compare Rudolph, who emends "that" to "this.")

c   The bracketed words are to be omitted. *G* at this point uses such words to introduce the oracle on Elam (*G* 25:14: "Jeremiah prophesied against the nations of Elam"). The words probably originated as a general title for the oracles against the nations (compare *M* 46:1). So Rudolph (Bright: "probably").

14a   Omit the verse with *G* (so also Duhm, Giesebrecht, Cornill, Rudolph, Bright; so Janzen, p. 122). Verse 14a is parallel with 27:7b: either the half-verse here was taken from 27:7b (so most), or else both passages arose from the same expansionist process (so Janzen, p. 122; compare 101–3). Verse 14b is similar to 50:29.

b   *G*, *V*, and *T* read "works"; compare v 6, note b.

Structure and Setting

Analysis of this passage presents great difficulty; the contrast between *G* and *M* for these verses and the rhetoric of both forms of text make it clear that the passage has undergone much redactional activity.

In *G* vv 15–38 are separated from the first portion of the chapter by the whole bulk of the foreign nations oracles, a circumstance causing a contrast in the numeration of chapters in the two texts from this point onward. This circumstance, and the fact that the contents of vv 15–38 (in general, the theme of the "cup of wrath") are separate from the theme of vv 1–14, make it necessary to examine vv 15–38 apart from vv 1–14.

Should vv 1–14 be examined as a whole, or divided? Some commentators separate vv 12–14 from vv 1–11 (for example Naegelsbach in the nineteenth century, Claus Rietzschel[1] recently). *M* of v 13 reads "that land," and in the context of *M* the reference is to Babylon. Rietzschel concludes[2] that "this book" must then have reference to Babylon, and that therefore the "book" must have been the oracles against Babylon, part of the oracles against foreign nations that follow in *G*. Most commentators reject this line of thinking, however. The superscription (v 1), which corresponds to the date of the dictation of the first scroll (36:1), suggests that "this book" in v 13 refers to that scroll, or to the second scroll (36:32). If that is true, then v 13 is brought into the orbit of what precedes in the chapter, and the passage may be understood as a conclusion of one or both scrolls rather than (in part) an introduction to something new. This is the case whether one believes that the present passage (in an earlier recension) is the authentic close of the scroll(s) (so Weiser, Bright, Thompson) or whether one believes that the passage is simply intended by an exilic redactor to be an appropriate close for the scroll(s) (that is, that it is the product of a "Deuteronomistic redactor," so Hyatt, Nicholson[3]). In either event vv 1–14 are taken as a unit.

The *G* text of the passage is appreciably shorter than that of *M*. To critical scholars at the beginning of this century (notably Duhm, Giesebrecht, and Cornill) it seemed clear that the plusses in *M* were redactional: many plusses mention Babylon, or become more specific in naming Nebuchadrezzar. In general, then, these scholars accepted *G* as the more original form of text. More recently scholars have admitted that the passage has been much reworked but have hesitated to specify the stages (so Rudolph, Bright); in part this hesitation has been encouraged by the complicated and not always convincing argumentation of Rietzschel on the origin of the passage. But more recently the pendulum has swung again. Thus Michael A. Fishbane has noted how *M* represents a redaction specifying the identity of the foe from the north;[4] Janzen has called attention to the fact that the wording of *G* in vv 3–5, by which Yahweh is the speaker, is the original wording, while *M* in these verses, by which Jrm is the speaker, represents a later redaction[5]—this detail of the identity of the speaker in these three verses was unnoticed by Duhm, Giesebrecht, and Cornill. When the text of the passage is examined and clear redactional elements are eliminated (most among them being the plusses in *M*), a text remains (hereafter called the "basic text") that interweaves diction appropriate to the first scroll and diction appropriate to the second scroll. When in turn the phrases appropriate to the second scroll are removed, what remains is rhetorically intact. This circumstance suggests that there is available a "first-scroll recension" and a "second-scroll recension," both authentic to Jrm, but the validation of this conclusion must be based upon a close examination of the evidence. (For the text of the "first-scroll recension," see after the present section, Structure and Setting.)

It must be noted in the first instance that *G*, in avoiding references to Babylon, to the Chaldeans, or to Nebuchadrezzar, reflects Jrm's own reluctance in the matter. One has only to recall 1:15, the poetic references to the foe in 4:6; 5:15–16; 6:22–23; and elsewhere, or the elaborate descriptions of battle in 14:11—15:9 and elsewhere, to recognize that reluctance, which has given rise to much speculation on the identity of that foe. In 20:6 we can be reasonably sure of Jrm's mention of Babylon, and then there is material in chapters 27—29 which mention Babylon, but the latter are to be dated to 594. One cannot be sure of the motive for this reluctance, but that fact that *G* reflects it should encourage the conclusion that one is in touch with Jrm's own words

1   Rietzschel, *Urrolle*, 33.
2   Ibid., 40–42.
3   Nicholson, *Jer. 1—25*, 209.
4   Fishbane, "Revelation and Tradition," 356.
5   Janzen, p. 100.

in the text of *G*. And Janzen's observation regarding vv 3–5 points in the same direction: he observes that the idiom of הַשְׁכֵּם with another infinitive (translated "speak [or send or the like] early and constantly") occurs ten times otherwise in *M* of the OT, always otherwise with Yahweh as subject (Jer 7:13, 25; 11:7; 26:5; 29:19; 32:33; 35:14, 15; 44:4; 2 Chr 36:15); only here (in *M* of v 3) is it used with Jrm as subject.[6] This datum suggests strongly that *G* of v 3 (by which Yahweh is the subject) is to be preferred.

In general, then, the basic text established here for the passage is that of *G*. The exceptions are as follows: (1) Though both *M* and *G* contain "and against all these nations around" in v 9, the phrase disturbs the preoccupation with Judah in the passage; as Rudolph points out, only Judah can be punished for the sin of Judah (v 8). The phrase seems to be an early addition based on vv 15–38. (2) Though both *M* and *G* contain v 12, that verse seems to be an addition looking forward to the suppression of the enemy once the time of exile is past (so almost all commentators). (3) In v 9 *G* reads "the tribe from the north" while *M* reads "the tribes of the north"; *M* is preferable (compare 1:15). (4) In v 10 *G* reads "the scent of ointment" against the preferable *M* "the sound of millstones" (see Interpretation). (5) In v 13 the demonstrative "that" must be excised (see Interpretation).

The plusses and alterations in *M* in contrast to the basic text are not all of a kind and doubtless represent several hands. Thus there is a series of changes in vv 1–5: first a synchronism in v 1, then a gloss in v 2 once the synchronism of v 1 was in place, then, on the basis of the gloss in v 2, the expansion "the word of Yahweh has come to me" in v 3, and therefore the alteration of verbs in vv 3–5 from the designation of Yahweh as speaker to that of Jrm as speaker.[7] In vv 6–7 the excess in *M* is evidence of a double text (see Text). There are expansions in vv 9 and 12 to specify "(Nebuchadrezzar) king of Babylon (my servant)" and "the land of the Chaldeans." Finally there are various expansions in vv 11–14 that are understandable in the exilic and postexilic periods: the shift in v 11 from the statement that Judah will serve among the nations to the statement that Judah and others shall serve the king of Babylon; an adaptation in v

13 of what seems to have been originally a title of the oracles against the nations; an expansion about the nations (v 14) drawn from elsewhere.

What remains (the basic text) is heavy with phraseology found elsewhere in the prose of the book, some of which, by the evidence of the present study, is authentic to Jrm, and some of which is redactional. To some degree, then, the evidence is ambiguous, so that the division of opinion among scholars for or against authenticity is understandable. There is here little of the striking diction or irony which is to be found, for example, in 7:3–12 or 11:1–14, and this datum weakens the argument for authenticity.

Nevertheless several matters point toward authenticity. First, the two added terms in v 10, "the sound of millstones and the light of the lamp," not found in the parallels in 7:34 and 16:9, are surprising, not at all what one expects of a redactor (see further Interpretation). The fivefold repetition of קוֹל "sound, voice" followed by a single occurrence of אוֹר "light" is comparable to the same phenomenon in 50:35–38, where the fivefold "sword" (חֶרֶב) is completed by the single occurrence of "drought" (חֹרֶב). This one detail by itself points strongly toward authenticity at least for v 10 and so by implication for the basic text of the entire passage.

Then there is the matter of the specificity of the notorious "seventy years" in v 11 (and its rather different use in 29:10: see there). Of course there is no reason why such a span of time could not be the invention of an exilic redactor. But both its specificity and the fact that in the course of time the span corresponded to no exact pair of dates tend to argue for authenticity. A redactor would be more likely to frame a *vaticinium ex eventu*.

There are several instances of striking word usage. Thus there is the word-play on "return" (שׁוּבוּ) and "remain" (שְׁבוּ) in v 5, noted by Volz and Rudolph. The verb "devote to destruction" (חרם hip'il, v 9), with Yahweh as subject, appears in the OT only here and in Isa 34:2, clearly a late passage[8] (the seeming instance in Isa 11:15 must either be emended with the Versions or referred to a second root חרם—so *HALAT*); the usage is then hardly the work of a redactor.

As already suggested, I propose that the basic text

---

6   This exception is noted also in BDB, 1014b, and by Joüon, *Gramm.*, sec. 123r, note 2.

7   See n. 5.

8   End of the sixth century: Wildberger, *Jesaja*, 1341.

interweaves diction appropriate to the first scroll with diction appropriate to the second scroll. Separating these is a risky procedure, particularly when so many of the phrases occur widely in the prose of the book. It is worth the attempt, however, to see what can be done.

The matter is clear for v 10: the parallels already cited (7:34; 16:9) both belong to second-scroll material (see Setting for each passage). It may be added that both 7:34 and 16:9 offer for "silence" the verb שבת hip'il (once as a perfect, once as a participle), while here in v 10 the corresponding verb ("extinguish") is אבד hip'il: that is to say, the diction here is not a carbon copy of 7:34 and 16:9.

Though the question is not so clear-cut for v 11, the prediction of "seventy years" fits the diction of sure punishment found in the second scroll more than the mode of warning found in the first scroll (compare the expression "a long time" in 29:28). The probability then is that v 11, like v 10, is part of the second-scroll recension.

The sequence "from the thirteenth year of Josiah son of Amon, king of Judah, to this day" + "I have spoken to you" (v 3) is appropriate to the first scroll (compare the narrative in 36:2 on the dictation of the first scroll, "from the day I spoke to you, from the days of Josiah until this day"). But the phrase "that is, twenty-three years" interrupts that rhetorical flow; it is surely an addition. Was it added at the time of the second scroll, to match "seventy years" in v 11, or was it added still later?

The phraseology of v 4 appears in 7:25–26 (second scroll). It also appears in 35:15 (the sermon about the Rechabites) and 44:4–5 (the sermon to the Jews in Egypt), in both of which passages the diction may be redactional. The components of the phrases in v 4 appear additionally. Thus "hear the words of my servants the prophets whom I send to you early and constantly" appears in 26:5: but that verse interrupts the flow between 26:4 and 6 and is redactional (so also Rudolph: see there). The other instance of the phrase (29:19) is to be dated to 594. "You/they have not heard nor turned your/their ear" occurs additionally in 11:8 (594), 17:23 (sermon on the sabbath, dated after Jrm's time), and 34:14 (narrative on the freeing of slaves, 588). There is

one more component, the idiom with הַשְׁכֵּם ("early and constantly"), which appears here not only in v 4 but in v 3 as well: the passages elsewhere in the book where the idiom appears have already been listed in the discussion above of the G text of vv 3–5. Apart from the sequence with "my servants the prophets" already discussed in this paragraph, the idiom appears in four passages: in 35:15 (see on 35:14 above); in 7:13, where it is redactional, being omitted in G there; in 11:7 (594); and in 32:33 (part of the redactional expansion, vv 28–35, on the buying of the field at Anathoth: see there). One may conclude that "early and constantly" in v 3 and the entirety of v 4 are additions appearing in the second scroll (or later).

The beginning of v 5, "Return each from your evil way and from the evil of your doings," occurs significantly in the narrative summary of the temple sermon (26:3) and in the narrative of the dictation of the first scroll (36:3, 7); couched as an appeal, then, the expression would seem to belong quintessentially to the first scroll. Of course one might argue that both the narrative of chapter 26 and that of chapter 36 were framed by a Deuteronomistic redactor (so Nicholson), but the wording of 26:4, 6 does not differ in intention from 7:3–12, and the contrast of purpose between the first scroll and the second scroll which chapter 36 sets forth,[9] a contrast reflected in rhetorically separable passages in the poetic sections, makes it plausible to use diction in these chapters also for the quest for authentic recensions in the present passage. The end of v 5, "and remain on the soil which I have given to you and to your fathers from of old, for ever," is synonymous with 7:7, again part of the first scroll: indeed the verb "and remain" here is relevant to the vocalization of the verb in 7:7 (see Text there), since the verb in 7:7 and the verb here in v 5 are synonyms, not identical (compare the use of synonymous verbs in 7:34 and 16:9 on the one hand and in v 10 here on the other, already discussed). In view of the word-play between "return" and "remain," already noted, v 5 may be attributed to the first scroll.

Two phrases in vv 6–7 are likewise from the first scroll: "do not walk after other gods" is one of the phrases in 7:6 (compare 7:9), and "to your own hurt" is

---

9   See "A Chronology of Jeremiah's Career."

likewise found in 7:6. But the remainder of the basic text there, "to serve them and worship them, so as not to offend me with the work of your hands" and "but you have not listened" are characteristic of the second scroll. Thus "to serve them and worship them" is found otherwise four times: 8:2 (a late midrash); 13:10 (in a redactional addition); 16:11 (dated here to 598); and 22:9 (the exilic period). "Offend me with the work of your hands" is comparable to 7:18 and 19 (second scroll); the sequence appears further in 44:3 and 8 (the sermon to the Jews in Egypt) and in two redactional passages, 11:17 and 32:29, 30, 32. "But you have not listened" is found consistently in second-scroll diction (so 7:13, the end of 36:31, and so the end of the redactional verse 26:5).

Verses 8–9 embody a divine judgment in diction similar to 7:13–15 (see there).

Verse 13 indicates that Yahweh will carry out all his threats; this is characteristic of the second scroll—see 36:31: in both passages one has the striking verb "bring in" (בוא hip'il) with "upon" (עַל).

At the beginning of the passage, v 1 is similar enough to 36:1 to be appropriate for the first scroll. The bulk of v 2, "which he spoke against all the people of Judah and the inhabitants of Jerusalem," appears to parallel and supplement v 1 oddly: there is no way to determine whether it, too, is an expansion for the second scroll, but the pairing of "inhabitants of Jerusalem and men of Judah" (the reverse of the normal order) in 36:31 suggests that the phrase here (with normal order but with the unique variant "people of Judah" for "men of Judah") is indeed an expansion to underline the destruction which is ahead (compare the expansions in 1:1–3).

The shorter text containing phraseology appropriate to the first scroll emerges as a coherent and persuasive utterance of Jrm's, a kind of generalization of the temple sermon which in prose sums up his message at the time (compare 36:1). Indeed if the conclusions of the present study are sound, there is nothing in the early chapters of Jer past 7:1–12 which was contained in the first scroll; therefore if the material here in the basic text appropriate for the first scroll closed off that scroll, these words would have followed directly on 7:1–12.

First-Scroll Recension

1/ The word which came to Jeremiah concerning all the people of Judah in the fourth year of Jehoiakim son of Josiah, king of Judah, 2/ as follows: 3/ From the thirteenth year of Josiah son of Amon, king of Judah, to this day, I have spoken to you 5/ as follows: Return each from his evil way and from the evil of your doings, and remain on the soil which I have given to you and to your fathers, from of old, for ever, 6/ and do not walk after other gods 7/ to your own hurt, oracle of Yahweh.

Form

The form of the components of the passage is easily established from parallel passages. Verses 1–2 embody the title for what follows (compare 1:1–3). The basic text of the balance of the passage reports the kind of parenetic appeal found in 7:3–12: an appeal for repentance followed (in v 8) by the statement of divine action consequent upon disobedience. The first-scroll recension is overlaid in the second-scroll recension by several expressions for the invincible disobedience of the people (for example in vv 4, 7) and for the punishment for disobedience (vv 8–11, 13); for the details compare Form for 7:1–15 and 11:1–17.

Interpretation

■ **1–2** The translation of the prepositions in these verses is not immediately clear. *M* has עַל before "Jeremiah" in v 1, though some MSS. give אֶל (compare 11:2 and 23:35); it is clear that the word is directed "to" Jrm. The translation of the occurrences of עַל before "all the people of Judah" in vv 1 and 2, however, will depend on one's understanding of the intention of each phrase. If the phrase in v 1 is a part of the recension identified with the first scroll, then "concerning" is appropriate, since that scroll was intended as warning (36:3); but if the phrase in v 2 is part of the recension identified with the second scroll, then "against" is appropriate, since the second scroll proclaims irrevocable destruction (36:30–31) (see further Structure and Setting).

■ **1** By the reckoning of the spring new year, assumed in the present study, the fourth year of Jehoiakim extended from March/April 605 to March/April 604. By that reckoning there is a difficulty in the synchronism with Nebuchadrezzar, since he assumed power in September

605^{10} and his accession year thus extended for the half year until the next Babylonian New Year's Day in March/April 604 and his "first" year will then have extended from March/April 604 to March/April 603. The problem is not only with this passage, but with the synchronisms in 32:1 and 52:12 as well; we evidently have to do with a redactor with a consistent understanding of chronology. The problem would be solved if one assumes an autumnal new year for Judah at this period, since there would then be an overlap of six months; but that reckoning brings other difficulties in its train.[11] One suggestion for the present passage is to see in the unique form of "first" here (הָרִאשֹׁנִית rather than הָרִאשֹׁנָה) the implication of "accession year," or else a corruption of the term for "accession year" (רֵאשִׁית, see 26:1).[12] If "accession year" were here corrupted to "first year," then the one-year errors in 32:1 and 52:12 might have followed.

■ **3–4** For the diction see 7:25–26.

■ **3** "The thirteenth year of Josiah" is the identical datum to that in 1:2 (see there), namely (by the reckoning of the new year in the spring) March/April 627 to March/April 626. As already noted, the fourth year of Jehoiakim would be from March/April 605 to March/April 604, only twenty-two years, so the gloss, "twenty-three years," is excessive by one year. One must assume either careless arithmetic (for example, Josiah "reigned thirty-one years," 2 Kgs 22:1, so that his reign included eighteen years of Jrm's life, plus one year until the first year of Jehoiakim, plus the four years of Jehoiakim—the problem being that Josiah did not fill out his thirty-first year) or else that what is intended is that Jrm is beginning his twenty-third year (so Naegelsbach).

■ **5** For the diction of v 5a, see 18:11. For the word-play between "return" and "remain" see Structure and Setting. For the diction of v 5b compare 7:7 (and, from a later setting, 23:8).

■ **6–7** For the diction see 13:10; 7:6; and 7:18.

■ **8** For the diction see 7:13.

■ **9** For the use of "tribes of the north" to refer to Babylon see 1:15. For the remarkable expression "my servant" for Nebuchadrezzar see the discussion in 27:6. The reference of the third-person plural suffix "them" shifts from "I shall bring them in" (that is, the tribes of the north) to "I shall dedicate them to destruction" (that is, this land and its inhabitants), but the context makes the shift clear. The verb "dedicate to destruction" (חרם hip'il) is not found otherwise in Jer, nor is its related noun חֵרֶם; and the usage here, with Yahweh as subject, is found only once otherwise in the OT (see Structure and Setting). The verb means to destroy, especially in war, something or someone excluded from normal private use.[13] The usage here may well be a reflection of Deut 13:16, where such destruction is decreed for an Israelite city which has resorted to idolatry. For "desolation and hissing" see 19:8; for "reproach" see 7:34.

■ **10** For the phraseology here, less the last two phrases, see 7:34 and 16:9.

For "sound of millstones" *G* curiously has "scent of ointment," which is clearly a less convincing reading (note that Rev 18:22 presupposes *M*). The "sound of millstones" and the "light of the lamp" are doubtless intended to signify the beginning and the end of the day, and thus all activity between (compare Weiser).[14] Cornill: "Since the supply of bread must be baked daily, the noise of the grinding of the hand-mill was to be heard wherever people dwelt and thus symbolizes the typical work and activity of daily life. Dead silence during the day, uninterrupted by any human sound, unearthly darkness during the night, unillumined by any gleam of a lamp—in its concise characterization this is a quite wonderful depiction of complete barrenness and desolation which could be achieved only by a poet of God's grace."[15]

■ **11** For the use of "nations" as a synonym for Babylon see 4:16.

Since the term "seventy years" is evidently original but does not fit precisely any pair of dates (see Structure and

10   See Wiseman, *Chronicles*, 27; the specific document is B. M. 21946, line 11; see Wiseman, *Chronicles*, 69.

11   Compare Malamat, "Twilight of Judah," 128 n. 11.

12   So first Julius Lewy, *Forschungen zur alten Geschichte Vorderasiens* (Leipzig: Hinrichs, 1925) 27; so likewise Malamat, "Twilight of Judah," 129 n. 13, and by implication Bright and Thompson.

13   For the practice see conveniently Pedersen, III/IV,

272–73, and Marvin H. Pope, "Devoted," *IDB* 1:838–39.

14   For the forms of millstones see H. Neil Richardson, "Mill, millstone," *IDB* 3:380–81, and for those of lamps see Robert W. Funk and Immanuel Ben-Dor, "Lamp," *IDB* 3:63–64.

15   Cornill, pp. 289–90: "Da der Brodbedarf täglich gebacken wurde, so war das Geräusch der mahlen-

Setting), one must assume that it was intended as a round number suggesting a normal life-span (Ps 90:10; compare Judg 1:7; 1 Sam 6:19; 2 Sam 24:15). But it may reflect an idiom wider than the OT: in the Black Stone of Esarhaddon it is the period of time during which Marduk shows displeasure toward Babylon; it thus evidently designates the proper period for an ancient Oriental city to lie desolate[16] (compare Isa 23:15). But as a calculation the datum entered into the discourse of the postexilic period (Ezra 1:1!): in Zech 1:12 it seems to refer to the period of the destruction of the temple after 587, since the completion of the second temple was in 516/515;[17] in 2 Chr 36:20–23 it refers (erroneously) to the period from the fall of Jerusalem to the edict of Cyrus in 538; and in Dan 9:2 it enters into the calculations regarding Antiochus Epiphanes, namely that it is to mean "seventy weeks of years" (Dan 9:24), that is, four hundred ninety years.[18]

■ **12** The intention of the second scroll (36:30–31) can hardly have included a concern for the punishment of Babylon (so most commentators); but since the skeleton of this verse is present in *G*, one presumes it was added early. For the form of the infinitive מְלֹאות ("completion")

see GKC, sec. 74h.

■ **13** If the skeleton of v 13 was present in the second scroll (so the assumption of the present study), then the "land" must have been Judah. The easiest assumption then is that the text was originally "the land" (compare v 11) and that the demonstrative "that" was added when v 12 was added, so that the reference of the verse shifted from Judah to Babylon (Rudolph's emendation of "that land" to "this land" has the same intention, but is less plausible).

Aim

A closing summary intended for the first scroll, then expanded for the second scroll, was thereupon expanded and extended by many hands. For the first scroll: Judah will be destroyed if she does not repent. For the second scroll: Judah will be destroyed, since she has not repented, and will be enslaved for seventy years. But then come fresh additions: after the seventy years are over, the enslaver will be destroyed. If God is the God of the living and not of the dead, then his Scripture must at all costs be kept current.

---

den Handmühle vernehmbar, wo überhaupt Menschen hausten und steht daher typisch für die Arbeit und das Treiben des täglichen Lebens. Des Tages Todtenstille, durch kein menschliches Geräusch unterbrochen, des Nachts schauriges Dunkel, durch keinen Lampenschimmer erhellt— eine in ihrer Knappheit und Charakteristik geradezu bewunderungswürdige Schilderung der völligen Oede und Verödung, wie sie nur einem Dichter von Gottes Gnaden gelingen konnte."

16 Daniel D. Luckenbill, "The Black Stone of Esar-haddon," *AJSL* 41 (1924–25) 167; so also Riekele

Borger, "An Additional Remark on P. R. Ackroyd, *JNES* XVII, 23–27," *JNES* 18 (1959) 74.

17 Geo Widengren, "The Persian Period," *Israelite and Judaean History* (ed. John H. Hayes and J. Maxwell Miller; Philadelphia: Westminster, 1977) 522.

18 For this reinterpretation see conveniently Norman Porteous, *Daniel* (Philadelphia: Westminster, 1965) 133–35, 139–44.

All the Nations
Will Fall to Babylon,
and Then Babylon Will Fall

Bibliography

Bardtke, Hans
"Jeremia der Fremdvölkerprophet," *ZAW* 53 (1935) 220–27.
Brongers, Hendrik A.
"Der Zornesbecher," *OTS* 15 (Leiden: Brill, 1969) 177–92.
De Roche, Michael
"Is Jeremiah 25:15–19 a Piece of Reworked Jeremianic Poetry?" *JSOT* 10 (1978) 58–69.
McKane
"Poison," 487–92.
Peiser, Felix E.
"Miscellen—Jer. 25,25," *ZAW* 17 (1897) 350.
Winckler, Hugo
"Zum Alten Testament—Jer. 25,25," *Altorientalische Forschungen* I (Leipzig: Pfeiffer, 1895) 292.

25

15 [For]ᵃ thus Yahweh, God of Israel, has said to me: Take this cup of wine [wrath]ᵇ from my hand, and give it to all the nations to drink to whom I am sending you, 16/ and they shall drink and retch and act crazed from the presence of the sword which I am sending among them. 17/ And I took the cup from the hand of Yahweh, and I gave (it) to all the nations to drink to whom Yahweh sent me: [18/ Jerusalem and the cities of Judah and her kings and her officials, to make them a ruin, a desolation, a hissing {and an object of contempt, as at this day,}ᵇ 19/ Pharaoh king of Egypt, and his servants, and his officials, and all his people, 20/ and all the rabble, {and all the kings of the land of Uz,}ᵇ and all the kings of the {land

Text

15a   The connective כִּי is lacking in *G* and is doubtless redactional, to connect the passage to vv 1–14 (so Rudolph).

b   *M* is impossible, since both "wine" and "wrath" have the definite article: either one must omit the definite article with "wine" and read the construct יֵין, thus "take this cup of the wine of wrath" (so *V*, *S*), or else "wrath" must be construed either as a gloss or as a variant of "wine," thus evidence of a conflate text (so a suggestion of Bright). The reading of *G* is τοῦ οἴνου τοῦ ἀκράτου, "of unmixed wine," and the occurrence of the same translation ἄκρατος in Ps 75:9 to translate חָמָר (a word which may need to be revocalized, see *HALAT*, 317a) raises the question whether the text antecedent to *G* did not have הַחֶמֶר "wine" (compare Deut 32:14) as the variant instead of הַחֵמָה "wrath." On the other hand Isa 51:17 has כּוֹס חֲמָתוֹ "cup of his wrath," so the variant occurring here is early.

18–20a   Verses 18–20 as a whole appear to be an expansion reflecting the events of 605–604: see Structure, Form, Setting.

18b   These words are missing in *G* and are evidently a redactional expansion (so Janzen, p. 45, and with caution Bright). Rudolph contrariwise believes that *G* deliberately omitted the words as no longer applicable.

20b   These words are omitted by *G* and are evidently redactional (so Rudolph, against Janzen, p. 117, who believes *G* here to be haplographic). The phrase does not fit the context of Egypt and Philistia (compare Structure, Form, Setting). Why is it here? Rudolph can only conjecture that it was originally associated with Edom (v 21) on the basis of Lam 4:21 and that the gloss became displaced.

of the)[c] Philistines—)and⟨[d] Ashkelon and Gaza and Ekron and the remnant of Ashdod,][a] [21/ Edom and Moab and the Ammonites, 22/ {all}[b] the kings of Tyre and {all}[b] the kings of Sidon and the kings of the coastlands which are beyond the sea,][a] 23/ and Dedan and Tema and Buz and all (whose hair is) shaven at the temple, 24/ {and the kings of Arabia, and the kings of the rabble}[b] living in the desert, 25/ {and all the kings of ⟪ "Zimchi" ⟫[c] } [b] and {all}[d] the kings of Elam, and all the kings of the Medes, 26/ and all the kings of the north, near and far, one after the other, and all the [b]kingdoms {of the earth}[b] which are on the face of the ground;][a] [and the king of "Sheshach" shall drink after them.][c] 27/ And you shall say to them, Thus Yahweh of hosts, the God of Israel, has said, Drink and be drunk and vomit, fall and do not rise, from the presence of the sword which I am sending among you; 28/ and it shall happen when they refuse to take the cup from your hand to drink, then you shall say to them, Thus Yahweh of hosts has said, No, you must drink; 29/ for look, in the city which bears my name I am beginning to do evil; and will you your- selves be exempt at all? No, you will not!—for a sword I am summoning upon all the inhabitants of the earth, [oracle of Yahweh of hosts.][a]

c   Omit אֶרֶץ with *G*. If the original text meant "all the kings of the Philistines—Ashkelon and Gaza and Ekron and the remnant of Ashdod," then when the ו before "Ashkelon" was inserted (or interpreted as "and," see note d), the word "land" may have been inserted to denote the territory outside the cities.

d   ו is missing in *G*: either it is original to the text, a *waw explicativum* (GKC, sec. 154a, note, [b]) in which case *G* rightly omits it, or else it is an erroneous addition to the text (compare note c).

21–22a   Verses 21–22 as a whole appear to be an expansion reflecting the events of 594; see Struc- ture, Form, Setting, and compare 18–20a.

22b   Omit "all" twice with *G* (Janzen, p. 45).

23–26a   Verses 23–26a as a whole appear to have been an expansion in the exilic period; see Structure, Form, Setting, and compare 18–20a and 21–22a.

24b   "And the kings of Arabia" is omitted in *G*. The double phrase in *M* is clearly a conflate text (וְאֵת כָּל־ מַלְכֵי עֶרֶב וְאֵת כָּל־מַלְכֵי הָעֶרֶב). Janzen's suggestion (Janzen, p. 13) is accepted here, that "and all the rabble" is original in v 20, that the phrase fell out by haplography at that point, was restored in the margin, and was reincorporated into the text here in v 24, perhaps attracted by the phrase "living in the desert" (compare 9:25), so the text of *G*; and that *M* represents a further expansion of two variant texts.

25b   Omit the phrase with *G*; it appears to be a variant of "and (all) the kings of Elam" (see note c).

c   *M* זַמְרִי gives no sense here. Two major sugges- tions have been made: (1) that the text must be emended to גמרי (doubtless גֹּמְרִי), that is, the Cimmerians (see Machteld J. Mellink, "Gomer," *IDB* 2:440a)—so first Felix E. Peiser, "Miscellen—Jer. 25,25," *ZAW* 17 (1897) 350; (2) that the text be emended to זמכי, an "athbash" cipher for עילם "Elam" (see Bleddyn J. Roberts, "Athbash," *IDB* 1:306–7)—so first Felix Perles, "A Miscellany of Lexical and Textual Notes on the Bible," *JQR* NS 2 (1911/12) 103, and *Analekten zur Textkritik des Alten Testaments* NF (Leipzig: Engel, 1922) 39, 100. It is the second suggestion which is accepted here (so also Rudolph): by this understanding *M* is a conflate text, with and without the athbash.

d   Omit "all" with *G* (Janzen, p. 65).

26b—b   Omit "of the earth" with *G* and *S*; the wording is doubtless evidence of a conflate text, the equivalent of "which are on the face of the ground." "Kingdoms" must be revocalized to the absolute form, מַמְלָכוֹת.

c   The clause must be omitted with *G*; since "Sheshach" is an athbash cipher like *"Zimchi" in v 25, both additions may have been made at the same time. The setting for the clause must be late in the exilic period.

29a   Omit with *G*.

Structure, Form, Setting

Verse 30 begins poetic material only secondarily associated with vv 15–29; vv 15–29 deal with the cup of wine or of wrath and make up a literary unit.

The passage offers many difficulties. There is no skeleton of poetry here, in spite of the analysis of De Roche;[1] form-critically it is a first-person narrative of a symbolic act (or of the vision of a symbolic act: see below), and such narratives elsewhere seem to be in rhythmic prose (*Kunstprosa*).

The listing in vv 18–26 interrupts this rhythmic prose: on these verses see below. Both form-critical analysis and content analysis of vv 15–17, 27–29 suggest that the narrative did not originate in one step. In this sequence v 17 is a problem. Form-critially v 15 is a divine command for action, and v 16 an associated prediction of the consequences to follow from this action. Analogously v 27 is a divine command for associated words which the prophet is to pronounce, and vv 28–29 are an associated prediction of the consequences to follow from the words. Verse 17, however, is the report of the prophet's performance of the command for action. Rhetorically vv 27–29 must be subsumed under the narrative introduction of v 15, "Thus Yahweh, God of Israel, has said to me." But v 17 is not subsumable under that narrative introduction; it is parallel to it. Form-critically there are no exact parallels to the present collection of categories: in narratives of symbolic actions elsewhere one finds either a command for action followed by a command for words (19:1–3) but without a report of performance of the action and/or words, or else a command for action followed by a report of performance of the action (13:1–7), but in these latter narratives there are no commands to speak associated words. In content vv 28–29 are considerably darker than v 17: v 28 speaks of a refusal of the nations to drink the cup, and the first part of v 29 offers unique phraseology which is really appalling (especially "do evil" with Yahweh as subject): see Interpretation. One notes further that the second-plural address at the end of v 28 and in v 29 is primarily to Jerusalem ("the city"; "be exempt").

The easiest solution is to see vv 15–17 and 27–29 as having originated in separate experiences some years

apart: v 15 can introduce vv 27–29 as easily as it can vv 16–17. One could imagine several models for the present existence of vv 15–17 and 27–29. An introduction similar to v 15 may originally have stood before v 27 and have dropped out by haplography; or such an introduction may have been omitted deliberately by an early copyist; or such an introduction may not have been thought necessary for the material in vv 27–29 by the original scribe (Baruch?) or even by Jrm himself. One might even ask: Did the earlier experience present itself to Jrm with the phrase "cup of wine," and the later experience with the phrase "cup of wrath," so that the present text of v 15 is a conflation of the two narrations?

Verses 18–26 raise just as many questions, though, as will be shown, this passage may offer clues for the contexts of the original experiences narrated in vv 15–17 and 27–29.

The question first must be, can some of the list be integral to the narrative of vv 15–17? De Roche includes vv 18–19 (plus "and all the rabble" at the beginning of v 20) as part of his reconstructed poem; on the other hand, Rudolph rejects all of v 18 as inappropriate in a passage devoted to foreign nations. It must be pointed out that v 29 states that the disaster will begin with Jerusalem and move out from there to the whole world; a listing therefore that begins with Jerusalem is not inappropriate (against Rudolph). On the other hand, the listing of the segments of Judah in v 18a is reminiscent of the gloss in 2:26b, and the wording of v 18b is conventional (compare vv 9b and 11a, and 44:6 and 22); one may safely assume the hand of a redactor here (against De Roche).

G offers a shorter text than does *M* in vv 18–26, but even the text of the passage in *G* must have arisen in several stages, as will become apparent.

One may begin with vv 21–22, a listing of Transjordanian and Phoenician states; this is precisely the group represented as making up the delegates to a conference with Zedekiah, evidently in 594, to discuss possible rebellion against Nebuchadrezzar (27:3–4). But that group conspicuously did not include the Philistine cities, which by then made up Babylonian provinces.[2] One may presume therefore that if vv 21–22 reflect that aborted rebellion, v 20 must reflect some earlier occa-

---

1   Michael de Roche, "Is Jeremiah 25:15–19 a Piece of Reworked Jeremianic Poetry?" *JSOT* 10 (1978) 58–69.

2   Malamat, "Twilight of Judah," 135.

sion. The evidence is not so clear, but I would suggest that vv 18–20 reflect the desperate hope prevailing in Judah between the battle of Carchemish in May or June of 605 and the sack of Ashkelon by Nebuchadrezzar in December of 604, the hope that somehow Egypt and the Philistine cities together could help Judah stem the forward march of the Babylonian armies: doubtless the oracles in chapters 46—47 reflect that period as well. The hoped-for rebellion of 594 occurred six or seven years after Jehoiakim burned Jrm's scroll (601, by the reading of *G* of 36:9): the bitter words of vv 27–29 are more appropriate to that period in which Jrm was convinced of the irrevocable punishment of Yahweh than before. One may tentatively conclude, therefore, that vv 15–17 narrate an experience before 601, perhaps, as suggested, the period in 605–604, while vv 27–29 narrate a parallel experience in 594. Perhaps Baruch added both vv 18–20 and vv 21–22 after 587 as his memory of the applications of the experiences narrated here.

Verses 23–26a reflect a late expansion touching on nations not directly concerned with Judah but those defeated by various campaigns of Nebuchadrezzar (see Interpretation and compare 49:28–39). Verse 26b will then be a later addition (again, compare chaps. 50—51).

What sort of experiences are recorded in vv 15–17 and 27–29? Though form-critically the material is identical with narratives of symbolic actions such as those found in 13:1–11 and in chapter 19 (see above), there are only two ways the present narratives can be understood, as Lindblom has pointed out: either it is only a literary parable, or else it is the reproduction of a vision. "The central role which the prophet himself plays in that which happens and the absence of all expressions which usually characterize a comparison speak in favour of the fact that we have to do with a real vision, and, moreover, with a vision of a markedly dramatic character."[3] There is no reason, of course, why a dream or vision cannot recur, and that is the suggestion of the present analysis.

For the symbolic background of the vision, see Interpretation on v 15.

Interpretation

■ **15** The image of the drinking of a cup of wine as punishment is widespread in the OT (Pss 11:6; 75:9; Jer 49:12; 51:7; in contemporary material—Hab 2:15–16; Ezek 23:31–33; Obadiah 16; Lam 4:21; in later material—Isa 51:17, 22; Zech 12:2) and is echoed in the NT as well (Rev 14:10; 16:19; 17:4; 18:6). These passages are discussed by Hendrik A. Brongers[4] and McKane;[5] the set of assumptions lying behind these passages is puzzling. It is hardly likely that there is a close connection with the procedure for ordeal outlined in Num 5:16–28, for that passage prescribes "water of bitterness" rather than wine. According to McKane, Helmer Ringgren has attempted to connect the passages with a hypothesis of an intoxicated (humiliated) god-king in the course of a New Year's festival, but this attempt founders: it is the enemies of Yahweh who become intoxicated in these passages.[6] Brongers assumes that the wine has been poisoned—he compares Hab 2:15;[7] but again this is questionable. It is clear that what is envisaged is a banquet (indeed an anti-banquet!),[8] and that drunkenness is considered a judgment: compare Isa 28:7–8 and 29:9–10, where it is not a matter of Yahweh's dispensing a cup but where drunkenness and staggering are expressions of judgment. It is also clear that one does not have to do here with an ordeal procedure from which some participants will emerge unscathed: all who drink the cup undergo judgment.[9] It is possible that the image is pre-Israelite: Dahood cites a painted vase from Ras Shamra depicting El with a cup in his hand,[10] but there is no way to be sure. The most that can be said is that Yahweh is depicted compelling his enemies to drink a cup to utter intoxication as a judgment, but whether some old cultic procedure is involved, or whether one has to do here simply with a custom by which a king entraps his enemies with wine at a banquet so that they may be killed, is

3   Lindblom, *Prophecy*, 131.
4   Brongers, "Zornesbecher."
5   McKane, "Poison," 487–92.
6   Ibid., 489–90.
7   Brongers, "Zornesbecher," 190.
8   McKane, "Poison," 488–89.
9   McKane's view on this matter, "Poison," 489, is not clear.
10   Dahood, *Psalms I*, 70.

uncertain (compare on v 16).

The adaptation of the image by which Jrm himself becomes the cupbearer is noteworthy; there is no parallel for this in the comparable passages, but it is analogous to the image of the prophet as the agent of burning fire (5:14) or as the assayer (6:27). The fact that "the nations" and "all to whom I send you" are phrases occurring in Jrm's call (1:5, 7) suggests that the narrative here deals with an experience close to the heart of his prophetic activity. For the experience understood as a vision see Structure, Form, Setting.

■ 16 The meaning of the second verb (געש hitpoʻel) is somewhat uncertain: V and T here render "be confused" and S "be stupefied," while G understands "vomit," translating here with the same verb as for the third imperative in v 27. The verb occurs in 46:8 of the rising and falling of the Nile, and in the hitpaʻel stem (are the two distinguishable?) in 5:22 and 46:7 similarly of the surging of waters. Traditionally the translation has been "reel," but the rendering in G and the parallel in v 27 encourages the translation "retch" (so NEB). The verb will then refer to the "surging" of the stomach.

The third verb (הלל hitpoʻel) occurs in 1 Sam 21:14 meaning "pretend to be insane"; here it is "act crazed."

Duhm and Rudolph delete "from the presence of the sword I am sending among them" as an expansion from v 27 which spoils the image. But if v 27 is in any sense a parallel with the present verse, then the phrase belongs here as much as it does in v 27: the preposition מִפְּנֵי does not necessarily mean "because of" here, but may more literally mean "from the face of" or "from the presence of." (Compare the remarks in the interpretation of v 15 on the image of the cup of wine.)

■ 17 For the position of this verse see Structure, Form, Setting.

■ 18–26 These verses list the nations understood by the redactor to be implied by "all the nations" in v 17. Verse 29 implies that the judgment begins with Jerusalem and spreads out to all the inhabitants of the earth. See Structure, Form, Setting.

■ 20 The opening phrase וְאֵת כָּל־הָעֶרֶב calls for consideration; the phrase is evidently secondary in v 24 but belongs here, and it belongs to the phrases dealing with

Egypt in v 19 as G and S have understood it, so that the punctuation of M is in error. The same word is evidently vocalized both עֶרֶב and עֵרֶב[11] and because of the identity of consonant sequence is easily confused with עֲרָב "Arabia" (so again v 24; compare 1 Kings 10:15 = 2 Chr 9:14, and compare the Versions in various occurrences of the word). The impression given by the word is of a marginal population, but interpretations differ, beginning with the Versions: G uses τοὺς συμμείκτους "those of mixed race"—the term in Greek implies those other than true citizens, and Jerome explains the Greek word as referring to people who do not belong to the region of Egypt but who are foreigners or visitors, but in his V he simply translates the phrase as "all in general"; S translates "all of those of his borders," and T "all the kings of his auxiliaries," leading Rashi to explain the phrase as referring to non-Egyptian client tribes upon whom Pharaoh depends by treaty. The word is used to refer to those attached to Israel coming out of Egypt (Exod 12:38) and to those foreigners attached to Israel in postexilic Jerusalem (Neh 13:3), and to those attached to the Chaldeans (50:37). These contexts make the interpretation of T and Rashi unlikely. One may conclude that the term refers to a miscellaneous population, some of whom are foreign and some of whom are of mixed descent, who attach themselves to a dominant population.

The reference to "Uz" is not original here (see Text), and the region is not well defined—an area in the Syrian desert southeast of Damascus.[12]

For the mention of the Philistines compare Structure, Form, Setting. The "remnant" of Ashdod is evidently a reference to the defeat of that city by Pharaoh Psamtik (Psammetichus) I (663–610) after an extraordinary siege lasting twenty-nine years (Herodotus 2.157).[13]

■ 21 For the distinctive designation "Ammonites" (בְּנֵי־עַמּוֹן) see 9:24–25.

■ 22 The designation הָאִי refers to coastlands and islands (the plural occurs in 2:10, which see); the whole phrase here indicates territories touched by the Phoenicians.

■ 23 Dedan and Tema are both tribes and locations in northwest Arabia; they are likewise linked in Isa 21:13–14. Tema is the present-day taimāʼ, 27°37' N, 38°30' E;

11   HALAT, 831a and b.
12   B. Davie Napier, "Uz," IDB 4:741a.
13   See in general William F. Stinespring, "Ashdod," IDB 1:248–49.

Dedan is probably the present-day *al-'ulā*, 26°38' N, 37°57' E. Both are oases and caravan crossroads, and they were trade centers at all periods.[14] The Babylonian Chronicle mentions a raid by Nebuchadrezzar in 599/598 against the Arabs ("and scouring the desert they took much plunder from the Arabs"),[15] but whether this campaign or some other lies behind the mention here of these tribes is impossible to say. (Josephus quotes Berosus as stating that Nebuchadrezzar "conquered Arabia," among other regions, but no details are given.)[16] Compare the remarks on 49:28–33.

The identity or location of "Buz" is unknown; the reading of *G* here is *Rōs*. If Buz is correct, one is led to an identification with the Akkadian Bâzu, mentioned in Assyrian inscriptions, in one of which Bâzu is clearly in Arabia.[17] For the phrase "all (whose hair is) shaven at the temple" see 9:25.

■ **25–26** There is certainly one instance here of the so-called athbash cipher (the substitution of Hebrew letters in reverse alphabetical order),[18] "Sheshach" in v 26, and perhaps also "Zimchi" in v 25, if that correction from the *M* reading זִמְרִי is correct (see Text). "Sheshach" represents Babylon (see also 51:41), and "Zimchi" would represent Elam. The phrases in which both these words appear are secondary additions: indeed "Zimchi," if correct, simply duplicates "Elam" adjoining it. Since the name "Babylon" occurs freely elsewhere in Jer, particularly in chapters 50—51, it is difficult to imagine what purpose the cipher serves here except as evidence of playfulness or love of mystery.

Elam and the Medes centered in what is now western Iran: Elam in the south, touching the Persian Gulf, with its capital at Susa, and the Medes in the north, with their capital at Ecbatana. In the period after the fall of Assyria, however, the Median Empire extended north and west into central Anatolia, allied with Nabopolassar and exercizing a protectorate over Elam.[19] Damaged lines in the Babylonian Chronicle[20] may refer to a campaign of Nebuchadrezzar against Elam in 596/595, but one

cannot be sure; compare the remarks on 49:34–39.

The phraseology of v 26a becomes vague. "All the kings of the north, near and far, one after the other" implies ". . . whether near or far from each other." "North" suggests a region of which Israel had no first-hand knowledge but out of which threatening powers might come (compare "Gog" in Ezek 38:15). "All the kingdoms which are on the face of the ground" completes the totality of political powers. All of these named are presumably threatened by the power of Babylon; but then ultimately Babylon too will drink from the cup (v 26b).

■ **27–29** These verses offer wording similar to that of vv 15–17 as they match the instruction for words to say with instruction for acts to perform. Thus the imperatives in v 27, "drink and be drunk and vomit, fall and do not rise," parallel "they shall drink and retch and act crazed" in v 16, and the reference to the sword is likewise parallel. For the form of the imperative קְיוּ "vomit" see GKC, sec. 76h. Verse 28 brings a new note: the refusal of the nations to drink, followed by the instruction to contradict their refusal (expressed by the use of the infinitive absolute with the imperfect, GKC, sec. 113p). But the address is not to the nations in general but primarily to Jerusalem (see Structure, Form, Setting).

The phrase in v 29, "the city which bears my name" (literally "the city over which my name is called") is here unique in the book, the normal phrase being "the house which bears my name" (7:10, 11, 14, 30; 32:34; 34:15); the phrase with "city" appears otherwise in the OT only in Dan 9:18, 19, and cannot be considered "Deuteronomic" here (against Weinfeld).[21] It corresponds nicely to the mention of "Jerusalem" first in v 18: the operative word in the first part of the verse is "begin" (חלל hip'il), a verb which does not occur otherwise in Jer. Yahweh's destructive work begins in Jerusalem and spreads out from there to the far reaches of the earth. The verb "do

---

14 For details of the location of the two, and the equivalents in Akkadian, Greek, and Latin, see Wildberger, *Jesaja*, 792, 800; more generally see Otto Kaiser, *Isaiah 13—39* (Philadelphia: Westminster, 1974) 134—35, and Simon Cohen, "Dedan," *IDB* 1:812b, and "Tema," *IDB* 4:533.

15 British Museum 21946, reverse, line 10; see Wiseman, *Chronicles*, 31–32, 71.

16 Josephus *Ag. Ap.* 1.19, sec. 133.

17 *ANET*, 284a, compare also 290a; see also Westermann, *Genesis*, II, 450.

18 See Bleddyn J. Roberts, "Athbash," *IDB* 1:306–7.

19 See Mark J. Dresden, "Elam," *IDB* 2:70–71; "Media," *IDB* 3:319–20.

20 Wiseman, *Chronicles*, 73, compare 36, 48.

21 Weinfeld, *Deuteronomy*, 325, no. 2.

evil" (רעע hipʿil), with Yahweh as subject, is likewise striking: the only parallel is v 6, where there is a negative, and where the text is dubious (see there). The common expression is "bring evil [= disaster]," בוא hipʿil + רָעָה, 4:6 and often, but the expression here is stronger.

The strong language continues in the sequence וְאַתֶּם הִנָּקֵה תִנָּקוּ לֹא תִנָּקוּ. The first part must be construed as a question, but it is a verb reinforced by both a subject pronoun and an infinitive absolute. The verb נקה nipʿal elsewhere may mean "be innocent" (so 2:35), but here punishment is at issue (Bright: "be let off scot-free").

Aim

On more than one occasion Jrm became convinced that there would be no safety for Judah in numbers of nations who might hope to band together to withstand Babylon: all would fall. That conviction was broadened after 587: nations to the south and east and north of Babylon would fall to her as well. Finally the passage affirms that Babylon too will fall: only Yahweh will remain, once he has summoned a sword upon all the inhabitants of the earth.

All Nations Alike
Will Stand Before Yahweh, and
All Will Be Held Guilty

Bibliography

Bardtke, Hans
"Jeremia der Fremdvölkerprophet," *ZAW* 53
(1935) 227–30.
Castellino, Giorgio R.
"Observations," 404–6.
Condamin, Albert
"La 'colère de la Colombe' dans Jérémie 25,38; cf.
46,16; 50,16," *Bib* 12 (1931) 242–43.
Girard, L. Saint-Paul
"La colère de la Colombe (note sure Jérémie 25,38
et 26,16; 50,16)," *RB* 40 (1931) 92–93.

25

30 For your part you shall prophesy to them
[all][a] these words, and you shall say to
them:
Yahweh from on high roars,
and from his holy abode gives forth his
voice;
yes, he roars over his sheepfold,
a shout like (grape-)treaders echoes
back
to all the inhabitants of the earth;
31 the uproar reaches
to the end of the earth,
for Yahweh has a lawsuit with the
nations,
he argues his case against all flesh,
the guilty ⟨are given over⟩[a] to the
sword,
oracle of Yahweh.
32 Thus Yahweh of hosts has said:
Look, disaster goes out
from nation to nation,
a great gale is stirred up
from the extremes of the earth.
33 And those slain by Yahweh shall be [on
that day][a]
from one end of the earth to the other;
they shall not be [lamented, nor][b]
gathered, nor buried,
dung on the face of the ground they
shall become.
34 Wail, you shepherds, and cry out;
grovel, you lords of the flock;
for your days are fulfilled for slaughter,
[. . .][a] and you shall fall like choice

Text

30a   Omit with *G*; see Janzen, pp. 65–67.

31a   Vocalizing נְתֻנִם, passive participle, a reading
suggested by the *G* aorist passive ἐδόθησαν, instead
of the *M* vocalization נְתָנָם "he has given them over."
Note *M* in Num 3:9, where the plural passive participle is written without yod, and note Deut 28:32,
which has diction much like the present passage.
The participle is parallel to נִשְׁפָּט (and to בָּא, if that
is construed as a participle).

33a   The phrase overloads the colon and is evidently a
gloss; note that the same phrase is present in *M* and
missing in *G* in 49:26 and 50:30. *G* in the present
passage reads "on the day of Yahweh."

b   *M* has three verbs here ("lamented," "gathered,"
"buried") while *G* has only one ("buried"). Janzen
assumes that *G* is correct and that *M* has expanded
the text by two verbs (Janzen, p. 45). I propose that
the verse is poetry and that two verbs stood here
(compare the pairing of "gathered" and "buried" in
8:2 and the pairing of "lamented" and "buried" in
16:4), the text of *M* having undergone expansion by
the influence of 16:4 and *G* having suffered by
haplography. "Lamented" is appropriate in 16:1–9,
but "gathered" is more appropriate to the diction of
the present verse.

34a   *M* here offers a word (וּתְפוֹצוֹתִיכֶם) missing in *G*;
traditionally it has been translated as a feminine
plural noun ("and your scatterings," so *V*) but the
form is dubious. It appears to represent a verb: it
has been suggested that it is a mixed form representing תָּפוּצוּ "you shall be scattered" (פוץ qal) and
וַהֲפִיצוֹתִיכֶם "and I shall scatter you" (פוץ hip'il)
(GKC, sec. 91l). But such a meaning does not
comport well with the motif of slaughter (and
compare v 35). Given the contrast between *M* and *G*
at the end of the colon (see note b), the verb under
consideration may be a distorted form of נפץ or פצץ
"shatter" (for example, וְנַפַּצְתִּיכֶם "and I shall shatter
you," נפץ pi'el) developed for the *M* "choice vessel"
(see again note b) as a variant reading for "and you

《 rams; 》[b]

35 flight shall vanish from the shepherds,
and escape from the lords of the flock.

36 The sound of the cry of the shepherds,
and the wail of the lords of the flock!—
for Yahweh destroys their pasture,

37 and the peaceful sheepfolds lie silent,
because of the hot anger of Yahweh.

38 He has left like a lion his thicket,
for their land has become a waste,
because of the cruel sword[a]
》and because of his hot anger.《[b]

shall fall." In any event the present *M* appears to be conflate and the word can safely be omitted (see Janzen, pp. 14 and 194–95 n. 17; and Bright, p. 159 note *q—q*.

b   Reading כְּאֵלִי with *G* for *M* בִּכְלִי "(like a) vessel." Ehrlich's suggested emendation of the phrase to בִּכְלִי חֶמְלָה "without mercy" (Ehrlich, *Randglossen*, 309) is ingenious but not preferable.

38a   Reading with some MSS., *G*, and *T* חֶרֶב for *M* חֲרוֹן. The phrase in *M*, as presently vocalized, can only be translated "the wrath of the dove" (see Bibliography), but with "sword" (which is feminine) the following word may be construed as the feminine participle of ינה "oppress." Is the article in הַיּוֹנָה an early pseudocorrection? "Wrath" is evidently here by attraction from its occurrence in the following colon.

b   This last colon is lacking in *G* and could be a late addition, dittographic from the last colon of v 37; but the structure of 4:26b suggests that *M* is correct here.

Structure, Form, Setting

This last portion of the chapter consists of poetry, at least to a large degree (most commentators take v 33 as prose); and it is clear that the material pertains to foreign nations ("the nations," v 31; "from nation to nation," v 32). Many of the phrases are reminiscent of phrases elsewhere either in Jrm's poetry or in the poetry of other prophets, so that there is uncertainty how much is authentic to Jrm here. And the references are often obscure enough (does אֶרֶץ mean "land" or "earth"? who are the "lords of the flock," vv 34, 35, 36?) that one's understanding of the verses is not easy.

The first question, as always, is the integrity of the passage: is it one unit or more? Volz has a complex theory that vv 30–31 + 34–38 represent a single poem, though he transfers the last colon of v 37 to the end of v 35; he thus excises vv 32–33 as a later insertion (so also Hyatt). Rudolph analyzes the material in two poems, vv 30–31 and vv 32–38, and Bright follows him in this. Both commentators agree that vv 32–38 are authentic to Jrm. Bright thinks vv 30–31 may be anonymous but Rudolph raises the question whether "his sheepfold" in v 30 does not suggest Jeremianic authorship. Thompson takes the passage as a single poem.

The diction of vv 34–37 is united by "shepherds," "flock," "pasture," "sheepfold"; vv 30–32 are dominated by terms for noise, commotion, and tumult. Within the early portion of the sequence one finds terms for lawsuit and judgment (v 31); v 33, between the "commotion" section and the "flock" section, is an expression of

slaughter. But one finds "sheepfold" in v 30 as well as in v 37: this link could be either that of an external catchword or a sign of internal unity.

There are no clear-cut indications of speaker in the sequence except for the rubric at the beginning of v 32 announcing that Yahweh is the speaker: one may judge that rubric either to be trustworthy or to be a secondary addition. The rubric at the beginning of v 30 correspondingly suggests that Jrm is the speaker. The call to communal lamentation in v 34 is best understood on the lips of the prophet (compare 4:8; 6:26); v 33 is not impossible as words of Yahweh (even with the third-person reference to him) but is more easily understood as spoken by Jrm. The least complicated solution then is to see all the verses spoken by Jrm with the exception of v 32, marked as a quotation of Yahweh, the declaration of his "lawsuit" referred to in v 31. These considerations lead to the view that the passage is a single unit, not two. Earlier commentators made much of the fact that the first two poetic cola of v 30 are an adaptation of Amos 1:2a, a circumstance which casts doubt on the authenticity of the verse. But Jrm himself frequently cited or adapted earlier material (see 4:3–4; 10:23–25).

The judgment that the entire passage is authentic to Jrm is strengthened if "his sheepfold" in v 30 refers to Judah or Jerusalem (compare Rudolph); one may compare "my possession" in 12:7, 8, 9. The last colon of v 30 must be translated "all the inhabitants of the earth," since v 31 refers to the nations. If "his sheepfold" does refer to Judah or Jerusalem, then the general movement of the passage is from Judah outward to all the nations of the earth. This movement is subtly reinforced if the verb in the fourth line of v 30 (ענה, normally "answer") suggests an echo (see Interpretation): Yahweh first roars over his sheepfold, and the echo resounds among all the nations. This outward movement matches that of v 29 and suggests the appropriateness of placing the passage directly after vv 15–29: both involve the same thought patterns. The present passage, by this understanding, will reflect the same general outlook as that proposed for vv 15–29; the resemblance of v 32b to 6:22 and 10:22, and v 33b to 16:4, material whose setting the present study assigns to the period from 600 to 598, suggests that Jrm is now generalizing to all the nations the fate of Judah that had been announced earlier; 594 is the appropriate setting (compare vv 15–29, Structure, Form, Setting).

Though commentators have taken v 33 to be prose, there is no reason, once two suspected glosses are removed, why the passage cannot be construed as a tetracolon. Verses 32 and 34 likewise fall into four cola and v 35 into two. By contrast vv 30 (after the opening rubric) and 31 must be taken as five cola each ("to the end of the earth" in v 31 matches "to all the inhabitants of the earth" in v 30 and "from the extremes of the earth" in v 32), and these groups of five cola are matched by the five cola of vv 36–37. The third colon of each of the group of five is introduced by כִּי, a circumstance that strengthens this analysis; and this circumstance in turn suggests that vv 36–37 close the poem and that v 38 is a secondary addition—this last verse is evidently a late adaptation of diction from 4:7 (see Text, Interpretation).

The poetic cola in v 30 open with an adaptation of Amos 1:2a (see above), a short poem in the form of a theophany:[1] the name "Yahweh" comes first in the Hebrew colon, and the imperfect verbs express a present event announced by the prophet. But whereas Amos 1:2a announces Yahweh's roar from Zion, here the roar is from heaven. This citation from Amos may be matched by the third colon in v 31, "for Yahweh has a lawsuit with the nations," an adaptation of a colon in Hos 4:1. Both citations have been "cosmicized," the one from Amos (as already noted) by the shift from Zion to

heaven, the one from Hosea by the substitution of "the nations" for "the land" (= Israel). These shifts reinforce the pattern of movement from Jerusalem out to the nations already discussed.

Verse 31 continues the prophetic announcement by describing the effect of that roar: the verse then is form-critically comparable to Amos 1:2b. The effect reaches to the end of the earth, and Yahweh's roar is specifically his accusation in his lawsuit against all nations. The quotation of Yahweh in v 32 will then be the sentence he passes on the nations. Verse 33 continues the prophetic description of the effect of Yahweh's action begun in v 31. Verse 34 (as already mentioned) is a call to communal lamentation;[2] the first half of the verse is the appeal proper, followed in the second half by the cause for lamentation introduced by כִּי. Verse 35 may be considered either a continuation of v 34b or a resumption of the prophetic description of Yahweh's action begun in v 31. Verses 36–37 round off the poem by giving Jrm's report of the sound of distress he hears in his prophetic ear: the explanation of that sound is given in the last colon of v 36 and in v 37.

Interpretation

■ 30 The instruction to Jrm begins surprisingly with an emphatic subject pronoun. This can only express a contrast with the second-plural subject pronoun in v 29. The implication of the two adjoining verses is then that "none of you will be exempt, but you, Jeremiah, must prophesy." But whether this contrast is intrinsic to vv 15–38, so that the present passage is linked to vv 15–29 from the time of its origin, or whether the instruction here was shaped secondarily to fit the context of the previous passage, would be difficult to say.

The first two cola of the poem, depicting a theophany, are based on Amos 1:2a (see Structure, Form, Setting), with terms for "heaven" substituted for "Zion" and "Jerusalem": for "his holy abode" as an expression for heaven compare Deut 26:15; Zech 2:17; Ps 68:6; 2 Chr 30:27. For "his holy abode" (מְעוֹן קָדְשׁוֹ) G evidently reads only קָדְשׁוֹ "his sanctuary," suggesting the temple; this is not an impossible reading (Yahweh would thus roar both from heaven and from his temple) but is hardly prefer-

---

1   See Wolff, *Joel and Amos*, 118–19.
2   For this form see ibid., 21–22.

able; it doubtless arose from haplography, perhaps influenced by the meaning of Amos 1:2a.

The expansion of the old word from the scope of Jerusalem to the scope of heaven is part of Jrm's sense of outward movement of Yahweh's judgment from Jerusalem to include the nations (see Structure, Form, Setting). The verb "roar" implies here, as it does in Amos, the sound uttered by lions (Jer 2:15). The confrontation between Yahweh and the nations is a climactic one.

"His sheepfold" (נָוֵהוּ) occurs in 10:25 in a quotation from Ps 79:6–7, there in parallelism with "Jacob." The noun נָוֶה is a poetic word for "abode, habitation," but it particularly pertains to sheep and shepherds (so 33:12) and is appropriate here in anticipation of "lords of the flock" in vv 34–36. The parallelism with "Jacob" in 10:25 and its context here suggests its application to Judah and Jerusalem (see Structure, Form, Setting; so also Rudolph). The preposition עַל may mean either "over" or "against"; "over" is perhaps safer, given the positional connotation of "on high" and the directional implication of אֶל "to" in the last colon of the verse.

The fourth colon is not altogether clear. The דֹּרְכִים are "treaders of grapes," and the הֵידָד is a "shout" associated with grape-treading (see 48:33) as well as of warriors in battle (51:14). But the verb ענה is normally translated "answer," a meaning not appropriate if Yahweh is the subject: its presence here led G to read a plural ("these shall answer like grape-gatherers"). Most commentators and translations assume that the verb here has a more general meaning "utter" and take "shout" as an accusative or as adverbial, but the solution of NEB is doubtless correct ("an echo comes back like the shout of men treading grapes"): "shout" is the subject of the verb—Yahweh roars over Judah and Jerusalem but a shout "answers" (that is, echoes) in the realms of the nations just as grape-treaders (plural) shout to each other. This interpretation is at least implied by V ("a shout like grape-treaders will be sung out together [concinetur]") (see again Structure, Form, Setting).

The noun אֶרֶץ in the last colon must mean "earth" rather than "land," given the diction of v 31.
■ 31 The expression בוא עַד means "arrive at" or "reach" (a place) (compare 2 Kgs 19:3 = Isa 37:3); the echo still resounds to the end of the earth. The "uproar" (שָׁאוֹן) refers typically to the sound of ocean waves or the tumult

of battle; both this word and "shout" (v 30) then suggest the context of battle which is made clear by "sword" at the last of the verse.

Given the fact that "argues his case" in the fourth colon is a nip'al participle, one is led to construe בָּא in the first colon as a participle as well (and to read the verb in the last colon as a passive participle, see Text). The verse then gives the impression of the echoes in progress.

The third colon of the verse is an adaptation of a colon in Hos 4:1, though there Yahweh has a lawsuit with "the inhabitants of the land" (יֹשְׁבֵי הָאָרֶץ, the context there defining אֶרֶץ as "land [of Israel]"). In the present poem, however, the occurrence of the same Hebrew expression יֹשְׁבֵי הָאָרֶץ in the last colon of v 30, here expanded in meaning to "inhabitants of the earth," allows Jrm to reuse the expression from Hosea, replacing "the inhabitants of the land/earth" by "the nations." Thus the prophet has expanded both Amos 1:2a (in v 30) and the colon from Hos 4:1 from a local to a universal denotation (see Structure, Form, Setting). For "lawsuit" (רִיב) see 15:10, and for the cognate verb see 2:9. As in 2:9 and Hos 4:1 Yahweh is the plaintiff who is also the judge; here the whole inhabited earth stands before him.

In contrast to Hos 4:1, where the announcement of Yahweh's lawsuit is followed immediately by a listing of the defendant's offenses (introduced by כִּי), here the cola are in parallelism and simply continue to describe the echoing sound of the cosmic assizes.

For the expression "argue one's case" (שפט nip'al) see 2:35: there, as here, the form is a participle. For "all flesh" see 12:12; in the present passage the phrase implies "all humankind." The implication is that "the nations," "all flesh" are held "guilty": for רְשָׁעִים in legal contexts compare 5:26 and 12:1. The passive participle of "give over," proposed here for the vocalization of the verb, is used in a similar context in Deut 28:32. This mention of the "sword" is the first specific indication of the punishment visited upon the nations to be heard in the poem, though the way is prepared by "shout" in v 30 and "uproar" earlier in the present verse. The theme is expanded in vv 33 and 34.
■ 32 The verse embodies the statement of Yahweh in the courtroom scene (see Structure, Form, Setting). The participle "goes out" (יֹצֵאת) forms a nice counterpoise to its antonym "reaches" (בָּא) in the first colon of v 31, the more so in that the normal verb for "disaster" (רָעָה) is

"arrive" (בוא): see 2:3; 5:12; 23:17; Mic 3:11. But this disaster does not come in, it goes out.

For "gale" (סַעַר) see 23:19. The last half of the verse is a variation on the diction of 6:22, and it resembles 10:22 as well.

■ **33** This verse, less two expansions, is easily construed as poetry (see Text, and Structure, Form, Setting): "on that day" does not match the immediacy of the rest of the poem, and "lamented nor" is evidence of a conflation. The verse begins nicely with the waw-consecutive perfect of "be" (וְהָיוּ) and ends with the imperfect of the same verb (יִהְיוּ). For "slain" (חַלְלֵי) see 8:23 and 14:18: the present usage is like 14:18 in that the genitive construction in Hebrew expresses the agent ("by Yahweh"). For the phrase "from one end of the earth to the other" see 12:12 (where it is translated "from one end of the land to the other": here is another instance in which Jrm has taken earlier expressions and enlarged their meaning beyond the land of Israel). For "they shall not be gathered, nor buried, dung on the face of the ground they shall become" compare 8:2; 9:21; 16:4.

■ **34–36** These three verses, remarkably, offer three times the parallelism of "shepherds" (רֹעִים) and "lords of the flock" (אַדִּירֵי הַצֹּאן); the latter phrase is not found otherwise in the OT, and thus the parallelism is not either. For the term "lord" (אַדִּיר) see 14:3; for "shepherds" as a designation of the leadership of a nation see 2:8; 3:15; and notably 23:1–4. The context here of the nations of the earth suggests that it is the whole company of the leaders of all the nations that is being addressed and judged.

■ **34** For "wail" see 4:8; the combination "wail" and "cry out" is characteristic of the call to communal lamentation (compare Joel 1:13–14, and see Structure, Form, Setting). For "grovel" (פלש hitpa'el) compare 6:26, the other occurrence in Jer. The present passage is the only occurrence in the OT without "in the dust"; the translation "grovel" is the suggestion of Driver.[3]

How ironic that the time has come not for the slaughter of the sheep (so the verb "slaughter" in 11:19) but of the shepherds! For "days are fulfilled" compare Gen 25:24 and often; compare "years" as the subject of the verb in v 12 of the present chapter.

■ **35** The colon "flight shall vanish from the shepherds" is a variation of the first colon of Amos 2:14, "flight shall vanish from the swift." As with the expression in Amos, the diction is an ironic reversal: one expects "the shepherds shall perish" but hears instead "flight shall perish" (אבד: compare 4:9, where the verb is likewise used metaphorically).

■ **36** For the exclamatory construction with "sound of," see 10:22. "Cry" and "wail" here are noun equivalents of the parallelism of verbs in the first colon of v 34 (צְעָקָה, a by-form of זְעָקָה, 18:22; 20:16; יְלָלָה). In 6:26 it was the foe from the north who is to "destroy" (שדד); here it is Yahweh himself. For "pasture" (מַרְעִית) see 10:21; in that earlier passage the noun is used for the flock that feed in the pasture.

■ **37** The sequence of five cola from v 36 continues. "Sheepfold" (נָוֶה) was singular in v 30 but is now plural: does this shift suggest again that what began with Jerusalem and Judah has now spread to the whole earth? The phrase "peaceful sheepfold" (נְוֵה שָׁלוֹם) occurs also in Isa 32:18 (part of a late passage); for the implication of "peaceful" compare "prosperous land" (אֶרֶץ שָׁלוֹם) in 12:5: here the phrase suggests meadows offering prosperity and security. They will now "lie silent" (דמם nip'al); the same verb occurs in 8:14. The last colon of the verse resembles the last one in 4:26.

■ **38** Rudolph believes that this verse has been added to the poem secondarily: the diction of 4:7, which is similar ("a lion has come up from his thicket . . . to make your land a desolation") refers to the foe from the north, while here the "lion" has become a simile for Yahweh. But the vocabulary of the first colon is different ("lion" here is כְּפִיר and functions in a simile, while in 4:7 it is אַרְיֵה and is a metaphor; "thicket" here is סֻכָּה, in 4:7 סֹבֶךְ). Furthermore the shift of agent from the foe from the north (4:7) to Yahweh is the same shift as that from 6:26 to v 36b here. In 4:7 "your land" is Judah, while here, from the context, "their land" has come to denote the various lands of the shepherds, the rulers of the nations.

If the text of the third colon is correctly understood, "cruel" is a participle of the verb ינה "oppress" (the hip'il stem of which occurs in 22:3). The context suggests that this "sword" is the same as that mentioned in v 31.

---

3   Godfrey R. Driver, "Studies in the Vocabulary of the Old Testament," *JTS* 31 (1929/30) 275–76.

Aim

The voice of Yahweh strikes Jerusalem like a stone splashing into a pond, whose ripples move steadily outward to the shore, intersecting and reintersecting: the divine summons to court reverberates through all the nations of the world. All alike stand before God, and all alike will be held guilty. The vision is an astonishing climax in the mind's eye of the prophet, a culmination of God's work in the world. Those who know themselves to be the shepherds of their respective flocks will be slaughtered as sheep are slaughtered, the pastures silent and dead. Yahweh will stand supreme, and alone.

OK Nov 24, 2015 JAS